THE CORN LAWS

The Formation of Popular Economics in Britain

Edited by
ALON KADISH

VOLUME IV

FREE TRADE AND RELIGION

Routledge
Taylor & Francis Group
LONDON AND NEW YORK

First published 1996 by Pickering & Chatto (Publishers) Limited

Published 2016 by Routledge
2 Park Square, Milton Park, Abingdon, Oxon OX14 4RN
605 Third Avenue, New York, NY 10017

Routledge is an imprint of the Taylor & Francis Group, an informa business

BRITISH LIBRARY CATALOGUING IN PUBLICATION DATA
Corn Laws: Formation of Popular Economics
in Britain
I. Kadish, Alon
941.081

Set ISBN 1 85196 410 X

ISBN 13 : 978-1-138-75889-6 (hbk) (Vol-4)

LIBRARY OF CONGRESS CATALOGING-IN-PUBLICATION DATA
Kadish, Alon, 1950–
The corn laws : the formation of popular economics in Britain / Alon Kadish.
p. cm.
Includes bibliographical references and index.
ISBN 1–85196–410–X (set)
1. Corn laws (Great Britain) 2. Free trade––Great Britain.
3. Anti-Corn-Law League. I. Title.
HF2044.K33 1996
v. 1. Whig free trade I –– v. 2. Whig free trade II : Free trade and Irish nationalism I –– v. 3. Free trade and Irish nationalism I : James Wilson and the economist –– v. 4. Free trade and religion –– v. 5. Provincial free trade I –– v. 6. Provincial free trade II : Free trade farmers.
382.7'3'0942––dc20 98–1232
CIP

CONTENTS

REPORT

OF THE

CONFERENCE OF MINISTERS

OF ALL DENOMINATIONS

ON THE

CORN LAWS,

HELD IN MANCHESTER,

AUGUST 17TH, 18TH, 19TH, AND 20TH, 1841.

WITH A DIGEST OF THE DOCUMENTS CONTRIBUTED DURING THE CONFERENCE.

PUBLISHED UNDER THE AUSPICES OF THE COMMITTEE.

SECOND THOUSAND.

MANCHESTER:
J. GADSBY, NEWALL'S-BUILDINGS, MARKET-STREET.

LONDON:
T. WARD AND CO., 27, PATERNOSTER-ROW;
R. GROOMBRIDGE, PANYER-ALLEY, PATERNOSTER-ROW.

1841.

According to Archibald Prentice[1] the conference of ministers held in Manchester in August 1841 began with a circular issued by George Thompson (1804–78), one of the main speakers for the anti-slavery movement, requesting the ministers of religion in Manchester to meet in the summer of 1841 to discuss 'the Christian means of obtaining a settlement of the Corn Law question without injustice or civil convulsion.' Twenty eight ministers responded and decided to call a meeting of ministers of all denominations from the whole of the United Kingdom.

The manner whereby the demand for the repeal of the corn law was restated as a religious issue may be found in a hymn composed for the occasion and sung to the tune of 'Old Hundreth Psalm' at a tea party given by the Young Men's Anti Monopoly Association for the conference.[2]

From the eternal throne above,
Look down upon us, God of love;
For suffering millions now we plead,
O hear us in this hour of need.

What tho' the earth her increase yields,
And plenty crowns the distant fields,
The selfish few, for love of gold,
By cruel laws thy gift withhold.

Give to the Senate of our land
Wisdom! henceforth to understand,
Thy heavenly will – that all be fed,
And eat untax'd their 'daily bread!'

Our trade and commerce, Lord, revive;
If thou dost frown, what land can thrive?
On Britain still in mercy smile;
O deign to bless our native isle.

Prentice's *Manchester Times* (4 September 1841) argued that all in all, counting letters of approval, before and since the conference, some 1,500 clergymen were committed to carrying out its recommendations. According to the *Nonconformist*, quoted in the *Manchester Times*, the conference

. . . has, once for all, taken the question out of the cold, clear, frosty region of political economy, and transplanted it to the sunnier climate of humanity and religion. The League has made it, as became them, the business of the head – the Conference makes it the Business of the heart. 'Every thing in its own order.' To

[1] Archibald Prentice, *History of the Anti Corn Law League* (1853), London: Frank Cass, 1968, vol. 1, p. 233.
[2] *Manchester Times* 21 August 1841.

reason the matter out, as a question of political economy, was necessary before it could be fairly addressed to the sympathies and religious principles of men. The League proves the genuiness and authenticity of the text, the Conference takes it and preaches it to the conscience and best affections of the nation. ... Thousands who treated the corn laws as a matter of mere speculative opinion, will henceforth identify them with national immorality, and will calmly, and on principle, go to work to destroy them.

ADDRESS.

No event in modern times has so excited local attention, or created such general interest in the country, as the convention of Ministers of religion, from all parts of the empire, to consider the operation of laws restricting the food of the people. The preliminary arrangements were happily crowned with gratifying success; the promise which attended the earlier arrangements has been far more than realised; and the completion of the admirable design has been more than equal to the most sanguine expectation of the gentlemen who at first contemplated the movement.

About six hundred ministers had promised their presence and co-operation, of whom, more than seventy were unable to realise their expectation: yet, when the conference had assembled, the members numbered six hundred and forty-five, who had convened from the remotest districts of Scotland, the retired and rural regions of Wales, the agricultural parts of England and Ireland, and from the mining and manufacturing, as well as commercial towns of the united empire.

The opening of the proceedings was characterised by much deliberation and care. The chair was temporarily occupied, and a provisional committee was appointed to consult and select office-bearers for the conference. When the President, whom they had chosen for the day, took the chair, the assembly exhibited the most inspiring and enthusiastic appearance; the whole area, as also the platform, were filled by men whose countenance expressed the deepest solicitude as to the issue.

Four days of prolonged inquiry and discussion were devoted to the proceedings: the two sessions of every day extending from four to five hours each, while the acting committees ceased not their constant attention till the hour of midnight. Men of highest reputation and eminent talent eagerly and with deep solicitude entered into all the responsible and arduous duties of the Conference, and came forward to address the members more anxious to establish the claim of the poor and the cause of the right than to gain reputation or applause. In no case did the momentary interests of party, or the claims of political leaders, divert the discussion from the *one question*. A dignified and high moral bearing characterized the proceedings throughout The deputations who were admitted, whether from mechanics, hand-loom weavers, the Operative Anti-Corn-Law Association, or the Council of the League, seemed to feel that not only was the occasion important and the cause great, but that the assembly was alike worthy of the national character it sustained, and the universal attention it had excited. No compromise of principle or sacrifice of duty was required throughout; but every one seemed to feel that in such a place and for such an object he was legitimately engaged. The doubtful were confirmed, and those who had been sceptical eagerly associated themselves in the generous enterprise.

The deliberations of the Conference have closed, and the result is before the world. We have now the pleasure to submit to our readers the report of proceedings, from which they will be able to judge both of the wisdom and seasonable character of the design, and the manner of its execution. The speeches and documents which are embodied are equally calculated to convey truth and instruction. The information whether statistical or philanthropic will meet and answer the inquiries of the statesman or the Christian minister, and may lead to the adoption of such measures as will ultimately effect the overthrow of every unrighteous monopoly that interferes with the provision of the poor or the employment of the industrious. A calm survey of the great principles involved in, or developed by this unique convention of benevolent men, will be more suitable when the excitement and commotion occasioned by such a phenomenon have subsided. In the meantime we commend the following pages to the thoughtful consideration of all who love their country and their fellow-men.

THE COMMITTEE.

NAMES OF MINISTERS

WHO ATTENDED THE

CONFERENCE.

Abbott, R.	Baptist	Newport Pagnell
Abram, R.	Independent	Martin Top
Acworth, James, A. M.	Baptist	Bradford
Adey, Edward	Baptist	Leighton Buzzard
Adkins, Thomas	Independent	Southampton
Alexander, W.	Independent	Churchtown, nr. Stockport
Allin, Thomas	Meth. New Con.	Altringham
Allison, John	Baptist	Ogden
Alsop, James	Independent	Birmingham
Archer, Dr. J., P. P.	Roman Catholic	Dublin
Archer, Thomas	Scotch Secession	London
Archer, F. J.	Catholic	Blessington
Armitage, Josiah	Independent	Elswick
Armstrong, George, A. B.	Unitarian	Bristol
Ashworth, J.	Unitarian	New Church, Rosendale
Ashford, Joseph	Baptist	Burton Latimer
Aspinall, R.,	Independent	Colne
Aspland, R. B.	Unitarian	Duckinfield
Atkin, Daniel	Independent	Leigh
Atkin, Thomas	Independent	Glossop
Atkinson, C.	Meth. New Con.	Leeds
Atley, H.	Independent	Frome
Auld, W.	Scotch Relief	Greenock
Baggaly, William	Meth. New Con.	Longtown
Baird, Archibald	Scotch Secession	Paisley
Baker, Charles	Baptist	Stockport
Baker, James	Baptist	Andover
Baker, John	Independent	Brampton
Bakewell, John	Meth. New Con.	Manchester
Balfour, A.	Countess of Hun.	Middleton.
Banks, James	Scotch Relief	Paisley
Bannister, J. T.	Baptist	Warwick
Bartlett, Benjamin	Baptist	Chenies, Bucks
Barfett, J.	Independent	Salisbury
Barrett, John	Independent	Lydiate, near Ormskirk
Barnett, John	Baptist	Blaby
Barton, Joseph	Independent	Ellesmere
Battersby, M.,	Scotch Relief	Hamilton
Baxter, M.	Meth. Association	Northwich.

Bayley, J.	Swedenborgian	Accrington
Bayley, R. S.	Independent	Sheffield
Beard, J. R., D.D.	Unitarian	Manchester
Beardsall, Francis	Baptist	Manchester
Bedford, William	Independent	Narborough, nr. Leicester
Belcher, Joseph	Baptist	Greenwich
Bell, Robert	Independent	Sowerby Bridge
Berry, Charles	Unitarian	Leicester
Bevan, W.	Independent	Liverpool
Bilson, James	Baptist	Whitehaven
Birch, Henry	Independent	Fording Bridge, Hants
Birt, John	Baptist	Manchester
Bishop, A.	Independent	Beaminster
Bishop, Francis	Unitarian	Warrington
Blakey, John	Baptist	Haslingden
Blackwood, William	Scotch Relief	Dumfries
Blair, James	Baptist	Dunfermline
Bloodworth, J.	Calvinist	Leicester
Boardman, W	Unitarian	Swinton
Booker, Alfred	Scotch Baptist	Nottingham
Borland, J. W.	Scotch Relief	Lanark
Bostcok, H.	Establishment	Aylesbury
Bowen, W.	Independent	Chorley
Bowen, S.	Independent	Macclesfield
Bottomley, J.	Independent	Sowerby
Boycott, Thomas	Meth. New Con.	Barnsley
Boys, James	Swedenborgian	Pilkington
Bonner, W. H.	Baptist	Bilston
Bradley, James	New Church	Manchester
Bramall, John	Independent	Stainland, near Halifax
Breeden, H.	Methodist Asso.	Manchester
Brewster, Patrick	Ch. of Scotland	Paisley
Brian, J. F.	Independent	Stalybridge
Broadbent, F. B.	Independent	Belper
Broadbent, Isaac	Prim. Methodist	Barnard Castle
Brooks, J.	Presbyterian	Hyde
Brown, J. T.	Baptist	Oakham
Brown, Richard	Independent	Wrexham
Brown, John	Independent	Wareham, Dorset
Brown, J.	Scotch Relief	Campsie
Brown, A. Morton	Independent	Poole, Dorset
Buck, William Foster	Independent	Burton-on-Trent.
Buckley, James	Independent	Peniston, near Barnsley
Buckley, W. E.	Meth. Association	Cheltenham
Buckpitt, James	Independent	Castle Donington
Buckingham, T. P.	Independent	Lye
Buckley	Baptist	Stand
Bulgin, Samuel	Baptist	Poole
Bull, Josiah, M.A.	Independent	Newport Pagnell
Bunce, John S.	Baptist	Devizes
Bunbridge, James	Town Missionary	Manchester
Bunn, H. J.	Independent	Abergavenny
Burchell, W. F. E.	Baptist	Rochdale
Burnett, N. T.	Baptist	Lockerby
Burdett, A.	Baptist	Long Buckley
Burdett, C.	Baptist	Broughton Astley
Burton, T. B.	Independent	Hyson Green

Burke, John, P.P.	Roman Catholic	Castle Pollard
Burder, John	Independent	Stroud
Butler, W.	Baptist	Heptonstall Slack
Butler, Mark	Independent	Stone
Byrne, P., P. P.	Roman Catholic	Castletown
Cairns, Robert	Scotch Secession	Paisley
Casewell, J. D.	Baptist	Oldham
Calvert, R.	Independent	Hyde
Calvert, D.	Independent	Sandysyke
Calvert, J.	Independent	Morley
Campbell, Alexander	Independent	Greenock
Campbell, George O.	Scotch Relief	Strathaven
Carlisle, James	Independent	Hackney, London
Carr, Robert	Baptist	Ossett Common
Carruthers, P.	Scotch Secession	Longtown, Cumberland
Cater, Philip	Baptist	Bath
Chaplin, W.	Independent	Bishop's Stortford
Chapman, William	Meth. New Con.	Manchester
Cheatle, George	Baptist	Birmingham
Cheetham, H.	Independent	Calderbrook
Chester, R.	Meth. Association	Sheffield
Clarke, William	Independent	Sutton
Clarkson, Abraham	Independent	Batley
Clapp, Jerome	Independent	Appledore
Claypole, Ed.	Baptist	Ross
Clunie, John, L.L.D.	Independent	Manchester
Cocker, W.	Meth. New Con.	Brighouse
Colcroft, W.	Baptist	Golcar, near Huddersfield
Colston, John	Unitarian	Wilmslow
Collins, J. J.	Roman Catholic	New Mills, Derbyshire
Cooke, J. H.	Independent	Gomersal
Cooper, James	Independent	Middlewich
Cox, F. A., D.D.	Baptist	Hackney
Crabtree, William	Baptist	Lineholme, Todmorden
Crichton, Hugh, A.M.	Scotch Secession	Liverpool
Crook, J.	Baptist	Hebden Bridge
Crumpton, D.	Baptist	Henley in Arden
Cross, W. J.	Baptist	Thornbury
Crossley, J.	Independent	Horwich
Cumming, J. T.	Independent	Hammersmith
Cummins, J.	Independent	Leeds
Currie, William	Baptist	Lockwood
Curtis, James	Meth. New Con.	Huddersfield
Curwen, S.	Independent	Reading
Darke, E.	Wesleyan Asso.	Manchester
Davies, Thomas J.	Independent	Tintwistle, Cheshire
Davies, J.	Baptist	Sheffield
Davies, Thomas	Baptist	Merthyr Tidvyl
Davies, W. P.	Independent	Ashburton
Davies, Daniel	Independent	Ilkeston, Derbyshire
Davies, Ebenezer	Baptist	Lewes, Sussex
Davies, Jonathan	Independent	Penuel
Davies, Joseph	Baptist	Willenhall, Stafford
Davies, J.	Independent	Daventry, Northampton
Davies, Stephen	Independent	Rhyl
Davies, T.	Independent	Glastonbury
Dawson, William	Meth. Association	Heywood

Dawson, James	Independent	Dudley
Deakin, James	Independent	Stand, nr. Manchester
De Fraine, R.	Baptist	Lutterworth
Dean, Henry	Baptist	Colne
Dean, James	Independent	Topsham
Dickinson, J.	Independent	Kilmarnock
Dobbie, James	Scotch Secession	Annan
Dorney, T.	Baptist	Falfield
Dowling, Cornelius	Roman Catholic	Stradbally
Downing, John	Independent	Buxton
Dowson, Henry	Baptist	Bradford, Yorkshire
Dawson, Thomas	Baptist	Bacup
Driver, Henry	Independent	Holden, nr. Clitheroe
Driver, John	Baptist	Water
Drummond, William	Meth. Association	Oldham
Dubourg, S. A.	Independent	Clapham
Dunn, J.	Independent	Nottingham
Dyson, Joseph	Independent	Halshaw Moor
East, T.	Independent	Birmingham
Earnshaw, J.	Independent	Altringham
Edgar, James	Wesleyan Asso.	Hebden Bridge
Edmonds, J.	Independent	St. Helens
Edwards, Edward	Independent	Hatherlow
Edwards, James	Independent	Brighton
Edwards, James	Baptist	Nottingham
Edwards, C.	Wesleyan Asso.	Nantwich
Edwards, W.	Independent	Brecon College
Ellery, Thomas	Meth. Association	Manchester
Elliot, J.	Independent	Bury St. Edmunds
Ellis, M.	Independent	Mynyddyslwyn
Ellis, S.	Independent	Bolton
Elliott, J.	Unitarian	Prescot
Evans, D.	Independent Meth.	Manchester
Evans, D. D.	Baptist	Pontehydyryn
Ewing, Alexander, M.A.	Independent	Halifax
Ferguson, W.	Independent	Bicester, Oxfordshire
Fernie, W.	Independent	Frome
Finlayson, Thomas	Scotch Secession	Greenock
Firth, B.	Independent	Wyke, near Halifax
Fletcher Joseph	Independent	Hanley
Fletcher, Richard	Independent	Manchester
Foster, Jonas	Baptist	Farsley
Fogg, John	Independent	Elswick
Ford, William	Meth. New Con.	Hanley
Ford, W. S.	Independent	Alresford
Fox, John	Independent	Oldham
Fox, Joseph	Independent	Morley
Frazer, Alex.	Independent	Edinburgh
Fraser, William	Baptist	Bolton
Freeman, J. J.	Independent	Walthamstow
Gadsby, William	Baptist	Manchester
Galland, Joseph	Independent	Greenacres
Galloway, J. C.	Independent	West Bromwich
Garner, James	Baptist	Dunham, Cheshire
Garner, James	Primitive Meth.	Manchester
Garvey, M. A.	Independent	London
Gaskell, William	Unitarian	Manchester

Garrard, William	Baptist	Blackburn
Gibbons, S.	Independent	Warrington
Giles, William	Baptist	Preston
Giles, J. E.	Baptist	Leeds
Giles, W.	Baptist	Liverpool
Gill, J.	Independent	Walmsley
Gill, Thomas	Baptist	Burnley
Gillman, Thomas	Independent	Newport
Glanville, John	Independent	Bristol
Glendenning, John	Independent	Huddersfield
Goadby, Joseph	Baptist	Leicester
Good, J. E.	Independent	Gosport
Gould, Daniel	Baptist	Dunstable
Goulty, J. N.	Independent	Brighton
Gravestock, J.	Independent	Old
Graham, John	Scotch Secession	Glasgow
Gray, William	Baptist	Northampton
Green, J.	Independent	Uppingham
Green, James	Baptist	Barnoldswick
Greenall, T.	Independent	Burnley
Greenway, Josh.	Baptist	Netherton
Gregory, James	Independent	Thornton, near Bradford
Griffiths, Henry	Independent	Stroudwater
Griffiths, J. P.	Baptist	Pendlehill
Griffith, D.	Baptist	Accrington
Griffith, John	Independent	Llanharmon
Griffiths, R. N.	Independent	Kirkham
Griffith, D.	Independent	Rhuabon
Griffin, James	Independent	Manchester
Guest, W.	Independent	Southport
Guenett, J. F.	Independent	Weymouth
Guthrie, John	Presbyterian	Kendal
Guthridge, J.	Meth. Association	Frodsham
Gunn, P., P. P	Roman Catholic	Fermanagh
Gwyther, James	Independent	Hulme, Manchester
Hague, William	Independent	Guisborough
Halley, Robert, D.D.	Independent	Manchester
Hamer, Richard	Independent	Spetisburg
Hamer, Thomas	Independent	Rotherham College
Hamilton, R. W.	Independent	Leeds
Hammond, John	Independent	Handsworth
Harbottle, Joseph	Baptist	Accrington
Hardacre, Samuel	Baptist	Long Preston
Hardy, R.	Baptist	Queenshead
Hardy, James	Independent	Wednesbury
Harper, Humphrey	Independent	Manchester
Harper, Thomas S.	Independent	Ormskirk
Harris, G.	Independent	Ringwood
Harrison, James	Prim. Methodist	Staley Bridge
Harrison, John	Unitarian	Chowbent
Harrison, Joseph	Baptist	Stockport
Harrison, Jas.	Independent	Barnard Castle
Harrison, Richard	Baptist	Melbourne
Harrison, William	Unitarian	Blackley
Harrison, J.	Meth. New Con	Manchester
Harvey, Alexander	Scotch Relief	Glasgow
Harry, N. M.	Independent	London

Hawkes, James	Eng. Presbyterian	Nantwich
Haworth, D.	Swedenborgian	Manchester
Hayden, J.	Independent	High Wycombe
Havnes, J.	Meth. N. Con.	Batley
Healey, Samuel	Independent	Hazelgrove
Hearne, Daniel	Roman Catholic	Manchester
Hellings, N.	Independent	Exeter
Hewitt, David	Independent	Rochdale
Hewlett, J. G.	Independent	Coventry
Hibbert, Randal	Presbyterian	Godby
Higson, John	Baptist	West Clayton
Hill, Robert	Primitive Meth	Manchester
Hill, W.	Swedenborgian	Hull
Hilton, John	Meth. New Con.	Manchester
Hinton, J. Howard, M.A.	Baptist	London
Hollgate, John	Independent	Orrell, near Wigan
Hollinrake, Henry	Baptist	Briercliffe
Holroyd, John	Independent	Delph
Hopwood, J.	Independent	Lutterworth
Horne, R	Primitive Meth.	Newcastle-under-Lyne
Horsley, John	Meth. Association	Appleby
Howorth, Franklin	Presbyterian	Bury
Howe, J.	Baptist	Macclesfield
Hoyle, G.	Independent	Staley Bridge
Hudson, T. H.	Baptist	Leeds
Hughes, E.	Independent	Holywell
Hull, Edmund	Baptist	Watford
Hunter, Hugh	Baptist	Nottingham
Hurndall, L. L.	Independent	Berkeley
Hurndall, W. A.	Independent	Huddersfield
Hutton, Hugh	Unitarian	Birmingham
Hutton, Thomas	Independent	Allerton
Hyatt, Joseph	Independent	Gloucester
Ingham, R.	Baptist	Bradford
Ingham, Richard	Baptist	Belper
Inglis, John	Scotch Secession	Hamilton
Isaac, D. L.	Baptist	Trosant, Pontypool
Ivy, Robert	Independent	Dukinfield
Jack, A.	Scotch Secession	Dunbar
Jackson, W. E.	Baptist	Heywood
Jackson, S.	Independent	Walsall
Jackson, Joseph	Baptist	Knutsford
Jackson, William	Independent	Rotherham College
Jackson, William	Baptist	Manchester
James, William	Unitarian	Bridgewater
Jeffreys, T.	Independent	Ebber Vale
Jenkins, E. C.	Independent	Bedwelldy
Jenkins, William	Baptist	Dolio
Jenkinson, John	Baptist	Kettering
Jessop, Richard	Independent	Greenacres Moor
Jones, John	Independent	Horwich
Jones, William	Independent	Bolton
Jones, C.	Independent	Dolgelly
Jones, William	Baptist	Reuben
Jones, Thomas	Calvinistic Metho.	Wrexham
Jones, H. W.	Baptist	Carmarthen
Jones, D,	Baptist	Liverpool.

Jones, Hugh	Independent	Tredegar
Jones, Samuel	Meth. New Con.	Oldham
Jones, Noah	Unitarian	Derby
Jones, E.	Independent	Oxford
Jones, Richard	Independent	Sirhowy Iron Works
Jones, Samuel	Independent	Lane End
Jordan, John	Baptist	Stanningley
Joseph, William	Independent	Earl Shelton
Jukes, Edward	Independent	Leeds
Katterns, D.	Baptist	Hammersm.
Keay, William	Baptist	Wellington, Salop
Kelly, John	Independent	Liverpool
Kennedy, James	Independent	Bury
Kennedy, C. J.	Congregatn. Meth.	Paisley
Kenney, Richard	Baptist	Macclesfield
Kent, Samuel	Baptist*	Biggleswade
Kent, M.	Baptist	Shrewsbury
Kirkus, Robert	Independent	Marple Bridge
Kershaw, John	Baptist	Rochdale
Kirk, John	Independent	Hamilton
Kirtland, Charles	Baptist	Newark-upon-Trent
Kluht, William	Independent	Melbourne
Knowles, F.	Unitarian	Near Wigan
Lace, Charles	Primitive Metho.	Leicester
Laidler, Stephen	Independent	Harleston, Norfolk
Laing, James Byres	Independent	Aberdeen
Lamb, William	Independent	Northwich
Langridge, John	Countess of Hunt.	Tyldesley Banks
Larom, C.	Baptist	Sheffield
Layhe, J.	Unitarian	Manchester
Lee, Thomas G.	Independent	Manchester
Legg, William	Independent	Reading
Leicester, R.	Independent	Chipping, near Preston
Leigh, Thomas	Baptist	Sutton-in-Ashfield
Leighton, E.	Independent	Loughborough
Leslie, Alexander	Scotch Secession	Near Wigan
Lewis, J.	Independent	Wootton-under-Edge
Lewis, E. C.	Countess of Hunt.	Rochdale
Lindsay, J.	Scotch Secession	Kilmarnock
Lord, Thomas	Baptist	Oldham
Lorraine, John D.	Independent	Wakefield
Lucy, William	Countess of Hunt.	Bristol
Machray, Robert	Independent	Dumfries
Macpherson, James	Baptist	Salendine Nook
Malden, W.	Independent	Chichester
Manderson, J. F.	Unitarian	Newcastle, Potteries
Mann, Thomas	Independent	Trowbridge
Marshall, W.	Independent	Wigan
Marshall, William	Scotch Secession	Leith
Martin, Robert	Independent	Heckmondwicke
Martin, Samuel	Unitarian Baptist	Trowbridge
Massie, J. W., M.R. I.A.	Independent	Manchester
Massie, Robert	Independent	Peterhead
Mather, Joseph	Baptist	Shrewton, Wilts
Matthews, Daniel	Baptist	Rowley
Maund, Thomas	Independent	Stonehouse
May, Richard	Baptist	Barnstaple

Mays, Thomas	Independent	Wigston Magna
M'Dougall, W.	Scotch Relief	Kilmarnock
M'Farlane, John	Scotch Secession	Glasgow
M'Farlane, Andrew	Scotch Secession	Edinburgh
M'Gilchrist, John	Scotch Secession	Edinburgh
M'Gill, M.	Scotch Secession	Rigg of Gretna
M'Phail, Archibald	Baptist	Huncoat, Accrington
M'Kean. W.	Unitarian	Walsall
M'Kerrow, W.	Scotch Secession	Manchester
M'Lary, Walter	Scotch Relief	Strathaven
Melson, Robert	Wesleyan Metho.	Birmingham
Mellor, Thomas	Baptist	Rushford, near Halifax
Mellor, S. C.	Meth. New Connex	Nottingham
Merchant, J.	Meth. New Con.	Ashton-under-Lyne
Miall, G. R.	Independent	Ullesthorpe
Miall, J. G.	Independent	Bradford
Middleditch, C. J.	Baptist	Frome
Middleditch, Thomas	Baptist	Ipswich
Midgley, John	Baptist	Shore
Milne, R. G.	Independent	Whitehaven
Milner, Thomas	Independent	Northampton
Mills, William	Meth. New Con.	Manchester
Moase, Charles	Independent	Bassingbourne
Monteith, John	Scotch Secession	Moffatt
Moore, Hugh	Presbyterian	Newtownards
Morrell, C.	Baptist	Stalybridge
Morgan, Thomas	Baptist	Birmingham
Morgan, D.	Independent	Llanfyllin
Morris, Edward	Independent	Stretford
Morris, John	Independent	Springhead, Saddleworth
Morris, Richard	Baptist	Burton-on-Trent
Morris, A. G.	Independent	Salford
Morris, J. W.	Presbyterian	Wilmslow
Mountford, William	Unitarian	Manchester
Muir, J. H.	Independent	Sheffield
Muir, F.	Scotch Relief	Leith, Edinburghshire
Mursell, J. P.	Baptist	Leicester
Murphy, Patrick	Roman Catholic	Dublin
Murtigh, Dr., P. P.	Roman Catholic	Dublin
Muscutt, Edward	Independent	St. Neots, Hunts
Nisbet, William	Scotch Secession	Paisley
Newlyn, Peter	Independent	Chalfont, St. Giles, Bucks
Newton, John	Wesleyan Methodist	Stockport
Nichols, Samuel	Independent	Over Darwen
Nichols, Abraham	Baptist	Goodshaw, Rawtonstall
Nicholson, William	Baptist	Halifax
Nolan, E. H.	Independent	Manchester
Normanton, James	Baptist	Great Driffield
Obery, J. Meeson, M.A.	Independent	Halifax
O'Connor, N.	Roman Catholic	Maryborough
Oddie, Samuel	Independent	Elland
O'Hanlon, W. M.	Independent	Chorley
Orme, G.	Meth. New Con.	Stalybridge
Owen, D. A	Independent	Smethwick
Owen, J. J.	Baptist	Castle Donington
Parry, John	Independent	Werne, near Wrexham
Parsons, B.	Countess of Hunt.	Ebley, Stroud

Payne, George, D.D.	Independent	Exeter
Peacock, D.	Baptist	Rotherham
Pearson, Ewan	Wesleyan Assoc.	London
Peddie, William	Scotch Secession	Edinburgh
Penkethman, John	Independent	Tockholes
Percy, J. W.	Independent	Warwick
Perrey, A.	Baptist	Reading
Peters, J.	Meth. Association	Rochdale
Phillips, S. J.	Roman Catholic	Woolton
Philips, Peter	Independent Meth.	Warrington
Pickles, J.	Inghamite	Winewall, Colne
Pierce, Thomas	Independent	Liverpool
Pike, J. G.	Baptist	Derby
Poore, J. L.	Independent	Salford
Pope, J. W.	Independent	Exeter
Pottenger, Thomas	Baptist	Bradford
Preston, J.	Independent	Warley, near Halifax
Price, David	Independent	Rhosllanerchrugog
Price, Stephen	Baptist	Abersychaw, Pontypool
Pridie, James	Independent	Halifax
Priestley, J.	Independent	Smallbridge
Probert, William	Presbyterian	Walmsley
Pulling, John	Independent	Deptford
Puller, T.	Congregational Ch.	Glasgow
Ramsay, P.	Independent	Haslingden
Ragland, John H.	Unitarian	Hindley
Redford, G., D.D., LL.D.	Independent	Worcester
Rees, W.	Independent	Denbigh
Rees, David	Baptist	Sheffield
Reston, David	Scotch Relief	Cupar Angus
Rhodes, H. G.	Independent	Fullwood
Richards, John	Independent	Stourbridge
Ridley, T. W.	Meth. New Con.	Stockport
Ritchie, J., D.D.	Scotch Secession	Edinburgh
Roaf, William	Independent	Wigan
Robberds, C. W.	Unitarian	Mansfield
Roberts, J.	Baptist	Liverpool
Robertson, John	Independent	Knaresbro'
Robertson, James	Scotch Secession	Edinburgh
Robinson, W.	Independent	Westhoughton
Robinson, Edwin	Independent	Park, Bury
Robinson, J. H.	Meth. New Con.	Halifax
Robinson, Thomas	Baptist	Basford
Robinson William	Baptist	Kettering
Rogers, T.	Independent	Prescot
Rogers, W.	Baptist	Dudley
Ronald, D.	United Secession	Saltcoats
Roper, H. Isaac	Independent	Bristol
Rose, William	Baptist	Slimbridge
Roseman, W.	Independent	Bury
Russell, Thomas	Primitive Method.	Middlewich
Rutherford, Alex. C.	Scotch Secession	Falkirk
Salt, William	Independent	Hinckley
Saunders, M.	Baptist	Haworth
Savage, J. A.	Independent	Wilsden
Saxton, G. P.	Independent	Moulton
Saxton, L.	Meth. New Con.	Stalybridge

Sayce, George	Baptist	Wrexham
Scales, Thomas	Independent	Leeds
Scholefield, J.	Bible Christian	Manchester
Scott, James	Independent	Cleckheaton
Scott, Walter, S. T. P.	Independent	Airdale College
Scott, W. P.	Baptist	Loughborough
Seavill, Thomas	Independent	Wareham
Sedgwick, Joseph	Baptist	Brighton
Senior, Amos	Baptist	Shelly
Sevier, C. T.	Independent	Warrington
Shadrach, E. L.	Independent	Dursley
Shanks, William	Baptist	Paisley
Shuttleworth, W.	Meth. New Con.	Manchester
Sibree, Peter	Independent	Birmingham
Sibree, John	Independent	Coventry
Simon, Samuel	Independent	New Mills
Simmons, James, A.M.	Baptist	Leicester
Simpson, J. P.	Countess of Hunt.	Preston
Skinner, Francis	Evan. Presbyterian	Blackbburn
Slack, James	Meth. Association	Bradford
Slate, Richard	Independent	Preston
Slater, George	Wesleyan Asso.	Stalybridge
Smethhurst, R.	Unitarian	Monton
Smith, J. Pye, D.D.	Independent	London
Smith, Thomas	Baptist	Stalybridge
Smith, T. H.	Independent	Denton
Smith, F.	Baptist	Beeston
Smith, William	Eng. Presbyterian	Stockport
Smith, John	Independent	Manchester
Smith, John	Baptist	Ashton-under-Lyne
Smith, Thomas, A.M.	Independent	Sheffield
Smith, George	Wesleyan Asso.	Manchester
Smithson, John H.	Swedenborgian	Manchester
Solly, H.	Unitarian	Yeovil
Somerville, Andrew	Scotch Secession	Dumbarton
Speakman, Joseph	Independent	Sheffield
Spencer, Thomas	Establishment	Hinton, near Bath
Spencer, G. S.	Independent	Ashton-in-Mackerfield
Spurden, Charles	Baptist	Hereford
Stacey, James	Meth. New Con.	London
Stanion, R.	Baptist	Melbourne
Starkie, John	Nazarene Church	Stockport
Start, J.	Primitive Meth.	Oldham
Statham, John	Baptist	Reading
Steele, William	Scotch Secession	Falkirk
Steven, William	Scotch Relief	Largs
Stevens, George	Independent	Totton
Stewart, James	Independent	near Bolton
Stirling, James	Scotch Relief	Kirriemuir
Stephen, D. R.	Baptist	Newport
Stevenson, Thomas	Baptist	Leicester
Strettles, J. B.	Bible Christian	Salford
Stoddart, G. H.	Independent	Sheffield
Stokes, William	Baptist	West Bromwich
Stone, Alfred	Independent	Wickwar
Stonehouse, G.	Baptist	Chipping Norton
Strachan, J. Y.	Church of Scotland	Forfar

Struthers, Thomas	Scotch Secession	Hamilton
Stuart, W. J.	Baptist	Inskip
Sturges, Thomas	Christian Church	Motram
Swan, Thomas	Baptist	Birmingham
Tarrant, Henry	Wesleyan Asso.	Birmingham
Taylor, James	Independent	Airdrie
Taylor, E.	Presbyterian	Rawtenstall
Thomas, D.	Independent	Wootton-under-Edge
Thomas, Thomas	Baptist College	Pontypool
Thomas, William	Baptist	Maiseyhampton
Thomas, Thomas	Baptist	Meltham
Thomas, W.	Independent	Dwygyfylch
Thomas, William	Baptist	Fairford, Gloucestershire
Thomson, D. M. N.	Baptist	Hull
Thompson, P., A. M.	Independent	Chatham
Thompson, David	Baptist	Chowbent
Thompson, Charles	Baptist	Swansea
Thompson, D.	Baptist	Foulsham
Thomson, J. M.	Scotch Secession	Maybole
Thorburn, W. R., A.M.	Evang. Presbyterian	Hallfold
Thornber, J.	Inghamite	Whalley
Thornber, John	Baptist	Sabden
Thornton, John	Independent	Stockport
Tidswell, Jabez	Meth. Association	Gosport
Tiler, William	Independent	Ossett
Tilly, Thomas	Baptist	Forton, Hants
Tod, Andrew	United Secession	Ballino
Todd, Simpson	Baptist	Ashton-under-Lyne
Tooke, T. H.	Independent	Clifton
Todd, John	Baptist	Carwent
Townend, Joseph	Meth. Association	New Mills
Townend, Thomas	Wesleyan Asso.	Leeds
Townley, H.	Independent	Finsbury Circus, London
Tunnicliffe, T.	Baptist	Longford
Tunstall, J.	Independent	Liverpool
Turner, James	Independent	Knutsford
Turner, W.	Independent	Hindley
Underhill, John	Baptist	Liverpool
Vardy, Charles F.	Independent	Hounslow.
Vaughan, R., D.D.	Independent	Kensington, London
Verrall. George	Independent	Bromley, Kent
Wadsworth, J.	Independent	Clitheroe
Waite, Richard	Primitive Meth.	Barnoldswick
Walker, J. W.	Christian Church	Hyde
Ward, Richard	Baptist	Clough Fold, Rawtenstall
Ward, John	Independent	Hexham
Ward, Samuel	Baptist	Calverton
Wassell, D.	Baptist	Bath
Watts, J.	Baptist	Coventry
Watts, J.	Baptist	Wootton-under Edge
Watts, H.	Meth. New Con.	Macclesfield
Watson, G. N.	Independent	Belfast
Watson, J. S.	Independent	Westbury
Watkins, William	Independent	Ryhmney Iron Works
Watmough, Edwin	Methodist Asso.	Manchester
Waterhouse, Thomas	Meth. New Con.	Dewsbury
Weaver, R.	Independent	Mansfield

Webb, Samuel	Baptist	Oadby
Webb, J.	Baptist	Arnsby, near Leicester
Wells, G. H.	Unitarian	Gorton
West, John	Independent	London
Wessley, George	Baptist	Devizes
Wheeldon, John	Independent	Manchester
Whittenbury, John	Independent	Liverpool
Whitewood, Samuel	Baptist	Halifax
White, Robert	Baptist	Hillsby, Gloucestershire
Whitehead, James	Unitarian	Ainsworth
Whitworth, C.	Independent	Manchester
Wigg, S.	Baptist	Leicester
Williams, D.	Independent	Kingswood
Williams, Edward	Welsh Baptist	Manchester
Williams, J. E.	Unitarian	Belper
Williams, David	Independent	Kingswood
Williams, William	Baptist	Weston
Williams, Robert	Calvinistic Metho.	Manchester
Williamson, Joseph	Independent	Horton-in-Craven
Wilson, S. Sheridan	Independent	Shepton Mallet
Wilson, James	Meth. New Con.	Stockport
Wilson, Alexander	Baptist	Sunderland
Winder, John	Independent	Edgworth
Winterbottom, J.	Baptist	Haworth
Wiseman, J.	Independent	Wick, N. B.
Wood, John	Baptist	Mansfield
Wolfenden, Richard	Inghamite	Todmorden
Wolstenholme, Joseph	Meth. Association	Sunderland
Wolstenholme, Robert	Independent	Carlisle
Worrall, J.	Meth. Association	Blackburn
Wright, Edward	Wesleyan Asso.	Clitheroe
Wright, D.	Baptist	Coseley
Yates, W.	Baptist	Stroud
Young, John	Baptist	Andover, Hampshire
Young, D.	Scotch Secession	Liverpool
Young, John	Scotch Secession	Catrine

The following Ministers signified their intention to attend, but were, from various causes, prevented.

Adams, H. L.	Independent	Newark-upon-Trent
Austin, James		Bradford
Adamson, J.	Independent	Charlesworth
Blow, —	Baptist	Brecon
Burns, R., D.D.	Scotch Church	Paisley
Burke, T. V., D.S.D.	Catholic	Drogheda
Blyth, A. T.		Bristol
Bateman, C. H.	Methodist	Kendal
Bond, James		Marsden
Barker, Thomas		Eccleshill
Bean, Henry	Independent	Heckmondwicke
Cockin, John	Independent	Holmfirth
Cunningham, M.		Chedworth
Causley, Stephen		Allerton
Chamberlain, R.	Independent	Swanage

Campbell, John, D.D.	Independent	London
Cousins, T.	Independent	King's Stanley
Dallas, John	Establishment	Manchester
Davies, T.	Baptist	Stockport
Davies, S. A.	Independent	Enfield
Dalton, T.		Addington
Davies, D. W.		Darlaston
Eckett, R.	Methodist Asso.	London
Ferguson, R.	Sailor's Society	London
Gregory, S.	Baptist	Bayswater
Glanville, J.		Prescot
Griffiths, J. W.	Baptist	Carnarvon
Ginetty, W.		London
Gallsworthy, T.		Roslewell
Griffith, D.		Long Buckley
Hewlett, A.	Establishment	Astley
Hughes, James		Dowlas
Harper, Josh.		Alston
Hawkins, W.	Baptist	Shrewsbury
Heugh, H., D.D.	Scotch Secession	Glasgow
Jackson, W H.		Macclesfield
James, Thomas	Independent	Woolwich
James, Robert		Glastonbury
Jones, J. A.	Baptist	London
Leifchild, J., D.D.	Independent	London
Lindsay, W.	Scotch Relief	Perth
Miall, E.	Independent	London
Martin, T.		Malmsbury
M'Evoy, John	Catholic	Genshill
M'Farlane, —		London
Murtagh, R. J.	Catholic	Kilcullen
Morrell, S.	Independent	Little Badow
Mayer, Thomas		Newcastle
Marshall, A.	Scotch Secession	Kirkintilloch
Newnes, J. M.	Independent	Matlock
Powell, D.	Independent	Nailsworth
Porter, S. T.	Independent	Darwen
Pryce, —	Baptist	Abingdon
Pearson, T. W.	Methodist Asso.	Carlisle
Pearce, —		Wrexham
Reed, A., D.D.	Independent	London
Robertson, J.		Wallsend
Russell, W.	Primitive Methodist	Stroud
Rees, W.	Baptist	Llanelly
Swan, R.	Scotch Relief	Bonhill, N. B.
Smith, Thomas	Baptist	Staley Bridge
Sheppard, J. B.		Bury
Spiller, Charles	Baptist	Eccles
Thomson, R.	Baptist	Perth
Thomas, Micah	Baptist	Abergavenny
Whitby, John	Independent	Ipswich
Waddington, John	Independent	Stockport
White, John	Independent	Northowram
Worrall, M.	Meth. Association	Blackburn

LIST OF THE OFFICERS OF THE CONFERENCE.

PRESIDENTS OF THE FOUR DAYS.

Tuesday.—Rev. Thomas Adkins, of Southampton.
Wednesday.—Rev. William Chaplin, of Bishop's Stortford, Hertfordshire.
Thursday.—Rev. F. A. Cox, LL.D., D.D., of Hackney.
Friday.—Rev. Thomas Spencer, A.M., of Hinton, Bath.

SECRETARIES.

Rev. J. W. Massie, M.R.I.A., Salford.
Rev. William M'Kerrow, Manchester.
Rev. Richard Fletcher, Manchester.
Rev. William Bevan, Liverpool.

EXECUTIVE COMMITTEE.

SUB-COMMITTEES.

Sub-Committee of Resolutions, to prepare Propositions, Motions, Addresses, &c.—The Revs. R. Fletcher, Manchester (secretary); T. Scales, Leeds; J. Acworth, Bradford, Yorkshire; J. Kelly, Liverpool.

Sub-Committee to communicate with Gentlemen of the Press, to conduct the Publication, &c.—The Revs. J. W. Massie, Manchester (secretary); Dr. Clunie, Manchester; J. M'Farlane, Glasgow; J. Carlisle, London; T. G. Lee, Manchester.

Sub-Committee of Documents, Statistics, &c.—The Revs. W. M'Kerrow, Manchester (secretary); J. Gwyther, ditto; Dr. Payne, Exeter; A. Harvey, Glasgow; J. Robertson, Edinburgh; A. Baird, Paisley; J. Burder, Stroud; T. Thomas, Pontypool; J. G. Miall, Bradford.

Sub-Committee of Executive, to whom were referred all Matters of Difficulty arising during the Sittings of the Conference.—The Revs. J. W. Massie (secretary); W. Shuttleworth, J. L. Poore, J. Thornton, J. Griffin, F. Beardsall.

STANDING COMMITTEE.

To effect Resolutions of Conference and watch Proceedings,—
The Presidents.—The Secretaries.

The Revs. Robt. Vaughan, D.D., Kensington; J. H. Hinton, M.A., London; J. Carlisle, Hackney; J. Beard, D.D., Manchester; John M'Gilchrist, Edinburgh; James Robertson, Edinburgh; Alex. Harvey, Glasgow; Thomas Pullar, Glasgow; James Gwyther, Manchester; F. Beardsall, Manchester; T. G. Lee, Manchester; and N. M. Harry, London.

PROCEEDINGS.

TUESDAY, AUGUST 17.

At about twenty minutes past ten, the Rev. Richard Fletcher, of Manchester, announced, that the order intended to be adopted with respect to their arrangements was, to appoint a provisional committee, who would select from the gentlemen present the different committees, the chairmen, and officers which would be required in the conference. He would then move, in the first instance, that Dr. Cox be called to the chair provisionally.

The Rev. Francis Beardsall, of Manchester, seconded the motion, which was carried by acclamation.

The Rev. William M'Kerrow, of Manchester, then read the names of the following ministers, which he moved as the provisional committee: —The Revs. Thomas Spencer, A.M., Bath; Dr. Beard, Manchester; James Gwyther, Hulme; James Griffin, Manchester; J. Peters, Rochdale; Dr. Halley, Manchester; William Fraser, Bolton; J. H. Hinton, London; R. W. Hamilton, Leeds; W. Bevan, Liverpool; William Shuttleworth, Manchester; D. Hearne, Manchester; J. L. Poore, Salford; F. Beardsall, Manchester; T. G. Lee, Manchester; John Thornton, Stockport; Francis Skinner, Blackburn; William Chaplin, Bishop's Stortford; Thomas Scales, Leeds; J. G. Pike, Derby; and John Sibree, Coventry.

The Rev. J. Gwyther seconded the motion.

The Rev. P. Brewster, of Paisley, said, he was not aware that the list contained the name of any gentleman from Glasgow, a most important locality; and therefore he would propose that the name of Mr. Harvey, of the Relief connection, be added to the provisional committee.

Mr. M'Kerrow—Permit me to state, that this committee is to retire for the purpose of considering what committees are necessary, and who are to be the gentlemen to act on them.

The proposed list was then put from the chair, and adopted.

The Rev. H. Townley suggested that the provisional committee should be empowered to nominate themselves.

The Rev. J. W. Massie said, the suggestion was not overlooked in the preliminary arrangements.

The provisional committee having then retired,

The Rev. William M'Kerrow, of Manchester, addressed the meeting as follows:—The Manchester committee of arrangements have done every thing they possibly could for the accommodation of their brethren and fathers assembled on the present occasion. ("Hear," and applause.) We are well aware, however, that in consequence of the very great number who arrived at a late hour last night, there must have been some mistakes committed; and I have now to announce, that we shall be most happy to remedy any mistakes which have occurred, and to make our friends who are strangers here as comfortable as we can during the period of the Conference. Out of about fifteen hundred replies we have received to our invitations, there have been only *six* decidedly opposed to the object. (Hear, and applause.) There have been about an equal number who have expressed hesitation with respect to the manner. (Hear, and applause.) But the vast remainder have cordially agreed in the important objects, as we consider them to be, which we have in view, and in our proposed conference. We have been disappointed by the absence of some distinguished individuals whom we had expected,—gentlemen who had intimated to us their resolution to be present. They have uniformly said, however, that they should be with us in spirit. Amongst those who cannot be present on account of ill health, are the Rev. J. Angel James, of Birmingham; Dr. Leifchild, of London; Dr. Heugh, of Glasgow; Dr. Andrew Reed, of London; and also Mr. Marshall, of Kirkintilloch. Dr. Wardlaw, of Glasgow, has been detained in consequence of his son's indisposition. I have selected a few letters with which to occupy your time during the period the committee is engaged down stairs. The first is from Dr. Reed, Hackney:—

"Hackney, August 13th, 1841.

"My dear Friend,—I deeply, deeply regret, that I cannot be with you. When I wrote you last, I expressed the fear of its being out of my power to be present at the Conference; but, on reflection, it appeared of so much importance, that I resolved, if possible, to bend circumstances to the occasion; but Providence has crossed my path, and forbidden me. I have been confined to a sick chamber these four days; and my surgeon says, that it is a physical impossibility for me to visit Manchester next week.

"Will you kindly explain the reason of my absence, as it may be necessary? Will you be assured, and assure others, that I am entirely present with you in spirit? Nothing, in my judgment, is so important at the present time as a right movement, on the great subject before you, to the moral, religious, and social interests of the whole people. Now that we are committed to a meeting, be sure to have a good one; I mean good and efficient in its results. In so great a service, should not the first day be given to fasting and prayer? May the hand of God be with you.—I am, my dear sir, yours most truly,

"ANDREW REED."

We have already published a letter from Dr. Wardlaw; but it is more than probable that the great majority of our friends here may not have had an opportunity of reading that letter, (hear,) and therefore I beg leave to read it now:—

"Barlanark, August 10th, 1841.

"My dear Sir,—I beg pardon of yourself and the committee, that even a second notice, which ought not to have been even required, should be still unanswered. The plain truth is, that I was very reluctant to say no; yet I could not, with any certainty, say yes. And now, I am sincerely sorry that the former monosyllable must be my answer. The answer should have been given in the end of last week, but that I was then occupied with the mournfully pleasing duty of preparing the funeral sermon for the late venerated and lamented Mr. Ewing. Not only do I feel duties of a public nature pressing upon me and demanding fulfilment—duties which I only can do, while there are multitudes to do the other, who may not happen at the time to be thus bound; but circumstances of a domestic character, which you can partly guess, but which I need not now detail, seem to require my being at home.

"I should deeply feel, however, that great injustice was done me, were my absence suspected to arise from any indifference respecting the great object of the proposed convention. It is not so. It is far, very far otherwise. Some of my brethren call it a political question, and object to a ministerial convention respecting it on this ground. That should not frighten me. Admitting it to be a question of political legislation, I cannot, on that account, regard it as the less a question of humanity. Granting it to be a problem of political economy, I dare not allow myself to forget, to what a vast extent it is a question of domestic economy, most seriously and fearfully affecting the condition of myriads of families, and the families too of those who must ever be the staple of a commercial nation's strength and prosperity. In such a view of it, it can never be out of the legitimate sphere of the servants of that Saviour who, while the great end of his mission was "to seek and to save the lost," manifested, in the fulfilling of that commission, so benevolent a concern for the temporal, as well as the spiritual interests of a sinful and suffering world; the one in such harmonious and beautiful keeping with the other. And why should the political aspect of the question overpower the interest which, as ministers of the gospel, we ought to feel in it as a question of humanity? Politics themselves are a branch of ethics. Properly viewed, they are the morals of nations. They affect the character and the well-being of the world. Indifference to politics, in this view of them, is indifference to their results—peace or war—plenty or starvation—virtue or vice—prosperity or declension—security to person, property, and life, or the jeopardy of them all. Surely such indifference cannot be a feature of character which the Bible requires, either in Christian man or in Christian minister. I am no meddler with politics; but my simple reason is, that, in doing what I can to diffuse the influence of Bible truth, and co-operating with fellow-christians and fellow-ministers in the endeavour to leaven the community with its influence, I am doing what I conceive to be my proper part in promoting and ensuring rectitude of principle in the management of public affairs; not that I regard the management of public affairs as a matter with which, as a minister of the cross, I have no concern. Although holding the essential distinction between the kingdom of Christ and the kingdoms of this world, I yet believe and am sure, that the spread and prevalence of the principles of the one are the best security for the application of right principles in conducting the affairs of the other.

"Your avowed object, moreover, is consultation;—the comparing of both sides;—the hearing of the *pros* and *cons*. Attendance pledges no one to a side. This is fair play. Excuse all this prosing. I am anxious that my absence from the conference may not be misunderstood. May a right spirit pervade all your deliberations, and divine wisdom and goodness grant a happy result!

"With best wishes to your associates, as well as to yourself, believe me, my dear sir, yours faithfully,

"RALPH WARDLAW."

"To the Rev. J. W. Massie, &c. &c."

The next letter is from Dr. Balmer, one of the professors of theology in the United Secession Church of Scotland:—

"Berwick, July 31st, 1841.

"My dear Sir,—In reply to your circular, permit me to say, that I approve most cordially of the object of the Convention of Ministers, to be held in Manchester, next month; but that my official duties in Edinburgh at that time will prevent my attendance. Hoping that the proceedings of the Convention will be conducted with Christian wisdom and firmness, and will be productive of much good—I am, my dear sir, yours sincerely,

"ROBT. BALMER."

He then said he would also read a portion of a letter from the Rev. W. M. Bunting. ("Read the whole.") He must call on gentlemen to entrust him with a discretionary power in this matter; and he read an extract, as follows:—

"I beg very respectfully to decline the invitation with which you have honoured me to join the ensuing Conference of Christian ministers on the subject of the corn laws. I hope I rightly estimate the pious and humane impulse which has led you to summon such a convention, and cordially sympathise in so much of your design as respects the relief of the suffering poor of our country. You will permit me to add, that the general principles so admirably embodied in Dr. Wardlaw's answer, of which I have been favoured with a copy, have long been, and will ever be, mine. But I am not able to bring within the range of those purely Christian polities, into which it is the peculiar duty of Christian ministers to interfere a much-disputed fiscal question."

There was also, Mr. M'Kerrow continued, a long letter from Dr. Chalmers, of which he would read a portion, as the letter would be referred to a committee, who would probably report upon it hereafter. He then read as follows:—

"I have read the various communications which you have done me the honour of sending, and deem them altogether worthy, not only of the most respectful attention, but of a full and explicit reply. The proposal is, that the attention of the religious public should be immediately directed to the subject of the corn laws; and that, for the furtherance of this object, a convention should forthwith be held in Manchester of the ministers of all denominations, from all parts of the United Kingdom. In your address to the moderator and other clergymen of the established Church of Scotland, among other arguments for their consent and co-operation in the prosecution of this design, you have referred to my own views upon the question, and have reported, with perfect accuracy, a sentiment to which I gave utterance some ten years ago, and which is still unchanged, that, for the sake of its moral benefit, I know of no achievement more urgently desirable than that of a free corn trade. This is the first sentence of an article on the corn laws subjoined to my work on political economy. On the perusal of the whole article, it will become obvious that I place on the foreground the *moral* benefit which would ensue from their abolition, because I look on the *material* benefit of the measure as insignificant, or as but temporary in its duration, and limited in its amount."

The Rev. W. Gadsby said, he had felt a little astonished that, in an assembly of that nature, seeking the benefit of starving thousands, it should not be introduced by prayer. To him it seemed a shame, as professed ministers of the gospel, not to think it worth while to call upon God to bless them.

A Minister said, he thought, as ministers, that on all questions that were deemed of importance to bring them together, they should acknowledge God.

The Rev. E. H. Nolan observed that, the importance of imploring the divine blessing was not overlooked. As one of the Manchester ministers, he felt it his duty to say, that, in previous meetings of the ministers, this subject had been considered; and that when the gentlemen composing the provisional committee had returned, and the meeting was regularly commenced, the proceedings would be introduced with prayer, or any other means they might think proper. The subject had been previously under the serious consideration of gentlemen in Manchester, and he had no doubt the gentlemen below were considering the matter while he was speaking. The subject would be decided when the temporary committee came before the meeting.

The Chairman said, in his mind the series of engagements to which they had devoted themselves should commence with prayer. He was told, however, that prayer would most likely be the course proceeded in, when the gentlemen who were appointed on the committee returned to the Conference. He confessed that this appeared to him a situation so serious, and the Conference, consisting of ministers of different denominations, so important, that it would be in perfect harmony with that meeting, and that preliminary meeting too, that they should engage in prayer. If it were important that they should present themselves before the throne of Divine Majesty, when, as it was said, they regularly commenced their proceedings, he saw no reason, convened as they now were, and while their committee was sitting, they should not in this instance, and while other business was preparing, first begin their work in prayer to God in that feeling of harmony in this object, which he trusted pervaded that assembly, for that blessing from on high without which nothing could prosper. He then called upon the Rev. Dr. Vaughan to engage in prayer.

The Rev. Dr. VAUGHAN then engaged in prayer as follows:—Almighty God, we trust we feel it right to acknowledge thee in all our ways and proceedings, that without thy blessing nothing can be done, without thee nothing can be strong, nothing can be holy. We desire to thank thee for the encouragement we have given unto us to look unto thee in all perplexity for guidance, in all difficulty for support; and we now cast ourselves upon thy promised help towards those who ask the accomplishment of thy will in the employment of means according to that will. In His name to whose ministry we have been called, we bow in support of this faith. Through him we look also to thee for that help by means of which we may be enabled to argue the great questions that shall come under our consideration, so as to feel towards them as we ought, and to come to such conclusions as shall be for happiness to our country, and for the honour of thy name. O God! deliver us, we beseech thee, from all that disturbing influence of feeling that may not be in accordance with thy pleasure. Preserve to our minds calmness, bestow on us ability to look wisely on the matters that may come under our notice. May we be solicitous only for the light that may cause our views to be just and humane, and acceptable to thee, and to be the instruments in thy hands in removing somewhat of the misery pressing on thy people, and of securing to them the comforts which thou hast provided, but which, as we fear, man has intercepted from his fellow man. O God! grant there may be shed upon us, indeed, that light in which we shall find safety; and may we and our children look back upon these solemn scenes as scenes in which thy hand was with us. We are nothing, less than nothing. Make us, we beseech thee, wise to serve thee, strong to serve thee; and all that we have we cast at thy feet as the result of the influences which have descended from thee. We pray thee, O God! for thy blessing on all the interests of our country. Look on the minds of our people in all the classes and connections in which they exist before thee, and remove false conceptions; bestow right views upon those who may now be influenced by wrong views. Impart generosity of purpose where it may not now exist; and, amidst all the devices of man's heart, may we find that it is thy counsel, the counsel of the Lord, that does indeed stand. Look on those especially who may have the control of our affairs, and impart to our senators wisdom. Bestow on them a generous patriotism, which may cause them to be mindful of the wants of their fellow-men; and may all that may come to pass, when they gather together for deliberation, be found to work for our nation's welfare, and the honour of thy name. And we would desire to pour out the fervent sympathies of our hearts in prayer for thy blessing upon her majesty the Queen. O God! shed upon her every good and proper gift. Bestow upon her that goodness that may enable her to look upon the interests of her people, and bestow upon her heart all that generous solicitude that shall sustain her in her course, that may render her days memorable for the blessings which thy hand shall have connected with them, and which, by her instrumentality, may be transmitted to the ages to come. Forgive all our trespasses for the Redeemer's sake. Amen.

The Rev. E. H. NOLAN, of Manchester, thought it right to say, that, privileged as they were in the society of members of the Society of Friends, of Roman Catholic clergymen, and even, he believed, of dignitaries of that church, it might be that some held views different to the rest in reference to the commencement with prayer. (Hear.) The Manchester ministers, feeling the responsibility resting with them, had not introduced this, lest even a slight difference of opinion should exist. They were all happy at what had taken place; and confident that all would feel it was no want of spirituality on their part, but a mere feeling of responsibility resting upon them previously to the meeting being fully constituted.

The Rev. JAMES BLAIR, of Dunfermline, thought what was just said very excellent; but he would suggest that one hour be spent in prayer every morning. If it was agreed for the Conference to meet at ten, let the prayer meeting be at nine, or as the Conference might think proper.

The CHAIRMAN said, that as no one seconded that suggestion, he might say that the general feeling around him appeared to be, that it was most desirable to wait the communication of the committee already appointed, who would probably take this amongst other subjects into consideration.

The Rev. B. PARSONS, of Stroudwater, suggested that those who wished to engage in prayer might do so previously to the meetings of Conference; perhaps a chapel in the town might be obtained for the purpose, where those who agreed in sentiment might meet to pour forth prayers to the Almighty for his blessing to rest upon these meetings. No person who felt the least objection would attend, and thus it would meet the views of all parties.

The Rev. D. CRUMPTON, of Henley-in-Arden: I think one great means of preventing discussion would be, if, during the sitting of the committee below, some of the brethren present would engage in prayer.

Dr. VAUGHAN suggested, that, instead of discussing the question, it was better to wait until the temporary committee had returned, and made their report; after which it would be open to every gentleman to express an opinion on the subject.

After the lapse of a few minutes the committee returned, and—

The Rev. T. SPENCER, the chairman of the committee, said, they had unanimously resolved to elect the following gentlemen as chairmen successively during the following days of the meeting of conference:—Mr. Adkins, Mr. Chaplin, Dr. Cox, and Mr. Spencer. (Cheers.)

The Rev. Mr. MASSIE then read the following as the names of the committee: Mr. Bevan, of Liverpool; Mr. Scales, of Leeds; Mr. Brown, of Wareham; Mr. Hamilton, of Leeds; Mr. Acworth, of Bradford; Mr. Hinton, of London; Mr. James Carlisle, of London; Mr. Beardsall, of Manchester; Mr. Shuttleworth, of Manchester; Mr. Jones, of Bolton; Mr. Gwyther, of Hulme; Dr. Halley, of Manchester; Dr. Payne, of Exeter; Mr. Poore, of Salford; Mr. Barfett, of Salisbury; Mr. Somerville, of Dumbarton; Mr. Bowen, of Macclesfield; Mr. Kelly, of Liverpool; Mr. Giles, of Leeds; Mr. Laidler, of Harleston; Mr. Robinson, of Halifax; Mr. Roaf, of Wigan; Mr. Pike, of Derby; Dr. Redford, of Worcester; Mr. Roper, of Bristol; Profes. Walter Scott, of Airdale College; Mr. East, of Birmingham; Dr. Beard, of Manchester; Mr. Gadsby, of Manchester; Mr. Spencer, of Bath; Mr. Hearne, of Manchester; Mr. Nolan, of Manchester; Mr. Harvey, of Glasgow; Mr. Hutton, of Birmingham; and Mr. Baird, of Paisley, with power to add to their number.

The Rev. Mr. SPENCER: I was also resolved that the following gentlemen should be recommended as secretaries—Mr. Massie, Mr. M'Kerrow, Mr. Fletcher, and Mr. Bevan. I now beg to move, "That the proceedings of the provisional committee be confirmed by the conference."

Dr. VAUGHAN seconded the proposition.

The Rev. W[illegible]LES: Gentlemen, in the list of names that has been read, I have not perceived the name of any gentleman from Preston. Ours is a large town, and there is a respectable independent minister present from that locality, the Rev. Mr. Slate, whose name I beg leave to move be added to the list.

The Rev. Mr. MASSIE: The committee appointed have power to add to their number. It has been arranged, that they should divide themselves into sub-committees,—one to be a committee of resolutions and addresses, another a committee of documents, another an executive committee, and the fourth a committee for publication. (Applause.)

The Rev. Mr. SPENCER: In consequence of an error in the writing, one of the chairmen of the Conference has been announced as Mr. Fox, instead of Dr. Cox. (Applause, and some laughter.)

The CHAIRMAN said, that the motion was, that the report presented by the provisional committee be adopted. It passed unanimously, on which Dr. Cox vacated the chair; and—

The Rev. THOS. ADKINS, of Southampton, took the chair, when the proceedings commenced *seriatim*. He said, in opening the business,—Men, brethren, and fathers, accustomed as I am to meet the public eye, having often been placed, during the course of a public life that did not begin yesterday, in circumstances that have required nerves of firmer texture than my own to bear, you will allow me to say, that at no period of my by-gone existence have I felt myself to be placed in a situation more tremendously responsible than that in which, by your unmerited, but, at the same time, highly flattering suffrages, I am at this moment. (Applause.) Called upon most unexpectedly, and as you will allow me to say, most undeservedly, to fill this important situation; being also from that very circumstance thoroughly unprepared to address you in a clear consecutive manner, I can only throw myself upon your Christian kindness and forbearance, and, at the same time, I look up to Heaven for strength above my own. Gentlemen, the history, the ecclesiastical history of the world, presents us with a numerous succession of synods and of councils, assemblies of ministers of religion for various purposes, with "all the pomp and circumstance" attending those events; but will you allow me to say, that the meeting of this morning is unprecedented and unparalleled? (Hear.) What, when I look up, do I see? I must confess that my heart thrills with unwonted feelings, as I see hundreds, many hundreds, of ministers of the religion of Christ, representing every section of the universal church; many of them bearing names dear alike to learning and to piety, all of whom have trod with a greater or less degree of success in that humble but most important path of benefiting their fellow-creatures. I see them convened from every part of this extensive empire. And for what convened? Not to place themselves in hostile array, sect against sect, and party against party—(applause)—within the narrow lines of sectarian demarcation; not to hurl at each other the *brutum fulmen* of excommunication, placing the unhappy delinquent under the ban of exclusion in this world, and consigning him to final perdition in the world to come; not to harmonize the jarring shibboleths of conflicting creeds; but, men, brethren, and fathers, occupied and interested by an object greater than which can hardly enter into the mind of the most eminent Christians, but less than which cannot satisfy ours. (Loud applause.) We are met together, then, brethren and fathers, at the call of suffering humanity; (applause;) and that call reaching us, not across the briny ocean, but through the green valleys and the populous streets of our own native land. We are, I admit, met at the very outset of our procedure by a query, "What have Christians, and, more than all, Christian ministers, to do with temporal politics?" But I have yet to learn that, when we become denizens of that kingdom which is not of this world, we are to forego the immunities and to forget the duties that relate to the present life. (Hear.) I have yet to learn how, when we begin to be Christians, we cease to be men. (Hear.) Admitting, as I cheerfully do, that Christianity, taking man in his actual condition, elevates him to a nobler sphere, and, in proportion to the vigour and intensity of its operation, makes him a blessing to the country in which he lives,—

I have yet to learn that that Christianity which is adapted by its divine Author, not only to the mental and moral, but also to the social constitution of our nature, denies to us the exercise of those social principles by which "heart is bound to heart, man linked to man." (Applause.) Besides, brethren, if this principle were applicable to a part of the community, it must be applicable to the whole; (hear;) for the precepts of Christianity are not partial or local; and the consequence would be, if carried to its legitimate extent, that civil government, with all its complexity of interests,—that questions of political economy, interweaving themselves with all that distinguishes and elevates man, as an accountable and immortal being,—I say, the consequence would be, that civil government—a question by far the most momentous that can occupy the attention of man as a citizen of this world, while performing his part as a probationer for the world to come—must be left to the hands of men of professed infidelity, or of mere men of the world; (hear;) a proposition so monstrous that it requires only to be stated in order to be scouted. For myself, men, brethren, and fathers, (and you must allow me to throw myself upon your paternal and fraternal feelings in the manner I do,) for myself, I must aver that, though during the lapse of more than a quarter of a century, of which my public life has consisted, I have stood aloof, sensitively aloof, and, as some persons may imagine, guiltily so, from the arena of political disputation, I do feel-that this heart would have been a recreant, not only to the cause of humanity, but to the cause of religion, if in the present instance I had not obeyed the summons to come to your crowded town, and in the second place have preferred my own private conviction to your expressed wishes, in occupying this important post. But, not to occupy you longer with any prefatory remarks; not to anticipate the observations which will be elicited to a greater extent, and adorned with far greater beauty, than those to which I can give utterance, I must, for the moment, call your attention to the actual position in which we are placed. (Hear.) Here is a country, and that country dear to every one's heart, because it is our own; (applause;) a country great in arts and great in arms; the school of science and literature, the mart of industry, the cradle of luxury, the emporium of the moral world; occupying a high position amidst surrounding nations, while, from her lofty brow streams of light and glory extend to distant lands; and yet, gentlemen, this country, possessing within itself inexhaustible resources, whilst it is the wealthiest of all countries, is, in one sense of the word, the poorest of all. (Hear.) It possesses within itself inexhaustible means for carrying, to an indefinite extent, the manufactures by which it is distinguished; "its merchants are princes," who, with noble adventureship, have launched their gallant vessels for every coast where commerce can win its way; aye, and here is a population, composed of the most energetic, ingenious labourers of those that compose the vast family of man; instinct with irrepressible ardour, capable of doing all that ingenuity can devise, or unyielding energy can carry into effect. And what, after all, is the condition of this land? Why, look around! You see our looms are silent; our manufactories are closed; our commercial men are looking each other in the face with consternation and dismay; (hear;) our poor, our artisans, and our peasants, an integral part of our national self, and what are they? Why, their lank arms hang idly by their sides; their grim visages are pallid with privation, and their care-worn forms are but the skeletons of men. (Hear, and applause.) And now, brethren, what do we fancy is the actual cause of this? (Hear, hear, hear.) I am not prejudging the discussion of this question; but the very fact that we are convened to consider a particular question will, I presume, permit me to say what we conceive is the cause. On the other side of the water is a land in which, either from the paucity of its population, or the fertility of its soil, there is bread enough and to spare. There they have the *pabulum* of life, sufficient to repay the labour of industry, and to supply the wants of necessity. Yes, gentlemen, for while I would use caution, I will not indulge in cowardice; (applause;) yes, gentlemen, and your starving population is willing to purchase that *pabulum* of life; not, indeed, with wealth, for, like the poor disciples of a poorer Master, they shake their tattered garments, and say, "Silver and gold we have none;" but they are willing to purchase food with the well-strained sinews of nervous industry, (applause,) with the sweat of their honest brows. (Hear, hear.) And why cannot they purchase that? Why is there not the working out of that simple, but no less effectual, arrangement in the economy of the universe, by which the various productions of one country may be reciprocated with advantage, by communications made from another? Why is this machinery, so simple in its construction, but so multifarious, and withal so benign in its results, why is it retarded? Pardon me if I say, it is because we see, or think we see, a busy, bungling hand, a cruel and clumsy hand, put on this delicate machinery, to retard its movements, and to frustrate its designs. (Applause.) We believe this, men, brethren, and fathers, or our convocation here this day is but a nullity and a farce. (Hear.) And how are these evils to be removed, but by removing that pressure that retards the advancement of this simple machinery, and frustrates its benevolent purposes? In a word, by seeking, not by clamour, not by political agitation, but by such means as men, as Britons, as Christians, and as Christian ministers—means equally scriptural and constitutional—we are permitted to employ. (Applause.) Now, brethren, the working out of this, its practical effect, whilst it may be anticipated in theory, will be stated to a greater or less extent, by those who, in the course of these most important meetings, will address you. Allow me, however, to say, that the prospective sagacity of many a gifted and holy man in the present assembly has seen the storm gathering on our political horizon. The cloud has been portentous and dark; it has gradually overspread our heavens; its advance is indicated by the low murmur of dissatisfaction, or the sullen groan of despair. (Hear.) And for what purpose are we convened? Why, that cloud contains a fiery element, which, like the element in nature to which we have referred, often strikes ere it is seen; (hear;) and always withers when it strikes; (hear;) and we are met, men, brethren, and fathers, not to swell the tumult and to increase the storm, but to give a conductor, a happy conductor, by which that electric fire, so vivid in its flight, and so tremendous in its consequences, may pass harmlessly by, (applause,) and, instead of devastating one of the fairest spots in this lower world, allow the agitated and sulphureous air to subside into quietude and purity. (Applause.) I have to apologize for the length of time that I have occupied your attention. ("Go on.") I have no less to thank you—which I do with the same sincerity with which I have yearned over the miseries of our desolated land—I have to thank you for the particular attention with which you have listened to these preliminary and general remarks. And now, will you allow me to say, that I have a request to prefer to you,—a request which I prefer in the name of the suffering millions whose cause we are met to consider, and whose woes we are desirous to relieve,—a request which I prefer in the name of our mother country, whose maternal bosom is heaving at this moment with unearthly throes. Nay, I go a step further, and I say, in the name of that adorable Being whose name is above every name—in that name which to all of us, whatever may be the distinctive features of our religious character, is professedly the common bond of our union, and the common centre of repose to our guilty and throbbing hearts,—in that name I do beseech you, that, in the conducting of the important, proceedings which concentrate in themselves the attention of the country in which we live—(for all eyes at this moment are fixed upon Manchester, and upon the scenes in which it is about to engage),—I say, then, in his name, and for his sake, I do entreat you to avoid, as much as possible, all that may commit you to a distinctive line of party politics, (hear, hear,) all that may compromise you in the eyes of the world, or discredit you as not being influenced by the unswerving principles of him whose gospel is peace—"peace to him that is afar off, and to him that is nigh." I do hope—and these are my concluding words, and they are the result of sober and earnest prayer—I do hope that such may be the case with respect to you. I do beseech you, men, brethren, and fathers, to blend in yourselves all that is intrepid and unflinching in principle, with all that is bland in a conciliating spirit; and to superadd to the courage of a lion, also the gentleness of a lamb. (Loud applause.)

Dr. Pye Smith then rose to address the meeting, but was interrupted by—

Dr. Vaughan, who wished to know if Dr. Smith intended to speak to the question as to the manner in which the proceedings should be opened.

Dr. Smith said, he was sure there could be but one opinion on that subject. He regretted to state that his hearing was so imperfect that (except through the kindness of a dear friend who wrote for him) he was perfectly incapable of understanding any thing that was said. He could not, consequently, take any part in the proceedings of a deliberative assembly. But, as he was informed before he came to the meeting that he would be expected to say something at the commencement of the business on the propriety of such a meeting, he had arranged a few thoughts for the purpose. He felt, however, that he could not trust himself, were he to attempt to speak in his ordinary manner; he feared his feelings would betray him, and that he should be in danger both of failing to say what he wished, and of becoming unduly prolix. He would, therefore, cast himself on the candour and charity of his friends while he read a few words which he had prepared. (Cheers.) The venerable doctor then proceeded as follows:—I feel myself deeply obliged to those Christian ministers, and other friends to their country and to mankind, who devised and have convened this meeting. I am sure, also, that my brethren who have come from their homes, and intermitted their sacred labours upon this occasion of solemn and imperative demand, will unite with me in acknowledging the ready hospitality with which so large a number of honourable families have welcomed us. We have come together in no capacity, assumed or implied, expressed or imagined, of authority. We are not a conclave, nor a synod, nor a convocation. We disclaim any pretension of a right to make laws or regulations, or any desire to bind the consciences of our fellow Christians, or to command their practice. We disclaim and abhor every thing that might savour of disaffection to our beloved sovereign and the constituted authorities of her realm, or of dictating measures to the legislature, or of fomenting discontent, or exciting to turbulence. We want to soothe, not to irritate; we look and seek, and pray to do good, and not evil; to promote harmony and beneficence, to invade no man's interest, to diminish no man's happiness, to "follow the things which make for peace, and things wherewith one may edify another." We have not assembled at the summons of any human authority. We are not here to do any man's biddings. We are not come to say with our tongues, or subscribe with our hands, any declaration or opinions with which our hearts do not accord. Our gathering together is the unforced act of each man's own will; and, so far from regarding this individual freeness of action as a circumstance to be regretted, we see in it an element of strength and success. We may apply to it, with eminent reason, the noble declarations of one of the most distinguished philosophers of our own or any other country, Professor Whewell, in his presidential address to the British Association, delivered not three weeks ago, at Devonport, July 29th. Speaking of efforts, by voluntary association, "to elevate and improve the condition of man," he recommended such efforts as "of that use, which, if we disregard, the condition of man forthwith becomes degraded, and his prospects a blank; of use in raising our thoughts and stimulating our exertions, so that we may become wiser, and better, and nobler, than we are. Is this a new doctrine?" asked the professor. "God be thanked," he replied, "in this country at least, it has long been familiar to men's minds, has been practically acted upon, and has been attended with the most blessed and glorious effects. Do we despair of great and good objects, because we live in a state of society where men act each for himself, unforced by supreme power? Feeling that we are free, and that it is our glorious privilege to act as free men, we attempt to realize our ideas, not by the power of the state, but by that power which, in such a state, and on such subjects, represents the conviction of the nation, *the power* of VOLUNTARY ASSOCIATION." We are come together as ministers and teachers of the Christian religion However diversely we may understand that religion, with respect to many, and those important points, of theological doctrine, and ecclesiastical order, in this we are all agreed, that true religion requires of us, and of all men, "to do justly and to love mercy," as well as "to walk humbly with our God;" we are all convinced that religion, virtue, and morality, cannot be separated from each other. We are drawn to this populous town, one of the most important in her majesty's dominions, one of the most vital and sensitive parts of the body politic, because we have heard "the voice of the cry of"—our country—"lamentation and bitter weeping; the harvest is past, the summer is ended, and we are not saved!" The cry of distress has pierced our souls. The woes of thousands and hundreds of thousands have demanded our sympathy. The fear of still greater evils has filled us with intense anxiety. We come to give vent to our fellow-feeling with the destitute and the sorrowful, and those that have no comforter. We come to raise a protest and a prayer on their behalf; and not more on their behalf, as a class of men, than on behalf of the rich and great; for we are convinced, that all the orders of society, however immeasurably diversified, have one common bond of interest; and that it is folly, as well as injustice, for any class to attempt to raise itself upon the depression, or in anywise the injury, of any other. But, while we disavow unfounded assumptions, we advance, indeed, a claim, but of a very different kind; we elevate another kind of authority,—the claim of reason and love; the authority of "the righteous Lord, who loveth righteousness," and whose servants we are, not for our own aggrandizement, but for the universal good of mankind. We are discharging an important and necessary part of our function as men consecrated to the teaching of religion, when we explain and enforce its nature and its obligations as demanding *universal righteousness*. We take our stand upon the foundation of both the law and the gospel, and we desire to impress every soul of man with the indispensable obligation of honestly obeying the divine commands, "That which is altogether just, thou shalt follow. All things whatsoever ye would that men should do to you, do ye even so to them. Whatsoever things are true, whatsoever things are honest, whatsoever are just, whatsoever are pure, whatsoever are lovely, whatsoever are of good report; if there be any virtue and if there be any praise, think on these things;" so think on them, as the undeniable meaning of the passage is, (ταυτα λογίζεσθε), as to *reason upon them*, understand them in their full comprehension, apply them fairly, and practise them faithfully. But we are impressed with the conviction that this great law of righteousness is contradicted and violated, and *rebellion* is thus perpetrated against the Majesty of heaven by doctrines and practices, which for many centuries have been current among nations civilized, or professing to be so, with regard to trade; that is, the interchange of commodities, the products of skill and industry, be tween the different families and tribes of mankind. The corn laws of our country have a deplorable pre-eminence in this class of unrighteous and suicidal legislation. They had their origin in the night of ignorant and barbarous ages; when men were trampled down by absurd and wicked monopolies and other usages, the outbreaks and badges of that insolent feudal tyranny which oppressed both nations and princes; and thus the human mind was abased to a low pitch of degradation; education and mental culture were extremely rare, knowledge and improvement had only a very slow and limited diffusion, and men in general were accustomed to respect no argument but that of brute force. The principle upon which those usages rested originally was merely the law of strength, the logic of the savage and the brute. Afterwards ingenious men set themselves to find out arguments in their favour; and this was the case, especially with respect to the corn laws, 500 years ago. Their fundamental error was a mistaken idea of independence The general ignorance, and the military spirit of the time, may justly account, and will apologize for the mistake, which was but a part of a gigantic system of prejudice and error. The advantages of any nation, tribe, or family, were viewed with jealousy and envy; were supposed to be at variance with the prosperity of every other; and rivalry, the most short-sighted and narrow-minded, was directed in all practicable ways, by each class of society against every other class. A candid apology may be made for our ancestors; but with us the case is different. Sound reasoning has long ago poured its light into this obscure region, especially from the time of the publication of Adam Smith's great work, "On the Nature and Causes of the Wealth of Nations." But practice has not kept pace with theory in this matter, as in many others. Prejudices of custom, ancient usages, and the blind alarm of misunderstood self-interest, have operated to this day to clog the wheels of improvement. But now we have the evidence of bitter experience to aid our convictions that those are not the doctrines of reason and truth, but of superficial thinking, and of that blind selfishness which is the very essence of SIN. The providence of God, by establishing the vast diversity of climate, soil, atmosphere, products of all kinds; and national capabilities, has abundantly demonstrated the intention that all the divisions of the human race should be *dependent* on each other. This is a constitution of the glorious Creator and Lord of all things, replete with wisdom and beneficence. In the giving and receiving of benefits, upon a system of unlimited progression, the evils of a rivalry founded on jealousy and enmity are made glaringly evident by the mutually hurtful consequences which spring from it; and, on the opposite side, kind affections are cherished, acts of friendship are called forth and encouraged, mutual rights are respected, justice is maintained, peace is loved and preserved, and WAR, that greatest scourge of mankind, the most prolific cause of guilt and misery, is seen in its pernicious character, and is disliked and avoided from the dictates of rational self-interest.—This course of sentiment and practice is most happily subservient to the great design of the gospel of our Lord Jesus Christ, which all real Christians believe and love, and whose first and indispensable lesson is, that we should "not bite and devour," but cordially love, and by love serve, one another: and this glorious gospel will not rest till it has shed its beams upon all nations; "and they shall beat their swords into ploughshares, and their spears into pruning hooks; nation shall not lift up sword against nation, and they shall learn war no more." Thus the doctrine and practice of *free trade* is in harmony with the essential principle and the benevolent design of the gospel. "Let nothing be done through strife or vain-glory; but, in lowliness of mind, let each esteem other better than themselves. Look not every man on his own things," his own selfish feelings and interests; "but every man also on the things of others," with a generous and liberal consideration. "See that none render evil for evil to any man; but ever follow that which is good. both among yourselves and to all men." To help forward this happy state of human relations, is the object for which we have here assembled. We do not flatter ourselves that our efforts can at once eradicate the prejudices and errors which are the growth of ages, or that we unaided can effect this desirable conviction in minds reluctant and inveterate. But these principles of morality are a part of "the whole counsel of God," which we are bound to teach, if we would be "faithful ministers of Christ." If we be supine and silent, we shall be partakers of the guilt of the evil that is so fearfully done; and we shall be answerable at the tribunal of God for its consequences. Some of those consequences, long foreseen and forewarned, have burst upon us in a manner, as to rapidity and extent, which may fill the stoutest heart with grief and fear. Are we not then called upon by our most solemn obligations, to oppose the evil which threatens to destroy us, and to promote the good which is so instrumental of temporal and spiritual benefit? The feelings which are now awakened, the attention which is widely excited, encourage our hopes. An opportunity is given for enforcing this branch of evangelical morals, with prospects of attention and success, greater than we have before possessed. What we have taught and inculcated in our own small circles, we hope, by means of this meeting, to lay before our countrymen in a way that will draw their more serious attention, and more effectually recommend the truth to their understandings and their hearts. Some persons may object, that this and its allied subjects belong to the science of politics and political economy, and that it is not befitting to the ministers of religion to give opinions or advice upon them. Against the spirit of this objection, I enter my determined protest. It can be advanced by only ignorance or unfairness. What are politics, but the knowledge and practice of the claims of *right* and the obligations of *duty* which belong to men as members of society? Is not this knowledge and practice an essential part of morality? And is there, can there be, any religion without morality? As teachers of religion, therefore, we are bound to be teachers of politics, and to guard the important subject against errors and abuses. Our object is to teach the politics which flow from piety, the politics of equitable benevolence, the politics of the gospel, the politics of Jesus Christ, our Saviour and Lord. We are deeply concerned that we and those to whom we minister should "render to all their due; putting to silence the ignorance of foolish men; as free, and not using our liberty for a cloak of maliciousness, but as the servants of God." We are most earnest to guard all persons, to the utmost of our power, against sedition, treason, rebellion, in any manner of degree, approach, or tendency. Be it also considered, that, while the people have their duties, they have also their claims, just and honourable claims; and that, if these be neglected, "the cries of the poor ascend' to the Just and Almighy One, who "will plead their cause." Also, to borrow the memorable admonition of a lamented Christian statesman—"property and rank have their rights, but they have likewise their duties." To the higher classes, therefore, even to the highest, we "have a message from God." But few of them will give us the opportunity of delivering it. They come not to our places of Christian worship; nor will they allow us to go to them, and tell them of "justice, temperance, and the judgment to come." Therefore, if we except, writing and publishing, an extraordinary measure, like this assembly is the only method left for our endeavouring to make the word of the Lord be heard in high places, as well as in low; in towers and palaces, and in the pits and cellars where want and woe, disease and death, and many a form of misery, have fixed their dwelling. It is the violation of religious obligation, by our laws and law-makers, which, working through a course of years, has at length come to a term. Those laws have now reached to an amount of oppression, injury, and aggravated cruelty, which can no longer be endured. The alternative is the abrogation of the iniquity, or the ruin of the nation. Wise and honest men, versed in the inseparable means of public prosperity, agriculture, manufactures and commerce, have long foretold this crisis. It has arrived. It brings in its train of terror bodily diseases which will not be confined to the hovel, but will spread over the land, and will mount to the most splendid mansions. A state of freedom from the extreme of misery is ordinarily necessary for the calm reflections and the exercises of piety; but that state is destroyed by hunger and destitution, winter's keen cold, which soon will arrive, famished families, and "the first-born of death." Desperation is engendered. The burning discontent cannot be always smothered. We are walking on the fires below. They threaten eruptions. Then will military execution renew its horrors; and the terrible catastrophe will befall us of a revolutionary anarchy, or a stern, revengeful, and unsparing tyranny. Ah! how little do the men reflect who have snatched the morsel of hope from the lips of the famishing millions, what retribution they have been preparing for themselves! In the event of a national convulsion (which Almighty mercy avert!) they will be among the first victims of infuriated revenge. In the righteous judgment of God often one terrible form of sin is the instrument of punishment to another. Measures proposed in the late parliament raised our hope of a blessed relief. We caught with joy and gratitude the gleams of a brightening dawn. But darkness has returned. Our hopes are dashed to the ground. "We looked for peace, but there is no good; for the time of healing, and behold, trouble." But, distressed as we are, and wounded to the heart, we would not yield to the sad forebodings which we cannot suppress: we would not, we will not, despair. We desire to show our brethren, our distressed and trembling countrymen, whose labours at the loom and in the factory are failing of their honest recompense, that there are some, there are many, who feel for them and with them, and would gladly employ any means in their power to administer encouragement and consolation. Our warm desire is, to see realized the beautiful passage of the book of Job, "So the poor hath hope, and iniquity stoppeth her mouth." We likewise indulge the hope, that the facts which will be detailed by the Christian ministers who can bear testimony to the state of the manufacturing and labouring poor, will, by their statements, be presented to the public notice in a manner which will obtain the merited attention of all classes, and in every part of the country. We cherish the hope that the evidence supplied by this meeting will avail to dissipate the pernicious errors which are current in some important circles, and which led one of the highest order of the peerage to say in parliament, that the efforts to obtain the abrogation of the corn laws, proceeded only from a few rich manufacturers, who wished to avoid giving just wages to their workmen. May the God of mercy grant, my honoured brethren, that your conversation, your resolutions, your holy example in the walks of daily life, your influence, and your *prayers*, may be efficacious for the averting of evil, and the acquisition of blessing, above all that we ask or think.

The Rev. J. W. Massie said, he had expected that the duty which he now rose to perform would have devolved upon another brother of the ministry in Manchester. He had consented to present himself on this occasion with considerable reluctance, yet not with so much reluctance as to cause any interruption in the proceedings which had been arranged. It was designed by those who had laboured, and, blessed be God, with success, to convene the ministers of religion on this occasion, to present to them, when so convened, the reasons of the Manchester ministers who had taken the lead on this subject, for soliciting the attendance of gentlemen from such distances, and for such a purpose. They did not anticipate that their revered friend, who had now addressed them, would have spoke prior to the explanation now to be given; but there was not one connected with the arrangements who did not rejoice that he (Dr. J. Pye Smith) had felt at liberty thus to address them, following up the eloquent and fervid appeal of their distinguished chairman by the clearness of his expositions, and the depth of his inquiries. He (Mr. Massie) had felt regret that, as he proceeded, it was not likely every person present heard all that Dr. Pye Smith said; but he had this consolatory assurance, that, as it was in manuscript, every eye would see it, and every heart would feel it and would echo it through the uttermost parts of our land, carrying truth and persuasion to the mind of the intelligent and the reflective in all classes of people in the country. It was felt that there was now a crisis in regard to the restrictions which exist by law on the food of the community, both as those restrictions operated to the destruction of our foreign commerce, and to the injury of our home manufacture. The ministers who suggested the convocation of their brethren in this conference, were convinced that there was something that became those who went in and out, not alone through the dwellings of the rich, but many times oftener among the abodes of the poor, to sympathize with them in their poverty, and ask relief for them when they were oppressed; that it was not enough merely to say, "Be ye warmed, and be ye clothed," and to neglect the means of enabling them to enjoy such comforts; but that any thing which they could do, it was not only their duty to do, but that now was the time to do it. They said *now*, because, from circumstances to which he need not here refer, but which they would understand, the question of free trade had been made a subject of national consideration; and because, through certain influences, there had not been that response from the country on the question which might have been anticipated, and which the benefactors of their race had earnestly desired. The conclusion had been forcibly impressed on the minds of the movers in this conference, and had been by some of *them* anticipated for months and years, that it was necessary, before the settlement of the great questions involved in free trade in the article of food could be effected,—it was necessary that the sympathy of the religious world should be brought into co-operation with the mere political economist, or with those who were regarded as selfish in the question. They looked to the effect of such an amalgamation on the question of negro slavery, and in redeeming from bondage the myriads of the African race who had been unrighteously enthralled. They regarded the proceedings of these generous philanthropists and enlightened Christians, so allied on that occasion, as fully compatible with their profession as ministers of religion; and, though now and then some of them were evil spoken of through it, and they were asked what authority they had to interfere, their exertions had been blessed by millions of their brethren, and would be by generations yet unborn. Feeling it was so in reference to that question, it might be so with reference to this. They felt assured that, if the same energies were devoted to this cause, the same result would follow, if they only *wrought justice*, if they only *loved mercy*, and only desired to *walk humbly with their God*. And it was on this ground, and this ground alone, that they had been convened. An objection to interfere might have arisen in the minds of some, because they were ministers of religion. They knew that it had been a matter long debated, whether ministers of religion should enter into politics; but, as had been said, *politics were but the morals of nations*. and those were only discharging a moral duty, who sought to understand and diffuse the knowledge of right principles in national politics, that the obligations which they involved might be discharged. It might be objected, that ministers of religion were here *alone* assembled in this convocation; but reasons were not wanting to authorise the experiment. The apprehension was not without force that, if delegates, who were laymen, were invited from different communions, there would be introduced party politics, or the peculiar views of political economists; and that there would not be that condensation, that concentration, and thorough singleness of object, sought for by those who invited this conference. They concluded still further, that the delegates from such a mixed convention would not have so much influence in this generous enterprise as was hoped for from a more unique and united assembly; but that, going forth in this divided character, the effect of the conference would be comparatively diminished. (Hear hear.) Such were their considerations, and such were their reasons for calling them together. They had invited ministers of religion under every Christian name. They excluded none bearing that name. They had openly and distinctly invited all; and, when they could not reach them by their circulars, they had sought to gain them by public advertisement. They rejoiced to be able to testify, that not fewer than 650 ministers had responded with a generous warmth and a ready utterance to their invitation, to say they would come; and, he believed, come they had. They had also to announce, that they had received far more than an equal number of letters, approving of their object, from gentlemen who could not come. And thus they had, in 1,500 localities, excited the attention, occupied the minds, and enlisted the sympathies of men bound by the most sacred obligations to use their influence for their starving countrymen; and they were convinced that if this conference were at that moment scattered to the winds, they had been honoured to excite or call forth an influence which would reach and rouse certain quarters they should like to see moved. There were ministers of religion present who had come, some 200, some 300, some near 500 miles distance, at their own expense, some on foot, that they might be here. Some ministers were present, whose incomes did not exceed £50 per annum, and whose congregations did not contain among them three persons whose incomes were more than 8s. a week. He should not do more than state, at this moment, what they had contemplated. They anticipated that the conference would confine itself to the one single question involved in the laws which restricted commerce in the food of the people. On that ground, and that ground alone, had this conference been invited. A respected brother, he anticipated, would speak after him. Then a gentleman whose name was associated with that great question, the emancipation of the negro, who had lent his name and influence as their honorary secretary, would be permitted to state what would acquit him of presumption. This having been done, they should be permitted to hear a delegate from the Anti-Corn-Law League, who would state clearly the questions on which they were met. He would be heard only as a counsel at the bar. After this, they desired that gentlemen who had come with information, should give it either by *vivâ voce* statements or written documents. It would then remain for the committee to state what they should think fit to recommend to the conference. He then read the following portion of the address calling the conference together, showing the *single object* to which their attention was to be directed, as chosen by the conveners from among the *causes* of national distress:

"We are brought to the conclusion that it is *our duty*, and the duty of all who fill the sacred office of ministers of religion, to look into the causes of our national distress. The conviction has been forced upon our minds, that the sufferings we deplore, and the calamities we would avert, may be traced, in a great degree, to the operation of the laws which produce a scarcity of the necessaries of life, by circumscribing the bounties of Divine Providence. But we need counsel and cooperation, that we may proceed wisely and efficiently. We therefore earnestly invite you to a free and friendly conference on the subject of the laws which restrict the supply of food to the people of this country, and the principles upon which such laws are based—to the end that we may agree upon the adoption of some Christian and constitutional measures for the removal of the ascertained causes of the increasing poverty and impending ruin of large classes of our fellow-citizens."

Mr. Massie concluded by proposing "That this conference should confine its considerations exclusively to the laws affecting the food of our people."

The Rev. RICHARD FLETCHER said, he had engaged to second the resolution without any observations. Indeed, he hardly thought such a resolution necessary, and feared that the bringing of it forward was calculated to raise the question whether or not other topics than the corn laws should be entertained, and that some who might have a wish to bring forward other questions might avail themselves of such an opportunity for doing so. (Hear, hear.)

Mr. MASSIE: Then I withdraw the motion, and leave the business of the meeting to be ascertained from the terms of the inviting letter. (Cheers.)

The CHAIRMAN: I am sure that those who have had the benevolence to assemble on this occasion, will have the discretion to confine their attention exclusively to the corn-law question; and, therefore, such a resolution is not necessary.

Mr. FLETCHER then announced, that a list of queries had been extensively circulated, and requested that any gentlemen who had prepared answers to them, would send them for examination to the committee sitting below stairs, as soon as possible. The committee thought it desirable that the meetings should commence each day at nine o'clock, and continue till one, at which hour they were to adjourn for dinner. He did not know whether those present were aware of the Manchester habit of dining at one o'clock. (Hear, hear.) A great inconvenience would be sustained by those families who had invited ministers to their houses, unless a punctual attendance at that hour was observed. Those gentlemen who wished for tea or coffee should get it immediately after dinner, in order to be at the meeting again at four o'clock, where they would sit till nine in the evening. The committee were to meet immediately after the adjournment for the arrangement of the subsequent proceedings of the conference. He was not present when the discussion took place respecting the devotional proceedings of the conference; but he was desired to state, that it was thought advisable that some devotional engagements might be attended to each day in such a manner as not to compromise the principles of any gentleman present. It was thought better not to make such engagements the act of the body, but the voluntary act of those ministers who wished to join in them. Arrangements could be made for prayer meetings in Lloyd-street Chapel each morning and evening. He thought it right to mention the matter, that it might be talked over in the interval. He fully concurred in the greater part of the statements made by Mr. Massie respecting the getting up of the meeting, and could only say, that the wisdom or folly of such a course could only be judged of by its results. It was one of that class of experiments which might be regarded either as a complete failure or a glorious revolution, just as it turned out. Considering the character of the auditory, and the class of gentlemen of whom it was composed, many of whom were well known to him, he had full confidence in the wisdom, prudence, and the religious tone which would pervade their discussions. He trusted that party politics, and every thing of a partizan nature, would be wholly excluded from their deliberations.

Dr. Vaughan rose to order. He did not intend to make a speech, and hoped he would have the attention of the meeting. He could fully appreciate the difficulties which the Manchester committee had to contend against relative to the opening of the meetings by prayer. He thought he could see a mode by which any difficulty might be obviated, and which made no invasion on the religious feelings or opinions of any party. The chair might be taken at nine o'clock, and the first half hour appropriated to devotional exercises. It would then be optional with those who could not conscientiously join in those exercises, to stay away until half-past nine. The reverend gentleman then moved a resolution to that effect.

The Rev. Mr. Fletcher suggested that the matter might be left to the decision of the committee.

The Rev. Dr. Cox considered the subject of such paramount importance, that he was unwilling to have it thrown back on the consideration of the committee. He felt as much respect as any man in the room for gentlemen composing the committee; but to no committee on earth should the meeting delegate the power of determining whether they should present their united supplications to the throne of Heaven. He would warmly second the motion of Dr. Vaughan, for he thought prayer to God should precede every other consideration.

The Rev. Timothy East supported the motion. He thought that those Christian friends who could not unite in those exercises of prayer, might not come at the commencement of the proceedings. If they met as a body without prayer, he was of opinion that they would be held up to public disgrace.

The Rev. R. W. Hamilton, of Leeds, said there was a simple method of reconciling the opinions of all—namely, by opening their proceedings with the Lord's prayer; in which a petition would arise very much in congruity with the object and feelings of the meeting—"Give us this day" (or "day by day," if you please) "our daily bread." (Applause.) Nobody could see any invasion of religious or political feeling in that prayer; but he was very much afraid, that, if they were left to the outpourings of extemporaneous devotion, some prayers, not very consistent with the feelings of some parties, might be offered—prayers which would be something like a political indictment. (Disapprobation.) He would therefore suggest, that they would open their meetings with that form of prayer which our Lord had taught his disciples.

The Rev. Dr. RITCHIE, of Edinburgh, thought the question should not have been mooted at all. He could not understand what that gospel minister was made of, who would refuse to unite with his brethren in the ministry of Christ in supplication to the throne of grace. He would, therefore, support the motion of Dr. Vaughan. He disagreed with the previous speaker respecting the character of the extemporaneous prayers which might be offered up. The meeting was not composed of such discordant elements, that no one could be found in it capable of making a suitable extemporaneous prayer. (Hear, hear.) He (Dr. Ritchie) also deprecated the drawing of a line of demarcation between those who could join in prayer, and those who could not. He wished it, therefore, to be understood, that the first exercise in which they should engage when they met was prayer; and that if, from any cause, any gentleman could not join with them, no distinction should be drawn—"To his own master he standeth or falleth." (Approbation.)

The CHAIRMAN then rose to put the question, but was interrupted by—

Dr. HALLEY, who objected on the ground that the meeting was composed of persons of different religious denominations, some of whom could not conscientiously join with others in such a sacred exercise. He was surrounded by several Roman Catholic priests; and he thought that, in fairness to them, if gentlemen of other denominations were allowed to offer up extemporaneous prayers, they (the priests) should be allowed to commence by the celebration of the mass. Before he would join in such a prayer-meeting himself, he would like to know who were the parties uniting with him. If, for instance, Mr. Beard, who was an unitarian minister, should be called on to pray, he (Dr. Halley) would not think it right to unite with him. But why should he be excluded more than him (Dr. Halley)? Why should those who agreed with him arrogate to themselves any right to conduct the religious services? Was it because they constituted a majority? He trusted the meeting would not be influenced by any such reason. They had met to consider the wants of the poor; and he hoped the apple of religious discord would not be thrown in to mar their efforts at removing them. Those who desired to pray might do so at their homes and respective chapels; and by this means ministers of different denominations might for once come together on common grounds, without having their harmony interrupted by the introduction of topics on which they could not agree. (Hear, hear.)

The Rev. FRANCIS J. ARCHER, P.P., of Hillsborough Hall, Blessington, said he had attended the meeting on the invitation of Mr. George Thompson, and begged to put his decided negative on a resolution which had a tendency to turn the attention of that great meeting from the question they had met to consider, by involving them in a religious warfare. As a Catholic clergyman, he acknowledged that prayer was good; but as the meeting was neither of a political nor religious nature, he thought it better to confine their attention to the question they had met to discuss—a question on which the happiness of so many thousands of their fellow-creatures depended. The object of the meeting was to consider and discuss the necessity and utility of the total repeal of those oppressive laws which grind down the poor by enhancing the price of bread. He was of opinion that God, the great Creator, who created man in his own living image and likeness, and who, as the word of God said, "created the earth and the goodness of it, that man might eat bread to satiety," never sanctioned the present corn laws. A more irreligious enactment, or one more at variance with the law of God, never was passed than the corn law. ("Question, question.")

The CHAIRMAN expressed his pleasure in finding such gentlemen as the last speaker associating with clergymen of other denominations in the conference, and that the subject of opening the meeting by prayer had come under discussion. If that discussion had not taken place, it might have been said by certain parties out of doors, who watched their proceedings with a cautious eye, that prayer was practically excluded from the meeting. As that was not the only place in which the divine blessing could be supplicated, and as certain difficulties attending devotional exercises in the meeting could not well be got rid of, he hoped the resolution would be withdrawn. Gentlemen might meet in their respective coteries for social worship, and thus have all the advantages which might be expected to arise from prayer, without any of the evils that would result from its introduction into such a mixed assembly. He hoped they would all be united to advocate the cause of suffering humanity, and endeavour to carry out their benevolent objects without any compromise of principle. (Cheers.)

Dr. VAUGHAN said, he would not have proposed the resolution, if he had thought it would have met with so much opposition. The resolution was then withdrawn.

Mr. M'KERROW said, that during the interval, between one and four o clock, arrangements would be made for the increased accommodation of the assembly. Gentlemen wishing to communicate with each other, could leave notice on the table at the top of the first stairs. If any gentlemen who arrived that morning had not found their way to residences, he would recommend them to proceed to them without delay, as they might find it difficult to discover them in the darkness of the evening. Those who had not made arrangements with regard to dining, were requested to apply to Mr. Massie, in the boroughreeve's room, who had cards of invitation for fifty gentlemen.

Mr. MASSIE hoped that those hospitable friends who wished to open their houses to particular gentlemen, would not feel slighted if others were sent them by mistake.

The meeting was then declared by the CHAIRMAN to be adjourned to four o'clock; and the gentlemen named on the committee were requested to remain a short time, and assemble in the boroughreeve's room.

AFTERNOON MEETING.

During the adjournment of the meeting, the seats in the body of the hall had been turned so as to enable their occupants, the members of the conference generally, to face the platform at the upper end. The space for the public at the lower end of the hall, next Cheapside, had been contracted, so as to afford more room for the numerous ministers; the barrier being placed further back, and up to the columns, so as to reserve for the members of conference exclusively the whole space between the two ranges of columns in the room. The morning being gloomy, there was but a feeble light in some parts of the room; but in the afternoon the sun shone bright, and the large meeting had a very striking appearance when the spacious hall was illuminated by the sun's rays. About twenty minutes past four, the Rev. THOMAS ADKINS, of Southampton, resumed the chair, and said that the committee were making arrangements for the subsequent proceedings as rapidly as possible; and he expected them every moment to lay the programme of the future proceedings before the meeting. Shortly afterwards, the CHAIRMAN called upon—

The Rev. THOMAS SPENCER, of Hinton Charter-house, who said, he was not about to make a speech on the corn laws, but merely to state a matter of business. We are assembled here (said the rev. gentleman) from all parts of England, as a jury, to try a particular question. We hear that trade is dead; we are coming to hold a coroner's inquest. (Hear.) We shall to-morrow, the next day, and the day after, deliver our opinions, and also give such evidence as we have collected from our own parts of England; but in the meantime it is very desirable to call a layman to our bar, and to give him permission to bring a witness, if he has one, from foreign parts; we think it desirable to hear a merchant at home, and also a person from abroad; and, therefore, I have to propose that conference do allow Mr. Cobden to address them on this particular question; (applause;) and, if necessary, in his defence of the cause, to produce a gentleman from America, to speak as to the state of things there, that conference should permit him so to do. I think no layman ought to be allowed to address the ministers present, unless with the express permission of conference. I believe in the House of Commons they would not allow ministers to be present; then surely in this house, which consists of 650 members, not of 658, we should keep the privileges of our house, and only allow laymen to speak at our bar by permission. (Laughter.) I beg to propose that Richard Cobden, Esq., the able advocate of the repeal of the corn laws, be permitted to address this conference. (Applause.)

The motion having been seconded by Dr. Payne, and passed unanimously, amidst much applause,—

RICHARD COBDEN, Esq. M.P., came forward, warmly welcomed by plaudits, and said,—Mr. Chairman and gentlemen, although it has often been my fate to address a public meeting in this Town Hall, I must conscientiously declare, that on no former occasion have I addressed an assembly here with the same emotions which I now experience, because on no former occasion have I seen an assembly in this Town Hall, the result of whose deliberations, I believe, may be of such vast importance to the great question which I have so much at heart—the repeal of the corn laws. I appear before you, not as an individual, but as a representative, on this occasion, of a numerous and tolerably influential body, designated "The Anti-Corn-Law League." I am deputed by that body to explain to you the grounds on which we advocate the repeal of the corn and provision laws. And, in doing so, do not expect from me any appeals whatever to your feelings or your sympathies. I am come, as Mr. Spencer has well observed, to give evidence in this cause, and my evidence must be facts. (Hear, hear.) When, about two years and a half ago, a large number of individuals, from all parts of the kingdom, assembled in Manchester, to take into consideration the question of the corn and provision monopolies, they entered upon a discussion of the question with no other view but to arrive at a true and just conclusion, without respect to party considerations, to expediency, or to class interests, or any other inferior considerations whatever. They tested the question, as far as they were enabled to do so, by the unalterable principles of truth and justice; and they came to the conclusion, that no tax whatever upon the bread of the people was just. ("Hear," and applause.) It is estimated, that every family in the kingdom, of the same number, will consume about an equal quantity of bread. I think, it might be said, that the poorer the family, the greater amount of bread will that family consume. It has been further estimated, by a very important body, the hand-loom commission inquirers, that the average of the working-class families of the kingdom earn 10s. a-week; and of that 10s. these gentlemen are of opinion, after very wide and careful considerations, of this 10s. every working man's family spends 5s. upon bread. (Hear.) Now, it must be computed, that, at the very lowest, our bread tax has raised the price of bread in this country from the time it has passed, full 40 per cent. above the price of the bread which would have been eaten by the poor without a tax at all. 40 per cent, then, is the amount of the tax paid upon bread; 40 per cent upon 5s. which the labouring man spends for his family on bread, or 2s. out of 5s.; 2s. out of 10s. a-week, is the income tax which the labouring man pays for his bread. 2s out of 10s., or 20 per cent income tax, is the amount which the labouring community pay for a tax on their bread. Ascending a little higher in the social scale, the better-paid mechanic, with 20s. a week spends no more for bread than the humblest hand-loom weaver with 10s., or 2s. a week, which, upon his earnings, was an income tax of 10 per cent. The man receiving 40s. a week paid 2s. for bread, or five per cent. income tax; and, ascending to the middle class with an income of £5 per week, the income tax they paid was only two per cent. But, ascending higher, till you come to the income of a nobleman, or *millionaire*, he spends no more in bread than the poor hand-loom weaver; and to estimate the amount of tax he pays for bread, you must go to a fractional coin less than we can compute in this country. (Applause.) Thus, while the bread tax levies a tax of 20 per cent on an average, on the income of all the unskilful labourers in this country, the duke with his £15,000 a year does not pay a thousandth part of one per cent. per annum. (Hear.) If it were proposed to lay a tax in these proportions, and so graduated, for the purposes of revenue, would not a righteous burst of indignation be raised through the land against such a proposition? But the bread tax is that, and a great deal worse; for it is just that amount of income tax which I have described, and, instead of going to the revenue, it is a tax levied upon the poor man's cupboard for the benefit of the rich man. (Applause.) I know of no country where a tax has ever been directly levied upon the bread of the people. I have travelled in the dominions of Mehemet Ali himself; and I can bear testimony to the fact, that there is no bread tax in Egypt, and I know of no worse government than that. We know of the extremities to which some despotic governments are reduced for revenues; we know of the yearly borrowing of Austria: it has abundance of corn; but, in all the abundance of Austria, no despot has yet dared to levy a tax upon the bread of the people. Nor would you have a tax upon bread in this country, if it had been levied directly, and if it had been understood by the people who pay it. (Hear.) These, and such as these, were our reasons why the Anti-Corn-Law League founded itself upon the principle of a total repeal of the corn and provision laws. But they did more. We had amongst our body a few of those philanthropic members of the society of Friends, who had belonged to the anti-slavery party, (hear,) and they raised another question. It might have been felt inconvenient at the time this question was raised; but these sturdy sticklers for principle raised the question, "If the total repeal of the corn laws be just, is not the immediate repeal of the corn laws just?" (Hear, hear.) These gentlemen argued, and I think fairly, that, acknowledging the bread tax to be unjust, and that it was an injustice of such a magnitude, and bearing upon the great mass of the people, that there were no considerations that could justify the continuance of such a tax for a day, that might not justify it for a hundred years. It was, therefore, by bringing the question to the principles of truth and justice, and setting aside all other considerations,—it was, therefore, on those grounds that the fundamental principle of the Anti-Corn-Law League has been the advocacy of the total repeal of the corn laws, and no other question can be entertained by the Anti-Corn-Law League. I apprehend, at all events, that the circumstances to which I have directed your attention, are circumstances to which you will look in order to come to a just conclusion on the subject. You will recollect that the bread tax affects the great body of the people. We are told, indeed, that the corn law has a tendency to keep up wages. It has been, I believe, an error on the part of those who passed the law; it has been a fundamental error on the part of many of them—and that error has become wide-spread, and exists at the present day—that by some means or other, the putting of a tax on the food of the people was a bar against a fall in the rate of wages. A more mistaken, a more monstrous idea, could never be entertained. The idea that the shutting out of foreign commerce would have a tendency to increase the rate of wages, and the amount of employment, must appear, on the first view of the question, to every enlightened mind, the most monstrous fallacy that could possibly be conceived. But we are told, when we advocate the repeal of the corn laws, that the object of that repeal is to enable the manufacturing capitalists to compete with foreigners in the prices of their productions. Why, gentlemen, we compete with foreigners now, even with the bread tax on our shoulders; or how could we export to every corner of the globe forty or fifty millions' worth of the products of this country? When these productions go abroad, do the inhabitants of New York or China make any allowance to us on account of the bread tax? Do they make any allowance to our manufacturers on account of the burdens borne by the people? No: we must put our goods alongside of the productions of the Swiss or American; and, if not sold in competition with them, they will not be sold at all. (Hear, hear.) And the price at which they will sell in China or New York is precisely the same as that in this country; for think you any capitalist would send his goods to the Antipodes for sale, if he could find a better price for them in this market? so that, with respect to competition, perhaps we have it now to the fullest and completest degree. The master manufacturer must sell his productions as cheap as the manufacturer abroad or his labour will not be called for. We are told that the price of labour here is higher than abroad. I deny it: if our labour here was dearer than abroad, how could we sell our productions cheaper? I have travelled in most civilized countries, and in some barbarous; and I think that a fallacious mode of comparing the price of labour in foreign countries, with its price at home, has been adopted. They take the labour of a day, or of a week, and compare its price with the labour performed in the same time at home; but they do not take the quantity of that labour. You have here a fine full-blooded racer, that will do twice the quantity of work that could be done in the same time by the steed of another country, and then you clap on him double weight; you make him carry fourteen stone against seven. (Loud cheers.) Why, gentlemen, if any other fact were necessary to show that labour in this country has no protection against labour abroad, I need not go further than to state, that thirty or forty thousand pairs of arms are going abroad every year to find that employment which they cannot procure at home. Think you they would transport themselves—think you they would subject themselves to the second penalty in our criminal code, if they found better employment at home, or any employment at all? But, though these fallacies are daily refuted, they daily sprout up again. We are constantly told, that the bread tax is a protection of the labour of this country against the labour of the continent; but this has not been proved. This assertion has been reiterated in the teeth of facts and the most conclusive reasoning. (Hear, hear.) But do not you think, that, before a Christian legislator sits down to pass a law, to raise artificially and legally the price of food sold to the labouring man, he should first of all settle by what means he would raise in proportion the price of the man's labour? (Hear, hear.) I have lately been in Nottinghamshire, for the express purpose of ascertaining the rate of wages and the condition of the frame-work knitters there. There are gentlemen here present who will be able to know whether I am telling you the facts truly. I found men employed in the stocking frame-work for 8s. a week; and they told me, that, in 1816 and 1817, immediately after the corn law came into operation, they had 18s. a week with less labour. And mark this: the stocking-frame is not, like the hand-loom, subject to interference from the power-loom and the steam-engine: it is the same now as it was one hundred years ago. There are stocking-frames now at work nearly a hundred years old. The stocking-frame is subject to no disturbing causes like other machinery. But if you go from the poor man's hovel to the rich man's demesne, there you will find a class in Nottinghamshire, on the borders of a young nobleman's estate (I will not personally allude to him by name); but, at the last election, he declared that the legislature must keep up the price of corn to 56s. or 58s. These men, who were fed from the productions of those fields at a price raised by act of parliament, presented a petition to parliament on behalf of their families who were famishing for want of bread. In that petition they said, "Give us a law which will keep up the price of labour;" but they are answered in this manner:—"Oh! these men are ignorant of political economy. It is quite impossible to keep up the rate of wages by legislative enactment; that is all settled by a law over which we have no control—the law of supply and demand." Is it not almost incredible that men should be found in this Christian country—ay, men who are themselves individually disposed to be amiable and excellent—to pass a law which would compel the poor man to pay a double price for his food, and at the same time not to pass a law which would give that man a double price for his labour? But we have a law in existence nominally for the purpose of protecting, as it is called, the labour of this country. We have a fiscal system which imposes a duty on foreign cotton goods coming into this country, and also on woollens, silks, iron, and the like. But, gentlemen, I should tell you that the people of Manchester, representing every staple in the country, have unanimously petitioned parliament that those protective laws, as they are called, should be abolished. They feel and know that those laws are no protection to them. If we can send our goods to China, and sell them cheaper there than the French or Germans, what have we to fear from the invasion of foreign manufactures? Besides, those protective laws, as they are called, are made the pretence for other protective laws, which, as I have shown you, are calculated grievously to injure every class of trade. To give you a specimen of the extent to which this kind of pretences is carried, there is an item on the statute-book making a duty of 40s. a ton payable for coals brought to Newcastle! (Cheers and laughter.) We have, gentlemen, viewed this question as one affecting the rights of labour, because there are 20,000,000 of people in this country who subsist on the price of labour, and which should have our primary consideration, even if they had not the additional claim which their poverty gives them. It is with regard to their interests, and not those of the capitalists, that the anti-corn-law leaguers advocate the total repeal of those laws. I am now departing from that ground which I would exhort you to make the primary and principal ground of your consideration, to consider a question of a commercial character. You are told, that the repeal of the corn laws would cause a consequent drain of gold to pay for wheat. There is no difficulty in answering this question, by referring to our trade in other commodities. We are importing from £40,000,000 to £50,000,000 of goods every year, consisting of silk, cotton, coffee, and the like, and yet we never heard of a drain of gold to pay for these commodities. During the last twenty-five years, you will be startled when I tell you that we have imported £1,000 000,000 of commodities, and that we have exported the same amount of commodities in exchange. But during that time we have had to import some twenty or thirty millions of corn, and then you have heard of those mighty perturbations of our exchange, and those fearful drains of specie to pay for it. And why? Because you have a law applicable to corn different form all other fiscal laws; because you have a law which shuts out from the honest merchant, who can deal in all the other commodities of the earth, the power of dealing in corn, and confines to a class of jobbers and gamblers, who make this article for the food of the people an article for jobbing and gambling, just as they do at Ascot or Crockford's. Make the law so as the merchant importing corn should know what he would have to pay for it, and you would have this country the granary of Europe. Why, you hear of statesmen and ministers going to the weather-glass; they talk of the moon's changes, and speculate on what kind of weather we should have; and why? Because there was only three weeks' consumption in the north. We are on the edge of a precipice. But what have we of cotton? At the present moment there is lying at Liverpool 30 weeks' consumption of cotton. But we are told that it is dangerous, it is not proper that we should be dependent on foreigners for the food we eat. I see in the law of nature, and the arrangements of Providence, that which would forbid us to be independent. I see in this arrangement the best guarantee for peace. I see in this arrangement, on the grandest possible scale, the means of carrying out that golden rule of doing to all men as we wish them to do unto us. But if this dread of independence be so great in the article of wheat, how is it that we find these men so willing to be the vassals of other nations for other things! I have not travelled in any country that I have not made it my business to inquire where their best commodities were sent to. In the Levant, in Arabia, in China, ask where the prime commodities—take any thing you please—and you will be told, that the best of every thing is going to England. And how is it, if you go to the plains of Poland or the prairies of America, and see the pigs sent into the corn-fields and ask, why is that wheat not sent to England? you are told, there is a law in England which prohibits the introduction of corn. Recollect that the productions we send abroad are the work of our operatives: what you export is chiefly the manipulation on raw materials brought from foreign countries. The value given to them is given by the labouring classes; and is it not a mighty injustice to the working classes that when their productions are sent abroad, they should be told that not one ounce of these productions that they and their families most stand in need of should be given to them? No, say they, we shall have them to ourselves; and when we have surrounded ourselves with foreign luxuries, with Persian carpets—drinking their sherry, and sucking the luscious grapes—and then, when we are doing that, we will sermonise on the propriety of being independent of foreigners. (Laughter.) Gentlemen, you have heard much said with regard to the effects which would be produced on the agricultural labourers by the repeal of the corn laws. I see before me many gentlemen who, much to their honour, have broken through the trammels of old prejudices, and have come from agricultural counties: I ask those gentlemen in the course of this conference to supply facts bearing on the amount of wages in agricultural districts; and if it can be found that agricultural labourers are receiving as much wages as unskilled labourers in my employ, twenty miles from here, then I will give up the question. But what is the fact? The classes which, according to the arguments of the corn-law men, the corn laws are for, are at the lowest state of wages; and, more than that, they would be reduced still lower were it not that the manufacturers and the commercial interests absorb the increase of population, and that the agriculturist goes into the neighbouring towns for subsistence. What better proof need you have that the condition of the agricultural labourers is not good? Then we are told of the lamentable employment of these immigrants. Why, have not those who speak of that established an emigration agent, Mr. Muggeridge, for the very purpose of bringing here the surplus labour of the agricultural districts? I do not stand here to defend the manufacturing class. I do not say that they are better than they ought to be, or so good; but, if they are what they are represented to be, what must they be who established an agent in Manchester to send their own population there? (Loud applause.) But, gentlemen, you have heard, and you will hear, much of the enormity of the manufacturing and trading class of capitalists. I hope that you, while you are staying here, will avail yourselves of those opportunities which, I am sure, the manufacturers of Manchester will afford you of seeing for yourselves. But, gentlemen, let us go on, and suppose that these classes of people are as bad as they are represented by those who wish to make their crimes an argument for the corn laws, what consolation can that be to the poor labourer, who is badly worked and badly paid, and has to submit to the bread taxer into the bargain? If the corn law is a protection to the labourer, I ask, what has become of that protection when we are told that the masters in the manufacturing districts are grinding the faces of the poor? Should it be felt that the corn law regulates wages, I would say that the corn law has no tendency to keep up the rate of wages. Then I will say every argument will show the injustice of that law which, in addition, takes away one-third of their food. I was alluding to the agricultural labourers, and will glance at that argument which says that the land of this country will be taken out of cultivation unless it be protected by the corn laws. Why, that means that the land is not cultivated at the expense of the landlords there, but at the expense of the people here. It is quite clear that we are paying an enormous sum of money, and in the most extravagant way, to keep up the cultivation of their land. And if it is come to that, if we must pay for the cultivation of their land, let it be done by a tax, and not by a circumvention. But I believe that the agricultural labourers have no fear of the land going out of cultivation. I know that some of our lecturers have found some of the labourers very apt in rebutting this fallacy. One of them was lecturing in Buckinghamshire. He spoke of corn being imported at 50s. a quarter, and one of the farmers said, "What will you do with our labourers? our land will be thrown out of cultivation." "Oh," said the labourer, "we will cultivate it ourselves." (Laughter.) Let it not be supposed that we are met here to advocate the agrarian system; this is only escaping out of that awful dilemma into which our opponents would bring themselves. If it be said, how are the agricultural labourers to be fed? the peasantry say, "Never mind us; we will cultivate the land for ourselves." One of our friends, travelling in Devonshire, said to a peasant who was carrying his carpet bag, "Well, my friend, what will become of you when these Manchester people have repealed the corn law? They are going to admit foreign corn, and then you will be thrown out of employment." The peasant, with a significant twinkle of his eye, said, "They *beant* a-going to carry away the land, be em?" (Laughter.) Many of you who come from agricultural districts are much better acquainted with these things than I am, though I am a farmer's son, and from the south myself. I know they will bear me out in saying, that there is a strain put upon all the land by the corn monopoly. The enclosures acts grew out of these corn laws, and were always unpopular with the labouring classes. One of the friends of the labourers, Mr. Fyshe Palmer, one of the members for Berkshire, who was always opposed to these enclosures acts, used to quote some lines which I will repeat:

> "The fault is great in man or woman,
> Who steals a goose from off a common;
> But who shall plead that man's excuse
> Who steals the common from the goose?"

(Laughter.) Mr. Cobden then said, that, though he ought to be in another place on Thursday next, he felt this conference of far too much importance to be limited by any consideration whatever to induce him to leave Manchester as long as the conference honoured us with their presence. He was sure his friends in Stockport would agree with him in his resolution to remain here; and he must hope, if at any time the conference wished him to renew the subject, they would call upon him to address himself to any part of the subject, to answer any inquiries, and to put at the disposal of conference all the information upon the subject which the League had at its command. He believed the oldest inhabitant of this district never knew so great or long-continued distress as now existed. It was a state of things which, had it come suddenly, would inevitably have led to convulsions; but the people had been gradually brought down from the palmy condition of five years ago, by slow stages, and so seemed to have lost all hope and all energy in their present prostrate condition. If any thing could revive their hopes, and give them a gleam of comfort, he believed it was such a meeting as the present. The conference was looked upon as the last resort of a suffering people; and he believed the labouring population of the country were looking with the deepest interest at every word and act of this conference. He felt confident, from what he had witnessed, that its proceedings would be of a nature, from their calmness, gravity, and Christian charity and decorum, to give greater influence to the cause than all the labours to which its advocates had been devoted for the last two years. He entreated the conference to look at this question as one of paramount importance to the highest moral and religious welfare of the state. They were accustomed to meet with the poor, and must be well aware that it is vain to try to instruct, to train, to evangelize them, while their minds were brooding over their distress. It had been somewhere said, that, put a boat-load of philosophers upon the Atlantic, without food, and, in six days, they will become a body of raging cannibals. So, if you put a community upon a stinted allowance of food, you beget, in the first place, brooding resentments, where otherwise would have existed the most genial and generous feelings; you set neighbour against neighbour, and even husband against wife, and wife against child; for they were contesting, at every addition to their family, for the pittance of food allotted them. This state of things could never co-exist with high moral or religious comfort. (Hear.) These were the interests committed to the charge of the meeting on this occasion; there wanted but the impulse which they could give by the decision of the meeting, to aid the convictions spread through the country by the appeals made to the reason and judgment of the country; there wanted but the mighty impulse this conference could give, the greatest impulse that could affect the human mind in any country, and infinitely the greatest that can move a religious country such as this; there wanted but that this conference, at the conclusion of its meetings, would declare that this bread tax, which was systematically contrived, and cunningly framed, to put the whole country in want of the first necessaries of life,—to declare that this law was opposed to the law of God, was anti-scriptural, anti-christian; and the corn laws would be from that moment virtually abolished. (Loud applause.)

The Rev. T. East, of Birmingham, then came forward and said,—Gentlemen, I am requested to move a vote of thanks to Richard Cobden, Esq., M.P., for the address which he has just delivered. (Cheers.) As I cannot attend any other evening but the present, this must be my apology for stating a few facts which have fallen under my notice. This day week I travelled with a brother minister, to attend an anniversary. He has been a labourer for many years in Suffolk, an agricultural county; and he stated to me, that upwards of 700 of his hearers were incapable of paying one penny a week to any religious institution—these 700 were all depending on the proceeds of agricultural labour. (Hear.) He also informed me, that 11s. per week is the largest amount of income supplied to the best hands in Suffolk, while the average income does not exceed 7s. 6d. per week. (Hear, hear.) Mr. Chairman, since I first heard of this most important meeting, I went from house to house in the neighbourhood of Birmingham—I went from one cottage on the roadside to another, and I did not meet with one single poor person who could tell me the price of animal food per pound. I did not meet a single individual of the labouring classes in the neighbourhood of Birmingham, within the last month, who had tasted animal food for many, many months. On Thursday last, on my way from Birmingham to Shrewsbury, I stopped at different places, and conversed with several agricultural labourers employed on the roadside; and I learned from them, that they had not tasted one bit of animal food for two years. One of them said he had six in family, and they lived upon potatoes with their own fat. "I suppose, sir," said he, "you know what that means?" I confessed my ignorance. He said, "we eat the potatoes with some of the water they are boiled in." I give it as my decided opinion, formed from having been brought into accidental contact with the unemployed labourers in the vicinity of Birmingham, that, unless something is done promptly before the winter sets in, it will be hazardous for any human being to dwell near the large half-fed population of this country. (Cheers.) They express their feelings very calmly. but with great firmness. "Sir," they have said to me, "do you wish us to be starved to death in the land of plenty?" (Hear, hear.) I can assure you that the houses in the neighbourhood of Birmingham are nearly exhausted of their furniture, the people having been obliged to pawn one article after another to keep themselves from starving. Their extreme distress surpasses all my powers of description. The statement given us this evening by Mr. Cobden, by no means went to the full extent of the truth. Mr. Cobden said, that the man who earned 20s. per week was paying 10 per cent. of a bread tax; and the man who earned 10s. per week was paying 20 per cent. The proportion is not correctly stated, because, in proportion to the paucity of the man's income is the proportion of bread he consumes. For, as his wages rise, he purchases a little meat, and other gratifications, and the use of these diminish his consumption of bread. The reverend gentleman concluded by observing, that a large number of his congregation were unable to attend to Christian ordinances from want of clothing, having been obliged to pawn their raiment to provide themselves with food. (Shame.)

The Rev. Mr. Hinton, of London, seconded the resolution, which was then put in a very complimentary manner from the chair, and carried unanimously.

Mr. Cobden said he felt himself by no means entitled to the flattering compliment which had been paid to him, or to the very kind but too handsome encomiums which his excellent friend the chairman had passed upon him. Having thanked the meeting for the kind manner in which they received the resolution, he expressed a willingness to endeavour to remove any doubts or scruples that any of the audience might entertain on the corn-law question. He entreated those who might have doubts on the subject not to go away without hearing the information which two or three years' attention to the subject had given to some in Manchester. He would be deeply indebted to any gentleman who would give him an opportunity of explaining any difficulties, as he was satisfied that such explanations would contain more information than a long speech delivered on points on which perhaps there might be no difference of opinion. (Cheers.)

The Chairman then announced Mr. Curtis, from Ohio, in America, as the next speaker, but was informed by Mr. Cobden that it was not that gentleman's intention to address the meeting until next day.

The Rev. Thomas Spencer, of Hinton Charter-house, near Bath, said, to-night was a night of facts and of documents. They had been invited by ministers of religion, in co-operation with the Anti-Corn Law League, to come to Manchester, to see whether their statements were correct; and they were expected to tell what was the state of the people in their own neighbourhood. It had been stated, that the agricultural labourers would suffer by the repeal of the corn laws. He never knew one who said so. It was quite plain, and there was no mystification until legislators made it so. When Jacob and his family wanted corn, there was no difficulty in knowing that it could be got from Egypt. But there had been so much mystification, that one could hardly believe one's own common sense, and, therefore, he had taken the trouble of sending the parish clerk, where he lived, to every house in the parish. He gave him the names of every householder, and drew up several columns. One was, whether they were for free trade and cheap bread. One was, what was their occupation; and another was as to their wages. Another was, what were their wages in 1835; another, do their wages rise or fall with the price of food? These were agricultural labourers chiefly. However, they had some farmers, some clothiers; for there was a cloth manufactory in their parish, and there was a sprinkling of artizans, as in other towns. Out of 144 householders in his parish, there were 126 entirely for the repeal of the corn laws. (Applause.) Of sixty agricultural labourers, there was only one that was for the corn-laws; and that one man said, at the same time that he was for dear bread, he did not wish to hurt the manufacturers, and that he should like free trade.

And therefore he had entered him as for free trade and dear bread. (Laughter.) There were in his parish 14 farmers; and, notwithstanding what was commonly said in the house of commons where men *could* not contradict them, and before great men where people *dare* not contradict, out of 14 farmers six were for free trade, three were for the corn-laws, and five had so much doubt on their minds, that they would not give an opinion. He did not go round himself: he asked no man his opinion, lest it might be said that to please him they had stated what they did not think There were, besides, 17 cloth workers and 4 weavers, and, as might be expected, they were all for free trade. Then, at Frome, eight miles from where he lived, he had the authority of a guardian of the poor, that, to his certain knowledge, from the operation of the corn laws, 50 clothiers had failed during the last 20 years, and he had actually seen some of these men apply for parish pay who were formerly master manufacturers. He had also made inquiries in the town of Bradford. He sent the same parish clerk: and, as no man should work for nothing, he paid him for his trouble; but he also knew, from personal observation, the state of that neighbourhood. In Bradford, in Wiltshire, the poor-rates had doubled, and the greater part of the people were out of work. It was expected that they would increase from 7s in the pound, which they now were, to 14s.; yes, and a gentleman had assured him that they would be 20s. before the winter was over. (Hear.) And mark this, that while some people thought the poor-rates were an inexhaustible fund, all the ratepayers were becoming paupers. He had also made inquiry respecting the Vale of Rodborough, and he heard that 2s. 6d. a week for the support of a family was a common thing in that neighbourhood, and that 1½d. a day was the average income of all the people in that neighbourhood. He understood also, that there had been three rates of 3s. in the pound, each made within a quarter of a year, which made 9s. in the pound; and a gentleman who came from that neighbourhood had told him, that it would be at the rate of 36s. in the pound, if this state of things were to continue. Now, there were gentlemen who held large possessions of land, who knew nothing of this. They lived in palaces, and drove about in carriages, but knew nothing of the poor; they could not believe in this state of things. But there were some honourable exceptions. There was the Earl of Radnor, who actually gave out of his own pocket, in different ways, for charitable purposes, £7,000 a year. (Hear, hear.) That was not commonly known; but he (Mr. Spencer) took this opportunity of making it known, because, if a man did not let his left hand know what his right hand did, it was right that his light should shine before men. He also knew that the Earl of Ducie would make his farmers improve themselves, as manufacturers had had to do. Let the farmer not spend his ten shillings a day in drink (as he had known some of them do): let him look after his farm; let not the cattle and sheep, through neglect, tread down the corn, and he should prosper; and if they did not prosper, he knew many who, if the farmers would not take the land, would be glad to get it. He knew there were some who had allotments for which they paid 30s. an acre, including rates and taxes; whereas, while the farmers had that land, they paid a pound an acre for it, and charged the labourers 30s. He was saying that the Earl of Ducie was going the way to make the farmers prosperous. He was the first agriculturist in this country, and had laid out £20,000, without getting any profit from it, in a manufactory of agricultural implements, where a farmer could go and buy an implement for £15, which would cost him £25, elsewhere. This was the way to keep up the agricultural interest. He knew a gentleman in the

Potteries, who had told him two cases of the strongest possible kind; and as that gentleman was a tory or conservative, perhaps the evidence would be of more importance. He said there had been a gentleman from America, who wanted to purchase 500 packages of earthenware, at £20 a package, if they would take corn in exchange; (hear;) "for," said he, "we cannot get money;" and this gentleman told him, that he was obliged to refuse the offer, because the corn laws would not let them take their wheat; and another gentleman near him had a permanent offer made to him, which he also was obliged to refuse. He could not see that any thing could be clearer than this; and if after that they made a difficulty of the question, the fault was with themselves. There were persons who said that wages rose when bread rose, and yet these persons were silent upon that subject now when bread had been raised. (Hear, hear.) In answer to all the inquiries which he had made, he was informed that wages did not rise with bread. They said that they had the same wages as in 1835. There was not a man among them who had the slightest idea that their wages would rise with the price of bread. He had had a good deal to do with the poor laws, and was instrumental in his own parish in reducing the poor-rate from £700 a year to £200 a year; and he was glad to see men turn from a state of idleness to industry. He was opposed at first by the farmers, because under the old system they had their labourers paid out of the rates; but, when they saw that this should be no longer, they all came round to him. And these farmers invariably, in 1835, said to the men, "Times are better with you now than they used to be; bread is cheaper, and therefore you ought to lay something by now." These were their own arguments then, and he did not see how they could back out of them now. The rev. gentleman said, he would read a statement drawn up by a worthy individual; one whom he knew so thoroughly, that he could say he scarcely knew a better man in the working classes. This statement was in the following words:—

I am by trade a weaver. I was brought up in a populous village in the county of Somerset, situate about five miles from Frome, five from Bradford, and five from Trowbridge, in Wiltshire. Before the corn law was in existence, this was one of the most prosperous villages in England. The trade consisted principally in fine woollen cloth and cassimeres. It was every way well situated for trade. There was a fine stream of water running by it; and very commodious dye-houses, and every accommodation for the convenience of trade, and four respectable clothiers, men of good capital, and that had been brought up in the business from their youth. About thirty years ago, there were three new factories erected, and propelled by water; and, since then, one has been erected, and propelled by steam. Before the corn law was introduced, I think there never could be a village in greater prosperity. I suppose there were nearly a hundred pieces per week made in the village and its suburbs. When the corn bill was brought before parliament, we got up a petition against it. I, for one, signed it, as did nearly the whole village; but our petition was not heard; the corn bill passed, our trade began to decline, our operatives were out of employ, distress and pauperism was the consequence, our manufacturers sunk in capital; one of them, that could not keep up his establishment, was driven to the desperate act of suicide; another of them failed, about forty thousand pounds in debt, and was supposed to die of a broken heart; another declined business, and embarked into agriculture; and the other was obliged to leave off trade, after sacrificing thirty or forty thousand pounds, and is since dead, and his son is gone to America, and there is not a single end of cloth made in the village; the factories are all shut up, and the machinery utterly spoiled, and an industrious people in a state of starvation. One of them told me, that he and his family had not had a pound of meat, butter, or cheese in his house, for the last two years. It is my decided opinion, that, had it not been for the corn laws, Road would still have been in a state of prosperity. I wonder how so wise a man as Sir Robert Peel can consider the present distress as only a temporary depression of trade. I cannot conceive a thing to be very temporary that has been so painfully felt for more than a quarter of a century. I can truly say, I have felt it acutely for more than twenty-five years. In 1815 I got settled in life, and I then had very flattering hopes of prosperity; I was young, active, and industrious; I had saved by my industry a nice little sum of money; I laid it out in purchasing furniture, and in things necessary for my trade. I then had plenty of work for myself and two or three journeymen, and had work not only from my native village, but from one of the first manufacturers in Trowbridge; and I verily thought, as peace was restored to us, we never should know the want of work again; but the corn bill passed, and before I had been married one year, I began to find the sad effects of it. In the spring of 1816, our trade was almost at a stand; and where I placed my chief dependence, I had but one piece for four months; and from that time to the present, I have been involved in difficulty; and from my heart I think I can truly say, corn laws have been the greatest source of my misfortunes. I have been driven about the country to get labouring work; I have walked twelve or fourteen miles a day, besides working, in order to maintain my family, and have had no more than 1s. 6d. per day to maintain a wife and six children. Before the corn bill passed, I had 1s. 1d. per yard for weaving, but, for many years past, I have had only 8d. I then could earn 4s. per day, and now I find it difficult to earn 2s. per day. My prayer to God is, that we may have free trade once more restored to us, that the industrious may be enabled to procure the necessaries of life, and provide things honest in the sight of all men.

Before I sit down, (continued Mr. Spencer,) I will just state what the agricultural labourers will tell you. They would not allow you to be deceived by the cries in parliament, that the corn laws are good for the agricultural labourers. I never saw the labourer, and I have lived fifteen years in an agricultural village, who would stand up for the corn laws; but they would tell you that the stagnation of trade is doing them a great deal of injury. A factory near Bath lately stopped, and the 800 men thus thrown out of employment went to seek employment in the fields, by underselling the poor agricultural labourers; and thus the poor agricultural labourer, the pet of the landlords, was almost brought to ruin by those corn laws. One poor man, who had been long out of work, and who had walked sixteen miles to a factory in vain search of work, said he was determined to revenge himself on the first rich oppressor he met. Mr. Spencer said, he reasoned with him, and relieved him; and he said that there were 800 like himself ready to go in a body to revenge themselves, many of them armed. He showed that he himself was armed, by producing a knife with a blade nine inches long. This man laid the whole blame of his condition on the corn laws. He was for free trade, because he thought it would bring work; he did not want to do mischief; but he said, "What can we do, if we are compelled to starve?" He afterwards came to Mr. Spencer, and confessed he had been wrong in his thoughts of vengeance; but he had been driven to them by extreme distress. He (Mr. Spencer) was a great opponent of physical force; but we could not keep these things back. Distress would lead men to do horrible things. It had been said, what would become of a company of philosophers, without food, on the ocean? and we all well knew that it was difficult to make "an empty bag stand upright." (Applause.)

The CHAIRMAN then read a resolution submitted by the committee of management,—"That the meeting of this evening be set apart for the special purpose of hearing members of conference from manufacturing and agricultural districts, to make whatever statements they have to make, simply and shortly, relative to the state of trade and the circumstances of the working classes in their respective neighbourhoods." He called on

The Rev. JOHN COLSTON, of Wimslow, who stated that in the

small village where he resided, in which were only 1026 individuals, with most of whom he was thoroughly intimate, there was a manufacturing mill which had existed there for upwards of sixty years, and during the whole of that period, till within the last four years, that mill had never worked short time, with one single exception For more than half a century that establishment had been able to give full employment to the people, with that one exception, and the change was attributed to the corn laws, for now numbers had been out of work for months, and seeking it in various neighbouring towns without success, their families meanwhile left at home depending for subsistence on the chapter of accidents and the tender mercies of their neighbours.

The Rev. Mr. SIBREE, of Coventry, said; I trust, Mr. Chairman and Christian brethren, that I shall not be charged with arrogance or presumption in attempting to address you on the present momentous occasion, as I do it in compliance with the urgent request of our esteemed brethren who have so zealously undertaken the work of convening this assembly. I cast myself, therefore, on your candour while I advance a few plain remarks on the important subject now under consideration. We have met here to-day as ministers of various religious denominations. We ave agreed to sheathe the sword of theological controversy, and to unite in promoting an object worthy of our best energies, and dear to every Briton, but especially so to every British Christian,—the welfare of our country and the happiness of our fellow men. Let "the priest and the Levite," the selfish and the inhumane, "pass by on the other side;" but let us, as "good Samaritans," gather around the wounded, woe-begone traveller, and "pour in oil and wine," and thus illustrate and answer the inquiry, "Who is my neighbour?" In many points of theology we may differ, but there is one doctrine we all believe —one principle we all support—one creed to which we all subscribe—it is that contained in the "golden rule," "Whatsoever ye would that men should do unto you, do ye even so to them." The subject which has called us together is of no sectarian character. The groan and lament of starving millions is not the cry of a sect or party. Catholic and Protestant, Churchman, Dissenter, and Wesleyan, feel alike the iron hand of the oppressive bread tax, which, in the infliction of its tortures, at least, is "no respecter of persons." The cry of the widow and the fatherless is not the cry of a sect, unless it be of that "sect," which, among their oppressors, has been always "spoken against," that of the injured and the oppressed. In the support and defence of this sect, at least, I hope we may all be sectarians, and we would glory in the name. May it be the object of the members of this conference to accomplish that for which, "when the ear hears them it shall bless them, and when the eye sees them it shall give witness to them; because they delivered the poor that cried, and the fatherless, and him that had none to help him." We are called to express our deep conviction of the sinfulness of those laws that restrict the food of the community. It is not required of me to argue the question whether the corn laws do, or do not injure and oppress the mass of the population. Every day's observation proves to us, that in our laws exists some deep-rooted evil that affects the nation at large; an evil that deprives the artisan of employment, and at the same time cuts off the supply of bread. This evil, whose moral character we shall now more especially consider, has been proved again and again, even to the conviction, if not the conversion of most of its supporters, to be, the restriction of the food of the people. This, we maintain, is a crime against God as well as against man. "By the law," says an inspired apostle, "is the knowledge of sin;" and "This is the first and great commandment, Thou shalt love the Lord thy God with all thy heart, and with all thy soul, and with all thy mind. And the second is like unto it, Thou shalt love thy neighbour as thyself." Let the existing corn law, which prohibits the importation of food to a suffering, starving people, be tried by that standard, and it must certainly be "*found wanting*;"—wanting in justice, in humanity, in mercy. No such divine precept, as love to God and our neighbour, could ever have entered into the minds or counsels of the men who suggested, framed, and carried that anti-scriptural, anti-christian, unjust, inhuman law. Selfishness, of the meanest and most unworthy kind, dictated and decreed the enactment. The authority of the Supreme Being was set at defiance, his sceptre was trampled under foot; and the men who passed that law, and the monarch who affixed to it the royal signature, said in effect "Who is the Lord, that we should obey him?" I was lately conversing with a gentleman, who appeared to be an advocate for the corn laws, and after he had attempted to parry off all my other arguments against the monopoly, I made this appeal to him: "Well, sir, you are a professing Christian, and you must confess that the word of God con demns the system of withholding the corn." He at once replied, "There, sir, is your strong-hold, I confess I cannot defend the monopoly from the Bible." "Well, then," said I, "that consideration ought to settle the question." It reminded me of the story of the witness, in a court of justice, who said he had a dozen reasons to assign for the non-appear ance of a certain individual at the trial; and being requested to mention some of them, replied, "Why, then, my lord, in the first place, the man *is dead*." So in reference to the corn monopoly; we have a thousand arguments to plead against it; but, in the first place, it is a *crime*; and to any Christian man, need we say any thing more? Let us, for a moment, refer to "the law and to the testimony." "What saith the Scripture? How readest thou?" The divine purpose in creation is unfolded in these words; "And God said, Behold, I have given you every herb bearing seed which is upon the face of all the earth, and every tree in the which is the fruit of a tree yielding seed; to you it shall be for meat." "Moreover, the profit of the earth is for all: the king himself is served by the field." But the passage of sacred Scripture which more directly bears upon the question, and which is as good as a thousand, is that well known and oft-recited verse in the book of Prov., "He that withholdeth corn, the people shall curse him; but blessings shall be upon the head of him that selleth it." I will here cite the commentaries on that passage of three distinguished expositors; one an Independent, the other a Churchman, and the other a Wesleyan. Let my Independent brethren hear what good Matthew Henry says; "See here, 1st, What use we are to make of the gifts of God's bounty; we must not hoard them up merely for our own advantage, that we might be enriched by them, but we must bring them forth for the benefit of others, that they may be supported and maintained by them. It is a sin, when corn is dear and scarce, to withhold it, in hopes that it will still grow dearer, so to keep up and advance the market when it is already so high that the poor suffer by it; and at such a time it is the duty of those that have stocks of corn by them to consider the poor, and to be willing to sell it at the marke price, to be content with moderate profit, and not aim to make a gain of God's judgments. It is a noble and extensive piece of charity, for those who have stores wherewithal to do it, to help to keep the markets low when the price of our commodities grows excessive.—See here, 2nd. What regard we are to have to the voice of the people; we are not to think it an indifferent thing, and not worth heeding, whether we have the ill-will and word, or the good-will and word of our neighbours, their prayers or their curses; for here we are taught to dread their curses, and forego our own profits rather than incur them, and to court their blessings, and be at some expense to purchase them. Sometimes '*Vox populi, vox Dei*,' the voice of the people is the voice of God." Now let my Episcopalian brethren hear what their judicious commentator, Thomas Scott, says on the subject; "When the poor are pinched through the dearness of provisions many will not sell in hopes that it will be still dearer, preferring their gain to the relief of their perishing neighbours; but such mercenary wretches will be justly execrated; they will generally be losers by their avarice; they will be liable to the condemnation of God, whereas he who sells at a moderate price, will be commended and prayed for by those who are relieved, and will best consult his own benefit as well as the public good." And now, finally, let some one convey to our *absent*, alas! absent Wesleyan brethren, the following brief commentary of their learned Adam Clarke; "He who refuses to sell corn because he hopes for a dearth, and then can make his own price, the people shall curse him; yes, and God shall curse him also; and if he do not then turn and repent, he will get God's curse, and the curse of the poor, which will be a *canker* in his *money* during *time*, and a canker in his *soul* throughout *eternity*." Our Wesleyan brethren prove both by their doctrines and their practice that they are no monopolists of the bread of life. They have opened ports on almost every shore for the importation of that food, and they sing,

"Enough for each, enough for all,
Enough for evermore."

And surely they can never, either collectively or individually, sanction a monopoly of the bread that perisheth! They know, as well as ourselves, that both in a temporal and a spiritual sense, "In our Father's house there is bread enough, and to spare;" and why should any of his children "perish with hunger?" That it is a crime to restrict the food of the community is evident from the anger which good men in all ages have felt at such practices. It appears that in the days of Nehemiah there existed a corn monopoly, and "there was a great cry of the people and of their wives" against the monopolists. And the anger of that "faithful man, who feared God above many," was excited, and he "rebuked the nobles and the rulers," and compelled them to remove the restrictions, and to supply the people with corn. We may learn a lesson on this subject from the example of our blessed Lord. He saw the multitudes destitute of food; he had compassion on them; and instead of *monopolizing* the "five barley loaves and the two small fishes," he *multiplied* them. We cannot, it is true, perform such miracles, nor need we desire the power. We have mercies, and we need not miracles. Let us only open our ports, and remove all commercial restrictions, and then heaven's bounty shall flow in, and again it shall be said of the famishing multitudes, "they did all eat, and were filled." Brethren, if the corn monopoly be not a sin, it is a virtue; if it be not an evil, it is a good. We should, therefore, pray for a continuance and an increase of that good. What, then, would be a suitable prayer for a corn monopolist? "O thou Father of mercies, keep up and increase the price of food! Let *our* 'barns be filled with plenty and *our* presses burst out with new wine,' but regard not the cry of the poor and destitute! Let our horses be fed with the best of our corn, and let our 'dogs eat of the crumbs that fall from our table,' but let our fellow-men, our fellow-countrymen, our neighbours, pine in their misery, and die for want!" Oh, how awful do men's principles and practices sometimes appear, when they are formed into prayers! The corn monopolist, we know, justifies himself by an appeal to the existing laws; but we cite him before a higher tribunal than the Britian senate, and condemn him by a higher authority. In vain does he tell me of laws that sanction monopoly. There is a law above all the enactments of human codes, the same throughout the world, the same in all times; it is the law written in the Volume of Inspiration; the law written by the finger of God on the heart of man. "To human laws," said a celebrated living orator in the senate, "did they of old refer, who maintained the African slave trade; yet, in despite of law and of treaty, that infernal traffic is now destroyed, and its votaries put to death, like other pirates. How came this change to pass? Not, assuredly, by parliament leading the way; but the country at length awoke; the indignation of the people was kindled; it descended in thunder, and smote the traffic, and scattered its guilty profits to the winds. Now, then," *mutato nomine*, "let the corn monopolists beware; let their assemblies beware; let the government beware; let the parliament beware! The same country is once more awake—awake to the condition of starving thousands; the same indignation kindles in the bosom of the same people; the same cloud is gathering that annihilated the slave trade; and, if it shall descend, they on whom its crash may fall will not be destroyed before we have warned them; but we pray that their destruction may turn away from us the more terrible judgments of God!" I have been compelled to take an interest in the subject which has convened us together on the present occasion, from witnessing the sorrows and sufferings which have long been endured by a large portion of the inhabitants of the city where, for the last twenty-one years, my lot has been cast. And, O! brethren, I could

> "A tale unfold, whose lightest word
> Would harrow up your souls;"

I could open a scroll which, like that of Ezekiel, is "written within and without with mourning, lamentation, and woe;" I could relate scenes of misery sufficient to call forth the exclamation from every patriot breast in this assembly, "O that my head were waters, and mine eyes fountains of tears, that I might weep day and night for the slain of the daughters of my people!" In reply to the inquiries which have been forwarded to me in common with my brethren, I beg to state,

1st. That the ribbon and watch trades are the principal manufactories of Coventry. The working classes are generally very inadequately employed; for a long time past a great number have been absolutely destitute. Wages of employed persons in the ribbon trade, for the most part, are not more than 7s. or 8s. per week, and in very many instances, not more than 4s. or 5s. per week; few earn more than 12s. In the watch trade wages are somewhat higher, but full employment is by no means regular.

2nd. Within the last 20 years, wages in the silk trade, on which the bulk of the population depend, have diminished, directly and indirectly, full 50 per cent. The system of employment has entirely changed.

3rd. Dear food has never increased the demand for labour. On the other hand, employment has uniformly been most plentiful when bread has been cheapest.

4th. There has never existed any symptom of wages being influenced by the price of food. Wages have always been considered least in danger of falling when bread has been cheapest, because the demand for goods is greater when food is cheap.

5th. The condition of the labouring population was never so bad as at the present time.

6th. Poor rates are high, but not higher than they have been occasionally at former periods, but there are local circumstances (eligibility to the franchise, and the charities) which deter great numbers from seeking parochial relief, and induce them to endure very severe privations rather than do so. One thing may be safely stated as a fact, that the difficulty of paying the poor rates was never so great as at present, the working classes being frequently summoned before the magistrates, a hundred at a time, to enforce the rates from them.

7th. Petty thievery, vice, and destitution are extremely prevalent.

8th. Coventry is not an agricultural district.

9th. The uniform complaint of the middle and trading classes is, that times were never so bad with them before as they are now.

10th. The funds of our religious and benevolent societies have been somewhat diminished, but not to the degree that the state of trade might have led us to apprehend.

11th. Many of the working classes, through their distress, have been unable to provide themselves with what they deem suitable clothing for attendance on public worship, and have also been unable to pay their pew rents.

12th. Inability to provide children with clothing, has prevented the parents among the working classes from sending their children to our Sunday school; some, however, have been withdrawn from our school by acts of bribery, money and clothes being given, by some of the wealthier classes, for this purpose; and, in a season of depressed trade, these temptations overcome principle, conscience, and consistency.

One of our principal ribbon manufacturers informed me, a short time since, that he had resolved, if possible, to give up business, solely because he could not endure to witness the heart-rending scenes that daily came before his notice. If the wise and righteous measures proposed by her Majesty's present ministers had not been thwarted by a selfish, interested faction; if there had been any expectation held out that there would have been opened foreign marts for our manufactures, and a reduction effected in the price of food; if, in short, there had been any prospect that justice and mercy, humanity and charity, would have been allowed to preside in the British senate, a happy impulse would have been given to our trade, masters would, even at a present sacrifice, have employed their labourers, and hope, like the bow of promise, would have gleamed on the darkness of the retiring storm, and told of brighter days to come. But now, both masters and men are constrained to settle down in black despair, saying, "Our bones are dried, and our hope is lost, we are cut off for our parts." What a strange and awful spectacle does this island of ours present at this moment to the eye of heaven! Should some blest messenger from the skies be commissioned for the first time to visit this earth, alighting on "the base outside of the world," as he beheld the bright reflection of the sun on this fair creation, and saw the waving crops and pleasant pastures, he would deem its inhabitants happy, at least in the possession of heaven's bounty, and would anticipate the sight of temporal comfort among them. But as he approached nearer in his downward flight, sounds ungrateful would assail his ears. The cry of the oppressed, and the last sighs and death-groans of the dying, he would hear ascending to the Lord of Sabaoth. Astonished at the contrast between the plenty which he had witnessed, and the exclamations of misery he now heard, he would hastily retreat with horror, imagining that, in his too hasty flight, he had accidentally approached the precincts of the infernal world, part of the punishment of whose inhabitants consisted in having ever before their eyes the richest dainties, yet never allowed to partake of them; tantalized by the sight of food, yet perishing with hunger. And now, my brethren, for I may call you by this name, since we agree in one common creed of justice, I have endeavoured, though feebly, to expose the sinfulness of these unjust, oppressive laws, and the misery which their operation entails. Your exertions must now begin. I charge you as men, as Britons, as Christians, and as Christian ministers, to use your utmost efforts to annihilate them. Say not that you are weak, and can do nothing. The

God of truth, of justice, of mercy, is on your side. And know you not, that

> "There is a tide in the affairs of men,
> Which, taken at the flood, leads on to fortune;
> Omitted, all the voyage of their life
> Is bound in shallows and in miseries?"

The storm is up. It is for you to guide it. Let the mental, moral, and ministerial influence you possess, be employed on behalf of the spiritual and temporal interests of our fellow-men. And, above all, let us look to Him

> "Who rides on the whirlwind, and directs the storm;"

"by whom kings reign, and princes decree justice;" and pray that he would "be merciful to us, and bless us; and cause the earth to yield her increase." The rev. gentleman was loudly cheered throughout his speech.

The CHAIRMAN said, from the list of names which he had before him, he anticipated that, intensely interesting as these statements were, they should not be able to receive all the documents that were ready. He, therefore, hoped, that if any gentleman were not called upon, he would send his document, with his signature, to the committee, that a general digest might be made of them. He then introduced

The Rev. Mr. BAIRD, of Paisley, the moderator of the Scotch Secession Church, who said, he was aware that the unfortunate town from which he came had excited a considerable portion of the attention of the public mind generally, and he had been asked to make a few statements relative to it, but it would occupy too much of their time to go through it. The town of Paisley had a population of 50,000 souls, and it had not been on the increase during the last ten years, or but very slightly so indeed. He might mention, that the trade of Paisley was a fancy trade; all manner of fancy work, in silk, being the staple trade of the town; so that it would be seen that a large population like that, dependent on a fancy trade, occupied a somewhat unfortunate position in times of an adverse kind. When goods were manufactured of a plain fabric, if the maker could afford to hold them till the next season, he might secure himself against loss; but the maker of fancy goods, if he did not sell them in this market or this season, might throw them into the fire, for if the fashion was gone, they would have become mere rubbish; and the consequence of that was, that whenever there was a breath of commercial convulsion, from any part of the country, their trade, like a sensitive plant, instantly recoiled from the blast. Now, there was another fact, that whilst there had been very great and recurring distress, for the last sixteen years, it was not to be understood that on that account the trade of the town of Paisley was a decreasing trade. It might appear strange that, instead of theirs being a decreasing trade, it was, in point of fact, a very largely increasing trade, and during the last sixteen years that he had lived in the town, he believed he spoke within bounds when he said that the trade of the town of Paisley had doubled, if not quadrupled, and yet they had witnessed great distress. They were all aware that immense improvements had been made in reference to machinery for weaving, and the consequence was, that the hand-loom weavers, finding it a hopeless matter to compete with power-looms, had, in the various towns and villages of Renfrewshire, Ayrshire, Lanarkshire, and even as far as Perthshire, had thrown themselves on the trade of Paisley finding that its trade was an increasing trade. It was a trade the fabrics of which were captivating to the eye, and, with the trade of the country in a healthy state, likely to increase to a large amount. Under these circumstances, the hand-loom weavers had thrown themselves in thousands on the town of Paisley. When he went to Paisley there was scarcely such a thing as a weaver employed out of the town; but now, most of the weavers were employed out. He noticed these things, because the increase of the trade of Paisley might be brought up in parliament to defeat sound arguments on the subject of the corn laws; and the distress might be traced in a measure to other causes, such as speculation, fostered by too great facilities of bank accommodation, and that, therefore, it had no connection with the existing corn laws. The truth was, the warehouses would soon be emptied of their goods, if the agricultural produce of America could be taken in exchange for them. Then that trade would take up very nearly all the hands dislodged by the improvement of the power-loom, and furnish to them the means of remunerative employment. (Hear.) The corn laws not only prevent this healthful expansion of the trade of Paisley, but they impose such a pressure on the trade and food of the country generally, that during seasons of general depression the manufacturers are afraid to make stocks of fancy goods, which might, in consequence of this depression, not be got quit of while the fashion of the season lasted, and would then, consequently, be utterly valueless. In these circumstances, the trade of Paisley, being a fancy one, not only languished, but it shrunk, suffered, and was all but annihilated with such a killing frost. Every two or three years came a season of distress in that trade. Four years ago Paisley was for four months almost without trade of any kind, during which time thousands were dependent for subsistence on charity. £8,000 were raised in that town alone in subscriptions. Although a town of 50,000 inhabitants, it was a town chiefly of an operative class, the manufacturers forming a very small part of the population; and in subscribing £8,000, they did an immense thing; but, with nearly six thousand souls depending on them, they could not raise another shilling, and a deputation went to London, had interviews with the government, and, through their subscriptions and influence with the queen, they obtained £4,000, which enabled them to tide over that time of distress. From that time to the present, which was another season of distress, much privation had prevailed. In the present commercial crisis, nearly half a million sterling could not enable the merchants of the place to meet their engagements. Thousands of the poor were walking about, without any subsistence but from credit or charity and assessments; and in this way 3,000 souls had been fed for months. Masses of the people were in a state of most consummate wretchedness. Human nature has limits set to its endurance, and it was well that the mighty of the earth should remember that important truth, and not permit suffering to press too heavily, lest the bonds which held society together might be snapt asunder. For every one soliciting aid in that town, three or four were suffering in silence. In these circumstances their ears were sometimes open to counsels not of the wisest kind, yet it was to a great extent a noble population, and maintained a conflict with great difficulties in a most heroic manner. (Applause.) Many families there had been out of work for months, not a shilling going in to them, which, to this moment, had not asked a farthing from parish or alms. One mother said to him, with tears in her eyes, "We have borne it before; we'll bear it again." There were multitudes of such cases. While the charitable funds were exhausted, the applicants were increasing; and the funds raised by charity were sometimes exhausted before the most deserving applied. The pastors of the churches, during former times of distress, made collections therein for persons not seeking aid, but suffering deeply. One of his elders visited a large family, months out of work, in which clothes had been pledged, and the members of which were not able to appear at church; and the elder found the head of the family exceedingly indisposed even to receive one shilling of the money taken to him. On the elder at length pressing him next day, the head of the family admitted they had been without food and fire thirty hours, and he said they must take something or perish. There were high principles amongst a suffering community, which threw a glory around the suffering homes of the poor seldom found in the halls of the wealthy. Another individual in similar circumstances was waited upon, and it was difficult to prevail upon him to accept of 2s. 6d. He got work that evening, and next forenoon he returned the half-crown, rejoicing that his independence was still unimpaired. (Cheers.) He was much struck, last week, with the complaints of a mother of a family, who brought under his consideration several distressing cases, where young ladies, accustomed to live in affluence, were reduced to the lowest extremities; they had to pawn their last gown, before they could bring themselves to acknowledge their distress, or demand workhouse relief. In Scotland it had been always the practice with industrious families to lay in large quantities of provisions; he had been informed of persons who had been so reduced by the operation of the corn laws, that they, according to the prediction of a Scottish poet, when the corn laws were passed, were obliged to go to the grocery shops for a pennyworth of oatmeal to save themselves from actual starvation. The influence of such a state of things on the education and religion of the people was most disastrous, but time did not permit to enter into detail.

The Rev. Mr. M'KERROW stated, that a vast number of valuable documents had been received, which it was important to bring before the meeting during the evening. For this purpose it was necessary that the committee of documents should retire to the boroughreeve's room, to arrange those documents that were to come before the meeting. The committee then withdrew, and the rev gentleman announced that it was agreed by some ministers to hold a prayer meeting each morning during the sitting of the conference in his chapel, Lloyd-street, from half-past eight to half-past nine o'clock. Gentlemen who had prepared resolutions to be submitted to the conference were requested to leave them in the boroughreeve's room at the close of the meeting.

The CHAIRMAN then introduced to the meeting—

The Rev. E. DAVIES, from Lewes, in Sussex, who said he would confine himself to the document which he was requested to lay before the meeting. But before reading it, he begged to state, that the object of the meeting had the most hearty concurrence of the people of Lewes, who had been most successfully employed in promoting the same end in a somewhat different way, having unseated two monopolists and brought in two anti-monopolists at the last election. He might also be allowed to observe, that, though his friends in Sussex were distinguished by their poverty rather than their riches, the moment they heard that a conference of ministers was to be held in Manchester, they determined to defray his expenses here, that he might take a part in its proceedings. The document stated, that "in Lewes, Sussex, and its neighbourhood, the working classes generally are not employed—that there is no proportionate increase of the wages to the increase of the price of food—that the greatest demand for labour has been when the price of corn was low." He could bear testimony to the distressed condition of many of the labouring classes; and if the time of the meeting permitted, although from the south, where the labouring classes were supposed to be better off than in other parts of the country, he could make statements of their wretched condition, which would harrow up their souls. (Applause.) During 1835 and 1836, this class enjoyed many comforts more than now. Their wages enabled them to purchase articles of comfort. At the present time there are 134 uninhabited houses, the proportion of 1 in 13, and those being generally of the working class. From 1811 to 1821 the increase in the population was 1,500; but at the last census the increase was 500, instead of 1,500. There were instances of small traders being obliged to give up their shops to prevent total ruin; and, if this state of things continued, that class would merge into labourers. Many could not attend places of worship for want of decent clothing; the attendance at Sabbath schools was smaller than it otherwise would be, from the same cause. In conclusion, he said, the high price of provisions produced crime, and these laws were at variance with Christianity.

The Rev. Mr. BAYLEY, of Sheffield, next addressed the meeting. He said, he should confine himself to two or three instances illustrative of the state of the town in which he lived. He was well aware, that facts were every thing; it was not their opinions, but facts, which would weigh with the government. They might all be acquainted with some things that others did not know; and he should propose, that they should take no more oral evidence, but that those who had statements to make should send them to the committee. Last Saturday evening, as he was going into the town (of Sheffield), he met a poor man, named Bradshaw; he said he had earned but 9s. that week; he had three children; he could earn 20s. if in full work; and he attributed his not having it to the corn laws. He asked him what was his prospect; to which the reply was, "If there is not a change soon, I will not say what will be the consequences." He could bear witness with the reverend moderator who had preceded him, as to the noble principle of the poor; but the moral effects of the corn laws would destroy that principle. He knew that the poor helped each other, much more than the rich helped them; but the power to do that was decreasing every day. He went to two pawnbrokers, and inquired of them if they would like to bring the members of the House of Commons to see the pawnbroker's shop. They took their views of life from palaces. He had taken his from the pawnbroker's shop. There was the father's watch, the mother's wedding-ring, and the child's garment, stolen from it perhaps by its mother, to gratify the means of indulging in intemperance, corrupted first by the influence of the corn laws. He went to a physician, and asked him what was the state of public health. He replied, that he scarcely dare think of it, and that he believed in God many a man was sacrificed every day from the want of sustenance; and that many a one who might have lived to be an honour to his country, perished from not being able to procure sustenance from the almost barren breast of the mother. I adjure you by the thousands who are starving around you; I beseech you in the name of those who suffer more by fear than by necessity; I beseech you to remember that there are those who, though children now, will be the masters of society in the course of eight or ten years, and will shape it how they please, and your children must take the consequences; it is in your hands now to adhere on the side of the poor particularly, as far as justice will allow; and remember that there is a mighty difference between the issue of this conflict to the poor and to the upper classes. Capital can retire to its bank; genius can emigrate to more favoured parts of the world; but where is poverty to turn? (Hear.) Where is the poor man to go? Where are the women worn to the bone with domestic sorrow, and the men whose spirits are broken within them by alarm and privation? what is to become of them—of our poor population, of whom and of whose high moral bearing so much has been said to-night? Gentlemen, we are not the men that should be the last to remember,—indeed, we should be the first to remember, the eternal, the universal, the individual connection between every item of morals and extreme poverty. (Great applause.)

The CHAIRMAN said, after having contemplated those graphic pictures drawn by an independent minister, he had to introduce the Rev. Mr. Hearne, a minister of the Roman Catholic church.

Mr. HEARNE said, he came forward as a clergyman long residing in one of those districts of Manchester almost entirely inhabited by our poorer brethren. Poverty had been taking the most awful strides there within the last three years. He noticed it towards the end of 1838, when, and during 1839, he had to witness the most painful distress. Towards the end of 1839, it became clamorous; the cries for bread were loud; a charitable committee was formed, and for the first time he was brought amongst the clergy of the Church of England, and he never saw a body of men work with such zeal for the poor as they did. Oh that these men were amongst us now! (Applause.) He had taken the opportunity of expressing his feelings on the subject to his own congregation, and he was happy in having now an opportunity of doing so amongst ministers of various denominations. There were then 2000 families without a bed to lie on. In one district 2000 families, 8666 persons, had only 1s. 2½d. per head a week; in another 5s. 3d., and in the third only 6s. 3½d. for each family to live on. And in consequence of the inability of these poor people to pay, two hundred provision dealers made bad debts to the amount of upwards of £24,000. The same distress still existed in the neighbourhoods of St. George's Road and Newton-Lane, and he was astonished at the patience of the people. It was well for us that Chartism had broken out two years ago, instead of at present. (Hear.) In 1839 the poor weaver had 5s. 6d. a cut for that for which he could not get 2s. 9d. now; and, with the price of corn, how could the people be otherwise than starving! In his sick calls, which he did not choose, in one cellar, 34, Thompson-street, he found 11 in family, and only the wages of two boys, together 6s., to keep them. In another case, the mother ill of inflammation, and the father sick, and all the family supported by the wages of one little boy, working four days a week, getting 3s. Another family of 8 persons, in Pilling's-buildings, had last week only six shillings, the earnings of one girl, to maintain them, and on Monday I found them at a dinner procured by the pawning of a gown borrowed from a relative in Oxford Road. If he could bring the hand-loom weavers through that room, and show them how much of bare squalid skin and emaciated bone their forms consisted of, the conference would at once pronounce a universal malediction on the corn laws. For three dozen of 3-4ths shawls a weaver would only get 6s. 9d., and out of that he would have to pay 1s. 9d. for winding. Must they not, in spite of the frowns of the aristocracy, say, as far as our influence goes, such things shall cease to be? One man said to him, "If anything stirs, I'll be up; for better die abroad than starve at home." It gave him (Mr. Hearne) infinite pleasure to see this assembly, for it was a proof that though they might differ about modes of faith, charity, the soul and essence of religion, was there; and when they appeared with their flocks before the judgment-seat of God, they might hear in reference to this cause, "I was sick and in prison and ye visited me; hungry, and ye fed me: naked, and ye clothed me. Well done, ye good and faithful servants; enter ye into the joy of your Lord." (Great applause.)

The Rev. Mr. STRACHAN, St. James's parish, Forfar, a clergyman of the Established Church of Scotland, then came forward and said, that the subject of the corn laws was of such vast importance; that these laws had such an influence upon the national resources, and upon the moral and physical condition of the people, that the most timid and diffident might well be justified in coming forward upon such an occasion, to advocate their total and immediate abolition. The Anti-corn-law Society of Forfar, in Scotland, had elected him to take a part in the conference of ministers; and the feelings of his own heart, and the condition of the labouring poor, made him all the more willing to travel nearly 400 miles, that he might join with those delegates from other quarters in pleading upon this momentous subject. When he considered the natural position of England among the nations of the earth, he was inclined to apply to her the language of the prophet to ancient Tyre, "The harvest of the river is her revenue, and she is a mart of nations." Whatever the land-owners might say, she depended more upon the sea than the dry land for her wealth and power, and if only justice were done to her, England could cope with the whole earth. And yet, notwithstanding her glorious natural position, and the skill and industry of her own people, he was constrained to say, that many of the labouring classes were in a worse condition than the widow of Zarephath, when she made the solemn asseveration to the prophet, "As the Lord thy God liveth, I have not a cake, but an handful of meal in a barrel, and a little oil in a cruze." For he had found more than one among the labouring poor in the town where he resided, who had neither meal nor oil. (Hear.) He could not suppose, that any minister who seriously thought on the misery and wretchedness which stared him in the face in his daily visitations, would hesitate to advocate the repeal of those laws which produced stagnation of trade, and would soon bring total ruin upon the country. He would bring forward a few cases to show that ministers were more deeply concerned with the corn laws than many people supposed. A woman of another parish, who thought herself dying, sent for him to visit her in preference to her own minister, and assigned as a reason for so doing, that when she was out of employment, and in want, he refused to give her any aid, or to use his influence to get any work for her. She could not think, she said, that he would have much affection for her soul, when he had so little for her body. This fact proved two things. It proved, in the first place, although the cold-hearted and affluent might sneer, and say that the corn-laws was a *political subject*, that the suffering poor considered it a *minister's subject*. And it proved, in the second place, that it was impossible for a minister in the proper discharge of his duty to confine himself to the spiritual, and to refuse to take any interest in their temporal condition. He must be their minister for the things of time as well the things of eternity, or he would soon cease to be their minister altogether. (Hear.) A member of his own congregation, after being three weeks without work, entreated him to use his influence to get employment for her. After se ral unsuccessful attempts, he at last succeeded. And was not this another evidence, that whatever the rich may say, the poor do not conside. that a minister steps out of his way when he looks into their temporal concerns? In the town of Forfar, which entirely depends upon hand-loom weaving, one-third of the people are entirely idle, and another third are only half employed. The capital of the manufacturers is rapidly leaving them, and wages are reduced about one half within the last 20 years, and one-third within the last five. In 1835 the four-pound loaf was only 4½d., whilst at present it is 7d. What a state of things! wages falling one-third, and bread rising nearly one-half, in the short space of five years! (Hear.) The Secession minister of my parish met the other day with an affecting instance of destitution—a poor man who was not able to work out his web for hunger; he could get nothing to eat before receiving payment for his work, and it was necessary for the minister to enable him to get food to strengthen him for his labour.

(Hear, hear.) The rev. gentleman then proceeded to detail some facts tending to show that wages did not rise with the price of food, but the contrary. He concluded by saying, that God registered in his book the doings of his ministers. And if the law of love was binding upon all men, it was especially so upon those who were the teachers of others; and how could this law be fulfilled, if men were allowed to perish without any effort being made on their part to remove those unjust and immoral laws which caused their distresses? (Cheers.)

The Rev. J. WINTERBOTTOM, from Haworth, commenced by observing, that he came from a part of the country which was the centre of the worsted trade, having Bradford as the great mart of that branch of manufacture. In that portion of the kingdom great suffering had prevailed for several years past, and the evils attending the accursed bread tax were more and more visible. Since 1816 the wages of the hand-loom weavers had sunk one-half, and the cost of provisions for the subsistence of the poor had increased. In the chapelry of Haworth subscriptions had been raised for the relief of the poor, and a grant from London of £300 had been added to those subscriptions; but all was soon swallowed up in the gulph of want and woe, which unjust legislation had created. Hundreds of families had been found, whose circumstances, as to clothing and beds, were truly appalling. The cause of this misery was attributed by those poor sufferers to the accursed corn laws, which enhanced the price of bread and shut up the avenues of trade. Interested parties might reproach the members of the conference as being political partisans—the press might open upon them all its time-serving artillery—but, having the Bible on their side, they would go forward with fortitude, and relying on divine assistance, they would soon see the abominable corn laws buried in the gulph of oblivion. To deter us in our course many things conspired. Timid Christians were afraid of defilement from political contamination, and would not come out to help in the great work now contemplated by this conference. Poor creatures! they had yet to learn what true patriotism is. He who loved his country, he who regarded the precepts of humanity, he who hated oppression, he who loved God, would take part in this cause. For the last twenty-five years he had unvaryingly opposed the accursed bread tax, and would do, so long as they disgraced the British statute-book. The powers of men, the threats of those who live by oppression, would never move him. There was a Master in heaven to serve, who had commanded all his ministers to plead the cause of the poor, and this duty he would, to the best of his power, fulfil, not only now, here, in the presence of this great assembly, but elsewhere, as he could. He concluded by expressing a hope, that the corn laws would soon be abolished, and the dishonour of British legislation, in taxing the poor man's bread, be speedily wiped away. (Cheers.)

The Rev. S. PRICE, of Abersychan, Monmouthshire, addressed the meeting to the following effect:—Mr. Chairman and gentlemen, the gentleman who last addressed us said, that as this meeting consisted of ministers from all parts of the kingdom, the place he came from was a part of the kingdom; and I think, sir, that Wales is a part of the kingdom, and should have a voice in this assembly. From this consideration I appear before you at present; for I should be very sorry for the principality not to be represented in this conference, which I hope will be done, as there are many ministers present who are far more competent to do so than myself. I labour in an iron manufacturing district of Monmouthshire; and I can assure this meeting that it is not the cotton manufactories alone that suffer from the badness of the times; the iron trade is also in a most depressed state. Within the last fifteen months, in the neighbourhood where I live, the wages for labour have been reduced full 25 per cent., while provisions have advanced 10 or 15 per cent.; and many who are willing to work cannot obtain employment. During the last month, in consequence of the benevolence of some kind friends, I have been enabled to administer some little relief to more than one hundred families, and I found many in as great distress as any of whom we have heard this evening. I would mention one very appalling case, which came under my notice—of a poor woman, who walked four miles for a loaf of bread from the relieving officer, and in a short time after she returned home, she was delivered of twins; this took place on Saturday: and on the following Monday, among many others, I visited her house, and found eight persons in that family, destitute of the necessaries of life. Gentlemen, I am happy to inform you that the people in the neighbourhood from which I come are opposed to the corn laws, and all monopolies in every form. They wish for free trade, and they are opposed to them on the principle of justice; for the corn laws are unjust in principle; they are a protection of one class of people, to the injury of others. They are no protection to the agricultural labourer; there are many men in Wales, with families of six or eight children, who labour all the week for the miserable pittance of five or six shillings; so the corn laws are no protection to the labourer. Neither are they to the farmers; they are rapidly retrograding in their circumstances. They are a protection to none but to the rich landowners of our country; and all know that they are no protection to the manufacturers. It was remarked by a gentleman, in the morning, that it manifested great zeal and disinterestedness in the ministers who had come from great distances to this meeting, and who have paid their own expenses; but I am happy to remind this assembly, that great credit is due to the people in Wales, who have come forward and have sent my brother and myself here, and have paid our expenses; we appear before you as their representatives. And, sir, I am glad to meet in this conference ministers from every part of the United Kingdom,—from Scotland, Ireland, Wales, and from England; and as a Welshman I give you my hand, determined never to relinquish the grasp till we obtain the abolition of the corn laws. (Cheers.)

The Rev. Charles Berry, of Leicester, was called on, but as he did not answer,

The Rev. S. Martin, of Trowbridge, Wiltshire, came forward, and stated, that he appeared on behalf of a numerous body of the suffering poor, who had deputed him to state their famishing condition to this conference. There were more ways of causing the death of the poor than by the hand of violence: he had known numbers of them starved by inches; and many, in their graves, would have been alive now, but for this accursed, abominable, corn law. He knew some families perishing for want of bread; one family, consisting of a father, mother, and six children, had but half of a small loaf for their support during the past week. In one house which he visited, last Christmas, there was only a little straw in one corner, and some rags in another, on which a boy and girl lay dying, he believed, of starvation. The mother, son, and daughter, were now in their graves, and the father was wandering about alone, an outcast and a beggar. How long was this state of things to continue? Truly it was high time for something to be done.

The Rev. H. Hunter, of Nottingham, conceived the evidence, when properly collected, would tell more forcibly on the government than any number of speeches, however eloquent or powerful. He had visited not only a number of the working people, but also of the large manufacturers themselves. One master said, within the last ten days, he was obliged to turn away 300 hands. Another employed 500 less than he did three months ago. There were now about 800 families without the means of providing food. He (Mr. Hunter) was connected with one of the largest churches in the kingdom, and when he visited the garrets and cellars, and told them that a number of ministers from all parts of the kingdom were anxious to see them righted, they were delighted. Those still in full work said, their wages, after all expenses were paid, were 6s. to 8s. a week, in the stocking trade, and the masters said the same. In the union workhouse he saw young men and women in perfect health, obliged to throw themselves into that place, and no doubt from the operation of the corn laws. A friend had told him he had goods locked up in a warehouse in America, which he could soon convert into money, if he could bring corn here in exchange for them. He believed ministers of all denominations would go hence more disposed than ever to work in the cause of God and of religion.

The Rev. W. Jenkins, Baptist minister, Dolio, in the principality, said, they were assembled to transport monopoly, not to any other climate, but 20,000 fathoms deep. Whatever he might be ashamed of, in leaving this life, he believed he should not be ashamed of coming 200 miles to Manchester. In Radnorshire there were 800 cottagers, and he came to represent every Baptist in that county. The gain of the craft was at risk, and the monopolists were afraid to lose it. They were like Demetrius and the silversmiths of Ephesus. (Laughter.) The feet of monopoly were of clay, like that of the image in scripture. Here were 650 ministers; let them take their weapons and use them against this monopoly. Welshmen's hearts were large; they wanted monopoly down, and commerce free as the air we breathe in. (Applause.)

The Rev. Mr. Stirling, of Kirriemuir, in Forfarshire, said, the same features of misery and wretchedness described in other parts of the kingdom, were common to his neighbourhood. There the average wages were 4s. 6d. a week of the manufacturing operatives; and, where the wages were more, it was by the employment of females. A respectable manufacturer said, that, not long ago, he saw two respectable women leaving the town with small parcels, and it was ascertained that these industrious women, supposed not the most destitute, were begging, and the parcels concealed old mantles, in which they begged where they thought they were not known. As to the effects of the corn law on our religious institutions, he must state, that, in consequence of those laws, the religious feelings of the people in his neighbourhood were becoming benumbed. Some had left off attending the church, and, as to those who remained, the prayer meetings, once numerous, were but thinly attended; the missionary societies diminished in funds; education was languishing; and the children of the poor were kept at home for want of decent clothing. The duty of visiting his people, in which he formerly delighted, was now becoming one of the most unpleasant nature; his feelings were tortured by the scenes of misery and suffering he encountered. He considered this one of the most important meetings of ministers that had ever existed. He rejoiced that the determination of this meeting would not be borne down by evil-speaking; and he also rejoiced that, whilst they engaged in calling the attention of government and the country to the state of the poor, they had determined also to take the cause of the poor before the Lord of Sabaoth.

The Chairman said, he thought he should have had to close the meeting at this period, though its proceedings had gone on increasing in interest, but he had to announce that in their midst was one of the nobles, the peers of the realm,—those who carried into the highest grades of society the principles of genuine benevolence. (Applause.) He need only mention to them a name which he was sure would stand associated in their minds not more for the exaltation of its rank than for the genuineness of its philanthropy,—he meant the Earl of Ducie. (Great applause.) He (the chairman) asked them to accord with him in an invitation to his lordship to address the assembly for a few moments. ("Hear," and applause.) He was sure it would gladden their honest hearts to know that they were not looked upon by the aristocracy as a whole with the eye of contempt and scorn; but that there was very hearty sympathy with this meeting, not only in the depths of the lowest degradation and woe, which they sought to remove, but also in the loftier ranks of society; and it was delightful to see all that was dignified in grandeur brought into association with all that was pitiable in wretchedness, there to relieve and commiserate it.

The Earl of DUCIE came forward amidst loud cheers, and said—Mr. Chairman and Rev. Gentlemen, I can assure you that nothing ever came to me more unexpectedly than the request which has just been communicated to me by your chairman, that I should address you. I had come here for the purpose of learning, and not of teaching. I came to hear from the mouths of those who may be supposed to be the best judges, because they have seen most of the misery of the labouring population. I was requested most unexpectedly, and had I followed my own inclination, perhaps it is a question whether I should not have declined to comply with that request to come forward on this occasion; but I am a fellow-labourer in the same vineyard with yourselves. (Cheers.) I feel as strongly as you do the oppressive nature of the corn laws. Having on other occasions expressed those opinions, and having devoted myself, with others in the same branch of the legislature with myself, in support of the same opinions, I felt it a sacred duty not to decline coming forward on any ground of my own private feelings. And, however unfit to address such an assembly as the present, I felt it a duty which I could not justly decline. I have for many years been of opinion that the corn laws, as they exist, are extremely oppressive to the labouring population, and injurious to every branch of society. Had I been a monopolist—had I been one of those who had voted for charging an additional price on the bread of the poor man, I am quite sure that the testimony laid before you to-day by the reverend gentlemen who have spoken, would have been enough to persuade me that I had been in the wrong. (Applause.) It would have been enough to persuade me that I should retract those opinions. (Hear, hear.) But my opinions have been always those good old-fashioned Whig opinions, (laughter and applause,) that that government was the best which gave the greatest amount of happiness to the greatest number of its subjects. I am satisfied that the present corn laws are not acting in that way. Gentlemen, I am aware that discussions on the corn laws, and on the general principles of freedom of commerce, are looked upon by many as a merely political, or rather, I should say, an entirely party question. But I look on the question in a very different point of view. It is not, in my mind, a question whether Lord Melbourne should preside over the government of the country, or whether Sir Robert Peel should preside over its interests; but it is a question deeply involving the morality of our population. I believe that to take an active part in the suppression or alteration of the existing corn laws, is to do much towards education—towards increasing morality, and the spread of religious instruction throughout the land. (Hear.) These are the motives by which I am guided in the line of conduct which I shall pursue as regards the corn laws; and, although the party with which I shall most probably vote in the house in a few days will be but small, I shall then see those on whom you may depend. (Applause.) Though that body may not be numerous, I am quite sure I am saying no more than you will believe, when I say that that minority will be active, (Cheers,) and that they are all actuated by the highest motives. (Approbation.) It gave me the greatest pleasure to hear the Rev. Mr. Spencer speak in the way he did of Lord Radnor, than whom there is no man to whom the country owes a deeper debt. (Cheers.) He, with the Earl Fitzwilliam, (Cheers,) are not actuated by party spirit—their support of the ministerial project is founded on the purest grounds. I know they feel as you all feel—as all the ministers of religion whom I have listened to with so much pleasure to-day—that the happiness, and moral position, and religious instruction of the community, depend much on the corn-law question. (Applause.) As regards what I have heard to-day, there are many arguments used by the opponents of this question—though, indeed, in parliament I have heard but two—one of them the fallacy regarding wages, and the second, which is equally false, that much land will be thrown out of cultivation if the corn laws be repealed. Indeed it was boldly stated that one-third of the land of this country would be thrown out of cultivation. I have been for many years a practical agriculturist. I have been thrown much amongst them, and although there is a great misapprehension amongst them as to their real interests, I believe a greater body of practical agriculturists is with us than many suppose. (Hear.) I can only add, from my own experience in agriculture, from my own knowledge, and what I can glean from those whose opinions I consider the best, that so far from an alteration in the present corn laws tending in any way to throw land out of cultivation, the more probable result will be to bring more land into cultivation, and that cultivation, too, of a higher character. (Hear.) I will not trespass upon you any longer, but I felt it a duty to respond to the call of the chairman; and I will only add, that any way in which I can advance that cause which you have met here to promote, I shall at all times throw aside all private feelings and interests; (applause;) you will always find me ready, and anxious, and willing, to work with you. (Great applause.)

The Chairman said, that those ministers who had not had an opportunity of giving their oral testimony with respect to this important object, would be kind enough to commit it to writing, that it might be placed in the hands of the committee of documents, in order to be reduced to a digest; because he was thoroughly satisfied that the publication of that which they were capable of communicating would be the death-knell and death-warrant of that dreadful evil which they all deplored, and which they were bound under the sanction of high authority, as well as by the evidence laid before them that day, by all sacred and constitutional measures to remove.

The Rev. J. W. Massie then announced the proceedings for the following day. The prayer meeting in the morning, for such as were pleased to attend it, would be held in Lloyd-street Chapel (Mr. M'Kerrow's), at half-past eight o'clock; and he hoped those who meant to attend would be punctual there, in order that they might be punctual in their attendance at the Town Hall, which would be opened for the gathering of ministers at nine o'clock; but business would not commence till half-past nine precisely. During the meeting of to-morrow (Wednesday), there would be submitted various propositions, which had been considered by the committee of resolutions, which committee was requested to meet immediately after the close of the present meeting in the boroughreeve's room. He read the names of the committee: amongst them were,—the Revs. W. Gadsby, D. Hearne, Richard Fletcher, Thomas Spencer, W. M'Kerrow, J. W. Massie, Wm. Shuttleworth, Blair. Banks Reaf, Swan, Carr, Maldon, Good, Parsons, &c. The Young Men's Anti-Monopoly Association of Manchester, rejoiced at this conference, had resolved to hold a *soiree* on Thursday evening, where they might entertain such ministers as chose to be present, the tea-party being given in honour of the conference; but he hoped ministers would not attend it in such numbers as to render the conference meeting inefficient that evening. In conclusion, he would propose, "That the most respectful thanks of this assembly be given to our respected chairman, the Rev. Thomas Adkins, for the manner in which he has presided over the laborious business of this day; the tact which he has displayed in the conduct of it, and the energy and spirit which he has thrown into its proceedings." The Rev. W. M'Kerrow seconded the motion, which passed with great applause.

The Rev. T. Adkins said, that, he highly estimated the undeserved expression of their approbation, in the first instance, in placing him in that honourable position, and in the second place, in awarding to him the testimony of their approval, an approval which he felt he did not deserve, but which he was conscious he had aimed to attain; and if he had in any measure succeeded in promoting the august object which had convened them on this occasion, he needed not the meed of human approbation to reward him; he had his reward in the testimony of his own conscience, and in the anticipation of the woes of their suffering fellow-countrymen being mitigated, if not wholly relieved and enfranchised from the monopolies which oppressed them.—The meeting he now declared adjourned.

The proceedings terminated, and the numerous ministers present separated, about half-past nine o'clock.

During great part of the evening, a numerous concourse of persons assembled in front of the Town Hall, and appeared to manifest much interest in the proceedings within that building.

WEDNESDAY, AUGUST 18.

The Rev. Mr. Chaplin, of Bishop's Stortford, the chairman appointed at the opening of the Conference to preside on this day, took the chair about twenty minutes after nine o'clock. He commenced by stating he entered upon the arduous engagement before him under strong encouragements from two considerations; one was a full conviction of the great importance of the object in view, and the other was a perfect satisfaction in his own mind of the propriety of their present mode of procedure, with a view to its attainment. He said that it was his opinion that a lengthened address from the chair on the second day would be out of place; and after the observations of his friend, who occupied the chair on the previous day, he should think it wrong to take up their time. Let it not be supposed, however, that he entered on the proceedings with half-heartedness. That this might be beyond the fear of misconstruction, he placed, then, at the front of the proceedings of that day his public profession that the cause was the cause of justice and humanity; words which, if they had banners, ought to be inscribed on them as their motto in letters of gold. But, though they had no banners on which to inscribe the words, they had what he deemed far better, hearts on which were inscribed what those words express. (Applause.) It was with great satisfaction and pleasure that he had heard on the preceding evening a noble Lord, who had favoured them with his presence on this great occasion, state that the question was not whether this or that statesman should hold the reins of power; it was no question of party politics; but they were met to consider the causes of prevalent distress, especially among the poor, and whether any legitimate means for alleviating that growing distress could be found and adopted by the ministers of religion. The rev. gentleman, after reading the rules adopted by the committee to regulate the proceedings, concluded by introducing to the meeting the gentleman announced on the previous evening from the United States.

Mr. CURTIS, from Ohio, U. S., was received with great cheering. He said he was sensible of the honour, and grateful for the privilege, of addressing such a convention as this; for he not only felt it to be an honour, as a lover of mankind, to engage in such a work as this, but, as an American, he was also thankful for the privilege, for his country had an interest in this cause as well as their own; and he did not wish to conceal from any individual that this was one source of the interest he felt in this great question. He did not propose, however, here to set forth the bearings which a repeal of the corn laws would have upon the interests of his own country; but, on the contrary, what advantages England might derive from a free and open trade in corn with America. In that distant land, across the wide Atlantic, they had communication with this country almost every day; they heard of the distress of the English operatives—of the depression of trade—of families starving—of misery, wretchedness, and want. (Hear, hear.) To them this would seem strange, if not aware of the cause; for, on the other hand, their granaries were filled, and their markets glutted with food. (Hear, hear.) Their great distress was, not that they had not sufficient to eat and drink, but they had so much that they did not know what to do with it. (Hear, hear.) He stood before them to bear testimony to the fact that his countrymen were ready and anxious to exchange their grain and meat, and every thing else Englishmen might want to supply the necessities or comforts of life, for their manufactures. (Applause.) It appeared most strange indeed to America, that when they came to the shores of this country, and offered food on reasonable terms, and offered it too not for money, but in exchange for that surplus produce which the starving manufacturers of England had to spare, they were not permitted to sell it. (Loud cries of "Hear.") The chief thing he proposed to dwell on was, the power of the new world to supply England with all the food she wanted,—to furnish her with an unlimited supply, and that too at a price which ought to satisfy all parties, labourers or landlords. The southern, or slave-holding states, lying in a body in the south part of the union, produce, as you are aware, cotton and tobacco as their staple. The northern, or free states, which are the most populous and wealthy, produced, as their agricultural staple, corn and all kinds of food. The settlement of these states commenced with the eastern, and more sterile portions, and progressed westward, at first by slow advances, and afterwards by more rapid strides. The people of that country might be said to have been occupied during the last few years with subduing and taking actual possession of that portion of the country known as the Great Mississippi valley—a valley which extended three thousand miles from the mountains, and an equal distance from the rise of its rivers to the sea—a valley which, in fact, equalled all that was ever said or sung of the ancient plains of Syria and Capadocia in the production of corn, and oil, and milk, and honey, and great and small cattle innumerable.

From this great western granary, Great Britain, if she would, might eat to the full, grow and increase as she might, for one century at least; and that was long enough ahead for one generation of men to calculate. (Cheers.) In the first place, the Americans had spent, in the last ten years, £25,000,000 to lay this region open to them. And, as the Providence which orders all things would have it, just in the hour of need, the power of steam had laid this country by the side of their own. It was as if from the beginning of time, this garden of the world had been reserved until now for the purpose of feeding Englishmen. The portion of America best adapted to the culture of wheat, and to which he wished to call their particular attention, was comprised in the six north western states and territories, Ohio, Indiana, Illinois, Michigan, Wisconsin, and Iowa. They contained more than 178,000,000 acres of land, chiefly arable. England contains 32,000,000 acres. That portion of these States, which may be called good wheat land, at three quarters per acre, would produce in a year, 200,000,000 quarters. (Hear, hear.) They were at present just commencing to pour the immense amount of bread and meat they are capable of producing into the markets of the world. Ohio, alone, last year had eight million bushels of wheat to export. Michigan, which never exported until 1839, has now a surplus of 250,000 bushels of wheat, and 300,000 barrels of pork. The population of these states is now 3,000,000. It had increased during the last ten years at the rate of 202 per cent. It had been estimated by practical men that the amount of their exports would be doubled or trebled by a good demand in two years. The face of the newer portions of the country was that of a rolling prairie interspersed with woodland. The expense and delay of clearing away an immense forest was not to be incurred. The men and the capital were all that were required to place any amount of the most fertile soil under cultivation. (Hear, hear.) Mr. Curtis proceeded to point out on the map the vast extent of the States, which he said afforded them 3000 miles of coast navigation, with 14,000 miles of steam navigation on lakes and rivers, besides 3,000 miles of railway and an equal length of canal carriage already completed, and he pointed to the communication of the wheat-growing region with the sea by the Mississippi and its tributaries, and by the lakes and the Gulf of St. Lawrence. Five great thoroughfares by canal and railroad had been constructed, or were nearly finished, to bring the produce of that region to the commercial cities on the sea-board. Through these, Boston, New York, Philadelphia, and Baltimore were contending for the trade of the west, and competition would always bring the growth of the west to the sea-shore at the lowest prices. From personal acquaintance with the wheat region and the wheat culture, he fixed the price at which wheat could be expected to be produced to any given amount at Chicago, at the south end of Lake Michigan, in the heart of the wheat region, at 75 c. per bushel, or per quarter. . 27s.

heart of the wheat region, at 75 c. per bushel, or per quarter				27s.
Freight, charges, and profits to New York, in the shape of flour,				10s.
Ditto	ditto	Liverpool	ditto	10s.
Delivered in Liverpool				47s. per qr.

The price would never vary much from this amount if the currency should remain as at present, for this would remunerate the grower; and on those immense plains competition would always furnish any amount at remunerating prices. But the American farmer would not produce wheat for any body at a much less price than this. He would turn his attention to other employments of which he would have enough at any time to turn his hands to. Between him and the English grain-grower there would always be, in the shape of cost of transit, a fixed duty of at least 20s. per quarter. Was not that protection enough for British landlords against cheap bread and Yankee competition? (Cheers.) But here arises an important question. What will the American take his pay in? Take his pay in! Why, the very things he wants, and you want to let him have. Your dry goods, your crockery, your hardware, which he has been anxious to get, and could not, for you are not suffered to take his wheat, and flour, and pork, &c. in exchange. Lowering your prices is not what he wants. Offer him your best calicoes at sixpence a yard, he would not buy of you. His reply would be, "Silver and gold have I none; take these stacks of wheat and pork, then I will trade with you. We do not want you to lower your prices, and lower your wages, they are low enough already; but take enough for your starving workmen to eat, and my life for it some of those big warehouses in Manchester will be cleared out with a speed that will perfectly astonish the *natives*!" (Cheers.) Take the wheat of those western Yankees, and he would warrant them to buy as fast as you can sell. He should like to see the man who would set a limit to their consumption and purchase of goods, short of their ability to pay for them; or to the ability of American industry to pour from those wide wheat-bearing plains streams of plenty to the door of every English artizan. (Applause.) He believed the Americans to be the most insatiable consumers in the world; but their enterprize and industry were as proverbially great, and that made them the best customers in the world. (Hear, hear.) Through all the western country a lazy man could hardly be found. Such a man was considered a disgrace to the community—a nuisance; and no one was considered creditable who did not contribute something to the support of society. (Hear, hear.) The consequence of this industry upon a virgin soil was production to an immense amount; and it was not gold they wanted in exchange. He believed it was a fixed axiom of trade, that no commerce can long be carried on between two nations, that does not consist of barter. (Loud cries of "Hear.") It was an acknowledged principle, that if money was paid on one side, and produce was given on the other, it was impossible to continue the trade. (Applause.) He had heard a great deal of competition with foreign countries, and that wages must be reduced here in order to be able to produce cheaper, for that purpose. This was a grand mistake. (Hear.) The Americans did not want English manufactures cheaper; what they wanted was to be enabled to pay for them in the only way they could pay—by barter. There was one fact to which he regretted the necessity of alluding; but it was not strange that, being descended from the English, the Americans should be a little jealous when they thought themselves hardly used. It was not strange that when restrictions were put upon their goods, there should be a feeling that it was a game that two could play at, and an increasing determination to play their part. What was true might as well be plainly told, and fully understood. Out of the slave-holding states the feeling was becoming almost universal, that if Great Britain continued her restrictions, congress should lay restrictions in turn on British commerce. (Hear, hear.) A majority of the American people were in favour of free trade; but they demanded that that freedom should be mutual. (Cheers.) There was also a powerful party in that country in favour of restrictions on trade as a permanent American policy. The example of England was constantly quoted by them. They represented that England owed her wealth and prosperity, not to the skill of her artisans, or her internal capabilities and resources, but to her prohibitory and restrictive laws, and they proposed to follow what they termed "the path of England's glory." (Oh! oh!) If Great Britain found the lessons she taught practised upon against herself, ought she to complain? He wished to allude to some of the arguments of these restrictionists. Used on different sides of the Atlantic, they formed curious counterparts to each other. He heard it said, that if a free trade in corn were resorted to the country would become dependent upon foreigners. In America, they said, "If you take English goods, you become dependent on England." (Laughter.) Put that and that together, and the argument would dispose of itself. (Cheers.) Again: he heard it said that all the coin of Great Britain, if the corn trade was thrown open, would go to America to pay for it. That, again, was the argument used by the sticklers for restriction in America, against receiving manufactures from England. If both arguments were true, what would become of the money? Would it meet half way across the Atlantic, and remain suspended in the air, like Mahomet's coffin? (Cheers and laughter.) Another monstrous fallacy advanced here was, that if food were cheap, wages would be low. If they would look at America they might understand the folly of this assumption. In the Western States, the wages of the unskilled workman were 4s. 6d. a day, and his wheat, as already stated, was 27s. a quarter; his beef cost him 1½d. a pound. Now, if wages were regulated by the price of provisions, how came it that the rate of wages was higher, while food was cheaper, in America than in England? (Hear, hear.) There was one other point to which he wished to advert, and he was sure it could not be out of place in such a meeting as that,—he meant the effect which a repeal of the corn laws would have on American slavery. (Loud cheers.) It must certainly gladden and invigorate the heart of every lover of his kind, to know its accomplishment would redound to the cause of oppressed and enslaved humanity in other lands. He could not go into the state of things in America at large, but a glance would show the bearing of the anti corn-law upon the anti-slavery cause. With a strange inconsistency, Great Britain in effect refused to trade with any portion of the United States except that which was slave-holding. Cotton and tobacco, they were aware, were the staple productions of the American slaveholder. In 1839, a year, too, in which Britain took more than usual from the free states, she imported of their productions, less than £500,000 value, although their agricultural produce is 130,000,000 dollars greater than that of the slave states; while of the slaveholders' produce she took more than £12,000,000 value. (Hear, hear.) Thus the northern freeman was driven to the slave market with his products, because he could sell it nowhere else, and the slave was driven to the production of cotton and tobacco, for the British market. They saw, at once, how the free states were thus placed under commercial vassalage to the slave states. But let England open a free trade in corn with the free north, and the power of the slaveholder, political and financial, in that country, was past for ever. Then, in the place of the jack-o'-lantern light of pro-slavery, from Manchester and Liverpool, across the wide ocean, and through all the great thoroughfares of the free states, the free spirit of anti-slavery would live and glow along the line of commerce to the farthest bounds of the green West. (Cheers.) England had the power to give a fatal blow to American slavery. Let her corn laws be repealed. (Cheers.) But while her present policy continued, how could she remonstrate against American slavery? (Hear.) When England, no longer in effect, paid a premium in America to support the slavery she fixed on the states when they were colonists—when she would place free labour food on a par with slave-grown cotton, then would the world be ready to acknowledge the consistency of English zeal for African liberty. But, the corn laws were only a part of the odious system of monopoly and restriction which set nation against nation. Why should two such countries as Great Britain and the United States of America treat each other as jealous rivals, and mutually deny to each other the good they might confer? (Hear, hear.) Their interests were not adverse, but the same. Belonging to the same race, speaking the same language, drawing their laws, their literature, and their religion from the same fountains, each with peculiar capabilities and resources which the other might aid to use and develope, hand in hand they might rise to such a pitch of prosperity and greatness as the world had never yet seen. And why should not all nations pursue the same course, and mutually let their comforts bless, their arts adorn, their knowledge enlighten, their civilization and religion exalt and purify each other, until wars should be impossible, and the whole earth be enjoyed as the common gift of God to the children of men? All this must take place before the herald Peace upon the mountains announce the coming of Him whose universal kingdom was to be in the abundance of righteousness and peace. (Cheers.) Mr. Curtis concluded by thanking the Conference for the attention with which they had listened to him, and retired amidst loud cheers.

The CHAIRMAN said he was not surprised that the meeting should express a strong feeling on what they had just heard: this important speech, he trusted, would go forth to the public, and go forth correctly. There was no palaver there, (hear, hear,) it consisted of important facts, and some, he believed, not very well known to the people of this country. He next introduced

The Rev. Dr. VAUGHAN, of London, who came forward to propose the following resolution:—

"That this conference, drawn together from various parts of the United Kingdom by a general conviction of the existence of long-continued and still-increasing distress, affecting the community at large, and bearing with peculiar severity on the industrious classes, finds this conviction deeply confirmed by various statements and documentary evidence now laid before them, which clearly prove that vast numbers are incapable of obtaining, by their labour, a sufficiency of the common necessaries of life for the support of themselves and their families."

When he came to this meeting, it was not with the expectation of taking any conspicuous part in its proceedings. His desire was to contribute, as far as his presence might do, his expression of approval with respect to the object of the meeting. (Hear, hear.) With regard to the question of the corn and provision laws, the history of our country for some years past had been such that it would be strange if any man of reflection had not made this subject a matter of some thought and study. So far as he could perceive, the great argument of the supporters of those laws was based on the importance of our being as independent as possible of other countries for the supply of food. But he regarded this doctrine as exhibiting about as striking an instance of folly as could well occur in the history of political science. The world had never seen so formidable a commercial power as that of Great Britain—a power possessing such a navy, and such wealth with which to command supplies from the granaries of the world. Yet Great Britain is the first commercial power in the history of the world that has been known to regard the danger of perishing from the want of bread as its great danger. (Cheers.) If we look to the ancient cities of Phœnecia, Tyre, Sidon, and the rest, whose "merchants were princes," and who were to the world in those ages all that such cities as Manchester and Birmingham have become since, we find that those cities never dreamt of raising their own corn. They had their navy, consisting of mere boats compared with ours, but the ocean was before them, and they never doubted that they might command supplies of corn to any required amount. If you cross from Phœnicia to Greece—Attica never raised corn enough to support its inhabitants; and Corinth, the arm commercial, and one of the most powerful of the states of Greece, never possessed a territory of more than eight miles in space, while maintaining a large commercial intercourse with the remotest regions of the east and west. If you visit Italy at a later period, there is Venice, a city which, at the time when her commercial greatness gave her the proud name of the "Ocean Rome," did not possess a single foot of land, save what she had worked up for herself from the depths of the sea. The other great commercial cities of Italy, as Florence and Genoa, were much in the same circumstances in this respect. Concern to raise their own corn was never one of their solicitudes. If you descend to the period when the Portuguese were the great commercial power, and when that power passed over to Spain, this anxiety about raising corn enough for their own support, with which we are so much beset, would never seem to have perplexed them. And if you come nearer home, to our neighbours the Dutch, a brave people, who not only wrested their liberties from the haughty power of Spain, but made themselves the sovereigns of the deep, and for more than a century the great commercial power of Europe, it may be doubted if they ever raised corn enough from their own land to support a single town. But they possessed a navy, they possessed wealth, and bold hearts, and the produce of half the world was always at their bidding. It is true, Spain and Austria would have cut off their supplies, and would have starved them if it had been possible; but France and the other powers of Europe had their reasons for pursuing a different policy, and the Dutch knew nothing, in consequence, of famine and scarcity. (Cheers.) This idea of the evils which may result to us from not raising corn enough for our own wants, supposes the probability that all Europe may be united against us, through the ascendancy of some one power awing all the rest into subjection. But this notion of the probability of a universal monarchy in Europe is most unreasonable. Let any thoughtful man look to the geography of Europe—to its beautiful intersections of sea and land, of mountain chains and winding rivers, and it will be seen that Europe has been mapped out by the hand of Providence to become the home of a family of separate, vigorous, and independent states. Attempts have been made to break in upon this manifest design of Providence, but the effect has been to show only more certainly that it is not to be permanently disturbed. Charlemagne made an attempt of this sort, but his genius was no sooner withdrawn from the fabric which he reared, than it crumbled into ruin. Charles V. made some advances toward a similar object, but even before the decease of that monarch did his great empire begin to waste away. Louis XIV. would fain have made himself master of Europe, but his path was crossed at every point, and the glory of all his achievments passed away. And within our own memory a concurrence of circumstances served to raise the power of France into a most undue elevation; but we have seen that fabric also break down, and Europe again assume its only natural posture—the posture, I repeat, of a territory designed by Providence to be the home of a family of independent and powerful states. (Cheers.) Now, is it not marvellous that Britain—a power raising more corn than commercial power ever did before, a power which could do without raising its own corn more readily than any power preceding it, should be the first to give expression to the cry of fear, as to the probable want of the means of subsistence if dependent at all on imported corn? (Cheers.) If I could believe that this fear was really that of the people of England, I should be ready to ask, How is it possible that a people of such narrow views, and unmanly fears, should have risen to such greatness? The policy of the supporters of the corn and provision laws is to fasten upon us a system which cannot fail to carry the present evils along with it, as the means of providing against the remotest of all possible contingencies. And this is wisdom! And we are to be counted as dolts or idiots, if not prepared to bow to it! Sir, we are not to be schooled after this manner. We will think and act on these questions for ourselves; and let men sneer or scoff upon us as they may, from high places or from low places, we will continue to pursue the course which intelligence and humanity have marked out. (Cheers.) It has been said that the patronage of our noble houses must ever be to the artist and manufacturer as the breath of his nostrils. But the home of our feudal chiefs was a very rude concern, until the culture of man resident in towns and cities began to act upon it. Men in commercial cities built such halls as this in which we are assembled, long before feudal mansions could boast of similar splendour. What they possess now of this kind, is theirs by adoption rather than invention. If towns and cities, as places of manufactures and commerce, are to decline, along with their decline must come the abstraction of ray after ray from all the splendour of aristocracy. It has been said we could not do the poor man good by all we could do; that what we gave in food we took away in wages. It was a dream, that where there was a permanent cheapness of food there would be a corresponding influence on labour. It is presumed to be not so with us, because the virtues of the sliding scale keep every thing slipping about! But if, where there was some lowering of the price of food, there should be some lowering of the price of labour too, it would be but momentary; the question, however, is, whether, under the change, men would not be able to command more food than now. Rents might fall, perhaps; but with free, open commerce, there would be a demand for labour opened, and men, on Saturday, would be able to know how to provide for the coming week. It was said to be un-English, and ungrateful to Providence to wish for a change of our laws. It was important to distinguish between laws and institutions, and what we possessed in spite of these laws and institutions. He could not see how it was possible for any one in a humane state of mind to act thus, or how a portion of our fellow-subjects could look at and act upon these questions as they had done. The proposal that had filled these with so much alarm was the proposal of an 8s. duty, which was in addition to 12s. the expenses of bringing foreign corn to England. It gave him pain and alarm when he looked at the state of mind with which we had to deal, for deal with it we must. (Applause.) We owed all that might be said to constitute our liberties to the progress of towns like this. (Applause.) He believed with Hallam, that our liberties had been bought more with the money and industry, than with the blood of our ancestors. They were amongst the achievements of commerce. The monies of the commercial class were to be given in all times as the price of buying off bad and unjust laws; and, if commerce were to sink tomorrow, back must we sink to the condition of lord and vassal. ("Hear," and applause.) But he saw no reason to fear this. When he looked at such men as Fitzwilliam, and when such men as Ducie came amongst us to call themselves our fellow-labourers, he had strong hopes for the future. If we find that there is prejudice and selfishness leading to combination against that which we believe to be just and essential to the salvation of our country, then against the combination to do wrong we must have all a constitutional combination to do right. (Immense applause.)

The Chairman said, it had been said the power of steam destroyed distances in bringing people together; and the power of benevolence was much of the same kind. They had just heard Dr. Vaughan from the southern metropolis, and he would now introduce the Rev. James Robertson, from the modern Athens. (Applause.)

The Rev. JAMES ROBERTSON, of Edinburgh, was then introduced to the meeting, and received with loud acclamations. Having briefly touched on the vast importance of the subject about which they had met to confer, and having disclaimed every thing of political partisanship on the part of the meeting, he proceeded to justify Christian ministers in identifying themselves with the agitation of the corn law question. On this subject, as well as every other, they should be examples to their flock. The interests of religion and humanity demanded their exertions to put an end to a monopoly which was the source of scarcity, disease, and demoralization, and in every respect opposed to the revealed will of God. The word of God pronounced a blessing on the man who considered the case of the poor, and also said, "He that hath pity on the poor the Lord shall reward him." The corn laws were not conceived in the spirit of such declarations; they were inconsistent with truth, justice, and humanity, calculated to derange and cripple commerce, and produce wretchedness and demoralization throughout the land. If those laws were once repealed, England would arrive at such a degree of commercial prosperity that the words of Moses to Israel might be appropriately applied to her, "Happy art thou, O England; who is like unto thee, O people, saved by the Lord, the shield of thy help; and who is the sword of thy excellency; and thine enemies shall be found liars unto thee, and thou shalt tread upon their high places." (Applause.)

The Rev. Dr. Cox then took the chair in the temporary absence of the president, and called on the—

Rev. JOHN RAGLAND, from Hindley, to address the meeting. He said, Mr. chairman and gentlemen, if it had been possible for me to have known beforehand the ability with which the subject of the corn laws would have been advocated, it would have been with the greatest reluctance that I should have obtruded myself on the attention of this meeting. But to this I am compelled by a strong and imperative motive. A few of the suffering poor have requested me to state their case to the conference, and speak a word for them. Now having promised to do this, if I were to return without having done it, I might perhaps in the still silence of my own dwelling hear a voice saying, you are an unfaithful steward, you had a charge which you have not delivered. Mr. chairman, you want facts, and in stating mine I will be as concise as possible. I live in Hindley, three miles from Wigan, and in that district the misery of man is great upon him. I have reason to believe, that in Wigan there are at this time out of employ and in a state of destitution from *seven hundred to one thousand* persons, without work, without wages, without food; and if you take in a circle of three or four miles round, I am informed the number of the destitute will amount to *two thousand*. I assure you, gentlemen, I can hardly sit down to take a meal in comfort. Before I have half finished there is a rap at the door; I find standing before it half a dozen, sometimes a dozen, able-bodied men begging for relief, and assuring me their wives and families are starving. I say to them; why do you not go and work? The reply is, we can get no work, nobody will employ us. I immediately conclude that such men ought not to starve. I say to them, as long as you roam about from place to place in groups of twos, threes, and sixes, you will do no good. You should collect the really destitute, all who have no work and no food, and in hundreds walk the streets in solemn silence, insulting no one, touching no one's property, abusing no one's person, but keeping always within the line of the law. Thus you will show the public that something is wrong in the state of society. If trade, if commerce were permitted to act for itself, it would work out such results as God and Nature designed. But God's blessings we know are capable of perversion by man's abuse, by being diverted from their proper channel. Mr. Macaulay, in a debate in the House of Commons on Free Trade, was once asked by one of its opposers, what he would have government do in regard to commerce? To which he replied, "Let it alone, all we ask of you, gentlemen, is to let it alone." Would to God that we could see British legislators acting upon this advice; then trade would flourish, commerce would revive, capital would find its own level, enterprise would show itself in ten thousand directions, and all would be prosperous and happy. That the commerce of this country is languishing there can be no doubt, and this in my opinion is mainly, if not entirely, in consequence of the untimely interference of partial legislation, in consequence of those restrictions, duties, imposts, those so-called regulations, protections, tariffs, or by whatever other deceptive names those who advocate them and profit by them may choose to call them. In consequence of such a system of blind and selfish policy I believe it is that commerce, which is one of God's gracious designs to bless the human race, is, by man's avarice, selfishness, and pride, turned into a curse, and that which was designed for the good of all, is so conducted as to benefit a comparative few. If what is called the dignity of crowns and thrones must be maintained; if immense armies, fleets, and navies must be perpetuated, and if large revenues and taxes must be raised to support such things, why tax trade and commerce? Why tax the necessaries of life? Why not tax in tenfold degree its unnecessaries, its luxuries? Why tax labour and industry? Why not tax a hundred fold splendid idleness? Why tax poverty? Why not a thousand fold tax property? Why should it be preferred to tax that which men cannot live without, and therefore must have, to those things which men can do without, but are determined to have? I believe that every legislative enactment which tends to cripple trade, to injure commerce, to lessen the demand for labour, and to diminish its value, that increases the price of provisions, and diminishes the price of toil, that is at variance with justice, mercy, and humanity, with the love of God and man, I believe, Mr. Chairman, that every such enactment is unwise, impolitic, unjust, cruel, inhuman, wicked.

The Chairman then put the resolution, which passed unanimously.

The Rev. B. Parsons, of Ebley, near Stroudwater, Gloucestershire, moved the second resolution in a speech replete with facts and observation. He said—Before he left his congregation he called together some of their more experienced labourers and manufacturers, men working in the various departments of the cloth manufacture for the last forty years, and thus, from their lips, he obtained facts which he should state. The power-loom there had been generally used. He inquired about wages, and he found them to be only half what they were years ago, before the corn laws came into operation. Wages had been reduced 50 per cent., in the first place, with those having work. In the second place, along with this reduction the men had not half work; so that here was another loss of 50 per cent. Then if they took into consideration that at the present time bread was more than double the price that it was in 1835—if it is taken into consideration that these men, many of them, have not 4s. a week to live upon, then, according to a calculation placed before them yesterday, here was a reduction again upon the poor man's income of 50 per cent.; so that the wages of these operatives are many times worse than they were a few years ago. (Hear, hear.) These were facts elicited from the people, and he wished those people were in this place, that the conference might hear the moderation and the sense with which they gave their opinions when stating these *facts*, on the laws in question. Many industrious able-bodied men were walking about the streets in absolute idleness, and but for the children of some of them bringing home a few shillings a week, they would be in a state of starvation. Had not some of them been of frugal habits they must have been in their grave long ago. Some of them, he might say, were in the deepest distress, and these, too, were men who were tee-totallers, and therefore it could not be laid to their charge that improvidence had any thing to do with their condition. One of his congregation told him on Saturday evening last, that he went to visit three families in his neighbourhood, and he found them without fire, and without bread, and without a penny to purchase even soap to clean themselves to go to the house of God on the Sunday. There were also in his neighbourhood a great number destitute of clothes. He had missed them at the Sabbath morning worship; but they would wrap themselves up in the evening, and come out under cover of darkness when they were ashamed to come out in the daylight. Nor were these feelings to be despised. They were modest, though suffering people, and ought not to be less cared for than the bold pauper who cried out his wants to every one. (Hear, hear.) There were those who said that it was political to take part in a conference like this; but he told them that there was this difference between them and some others he could mention—that while they were what was called politically religious, those who came to the conference were only religiously political. (Cheers and laughter.) The day in which we lived was the day of scare-crows. (Laughter.) He often smiled when he saw a scarecrow hanging in a field, to think that if the crows really knew what it was, how little they would be frightened at it. (Laughter.) Well, their moral opponents wanted to frighten them from this conference, and they put up this scarecrow of "political ministers." (Laughter.) And the political ministers who had no souls had been frightened. (Laughter, and loud cheers.) Those who had souls, however, only smiled at the trick; and they would continue in the path of right and benevolence, be the consequences what they might. (Cheers.) Why, if it was political to take part in this question, it was political to eat; (Laughter;) and, then, if it was political to eat, perhaps it would be said that it was political to be hungry. (Great laughter.) He was looking, before he came in, at Johnson's Dictionary, for the meaning of the word, and he said that it was "prudent, artful, cunning." But he (Mr. Parsons) did not find that Johnson any where said that it was political to be hungry. (Laughter.) According to this notion, it was political to be humane. (Hear.) According to this doctrine, Christ was political when he fed the five thousand. (Cheers.) The following is the resolution:—

"That, in the judgment of this conference, the prevailing distress painfully tends to arrest the progress of education, to prevent the exercise of domestic and social affections, to induce reckless and immoral habits, to prevent attendance on religious worship, and to harden the heart against religious impressions."

The Rev. Charles Berry, of Leicester, was sorry not to have been present when called on last evening. As they were here to make contributions of facts, he would explain why he was present. When he received an invitation, he declined to attend; but a few days afterwards, a member of his congregation told him they thought it better he should attend; and he was unanimously requested to come. The numbers, spirit, intelligence, and zeal of this assembly had overruled all the objections he had had to this conference, as a convocation of ministers. (Hear.) His congregation contained some of the largest manufacturers in

Leicester, and some considerable landowners; and, without exception, all were convinced of the necessity of a change in our commercial code; and, while they approved of the ministerial measures, they regarded them only as the stepping-stones to the total abolition of all monopolies. (Applause.) He had addressed thousands in the market-place of Leicester and in crowded theatres on the subject of the corn laws; and, by way of enlivening the dulness of his speech, he would relate a little anecdote. The late celebrated Robert Hall, of Leicester (said Mr. Berry), who, though he detested heretics, was courteous and kind to some whom he deemed so, was many a time a guest at my table; and I have often conversed with him, while he smoked his pipe, to my great instruction and benefit. I remember, on one occasion, we were talking about the expedition to Copenhagen, when Lord Nelson captured the Danish fleet in the harbour of Copenhagen; and I made some observation, perhaps by way of argument, in order to show that the government were not so much to blame for that as was supposed. Mr. Hall said, "Sir, I am sorry to hear you talk in that manner. If the angel Gabriel were to come down from heaven, and endeavour to impose upon me by such sophistry, I would knock him down directly." (Laughter.) And if an angel were to come down, to say that it was right to tax the poor man's bread to put high rents into the pockets of the landowners, he (Mr. Berry) would reply, "Go home again to your celestial regions; you don't understand our affairs on earth." (Laughter.) Leicester is the seat of a very important branch of manufactures, and by the last census contains about 50,000 inhabitants; but it had been supposed to contain more. Of that number, about 10,000 persons were employed in various branches of our trade; and he was sorry to be obliged to state, that never in his time had he seen the trade of Leicester in a more depressed state, and the population, in greater destitution and distress. The prospect of winter, he was authorised to tell them, was fearful. Up to within the last two years, Leicester was one of the most thriving towns in this kingdom, in respect of its property, its size, and every thing else which was the sign of commercial and manufacturing prosperity. (Hear.) Perhaps one reason was, that the fabrics manufactured in Leicester were of the coarser sort—worsted stockings, woollen goods generally; and therefore the population had not suffered so much as the trades of Nottingham and Derby, whose manufactures were of the finer sorts of cotton and silk. Nevertheless, a large number of the working population of Leicester, at this time, were out of employment. A great many had only half-work, and very slender wages; and he could say, from the testimony of some of the most respectable manufacturers in the town, that unskilled artisans, when fully employed, received about 6s. or 7s. a week for 12 or 14 hours' work a day; and those who were more skilled got 9s. 10s. or 11s. a week, and he was not very sure whether he had not to deduct 1s. or 1s. 6d. a week for frame rent. (Cries of "Certainly," and "more.") That was the state of things in the town of Leicester. The census, taken within the last few weeks, reported that there were 1,100 houses in Leicester uninhabited; which number, with the usual average of five individuals to a house, might, if occupied, afford accommodation to more than one tenth of the whole population of the town. What had become of those people,—whether they had emigrated, or whether they were sent to distant parishes, or whether they were more crowded together, in consequence of not being able to pay the rent,—he could not say; but he regarded these eleven hundred houses being empty in the town of Leicester, as an indication of the decline of its prosperity. He had a still more important fact to state: he was conversing the other day with one of the most influential hosiers in the town, one of his own congregation, who had acquired a handsome fortune in the trade, and was still in some measure connected with it. He told him that in Saxony there were more stocking frames than in Leicestershire; that he had carried on a profitable business with Belgium and Saxony, but that he feared these markets were closed against the Leicester trade, never to be re-opened. Another friend showed him, not long since, a dozen pairs of gloves, received from his correspondent in London, made in Germany, and charged to him at 2s. 8d. per dozen, although there must have been two profits upon them, and an import duty of 20 per cent. He added, that the cost of the materials was very nearly the same, and that it was not possible to manufacture them at that price here. A great trade in gloves was carried on in Leicester, but how could it stand against such a competition? The prosperity of the town of Leicester, and of all other towns must decay, if foreign rivals were to be allowed such advantages as our provision laws afforded them. Though he hoped he had a proper sense of justice, yet somehow or other he had been very blind on this subject till lately. He had an idea formerly, that our machinery, minerals, capital, and industry were such, that we could defy all competition, even after the cessation of the war; and he thought that England was destined to be always the first great commercial country of the world. For a long time it did seem so; but facts had since shown that it was otherwise. His mind was opened to a consideration of the subject, by the distress which took place in Leicester last Christmas twelve-months, when there was a great stagnation of trade, and many thousands were thrown out of employment. In addition to very heavy poor-rates, they raised somewhere near £5,000 for distribution amongst the poor. He had a district for the purpose of distributing small sums, and that occupied him six months, before there was any revival; and the poor were in a state of almost utter destitution during that period. Every Saturday he went amongst from 30 to 40 families, giving to each 2s., 3s., 4s., or 5s.; and he should never forget the heart-rending scenes which he saw. Many of them told him (and this was one reason why the poor-rates were not heavier), it might be a prejudice, but they said, "I would sooner die in the streets, than I would go to those cursed bastiles;" and that was the reason why the poor-rates did not press so heavily upon them as they otherwise would do. This being the general state of Leicester, he would declare, having resided in that town nearly forty years, that he had never seen it more depressed; or its manufacturers in a state of greater alarm. He believed conscientiously, though his congregation did not contain so many poor as some, that many poor persons, who were inclined to attend places of worship, abstained, because they had not decent clothing to appear in; and many children kept away from day schools, infant schools, and every other kind of schools, because of the utter destitution of their parents. Only the day before he left Leicester, he met a gentleman, not of his own congregation, but of the Church, who said he was glad to hear that Mr. Berry was going to the conference at Manchester. He asked this gentleman what he should say there as to the state of the trade of Leicester. The gentleman replied, "Tell them that part of the trade of Leicester is gone; that the rest is going; and that, before long, if the present state of things continue, it will be done for altogether." If things continue as they are, it will lead to insubordination and rebellion. (Hear, hear.) He would not reason upon the subject; why should they reason upon it? It had been fully discussed in the newspapers, and many able publications had appeared on the subject. He would recommend to them the pamphlet of Mr. Whitmore, late member for Bridgenorth; for there could not be a better piece of reasoning than his address to the agriculturists of Shropshire. He would advise them to read the tract of the Hon. and Rev. Baptist Noel. (Hear, and applause.) He would also recommend to their notice the pamphlets which were sometimes issued by the Rev. Thomas Spencer, of Hinton; and one pleasure he had experienced in attending this meeting was to shake that gentleman by the hand. Mr. Spencer did him the honour generously to send him one of his pamphlets, and the moment it came into his hands he read it with avidity and delight; (Hear;) and he would say, it was an honour to a man who, in his (Mr. Spencer's) particular profession and station, laboured for the public good with so much disinterestedness. The proper object of all government (for he was speaking to patriots, Christians, and Christian ministers) was to promote the happiness of the people. (Hear, hear, and applause.) That was not a political or factious sentiment, but the sentiment of a Christian minister. And, if an enlightened and just government considered the happiness and interest of any class of the people more than another, that class should be the largest, the weakest, and the most destitute; that is, the poor. (Cheers.) Sir Thomas More said, that, from the recollection of all past history, he was sorry to say, that the general design and effect of all government had been to magnify and cherish the rich against the poor, the few against the many, and the powerful against the weak. He (Mr. Berry) would say, that, generally speaking, the course of past legislation had been to degrade, to oppress, and neglect the poor. (Cheers.) He agreed with the sentiment expressed the day before, in the discourse of his tutor, Dr. Pye Smith; for his tutor he was, though he (Mr. Berry) had deviated from his doctrine; perhaps had erred in doing so; but he was sure that if ever he had departed from piety and integrity, he had deviated from his venerable instructor's example. (Hear, hear.) The sentiment was, that if something were not done to promote the happiness of the people, and give them a sufficient supply of food, anarchy and disorder would come upon us; or the alternative would be, that we should experience the vengeance of a reckless despotism, under whose sword all our liberties would be extinguished. (Hear, and cheers.) He would warn those present, and if his voice could extend further, he would warn all the magnates and nobles of this country, that if our commerce were to pass away, they would be in the greatest danger; for, as Mr. Burke said in one of his orations, "If a great storm rage upon the coast, it will cast the whales upon the strand, as well as the periwinkles." He would make one remark more, as to the difference between this question, and many others on which public opinion had operated, and successfully. He was a great believer in the force of enlightened public opinion; and he thought this conference would have a great influence upon the country at large, when they returned home. At the same time there was this difference, that in all former measures—the emancipation of the catholics, the abolition of the test and corporation acts, the extinction of negro slavery, and the municipal corporation acts, and other things—the people could have waited a little longer. He would grant that every delay of a good measure was inconvenient; but, in these cases, the people might have waited. But if just legislation was not speedily enacted with regard to the industry and the food of the nation, good measures would be passed in vain some years hence. (Hear.) There was an important distinction between this and all other questions. He considered, as he had said a portion of the trade of this country had already gone; another portion was preparing wings for flight, and the rest would go after it; and if once our industry, our skill, and our mechanics departed, adieu to the glory of this country; its commerce and prosperity would pass into perpetual exile. (Applause.) He would exhort them, when they returned home, to exert themselves speedily, in order that it might be effectually; and, if the restrictions were removed from our industry, he believed we might yet be greater than any nation in the history of the world. He believed the spirit of patriotism, of candour, and of enlightened benevolence, actuated this assembly. Let it burn brighter and stronger, and it must have great influence and power. He prayed God to give his blessing, and that it might attend all their exertions for the general happiness of mankind; and, if ever they were disposed to relax in their exertions—for sometimes even patriots and Christians were tempted to despair—let them think of that beautiful sentence,—"Blessed is he that considereth the poor: the Lord shall deliver *him* in the time of trouble. (Applause.)

The Chairman then put the motion, which passed unanimously. He next announced the names of the parties to speak at the evening meeting, and the meeting then adjourned a few minutes before one o'clock to four o'clock.

AFTERNOON MEETING.

There was, amongst the public, a large number of ladies, this afternoon. The chair was resumed at ten minutes after four; but it was twenty-five minutes after four o'clock, before the business commenced.

In the absence of the Rev. T. Spencer, of Bath,

The Rev. C. Thompson, of Swansea, was called on to move the third resolution. He said—Mr. Chairman, and Brethren in the Ministry,—We have been listening to much, since we came together, on the subject of monopoly. As I crossed the platform, the word fell on my ears, and my feelings tell me, that there is somewhat of monopoly in my situation, called upon, as I am, to move this resolution, instead of seconding, as proposed. I hope, however, that you will not find me a monopolist of time. We have been cautioned on that point; and I shall bear it in mind. One thing has impressed my mind—the necessity of simplifying our object and our agency. I cannot fully agree in the general principles which have been laid down by some of the speakers; nor is there that unanimity in the movement under which we are now convened, that some of the gentlemen have avowed. But this is not from opposition so much as an impression that the question requires elucidation. Now, it appears to me that the whole subject is comprised in a very simple and intelligible proposition, viz., Man is to subsist by his labour; he ought to be at liberty to take that labour to the best market, and to procure his food at the cheapest rate. This is the principle. In pursuing some inquiries on the subject in my own neighbourhood, I applied to a gentleman of great intelligence and influence, who placed a document in my hands which I cannot do more than refer to. The county in which I reside is one rich in mineral productions; and in answer to an inquiry which I made of that gentleman, whether the corn law were injurious to trade, he said it was; inasmuch as the coal, immense quantities of which could be produced and exchanged for wheat with France and other places, was held back, as the duty on corn prevented the interchange. If, however, man can buy food cheaper abroad than at home, God and man, truth and justice, declare he ought to do so. (Applause.) While listening to the address of Mr. Cobden, which was a most excellent one, I had hoped to hear from him or some other gentleman, an exposition of the averages. Now, in some parts of the country, wheat is selling at 70s., 75s., 79s., and in one place at 80s.

I myself did not understand the subject thoroughly until a few weeks ago, when I found, from the speech of our borough member, who is an out-and-out repealer, that corn dealers played into each other's hands, and sold the same grain five or six times over, for the purpose of influencing the averages. (Hear, hear.) It is important that we should understand this and other matters, in order that we may work on the mind of the public afterwards. A person in Swansea had recently received a very large order from Russia, on condition of taking wheat in return; owing to the state of the market he could not take the order; had he done so, he would have been ruined. This is a state of things which ought not to exist, that a British subject should be liable to ruin because of free intercourse. The question was a national one; but why might not we as well take a portion of the country, say the town of Manchester, wall it in, and compel the inhabitants to subsist on the corn that would be grown in their own flower-pots, before they were allowed to buy any elsewhere? The authority on which I submit this statement, requested me to say that they were steadily advancing to ruin, under the operation of the corn laws; and all they wanted was that ministers should exert themselves to influence public opinion and the legislature. (Applause.) We come here to seek information, and we shall depart to diffuse that information, and arouse whilst we enlighten. (Cheers.) We have heard of two parties, monopolists and anti-monopolists, but these two will be found to agree in one main point. The one says, the corn law agitation is a desolating torrent; the other says, it is a fertilizing stream: both then agree in this, that there is a current rolling, and I say he that does not go with it will perish in its depths. (Applause.) I must now conclude by moving,

"That, influenced at once by feelings of sympathy for the suffering poor, with whom their official duties bring them into daily contact, and by a deep interest in the success of that religion whereof they are ministers, this conference feels itself only acting from a strong sense of duty in examining into the causes of the existing distress, and, after the example of the Saviour himself, in employing its utmost influence to alleviate or remove it."

The Rev. Thomas Spencer, of Hinton Charter-house, near Bath, was called on, and was received with much applause. He said—Mr. Chairman and Gentlemen,—I ought to apologise for not having been here at the commencement of the meeting (he was expected to have moved the resolution); but the mistake is not my own, for I was told by the committee to be here by half-past four. Before I make any remark on the corn laws, the meeting will allow me to congratulate them on the proceedings of this conference up to this point. I have seen many public meetings; I am frequently at public meetings; but I do not know that I ever witnessed an assembly that commanded such a feeling of respect in my own mind as the present conference at its sittings yesterday and to-day. (Applause.) I recollect the interest with which we read of the first Christian disciples, when the Holy Spirit descended upon them as in cloven tongues of fire; and I cannot help thinking that there is a holy spirit upon this assembly; and in the varying of tongues that we have from different parts of England, Scotland, Wales, and, as we shall have, from Ireland, I believe there is a degree of fire about them that will really kindle a flame upon this subject in this country that will not be easily quenched. (Applause.) There was, indeed, one critical moment, yesterday, when our fears were to a certain extent excited; and had that critical moment occurred in another house, and another assembly, I believe that uproar would have been the consequence. But it was because they were ministers of religion, men of sense, and men of self-denial, it was because of their great zeal for a great object, which made them overlook all minor differences, and not allow themselves to be disturbed or diverted from the great object for which they had assembled. (Loud applause.) The resolution which I have in my hand, and which has just been read to you by Mr Thompson, declares that it is our duty, as ministers of religion, to feel for the distresses of our people, to sympathise with them, to examine into the causes of their distress, and to use our best efforts to put those causes away. Now, upon that depends the whole of our right to be here. Are we not bound to sympathise with distress, and bound to relieve distress? And if the corn laws produce distress, it must forthwith become our business—it is our business—to remove them. (Applause.) We have frequently heard the quotation, and it cannot be too often repeated, "Blessed is he that considereth the poor and needy." But it is not for us to end in mere consideration. (Applause.) He that considereth the poor and needy is not blessed unless his consideration comes to some good purpose. He goes into their cellars; he sees the tens of thousands of Liverpool, of Manchester, and of Glasgow, all but starved to death; he considers the cause; and if he were to go and sit down and enjoy himself after that consideration, and never move a step to redress their wrongs, I cannot conceive that the blessing would belong to him. Blessed is he that considereth the poor and needy, so as to discover the cause of their poverty and need, and to remove it. (Applause.) We have frequently referred to the petition which our Lord himself taught us to use—"Give us this day our daily bread." But as we should blame the idle labouring man, who should offer up that prayer, and not go forth, and sow, and reap, in order to get that bread, so when we pray for others that they may have that bread along with us, we should deserve the same censure were we to confine ourselves to the prayer, and never take steps to give this daily bread to thousands, if we know of any steps that would have that object. Therefore, we are bound to understand that prayer, and to carry it out. (Applause.) In the same manner we are told that pure religion, whether it be for ministers or common men—and I for one think that ministers are very much like common men. (Applause.) I for one am very much against the heresy of a human priesthood. (Loud cheers.) I believe that, as I am a citizen, I am bound to earn my bread by the sweat of my brow, and every day to labour to render useful service to my fellow-creatures, to earn my food before I eat it, as much as if I were labouring in the field; were I to get up in the morning, and lie down at night, without rendering any valuable service, I should feel that I was but a barren fig-tree that cumbered the ground. (Loud applause.) Therefore, for a minister, and for every other man, "pure religion before God and the Father, is this, to visit the fatherless and widows in affliction, and to keep himself unspotted from the world." To visit the fatherless and the widows, there are plenty of opportunities in Manchester; but what should we say of a man, who should so use and interpret scripture as to be satisfied with merely walking into the rooms of the fatherless and widows, that is to say, those who are destitute and suffering, those who are grieved, and are suffering affliction of a temporal nature, and after visiting them, should never take any steps to relieve them? (Applause.) And if it is right to relieve one fatherless person and one widow, it is right to relieve twenty fatherless and widows; but how much more beautiful must it be, if, by any act or deed of ours, we could relieve a million fatherless children and widows at once? (Cheers.) This is the best kind of charity; we advocate charity to the thousands, the millions. This is the charity which is ever parallel with justice; and justice is better than charity, any day; at all events, it should go before charity. "Do justly; love mercy;" be just before you are generous. I have no idea of any man's character who is not just in all his dealings with his fellow-men. (Applause.) Another passage has been referred to, (and I delight in that passage, because I believe I have called the attention of many to it; I preached upon it in my own country church two or three years ago), "He that withholdeth corn, the people shall curse him; but blessing shall be upon the head of him that selleth it." (Applause.) Now, surely, every minister, and any person of experience who is not a minister, will perceive that "he that withholdeth corn" is not merely the man who locks it up in the granary, and keeps it by restrictive laws from the people; but he who allows the thing to go on when he might prevent it; he who renders himself a party to it is himself guilty of the deed, almost as much as the man who does it. In former times, people were so ignorant, when there was not bread enough, as to blame the baker and the miller; and I know, and perhaps you know too, the lines that were put upon the walls of a town against the millers, accusing them of having starved the people:—

"Two millers thin,
Called Bone and Skin,
Have starved the town, or near it;
But be it known,
To Skin and Bone,
That flesh and blood won't bear it."

(Cheers, and laughter.) In the degree of light which we now possess, we know it is not the millers nor the bakers; the skin and bone we will call some one else. (Cheers.) But be it known, whoever be the parties, be it known to skin and bone, that the ministers of religion won't let the people bear it. (Loud cheers.) And if it is a curse to be a party to the withholding of corn, to sanction it by our voice and vote, or to sanction it by our guilty silence, so also it is a blessing, not only to be sellers of food, generously, at a fair and equitable profit, which every man ought to have, and no more; but it is also a blessing for those who try to have it so sold, who carry out the principle which will cause corn to be so sold. Therefore a blessing shall be upon the head of you, if you cause corn to be sold from those parts of the world where it is grown, to those where it is wanted. (Applause.) This is the blessing which we seek, and the blessing which we hope to have. (Cheers.) And now, ministers of religion, it will be declared, I have no doubt, by some papers when we see them, that you have stepped out of your proper business; that you have got into the arena of politics; that you have left your pulpits, and come into the common ground of common men. Well, if common men be honest men, I, for one, like to be with them. (Applause.) However, though "an honest man is the noblest work of God," yet still, if they will have us to be tried by the rule of the clergy, let us look at what they do. I was myself for many years a fellow of a college, until I married and lost my fellowship; and I will tell you this, which is no secret, because all who know college affairs know it very well; and if the masters and fellows of the college were present, I would say it before their faces; the fellows of the college are generally clergymen; and what sort of things do they meet about? The bursar of the college is a clergyman; he manages the whole of the college estates; he receives the rents and sets the property; and sometimes the bursars of colleges have so much to do that they even keep their books on Sundays. (Applause.) And will they say that we are agitating for a worldly object because we conceive it our duty to relieve the poor? (Cheers.) When there is a large college estate to be let to any large farmer, how do they proceed? I have been at the letting of estates many times, and have received one or two pounds as my share of the fine, as they call it; sometimes it was two or three pounds; the sum was divided among the sixteen senior fellows who happened to be present. Where do you think this was done, and by whom was it done? When an estate belonging to the college was to be let, the sixteen senior fellows were summoned into the college chapel; they heard the lease read from the reading-desk, containing the rent, the names of the parties, and other matters, all connected with secular affairs. (Applause.) All that is read aloud by some of them; sometimes it is so long that they take it in turns, one and another gets up; I have very often had to read part of a lease from the desk of a college chapel. Then, when read through, the seal was affixed to it; and all this was done in the college chapel, and by clergymen. (Hear.) Now, I ask, is our object more secular than that? Ours is for the good of others; theirs is for the good of themselves. (Laughter.) Some have called our conference a convocation, and I do not care for words; a convocation is a calling together; and we are called together. There used to be a convocation which I respect infinitely less than I do this; for I have such a bias on my mind in favour of liberty, and I prefer being where there is a variety of sentiment, to being with those who are all of one mind; I like this approximation and tendency to one common centre—it is the best sign in our day. (Applause.) And if this object for which we have met will not draw men together, and cause them to lose all party spirit, all bitter hatred and malice towards one another, I don't know what will. (Cheers.) But there used to be a convocation of archbishops, bishops, deans, archdeacons, and priests; they formed two houses, the upper and the lower; they were entirely clerical, entirely spiritual, and what did they talk about? If any one will read Bishop Burnet, who wrote about these things, he will find that they discussed how much tax should go to the king, and how much they should tax themselves, while the parliament taxed the people. And I think that considering the subject of taxes was not at all less secular than considering how we are to feed the hungry. (Cheers.) But they have gone beyond this, they were worse than this a great deal; there were clamour, disputation, and quarrels amongst them; sometimes they were at dagger's-drawn almost, and the upper house quarrelled with the lower. So uproarious and unpleasant were these convocations, that lately the sovereign has never liked to set them to business. By law, the convocation must meet whenever a new parliament meets. They do meet, and they have an anthem sung, and a long speech made; but the order is that they cannot proceed to any business, however small, without the consent of the sovereign; and as the sovereign does not give that order, they go home without doing anything. Now, we meet for business, and we shall do something before we go home. (Applause.) We meet for business, secular, if you will, but not so secular, and not with such secular spirit as theirs was. (Applause.) We will carry religion into our secular affairs; we will bring down the Spirit of the Most High, as he once descended upon an enslaved people, when he said, "I have surely seen the afflictions of my people; I have heard their cry, for I know their sorrows; and I am come down to deliver them." (Applause.) Yes, and I think that when six hundred and fifty ministers of religion come from all parts of the kingdom, surely they must be a proof, a standing proof, and a witness to all mankind, that God is indeed coming down to deliver the people. (Great applause.) But why are ministers of religion to be more thought of than any other men? I answer, Why are members of parliament to be more thought of than other men? Merely for this; that they represent other men, they are chosen by other men; they embody, they are the essence of a large number of other men; and if there is a bad house of parliament, it is because the electers are bad; if there is any thing wrong, the electors are to be blamed, because they choose them. Now, it is on this ground that we respect the ministers of religion—because each of them is a congregation. All the congregations cannot be admitted here; we could not have 650 congregations in this hall; therefore the people say to their ministers—"Go you, and be in our place and stead." Therefore is there a weight attached to the ministers of religion in this business which could not attach to any other men; especially is it so in those cases where the ministers of religion are chosen by the people themselves—(applause)—especially is it the case when those ministers of religion are particularly requested by their congregations to be here present; especially is it the case where the congregations have raised money and defrayed the cost of their being here. (Applause.) Now, if here be 650 ministers, and each represents a congregation, and if there be, in the towns from which they come, 1000 persons, on the average, interested in these questions, then this assembly of 650 ministers of religion represents 650,000 men. (Applause.) It represents also their children, the posterity yet unborn; it represents all who shall suffer if the corn laws continue; all who will be blessed, if we succeed in doing them away. (Cheers.) And, now, have we any authority, from the examples recorded in scripture, to act in this way? Did the ministers of God, in old times, ever meddle with such things? Why, they were the very men that did. When Israel was to be delivered out of Egypt, it was Moses and Aaron who were to do it; Moses was the man who was to conduct them when no bread was to be got but what was rained down from heaven. And when corn was to be provided in Egypt for Jacob's children, Joseph, the best of his sons, the prophet, the interpreter of dreams, the favourite of the Most High, was the very man that was to use measures to get all the corn together while corn was to be had. (Applause.) And when Israel was sinning against God to a degree almost beyond bearing, and their was to be a famine, Elijah, the prophet, was to be the instrument for effecting it; and though many are angry with the corn-law repealers when they smile at bad weather, and say that it rains repeal, and that it will do good, yet Elijah, to bring about an ultimate good, prayed that there might be no rain, and there was no rain for three years and a-half. And when the end of his judgment was answered, it was Elijah that brought the king to his senses, that brought the people in humble obedience to the footstool of their God, and reconciled them to the true religion. (Applause.) If Elijah, therefore, acted in this way, shall we be blamed for supposing that such a dispensation as a bad harvest, by causing greater suffering at this time, may be the means of joy and prosperity for hundreds of years to come? (Applause.) And, now, if we look at the New Testament, when there was a famine in Judea, and the early Christians were suffering, who was the man who went and got corn from foreign parts, or what was the same thing, he got money, and money is corn? Why, it was the apostle Paul—he, whose time was so valuable, that one would have supposed he did nothing but preach—he, who was determined to know nothing among men but Jesus Christ, and him crucified,—he, above all other men, went round from country to country, collecting subscriptions to supply the wants of the Christian Jews in Judea. He gave months of his time to travelling about, when they could not travel by railways. (Hear, hear.) We do not lose so much of our time now, and surely we need not be grudged a day or two. I, as a minister, have not been absent from my parish on a Sunday, above two or three times a year, for several years past; and if I am absent now on the week-days, I shall be there again next Sunday, as I was last Sunday. (Applause.) But the apostle Paul, when he could not travel so fast, spent months in journeying, for no other purpose whatever but to supply the wants of those who were suffering from famine. They tell me I am a successor of the apostles. (Loud cheers, and laughter.) Why, then, if I were to spend months in journeying, in order to get corn for the people of Manchester, or, what is the same thing, to get them trade, by which they could get work, and thus obtain money to buy the corn,—if I were to spend months in doing this, I should only do as the apostle did, whose successor I am. (Cheers.) There is another good successor of the apostles, the Hon. and Rev. Baptist Noel; (cheers;) and it gives me pleasure to announce to those who have not yet seen it in this day's paper, that our gracious Queen has made him one of her own chaplains. (Loud cheers, and waving of hats, which lasted for some time.) If any minister of religion doubts whether we shall have sound doctrine, whether we shall have the good of the poor remembered in high places,—if any one doubts whether we shall have the sympathies and affections of our gracious and beloved Queen in this matter, let him look at this fact. (Enthusiastic cheering.) Now, all this goes on the supposition that the corn laws produce distress: supposing any one contradicts this, what shall we say? Why, when there is a tax upon windows, and the poor man is obliged to shut up almost every window in his house, and can hardly see because of the darkness, every one can understand that he suffers, because he has not a sufficient supply of light. Suppose that in a particular town, (and I know such a case,) the wells are not sufficient to supply the inhabitants with water, and that there is a plentiful spring in a hill outside the town, whence the water could easily be conveyed into it, but the interested parties in the town, who sold the water, and who had power to oppose and prevent the enlarged supply, should do so, and argue that it would be a waste of the public money to bring more water to the town;—does not any one see that, as the population increases, they must suffer, and that it would be a good thing for them if they could have a "free trade" in water from the hill adjoining? (Cheers.) Now, in this little island of ours, cannot we understand that though there may have been corn enough for ten millions of individuals; though there may have been enough to feed fifteen or twenty millions, yet, that now we are thirty millions of people, and increasing at the rate of a thousand a day, is it not possible that there may not be corn enough in the country? And if that is possible, ought we not to be allowed to get corn from foreign parts? (Cheers.) And if it is true, at the same time, that those foreign parts are equally in want of our goods, as much as we want their corn, and that the making and selling of these goods would employ hundreds of thousands, yea, millions of our population at home, and give them constant work and wages, so that they would be able to purchase food, is it not a clear case that those who are interested in preventing the supply of food are acting on the same principle as those who keep away the supply of water, in order to profit by the sale of their own wells at home? (Loud cheers.) Surely, then, the corn laws may be, and clearly are, the cause of commercial distress. (Applause.) But they say that we speak against agriculture; they say that we are enemies to one of the most respectable and important portions of the community. I deny it; (Applause;) Earl Radnor denies it; the excellent nobleman whom we had here last night, Earl Ducie, denies it; and, as I heard him say the other day, the reason why agriculture is at so low an ebb, the reason why the farmer cultivates his farm so badly, and does not apply the discoveries of science to his farming, is because of the corn laws, partly because they do not allow of the competition which is so good for us all, and partly because the sliding scale makes prices so uncertain that he does not know what he has to look to. (Hear.)

But agriculture and manufactures are, in one sense, the same thing; (Hear, hear;) and when they are separated and opposed to each other, it is a house divided against itself, which cannot stand; and I think that those ministers of religion who will go with me, for a minute or two, into the history of the case, as set forth in Scripture, will perceive it to be so. The first man was sent out of Paradise to till the ground; that was thenceforward to be his business and the business of his descendants; and I maintain that all afterwards, to this very day, have been doing nothing else; I maintain that there is no occupation on the face of the earth but tilling the ground from whence we are taken; and I will make it out in this manner. Adam, after the sentence was passed upon him, divided the labour between his two sons, Cain and Abel; one took care of the sheep, the other tilled the ground; but they were all agriculturists; though the labour was divided into two, they were all engaged in the same thing. When the sons of Cain and Abel began to multiply on the face of the earth, there would be opportunity for greater division of labour, and greater variety of employment; and, as they extended over a greater surface of ground, they would want some to make baskets, wheelbarrows, carts, and so on. But were not those made for the purpose of helping to till the ground? are not the man who makes, and the man who drives a cart, equally helping the farmer to till the ground? For how is he to do without them? The carpenter, therefore, is helping to cultivate the ground, and the farmer cannot do without him; he is equally essential to the farmer, with the boy, whose business it is to catch or drive away the birds that would otherwise eat up the seed as soon as it was sown. As the families of Cain and Abel increased, while some were employed in the different departments of tilling the ground, others would be employed in preparing food for them when they came home; but who does not perceive that this would be all one great work, one great concern, one great partnership? The actual tilling of the ground, and the making of carts to be used in that purpose, and the making of coats of skin for those so engaged, was all one great concern. Then they would have their bearers of messages from one part of the grounds to another—a sort of rude post office; and others would be employed in making roads, in order that their conveyances might pass along quickly. All these would be parts of one great work; and whoever did their portion most quickly, and with the least delay, would most promote the interests of the family; while those who placed impediments and restrictions in the way, who were idle, and who neglected to convey things from one to another as quickly as possible, would be disturbing the general prosperity, and would be hurtful to the common family of man. Now, though we have multiplied so much, and though we are divided into different trades, much more than they were, yet still I maintain the principle is the same; it is the same thing still. The inhabitants of different nations of the earth have a common interest; we in the same nation have a common interest; and it is not for the interest of the many that one man should be protected, and that any should enjoy particular monopoly. If that be so, and I am sure it is, as well might Lancashire seek to be protected against Yorkshire, and Somersetshire against Wiltshire, or the people in one street be compelled to buy all their goods on a shop in that street. But the more we consider the family of man, the more we shall see that its prosperity arises from free intercourse, and the more we shall see that we must be at peace; if we depend for prosperity upon one another, the more for the good of all is it that trade should be free, and commerce without any possible restrictions. (Applause.) But if there are interested parties, if commerce and agriculture are opposed to each other, which ought to give way? I stated last night I sent the parish clerk to 144 houses in my own parish, in order to get their opinions on the subject; and 126 of them were for free trade. Now, ought the 126 of the 18 to be considered? Of the latter, a considerable number were of doubtful mind, and wished not to give an opinion. I am for the greatest happiness to the greatest number; and those who love their fellow-creatures ought to do them the greatest good they can. (Applause.) As in my own parish, so in England at large. There are 30,000 landowners and thirty millions of people: which ought to be considered? Supposing their interests to be opposed, which I do not allow, I maintain that we are working for the good of the farmers and landowners in the end, and that after a very few years too; but, supposing there were conflicting interests, which ought we to consider,—the 30,000, or those who are a thousand times as many, the 30 millions of the people of England? I maintain, therefore, it is a very selfish argument to say, that 30,000 would be injured, and that we ought not to proceed; when 30 millions will be benefited, we ought to proceed. (Applause.) But many say it is not self-interest; but that the landowners understand these things better than the manufacturers. Now I take them at their word, and out of the mouths of the landowners will I condemn them. If they are best judges, we must not permit them to include themselves only, but the landowners of Germany and America, and other countries. They all declare our corn laws to be unwise, impolitic, and hurtful; because they prevent those countries from taking our goods in return for their wheat; therefore we have the evidence of the landowners on our side. (Applause.) I have, on a former occasion in Manchester, referred to a prayer in the Prayer Book of the Church of England, as being entirely on our side; and to this day I never met with a person who could answer it. (Applause.) I know that the clergy don't use these prayers generally; I know that during a late rain they have been using the prayer for fine weather, (hear, hear,) but they do not use the prayer for cheapness and plenty. (Applause.) Then, I say, I am a better churchman than they are; I am more a successor of the apostles than they are. (Cheers and laughter.) If a man is a churchman, and really wishes for the welfare of his fellow creatures, he ought to desire with all his heart and soul cheapness and plenty. (Applause.) I will not occupy your time longer than to declare my firm conviction that if the corn laws were repealed, it would be in the first instance beneficial to the manufacturer; in the next to the labourer; and in the last instance to the landlord himself. (Cheers.) And whilst I mention these classes, I would include also a numerous class which they are apt to leave out. When they talk of wages rising and falling with the price of provisions, they are apt to forget the thousands that have no wages at all; the poor widows who receive not variable sums, but a small fixed income by way of annuity, and upon whom the price of bread doubtless must have a very melancholy effect. (Hear.) I do believe, and I stand here solemnly to declare my conviction, that if we succeed in getting the corn laws repealed, it will be beneficial to every class of her Majesty's subjects. (The conclusion of this powerful and eloquent speech was followed by a loud burst of cheering.)

The Rev. J. W. Massie then stated, that, from communication which had been made, there were not fewer than fifty ministers who had been deputed to speak by their people, who had paid their expenses, and who were crushed and bleeding from the operation of the corn laws. He would urge upon those who had to speak to bear this in mind, and take up as little time as possible. If the succeeding speakers were to speak at the same length as those who had spoken, there would require a conference for three months; and they must beg her majesty to defer the opening of the parliament. It was their intention to propose an address to the queen, and to petition parliament; and would that every minister would put his name to it! Then there was to be an address to the people, which would be, in effect, an address to every congregation that had sent a minister, to 800 congregations whose ministers could not come, and to the methodist conference, whose ministers would not attend though they could. (Loud applause.) 350,000 Methodists were associated under the Wesleyan conference, but they had not one representative in this assembly. To-morrow they were to have the address proposed. What they wished to do was, that the resolutions to be proposed as the bases of those addresses should be passed this evening; and that those who had to speak would confine themselves to a quarter of an hour long. There were nine resolutions altogether, and three had been moved.

The Rev. S. J. Phillips, of Woolton, near Liverpool, next addressed the meeting, and expressed his gratification to see gentlemen of such various theological opinions, uniting so harmoniously in the cause of the poor. He had been 21 years a catholic priest, and had witnessed during that period several seasons of distress, but none so great as the present. His heart boiled with indignation at the consideration that myriads of his fellow-creatures were pining in wretchedness and want, and the blessings of Providence denied to them by hard-hearted monopolists. Was it possible that a monopolist ever read the word of God? If so, what answer could he make when called on to appear before the solemn tribunal of his God? Then the Saviour would invite those who had ministered to the wants of the suffering poor to enter into eternal blessedness; while, turning to the monopolists, he would apply to them the sentence on those who fed not the hungry, and clothed not the naked. As ministers, they were in their appropriate position in denouncing monopoly. The duties of their vocation brought them so frequently into contact with those who were experiencing the evils of the present restrictive system, that it was their peculiar province to come forward, and boldly denounce the evil. This country was once called "Merrie England," but that name was not the most suitable one at present. However, he trusted, that, when monopolies were abolished, England would once more have "happy homes and altars free." (Applause.)

The Chairman then put the resolution, which passed unanimously.

The Rev. Dr. Payne, of Exeter, said that the severe indisposition under which he laboured would not permit him to exceed the prescribed limits; yet he could not forego the opportunity of recording his conviction that the laws which they wished to abolish had brought the country to the brink of a precipice, and that nothing but instant retreat would save it from destruction. (Hear, hear.) He wished to express his fervent gratitude to God for bringing so many ministers together, from all parts of the country, without the slightest accident; and his cordial congratulations to the Manchester pastors, that the call made by them had been so generally responded to. When he thought of the obstacles to their meeting, resulting from distance, expense, &c., he felt that they could only have been drawn together by the power of principle—principle which must ultimately triumph. (Applause.) When he remembered the immense numbers which this conference represented, the constitution of the meeting, the characters of the men composing it, their integrity and single-mindedness, their devotion to the glory of God and the good of man, their intelligence and education, their powers of thought and addition to thought, their ability to grapple with any difficulty; and, especially, when he thought of the wonderful unanimity of opinion and feeling that pervaded the meeting, he could not but conclude that the movement was of God. (Applause.) They had been convened, (he said) to consider the operation of the corn laws. The presence of any individual there, did not, then, commit him to an opinion that that operation was baneful. Any one who had not reached that opinion might have been present, and perhaps ought to have been present, that he might be aided in forming his conclusions. The meeting had first heard evidence on the case; and that evidence had been so abundant and conclusive as to convince the doubtful, and to strengthen the convictions of those who had previously reached conviction, that all protective duties, whether of corn or of any thing else, were a blot upon our statute book, and that it became us to unite, as with one heart and soul, to get them expunged from that book. He had long ago reached the conviction that any tax but for the single purpose of raising the revenue necessary for defraying the expenses of government, was wrong in principle, and, of course, baneful in operation. (Hear, hear.) Government, he said, had been in the habit of giving us too much of government, (Laughter,) of intermeddling with things which were better left to be regulated by the great principles of human nature and the wise and merciful providence of God. Only let them leave science, and religion, and commerce, and trade, alone, and they would prosper better without protection than with it. (Applause.) Never did government commit a greater blunder than in establishing the present protective duties on corn. His resolution expressed a conviction that the existing misery of the country resulted, in a great measure, from the operation of the corn laws. He believed it. It was their duty accordingly to seek an alteration. But it is objected (he said) that this is a political question, with which Christians and their ministers have nothing to do. He would have entered upon this point at large, but it had been well considered by his reverend friend, Dr. Smith. Still he must be permitted to say that, in his opinion, ministers had much to do with politics. (Hear.) They had to show how the great principles of the gospel should influence political measures and movements; and a Christian minister not capable of doing this was so far incapacitated for the discharge of his duties. (Applause.) Immoral political measures and movements might (he said) involve the whole country in guilt. We should not be legally responsible, but who shall say that we should not be morally responsible, if we did not demonstrate against them? Suppose that a profligate government were to attempt the reestablishment of slavery, or to plunge the country into a war deemed unlawful by the great body of the population, would not God hold them to be guilty, if they raised not their voices against the measures? It was the same (he said) with regard to the corn laws. (Applause.) It is again objected that the question is within the domains of political economy, and that Christian ministers are not competent to grapple with such questions. He denied it. They were as much level to their comprehension as to that of those who made the objection. He thought that the qualifications of ministers, their habits of close and consequential thought, positively fitted them for such duties; while the importance and practical bearing of the great principles of the science demanded attention from them. They had important aid (he said) in the writings of Malthus, Ricardo, M'Culloch, and especially in the work of that able and excellent man, Professor Wayland. He ventured to recommend the book to his brethren, and moved—

"That, in the face of the facts which have come under their notice in their own respective neighbourhoods no less than by statements laid before them, the ministers composing this conference cannot avoid the painful conviction, that much of the wide-spread distress of the present time is attributable to provision laws, inasmuch as they limit the supply, and, thereby enhancing the cost of the common necessaries of life, fetter industry, repress enterprise, divert the legitimate employment of capital, and spread discontent and heartburning through the land."

The Rev. J. Harvey, of Glasgow, seconded the motion. He said it was long since he had agitated for the repeal of the corn laws. He had become so familiar with abuse, that he felt perfectly indifferent to its most copious outpourings. "Political dissenters" sounded no worse than "political churchmen," and was certainly neither more unbecoming nor dangerous. It was twelve years since he began to lecture against the corn laws, and he was not likely, if health were granted to him, to cease to agitate till they were totally repealed. He might say that he not only represented his own congregation but likewise the Anti-Corn-Law Association of Glasgow, at whose special request he had come to the conference. His own congregation had petitioned against these laws three years in succession; and in May last the petition had above seven hundred signatures attached to it. The time necessarily allotted him did not admit of a full discussion of the influence and tendency of these laws. It might be demonstrated that they were pernicious in all their bearings. They were impolitic, agitating the country, and disturbing its peace—ruinous to trade—imposing an immense tax, yet yielding little revenue to the government; they violated every principle of justice, and set at defiance all the precepts of religion and all the claims of humanity. He would restrict himself to their influence on the price of food. He firmly believed that the direct tendency of these laws was to raise the price of food, and that it was for this very end they were enacted. No law had assumed so many Proteus shapes as the corn laws; they had never met the expectations of their enactors; and never would do good; because they were founded in essential injustice. While they bear with peculiar severity on the industrious classes—diminishing wages, and raising the price of food, they do not benefit the agriculturist. They are a fathomless sea, engulphing the energies of the nation with little advantage to any. Though the corn laws are most extensively pernicious, they stand not alone in the scale of iniquity—every article of food which can be imported is included in the list, from raw grain to manufactured sausages. (Applause.) The working classes can not only procure a smaller supply of the delicacies of life than the wealthier, but actually require a much larger amount of food than those who do not give their bodily energies for the production of wealth. The man who labours with his mind may be a very hard worker, and a most useful member of society; but from the very nature of his employment he does not require so much food as the operative. Hence a tax on corn bears with peculiar severity on the labourer: he is compelled either to support himself and family on an insufficient quantity of food, or to subsist on inferior articles of diet, or to deprive himself of a comfortable and healthy dwelling, or to go half clad, or to neglect the education of his children, and to send them to work at an age when labour is utterly unsuited to their years. For a time he may struggle on and make his selection among these expedients, but by and by they will all come into operation, and sink that portion of the community, which ought to be the ornament and pride of the nation, into wretchedness, immorality, and crime. To this alarming condition is our population rapidly tending. Parents are compelled to send their children to work before they are educated; and, although night-schools have been provided for such, little good can be accomplished by their instrumentality. Can it be expected that children of ten or twelve years of age, after having toiled from six in the morning till seven in the evening, in a heated atmosphere, can be in a fit state to receive instruction after that late hour? Often with a bleeding heart had he seen these toiling children drop asleep on their seat and tumble upon the floor through perfect exhaustion. The consequence is, the present generation is rising up comparatively uneducated, and a great quantity of labour is prematurely brought into the market, the tendency of which is to lower wages; thus food is raised in price, and wages lowered at the same time, making the pressure bear with double the severity on the industrious portion of the community. (Applause.) Besides, the corn laws have the effect of limiting the demand for manufactured articles. Our market is limited in two ways—limited by a deficiency of home consumption through dear bread; for it will invariably be found that when provisions are dear, manufactured goods are in less demand, and limited for want of a foreign market. Hence many are thrown out of employment entirely. Not to mention the weavers, many of whom have no work at any price, and when employed cannot, with the greatest exertions, earn half wages, the spinning and weaving factories and the printing establishments of Glasgow are on short time, and some of them entirely at a stand. In Calton, one of the suburbs of Glasgow, with which he (Mr. H.) was more immediately connected, there is the deepest wretchedness. In proof of this he mentioned a circumstance. A missionary had been employed by his congregation to visit the families in the district around his place of worship. He was a most diligent and active person; but such was the depth of the poverty of the great majority of the families, that he became convinced that it was in vain to attempt to communicate religious instruction to them till their temporal condition was improved, and he gave up his labours in despair. (Hear, hear.) In many of their dwellings there was not an article of furniture—not a stool to sit on, and only a little straw in one corner of the wretched apartment, on which the miserable inmates huddled themselves together in their ordinary clothes for a little sleep. To talk to persons in these circumstances on religious subjects, without first relieving their temporal necessities, is to insult them. It is virtually to tell them they may die of hunger, and starve through cold, and Christians care not. Their only concern is about the soul, but the people themselves must provide for their bodies in the best way they can. It may be said, why not apply to the parish? It is useless. The tedious forms adopted professedly to prevent imposition, but in reality to starve the destitute, render such application almost needless. But even although successful, to what does the relief granted amount? To not more than a penny or three-halfpence a-day, which can only prolong life in lingering starvation. (Applause.) Bad as the poor laws of England are, those of Scotland are yet worse, if not in the letter, yet in their administration. The famishing may get into the union or parish workhouses of England, and have food and comfortable shelter; but not so in Scotland. The poor laws there are a system of starvation throughout. The minister who confines his visits to his own flock can form no conception of the wretchedness of a large portion of the community. It is always the more comfortable class of operatives who attend church, and when they sink below a certain scale they are compelled to give up attendance for want of clothes. He (Mr. H.) had known instances in which attendants on his ministry had, through the depth of misery to which they had been reduced, without complaining, secretly retired to some deeper sink of wretchedness that they might suffer unknown by those who had known them in their better days. This feeling may be called pride; but if this feeling of honest independence is crushed, and beaten out of the breast of our countrymen by oppression, woe to our native land. (Applause.) One class of the community is at present, and has been for a considerable time, in deep distress—he meant solitary females, a little advanced in life, and widows, who had once known better days; their case was peculiarly pitiable, and the corn laws bear with tremendous severity against them. Their children had died, or emigrated to a foreign shore, and friends they had none, and they had no hope but in the grave, or in the haven beyond it. Facts the most numerous and well attested might be adduced to prove that something must be done, and that speedily. But they had already a sufficiency of facts, and enough of speaking. We have come here to act, and we will act till we have rescued our beloved country from the oppression that is sinking her in misery. We have been told that we all believe in the beautiful precept of Jesus, that "we should do to others as we wish others to do to us." He doubted it. Faith, without corresponding conduct, is dead. Let all act on this rule, and then the misery that now assails us will soon flee away—the injustice which grinds the faces of the poor will no longer be practised—the discontent that now mourns in our streets will no longer be heard, but peace, contentment, and plenty, will bind the whole community together in one happy brotherhood. (Applause.)

The CHAIRMAN said he had received a private communication from several gentlemen, requesting permission to address the meeting on various resolutions. He feared he could not grant the request in one case and refuse it in another, much less could he consent to take the matter out of the hands of the committee. (Hear.) It had been intimated, that there were no Wesleyan methodists in the room. A methodist minister, though not a Wesleyan methodist, was present—a minister from Paisley, in Scotland.—The fourth resolution was then put, and carried *nem. dis.*

A MINISTER, in the body of the meeting, protested against the rule laid down, that no one should address the meeting unless the mover and seconder appointed by the committee.

Another MINISTER, in the body of the room, said that there were twenty ministers present belonging to the methodist new connection (Cheers.)

The Rev. Dr. RITCHIE rose to propose the following resolution:—

"That, believing the law of Almighty God, as revealed in his word, ought to be, in all cases, the rule of human action,—that any allowed deviation from it, either in individual conduct or in the affairs of nations, must incur the Divine displeasure,—and convinced that a monopoly in bread is anti-Christian in its principle—this conference, while it seeks the abolition of the provision laws, on other high and important grounds, more especially deprecates their continuance as a great national offence against that Being by whom kings reign, and princes decree justice."

He felt great pleasure in addressing the assembly; and he trusted that on every occasion, when a meeting was convened for an equally laudable purpose, he should be one of the number. He had laboured forty years for the abolition of slavery; and, with 339 delegates, he told Lord Althorp, in Downing-street, that Scotland was up in arms against slavery, and would never sit down till it was abolished. Slavery had been abolished, and monopoly would soon share the same fate. All the members of the body politic had a mutual sympathy for each other; and, as in the body natural, whenever a member became diseased, amputation, if necessary, should be resorted to for the salvation of the rest. He did not care what limb might require such treatment; but the safety of the whole system should be consulted. He could not recognise any line of demarcation between nations, inasmuch as God had "made of one blood all the nations of the earth." (Applause.) God and nature had condemned the corn law; and if the nation expected the blessing of the Most High, it should put forth its most energetic exertions for the abolition of that accursed enactment. (Applause.)

The Rev. JEROME CLAPP, of Appledore, Devon, seconded the resolution by saying—Gentlemen, I need not detain your attention but a very few minutes to second the resolution, the spirit of which must so approve it to us all, as ministers of the gospel of Christ, that it must be its best and most powerful recommendation. After the eloquent and forcible address by which it has been moved, I need but say how devoutly I rejoice in the purely religious character which this resolution gives to our proceedings,—a devotional and moral character, which is at once most consistent with our feelings and our office, and which will constitute our best security of ultimate success. Some of our congregations have possibly asked us wherefore we were coming to this meeting; and some, on our return, may ask us what we purpose to effect. Let this resolution be our answer—that, because we perceive these laws to be contrary to the spirit and purposes of God, we set ourselves to their removal. Brethren, let me say to you, in the language of the angel to Gideon, "Go in this your might, and ye shall prevail;" clothe yourselves in this impulse of godly principle, and nothing can withstand you. Lord Stanley, I remember, said, in introducing the bill to parliament for the abolition of slavery, that when the Christian public of this country spoke out in the deep conviction of their religious principle, it was with a power which no parliament nor cabinet could neglect or despise. Let us, on the same convictions and from the same holy impulse, speak again for God on behalf of the poor, and it shall be with an immediate and like success.

The Rev. J. E. GILES, of Leeds, moved the following resolution:—

"That the laws which restrict the importation of the prime necessaries of life are, in the judgment of this conference, essentially and manifestly unjust, and operate with peculiar hardship on the operative classes, by at once depriving them of a market for the disposal of the fruits of their labour, and raising the price of food when they are least able to procure it."

In moving that resolution, it was by no means his intention to say that every agriculturist in the land was unjust, while there were many of them, who, like the noble Earl who had favoured them with his presence, had risen above the dictates of a blind selfishness to advocate free trade. He would not venture to charge even the framers or supporters of the present corn laws with acting upon principles of known injustice; since he happened to know, among the latter, not a few who were distinguished for benevolence and integrity. But if, instead of being led by interested party guides, they would carefully examine the operation of those laws for themselves, he felt assured, just in proportion to the confidence he had in their characters, that their hearts would bleed for the miseries which they had been unconsciously inflicting. From the year 1463, when the system of protection (so called) first began, what had been the history of the corn laws, but the history of injustice? what was the object of those laws but injustice? what their operation but injustice? injustice *first*, injustice *last*, injustice *midst*, and *without end!* To this statement, however, the law of 1763, which fixed the duty at 6d., ought to be mentioned as an exception. But the legislation of that period was too just and rational to be allowed to continue long; so that, for nearly 400 years, the country had groaned under a system of laws, in which the interests of only one party were consulted; and whether he looked at the duties imposed to make bread dear or the bounties given to prevent its becoming cheap; whether he looked at the price at which the duty was fixed or the manner in which the average price was determined, he saw that the question asked by the legislature had never been, what did justice to the people demand? but how much injustice and famine would they bear? After various transmigrations, the spirit of monopoly had snugly embodied itself in the present corn law bill, which received the royal assent, July 15th, 1828; and by that bill it was determined, that at 73s. per quarter, the duty on wheat should be 1s., which should progressively rise till the price should sink to 66s. when it would become 20s. 8d.; and that below 66s., the duty should increase 1s. with every decrease of a shilling in the price of corn. Now, though this law had been extolled as a profound contrivance, to preserve a beautiful equipoise between production and price, that should protect or rather benefit all classes, he would venture to denounce it as so much unmitigated injustice and oppression. It was sometimes said that the amount of duty paid on corn was but small, because there was no great quantity imported; that, however, was not reasoning, but only an artful and evasive piece of sophistry, which could impose upon none but the grossly ignorant; because the duty must be regarded as added, not only to the corn imported, but to every quarter consumed; so that, probably, not less than fifty millions of pounds annually are taken out of the pockets of the people, and handed over to the proprietors of land. And when he considered the way in which the corn laws operated to make bread dear, not only by adding the duty to the price of growth, but by discouraging the growth of corn in other lands, for the British market; by producing a fluctuation in price, which rendered it impossible that growers should know when to grow, or speculators when to buy; by narrowing the surface from which corn could ever be imported, through fear that the price should fall and the duty should rise, before it could arrive; by protecting the growth of corn on improper lands at home—and by persons with whom agriculture was a mere pastime and sport—he could not but regard them as a monopoly, not only of British produce, but, as far as we are concerned, of that of other lands; a monopoly not of land only but of the winds and waves; a turnpike across the great highway of nations, to keep from our shores the varied blessings of the earth. It was well known that, in consequence of the length of time it had been kept in bond, 899 quarters of Russian wheat were spoiled and thrown into the Thames, in 1839; the very year in which the Highlanders were dying for want of bread. But the worst feature of that unrighteous system remained yet to be exposed. The duty was determined according to the average price, for the purpose of ascertaining which, the law selected 150 towns, in which corn dealers are enjoined to furnish the amount and price of their purchases, to certain inspectors, (the London dealers give the price of their sales) who transmit them to the general receiver of returns, in London; whose business it is, weekly to strike the average of the last six weeks, and publish it in the *London Gazette*. Now, he complained of this enactment on two grounds, first, because instead of taking the average of the whole world, it took the average of England only; and, next, because it enabled the corn monopolists to make the average just what they pleased. If they wished to get up the price, four or five dealers, in the several towns, meeting in a room, A, supposing the previous price to be 60s., would enter into an understanding to sell to B for 61s.; B to C for 62s.; C to D for 63s.; and D back to A for 64s.; and, though not a grain of wheat might be interchanged among them, they would hand over the several amounts of these fictitious sales, as genuine returns, and thus raise throughout the kingdom the average price. In the same way, when threatened with importation, they frequently managed to shut the ports by lowering the price. The sliding scale, therefore, was nothing but a piece of sliding injustice; the very see-saw of iniquity:

> "Here we go up, up, up,
> Here we go down, down, down,
> Here we go backwards and forwards,
> And here we go round, round, round."

It was very well for children to play at such games; but was it right, he would ask, that statesmen and noblemen should so amuse themselves, when the music to which they were dancing was the groans and execrations of dying millions? Whatever they might think upon that subject, he would assure that audience that the present system placed the very gates of life and death in the hands of men, who were in the habit of gambling with the bread, and therefore with the lives of the people. It had been urged on the opposite side of the question, that the people would be no gainers by an alteration of the corn laws, partly because it would throw much land out of cultivation, and partly because wheat, at a moderate fixed duty, could not be imported cheaper than it is sold now. Now he would say, that he had nothing to do with a moderate fixed duty; for a moderate fixed duty was, in his opinion, a moderate fixed injustice. But looking at the objections as they were offered, he would say, first of all, to the monopolists, "If you really believe that the price of corn will not be lowered by the repeal of the corn laws, why, unless it be merely for the sake of opposition, do you resist that repeal?" And next he would urge, that the two objections could not stand together. If corn could not be imported cheaper than it is now grown, no land could be thrown out of cultivation; but if land would be thrown out of cultivation, it could only be in the ratio in which it would be imported cheaper than it is now grown; so that gentlemen using such logic might expect, like Actæon, to be hunted to death by their own dogs. But he would contend that the corn laws not only robbed the nation of its golden eggs, but killed the goose which laid them, by their ruinous effect upon our commerce. As the people, generally, had so much less to lay out in manufactured articles, in proportion to the dearness of bread, the tendency of all duty on corn was to injure our home-trade; while, by keeping the produce of foreign lands from our shores, it cripples our commerce abroad; other nations, either through necessity or on a principle of retaliation, refusing to take our goods unless we took their corn. Thus foreign nations had been converted from customers into rivals; and to expect the British merchant to compete with them under the existing system, was to expect men to run in sacks as fast as those whose limbs were free. But the worst effect of the present system upon commerce remained yet to be considered. Owing to the rapid fluctuations in price, and consequently in duty, which it produced, the speculators, at a time of scarcity, were obliged to buy as much and as quickly as possible, lest the price sinking, and the duty rising, should expose them to a double loss before their importation could arrive. But, as in foreign lands there is no sudden demand for foreign corn, the purchases were necessarily made with gold. And what was the consequence? Why, the Bank of England, drained of its bullion, began to draw upon the banks in the country, they upon the merchant, the merchant upon the tradesman, and the tradesman upon every other class; and thus consternation and ruin were spread through the land. While, on the one hand, everything sank in value, in consequence of forced sales for ready money to meet unexpected demands; on the other, every person, from the scarcity of money, became afraid to sell or to buy. The merchant having no demand on the manufacturer, nor the manufacturer on his workmen, nor the workmen, for want of employment, on the tradesmen, all things were thrown into confusion; so that respectable men found themselves suddenly ruined in the midst of buildings and goods which they had a right to think their own, while the workmen went, hungry and in rags, under the very walls of those factories that were capable of producing clothing for the world. Thus he had seen many an affluent and noble-minded man reduced to very moderate circumstances, and many a man of moderate condition reduced to beggary and want. To obviate the force of this reasoning, it was sometimes said, on the other side, that our commercial embarrassments were not real, and the largeness of our exports was referred to in proof of the flourishing state of our trade. Amongst other reasoners of this class it would be recollected that Lord Stanley, condescending to amuse himself with our commercial distress, had said that the merchants of Lancashire were like the old woman selling matches, who said, "though she lost by every bunch, she thanked the Lord a great many bunches had been sold." Such was his Lordship's elegant and benevolent allusion to men who had nothing before them but bankruptcy, embarrassments, or loss. But turning from his Lordship to the general argument of the monopolist, where, he would ask, was its force? It was not by the amount, but by the profits of our exports, that we were to estimate the value of our trade; and the wealth of a nation must be determined, not so much by what it sends away, as by what it keeps. It was well known that our goods, for want of sale at home, had been sent at ruinous prices abroad; and that, of those which had been sent, large quantities had been spoiled in foreign lands, or thrown back upon the hands of our merchants, because the productions of other countries could not be taken in exchange. If, independently of the profit which it brings, a large exportation were a proof of prosperity, no country was in a more flourishing state than Ireland, which not only exported all her oxen and pigs, but a great proportion of her potatoes and corn. But while, by some, our commercial distress was denied, there were others who contended that overtrading, and not the duties on corn, was the cause to which it ought to be ascribed. That there had been too much speculation and trading on fictitious capital, he would willingly admit. But at the same time he believed, that nothing had so much contributed to injurious speculations in trade, as those unnatural fluctuations which arose from the duties on corn, and gave an artificial impulse at one time, while they created an unnecessary depression at another. But supposing this were not the case, was it to be endured that, by a selfish monopoly, the manufacturer should have every market in Europe closed against his goods, and then be told, by the advocates of that monopoly, that he had manufactured too much? If there had been an overflow, it was not that the land-springs of our industry were too full—it was not that the stream of production was too large for human wants; but because it had been artificially contracted and dammed up, instead of being allowed to roll on between its native banks, widening and deepening in its flow, towards that boundless ocean where mingling tides and currents find their common level, beneath the great commanding law of the God of Heaven. Such, then, being the operation of the corn laws, he would ask, what right had any man or set of men to enact or support such iniquitous and oppressive measures? In reply to this inquiry, they were frequently told, that those laws were essential for the protection of "British interests." There was sometimes a world of meaning in a word; and he believed that the term "British interests" implied, that nothing belonging to commerce ought to be considered "British." Gentlemen at Manchester and other great commercial towns had amongst them factories, steam-engines, and spinning-jennies, constructed with consummate ingenuity and immense expense; but these were no doubt imported from China or the Georgium Sidus, for none of them were "British;" they might have among them men of science, such as Dalton and a Henry, who had astonished the world by their discoveries; they might have among them merchants who were princes, and artisans unrivalled in industry and skill; but what were all these but a kind of Jews, heretics, or "aliens in blood," who ought to be left to the uncovenanted mercies of the British senate, and to be thankful for toleration on the British soil? Begging leave, however, to differ from such exclusive notions, he would ask, were not our workmen British, and if so were not they to be protected? Supposing, however, for the sake of argument, that the landowners had a right to monopolize the word "British" to themselves, what protection he would ask could they fairly need beyond that which they derived from our insular situation and the difficulties of transporting corn? Dantzic wheat, we were told on unquestionable authority, could not be obtained for less than 35s. per quarter, to which must be added, charges of shipment and freight, a profit to the importer, and the expenses after it reaches our coast, of inland conveyance; and if, with all these advantages in his favour, the home grower could not compete with the foreigner, he would say that England should grow no corn at all. Some lands, it was true, might, if the restrictions on the importation of food were removed, be no longer used for the growth of corn; but it was well known that it was now grown on land totally unfit for such a purpose. He himself had seen, last spring, a man employed with a breast plough, on the top of a barren mountain, in Worcestershire, which looked like a twin brother to the highest of the Malvern hills; in a soil, through which the rock was every where projecting, and in a situation to which a wheel-barrow of manure could scarcely be driven. On asking his agricultural friend, who stood near him, how soil could be procured for the growth of corn on such a wilderness of stones and moss, to which it was impossible to convey manure, he was informed that it was the practice, in such cases, to burn the turf to ashes; which answered the purpose for two or three years, when the land sank back again into its barren condition. Thus, at a ruinous expense to the people, was the cultivation of bleak mountain-tops, in England, protected; while the fat, black soils of Poland were left untilled; and while other more productive mountain-tops, in Wales and Yorkshire, mountains of inter-stratified coal and iron, were thrown by the corn laws out of cultivation. But then it was asked what would become of the poor? He hated hypocrisy of all kinds, but especially hypocrisy under the mask of benevolence, he looked, however, upon the objection as an omen for good, believing that nothing but the torment of a justly anticipated repeal of the corn laws, would have induced the landowner, like Dives, to call Lazarus to his help. It was of importance to remember, however, that it was not their starving artizans, but such paupers as his *poor* Grace the Duke of Buckingham, the *poor* Right Honourable Member for Tamworth, the *poor* noble Lord who represents, or misrepresents, North Lancashire, who were the real objects of the monopolists' solicitude. As to the other poor, the fact that poor-rates were heavier in agricultural than in manufacturing counties, served to show that commerce was the poor man's friend, and that it kept him from the workhouse by finding him employment. In answer to the objection that the repeal of the corn laws would make us dependent on other countries, he would say that we were dependent upon them now; for what, he would ask, would become of Lancashire were America to withhold her cotton from our shores? It was consolatory, however, to know that the seller was as dependent on the customer, as the customer on the seller; dependence was mutual; America could not starve Lancashire without first starving herself; so that commerce, if free, would be the great peace-maker of nations; and he could not but look upon that Conference as a great peace society. It was customary, when all other arguments failed, to charge the working classes with a disposition to indulge themselves, without cause, in a spirit of dissatisfaction and complaint. But he, for one, would repel the slander, and say that, as a whole, they were not a complaining race. Britain ever had been, and was still, the land of heroes; but there were heroes at the anvil and the loom, as well as on the "tented field" or the quarter-deck; and, if a calm endurance of unavoidable hardship and toil could constitute a hero, such might every where be seen. That the working classes were now in a state of dissatisfaction, was certainly true; but of what did they complain? Was it that they were called to labour in wet dye-houses or hot drying-rooms, oppressed with heat or saturated in water? No! It was that through cruel and oppressive laws, their willing hands hung idle at their sides, and that they were doomed to wear the sluggard's rags, and to hear their children cry in vain for bread. And did Sir Robert Peel think it right or safe, that such complaints should go unheeded and unheard? If so, he could only tell the Right Honourable Baronet, that, were he, like Phaëton, to leap into the Chariot of the Sun, he could not kindle a more dreadful blaze, nor meet with a heavier fall, than must result from his taking the reins of government, under a pledge to the sliding scale. The rev. gentleman was listened to with intense interest, and was loudly cheered throughout his speech.

The Rev. F. J. Archer, of Blessington, county Antrim, Wicklow, seconded the resolution. He said he lived in a locality of 7,000 or 8,000 individuals, and should confine his observations to that. He declared that the average weekly wages paid to common labourers did not exceed 3s. 6d. to 5s. a week. In the county Kildare the lowest rent of poor land was 38s. to 60s. per British acre, the produce of which never fetched more than 12s. 6d. a barrel. The rate of wages was continually diminishing from 1d. to 2d. a day; excellent labourers could be hired for 5d. a day; and at the present time the price of the quartern loaf was 10d., and the earnings of a poor man and his family were at the most 11d. a day; they paid 10d. for their loaf: what were they to buy their potatoes with, which were 8d. a stone? (Cheers.) Let them conceive how destitute must be the condition of such families. It was asked if the price of labour rose with the price of food: in his locality wages never rose, they were permanent; the grasping aristocracy, who told their wealth by thousands and tens of thousands, would do nothing to raise the price of labour. (Cheers.) He rejoiced to know that the people had got the smell of cheap bread in their noses; he trusted they never would rest till they had gratified their taste also. (Cheers.) He was delighted to have an opportunity of raising his voice in an assembly which comprised men of such learning, information, piety, and public zeal, and he referred, above all, to the information and public spirit evinced by the truly "apostolic" minister who had addressed them. (Cheers.) He rejoiced that he, the least among his brethren, had an opportunity of being heard in such an assembly. (Hear, hear.) He trusted that a voice would go forth from the meeting which should make the Tory aristocracy surrender their unjust advantage, and should drive monopoly to its last home, and bury it, overwhelm it, in the public indignation. (Cheers.) Yes, a sound will go forth from *this Hall*, which will be carried to the utmost verge of this great Empire, *proclaiming* in behalf of *famishing thousands*—that the "*Corn Laws*," the baneful source of so much national misery and degradation, must be *repealed*. Our cry will be—"*away* with them—*away with them!* Give the people *cheap bread* or the fate of mighty England may *be risked* on this question alone" But *they must, they will* be annihilated, by *the outpouring* of universal condemnation (Loud cheers.)

The Rev. T. Swan, of Birmingham, stated, that the hearts of the men of Birmingham, he doubted not, beat in unison with those of the men of Manchester on this question. The men of Manchester occupied a most elevated position; but it was one of tremendous responsibility. The eyes of the world were upon them, and so were those of the newspapers; the *Watchman*, the vigilant and trustworthy *Watchman*, had its eyes upon them—(cheers and laughter)—also that veracious, consistent, and respectable journal, the *Times*. (Loud cheers.) The object of the meeting was to set free the white slaves—the suffering class, he would not call them poor, for their ambition was to obtain their bread by the sweat of their brow. (Applause.) He was prepared to corroborate the statements which had been given by Mr. East. He had been sent by the unanimous vote of a church of 800 members; and he would assure them that many of their pious friends were suffering severely from the oppression of what he would call the "accursed" corn laws. (Hear, hear.) Many had been compelled to relinquish their places in the sanctuary for want of sufficient clothing, and many young men had had to expatriate themselves for want of employment. He acknowledged it was his belief that their people were in advance of them on this question; for his own part, he had been wafted into this august assembly by the popular will. (Cheers.) It was not the duty of ministers to sit still and do nothing, to give up the question as one which they knew nothing about. Had not the facts adduced by Mr. Cobden shown them their duty on this subject? They ought not to despond; for God himself would fight for them. It was not their duty to become the tools of factious or interested politicians; and had he supposed that this was a mere affair connected with whiggery, or aught of that kind, he would not have countenanced it. Let them do nothing either to keep in whigs or tories; he was of no party, either whig, tory, or radical, but was for justice and righteousness. (Cheers.) Their duty unquestionably was to take the side of the oppressed. Were not many of them their own people, to whom they had been useful, and who looked to the ministers as their natural guardians and their last hope; and let them not look in vain. (Applause.) It was their duty, further, to strive to avert God's judgments; and if iniquitous laws were not repealed, God's judgments might be expected to come upon the land. The operatives of this country seemed, like the Saviour, to be crucified between two thieves; be it their duty to strive to save both the operatives and the thieves, both the oppressed and the oppressors (Cheers.): It was their duty to agitate; for nothing was done without it, either in the natural, moral, or the spiritual world. He rejoiced that so many were committed to this agitation; they must not only agitate here, but they must keep it up when they got home amongst their friends, their congregations, and the youth of the country. A sliding scale and a slippery politician would never do in these days; they must get up the pressure from without against it, and must never rest till these laws were removed. They were moreover like the Scotchman, "to tak a part, and ask for mair;" they would accept a fixed duty, but would seek for something better. (Cheers.)

The Rev. Wm. M'Kerrow said, it was impossible for all who wished to speak to be gratified; but he trusted that the meeting would not think they were despotic in exercising a discretion. Mr. George Thompson, the enemy of slavery in all its forms, would address them to-morrow.

The Rev. J. W. Massie then stated, that, as some of the ministers might have to leave the town the following morning, the memorials which it was intended to bring before the meeting were prepared, ready for the signatures of those ministers who wished to give effect to their assembly.

The Rev. Thomas Adkins moved the following resolution:—

"That, in the undeniable fact of the reciprocal dependance of the several branches of the human family, this conference, recognising the admirable provision of the all-wise, beneficent Creator for securing their individual happiness, maintaining their peaceful intercourse, and enhancing their collective welfare, in consequence feels itself solemnly bound to declare its uncompromising hostility to those legislative enactments which prevent the ever-increasing population of this country from exchanging the products of their manufacturing industry and skill, which they are especially enabled to proffer, for the food which they so much need, and which other countries are so well able and most anxious to give in return for them.

He had a heartfelt request to prefer—that they would permit him, having moved the resolution, to commit it to other hands.—("No.")

The Rev. Jas. Edwards, of Nottingham, seconded the resolution. He said he was just retiring from the room through indisposition, when he heard his name called on. He thought there could not be a more animating vision under heaven than that which this meeting presented. It was delightful to see so many hundred Christian ministers assembled together to consult the interests of the suffering poor, and to combine their counsels and influence for the destruction of one of the most baneful monopolies that were ever sustained by the sanctions of legislation, or permitted in the inscrutable providence of God, to spread desolation through the land. Much had been said by the preceding speakers of the mischievous working of the provision laws in producing commercial embarrassments, and in subjecting multitudes of our industrious population to misery and starvation. Under the influence of these unjust laws, it might with propriety be said,

"Life dies, death lives, and nature breeds
Perverse, all monstrous, all prodigious things,
Abominable, unutterable,
And worse than fables yet have feigned, or fear conceived."

A few days ago a working man of Nottingham told him, he was glad to hear of the meeting which was about to be held in Manchester. He said, he had long thought the dissenting ministers had but little sympathy with the sufferings of the working classes of this country. When the negroes were in bondage, he said, "you fought for them and broke their chains, but there are thousands of us who are much worse off than the slaves were, and yet you do nothing for us. I believe if you take up our cause you will succeed, and you may depend upon it we shall rally around you with all our hearts." In the autumn of 1839, he visited Madeira and the Canary Islands, and there he witnessed the injurious effects of the corn and provision laws of England. In consequence of the large and unexpected purchases made by the British vessels calling at those places, provisions became scarce, prices advanced, and much distress followed, especially among the poor. In Santa Cruz, the inhabitants were apprehensive that they should be subjected to a famine, and having ascertained that some extensive purchases of wheat had been made for shipment to England, the alarm became so great that the authorities were compelled to interfere, and prevent the corn leaving the island. In his own neighbourhood, he had been informed, that thousands were prepared to adopt and act on the plan that was resorted to at the time of the passing of the Reform Bill, by placing on their doors the words, "No taxes paid here till the corn laws are repealed."

The CHAIRMAN next introduced the Rev. Robert Melson, who, he stated, was a Wesleyan Minister, and "one of the hundred." (Applause.)

The Rev. ROBERT MELSON, of Birmingham, said—It was true he had the honour of being a member of "the hundred" that constituted the Wesleyan Conference, but he represented not that body. Their committee had addressed the Wesleyan Conference, and their letter was read on Friday last and considered; but it was thought that the conference ought not to come forward as a body, and where was the body that would? (Cheers.) But, Sir, said he, if the church of England would come forward with all her ministers, her bishops, and her Majesty, (who is its head,) no doubt the Wesleyan Society would then follow as a body. (Loud cheers.) He must confess, however, that as an individual he should have been delighted had the Conference sent a deputation to their body, for he was a lover of mankind, and rejoiced to promote the welfare of his fellow-creatures, though he represented no people, unless, indeed it might be said, that on this occasion he represented the great and suffering masses of the poor. On entering the room he had no intention whatever of addressing the meeting, and was quite unprepared to address so large, learned, and respectable an assembly of divines; but after attending the Wesleyan Conference for three weeks, he had thought it right to see this Conference before he left Manchester. Even on entering the room he had it in intention to return home that very evening, but having heard so many forcible and eloquent addresses, he had now formed the resolution not to leave Manchester so long as this Conference held its sittings. On Saturday last he took a journey of about twenty miles into the country, and meeting with a gentleman, who travelled with him in the coach, they got into a very free conversation, until coming near to the place of his residence the gentleman pointed it out to him, and told him that there he was born, that it had been for many years the residence of his father, and that in the adjoining factory they had been in the habit of paying upwards of two thousand pounds a month as wages to their work-people until last Christmas, when, in consequence of the depression of trade, he had been under the necessity of closing his factory and dismissing all his hands, since which time they had been deprived of employment, and his extensive machinery had been gradually deteriorating in value. The same gentleman stated that the large factory on the other side of the road was also recently closed, by which event several hundreds of persons had been deprived of their daily employment. After stating other facts illustrative of the distress which prevailed throughout the country at large, and in the vicinity of Manchester in particular, he said that he did not feel himself justified in occupying more of their valuable time at so late an hour in the evening, and begged to conclude by supporting the resolution. (Prolonged applause.)

The Rev. R. W. HAMILTON, of Leeds—Mr. Chairman, and Reverend Brethren,—Is there one of you whose spirit within him now lusteth to envy? (laughter;) one who covets my present position? The clock will in a moment strike the ninth hour after "a summer day" of absorbing interest and oppressive attention. (Laughter.) If such a one there be in this assembly, gladly will I exchange my lot with him, upon the honest principle of that barter which we are here to explain and recommend. (Laughter.) Nor can I forget in what succession I appear. After a member of the hundred! Who is he that cometh after the king? (Laughter.) Then what is my temerity in following the centurion? (Laughter.) What are the most colossal forms and depositories of power compared with this? Let sceptres vibrate and thrones quake. (Loud laughter.) Many are the reasons which justify this gathering with whatever name friend or foe may distinguish it. If this be new, not less new is the exigence. The Christian pastor sees the coil of the strait and famine, which I most surely believe to be the consequence mainly of these cruel impositions on trade and capital, in more obvious and appalling forms than most other men. We can no longer keep to our "course in the temple." We pierce the masses and pursue the haunts of our population. Is our experience nothing? Long collected and arduously obtained, may it not be of some avail to statistical science and political economy? We can bear witness, as few can do, to a pauperization of the people, so rapid, so fearful, that we believe it to be in both these qualities, without parallel and without precedent. It may be a false scrupulousness, but it is well known that a great number of religious, truly Christian men, object to our taking part in political meetings. I do not see myself that the Christian minister should forego civil rights, or decline social duties, because of his office. But thus is it often *ruled*. Where, then, may we speak? We have sought a quiet enclosure of our own. Avoiding the theatres of party strife, we have selected these "mollia tempora fandi." Are we to be refused the privilege of this sanctuary and this season to which we are almost compelled? Shall we be suffered no opinion, and no medium for its articulation? Must we be annihilated to a caprice of taste? And though we are working men, and unquestionably belong to the industrious classes, yet our products are not those which society recognizes in the way of profit and gain. "Nos numerus sumus, et fruges consumere nati." It is therefore the more incumbent on us to protect the men who labour to create those commodities to which we cannot contribute, but the amount of which we cannot but reduce. (Cheers.) Were it only the perjury which the present corn law fosters and too safely screens, they who believe that there is a God that judgeth in the earth, that because of swearing the land mourneth, that lying lips are an abomination, would feel themselves solemnly required to put away the occasion of offence—all moralists and juris-consults are agreed that a law, which necessarily tempts to its evasion, and provides a security for its transgressor in itself, is essentially evil: both practically and philosophically it must be indefensible. (Hear, hear.) It is not requisite to meet the objection, that, as we respectively disapprove of all legislative restriction on the food of the people, we add nothing to the weight of that disapproval by this combination. This is inconsistent with all we have ever known. You may not increase the integers, but by a closer contact and a more systematic arrangement, you may give them greater influence and strength. The burning glass forms not a ray nor fervor, but it collects them, it concentrates them, into manifold splendor and intenseness. But let us, reverend brethren, with this justification of our conduct, advance to this vital question—the question of our day—the question of our country. Little are the difficulties which hamper its settlement understood. The merchant, it may be, has realized his fortune. What shall he do? How shall he invest his property? Land offers a poor rate of interest, but that interest is steady and secure. His argosies no longer ride upon the treacherous deep. His markets no longer alternate with ruinous fluctuations. Disinterested millionaire! Without a pun, he sets his all upon the moveless soil. Amidst this generous sacrifice some comfort cheers him too. Trade is not genteel or aristocratic. He escapes the stain; yet may he sell turnip, mangel-wurzel, and coal: but this is not trade. (Laughter.) He is recommended to the commission. He is pricked for the shrievalty. He stands for the shire. He shuffles off his mercantile coil and slough. He has slipped his caste. Who is such a zealot for monopoly as he? Who, like himself, treads the trading community? The great proprietors are generally with us: it is this upstart race, these novi homines, who adopt the imperious tone and display an unfeeling insolence. This is not all. Capital, we might have supposed, would have taken the part of trade, and in any conflict between it and their putative interests of agriculture, would have thrown over it the mighty shield of its protection. Is it so? The monetary crisis comes. Capital has to decide for its own safety. It holds largely in mortgages and annuities upon the estates of the country. How few of these are disencumbered! Its natural leaning is paralyzed. It has a strange, unlikely state. It is alarmed, in turn, when the idea of cheap provisions is entertained. The scale, with such incongruous, but preponderant weights, is dashed to the earth. (Applause.) The complaint (for theirs is not the rural contentment which poets sing) of those who possess the ground has commonly been, that without protection they cannot till it to a profit. If true that were to be deplored. Others would be ready and glad to try for themselves that experiment. But when the manufacturer cannot find a profit, does the legislature instantly interfere? The poor skilled labourer toils day and night, and cannot work to a profit; (hear, hear;) does the senate immediately raise it? Why this favouritism? What is the rule of these arbitrary distinctions? Let us not take for granted that this is any question of the tenant. That, notwithstanding, we will pass. Is it any question of the farming labourer? You, reverend gentlemen, come, many of you, from the corn-growing districts. Can you tell us of that happy people? Can you describe them feeding on the finest of the wheat, and rioting in fulness of bread? Can you report their cottage-home of comfort, their board of plenty, their love to patriarchal lords? (Laughter.) How works the law for them? Are they not, in many instances, abject as the serf? Until of late, was not the poor-rate often robbed to eke out the wages they were grudged? Out upon that hypocrisy which feigns a paradise where man, instead of kind treatment, is worn out by harsh exaction, and, instead of being encouraged to a noble independence, is teazed into servility soul-less as that of the flock and herd! (Cheers.) We may most certainly stand upon this position: that all kinds of labour suffer pretty equally the same; that the artizan does not pine to help the agricultural servant; that the pressure of the wrong is well-nigh common. And can aught in cruelty be conceived more unjust and reckless than to come between the labourer, whatever his province, and the remuneration of his labour? Labour is his only capital. Is that the pittance which a needy commonwealth should first impound? It is to muzzle the mouth of the ox that treadeth out the corn! (Cheers.) If this be the moot-point,—Are the poor thus pinched and curtailed by the operation of the corn regulation? To it let us now address ourselves. There is a plain fact which all must know: that the poor man, in proportion, consumes more corn than the rich. It is a necessary, and beyond it his means but very partially can reach. Animal food is a luxury which is greatly denied him. Other articles of gratification are peremptorily excluded from his diet. Whatever makes corn dear must, consequently, affect the eater of mere corn more than those who wanton on their superfluities. (Applause.) But ought he to be singled out, and his crust be taxed? What is the influence of these statutes? Examine the corn law of the year 1791. The quarter was the following year at 42s. 11d. The next year it rose to 48s. 11d. Mark its increase until 1796, when it stood at 77s.! In 1800 it was 113s. 7d.! In 1801 it had mounted to 118s. 3d.! This might have contented the growers. (Laughter.) Peace then came, and in 1802 it descended to 67s. 5d. The next year it fell to 56s. 6d. The grower was alarmed, and there was a new corn bill! (Renewed laughter.) From that time until 1814, though it had stood as high as 125s., it never sunk under 73s. Peace returned; and, in 1815, the price was 66s. 3d. The grower was ruined: another corn bill must be obtained! (Much laughter and cheering.) It has kept up what must have otherwise been greatly cheapened. Peace has scarcely been since interrupted Abundant harvests have blest us. Trade, for a time, modified the hardship. But has the restriction ever favoured the consumer? The corn law of 1828, with its slide, has it been once even-handed between the grower and the buyer? But while the importation is prohibited, the grower can, at any time, without a fraction of duty, export all his stores! Can a doubt be felt, that all such legislation is intended to keep up prices, and that it has always succeeded in doing it? But it is contended that the poor can scarcely feel such an atom-impost. This we are not prepared to admit. Still were it so—and in this stage of the argument we can afford to allow that this is the lightest pressure of the law upon the working man,—what is its influence upon his supply, not of food, but of work? The manufacturer can only obtain returns for his goods in corn. This he may not receive. Trade stagnates. The factory is shut. The workman is thrown out of employment. And yet it is asked, what injury he suffers? His loaf costs more: and then the principle which has fixed that cost, cuts off the labour by which he could with the utmost effort purchase it. The indirect operation is more fatal by far than the direct influence of such a system. (Cheers.) There is a very natural temptation, during a state of agricultural alarm, to lessen the extent of our claims. To lull that alarm it is pretended that we do not anticipate any large advantage. This may be amiable, or it may be simulative: certes, it is illogical and ruinous to the argument. Is the result so trivial, so inappreciable? Is it then worth this grave and serious contest? Why the alarm if there be little to lose? Why the contest if there be little to gain? The alarm must be the standard and warrant of our expected benefit. (Cheers.) What are the grounds taken to bear out this extenuating hypothesis? The standard price of foreign wheat is reckoned at 35s. per quarter. For freight 10s. are included: 8s. are the recently proposed duty. For profit 3s. may be allowed. The whole would be 56s. charge. But for a ten years' average, wheat might have been bought at 57s. at home. Now we ask is this a fair estimate of the price of continental wheats? Dantzic corn is known to be the best, perhaps, in all the world. It fetches 3s. more than the finest British; but there is a great range between the different sorts of our native grown, this comprehending all Scotch and Irish. Is this calculation, fixed upon the price of the highest quality of foreign wheat, a just one? (Hear.) On a ten years' average, Hamburgh corn was 27s. Amsterdam 31s. I make the figures whole. These would resemble our common growths. But what would be the price in particular years? In 1826 Hamburgh was not 19s. In 1824 Amsterdam was not 21s. Put the gross and common price of wheats abroad, quite equal to what is produced at home, at 31s. Add the projected duty and make it 39s. (Cheers.) Now comes the fallacy of freight. This must be 10s.! Two voyages may, perhaps, require as much. Then one would only require 5s. But only one would be wanted. The outward, carrying goods, would pay itself. The homeward, with its exchange of corn, would bear no other charge. How is it now? The ship goes out empty when corn may be imported; all until it gets its cargo is expense and loss. Hence the rate of carrying! Make it a regular trade—a trade in which our merchant-princes can honourably embark—a trade of legitimate interchange—not of trick and chance, not involving the sudden withdrawal of capital from other channels, not causing a sudden drain of gold; and nothing will be more healthy than such a right arm of our national merchandise, and you may leave to its nautical enterprise the bringing over of those vast crops which Europe yields beyond its necessities. (Loud cheers.) But will it be endured that *this* shall be the *duty?* Eight shillings have been talked of, have been proposed. Who is the statesman that will reiterate it? Time was when the bargain might have been struck. The idea of duty, save for the shortest interval, is for ever exploded. Our petition is for the food of the people unburthened by condition or restraint. We demand the unstipulated removal of every provision law. (Cheers.) Corn free in every sense, degree, circumstance! If men would not accept the proffered bounty, there is no reason for opening the negociations and pressing it again. The sybil was refused her terms: they are advanced. King Log was rejected: he is succeeded by king Stork. (Cheers.) I leave to others to dwell upon remaining evils of this law. Let others tell of the prevention of barter, for we might clothe the world if we would accept payment in what we want to feed a starving people. Let others tell of the retaliation of Tariff, threatening to prohibit and spurn our exports. Let others tell of the convulsions of our monetary system, aggravated if not entirely caused by the efflux of our bullion to quarters which will only sell us on these terms their grain. Let others tell of the exchanges kept in fearful oscillation, holding nations in dismay. Enough for the plainest man to know, that the very theory of the corn law is, to *make bread scarce and therefore dear.* (Cheers.) Deeply is it to be deplored that a sophism has been tried upon the labouring poor, and with too full success. They have been taught that low priced food will depress their wages. The effect is, however, nearly passed away; how simple is the proposition, that wages must rise with the demand for labour. But cheapness in provisions will increase that demand for labour; the benefit is double; Manchester could testify to its prosperity in 1835; never was food, for years, so cheap, nor wages so ample. (Cheers.) Then how humiliating is it that corn should be so variable, that it which might constitute a safe standard and index of value, can furnish no fair criterion of profit to the honest trader. He leaves his country; at its current price he judges that his adventure will reimburse him. He returns; he cannot sell, his wheats lie up in bond, then their value is reduced; and the owner, it is likely, ends in insolvency. (Hear, hear.) And by false returns, by nominal transactions, the uncertainty is constantly augmented; the averages are jockeyed, and this great nation, with her diadem of power and zone of dependencies, is incessantly cheated by the finesse and false swearing of higglers and jugglers, whom justice must indeed be blind if she cannot see; and punishment must indeed be lame if she cannot overtake. (Laughter.) It is said by some, and not without deep scorn, how is it that you have come to the sudden discovery that corn restriction is so destructive? It will suffice to reply, that our patriotic senators protested against it from the first. The people, competent always to discern their own interests, broke forth into acts of outrage when it passed, and *proved*, however illegally, their horror of it. (Loud cheers.) Petitions, from all parties, inundated the houses of parliament, but only to be derided. It is not denied that the evil, which the sagacious always saw, was for a time hidden from the national eye, and was not numbered very distinctly among the national burdens. But all along it was at work; foreign rivalries were fomenting; we have reached the precipice; is it not instinctive to recoil? Warning was never wanting, had the country but listened; the omen was always discerned, but present prosperity deluded the nation; we need not recriminate; the danger is now at our gates; it is for us to determine whether to meet and vanquish it, or suffer it to ride over our heads. (Cheers.) Parley and compromise can but embolden the arrogance and assist the malignity of the foe. What has caused this unexampled revolution in our trade? What is its unutterable aggravation? The corn laws filled the cup of our misery, and it is the corn laws which now embitter it and make it overflow. And now, for our famishing population what hope have we of providing? Where are the funds? The poor assessments? It is paid by those who are among the very poor; the workhouse is maintained by thousands who are strangers to its comforts. (Hear, hear.) This impost will not bear another strain; charity may at last go beyond itself; and all the while, what is the demoralization of their weekly dole? Could you feed a people with these eleemosynary grants, do you not at the same time degrade their sentiments and vitiate their habits? Many a reverend speaker has informed us of principle so lofty, of magnanimity so proud, among the poor whom they have visited, that my heart misgives if I must report to you another testimony. But I have seen their spirits broken down; I have seen the industrious reconciled to mendicancy; I have seen the short-lived generation pass onward in despair. Deal I a censure? It is on ourselves. If we make a slave, we destroy the soul within him, and we are as responsible for debasing his mind as for shackling his limbs! (Loud cheers.) I know not, reverend brethren, but that the evil is gone too far, to be thoroughly retrieved. The opportunity is all but past; the world is fortifying itself in resentment of our monopolies; yet, if there came, in the change of measures, no physical relief, what would be the reviving of the poor man's mind! The attempt, he would see, was made to retrace our infatuated course. There would spring up in his bosom a resignation to some necessity; but not that of unrelenting injustice. He would yield, not to earthly misrule persisting in its blunders, but to that which human power could not then undo. He would learn to meditate on heaven's inscrutable wisdom, perhaps righteous displeasure. Though the project of the remedy came too late, what burdens would it lighten, and irritations would it heal! [Loud cheers.] Our business is to lift the population which has sunk, and bid them hope; we must cause our voice to be heard in high places; to open the sources of industry must be the earliest measure; they must learn a self-respect; the nation must also learn that population is wealth and strength. Government, in its sympathies, but likewise in its duty, must stand forth, an expedient not of *interests and classes*, but the vast contrivance for the good of all. [Hear, hear, and loud cheers.] The earth, which is full of divine riches, will develope them to the competitions of those that cultivate it. In the inter-community and subserviency of nations, peace will find its guarantee; agriculture shall bind its luxuriant sheaves and commerce shall waft its noblest spoils. But, if oppression will not alter, nor injustice pause, the sighing of the needy shall prevail, the poor who hath no helper shall be heard of God who judgeth righteously; and in their neglect, destitution, and utter extinction, we may read our guilt and suffer our punishment. *We*, at least, have striven to turn the public thought and commiseration towards our naked, hungry brethren, and if we have failed, we may have failed in our weakness; could sincerity have redeemed us from our weakness, in our sincerity we should have been strong, and virtuous. [Loud Applause.]

"Princes and lords may flourish or may fade,
A breath can make them, as a breath hath made;
But a bold peasantry, the nation's pride,
When once destroy'd, can never be supplied."

The Rev. J. W. Massie, in the absence of the Rev. P. Brewster, of Paisley, seconded the resolution, which was put to the meeting, and passed.

The Rev. J. J. Freeman,* of Walthamstow, then, in a speech of great point and power, moved the following resolution:—

"That this conference, deeply interested in the maintenance of the various benevolent and religious institutions which exist in our country, and which depend for their support on the general prosperity of the community, is penetrated with the conviction that the resources of many of those institutions have been already materially affected by the prevailing distress; and fears that, unless that distress be speedily and effectually alleviated, Christians, instead of enlarging, must contract their sphere of benevolence."

The Rev. Mr. Carlisle, of London, as the sincere enemy of all monopolies, was determined to devote all his powers of body and mind to the abolition of all monopolies.

The Rev. J. W. Massie announced that application had been made to the committee for permission that a few of the poor heart-stricken objects of compassion might appear, and tell their own tale. No one, he was sure, would say "No" to them. (Hear,) He proposed the thanks of the meeting to the Rev. Wm. Chaplin, for his conduct in the chair during the day. It passed unanimously.

The Chairman thanked the meeting for their kindness and conduct throughout the day.

The meeting then adjourned at half-past nine o'clock.

* The admirable speech of Mr. Freeman will be found at the conclusion, having been received too late for insertion here.

THURSDAY, AUGUST 19.

From nine to half-past nine o'clock, the hall became gradually filled with ministers; and, in the part allotted to the public, with ladies and gentlemen.

At twenty minutes before ten o'clock, the Rev. F. A. Cox, D.D. LL.D., of Hackney, the president of the day, took the chair; and, shortly afterwards, the proceedings commenced.

The Chairman, in opening the proceedings, said,—Gentlemen and Christian ministers, I am fully sensible of the distinguished honour of being called upon to preside, on this occasion, over one of the most remarkable, one of the most important, meetings that ever was convened in our country—*remarkable* for the number of ministers of religion assembled from every quarter—for the sublime spirit of philanthropy which is displayed—and for the sobriety, harmony, and dignity of its proceedings; (cheers;) *important* for the moral influence it must exert through its individual members, who will carry the sparks of holy fire from this central conference to their respective localities; important for the moral force with which it will push forward the settlement—the inevitable, (cheers,) the satisfactory, and the speedy settlement, of one of the greatest questions before the country; (cheers;) the practical exemplification it will afford in the eye of mankind of the might of principle—(cheers;) in its self-denying, self-sacrificing, and potent effects, when wrought into benevolent combination; and for the influence which it cannot fail of exerting over the present generation and far distant times. (Loud applause.) Gentlemen, if such an assembly as the present were to fail of producing great and good effects, then I should begin to despair of my country. (Hear, hear.) I should begin to think that despotism, in that case, was likely to restore the darkness of the middle ages—that society would be on the eve of retrocession, and the bright era of the nineteenth century likely to suffer an eclipse. (Cheers.) Depend upon it, that the period of a nation's decline must be at hand, whenever the popular voice cannot be heard in high places—whenever the public sentiment and private feeling are disregarded—whenever legislation *dares to* be indifferent to the woes and the wailings of a suffering people. (Applause.) It is fearfully ominous when the lightnings of a nation's indignation begin to glare, and when the thunders of a troubled, tormented, united, but afflicted people begin to roll. (Cheers.) We have been asked the reason why we are here. Why, gentlemen, we are here at the call of groaning humanity; at the voice of afflicted patriotism; at the cry of outraged religion. (Cheers.) The monster monopoly stalks through the length and breadth of the country—bleeding millions are trodden down by the giant foot, and are perishing by the iron gripe that digs into the very soul. (Hear, hear.) Abject misery, starvation, and vice, in every hideous form and multiform variety, compose the train; and shouts of agony and shrieks of woe attend the direful march over our desolated land. Gentlemen, why should we be here? I ask why should we *not* be here? (Loud cheers.) Is any principle sacrificed? (No.) Is any duty neglected? (No.) Are the mere interests of a party, political or theological, subserved? (No.) Our *principle* is to love God supremely, and our neighbours as ourselves. Our *duty* is to do good, by whatever mode we can accomplish it. Our *party* is our country. (Applause.) "I see," as Lord Fitzwilliam said, "my countrymen in distress, and my country in danger." (Cheers.) We are all sufficiently convinced of this, that misery exists. The cause of that misery it is important for us to ascertain, in order that we may, if possible, remove it. The fact is, that Providence gives the people bread, and monopoly gives the people a stone. (Hear, hear.) It is easy enough to sit in the aristocratic chair, or move heedlessly along the avenues of splendour, and indulge in the carpeted magnificence of superior life, and amidst luxury to forget poverty; but starvation prevails—there is the horror—it meets us on every side. (Hear, hear, hear.) This is a question, therefore of the utmost importance to our country. The details we have already heard tend to show, not only the danger of the state, when men are driven to desperation by their sufferings, but the true character of the present meeting. And what is it? It is a *shield*—a shield against the encroachment of aristocratic power on the one hand, and the faction and fury of mob-democracy on the other. [Cheers.] We say on the one hand, from this great meeting, that the aristocracy *shall not* oppress the people. [Prolonged cheering.] We say, on the other, that the people *shall not* rebel against the constituted authorities, nor act inconsistently, if we can prevent it, with the great principles of the constitution. (Renewed cheering.) We say to the aristocracy, "You must *come down* to a right state of feeling and sympathy with the condition of the poor of the land;" and we say to the poor, "You must *come up* to right sentiments—to just views—to a feeling of submission to the inscrutable dispensations of Providence—and cherish a serious, solemn, and pious concern to do your duty to God and to man." (Cheers.) At present, gentlemen, a great portion of the higher classes have stood aloof in their eminences—a great gulf has been between them and the people; but it *is* our object to link them together—to bind them by common sympathies. The prejudices and the passions of both have kept them asunder for ages. Wrong views, petty self-interests, and mutual aggression, have separated them. (Hear.) The laws that have been enacted have been inapplicable to the actual condition of society, hostile to the interests, and aggravating to the feelings of the people. (Here a loud and prolonged cheer announced the entrance of Earl Ducie.) Gentlemen, I hesitate not to say—and I say it with peculiar pleasure, now in the presence of one of our illustrious aristocracy, (cheers,) that it is most obvious a moral revolution is at hand. (Hear, hear.) A moral revolution has begun—we must direct it. (Cheers.) We are the intercessors for the people. We seek their confidence; and we will plead their cause. (Cheers.) Gentlemen, when hostile arms were opposed to our countrymen in former days, one of our most illustrious admirals—indeed, the most distinguished that ever belonged to this country—on the eve of battle said, "England expects every man to do his duty." I say, gentlemen, that England, and the poor of England especially, expect every minister to do his duty. (Cheers.) We must not blind our eyes to the fact, that we have a great contest to maintain; but, trusting in the power of the Most High, and the grace he shall dispense to us in answer to our fervent prayers and supplications, I look to the period as not far distant when we shall return from the contest crowned with victory, and having inscribed on our banners, "Monopoly has fallen," [applause,] "Britain has risen." [Cheers.] Britain's queen, not coming from afar, like the queen of Sheba, to contemplate the magnificence of Solomon, shall pass through the length and breadth of her own blessed isle, to contemplate a glory far greater than that of Solomon —the land filled with plenty—the cottages with joy, [cheers,] gratitude in every poor man's heart, [cheers,] and a *cheap loaf* in every poor man's hand. [Loud, continued cheers.] Gentlemen, permit me to state, that Mr. M'Kerrow will now introduce a certain deputation, who are about to present themselves to this meeting; after which, individuals wishing to address the meeting will be called on to hand up their names to the chairman. They will address the meeting in the order in which their names are handed in, and give such statements of facts as they may have collected in the different districts from which they have come. We shall hear them until those measures are ready for introduction, which the committee are preparing to bring under our notice. Memorials, petitions, and addresses are in the adjoining room; and gentlemen who are about to leave town before the conference concludes its sittings, are requested to sign them before their departure. I hope all will be over to-morrow, at the farthest. Those gentlemen who may leave town this evening are requested not to transfer to any one their cards of admission It is hoped that the memorials, &c. alluded to will be read to the meeting this day. [Applause.]

Th Rev. J. W. Massie thought it but justice to those ministers whose names were already given in, to take precedence of those whose names were not given in.

The Rev. W. M'Kerrow introduced a deputation of workmen from the establishment of Messrs. Sharp, Roberts, and Co., with an address from the workmen;—the deputation consisting of Mr. Fothergill and three workmen, who were invited upon the platform, and cordially welcomed with applause.

Mr. FOTHERGILL said, he was one of the managers in the establishment, and had been requested to present an address. The workmen did not wish in any way to dictate to the conference in what way to effect the object they all had so much at heart; but they wished to express their deep sympathy with their fellow-workmen around them, whom they were often called upon to assist. (Great applause.) [He then read the address, which was signed by himself, as chairman of the committee, and 614 other individuals.] As many ministers of religion were assembled who were not acquainted with the nature of the establishment in which these workmen were employed, he might state, that their employers were extensive manufacturers of locomotive engines, both for this country and several places on the continent, employing several hundred hands. The deputation were much obliged to the chairman, and to the rev. gentlemen, for their own reception, and that of their address. The workmen, any more perhaps than the ministers, did not mean to say there were no other bad laws than the corn laws. [Hear.] He thought the address breathed a spirit of Christian charity. [Hear.] Prophets had told us, that righteousness—"right-wise-ness,"—should cover the earth as the waters cover the deep. [Applause.] They hailed with pleasure the meeting of ministers, and wished them "God speed," and hoped their efforts would be crowned with success. [Great applause.]

"*To the National Conference of Ministers of Religion, assembled to discuss the taxes on food.*

"We, the undersigned workmen in the employ of Messrs. Sharp, Roberts, and Co., engineers and machine makers, are desirous of respectfully addressing to the conference our full concurrence in those views of the injustice of all laws which restrict the supply of food, which have led to their meeting; and our admiration of the courage and devotion to sound principles which have brought so many hundreds of ministers from their usual retirement to meet in conference upon this vitally important and all-interesting subject.

"We have long been deeply convinced that the food monopoly is unjust, unchristian, and oppressive. Our situation as workmen in a very large manufacturing establishment has given us many opportunities of witnessing its destructive influence on trade, although, owing to the peculiar position and extensive connection of our respected employers, we have not hitherto (comparatively) suffered from its direful effects to the extent that others have; yet our familiarity with the homes and circumstances of the working population in this town enables us to affirm that the amount of misery and want which the corn laws have produced among us is heart-rending and appalling.

"We rejoice in all efforts to put an end to a system which we hold to be so wicked and demoralizing, and hail with peculiar satisfaction the present combined exertions of men whose frequent intercourse with the poor leads them to feel for their distress, and whose just influence in society adds weight of their sentiments.

"We believe that ministers of religion cannot devote their talents and valuable time to more blessed or more important objects than in advocating the rights and exposing the wrongs of their suffering fellow men. We welcome your assembly with heartfelt pleasure, we sympathise with you in feeling, and we trust that your efforts will be sustained in hopeful perseverance that more and more of your profession will soon feel constrained to join with you, and that a glorious success will ere long be your gratifying reward.

"The prayers of many who are ready to perish are with you; and their blessings are upon your endeavours to aid in procuring for them that share of the means of subsistence which was designed and is provided by the Creator of all things.

"We are, with sincere respect, &c. &c.,

(Signed) "BENJAMIN FOTHERGILL, Chairman.
"JOHN ALLEY,
"R. TENNANT, } Secretaries."

[Signed by 614 workmen.]

The Rev. Mr. CARLISLE, of London, moved,

"That the gratifying address just read be gratefully received by this conference, and that it be inserted in the minutes of their proceedings."

The Rev. J. CLUNIE, LL.D., Manchester, seconded the motion, which passed unanimously, and then the deputation retired amidst great applause.

The Rev. WM. M'KERROW said he had now to introduce a deputation from a class of people whose privations and sufferings were beyond description.—The deputation, consisting of Edward Curran and F. Moore, were upon the platform.

The Rev. J. W. MASSIE suggested, that the address of the hand-loom weavers should be received in solemn silence as expressing the depth and sorrowing character of our heartfelt sympathies in their mournful condition.

The CHAIRMAN then said to the deputation, that their address might now be read to the meeting; and he hoped, that the time would come, when, instead of receiving them with tearful sympathies, it would be with grateful and rejoicing satisfaction.

"*To the Rev. Gentlemen assembled in the Town-Hall of Manchester this 18th day of August*, 1841.

"Rev. Sirs—It is with feelings of regret that we are compelled to call upon you, gentlemen, ith a view to obtain your sympathy, and prevent our suffering and starving families from a premature grave.

"Rev. Sirs—For years past we have been applying to Parliament for a redress of our grievances, and to make such alterations in the corn and provision laws as in our humble opinion would not only improve our condition but would benefit the country at large; for, though poor and wretched in our present deplorable situation, we should be sorry to ask for any favour from the government of our common country that was likely to be injurious to any portion of her Majesty's subjects. But, after all, and upon a principle of common justice, we do think we should receive, in return for our labour, *food*, *shelter*, and *clothing*.

"Rev. Sirs—Considering you, gentlemen, as the faithful servants of your Divine Master, and having heard of the god-like purpose for which you are assembled, we trust you will pardon us for thus calling upon you, in the name of God and justice, to rouse public sympathy in our favour, and prevent us from being reduced to the necessity of concluding that we have no hope to lean upon but the *grave*, that bed in which the greatest of our land will, after all, be but equal to ourselves in the sight of a just God, in whose presence there is a fulness of joy.

"Rev. Sirs—In 1831 we sent our petitions to Parliament praying for the repeal of the tax on bread. Henry Hunt, the honest friend of his country, presented the said petitions for us; in his place in Parliament he told the members then present the ruin that would overtake us as a nation if a different line of policy was not pursued in connection with laws that affected our commerce. But, alas, gentlemen, up to this hour the same wicked and unchristian laws are in existence, and, unfortunately for us, we feel their bitter effects when we hear our children crying for bread, and have none to give them.

"The following is a copy of the prayer of the above-mentioned petitions presented from us in 1831:

"'Your petitioners pray your honourable house not to counteract the will of Omnipotence, and goad a generous people to madness, by the continuance of this system of starvation; but, as Christianity is part and parcel of the law of the land, to obey its heavenly precepts—to do unto others as you would they should do unto you—to quash every enactment that is contrary to its mild, equitable, and conciliating spirit; and, in fine, to reinstate your honourable house in the favour of the British nation, by repealing at once the obnoxious and infamous corn law.'

"In conclusion, reverend sirs, we hope you will see, from the spirit of the prayer of the petition just quoted, that we were not impelled by improper motives in our plain and humble way of making our case known; and, at the same time, we hope that this our appeal to you, gentlemen, will not be made in vain, trusting that, with your assistance and that of your Divine Master, the great God of heaven, who gave us this earth for our inheritance, that we will yet be enabled to obtain the repeal of all laws that prevent the plentiful supply of food to the producers of the nation's wealth, viz, the working classes; and, most earnestly praying that your meritorious labours may be crowned with success, we subscribe ourselves, on behalf of the hand-loom weavers of Manchester, most respectfully yours, &c., &c., the deputation.

"EDWARD CURRAN, 6, Heyrod-street,
Great Ancoats street.
"JOHN JOS. FINNIGAN, Meadow-street,
St. George's-road.
"RICHARD MOORE."

EDWARD CURRAN, having read the address, said he hoped that no effort would be wanting in the poor hand-loom weavers, to aid the ministers in their efforts.

The Rev. W. M'KERROW said, he felt, if possible, more sympathy with this address than in the preceding one. He thought it right that there should be no distinction; and he therefore moved,

"That the address be received, and entered on the minutes of proceeding."

The motion was seconded, and unanimously passed.

EDWARD CURRAN said, the number of hand loom weavers, on whose behalf this address was presented, was about 7,000. [Hear, hear.]

The Rev. THOMAS ADKINS asked permission to put a few queries to the deputation—How many do you represent?—CURRAN: 7,000.

What is their condition?—About one-third out of employment, and destitute of means of subsistence, either from public sympathy or otherwise.

How are they kept alive?—That might be better imagined than described.

Can you tell what is the state of the health of this one-third, between 2,000 and 3,000 individuals, with their wives, amounting to 4,000 or 5,000 individuals?—Very bad indeed.

What diseases prevail amongst them? Fevers.

MR. SPENCER: Are all these destitute persons receiving any thing from the poor rates?—Some portion of them.

Will you tell us something that can be described of their destitution?—CURRAN: I can only say, that thousands of those unfortunate people are living in cellars and garrets, without scarcely a blanket to cover them, or a vessel, if they had food, to boil it in. This condition has been brought about by its getting worse and worse year after year. Where they have lived, being unable to pay their just debts, they have been sold up, and so driven to the state I have described.

Mr. SPENCER: What is the kind of food which these persons generally eat?—Potatoes, if they can get them, and gruel.

Are you aware that they go a long time without food?—I am aware that there are persons in this town who did not taste yesterday, and don't know where to get food to-day. I met some men this morning, in St. George's Road, and they begged me to impress upon your minds the necessity of doing something temporarily to save them from the grave.

Will you tell us whether, among these thousands, it is the common opinion that the corn laws are the cause of their distress?—It is generally the opinion among the hand-loom weavers, that the corn law is one of the greatest evils this country has to complain of.

Is it your opinion that, if the corn laws were repealed, these men would be of an honest, sober, religious turn of mind?—I have no doubt of it; and I think there is sufficient evidence before the country, that they are the most peaceable and well disposed men now, amidst all their privations and sufferings; and it is not to be told, that the hand-loom weavers of Manchester ever disturbed the public peace. (Applause.)

Mr. SPENCER: I will say one thing to this worthy man. I hope, whatever be the return of this conference to that address, that he will inform his brethren, that there are men here, who would rather have the heart's affection of that class of men, than the smiles of the rich and great. (Great applause.)

The Rev. T. ADKINS, of Southampton: I wish to learn whether those out of employment and in destitution are in the habit of attending places of worship; whether they are in a condition, from clothing, &c., to avail themselves of public worship?—CURRAN: I believe there are hundreds and thousands that would most anxiously attend places of worship, but they have not a shirt on their backs, nor a coat or shoe to wear. (Hear.)

The Rev. Mr. YOUNG, of Andover: How long has this state of destitution existed?—CURRAN: since 1815, when this corn law was passed the condition of the hand-loom weaver has been getting worse and worse, till it has become such as I have described.

Mr. YOUNG: Do you remember, in a time when bread was cheap, say in 1835, what was the condition of this class?—CURRAN: in 1835 there was certainly a dawn of hope let upon us; and we expected, from the sudden change that then took place, that our condition was likely to be improved, because our food got cheaper, and our wages increased. (Hear.) Every article of consumption was cheaper then, than for years before or since. I myself and my brother workmen received better wages that year than in the last 15 years.

The CHAIRMAN: How many of the employed are fully occupied?—CURRAN: Not more than one-third at the outside are in that condition and one-third partially employed.

What are the weekly earnings of the average of those who are partially employed?—CURRAN: I can be borne out by the most respectable manufacturers in Manchester, that they will not average more than 1s. a day when fully employed.

How many hours a day?—Fourteen hours a day.

What is the average wages procured by each family?—To that question I cannot distinctly answer, because of late years many families have been endeavouring to send their children to factories, and in consequence of the diminution of factory labour at present, their wages are materially deteriorated; and those families depending wholly on hand-loom weaving are receiving no more on an average, taking them to have three or four looms each family, than 12s. at the outside, for five or six individuals.

Is it your opinion that the introduction of machinery, or the operation of the corn laws, has done the most harm?—That the introduction of machinery, as at present regulated, has been an injury, is without doubt, indirectly it has; but if the corn laws had been repealed, it never could have affected us.

What is the difference between the rate of wages now and five years ago, '35 or 36?—At least they have been from 20 to 30 per cent. reduced. There is a variety of work, some that machinery can never reach, consequently there are some branches that have not undergone the reduction that others have; so that, while some have been reduced 30 per cent. others have not suffered more than 20 per cent.

The Rev. James Dearin, of Stand, said he lived in the midst of power-loom weavers, and pledged his character that there was no exaggeration in these statements. He had gone from house to house in his own neighbourhood. Hundreds and thousands were only earning 1s. a head on the average daily; living on water-gruel, with nothing to eat.

Mr. John Brown, of Wareham: What influence have the circumstances on the education of your children?—Curran: In the first place, it is out of our power to educate them ourselves; in the next place, it is out of our power to clothe them decently to send them to school, consequently they are destitute of education. [Hear.]

The Chairman: Is the condition of fancy weavers better than your own?—Curran: Such is the expense of *gaiting* the fancy looms, which falls to the weaver to do, that though he may make a decenter appearance, and at some seasons recover himself a little, yet in the winter he has scarcely any thing to do. [Hear.]

Can you tell the difference between wages now, and at the time when the corn laws were introduced?—Curran: I think a friend of mine here can answer that better than myself.—Moore: In 1795, the weaver of the 100 reed was paid 1s. 8d. per yard; in 1800, 1s. 4d.; 1812, 10d.; 1815, 9d.; in 1816, 4½d.—[hear]—that was the year the corn law was put on.

What is it now?—Why, 2½d. (Hear.) I was out of employment three months this summer, and I have just got a warp of the same sort, 50 yards for 10s; and it will take me a fortnight to do it. I cannot do it under. Threepence goes out of every shilling, which makes 3s. 9d. per week; and I have not got on an average for the last four years more than 3s. 6d. a week, and still I have lived. But there are people far worse than me. If I had a wife and three or four little children how could I have kept them? There are hundreds in this situation with families; how they live I cannot tell; they do not live, (Hear,) they barely exist on water gruel and dry potatoes.

Rev. Mr. Watson: Does it take as much time now to weave a piece as at the period referred to?

The Chairman: Say in 1815.—Moore: I find twist worse now than in 1815, consequently it is more difficult to weave now than then. I have been a weaver fifty-three years. I began to weave cotton when that was in its infancy, and I can trace the prices for fifty three years down to the present time; and I find that the prices of provisions have nothing to do with each other, for in 1815, when flour was 6d. a lb., wages dropped lower.

Some questions were asked which the general feeling of the meeting deemed unnecessary to be put or answered.

The Chairman said the questions and answers already given went to the very heart of the question and they were now taking a course to obtain that information, more extensive and minute than they could obtain till now, from the individuals themselves, (and not merely from the printed page,) which it was important they should receive, first, because coming directly from themselves; and next, because meeting them here, these individuals would be convinced that our sympathies operated in the midst of their destitution, and our desires were for their improvement in their situation in life, as well as in their moral character, which, he feared, was deeply affected by the operation of the corn laws.

CURRAN said a gentleman had asked if the deputation were themselves out of work. He was employed by one of the most respectable firms in Manchester, [Mr. Wm. Walker, of Cannon st.,] and was in full employment, but his less fortunate fellow-workmen had requested him to represent them, and he could not refuse their request.

The Rev. T. ADKINS thought the deputation had demonstrated that they had not only hearts to feel, but minds to think. ("Hear," and applause.) He looked on them as brethren; he felt honoured by the fraternity; and these questions had been put, not to lift the rags that conceal the miseries behind, but that we (the ministers) might communicate to the sympathies of our loved country the astounding facts, that, while many were living in all the luxury that wealth could purchase, there were those at their very doors sunk to a state of wretchedness that must melt a heart of stone. He submitted that, with thanks to the deputation for their intelligence, and the humble and unpretending, but explicit, replies which they had given, they might be allowed to depart.

The deputation then withdrew amidst encouraging plaudits from the assembly.

The Rev. J. W. MASSIE said he had twenty-four names down of gentlemen who wished to speak, and it would be absolutely necessary that those who did speak should not occupy more than ten minutes, unless they were monopolists. (Cries of "Five.")

The Rev. W. FORD, of the Methodist New Connexion, then addressed the meeting. He said he knew there were a great number of the community to which he belonged thought they should not go forth as the friends of monopoly, but as responding to every sentiment which had been expressed as to the distress which prevailed, and as to the injustice of the corn laws. His heart's desire and fervent prayer—and he was sure they would all join him—was that these laws, accursed as they had been properly called, should be blotted out from the statute book. He rejoiced that circumstances had called them together in this way, he represented a very numerous constituency who were most anxiously desirous that these laws should be abolished.

The Rev. G. N. WATSON, of Belfast, said he believed, and he was sorry for it, he was the only protestant minister present who represented Ireland. Before he came here he called on a manufacturer who told him that instead of employing, as they did six months ago, 1600 persons, they only now employed about 500. He should go back from this conference prepared to give every information calculated to promote the object they had in view.

The Rev. Dr. REDFORD, of Worcester, was then called upon, and, alluding to the interesting scene which had just taken place, he said the evidence which had just been elicited would go forth to the public and tell unspeakably more than all the speeches that had or could be made on the subject. He went on to describe the state of trade at Worcester, where, he said, in the staple trade not more than half of the hands were employed, as comparing the present time with a few years past. Some gentlemen might wish to know what amount of population were employed in the leather glove trade throughout the country. He had no certain means of knowing, and could not give the estimate with accuracy; but, to make a rough guess, he should suppose that in Worcestershire, Herefordshire, and other places, there might be somewhere about 100,000; he referred to Woodstock and Yeovil, as well as Worcester and parts of Devonshire. The earnings of these workmen also had been found to decrease with the rise of provisions, the decrease in wages being from 10 to 15 per cent.—[The more minute and elaborate details prepared by Dr. Redford, as well as other ministers, will be digested and given as the Appendix.]

The Rev. J. Blair, of Dunfermline, said, that his being from a town where the manufacture was so different from any that had been brought before the meeting was the chief reason for his appearance here. He had the honour to reside in an ancient town, which had been famous as the residence and the burial place of kings. The staple manufacture was Damask or table linen, in which trade in 1840 there were 3,600 looms engaged. Their number had been doubled in the preceding 22 years. They now experienced great dulness and oppression. He was authorised to state that the looms were, on an average, from one-fourth to one-third of the working time idle. A table, framed from documents taken from the books of several manufacturers, and admitted by them as correct, states the average wages of journeymen, in 1835 or 1836, to be 7s. 6d. per week. Now if the medium betwixt one-fourth and one-third be deducted from 7s. 6d. you will have 5s. 3½d. only remaining as the present average weekly income of a journeyman operative, in the table-linen trade of Dunfermline; a pittance, gentlemen, far from being adequate to the keeping of a single man in any state of self-respect; and what must it be when a family is in the case, but a kind of unkilling starvation? Our population is a most intelligent one; but this cannot be long the case in this state of things, when, although cheap, or even gratis, education is provided, parents cannot clothe their children so as to allow them to attend to enjoy it. I am a friend, Mr. Chairman, to the five minutes' allowance to speakers, and only wish that it, or something like it, had been adopted sooner. Of all men, we, who are met to put down monopoly, should not be monopolists ourselves, of that most precious earthly blessing, *time*. One word and I conclude. Beloved brethren, there is one passage of the sacred word which I have not heard adduced on this occasion, but which has been much impressed on my mind in relation to the subject before us, and that impression has been rendered infinitely greater, sir, by the heart-rending statements we have just heard. [Alluding to the deputation of the hand-loom weavers.] The passage I refer to is, "If thou forbear to deliver them that are drawn unto death, and those that are ready to be slain; if thou sayest, behold we knew it not, doth not he that pondereth the heart consider it; and he that keepeth thy soul doth not he know it: and shall not he render to every man according to his works?"

The Rev. Wm. Macdougal, of Kilmarnock, said, there was scarcely any employment in that town, and 600 hand-loom weavers were out of work. Wages had decreased 25 per cent within the last 14 years, and the condition of the working classes was becoming worse. Disease was prevalent, and there was never known so much fever; and, when fever entered a family, there was such a want of the necessaries of life, that it was generally fatal.

The Rev. S. S. Wilson, F.S.A., of Shepton Mallet, spoke much as follows: Sir, almost immediately after my return from Greece and Malta, my nerves received a shock, from which I have never entirely recovered, even to this day; so that I might almost say, with the venerable William Jay, "I was not born under the platform dispensation." It hence results, sir, that though in the pulpit I am a child at home, yet, as often as I am placed in a novel position, I am the victim of a momentary trepidation. Why these personal allusions, when only five minutes are allowed to each speaker? Simply, sir, to gain time; I wished to get *calm*, and now that the calm is come, I will venture to float my little argosy. Small, indeed, is the cargo: yet, if all the captains of the thousands of Israel who this day sail into the port of conference, will disembark even an equal amount of fact and argument, we shall produce an immense moral effect upon the nation. Sir, I appear here as the representative of the independent church and congregation of Shepton Mallet. I am also requested to represent a church of primitive methodists, who are most cordial foes to the unrighteous laws of starvation. So you see, sir, that *all* methodists do not desert the interests of the poor, and I am much in error, sir, if a storm be not gathering around the Wesleyan bark, from which all the *bunting* on board must fail to save them. Sir, we appear in this arena as the firm friends of international *peace*. Not long ago, a lucid spark was struck out of the elements of strife, lying between Washington and London. The demon of war saw the flash, raised his head, and prepared to unchain the furies. Just then smiling Commerce passed by, a *machine* in one hand and *corn* in the other. She frowned, she reasoned, when the demon laid down his head in the dust, and the furies fell back on their lairs. Sir, are my five minutes gone? for though I detest the five *mile* act, I revere the five *minute* act.

CHAIRMAN: Your time is out, sir.

The Rev. JOHN YOUNG, of Andover, said, Mr. Chairman, we have been assailed for taking up this question, upon the ground that ministers have nothing to do with politics; I am of opinion that, as fathers and husbands, as citizens and patriots, we are called upon to labour for the happiness of all around us; and that for the discharge of these duties, we are under a solemn responsibility to God and our country. The corn laws interfere with the dearest rights of humanity; there is no possession so peculiarly a man's own, as his labour; the fruit of men's labour is the means of their existence, and when law interferes with that, it touches the very *life* of the community. The manufacturer can call useful fabrics into existence, for which other nations would give him food, but the corn laws compel him to starve, rather than receive that food at their hands; upon the heads then of the upholders of these laws, will lie the blood of these thousands, who may die from poverty and starvation, during the coming winter.. These laws also interfere with the beautiful arrangements of Divine Providence, in scattering blessings variously up and down, throughout the earth; by the interchange of these blessings the scattered tribes of men are brought into contact, and nation is interlinked with nation for the civilization of the whole; but we have been fencing ourselves about by protective duties; building a fortress in which national selfishness and injustice might intrench itself, and refusing to take full advantage of God's goodness in throwing the highway of the ocean around our islands. I am an Irishman, and I cannot sit down without noticing what effect a repeal of these laws would have on that country. The curse of Ireland is an overwhelming agricultural population, who cannot find employment for one half of their time; yet their country is surrounded with ports and harbours, situate in the very pathway of trade and commerce; pierced by noble rivers, and possessing glorious capabilities of manufacturing industry. The increase of manufacture is what Ireland wants; this would give employment to her starving peasantry, and by drawing off the surplus hands from agriculture, the people would be rescued from the tyrannical grasp of their *cruel landlords*, and placed in a situation of noble minded independence.

The CHAIRMAN requested that no speaker would indulge in severe reflections on other bodies.

The Rev. THOS. MORGAN, of Birmingham, said, he was there because he was sent by his people. They were in great distress, and he could go on making statements in perfect harmony with those who had preceded him, and he trusted they would all go away determined to act with fresh vigour to get the repeal of those laws.

The Rev. J. E. GOOD, of Gosport, said, he had come not alone to exercise his own sympathies with the suffering myriads, but also to convey assurances of sympathy from some who were rich and benevolent. Admiral Bouverie and Sir George Staunton had wished him to express their admiration of this ministerial conference. But now he should confine himself to answering the questions in the circular. The agricultural labourers in his district had from 9s. to 11s. wages. The working men consisted principally of watermen and fishermen, who suffered severely from the high prices of food. The poor-rates had increased as much as 20 per cent, and the condition of the small tradesmen was continually getting worse.

The Rev. J. BARFETT, of Salisbury, said, it was impossible for any one to listen to the speech of Mr. Giles last evening, and not to feel that the great cause of the national distress was the corn laws. It was impossible to listen to the address of Mr. Curtis, from America, without feeling that if we had not a single grain of corn grown here, we could be fed, if we had anything approaching to reciprocity. He resided in the midst of an agricultural community, which was in a state of retrogression, and in the city of Salisbury, where, five years ago, scarcely a house was to be got, but now there were 150 uninhabited. The trade of the city is fast declining,—provisions of every description dear, wages low, employment scarce, and the poor rates increasing. All this, in the very centre of one of the largest agricultural districts in England.

The Rev. WM. FERGUSON, of Bicester, said the town he came from had a population of about 9,000 souls. It was one of the most fertile parts of the country, yet the poor were in the most wretched condition. 7s. 6d. was the maximum weekly wages of the labouring classes; the second class earned 5s.; and the third, only 2s. 6d. The maximum wages of skilled artizans was about 13s. a week. The wages of the agricultural labourers were as immutably settled as the laws of the Medes and Persians. The labourers lived in the most wretched manner, and their distress was entirely attributable to the operation of the corn laws.

The Rev. W. GILES, of Liverpool, said he expected to find in Manchester numerous illustrations of the hydraulic power, but did not expect to be subjected to the operation of a pneumatic press, occasioned by the fact, that while his bosom, in common with others, was almost bursting with the accumulation of the heart-paining truths that this great conference had brought to light- five short minutes alone were allowed to each speaker to give vent to his feelings concerning them. It was his unhappiness to have to state, in reference to Liverpool, that great distress existed there; numerous ships were lying idle in the docks, and scenes of wretchedness were daily to be witnessed in families torn from the endearments of home, and driven to foreign lands, to obtain a subsistence denied them in their own, mainly through the working of the man-destroying and God-dishonouring corn law. (Hear, hear.) It was told of a notorious felon and an equally notorious chimney-sweep, when riding together for execution in the same cart, that the former commanded his sooty companion to keep his distance. "Keep my distance!" rejoined the sweep, "I'd have you to know that I have quite as much right here as yourself!" (Laughter.) Now he (Mr. Giles) was of opinion, that, reversing the order of the illustration, the corn law monopoly had quite as much right to public execution as colonial slavery; and that, to say the least, they ought both to have perished on the same day. ("Hear, hear," and cheers.) He trusted that neither his brethren present nor himself would grow for a moment supine in that great and good work for which they had assembled—that they would constantly place before their eyes the old motto, "*Perseverentia omnia vincit*," and not suffer a single day to pass without giving a vigorous stroke at the root of the baneful upas tree, monopoly. (Cheers.)

[A discussion took place at this time, whether the memorials and addresses should be read before dinner; and it was finally agreed that the ministers should proceed with their statements, and that those documents should be brought forward at the evening meeting.]

The Rev. J. N. Goulty, of Brighton, said he had in his hand 30 communications from ministers in Sussex, the substance of which was in accordance with the sentiments previously expressed in the meeting. Twenty of those communications were from ministers, eight of them from landowners, and the other two from relieving officers, and all of them attributed the existing distress to the corn laws.

The Rev. A. Perry, M.D., of Reading, said he felt happy that evidence had lately reverted to the agricultural districts. His was an agricultural neighbourhood, and he was able (though with little previous preparation, or opportunity to investigate) to bear his testimony to the amount and severity of distress in that vicinity. Not far from Reading there was a parish in which formerly there were ten farms, all freehold property, their owners possessing capital to the amount of from five to forty thousand pounds. At the present time those farms were reduced to two, and neither of them in a state that could be considered prosperous. At Peppard, also, about five miles distant, there were, before the corn laws came into operation, twenty-five farms, which have been reduced to five; and one of the present occupants lately said, he was in such distress that he wished he had been transported fourteen years ago; he had worked hard from four o'clock in the morning till nine at night, and could not make it do. The same distress pervaded the town of Reading, especially among the smaller shopkeepers and middling class of tradesmen, as he (Dr. P.) was authorised to state, on the evidence of one of his friends, who had been both an overseer of the poor and a churchwarden in one of the parishes. He had been informed that for nearly twenty years such depression in trade had been unknown; that one who was accustomed to take as much as £10 on a market-day now seldom took more than 10s.; that a respectable tradesman had passed a whole week without receiving a single shilling; that another had solemnly declared that he had been losing £10 per week for a considerable time; and that a third instance afforded full evidence of the diminished rate of profits, for from his account it appeared that he formerly returned more by £250 per annum, with two hands, than he does at the present time, with seven hands, and a larger stock in trade. That the rate of wages does not rise and fall with the price of wheat is clear, by the wages now actually paid in that neighbourhood, viz., 8s. or 9s. per week to men, whether with or without families, 8d. per diem to women during harvest, and 4s. per week to boys. These have been the usual wages for a considerable time past, or, if any change has been experienced, it has been to lower the rate rather than heighten it, in times of scarcity and high prices. Many of the poor, during the last winter, were obliged to live on potatoes for days together; and many able-bodied labourers have been out of employ, because the farmers either cannot or will not employ them. He was going on to say that the poor rates had increased, and, in some parishes, doubled their former amount, but the time had elapsed, and the speaker somewhat abruptly concluded.

The Rev. H. G. RHODES, of Fullwood, spoke as follows:—Sir, I have taken from the *Sheffield Iris*, of March 21st, 1815, then published by James Montgomery, the following statements. When the corn laws, which have produced such a great amount of misery, were passing through the houses of Parliament, there were 1,848,000 petitioners against them; for them 210,000, and the majority of petitioners against them was 1,638,000. And in the *Iris* of March the 28th, there is the following resolution advertised, which was unanimously passed at a public meeting of the inhabitants of Sheffield, held in Paradise-square, on Monday, the 27th of March. Paul Bibbs in the chair. "It was unanimously resolved, that the object for which this meeting was called having been rendered abortive, by the rapidity with which the corn bill has received the royal assent, it behoves the people at large to take such steps as in their opinion may tend to remedy the evil complained of." And, sir, not only had the bill a rapid course through the houses of Parliament, but the supporters of it had to be guarded to and from the house; so that it became a law under the protection of bristling bayonets and prancing dragoons. I learned yesterday, that the Duke of Kent's name is affixed to the protest against the bill in the house of lords. It is then left to the meeting to say to the illustrious Individual on the throne, "Honour thy father." I learned lately from a knife grinder in Sheffield, that these laws were breaking up their union. These grinders support their own poor, so that the members of this club have never received any thing from the poor rates. But if the corn laws continue much longer, they will break up such associations as these. I purchased a bible from one of the pawnbrokers of Sheffield, and on the blank leaf in the front there is recorded the date of the marriage of the parties who did possess it, the date of the births of their children, and the date of the deaths of some of them. There are marks in it of its having been very diligently used. It must have been dire necessity that forced this bible into the pawn shop.

The Rev. H. ATLEY, of Frome, said, he felt proud in standing before the meeting to represent a body of 400 hand loom weavers, in the same condition as those who had already appeared before the conference by their deputation. He knew some of them who, for twenty-four hours, subsisted on one meal of potatoes mixed with their poisonous water; others who had not possessed a bed for six months, and when they did lie down at night their only coverlid was the clothes they wore by day. He knew instances of persons who had not entered a place of worship for years owing to the want of clothes. He dare not mention names for it would be attended with loss to the parties. The average wages did not exceed 8s. a week; and families of five, six, and, in some instances, ten had to be supported on that miserable pittance, deducting rent. On their behalf he claimed the sympathy and co-operation of the conference.

The Rev. W. P. DAVIES, of Ashburton, Devonshire, said, he had not only represented his own congregation, but three others in South Devon. The working people of Ashburton were half their time unemployed, and in a state of great destitution. He hoped the labours of the meeting would be beneficial.

The Rev. RICHARD SLATE, of Preston, said, the hand-loom weavers of Preston were as much distressed as those in Manchester; much of their misery was productive of immorality; for, in some instances, no less than eight individuals were lying together in the same bed, without any covering but their daily clothes. Brothers and sisters, fourteen and sixteen years of age, had to lie in the same bed. The poor-rates amounted in 1836, to £4,725; but in last year they had increased to £7,229. A proportionate increase had taken place in the number of persons admitted into the dispensary. In 1836, the number was 1911; but in 1840, it was 3,072. The increase of deaths, within the union, in 1840 as compared with the preceding year, amounted to 462, and in the last quarter the number of deaths had increased in a greater ratio. These facts so excited the attention of the registrar-general, in London, that he wrote to the clerk of the union to ascertain the cause. The rev. gentleman read a copy of the clerk's reply.

(*Copy of the letter read.*)

"Preston, July 28th, 1841.

"Sir,—I have to acknowledge the receipt of your letter of the 24th inst., requesting I would inform you to what causes I attribute the increased number of deaths registered in the Preston Union in the year 1840, as compared with these in the year ending June 30th, 1839.

"I beg to state in reply, that the cause in a very great measure, in my opinion, undoubtedly is owing to a want of sufficiency of food, of a good quality, by the labouring classes, which has tended to engender death; inasmuch as these classes especially have been exposed to high prices for provisions, and those of an inferior kind, whilst at the same time they had only decreasing wages to provide a sufficiency thereof, as well as clothing and fuel. The evils but too evidently spring from the operation of the *corn laws;* from which also result bad and unprofitable trade, labour reduced in price, and, moreover, employment made scarce,—a situation deeply to be deplored. These laws too are, in my opinion, not only undermining the industrial and commercial interests of the empire, but which must eventually lead to the destruction and extinction of its property, beyond all manner of doubt, unless something be effectually done to beneficially alter them. Should the ensuing crop prove below an average one, the poor man's condition must be hopeless.

"Joseph Thackeray,
"Clerk to the Preston Union."

The Rev. Thomas Mann, of Trowbridge, Wilts, said, he was the representative of a large number of the inhabitants of that place, which had about twelve thousand inhabitants engaged chiefly in the manufacture of kerseymere and broadcloth; and the whole town was supported by the profits of that business. The great outlet for the trade had been for America, though, to some extent, they had depended on home consumption. The corn laws had operated severely on this trade; the exports were now so small, and the returns so uncertain, scarcely any business was now done. Many individuals were unemployed, and scarcely any employed were adequately remunerated. Numbers were in a state of gradual starvation, and last winter many were actually starved to death. (Hear.) His congregation collected the money to send him here; and another minister was present from the same town. The British School was reduced from 500 to 200 children. Poor-rates (which were in 1835:—4s.) had risen to 8s.

The Rev. D. Ronald, of Saltcoats, Ayrshire, had been sent by the people of his locality without any previous concert on his part. So anxious were they that some one should appear for them, that, of their own accord, they convened a meeting and undertook the entire responsibility of his delegation; and it was no wonder they felt so interested, for those who sent him were a people depending mostly for employment on weaving. There were 900 looms for weaving cotton, and the average weekly wages was not more than 4s. This had its effects on their health, clothing, physical and moral condition, their attendance on divine worship, and in various ways. The distress, it was generally believed, was owing to the corn laws.

The Rev. THOS. SMITH, A.M., classical tutor of Rotherham College, said he had come on his own account, though he was assured he had the concurrence of his people. Many objections which had existed in his mind had been removed since he came here; and, if the conference were adjourned, and to meet again in London when parliament met, he had no fear that they would entrench upon politics. He was acquainted with the condition of Glasgow, and he knew that much misery and distress prevailed amongst the hand loom weavers there; and being well acquainted with Sheffield, he could state that it existed there also, and he had known as many as 50 persons even leave that town at once for Canada, where they could get a supply of food.

The Rev. J. G. MIALL (in the place of the Rev. WALTER SCOTT, of Airedale College) said, that ministers might be assured that, in that institution, nothing like monopoly would be inculcated. He had a table which had been carefully prepared by Mr. Scott showing the prices of food and wages at Bradford; and while flour was from 2s. 10½d. to 2s. 5½d. weaving wages rose from 2s. 0½d. to 2s. 3d. From 1836 to 1837, flour rose 2½d. per stone, and weaving fell 2s. 6d. per piece. From 1831 to 1834, a fall in corn, accompanied by a rise in wages; and from that time, a rise in corn, and a fall in wages. In Bradford the distress was as great as it had been represented in any other district.

The Rev. J. PETERS, of Rochdale, of the Wesleyan Association, (and the only member of that association who had yet spoken,) said: Mr. Chairman, my object, in addressing this meeting, is simply to state one or two facts. I am here to represent the Wesleyan Methodist Association of the town of Rochdale. The society whose opinions and wishes I am here to express, numbers upwards of 1600 members. These are almost, if not altogether, unanimous as to the injustice and wickedness of the corn laws. The leaders of the society, specially convened to consider the propriety of the intended convention of ministers on the subject of the corn laws, passed a resolution, *unanimously*, to the effect that the restrictions on the food of the poor are alike opposed to the law of God, and subversive of the power, morality, and happiness of the community, and that it cordially approves of the meeting which we are now holding. But, sir, there is another class of officers in our society, denominated with us, as in the Wesleyan Connexion and all its other branches, local preachers. These men have not satisfied themselves with merely giving an expression of their opinion in common with their brethren; they have met in their separate and official capacity, and have forwarded an address on the subject, which I have handed over to the committee of documents, expressive of their decided conviction of the impoverishing and demoralising effects of the laws which enhance the food of the poor. They most cordially approve of this meeting, and their earnest aspirations are that it may be very influential in accomplishing the destruction of the monopoly of bread. And now, sir, may I be permitted to express my regret at the absence of the ministers of one large and influential section of the church from the convention? While we indulge in no severity of reflection, yet may we not, without offence, express our regrets? But, sir, in that body, as in that to which I belong, there are local preachers—men of sympathy and compassion—men of high moral worth and extensive influence in their respective societies. To these men we may look in hope, and I am persuaded that, if only appealed to, our appeal will not be in vain. Whatever influence may operate to prevent others from following their convictions or forbid their co-operation, these men—these pious, useful, and devoted men—are under none which can prevent their coming forward to give their assistance. Many of them, I know, are heartily with us, and multitudes of the members of that church may be confidently reckoned among the friends of repeal. I wished, sir, in justice to the society which I represent, to state their views and feelings. I shall not further trespass upon the time and attention of this meeting.

The Rev. JAMES ACWORTH again requested that ministers would not leave before the conference terminated, or if they did, that they would sign the petitions, memorial, and address.

Some members had already left Manchester without doing so.

The Rev. J. W. MASSIE read the names of ministers who desired to speak, but had not, in consequence of the pressure of business and the brevity of time, been permitted to do so:—The Rev. J. H. Muir, from Sheffield; the Revs. Mr. Cooke, Mr. Orme, Mr. Stevens, Mr. Lindsay, from Kilmarnock; the Rev. Mr. West, from Bethnal Green; and the Rev. J. M. Thomson, Maybole.

A MINISTER asked if the conference would close on Friday.

The Rev. W. BEVAN, of Liverpool, said that nothing but necessity would have induced him to retire now from performing the duties of one of the secretaries of the conference.

The Rev. Wm. M'KERROW said the Young Men's Anti-Monopoly Association had issued 100 additional tickets for their tea party that evening, and those ministers who wished to attend were requested to apply for them.

The CHAIRMAN expressed his regret that Mr. West, of Bethnal Green, had not been heard. He (the Chairman) had himself kept back details of facts that other ministers might be heard.

In reference to the question as to the time of closing the conference, the Rev. T. SPENCER suggested that conference should terminate on Friday evening, and that if any documentary facts remained to be examined the committee should sit next week.

Dr. RITCHIE expressed concurrence with Mr. Spencer, and

The CHAIRMAN then adjourned the meeting to four o'clock.

AFTERNOON MEETING.

The Rev. Dr. Cox took the chair at four o'clock precisely, and Mr. M'KERROW opened the proceedings by announcing, that the committee had received a number of interesting letters from various quarters; but it was not considered necessary to bring them all before the meeting. Nevertheless, it was important that some of them should be read, on account of the denominational influence of the parties from whom they had emanated. Letters had been read, on that account, from Dr. Chalmers, Mr. Bunting, and others; and he would now read one from Mr. Candlish, a distinguished minister of the church of Scotland, and one of the leaders of the non-intrusion movement in Scotland.

The letter from the last-named gentleman was then read, and was received with loud cheers.

The Rev. JAMES ACWORTH, A.M., President of the Baptist College, Bradford, was first called on. He regretted not having had the opportunity of listening to the facts stated in the meeting, owing to his engagements on the committee. But it was thought that they had now heard facts enough, and ought to proceed to action. In conformity with this view, he had to submit an address to be presented to her most gracious Majesty the Queen. (Cheers.) It had been the most anxious and sedulous endeavour of those who drew up the address, to avoid all allusions to party politics. They would have liked to epxress their approbation of the progressive and general tendency of the late measures of ministers; but, feeling that such would be improper, and perhaps hazardous, they had avoided it. He then read the address, of which the following is a copy:—

"*To Her Most Gracious Majesty.*

"May it please your Majesty—We, your Majesty's dutiful and loyal subjects, being Christian ministers of various denominations, and from different parts of the United Kingdom, assembled in Manchester the 17th, 18th, 19th, and 20th days of August, 1841, to consider the laws restricting the food of the kingdom, beg permission to approach your Majesty with an expression of our sentiments in relation to the momentous subject which has thus brought us together.

"In craving this indulgence we beseech your Majesty to believe that we are influenced by an affectionate veneration for the person, and an ardent attachment to the throne of your Majesty, as well as by a deep heartfelt interest in the subject itself.

"Our unceasing prayer to the Supreme Ruler is, that he will continue to smile on your Majesty, your august Consort, and your illustrious offspring, preserving your Majesty in the uninterrupted enjoyment of health, surrounding you with all the endearments of domestic life, and after rendering you, through a long course of years, a blessing to your people, giving you in the realms of Eternal Glory a crown that fadeth not away.

"Brought by our professional avocations into daily intercourse with the more numerous classes of our fellow-subjects, it is, as it has for some time past been, our painful lot to witness scenes of wide-spread, heart-rending, and ever-deepening distress, arising mainly—as alas! is too obvious—from a want of adequate employ, and a consequent destitution to a very great extent of the common necessaries of life.

"In endeavouring to ascertain the cause of this most deplorable state of things, we beg to assure your Majesty that after patient and dispassionate investigation, we have been constrained to admit the conviction, that it is to be found primarily and chiefly in those laws which, by unrighteously interfering with the arrangements of our beneficent Creator, produce an artificial scarcity of food, impose shackles on trade and commerce, cramp the efforts of industry, and, even where they seem to benefit, occasion only a delusive advantage.

"Encouraged by the parental solicitude which your Majesty has uniformly manifested for the well-being of your subjects, we humbly, yet most earnestly solicit your Majesty's gracious interposition on this behalf, so far as it can be constitutionally rendered; assured that nothing more becomes the dignity or answers to the office of Princes and Potentates, than an imitation of the Soverign Ruler, 'who is good to all, and whose tender mercies are over all his works.'"

He had very great satisfaction in submitting the address now read for their consideration and, if approved of, for their adoption. The committee had not thought it necessary to prescribe the mode of presenting the address; there are two modes,—one through the home office; the other, the more dignified one, to present it at a levee. He knew not whether their London brethren, now present, belonging to the three denominations, could obtain the privilege of presenting it to her Majesty on the throne; if so, he should prefer their being requested to do it; but he would move that the mode of presentation should be left to the secretaries of the conference. Enough had doubtless been brought forward by the brethren who had already spoken, to evince the injurious working of those laws which they were so anxious to have abrogated, and he would not, therefore, detain them by a recital of any of the facts which had (illustrative of the same point) come under his own notice, especially as in doing so, he might be merely reiterating what had been again and again stated by preceding speakers. But, in sitting down, he would just advert to the fact, perhaps not yet noticed, that in the institution over which he presided, and, of course, in all similar institutions, a greater number of men might be prepared for the Christian ministry, with the same amount of pecuniary means, derived entirely from voluntary contributions, provided only the necessaries of life could be procured at a cheaper rate. And who, looking abroad on the country or on the wide world, could deny that there was the most lamentable spiritual destitution, which it was exceedingly desirable to meet and relieve, no less than that other kind of destitution which they were now seeking to remove? (Applause.)

The Rev. RICHARD FLETCHER seconded the motion. He hoped her majesty would be enabled to act in accordance with the wishes of the great body of her people, and that the most beneficial results might flow from the proceedings of the conference. So far as he could judge from what had taken place since the sitting of the conference, he had reason to believe, that the movement had been sanctioned by God, and that the best effects would be produced. The opinions advanced by the conference were a fair expression of the sentiments of the religious public who had given their attention to the subject, and this convention would be the means of enlisting the cooperation of that portion of the religious community who had not hitherto thought upon the matter.

The Rev. S. S. WILSON, F.S.A., suggested, that as it was a deliberative assembly, it would be well to have the address sent to the press, and copies of it distributed among the members of the conference before it was adopted. This suggestion not meeting with the approval of the meeting,

The CHAIRMAN then put the motion that the address to the queen embodying the opinions of the conference be adopted; and it passed.

The Rev. THOMAS SMITH, A.M., then moved, "That the chairmen of the conference, the Rev. Dr. Cox, and Messrs. Adkins, Spencer, and Chaplin, with the secretaries, be requested to present this memorial to her Majesty the queen." He said, a great portion of the people of Scotland were within a hair's breadth of the starving point, and many persons had nothing but bread and water to live upon. Any change, he was convinced, would be for the better, for they could be no worse.

The Rev. Dr. VAUGHAN seconded the resolution, which was put and carried.

The CHAIRMAN then stated, that the next business would be the consideration of the address to the people; Mr. George Thompson was expected to speak to it, but he could only do so by the permission of the conference. (Cries of "Speak.")

The Rev. J. W. MASSIE said, as no other persons except ministers had been permitted to speak without a deliberate resolution, he moved that Mr. George Thompson be allowed to address the meeting.

The Rev. Mr. MANN seconded the resolution, which passed with applause.

GEORGE THOMPSON, Esq., then presented himself, and was enthusiastically cheered. He said: I am sorry, sir, that a moment of the time of this assembly should have been occupied in settling the question of my competency to address this conference, as I do not feel myself able at present to say anything to this audience beyond that which is contained in the paper which I have the honour to hold in my hand. Should you permit the vote which you have so kindly passed, to remain upon your books, I shall be willing at some subsequent stage of the business of this conference to avail myself of the opportunity which you have placed in my hands. [Hear, hear, and "Now, now."] But I beg to assure those by whom I am surrounded, that I do not possess sufficient strength to do more than to read the address which has been entrusted to me. I will, however, take this opportunity of saying that, gazing upon this unexampled assembly, I do give thanks to God, on behalf of the perishing poor of our country. [Applause.] I proceed, Sir, to read the address, which will be formally submitted to you by a motion, proposed and seconded by members of the conference. It is as follows:—

"*To the People of the United Kingdom of Great Britain and Ireland.*

"Fellow-countrymen! An assembly of Christian ministers, unprecedented in its numbers, and embracing almost every denomination; yet, united as one, by the object which has brought us together, we proceed, in the discharge of our duty, to lay before you the result of our deliberations.

"Suffer us to claim for our present very brief address the calm and earnest attention which the importance and solemnity of the subject demand.

"We were convened for the purpose of considering the laws restricting the food of the community.

"We have endeavoured to approach this subject with minds uninfluenced by party feeling or sectional interests, and to try all questions submitted to us by the unerring standard of Christian morality.

"Our attention has, in the first place, been directed to the principle upon which the corn and provision laws of this country are based. The immediate effect of these laws is, to make the food of the people dear. It is demonstrable that this can be done, only by rendering food scarce. From the artificial scarcity so created, the different classes of consumers escape, in proportion to their wealth, the evil pressing with accumulating severity upon the humbler classes, exactly in the degree of their inability to sustain the burden.

"These laws operate with continually aggravating force, in consequence of the natural and progressive increase in the numbers of the people.

"The most painful evidence of the truth of this principle has been laid before us from all parts of the kingdom, proving the poverty and privations of the labouring classes, whose general fortitude under their augmenting wretchedness has awakened our sympathy, and called for our present interference in their behalf.

"In addition to the existence of domestic suffering, often in the most distressing forms of misery and disease, proof of an increased mortality has been forced upon us, and we have had the appalling fact disclosed, that famine is already doing its deadly work among the most destitute portions of the community.

"The moral effects of the corn and provision laws have occupied our serious consideration.

"It has been proved to us, that the physical deterioration of multitudes of our countrymen has produced an alarming amount of demoralization. Under this aspect, these laws have appeared to us to require the most anxious attention of all who are concerned for the advancement of the spiritual and eternal interests of their fellow-creatures.

"As Christian ministers, prizing above all other considerations the interests of morality and religion, we have been unable to anticipate, without apprehension and dread, the growth and development of those passions, which are stimulated and called into action by hunger and destitution.

"Fellow-countrymen! We have asked ourselves, if the calamities we have been called to contemplate and the more dreadful consequences with which we are threatened, are to be regarded as the just judgment and visitation of the Almighty; and our unanimous answer is—No. We have sought instruction in the word and through the works of God, and have been taught by both, that a bountiful and unfailing provision has been made, for the wants of every living creature. We stand forth, therefore, to assert and vindicate the divine wisdom and beneficence. We charge existing misery and impending danger upon the selfish or ignorant inventions of man, which have frustrated the merciful designs of the Ruler of the universe.

"The chastisements we are enduring are self-inflicted; our national distresses are the results of a departure, by human legislation, from the spirit and mandates of the divine law; and our strong conviction is, that our present deliverance and future safety, are to be secured only by recognising and observing the unerring and clearly revealed will of a beneficent Creator.

"Our duty, then, as ministers of religion, is plain. On scriptural grounds, we are called upon to denounce all human restrictions upon the supply of food to the people, and to employ all appropriate means, to place the fatherly provision of God, within reach of his suffering and famishing children.

"In the attainment of this object, we affectionately call upon the Christian public to aid us, by an instant, a combined, and a vigorous effort. The case is one of extreme urgency. The poor are daily perishing; and, though we commend the exercise of individual charity towards those who are at present suffering from want, we must declare our solemn conviction, that all assistance will prove ineffectual to the relief of prevailing wretchedness, during the continuance of laws, which impiously interfere with, and limit the enjoyment of the all-sufficient bounties of divine Providence.

"Our first advice to our brethren and friends throughout the country is, to investigate the subject now before them.

"Let every one convinced of the justice and necessity of abolishing these laws, do all in his power, in the spirit of meekness and love, to enlighten and convince those who are around him. Under the responsibilities of citizenship, let every opportunity be embraced, of bringing the nature and effects of the corn and provision laws under the notice of the legislature.

"We would, also, earnestly exhort such as are suffering from the operation of these laws to continue peaceable and loyal, and to cooperate in all Christian and constitutional efforts, to effect their extinction; relying with patience upon the sympathy of their friends and the blessing of the Most High.

"Finally, let unceasing supplication ascend, that it may please the God and Father of us all to give our law-makers the wisdom that is profitable to direct and to incline their hearts to do justice and love mercy."

The address, which is from the pen of Mr. Thompson, seemed to express the feeling of every heart, both in its sympathies with the people and in the sentiments which it avowed. It was listened to with profound attention, and on its conclusion, a deafening burst of acclamation arose.

The Rev. J. H. Hinton, of London, moved the adoption of the address. He eulogized both the beauty of its composition, and the excellence of its sentiments. He dwelt particularly on its assertion, that the conference had not assembled to support any sectional interests. It was often said that the opponents of the corn law were upholding the manufacturers against the agriculturists; but it was not so. For himself, he sought equally the benefit of both. He believed that the interests of both were threatened, and that what would ruin one would ruin both. Certainly it could not be for the interest of the British agriculturist that British manufactures should decay. Who was to consume the produce of the British soil, but the people of Great Britain? The present laws shut out our corn-growers from the market of the world, by raising it to a price which they could not get for it any where but in England. The home market was the only market they had; and it must, therefore, be to their interest that the demand here should be large. The better the people were off, the more food they would buy—in other words, the better for the farmers. If manufactures were to decay, the effect of it would fall directly on the agriculturists. An impoverished population must reduce its purchases of food to the smallest possible quantity; and population itself, instead of increasing rapidly, as it had done, must be checked, and ultimately diminished. In allowing the decay of British manufactures, the agriculturists would be destroying their own and their only market. In addition to the consumption of food, immense quantities of agricultural produce were employed in manufacturing processes. He would not now mention wool, but would speak of flour, of which he was assured, on good authority, that not less than 240,000 bags were used annually in the manufacture of silk, woollen and cotton stuffs. A large quantity—perhaps as much—was used by the calico printers. He knew a single calico printer whose consumption of British agricultural produce amounted to £10,000 per annum. He considered, therefore, that thriving manufactures were essential to the prosperity of agriculture, and that the agriculturists, by clinging to the corn law, were cutting their own throats. Besides, agriculture itself would be benefited by the repeal of the corn law. To protect a manufacture was the way to ruin it, and it was monopoly that ruined agriculture. Competition was necessary to the success of both manufacturing and agricultural pursuits. It sharpened intellect, increased ingenuity, elicited skill. It had made our manufactures what they were. It had even rendered service to agriculture. Competition existed between the more difficult agriculture of Scotland, and the more easy agriculture of England. Under this stimulus the agriculture of Scotland had far outstripped that of England, and southern lands now got their best farmers from the north. Let British agriculture generally come under the same beneficial influence, and it would become the glory of the world. The apprehension that there would be a deficiency of demand, while our population was increasing at the rate of a thousand a day, was preposterous, and showed the agriculturists to be blind to their real interests. He then adverted to the character of the address as an appeal to public opinion, which was now, in this country, the ruling power. As an expression of public opinion the conference would have great effect; and if they could influence public opinion generally, they would carry their point. He approved of the address also, because its sentiments eminently befitted them as Christian ministers. It called for inquiry and reflection, and particularly for the study of the bible and for prayer. He delighted to think that the study of the bible was adapted of itself to settle the corn law question, and to settle it with ease and harmony. It would not lead into intricate questions of political economy, or long lines of figures and calculations, but it would bring us into the presence of clear and irresistible moral obligations, to which any upright man must bow. All differences would vanish before a universal reference to the word of God, and when all should be united in the study and practice of the precept, "Whatsoever ye would that men should do to you, do ye even so to them." Agreement in this principle would secure the extermination of the corn laws for ever.

The Rev. J. W. MASSIE seconded the resolution. He acknowledged himself oppressed with an overwhelming feeling of gratitude to the Disposer of all hearts, for the prosperous issue which had attended the convocation of this conference; that so many had assembled from distant quarters, and, sacrificing personal indulgence, rival jealousies, or selfish interests, had responded to the invitation to meet for counsel and co-operation in the cause of our common country and our suffering poor. He was thankful that their deliberations had been conducted in harmony with the great object of their meeting, in a spirit of expansive liberality and Christian charity, and in feelings of generous sympathy with the afflicted myriads whose cry had pierced their ears and summoned them to this benevolent enterprise. It was cause of heartfelt and mutual rejoicing that every proposition which the committee had submitted had been readily, cordially, and unanimously accepted by the conference; not with a blind confidence or a servile submission, but after independent and mature reflection. Spontaneous and general unanimity, not alone in the object and motive, but also in the principles and measures recognised, had given character and efficiency to the conference. He now exulted and gave God thanks for the full realization of all that he had anticipated when contemplating from the first this assemblage of the people's ministers. The committees appointed by this convention had severally proceeded to examine apart, and consult together, what principles were involved in the great question and what measures had been suggested to attain the object by the conveners; and after a strict and ingenuous examination, after carefully weighing every expression, and analysing every sentiment, for which they deserved the gratitude of all, (and none were more vigilant and indefatigable than the gentleman who moved this resolution, who with his wonted sagacity and eagle eye, watched as from his *eyrie* every principle whether in expression or in detail), they brought forward the resolutions and addresses which had now been submitted. (Cheers.) Thus men of sound judgment, cautious eye, of scrupulous inquiry, had convened without previous arrangement or concert as to any scheme to be followed; but each judging for himself, had frankly declared and as one man had resolved that there was no time to be lost in freeing our trade from restrictions which trammelled commerce, impoverished the people, and paralysed industry. They spoke to the men of their time and of their country in accents of tenderness, of assuring sympathy, and cheering counsel. They cautioned them against the evils by which they were threatened, and gave token to them of zealous and energetic cooperation in every legitimate means for the overthrow and utter annihilation of the odious enactments which had dishonoured the government and prostrated the national energies; and they proclaimed to the nations afar off, that England was determined to release herself from the state of bondage in which she was placed, while they declared that the bread of the poor should be freed from the oppressive impost under which it had hitherto laboured. It was his honour to have been associated, from the first conception of this measure and the first deliberation for effecting such a movement, with his distinguished friend, Mr. Thompson, the hon. secretary of the preliminary committee, whose name had become the common property of philanthropy, benevolence, and patriotism. (Cheers.) It was to avoid the appearance of any tinge of sectarianism that the invitations to this meeting had been issued under his name instead of that of the original promoter of the conference. (Applause.) After a few further explanatory remarks, Mr. Massie concluded by seconding the acceptance of the address, and resumed his seat amidst much cheering.

The adoption of the address was then put by the Chairman, and carried unanimously by the conference, with tokens of most cordial approbation.

The Rev. T. Scales of Leeds said, Mr. Chairman and Rev. Brethren, Were I to select for myself a motto to describe the nature and duties of the high and sacred office, which in common with you it is my privilege to hold, it should be this, "*pro Christo—pro patria—et pro mundo*;" and this too should be my vindication, my laconic answer to any who might dispute or question the propriety of my attendance at this meeting. I feel that so far from being a recreant here to any of these interests, I am on the way of promoting them all in a most happy combination. (Cheers.) My brethren and fellow-countrymen of England and Wales, of Scotland and Ireland, I am exceedingly happy to meet you on so great and august an occasion, and for the promotion of an object so just and humane; and I am happy to find myself among you, to take a part, however humble, in your truly Christian, truly patriot, and truly philanthropic proceedings. I would not have been away from you, but through the direst necessity; although I have had little but the duties and toils of one of your working committees from the moment of my arrival in Manchester; and though while you have been listening to the eloquent addresses of your brethren, I have been fagging, I might say almost day and night, to prepare with my worthy coadjutors the business to be brought before you. This, however, is a duty which I know from a rather lengthened experience in public meetings, must devolve somewhere; and when I can serve a good cause, and my brethren have been pleased to call for my services, I have never shrunk from the labours of it. The consequence of this however has been an apparent neglect of the affairs and interests of my own town, in relation to the objects of this conference; but as my brethren, Hamilton and Giles, Jukes, Cummins, Fox, Atkinson, and others are present, and some of them have addressed you, it is not necessary that I should go at this time into any details. Had the opportunity been afforded me, I might have availed myself of it, to show you that our town and neighbourhood are sharing with other parts of the kingdom in the prevalent distress; and to tell you the tale of unprecedented embarrassment and difficulties; of the failure of our merchants and traders; of the sufferings of our artisans and mechanics; and but for the other duties you have been pleased to impose upon me, I should have been prepared to take my place amongst the great cloud of witnesses who have encompassed you. These details I wil present to your committee of documents. Just let me say, however, of the general character of our towns-people, especially the working classes, that I never knew a population anywhere so well-conducted, so forbearing, so uncomplaining, even in the worst of times, and under the most grievous sufferings; but though little may be said about their present distress, and their complaints may not be heard in loud tones, yet I fear, nay I am persuaded that distress and suffering are now widely spread, and wasting and destruction prevail to a fearful degree amongst them. But, sir, it is not to the humbler walks of life that distress is confined, or amongst our workpeople alone that the pernicious, impoverishing, and withering influence of an unnatural and unrighteous system of monopoly is felt. Their employers, our merchants, our capitalists and commercial men, are suffering in various ways as its victims. I was struck by a remark of that learned, holy, and philanthropic man of God, Dr. Pye Smith, in his admirable address—that the diseases engendered by this ruinous system will not be confined to the hovel. There has been for some time past a more than ordinary amount of sickness, I believe, in our town; and I have been assured, Sir, that some of our most experienced medical practitioners, ascribe it in many cases to the prevalence of commercial embarrassment, and the depression and anxiety consequent upon it. (Hear.) In various instances occurring in their practice they have not been able to trace it to any other source, or to account for it in any other way. The condition of our tradesmen too, not merely of the small shopkeepers, but of those hitherto in a more extended and profitable line of business, is becoming daily more and more distressing; and I believe I am telling no secret, when I say that unless there be a speedy change, the downfall of many is fearfully expected. But, sir, I am afraid to trespass on the time of the meeting, and I will come at once to the business for which I have risen, to submit the copy of a petition to both houses of parliament, founded on the resolutions and statements which have been already brought before you. And as the principles which it asserts, and the points on which it touches, have been so fully and, I doubt not, though this is a matter of faith, not having been able to hear many of the addresses of my reverend brethren, yet I venture to say, ably and eloquently discussed, I will merely read the petition, and then propose that it be adopted as the petition of this conference.

"*To the Honourable the Commons, &c.*

"The humble petition of a conference of ministers of religion, of various Christian denominations, and from all parts of the United Kingdom, held in the town of Manchester, on Tuesday, August 17, and following days,

"Showeth—That your petitioners are ministers of the God of love and mercy, who have assembled to consider the laws which restrict the supply of the food of the people.

"That, to your petitioners, dwelling in the midst of their respective charges, and, by habits of frequent and pastoral intercourse, familar with their actual condition, and still further informed by the evidence submitted to this conference by unimpeachable witnesses, it is most unquestionable that evils the most serious are preying on the vitals of the country, and that the labouring classes throughout the kingdom are sinking into the lowest condition of physical suffering, and pining away under a wasting destitution of the necessaries of life.

"That your petitioners would feel themselves most unworthy of the office they sustain, and the Master they serve, were they to view such a state of things with indifference, or to allow it to become daily more and more aggravated, without directing their attention to its cause, and seeking the means of its alleviation.

"That, to your petitioners, it appears obvious beyond all doubt, that whatever other causes may have contributed to the frightful amount of misery which they deplore, the principal has been the provision laws, which make the very necessaries of life scarce and dear, and, by their mischievous operation, have, at the same time, enhanced the price of food, and diminished the ability to purchase it; and that as obviously the remedy for this evil is, the abrogation of the laws which have produced it.

"That, to your petitioners, it is manifest any law tending to produce a scarcity of the food necessary to sustain the life of man, or to increase its price, and so to throw difficulties in the way of procuring it, is a wrong done to society at large, and a direct and glaring violation of the will and law of the universal Parent of mankind.

"That your petitioners are only acting in the spirit of their office when they remind your honourable house that laws of human legislatures should be framed in strict accordance with the declared will of God and the beneficent designs of his providence; and that all laws which contradict his will and counteract his bounty, must, of necessity, be wrong in principle and injurious in their tendency; and that it is the deliberate and solemn conviction of this assembly that this is the unrighteous character of the operation of the provision laws of this kingdom, under whose baneful influence our beloved country is severed from profitable intercourse with other countries which are ready to exchange their products for our manufactures—the skill and labour of the industrious classes of our countrymen are rendered of less and less avail to their own subsistence, whilst immense numbers of them, from day to day, are thrown out of employment, and reduced to a state of utter destitution, or cast upon the rapidly decreasing resources of the humane and charitable, who, in their turn, are sinking down into the abject condition of paupers; and famine, disease, and death are spreading with fearful desolation throughout the length and breadth of this once prosperous and happy land.

"Your petitioners, therefore, convinced of the sinfulness of these laws, which violate the paramount law of God and restrict the bounty of his providence; of their injurious operation on the domestic comforts, and the social, moral, and religious condition of the people of these realms; of the vast amount of evil which they have already produced; and of the fearful rapidity with which they are driving on their injured and suffering victims to despondency or desperation, and threatening the peace and safety of the empire, implore your honourable house, as you fear that God who is the friend and avenger of the poor, as you love that country whose interests are committed into your hand, to take into your early and most serious consideration the provision laws, and especially the corn laws, which have wrought this enormous amount of evil and misery, for the purpose of devising such means as to your honourable house may seem meet for their abolition.

"And your petitioners will ever pray," &c.

The Rev. WILLIAM M'KERROW seconded the resolution. In the documents that had come under his consideration as secretary of the documentary committee, his convictions of the injustice of the corn laws had been abundantly strengthened. He had thought he had known somewhat of the distress of the country, but he had had no idea of the awful reality. They had received 460 documents, worth at least a thousand of those usually issued by parliamentary committees. These came from all parts of the empire, and he looked through them in vain for some gleam of hope struggling through the gloom. When these were arranged and published, it would create such an impulse as must issue in the removal of those accursed laws: it was impossible they should continue; the feelings of humanity forbade it, the God of nature forbade it, every consideration that could affect a rational mind forbade it. (Loud cheers.)

The Chairman put the resolution to the meeting, and the petition was unanimously adopted by the Conference.

The Rev. W. JAMES, of Bridgewater, rose to propose a question to Mr. Cobden respecting a branch of the great subject which they had been convened to consider, and to which, in his view, sufficient attention had scarcely been paid. It had been stated in the circular letter by which they had been invited to the present conference, that they were to regard the question of the corn laws in all its various bearings, and to inquire how it might be settled, so as to promote the interests of all classes of the community. Now, he was anxious that this should be borne in mind. He would not that it should go forth to the world that they had been listening there merely to ex-parte statements. He wished fairly and candidly to examine this great question, so as to arrive at right and just conclusions respecting it. He was from a large agricultural district, and it was common to hear it said there that a repeal of the corn laws would be the ruin of all who were engaged in agricultural pursuits. This objection it was necessary to meet; and, however much had been said and written on this branch of the subject, it was certainly, in his view, important that it should not be passed over by the conference. Mr. Cobden having courteously offered to place any information which his long acquaintance with the question had given him, at the disposal of gentlemen present, he (Mr. James) would ask him—"Is it your opinion that English agriculturists would, on an entire repeal of the corn laws, be enabled to compete with foreign corn growers in our own markets; and if not, would there be, in your judgment, any adequate and profitable employment for the land of this country?

Richard Cobden, Esq., on presenting himself was most loudly cheered. He said he agreed that the agricultural view of the question had been rather lost sight of. (Hear, hear.) He should take blame to himself, probably, for having, too summarily, and, perhaps, not with sufficient gravity, dismissed that part of the question. But he had expected that, in the course of discussion, that part of the question would have been frequently mooted by gentlemen from agricultural districts, and that information would have been elicited from them better than he was able to afford. He was asked whether, in the case of an entire repeal of the corn and provision laws, the land of this country could compete with other countries. He supposed that the question meant—Could the agriculturists of this country afford to sell their corn in this market as cheap as the agriculturists of other countries could bring it here for sale? (Hear.) He had never, in discussing this question, ventured much into the field of prophecy; but the prophesies we had had on the other side afforded almost a proof that our agriculturists might compete with foreign agriculturists, provided the narcotic of protection, which lulled them to sleep, were removed from them. In 1815, during the discussion on the corn bill, which then passed, the almost unanimous opinion of the landowners and farmers was that they could not possibly produce corn in this country at less than 80s. or 90s. a quarter. In the course of five or six years, however, corn went down to nearly half that price, and yet the people were fed from the land of this country. In 1828, when the present corn law came into operation, the almost unanimous declaration was that corn could not be grown and sold for less than 63s. or 65s. per quarter. In 1838, the average price of wheat was 39s. 4d., and yet, so far from having the land thrown out af cultivation, in that very year four acts were obtained for enclosing waste land. (Applause.) It was as presumptuous as it was fallacious for them, or any body of men, to sit down in any year, and say what was the price at which we should be enabled to produce corn. (Hear.) If those who supplied the corn were allowed to decide, there would be no difficulty; they would be sure to fix the price high enough. (Applause and laughter.) He was happy to be able to call to the aid of the conference on this question the opinion of a nobleman, who, when he uttered the sentiment, did not expect that he was giving an argument in favour of the repeal of the corn laws; he alluded to the speech of Lord Stanley at the agricultural dinner, at Liverpool. (Hear, hear.) His lordship said, "The man who should at this time form an accurate estimate of those improvements in the capabilities of our production which I believe will be seen within a century hence, would be deemed, not a rational calculator, but a visionary enthusiast." (Applause.) Entertaining such opinions, he thought the Conference would not have the presumption to sit down and say at what price the agriculturists might produce their corn five years hence, provided they made use of those stores of the scientific world which the manufacturing capitalists were compelled to resort to; (Applause;) and provided always that they were stimulated by that wholesome competition of the world's markets which the manufacturers were subjected to. (Applause) When they had ascertained what was right and just in the abstract, they might fairly leave the consequence to the God of justice. (Cheers.) But, as he presumed their sympathies were directed primarily to the condition of the agricultural labourers, let them see what was the effect of low priced food upon their condition; and here he was happy again to draw arguments from the quiver of their opponents, from the evidence given before the poor-law committee, in 1839, the year after that in which the average price of wheat was 39s. 4d. Mr. Stairs, a farmer and miller, said, "I paid my men from 8s. to 10s. a week in 1829 and 1830, when wheat was 10s. a bushel; I pay them now from 9s. to 13s., when wheat is 5s. a bushel." (Applause) Mr. Goldsmith, a farmer, said, "A rise in the price of corn is prejudicial to the agricultural labourer; it is beneficial to the agricultural labourer to have corn cheap." (Applause.) Mr. Clement Hoare, a farmer, said, "In my neighbourhood, wages have risen, but nothing like in proportion to the rise in the price of provisions." (Applause.) Mr. James Ford, a farmer, giving his evidence on the same committee, said, "Twelve shillings a week was the highest wages I paid, in Petworth, during the war, with wheat at £40 a load; but we pay 10s. now that wheat is £15 a load." (Cheers.) Mr. Woods, a farmer, said, "Although wages have nominally increased, the labourer has not the same income now as when wages and bread were lower. (Applause.) And if they wanted further evidence, he would take the highest authority amongst the nobles of the land, and give them proof positive that the high price of food, instead of benefiting the agricultural labourer, plunged him down to a lower depth; it was a resolution passed by the Grantham Board of Guardians, of which the Duke of Rutland was the chairman, in 1839. (Applause.) It was—"Considering that during the high price of bread corn, the independent labourers are generally consuming barley bread,—resolved, that the bread given to the paupers shall be of the same quality as that now generally consumed by the agricultural independent labourers in this union." (Applause.) He supposed this would only be adding to the testimony which every gentleman from a purely agricultural district could afford, that the wages of the labouring peasantry were not really so good in dear years as in cheap years. (Applause.) Thus, then, they had evidence in their own experience to show that the labouring class were especially interested in cheap food. But the gentleman who asked the question had assumed that a low price of food would arise from the importation of corn and provisions from abroad, and he asked what then might be the effect of it upon the labourer here? The land *now* supported the agricultural labourers the farmers, and the landlords, who lived in splendour in Paris or of Naples; and the landlords insisted that the land should not only support those classes, but should support the manufacturing classes too. Did it require any argument to prove that if the manufacturers were to draw their food from the rich prairies of America, by exchanging our manufactures for their corn, the land which now supported all classes, would still have virtue enough left in it to support the agriculturists? and if it should come to the worst, until the landlords lost their rental, the labouring classes must be as well off as they were now. If the landlords lost their rental, if the Duke of Richmond put into execution the threat he threw out a year or two ago, that he would emigrate to America or some other country,—without wishing to maintain an agrarian system, he maintained that the land, which they could not take away with them, would always support those who were left behind. ("Hear, hear," and cheers.) But they were proceeding on a fallacy, on the assumption that the people were sufficiently and abundantly fed. Had they not had evidence enough to prove that this was not the case? He would state from his own knowledge, that, compared with the labouring classes of the United States, the labouring population of this country were not half fed. (Cheers.) By giving the stimulus to their labour which free trade, and free trade only, would give, they should in an instant call into activity fresh wants, fresh desires, new ambitions; and if they did not purchase more bread of the landlord here, they would purchase more milk, more butter, more beef, more pork, and every thing else. (Cheers.) He repeated it was his conviction the repeal of the corn laws would not injure ultimately either the landlord, tenant, or peasant, but that it must, on the other hand, contribute very much to their benefit, as that of other classes. (Hear, hear.) He would not for a moment say that the transition state would not have its inconveniences; he would not say that no legislative measure would be necessary to provide against that, and to aid them in that transition state, especially to protect the labourers; but he maintained that a free trade in corn must ultimately add to the value of land. (Applause.) To those landlords whose estates were deeply mortgaged, and who had large fixed money payments to make upon them, he did not say that this measure would not be attended with inconvenience, but they did not come here to consider class interests; *they* might be embarrassed by the measure; but if we left them all they were in right and justice entitled to, and if then they could not do, they must fare as men in our own walks of life do. (Hear, hear,) So far from a free trade in corn tending to depreciate the price of land, if we looked at the example of Switzerland we should find that the very contrary was the case. You might drive your waggons of corn from the plains of Swabia into her cities, and no interference would take place lest it should injure their own agriculturists. The fact was, that manufactures had given a value to land in Switzerland far beyond, indeed more than threefold, the value of the land whence they derived their corn, in Germany. (Hear, hear.) We were told that land was highly burdened in this country by taxation. But he contended that that was not a question for discussion here; that was a subject for consideration in another place. If such was the fact, let them make out a case, and there was the power and the disposition to set them right; but surely it was not a justification for taxing the bread-loaf of the hand-loom weaver. (Cheers.) He thought he need not longer occupy their attention, as the subject was in itself so clear; and if looked at in reference to the great body of agriculturists, it would be found that they had nothing to fear. He did not call a landowner an agriculturist any more than he called a shipowner a sailor. (Loud cheers.) The agriculturists were the labourers and farmers; they were too apt to mix up these terms; but so far as the labourers were concerned, there was nothing to excite their sympathies on that occasion. He would, however, leave the matter in the hands of gentlemen who had better opportunities, in their own immediate neighbourhoods, of inquiring into the condition of the agricultural labourers. He asked them to inquire what were their regular and uniform wages, and it would be found that they were at the lowest point in the scale in this country. Let them inquire the present, the past, aye, the inevitable rate of wages in the agricultural districts. It was 8s., 9s., and 10s. per week. (Hear, hear.) He himself employed 600 people; he had hundreds of unskilled labourers, and not one in his employ received less than 12s. a week. This was not in a town; it was twenty miles from here, and was in a rural district. He challenged them to say whether the agricultural labourers in Devonshire, Dorsetshire, and Sussex were so paid; and if not, let them ask what benefit the agricultural labourers derived from the plunder of the corn laws. (Cheers.) Having tendered the meeting his thanks for the interest which they had taken in the subject, Mr. Cobden observed, that if 28 ministers of the gospel in Manchester had succeeded in assembling 700, what might be expected if these hundreds of ministers would send out a similar invitation to convene a meeting in London? (Cheers.) Why should not such a meeting be got up in Exeter Hall? Let ministers meet there, and let them bring their congregations with them, (Cheers,) and let them be congregated in the neighbouring streets. (Applause.) Why should not Exeter Hall, which had so recently resounded with the acclamations of those who were seeking to strike the fetters off the slave be also used for striking the tax off the bread of the poor. (Applause.) Where was the difference between freeing a man from his fetters, and restoring to the freeman the fruits of his labour? (Cheers.) After some further observations, Mr. Cobden resumed his seat amid loud cheers.

The Rev. D. WASSELL, of Bath, addressing Mr. Cobden, said it might be a good thing to promote the interests of the landowner, according to the tenor of the question put by our friend from Bridgewater; but if this cannot be done without injury to others, is it your opinion that the end will sanctify the means? Or, if it be not your opinion that the end will sanctify the means, ought Christian ministers, meeting on Christian ground to carry out a great question, to raise a question concerning the interests of any particular class of the community?

Mr. COBDEN: I am not at all a good casuist to settle matters of conscience. (Cheers and laughter.)

The Rev. Mr. SPENCER inquired if the gentleman who had put the first question to Mr. Cobden was satisfied with the answer.

The Rev. Mr. JAMES replied, that he had asked the question which he had proposed not so much for his own satisfaction as to bring the subject to which it referred before the conference. It was his desire that the benefit resulting from their meetings in Manchester might be felt in their various localities, and in order to this it was important that the question should be thoroughly understood. He agreed, generally, with what Mr. Cobden had said, and especially in that part of his speech which had reference to the transition state. He believed, from all the attention that he had given to this subject, that there would probably be some inconvenience and injury sustained by agriculturists on the first changes consequent upon a repeal of the corn laws, but that the prospective advantages were great; and it was in his opinion the duty of the conference, fairly and candidly, to admit this. He had no doubt of the abstract injustice and unreasonableness of the corn laws, and, believing this, it would be his duty to lend his full aid to their ultimate repeal, leaving the consequences to the Almighty.

The Rev. E. H. NOLAN then moved that the petition to the House of

Commons be presented by the members for Manchester, and that Mr. Cobden be requested to support it. He (Mr. Nolan) said it was an axiom in political economy, that labour was capital; the meeting was, therefore, an important one, as there were no labourers in England who laboured so hard and so effectually—he almost said as the protestant dissenting—but, he might certainly say, as the religious ministers of England. It was important in another respect, they were the ministers of congregations of the poor. The lightning did not always strike from the overhanging cloud; it sometimes shot upwards; and so it was, that from the class of society deemed the meanest, there sometimes went up an electric power which was felt by the highest, before which senates and thrones themselves might well tremble. The aëronaut, while he soared far above the smoke and dust of the world beneath, was still kept within the sphere of attraction which linked him to the earth. Ministers also arose in their holy calling above much of the turmoil and strife of time; but the sympathies of the poor kept them within the power of an attraction which they should always own. (Cheers.) He rejoiced that Mr. Cobden, the anti-corn-law agitator, *par excellence*, would soon be representing their agitation in St. Stephen's, and concluded by proposing the resolution:

"That the petition be presented to the House of Commons by the members for Manchester, and that the members for Stockport and Salford be requested to support it."

The Rev. P. Brewster, of Paisley, a minister of the Church of Scotland, seconded the resolution. His instruction, on coming to the meeting, was not to agree to any tax on food. These instructions corresponded with his own feelings. Such a tax would be most severely felt by the poorest, who would have to pay 20 per cent. for their bread, according to the present corn law. He was, therefore, decidedly opposed to any, even the smallest, tax on the food of the people. He was astonished at the question which was put to Mr. Cobden. Was not the fact of their being there to use all constitutional means to repeal those laws a sufficient answer?

The Chairman then put the motion, which passed unanimously.

A Minister stated, that the address would not only represent the opinions of the 600 or 700 ministers who might sign it, but of 2000 congregations.

The Rev. J. P. Mursell, of Leceister, said, he was anxious that the meeting should have some practical result; and he should be sorry if it should be said that they met to discuss a secular question, without doing something in their religious capacity. He had therefore great pleasure in moving,

"That this conference earnestly recommends, to all who may approve of it, to set apart Monday the 6th of September next, as a day of humiliation before Almighty God, on account of our sins, and of solemn prayer, that it might please Him in his all wise providence to remove the distress which at this time afflicts the nation, and which especially bows down the hearts of the suffering poor, and that He would endow our senators, at this crisis, with that "wisdom which is profitable to direct.'"

The Rev. J. Webb, of Arnsby (Leicester), seconded the resolution, which was carried.

The Rev. Andrew Somerville, of Dumbarton, moved the following resolution:—

"That, while this conference declines to prescribe any distinct and specific plan of operations to be followed by the members after this meeting breaks up, we pledge ourselves that, by all such means as may be deemed by the individuals themselves best fitted to promote the great cause in which we are engaged, we shall never cease our efforts till these unjust and unscriptural enactments, which restrict the supply of food, are expunged from the statute book."

It is not necessary, sir, for me to say much in support of this motion, as I have no doubt that it will meet with the cordial approbation of all present. We have, sir, done much since we assembled. We have collected a vast number of important facts respecting the extensive distress that exists among the people: we have been unanimous in attributing that distress mainly to the operation of the corn laws, and we have passed resolutions, and have proposed and issued documents, that embody our opinions both with regard to the evils and the remedy, and that we designed to make these opinions known to the country, the legislature and the throne. We have done much; but the evils still exist in all their magnitude. We cannot remain here; our sacred duties demand that we return to our homes, and were we to abide here, we might exhaust the benevolence of the generous inhabitants of Manchester, great and wonderful though that benevolence is. But, sir, shall we separate without putting on record a solemn pledge, that we shall never cease to agitate peacefully, but earnestly, till the sufferings of the people are relieved? Shall we sow the seed and not look after the fruit? Shall we give our opponents occasion to say, The phalanx was numerous; it was firmly united and formidable, but it is divided and dispersed: the cloud was dark and portentous, but it has passed away? No; let us tell them that we have gone home to prosecute the work—that we have retired, like the refluent wave, only that we may return, if need be, with greater power and in greater numbers—that we have gone to gather those rills of public opinion that are flowing in all parts of the country, unite them into one great current, and make that current beat with increasing force against the edifice of oppression and monopoly, till the unhallowed structure be laid in ruins and swept away for ever. Those same high and holy principles which brought us to this conference, bind us to continue our efforts. The claims of justice, humanity, and mercy, the cries of starving millions, and our consistency, all imperatively demand that we persevere in this benevolent enterprize. We have buckled on our armour and we cannot put it off, so long as these laws are crushing the people to the earth. It is scarcely possible to prescribe any plan of operations that would suit all parties and all localities. All that the motion imposes on those who adopt it is, that we shall consider ourselves bound to follow those methods which each of us may deem most expedient and most effective. It assures the country that our present meeting is not a single effort which is to be succeeded by inactivity, but that, stimulated and encouraged by what we have now heard, we are resolved to be more zealous, energetic, and untiring in this cause than we have yet been. Sir, I have never despaired of the growing prosperity of this country. The intelligence, the piety, the skill and the industry which prevail among its population, forbid such a feeling. I have been accustomed to cherish the most ardent hopes with regard to its increasing greatness; and all that I have heard here, tends to strengthen such expectations. It is true that the people are suffering, and that evils exist, which will, should they continue, effectually undermine and destroy our strength. But then the causes of these evils are so obvious and the remedy is so palpable, that we cannot think it will be long ere they are removed. The laws of which we complain are so bad, that they cannot be defended—the consciences of their supporters will soon remonstrate against the very attempt to do so. It needs but the enlightened, the unanimous, and the decided voice of the people to secure their abolition. No interest, however extensive, no power, however venerated, and no class, however protected, can long and safely withstand the demands of a united people. And do not the bosoms of all here beat with anxious desire to make known to the people the facts, statements and principles which we have heard, and to call upon them to petition for the redress of their wrongs? Let us tell them that the money of which these laws rob us, does not go into the national exchequer; for were this the case, all other taxes might be abolished. It is received by the landowners, and all that the government gets is only the trifling sum that is *actually* paid on imported grain. Let us tell them that the nature and operation of these laws are such as that, though not a bushel be imported from abroad, they rob us of forty or fifty millions annually, as we are compelled to give all that more for our corn than we should have to pay were a free trade in grain allowed. Let us tell them, as a plain proof that we have discovered the cause of their misery, that were the money which we have paid by reason of these laws, during the last year, in the pockets of the people, it would be enough to relieve all the suffering that exists, and to afford abundant employment to all that want it. Throw fifty millions—the cost of these laws—into the home market at this moment, and the distress under which the working classes labour would disappear at once. Then let us exert ourselves to the utmost—let us never pause in our labours, till ignorance, disease, want, and misery are removed, and till abundance and prosperity bless every family, joy shine on every countenance, and gratitude beat in every heart. (Cheers.)

The Rev. Dr. HALLEY, in seconding the resolution, said, from his education, he had a great fear of clerical convocations; and he believed, if that convocation did good, it would be the first that had. He had had much doubt whether he should attend this conference, and his doubts were strengthened by letters from some of his own connection. However, he determined to attend, and oppose anything he might dislike; but he had heard nothing of which he disapproved, and most cordially did he second that resolution. There were two popular arguments which were used against the repeal of the corn laws. The one was that a large quantity of land would be thrown out of cultivation; but he held that not an acre of land which was now cultivated would be thrown out of cultivation. If five bushels of corn were consumed in cultivating a certain portion of land which produced seven bushels, no act of parliament would ever throw that land out of cultivation, though he admitted that the *money* profit of the cultivation might be lost. The other argument was, that wages rise and fall according to the means of subsistence. But he believed it could be demonstrated, that wages would depend on what the people consumed, and the means of subsistence; and that if they considered that flour and beef were necessary, and they could not get them here, they would emigrate to other countries where they could. Wages had fallen in Ireland because the people of Ireland had found out that they could live upon potatoes. The best way of keeping up wages would be to inspire them with a dread of finding out upon what inferior diet they could subsist. The resolution was then passed.

The Rev. Mr. CAIRNS, of Paisley, proposed the next resolution:

"That the following gentlemen constitute a committee to superintend the printing and circulation of the address to the people of the United Kingdom, to effect publication, in a revised and authentic form, of the proceedings of the conference, and to attend to any other business which may be left in an unfinished state, or which may arise out of its proceedings, with power to fill up vacancies: Revds. W. M'Kerrow, R. Fletcher, J. W. Massie, P. Beardsall, T. G. Lee, J. Gwyther, F. A. Cox, D.D., L.L.D., J. Carlisle, J. H. Hinton, N. M. Harry.

Mr. Chairman and Christian Friends,—I had no idea until a few minutes ago that I should be called upon to speak in this meeting. I am exceedingly happy, however, that this opportunity has been presented, and that I am allowed thus to testify my interest in the cause of the suffering thousands in this land. The times in which our lot has fallen are full of interest to every reflecting mind. All the nations seem to be in the attitude of expectation. Human beings are everywhere looking out with solicitude for coming events in the providence of God. In our own land public affairs present a spectacle of appalling interest, and we are evidently on the borders of a most momentous crisis. The advocates of monopoly and selfish measures have been mustering their forces and preparing for the contest; and, on many accounts, the prospect before us is of the most discouraging character. The present state of our manufacturing districts is most alarming. The wheels of our commerce, which have long been turning heavily, seem as if they were about to stop. A storm has burst with a blighting influence on our mercantile speculations. This has been especially the case in Paisley, the town where I reside; and throughout the whole country trade and commerce have been in a very languishing condition. The current of distress is still rising higher and higher; and although it may partially subside for a time, there is reason to fear that, without some important reforms in our national legislation, the clouds will speedily gather and burst again, and the rains descend, and the dark stream of misery roll yet more furiously through the land. I felt exceedingly interested, as I am sure every member of the conference did, in the case of those poor men, the hand-loom weavers, who were with us in the forenoon, and conducted themselves in such a masterly and creditable manner. (Hear.) Why should those excellent persons be doomed to labour in a damp workshop, fourteen or sixteen hours a day, for the paltry pittance of a shilling! Why should they be obliged to toil from week to week, (when work can be had,) for wages scarcely sufficient to procure as much provisions as will keep body and soul together? Why should such misery exist in our country, where our merchants are so enterprising, where our workmen are so skilful, and have such a facility of production in their several departments of labour? (Hear, hear.) Why is it that we have so many seasons of depression, and that our manufactures and commerce are in such a languishing and decaying state? It is obvious that many causes may be assigned for this, but probably all originating in one cause, *misgovernment*. Monopolies are rife amongst us, and monopolies of every kind are bad; but the corn-law monopoly is especially to be condemned. If our trade has been fettered and restricted, if employment has been scarce, if wages have been low, if provisions have been high in price, if families have been reduced almost to rags and to the starving point, these unjust and obnoxious laws have in a great measure been the cause. Yes, Mr. Chairman, these laws we condemn as unjust in principle, cruel in operation, opposed to the Divine benevolence in the bounties of providence, injurious to morality, a prominent cause of disease and distress, and the fruitful source of discontent and disaffection in the community. God, the almighty and benignant Creator, has given fertility to the soil, and, year by year, enriched the world with his bounty. The occasional failure of the crop in one place has been amply compensated by a luxuriant harvest in another, and thus provision made for the necessities of man. But the corn monopolist has with a daring effrontery, and recklessness as to the misery occasioned by his selfishness, attempted to put his veto on the benevolent designs of God; and in filling his own coffers, he has spoiled the habitations, and the homes of millions of his fellow-men, of almost every thing that deserves the name of comfort. I feel thankful for the opportunity of expressing my sympathy with the suffering thousands of our countrymen. Since I went to Paisley five years ago, I have observed a gradual falling off in the comforts of the operatives. I might go at length into harrassing details of this matter, but as my brother, Mr. Baird, did that so well and so effectively on Tuesday evening, I shall not trouble you with many remarks. It is distressing to witness the destitution of the operatives in that town; and a destitution which is incessantly on the increase. Industrious and well-doing families are on every side struggling with the adversities of life; and after all can scarcely gain a scanty subsistence. In many cases, the furniture, which was wont to indicate comparative comfort, has been parted with for monopoly—high-priced provisions, and now they cannot replace it. In numerous instances, the clothing with which they could appear respectably in the market, and in the house of God, is gone, and they cannot get a new supply. They have parted with these to save them and their families from starvation, in such seasons of depression as the present, and what are they now to do? In hundreds of families, the parents are dispirited, they have been overwrought, they have been under-fed, they are ill-clothed, they are stripped of almost every comfort. And, sir, distressing as all this may be, they might bear up under their sorrows, if they alone had to bear them. But their hearts bleed for their poor children, whom the necessities of the household subject to labour, so early, that they are rising up without education, and apparently to be crushed down to the very dust, by that increasing load under which their parents have long been groaning. Mr. Chairman, I rejoice in this assembly, and anticipate very much good as its results. It is the proper position in which, as ministers, we should be found. But, O sir, when we look at the distress in our own localities, and throughout the country, I feel that we have been too tardy in our movements; we should have taken this step long ago! but, now that we have come out to give expression to the feelings which we always cherished, let us be resolved that we will determinately hold on our way; and let us make it evident to the country, that while the poor have hitherto been oppressed, we are determined that we will on every occasion lift up our voices in their behalf; and that, in so far as our energies go, they shall be free from their misery, and safe from the oppressor. (Cheers.)

The Rev. William Robinson, of Kettering, seconded the resolution, and hoped that the unfinished business alluded to in the resolution, might not include any thing unconnected with a total and immediate repeal of the corn laws. He rejoiced that the proposition of Lord John Russell had not been accepted by parliament, as it would be imposing a burden on the shoulders of the people, which they could not hereafter easily get rid of. (Cheers.)

The Chairman then introduced a deputation from the Operative Anti-Corn-Law Association, consisting of Messrs. Edward Watkin, D. Hargreave, J. J. Finnigan, Stephen Neild, Jas. Daly, and J. S. Oswald.

Mr. Edward Watkin, one of the deputation, read the address from the association, which was as follows:

"*To the President and Members of the Conference of Ministers of the Gospel on the Corn and Provision Laws.*

"Reverend Sirs,—We cannot allow the present opportunity to pass, without publicly thanking you for your patriotic and Christian efforts on behalf of the interests of the country generally, and more especially of the numerous, important, and useful, but unfortunately suffering class, of which our association is almost entirely composed. We thank you on behalf of the working men of England, Ireland, Scotland, and Wales.

"We need not enlarge upon the sufferings which, for a long period, it has been our lot to experience amongst ourselves, and to see amongst different portions of our working brethren. These sufferings have been steadily increasing. The details of privation and misery which have been laid before the Conference by reverend gentlemen, of all sects of Christians, ministering in almost every part of the empire, are unparalleled in a civilized and enlightened community; and they sufficiently demonstrate, not only that you are well aware of the miserable condition of the poorer classes, and of the main cause of their distress, but also that you have well and faithfully fulfilled one of the most important duties of the sacred trust delegated to you,—that of searching out the sorrowing beings who are crushed to the earth by poverty and want, and of carrying the hopes and consolations of religion to relieve and sustain those who, without them, would fall victims to the blackest despair. We have, therefore, no occasion to prove to you, that the unrighteous corn and provision laws produce an incalculable amount of distress amongst the working classes, and that at present the baneful influence of those laws is acutely felt throughout the whole country. Suffice it to assure you, that the working classes know full well from what source their sufferings proceed, and are resolutely determined to do all in their power, by moral and peaceful means, to produce a radical change in the present wicked and cruel system. Such a change cannot, in their opinion, be effected, without a total and immediate annihilation of the monopoly of food.

"By your timely assistance, you have invigorated our hopes of a speedy improvement in the state of our affairs; you have shown, that you hold in just contempt the sneers and opposition of those who appear to rest satisfied with promulgating the precepts, without enforcing obedience to, or denouncing the violation of, that Christian charity which forms the practice of the real disciple of Jesus. You have caused thousands, who could only see a reinstatement of their prosperity through the bloody vista of revolution, to stay their unhallowed thoughts, and to withhold their hands from violence. Your reward hereafter will be great. Here you will receive, at least, all that the people have to offer,—the heartfelt thanks and sincere prayers of millions who rejoice in your aid; amongst whom the members of the Manchester Operative Association desire to be considered not the least sincere.

"On behalf of the Association,

"JAMES MORRIS, Secretary.

"Passed at a meeting of members, August 19, 1841."

J. J. FINNIGAN, at the request of the chairman, then addressed the meeting in very suitable and appropriate terms.

The Rev. Mr. M'KERROW moved the adoption of the address.

The Rev. Mr. MASSIE seconded the motion, and hoped the operative association would not cease their efforts against monopoly until they were crowned with victory.

The CHAIRMAN having addressed the deputation in very appropriate terms, and given them the right hand of fellowship, they retired amid loud cheers.

The Rev. Mr. MASSIE requested that gentlemen would, on the following day, furnish the meeting with statements respecting the condition of the agricultural districts, in order that the fullest consideration might be given to the subject.

The Rev. WILLIAM JONES, of Bolton, moved a vote of thanks to Dr. Cox, for his conduct in the chair; which was seconded by the Rev. T. THOMAS, of Pontypool academy, and carried with applause.

Dr Cox acknowledged the compliment in suitable terms, and said, though he could not properly put the last resolution, there was another which he could state, and that was that he would use his utmost exertions to carry out what had been so clearly demonstrated to be the wishes of the conference, if necessary, in London, for a similar purpose.

The conference then adjourned, about a quarter to nine o'clock, till the following morning.

FRIDAY, AUGUST 20.

The doors were opened shortly after nine o'clock, for the admission of ministers and the public; but it was half-past nine before the hall was half filled, a great many of the members having returned home. At a quarter to ten o'clock the chair was taken by

The Rev. THOMAS SPENCER, A.M., of Hinton Charterhouse, near Bath, the president of the day. He said, if they concluded the last day of the conference as well as they had concluded every other day, he for one should be perfectly satisfied. (Hear.) There was one thing on taking that chair that he regretted, and that was, that if the church of England was to be represented in this conference, it had not been represented by a man who, in his opinion, ought to be in this chair, and that was the Archbishop of Dublin, an enlightened and zealous corn-law repealer. He knew there was not a man in England who had clearer views on this subject than Archbishop Whateley. He had learnt, from a person living in his house, that, were it not for his being fettered as he was by the bonds which churchmen were bound with, he would take a conspicuous part in this subject; but, situated as he was, he could not. That excellent man said, that, if they were in conversation with any one, and wanted to know if he were an honest and intelligent person with whom they conversed, introduce the subject of the corn laws. If that were the test of honesty and integrity, he was glad they could stand it. However, this conference had acted so well, and had got so much respect, that it would not be the last conference unless the corn laws were repealed. If they did not wish to see a conference in London—if they did not wish to see every minister attended by three or four of his congregation—if they did not wish to see Exeter Hall filled by 5,000 people, they must repeal the corn laws. He wished the young men of Manchester, the Young Men's Anti-Monopoly Association, could spare money to go up at the same time. For he was sorry to say that there was a gin-drinking public opinion, and a freeman's public opinion in London, that wanted to throw out Lord John Russell. And the licensed victuallers also wished to throw him out, because he wished to restrict them; and they cared more about selling strong drink, than for the liberties of the people. He could like to draw a little public opinion from here, that when her majesty went to parliament, she might go waffed on the breeze of free trade And let the lords spiritual, who did not think it too secular to attend to politics in the house of lords, though they thought it very secular to meet on the corn laws, consider these things. (Hear.) If these young men went to London, and lined the approaches to parliament, instead of the idle mob who went for mere curiosity; if they had a few of the young suffering men of Manchester there, to call out "No corn laws!" he thought the present session would see the corn laws destroyed. However, whether the young men of Manchester would go up or not, they, the ministers of religion, would pledge themselves to answer the first call. They had entered into the work; for, whether popular or unpopular, they were in for it. (Laughter.) As for himself, he had been advocating certain sentiments with respect to the new poor law and teetotalism; for he appeared there as a Rechabite, and had encountered much opposition, and therefore it would take a good deal to intimidate him; and his own opinion was, that if a man thought freely and acted freely, every person would allow him to do so. If they were summoned to meet in council in London as in Manchester, he thought the ministers of religion would be in their proper position, and which few of them had never been yet. It was their business to stand in the gap. Why had noblemen so many chaplains, but that they should occasionally reason respecting righteousness? Why had they clergymen for gaols, and ministers of religion in all directions, if they were not to declare the counsel of God to all alike? And when he read of John the Baptist (who was a teetotaller), telling Herod that it was not lawful for him to have his brother's wife—when he heard of Knox telling kings of their faults, and nobles of their crimes—of a Latimer preaching until his offence was such that he was required to recant—when he heard of the giants of those days, he was ashamed of the small men of our time. He was wishful that there should be giants also in our time—that the ministers of religion of our days should be fearless in speaking the truth. He had to make a remark on the business of this day. Hitherto there had been a little restriction, and it was necessary. All law was the giving up of personal liberty for the public good, and he admired the conduct of the committee in this respect. But they had now got through their resolutions; they had carried the address to the people and to our beloved queen. They had carried their petition to the parliament, whom they would love if they would let them, but not unless they did right. And now, if there were gentlemen who had not expressed their opinions, and they thought they ought to be expressed,—if there were those who had yet difficulties or arguments which they wished to urge, they had Mr. Cobden to answer any questions. If there were any such, this would be a day of liberty and freedom; and this meeting should be a lesson to the other side. This was no hole-and-corner meeting. The people of Manchester said, "If you have any doubt as to the distress in Manchester, we don't want you to believe us; but make inquiries for yourselves; and if you do not see it, we are here to answer any questions; and if we do not satisfy your minds, decide against us." This was the way in which a man of truth always acted; for when they saw a man seeking the light, they might be convinced that he was right.

The Rev. J. W. MASSIE said, it was considered desirable to make a small addition to the committee to wind up the affairs of the conference; and that four gentlemen should be put upon it from Scotland. He moved,

"That the following names be added to the executive committee already appointed: The respective chairmen, viz., the Rev. T. Adkins, the Rev. William Chaplin, and the Rev T. Spencer, (Dr. Cox being already named;) with Dr. Vaughan, of London, the Rev. John M'Gilchrist, and Rev. James Robertson, of Edinburgh; and the Rev. Alex. Harvey, and Rev. T. Pullar, of Glasgow."

The Rev. G. HOYLE, of Stalybridge, said: Mr. Chairman, after all that has been said of the great distress which is prevailing in various parts of the country, you and the meeting will be surprised when I say there are in the north-eastern districts near Manchester 200,000 souls for whom no one had yet spoken,—Stockport, Ashton, Stalybridge, Dukinfield, and Oldham. When, ten years ago, the providence of God led me to Stalybridge, all was prosperity; each man had labour for his hands and wages for his labour, but now it is quite the reverse. In my adopted town we are not yet reduced to that distressing state of privation and misery of which we have heard, but we are on the highway to it. There is distress, and that very great, which I have witnessed. I entered a poor man's house the other day, and on going up stairs I found in one corner of the room a young man laid in a bed, and the mother in another, both under a wasting disease, and no one to earn a farthing for them. There were numbers also walking the streets without employment. I think there was a mistake as to the way in which this question has been discussed. There has been too much time spent in considering whom repeal would injure. The question to me seems to be whether the corn law is just to the community in general; and, if not, down with it; it ought to be repealed. It never entered into my mind to suppose that wages were regulated according to the food a man eats, but according to the demand for labour. The spinners would say, "Only let us have work and we shall have wages. When trade was good, placards were seen upon the walls, so many hands wanted, and liberal wages given."

The Rev. PETER GUNN, Catholic parish priest, of Eastern Temple, county Fermanagh, said, he came to tender conference the moral energies and determination of 3,000 people in Ireland against that inhuman law, which destroyed thousands for want of food. If the Irish people knew conference as well as he did, who had not set foot in England till Monday last, they would unite heart and hand. He trusted that the end of this beginning would be, that England and Ireland would know each other better on the subject of the corn laws. When Mr. Spencer, last night, at the tea party, said there were Roman Catholic priests attending this conference, it was received with a burst of cheering, for which he returned his most cordial thanks. The editor of the *Evening Mail*, Dublin, though he had a sister a nun, and had been a catholic himself, blackguarded the catholics, lest he should not be thought a good Protestant. (Question.) A hired scribe had recommended to the incoming government, to seize all the catholic priests of Ireland, and transport them; but the scribe little knew that those who attempted to carry this into effect must climb to the task over the corses of seven millions of the people of Ireland. There was no utility in the corn law; it alienated the affections of other countries from England; they thought her a proud and monopolising nation; it starved the poor of England; it profited only the pampered few. The *Times* was beginning to say, that the sliding scale was a corrupt system. As to Ireland, that oppressed country, with high rents, heavy taxes, and tithe to pay, it was said if the corn laws were to be repealed, then rents would fall, and distress would come upon the country. No; he would say not upon the people, but upon a few landlords, there might be some reduction of income. The rents must come down. (Hear.) In Ireland the daughters and sons of the farm tenant did the agricultural labour, instead of hired labourers as in England, with no wages but their humble fare; and, but for this, these high rents could not be paid. There was poverty in every valley; the people were so naked and miserable, that perhaps one fourth staid at home, though taught their duty by the church to attend divine worship, because of their rags.

The CHAIRMAN said, with so many persons to address the meeting, something must be done to keep each speaker within a limited time. Some thought that the persons whose names were called were desirous to speak; that was not so; they were requested by the committee, or recommended by some friend, while others were charged from home to deliver a message for their people, and would be ashamed to return without delivering it. In future, no speaker would speak more than ten minutes. He hoped that none would use vituperative language against any man: our desire was to do good to all.

The Rev. G. Harris, Independent minister, of Ringwood, Hants, came by the wish of Mr. Cobden, to make a few statements as to the condition of the poor in his neighbourhood. It was remarkable that, during conference, not a single communication or statement had been made as to the state of the people in the great corn-growing counties of Norfolk, Essex, Sussex, Kent, Surrey, Dorset, and Hants. He thought it might be shown, that the agricultural labourers in some of these counties were suffering greatly. The other side of Southampton, the labourers did not work 12 hours a day, and got wood and turf cheap from the New Forest. A few of the farmers allowed their labourers to purchase wheat at 6d. per bushel less than the market price. Potatoes they were allowed to grow in the farmer's fields at 4d. per rood. One clergyman told him, that the farm men who took care of the horses got 9s. a week. The average amount of wages was not more than 7s.; the common wages were 8s.; but, as there was little work in winter, 7s. would be the average of the year. Deducting £3. 10s. for rent of their cottage and garden, this would leave £18. 10s. or six shillings a week to the labourer; and, if six persons in family, that was not quite 2d. per head. These were the wages throughout the whole agricultural district in which he lived. He would ask the chairman, what provision will be made for the use of any communications that might be sent hereafter from the country?

The Rev. William M'Kerrow said, that many had been received from agricultural districts, of which a digest should be made.

The Chairman said, gentlemen were about to speak from those very districts, and he would call upon the Rev. Mr. Good, of Gosport, Hants.

The Rev. John Everett Good, of Gosport, spoke as follows:—Before I enter upon the general question, I beg, Mr. Chairman, to state in reply to my friend Mr. Harris, that there was given yesterday to this meeting a brief report of the state of the poor in the district from which I come; and I regret to say, that their condition is very deplorable, partly from the want of employment, and partly, and more especially, from the high price of provisions. I beg to offer my congratulations to the meeting in seeing you, sir, occupy the chair on this occasion. If there be one gentleman more than another to whom the success of the anti-bread tax movement is indebted, you, sir, are that gentleman. If the auspicious day should ever arrive when you occupy the episcopal see of his Lordship of Exeter, or any other on which you would shed lustre and confer dignity, I shall regard the elevation as your desert. I have been anxious to say a few words on this occasion, that I may discharge the duty I owe to my constituents. I have to state the sympathy of a gallant admiral, the brother of the Earl of Radnor, (who, like the noble earl now on the platform, is distinguished by his zeal in this great cause.) with the object of this convention, and to express his belief that it cannot fail to do good. Of this gentleman it is only right to say, and I will say this only, that a more noble-minded man, or a warmer friend of the Anti-Bread-Tax Society does not exist. I may say also, that that most excellent man, Sir G. T. Staunton, Bart. M.P. for Portsmouth, the faithful friend of the late Dr. Morrison, of China, cordially sympathises with the measures of free trade, and hopes that great good will result from this meeting. I am also authorised to state that the Catholic priest and Wesleyan minister of my town, are entirely concurrent with your great purposes. One gentleman, a farmer, has furnished me with a scale, showing the different prices of wheat between

Berlin and this country for the last fifty years. This gentleman, who was a *rara avis in terris*, has expressed his willingness to make any sacrifice for the destruction of the corn laws. We have been honoured with the condemnation of an opposing press, and charged with becoming meddling politicians. I regard the charge with the most perfect indifference, and take it for what it is worth. It cannot be of much consequence what that scribe may say who will justify the interference of the church, so as to determine the character of the last elections, and yet to condemn ministers of religion for meeting calmly to discuss the sufferings of the poor in connexion with high prices of food. (Hear, hear.) But how stands the case. I turn to the patriarchal age, and the first great promise of mercy after the deluge, was that seed time and harvest should continue to the end of the world. I look to the Levitical dispensation, and there I find that the corners of the field of corn were to be left for the poor. If a sheaf were to be overlooked by the proprietor, it was to be left for the poor. When Nehemiah the reformer read the book of the law, it was to be followed by a feast to the people, and portions were to be sent to those for whom nothing was prepared. The first question for discussion in the primitive church, was the distinction between preaching the gospel and serving the tables of the poor. The highest commendation bestowed on the apostolic churches was their forwardness to minister to the wants of the poor, especially poor saints. This was the cause of the apostles, and they are the true successors of these holy men who tread in their steps of benevolence and charity. Believing, as I do, that the corn laws are amongst the most prolific causes of the distress of the poor, I am decidedly opposed to their existence. I believe they are at entire variance with the spirit of the gospel. I am happy that this meeting has avoided allusion to party politics, as much so, perhaps, as it was in human nature to do. I hope the cause will now progress without interruption. We must take care that it does not settle down on the cushion of slumber, as many others have done which once promised great things to the world. Let us be firm, cordial, temperate, and persevering, and we shall be among the greatest benefactors of the land. This is the first time of our meeting, it must not be the last. We this day put our hands to a cause which we dare not abandon till we triumph, and then we shall see our favoured country great glorious, and free. (Applause.)

During Mr. Good's speech, Thomas Gisborne, Esq., M.P., entered the room, and was invited upon the platform.

The Rev. Mr. Malden, of Chichester, Sussex, was not ashamed, to avow himself a political dissenter; he considered this was a politico-religious meeting on a politico-religious question. He had been in Chichester 15 years; he had been sent by his people who had paid his expenses, and he came with the good-will of the citizens generally, and the Wesleyan minister there said, he too should like to go, but he could not. The mechanics of Chichester, if they had constant employment, would be satisfied with their wages; but they were without work during four months every year, and suffered much, being above seeking parochial pay. The labourers' wages were 2s. or 2s. 6d. a day; but they were out of work five or six months of the year, and were supported by the parish and private charity. The most respectable agricultural labourers around Chichester and in Western Sussex, were two thirds of them in constant employment, getting from 11s. to 12s. a week, but notwithstanding this, they were much distressed in consequence of the high price of corn; for although their wages had been raised one sixth, they had to pay more than double for their bread! (Hear.) Since the poor law they had lost their "bread money," an allowance in proportion to the number of children. The labourer could not buy meat or bacon, and lived much on bread and potatoes. The wages must be regarded as charity wages; for no agricultural labourer could make a bargain with his employer; and in harvest the labourer did not know what he should get till his work was done. [The speaker, referring to the new poor law, cries of "Question" interrupted him, and the chairman decided that he was out of order.]

The Rev. M. A. Garvey, of London, said, many facts have been laid before the conference demonstrating the frightful effects of the corn laws on the comfort and health of the manufacturing population. Permit me to direct your attention to the equally ruinous consequences they have had on the agricultural people. Ireland is principally an agricultural country, but have the corn laws protected the happiness of her children? Far from it. I tell you, rev. fathers and brethren, that those pictures of British wretchedness which have been laid before you are comfort itself compared with the misery of Ireland. (Hear.) A friend of mine, on going into one of the hovels of Ireland, observed a pig in the principal living room, and on asking why it was permitted, received the reply, "Arrah! an' sure who has a better right to it? isn't it himself that pays the rint?" (Laughter.) And so it is. The wretched cottier of Ireland is obliged to sell his pig, his corn, his everything, in order to retain a few potatoes for his miserable subsistence. Many more facts might be laid before you, but you yourselves present the most striking, the most emphatic and conclusive evidence of the iniquity of the corn laws. What strange and powerful impulse is it which has collected you together from the most distant parts of the empire, and drawn you from the retirement and tranquillity of your usual avocations? It must be something singular, for the present convocation is unique in ecclesiastical history. Our enemies say we are interested parties, that we fear for our own livelihood. This cannot apply to the great majority, who have been deputed by their people. But though it could be said of all, is not the objection a two-edged sword, that cuts both ways, showing at the same time our selfishness and the oppression we suffer from those unmerciful laws? I am anxious, however, that the Conference should tell the noble earl and the hon. member on the platform, that they should tell the country and the senate, that it is our boast and glory that we dwell in the affections of our people, (Applause,) that upon the affectionate relationship subsisting between us and our people depend much of the comfort of our lives and the usefulness of our labours, (Applause,) that they surround us with a barrier of kindly and tender feeling, and that in seasons of adversity they will suffer to extremity before they will allow that adversity to touch their minister. If, therefore, according to our enemies, we feel the effects of these laws, how constant and urgent must have been the sufferings of our people from the same cause when the tide has at length overflown that barrier, and driven us together in alarm to consult for our personal safety? The corn laws are called protective laws. Whom do they protect? Who are the belligerents? Are they two parties of unequal power, so that one requires to be protected from the grasping ambition of the other? Does the party requiring protection fear that the other will take away its natural and inherent rights, and leave it forlorn and destitute? No; it is the powerful and mighty, the rich and haughty that require protection from the weak, and humble, and wretched. Those, whose eyes stand out with fatness, who have more than heart can wish, require protection from those who are perishing with hunger. They fear lest their luxuries and superfluities should be taken away and turned into bread for the perishing and destitute; and because they thus fear they enact laws which aggravate the primary curse, and declare that man shall not eat bread even in the sweat of his face. (Applause.) I am glad to find that an adjournment of the conference to London has been suggested, without this, your proceedings, though not nugatory, will have a smaller effect than they would if the powers that be should see you prepared to take another step in that course of which this is the initial. (Applause.) We have the people with us, we have a large portion of the senate with us, and, from the significant intimation given to the country by the recent appointment in the chapel royal, we may safely infer that our cause is looked upon with favour in high quarters. (Applause.) We have every thing, therefore, to encourage us, and nothing to fear. Let us go forward in the strength of the Lord, and not cease our exertions till our benevolent and Christian object be fully accomplished. (Applause.)

Mr. M'Kerrow said there had been no motion as to the adjournment to London. It was a subject which required serious and calm deliberation in committee.

The Rev. George Armstrong, of Bristol, said, that having been desirous of introducing a proposition to the notice of the meeting, which the committee had thought it inexpedient to embrace,—he now rose, although without any specific object, to express in a few words the gratifying impressions he had derived from his attendance on this great and instructive meeting. With respect to the question of the corn laws, after the discussion it had had, there was in truth nothing to add. It had occurred to him that, in a certain sense, this meeting had converted them all into tillers of the soil; for clear it was, that they had effectually winnowed the subject of every fallacy, and from the determination evinced, no less clear it was, that having put their hands to the plough, they would never look back, until, by the blessing of the Most High, they had finished their work, and carried it to that victory, which none more gladly than Victoria herself—auspicious name—would sanction and secure for her suffering people. He regretted that more of the denomination to which he belonged, had not responded to the call which had been made to them. Had they done so, their impressions would have been not less happy than his own. They could not but have admired the eloquence, they could not but have loved the philanthropy, they could not but have acknowledged the accurate and extensive acquaintance with the subject, which had been exhibited, and not least, would have been honoured with the demonstrations of sympathy which had been afforded by the presence and aid of a nobleman, high in rank; but higher still in the virtue and patriotism by which he was actuated. One word more he could not forbear from adding. Their Rev. Chairman, on the first morning of their meeting, had read to them some passages from the authorised prayers of the established church, in order to prove how much in accordance with the principles they advocated were the sentiments and desires expressed in those prayers. He had himself been a minister of that church; but though it had been his fortune subsequently to dissent from her doctrines, he could not but retain a reverence and affection for many portions of the Book of Common Prayer, from which he would now read but two short extracts, and then, with thanks for the kindness of the meeting, resume his seat, and give place to others. And now there remained a petition to be added, in which he could not but anticipate the affectionate concurrence of every heart present. It was in behalf of one whose name was allied with every thought of dearest interest to them as men and citizens,—of her whose political travail had already commenced, and whose anxieties of a different nature were so soon to ensue:—

"Almighty God, the fountain of all goodness, we humbly beseech thee to bless our gracious Queen, Victoria. Endue her with thy holy spirit; enrich her with thy heavenly grace; prosper her with all happiness, and bring her to thine everlasting kingdom, through Jesus Christ, our Lord."

Mr. Massie announced that there were a few resolutions as matters of detail and arrangement,—one concerned the magistracy by whose liberal kindness we had been permitted to assemble in this magnificent and commodious hall, and another the domestic hospitality which the ministers have received while attending the conference; one regarded the subsequent proceedings of ministers who had attended conference, which the committee would suggest as expedient to be adopted, and another had reference to the Manchester ministers who had convened this conference; the last, and most important, he believed, regarded the Council of the Anti-Corn-Law League, who had so efficiently aided our movements, co-operating whenever it was necessary, with a liberality which never said "No" to any thing of expense relating to this conference, and were about to present an address to the conference, in company with Mr. George Thompson.

The Rev. W. Giles, Baptist minister, of Liverpool, rose, amidst cheers and cries of "Spoke." He said he had waited anxiously expecting that some of the delegates from the second sea-port in the world, containing a population of about 300,000 souls, would have spoken to the question; but, as this had not been done, he begged to be heard, especially as he had been limited to five minutes yesterday, and had some important fact to communicate, both in respect to Stockport and Liverpool. He had just been informed, that in the former place nine hundred hands had been thrown out of work from Messrs. Kerr and Co.'s, and that by next week eleven hundred would share a similar fate from the firm of Messrs. Lane and Co.'s. which, at an average of three persons to a family, would leave six thousand individuals destitute of the means of subsistence,—a startling fact. In Liverpool it was computed that sixty thousand of the inhabitants were doomed to drag out their existence in cold, damp cellars; and freights brought only about one-half the remuneration to the ship-owner that they did three or four years ago. It was, moreover, the easiest thing possible to show, that the corn law was anti-philanthropic, anti-patriotic, and anti-Christian. (Hear.) Anti-philanthropic, because it robs, at the rate of several millions per annum, by far the most numerous, by far the most taxed, and ten thousand times the poorest part of the nation, to enrich those who, at the very enactment of this iniquitous impost, were rolling in luxury. (Hear.) Anti-patriotic, because it endangers the peace of the nation and the safety of the British constitution. (Hear.) Did we wish our patriotic Queen to reign? Yes! Did we desire that her throne may be adorned with the olive branch of peace and the horn of plenty? Yes! Then that throne must rest upon the basis of inviolable justice to *all*. He, for one, joined heartily in the national wish, that Britannia might *rule* supreme amongst the nations; but, he said, let her rule in equity and righteousness, like the God who rules the universe. (Cheers.) That the corn law was anti-Christian had again and again been shown, by its direct opposition to the spirit and testimony of God's most holy word. He had perceived, with grief, that the details which this great conference had educed served to prove the accuracy of a statement made to him some time ago, by Mr. Chas. Dickens, the distinguished Boz, whom he was proud to name as an old pupil. While speaking to him of his graphic description of a poorhouse, in one of his most talented productions, Oliver Twist, he said, "Charles, the world says you must have spent your life in a poorhouse, to have described it so strikingly." Mr. Dickens smiled, and replied, "I never entered what is called a poorhouse in my life; but the whole nation is a poorhouse, and you need not go far from your own doors to see faithful illustrations of what I have written." (Hear, hear.) As the time assigned him had now just expired, he would conclude with a new version of a stanza in the National Anthem, the spirit and prayer of which he hoped both his brethren and himself would take with them:—

O Lord, our God, arise,
Destroy monopolies,
And corn laws sore:
Confound such politics,
Frustrate all knavish tricks,
On thee our hopes we fix:
God save the poor!

The Rev. JOSEPH SEDGWICK, Baptist minister, of Brighton, said, he was sent here by the poor of a people that felt deep distress; and, in consequence of the fear of God, and on the principles of humanity alone, did they send him here. And his earnest hope was, that he should go home praying, not only for the destruction of monopoly, but of covetousness also of every kind.

The Rev J. W. MASSIE then moved, and the Rev. W. M'KERROW seconded a motion, that Mr. Thomas Gisborne should be requested to address the conference.

A momentary misapprehension occasioned here some interruption, which ceased after the cause was explained.

Mr. GISBORNE then came forward, and said, I beg to assure you that I did not come into this room with the slightest idea that I should be called upon to address this meeting. I do not stand now before you with any wish to address you, if disagreeable to any portion of the meeting. (Applause. "Go on.") It has happened to me both to hear and to read in print many calumnious statements with respect to the objects of this meeting. (Hear.) I have heard their very right, their object, and the motives that suggested this meeting very much calumniated, and when I did so, I said, I have entertained so different an opinion on all these points, that at least I will do myself the pleasure of going amongst these gentlemen and judging for myself. It is true that we are here all agitators together, and our agitation has been denounced in very high places, at least by those who we expect will be in very high places speedily,—for I have heard men who are expected to be high in office in a very short time, state that it was inexcusable to excite the people on the subject of their food. Dry bread, then, is so exciting a subject to the British people, that it must not be mentioned amongst you. (Applause.) You must not even suggest to the people of England, that any course of legislation can take place under which they should have a sufficient supply of dry bread. I dare say you may tell the working people about such things as stamps and conveyances on real property; but to suggest to them that under any system of legislation they and their families should have a sufficiency of bread for their support,—those who venture to do so,—this Conference and the Anti-Corn-Law League, are denounced altogether as unprincipled agitators, because they bring this subject before the British public. One reason why I approve of this conference is this, when we see ministers of the Christian religion of all denominations called together, coming together, sent by their people, coming willingly no doubt, but sent and their expenses paid by their people, to agitate such a subject as this, we have a great security that it will be agitated in a manner not unworthy of that profession which they adorn, and who, instead of bringing danger, would bring security into the agitation of this subject. We are told that these corn laws are for the protection of the landed interest, and on that point I have a personal quarrel with these laws, because they don't protect me. I am a large farmer; I occupy 500 acres of land at the present time. These corn laws are made in order to enable the farmers in Lincolnshire and in Essex to grow corn for the supply of the British people. A price of between 60s. and 70s. is necessary for that purpose; but I cannot grow corn at 60s. or 70s. If I were to attempt to do that in North Derbyshire, I should be ruined. Now I want to know why, if the principle of protection is good for the farmer in Lincolnshire and Essex, why am I not to be protected also? (Hear;) why should they raise the farmers of Lincolnshire and Essex just up to the thawing point, and leave me below zero? (Hear.) That very thing proves that the principle is just good for nothing; for it is not applicable even to all the agriculturists of this country. Suppose you try to apply the principle of protection to trade and manufactures; and then I want to know why, many years ago, the old women who, by dint of great labour and saliva, spun twist, were not protected against the spinning jennies. Why did you not say to them, "Never mind; let foreigners adopt these new-fangled things if they please; we will secure to you that best of all markets, the home market. None of these stuffs spun in this new way shall come in to interfere with you. We will protect British industry; you shall spin by the distaff as before, and shall have the command of the home market." (Laughter.) What state would our manufactures have been in now, if such had been the protection to them? Let me tell you, as a British farmer, that agriculture, if not quite in that state, is verging towards the same state, on account of this protection. It is said, that the corn laws are for the protection of agriculture; I tell you that these corn laws are for the destruction of good agriculture. Their object is to give the *maximum* of rent and of produce, with the least possible production; (Hear, hear;) it is to enable people to farm badly, in order to keep up and maintain that most cherished of all the fancies of British landowners, to have their tenants thoroughly dependant upon them, by never granting leases. (Immense applause.) British agriculture would flourish, ay, and Britons would be able to grow corn, in competition with any other kingdom in the world, if it had a fair chance, if it were not for this protection. Why does no man think of embarking any considerable capital, and very few any considerable degree of skill, education, or enterprise whatever, in agriculture? We all know, that in all the midland counties, at least, (there are some counties, certainly, where they grant leases,) almost anything is enough to set a man up in a farm. A discarded gentleman's servant, or any man, who has saved a hundred pounds, without knowing anything at all about the business, if he can buy two or three cows, can set up a farm. (Hear.) That is the reason of the miserable state in which agriculture exists, throughout a great part of this country. If they were obliged to enter into competition with all the world, they would be enabled to do it just as our manufacturers have done. Why should not the same skill and advantages apply in agriculture as in manufactures? (Hear.) It would be exactly the same in both; but you make laws against good agriculture, against good occupation of the land in this country, which discourage any man from embarking his skill and capital in agriculture; for what man in his senses would embark a large capital or much skill in agriculture, while this *vexata questio* of the corn laws is hanging over it? So that, instead of being a farmers' question, it is merely a question which keeps the farmers in a state of dependance. (Hear, hear.) I am quite aware that there must be a struggle while the thing is getting to its natural bearings; but afterwards we shall all do well. The question of the corn laws cannot regulate profits; that will regulate itself; it will bear proportion to the same skill and capital applied in other lines of business; but the farmer then, taking a farm under such circumstances, would feel that he was treading on secure ground; men would educate their children to be farmers, as has been done in manufactures; men of capital would embark largely in farming; and British agriculture would be able to compete with the world; at least, from long experience in farming, these are my opinions on the subject. (Applause.) There is only one other point upon which I will say a word. You have heard much of how necessary it is that we should be independent of other nations for our food. Does not every one of us—does not every one in the higher and middle classes, every one above the poorest class—when he sits down to breakfast, call three quarters of the world to his assistance? Does he not call upon Asia for his tea, on America for his sugar, and on Africa for the labourers to grow it for him? (Hear.) Then before we apply this rule of independence of foreign nations to the lower classes, we should give them an option; we should say to them, "*We* don't take a meal for which we are not more or less dependent on foreign nations; and we give you your choice, whether you will be dependent like us, or independent." (Hear, hear.) Suppose a man of the lower classes comes to a legislator, and says, "Now, there is no corn in England; at least if there is, it is so dear that, with my means, I cannot acquire it; let me go to Hamburg, where it is much cheaper, there to buy some for myself and my family." The legislator says, "Oh, no; you must be independent of foreigners; take, my word for it, independence and an empty belly is the thing for you. (Laughter.) We don't practise it, but it is the only thing for you." I say the legislator is not the man to choose on that subject. We ought to have a parliament elected by universal suffrage, just to set at rest this question; for everybody who has a mouth ought to have a voice upon it. (Hear.) Universal suffrage may be a very bad thing in general, but I think it would be a very right way in settling this question; for, without aiming at a pun (though I think a pun is not a bad thing in its way) universal suffrage is a much better thing than universal suffering, (Hear,) and it is a better thing, also, than a general insurrection, (Hear,) and we may have our choice to take between the two. ("Hear," and applause.) In conclusion, thanking them for the reception they had given him, Mr. Gisborne said, I shall derive this gratification at least, that, in consequence, perhaps, of the few words I have addressed to you, I may be known to have cast my lot in amongst you, and to have given my approbation, both to the object and the means which you have adopted for carrying it out; and I wish most sincerely that the result may be commensurate both with the energy and ability, and also with the honesty and praiseworthiness of the motives which have called you together. (Great applause.)

The CHAIRMAN said, the meeting would see that they were only doing their duty in hearing the opinions of Mr. Gisborne, a landed proprietor. However, he should wish them to be unanimous, and therefore he called on the gentleman who made the objection, and who wished to say a few words in explanation.

Mr. MALDEN said, he had not intended to oppose Mr. Gisborne being heard; he was glad that they had heard Mr. Gisborne; but he thought they were hardly acting fairly in putting him down, from West Sussex, when speaking, as he had thought, to the question, and hearing one who was not of the conference. He was anxious to preserve their convention from any appearance of being too much tinged with whiggery.

The Rev. WALTER SCOTT, President of Airedale College, near Bradford, said—I have been called, altogether unexpectedly, to address this large and highly respectable meeting. I had prepared a few facts to state to the conference, and sent in my name yesterday to the chairman as one who wished to speak; but I was obliged to leave before my turn came; in consequence of which, I left a statement of some of those facts with a minister from Bradford, by whom, I presume, they have been presented to you. I am glad, however, of this opportunity of saying a few words, because I may be considered as the representative, not only of my own congregation, but also as one of the representatives of the anti-corn-law association at Bradford, who highly approved of this meeting, and have signified their approbation, by letter, to all the ministers of the town who intended to be present at the conference. I believe, also, that the students of Airedale College, had they been at home, would have sent me as their delegate. (Hear, hear.) I must own that when I heard of this meeting I hesitated, for a time, whether or not to send my name, as approving of its nature and object, to those by whom it was called. It was so novel; it might be viewed in so many lights, was capable of so many constructions; it was sure to give offence in certain quarters, and would certainly be very much misrepresented. I did not, however, hesitate long; and, I must own, I should now have been very sorry if my humble name had not been found in the list of its members, and associated with the many much more respectable and influential names that it will record. (Cheers.) There are some denominations of Christians who glory in providing "the poor man's church." I do not say this sarcastically or invidiously. In proportion as they do so, they are worthy of praise; and they so far subserve the purpose for which the gospel was appointed to be preached; but, whatever claim they may have to this honour, the Bible is much better entitled to the epithet of "the poor man's book;" for amongst the many peculiar characteristic properties by which it is distinguished from every other book in the world, and exalted infinitely above them, the following is one:—the great importance which it attaches to the condition, to the sufferings and enjoyments of the poor, and to the treatment which they receive from the community to which they belong. With how much eloquence does it plead their cause! How valuable the promises which it makes to those who pity and relieve them! How terrible the threatenings which it denounces against their oppressors! It is not too much to say that, by its representations, God throws the whole weight of his authority and character into the scale of the poor man's rights and claims: yes, for he assures us that those "who oppress the poor, reproach their Maker;" that "those who give to the poor, lend to the Lord," &c. (Applause.) I could detail many heart-rending facts respecting the poor at Bradford. The following is only a specimen. A short time since, I went, by chance, or rather providentially, into a cellar about perhaps ten or twelve feet square, almost destitute of everything that deserved the name of furniture, the only home (no other rooms or chambers belonging to it) of a family of five (if not six) individuals,—a father, and mother, and three children,—all dependent, at that time, on the earnings of one child, a daughter, of about fourteen years old. She had just come home to dinner. I saw no signs of provision made for her. I thought that she looked very grave and dejected; and I found, on inquiry, that there was literally no dinner for her, and that she must have returned to the mill as she came. Another day when I called, I found that the family had nothing on which to dine but a few potatoes which had been sent to them by a charitable individual. I could relate many facts of a similar nature. At Bradford, many of the combers are in almost as wretched a state as the hand-loom weavers; and many even of the carpenters and masons find it difficult to obtain work. It is easy to prove, it has often been demonstrated, that this is owing to the operation of the abominable corn laws. But this is not merely a poor man's question. (Hear.) These laws affect very injuriously, and that in many ways, the more wealthy classes; and the skill, and thought, and capital, and enterprise of their employers, are as necessary to secure the welfare of the poor as are their own labour and industry,—a fact, I am sorry to say, of which many of the poor are not sufficiently sensible. I have to move—

"That this conference, without wishing to exercise any authority that its constitution does not give, or to prescribe any course to be pursued by its members after its dissolution, must believe that considerable efficiency may be given to its proceedings, if those of whom it is composed will, in their different localities, avail themselves of the press to promote its object, and induce their congregations to send petitions to both houses of parliament."

It is with great propriety that this conference disdains all authority and presumption; but I trust that it will exercise something much better and mightier than mere authority,—the moral influence of knowledge, and argument, and truth, and justice, before which no bad law can stand (Applause.) I have great pleasure in presenting the resolution to the approval of the meeting.

The Rev. H. SOLLY, Unitarian minister of Yeovil, on rising to second the resolution, said that, whilst many meetings were of merely temporary interest, the results of that meeting would reach through eternity; and though he individually would not monopolize much of their time, he trusted the proceedings would not be hurried. Whilst some gentlemen present had come from manufacturing, and others from agricultural districts, he (Mr. Solly) came from a population which combined the miseries of both. The people whom he represented said, "We are miserable, we are starving, we are crushed, we cannot speak for ourselves—speak for us;" and he, in reply, had declared that, by the blessing of God, he would speak. The higher-minded amongst the manufacturing population of the district whence he came, felt that the physical evils of their condition, sad though they were, were not the worst to which they were subjected. They had within them immortal spirits, which were cramped and blighted by excessive toil and privation. They were degraded, and they knew it. But there was another class, from whom, though they spoke not to him as these had, there came a voice still more mournful,—the voice of *unconscious* degradation and sin. There was one evil resulting from the scanty employment and remuneration of the working classes, in his neighbourhood, to which he could not help alluding. The absolute dependance of the male workmen on their employers was bad enough, but its effects were too often of a more deplorable nature with regard to the females. He need not dwell on this point; but he would ask, should their sympathies have been roused in behalf of female purity in the slave states of America, and would they refuse to interpose in behalf of the victims of oppression at home? (Hear, hear.) But to turn to the rural population. He could in a few words give them a picture of destitution and wretchedness seldom surpassed. (The rev. gentleman here referred to some statements, furnished him by the surgeon of Ilchester gaol, in reference to the increase of crime consequent on extreme poverty. After detailing these cases) "Good heavens!" (exclaimed Mr. Solly) can it be that such enormities as these are occurring daily before our eyes, eighteen hundred years after the promulgation of the gospel of mercy and love! Surely it is time an end should be put to such a state of things!" (Applause.) It had been said, in reference to the oppressive system they were then assembled to check, that, admitting the corn laws ought to be repealed, the landlords were entitled to compensation, on the same ground as the West India proprietors. He must say that he thought this a most unfortunate position to take, inasmuch as it appeared to him neither the one nor the other had a rightful claim to compensation. He was at a loss to understand how men could dare to ask compensation for the loss of property made valuable by a systematic infraction of the eternal laws of justice and of right. (Whilst arguing this point, the chairman having intimated to Mr. Solly that his time was expiring, he said:) He must conclude, then, by delivering to the conference the message with which he had been entrusted. The people who sent him were anxious to express their deep conviction, that, whilst they regarded the corn laws as oppressive and unjust, no remedy for the wide spread and increasing sufferings of the country could be effectual, till that political system under which the corn laws had grown up and flourished, had undergone an entire renovation. They said, how could the manufacturing classes expect justice for themselves, while they refused it to those beneath them? The monopoly of food was bad, but the monopoly of legislation was worse; and upon no measure of half justice could the blessing of God be expected to rest.

"Hear it, ye senates, hear this truth sublime:
He who allows oppression shares the crime.

(Applause.) He begged to second the resolution, which he thought calculated to do much good, and then resumed his seat.

The Rev. Thomas Jones, Welsh Calvinistic Methodist, of Wrexham, said, they had heard a great deal about the agricultural and commercial, but nothing had been said about the mining interests. He came from a mining district, and was sorry to have to testify that it afforded no exception to the remark of a preceding speaker, that "England was all one poorhouse." It was the case with persons of little mind and small acquirements, that they might be restricted to a small sphere of action without injury; but larger and more cultivated minds must have a wider sphere, their energies must not be cramped; they would prey upon themselves. As it was with individuals, so it was with nations. It might do to restrict the lethargic Ottoman to his own boundaries, but not the active Briton. It might have been possible, a few centuries ago, to restrict the energies of British enterprise, but now that she has made, and is making, such immense strides in improvement, you must either stop the march of intellect, check the increase of knowledge, and stay the spirit of invention in Great Britain, or you must throw open the whole world for her operation, otherwise her energies will prey on themselves and on each other, as in fact they now do, and great will be the desolation. It might have been expected that the iron trade would have long flourished, from the impetus received by the increased use of machinery, and the rage for railways, &c.; it might have been thought that this trade would not so soon and so suddenly have partaken in the check to its expansion which arrested the onward course of our manufactures and exports, viz., our illiberal and exclusive and impolitic tariff. But so it is. Owing to the restrictive duties checking consumption, and the speculations in corn disordering the currency, great depression has succeeded the temporary (might have been, with better policy, permanent) activity in this trade, and the many furnaces which, a few years ago, were lighted all over the country, are now being blown out, one after the other; and, at each monthly or fortnightly settlement of wages, scores, and, in some instances, hundreds of workmen are discharged. In the neighbourhood of Wrexham there were now many hundreds out of work, who, with their families, must famish but for the charity of the humane and benevolent. They were continually begging at the doors in parties of from two or three to a dozen together. A few weeks ago about 700 colliers came in a body to solicit relief from the board of guardians at Wrexham. There was great alarm at the circumstance, and a party of soldiers was sent for. But the men were quite peaceable; many of them were intelligent Christian men, and teetotallers. They manifested not the least inclination to violence; all they wanted, they said, was WORK. The board of guardians could do nothing for them, but to receive as many as could be admitted to the workhouse. About 200 had tickets of admission; the rest returned home unrelieved. Many of these men have gone the round of the other mineral districts in the country to seek employment, and have returned home after a fruitless journey. Very great distress prevailed and it was the general impression amongst the sufferers that it was mainly owing to the corn laws. He (Mr. J.) thought that ministers of religion were very much in their places in agitating this question. It was a question of *justice*. The injustice implied in the unequal legislation and the oppression of the poor which characterised the corn laws brought a slur not only on the British nation, but also on that Christianity which was preeminently associated with the British name. It was a question of *charity*, and he hoped that, in addition to making this effort for obtaining legislative and permanent relief for the poor, that the various ministers would raise subscriptions amongst their congregations for the temporary relief of the more distressed districts. At any rate, let us all endeavour to carry home the feelings excited by this meeting. Let us remember that the success of this conference depends not only on its influence in the aggregate as a united body, but also on the exertion of the individual influence of each member in his own sphere. (Hear.) Let each consider himself pledged, firmly pledged, by his presence here, to set his face in earnest against the oppressive corn laws, and not to relax in his efforts until their downfall is accomplished, our commerce free, and the permanent prosperity and ascendancy of the British nation in a great measure secured. (Cheers.)

The Rev. T. SMITH, A.M., Theological Tutor of Rotherham College, moved,

"That the heartfelt thanks of this conference be returned to the gentlemen with whom it originated, and by whom its preliminary arrangements were executed.

He had, with many others, thought that the conference originated with their eloquent friend, Mr. Thompson; but he had since heard that he only lent his name, which was the common property of the church and the public; and that it took its rise from gentlemen whose names he did not know. He conceived that these men were highly honoured in having been permitted to conceive so great a design. In a most beautiful and eloquent parallel, drawn from the history of Columbus and the origin of Gibbon's work on the Roman empire, he eulogised the conception, and the man honoured in giving it birth. And he trusted, as had been said by Dr. Halley, that this would be the first ecclesiastical senate that had ever done any good.

The Rev. WILLIAM AULD, Scotch relief minister, of Greenock, in seconding the resolution, said, he was sent by the united voice of the elders of his church; and he had no doubt that, when he came to give his report to them, it would be highly satisfactory, and that congregational petitions would be sent. Their thanks were due to the gentlemen who had designed this conference; and he trusted that no exertions would be wanting on their part to give it effect.

The motion was then passed.

The Rev J. W. Massie said, perhaps it might be proper that the originators of that conference should acknowledge the compliment which had been paid them. Himself and his brother Mr. M'Kerrow had, in some measure the responsibility of the parentage; (Applause;) and they would defer making an attempt at a suitable acknowledgment until the afternoon.

The Chairman then adjourned the conference to half-past four o'clock.

AFTERNOON MEETING.—CLOSE OF THE CONFERENCE.

The body of the hall presented a novel appearance at the re-assembling of the conference this afternoon. The greater part of the seats previously set apart for members only, exhibited a large sprinkling of ladies and laymen. The hall in every part was densely crowded, though fewer ministers were present than at any former sitting.

At twenty minutes to five o'clock, the Rev. Thomas Spencer resumed the chair. He said, a few more gentlemen might address the meeting for five minutes each.

Mr. Brown, of Wareham, moved,

"That the most cordial thanks of this conference be given to the worshipful the mayor, and the boroughreeve of this borough, for the kindness with which they have granted the use of the Town Hall for its accommodation."

He was no "reverend," but a layman, invited in consequence of his exertions in the cause. He pitied those who from *sickly* considerations had remained at home, instead of attending this conference. Ministers were met to liberate the people from a torture worse than that of the thumb-screw; for the sliding scale was nothing more nor less than Satan's starvation screw. (Laughter.) He wanted to see the subject cleared of all the dust which monopolists threw in our eyes, and made so clear that any Sunday scholar of fourteen could understand it. It was no such profound question, whether they should not have the right to buy their bread where they could get it cheapest. (Hear.) God had willed longevity to be a blessing to the human race; but the corn laws cut down the finest specimens of humanity.

The Rev. James Gwyther, independent minister, of Hulme, seconded the motion, and congratulated the meeting that his brethren were actuated by principle rather than expediency; and, while some *bats* were waiting to see which was the right side to take, they had decided at once on the side of principle. (Applause.)

The Rev. A. Morton Brown, Poole, Dorset, rose and spoke nearly as follows: I feel great pleasure in rising to support this motion. We owe a deep debt of gratitude, as ministers, and as a Conference, to the worshipful the Mayor, and to the Boroughreeve of Manchester, in granting us the admirable accommodation throughout our meetings of this magnificent hall. I speak, Sir, I know, only the feelings and the gratitude of the ministers present, as well as of those who have left us, when I say this much. (Cheers.) But, Sir, as I am the only delegate from the county of Dorset who, throughout this Conference, had an opportunity of giving expression to the feelings, the opinions, and the wishes of the large majority of the people in that southern part, I hope you will excuse for occupying your attention for a few minutes. My speech will be a speech of facts (Hear.) Having lately been appointed by the County Association of Independent Ministers to visit all the Home Missionary stations in the eastern part of the county, I have had an enlarged opportunity of ascertaining the sentiments and of seeing the condition both of the farmers and labourers. (Hear, hear.) There is, Sir, a considerable tract of country, running throughout the southern part of Dorset, almost as sterile as the pure sand by our sea shores. On this district of country there are located a great number of small farmers. They pay for their poor and barren fields, I might say, an exorbitant rent. (Hear.) They can only pay this rent by rearing vegetables in their gardens, the only well-cultivated and fruitful parts of their petty farms, and by supplying with these the neighbouring and more distant markets. Here and there may be seen a thin field of wheat or barley, or considerable plots of potatoes, almost all of which are necessary to afford to the farmer and his family sufficient to keep themselves. The land is scarce worth the labour, (Hear,) and yet these men, till lately, were in favour of the existing corn law. (Hear.) But, Sir, I have reason to know that now, to a considerable extent, through the influence of the lectures delivered by the lecturers sent out by the National Anti-Corn-Law League, many of them have been converted to our ranks, and are shouting as loudly as we are for the abolition of the corn laws. (Cheers.) And what is the reasoning which has prevailed on this subject with these men? (Hear, hear.) Why, this. They say that if the trade and commerce of our country prospered, some of the branches of our families, now unable to be supported, or badly supported, by what is tortured out of our barren soil, would then be draughted into our towns and cities, find employment and an adequate return for their employment there; and those that remain behind would then have a comfortable subsistence and a happy home, instead of idleness, destitution, or the workhouse. (Cheers.) I conversed not long ago with one of these farmers. "I have three sons," said he. "My eldest son I can employ with myself, and can support by his cooperating with me in tilling my little ground. But what of my two other sons? I do not need them; my farm does not need them; and after I have paid my rent and rates, I cannot keep them. (Hear, hear.) But let trade and commerce thrive, and they can be engaged in some other part of our common country, find sufficient to engage them, and, instead of reducing all of us to poverty and distress, they can do themselves good, and help me. (Cheers.) Not so now." And these little farmers in many parts of our county are amongst the greatest sufferers of the whole community. (Hear, hear.) As for the labourers, I have read faithful descriptions of the Irish cabin, peopled with its too numerous but generous hearted inhabitants; I have seen the Highland hut, with its sturdy and brave-hearted inmates; but, Sir, never have I seen more destitute or more deplorable scenes than those we may daily witness in the clay-built cottages of some of the districts of Dorset. (Hear, hear.) Their wages, after careful inquiry, average not more throughout the year to support a wife and family, than between seven and eight shillings per week. (Hear, hear.) And what, Sir, is the state of the towns of Dorset? I hold in my hand a document sent me from a committee of respectable gentlemen from the town of Bridport, a town till within a few years the most flourishing and wealthy in the whole county. Let that document speak for itself.

The state of trade in Bridport is extremely depressed.

In many branches of the trade, there is not more than *half* the usual employment for the operatives.

Bridport is largely engaged in foreign commerce, a considerable portion of which is with the United States. The present corn laws seriously operate to prevent that exchange of commodities which would take place if a free trade in corn were established.

One important branch of the trade of the town is the weaving of sail-cloth. A free trade in corn, by increasing the shipping interest, would materially encourage its manufacture, and consequently give employment to a large number of operatives.

The rate of wages is entirely dependent upon the demand for labour, which is always diminished by the high price of the necessaries of life.

Wages in Bridport are lower at the present period than during the years 1835, 6, and 7, when employment was abundant, and food at its minimum price.

The wages of the agricultural labourers do not average more than 7s. 6d. per week.

One word and I have done, in reference to the town whence I come, the sea-port town of Poole. There live in it men, and men who have told me, that they have seen in its harbour 20 and 25 vessels at a time with foreign corn. Now, the ships of that port go to victual at Hamburgh. Its storehouses are shut up—many of its inhabitants are unemployed, and all but starving. There are now, it is said, between 200 and 250 houses shut up, and nowhere in the country are poor-rates more burdensome than in Poole. Property is depreciated, and scarcely worth preserving, which might soon be most valuable if we had only free trade. (Cheers.) I inhabit a house at this time which formerly would have brought an annual rent of £50 or £60 I rent it now for £25, and my rates and taxes for the last year were, for this same house, between £34 and £35. (Cheers; hear, hear.) I might have mentioned many similar cases had time permitted. (Cheers.)

The CHAIRMAN put the motion, which passed unanimously.

The Rev. J. N. GOULTY, Independent minister, of Brighton, moved,

"That the grateful acknowledgments of this conference be rendered to the friends and families in Manchester, for their generous and hospitable entertainment of the members of this conference, during the protracted and eventful proceedings for which it has been assembled."

On inquiring amongst several agricultural labourers in Sussex, he found that when they had paid for their rent, and bought flour on the Saturday they had not 1s. left for anything else; and some of them were almost in a state of vassalage, and, in their opinion, the sooner the corn laws were altered the better for them. The landowners too believed that, could their beautiful downs be restored to a state of pasture, instead of being turned up by the plough, it would be better for the country and for themselves. ("Hear," and applause.)

The Rev. ALEX. CAMPBELL, Independent minister, of Greenock, in seconding the motion, said he was the only minister of the congregationalists, in Scotland, who had taken part in the proceedings; and, moreover, he was the only one who represented the highlands of Scotland. (Hear.) It was well known that £8,000 was collected last year, in London, for the relief of the poor, which proved utterly inadequate. The manufacture of kelp had lately declined, and had thrown thousands out of employment. The agriculturists in the highlands had found it more profitable to convert the land into pasture, to supply the lowlands with animal food. People were thus thrown off the land, and the distress was generally attributed to the operation of the corn laws. He had great pleasure in seconding the resolution.

The CHAIRMAN, in putting it, said, he was certain every minister would do every justice to the hospitality of Manchester. The motion passed by acclamation, all the ministers rising in honour of their hosts.

The Rev. JAMES GRIFFIN, Independent minister, of Manchester, looked at the present as a case of extreme emergency, and because distress was extreme, and rapidly increasing, he thought it incumbent on ministers to do what they could to lessen this distress. He moved,

"That the Council of the National Anti-Corn-Law League be admitted to address the conference, according to their request.

The Rev. JOHN WISEMAN, Independent minister, of Wick, near Caithness, (and, as he said, within a few miles of the far-famed John o'Groats,) stated, that the occupations of the people there were wholly confined to farming and fishing, and the wages of agricultural labourers in Caithness were only 1s. a day, without food, and they had employment during only nine months in the year. A first-rate ploughman had only £7 a year, with potatoes and coarse meal; if he had a wife and family he was allowed a hut to live in; some of them had families, and how they fed them out of £7 a year was a mystery to him. (Hear.) The condition of the small farmers was miserable; their houses were mud huts. they reared black cattle, pigs, and poultry, but ate none of these themselves; (Hear;) they lived on barley bread and potatoes, and when the harvest was bad they were on the point of starvation. The first rate coopers in Caithness had only nine shillings a week wages. The fisheries might be prosecuted to any extent, if they could find a market. To Wick, in one week, was brought 150,000 barrels of herrings. Russia would take the fish if we would take their corn. (Hear.) In Russia a prohibitive duty was imposed upon British fish, by way of retaliation for our corn laws. (Hear.) If the corn laws worked well for any one in Caithness, it was only for the landlords; and, with only two exceptions, every landlord in Caithness was over head and ears in debt. (Hear.)

The motion passed unanimously, and with applause.

The deputation was then introduced by Mr. MASSIE. It consisted of the following gentlemen: – Sir Thomas Potter; Messrs. George Wilson, (chairman of the council,) Alderman Walker, Elkanah Armitage, Alderman Kershaw, Alderman Cobden, Thomas Bazley jun., William Rawson, Archibald Prentice, George Thompson, William Bickham, and James Howie.

The CHAIRMAN, addressing the deputation, said, this meeting of ministers and laymen, on this occasion, was one of the happiest unions of church and state. (Applause.) They only conspired together for the public good, not only for the benefit of the manufacturers, but for the general good of the labourers, and the agriculturists, and the landlords themselves. The conference served no political party in the state; they desired food and support for the labouring classes, without driving them to parochial relief or starvation. (Hear.) As the conference understood the Anti-Corn-Law League wished to address them, they would be most happy to receive the address. (Applause.)

Mr. COBDEN then read the address, which was as follows:—

"*To the Christian Ministers of all denominations in conference assembled, for the consideration of the laws restricting the food of the people, the Address of the Executive Council of the National Anti-Corn-Law League in Manchester.*

"Reverend Sirs,—We beg respectfully to tender you our earnest and grateful thanks for the zealous and truly Christian services which you have rendered to the cause of suffering humanity; and to express our acknowledgments for the sanction which your dignified proceedings have given to our past labours, and from which we shall derive increased encouragement and a new stimulus to our future efforts.

"The religious world will regard the acts of your conference as a noble illustration of the true spirit of a Christian ministry, whose benign influence can never be more consistently exerted than when vindicating the cause of the poor and destitute.

"We highly appreciate the minute and startling array of evidence brought by you from all parts of the empire, proving on such inforpeachable testimony the physical and moral degradation of great numbers of the people, as well in the agricultural as in the manufacturing counties. You have thus made it manifest that, during the long continuance of extreme scarcity and dearness of provisions consequent upon unwise and unjust legislation, the condition of the labouring classes has rapidly deteriorated, that the demand for labour has declined, that wages (notwithstanding the assertion of the monopolists to the contrary) have materially decreased, and that, from these causes, multitudes of our industrious fellow-countrymen have been cruelly and needlessly subjected to all the evils of misery, disease, and premature death.

"Sympathising with you in the still augmenting distress of our poorer brethren, and fortified by the facts with which your testimony has supplied us, we shall continue to advocate, and with renewed energy, the abolition of those impious laws, which, by limiting the food of the people, and restricting the demand for labour, have been the main source of the manifold ills now afflicting the community.

"Whilst giving expression to our grateful acknowledgments of the inestimable value of your present labours, permit us to beseech your continued efforts in furtherance of the righteous and philanthropic work in which, as Christian ministers, you have engaged.

"We would earnestly entreat you, in your respective spheres of usefulness, individually to use the influence of your sacred calling in awakening the public mind to the national importance of this great question.

"We rely on the moral weight of your example; we trust much to the efficacy of your pulpit exhortations; we feel that to your supplications at the throne of the Most High the poor and wretched may yet look with humble hope, and to the Christian confidence that justice, so long denied, will at last be rendered them; and resting with firm reliance on your patriotic efforts, we look forward with well grounded assurance to the early and triumphant issue of a struggle on which depends the happiness or misery of millions of our fellow-creatures, and the irretrievable ruin of our beloved country.

"By order of the Council,

"GEORGE WILSON, Chairman."

Having read the address of the Anti-Corn-Law League to the conference, Mr. Alderman COBDEN, M.P., addressed the conference as follows: It has been suggested that now is the time if any member of our deputation wishes to address the conference to do so. I have been requested merely to state, in the behalf of the Executive Council of the National Anti-Corn-Law League, one or two points. In the first place, I wish to impress upon you the principle on which we are leagued together. I may mention, that at not merely one of our meetings, but at every meeting, we have passed and confirmed that resolution in favour of the total and immediate repeal of the corn and provision laws. (Applause.) I may add my own conviction, that it is to the abstract truth of that principle that we owe our long existing union as a body, that we owe much of the success of our past efforts, and to which principle alone I feel assured we are indebted for this assembly of ministers, aided as they are by this assemblage of the fairest portion of creation, who would not have joined us here now in any thing which has not for its basis justice and truth. And now I may be allowed, from past experience, to offer a word of observation to the rev. gentlemen present. I would entreat them, on departing to their several localities, that they would take care to guard themselves against entertaining the question of the corn laws on any other ground than that of abstract right and justice; (Hear;)

that once settled, the morality of the question once vindicated, you may safely leave all the details and expedients necessary to carry out the principle to others, with the assurance, that what can be demonstrated to be morally right will never in the end prove to be politically wrong. I may warn you, gentlemen, that attempts will be made by those who well know the strength of this position, to draw you forth from that impregnable standing, and endeavour to engage you on ground less favourable to you, and more so to the enemy. You may have placed before you difficulties, ambiguities, mysteries with which you may not be prepared to grapple; it may be proposed to you to discuss this question with reference to other questions; you may be asked to discuss whether this question be of itself greater or more entitled to consideration than other questions. Let me warn you from taking up any such position; for, by so doing, by making this question to revolve round party politics or expediency, you will be engaged in an endless controversy, from which no possible good, so far as the interests of truth are concerned, can ever result. One other point I wish to state in vindication of the proceedings of the National Anti-Corn-Law League. At our first meeting, when we mustered a body of between 200 and 300 individuals, assembled from all parts of the kingdom, representing every large manufacturing interest in the kingdom, there was a resolution passed and recorded, that inasmuch as we claimed as an act of justice the removal of all restrictions on the importation of corn and provisions, we were bound at the same time to express our willingness and desire, that all laws for the protection, so called, of the manufacturing interest, should be at the same time abolished, and that all impediments between the free interchange of the commodities of this country for the protection of others should be entirely removed. This it was thought necessary to state, in order that we might appear before the legislature and the country with clean hands. And those, therefore, who argue that we have protection, the monopolists, who set up a right to protection for corn, because, as they assert, we are protected in our manufactures, are answered at once by our resolution, which has been passed and repassed at every successive meeting we have held, in which we have declared our willingness and anxiety for the removal of all these restrictions. And now it may be interesting just to hear what we have done in the way of petitioning since we began our movements in 1839. In 1839, petitions were presented, 436 in number, with 527,334 signatures, praying that the petitioners might be heard at the bar of the house to state their case. In 1840, petitions for the repeal of the corn and provision laws, 3,923 in number, with 1,459,545 signatures, were presented. In 1841, a session of parliament, which you are well aware was brought to a premature close, 6,169 petitions, with 1,756,645 signatures, were presented. (Applause.) This, however, is not the most gratifying view of the question of petitioning. I will now glance at the array of petitions which were presented from our opponents. In 1839, when no efforts had been made to enlighten and rouse the public mind on this question, 3,068 petitions, with 318,723 signatures were presented in favour of the corn laws. In 1840, after we had been a twelvemonth at work in agitating this question, though the number of petitions had increased to 3,376, yet the number of signatures had declined to 240,800. (Hear.) In 1841, notwithstanding the strenuous efforts of our opponents, the progress which had been made in public opinion, in the cause of justice and humanity, was still more manifest. In 1841, the number of petitions for the corn laws had decreased to 1,791, and the number of signatures amounted only to 113,800. (Hear.) The summary of these petitions is this. The total of signatures for petitions against the corn laws, for three years, 1839, 1840, and 1841, amounts to 3,743,524 · the total of the signatures *for* the corn laws is 672,910, leaving a majority in favour of repeal, of 3,070,614. (Applause.) I need do no more than point out these statistics, in answer to the assertions that will be made, consequent upon the late general election, that the people of England are in favour of dear bread and monopoly. (Hear.) One word upon a subject upon which we have been very considerably and systematically misrepresented. After we had been refused to be heard at the bar of the house of commons, for the purpose of stating what were the views, the objects, and the expectations of the parties who move in this question, our enemies took upon themselves to describe for us what were our motives, intentions, and prospects; and we are told now, forsooth, that the object of the Anti-Corn-Law League is to reduce wages. (Hear.) This is the assertion of Lord Stanley, made at his late election at Lancaster, in my own hearing; and this I see repeated in the leading article of the *Times* of yesterday, and it is in italics. I do not know whether I may be censured by some of the sterner political economists who surround me, if I were to say at once that the members of the Anti-Corn-Law League do not wish or expect to reduce wages, because they all know, though Lord Stanley does not, and the *Times* will not, that manufacturers have not the power to reduce wages, (Hear,) that the law which governs the rate of wages is as independent of the will of the master manufacturer, as are the tides of the sea themselves. I will state what is my own belief, and what is the belief of those gentlemen with whom I act. It is, that the repeal of the corn laws only can maintain wages; that by the repeal of the corn laws alone can wages be increased. I am sure that, if it were the object of the manufacturers of this country to reduce wages, past experience would tell them, that the most certain way of effecting their object would be, to maintain the present corn laws, under which wages have constantly and will continually decline. But, gentlemen, the Anti-Corn-Law League, at its various aggregate meetings, both in Manchester and London, have declared what their object is in seeking the repeal of the corn laws. They have declared, that their object is to possess the right they claim, as the natural right of mankind, to exchange the products of their industry for the corn and other provisions of foreign countries; and they know that the effect of this repeal would be to give a great augmentation to the present amount of our trade in this country; they know that besides the trade which we now have in coffee, cotton, tea, and the like, we should have an additional independent traffic in the article of corn; that that additional trade could only be carried on by raising and producing commodities for the exchange of these products; and they know that increased productions cannot go on without calling into activity an increased amount of labour, and therefore raising the wages of the manufacturing labourers. (Cheers.) We do not desire a reduction of wages: we are, I hope, sufficiently informed upon our own interests to know, that the best customers of all manufacturers are the labouring class. It has been well said by Burke, that we are all the pensioners of the labouring class; and we know, that in order to maintain a prosperous and flourishing trade at home, it is absolutely necessary that the great mass of the people should be well employed, at good remunerative wages. But this misrepresentation has been backed by another charge, that we only seek the repeal of the corn laws, in order that we may compete with foreigners in foreign markets. I told you the other day, and wish it to be emphatically borne in mind by every gentleman present, that we do now compete with other manufacturers all over the world in every thing we produce, in all our staple commodities. We do so, notwithstanding we have this enormous burden of monopoly-taxation; and we do so in spite of the burden of our immense state-taxation. And, if we do so now, will any one pretend for a moment that the labouring class, who now, by their great and, I will say, unequalled exertions, rival the labourers of other countries, that they will not be a great deal better able to rival them, if they had this tax on their bread removed, and be able to eat their daily meals at nearly the same cost as their Saxon and Swiss rivals? I have answered this assertion by the quotation I gave you from our own published declarations, that we have never said,—and no one can point to one syllable of any authorized document of the Anti-Corn-Law League—that we wish to repeal the corn laws in order that we may compete with foreigners. It is known,—though it may not be known to those who judge of us in ignorance,—that we do compete now; and we know that, so far from foreign competition ceasing, we must go on competing, inasmuch as three-fourths of the cotton that is brought into England is sent abroad again, to be sold in foreign markets. I am sorry to have trespassed so long; I need not proceed, but I shall conclude by calling your attention to the observations you heard from Mr. Curtis, of America, the other day. He told you, that the Americans will take any amount of your manufactures for any amount of their grain, cotton, and pork you are inclined to take. He tells you he does not want your goods cheaper than they are now sold. He tells you he does not want your wages to be reduced; he says that they are already low enough, and so I say. But he tells you, that, unless you take corn and provisions from the settlers in the western prairies of America, even if you sold the goods at half the price you do now, unless you would take their corn and provisions they cannot buy them at all. There is one other fallacy that Mr. Curtis answered, and I am glad he did so, from his individual experience. You will be told of this, the standing fallacy of the monopolists, that we want to import foreign corn in order to bring the wages down here to the level they are in Poland, and elsewhere on the continent. I told you, that wages here, for a given amount of labour, were as low as in any part of Europe, and that they must be estimated according to the amount of labour done. What should we say of the merchant who went into the market to buy a piece of calico, and one piece was offered him at 6s. and another at 12s., and he decided that the piece at 6s. was the cheaper, without looking to see whether one was better or worse than the other? And so it is with wages. I believe there is not a town on the continent, of any size, from Calais to Moscow, in which there are not a number of English artisans receiving higher money wages than they can get at home, or you would not find them going hundreds of miles from you. But when you are told that you would bring down the price of wages, because the price of wages falls with the price of corn, and, therefore, that by getting corn from Poland you would bring down wages here to the rate of wages in Poland; when you are told that, tell your hearers that you have seen an American gentleman from Ohio, one who has himself held the plough, and who has employed labouring men, and that he told you the daily wages there were 4s. 6d. for unskilled labourers; and therefore, if the importation of corn should bring to a level wages here with those of the countries where cheap corn is grown that you have the happy prospect before you of seeing your labourers here receive the wages of the American. (Cheers.) I have only to thank you, in the name of the Anti-Corn-Law League, for your favourable response to the sentiments of this address, and in their name, and in the name of the people of England, to thank this conference of ministers for having set a glorious example, an example that is without precedent; and I think they will have the blessings of unnumbered millions for their exertions. (Loud cheers.)

The Rev. T. Middleditch, Baptist minister of Ipswich, moved:

"That the address of the League, now read, be entered on the minutes."

He could bear testimony to the beneficial results of the labours of the Anti-Corn-Law League even in the agricultural districts. Their lecturers had gone through the country diffusing information on this important subject, and the fruit of their labours was seen at the last election at Ipswich. The people would not have been aroused to support a mere Whig or Tory; but when the candidates came forward and avowed themselves anti-monopolists, they rallied round them, and returned them by a triumphant majority. There was no adequate rise in the wages of the agricultural labourer when corn was dear, so that they were much worse off in dear than in cheap years. He rejoiced that he had been present at the conference, and he should go back with increased determination to use his efforts to obtain the repeal of the obnoxious laws, and to forward the righteous cause which brought them together.

The Rev. THOMAS STRUTHERS, Scotch Secession minister, Hamilton, in seconding the resolution, said, that there had long been an incalculable amount of distress amongst the poor in his neighbourhood. The ministers present could not withdraw from this cause without sacrificing their honour; they had passed the Rubicon, and "Onward!" must be their motto. (Applause.) Twenty-four years ago, he was associated with the late Rev. Rowland Hill, at an anniversary, in the neighbourhood of London; and, in the course of his sermon, that venerable man said, "This is the fourth time I have preached this week, and they will call me 'methodist,' and twenty *bad* names; but hard names break no bones." (Laughter.)

The motion was then passed unanimously.

The CHAIRMAN having called upon Mr. George Thompson to deliver his farewell address to the conference, that body being about to terminate its sittings,

Mr. GEORGE THOMPSON having been called upon to deliver a valedictory address to the conference, came forward amidst loud and long-continued cheering. He said, Mr. President, ministers of the conference, and ladies and gentlemen—In the whole course of my life, I never felt a stronger desire to acquit myself worthily than I do upon this interesting and solemn occasion. I have to address to you some remarks suited to the close of those important and all absorbing proceedings, in which you have now for four days been engaged. But I, unhappily, labour under a consciousness of inability equal to the intensity of my desire to perform the task assigned me in a creditable manner. One thought, however, affords me comfort; it is that no necessity is laid upon me to discuss any branch of the great question which has been brought under your consideration. The hour for argument and deliberation is past; and it is my duty to review the transactions in which you have been engaged, and to express my opinion of the probable influence which those transactions will exert upon the issue of the momentous struggle in which the friends of the poor are engaged with the powerful monopolists of the bounties of an all-wise and ever beneficent Creator. (Loud cheers.) Your assembly has been one unprecedented in its character and unexampled in its numbers. (Hear, hear.) But these are not the most gratifying characteristics of this conference. The sublime spectacle has, for the first time in the annals of the world, been presented of seven hundred ministers of religion of widely varying theological opinions assembling together, not only without discord, contention, and animosity, but with a degree of brotherly love and delicate courtesy and consideration, one towards another, deserving the highest admiration, and furnishing the demonstration, that, where the good of our common humanity is sought, men can merge the differences which divide them out of doors, in a generous and combined effort for the rescue of their suffering brethren. (Loud applause.) Your conference has been distinguished by catholicity without compromise; by a stern maintenance of the cardinal principles of Christian morality, without the slightest abatement of your attachment to those peculiarities by which, as sects and religious parties, you are known. (Cheers.) The talent that has been exhibited has been of a high order; convincing arguments, sound reasoning, affecting statement, pathetic appeal, and earnest exhortation, these have been the weapons you have resorted to, for the purpose of enlightening and confirming one another, and of dissipating any lingering prejudice or doubt in the mind of any undecided or hesitating member of your body. (Hear, hear.) The principles you have proclaimed have been of the loftiest and purest kind—your sentiments those of Christian charity and universal benevolence, and your measures, as far as any have been adopted, measures in perfect keeping with the character you sustain, both as ministers of Christ and loyal subjects of a patriot Queen. (Loud cheers.) I have marked with watchfulness and deep interest the responses that have been given to the speeches that have been delivered, and I have been gratified beyond measure to perceive, that just in proportion as the respective speakers have taken their stand upon the high ground of immutable justice—just in proportion as they have spurned all compromise with the dictates of a temporary and time-serving policy—just in proportion to the determination they have shown to carry out with inexorable resolution the great laws of nature and of God, given to regulate the intercourse of man with man throughout the world, they have been met with the deep-toned and assenting acclamations both of their brethren around them, and of those who have been permitted to be spectators of the business of this conference. (Cheers.) Sir, the numbers, the spirit, and the unanimity of this conference, will strike terror into the hearts of those, if such there be, who from selfish or malignant motives are standing in the way of a settlement of this question. They will look with dismay upon this extraordinary gathering, and will read in your determination the sentence upon their cherished monopoly of the bread of the poor. [Hear, hear.] Sir, I consider the holding of this conference to be one of the most seasonable and happy events that could possibly occur in the present trying crisis of our country's affairs. [Hear, hear.] The conduct of the cause in which you are now engaged, has hitherto been chiefly in the hands of men engaged altogether in secular affairs, or under the influence of cold and calculating political economists, who have little to do with the discussion or application of those great religions principles which lie at the foundation of public morality and national prosperity. Long and earnestly have the friends of the poor desired to see the religious feeling of the country enlisted in the cause to which you are now, I rejoice to know, irrevocably pledged. To bring about a consummation so devoutly to be wished, some five weeks ago it was resolved by a few humble individuals, without name, or influence, or note, to issue a circular calling upon ministers of religion of every denomination to assemble in this town, for the purpose of considering, in the fear of God, the subject of the laws restricting the supply of food to the community. I can bear witness, that that circular was penned with a trembling hand, and issued with a faltering heart. [Hear, hear.] Not only were no extraordinary means employed to give effect to the invitation, but, those usually resorted to, were, in this instance, almost wholly dispensed with. Yet, I will not say in obedience to that call, but rather say that, prompted by a feeling of humanity, inspired by the genius of the gospel, and touched with pity for the miseries of those around them, a noble army of seven hundred men—the soldiers of Christ—the preachers of righteousness—the friends of the poor and the perishing—have left their homes and the altars at which they minister, and have come up to the help of the Lord—to the help of the Lord against the mighty. [Hear, hear, and applause.] There have not been wanting those who, by anticipation, have poured contempt upon the noble effort. Predictions of failure, charges of incompetency, the imputation of low and sordid motives, have been plentiful. But your numbers, your demeanour, the spirit you have displayed, the wisdom you have brought to the task, the absence of every petty and party feeling by which all your doings have been characterised—these, have scattered the fears of the timid and the hopes of the wicked to the winds, and have given the friends of perishing humanity assurance, that the ministers of religion in Great Britain, from Caithness to Cornwall, and from Cape Clear to Holyhead, are men who can, when necessary, bury in one grave their polemical animosities and their partizan predilections, and, as brethren, unite to assert the rights of the poor and justify the ways of God toward the children of men. [Hear, hear, hear.] Oh, sir, when those who are now wretched and almost bereft of hope shall hear in their cells of poverty of this your glorious meeting, they will take courage, and look up, and believe that the day of their temporal deliverance draws nigh. [Hear, hear.] Gentlemen of the Anti-Corn-Law League, now present in this conference, I congratulate you from my inmost soul upon the position of that cause in which you have so long meritoriously struggled. Where is that cause now? In the sanctuary of the Most High. It has been bound in faith and prayer to the horns of the altar. It has been carried by the ministers of religion to the footstool of the throne of Him who is good to all and whose tender mercies are over all his works. [Hear, hear.] Divested of its secular complexion, your cause has been demonstrated to be the cause of justice, and men whose privilege and high prerogative it is to be the defenders of the law of the ever-living God are now the consecrated and self-devoted champions of the interests and rights of the poor. In the address to our beloved queen which has been adopted, in the petition to parliament, and in the appeal to the people of this country, the question has been placed upon the highest ground. You have given the opponents of cheap bread that to do which they will find it hard to accomplish. You have called upon them to show the accordance of their niggardly and starving system with the principles of immutable justice and that law which is above all other laws, by which man asserts the right to obtain by honest industry a share of the bounties of our common Father. (Cheers.) This is as it should be. This has given a complexion to the question more important than it has ever worn before. Sir, the bearings of this great question have, in the most able manner been unfolded during the progress of your deliberations. The question has been linked by the most obvious and indissoluble ties to all the interests of humanity, and all the hopes of our country and the world. It has been shown that that question is one intimately connected with the cause of domestic happiness, with the health and self-respect, the purity, the education, the independence of the people of our native land. It has been shown that the interests of national morality sternly demand the equitable settlement of the question of the corn laws. It has been shown that the way to disenthral the commerce of the country, and to make it the sanctified means of elevating, uniting, and fraternizing the various tribes of the human family, is to abolish at once, and for ever, those unnatural and unjust restrictions which prevent men from exchanging the fruits of their handicraft-skill for the bounties of the teeming earth. It has been shown that that is the cause of peace; that the directest way to sheath the weapons of inhuman warfare, and to bring about the time when men shall beat their swords into ploughshares and their spears into pruning-hooks, and learn the arts of war no more, is to teach them the great truth, that it is the design of the *God* that created them, that they should be mutually dependent, and make their individual interests one with the cause of universal brotherhood. (Cheers.) Yes, sir, this is the cause of international amity. The poet has said,

> "Lands intercepted by a narrow frith
> Abhor each other: mountains interposed,
> Make enemies of nations, which had else,
> Like kindred drops, been mingled into one."

Sir, it is not the design of God that this should be the case, and you have had the evidence furnished you during this conference that it need not be. (Hear, hear.) A missionary has come to you from the other side of the Alleghany mountains. He has left his peaceful dwelling upon the margin of those mighty waters, midway between the Atlantic and Pacific Oceans; he has travelled with the speed of one of your own majestic and unrivalled steam-ships, and has arrived in time to tell you that a noble race of Anglo-Saxon farmers, the sons of the pilgrim fathers, who have emigrated from the sanctified soil of New England to the Prairies of the far west, and are there building up an empire destined to be the glory of the whole earth, are waiting to exchange the produce of their free adopted soil for the fabrics and implements created by the skill of the inhabitants of their fatherland. (Great applause.) Shall this ambassador of peace and plenty return to tell the tenants of the western wilds that the law which defaces our statute book is irreversible, and that there is no power in Britain to compel the titled legislators and lords paramount of our country to revoke the decree that has gone forth, that the poor of the land must perish in poverty, or expatriate themselves where no corn law frustrates the beneficent intentions of the Creator? [Tremendous cheers.] No; rather bid him tell those from whom he comes that the ministers of the Most High have risen in the name of their master to reverse the mandates of unrelenting power, and, with a Christian people by their side, are resolved to demand that the blessings which have been provided for the poor shall be no longer withheld by a sordid and self-willed confederacy. [Cheers.] It has been further shown that our country's reputation in the eyes of the civilized world is deeply suffering from the laws which have been denounced, and that the moral influence of the nation is circumscribed and crippled by the odious enactments which limit the supply of food to the people. [Hear, hear.] What is the langurge of the nations around us? The other day a friend to our cause and a friend to mankind—the estimable Joseph Sturge [cheers]—undertook a mission to his anti-slavery brethren of America, not, however, without leaving behind him his munificent contributions to this cause, and his heart's best wishes for its success. [Hear, hear, and applause.] On touching the trans-Atlantic strand he was told by the press of New York to return to the land from whence he came; and before he undertook to counsel the people of the United States to do justice to the manacled slaves of the South, to bring to a sense of justice those who are grinding the faces of the poor in England, and by their cruel laws making abject paupers of those who otherwise would be loyal, independent, and grateful labourers in the promotion of their country's prosperity. [Cheers.] Such is the well-merited taunt of proud, republican, slave-holding America. [Hear, hear.] Take another instance. A gallant commodore, whom the people of Manchester have delighted to honour in the hall in which we meet, undertook to school the bearded Pacha of Egypt on the subject of his restricted policy. What was the answer of Mehemet Ali? "First, let England, the huge monopolist, abolish her own corn laws. [Deafening cheers.] Let her trample under foot the gigantic engine of injustice which is crushing her own people into the dust, and then you shall find me willing to sign the death warrant of the monopolies which I uphold. Let the mistress and mother of monopolies do her duty, and then Mehemet Ali, who with a soldier's sword, has hewn his way from poverty and obscurity to the pachaship of Egypt, shall not be slow to imitate the example of your great and invincible empire." (Loud cheers, which were several times renewed.) And what, Sir, is the withering rebuke which polished France administers? (Hear, hear.) Speaking through one of her most popular organs, the *Nationael*, she says, "Britain! raze from your shield the lordly lion, and put in its place the starving operative, vainly supplicating a sufficiency of food." (Renewed and long-continued cheering.) Say I not truly, then, this is the cause of our country's honour, and that if we would not be a by-word and a hissing amongst all nations, we must hasten to put away the corn and provision laws, and become the friends of the impoverished poor of England, ere we can preach clemency and liberal principles to the less favoured countries of the world? (Hear, hear.) It is a deep reproach to our country, that while millions of our hard-earned money are every year expended in the purchase of an article reared exclusively by the hands of wretched slaves, in defiance of every principle of justice, human and divine, we exclude the produce of the same country, though grown by freemen, and offered for the support of our perishing fellow-countrymen. (Hear, hear.) Let Manchester and Liverpool look to this. (Hear.) Perhaps some solution of our present difficulties may be found in this fact; perhaps it is not too much to say, that the calamity and curse under which we are groaning, may be traced to this circumstance. The laws of Christian England welcome to these shores the cotton that is reared by the slave: they say to the tyrant master, "You cannot flog too much, or drive too hard, the wretched victims of your avarice, for we are ready with greediness to purchase and consume the blood-stained produce of your fields;" while the same laws refuse admission to the corn of the free, and put under impenetrable bond, the fruits of those harvests which have gladdened the eyes of the hardy and enterprising yeomanry of the noblest republic on the face of the earth. (Cheers.) So much for the bearings of this question, as they have been elicited in the course of your discussion. A word now with regard to the purposes which have been answered by this convention, in addition to the important developments to which I have already referred. Who can calculate the good that has been done by the gathering together of seven hundred men, whose hearts have been made one in the cause of humanity, who have mutually animated and informed each other? Opinions have been settled which before were unstable; resolutions have been formed which before were incipient and unexpressed. A position has been taken previously doubtful and undetermined; men have committed themselves collectively and irrevocably to a cause of which they were before isolated, unknown, and perhaps uninfluential friends—a cause, branded as secular and selfish by those who are themselves the most worldly and exclusive of mankind, has received the solemn *imprimatur* of an assembly composed altogether of men whose profession and practice is religious. And in addition to the presence of those who are here, we have received pledges of concurrence and cooperation from a still larger number, (hear, hear,) who have been prevented by providential circumstances from giving their personal attendance. Again, sir, the calling of this conference has originated throughout the country a discussion of the merits of this question more general and more useful than any that has before taken place. It has set all heads thinking, and all pens writing on the subject; and above all, it has urged that class of the community to bestow attention upon the subject, who had previously considered it either beyond the limit of their legitimate cognizance, or inconsistent with their religious character. (Hear, hear.) This conference has answered another high and excellent purpose; it has shown that there is an intimate connexion between the abolition of the laws that have been brought under our notice, and the spread of that religion whose ministers are here assembled. And here, sir, I must break the thread of my remarks to dwell for a moment upon the most striking feature of this conference. It is a conference of Christian ministers assembled in the heart of Great Britain, at the seat of science and manufactures, in the year 1841 of the Christian era, at the moment when Britain occupies the highest eminence she has ever scaled, conspicuous in arts, invincible in arms, famed for learning, mistress of the seas, with one hundred and fifty millions of subjects; colonizing with her children the untrodden wildernesses of the world, embracing in her christian sympathy all Pagan lands, and not unjustly claiming to be first on the list of civilised nations. (Hear and cheers.) At such a period of time, and in such circumstances, have you assembled, but for what? (Hear.) To exult in the manifold blessings enjoyed by those who inhabit the home of empire, and the sanctuary of religion? To devise measures for directing from this, the fountain head of knowledge, refreshing streams that shall carry truth and salvation to the uttermost bounds of the globe? To turn the power and dominion which have been acquired, to the purposes of human improvement in distant countries? Nothing of the kind. (Hear, hear.) The phenomenon is presented, of seven hundred ministers of religion, called from their homes, to sit in solemn council upon the state of their native country, in which millions are perishing for lack of bread. (Hear, hear, and applause.) Oh, Sir, what will the heathen think of us when they shall know this? You send your missionary with this book (the Bible) to the barbarous nations of the world, to preach amongst them the unsearchable riches of Christ—to give them the volume that is to make them wise unto salvation. That book, translated into their vernacular tongue, is placed in their hands, and they are told it is the word of God. They reverently open it, and on its first page they read, that, when God had formed man out of the dust of the ground, and breathed into him the breath of life, he said, "Behold I have given you every herb bearing seed which is upon the face of all the earth, and every tree in which is the fruit of a tree yielding seed; to you it shall be for meat. And to every beast of the earth, and to every fowl of the air, and to every thing that creepeth upon the earth wherein there is life, I have given every green herb for meat, and it was so." (Loud applause.) He reads onwards; he listens to the thunders of Sinai, most awful, when denouncing the oppression of the poor, and the withholding of bread from the hungry. He advances towards the dawning of the gospel dispensation, and at last he sits at the feet of Christ and his apostles. From lips that spake as never man spake he learns that the very hairs of his head are all numbered, and he reads the precept whose character stamps it as divine; "If thine enemy hunger, feed him; and if he thirst, give him drink." (Very loud applause.) The missionary points him to the prayer which, with every sunrise, he is to present at the footstool of eternal mercy,—"Give us this day our daily bread." (Hear, hear.) The holy man shows him the answer to this prayer in the fertility of his native land, in the "cattle upon a thousand hills," and in the provision that is made alike for the sparrow that falls at his feet and the raven that cries for food above his head. (Deafening cheers.) He asks the missionary from what blessed land he has brought him these glad tidings, and he tells him from a land where the gospel shines brightest, where Christian ministers most abound, where every hamlet is adorned with a Christian temple, and where the statutes of the book he has given are part and parcel of the constitution and the law. (Hear, hear.) "O happy land!" exclaims the converted heathen, "just on the verge of heaven; would I were there, that I might participate the blessings which the gospel has conferred upon it!" Yet, a little while, and the sad truth shall reach the ears of that unsophisticated convert, that in that very land from which the message of his salvation has been sent there are millions who, by so-called Christian legislators are deprived of the benefits of that provision which God has made for every living being. (Loud cheers.) May not the Christian patriot exclaim, "O! tell it not in Gath; publish it not in the streets of Askalon, lest we be covered with the scorn of the barbarian, and see our religion rejected as a fable? But, let it go forth. Let the rebukes of the civilized and the savage be heaped upon us till those who will not yield to the cry of the wretched are constrained by very shame "to do justly and to love mercy." (Applause.) Let it be published that the emigrant who leaves the land of his nativity with an aching heart to find an asylum in some more genial region—in some region where the laws permit him to enjoy the fruits of the earth—may not send to the starving parent he has left behind, the smallest contribution from the bounty of another clime in the shape of food to save that parent alive. [Hear, hear.] Should the donation of filial piety, in the form of a barrel of flour, be sent to the shores of this country, the demon of the corn laws would meet it on the beach, and, raising the gaunt arm of famine, would say, "Hitherto shalt thou come, but no farther," and the agents of that accursed law would deprive the venerable sire, famishing at his fireless hearth, of the benefit of the supply which reverent love had devised to keep the old man alive. [Tremendous cheering.] Oh, Sirs, it is time to rise at the stirring call of nature, and put down the abomination which maketh desolate. [Cheers.] To-day beholds you in your right place. [Immense applause.] You are treading in the steps of holy men of old, who did not hesitate to rebuke the iniquities of unrighteous law-makers. You are imitating the example of Him who went about doing good. The poor have a right to claim you as their friends. You are the heaven-commissioned guardians of their rights. Your message is to them. Your duties are amongst them. You stand between the oppressor and the oppressed.

> "By you, the violated Law speaks out
> Its thunders; and by you, in strains as sweet
> As angels use, the gospel whispers peace."

Cry aloud, then, and spare not. Say to those who, while professing a zeal for religion, neglect the weightier matters of the law,—"Is not this the fast that I have chosen? To undo the heavy burdens, to deal thy bread to the hungry, and to satisfy the afflicted soul?" Rebuke the ignorant unbelief, that pretends to advance the interests of the poor by transgressing the commands of the Most High. Say to those who are robbing God, by robbing his poor, "You are at war with your Maker; you are in the road to retribution and ruin." Remind such of the promises given to those who obey the Divine injunction, and have faith in the providence of God—"Prove me now herewith, saith the Lord of Hosts, if I will not open you the windows of heaven, and pour you out a blessing, that there shall not be room enough to receive it." [Loud cheers.] Sir, we have had the state of our country described; we have been told, and the proof has been forthcoming, that there are six millions of our countrymen who know not the taste of wheaten bread; that there are millions more, whose supply is scanty and insufficient; in fact, that the whole nation has been put upon short allowance, and that discontented hunger prowls through our streets, devising plans of mischief, and ready for deeds that menace the existence of our dearest social institutions. [Hear, hear.] Those who have ascertained these facts, have asked themselves, if this state of things is to be charged to the account of a judgment and visitation from the Almighty? And they have rescued the sacred name from impiety and profanity, by declaring, that our chastisements are self-inflicted, and the evils we deplore, the result of an unbelieving and wicked departure from the spirit and mandates of the Divine law. They have vindicated the veracity of God when he gave to man the promise, "Thy bread shall be given thee, and thy water shall be sure; seed time and harvest, summer and winter, shall never fail." ["Hear, hear," and loud cheers.] You, reverend sirs, have—I was going to say, *exonerated* the Deity from the impious charge of being the author of prevailing misery, but I retract the word—you have asserted and vindicated the Divine beneficence. You have declared, that in the provision which God has made for his creatures there is enough for all, enough for each; an unfailing, an everlasting supply. [Loud cheers.] You have laid the complaints of the poor, where they are justly chargeable,—at the door of unchristian legislation. You have called upon the oppressors of the poor in high places to beware lest, by their continuance in wrong doing, they involve *themselves* in the ruin in which they have already plunged so many of their humbler countrymen. You have done well. Never have you appeared more like the disciples and followers of your benevolent and sympathising Master. Permit me to repeat it; you are in your right place. Methinks, the gospel will not sound less sweetly in the ears of those to whom you preach, when you shall return from this place, after having met to devise means for bringing the bread which perisheth within reach of those to whom you are accustomed to break the bread of eternal life. [Loud applause.] You are treading in the steps of Him who, if partial at all, displayed his partiality in acts of charity to the poor; who exerted his wonder-working power to feed the famishing multitude; and who, when he comes to judgment, will say unto you, in consequence of the deeds you have this day done, "I was an hungered, and ye gave *me* meat;" and when you shall say, "Lord, when saw we *thee* an hungered and fed thee?" shall reply, "Forasmuch as ye did it to the least of one of these my brethren, ye did it unto me." ["Hear, hear," and great applause.] Sir, it now remains to be seen what influence your counsels and measures will produce upon those who are entrusted with the tremendous power of making laws for the people of this country. And here I must observe that it is with peculiar pleasure I have remarked the sensitive regard which has been shown to the interests of all classes of our fellow-subjects. You have stood forth, not as the advocates of the claims of a particular class, but as the vindicators of the rights of *all* your fellow-countrymen. Aware that the existing laws have been defended on the ground that they were essential to the maintenance of agricultural prosperity, you have directed your special attention to the condition of those who are engaged in *rural occupations*, and to the operation of the present laws upon their welfare. Overwhelming testimony has been adduced, proving that the interests of the manufacturer and the artizan, and the interests of the farmer and the labourer, are one and indivisible. [Hear.] You have demonstrated that the wretchedness which is the lot of the former, has already overtaken and threatens to swallow up the latter. [Hear, hear.] I have myself, in perusing the vast number of letters that have passed through my hands, as your honorary secretary, been affected by the frequent assurances given by ministers of the gospel in agricultural districts, that they are firmly persuaded themselves, and are supported by the convictions of the members of their congregations who are engaged in agricultural pursuits, of the justice and necessity of a repeal of the present corn laws. [Cheers.] But, they at the same time lament their inability to give any open and avowed assistance to the cause in which we are engaged, because of the bondage in which they are held to the proprietors of the soil, who exercise an arbitrary and despotic control over the condition of the occupiers and tillers of the land. [Hear, hear.] The fact has been made abundantly apparent, that though the consciences of hundreds of thousands of the agricultural population are with us, their votes have been directed against us, in consequence of their abject dependance upon those, whose will can at any time dispossess them of the means of their subsistence. [Hear, hear.] Sir, the fact must not be disguised. The farmers of our country are under the relentless domination of the titled and untitled lords of the soil; who not only claim the fee-simple of the broad acres they possess, but the votes of those who are their tenants at will. Freedom of election, in the counties of England, there is none. The horned cattle in the stall are not in a condition of more abject submission than are that class known by the name of the "bold and independent yeomanry of England." ["Hear," and cheers.] Out of a multitude of letters bearing upon this point, I will read you one. The names that are mentioned I must, for reasons which will be obvious, conceal; the writer is a minister, in connection with the church of Scotland, officiating in a certain part of England. [Hear, hear.]

"I have received your circular, very kindly inviting me to a meeting of ministers and others, to be held in Manchester, on Tuesday, the 17th current, to take into consideration the laws respecting the monopoly in food; and, in answer, I beg respectfully to assure you that you have my best wishes, and the best wishes of thousands in this district, but as my congregation is chiefly composed of ——— farmers, it would be madness in me, nay, it would completely destroy my usefulness as a minister, to take any open part in the repeal of these laws, or at your meeting. All I can do, therefore, is to send you my best wishes. Nor are you to suppose, from this, that the farmers here are against you. Hundreds of them, and these, too, the largest and most intelligent, are your decided friends, but they dare not show it, or they may leave the district. They must do as ——— bids them, and their excuse is, and it is the excuse both of minister and people, that as the public cannot and will not protect them, therefore they cannot reasonably be expected to sacrifice all their own private interests for its weal. In these circumstances we dare not countenance you openly, but you have our best wishes, and should you ever come this way agitating the subject," [and this, I think, I shall be inclined to do,] (Loud cheers,) "we will do you all the good we can. More, at present, we cannot do, with safety to ourselves and families. Trusting, therefore, that you will take courage, and be as successful in this as you were in the slave agitation question, I am, my dear Sir, yours very truly,

———

"Minister in connection with the Church of Scotland.

"Geo Thompson, Esq."

Yes, gentlemen, with your efficient aid, and the blessing of the God you serve, we shall be as successful in this as we were in that sacred cause to which reference is here made. (Loud cheers.) The yeomanry of England must be emancipated from the thraldom of a tyrannical land-holding aristocracy. (Very loud cheers.) I said, it remained to be seen what influence your conference would exert upon those who sit in high places. You have had your Parliament. (Loud cheers.) It was a glorious sight to witness, on the first day of your assembling, more than the number of those who constitute the Commons of Great Britain. (Cheers.)

Yes, this hallowed Parliament of England's best and purest minds—the representatives of weeping and famishing misery—the friends of starving attenuated operatives—the pastors of impoverished congregations—on the first day of its meeting, numbered more than the sum-total of those who are wont to assemble in the Chapel of St. Stephen. (Cheers.) Would that the destinies of this question had been committed to your hands for final adjudication. (Loud cheers.) I think it might have been, with quite as good a chance of a wise and equitable decision, as that with which it is likely to meet in another place. (Very loud cheering.) I think, the suffrages by which you have been returned to this Parliament, are quite as extensive and independent as those of many honourable members. (Laughter.) I think the means which have been taken to return you, are quite as pure and unexceptionable as those resorted to in many of the constituencies of the empire. (Cheers and laughter.) I think, you are quite as respectable in calling, and *almost* as wise in understanding, as either the hereditary or elected law-makers of the land. And I think that you would have settled this question upon principles quite as sound and as patriotic as those who are likely to guide the decisions of either house of Parliament. (Loud cheers.) I think you would have come to the work of legislation with minds quite as disinterested, and hands quite as clean, as another Parliament, which is notoriously a Parliament of landlords sitting in judgment upon their own case, and legislating not for the benefit of the poor but for the benefit of their rent-rolls. Could you have had the making of the law, it would not have been like the present one—resembling the scroll of Jeremiah, written within and without with lamentation and woe—it would not have circumscribed the bounties of Providence—it would not have withered the hopes of the widow and the orphan—it would not have perpetuated the misery of millions of half-starved labourers; No. Yours would have been a law based upon the demands of justice—a law which would have opened the storehouse of the Divine liberality—a law which would have rekindled the hopes of those who are ready to perish—a law that would have caused the widow's heart to sing for joy, and carried contentment and gladness to every home in Britain. (Cheers.) And, then, it would have been carried without anger and without hatred. What glorious unanimity there would have been! Not a miserable majority of two or five, but a law passed by a Parliament united as one man. (Cheers and laughter.) But though you are denied any legislative power, of this be sure, that no opinion which will be advanced elsewhere, will have half the weight with the community of that which you have expressed in your deliberate and solemnly attested documents. And, I will venture to say, that the statesmen of the land, and those at their head, whether meditating upon the state of things and the signs of the times, at Brocket Hall, or Drayton Manor, will regard, with an intensity of interest which cannot be exaggerated, the transactions in which you have been engaged, and the conclusions at which you have arrived. (Cheers.) God grant that your decisions may produce their rightful influence, and turn the scale in favour of justice to a starving population. (Hear, hear, and applause.) One word with regard to practical measures, and I have done. From this time forth you must be the ministers and missionaries of truth upon the great question which has brought you together. (Hear, hear.) You must be instant, in season and out of season, in the work of enlightening, purifying and directing the minds of all who are around you. (Hear, hear.) You must be prepared to attend another conference, and to that conference you must come accompanied by the laity. (Hear, hear.) Pastor and people must appear together (Loud cheers.) The next circular that goes forth must be not with the authority of twenty-six ministers in Manchester, but of the seven hundred who assembled in open conference in this town. (Renewed cheers.) And, sir, if twenty-six men, making their appeal to their brethren, could convene such an assembly as that which we have witnessed, what may we not expect when seven hundred shall send forth the rallying cry, and muster the armies of Israel to this holy war? (Hear, hear, hear.) Why, sir, we may expect to see a gathering of seven thousand men, clothed in the panoply of justice, who will not bow the knee to the Baal of a cruel monopoly, but fight until they vanquish the monster that is preying on the vitals of the country. (Deafening cheers.) There is another element of society, the purest and best, which must be brought into action. Sir, we must enlist in this cause of holy domestic charity the women of Great Britain. (Tremendous cheers.) Seven hundred and fifty thousands of the maids and matrons of this country carried their petition to the footstool of a maiden Queen in behalf of the manacled slaves of our colonies. (Hear, hear, hear.) Let this reverend assembly speak the word, and I believe that double the number will lay a petition at the feet of our beloved monarch, now a wife and a mother, (renewed cheers,) in behalf of the cause of famishing humanity, and that petition will be graciously received, and all that a monarch may constitutionally do, who loves her country, and desires the happiness of her people she will do, to restore the reign of contentment, and shed the light of joy and gladness upon every cottage throughout her kingdom. (Deafening cheers, which were renewed and renewed again.) Finally, suffer me to say to you, be strong and of good courage. You have every thing to hope, and nothing to fear, in the work upon which you have entered. (Hear, hear, hear.) The patron of the cause you have espoused is the God who considereth the poor. (Hear, hear.) On earth, the sovereign to whom in loyalty and love you are attached leads you onward in your career of mercy. (Hear, hear, hear.) The choicest of England's nobility is with you, and the presence of one of the hereditary peerage of the land who sits by my side at this moment (Lord Ducie), a pledged fellow-labourer in your hallowed enterprise. (Great cheering.) Yes, you have a Radnor, (cheers,) a Spencer, (cheers,) a Fitzwilliam, (loud cheers,) a peerless Brougham, (renewed cheers,) and a Cleveland. (Cheers.) In the House of Commons you have men who have been faithful and true for many years; (hear, hear;) and you are about to have one there who though untried in parliament has proved himself out of doors the most steady and talented supporter of the cause. Here he is—need I name Richard Cobden! (Vehement cheering.) I know not whether to be glad or sorry that that gentleman is now a member of parliament. Warwick was called a king-maker, and Mr. Cobden might justly be called a member-of-parliament maker; and I do not know whether he would not be better employed out of doors in manufacturing members of parliament, (laughter,) than, as I am sure he will always be employed, soundly counselling them within the house. But he is there, and there will not be in that assembly one who may with greater confidence say, "I am supported by the prayers and the hearts of the people of England." (Applause.) Let the county members boast of the purity and freedom of election which has sent them there. (Laughter.) Mr. Cobden can do better; he represents, not the constituency of Stockport alone, he represents the suffering community of our native land; and, if human misery can make him strong, he carries with him there the tears of the suffering poor, and will be omnipotent. (Cheers.) Or, if he be not, ministers of the gospel, let him have your prayers, and his triumph is at hand.

Again I say, be of good heart. When you would gather courage, think of the goodness of your cause; think of the imperishable nature of the principles on which your cause rests; think upon the power of Him who has the hearts of all men in his hand, and is emphatically the God of the poor. And now, reverend sirs, for a while we must part. You are going to your respective scenes of labour; the blessing and prayer of the perishing go with you! Nations are looking on, and will applaud every effort that you make to place the bounties of Divine Providence within reach of a suffering people. [Cheers.] The testimony of your own consciences will support you amidst all the reproaches which may be heaped upon you. It will not be long ere the moral power of the country will rise in its might and magnificence, and overcome every obstacle which selfishness and ignorance have placed in the way of your success. [Loud cheers.] In the words of apostolical valediction, therefore I bid you "Farewell, and God speed!" saying, "Be steadfast, unmoveable, always abounding in the work of the Lord, for as much as ye know that your labour shall not be in vain in the Lord." [The eloquent speaker then sat down amid the most enthusiastic cheering.]

After the oft-renewed plaudits which succeeded this speech had subsided,

The CHAIRMAN said, he thought he saw in the ministers assembled, a right conformity with the Saviour's prayer, "I pray not that thou shouldst take them out of the world, but that thou shouldst keep them from the evil." They were not taken out of the world; but they were also told that "a little leaven leaveneth the whole lump," and they would endeavour to keep themselves and others from the evils of the corn laws, and other evils of the world. (Hear.) Those had met face to face on this occasion who had never met before, and he felt almost sorry at parting. Till now many differences of opinion had kept them apart from each other. He had never seen Dr. Pye Smith, or Dr. Vaughan, or his colleagues around him, or the greater part of the ministers, and of the present assembly before; but during this week they had spoken together, and he hoped had also agreed in that other characteristic "the fear of the Lord." And if they had spoken in that fear there was one who had hearkened and heard them, and who would prosper the work when they were gone. When infidels heard and knew that men of all denominations, and principles, laying aside party feeling and sectarian prejudices, had met together with one accord and mind, after the manner of the first christians, and had not only given to each other the right hand of fellowship, but the hearts of brothers too, they would say, "Surely there is something of a truth in this." And those who sneered at religion, and asked, "What good can the ministers of religion do us?" when they find that through their instrumentality, bread was made cheap, and trade was made free, and that they had again got an honest trade, or honest work in the world,—they would say, "Of all men in the world, the ministers of religion are the men for us." And ought it not to be so? The very name of "ministers" meant "servants." They (the ministers) should be the servants of the people, and especially ought they to be the servants of the poor; and they wished such to be the result of this conference, that that saying should in them be verified—that the poor had risen up and called them blessed. He prayed that the Almighty might pour his blessing on every one who was, and had been assembled in that place. Like an American Indian who, at a large meeting, said he could not shake hands with all present, he (the chairman) would declare from the spot where he stood, he shook hands with them all at once, and he now declared this conference dissolved. (Applause.)

The Rev. J. W. Massie then moved a vote of thanks to the chairman, which was carried by acclamation.

A Minister proposed a vote of thanks to the ministers of Manchester for convening this conference, which passed amidst cries of "seconded by all," and great applause.

A vote of thanks was also proposed and passed with like applause, to the several secretaries of the conference.

The assembly then separated about half-past seven o'clock, and thus the four days' memorable proceedings of this extraordinary convocation closed.

The Speech of the Rev. J. J. Freeman, of Walthamstow, one of the Foreign Secretaries of the London Missionary Society, on the ninth resolution. (*See page* 109.)

Mr. Chairman,—While I cordially move the resolution which I have the honour of reading to this meeting, I feel that I dare not, at this late hour, offer more than a few brief remarks. The sentiments of the resolution appear to me as obvious as they are true. They commend themselves to our judgment and carry with them their own evidence. The argument is, that our benevolent institutions depend, in no small measure, for their pecuniary resources, on the liberality of the industrious classes. If, then, the resources of those classes are exhansted, or limited to the amount of their own bare exigencies, of course they can no longer aid those benevolent institutions. *These* must suffer in proportion to the amount in which the industrious and labouring classes are straitened. How much our institutions are dependent on those classes, I am not able to say exactly, but I apprehend that I am quite within the range, if I suppose that *one third* of the incomes of our public institutions of a religious and benevolent character, may be derived from the sources which we are now reviewing. And, sir, the prospect of being deprived of one third of such incomes, is a very serious matter, when we are rather in need of increase and augmentation on every hand. And that there is reason to fear a decrease of contribution from the parties I refer to, the industrious classes, is but too manifest. If they have not occupation they have not wages—and can then give nothing. With but partial employment, they can obtain but partial wages—at most but just sufficient to meet the necessities of their suffering and half-famished families. And I for one, sir, am not prepared to go to the half-famished family of the industrious poor, and ask him to contribute from his extreme poverty to the cause of universal benevolence, noble as that cause is. But then, sir, let me ask, who is the sufferer in this case? Surely not just the society which is no longer favoured with the amount of the poor man's contribution, but the poor man himself who is no longer able to contribute. The sympathies and charities of human nature dwell in the bosoms of the poor and industrious classes as richly as in those of other classes, and whatever state of things deprives them of the means of indulging those sympathies and exercising those charities, it is at variance with the established principles of human nature and the merciful arrangement of Divine Providence. Besides, sir, it is in the very nature of Christianity that "it is more blessed to give than to receive;" and why are the industrious classes to be deprived of that "blessedness" by being deprived of the means of "giving," the means of exercising Christian beneficence? I feel, therefore, that in pleading for our benevolent societies on the basis of the principle contained in this resolution, I am also pleading for the best interests of the industrious classes themselves. Far distant be the day when all that they can earn shall be demanded for their own mere physical wants, leaving them no opportunity of proving their sympathy with the necessities of others, the claims of the Saviour, and the wants of a fallen world. (Cheers.) Our benevolent institutions are blessings to our own land in sustaining them, as they are to the world, for which they were formed. The more they are supported and enabled to carry out their great designs, the more will they return to us of prosperity at home. These positions might be fully established and illustrated; but I can merely advert to them, and commend them to the intelligence and good feelings of the vast assembly I have the honour to address in moving the resolution now read.

CORRESPONDENCE.

(From the Rev. Dr. Bennett, of London.)

My dear Sir,—Having lately visited Manchester, on behalf of missions, my duties now call me in another direction; but I am anxious to show, by letter, that I feel an interest in your meeting, which, however, some may affect to treat as political, is truly an affair of justice, benevolence, and religion:—

For the present corn laws bid defiance to that God, who made of one blood all nations, and so distributed his blessings among them, that they should, by promoting each other's welfare, advance their own. But as every attempt to oppose the selfish to the cosmopolite principle, is, by the omnipotent Governor of the world, made to recoil upon its author, so we are the last people on earth that should meddle with this rolling stone: Since we are at the extremity of the corn growing countries, and are touching the *ne plus ultra* of all efforts to supply ourselves. We already are forcing lands to produce corn that are fitted only for pasture; and while we may admire the talent and industry of the Scotch, every one may see that they are struggling against Providence; raising corn in spite of nature.

The wet and uncertain climate often destroys our harvests, and bids us look to other lands, still uncultivated; where a warmer sun gives greater security for the ripening and housing of crops. But we prefer fighting with the laws of latitude.

God has given us, in such abundance, minerals, that are independent of weather; and has so distinguished us by manufacturing talent and industry, that we are bidden to exchange the *quid pro quo*, and furnish the world with that which *it* has not, that it may have the motive *for* producing from other soils what *we* have not, and cannot have, but by exchanging.

For while the census shows that our millions are increasing, as our acres do not increase, it is madness to expect to persevere in our present course. We must, at last, grow wise, though it may be too late to avert the ruin we have courted. We are avowedly labouring to keep up the prices of agricultural produce; while in manufactures we are compelled to bring down prices, in order to find a market. We are thus exhibiting the ludicrous spectacle of a people, one half of whom are pulling in a direction opposite to the other, to bring us to a dead stand-still.

* * * * *

We are also attempting to isolate ourselves among nations; as if we could keep up a portion of water in the middle of a lake, above the level of the rest. If there were ever any chance of success by this system, it would be in a nation that is shut up within itself, and has no intercourse with the rest of the world; while we, who are the manufacturers and merchants for the world, are the last people upon earth to succeed in an isolating scheme.

The real landowners are not the cause of this mad course, for they say that if the nominal rents must come down, their establishments would cost them less; but the evil is supported by nominal landlords, whose estates are mortgaged and burdened with charges for various branches of their families, calculated at old prices, which make them dread all reduction of rents, lest it should leave them little but the name of the proprietor. But manufacturing property has now become nominal; and bankrupt landlords can no more fight against the course of human affairs, than bankrupt manufacturers; for notes in a landlord's parliament will not change the nature of things.

Nothing can break the fall of all classes, but a timely retreat to equitable and liberal principles of intercourse with the rest of the world; for, if manufacturers are hurled to ruin, the land must, in spite of any system of poor laws, maintain the paupers. We may throw millions into starvation, but we must supply them with food, in some form or other; though we deprive them of profitable employ.

That your deliberations may produce a happy result is the prayer of, reverend brethren, your fellow-labourer in the cause of justice and humanity,

JAMES BENNETT.

5, Mountfort Crescent, Barnsbury Park,
London, Aug. 16, 1841.

(From the Rev. Hugh M'Neile.)

Sir,—Your letter of the 10th instant was re-directed to me to Ballycastle, and from thence to this place, where I received it last night.

I thank you for the friendly terms in which you invite me to take part in the proposed conference, assuring me of "a courteous reception and a respectful audience, even to hear me in opposition to your opinions;" independent, however, of now impracticable distance, and apart from the merits of the question to be brought under consideration, I am compelled to decline, by the terms of your printed address convening the assembly. In it you say, "For a while let us lay aside our sectarian and partisan differences, and on the hallowed ground of Christian charity assemble for the purpose of bettering the condition of famishing multitudes."

In what you call our sectarian differences are involved all the eternal truths of the Christian religion; truth from which *alone* can emanate anything deserving the name of Christian charity. To admit the possibility of meeting on the ground of *Christian* charity, without reference to christian truth—nay, on the express condition of laying aside for a while all that many among us consider to be God's own word, would, in my opinion, be to countenance the infidel liberalism which implies that revelation is useless, without having the honest boldness to say so. Believing, as I do, that all scripture is given by the inspiration of God, I feel bound, whatever enterprise I undertake, whatever subject I discuss, to do all on christian principles, or, in the language of the apostle, to "do all in the name of the Lord Jesus," and therefore I cannot consent to place myself in any circumstances where I must lay aside for a while all reference to these great and glorious truths, which Christ lived, and died, and rose again to establish and promulgate.

The corn-law question is a *national* one. It may be discussed on scriptural principles; and our Saviour's prophecy that, until his coming again, "nation shall rise against nation, and kingdom against kingdom," may preserve our christian statesmen from the flattering delusion of abjuring patriotism as a prejudice, and embracing a cosmopolitan phantom which they would in vain persuade the statesmen of other nations to embrace; while the apostolical injunction to "provide for our own, especially those of our own house," may suggest to a paternal government the wisdom of not exposing the multitudes of our fellow-countrymen to the risk of famishing by leaving their provisions dependent upon foreigners. But you must excuse me when I say that I anticipate no benefit to the world, to their own country, or to themselves, from a conference of men who stipulate for the exclusion, during their conference, of all the essentials of scriptural truth, under the name of sectarian differences.

This is not too strong; for your printed address is to "the ministers of *all* religious denominations throughout the united kingdom," and no arguments are required to prove that their sectarian differences involve all the essentials of scriptural truth, including the inspiration of scripture itself. I have the honour to be, sir, your obedient servant,

HUGH MC. NEILE.

Killarney, 18th August, 1841.

(From Dr. Harris, President of Cheshunt College.)

My dear Sir,—If I do not write to you at any great length on the subject of the corn laws, it is not because I do not deeply feel its importance, and am not concerned for the success of your movement; but because your hands must be already filled with correspondence of greater interest and weight than mine can be; and if I do not attend the meeting, it is only because pre engagements in another direction absolutely forbid. You do me but justice in supposing that I truly sympathise with your effort. I sincerely wish that it had been made earlier, and when it might have been of more immediate effect. Still, as no useful act is ever entirely lost, though you should fail of speedy success, justice, whenever it shall triumph, will triumph partly as the result of your present endeavour. Meanwhile, you will carry with you the sympathies of the poor, and "the blessing of him that is ready to perish," and the approbation of Him who is the Creator of corn, and the God of the poor.

May I be excused for adding my conviction that you would have enlisted more ministers, if, by circular or otherwise, you had shown in what respect the corn law question differs from a merely political subject; or how a minister who does not wish to commit himself to politics, may yet consistently throw himself heart and soul into the subject. This, I think, might have been done; and would have induced some to join you who may now deem it their duty and their "strength to sit still."—I am, my dear sir, faithfully yours.

Cheshunt College, Aug. 13, 1841. JOHN HARRIS.

(From the Rev. Dr. Leifchild, of London.)

My dear Friend and Brother,—I requested my son, ere I left town, to inform you of the cause of my absence from the proposed convocation on the 17th instant. I was myself unable to write, in consequence of the nervous agitation of my frame, produced by a disordered state of the circulation; but, having recovered a little at this place, on my way to the continent, I cannot leave England (which I purpose doing, in a few days, for a short time) without stating to you, as one of the appointed organs of communication, my opinions and feelings in reference to the said meeting.

Upon the receipt of Mr. Thompson's letter, I wrote a few lines expressive of my intention of being present. I had no opportunity of ascertaining the views of my brethren on the subject; but my own mind decided at once on the propriety of the measure in contemplation; and in this decision I have only been confirmed by all that I have subsequently read, and heard, and thought upon the subject.

I might have objected, in the first instance, to some points in the arrangements; but all could not be consulted. Some step was to be taken; some plan to be framed and acted upon. This had been done by men of some judgment and piety; and it became, therefore, the duty of all, for the sake of concurrence in a great object, to sacrifice their particular opinions or minor points.

I take the meeting to have for its direct object the vindication of the rights of suffering humanity; to plead the cause of the poor against those who would oppress them; and to demand attention to be paid to the crying misery and appalling destitution of a large portion of the population by those, who have it in their power to devise and afford the means for their relief, and who are responsible for their conduct in this respect both to God and man.

What but the bitterness and blindness of party zeal could lead men to represent this as an object unsuitable for the deliberation of Christian ministers, and to endeavour to fasten upon it the charge of a busy meddling with the intricacies of worldly politics? But they knew better; they knew that the character of the men who were pledged to conduct these deliberations afforded no ground for such a charge. They hoped, however, thus to discredit the proceeding, and to deter the timid and irresolute from giving it their countenance. I am happy to observe, by the list of honourable names who have responded to your invitation, how powerless they are become in their attempt to mislead, disguise, and, terrify; and I imagine the result will be such as to make every member of our body who is voluntarily absent (to say nothing of a whole denomination who stand aloof) regret that he deferred to lend his individual aid, in the first instance, to the impetus of what may prove a mighty movement on behalf of our fellow countrymen.

I shall be present with you in spirit, and my prayer shall ascend to God, at the time of your meeting, for a large supply to be afforded you of the spirit of wisdom, of unanimity, of boldness, and of a sound mind. You will have some choice spirits with you from a distance, as well as from your own neighbourhood; and you, I doubt not, will bear your part manfully through the whole of the proceedings.

Pray inform me, from time to time, how affairs go on; and assure the meeting, from me, that whatever measures they adopt and recommend, I will do my utmost, in the sphere in which I am placed, to carry them into effect.—Yours sincerely,

Dover, August 13, 1841. JOHN LEIFCHILD.

(From Dr. Burns.)

To the Congress of Ministers at Manchester on the Corn and Restriction laws.

Gentlemen,—Although I have some doubts of the expediency of Christian ministers meeting by themselves, and apart from all other classes of citizens, to discuss public questions, I have no doubt whatever of the moral dignity and vast public moment of the particular question which has convened you together. I do not look upon it as a question of party politics at all, but as one of humanity and national morals. It is one of humanity, inasmuch as it has to do with the main elements of human comfort. It is one of national morals, inasmuch as it resolves itself into the problem, whether or not shall the provision made by the God of nature for the sustenance of his children, and the arrangements of providence for its wise diffusion, be diminished and counteracted by the short-sighted selfishness and monopolising policy of man? It does not appear to me that you are met for the purpose of suggesting fiscal regulations on commerce at all—that would be to intermeddle with politics; but rather to show cause why all such regulations ought to be looked on with a jealous suspicion, as at variance with the wise and benevolent arrangements of the Author of all. In prosecuting your inquiries, every member of your congress may be expected to contribute his quota of information regarding the actual condition of the people with whom he has to do, and thereby a most valuable store of useful materials may be gathered for the use of the philanthropist and political economist. The bearings of a right moral and political economy on each other may be thus calculated and ascertained. A practical evidence may also be supplied of what has long appeared to me a great desideratum; the evidence I mean of the fact, that clerical men are not so occupied with their peculiar studies, or with their sectarian differences, as to overlook the claims which the distresses of the working classes of the community have on a portion of their time and benevolent sympathy. With the minuter details of such questions as come before you, ministers of Christ may not have much to do, but with the broad features of the case we have all to do; and whatever stands in the way of the physical comfort of our humbler brethren, must necessarily affect their moral and religious state. The experience of many years has convinced me that interested monopolisers of all kinds have uniformly started the cry of "politics" on every question of humanity or principle that has been mooted; and in this way they succeeded long in blinding the eyes of many, and especially of ministers, to the essentially moral features of the struggles for negro emancipation, and for the repeal of the Test and Corporation Acts. Many pious and worthy men have been kept back from the post of active duty they were well qualified to fill, by the senseless cry of "politics;" and great principles have been compromised, and measures of enlarged benevolence have been lost, by this species of puling sentimentalism. If the working classes and the poor are to have advocates at all, where should they look for them save among their professed spiritual teachers? and if *they* shall stand aloof as unconcerned spectators, at whose door shall we lay those prejudices against the gospel which are strong enough by nature, but which will thus be progressively increased? No: let us prove that we care for our fellow-creatures under every aspect of their condition, and our path to usefulness, in regard to their noblest interests, will be thereby opened and smoothed. Let us assert and vindicate great principles, leaving the working of them out to others. Let us seek to dissipate delusion by the light of evidence, and let us assist one another by our collection and contributions to a common cause.

It gives me great pleasure to see that Dr. Chalmers has, within these few weeks, published to the world his matured judgment on the subject which has convened you together. In the twentieth volume of his works he has given it as his opinion, that "there are certain attendant moral benefits which render the adoption of the free trade system one of the best and wisest achievements of an enlightened national policy." He speaks the substance of volumes when he says of it—"It is on the side both of internal and external peace. It would quiet many a discontent within our own territory, and dry up the teeming fountain of most of our modern wars." Of the particular case of the corn laws, he thus opens his mind—"For the sake of its moral benefits, we know of no achievement more urgently desirable than a free corn trade. There is not a more fertile topic of clamour and discontent all over the land; and were it but effectually set at rest, we are aware of nothing which might serve more to sweeten the breath of British society.—(Works, vol. xx. p. 100-103. 1841.) And what hinders it from being "set effectually at rest?" The presumption is strong against all restrictions either on the productions of nature or on the commerce of men. It is monstrous to affirm that, while Britain depends on all lands, and on all climes, for her luxuries, and not a few of her comforts, she ought to be doomed to her own unaided resources for the very necessaries of life. The original principle of all commerce is barter; and what can be more ridiculous than to maintain that, while our manufactured products shall be sent to Germany or to the United States, we shall not be permitted to exchange these freely with the inhabitants of those countries for the corn and the provisions which are *their* appropriate products, and of which they have enough and to spare. Has not the God of heaven, by many infallible evidences, demonstrated that the peculiar province of Great Britain is that of a manufacturing country? Do not our canals, our rivers, our railways, our vast coal-fields, our wealth, our free institutions, and, above all, the enterprise and ingenuity of our artisans, evince this? Have not other lands looked to us in this light till they were tired in looking, and disgusted by the restrictive policy which deprived us of the benefits hence to be derived? Does not the lapse of twenty years, and with all the advantages of the corn and provision restriction acts, prove that the number of our agriculturists has been diminishing, while that of our artisans is rapidly and progressively increasing? And, as a melancholy set-off to this, is it not proved by every commercial document and trade report, that our export of manufactured goods has been for the same period rapidly and regularly diminishing?*

The dangers of interference with the fair and free progress of trade were strikingly exhibited in the commercial crash of 1810, the direct result of an unfriendly and restrictive policy on the trade of the United States. Britain took offence at the enterprise of America in first purchasing the products of our manufactures at a good price, and then selling them over again to the new states of the south. "May not we," said John Bull, "keep the profit of both?" No sooner said than done. Forth came fiscal regulations to check the trade of the United States with the old and new kingdoms of South America, and forthwith rushed our manufacturers and merchants to that field which Jonathan knew how to cultivate, but which John Bull did not. The issue was, plenty of goods sent, but scanty returns in money; large credit unredeemed, and a general crash. Thus was created, or fostered rather, the jealousy betwixt the mother country and her daughter, which ought to have been consigned to the tomb of the Capulets. Then followed the second American war; and then, in the year 1815, was passed, as a boon! to the landowner, the amended corn-law act, with its sliding scale, the

* An article in the *Leeds Times*, a few days ago, exhibited the appalling fact of the decrease of the woollen exports from £427,288 in 1820, to £258,942 in 1840. The same thing is evinced as to other articles, and other places, by the printed testimonies of the most unexceptionable witnesses on the export laws. Can any man read these without trembling for fear lest "Ichabod" should soon be seen in legible characters on the ruined walls of our noble manufactories?

fertile source of endless speculation, of demoralising chicanery and cheating, and of international hate. From that day to this, the noblest outlet for our manufacture has been, in a great measure, shut out from us. The Americans have, in retaliation, first imposed a tax of from 20 to 50 per cent. on various species of our goods, and then, very fairly, have begun to manufacture for themselves. In the meanwhile that vast continent has, in the progress of human discovery, and in the kindness of an over-ruling Providence, approached to within a fourth of its former distance from our shores; thus inviting us to the closest commerce; while her inhabitants are rich, enterprising, and free; "bone of our bone;" speaking the same language; professing the same religion; cherishing the same institutions; and vying with us in helping on the Christianity and civilization of mankind. And yet their flour we must not touch! and our colonies must retain to them the aspect and attitude of repulsion: and two great families, whom the common Father has blended into one, must be kept at arm's length from each other, to gratify the lovers of a wretched and crushing monopoly!

And now for a little episode about Paisley,—my "ain gude toun." Gentlemen, you all know that few, aye, few of our staple goods, can be allowed free entrance into the States, just as few as any of *their* growth of goods,—the products of their indefinitely expanded and rich soils—can be allowed free ingress into our ports. But so it happened, there was one species of Paisley manufacture which had not come under the paralysing arm of man's sinful interference with the rights of God. Worsted goods had made an escape even under the Argus eye of our fiscal men, and in these goods our worthy manufacturers and merchants have been for years making a fair traffic. It was not to be supposed that brother Jonathan would ever look on with cool indifference. No he has for some time past had his hand lifted to the tune of twenty per cent. on worsted imports into his territories; and congress has paused a little, just to see whether the enlightened and liberal proposals of the ministry that is going out shall be taken up by another party, (whether with due acknowledgments or not, is to my argument of no consequence,) or whether the paltry, puny, inhuman, unchristian, and impolitic regulations of the "good old times" shall be indefinitely re-enacted. Nor does America stand alone in this; but I mention that country because it is the noblest outlet for our goods. And yet, such is the ignorance and infatuation which prevails, that I could name more than one of those merchants that have suffered by our recent failures, who actually gave their votes, as electors, to the support of that political party who grasp at office on the avowed plea of resisting the reckless novelties of the Whigs, and of keeping things as they are. When is this delusion to end? If the meeting at Manchester will help in dissipating this delusion and opening the eyes of the people to their true interests, it will deserve well of every philanthropist, though it should entail upon it the imprecations of a faction which has ever been the sworn foe of the liberties of mankind.

Calling, last week, on one of my hearers, and conversing together on the distresses of the times, the mistress of the house remarked to me, "Ah, sir, well do I remember a conversation between my grandfather, a much respected man in the Causeyside, and three ministers, who happened one day to meet in his house, Dr. Findlay, Mr. Gillies, and Mr. Kinloch; when they got upon some laws, then (1804) passed in Parliament regarding corn and articles of food: and they all cried out against it as sinful, and one of them (Dr. Findlay of the High Church) said "We may not see at once all its evils, but our children will." "Andrew," said I, "things are changed. There your wife tells us of three ministers, all taking an interest in what affected the food and comfort of the people; and now, when one of us puts out a 'tippenny tract' about it, the cry is—keep to your pulpits; you have nothing to do with politics." "Ah," said Andrew, "you are right, Sir. These are not politics at all; they go deeper; and I wish all our ministers would do as you have done." The ministers above-named were eminent in their day. Mr. Gillies, a predecessor of my own, was the son of the distinguished Dr. Gillies, of Glasgow, and, while health was allowed him, an able and faithful pastor. Dr. Findlay was forty years minister of the largest church of the Establishment in this town, and a man whose name is dear to many still alive, who trace to him their first and best impressions. Mr. Kinloch was the venerable minister of the Associate Secession Church, and the predecessor of my late noble-minded Dissenting colleague, Mr. Smart. In those days, the "Voluntary" controversy was unknown, and the ministers of all denominations in Paisley vied who should do most good to the temporal and eternal interests of man. It may be proper to add, that my friend Andrew is an elder of the Church, and a man of intelligence.

Before I conclude, allow me to say, that the diffusion of intelligence up and down the land should be your first and greatest object, and, with this view, try and engage as many of the periodicals as possible. This should be no question of Whig, Tory, or Chartist. But if Whig and Tory, Churchman and Dissenter, should unite in "burking" the question, they will infallibly succeed in making the people all Chartists together.

With best wishes for success to you in your disinterested "labour of love," and in all your efforts for the real good of that great family of which our heavenly Father has called us to take the guardianship, I am, Gentlemen, faithfully and affectionately yours,

ROBT. BURNS.

Paisley, Aug. 16, 1841.

(From the Rev. R. Burls, Maldon, Essex.)

My dear Sir,—I was glad to hear from Mr. Craig of your intention to be at the Manchester Meeting.

In your letter to me you mentioned it as a probability: now I find that circumstances have fully determined your mind. The committee have sent me two pressing invitations to attend, but I do not expect to be there: not that it would be contrary to my conviction of duty or propriety, nor that my friends would object, but because I am so engaged at Parnden as well as Maldon, that time can ill be spared. You know that I live in the grand wheat district of Essex, near the part from which so much of the surplus corn of Essex is conveyed to the north of England. Some of the first corn factors belong to my congregation, and some farmers; yet most, if not all, are friendly to a change in the corn laws. In proof of this feeling, I need state nothing more than the fact that at the late election, Mr. Abdy, the third candidate, came forward on the proposal of ministers, (substantially,) and was well supported by my friends, united with some liberal churchmen, and when the poll closed he was only 34 votes behind. There was the most manly and principled voting in his favour which I ever remember. The farmers in my congregation were at first somewhat confounded, but I believe they all did right at last. I have never concealed my opinions—have always told them that a much lower duty would be just, and that it would in the long run be most to the advantage of the farmers, as his profits would be more ascertainable, and would rest upon a more regular and permanent basis

As it is, a season of great depression is sure to follow a season of prosperity: while millions are in a state of semi-starvation. *We want prices to be kept up by consumption, not by high duties.* Bread is now so dear that the masses cannot get it, and should the harvest be unpropitious, and the duty go down to 1s., still the corn which would then come in must be bought at so high a price abroad, on account of the great demand, that bread would still be as dear; and so whether the duty be high or low—the scale being so sliding—the people pine for want of food.

Most of the farmers in this district are hostile to a change: we saw enough of this at the election. They are foolish, headstrong, selfish, and willing to isolate their interests from those of the manufacturers, not considering how much the arts in their practical working have promoted the growth of their own prosperity, and how certainly this will decline if they fail of encouragement. In this part of the country the poor are certainly not without employment. Farmers are able to employ them to great advantage to themselves; and they are better paid here than they are about Dunmow and Thaxted, in a ratio of three or four shillings per week more. Still their privations are many, as any one must know who estimates the worth of 12s. a week in food, clothing, &c. for a family of four, five, or six persons.

What created a doubt in my mind at first, as to the propriety of such a meeting of ministers for such a purpose, was probably the same as impressed other minds! namely, the seeming interference of such persons in their *official character* with political questions. It is a great moral question, as was the abolition of slavery, and calls for the efforts of the ministers of the gospel. To me such efforts commend themselves. I have acted in the character of a politician as well as in that of a Christian minister, in the town in which providence has placed me; feeling assured that in regard to all relative duties, and these considered on the largest scale, Christianity is not privative but emulative. There is no need to be a meddler, but there are reasons now and then recurring when the friend of political truth and righteousness will do his best to serve the cause of humanity, notwithstanding the addition of the clerical to his character as a citizen. I believe some of our brethren rather fear giving offence; I have none of this feeling though I respect theirs, and there may be many cases in which even Christian prudence would keep a minister silent and at home.

That you intend to go is to me a great satisfaction. Your age, standing, character, &c. fit you for such a service. I trust divine wisdom will direct the meeting, and make it subservient to the common good. It *must* shed a moral influence. *May God prevent what seems to be at hand—a fearful crisis.*

Excuse such a letter. When yours arrived I was at Parnden, and I have but just returned from Bocking. Yours, &c.

R. Burls.

Maldon, Essex, Aug. 9, 1841.

(From the Rev. S. Jones, of Burford.)

Dear Sir,—I write these few lines to assure you again that my heart is with you, and would have been very glad, if circumstances permitted, to be one of your number. I have prayed for you both in private and in public, that the wisdom of omniscience may guide all your deliberations, and that these deliberations may have the most beneficial tendency on the population of our country at large. The present aspect of things I consider truly ominous; the Lord only knows what the result will be. If you consider the following information of any advantage to the cause, it is at your service to use it in any way you deem best. I live in an agricultural district where wages are very low, averaging from six to ten shillings per week, and of course the poor are very badly off; and I see very plainly that the rise in the price of corn does not cause anything like a proportionate rise in wages. I have, belonging to my congregation, a farmer and a landowner to some little extent, who is a sensible and rather an intelligent man, as I think you will judge him to be when I tell you what he has repeatedly told me, which is as follows:—"I do not know but what the repeal of the corn laws may cause me a loss of one thousand pounds or more; nevertheless, I wish them repealed with all my heart, for I am a strong advocate for *free trade*, for I see very plainly that no trade but that is just, and that no trade but that is safe either." I wish, dear sir, that all the farmers and landowners in the country were like minded with this man, but I fear that he is a *rara avis in terris*. The *Patriot* newspaper speaks of having a list not only of those ministers actually present at your meeting, but also of those ministers who would have been present if circumstances admitted, and you will please to place my name in that list.

Samuel Jones.

Burford, Oxon, Aug. 16, 1841.

(From the Rev. T. Dawson, Bacup.)

Dear Sir,—During one of my pastoral visits among the poor of my congregation, the following case of want came under my own observation. In a family consisting of husband and wife and four children, I found their income at most did not average more than ten shillings a week. Out of this, rent, coals, food, and clothing had to be provided. I said to the mother, "How do you live?" She burst into tears, and gave me the following narrative. "Last winter," she said, "most of my children were ill; we had nothing to eat for nearly two days, and I determined upon destroying myself; and for this purpose I had purchased some arsenic, under the pretence of destroying vermin. It so happened, however, before I took it, that a part of scripture came with much force,—'Fear not! for I am with thee,'—which was the means of preventing me." I hope this may lead to some beneficial result. I had some pleasing conversation with her on spiritual things; and she would now thankfully attend the house of God, if a want of clothing did not prevent. Her children attend no school for the same reason.

Almost adjoining my own house there is a family whom we have often supplied from our own table. As many of them as can are now in full employ. The father is a sizer, and two of the children work in the mill. The full amount of their income is 18s. a week. Out of this, 1s. 2d. goes for rent, and 7d. a week for coals, leaving for food and clothing 16s. 3d. Out of this, husband and wife and six children must be maintained. Into sick clubs they pay 8d per week, leaving 5d. less than 2s. a week for each. This is not an extraordinary case, and would not, I believe, be below an average, in families placed under similar circumstances as to the age and number of their children.

Twenty years since, I have been informed by the parties themselves, on whose statements I can place a full confidence, they received 21s. 6d. for a piece of cloth; now, for the same work, they are only receiving 12s. Then, a load of flour cost 38s.; now it costs 50s. They had then two small children, and did, for some few years, save out of their earnings £20 a year.

Thomas Dawson.

Bacup, August 11, 1841.

(From the Rev. J. Reynolds, Romsey.)

Dear Sir,—I trouble you with a very few lines for the purpose of conveying, through you, to the great and awful convention, to be assembled at Manchester on the 17th curt., the expression of my deep and sincere regret that circumstances, over which I have no control, and engagements formed before the issuing of your circular of the 8th of July, and of the address of the 13th of that month, combine to render my appearance at that meeting altogether impracticable. But I should consider that I forfeited all title to the character of a Christian minister and a true patriot, if I did not sympathize, to my heart's core, with the great principles and purposes which are to be exhibited at that assembly. Though absent in body, I shall be present in spirit: and my heart's desire and prayer to God shall be, that a very eminent measure of divine wisdom and love may be vouchsafed to the great convocation; so that results may follow for which our beloved country, and the church of Christ, shall have cause to bless the originators and the conductors of this august exhibition of Christian benevolence.

If I might be permitted to offer one suggestion, I should say, I hope that the conference will not separate without setting apart a day for solemn humiliation and prayer in behalf of the great topics which will be brought before them.—I have the honour to be, dear sir,

Yours most gratefully and respectfully,
JOHN REYNOLDS,
Bishop of the Independent Church in this town.

Romsey, Hampshire, August 14, 1841.

(From Mr. J. Morris, London.)

Dear Sir,—At the request of a highly esteemed ministerial brother, the Rev. Mr. Gilbert, of Islington, who, like myself, feels deeply interested in the contemplated proceedings of the Manchester convention, but who cannot have the desired pleasure and honour of being present with you, I beg thus most respectfully to address you; and more especially, because, during my late residence at Olney, Bucks, I held a farm of nearly 300 acres from the close of 1832 to the close of 1839, a period of considerable fluctuation in the price of corn, and especially of wheat. In the year 1836 I took a lease for fourteen years at £420 per annum, or about 30s. 6d. per acre, principally extra parochial, so that I was but little benefited by the new poor-law bill. Under these circumstances the frequent agitation of the corn-law question alarmed me, and, in some measure, influenced my determination to relinquish the farm, which I did in 1839. But, to address myself to the series of questions proposed in the *Patriot* of the 9th inst., I am informed that the working classes in the town and neighbourhood of Olney are not well employed; not a few able-bodied and steady labourers being out of employment, and exposed to much privation and suffering.

During my own observation up to 1839, stout useful young men of sixteen, able to do almost any ordinary work on a farm, seldom receive wages exceeding 5s. or 6s. per week. Boys at ten years, to drive plough (horse), 1s. 6d.; twelve, 1s. 8d.; thirteen, 2s. 6d. Second-rate labourers 8s. or 9s. First-rate men 10s. per week, and when employed at task-work, at draining, hedging, and ditching, or thrashing corn in the barn, from 11s. to 13s. per week. Within my experience their wages, on the whole, have increased about from 1s. to 2s. per week.

When corn is high, farmers generally employ a greater number of labourers than when prices are depressed.

Wages rise, when corn maintains for a few weeks an advanced price, about 1s. per week; say from 9s. to 10s., from Lady Day to hay term, when 1s. more is occasionally paid, and boys' wages in a small proportion are advanced.

During the winter months the inferior boys and labourers are generally discharged, and mostly the wages of day labourers reduced about 1s. per week, and boys in proportion.

To the comparative condition of the labouring classes I cannot speak with much confidence, but my impression is, that in the neighbourhood of my late residence it is much worse than it was twenty-five years ago, and house property has deteriorated within that period 30 per cent. or more. To the latter fact I speak confidently.

The rates on land and house property have certainly, since the new poor-law act, been reduced one-third or more. I remember to have paid twelve rates per annum, while now seven often meet the demand of the year.

Of prison reports, &c., I have no knowledge, but I can testify that the poor there are miserably so indeed. How they live is a mystery to many. In no case do I remember wages, since the said new act, to be regulated according to the number of a man's children, except when benevolent and private considerations influenced the employer.

The state of the small traders, bakers more particularly, is very trying. All traders suffer much, but the poor have very little to spare for any thing besides bread.

Perhaps the town of Olney is rather remarkable for the number of persons disposed to attend public worship campared with the population; but even of those many are prevented from want of decent apparel. I have met with an instance, of a widow and her daughter who were in the habit of using one pair of shoes alternately (the only decent pair they had between them) to attend public worship.

The attendance of children at the Sunday school has been of late years rather diminished, mainly from destitution of clothing, and but for charitable efforts many more would certainly be prevented from attending. The infant school has also suffered from a similar cause.

With respect to the comparative advantage of a "fixed duty" over the "sliding scale," I well remember the remarks of thinking and reading intelligent farmers stating their conviction, that the former would be decidedly preferable to the latter, as it is a fact that has fallen under my own observation, that wheat of the same quality has fluctuated (in one year) from 4s. 6d. per bushel to 8s. or 8s. 6d. per bushel. I think it was so in 1836, and in 1838 it was 11s. and 12s. per bushel.

To a total repeal of the corn laws no farmer could be brought to accede, without the admission of certain ruin to his property*; although even such a measure may, in a national view, be *ultimately* allowed to be beneficial, from the hope that foreigners would be our customers for manufactured goods in exchange for corn. The sliding scale places in the hands of the wealthy factor of Mark-Lane the command of the market—the means of degrading the revenue, by nominal sales in which neither corn nor money changes hands, but which are entered in their mutual books, merely to affect the averages, and is in every point of view a crying abomination, seldom of benefit to any except the rich among farmers, who can retain their stacks in the yard, for one, two, or three years. With regard to a fixed duty, I wish to speak very modestly, that in my opinion it would be decidedly advantageous to the farmer on the whole, as he would sow and reap with some degree of certainty as to the result of

* On this point we have inserted proof sufficient that Mr. M.'s assertion is erroneous in every sense.

his general calculations for the year, which he never can do under a sliding scale. I have calculated the general price of wheat in the continental corn markets, freightage, insurance, unloading, warehousing, merchant, and miller's profits, &c.; and conclude that foreign wheat could scarcely be brought into this country under from 6s. to 6s. 9d. per bushel, which with a reduction of about 20 per cent. in rent, and a small reduction, say 1s. per week in labourers' wages, would enable the English grower to compete with the foreigner, promote our exportation of manufactures, greatly benefit at least the shipping interests of this country, and restore it to the position of being the leading manufacturer for the civilized world.

Desiring to express my full concurrence in your noble object, and fervently praying you and all the dear brethren and fathers assembled, may be richly favoured with that wisdom which is from above, and eminently blessed in all your consultations to promote the good of the nation, I remain, yours, &c., JOHN MORRIS.

27, Bermondsey Wall, London, Aug. 14th, 1841.

As a delegate from the church and congregation assembling in Legge-Street, Birmingham, I beg leave to state, in addition to the oral communications of the Rev. T. East and the Rev. T. Swan, already given to this conference, that I have personally visited several hundred families residing in the most destitute parts of the above town, and can bear mournful testimony to their wretched condition. Our poor rates, compared with former periods, are doubled, and the situation of the labouring classes and many of the smaller tradesmen is worse than at any previous time; and the strong conviction of many of the suffering constituents in my congregation is, that their condition would be greatly alleviated by the total repeal of the corn laws. With them I am bound to sympathize, having in the neighbourhood of my chapel seen some of my fellow-creatures in the most abject state of destitution. Though the numbers of the distressed are not equal to Manchester and other places, yet I have found some of them lying on no better beds than straw or shavings, in the miserable garrets of the courts of our towns, and almost in a state of starvation. One respectable manufacturer in my district, and who employs more than 200 men, declares that besides the great reduction in wages among his operatives, the proceeds of the club connected with his factory for provident purposes, only realizes half what it formerly produced.

There are two spacious chapels belonging to the respectable body of the Wesleyans in this neighbourhood, which some time ago had not a single sitting to let, but which are now, through the distressed state of the labouring classes, vacated by more than 300 persons. And I can bear my humble testimony that the absentees from religious worship in my own chapel, have borne an almost similar proportion, and may be attributed to the same causes.

A button manufacturer in my own congregation, with a large family, has received no orders for some months, his factory has been closed, and he is now looking, with thousands of others in the same deplorable situation, to the important deliberations of this conference, as a dernier hope that something will be done to render his condition and that of his neighbours, supportable. I only briefly add, that the reports of our town missionaries afford melancholy and abundant proofs from Birmingham that the situation of the poor is most distressing, and supply the most powerful argument for the immediate removal of the unjust and unscriptural restrictions on the food of the people.

Birmingham. P. S.

My dear Sir,—I did not see the queries to be answered at your conference until yesterday. I was very glad to find that I had met some of them, though not to that extent which I might have done, as I feared that I might be going wrong. Wishing to help your good work as much as possible, I beg leave to add a little more. I am the only dissenting minister in the midst of many parishes, and I am regarded, indeed, with a most jealous eye by the land and tithe-holders. A farmer, about two and a half miles from us, has a farm of his own in one parish of about 1100 acres, rents one of about 1200 acres in another parish, and is lord of the manor in a third parish, where he is buying up all, and turning out the small tenants with their families, who know not where to go or what to do, and in the end their families must come to the poor rate. Under such power the poor, and all, suffer. Such landlords pay the labourers just what wages they please, from 4s. 6d. to 8s. a week to those with families, let the price of the loaf be what it may. A poor woman of our poor congregation has a stout healthy son, about fourteen years of age. The farmer who employs him gives him no more than 4d. a day. His mother went to beg a little more, as she could not provide for him with what he had. The farmer told her that he would not give any more. She then said that she should be obliged to get another place for her son. The farmer said that if she did so, he would turn her father and brother (who worked for him) away. These men had large families; the farmer was proprietor of all the land in the parish; and what could be done by these poor depending creatures? These very persons wish to go to hear the gospel, and to judge for themselves; but when they attempt to do so, they are watched, and cursed, and threatened with having no work. What a high state of slavery! and how very difficult for our poor people to stand their ground!

Some time before I came, our Sabbath school was completely swept away by the hostile influence, which is very great indeed. However, we have had courage to begin it again, with a view to take what the Church cannot accommodate, and the children are coming back as fast as they can. Where there is no school, the hunting clergy and their ladies, who have got all the money, and, of course, all the influence, buy the poor children by paying for their schooling, and by other favours. Trade is bad amongst the middle classes. Some time ago we had a dreadful fire, by which fourteen houses were destroyed in two hours, and little tradesmen suffered much. One of our people, whose house was burned, sustained great loss. A subscription was opened, and, when it might have been a very good one indeed, it was closed, and the money locked up in the bank. And why so? To drive such people out of the place. As for crime in public, it exceeds everything. Last Sabbath, I was forced to call in the aid of the constable. I am threatened with some disturbance next Lord's day, but I do not yet know what it will be. All this is in a free and Christian land, because the people are left in ignorance and crime, although so many thousands of pounds are paid to teach them better. Many of our people are obliged to take up such a heavy cross that one is ready to think we must be crushed in the end.

Wishing that your plans may be so effectual as to raise a powerful voice, that must be heard, I remain, yours most respectfully,

P.S.—I long to hear of the triumph of your proceedings.

Maiden Newton, Dorset. T. D.

Dear Sir,—Last week, I entertained some hope of attending the meeting of ministers, at Manchester, but as I have not been able, I write to say that I cordially approve of the meeting, and believe that great good will result. I have carefully examined your questions, and beg leave to state a few things, as general answers to them.

There is no manufactory in the town of Huntingdon, or in the county, so that we are not affected in that marked degree, in which the manufacturing districts are. Yet persons in trade generally complain of having very little retail custom, the poor having nothing to lay out, *but* for the necessaries of life. The assertion that "farmers never raise the wages of labourers in proportion to the price of corn," is fully supported in this county. I have sat at the board of guardians in this town, and able-bodied men from the villages around, with families of six and seven, have declared that their wages were only 10s., and, in some cases 9s., a week. On examination, these statements were found to be correct. The sum generally given, is 12s. a week, for the most able men.

The increase in our jails and infirmaries has not been great; nor does there appear to be a decrease in our congregations, or in our *religious* funds, from the high price of provisions; or if there be, it is but *trivial.*

There is no attention paid to the number of children in a family, in the payment of wages. I consider the circumstances of the poor generally, in the town and county, to be very indifferent; and that some of them are suffering great privations. Any decrease that may exist in our congregations, or in our religious funds, is obviously in the attendance and contributions of the *poor.* Our towns in this county are small, and the symptoms of deterioration are not striking and urgent as in some places.

These general statements may be relied on, and I transmit them for the furtherance of the great object of the meeting, as a mite towards the mass of information about to be collected.

I am decidedly opposed to the present corn laws, and for many reasons think Lord John Russell's plan the best, that could be adopted under *present* circumstances.

Huntingdon. W. W.

(*From a large proprietor and occupier of land.*)

My dear Friend,—I have your circular with your note, and hope you will be successful in calling the attention of the ministers of this county to the important subject of the corn laws, and inducing as many as can to attend the conference to be held at Manchester. With respect to the queries in your note, I do not know that I can give you any information which you do not already possess; however, as you wish it, I will endeavour to state my views on the subject as briefly as I can.—First, As to the probable effects on the owners of land: I believe the present corn laws were especially designed to keep up the unnaturally high price which land, and consequently rents had attained during the war, and that they have most effectively answered that purpose to the great injury of every class except the landowners and the clergy; and supposing them to be altered as proposed by Lord John Russell, the value of land *will be reduced* and *rents must fall* to a more natural level; but not to the ruinous extent which many persons affect to believe.—1st, Because, from the rapid increase of population, there must necessarily be a much greater demand for the produce of the land, provided the people can obtain employment, and indeed whether they can or not they must be fed.—2d, If we consent to take foreign corn at a moderate duty, it will in a great measure, if not wholly prevent that accumulation of corn in foreign ports which has caused the low price at which it can be purchased when our ports are closed against it, and there can consequently be but little demand for it. 3d, That it will in all probability produce a regular trade in which the corn imported by us will be paid for in manufactures instead of specie as at present, thus preventing that drain of gold which occasions the commercial difficulties and ruin which we have so frequently witnessed of late years. That while a regular supply of foreign corn in our markets has a tendency to keep *down the price* here, it at the same time tends *to raise it on* the continent, and will thus place our manufactures more on a level with the continental competitors, who will not then be able to undersell them in neutral markets as at present, and the manufacturing population being fully employed will occasion a further increased demand, so as to prevent the price receding below a remunerating level.

Second, As regards the occupiers of land, the decrease in the value of the produce will be met by a reduction of the rent and tithes, and also, which is a very natural item, a considerable reduction in the parochial rates, by a general diminution in the price of most of the necessaries of life. I do not myself think the reduction will be to such an extent as materially to affect wages; if it does at all, it will be only in some agricultural districts. When I sold wheat at £9 per load I gave 10s. per week wages; since then it has been as high as £19, and not less than £14 per load, and I now pay 12s. per week. I think £9 is much less than it is likely to be on an average of years; but I am persuaded that if it had continued at that price the payments of the farmer would have been adjusted to it.

The labourers must evidently be gainers by the reduction in the price of wheat; their wages are not raised in proportion to the advance of corn, neither are they lowered in the proportion to the decrease in price, as is evident from the above statement. The benefit to the manufacturing labourers cannot be doubted, inasmuch as their wages are not affected at all by the price of food. but by the demand for labour; they must therefore be doubly gainers, as the measures which will lower the price of bread are the most likely to procure them employment.

For my own part, I am persuaded that whatever party may be in power, an alteration in the corn laws must be made; the sooner the better for the welfare of our country. I trust the conference at Manchester will promote and hasten so desirable an end, therefore most heartily wish you God-speed, and am, my dear friend, yours faithfully,

J. V., jun.

Hurst, 13th August, 1841.

My dear Sir,—So far as I have considered the subject, it appears to me that the existing corn laws have proved exceedingly injurious to the nation; and I feel persuaded that, so long as they are in operation, poverty and misery will continue to increase. As a minister of Christ, I feel myself bound to unite with my brethren whose object it is, by all legitimate means, to aid in the removal of these baneful laws; especially as they interfere most seriously, in their practical bearings, with the spiritual interest of the poorer part of the community.

I must confess that I am not qualified to give an opinion as to a fixed corn duty, but I am inclined to think that in proportion to our encouragement of foreign growth, will be our commercial prosperity: assuredly it would render nations so dependent upon each other, as either to prevent war, or to lead them to engage in it from absolute necessity alone?

As to the means of providing for our rapidly increasing population, it is perfectly plain, from the calculations which have been made, that only a small portion could be maintained by agriculture, and that emigration would not meet the necessity of the case; but if laws were enacted which would encourage an abundant supply of foreign corn, our commerce would in all probability be so much increased, as to furnish means for the employment of the surplus population; and, in a variety of ways, to confer essential benefit upon the community at large.

I have thus expressed my humble opinion upon the subject. I had intended to write to our friend, Mr. Thompson, but it occurred to me that, as you are collecting information from the country, and intend to visit Manchester, it would be better to convey my sentiments to you. Please present my kind regards to Mr. Thompson. Accept my thanks for Baptist Noel's excellent pamphlet, and allow me to remain, my dear sir, yours very sincerely,

J. P. W.

Hers monceux, August 9th, 1841.

(*From an occupier and proprietor of land.*)

Dear Sir,—Yours with the circular I duly received, and am obliged. I do not exactly agree with all the statements made therein. On the whole, the arguments are good, but must confess I have not sufficiently thought on the subject to furnish much, if any, information relative thereto. From past events in the corn duty, or what is called the sliding scale, I think it has not generally worked as was expected; the consequence is, in my mind, the capitalists and large importers now bring as much corn as suits their purpose and profit, and bond it; when here safe bonded, the same party set about getting up the price to take it out at the lowest average; after which, it appears, when released, it is brought into the market and used; but the question is, who has been benefited? in my mind *the merchants* have realized *the largest* profits by far. Now if we had a fixed *moderate* duty, the corn, when imported, would be likely to be brought into the markets regularly, which I think would operate against existing high prices, which benefit no one except the moneyed growers who have the means to hold back till it reaches his *fixed* price for selling. I was in conversation with a large farmer in this quarter this day. This gentleman has been opposed to a fixed duty; but to my great surprise, he strongly advocated admitting corn without duty. Make it an article of mutual trade, send goods of our manufacturing for corn, and, in his opinion, the price would find its level. If corn did not pay so well as grazing and fattening cattle, the farmer must turn his attention to this, and if that lowered in profit, they must plough again; so that, after a fair trial, the farmer will cultivate his land in the best way he can for profit, the same as every other person does who has a business to attend to. I have no doubt the present sliding scale has enriched the *large merchants* and *importers* to an amazing extent, and some plan should be arranged to supersede this; but I cannot point out the way, or even see how, only by a low fixed import duty, or admitting it without duty. If corn be admitted without, and price comes down below what the cultivator of the land can live at, from present high rents, it appears to me it will be a path of duty of the landlords to meet the case by *lowering* his rent in proportion to the low price of corn. I wish I could give you better information on this subject. I am, dear sir, yours respectfully,

W. A.

Arundel, August 10, 1840.

(*From the Rev. John West, Bethnal Green, London.*)

I regret that amidst the many interesting and deeply affecting details, which, during the course of yesterday, were presented to the conference, none were presented from any of the densely populated, and most afflictingly wretched parts of the *metropolis*. Coming, as I do, from the parish of Bethnal Green, containing a population of 74,000 souls, most of whom are in the weaving trade, I could, if it were necessary, exhibit a picture of actual suffering as existing at the present time in that locality, which would harrow up every feeling, and awaken every sympathy of the benevolent heart. There are at this time from 30 to 40 per cent. of the working classes out of employ, and the rate of earnings to those in work is from 5s. to 12s. per week. Prices have very much decreased within the last twenty years on all kinds of work, and during the last year there has been a reduction in the branch of the velvet trade to a considerable amount. The demand for labour in this locality is by no means affected by cheap or dear food, and wages have not risen or fallen with the rise and fall of provisions. There is scarcely any comparison between the condition of the operative classes now and formerly. There has for some years past been a gradual deterioration; but never were they in so deplorable and abject a state as they are at present. The scenes of squalid poverty and appalling wretchedness, of utter destitution of the comforts, and even necessaries of life—the disease and suffering of the poor which comes before the view of our Christian instruction, and city mission agent, are beyond all description. The want of employment is literally starving whole families; and, but for charity or parochial help, they must perish by hundreds. As the necessary consequence, the poor-house is crowded; so much so, that while the average number within its walls during the summer months, ordinarily, is only from 300 to 400, there are at this time between 800 and 900. The small traders in the neighbourhood say that they never knew things in so bad a state as they now are. Multitudes are unable to pay their rents, and are fast merging into pauperism themselves. Although the state of *our* religious and benevolent societies has not yet suffered to any great extent; nor the numbers of attendants at public worship and children at the Sabbath school actually decreased, yet we find that individuals decline their subscriptions, and vacate their sittings, and keep their children at home, on account of the want of employment and suitable clothing; and these instances are getting common beyond all precedent, so that unless some beneficial change be effected soon, there can be no doubt that we shall feel the consequences to a very painful extent. In conclusion, I would say, that the prevailing opinion among the operative and middle classes in our neighbourhood, is that the laws restricting the importation of corn have much to do with the existing misery, and that the effect of their removal would be the improvement of trade, and the consequent enlargement of the means of subsistence and of comfort.

(*From Spitalfields, London.*)

Dear Sir,—I send you enclosed with this a statement of the prices which are paid for different sorts of silk goods at the present time, and also of some a few years back. The works, which are of the date 1841, are making at the present time; and the others are also actual works, which were made at the dates affixed. I could not get any correct account for the year 1835, but the prices were about the same as in 1836.

A man in 1824 would make 4 or 5 yards of 8 thread satin per day, at 70 shutes; now he cannot do more than 2 yards at 184 shutes. Consequently his earnings at that work were about 6s. per day; now, for the same time, he earns 1s. 6d., or about a quarter of what he could earn in 1824.

In velvets, in 1824, a man could make 1½ to 2 yards per day; his earnings then were from 6s. to 8s. per day; now it does not exceed 4s. or 5s., with good silk.

In gros-de-naples and other plain goods, the price is rather less than half what it was in 1824, for the same length of work, with an extra quantity of shute per inch; so that, from what I can ascertain, the prices now paid for work in general average rather less than one-third of the prices paid in 1824.

We must also take into account, that the silk used at present is much more difficult to work than that used previous to the reduction, which, in many instances, especially in velvets, will make the price earned much less than I have stated.

The prices in 1824 were moderately stationary; but they very soon began to fall, and they have gradually become lower and lower, till they have arrived at the present prices; and from the present depressed state of trade, there is reason to believe they will be still lower; for, besides the low prices I have mentioned, the weaver has a great deal of *play*: that is, waiting for work or having nothing to do.

The working hours of a working day are also more than they were; for a weaver is at the present time up and at work at five or six o'clock in the morning, and works on, with not more than an hour at meals, till dark. Next week they will begin their *allumer*, or (as they call it) *hollymosh*; that is, to work by lamplight, when their time of working will be extended to ten or eleven at night; and through the whole of the winter they begin to light up in a morning at six and seven o'clock, and so work till ten or eleven at night.

In 1824, and previous to that, they did not work so close as they do now; not that they were less early at work, but they had more time for their meals, and more time to spare in an evening. Now, with the exception of about three months during the summer, the whole of their time, from Monday morning till Saturday night, is employed incessantly at work, while there is any to do, to get a living.

Previous to 1824, it was an uncommon thing for the wives and daughters of weavers *not* to have periodically a silk dress made by themselves; now, they are so poor it is an uncommon thing for them to have one at all.

In addition to these things, there are a great quantity of tradespeople who are dependant upon the well-doing of the weavers, and who experience very great reverses in trade, in consequence of the very depressed state of the trade.

I will now take notice of a very great fallacy which most political economists are in the habit of upholding, and which is the subject of very great error, that is, that if there is a greater amount of goods made, that, therefore, the persons employed in the manufacture, must, of necessity, be better off, and the hon. and rev. Baptist Noel, in his excellent pamphlet, "A Plea for the Poor," appears to be of the same opinion; for, according to his account, and I suppose he is correct, he states the average consumption of raw and thrown silk in the ten years preceding 1824 to be 1,940,902 lbs., and the average consumption of the twelve years following 4,144,444 lbs. Now if that is a proof of the flourishing state of the trade, how is it that the journeymen are in so depressed a condition as they are at present; for if the increased consumption, as above shown, is any proof of the increased prosperity of the trade, wages should at least have doubled; but, strange to say, the fact is quite the reverse; for, instead of being doubled, the wages are not one-third of what they were in 1824. But these gross amounts give you no information whatever as to the state of wages or of profits in any manufacture; if you want to find them out, you must apply to the operative and to the manufacturer, you must enter their workshops and their warehouses, you must be in some measure intimately acquainted with both, and you must also know something about their operations before you come to a judgment to which such gross amounts will appear to lead you.

I have endeavoured to give you a short account of how things are at present in the silk trade, in the Spitalfields district, and I hope it may be of service to Dr. Cox at the approaching meeting.

Year.	Price of corn.	Description of work.	Price per yard.
1835....	39s. 6d....	The prices were about the same as 1836.	
1836....	49s. 6d....	1100 6-thread satin, 96 shutes per inch	....7d.
1837....	56s. 0d....	1200 6 do. 96 do.	....8d.
1839....	71s. 0d....	1000 8 do. 130 do.	....9d.
1840....	68s. 0d....	1000 7 do. 130 do.	....9d.
1841..	70s. 5d. is the average of last week	1070 8 do. 170 do.	....9d.
		1000 7 do. 184 do.	....9d.
		1640 4 do. 120 do.	....7½d.

In 1824, and previous to that, the number of shutes per inch in satins were from 70 to 80; and a double number of shutes per inch will take up nearly double the time to make the same length of work.

Description of work.	Price in 1840.	1841.	1824.
1000 velvet....	3s. 0d....	2s. 9d....	4s. 0d.
1200 do.	3s. 6d....	3s. 3d....	4s. 6d.
1300 do.	3s. 9d....	3s. 6d....	4s. 9d.

The number of shutes in velvets is about the same as previous to 1824.

Gros-de-Naples were paid, in 1824, from 11d. to 1s. 2d.; they are now paid 6d. per yard. And there is about the same reduction in every description of work; and with this addition, (with the exception of velvets,) the number of shutes per inch is very considerably increased, which lowers the price of the work very much to the weaver.

J. P. G.

August 13, 1841.

When I wrote to you last week I wrote the few remarks in haste. Looking over some papers, I found an account of three parishes, as they were about the year 1761; my informant died about two years since, aged eighty; he began with his own parish, where born. He has given me the names of twenty-two farmers, all known to him, the number of acres each farmed; in the whole, amounting to 425. The whole of the land in the parish he states about 1000 acres; number of inhabitants, about 200; at this time, the poors-rate from 1761 to 1770, was from £20 to £25 per year: at the present time, £289 7s., one of the most degraded parishes we have. One, a highly respectable and sober one, had, to their misery, a beer-shop or two in the parish, and men were unhappily drawn there and spent a part of their 7s. or 8s. per week. He gave me an account of two other parishes, similar; and I have an account of two more much in the same state. And until some alteration takes place, miserable must be the circumstances of hundreds of the working class, as well as the middle men. The working man, with 8s. or 9s. per week, after providing for self, wife, and three, four, or five, and some six children, cannot have money for many things necessary. My informant told me he lived with his grandfather, the people used to come and buy malt of him; and he sold his barley, 11s. per quarter; malt, 6½d. per peck; hops, 1½d. per lb. He recollected hearing one man say he sold twenty loads of wheat to a factor, at Poole, for £100, and said he thought he had made a good day's work. This was an old farmer in the parish, in the year 1737; but what have our ruinous, unhappy laws done for us! Well may Bishop Porteus say, "Ah, why should kings forget that they are men, or men that they are brethren?" I do not wonder, for the apostle Paul tells me wars and fightings come from men's lusts. Hoping all deliberations will be conducted amidst harmony and peace.

Blandford. J. R.

Dear Sir,—I am sorry that I was forced to delay my communication, from not being able until last night to obtain the sums expended by some of the trades, which I considered essential to the object in view, as far as Sheffield is concerned. The great sums paid by these workmen had partly been saved during the years 1834, 1835, and 1836, when bread was cheap and trade good. These funds are now exhausted, and the number of workmen receiving aid are continually increasing, and those who have to pay daily diminishing. This may appear from these returns somewhat paradoxical, as the sums paid do not appear to have much increased. The reason is that the weekly scale paid to the unemployed workmen have been decreased one-third, and in some cases one-half. Some trades are paying 3s. for a man, and a shilling per head for the rest of the family. Of the situation of these families (many of whom have lived in great respectability) some estimate may be formed, when, from this small pittance, rent, clothing, fuel, &c., is to be provided. As one fallacy is continually attempted to be imposed upon the people of this country, viz., that on the continent, where bread is cheap, the people there have very low wages, and live on the most miserable diet, I have enclosed you my letters to Dr. Holland, and a manufacturer; in these you will find references to Mr. Porter of the Board of Trade, Jelinger J. Symonds on arts and artisans, which may possibly be of some use to you. If you got the rates from Mr. Crosland the vestry clerk, descanting on the misery and increase of pauperism, it would be well to contrast the casual poor list for the year 1834, 1835, and 1836, against the sums paid in 1838, 1839, 1840, and the year ending April, 1841. You may then point out what those rates most probably would have been, had not the heavy sums paid by the workmen contributed greatly to lessen the amount of those rates.

There are many who, having been in good circumstances, are now in a state of starvation, and can scarcely get food to keep soul and body together. A person who works in the same factory with me, an excellent workman in the scissor line, for a great length of time has not averaged above 4s. per week. From this he pays 2s. for lodgings, 2d. washing. His principal food is potatoes and a little bread; to this he drinks mint or balm tea without sugar twice a day. In this manner hundreds subsist; the falling off in the consumption of that necessary article, sugar, will clearly show the deprivation of the working classes. In my address to the operatives of the United Kingdom on the corn laws, you will find some calculations of the effects of high prices on the home trade, as the high price of provision takes away the means of the industrious classes to purchase clothing, furniture, &c., the produce of the labour of the artisan.

The effects of these laws are driving great numbers of our best workmen in the grinding department to seek refuge in America and the continent. This will be an irreparable misfortune. How can we long compete with these men, when established in countries where provisions are not one-half the cost we pay for them here? If these laws continue in force a few years longer, the sun of England's manufacturing superiority will set for ever, and her naval and military strength must decline, from want of resources and a sufficient and flourishing revenue.

I got the following returns from the several branches; some others do not meet more than once a fortnight; and as the keys of their boxes with their accounts are generally held by four or five different persons, I could not obtain their accounts without considerable trouble and expense.

The table-knife grinders, who are the most numerous body of the heavy grinders, paid to their unemployed workmen, from January 1st, 1837, to January, 1838, £3901. 7s. 7d.; to January, 1839, £2801. 8s.; to January 1st, 1840, £2683. 8s. 6d.; to 1841, £3528. 17s.; and up to June 24th, of the present year, £1857. 2s. 9d. Their scale has been reduced twice, and they have paid in that period £14,771. 3s. 8d. The saw-grinders paid from October 31st, 1837, to July 1840, £2247. 2s. 6d.; the edge tool-grinders, from January 1838 to January of the present year, £1560. 18s.; and the file-grinders, during the last four years, have paid £1416. 10s. 9d. These are but a small number of the trades; but it may be considered what a vast number of individuals are out of employment. To the casual poor list of Sheffield township should be added Ecclesall, Bierlow, and the other out townships of the parish of Sheffield. Some idea of the mass of human misery caused in this place alone, may be gathered from the fact that the majority of trades do not allow more than the parish scale.

Sheffield.

(From the Rev. J. Davies, Sheffield.)

Dear Sir,—I write principally to convey to you a little information as to the operation of the corn laws in this town. I have only of late become a resident here, and can therefore testify nothing as the result of my own observation or experience. I have, however, instituted inquiry in quarters where information was likely to be gathered, and now hand you the replies with which I have been furnished.

1. [Furnished by Mr. Ibbotson, a highly respectable manufacturer in this place. the chief friend of Mr. Buckingham, and a leading and highly efficient agitator on the question of the corn laws; having in the year 1837 published a useful book on the subject.] The working classes are very inadequately employed. A small portion of the workmen may not have been much reduced in their scale of remuneration, but a large portion have been fearfully reduced.

2. [By Mr. Ibbotson.] The wages of manufacturers depend on the price of food, and more extensively than has generally been supposed. But the price of food operates in a way the very reverse of what is generally stated by the supporters of the present corn law. The high price of corn has a tendency to lower wages by lessening the demand for goods. On the contrary, the low price of corn has a tendency to increase the demand for goods, and therefore to raise wages. From the year 1820 to 1823 wheat fell to an unprecedentedly low price, and the demand for manufactured goods was unprecedented likewise. From 1832 to 1835 a similar case occurred, and similar results followed.

3. [By Mr. Ibbotson.] The general answer to this is to be gathered from the statement made in reply to the previous question. The amount of wages is always affected by the demand for labour; and the demand for labour always varies with the cheapness or dearness of food.

[By Mr. Norton, a respectable medical practitioner in the town, and a leading man in the Wesleyan Association.] In 1835-36, when bread was cheap, wages were good; bread is now dear, and wages are at a low point.

4. [By Mr. Ibbotson.] The prostration of the labouring class is greater than has ever been known.

[By Mr. Norton.] Worse! sober and industrious people find it hard work to make both ends meet.

[By Mr. Crosslynn, governor of the workhouse, and superintendent registrar for the district.] There is greater distress in Sheffield than has been known for the last sixteen years; the number in the workhouse is greater than informant has ever known it.

5. [Extracted from the accounts of the parish of Sheffield.]

Amount of Poor-Rates for each Year (ending at Lady-day) from 1815 to 1841.

For 1815	£16,900	For 1830	£18,600
— 1816	18,100	— 1831	17,000
— 1817	24,200	— 1832	17,300
— 1818	35,500	— 1833 (the year of the cholera)	22,500
— 1819	26,400	— 1834	17,600
— 1820	36,800	— 1835	16,000
— 1821	36,200	— 1836	11,400
— 1822	20,100	— 1837 (the least sum ever known)	10,500
— 1823	15,600	— 1838	14,000
— 1824	16,700	— 1839	15,600
— 1825	16,600	— 1840	18,000
— 1826	12,900	— 1841 (highest amount since 1821)	28,800
— 1827	14,200		
— 1828*	15,900		
— 1829	20,500		

The following returns have been collected from the columns of the "*Independent*," a weekly paper published here. They exhibit the amount of moneys paid in various weeks from 1831 to 1841, to the casual poor; a class mainly consisting of persons thrown out of employment, and seeking only occasional assistance from the parish. They thus furnish a more accurate test of the state of trade than can be implied by reference to the gross amount of poor-rates, as the rates in general are influenced by various causes apart from the state of trade, while the amount of moneys paid to the casual poor depends in a great measure, if not entirely, upon the state of trade.

Amount paid for the relief of the casual poor in the parish of Sheffield, for the week ending

	£	s.	d.		£	s.	d.
Jan. 16, 1831	50	0	9	June 25, 1837	18	11	3
June 19	48	5	6	Jan. 26, 1838	63	15	0
Jan. 29, 1832	57	13	6	June 16	49	12	4
June 24	65	5	0	Jan. 25, 1839	38	7	6
Jan. 27, 1833	80	7	0	June 29	24	15	6
June 23	73	14	7	Jan. 24, 1840	93	11	6
Jan. 26, 1834	40	16	0	June 26	151	13	0
June 29	43	19	0	July 16, 1841	116	12	6
Jan. 25, 1835	35	16	0	—— 23	125	19	0
June 26	19	2	6	—— 30	111	10	0
Jan. 29, 1836	3	11	6	Aug. 6	114	17	0
June 26	11	10	0	—— 13	135	1	0
Jan. 29, 1837	10	17	6				

It is worth remarking, that in collecting the foregoing returns, no principle of selection has been adopted with a view to the purposes of mere argument. For ten years one week in January has been taken, and another in June, generally the last in each month. The returns copied for 1841 were published together the week before the conference took

* During the years 1828 to 1835, the purchase of the present workhouse, which cost £12,000, took place.

place, and strangely illustrate the depression at this moment so sadly prevalent among us.

6. I can only say here, that the editor of the *Independent* suggests, that the recent enlargement of the prison at Wakefield illustrates the progress of crime; while Mr. Turton informs me, that he has of late observed a great increase in the number of applicants at Sheffield dispensary.

7. I sent this inquiry to three friends of mine residing in the county of Buckingham, and received replies as below.

"The labourers in this neighbourhood, (Princes Risborough) are not paid according to the number of children they may have; nor do I think it is now much the practice, though common some few years ago. The average weekly amount for able-bodied men is 10s.; some give 1s. more, and some 1s. less."

"At Olney, able-bodied men have 10s. and 11s. per week—less able from 7s. to 9s. The number in family makes no difference as to amount."

"Our agricultural labourers [at Haddenham] have no manner of allowance in their pay for children, so that a man and wife, and six, or seven, or eight children, can only realize eight, nine, or ten shillings per week. The only difference is this. Some humane masters will, at certain times, let the men, half-starved, have work; so that, being without food, they must work more hours in a day to obtain some few pence more in a week, seldom more than 1s. or 2s."

8. [Mr. Turton.] Greatly deteriorated. It is hard to get medical fees from honest people.

[Mr. Ibbotson.] The middle classes in this neighbourhood are in an awfully suffering condition. Things were never known much worse. Complaints would be louder; only people naturally wish to keep up their credit.

To this I may add that I was conversing only yesterday with a person on this subject, who assured me that it appeared to her as if matters were getting worse every day. She is continually receiving applications for credit from poor people, to which she is compelled to turn a deaf ear, in order to prevent the almost inevitable multiplication of bad debts. She added that this state of things was not to be wondered at, while scissors made in Germany were offered for less money than their mere manufacture would cost in Sheffield?

9 to 12. It is difficult to answer these questions satisfactorily, so far as the interest with which I am connected is concerned, as many causes are at work besides those contemplated in the inquiries. It is often said, however, that our attendances on public worship would be larger if the people were in a better state; while cases are constantly occurring in which children are absent from the Sabbath schools for want of decent clothing.

I may add that I learn from Mr. Turton, that, at the conference of the Wesleyan Association, for this year,—a body comprising 26,000 members,—complaints were made, from every quarter, of impediments to the progress of the connexion, arising from the growing poverty of the people. Our town missionary here also informs me that he is perpetually coming into contact with cases in which persons plead their want of clothing as an excuse for not attending places of worship; and among these are many who were once members of religious communities.

In answer to several inquiries as to funds, I find that it is a general impression that the amounts raised for religious purposes are not much smaller than in former years, but that the moneys come more from the wealthier classes, and less from the middle and lower. In my own congregation, including no members of the higher classes, complaints are heavy of inability to do as friends have done heretofore, and as they long to do again.

You will be pleased to learn, if you have not heard before, that on Tuesday evening we had a meeting in our largest Independent chapel at which the ministers of Sheffield who had attended the conference gave some account of its proceedings, and dwelt largely on practical deductions. Mr. Smith, at whose chapel, "Nether Chapel," we met, took the chair. There were certainly 1500 persons present, and probably many more. We met at seven, and kept the meeting up till ten. An intense interest was awakened, and I think great good must have been done. The temper of the people seemed to be excellent. They acted like a company of enlightened, calm, determined, hopeful men; and by the way, we had but few ladies in the assembly. As opportunity may occur, we intend to agitate the matter again, and probably shall have occasion to do so very soon. Much is gained here, and must be gained everywhere, by identifying the cause with religion and its ministers. It is thus taken out of the hands of mere politicians or demagogues. It is placed under sacred influences. It will henceforth be worked by men who will act towards the people as our West Indian Missionaries acted towards those who were once slaves, by men who will at once fight the battle of the people, and keep them quiet till the victory is gained. This is one great point gained by our glorious conference—and gained by our first movements. Who shall say what results, beyond the mere abolition of the wicked corn laws, shall ultimately be realized? or how far these results shall extend?

But I feel that I am trespassing. I only add, that I am deeply thankful to Him who put it into the hearts of the brethren at Manchester to summon our great gathering; and that, though it is but little that I can do in promoting our grand object, that little will always be cherfully contributed. I remain, dear brother, very truly yours,

J. Davis,
Minister of Portmahon Chapel, Sheffield,

Session met in the vestry and was constituted; the Rev. J. W. Borland moderator. *Inter alia*, it was resolved,

1. That we regard the bread tax as an impolitic and odious impost, operating most injuriously upon the health, comfort, and energies of the productive classes of the commonwealth, and on these grounds imperiously demanding immediate and entire repeal; and especially that we deem all legislation tending to diminish or deteriorate the food of the people as an impious and unwarrantable interference with the will of him who has granted the produce of the soil to man as his natural birthright; and taught us constantly to pray, "Give us this day our daily bread."

2. That the impoverished and starving condition of millions of our countrymen, our neighbours, our kinsfolk, at the present moment throughout the empire, arising mainly from the injurious effects of monopoly, especially that in corn, suffers us no longer to be silent; but requires us, in terms of our former congregational protest and complaint, to lift high our united voices against this evil, and to persevere in our respectful but unvarnished remonstrances and strenuous efforts till the object in view shall be gained.

3 That, in accordance with these views, we hail the approaching wider discussion of this great question, and approve highly of the convention of ministers of all religious denominations, proposed to be held at Manchester, on Tuesday the seventeenth current, and succeeding days; and will very cordially enter, so far as circumstances may permit into any scheme which may seem likely, on christian principles, to secure the end in view.

4. That for the purpose of expressing more fully our feelings in this matter, we depute and appoint the Rev. John W. Borland, our pastor, to proceed to Manchester, and represent us in the contemplated conference.

Extracted from the minutes of session by

JAMES MARTIN, Session Clerk.

Lanark First Relief Church, 6th August, 1841.

Deaths and Crime from Starvation, Bolton.

1st. A man who resided in Haslam's-court, bottom of Bradshawgate, with a wife and six children. I visited the case, and found two of the children lying sick in a corner of the room on a small quantity of straw. Found the husband laid dead up stairs on a board. They had neither bed, bedding, nor any kind of furniture in the house. When I came out the neighbours gathered round me, and told me that the man had died for want of food. He said he wished he could have a little bread and cheese the day before he died. This family belong to a parish in the south of England who sent the letter of application for relief back to Bolton without opening!

2nd. A man residing in a cellar in Howel croft. Wife and two children out of work. His own earnings were four shillings per week. The neighbours came to tell me, as one of the guardians, that the man had died of hunger. I immediately visited the case along with the relieving officer and assistant overseer, and found the man laid out on one of the looms, there being neither bed nor bedding in the cellar. I assisted to get an inquest on the body, when it was clearly proved to a respectable jury that the man had died from want. The family did not belong to Bolton.

3rd. A woman applied to the Board of Guardians for relief with a child at her breast. The Board was breaking up, but I induced two of the Guardians to stop and give her an order for the workhouse. She had neither work nor home, and no milk for the child, owing to the want of the necessaries of life. Next morning, on visiting the workhouse to know if they were alive, the governor informed me the child was dead. I told him it had died of hunger. He said he understood so.

4th. I received a letter from Mr. Adam Dale, then Guardian for Rumworth, stating that a family, residing at the Willows, belonging to Great Bolton were in a state of starvation. I went to the place, and found they had been sold up the day before for rent, and had removed to his father's near Dobil Bar, to which place I followed them, and found the man and his wife with four children, along with two brothers, one having a wife with three small children, and the other also having a wife and one child, the men out of work, and their wives all pregnant, and near their time of delivery. They were all in one house with their old father and mother, the cottage being only four and a half yards square. I requested to see where they slept, and was shown into a room above, the same size, chiefly furnished with straw, where these poor women in all probability must have had their accouchement had I not visited them, and ordered them to apply to the Guardians. Do not such cases as these demoralise the rising generation?

5th. A man, formerly a spinner, applied to the Board with a wife and three small children, he being unable to spin in consequence of bad eyesight. The Guardians bought him a wheelbarrow so that he might go about selling salt, but not being able to procure a livelihood by this, one morning, his children being without anything to eat, he ordered his wife to go out and beg something for them. Not being able to procure anything by begging, she was induced to steal a piece of meat, and, being detected, was sent to the New Bailey. Thus poverty begets crime and fills our prisons.

6th. Mr. Eden, then Guardian for Sharples, stated, at the Guardian meeting, that eleven or twelve hundred people were in a state of starvation in consequence of the stoppage of Garnet Taylor's works. This induced myself and Mr. Thomas Evans, another Guardian, to go to the above-named place. We visited one hundred and thirteen people, whose earnings, including relief, amounted to one penny farthing per day. Many of them were without either bedding, clothes, or anything to eat. We have the documents by us with the names of the parties. I visited all those cases myself whilst I was a Guardian, in the space of eighteen months, along with scores of a similar nature. They all appear in the relieving officer's books with the exception of those at Sharples.

W. N.
W. J.

Bolton in 1773 contained a population of 5,300; in 1821, in consequence of its manufactures, it increased to 31,200; in 1831 it was 41,195; at present its population is full 50,000, and the parish contains not less than one hundred thousand persons.

In 1834, 5, 6, houses were not to be obtained; they were taken as soon as the foundation was dug. All hands at that time were fully employed; now there are 1,328 houses untenanted, and most are depreciated in value nearly one-third.

The poor-rates are an index of the state of a community. In the three years 1834, 5, 6, the rates levied for both townships amounted to £16,466 15s. In the year 1840 they amounted to £16,040 0s. 9d., but we established a relief fund in February 1840, for the relief of those who resided in the town, but had not their settlement in it, consequently having no claim upon the parish. That fund, amounting to £2,800, must be added to the £16,040 0s, 9d., which will make £18,840 0s. 9d: —one-fourth of the rates levied cannot be collected, in consequence of the poverty of the people.

Trade never was known to be worse; last week was the worst week ever known in Bolton. A shop keeper paying 40 pounds a year for rent, on a market day did not take a single farthing. In a street, one of the most public in the town, containing 34 shops and houses, where different descriptions of trade are carried on; out of these 34, there have been sold up 19 persons during the last 17 months.

The depression extends not to one but *all* trades. This state of things is without a parallel. In 1834, 5, 6, we were *compelled* to obtain hands from the agricultural districts.

The people of England are paying about 50 millions a year more for food than they did in 1835. Wheat was then 39s. What amount more were the people in the Bolton Union paying for their food in 1840? Not less than £195,000.

Independently of the general indexes I have adopted, I have employed another method of obtaining information, upon which undoubted reliance can be placed. I have seen the grocers, provision dealers, and pawnbrokers, and made inquiries of them.

The grocers used to sell their goods in large quantities, as pounds, half pounds, &c.; now their principal trade amongst the lower classes will be no more than pennyworths of sugar, tea, butter, &c. A father and mother and five children sleep in one bed. There are many such cases; 16 persons, young and old, were lodged and slept in an apartment only four yards and a half square.

Bad times for trade are the worst times for the pawnbrokers, whose shops are stocked with goods that cannot be redeemed. They will not lend more than 24s. upon what cost *two pounds*. Persons are in the habit of pledging their bedding, which they redeem at night by their clothes, and in the morning they redeem their clothes again with their bedding. Many persons do this; they are not paupers. All the pawnbrokers can testify to this fact.

After inquiries made of the leading manufacturers and the weavers themselves, as nearly as possible taking all together, the average amount of income is not more than 5s. 9d. per week, out of which they pay for rent 1s. 10d., preparation 10d., winding 5½d., coal 8d., soap 4d., tear and wear, 4d., leaving for subsistence 1s. 3½d. per week. Suppose a man to have five in a family, which is the average, then 3½d per week for each individual is the average.

To show how the taxes upon food affect the wages of an able-bodied weaver, without wife or child, let me refer you to the following calculation. Grant him to work fancy work; then he takes from his warehouse 7s. 6d. After deducting for his lodgings and preparation 3s. 3½d., he has left to support himself 4s. 2½d. He spends it in the following way. He pays for

Six breakfasts of oatmeal ..	6d......	tax, 2d.
Tea and Coffee	2d......	do. 1d.
Bacon	8d......	do. 3d.
Bread	1s. 1d......	do. 4d.
Milk	3d......	do. 0d.
Sugar	4d......	do. 2d.
Butter	4d......	do. 1d.
Flour	1d......	do. 0d.
Potatoes	5d......	do. 0d.
	3s. 10d.	1s. 1d.

One shilling and a penny is the amount of tax on this poor man's food! Deducting the 3s. 10d. from his 4s 2½d., what has he a week to spend in cloth or for shoes, or for the maintenance of a family, &c.?

Thousands of these persons are starving—actually starving; and deaths from starvation are constantly occurring. A poor law guardian asserts that they are numerous; two cases have been narrated that came under his own observation. James Birstal, a native of Wiltshire, with a wife and six children, could get no employment. When visited they had nothing—there was no article of furniture in the house. The man was found dead up stairs, and an old rag thrown over his naked body. The last words he was heard to utter were two days before he died "O that I had a little bread and a small piece of cheese!" There was another found stretched dead upon his loom. A jury brought in a verdict in this case, of "Death for want of food!"

Statements regarding the state of the labouring population, in that district of the parish of Rochdale, comprehending the villages of Whitworth, &c. &c.

The working classes are employed chiefly in cotton and woollen factories, stone or flag quarries, &c. They are, generally, employed at the present time, though, during the last two or three years, the factories have, now and then, worked short time, and I believe the stone trade is not so good, just now, as it usually was. Fears are very generally entertained by those capable of judging, that, unless some salutary change take place very soon, the demand for labour will be very much diminished.

Of those employed in the factories, the average weekly wages of the unskilled operatives is about 7s. or 8s., and of the skilled, 12s. or 16s. And of the employed in stone quarries, the one class called feighers or borers, have not, for the last year, earned more than 11s. weekly, and the other class, called dressers, 15s. weekly, on an average. It is to be recollected that, in common with all out-door labours, they are liable to serious interruptions, arising from the state of the weather. For instance, at the beginning of this year, the snows were so heavy and long continued as to prevent all work in the quarries for more than a month—a circumstance peculiarly calamitous to men who too generally spend such time in intemperance.

The amount of earnings has been diminished. Power-loom weavers, when employed full time, are not able to earn as much as formerly (say from 1832 to 1837) by 3s. or 4s. per week. Some, who have had longer experience, say 6s. or 7s. per week. And the quarry-men get from 6d. to 9d. per day less than they did in the period above specified.

It is my decided opinion that the demand for labour is affected by the price of food. It has been so, without denial, in this neighbourhood. For instance, during the years 1832, 33, 34, 35, 36, food was cheap, the demand for labour very urgent. Flour sold at 3s. per 20lbs. and (I believe) every other necessary of life was proportionately cheap: and so great was the demand for labour, that families, (called *foreigners* by the natives of Lancashire) were imported from the southern counties, as Suffolk, &c. On the other hand, during the last four or five years, (from 1836 to 1841) food has been dear and labour scarce. Flour has been selling on an average at 4s. 4d. per 20 lbs., an increase on the former price of 44 per cent. Every other article has been high priced in proportion, and labour has been scarce—many operatives unemployed or partially employed.

An individual of considerable experience assures me, that in no case within his knowledge have the wages risen with the rise in the price of food, but the reverse; when food has been dear, labour has been cheap. And it is a fact, that from 1832 to 1836 we had low prices and high wages, and from 1836 to 1841 we have had high prices and low wages.

In one view the condition of the labouring population may be said to be improved. The hand-loom weaving, which once constituted the principal employment, has sunk almost to the starving point. The factory system, which has extended itself very much in this neighbourhood of late, has, in some measure, rectified that which would have been found, ere now, a grievous evil. But, under the factory system, the condition of the labouring population, at the present time, is not improved, as compared with former periods. Several friends agree in assuring me that it is decidedly worse. I may subjoin the testimony of one of them: "I know a man that is employed on one of the lowest descriptions of factory labour. He has stated weekly wages, which are very low, and are nearly the same now as they have been for several years past. He has a wife and four children. During the years 1832-6 he and his eldest daughter, who at that time commenced working at the factory, were able to maintain the family in some degree of comfort, having a sufficiency of food, and also a trifle to expend on clothing. Within the last four years another child has arrived at the age when young persons are admitted to factory labour, and she also has been sent to work; but the united earnings of the *three* are not sufficient to procure the same amount of the necessaries of life now, as the earnings of the two procured during the years of comparatively cheap food. During the last year, when working short time, the family had to do, generally, with only two meals per day.

and these consisted of oatmeal porridge and treacle beer, or something little better. Numerous families are no better in their condition. I have just conversed with the father of a family, consisting of eight, who says that he and his family, when working reduced time, had to do with a meal less than usual. Besides, he says, they are now very seldom able to get flesh meat, or to have any beer. In addition to such and similar privations which families endure, there are very few indeed who are not seriously in debt. The representation is not founded on any extreme cases."

Poor-rates in this parish have increased, but in what proportion I know not.

On the state of the small trader, I subjoin the following testimonies of two respectable individuals of the class. The state of the provision dealer is very bad indeed. The credit system obtains to a very considerable extent here; and, as a necessary consequence, when the operative is out of employment, or working short time, or his wages low, he runs into debt with his shopkeeper; the shopkeeper, in his turn, runs into debt with the wholesale merchant; and thus the greater part of the shopkeepers here are in a state bordering upon insolvency. Many of them are not able to maintain their families without betaking themselves to some other employment. Some shopkeepers have book debts, owing to them by the operatives, to the amount of some hundreds of pounds, for which they would be very glad to find purchasers at 20 per cent. upon the whole amount. The small trader is regularly getting worse and worse, and ruin to him is certain, if the present state of things continues much longer. The labourer has not wherewith to pay for the maintenance of himself and his family, if he has one.

I am not sure that I can give any very definite answer to the question which regards the relative price of food and the state of the funds of our religious and benevolent societies in this neighbourhood. It is a *fact*, within the range of my experience here, that when food was low-priced our funds were greater, and our pecuniary efforts more spirited and successful; and now, when prices are comparatively high, there has been a slight diminution in our funds. I dare not say, however, that the variation in the price of grain has been the *sole cause* of the specified variation in our funds. There may have been other concurrent influences. But I believe the price of grain to be one cause.

I do not think that there is any very perceptible falling-off in the number of our congregation here, in consequence of high-priced food and the distress which it occasions. But there have undoubtedly been some instances of this kind. For instance, I know two very respectable individuals, who had been consistent members of a Christian church, situated ten or fifteen miles from this place. They came to reside in this place, and attended my ministry with exemplary regularity for a considerable time. At length, they gave up; and they themselves ascribed the painful change to the pressure of destitution, and to the existence of honourable feelings that they could once gratify and could not now wholly suppress. It is painful to add that, so far as is known to the minister, they attend no other place of worship. I know another respectable individual, withal sober, industrious, and economical, who was obliged to give up his attendance on religious worship for want of a necessary article of dress. And it is my conviction that there are not a few in this neighbourhood who are prevented from attending the means of grace, in consequence of the high price of food, and consequent inability to secure food and clothing which are needful for the body. Can it be reasonably expected, can it be religiously insisted on, that men and women, scantily fed and inadequately clothed, should wait upon the Lord without distraction? The religion of benevolence says, No. Thus, the system which starves the bodies of men tends also to starve the souls. The system which beggars man in this world, tends to ruin him in the next. There are many I know, who falsely plead poverty as an excuse for neglecting religion, and falsely say, that if they had this and the other thing they would attend the house of God; but their cases do not affect the accuracy of the preceding statements.

That our Sabbath schools suffer from the high price of food, I have no doubt. I submit the opinion of one of the superintendents, who is well acquainted with the whole matter. "There is a decrease generally in our Sabbath schools; parents, in many cases, are not able to send their children decently clad to the schools: many such cases the writer of this is acquainted with, and he believes the cause to be the high price of food and low wages."

DOCUMENTARY EVIDENCE.

QUERIES TO BE ANSWERED AT THE CONFERENCE.

The following were the Queries to which answers were requested. The numbers prefixed to the various replies will refer to the corresponding questions.

1. Are the working classes in your neighbourhood generally well employed, or otherwise? State the average weekly wages paid, distinguishing between skilled and unskilled labourers.

2. Has the amount of their earnings been increased or diminished within your experience? and how much?

3. How have you found the demand for labour to be affected by cheap or dear food?

4. Have wages risen with the rise of the price of food, and fallen with its fall? and in what proportion?

5. Is the condition of the labouring population, as a class, better or worse now, as compared with former periods within your experience?

6. What proportion do the poor-rates in your parish bear to those of former periods?

7. Refer to prison reports, and to reports of infirmaries, dispensaries, and other charities, for statistics of the state of crime, disease, and destitution in your neighbourhood now, as compared with former periods.

8. If your experience lie in a rural district, state whether the wages paid to agricultural labourers are regulated according to the number of their children.

9. What is the state of the middle class in your districts, such as the small trader, &c.? Is their condition improved or deteriorated now, as compared with former periods within your experience?

10 Have you perceived any connection between high and low-priced food and an increase or diminution of the funds of your religious and benevolent societies?

11. Have you found any falling off in the numbers of your congregation in consequence of the distress occasioned by the price of food?

12. Has there been any decrease in the attendance of the scholars at your Sunday schools? and if so, to what cause do you attribute it?

SCOTLAND.

DUNFERMLINE.—Poverty and crime are making rapid progress in this place. As one proof, no fewer than fifteen to seventeen pawnbrokers, of the worst kind, are in a flourishing trade; a number of them have been convicted of receiving stolen goods, and purchasing from persons of very doubtful character. Now all these houses have been opened within a very few years, and many of them within a year.

Provisions are rising in price, and wages, although in many cases the same, are in *reality* in most cases reduced; in some cases the whole wages must be taken up in goods, and often at prices, of kinds and qualities, unfavourable to weavers. There are other evasions, by which labour is reduced in value; and besides this, work is much more difficult to be had, many looms are standing, and it is to be feared many others will be paid off. Many a poor family is suffering most severely, and a great part of the misery and crime may safely be laid to the debt of the corn and provision laws. You know a great portion of our manufactures go to America, where the people would be glad to purchase, could we take their produce.

DUMFRIES.—1. The working classes, as skilled labourers, or rather workmen, are very ill employed. The mere labouring classes are generally well employed.

The wages of unskilled labourers, when employed winter and summer, will not exceed, in the average, 8s. weekly. The skilled vary, and therefore may be distinguished as under:

	£	s.	d.
Black and whitesmiths, and tailors	0	12	3
Joiners, or house-carpenters (ill employed)	0	12	0
Coachmakers	1	0	0
Tailors (only casually employed)	0	14	0
Shoemakers................................	0	7	0
Weavers	0	4	0
Fleshers ....(besides meat)	0	4	6
Bakers .... (besides bread)	0	5	0
Masons (when employed)	0	16	0
Stocking-makers (very ill employed)	0	12	0

2. The earnings of the unskilled have been stationary for some years. The wages of skilled workmen have greatly diminished, and employment very precarious.

3. Every description of productive industry has been suffering for two or three years back, more than formerly.

4. Wages have neither risen nor fallen with the price of food.

5. The condition of the working classes is worse, as compared with former periods.

6. The nominal rate is the same as it has been for some years, but the poors' board is running into debt; whilst the demands upon the board are most urgent and claimant. The allowances in most cases are a mere pittance, quite unequal to the wants of the poor, who are driven to eke out a subsistence by begging.

7. Aggravated crimes are greatly on the decrease; general destitution on the increase. Fever has been general and fatal during the present year.

8. Agricultural labourers, male and female, are badly paid.

9. The condition of the middle classes is decidedly materially deteriorated.

10. The effect of high priced provisions is invariably attended with a diminution in our funds for religious and benevolent purposes; whilst that of low priced food has generally a kindly, reactive influence.

11 & 12. To the last two queries, we reply in the affirmative; for when food is dear, there is no surplus fund for procuring suitable clothing; and thus parents are prevented from attending religious ordinances, and children at our Sabbath classes; for parents like not to appear in garb unseemly, or to see their children do so. We ascribe the causes thereof to the enactment and continued existence of the corn laws, which we and the locality we represent in your conference, regard as the greatest anomaly in legislation; and as loudly and unequivocally condemned by the voice of nature, of reason, and of God; and therefore ought speedily to be abrogated by our legislation, if they would behold our country in the full possession of that prosperity and plenty, which inherently belong to it.

PAISLEY.—1. The working classes in this town and neighbourhood have been but very partially employed, and at low wages, for the last *four* years. During the last three months in particular, there have never been less than from *one to two thousand males* idle. At present, from *seven to eight hundred*, with about *fifteen hundred* dependants, are living on subscriptions raised from the charitable as their only means of support; while, at the same time, several hundreds have emigrated during the period referred to. The number of weavers—manufacturing being the staple trade of the town—have diminished to the extent of eleven hundred during the last ten years. Men in the prime of life may earn about 9s. per week, while the weekly average of those who have passed that period will average only from 3s. to 5s.

2. The earnings of the working classes in this town have greatly diminished in amount within the experience of the present generation; and for years past they have been so very low that able-bodied men are incapable of earning even a bare subsistence.

3. The demand for labour has always been abundant in years when food was cheap. This was particularly the case in 1822, 1835, and 1836.

4. Wages have been affected by the price of food. When food is cheap, labour is abundant, and wages high. When food is dear, labour is scarce, and wages low.

5. The condition of the labouring population is greatly inferior to that of former periods, and is gradually becoming worse. The great mass of the weavers being sunk to a condition worse than that of ordinary paupers. They are, in a great measure, deprived of both furniture and clothing, having had to dispose of these articles during the late years of depression, to preserve an existence.

6. The poor rates on the town and neighbourhood have been gradually on the increase for several years past.

8. This is a manufacturing district, and the workmen are paid according to the labour performed.

9. The trading and middle classes in this district are gradually losing their capital, and sinking into poverty. During the last three weeks, upwards of thirty failures have taken place in the town of Paisley, and the amount of the engagements of the insolvent parties is above *half a million* sterling. Shopkeepers and small traders have been driven out of business in large numbers, and the greater portion of those who continue are verging into bankruptcy. Many proprietors of houses also, have been deprived of their property, on account of the inability of their tenants to pay rent; and these houses have been taken possession of by the bond-holders, who are also unable to obtain a return for their money.

10. For several years past, the working classes, and persons with small incomes, who are affected by the price of food, have been so reduced in their circumstances as to be altogether unable to contribute materially either to religious or benevolent societies. A great portion of

the friendly and benevolent societies have been broken up, from the poverty of the members, and the whole of those in existence are rapidly declining in numbers, from the inability of the members to pay their contributions.

11. Owing to the high price of food, and low rate of wages, a great proportion of the population are unable to attend a place of worship from want of clothing. Among some of the wealthier congregations, contributions have been made to supply clothing for the poorer members. But even these contributions have been insufficient to supply the demand. The less wealthy congregations have been greatly diminished in numbers, on account of their members being unable to attend public worship from want of clothing.

Kilmarnock.—1. Ill employed. There are 570 weavers idle, and 200 more are expected to be so the next week. This is exclusive of the carpet weavers and other trades, many of whom are expecting not to have employment. From 7s. to 8s. is the average rate of wages, 8s. is a fair average, including *all trades*. The hand-loom weavers are much lower.

2. Diminished from 25 to 30 per cent

3. Universally when food is cheap labour is in greater demand. The demand for labour is that which increases the wages. When food is dear there is less demand for labour, and consequently wages fall.

4. Not so, but the reverse in Kilmarnock.

5. Considerably impaired, and gradually becoming worse.

6. In 1831 the assessment was £1210; in 1841 the assessment was £1800.

7. *Crime* increased as the population increased, though not many serious offences, but for the last two or three years crime has been rather on the decrease. Reasons of this—1. Decrease of the population. 2. The decided influence of the temperance and tee-total societies on the lower classes; many who often appeared in the police court are now reformed, and are good members of society. *Disease*, especially malignant typhus and scarlet fever, very general, and the latter very fatal. Destitution very general, and this destitution tends in a very great degree to propagate disease, owing to the want of the necessary comforts.

8. No, this rule is not followed in the county of Ayr.

9. Greatly deteriorated, complaints very general, and many almost in a state of insolvency.

10. A very decided connection, there being when food is dear a falling off of from one-third to one-half.

11. Yes, very many in Kilmarnock cannot attend public worship for want of clothes; in their distress they have had to part with them.

12. Many of the parents say that they cannot send their children to school for want of clothes.

Bannockburn.—The working classes in this place are generally well employed. The leading branches of manufacture are carpeting and tartan. When in full employment as at present, the average weekly wages of a carpet weaver is 12s. 6d., and that of a tartan weaver 6s. 6d. However, these branches are liable to occasional depressions, when the workmen are put on restricted time, which on an average of twelve years will amount to about an eighth part of their hours of labour.

The wages of carpet weavers have during the last twenty years been reduced 10 per cent., and that of tartan weavers for the same period about 25 per cent.

The demand for carpeting and the rate of wages we do not find to be affected by cheap or dear food. The condition of the labouring population as a class we consider worse now than as compared with former periods, because the heads of families, in order to make up for the decrease in their incomes, are necessitated to take their children from school, and put them to work at an earlier age than formerly.

Our congregation, though not finding it convenient to send a representative to conference, yet, as they approve of its object, have agreed to forward the above local information.

As our existence as a congregation is but of recent date, we have yet no means of determining the influence which variations in the price of labour exert upon the funds of our religious societies.

PERTH.—1. Not *well* employed. Weavers, unskilled, 6s. 6d.; skilled, 10s. 6d.; weaving being the staple trade of the place.

2. Diminished one half.

3. The demand for goods for home consumption, and consequently the demand for labour, invariably increased by cheapness of food.

4. Wages generally found to fall when the price of food rose, and *vice versa*.

5. Decidedly worse.

6. Much higher—nearly doubled.

7 and 8. Cannot answer decidedly.

9. Much deteriorated.

10 and 11. Cannot answer decidedly.

12. A decrease, partly through want of clothing, arising from the pressure of the times.

To these I may add that, from my own observation, as well as from the testimony of others who have occasion to know the state of the poor, fever and diseases of various kinds are lamentably increased through want of sufficient food, clothing, and lodging. At this time one family, consisting of father, mother, and five children, are all ill of typhus fever. They all lay on the floor amongst a bundle of shavings, with only one blanket and coverlet for the whole. Four of them have been taken to the infirmary, where they will be attended to. Such is one instance out of many.

Nothing seems to me more hypocritical than the cry respecting the throwing of land out of cultivation, for when it suits the landowners it is done without hesitation or remorse. The process has been somewhat like the following:

By the aid of their retainers and followers, our great men got possession of immense tracts of country; so long as these retainers were of any use to them, they kept them about them, and gave them small portions of land at a certain rent, but as soon as they found they could do without them, or that the land would yield a better rent in a state of pasturage, the miserable tenants were immediately dispossessed, and their lands were let to some wealthy sheep farmers, i. e., they were thrown out of cultivation, as many 10,000 acres in Scotland can testify. But if some portions still yielded a better rent under tillage, they were continued so, till at length the £50 clause required several small holdings to be turned into a £50 farm, and now to increase the voters in the laird's interest, hundreds of poor families are driven from the places in which their forefathers have lived from twelve to fourteen generations. And what has become of the persons thus driven away? The lairds neither know nor care, but others know that while multitudes have been compelled to emigrate to distant lands, multitudes more have been driven into the towns and while many of them have nobly struggled against difficulties, and overcome them, many others have been reduced to absolute poverty; while at the same time the increase of labour has reduced many besides themselves to a similar state of destitution. And to complete the tale of oppression, it ought to be known and proclaimed throughout the land, that while the poor, that is, the disabled and friendless poor, are only allowed from 6d. to 1s. 6d., and in rare cases 2s. a week, without any allowance for rent, coals, or clothing; an abominable law prevents them from begging in the country around. The able-bodied poor, however destitute of employment, have no legal claim on the poor-rates, and by the above most iniquitous regulation, they dare not beg, on pain of being taken up and imprisoned as vagrants.

Thus the lairds drive their poor tenants from their holdings; they will not provide for them in their poverty, they will not permit *them to beg*, and if they scrape a few miserable pence together, they will not suffer them to lay them out on the cheap corn of other lands, but will *force them to buy their own dear corn or starve.*

On such proceedings what can be expected but the vengeance of a holy and righteous God.

WICK.—The county of Caithness is an agricultural and fishing district wholly without manufactures; and the state of things thence affords a very striking illustration of what this great country would be but for our trade and commerce; the very existence of which is evidently put by the iniquitous corn laws in the greatest peril.

1. The working classes are very ill employed, agricultural labourers have not any thing like full employment; and coopers, (barrel-makers for the fisheries) who are the principal part of our trades men, are generally idle three months in the year: frequently for six months. The average weekly wages of agricultural labourers is six shillings per week without food. A good ploughman has £7 per annum, a house, and an allowance of oatmeal and potatoes, and milk sufficient for one man. Many of them have families; how they are able to support them has often been a mystery to me. Coopers have from 8s. to 10s. per week. A foreman as he is called, that is, a person who manages a fish-curer's business, taking the charge of the cooperage and the curing, and who in addition to his being a practical cooper, must be able to write and keep accounts, has from £26 to £40 per annum.

2. The amount of a workman's earnings has been greatly diminished within these few years. The wages of coopers have fallen from 16s. per week to 9s.

3. The demand for labour is not increased by dear food, nor do wages rise with its rise.

5. The condition of the labouring population as a class is very rapidly deteriorating.

6. We have no poor-rates in our district.

7. Though we have a prison, no report is issued; and there is neither infirmary, dispensary, nor other charity.

8. The wages are not regulated according to the number of children.

9. The middle class in our district consists of merchants, fish-curers, and small farmers: though the last, strictly speaking, belong rather to the lower class. In regard to merchants, nearly a half of those in Wick have within the last few years become bankrupts, and some are now in the course of winding up their business, having induced their creditors to give them six or nine months' time to do this, in order to avoid bankruptcy. An immense number of fish-curers have also become bankrupts during the last few years, and been obliged to withdraw from the trade. And in regard to the small farmers, their condition is wretched in the extreme. Their houses are mere huts, being built for the most part of land stones, and turf without a single particle of lime either on the inside or the outside of the walls. These houses are miserably furnished, and for the most part the whole household, male and female, sleep in one common low-roofed ill-aired apartment, having very seldom a fireplace in it. Their small patches of land are held at a rack-rent; their food is for the most

part oatmeal, bean meal, and potatoes with milk, and occasionally a little fish. They rear black cattle, pigs, poultry, &c.; but as they must sell as much of these as they can spare to raise the *laird* his rent, animal food is seldom tasted by them. This is their condition in the best seasons, and when a bad harvest comes, a thing of by no means seldom occurrence in our ungenial climate, many of them are in a state of the greatest destitution, having hardly a meal of nourishing or wholesome food for months together.

How the corn laws operate in producing this misery, or at least a great part of it, is easily explained. Were it not for them, Russia would afford a market for salt herrings to an almost unlimited extent, in which they could be disposed of at a price that would remunerate both the fisherman and the curer. This market the corn laws absolutely shut up; partly because fish will not be taken by the Russians unless corn be received in exchange, and partly because, as a retaliative measure, that government has imposed a duty upon British fish, so heavy that it amounts to a prohibition. The foreign market being thus shut up, all the fish cured must, of course, be sent to the home market, and as this is often glutted, they must be disposed of at a price ruinous first of all to the curer, and ultimately to the fisherman. Our government pretended at one time to be anxious, for the sake of training seamen, to extend the British fisheries, and actually gave a bounty as high as 4s. per barrel on properly cured herrings, and this when the curer could readily get for them £2 or £2 10s. per barrel; now, when the price is seldom as high as £1, and often as low as 16s. they shut up the foreign market against him, and will not allow him to carry them where he could dispose of them at a remunerating price. But for this obstacle, the fisheries could be extended almost without limit, and afford a profitable employment to the surplus population. Numbers being thus prevented from obtaining a livelihood from the sea must seek it from the land. This both lowers the wages of agricultural labourers, by bringing too large a supply of labour into the market, and raises the rent of small farms, because there are more who wish to obtain farms than there are farms to occupy.

The above statements afford an outline of the working of the corn laws in our far distant region. They show that if these laws work well in one quarter it is only for the landowners. It would seem, however, that they do not work very advantageously for them either, for, with one exception, or at the most two, the landowners of Caithness-shire are over the head and ears in debt.

LANARK.—1. Hand loom weaving is the staple trade. There are 770 weavers in the parish, and from 1200 to 1300, including the immediate neighbourhood. Of these, 200 are entirely out of employment; and about one-sixteenth of the whole may be employed at agricultural labour.

2. The following is the average income of hand-loom weavers, when fully employed for the last ten years—supplied from the books of an agent who employs from 300 to 500 persons:

AVERAGE WEEKLY INCOME FROM 1831.

1831	1832	1833	1834	1835	1836	1837	1838	1839	1840	1841
S. D.	S. D.	S. D.	S. D.	S. D.	S. D.	S. D.	S. D.	S. D.	S. D.	S. D
6 1	5 0	4 10	5 0	5 7	5 3	5 0	4 3	4 9½	5 3	4 6

A decrease on the whole of 25 per cent. A statement presented by another agent of long standing is a shade lower than the above.

4th. The following is the price of oatmeal and potatoes, the common article of food, for the same period, fully disproving the assertion that wages rise with the price of provisions:

AVERAGE PRICE OF PROVISIONS SINCE 1831.

	1831	1832	1833	1834	1835	1836	1837	1838	1839	1840	1841
	s. d.	s. d.	s. d.	s. d.	s. d.	s. d.	s. d.	s d.	s. d.	s. d.	s. d.
250 lbs. oatmeal	30 0	31 0	29 0	30 6	31 0	37 0	35 0	32 0	42 0	37 0	36 6
4 cwt. potatoes	5 6	5 6	5 9	5 6	5 6	8 0	..	11 0	13 0	10 0	expected 8s. or 9s.

RESULTS APPARENT.—Oatmeal advanced in price 20 per cent. since 1831; potatoes from 80 to 100 per cent. Wages decreased 25 per cent. Beef was 5¼d. per pound in 1831, 5d. in 1835, 6½d. in 1841; increase, 20 per cent

9th. Females winding yarn for three looms, occupying their whole time, make from 2s. 6d. to 2s. 11d. per week. Hand-loom weavers work from twelve to fourteen hours a day. Their condition is most lamentable. Many of their beds are without blankets; the houses without even a chair to sit upon; their children uneducated and in rags.

10th. All our benevolent and religious institutions have suffered very severely from the existing depression. Indeed, it is useless toil, in the majority of cases, to ask for contributions from hand-loom weavers.

11th. Not a few persons who were, a few years ago, regularly in attendance upon divine ordinances, are now prevented from being present for want of clothes, whilst disease, poverty, and wide-spread wretchedness are greatly on the increase.

HAMILTON.—Since the year 1815 there has been a gradual reduction in the wages of tradesmen, the fabrics then paid at the rate of from 18d. to 20d., being now paid at the rate of 7½d. per ell of five-fourths. This was the best sort of work, but it is now almost entirely withdrawn from the town, having been supplanted by various other sorts of inferior work, on which, of late years, there has been a reduction of about 50 per cent. After the examination of the book of eight different agents, it is found that the average weekly wages of a hand-loom weaver is at present not more than 5s. 7d., subject to a deduction of about 1s 2d. for loom rent, &c., leaving only 4s. 5d., exclusive of perhaps a fifth of their time while waiting on work, there being such a scarcity of it. In Hamilton and its vicinity there are 1000 or 1200 females employed in lace tambouring. In 1831, their weekly wages, working 12 hours, were about 8s.; at present they do not exceed 3s. 6d.

WALES.

PONTYPOOL WELCH CHURCH.—1. Underground-men, from 12s. to 25s., and firemen, from 15s. to 35s. per week. 2. Diminished 20 per cent. within the last two years. 4. No. 5. Worse one-fifth within the last two years. 6. Quite twice the amount paid. 8. I think not. 9. Deteriorated. 10. No. 11. As usual.

FOREST OF DEAN.—This is a mining district,—the population generally employed in collieries, iron mines, and at blast furnaces; a small portion being employed in the forest plantations, and in agricultural labour.

1. They have been for the most part well employed of late years, but are now suffering greatly from the general depression of trade. The

wages vary from 12s. per week for inferior hands, to about 24s. per week for the most skilful workmen; but at present they have only about *half work*, three days per week.

2. Their earnings are consequently diminished by one half.

3. The demand for labour is not affected by cheap or dear food, except as the high price of provision *lessens the demand for articles of manufacture;* in such a case it must obviously *lessen the demand for labour* in a mining or manufacturing district.

4. Wages have *not* risen with the price of food; on the contrary, while provisions have risen, wages have been greatly reduced.

5. The condition of the labouring population, as to their physical wants, is, at the present time, decidedly worse than I have known it for some years past. In this district we have had much religious and moral improvement, but *in their temporal condition* the poor are now *very badly off.*

6. The Forest of Dean being extra parochial, we have no poor rates; and the inhabitants have no parochial relief, except where they have gained a settlement in some parish. The surrounding parishes complain of an increase of poor rates, which is said to be occasioned by the building of union workhouses.

8. The wages of agricultural workmen are *not* regulated according to the number of their children.

9. The state of the middle class, such as the small tradesmen, is, in my opinion, greatly deteriorated as compared with former periods. No one, who is not extensively acquainted with commercial affairs, can form any just conception of the overwhelming difficulties and distressing anxieties to which the middle class are subject, in carrying on their business in these times.

I am the agent of a concern in which a thousand families are employed—and I know there is much distress among the labouring class—but I believe there is far greater mental suffering endured by thousands of the middle class, who are rapidly hastening to ruin under the operation of our iniquitous laws.

I am decidedly of opinion that a repeal of the corn laws would afford most effectual relief. I may mention one *fact* in proof. I could have sold a large quantity of coal to the continent, this year, (which would have kept our colliers fully employed) if *corn* could have been taken in exchange.

PONTRHYDYRYN.—1. For a long time past the working classes in this part of the country have been unusually well employed; wages differ materially; agricultural labourers, from 8s. to 10s. per week; labourers connected with the manufacturing district, from 12s. to 15s. per week; mechanics differ still more, working by the piece and earning from 20s. to 40s. or 50s. per week.

2. Wages have invariably been regulated by the price of the manufactured article, and *that* has been regulated by the demand. Labour is now considerably reduced, in comparison with what it was a *few* months back.

3. The demand for labour is entirely dependant upon the demand for manufactured goods.

4. I am not aware that the price of food has ever formed a consideration in advancing or reducing wages. Demand *for* the manufactured article, and consequently its price, are the only ingredients that regulate wages.

5. It is now greatly worse than it has been; but still not so bad as it has before been in times long gone by.

8. Since the introduction of the new poor law, the poor-rates have been greatly reduced.

9. The small shopkeeper is of course almost entirely dependant upon the labourer, and is now suffering severely from the general depression.

11. Only inasmuch as it affects the employment of the labourer.

PONTYPOOL.—1. The working classes in this neighbourhood are by no means well employed. Trade is in an extremely depressed state, and hundreds of families have, within a few months, been reduced to the deepest distress; to relieve which, congregational collections have been made, and private charity has been exerted in an extraordinary degree. Many houses are unoccupied in the town, and many more, chiefly from local causes, in another part of the parish; and the population of the parish has been reduced, within two years, from 17,000 to little more than 14,000 persons. The weekly wages are nearly as follows:—

Agricultural labourers (Mr. Leigh's estate 13s.)	12	0
Do. at a distance of 20 miles, average	10	0
Do. in the immediate vicinity of iron works ..	15	0
Colliers and miners, about	16	0
but a considerable deduction to be made for candles and powder.		
Navigators and other labourers	15	0
Loss of time to be deducted.		
Plasterers	21	0
Painters	27	0
Pudlers and men working at the rollers.		

The *actual* earnings of these classes of labourers are considerably below the sums above-mentioned, because many who are employed are not in *full* work. The condition of those who are employed in the tin works is tolerably good.

2. The amount of wages has been *diminished* within the last two years, in some cases one-fourth, and in some one-third.

3. I cannot ascertain facts to enable me to determine whether "the demand for labour is affected by cheap or dear food."

4. Wages have *not* risen with the rise of the price of food nor fallen with its fall. The *reverse* has been the case for months past in this neighbourhood. The most obvious facts fully sustain the conclusion that wages in this district are never regulated by the price of food, but by the demand for labour.

5. The condition of the labouring population, as a class, is very far worse now than at any former period within my limited experience of five years in this town.

6. As to the proportion of the poor-rates in our parish to those of former periods, an overseer in 1835 to 1838 states that three fourpenny or not exceeding sixpenny rates sufficed for two years, but these last two years two shilling rates are made and one sixpenny, and property valued at rack-rent.

7. The board of guardians issued orders lately for the admission into the poor-house of about 200 persons, but few availed themselves of the regulation. Still that number of persons might be seen in a small part of one parish comprehended in the union in a state of extreme destitution and want, many of whom received temporary relief from Christian charity. Crime increases to an alarming extent in the county. See Mr. Justice Coltman's charge to the jury at the late assizes, at Monmouth.—*Beacon*, August 7th.

8. Wages are not paid, according to the number of children, to agricultural labourers.

9. The state of the middle class, as the small trader, &c., is sadly deteriorated within the last few years, or rather within the last year or

two. Almost every tradesman bitterly complains, though a few branches of trade may not have been seriously affected by the general depression. But builders, grocers, carpenters, ironmongers, painters, and drapers greatly feel the stagnation of business. Some confess their trade to have been diminished two-thirds. others one-half, others one-fourth, and those who have property in workmen's cottages suffer a great diminution of income.

10. The income of religious societies has been kept up, despite unfavourable circumstances; but I have good reason for thinking, that with the efforts used a great increase would have occurred, but for the melancholy state of trade and of the working classes.

11. I have not perceived any falling off in the congregation I represent in consequence of the high price of provisions.

12. There has been a decrease of scholars attending one Sunday school, and the poverty of parents has been, in more cases than usual, assigned as a reason, but whether this be the sole reason of the decrease I am unable to determine.

Talywaen, near Pontypool.—The stoppage of the Varteg Iron Works, in our parish, has thrown about 1600 or 1700 men out of employment, and from 500 to 600 men employed at the British Works, Abersychan, in the same parish, have been a considerable time out of work; and though local causes may partly account for the ruinous state of our trade, although we hope shortly to see a slight improvement in the neighbourhood, yet we despair of an effectual remedy so long as the present corn laws exist. Scores of families are now, and have been for many weeks past, in a state of starvation, and several congregations have been constrained to make special collections for their relief. Some idea of the general distress in this parish may be formed from the fact that out of fourteen furnaces there are now but five on blast, and all the mills, where the iron is manufactured, in our vicinity, are stopped. Where men are at work their wages have been much reduced, and the price of the necessaries of life has long been exceedingly high, and flour especially has just risen to 12s. 6d. per bushel

Abersychon.—1. The working classes in our neighbourhood are not well employed, according to the testimony of the relieving officer; and they all have not anything like full work. Average wages: firemen, £1 a week; miners and colliers, 15s. a week; day labourers, 12s. a week; mechanics, masons, carpenters, 18s.

2. The amount of their earnings has been greatly diminished. In one work within this last month, wages have been reduced 20 per cent.; and in another they have been reduced 25 per cent. in these last fifteen months; and much more than that, when we take into consideration that there is not full employ.

4. Wages have not risen with the price of food, but, on the contrary, at this very moment, when wages are reduced 20 per cent., provision is advancing, and is, according to the testimony of respectable tradesmen, 25 per cent. higher than it was six years ago.

5. The condition of the labouring population is much worse than I remember it to have been in former periods. I have, within this last month, witnessed more poverty and distress than ever I before beheld in my life.

6. I cannot exactly say what proportion the poor-rates bear to those of former years; but all greatly complain of them, and many are not able to pay them.

9. The small traders are in a most deplorable state; great numbers have failed, and others can scarcely rub on.

10. Our funds have been greatly diminished, or rather our resources

cut off, by the depression in trade; and we have no doubt but that the high price of food has operated as one cause.

11. Every congregation in the neighbourhood has suffered from a variety of sources; but all arising from a want of employment and, we believe, from the high price of food, as some have told me that they had pledged their clothes for food, and could not come to a place of worship.

12. There has been a decrease in the attendance at our Sabbath schools; the parents probably have left, and doubtless the children have been prevented from attending, for want of suitable apparel.

LLANELLY.—The state of trade in this place is deplorable, scores of the best workmen are now out of employ, and hundreds, according to present appearances, will be thrown on the wide world. One of the two copperworks is about stopping; the colliers are almost at a stand, as there is no demand for coal, the shipping has not been nearly half what it used to be. The most extensive coal and copper master in the place has now from 25 to 30,000 tons of coal in his yard; in consequence of this, he has lowered the workmen's wages 2s. in the pound, about a month ago; and now, although the most humane and feeling master of workmen, has given notice to stop, so that several extensive collieries are likely to cease to be worked. We look to God, and trust that he will overrule in his providence and spare us The appearances of things are now very gloomy indeed. The wages of colliers used to average from 2s. 6d. to 3s. daily, now it is no more than 2s. 8d. to the best; coppermen average from 15s. to 22s., mechanics from 12s. to 18s., labourers from 10s. to 12s. per week. I speak of wages as they have been this year until now. As far as my observation went, the most prosperous years were those in which bread was cheap and plentiful. The poor-rate is higher than usual, and has been higher for some time than in former years. Small tradesmen are often ruined by a stagnation of trade in mineral districts; many workmen are rendered unable to meet their debt on the shop book. Such a state of things materially affects our Sunday schools, our best teachers and most useful men in the church are obliged to wander from their homes; the parents are unable to furnish their children with clothes to go to the Sunday schools.

ENGLAND.

BEDFORDSHIRE.—LEIGHTON BUZZARD.—1. The working classes (particularly agricultural) are not fully employed. Wages of agricultural labourers, 10s. to 12s.; mechanics, 21s. per week. 2. They have been nearly stationary for some years. 3. Cheap or dear food has not materially affected the demand for labour. Cheap food is, however, the most calculated to create a demand for labour. 4. Wages have not risen with the rise in the price of food, although there was some reduction when it fell. This applies more particularly to agricultural labour. 5. The condition of the labouring classes has not varied much; but, from the greater economy and self-support produced by the new poor law, it is, if any thing, improved. But there are many cases of great destitution. 6. The poor-rates have been reduced nearly 50 per cent. on an average, since the change in the poor-laws. 7. Without reference, I should think they are not increased, or much altered. 8. The wages are less regulated by the number of children than formerly. 9. The middle classes complain of want of trade, from the high price of bread, and consequent inability in the labourer to purchase other articles. 10. No.

BERKSHIRE.—READING.—1. Generally well employed, this being an agricultural district; some out of employ. 2. During the last seven years diminished at least 2s. 3. When bread is cheap a greater demand for labour, except as it refers to agriculturists; probably the demand for labour is greater as corn is dear. 4. Instead of advancing the price of labour whilst corn has been rising during the past year, the farmers have generally lowered the wages of their men 1s. per week; all other classes have been lowered rather than increased as food has risen, their employers, that is, the farmers, taking strict account and advantage of the fall in the markets, but forgetting the rise. 5. Not so good as formerly. 6. About one third less since the new poor law came into operation. 7. No means of ascertaining. 8. Formerly, that is, whilst the old poor laws were in operation, they were, now they are not; but now, if there be not full employment for all, those men of good character are preferred who have large families, because, if not employed, their families become chargeable upon the parish. 9. Their condition is decidedly worse; this arises in some measure from the system of giving parish relief in bread instead of money, so that the poor have nothing to spend. In consequence of the small traders being thus reduced in circumstances, it is thought they have been more susceptible of bribery at the election than they were before. 10. Not in stated annual subscriptions, but public collections have decreased in amount, in proportion as food has been dear. 11. In some instances, when provisions have been dear, the poor have given a reason for their non-attendance that they have been unable to procure clothes sufficiently decent to come to the house of God. 12. There has been an increase in the number of scholars, arising from increase of population in the vicinity of the place of worship, but some children have been prevented from attending for the same reasons as given in answer to the preceding question.

High Wycombe.—1. The working classes in this neighbourhood are not generally well employed. The average weekly wages of skilled labourers or husbandmen, is 10s.; for unskilled labourers, 8s. The average weekly wages of operatives or mechanics, 15s. 2. The chair trade has diminished within the last seven years, at least fifteen per cent the paper trade at least twenty per cent; and the lace trade at least twenty per cent. 3. When food is dear, there is less demand for labour. 4. Wages have not generally risen with the rise of the price of food. 5. The condition of the labouring population is decidedly worse. 6. The poor-rates are about the same. 7. There is less crime: disease is not increased; and the destitution is greater than in former periods. 8. The wages of agricultural labourers are not regulated according to the number of their children. 9. The state of the middle classes has materially deteriorated. 10. No. 11. No. 12. There has been an increase in the attendance of the scholars at the Sunday schools belonging to Creedonlane Meeting house, and to Ebenezer Chapel. The above embraces a period of seven years.

BUCKINGHAMSHIRE.—Newport-Pagnel.—In ten villages taken promiscuously in the neighbourhood of Newport-Paghel, Buckinghamshire, there is a considerable number of able-bodied, well-conducted men, out of employ. In the village of *Linford*, containing a population of about 400, 17 men went to the squire of the parish, on Monday week, August 9th begging for employment; he could do nothing for them. About the same time, 17 men applied for work at a farm, at *Chickeley* parish, a circumstance which never before occurred to the knowledge of the parties. In *Sherrington*, the population in 1831 was 804; from 30 to 40 men were out of employ last week, and cried themselves about the village for anything that might be offered them, but without success. The wages of those who are employed are from 8s. to 10s. per week. More hands will be employed during harvest, but it is supposed that after that time, the destitution must be very great; and that at least one third of the labouring population will be without work.

The women are generally employed in making pillow lace, at ruinous wages; 2s. 3d. per week being the average price they receive; working from 12 to 16 hours per day. Mechanics are mostly employed and receiving their usual wages.

2. Farm labourers have received 1s. additional since the rise of corn; but this has not met the additional expense, for in one instance an individual stated that the increased cost of bread and flour was 3s. per week.

5. Worse. When things were in a better state, the labouring classes would buy the best of articles, in meat, grocery, and clothing; purchasing tea and sugar, for example, of a better quality than that used by tradespeople; but now they ask for what is cheapest, and purchase far less in quantity. Parties who have worked 30 years for the individual making this statement, are grown in these respects much more destitute, and were never in a worse condition than at present.

6. They are reduced nearly one half since introduction of the new poor law; but they must either rise again or the poor starve, which many perhaps would rather do than go into the house.

7. There are none in the immediate neighbourhood.

8. They are not since the introduction of the new poor law.

9. Far worse than formerly. They are purchasing the smallest quantities of goods to sell again; they are as bad or worse off than the labourers, having rates and taxes to pay, and being obliged to keep up a somewhat respectable appearance.

10, 11, & 12.—Nothing definite can be stated on those three points; our district being agricultural. We have not been sensibly affected by the distress of the poor in these respects.

CAMBRIDGESHIRE.—Bassingbourn.—This parish is in the midst of a district exclusively agricultural. The population of the parish amounts to 1419; 164 above population in 1831. 1. The working classes here are generally well employed. The average weekly wages is about 10s. per week; but the more skilled workmen frequently earn 15s. per week. 2. The amount of their earnings have increased from 8s. to 10s. during the last twelve years. 3. The demand for labour is somewhat quickened since the rise in the price of corn. When the price of grain is low the farmer is sparing of all labour that he can dispense with. 4. Wages have, to some degree, risen with the price of food, but in nothing like a corresponding degree. All admit that other considerations determine the price of labour. A most respectable working man has just told me that when half a sack of flour cost him 13s. 6d. his lowest wages were 8s.; now the same quantity of flour sells for 27s. 6d., and his wages for day labour do not exceed 10s. a-week. 5. The condition of the labouring population is improved of late years. This is owing to various causes. The adoption of the cottage allotment system was the first. The operation of the new poor law has also been beneficial. By encouraging industry, forethought, and good conduct, and leaving sloth, intemperance, and improvidence to suffer their natural effects, this law has effected much good. And in this parish and neighbourhood the increased influence and extension of religion has conspicuously improved the character, habits, and circumstances of a large proportion of the labourers. 8. Wages are never regulated according to the number of children. 9. The middle class, such as small traders, are not in a prosperous condition; now bread is dear. 11 and 12. There is an unquestionable tendency in high priced food to diminish congregations, schools, and the funds of religious and benevolent societies. I have known many instances of it.

CHESHIRE.—Duckinfield.—1. At the present time the people in this neighbourhood are, generally speaking, employed; this however has not been the case till within a short time. The mills here, as in most of the manufacturing districts, have worked short time for several weeks, and I am informed that there is a probability of their doing so again in the course of a few weeks; so that the prospects of the labouring classes are of the most gloomy and discouraging nature. The average weekly wages paid to those in the best department of mill labour, may be from 20s. to 25s., and the others from 10s. to 15s. 2. The decrease of their earnings since my residence in this district, is very considerable. I am informed in many cases a fourth at least. 3. It is my firm conviction that the demand for labour is materially affected by the high price of provisions, and that if means are not adopted to remove the laws which restrict labour and keep up the price of food, the whole of the manufacturing district will be placed beyond remedy, a thing which every friend of humanity must deeply deplore. 4. From my inquiries, I find that wages have not advanced with the rise of the price of food, but that, whilst provisions have been increasing in price, wages have been gradually decreasing; indeed, I believe it will be found on examination, that wages seldom gain their former scale, though there may be, on some occasions, an improvement in trade. I pretend not to state who are to blame on that account, but the poor are always the sufferers. 5. I can confidently affirm that the labouring classes are much worse, compared with former periods. Within my experience, to state one case well known in this district, a man, a widower, with a family of six children, had, after the deduction of house rent, at the end of a fortnight, only to receive 3s. This was principally occasioned by short time; and I am disposed to think that there are many cases, if not as distressing as his, yet of the most heart rending character. 6. With respect to the poor rates, they are about a third more than they were in 1836. 9. As it regards the small tradesmen, they are much to be pitied. By the existing state of things, many of them have been sold up, and thus have lost their little all; for however willing and desirous that class may be on whom they depend for support, to pay their just debts, they are incapable of doing so. 10. With respect to the funds for religious purposes in this neighbourhood, they have decreased, and must do so if some change for the better, among the labouring class, does not speedily take place. 11. I am sorry to add that there has been a falling off in the attendance on the means of grace, owing to the people not being able to appear as formerly, and to pay their seat rents; and I fear that this will still be found to increase, unless those laws are crossed from the statute book that prevent free trade, and keep up the price of the most common yet the most necessary article of life.

Stockport.—The working community in the borough of Stockport is now inefficiently employed. Sixteen mills are standing, and it is computed one-third of the operatives are unemployed. The total amount of steam and water power is equal to 4000 horses; 500 horse power is now dormant, the average number of persons to each horse power is at least five. Some of our mills have been closed three and four years. The factories at work are working short time three, four, and five days in the week, and the loss of employment occasioned thereby may be considered as equal to one full fourth of the power and labour now in action.

Besides the want of employment occasioned by the mills being stopped and working short time, there has been a considerable reduction in wages within four years; in one mill, as an instance, the wages of the general hands have been reduced 6 per cent., and that of the weavers 12½ per cent.; 3d. in 1s. 11d. These reductions in factory labour have diminished the circulation of money at least £800 per week, upon the limited work done, which would have amounted to £1200 per week were all the factories in the borough working full time.

The state of trade is essentially affected here by the price of food. When food is high the home trade is proportionably diminished, and consequently there is less demand for labour, and wages fall. Stockport pays for provisions £2000 more than in 1835.

Wages have been falling whilst food has been rising. Wages are 9 per cent. less, and food is 35 per cent. higher; and whilst at this time corn is still on the rise, there seems no chance of any rise in wages, but the apprehension of still further reductions.

The number of houses in the borough is about 12,000, and of these 2000 are unoccupied; and of the 10,000 tenanted, such is the reduction and the non-payment of rent, that the owners have sustained a loss as though 4000 shops, taverns, and houses had been entirely empty during the last five years. Numbers of our best artizans are leaving the town every week for the continent, the colonies, United States, &c.

The pressure of the poor rates in the borough of Stockport is now exceedingly severe. On the 9th of this month there were 1900 defaulters of the last and former rate. Of the cases of 1026 defaulters on the poor rates, lately investigated by a joint committee of guardians and overseers of the poor, it was ascertained that hundreds of families had to subsist on a daily income not exceeding twopence per head. It is also well authenticated that very many who paid their rates were under the necessity of pledging their articles of furniture and clothing to do so. The testimony of pawnbrokers as to the existing depression, confirms the opinion held by many that the condition of the town, as it regards the middle and lower orders, is unprecedented.

There are 9000 in this borough living in cellars, many in circumstances of destitution that defies all description. I have visited very many of the tenants of these abodes, who, at the time of my visit, had no furniture, nor food, nor money, nor fire.

No fact will more clearly manifest the change in the circumstances of the population than the following. In the year 1835, there were 260 beer-houses and 120 public houses, which, with few exceptions, were doing well. The beer-houses are reduced to 120, several taverns are closed, and the publicans of both classes are in great distress.

Knutsford.—In this town, manufactures have been less encouraged than in any other within the same distance of Manchester; but, when times were very prosperous, they forced themselves, to some extent, even into this place; so that, at one time, there were two small factories,—one of silk, the other of cotton; and the hand-loom weavers amounted to several hundreds. The factories have been discontinued for a number of years past; and, as the times have become worse, the number of hand-loom weavers has been much diminished. A considerable number of them have removed to larger towns, where they have found it more easy to obtain employ. The condition of those who remain is most distressing. When it was known that I intended to be present at the corn-law conference, a statement was sent to me, from our part of the town, which I enclose, and from which it appears that out of forty-one hand loom weavers, only six are in employ. Some of these, as they state, are living, or rather dying, upon *one* meal a day; others of them get a little employ during the harvest; but their prospect for the winter is most frightful. The condition of the farmers and of the agricultural labourers is far from being prosperous. The Chairman of the Quarter Sessions held in Knutsford, an intelligent Cheshire gentleman, stated, some time ago, from the bench, that formerly it was a common notion and statement that a farmer ought to realize *three rents*,—one for his landlord; one to defray all his other expenses of housekeeping, servants, taxes, &c.; and *a third for profit* and interest upon the capital necessarily embarked; but, he added, that one of the three (the last mentioned) had now become *quite extinct*. The farmers employ very few labourers: so that there are a number of persons of that description about the country, either out of work or able to get very little. Coeval with the first operations of the corn law, was the erection of the new House of Correction, at Knutsford, for the county of Chester. Up to that time, the old House of Correction, at Middlewich, had never contained, at once, so many as one hundred prisoners; but, in the new prison, the numbers have been regularly upon the increase; so that now, I believe, there are never less than three hundred, and they frequently amount to nearly four hundred. When I came to Knutsford, upwards of thirty years ago, the Quarter Sessions commenced on one day and almost invariably concluded the next. They had then only one court; now there are two; and the business takes up generally about five days, and, on some occasions, has lasted a full week at least. On occasion of the sessions lately, I dropped into conversation with a worthy beneficed clergyman, who told me that he had just been conversing, on the awful increase of crime, with a respectable solicitor who had great opportunities of seeing how it originated, being a clerk to several magistrates, and who said that he could not but often feel great sympathy for the prisoners committed for trial, as they were thrown upon the public for want of employ, and were, in a great measure, under the necessity of betaking themselves to dishonest courses.

MACCLESFIELD.—A family of eight (parents and six children), the children being from three years old to fourteen, will consume weekly full five pecks of flour, at 1s. 10d. per peck, 9s. 2d.; barm, 4d.; baking, 5d.; making 9s. 11d., say 10s. The husband and father, if a skilful man, *i. e.* a good hand, will get at an average 12s. 6d. per week. A widow, with three children, require 5s. worth of bread weekly. This said widow, by "doubling," will, by working *seven* days a week, get 4s. In 1835, the same widow got 12s weekly. The working classes generally live on bread almost entirely. Butcher meat is out of the question, their daily bread being emphatically their staff of life. I infer, as a matter of opinion, that the entire wages of the employed, considering the numbers unemployed, would go little, if any further, at present, in our town, than to provide *bread alone* for the whole body of our operatives, 25,000, at least, including their families; bread and sugar I do not believe they would procure. Such is the state of things, generally; but there are many special cases of the most heart-rending description.

CORNWALL.—FALMOUTH.—Neither the demand for, nor the price of, labour has been at all affected by the price of grain in this neighbourhood, nor are the wages of the agricultural labourers at all regulated by the number of their children. The present state of the middle traders is much worse than formerly, and the poor are suffering extreme distress from the present high price of food. Our poor-rates have been increasing for some time; and I believe we have a large number of persons unable to attend any place of worship for want of decent apparel.

CUMBERLAND.—CARLISLE.—The working classes are not well employed; no time has been known scarcely in which their prospects on this point have been more gloomy. In reference to the weavers, I know from the statements of the workmen themselves, as well as from those of some of the masters, that skilled labourers do not earn more than from 6s. to 8s. per week; and unskilled, 3s. 4s., or 5s., even when fully employed. I knew one man with a wife and family of five children, himself the only worker in the family, who laboured from the close to the commencement of the Sabbath after, and could not earn upon an average more than 5s. per week. He told me with tears in his eyes he would be quite content if he could only get potatoes for his family. With the wages of other trades in Carlisle I am not acquainted. 2. To your second question I should say, diminished. 3. The demand for labour has risen with cheap and fallen with dear food. 5. Decidedly worse. 9. Their condition is far worse. The pawnbroker has his rooms crowded out. Many of the shopkeepers receive clothes in pledge for payment. 11. Some have left us for other lands in consequence of the prospect of starving in this country. 12. In winter the attendance falls off greatly; the parents being totally unable to provide clothing for the children; and even in summer some cannot come on this account, and many who do come are miserably clad.

WHITEHAVEN.—1. No, they are not. Average wages for labourers 8s., mechanics 16s. 2. Much diminished. 3. When provisions are cheap the labourer has generally plenty of work, and consequently his circumstances are easy, but it frequently occurs that when provisions are dear, there is a scarcity of employment. 4. No, No! 5. Worse considerably. 6. An increase, but cannot say to what amount. 7. Very great improvement, from the increase of teetotalism. 8. We are not in a rural district. 9. Very great depression in every branch of our trade, which has much deteriorated the condition of the small trader, &c. 10. Yes, and also a diminution in both the religious and benevolent societies. 11. Yes. 12. Yes! attributable to the want of clothing, which they cannot obtain from the very high price of provisions and great scarcity of employment.

DERBYSHIRE.—MELBOURNE.—1. This is a manufacturing town, in the midst of an agricultural district; and when speaking of the labouring population, we find it necessary to distinguish not only the farmer's labourer from the mechanic, but to state particularly to what branch the mechanic is devoted; for the several branches are not only unequal in their demand for labour, but also very unequal in the rate of wages given. 2. The staple trade was, until lately, the manufacture of blond lace; besides which, a great number of hands were employed in stocking frames. Both these branches have declined; the hands who could get a few years since from 25s. to 30s. per week, cannot now earn more than 7s. or 8s. per week. The blond hands were receiving, no further back than 1838, 2s. 0½d. per yard; but now the highest price paid is only 11½d. for the same. Against the above we may place the fact, that two or three spirited manufacturers have introduced the fancy silk glove trade during the last two years, which has given employment to a great number of hands, men, women, and children; and had it not been for this, the whole labouring population would have been in an awfully distressed condition; but this is now declining, many are out of employ, and it is expected that in the course of a few weeks, nearly the whole will be without work. 3. Farmers may increase their hands when food is dear, but it is clear that it is not to any considerable extent, from the fact that while the population in one manufacturing town has been increasing, and there has been a greater demand for the products of the earth, our agricultural villages have rather decreased; in proof, we refer to the Melbourne registration district, which shows a decrease, in five villages, of 219 since 1831; and in two others, an increase of only 18, in the same period. 4. The manufacturers state that high priced food tends to diminish the demand for labour. 5. The condition of the labouring population is nearly the same as it was a few years since; this is owing to the introduction, as we have said, of a new branch of trade, which has given employment to the wives and daughters of the labourers; but had it not been so it would have been very much worse. One manufacturer states that owing to the restrictive duty upon food, he cannot compete with the French, who are now supplying the American markets with the article that he formerly sent; but if he could bring home corn at a very low duty, he could keep his hands at work, and supply the Americans with as good an article, and at as low a price, as the French; but as it is they can neither make fresh purchases, nor pay him for the goods received five or six years ago. 6. The poor-rates are lower now than formerly, for in 1819 the parish expenses were £2,233 4s. 2d.; but during the year 1840 they were only £478 7s. 9d. This may be attributed. partly, to the operation of the new poor law, and partly to the fact that the women and girls have been pretty well employed; by which their husbands and fathers have been kept from applying for parochial relief. 8. The rate of wages depends more upon the skill of the labourer than the number of his children. 9. Shopkeepers complain that when food is dear they suffer. 10. The funds of our societies have not fallen off, but this we attribute to the enlarged views now taken of christian obligation. 11. A few instances have been observed when persons have absented themselves from chapel owing to the want of clothing in which to appear, but these have not been numerous.

Derby.—1. They are not. Weekly wages for unskilled labourers at present average about 12s.; for skilled, from 18s. to 22s. Framework-knitters are earning on the average not more than 7s. 2. Diminished—particularly of those of the skilled labourers. 3. Generally when food has been dear, we have found work scarce; and on the contrary, when food has been cheap, the demand for labour has been good. 4. No; we have not perceived that the rate of wages has been thus affected by the price of food. 5. Worse. 6. About the same upon an average, in Derby, as they have been the last ten years. 7. We are not possessed of sufficient information to reply to this. 9. Much deteriorated—and many of them are fast sinking into a state of pauperism. 10. The income of our particular church, for years past, has been pretty steady; but though the number of our members has considerably increased, the amount of our funds has not increased in proportion. Our limited knowledge of other societies in the town will not permit us to answer the question as it concerns them. 11. We are not aware of any particular decrease in any of the congregations in Derby, occasioned by distress. 12. Our Sabbath schools are attended at present, much the same as formerly.

Belper.—This town may be considered to depend on three branches of trade, nail-making, cotton spinning, and hosiery. From each of these branches reports have been obtained, and the respectability of the sources whence they have been derived is a guarantee for their accuracy, so far as they go. The manufacture of horse nails. Answers to the queries which have been proposed. 1. The operatives in this department are stinted in their work; the difference between being stinted and having full work will amount at least to 5s. per week. The stint is generally directed according to the number of the family, i. e., the number incapable of working or unemployed. There is a little variation among different firms in this respect. The average weekly wages for those under the greater stint are about 7s. 6d., and those under the least about 10s. 2. The stint has been in operation ten years or upwards; there have been short intervals within that period when they have been fully employed, but they were few and long between. The same quantity of work is now done for less money than it was ten years ago, but the greatest diminution in the earnings of the operative arises from the stint. 3. Cheap food has increased the demand, and dear food the contrary. 4. Wages have not risen with the price of food nor fallen with its fall. If there has been any difference at all, it has borne no proportion to the rise or fall in food. 5. The condition of the operatives now is much worse than it was five years ago, and the tendency is still downwards. 5. The poor-rates—the amount in 1839 was £837 2s.; in 1840, 781 10s.; in 1841, 955 13s. The average amount for the three years preceding the introduction of the new poor law was £1177; for the last three, £858. 7. We have no prison, infirmary, or dispensary in our town, and are unable to reply as to the state of crime. 1. Ours is not a rural district. The wages here are not regulated according to the number of the labourer's children. 9. If the periods during which extra work has been carried on be excepted, for instance, the making of the railway, their condition is deteriorated. 10. Our funds to the present have not been materially diminished. The means, however, of contributing have been diminished. That they have not been actually diminished must be attributed, we think, to the strength of religious principle and the increase of population. Powerful appeals have also been made to prevent a falling off. 11. In this locality we have not perceived any material falling off on the account mentioned. 12. No decrease at present. As to other kinds of nails besides horse nails, the average earnings are about 5s. per week, this work being done by inferior operatives and children; it is much reduced, and there is some fear lest it be superseded by the production by power.

Another report states that the silk hosiery branch is nearly extinct. One house which formerly did nearly £35,000 per year, has passed through the *Gazette*; another has decreased from £28,000 to £5,000; and another, that did £25,000, has ceased to manufacture.

DEVONSHIRE.—MODBURY.—This is a small town, supported entirely by agriculture. There was at one period a manufactory, but that has been stopped several years. The answers to the questions have been furnished me by a farmer who is a member of my congregation. 1. They are not so well employed as one would wish, because the renting farmers are unable to pay their wages on account of the high rents of their farms. The average weekly wages are 9s. for able-bodied men. 2. Able-bodied men have received 9s. per week for the last twenty years. 3. The demand for labour has been equally great when food was cheap as when dear. 4. The price of food has had no effect on the rate of wages. 5. It is somewhat better than a few years since. 6. The amount of rate paid by the farmer has increased of late years. 7. There is far less crime than formerly. 8. The wages bear no proportion to the number of children; 9s. per week are the fixed wages. When a man has more than four children, the Board of Guardians, if applied to, will allow something, or take one of the children into the house, as the case may require. 9. The middle class is, generally, in a worse condition than formerly. The small tradesman is badly off on account of the difficulty in collecting money for his goods from the labouring classes. The late advance in the price of bread will be very severely felt here if it continue.

DEVON.—1. Agricultural labourers are generally well employed at from 7s. to 8s. per week, with one quart of cider or ale per day, except in the winter, when we have a surplus of one-fifth of labour. But it must be observed that the making of new roads has found employment for very many of those in work, and consequently, as the new roads are nearly all completed, we expect a vast proportion of our poor to be out of employment the next winter. In our manufacturing towns many hands are quite out of employment as manufacturers, whilst the machinery works but four days per week, and in some manufactories even less. When in full work, the wages are, on an average, taking good and bad hands—combers 11s. per week, women in factories 5s. per week, women weavers 3s. 6d. per week; that is, at the best times and in full employ. Four days per week in proportion. 2. The earnings of agricultural labourers have been nearly the same for the last twenty-five years, whilst among manufacturers the price never alters; but labour is increased or reduced according to the demand for the article. 3. Agricultural labourers very little, and manufacturing labourers not at all, only inasmuch as trade is often bad through provisions being dear. This was particularly the case in 1839-40. 4. No. 5. Much the same, except the able-bodied poor and weavers, who are worse off 6. About the same for the last eighteen years. 7. Crime about the same; destitution about the same. 8. No. 9. Worse off. 10. Considering the increase of our members, rather worse. 11. Not any decrease. Let me add, as ours is principally an agricultural district, we see the effects of the corn laws to be vassalage on the part of the labourer toward his employer, and vassalage on the part of the tenant toward his landlord. Hence the enfranchisement is a mere farce—a complete misnomer.

A copy of the statement of the wife of G. H., agricultural labourer, of the parish of Frittlestock, in the county of Devon.

I have four children all under seven years old; my husband's wages are seven shillings per week; my house rent is £3 3s.; his wages never rise or fall; we buy a little pig and rear it up to sell to pay our rent with; always eat barley bread; we buy 1 lb. of bacon per week, for myself, husband, and children; we settle with my husband's master once a month; I am always expected to purchase of my husband's master what things I may want in the eatable way at the end of the month; I receive sometimes two or three shillings, other months nothing; as it has all been taken out in potatoes and other things. I consider myself as well off as any labourer's wife in the parish; no labourer gets more wages per week than my husband; many labourers get but tenpence to one shilling per day; labourers generally are expected to have from the farmers what barley, &c., they want.

A copy of the statement of J. L., agricultural labourer, of the parish of Shibbear.

Able-bodied labourers get seven shillings per week in my parish; others only six shillings per week; labourers generally get their corn of their masters at the following prices: eight shillings per bushel for wheat, and 3s. 6d. for barley; the labourers are allowed one bushel of wheat and one bushel of barley per month; if they want more they must pay the market price for it; our house-rent is £3 per year; we scarcely ever taste meat; we buy 1 lb of suet per week; that we have to fry potatoes with and make into broth. If the labourer can buy a small pig he rears it, and then sells it to pay his rent with; others have to work for the person that they rent their cottage off one day per week. About 100 left this parish last Lady-day for America. The labourers generally want work, although so many have emigrated lately. I will instance a family whom I am well acquainted with how they lay out their seven shillings; J. A., wages 7s. per week, wife and four children; 1 peck of wheat 2s., 1 peck of barley 10½d., 1lb. of suet 7d., rent per week 1s. 3d., firing 1s. 3d. per week; after the above outlay he has left 1s. 0½d. to purchase tools to work with, and other necessaries for clothing, &c. if he can raise any. All J. A.'s children are under five years old. I consider him as well off as labourers generally are in my parish. I am 56 years of age. Labourers were a great deal better off some years ago than they are now. I do not know of any more than 7s. per week being given in any parish. I am acquainted with labourers of twenty different parishes, and 7s. per week is the highest wages which any of them receive. Coal in my parish is 1s. 3d. per cwt. No labourer is allowed to gather fire-wood. There is a society formed which gives a reward for information on any person who is found cutting wood.

Statement of P. M. agricultural labourer.

I have a wife and three children. My wages are 7s. per week; and I give 4s. per bushel for barley. I am idle many days on account of bad weather, and never get paid for these days. My wages do not average 6s. per week. My rent is £3 per year. No labourer that I know gets more than 7s. per week.

Statement of P. S., of the parish of Great Torrington.

I am a grounder of leather by trade, but, owing to the decline of my business, I am obliged to break stones on the parish road, for which I am paid 5s. per week. I have to walk four miles and a half every morning to my work, and return the same evening, making, on the whole, fifty-four miles per week. I must break, for my week's work, 72 barrows of stones. I have a wife and one child. My rent is 1s. 3d. per week, which I must pay regularly; the remainder of my wages we have to live upon. I scarcely ever taste butcher's meat; sometimes I get a salt herring. I take with me to my work a piece of dry barley bread, for my breakfast and dinner. There are from 40 to 50, of all trades, breaking stones on the roads. Some of the men, who have large families, are allowed 10d. per week more than I have, and many of the men are only allowed 2s. 4d., so that the wages vary from 2s. 4d. to 5s. 10d. per week. When I had work, I could earn at my own business from 12s. to 18s. per week.

DORSETSHIRE.—Bridport is largely engaged in foreign commerce, a considerable portion of which is with the United States. The present corn-law seriously operates to prevent that exchange of commodities which would take place if a perfectly free trade were established. One important branch of the trade of the town is the weaving of sailcloth. A free trade in corn, by increasing the shipping interest, would materially encourage its manufacture, and consequently give employment to a larger number of operatives. 1. The state of trade in Bridport is at present extremely depressed. In many branches there is not more than half the usual employment for those engaged therein. The rate of wages, when in full employ, is as follows:—weavers, 11s. per week; hecklers, 15s.; labourers, 10s.; master spinners, 14s.; carpenters, 14s.; masons, 12s. The wages of the agricultural labourers in the neighbourhood do not average more than 7s. 6d. per week. 3. The rate of wages is entirely dependant upon the demand for labour, which is always slackened by high prices of the necessaries of life. 4. Wages in Bridport are lower at the present period than during the years 1835, 1836, and 1837, when employment was abundant and food at its minimum price.

Beaminster.—The above statements apply equally to the adjacent town of Beaminster and the neighbouring country, in which a similar depression of trade, and scarcity of employ, exist; productive of semi-starvation to the operatives, great difficulties to persons in retail business, increase of poor rates, and the prospect of a distressing winter.

DURHAM.—Barnard Castle.—1. The operatives of Barnard Castle, the staple trade of which is carpet weaving, have not had more than half employment for the last six months. The average wages of the carpet weavers do not amount to more than about 7s. per week. 2. During the last twenty years the amount of their earnings has diminished as much as 30 per cent. 3. It has been found that dear food acts alike injuriously on the artizan and on the agricultural labourer. 4. It has also been observed that wages have fallen in proportion to the rise in food, to the degree of about 40 per cent. 5. It can be truly affirmed that the condition of the labouring class is considerably worse now than at any period during our experience. 6. Poor rates are higher. 8. The wages paid to agricultural labourers are not regulated according to the number of their children. Children are never taken into account. 9. The state of the middle class in this district, such as the small trader, is extremely bad. 10. An intimate connection has been observed between high and low-priced food and the funds of our religious societies. When food is reasonable in its price the contributions are good, but when provisions are high there is an evident diminution. 11. Owing to the prevailing distress a considerable falling off has been witnessed in the attendance upon religious worship. 12. There has also been observed a decrease in the attendance of children at our Sabbath school, owing to the want of decent clothing.—There have been a number of failures in the town. Property has decreased in value to the amount of between 40 and 50 per cent. There are at present sixty-one houses unoccupied, and the number of the population has not increased since the last census. The population is, 4452. The above facts were ascertained by a committee of gentlemen, who were highly competent to form a correct opinion of the commercial state of the town, and who gave their testimony as the result of careful inquiry.

EXETER.—Exeter.—1. The working classes in the city are generally well employed, although it is otherwise at present. Wages: artizans from 15s. to 30s. per week; labourers from 10s. 6d. to 14s. 2. Their earnings are subject to little variation. 3. The demand for labour is not much affected by the price of food. 4. Wages have not risen in proportion with the rise in the price of food. In the rural districts, about sixty years ago, the wages of labourers were 6s. per week; corn was then 4s. per bushel, and butter 4d. per lb. and other things in proportion. Wages are now about 7s. 6d.; corn nearly 10s. per bushel, and butter 1s. per lb. 5. The condition of the labouring population in the rural districts is much worse. 6. The poor rates in the city are lower than those of former periods. In the rural districts, the poor rates are higher than they formerly were. 7. The city prison report states an alarming increase in crime. Criminals in 1835, 35; in 1840, 82. In the house of correction there has been little variation. The dispensary, in 1820, patients admitted, 897; 1830, admitted, 1114, 1840, admitted, 1728. 8. Their wages are not regulated according to the number of their children. 9. The state of the small trader, &c. is not improved. 10. The funds of our religious and benevolent societies have been affected, in some degree, by the altered circumstances of members of the congregation. Some have left the city in search of employment. 11 Some parents have complained that they have not been able to send their children to the Sunday school for want of clothing.

ESSEX.—Earl's Colne.—I reside in a rural district in the above-named great agricultural county, ten miles from Colchester, and nine from Braintree. Full three-fourths of my congregation are agricultural labourers. The condition of the working classes, generally, in my neighbourhood is indeed deplorable. The eight pound loaf is now 1s. 6½d., and flour is 12s. 4d. per bushel. The general rate of wages is 10s. per week. I know of but one farmer in the neighbourhood who gives 11s., and another very large farmer whom I know gives but 9s. per week. Boys from the age of twelve to sixteen are paid from 1s. to 4s. per week, and such boys are generally employed on the Sundays as well as week days. It is the general custom of the neighbourhood to give the men £4 for the month's harvest. The average rent of the cottages occupied by working men is £4 per annum, in addition to which they have to pay 8s. or 10s. per annum for poor rate! The poor creatures always look to their harvest wages for the payment of their rents. I have now resided at Earl's Colne for twelve years. Six years ago the average price of flour in this neighbourhood was 6s. 4d. and 6s. 6d. per bushel. The general rate of wages then was 8s. per week. This year, the average price of flour has been, till of late, 11s. per bushel, and the general rate of wages 10s. per week. I never knew less than 8s., and never more than 11s. being paid. In reply to inquiries which I have made, I have been informed that not less than one bushel of wheat is sufficient to supply a working man, his wife, and a family of five or six children from two to fourteen years of age. Every poor family at least requires fifty-two bushels of coals for the year, taking one year with another and the lowest price of coal in this district is 1s. per bushel. The condition of the labouring population, as a class, is much worse now as compared with former periods within my experience. The wages paid to agricultural labourers are not regulated according to the number of their children. The condition of small traders is much deteriorated now as compared with other periods. Up to the present week (harvest having now commenced) considerable numbers of persons were out of employment. The allowance to the infirm and disabled poor out of the union house is 2s. 6d. per week, part in bread and part in money. Some of my hearers, able-bodied men in regular work, have not been able for many months to attend any place of worship on account of their having nothing decent to put on, and no means of procuring anything, the whole of their wages being absorbed in procuring a scanty supply of bread for themselves and their large families. I have perceived, and felt too, and do still feel, a very material connection between the high price of food and the diminution of our religious funds. We have during the last three years lost about one-third of our Sunday scholars, the bread monopolists having succeeded with the poor parents to send them to the parish church school, where they learn nothing good or useful. The means employed to get the children from our school were fair promises to give them a new frock, or some other little article of dress, on the condition of compliance with the temptation. It appears to me but too evident that there is nothing which the monopolists dread more than the spread of useful knowledge among the labouring population. From the above facts you will be able to form a conception of the effect of the unrighteous bread tax in this rural district.

GLOUCESTERSHIRE.—Wickwar.—1. The working classes are not generally employed in this neighbourhood. The average weekly wages paid to skilled labourers is 9s., to unskilled 7s. 2. The amount of their earnings has not been increased or diminished within my experience, which is very limited 3. I have not found the demand for labour to be affected by dear or cheap food. 4. Wages have not risen with the rise of food, or fallen with its fall. 5. The condition of the labouring population is worse now, as compared with former periods. 6. The poor-rates are more in this parish than at former periods. 8. The wages paid to agricultural labourers are not regulated according to the number of their children. 9 The state of the middle classes is much worse now as compared with former periods. 10. I have not perceived any diminution of funds for religious purposes, but I am sure such is the case from undoubted facts. 11. Many do not attend the ordinances of religion, in consequence of the high price of food. 12. Many of the children are kept from Sunday schools, and many more from our grammar schools, in which they might have, gratuitously, a liberal education, in consequence of the extreme poverty of the parents, arising from the high prices of food. The children, as soon as able to do anything, are obliged to labour in the fields or at the factory.

TEWKESBURY.—We have in this town between 700 and 800 stocking frames. 15 years ago the average wages of the stocking makers was 15s. *per week*, the present average is 3s. 6d.; they have long been "stinted" to a fixed amount of work; without the "stint" they could earn hardly 7s. per week. We are assured that unless trade is improved the greater part, if not the whole of them, must be thrown out of work before winter. Many of them are already out of employment; the stock of the hosiers is unusually large, and they are *sinking their capital daily*. In our lace manufactory, 15 years ago, the men earned on the average above £3 per week; they now earn 15s. If not stinted they could get only £1 weekly. Many of the valuable lace machines are *still;* and though the lace made is far superior in texture and beauty to that made formerly, the men are getting but *one-fourth* of their *former* wages. Our labouring population are in a miserable state of poverty, and the trade of the town generally is deeply depressed. The funds of all our religious institutions are decreasing.

DURSLEY.—1. The working classes of Dursley and the villages of Cam and Uley never had so little employment as at present. Many of them, with their wives and families, are prolonging their existence by means of potatoes and salt only rather than enter the union workhouse; but they must enter ere long, if they have no work, or starve. I am informed that there are at this present time more persons out of employment than during any of the severest past winters. 2. Considerably diminished; I should say half at least, if not two-thirds, from the earnings when the clothing trade was good. Many able-bodied men would now work for 6s. per week if they could get it, and struggle to live with their wives and children without aid of the parish. 3. When the necessaries of life are dear, there are more persons seeking labour, especially boys of a tender age. 4. Wages in my neighbourhood do not rise with the rise of food, but fall, if any difference, labour being scarce and labourers more plentiful. 5. The condition of the labouring class never was so deplorable as at present, it has been gradually getting worse for several years past. 6. Considerably higher, but what proportion I am unable to state; during the last year the rates amounted to 9s. 2d. in the pound. 7. There is no prison in the immediate neighbourhood, but our county gaol has had more prison within its walls already this year than at any former like period. I hear in the last January sessions 125 were tried, at the March sessions 124, at the spring assizes in April upwards of 100, at the Easter sessions 14, at the July sessions 119, and now at the assizes just over 66, altogether 500, being an increase of at least 30 per cent. on any former period, and this too, without any riots or great public disturbance in the county—therefore a steady increase of crime. 8. Some portion of my district is agricultural; the wages paid to agricultural labourers are *not* regulated according to the number of their children. 9. During my experience, for seven years past, the condition of the tradesmen and respectable artisans have been gradually getting worse; many of them are now, and have been for some time past, living upon their capital; and unless something can soon be done to increase trade, they cannot maintain their present state and pay rents and heavy poor-rates. 11. Many of the labouring classes are prevented attending a religious place of worship, because they have been obliged to pledge their wearing apparel to buy food, rather than go into the union work house. There are, or were, twelve woollen cloth mills at Dursley, capable of employing nearly 3000 hands, but only about 200 are now at work therein; and it is expected that during the winter, more will have to stop. Some of the mills have been closed for several years.

ULEY.—Houses worth £10 per year when trade was good, may now be purchased, *with the freehold*, for from £10 to £15.

STROUD.—1. Not well employed; average wages of weavers 6s. per week. 2. Reduced from 10s. to 6s. during the last ten years. 3. When provisions are dear, the poor man spends his little all in bread, and has nothing left for clothes. Thus, first the retailer, next the manufacturer, and lastly, the workman suffers. 4. No. 5. Worse. 9. Deteriorated. 10. The high price of provisions in connexion with the scarcity of work and the lowness of wages greatly interfere with the prospects of religious and benevolent institutions. 11. Scores of persons are kept away from places of worship for want of clothes. 12. Scores of children are kept from Sunday schools for want of clothes, and many children from British and other day schools, from the poverty of the parents, not allowing them to pay 2d. or 1d. per week.

HANTS.—FORDINGBRIDGE.—1. During the principal part of the year, we have in general a considerable number out of employment. 2. At the present time *able-bodied* men do not receive more than 9s. per week, and the average would not be more than 8s. 3. We never knew less than 7s. per week given to active labourers, when wheat was from 36s. to 40s. per quarter. 5. The condition of the labouring population as a class, is much worse *now* than in former periods. 6. The poor-rates within the last few years have increased about one-fourth. 7. The wages paid to agricultural labourers in this parish are not regulated by the number of their children. 8. The condition of the middle classes is now much worse than formerly, in consequence of nearly all the money being expended in bread.

WHITCHURCH.—1. At present they are nearly all employed, but in the winter and spring numbers are unemployed. 2. Nine and ten shillings per week has been the price of labour for some years past. 3. We are not aware that the demand for labour has at all been affected by the price of food. The farmers will never employ a single hand more than they actually need. 4. A shilling a week more than the sum above stated was given, on account of the dearness of food, for some time, but it soon reverted to the usual sum. 5. Much worse; as their wages are, in most cases, insufficient to secure the common necessaries of life. Things have been getting worse and worse ever since the enactment of the new poor law. 6. Since the alteration of the poor laws the rates have somewhat diminished, say about one-third. 7. Crime is nearly as prevalent, and disease as much so as ever, and there is a greater amount of destitution. 8. Wages are not regulated by the number of children. 9. The small traders are much worse off than formerly, from the inability of the poor to pay for the articles they need. 10. Our religious and benevolent societies are much affected by the price of provisions. Many who once subscribed to our "Sick Man's Friend Society," our "Missionary Society," &c., as well as towards the support of the minister, have been compelled to discontinue or reduce their subscriptions.

GOSPORT.—1. Labourers receive from nine shillings to eleven shillings per week. 3. The working men in this parish consist principally of watermen and fishermen. These suffer much from dear food; and trade suffers much from the same cause. 4. The alteration in prices of food make but little difference in the amount of wages or the demand for labour. 6. The poor rates invariably increase with high prices in food—sometimes as much as 20 per cent., and when very high, more than that. 7. Crime, in this parish, is less in amount than in most other districts. 8. Members in families have no bearing on amount of wages paid to labourers. 9. The state of the middle classes and little traders is getting worse every year.

ANDOVER.—1. The working classes are not well employed, particularly in the winter months, when great numbers are totally unemployed. The average amount of pay to agricultural skilled labourers is 9s. per week. 2. The amount of wages previous to the year 1830 were seven shillings per week, but at the time of the rioting in this part of the country the wages were increased to twelve shillings per week, and were afterwards gradually reduced to the present pay of nine shillings per week. 3. The increase in the price of food has a tendency to decrease the demand for labour. 4. Wages do not rise in proportion to the price of food. 5. The condition of the labouring classes is considerably worse, more particularly so since the introduction of the new poor law. 6. The amount of rates collected are nearly the same, but the proportion paid to the poor considerably less since the new poor law was introduced. 7. Disease considerably on the increase among the poor, arising from their present state of poverty and destitution. 8. The wages paid to labourers are not regulated according to the number of their families. 9. The middle class and small traders are considerably reduced in circumstances, more particularly so in the rural districts; the small shopkeepers are, generally speaking, reduced to a state of pauperism. 10. The present depressed state of the poor in Andover, arising from the want of employment, has been injurious to our benevolent societies. Many of the poor are quite unable to send their children to school, not having wherewith to pay for their education. The last two queries must be answered in the negative, as ours is a rising interest; but our progress would be much more rapid were it not that many of the poor are forced, by want of employment, to remove to London and some other large towns. Andover is a town of five thousand inhabitants in a purely agricultural district. The above answers were prepared by a number of practical men, viz., farmers and men of business, to whom I submitted the queries. The most complete reliance may be placed on their correctness.

LOCKERLEY.—1. The labouring classes are all well and fully employed, in this locality; the average weekly wages vary from eight shillings to ten shillings per week; having regard to the skill and efficiency of the parties employed. 2. The earnings of the labourers in this and the proximate parishes, for these last twenty years, have not fluctuated more than from one to two shillings per week, *either way*. 3. There has not been any relaxation in the demand for labour, or in the industrious habits of the labouring classes, comprehended in this and the immedi-diately adjoining parishes, by cheap or dear food. 4. Better decidedly. 8. No regard is paid to the number of children of agricultural labourers, as to regulating their wages, in this parish. 9. Tradesmen and shopkeepers always find trade more flourishing, and their customers more prompt in their payments, when bread is cheap; and, consequently, their business fluctuates with the rise and fall of bread. 10. The funds of our religious and benevolent societies are, unquestionably affected by high and low-priced food. 11. Fewer persons attend when food is high priced, at our place of worship, which is mainly attributable to the insuperable difficulty of purchasing decent and proper clothing; that is after supplying nature s wants. The same answer equally applies to our Sunday schools.

HEREFORDSHIRE—HEREFORD.—1. Agricultural labourers wages, 8s. to 9s. per week, with from two to four quarts of cider per day; in harvest time, what they can earn extra, by piece work. 2. In some few cases, on farms belonging to liberal persons, wages are 10s. per week, when wheat is 8s. per bushel, or under; 9s. per week when it exceeds that price. 4. The testimony of the minister of Gorsby, whose congregation is composed of labourers, is that in 1835 when wheat was at its lowest price, wages were 8s. per week; now they are 9s. 6 The poor-rates in the Hereford union of forty-seven parishes have diminished, comparing the three years ending 1840 with the three ending 1836: increase in eight parishes, £82; decrease in thirty-seven parishes, £2759; decrease £2677. 7. From the reports of the infirmary and dispensary, a gradual increase has taken place from 1825 to 1840 in the number of persons relieved, without any increase in the amount of annual subscriptions. Crime, from the accounts of the city and county prison, is not on the increase. Information furnished by the superintendent of police: number of persons brought before the magistrates in 1836, 644; in 1840, 485. 8. Labourers' wages are *not* regulated by the number of children, but handy boys can earn 6d. per day. The population of Hereford, in 1831, was over 10,000; in 1841, it was under 11,000. It is often difficult for casual workmen to find employment from the end of October to the turn of Christmas. Farmers, many of them, do not employ on their farms as many men all the year round now as they did sixteen years ago.

HERTFORDSHIRE.—BISHOPS' STORTFORD.—1. There is some excess of supply of labour over the demand in this neighbourhood, so that a proportion of the labourers are often out of employ, or only partially employed, doing perhaps four days' work instead of six; of course these are generally not the best workmen; the best are commonly in full employ. The most common rate of wages for agricultural labourers, who are paid less than any others, is ten shillings a week. The wages of others vary with the nature of their employment. 2. A rise of about a shilling per week since 1835. 3. There is no doubt that a high price of agricultural produce tends to encourage the employment of labour by the farmers. There are no other kinds of employment in this neighbourhood which appear to be sensibly affected by the price of food. 4. (See No. 2.) It is the practice for the farmers to raise the wages a little when a large rise takes place in wheat, or rather in flour, for this is what is looked at; the increase of the labourer's expenses, not of the farmer's profits. 5. Worse than when wheat was six shillings per bushel. The rise in wages is by no means equivalent to that in food; but the operation of the new poor law has improved the condition of the poor, by inducing habits of greater care and industry, and has taught them to look more to their own resources and less to public charity; and the introduction of cottage gardens, by providing them with other articles of food besides bread, has made them less dependent on the price of wheat. It is evident that the more they *rear* their food, instead of *purchasing* it, the less they feel variations of price in the market; if they could grow it all themselves, the market price would be quite indifferent to them. 6. The poor rates are about one-third of what they were during the few years preceding the new poor law: No very material change during the last three years. 8. To the extent of giving men who have large families the most lucrative kinds of work, the wages do depend on the number of children; but the absurdity of setting two men to do the same work, and paying them differently is now generally seen, and the practice, it is hoped, discontinued. 9. Worse than when food was cheap. The small trader depends on the money the labourer has left after providing his supply of flour for the week, and always feels the diminution of this surplus by any aggravation of the price of flour.

——— 1. In a town population where the manufacture of malt is extensively carried on, and one or two other manufactories of articles of every day consumption, employment is not so fluctuating as in a strictly manufacturing district; and, being surrounded by an agricultural population, there is no great variation of wages. 2. The amount of wages is nearly stationary. Though an advance of wages is given to better skilled workmen than formerly, the longer time occupied to produce a better made article prevents a greater amount of weekly earnings. 3. The demand for the labour of those who supply the agricultural poor with clothing, &c., is affected by the price of food; dear food depriving the labourer of the means of providing himself and family with many of the necessaries of life. The lessened demand for articles furnished by the mechanic or artizan, deprives them of the means of purchasing from each other those common necessaries they are ready to supply each other with, whilst all who labour are compelled, to the extent of their means, to purchase the high-priced produce of the agriculturist. 4. Wages can scarcely be said to bear any comparative relation to the price of food. In agricultural districts, as in all others, the supply and demand for labour regulate the amount of wages, not the price of food. Through the excess of supply beyond demand the agricultural employer reduces the rate of wages when the price of corn is low, and is not pressed with the necessity of raising it when food is dear. 5. From local circumstances, the condition of the town labouring population is not any worse than formerly, except as it is affected by the causes as described in answer to third query; but the condition of the agricultural labourer is worse than formerly. Their moral principles, and that self-respect which would deter from falsehood and dishonesty, are fast waning away, before the pressure of circumstances they are not able to control. Their only capital—their labour—does not meet with that remuneration which will leave them a sufficient surplus to promote decent and cleanly habits, after supplying themselves with that quantity of bread necessary to existence. 6. A better system of relief to the poor, under the New Poor-Law Amendment Act, has reduced the amount of the rates compared with periods previous to the operation of that act; but the reduction has sunk to its lowest degree, and an increase upon the expenditure is to be expected. The reason to be assigned is this: It was expected by the refusal to grant relief to able-bodied labourers, many would be compelled to locate themselves in manufacturing districts, where there would be a demand for their labour, thus lessening the supply of labour in the agricultural districts, which would have effected an advance of wages for the labour that was left. This expectation *has not* been realised; this intention or proposition of the framers and supporters of that act has been completely nullified by (we conceive) those *fiscal* arrangements which have operated upon the markets of foreign countries, partially or entirely closing them against the manufactures of our own country. The surplus labour from the agricultural labour market, which ought to have been profitably employed in manufactures, remains as a surplus; privations to a great extent are endured; the workhouse is resorted to as an asylum from want; privation and destitution increase with the increased price of food, coupled with the stationary rate of wages. Under such circumstances the poor rate must tend to an increase, compared with the first few years immediately after the New Poor-Law Amendment Act came into operation. 8. The wages of agricultural labourers in this neighbourhood are not regulated by the number of their children. The farmer does not apply the *same* rule in the payment of wages, as when the overseer from the poor rate made up for the deficiency in the payment of labour. *Then* the *sliding scale* for payment was highly appreciated, and faithfully acted upon; *now* the principles of *free trade*, in this respect, are thoroughly understood, and carried to their fullest extent; degenerating even into acts of oppression. Not unfrequently, youths, from sixteen to twenty years of age, are paid no greater amount of wages than those usually paid to boys from twelve to sixteen years old. 9. The state of the middle class in this neighbourhood is, year after year, deteriorating from its former advantageous means of securing a profitable return upon the employment of capital. This may be partly owing to competition reducing the profits upon the amount returned, &c.; but it is *much affected* by the reduced state of the small trader, compared with his former means of purchasing, either to manufacture or to retail. Instances, not a few might be adduced, of small traders, who a few years ago were tending to rank among the middle classes, but who now are fast sinking to a level with the labouring poor. This state of the small trader is greatly aggravated by the high price of food and provisions. The agricultural labourer has now exhausted the means of obtaining upon credit from the small trader necessary articles of clothing, &c.; and not only can the latter not afford to give credit now, but by his having done so in time past, he has by this been drawn into a condition of equal poverty and more painful circumstances than the labouring poor, and the future for him beams with no hope. To whatever causes these circumstances of the small trader is to be attributed, or from what moving power such a vicious state of things has been induced and is spreading; it is here that the *degrading* and *demoralizing* working of adverse circumstances are most plainly seen. None but those who have dealings with the small trader and the labourer can conceive of the decline of principles of common honesty, compared with former years; and it is with painful emotion they can bear witness to the severe ordeal to which the honest and upright are subjected. The present social condition of the small trader and labourer may be aptly described as one in which they bite and devour each other, and are in danger of being consumed one of another.

LANCASHIRE. — Preston. — 1. Employment is exceedingly scarce. If a man get out of a situation, it is almost impossible for him to obtain another. I should think there are above 1000 persons, from the age of 16 years and upwards, out of employment. 2. In all trades excepting those which are sustained by strict unions, the wages have been reduced during the last four years. 3. During the period of 1835 and 1836, when food was cheap, there was a great number of factories built and projected; and a great amount of labour for the people, compared with the present time. 4. Wages have greatly declined for the last four years, although food has not been cheap. 5. Never was there a more general sinking in the condition of the working classes. Above twelve hundred houses are unoccupied, including many shops. Poor people's goods are daily sold by auction for debts or for rent. 6. I am not aware that there has been any considerable increase in the poor-rates, but this is to be attributed to the extent practised of offering the workhouse to poor people instead of out-door relief, which leads many to the practice of begging; and others submit to the greatest privations, rather than go to the workhouse, which is crowded to excess. 7. Many suffer their extreme privations with great patience; others are discontented and sullen; many give up all in despair; while not a few are confident that an open rupture will relieve them. A great indifference is felt towards constitutional efforts, such as petitioning, &c., for the purpose of obtaining relief from their distress. Many of the hand-loom weavers live almost entirely on water-porridge, and are distressingly destitute of clothes and bedding. 9. The small traders, indeed almost all the shopkeepers, complain that they are sinking the little property they have, and that with very few exceptions. 10. Since the years 1835 and 1836, provisions have much advanced. During this period our congregation has decreased, owing to many having been obliged to leave the town to seek employment; some are kept back from attendance through the want of clothing. 11. The current income of our place of worship has decreased through the distress of the people 25 per cent. within the last four years, and all other occasional collections in proportion. The above information has been obtained from my own observation and application to a gentleman exceedingly well acquainted with the condition of the working classes. One of my members informed me last week, that when he could purchase eight pounds of flour for 1s., his wages were more than they are now, when he can obtain but four pounds and a half for 1s.

Liverpool.—1. A deacon of my church assures me that out of 300 householders visited by him every Monday, one-third are utterly unemployed, and the remainder only partially so. The wages of first-rate workmen have of late greatly decreased, and a fair working carpenter is often induced to work for 1s. per diem. The amount of wages does not influence the price of food. The overseer of the parish of Everton informed me that the poor rates have been increasing for the last four years in the proportion of 5, 6, 7, 8, and will be assuredly higher the next year.

Ashton in Mackerfield.—This is a township in the parish of Winwick, and contains 5411 inhabitants, employed, for the greater part, in manufactures and mining. Several extensive collieries are, I think, pretty well employed. Generally, the average wages of the men are, for day-men, 11s. per week; Colliers, 15s. to 17s. For smiths employed in hinge-making, chainmakers, and nailors, the average wages will be; hingemakers, 10s. to 12s.; locksmiths, 12s. to 13s.; chainmakers, 10s. to 12s., and limited to quantity; nailors, 7s. to 8s., but they work generally 14 hours per day. Silk weavers are scarcely half employed, and are subject to capricious and arbitrary abatements, amounting to 30 per cent. at least, averaging not more than 9s. per week when employed. Cotton weavers are still worse employed, and do not get more than 4s. per week when in work. Agricultural labourers have from some farmers 2s. per day; but Sir John Gerard, Bart., gives only 1s. 8d. per day to those employed by him on his estate, and to some only 1s. 6d. Spinners are not fully employed, and, on an average, have not earned 12s. per week for two years past. 2. Every branch seriously diminished. 3. Since 1835 the demand for labour has greatly diminished. Fifty cottages have been pulled down, and the inhabitants scattered. 4. The very reverse. Wages rise with the fall of the price of food, and *vice versa*. 5. Much worse in every branch. 6. Doubled in three years. Several persons have perished for want of the common necessaries of life, yet receiving parish pay. Thomas D—, John H—, and a poor Irishman perished by the roadside. 8. It does not. They are not so regulated. 9. Business is passing into the hands of a few large traders, who are perfect monopolists. The small tradesmen are disappearing; shoemakers, tailors, &c., are especially suffering; and small manufacturers are quite broken up. 10. I have inquired of an office bearer of the Independent Order of Oddfellows, who states the number of applicants for relief is doubled within the last year; much difficulty is found in obtaining the usual contributions to the box in consequence of the present state of trade here. A member in the united order states their funds are greatly diminished. The religious funds are decidedly less in amount as compared with 1835. The poor's fund, library, and collections for various purposes are now most decidedly less, almost to annihilation. 11. The excuses generally given are the want of clothing, and distress through poverty. Some families have been constrained to absent themselves from the public ordinances. There is one point to which I can bear strong testimony, the awful feelings of desperation abroad in the minds of the poor. R. T., plasterer, states that his business was never so bad as at this time since 1826. During last year, he had twenty-two houses to plaster and finish; up to this day, August 16, he has only had two, and knows of but three more for the remainder of the year. One house, and that not of a large size, and four small cottages are all the buildings erected this year throughout this township.

Heywood.—1. Less than four-fifths employed; skilled labour, 15s.; unskilled, 7s. per week. 2. The amount has been diminished from 20 to 30 per cent. Hand-loom weavers, 60 per cent. since 1836. 4. In our district dear food universally lowers wages, and cheap food raises them. 5. Worse than at any former period. 6. The poor-rates are 55 per cent. more than at any former period. 9. Many of them have become bankrupt, and most of those that remain are on the borders of bankruptcy, and compelled to cease the trust system; their condition was never so deplorable as at present. 10. When provisions are high, there is generally a falling off in the funds. In our village there are at this time eight factories unemployed, which are valued at about £80,000; they would engage 1,060 hands, the weekly wages of whom would amount to £424; besides several factories running short time.

Bury.—1. The operative classes, as a whole, are little more than half employed. In the township of Heap there are upwards of 2000 out of employ. The wages of the skilled labourer are reduced to a greater extent than the unskilled. 2. Decidedly decreased, and at this moment it rests entirely with the master to say what he will pay. 3. We have always found that in times of abundance, when provisions are low, wages have no chance of being reduced; men are more independent, and wages have, during our experience, invariably tended to rise when provisions were cheap. 4. Never within our knowledge did wages rise with the advance of provisions, but, on the contrary, the wages of labour invariably are depressed when food is at a high price. 5. Certainly worse, and that to a lamentable extent. 6. Double. 9. The masters are carrying on at but a profitless business; the shopkeepers are being ruined.

Denton.—The staple manufacture of the district is the manufacture of hats in its various branches, which only gives full employment about six months in the year, and which is principally a home trade, for, before the passing of the corn laws, many hats were exported from Denton to America; since then a prohibitory duty has been imposed. 1. Not well employed. In some branches of the trade skilful workmen, when in full work, can earn from 18s. to 40s. per week; the unskilled from 12s. to 18s. 2. Some branches, *i.e.* ruffers, body makers, and trimmers, have decreased as much as 30 per cent. 3. Abundance of labour when food is cheap, and the reverse when food is dear. 4. Wages invariably fall with the rise in the price of food, because then men will take out work at less than the regular wages to support their families. 5. Considerably worse. 6. About a quarter higher. 9. Very much deteriorated; the shopkeepers and little hat manufacturers badly of. 10. A diminution in collections for religious objects. 11. Many persons have stated their inability to attend on the public worship of God, because they could not appear so respectable as formerly, and could not give so liberally as formerly to the cause of God. 12. Many have neglected in consequence of not having suitable clothing, the parents with difficulty being able to procure food.

Wigan.—1. The working classes in the neighbourhood of Wigan are not well employed. The generality of labourers earn from 3s. 6d. to 7s. 6d. per week; in a few instances, skilful workmen obtain 10s. to 13s. per week. Hand-loom weavers do not earn on an average, clear of expenses, more than 4s. 6d. per week, but in very many instances much less. 2. The amount of their earnings, within my experience, have decreased full one half, and in many instances three-fourths. 3. From my own observation, I find the demand for labour invariably decreases when food is dear. 4. Wages fall when food rises, and rise when food is cheap—but in what proportion it is hard to ascertain. 5. The condition of the labouring population is very much worse than it was formerly. 6. The poor rates now, as compared with seven years previous to 1839, are fully *double*. 7. Wigan has no prison: the state of crime, from the number of prisoners committed to Kirkdale, appears to be much the same as for several years past, but rather upon the increase. Disease and destitution have very much increased, and the dispensary is by no means able to meet the wants of the poor. 9. The state of the middle class never was so bad in my remembrance as at present. 10. When food is high, our *funds* decrease. 11. A very considerable falling off among the working class. 12. A decrease in the attendance of our Sunday scholars for want of clothing.

There are at the present time two thousand and upwards persons out of work in Wigan; all the factories that are at work, except two, are working short time; half of one, and the whole of four others, are standing still altogether. The number of factories in Wigan is, I think, 22. There are about 330 houses uninhabited.

MIDDLETON.—Taking silk weavers for the last six months, they have not been employed above three-fourths of their time. The averaged weekly wages for skilled labourers will not exceed more than ten shillings per week. The unskilled labourer will not average more than six shillings, and in numerous cases not more than four shillings per week. 2. In the year 1825, plain sarsnet 2000 three-thread was elevenpence per yard for weaving; in this present year, 1841, the same description of goods are wove at fourpence-halfpenny; cotton goods have been reduced. 3. It is a generally admitted fact, that when food has been dear labour has invariably been scarce; when a rise has taken place in the market (of food) work has invariably decreased, and contrariwise, when the markets have lowered work has been more plentiful. 4. The condition of the labouring population, as a class, has for the last sixteen years deteriorated, but more particularly so for the last six years. 5. With reference to the poors'-rate, the amount actually collected from March 25th, 1836, to 25th March, 1837, was £613 15s., and for the year ending 25th March, 1841, £1358 12s. 10¾d. 8. The middle class, such as the small trader, &c., in the township of Middleton are much reduced for the last five years; there has appeared to me as a collector to be a general sinking among them, and more especially in the last year.

LEICESTERSHIRE.—ASHBY-DE-LA-ZOUCH.—1. Well employed only for two months, from May harvest to the end of corn harvest. 2. Some few raised wages 1s. a week in 1838 and 1839. The rate of agricultural wages for the whole of the division of South Leicestershire is 10s. winter, 12s. during harvest work, but some give 11s. all the year round. 3 No reduction in cheap years; no advance in dear years. 4. The rise but partial; I never heard of a *fall* with the *fall* of wheat. 5. The condition is worse; my parish consists of colliers, framework-knitters, and agricultural labourers; and the light work on the farms is mostly done by women at 8s., in harvest 10s. It is a matter of course that when wages do not advance in proportion to the price of wheat, the condition of all must be worse; and the order of their deterioration is,—labourers bad, colliers worse, and framework knitters worst; theirs is wretched indeed, and their net earnings, when in full employ, are hardly more, on the average, if so much, as 1s. a day. 6. There is a trifling decrease, caused by the depression of trade for the last three years. Some of the remaining questions it is not in my power to answer. I may, however, observe, that wages have never reference to the number of a man's children; that in a county where manufactures exist, the wages of agricultural labour do not fall with the price of wheat, because contemporaneously with it, trade is, as it might be expected, naturally better, and, therefore, the surplus hands are carried off to other employments. In the parish with which I am connected there are too many labourers already, and if the trade of the country should continue to decline, there must be a recoil, and the wages of farm labourers be reduced, through the manufacturers not taking them off.

LEICESTER.—1. The working classes in the vicinity of Leicester are not half employed. The average wages paid to the frame-work knitters for the manufacture of wrought hose are about six shillings per week. A skilled workman can earn, clear of expenses, about eight shillings per week: an unskilled workman can earn about four shillings and sixpence or five shillings. But a great deal depends on the particular branch of the manufacture in which each individual is employed. 2. The amount of wages has greatly diminished within the last few years, and is continually diminishing. 3. The demand for labour has always risen with cheap food. 4. Wages have never risen with the price of food among the Leicester operatives. 5. The condition of the working classes is much worse than it was ten years ago. The agricultural labourers have suffered greatly for the last six months from the want of employment. Their work has been done to a great extent, and at a reduced price, by the unemployed operatives. 6. The present poor rates bear a great and perpetually increasing disproportion to those of 1838. In one parish in my circuit a farmer recently informed me that he had paid £50 in poor rates alone for the last twelve months. Another farmer in another parish solemnly assured me that his rates for the last year had amounted to more than his rent. By the word rates he meant rates of every kind, but among these the poor rates were by far the most burthensome. In both these parishes many unemployed operatives had fallen on the poor rates for maintenance. 10. A partial diminution of the funds of the religious body with which I am connected has been the invariable result of high priced food. 11. I have found a small falling off in the members of my congregation, in consequence of their inability to purchase suitable raiment, inability arising from the scarcity of employment, the low scale of wages, and high price of food. There has been a considerable decrease in the attendance of children at our Sabbath schools from the cause which I have named in my answer to the last question.

—— 1. Not above two-thirds fully employed. Unskilled labourers from 6s. to 7s. 6d., and skilled ditto from 12s. to 15s. per week. 2. Diminished 20 per cent. or more. 3. In cheap food years the demand for labour is greater, and wages rise. This was the case here in 1835-6, when corn was at half the price. 4. In dear years, as in the three last years, the demand diminishes, a want of employment ensues, and wages fall. 5. Infinitely worse; all are sinking into the class of extreme poor. Never knew it to be so bad for thirty years. 6. Rates are not as they were once, correct data by which to judge of destitution; the poor here, as elsewhere, will suffer the greatest privation rather than go into the poor house. 7. Needless; destitution meets us daily; here, however, crime in consequence of it has not yet increased to any extent. 9. The small traders are barely getting a livelihood now. If their concerns were wound up most of them would be found insolvent. They have credited the most trustworthy of the working classes while out of employment, and the debts incurred, even if they were to get into full employ, which is hopeless, they would be unable to pay off for a long time. 12. A decrease of scholars, and the total annihilation of the funds dependent on the weekly contributions of the children.

HINCKLEY.—We seldom hear of farmers failing in our neighbourhood, but failures of tradespeople are very frequent. Red herrings, and sometimes a little Irish bacon, form the principal food, in addition to potatoes and bread, during the bad trade; most of the poor people eat their bread yet hot from the oven. The truck system most extensively carried on here. We have but 400 rate payers in our parish: our population is upwards of 6400. Prostitution and obscene language much on the increase. Assize of bread not enforced here, which operates much against the interest of the poor. The hosiery trade, principally of cotton hose, is the only branch of manufacture. Coals from 10s. 6d. to 13s. per ton: rents from 1s. to 2s. 9d. a week: unoccupied houses 157. Petty depredations very frequent: crimes of greater magnitude very scarce. The moral education of great numbers altogether neglected, and society reaps the consequences. There are a great number of alehouses. Fathers and mothers, with from four to seven children of both sexes, sleep in one room.

ARNESBY.—1. They are most of them, *just now*, employed; but during three or four months in the year, many are destitute of work. Our skilled frame-work knitters earn about 7s.; and the unskilled 4s. per week. 2. Diminished within the last twenty years, in the stocking making branch, full 40 per cent. 3. Generally when provisions are dear, trade is bad and wages low. 4. Not in manufactures, and only in a slight degree in agriculture; and the rise in wages has, in this department, been partly occasioned by the demand which the construction of railroads has created for labour. 5. Much worse. I am often called upon to relieve families that are absolutely without bread. There are certain cases of such horrible destitution and wretchedness, that in consequence of the absence of sufficient beds, bed linen, &c., lead to results involving a violation of decency too gross to mention. 10. I have perceived a sensible connexion between them. The poor of my congregation, connected with manufactures, cannot get bread enough; they have not a penny to spare for religious purposes. The long depression of trade in my village has sunk the great body of frame-work knitters into a state bordering on despair. Several of the best men, and the best workmen, are thinking of emigrating; and almost all would, I believe, if they could raise the requisite funds.

LUTTERWORTH.—The hands are not fully employed more than nine months in the year. The first in skill gets not more than 7s. per week; the second in skill 5s. 6d., and the third in skill 4s. I came to Lutterworth in 1809. The average price of labour was then from 13s. 6d. to 14s. 6d., and continued so till the year 1815. After that time there was a decrease till 1836, and in the same year corn was sold from 40s. to 46s. per quarter. When corn was cheap, in 1836, wages rose from 7s. to 9s. per week. A hand must work from six o'clock in the morning till ten at night to get the above wages. In 1811 I had for making one dozen of hose 9s. 6d., but now at this time I can only get 9s. 6d. for the worsted and labour as well. The worsted for this dozen of hose cost 5s. 10d., which leaves for labour 3s. 8d.

LOUGHBOROUGH.—1. The working classes are not fully employed; indeed, great numbers of them, during the last three years have had but an inconsiderable portion of employment. Those employed in the hosiery business are on the stint, that is, only a restricted quantity of work is allowed them; and this has now been the case for the greater portion of the last two years. The average rate of wages for lace hands is 12s. per week. Adult frame-work knitters, 8s. per week, when fully employed. Agricultural and day labourers 10s. per week, with but very uncertain employment, many of the latter (agriculturists and day-labourers) being out of work for as much as three months in the year. 2. The wages of all classes considerably diminished within the last 25 years. In 1815 agricultural labourers in this neighbourhood received 15s. per week; the average rate of their wages now is 10s. per week. Even so late as 1824, lace hands, with six hours' daily work, could earn from 69s. to 70s. per week, and at that time 1s. 5d. per rack was paid for the net made in the 8-quarter 12-point twist lace machine; and now the price for the same article in the same machines is 1¼d. per rack, and the workman must work sixteen hours per day to clear the sum of 10s. per week. The wages of stocking-makers have, since 1815, suffered a reduction of more than one-half. In 1815, at the termination of the French war, and the year of the passing of the corn laws, the wages of this class were on the average about 18s. per week; but immediately after the passing of the corn laws a considerable reduction took place, and the prices fluctuated; but the advance seldom was so great as the previous reduction, so that in fact, on the average of years, a reduced rate of wages was received. In 1828-9 another considerable reduction took place in the prices of making hosiery goods, and since then they have but slightly varied in nominal rate. In 1835-6 they rose, till in 1836 they reached the highest point attained within the last twelve years: this was owing to the great demand for goods, chiefly caused by the cheapness of provisions during those years. 3. Have always found employment most scarce when food is dearest. In 1835 employment was very abundant. In the warp trade, which is a branch of the hosiery business, 1s. 8d. per lb. was paid for the making of cotton Berlin web, and 4s. 6d. for the medium size and quality of warp hose, with abundance of employment. Flour was then 1s. 6d. per stone of 14lbs.; flesh meat 4d. to 4½d. per lb., and other provisions equally cheap. Now, with flour 2s. 8d. a stone, and meat 6½d. per lb., the same articles are 11d. per lb. for the Berlin web, and 3s. 3d. per dozen for the hose; and the manufacturers have just stopped, during harvest, the bulk of the hands engaged in making those. Other branches of the trade have been affected nearly in the same proportion. 4. Wages in this neighbourhood are not regulated in the least by the price of food, but wholly by the demand for labour. 5. Have invariably observed that, when food is cheap, the physical condition of the people is beneficially affected, and that they dress in a superior manner, and are cheerful and contented; whilst in dear years, as in 1839, 1840, and at the present time, the reverse is very apparent: a gradual deterioration has, during the last-named period, taken place, and they are in the mass, at this time, to an unparalleled degree, distressed. 6. Poor rates are now much higher than in the years 1835 and 1836. I am not able to state the difference in the amount of the poor's rate in the different periods of cheap and dear years. The rates are now increasing. A few weeks back the overseers issued a notice stating that all those who did not pay up the rates would be served with a summons from the magistrates. In several instances the goods were seized for poor's rate; but this plan did not answer, as the persons whose goods were then sold were obliged to enter the workhouse as paupers in consequence. 8. Not the least consideration is paid to the number of the agricultural labourer's children, when fixing the amount of his wages. 9. The condition of the shopkeepers is deplorably bad. They all complain of the great decrease in the amount of their business; the reason they assign is the high price of food and the low rate of wages. 10. Has been a decided falling off in the funds for religious purposes during the last eighteen months. 11. To some extent. 12. Attendance at Sunday school is considerably lessened by the distressed state of the working classes.

ULLESTHORPE.—1. Employment among the working classes has very considerably fallen off, many having no occupation for their stocking frames, and the average earnings not being more than from 6s. to 8s. for skilled, and 3s. to 5s. unskilled. 2. During the four years of my experience, earnings have diminished at least 2s. per week. 3. When food has been dear the demand for labour has been invariably less. 4. Wages have *not* risen with the rise in the price of food. 5. The condition of the labouring population has decidedly deteriorated within the last four years. 6. Our poor rates have increased at least one-third within the last twelve months. 7. The mass of the skilled labourers seldom taste meat once a week, and many of them not for months together. 8. The agricultural labourers are not remunerated according to the number of their children. 9. The small trader, unless an alteration takes place, will be ruined, or brought down to the level of the labourer; the demand is less, and the probabilities of payment very uncertain. 10—12. The benevolent societies, congregations, and Sunday school have all been only slightly affected by the high price of food, as our congregation is partly agricultural and partly manufacturing. The general tone of the labouring population is very unhealthy; murmurs of deep-seated discontent are everywhere to be heard, and unless matters mend the consequences may be terrible to contemplate. In our article it is right to state, that the agricultural labourers' condition is certainly superior to that of the skilled; their wages average from 10s. to 11s. per week.

MIDDLESEX.—ENFIELD.—The day labourers in our neighbourhood are, generally speaking, very well employed; their average weekly wages are twelve shillings all the year round, but skilled labourers have fifteen shillings with the advantage of working occasionally by the piece, when they earn something more. In harvest they can earn twenty shillings and upwards. 2. The amount of their earnings has not been increased within my experience, but there has been a greater facility of obtaining work since the new poor law, the poor rate having been lessened, and the payment for labour increased. 3. The demand for labour is very little affected by cheap or dear food, if at all. 4. Wages do not rise with the price of food, nor fall with its fall. 5. The condition of the labourer is certainly improved by the increased facility of obtaining work which gained in our parish before the new poor law, through the principle of that law having been previously acted on. 8. The wages are not regulated according to the number of children. 9. The state of the small trader is perhaps slightly improved. 10. The funds of our societies are but slightly affected by the price of food, inasmuch as they are furnished by the labouring classes only in a very limited degree. Our congregations are somewhat affected by high prices. 12. The attendance at our Sunday schools is not diminished.

SPITALFIELDS, LONDON.—1. They are not well employed. The labouring classes in Spitalfields are employed in the manufacture of silks. Skilful workmen, employed in the best parts of the manufacture, can earn 25s. per week; but this class bears a small proportion to the total number; say as *one in twenty*. The next class will earn about 15s. per week; of this class, the proportion is about one third, or four in every twelve. The remainder earn 7s. or 8s. per week. 2. Decreased, at least 20 per cent. 5. Worse considerably than during the last ten years. 6. In the year 1834, they were 9d. in the pound for the quarter; they are now 1s. 3d. in the pound for the quarter, which is scarcely sufficient to cover the current expenses. There are more of the poor applying for relief at the present time, than have been known for the last ten years; at this season of the year. When bread is cheap, the poor weaver can just manage to live; when it is dear, he cannot obtain wages sufficient to procure it; hence the numerous applications for relief, and the consequent increase in the amount of the rates. 9. Very much deteriorated.

NORTHAMPTONSHIRE.—DAVENTRY.—1. The working classes are not well employed. The principal shoemakers in the town assured me, last week, that they have an unusual stock on hand, for which they can find no market; in consequence the men have not during the week more work given them than they could with ease accomplish in four days. The average wages of our shoemakers is between 9s. and 10s. a week, the whole of which is, in many instances, spent in the purchase of bread alone. 2, 3, and 4. The amount of their earnings has rather *diminished* than otherwise since 1835, which proves that wages have not risen with the rise of the price of food. 5. The condition of the labouring population, as a class, is necessarily worse now than in former periods; as a proof of which, parents with large families have been compelled to send some of their children to the union workhouse, not being able to obtain for them the means of support. 10. The funds of our religious and benevolent societies have been considerably affected by the high price of food. Many in my congregation, who once cheerfully subscribed their penny a week to missionary and other societies, are now necessitated to withhold their subscriptions. 11 and 12. Some, in consequence of their deep poverty, are not able to attend public worship; and the same cause has operated in diminishing the number of children in our Sabbath school. The agricultural labourers in our neighbourhood must also endure many severe privations, their wages being about 10s. a week. Whole families, I have ascertained by personal inquiry, have not tasted flesh meat for twelve months and upwards.

BRYBROOKE.—1. The majority are fully employed during summer, but there are some exceptions, and in winter very many have much unemployed time and consequent distress. Several are obliged to seek work at a considerable distance, say from twenty to forty miles, on the railroads. Farmers' labourers receive from 8s. to 10s. per week, with the addition of their board during harvest. A few skilled hands may occasionally get 12s. 6. The poor rates now do not amount to more than two 1s. rates in the year, whereas there used to be eight. This alteration is partly owing to the operation of the new poor law, but chiefly to the fact that there are two miles of the railroad in this parish for which rates are paid to the poor. 8. Wages are not regulated by the number of children. 9. The condition of small traders, or shopkeepers, is deteriorated partly by the fact that when sickness or other causes increase the expenses of the poor, the loss must fall on them in the form of bad debts. 10. A considerable reduction in the amount of contribution has occurred, it is said, from this cause. 11. There has been no falling off from this cause. 12. The attendance at Sabbath schools was never better. The fact that the females are generally employed in making pillow-lace, though their earnings are small, preserves the poor from the distress and destitution which they must endure I have three village stations in adjacent parishes in which the poor are less favoured than in this. In two of them considerable help is obtained from endowed charities connected with the state church, but these have generally a debasing and demoralizing effect upon the recipients.

NOTTINGHAMSHIRE.—SUTTON-IN-ASHFIELD.—1. For the last twenty years they have, been exposed to frequently-recurring gluts and panics; for the last five years, (with the exception of the last six months) two-thirds have not had half employment; and their average earnings, including skilled and unskilled workmen, have not been more, when fully employed, than from five to eight shillings per week. 2. The amount of their earnings have decreased, within my experience, at least three-fourths. 3. We have not found the demand for labour to be affected by cheap or dear food, only with one or two exceptions—peace of Paris, &c. 4. Wages have not risen with the rise of the price of food. The average price of flour has been for the last twenty years, 2s. 6d. per stone, (14lbs.) and wages gradually on the decline. 5. The condition of the working classes is wretched indeed, and bears no comparison with former years. 6. The comparison which poor rates bear to former years, within my experience, is three to one. 8. The wages of agricultural labourers are not regulated by the number of their children. 9. The state of the middle class, and particularly the small trader, is much deteriorated by competition, bad debts, and small profits. 10. We have experienced a diminution in our religious funds of more than one half, owing to high-priced food, want of employment, and low wages. 11. We have not experienced any falling off in our congregations, but we believe many more would attend, and religion would prosper amongst us, could the people obtain decent clothing, and the mind be disburthened from the weight that presses upon it. 12. With regard to our Sabbath schools, all our energies are cramped. Want of school rooms, want of funds, want of more employment and better wages, and high prices of food, place parents and children, teachers and supporters, in the most deplorable situation.

Beeston.—1. The people are not generally well employed. The greater part of the population are employed in manufacturing cotton hose; the other part in the manufacturing of lace. The average weekly wages of the former, skilled workmen, do not amount to above 8s.; while the wages of the lace makers are averaged at about 17s. per week. 2. The amount of earnings are diminished, I cannot say how much. 3. The demand for labour has been less when the price of bread has been high than when otherwise. 5. The condition of the labouring poor is worse now, as compared with former periods, within my experience. 6. The poor-rates are double to those of former periods. 8. Agricultural labourers' wages are not regulated according to the number of children. 9. The condition of the middle class is rather deteriorated. 10. Our religious funds have suffered from the high price of bread. 11. Several of our congregation are unable to attend divine service on account of scarcity of employment and the high price of food. 12. Several children cannot attend our Sabbath school from want of clothing.

Lenton.—Our report from Lenton is similar to the above. It concludes as follows: "We never remember a period when the middle class had so much to contend with as at present; many of them have already merged into the labouring class. We regard the corn laws as a great national grievance; they tend to increase the price of all agricultural produce, and diminish the wages of the mechanic and artisan; inasmuch as it is evident that, by their operation, the poor man, with a fixed rate of wages, has less to spare for necessary comforts, such as apparel, repairs, fuel, &c., than he otherwise would have if the price of his food was unfettered by the removal of 'protective duties.' He would then be enabled to give more employment to his neighbour; labour would be in greater demand generally; and, consequently, increase in value."

Hexham.—1. The staple trade is the manufacture of gloves of a kind peculiar to the place, which is at present quite at a stand, principally owing to the state of the American market. The wages of the operatives in this department are from 12s. to 18s. per week when in full employ. 2. The earnings of glove-sewers are reduced 30 per cent. 3. If in the decided opinion of an extensive glove manufacturer, that there is more demand for labour when provisions are cheap. 4. In general the wages do not keep pace with the price of food. 5. They are certainly worse than formerly, according to the opinions of their employers. 9. The small traders complain of difficulty in getting pay for what they sell, which is consequent on the want of employment among the labouring classes. 10, 11, 12. Our congregation and schools are in a prosperous state.

SOMERSETSHIRE.—FROME.—I have been acquainted with this town only four years and a half, during which time no great alteration has taken place in the scale of wages, but testimony is given that not more than 25 years since, wages were paid to the amount of a guinea where only about twelve shillings are now given. Great diminution of earnings is, however, occasioned by the want of constant and uninterrupted labour, though the scale of wages has not been much altered. 4. When provisions have been dear, the mechanics, and especially the weavers, have been compelled to work more hours in the day, in order to obtain the necessary support for their families. 6. The poor's rate for 1837 was 2s. 10d. in the pound; for 1838, 4s. 4d.; for 1839, 5s.; for 1840, 5s. 4d. The condition of the small trader is considerably deteriorated in this town; there were here formerly a large number of small clothiers, of whom not more than one half, and probably a much smaller number, now remain. 10. Many who used to subscribe to religious and charitable institutions have been compelled to decline or to diminish their contributions. 12. There are many who are prevented from attendance on religious worship from want of clothing.—Another report says that the working population are not more than half employed; and that cheap food has always increased the amount of work.

SHEPTON MALLET.—1 Excepting in the winter months the agricultural labourers are generally employed at wages varying from 7s. to 9s per week. During the hay and corn harvest robust labourers, skilful in mowing and reaping, can earn from 2s. 6d. to 3s. per day, with one meal daily and sufficient drink. At these times, however, they are frequently idle in consequence of rain, and they assert that, on an average, after paying for tools and other contingent expenses, their aggregate wages very little, if any, exceed the highest amount paid to weekly farm labourers of the best class, say about 9s. per week. In winter they are frequently much distressed for want of employment, and many seek an asylum in the union workhouses. 2. Wages have fallen within the last two years about 15 or 20 per cent. amongst skilled labourers. Amongst unskilled labourers it has been stationary; 1s. 6d. per day to such, if not in constant places and regularly employed, is considered top wages. 3. Periodical stagnation of trade reduces the demand for labour. 4 Certainly not; the price of labour appears to be regulated by the demand, and supply, and cost of production. 5. The condition of the labouring population is decidedly worse now than when provisions were lower, some two or three years ago; their earnings are so absorbed in purchasing food that they cannot spare money for other purposes. The country linen drapers and ready made clothes sellers feel the difference most sensibly, and can give more direct and positive evidence than any other class. 6. The poor rates were rather higher before the passing of the poor-law amendment act. They are now full 30 per cent. upon the rental of the parish, and have in nearly all the unions in the county been steadily advancing for the last three or four years at the rate of 10 per cent. per annum above the preceding year on the relief actually given to paupers, and this estimate is made to show that the increase is not occasioned by expenses of management. 8. In this neighbourhood so vicious a principle is not openly advocated or acted on, although it perhaps operates to the disadvantage of a man with a large family, and it is unquestionable that there exists a strong repugnance in the minds of very many young labouring men to marriage. As a general fact it may be safely asserted that the profits of trade amongst the smaller class of traders will hardly enable them to bear the pressure of taxes and provide for their families, and the difficulties appear to be increasing. House rent has declined within the last two or three years 20 or 30 per cent. in all new lettings where the former tenants have left, and many shops and cottages are vacant. The food of the poor is principally potatoes which are grown in the neighbourhood, of very superior quality, and sold, on an average, at about 3s. 6d. per cwt. They rarely purchase animal food, except a little bacon, and, in the spring months, small quantities of very young veal hardly fit for food; they also, in the autumn months, some seasons when cattle are plenty and fodder scarce, expend a few pence in portions of cow beef of the most inferior description, supplied by the lowest class of butchers, who purchase of the dairy farmers cows no longer profitable in the dairy, and too old to fatten, and very many of them half dead of diarrhœa and affections of the liver. Coarse bread is not much used, most poor families preferring the better qualities and potatoes. Coarse bread is too often compounded of various kinds of corn, the miller exerting his ingenuity to make it appear like wheaten flour, and at the same time using the least possible quantity of wheat. The rent of factories in this town have fallen so much that some vacant ones may be rented at any price parties may choose to offer.

Bristol.—I have never known, (except in the depth of severe winters) employment so scarce as at present. 2. Diminished fully one-fourth. Trades which within my memory regularly earned 24s., and even upwards per week (beside the advantage of working overtime, sometimes making eight or nine days in the week,) now receive only 18s., and work so scarce, that if discharged from a regular place, there is considerable difficulty in obtaining employment. 3. Those branches of trade engaged in manufacturing and selling articles of clothing, furniture, and those things generally termed "comforts" always suffer very severely when food is dear, and are so especially at this time. 4. No. I know of no single instance in all my experience (both in town and country) of wages being raised on account of the high price of food. 5. Decidedly worse, as employment is scarce, wages low, and provisions excessively dear. 9. The condition of small tradesmen is decidedly bad, as from decreased consumption, and increased bad debts; their income is in many cases decreased from one-third to one-half, in some cases more. Many who a few years ago were doing considerable business at good profits, are now fast sinking into a state of insolvency. 10. Yes. Many of these institutions are now languishing and crippled in their efforts for want of means, and those whose incomes are kept up to anything approaching their average amount, are kept so by extraordinary efforts, which can only have a temporary duration. The highest wages usually paid to agricultural labourers is 9s. per week, excepting in the time of hay, and wheat harvest, when they may earn 2s. per diem; but in the winter their wages do not average one-half the first amount, as more than one half of their time is unemployed. I have been eye-witness to scenes of the greatest wretchedness and privation. A family of six or seven children, the father and mother sick, and for days with no other food than potatoes; nor is this a solitary instance, for many others of a similar kind might be pointed out. In one district, with which I am intimately acquainted, if it had not been for the praiseworthy course pursued by one gentleman who holds several large farms, in letting out small allotments of ground to the labouring poor for the purpose of raising potatoes, I firmly believe that many families would have been in a state of actual starvation.

YEOVIL.—This is a manufacturing town; staple, kid glove manufacture; 7000 inhabitants. 1. Badly employed. Four days' work in the week considered very good employment; many have no work for week together. Unskilled labourers average barely 7s. in the rural districts; mason's assistants, gardener's ditto, and so forth, in the town, 8s. or 9s. Women formerly earned for sewing the gloves 3s. 6d., for what they now receive 2s., or even 1s. 3d. 2. The reduction in price of skilled labour has been taking place during the last fourteen years. 3. Certainly diminished by dear food. 4. Rate of wages unaffected by price of food. 5. Much worse both in town and country. There are about 150 uninhabited houses in Yeovil, though the population has increased one-seventh since 1830; the former occupiers of houses are now crowded into apartments. Food was formerly much cheaper and wages higher. Bacon, since 1800, and before the close of the war, was 6d. per lb.; it is now 9d. Cheese was then 1½d. per lb., and butter 4d.; they are now 4d. and 1s. The farm labourers seldom paid rent, and purchased no coal, being allowed faggoting; they often had right of waste land. But it is within the last ten or fifteen years that a class of poor have entirely disappeared, who were a most respectable body. These folks had generally one or two pounds in the house, a pig, or even a cow and a few geese, and generally attended the autumn fairs, with a little stock kept on waste lands through the summer. At Compton, three miles from Yeovil, a sail-cloth manufacturing village, at least forty of this class have disappeared within the last few years. 6. Just double what they were under the old law. 7. The surgeon of Ilchester gaol informed me that crime is on the increase. I asked him the cause. He replied "Poverty! the increase being in petty thefts of provisions, vegetables, &c," and then gave me two or three melancholy cases out of a great number. 9. The small traders are gradually sinking through decreasing custom. Bankruptcies and insolvencies 20 years ago were almost unknown. There have been three melancholy failures in this class within the last four months. In the higher class of manufacturers, from 1800 to 1821, their were four failures; from 1821 to 1841 there were 37. 10 and 11. Certainly. High prices and low wages are a heavy discouragement, and check every effort at advancing the spiritual interests of the poor, and promoting benevolent objects. 12. Children are frequently absent from want of clothing, particularly of shoes.

BATH.—1. Not being a manufacturing place, Bath is not subject to great fluctuations. 2. The amount of earnings, I am informed, have been gradually diminishing for several years past. 3. Never. 4. The price of labour appears to be regulated by the amount of supply and demand. 5. A gradual deterioration has taken place, there being fewer persons in what is called constant situations, that is, having full work throughout the year. 6. I cannot positively say, but I think they are less now than under the old poor law.

STAFFORDSHIRE.—WALSALL.—The staple trade of this town is in saddlers' ironmongery, the prosperity of which depends quite as much on home as on foreign demand. It has been for some time past, and is at present, in a deeply depressed state. Masters are on the brink of ruin, and workmen are already ruined. Numbers of houses and shops in every street are closed, and many of the poor are in a state of starvation. Mr. B., a chainmaker, informed me, that two years ago he employed 30 men; now he has only two, and has great difficulty in finding employment for them. Many of those whom he formerly employed are, with their families, in a state of the most abject poverty. He states that a man who could earn 20s. a week two or three years ago will now get only 14s., when he has full work; unskilled workmen will not get more than half that sum. The demand for labour he says he has found invariably to increase with the cheapness of food, and to fall off as food has risen; and the same with regard to wages. Articles, sold for 9s. when food was cheap, will now not bring more than 3s., nor is there much demand even at that price. One of the most respectable houses in Birmingham, which two years ago usually ordered 100 gross, will now not order more than 6 gross. The condition of the middle class, consisting of the small trader, is, he says, pitiable beyond description. Mr. C., saddlers' ironmonger, states, that workmen generally are not half employed, and that he has constantly applications from men, earnestly imploring him to give them work at prices at which it would be impossible for them to earn anything like a proper living. W. K. could, a few years ago, employ 20 workmen; he would now be thankful to get work for himself and family. Last winter they were compelled to go into the poor house, and there seems no other prospect for them the next. This man is a member of the church to which I minister. Innumerable cases of a similar kind might be furnished, but the above may be considered as fair specimens of the classes to which they respectively belong. The people's hearts are failing them through fear. Their condition is fearfully bad, and their hope is almost cut off. Unless something be done, and that speedily, the inhabitants generally will be overwhelmed in one common ruin. To the restrictions on food the people are convinced the depression of trade may be attributed, and, consequently, their destitution.

Stafford.—1. A greater number of the working classes of this neighbourhood are at the present time destitute of employment than perhaps at any former period. Until recently the condition of the labouring classes has been better than in many other places, but in consequence of the stoppage of four cotton mills, which have given employment to upwards of four hundred hands, and paid about £200 per week in wages, the town is in a very depressed state. 3. Apparently cheap food has increased the demand for labour; dear food has tended to decrease that demand. 4. Wages have not risen and fallen equal to the rise and fall of the price of provisions. 5. The condition of the labouring classes is worse than at any former period. 8. The wages paid to agricultural labourers in this district are not proportioned to the number of their families. 9. The condition of the middle class, or small tradesmen, has been very good, but the stoppage of the cotton factories has materially affected them.

West Bromwich.—The chief trades of West Bromwich are in coal and iron. 1. The workmen generally are very ill employed at the present time. 2. Less by 20 per cent. than it was two years ago. Ten years ago, colliers could obtain 5s. a day, and six days work a week; now only 4s. a day, and not more than four days work a week. Forgemen, within the last four years, have been reduced 2s. per ton. Mechanics, that used to have 4s. a day, now have 3s. or 3s. 6d.. 4. Quite the contrary: when colliers had 5s. per day, flour was 8s. per bushel, cheese 6d.; meal 5d.; butter 13d. Now flour is 12s. per bushel; cheese 9d; meal 7½d.; butter 16d. 5. Much worse: many families that used to have meat every day, now taste it only once a week—many not even that. 6. Double during the last eighteen months. 9. All complain of bad business. It is the opinion of an agent of a large firm in London who visits this neighbourhood regularly that two-thirds of the tradesmen, at this time, are not able to pay their creditors. 10. Our congregation is on the increase, and their general disposition to exert themselves is much improved; still I do not witness, by any means, a proportionate increase in their contributions. There is some falling off in this respect. 12. In such an increasing population, an increase of attendance at the Sabbath schools may be expected. Still many—many children, as well as adults, absent themselves from places of worship, in consequence of not having what they deem suitable clothing.—Another report states that trade is very bad; that property of all kinds connected with trade has deteriorated at least 25 per cent.; and that the poor rates, from March, 1837, to March, 1838, was £1975 10s. 2d.; and from March, 1840, to March, 1841, £4081 17s. 4d.

HANLEY.—1. During the last eighteen months the working classes in our neighbourhood have not been employed more than half their usual time, or, on an average, three days per week. 2. Most certainly the amount of earnings have been diminished, but I am not prepared to state to what extent. 3. When food is cheap I have invariably observed a greater demand for manufactured goods, more particularly for home consumption, and consequently a greater demand for the labour of the artisan. 4. Within my own experience wages never have risen with the price of food, nor have I ever witnessed a reduction of wages in consequence of food being cheap. 5 The condition of the labouring population at the present time is worse than at any former period within my recollection, arising principally from the want of employment, if not altogether so.—Another report states that the food of the working classes is greatly reduced in quality; that hundreds of families live upon potatoes, with only a little bread, seldom tasting meat; and that the Sunday schools are but thinly attended compared with what they would be but for the high price of provisions.

SUFFOLK.—BURY ST. EDMUNDS.—I live in the midst of an agricultural district, and have conversed with ministers, merchants, farmers, shopkeepers, and labourers, in order to ascertain their views and state. Farmers, in general, know but little about the bearings of things, only they get a high price for their grain, and they are satisfied. Small shopkeepers find it difficult to live, because the poor have no money to lay out with them. The labouring class have no increase of wages at all proportionate to the high price of grain; many of them who have families are in deep distress; children crying for food and the parents obliged to stint them that every one may have a little. I myself have seen six or seven children in a family, whose parents were moral and religious, having nothing to eat at night but a few cold potatoes left from noon, and not enough of them. Ministers of religion know enough of the distress of the poor, without much inquiry; it is forced upon them, and many of them, like myself, have frequently to return to their studies in tears. And yet we are told that it is no business of ours to meddle with these matters. Is it no business of the shepherd whether he see his flock starve?

—— The average wages of agricultural labourers in Suffolk are about 9s. a week; some think 9s. or 10s., and all agree in the opinion that wages do not rise in proportion to the rise of corn. In the town of Bury the average wages of skilled labourers are 13s. or 14s. per week; of unskilled labourers 9s., and some of the latter receive parish relief in winter months. In Suffolk the high price of corn increases the demand for agricultural labourers, and also for labourers in town, but to a slighter extent. The condition of the labouring population in Suffolk is *worse* than it was five or ten years ago, and the state of the *small trader* is unquestionably *deteriorated*, and, in the opinion of some, deteriorated "very much."

SUSSEX.—LEWES.—The working classes generally are not well employed; there is no proportionate increase of wages to the increased price of food; and the greatest demand *for* labour has been when the price of corn was low. I can also bear painful testimony to the distressed condition of the labouring classes generally, the whole amount of their earnings being consumed in purchasing the bare necessaries of life; even these are not always attainable; and I am decidedly of opinion that the many deprivations they at present endure would be removed by provisions being at a lower rate. At the present time there are 134 houses uninhabited, being a proportion of 1 to 13; and the increase of population which, from 1811 to 1821, was 1500, is only 500 from 1831 to the present year. There is no spirit of enterprise, nor stimulus to trade, and the prospect for the approaching winter is deplorable in the extreme. There is neither infirmary nor dispensary in Lewes. The increase of crime has been fearfully great, and we have had upwards of one-third more commitments to our jail within the last few years. The inevitable consequence of a continuance of the present state of things must be, that the class of small traders will be merged in that of the labourer. It is with pain I bear testimony to the fact, that the want of employment, with the disproportionate amount of wages to the price of provisions, prevents many from attending the house of God from want of decent clothing. The attendance of children at our Sabbath schools has been prevented from the same cause; and it is a common reply, when we are urging parents to send their children, "We cannot send them; we have no clothing to put upon them." The degradation of the people, arising from the present general depression caused by the high price of provisions, naturally produces great increase of immorality and crime; and the claims of the gospel are less readily recognized by a people suffering from the laws of a legislature professedly Christian—laws which are at direct variance with the principles of that Christianity which they believe to be divine.

Brighton.—During the summer months few are unemployed; those who are out of work have found it on the railways. In winter many are without work, especially unmarried men. Single men get from 5s. 6d. to 9s., and married men from 9s. to 12s. 2. Under the old poor law the labourer's wages were very low, and it was made up to him by parish relief, according to the number in family. Under the new poor law wages have increased for married men with a family. 3 & 4. During 25 years' residence in this county I have not known that dear food increased the demand for labour, or that wages rose or fell with the price of food. 5. The condition of the labouring population in this county is worse compared with former periods. 7. Crime has greatly increased and is increasing, and disease also. 9 & 10. The condition of the small trader is much deteriorated compared with former periods. What with lowness of wages, the high price of provisions, and the increase of pauperism, and no out-door relief, they have great difficulty in paying their way, and consequently they have little or nothing to give to religious or benevolent societies. While the poor are thus suffering we cannot expect, nor do we find, that they will respect moral or religious instruction. Generally speaking, very few of the labouring class frequent the parish churches.

WESTMORLAND.—Kendal.—A sober man and good workman told me that for 10 weeks he had only earned 30s. The fact is, that the working classes here are not half employed. I very much doubt whether they are one-third employed, and I think I know their state. The manufacturers here have not generally reduced the wages of weavers, and the consequence is, that though they get the same amount for their work done as in 1835 or 1836; such is the scarcity of work, that they do not earn half as much. The pale countenances of the weavers and working men as a class, and their humble deportment, I was almost going to tay cringing deportment particularly to their employers, betoken the spirit-breaking tendency of their course of gradual starvation. This is a question, the answer to which we all know from experience. Many of the Fellside school scholars are absent for weeks together for no other reason but the want of shoes, or a change of clothing.

WILTSHIRE.—DEVIZES.— —— has a wife and five children to maintain on 9s. per week; but he is frequently out of employment; and for the last week he has been without work. His children look the very picture of squalid poverty; their shoes were eating mud and drinking water; and the clothes which the poor things had to cover their nakedness were more fit to be in the field scaring crows. His mother-in-law, when asked what she thought of the times, replied, that they were "shockan bad," and that "if it were not var a vew tatees, they wad be half starved." Whilst conversing with the old woman, a young man, 17 years of age, came up to the door. I asked him if he had any work. He said that he had not any, and would be glad to get some. He informed me that a good many in the parish were then out of employment. I stopped in the road for a minute or two to insert a few notes, when the eldest of a group of children who had followed me called out, "Set my name down too, measter: I want some victuals too." One little girl among the group was sipping something out of a basin with a tea-spoon; and when I asked what she had got, she said, "Tea;" and upon my inquiring where her bread was, she replied, "I ha' not got none, sir."—I shall pass over some others, and come to ——, who has a wife and seven children to maintain on 8s. per week. Two of them earn 1s. 6d. each per week. Their poor father has the misfortune to be out of employment occasionally. He pays £3 13s. 6d. per annum for his cottage, and rents 40 perches of land in a field, on which to grow potatoes for his family. His wife told me that they might have half a pound of bacon in the house once a quarter; but, then, it was a hard matter to part it among them; that, had it not been for potatoes, they would have been starved; and that, if they could get some bread and potatoes for the family, they would think themselves well off. —— of the same village, was turned out of a cottage, with his wife and seven children, last midsummer; since which time, up to the last three weeks, they lived in an open shed; but they are now the inhabitants of a stable. They left their last residence because they could not pay the rent. They made their case known to the magistrates, the guardians, and the overseers of the parish; none of whom would do anything for them. One night they stopped in the churchyard till nearly twelve o'clock at night, when the rain came into their hovel (shed) in torrents. There is no fire-place in the stable; and they are indebted to a kind neighbour for allowing them to cook their food, principally potatoes. I can solemnly assure you that the appearance of the peasantry is very miserable indeed. On my way home, I called at a wretched looking cottage, and was given to understand by the mother of six helpless children, that her husband had been from home in search of work for a fortnight; and that she had not had a morsel of bread within her house, for herself and children, for the last week. When I asked her how she lived, she replied, "I don't call it livin, sir; it's starvin." "But how do you subsist at all?" said I, "we live on garden stuff, sir," was her answer. This statement appeared to me so very extraordinary, that I called upon a respectable neighbour, and asked her if she thought the unfortunate woman's story was true; she said it was her belief that she had told me nothing but the truth.

TROWBRIDGE.—Our tradesmen in general are doing very little, and there are very many who, if the balance sheet was struck, would not be level with the world; as to others, there are very many who have no employment, and half of those who are employed do not average more than 10s. per week, to support their families. Our poor rates are very heavy, and a great many are compelled to pay them who have not half sufficient to support themselves. My friend, the overseer of the parish, informs me, that it is truly distressing to go round collecting the poor rates and taxes. At the last quarterly parish meeting, there were about 300 forgiven the rates, having no means to pay the same: there were about 40 or 50 others summoned before the magistrates, to give a reason why they did not pay their rates; many of them were forgiven, the others were obliged to sell their things to pay them. To say nothing of the half-starved condition of hundreds that are on the parish books, there are numbers no better off who will not make their condition known. And in consequence of the distress of the people, there are many whose circumstances render it impossible for them to appear in the house of God on the Sabbath day, because they have no decent clothes, or money to pay their sittings. There are many others who deprive themselves of the necessaries of life to enable them to do so.

WESTBURY.—This borough contains a population of about 8,000 inhabitants spread over a surface of about seven miles, most of whom are employed in the clothing trade, and, of course, some in agriculture.

If the working classes had with us full employment, with the present *rates* of wages and *prices* of provisions, they must live principally on potatoes to make both ends meet.

At present they have not *one-third;* consequently butter, cheese, sugar, &c., they cannot get; butchers' meat they do not, and cannot, get once a month; bread is an occasional treat, and potatoes form their daily meals. Hundreds of honest and pious men here are in this state.

It is not the general practice to turn off hands when labour is wanting, but reduce them to half, one-third, and sometimes less. Having occasional work they cannot go into the poor-house, or obtain temporary relief.

Their own statements are as follow:—We have not half employ at best, never knew trade worse—prices never rise with bread—have been falling for years—the best time for us was when there was no corn-law—machinery reduces our work—we are degraded every year, and must soon go to the union workhouse—never knew wages so low and work so scarce as now; many go from day to day ill-clothed and half-fed. Morals are declining, the bonds of society are dissolving, and a spirit of reckless indifference is enkindling.

That the people want *work*, and not charity, is evident from the following facts:—They hire and cultivate small portions of land at the rates of from *five* to *ten* pounds per acre, while farmers complain of thirty shillings.

Nearly *one* thousand out of *eight* are existing on parish-supply; rates are one-fourth more than in 1835. The poor law tells them they must earn their dinner before they eat it, and the corn laws say they shall have but little and sometimes no work to do.

All the congregations suffer considerably, and the Sunday schools would be much better attended if the parents could provide suitable clothing.

Agricultural labour is wanting, and the average wages do not exceed 7s. 6d. or 8s. This statement I have from a practical farmer, whose intelligence raises him above many, and he being a pro-corn-law man.

WORCESTERSHIRE.—WORCESTER.—The working classes in this town, particularly in the staple trade, which is that of leather glove manufacturing, are scarcely more than half employed; the earnings of men who are in partial work with those in full work, would not, I imagine, average more than 13s. per week; skilled workmen could earn 20s. per week; unskilled, about 15s. Men employed in the porcelain manufacture, are better off for work than glovers, though the number employed is much less than ten years ago; skilled workmen could earn 24s. per week; unskilled, about 16s. The amount of earnings in the glove and porcelain trades has decreased from 10 to 15 per cent. The condition of the labouring population is very much worse now than formerly, owing to the deficiency of work. The state of the middle classes, dependent on business, is very much worse than formerly, and particularly the manufacturing part; although shopkeepers and others, of course, feel acutely the pressure of the times.

YORKSHIRE.—HALIFAX.—The working classes are better employed in Halifax than in many other parts of the kingdom.—Mechanics, in 1835, received from 28s. to 30s. per week; now they receive from 18s. to 22s. per week. Mechanics may now be had at almost any price. Woolcombers earn from 7s. to 12s. per week; in nine years their wages have been reduced from 18s. to 12s. per week. Weavers' wages have been greatly diminished during the last twelve years. In worsted goods nearly 16s. have been taken from one piece. The price of weaving a best piece fourteen years since was £2. 2s., now it is £1. 4s. 6d.; the price of weaving a middle piece was £1. 1s. 6d., now 11s. 6d.; the price of an inferior piece from 8s. to 9s., now 4s. 6d. When meat was 4d. per lb. they had plenty of work at the higher rate of wages; now the price of meat is nearly doubled they have little more than half the wages. Wages have not risen, but declined, with the price of food. Poor-rates, in 1836, £4,964; 1840, £5673. The number of persons imprisoned for debt during half-year ending 31st July, 1839, was 164; ditto, 1840, 264; ditto, 1841, 359. In many instances I have found persons unable to contribute to religious institutions through their poverty. Many children are kept from our Sabbath schools through the want of clogs and clothing.

BRADFORD.—The wholesale shopkeepers complain that their returns from the small shopkeepers are falling off weekly; the small shopkeepers state that their returns from their weekly customers are weekly declining. The reason assigned is, that whilst provisions are rapidly advancing wages are declining, and great numbers are totally unemployed.

—— The wages of working men are considerably less at the present time than they were four or five years ago, when corn was lower in price; and I have found it an invariable rule, that as corn advanced workmen were thrown out of employment, consequently there was more competition amongst them, and wages were lowered. During the years that corn was 40s. and 50s. per quarter, wages were good, and whenever corn has been, for a long time, above that price wages have been sure to come down, and want of employment has followed. 6. Poor rates are higher by one-third than they were a few years ago. 10. No material alteration has taken place in the funds of religious and benevolent societies, but they are a little reduced by high priced provisions. Owing to their provident habits religious people suffer less than others from the pressure of the times. 12. Congregations and Sabbath schools suffer in the attendance of adults and children for want of clothing.

OSSETT.—1. The people of the township of Ossett are, generally, pretty well employed at present, though trade has for a long time previously been very stagnant. The prospects of the harvest are very unfavourable for the continuance of the present average of employment. The average of wages for skilful labourers is from 12s. to 15s. per week, of unskilful from 8s. to 10s. per week. There are many, however, still out of employment, and the present trade is expected to stop every week, on account of the prospects of the harvest. 2. The amount of earnings, within the last four or five years, has *diminished* 4s. per week, from the quality of the goods made being of a very inferior description. 3. Dear bread sensibly *diminishes* the demand for labour, and cheap bread as sensibly *increases* the demand. 4. Wages are fixed by a *certain standard*, so they are not affected by the price of provisions. 5. From the description of work now done, more hands, of *women* and *children*, are employed to do what fewer hands could previously accomplish, consequently, though more in a family are often occupied in trade, the condition of the labouring class is decidedly worse than it was a *few years* ago. 6. The *poor-rates* are much lighter than they were some years ago, because the poor labourers on the highways, who were previously paid out of the poor-rate, are paid out of the *highway-rate*; but this is only shifting the burden, for the general rates are heavier considerably than they were at any former period. 9. Mealsellers, shopkeepers, cordwainers, and others suffer exceedingly from the distresses of the poor. Many of the poor are indebted to these traders from £10 to £20, with no means of payment; and chartists expect a levelling day, and they are careless about payment. 11, 12. Many are induced to absent themselves from the house of God from the want of decent apparel; and the visitors of the absentee scholars give the most distressing account of the destitution of clothing that prevents many of the scholars from attending the school or the house of God. The distress and destitution upon this subject are so great that it renders all attempts to relieve it quite hopeless. Want of clothing is the universal reply to the question as to the cause of absence from the Sabbath school.

HAWORTH.—Our district is nearly wholly in the stuff or worsted trade, and we are, generally, rather better off than we were a year and a half ago. In the beginning of last year, I was one of a committee for distributing a charitable fund, and I then investigated a great part of the township. We found 200 families whose means of support did not amount to 2s. per head per week, and many not half of it. Their beds were most deplorable, and their apparel not much better, and everything in their houses betokened wretchedness and misery. In some instances I was struck with the simple, honest replies of the poor sufferers. When I have found a family without the apparent means of procuring food to support life, I have asked, "How do you live, or get on?" "Why, Sir," was the answer, "we go to bed without supper, and we get up without breakfast; hungry we lie down, and hungry we get up." Others have tied bandages round their bodies to lessen the gnawings of hunger. I have been credibly informed that some have even robbed the pigs of their grains and their wash. I could mention other appalling facts, but, as my district, generally, is not so bad as some others, owing to our particular branch of trade, and the generosity of the masters, I forbear. The corn laws seem the giant evil. There is a solemn murmur of discontent truly ominous. During my acquaintance with the locality for 18 years, I never saw such cause for alarm as at present. We only want a spark to set the country in a blaze.

SOWERBY BRIDGE.—Perhaps there is no village in England that has been more highly indebted to trade than this. During years of commercial prosperity its growth in population and wealth was very considerable. But its interests are at present declining in a marked degree. The following particulars may give some idea of the change for the worse which is now taking place. Manufactures in the cotton, woollen, and silk trades are much embarrassed, while the operative is employed little more than half time. Instance: One manufacturer paid in weekly wages, in the years, 1837, 1838, and 1839, as much as £250, and is now paying from £50 to £100 per week. Wages have suffered in some branches of manufacture considerable reduction. The average earnings are not more than from 10s. to 12s. a week. The item of provisions is very painful. Family after family confess the entire absence of animal food, and of white wheaten bread. Oatmeal made into porridge is the principal food, and of this, in many cases, there is a very inadequate supply. A poor family was visited where the father had long been confined to a sick bed. The mother had been delivered of a child three weeks before. They were alike helpless and destitute. On food being supplied it was eaten so voraciously that disorder of a very alarming kind was the consequence. Poor rates very high. In one locality there are many houses untenanted to the extent of one to every tenth house. The removal of many from the neighbourhood has made the burden fall more heavily on the remaining rate-payers. Sabbath schools and congregations much and increasingly thinned and depressed, from the want of decent clothing to appear in, in the house of God. It is ascertained that, in the Halifax union, in 1840, there is a falling off in marriages to the extent of one-fourth. In the same year a proportionate increase in the number of deaths. Prospects disastrous in the extreme to all classes, if not blessed soon with a more favourable state of things.

Thornton.—Very similar to Halifax, as to wages and employment. Crime has been very rife; disease and general destitution have for the last three years been very prevalent. During the year 1837, there was collected in the township of Thornton-with-Denholme, £900; during the last year, £1,300; population, 7,000. Amongst a number of honourable and respectable tradesmen, great difficulties have been experienced, capital has diminished, and insolvency in many instances has been the result.

Golcar, near Huddersfield.—1. The working classes in our neighbourhood are scarcely half employed. The average wages paid to labourers, taking the best and worst workmen together, will not exceed 8s. or 9s. per week. 2. During the last four or five years, wages have been reduced 5s. per week. 3. When food has been dear, the demand for labour has been less than at other times; and the same with wages. 5. The condition of the labouring population was never known so bad as it is at present. 6. The poor rates, with us, are greatly increased, but in what proportion to former periods I cannot state with accuracy. 9. The state of the middle class of persons, such as small tradesmen, is very deplorable indeed. Many of them are ruined, and most of them are unable to meet their creditors. 10. Have not perceived any connection between high and low priced food, but there has been a serious falling off in the funds connected with the chapel at Golcar. 11. The distress arising from the high price of food has caused many to absent themselves from public worship among us.

It has been found by "the committee on documents" to be altogether impracticable to form *so full and satisfactory a digest* of the communications which they have received, as they contemplated should appear with the official report of the proceedings of the ministerial conference. Hence the plan has been adopted of giving at present merely a few extracts from the statements and invaluable documents which have been considered by the committee. It will be seen that these extracts refer to the condition both of the manufacturing and agricultural population of various counties in England, Wales, and Scotland. There is a mass of evidence of which use yet remains to be made, that is scarcely less interesting and affecting than the portion which is now published. An elaborate digest has been drawn up from the documents, and sustained by deeply interesting facts of a personal nature. The publication of this digest and other documents now depends upon the sale of the present report. The friends who have furnished the information by documents and letters will please to accept the acknowledgments of "the committee," and to rest assured that it will in some form be made available to the important object for which it has been sought.

PRELIMINARY PROCEEDINGS OF THE CONFERENCE.

Copy of a Circular addressed to the Ministers of Religion in Manchester and its vicinity.

15, Lever-street, Manchester, July 8th, 1841.

Dear Sir,—The present communication has its origin in the deliberations of a few friends, who, being deeply interested in the physical and moral condition of the poor, and in the general welfare of our country, have come together to consider what is our duty at the present crisis.

The aspect of public affairs, at this juncture, is fearfully ominous of collision and animosity between the different classes of the community, and seems to demand the prayerful interposition and cooperation of all who desire the peace of our population and the prosperity of the empire.

Our consultations have brought us to the unanimous conclusion, that the attention of the *religious public* should be immediately directed—

To the effects of the monopoly in food;

To the principles upon which the law of that monopoly is based, and

To the most legitimate and Christian means of obtaining an equitable settlement of the question, without civil convulsion, and without injury to the just interests of any class of our fellow-citizens.

We are fully persuaded that these inquiries may be most beneficially prosecuted in a free and friendly Conference of Ministers of Religion, from all parts of the United Kingdom; and that such a Convention might, under the blessing of God, exercise a salutary and decisive influence.

With these views, we respectfully and urgently solicit your cooperation and direction in regard to such a movement; and shall feel obliged by your attendance at a meeting of the Ministers of this town and neighbourhood, to be held in the Boroughreeve's Room, Town Hall, King-Street, Manchester, on Monday morning next, the 12th instant, at eleven o'clock precisely.

I am, dear Sir, yours respectfully,

Geo. Thompson.

The meeting, convened as above, was attended by twenty-eight ministers, viz., from Manchester, John Birt, John Dallas, Richard Fletcher, Dr. Halley, Frederick Langhorne, Thomas G. Lee, W. M'Kerrow, D. Hearne, James Scholefield, J. H. Smithson, Robt. Williams; Salford, John R. Beard, David Haworth, James William Massie; Rochdale, W. F. E. Burchell, David Hewitt, John Peters; Stockport, John Thornton, John Waddington; Ludlow Salop, Theophilus Davies; Oldham, Wm. Drummond; Halshaw Moor, John Dyson; Greenacres, Josh. Galland; Hazel Grove, Samuel Healley: Stalybridge, G. Hoyle; Dukinfield, Robert Ivy; Greenacres' Moor, Richard Jessop; Stretford, Edward Morris.

The origin and object of the meeting having been briefly explained, a full discussion of the subject took place, at the conclusion of which the following resolution was passed: Mr. Langhorne being the only dissentient;

Resolved—That it is the opinion of this meeting that the conference contemplated in the circular, issued by Mr. George Thompson, is desirable. that measures be adopted to convene the ministers of religion, (who may be able to assemble,) from all parts of the United Kingdom, to deliberate on the questions suggested for consideration; and that the convention be held in the week between the 15th and 22d of August next

A Committee of nine gentlemen, with power to add to their number, was appointed to carry this Resolution into effect. The following is their

Address to the Ministers of all Religious Denominations throughout the United Kingdom.

Gentlemen,—Receive the present address as if from friends of the suffering poor, and the lovers of peace and righteousness.

We are surrounded by scenes of want and misery, over which our hearts have long mourned, with the power of affording little beyond the consolation of mere words.

We are brought to the conclusion, that it is *our duty*, and the duty of all who fill the sacred office of Ministers of Religion, to look into the causes of our national distress.

The conviction has been forced upon our own minds, that the sufferings we deplore, and the calamities we would avert, may be traced in a great degree to the operation of the laws which produce a scarcity of the necessaries of life, by circumscribing the bounties of Divine Providence.

But, we need counsel and co-operation, that we may proceed wisely and efficiently. We therefore earnestly invite you to a free and friendly Conference on the subject of the laws which restrict the supply of food to the people of this country, and the principles upon which such laws are based—to the end, that we may agree upon the adoption of some Christian and constitutional measures for the removal of the ascertained causes of the increasing poverty and impending ruin of large classes of our fellow-citizens.

Conferences on debateable and difficult subjects have already been productive of the best results, whether for conviction in the minds of inquirers, or for constraining unwilling parties to fulfil the demands of justice. Anti-slavery conventions, in recent times, produced effects which warrant our hope as rational and well founded that this conference will become influential and decisive.

We think we may be permitted to say, that, to no body of men ought such momentous questions be submitted with a better prospect of a calm, an enlightened, and an honest solution, than to that body which we desire to convene—a body composed of men who, while deeply sympathizing in the wants and woes of the poor, profess to respect the just rights of all, and to be guided equally by the feelings of a disinterested benevolence and the dictates of an uncompromising morality. We cannot doubt that the decisions of such a body would exercise a benign and beneficial influence over the nation at large.

We feel persuaded that we need employ no arguments to prove that the cause in which we would enlist your individual and combined exertions is associated with all the nearest and dearest interests of those to whose welfare you are devoted, or that the ends of morality and pure religion would be much promoted by the alleviation of the existing wide-spread wretchedness. But one thing is certain; we shall be fulfilling the behests of that religion whose ministers we are, by demonstrating our desire and determination to do what we can for the physical as well as the spiritual benefit of our fellow-men.

Accept, then, our invitation, and unite with us in an effort for the common weal and general safety. For a while let us lay aside our sectarian and partizan differences, and, on the hallowed ground of Christian charity, assemble for the purpose of bettering the condition of famishing multitudes.

As the friends of humanity, let us plead the cause of the poor.

As the expounders and defenders of the principles of immutable justice, let us protest against laws, under whatever form, which deny to our necessitous fellow-countrymen a share in the bounties which the Creator has provided for the wants of all his creatures.

As the ministers of religion, let us remove, if it be possible, the causes which are engendering a frightful amount of immorality and impiety.

As patriots, burning with a love of country, let us make an effort to put away the occasions of disaffection and animosity, and so restore peace and harmony to a now unhappily distracted people, and may the blessing of God rest upon our meeting!

Not only are those invited whose minds are made up, but those also who have conscientious difficulties, which may possibly be removed by candid and full discussion.

Every effort will be made to provide hospitable accommodation for accredited individuals attending the conference.

Those who intend to accept this invitation, are requested to take counsel of their congregations, how they may best facilitate the object of the conference; and provide funds necessary for the journey.

The Conference will commence its sittings on the morning of Tuesday, the 17th of August, at ten o'clock, at the Town Hall, Manchester.

Communications to be addressed to the Hon. Secretary, 15, Lever-Street, Manchester.

On behalf of the Committee,
GEO. THOMPSON, Hon. Sec.

Manchester, July 13th, 1841.

The following is a copy of a letter which was sent to the president and ministers of the Wesleyan Methodist Conference:—

TO THE PRESIDENT AND MINISTERS OF THE WESLEYAN DENOMINATION, IN CONFERENCE ASSEMBLED.

Dear Sirs,—It may occasion to you some surprise to be addressed by us in your denominational character. Our reasons for doing so are the following: It was designed that the enclosed circular should appear as an advertisement in the pages of your magazine, but it was found that our communication was too late to be inserted next month. We then anticipated the presence of a large number of your body, as the representatives of the whole, at your meeting of conference to be held in Manchester, and therefore have deferred our address till this time.

We appeal to you especially, because, like ourselves, you have sprung from the people, and with them it may be presumed that your interests and sympathies are identified. Your ministerial labours are devoted to the interests of the people, and frequently your duty requires you to enter into the sorrows and sufferings of the impoverished and working classes. The community with which you are associated in name and fellowship, are chiefly composed of the industrious portion of society depending on trade and commerce for the supply of their temporal wants. You have been singularly successful in your benevolent exertions to teach and elevate the masses of the people. For the resources of your charitable and religious operations you are indebted to the regular contributions of the humblest, and, oftentimes, the poorest members of your connection. By their weekly, or otherwise periodical sacrifices—sacrifices in many cases made at the expense of their temporal comforts, but cheerfully and generously made—your denomination are enabled to undertake great things for the improvement and happiness of mankind. The principles which you inculcate are professedly derived from Him who was eminently the friend of the poor. The blessed Saviour was moved with pity when he looked on the scattered and famishing multitude, and said, "I have compassion on them!" and he has encouraged his followers to trust that he will reward them for deeds of kindness to the hungry and the naked, as if done to himself.

We claim the testimony of Scripture in behalf of the movement which we contemplate. If it be a religious duty to provide for the destitute, it is surely no less a duty of religion to endeavour to prevent the honestly industrious from sinking into indigent helplessness. We are taught to seek the moral amelioration of those who are criminal, and to rejoice in their restoration to virtue; does it not equally become us to do what we can to protect the virtuous from temptation and the snares of sin? That the corn law system has an impoverishing, debasing, and demoralizing tendency, is abundantly evinced by the enclosed documents.

If Jacob and the patriarchs sent even from the promised land to Egypt for corn; if the Jewish people travelled in times of famine to the surrounding countries to obtain supplies of food; if Solomon bartered with Hiram, giving him wheat and oil for his timber and the labour of his men; if Nehemiah rebuked the nobles because they oppressed the people, and brought them into bondage by keeping up corn; and if, by the prophet Isaiah, the God of heaven and earth has taught us that the fast which He has chosen is to undo the heavy burdens, to let the oppressed go free, and to deal bread to the hungry; then, surely, ministers of religion are only legitimately fulfilling the duties of their province when they take counsel how food may be obtained for the necessities of their fellow-men.

We therefore urge it upon you as a "conference"—we urge it upon you as ministers in your several spheres—we urge it upon you, as members of the great national community, to take into mature deliberation, and, if possible, give your aid to the contemplated movement in reference to the corn law. We invite every one of you to our convention. You will there meet ministers of other religious persuasions equally consecrated with yourselves in the cause of humanity and of God. It is designed to fetter no man's conscience—to pledge no one who does not approve of our principles and measures, but we ask the consultation and advice of all.

We respectfully solicit, through your president, an early answer to this application.

We are, on behalf of the commitee for arrangements of the ministerial conference on the corn laws,

Your faithful servants,

Wm. M'Kerrow,
James Wm. Massie,
Richard Fletcher.

Manchester, July 28th, 1841.

ERRATA.

Page 30, Mr. Bayley's speech: for the sentence, "He went to two pawnbrokers, and inquired of them if they would like to bring the members of the House of Commons," &c.; read, "and inquired of them the state of trade, and said he should like to bring the members of the House of Commons," &c. [Mr. B's revise of his speech, with several others, arrived too late.]

Page 228 in *part* of our impression, for "Leighlon Burzard," read "Leighton Buzzard."

J. GADSBY, PRINTER, MARKET-STREET, MANCHESTER.

THE

CORN LAWS CONDEMNED

ON ACCOUNT OF THEIR

INJUSTICE AND IMMORAL TENDENCY,

BY UPWARDS OF

FIVE HUNDRED MINISTERS,

OF DIFFERENT DENOMINATIONS,

RESIDENT IN SCOTLAND.

EDINBURGH:
ADAM & CHARLES BLACK, NORTH BRIDGE.

MDCCCXLII.

The Corn Laws condemned on account of their Injustice and Immoral Tendency (1842)

The conference of ministers in Manchester in August 1841 was followed by one of some forty ministers in Caernarvon on 30 November at which Revd J. W. Massie and Colonel Thomas Perronet Thompson (1783–1869) represented the League,[1] and by the conference of Scots nonconformist ministers in Edinburgh in January 1842. In addition to the distinctly anti-establishment tone of this activity it was purely provincial, a point noted by a Yorkshire paper quoted in the *Manchester Times* (29 January, 1842).

> The country have waited with some anxiety to discover would any arrangements be made, as have occasionally been suggested by ministers in London, to centralize a movement which would bear on the parliament and the court. Hundreds of congregations are preparing their petitions, and thousands of females are enrolling their neighbours as memorialists for the abolition of the ruinous unrighteous laws which beggar the nation and famish the multitude; but they look in vain for any active sympathy and co-operation among *anti-slavery* champions, or friends of foreign slaves and perishing idolaters. [i.e. the Anti Slavery Society]

In addition to the organization of religious congregations as part of the repeal campaign the paper suggested a long term educational effort, especially in Sunday schools.

> Let *free trade*, as the policy of justice and equity, be lisped in numbers and taught in nursery rhymes; let it be made to flow in the streams of elementary instruction, and imbibed under the auspices of Christian Sunday Schools; let the operation of its antagonist form, in a provision monopoly, begin to be understood and denounced among the myriads who assemble within these schools, and actuate the sympathies and direct the moral energies of almost two hundred thousand teachers; and the issue will be speedy and complete. Within such spheres are found the paramount influence of the Christian Pastor, and his most powerful means of popular influence.

Thus it was the combination of religious instruction and congregational mobilization in the service of the campaign for the repeal of the corn law that largely established free trade as a semi-religious gospel within British popular political culture.

[1] Prentice, *History of the Anti Corn Law League*, vol. 1, pp. 276–77. See also Thomas Thomas (President of the Baptist Theological Institution), *A Proper Consideration of the Cause of the Poor, a test of a righteous Character. A discourse designed to advance the objects of the Manchester Conference: delivered September 12th, 1841, at Pontypool*, London: Ward & Co., 1841. On the League in Wales see Ieuan Gwynedd Jones, 'The Anti Corn Law Letters of Walter Griffith', in *Bulletin Board of Celtic Studies* 28 part 1 (1980) pp. 95–128, and Ryland Wallace, 'The Anti Corn Law League in Wales', in *The Welsh History Review*, vol. 13, no. 1, June 1986, pp. 1–23.

CONTENTS.

APPENDIX.

INTRODUCTION.

THE following Answers, from five hundred and eighty-eight ministers, in the different districts of Scotland, expressive of their own opinions, and also of those of their people, regarding the Corn and Provision Laws, were brought under the consideration of an adjourned preliminary meeting of Ministers and Members of Dissenting Churches, residing in Edinburgh and neighbourhood, held in Broughton Place Session-house, on the 20th December 1841. This Meeting had been called to receive these Answers, and consider the propriety of calling a public meeting of Ministers and Members of Dissenting Churches, from various parts of Scotland, to be held on the 11th, 12th, and 13th January 1842; and after much consideration, they unanimously adopted the following Resolution, directing the Answers to be published:—

'That the answers already received from upwards of five hundred Ministers, residing in all parts of Scotland, to the Queries circulated on the 7th instant, requesting to know their own opinions, and those of their Congregations, regarding the Total Abolition of the Corn and Provision Laws, contain, it is believed, a more accurate and valuable digest of public opinion on this question than has ever been laid before the public; that the tendency of an immense majority of these answers is to show that the middling and working classes in Scotland, not even excepting the agricultural districts, are nearly unanimous in regarding the Corn and Provision Laws as unjust in principle, vexatious and oppressive in their operation, and the main cause of all the distresses of the country—and in advocating their Total Repeal and the establishment of an entirely Free Trade in Corn; that the Ministers of Religion, to whom the Queries were addressed, generally concur in the same opinions, and likewise condemn these Laws as being alike opposed to the principles of Religion and the precepts of Morality; that the publication of these Answers could not fail to produce a very powerful impression in favour of the cause of Total Repeal; and that the Meeting, therefore, direct the Committee to take all proper steps for their early publication, but enjoining them *not* to publish the names of the individual Ministers, or of the separate religious bodies by whom the Answers are severally given, or of the places from which they are severally dated, or of persons or places referred to in them by which the answers of one Minister could be distinguished from those of another,—and to arrange the whole Answers into Counties or clusters of Counties, distinguishing the trading from the agricultural, and blending the Answers of all the different religious bodies together, without distinction of sects,—these restrictions being considered by this Meeting indispensable, in consequence of the Answers having been written without any view to their publication.'

In compliance with this Resolution, the answers are now published in their present form. The Schedule, with queries as originally circulated, will be found in the Appendix (p. 60–63). It contains six queries, the first and second of which were framed to ascertain the opinions of the ministers and people regarding the Total Abolition of the Corn and

Provision Laws, and the establishment of an entirely Free Trade in Corn. The answers to these two queries have been given *verbatim*, with the exception of a few instances—certainly not exceeding thirty—in which unimportant corrections have been made. These consist chiefly of the omission of the names of places, and of circumstances calculated to lead to a knowledge of the particular ministers and congregations by whom the answers were given; and others of them consist of the correction of inaccurate or inelegant expressions, by substituting others of the same import. But in no instance has the meaning of the authors been changed, even to the very slightest extent. The third and fourth queries (p. 63) were intended merely to ascertain whether the ministers, or any of their people, would attend the proposed Meeting; and as the answers regarding these points,—when the names were directed to be withheld,—could not possess any degree of interest, they have been altogether omitted. The fifth and sixth Queries (now compressed into one, and marked No. 3) were intended to ascertain whether the ministers approved of the plan of the proposed meeting, and whether they could offer any suggestions for its improvement. These Queries led, in many instances, to long answers, and to digressions not very much connected with the subject of the inquiry. It was, therefore, found necessary, in not a few instances, to abridge them, in order to prevent the publication from being swelled to an immoderate bulk; but in every such instance it was anxiously desired that the abridgment should fairly indicate the nature of the objections or suggestions offered by the different writers; and it is believed the true *import* of every objection and suggestion has been faithfully given, although not in the precise words of the author. Not one answer or opinion has been suppressed, however adverse to the views of the Committee or the compiler of the documents. Any other course would have greatly lessened the value of the publication as an authentic record of public opinion. The answers of the ministers who were conscientiously opposed to the plan of the meeting, will be found as faithfully given, as those of the great majority who gave it their cordial support; at least such was the honest intention with which the whole documents were prepared for the press. A few instances occurred, in which persons decidedly hostile to the plan of the meeting, gave long answers, prophesying nothing but evil to the cause of dissent and to that of Total Abolition, from such a meeting as that contemplated, and pointing out the various modes in which they imagined those evils, real or imaginary, would be inflicted. It was thought that the publication, by the Committee, of such passages, would appear somewhat like suggesting the propriety of inflicting the contemplated inquiries; and it was therefore resolved to omit all such matter, at the same time taking care to indicate the nature of the objections, or suggestions, even in cases where the arguments and illustrations are omitted; and, indeed, in the process of abridgment, the instances are very few in which other words have been employed than those of the authors of the Answers.

As a help to the memory, the *import* of the three Queries to which the Answers are published, is placed in small type, at the top of each page, numbered 1, 2, and 3; but the original Queries (p. 63) should be read, in order fully to understand the import of the Answers.

The various documents, showing the origin and objects of the Queries and Answers, and the results to which they led,—the holding of a great Anti-Corn Law Meeting and Soiree on the 11th, 12th, and 13th instant,—will be found in Appendix No. III. One of these documents, the Minute of 20th December last, shows the general plan of the Meeting, and the conditions according to which its proceedings are to be regulated. It likewise shows the results of the Answers, so far as they had been received up to that date: but a considerable number are now printed which were not then received, including all those which arrived up to the 30th December; and consequently, these results, although accurate when the Minute was framed, do not agree in all respects with those shown by the Answers as now printed; but they approximate so nearly, that it was not thought necessary to undertake the labour of making a new analysis; and, indeed, the time of publication did not admit of the additional delay which, in this case, would have been required.

It will be noticed that the chief ground on which any material difference of opinion existed, was the propriety of inviting the ministers of the Established Church to the Meeting; and that, both at the Committee and General Preliminary Meetings, it was *unanimously* agreed that, in the circumstances, it was unnecessary to invite them, as it was well known they would not attend. This part of the Minute is here quoted, to show that the decision was not arrived at from any sectarian feelings; but that, on the contrary, a resolution was adopted, pledging the Members present at the Preliminary Meeting, cordially to co-operate with the Established Ministers, or others, in getting up a similar meeting, based on the broad ground of citizenship, as soon as any disposition shall be manifested by them to join in the movement:—

'The Committee reported that upwards of thirty* Ministers in answering the Queries, had more or less strongly expressed a wish that the invitations should be extended, so as to include the Ministers of the Established Church, but that after giving the subject the most mature consideration, they were unanimously of opinion, that it was unnecessary to make the proposed alteration. It was explained to the Meeting, that during last autumn a preliminary meeting was called of all the Established and Dissenting Ministers in the city and neighbourhood by circular letters addressed to each, with the view of inducing them to co-operate with the Manchester Anti-Corn Law Conference then about to meet; and that, although these circulars were signed by several of the Edinburgh Ministers, including one belonging to the Established Church, not one of the latter body attended the Meeting, or sent any apology,—not even the Minister who had signed the requisition calling the meeting. It was likewise explained, that although all the 1200 Ministers of the Scotch Established Church were invited to the Manchester Conference, only two Ministers attended, and other two wrote friendly letters; that as a body they had a deep pecuniary interest in maintaining Corn at the highest possible price, because their annual stipends were, with comparatively few exceptions, payable according to the price of certain fixed quantities of Corn; and that these facts proved that it was in vain to invite the Established Clergy to the proposed Meeting, or expect them to attend.

'The meeting having heard these explanations, unanimously resolved that it was unnecessary in the circumstances, to solicit the co-operation of the Established Clergy, but that if they shall afterwards show any disposition to join in the movement, this meeting will, at any time, most willingly co-operate with them in promoting a meeting of ministers and members of all religious denominations, to express their opinion of the injustice and immoral tendency of the Corn and Provision Laws, and to Petition for their Total Repeal; and that this meeting entertain no doubt that an immense

* This number is exclusive of those who stated, that *they approved of the plan as it was*, but who added in substance that they would have been still better pleased with it, if the Established Ministers had been invited.

majority of the *Members* of the Established Church would cordially agree with them in approving of such a movement, or of any other measure calculated to promote a cause in which the great body of Churchmen and Dissenters are equally interested,—Total Repeal and Free Trade.

'The Committee reported that a few of the Ministers, in answering the Queries, had expressed a preference for a Meeting consisting of Deputations from Anti-Corn Law Associations and other public bodies, to one composed of Ministers and Members of Dissenting Churches. The Meeting having deliberated thereon, resolved that the two objects were not opposed to, but perfectly compatible with, each other; and that, although Ministers and Members of Dissenting Churches assemble at the proposed Meeting to express their opinion of the moral and religious bearings of the question, they are not precluded from afterwards co-operating with other parties in attending Meetings, based on the broad ground of Citizenship, for considering the bearings of these unjust Laws in other points of view; and that they will most cordially co-operate with other Citizens in promoting such Meetings whenever they shall be thought advisable.

'The Committee reported that the answers to the Query requesting suggestions, with the view of improving the plan of the meeting, had elicited a great variety of suggestions having that object in view; that they had carefully considered these answers, and, in terms of the powers formerly conferred on them for that purpose, had amended the resolutions, so as to include all those which appeared to them calculated to remove well founded objections, or to render the plan or details of the Public Meeting more perfect.' [The Resolutions will be found in the Appendix, p. 65.]

It is now known that the reasons stated in the preceding Minute have satisfied many of the objectors, of the propriety of the decision to which the Preliminary Meeting came, with regard to the Ministers of the Established Church; and it is very satisfactory to know, that their decision has likewise met with the entire approbation of the friends of Total Repeal in Manchester, as appears from their organ, the Anti-Bread Tax Circular of the 30th December last:—'We think the course pursued by the Edinburgh Committee is wise and justifiable. Apart from the experience we have had of the state clergy, they are not in a position to be impartial judges of the question to be brought before the Edinburgh Conference. They would be excluded from a jury-box, or witness-box, in any civil court in a cause where their own interests are at issue. How, then, can they be competent witnesses or judges in the cause of the people against those who profit by the Corn Law?'

The whole responsibility connected with the preparation of the Answers for the press having devolved on a single Member of the Committee, the only guarantee which, in these circumstances, it is possible to give for the fidelity with which the work has been executed, or the accuracy of its statements, is by affixing his signature to the publication, since no other person has read the Answers or proofs. This guarantee he thinks it his duty, in the circumstances, to give, although, for many reasons, it would have been much more agreeable to him if that duty could, with propriety, have been devolved on some other individual.

D. M'LAREN.

2, *Ramsay Gardens, 7th January* 1842.

I.

ANSWERS

FROM

THE FOUR LARGE BODIES OF DISSENTERS—THE SECESSION, RELIEF, INDEPENDENT, AND BAPTIST CHURCHES, DIVIDED INTO COUNTIES.

To the churches in Scotland belonging to the above bodies 602 circulars were sent, and from them 479 answers have been received. It appears, from the Minute of the 20th December, that, at that date, 207 of their Ministers, and 469 of their Members, had promised to attend the public meeting—making a total of 676, or nineteen-twentieths of the whole number who had promised to be present.

COUNTY OF ABERDEEN.

Answers from 29 Ministers.

Questions.—1. Are you in favour of an entirely Free Trade in Corn? 2. Is your congregation nearly unanimous in wishing an entirely Free Trade in Corn? 3. Do you approve generally of the plan of the Meeting, or have you any suggestions to offer?

Answers.—1. Yes. 2. I believe they are nearly unanimous. 3. Yes.

1. Certainly. When connected with the country in the very den of Toryism, I was wont to get up petitions addressed to Parliament against the Corn Laws, and that more numerously signed than could be got up by all the farmers united in the whole parish. 2. I believe my present congregation are all united in utter abhorrence of the Corn Laws. 3. I have some doubts as to the real value and effect of such a plan, though I cannot at present suggest a better. Seceders in the country, who are farmers, are generally as averse to Free Trade in Corn, as any class in the kingdom, at least in Aberdeenshire. The sending out of small tracts on the subject of the Corn Laws, and answering objections to a Free Trade in Corn, would do immense good. Every one, who is a farmer, in this quarter, views any alteration in the Corn Laws as certain destruction to himself and his profession, and he fights for these laws as he would do for his very existence. Light! light! light! is wanted.

1. I am decidedly. 2. They are not nearly unanimous. The majority, perhaps, are friendly to the present Corn Laws. 3. I do approve very much. For my own part, I detest the Corn Laws, and declare my opinion of them freely in private to all sorts of people. But my congregation consists either of agriculturists, or of tradesmen dependent on that class; and I could not bring the matter before them without the risk of exciting unpleasant feelings, and perhaps creating prejudices that might abridge my power of being spiritually useful, at least, to a portion of my people.

1. I am. 2. The congregation here are unanimous in wishing the Total Abolition of the Corn and Provision Laws, and the establishment of an entirely Free Trade in Corn. 3. We do.

Questions.—1. Are you in favour of an entirely Free Trade in Corn? 2. Is your congregation nearly unanimous in wishing an entirely Free Trade in Corn? 3. Do you approve generally of the plan of the Meeting, or have you any suggestions to offer?

1. I think that there ought to be Free Trade in all the necessaries of life, and that all Provision Lords, as well as Corn Lords, are the enemies of man. 2. Consisting of Tories, Whigs, and Radicals, there is a diversity of sentiment among my people on the subject. 3. As the matter is so mixed up with politics, is so extensively regarded as exclusively political, and is so connected with the change of Ministry from semi-Reformers to ultra-Conservatism, I cannot satisfy myself of the propriety of ministers of the gospel being its avowed agitators. I presume to think that petitions signed by anti-monopolists generally preferable to exclusively dissenting petitions; and I regard it as bad policy for dissenters to shew face against such a powerful body as the *Aristocracy* and *the Church*, unless in their own defence, and on party interests.

1. Yes. 2. Nearly unanimous. 3. Yes, generally.

1. I am a decided enemy to the Corn Law, and to all monopolies. But it will be impossible for me, in present circumstances, to do any thing in reference to the projected convention. 2. I presume that, with few exceptions, my people are as hostile to the existing Corn and Provision Laws as myself.

1. Yes. 2. The great majority are so. 3. I approve.

1. I most certainly am. The Corn Law I have long regarded as a most iniquitous piece of legislation. 2. So far as I know the sentiments of my congregation, and for some time past I have been using the means of becoming acquainted with them, I think they are nearly unanimous in wishing the abolition of the laws referred to. It will not be in my power to be present. 3. The plan appears to me calculated to despatch business, and to promote that decorum which should characterize every such meeting; but they who have seen such meetings conducted, are better fitted to speak on the propriety of the plan, and also to suggest improvements, than I can be expected to be. Wishing you, Sir, and your coadjutors, all success in your efforts,—I am, &c.

1. Decidedly favourable. 2. Nearly unanimous. 3. I do.

1. I am in favour of the Total Abolition of these Laws, and the establishment of an entirely Free Trade in Corn. 2. So far as I am acquainted with the sentiments of the congregation in this place, I think I am warranted to state, that a majority of its members are in favour of the Total Abolition of the Corn and Provision Laws, and the establishment of an entirely Free Trade in Corn. I am aware, however, that a few of them are against any alteration in these Laws; and some prefer the adoption of a low fixed duty in Corn, to an entirely Free Trade in it. 3. I approve of the plan.

1. I am. 2. They are ENTIRELY *unanimous*. 3. I do, most cordially.

1. Decidedly so. 2. Certainly. 3. I do.

1. Yes; decidedly so. I have been delivering lectures on the subject of late, and have put into circulation a number of Anti-Corn Law Publications. 2. Yes; but I am requested by a meeting held this evening to state, that they are decidedly hostile to all 'class legislation;' and, considering the state of parties in the empire, they have little hope of seeing the Corn Laws repealed, except as the result of a law granting, what Joseph Sturge of Birmingham calls 'complete suffrage,' and would not unite with any party in seeking the repeal of the Corn Laws, so long as that party refuse to aid in seeking to obtain 'complete suffrage.' 3. Yes. I beg leave to suggest that the grand object would be better promoted, by having something like county meetings, or at least one in Glasgow, Dundee, Aberdeen, and Inverness. The aggregate number who would *attend* would be much greater, and the interest excited throughout the island generally would be greater, owing to the attention that would be awakened by local influences.

1. Yes. 2. It is. 3. Yes.

1. I am in favour of the Total Abolition of the Corn and Provision Laws, and the establishment of an entirely Free Trade in Corn. 2. I am of opinion that they are nearly unanimous in wishing the Total Abolition of these Laws, and an entirely Free Trade in Corn. 3. I approve.

1. Yes. 2. I have good reason to believe that they are. 3. I do.

Questions.—1. Are you in favour of an entirely Free Trade in Corn? 2. Is your congregation nearly unanimous in wishing an entirely Free Trade in Corn? 3. Do you approve generally of the plan of the Meeting, or have you any suggestions to offer?

1. Yes. 2. It is not only my opinion that these are the sentiments of my people, but by a unanimous vote at a meeting called for the purpose last night, they expressed their wish for the Total Abolition of these Laws. 3. I approve generally of the plan of the proposed meeting. Every thing preliminary should be left to the discretion of the Committee named in the minute.

1. I am. 2. I know only of one person who has doubts about an *entirely* Free Trade, and he is anxious for a change of the present system. 3. I do, with the exception that I entirely disapprove of making the proposed meeting a Dissenting one. The connexion of ministers of the Established Church with corn-growing, or their feelings towards Dissenters, might prevent most of them from accepting the invitation; in fact, I should anticipate the presence of but very few indeed of the Established Clergy. Still I would open the door; and I do think that the influence of the assembly will be very much injured by making it exclusively Dissenting. I hope this matter will be very maturely considered, before the meeting is finally called.

1. Yes; decidedly. 2. Although the greater part of them are farmers, the *general* feeling is against the Corn Laws. 3. Yes; it seems to me better than a conference of ministers exclusively. I heartily wish success to the endeavour. The means taken to ascertain the sentiments of friends in the country, will, I hope, secure unanimity.

1. I am. 2. A considerable portion of the congregation are farmers, holding leases, and paying rents proportioned to the prices designed to be maintained by the Corn Laws; yet I have found none disposed to vindicate these Laws, nor am I aware that any member of the congregation would oppose their Total Abolition. 3. In the plan I have observed nothing objectionable.

1. I most heartily wish the Total Abolition of the existing Corn Laws, and all restrictions upon trade. 2. A number of them are, but I have not had an opportunity of knowing their minds individually, as they are wide spread. 3. I do most cordially approve of the plan of the proposed meeting. It is hoped, if the proposed meeting take place, joint and continued prayer to Him whose kingdom ruleth over all, and who can turn the hearts of kings and all men whithersoever He will, will be recommended to all who feel interested in the object of the meeting. The command is, 'Be careful in nothing, but in every thing by prayer,' &c. It might be seasonable, if possible, to publish something to the suffering class, to remind them that sin is the cause of all that is afflictive in the lot of man, whoever be the instruments of it. It might also be the duty of the meeting to remind those in power of their responsibility to the Judge of all, and of the threatenings in the word of God against all oppressors.

1. I have always been favourable to this. 2. Only a few are of this mind 3. So far as I am able to judge, the plan of the proposed meeting seems well adapted to answer the end intended. Much will depend on the Committee appointed by the meeting to frame the resolutions, and superintend the order of public business. I would most readily co-operate with all who wish their entire Abolition, and the establishment of Free Trade in Corn; but in this remote district of country where my lot is cast, the political feeling in regard to these laws is almost entirely on the opposite side; so that, in the present state of society here, I do not think it would be wise for a few individuals to provoke the hostilities of feudal lairds and landlords, for all the advantage that could be gained. But should the meeting proposed take place in Edinburgh, and unanimity be found to prevail on the subject among the Dissenters of Scotland, and should your Committee favour me with a draft of a petition to Parliament for the Repeal of these unjust laws, I shall not hesitate to sign it myself, and procure as many other signatures as I can.

1. Decidedly so. 2. So far as I know, the congregation here are, to a man, Corn Law Repealers. 3. I think it is only by such demonstrations that there is any hope of the Corn Laws being repealed. Provision should be made for securing the meetings from interruption by a section of the Chartists.

Questions.—1. Are you in favour of an entirely Free Trade in Corn? 2. Is your congregation nearly unanimous in wishing an entirely Free Trade in Corn? 3. Do you approve generally of the plan of the Meeting, or have you any suggestions to offer?

1. Decidedly. 2. I have reason to believe that they are quite unanimous on the point. 3. I cordially approve both of the plan and purpose of the meeting.

1. I have been in favour of both these for many years. 2. It is my impression that my congregation are perfectly unanimous on that point. 3. I consider the plan admirably adapted to the circumstances of the case. May Almighty God crown with success the efforts that are making for bringing down that system of iniquity—the Corn Laws.

1. Decidedly so. 2. We are unanimous. 3. I approve, and I have good hope of the meeting being of great use to the cause, and think the friends interested in promoting it well fitted for the task.

1. Yes. 2. I believe the congregation are nearly, if not entirely, unanimous in wishing the Repeal of the Corn Laws, and an entirely Free Trade in Corn. 3. I do.

1. Yes; decidedly so. 2. Not nearly unanimous (I fear); my congregation being composed chiefly of farmers and their dependents; but I am fully warranted to say, that upwards of two-thirds of their number are decided in wishing the Total Abolition of these laws, and an entirely Free Trade in Corn,—the membership being nearly 300. 3. I decidedly approve of the proposed meeting, and of the plan generally, as explained in the circular and minute sent; and remain, with best wishes for the abundant success of the proposed demonstration, in aiding the downfall of such unjust and unscriptural statutes as the Corn Laws,—the Committee's most obedient, &c.

COUNTY OF ARGYLE.*

Answers from 14 Ministers.

Answers.—1. I am in favour of the Total Abolition of these Laws. 2. In this neighbourhood there is a growing wish for Total Abolition, as people become acquainted with the subject. The members of the Congregation are nearly unanimous for Total Abolition. 3. I approve.

1. I am. 2. So far as I know, they are entirely unanimous. 3. I approve most cordially of the plan proposed.

1. I am. 2. A large number of them are farmers, who, although they may be favourable, are deterred by the fear of the landlord from expressing their sentiments on the question. Several are against Repeal. 3. If the discussion be confined to the moral bearings of the question, I can approve of such a meeting.

1. Yes. 2. Such of them as understand the question; it is my firm belief that they wish their Total Abolition, and an entirely Free Trade in Corn. 3. Highly. Our principal merchant says, that neither the farmers nor the landlords gain by the present laws, but only the jobbers in grain.

1. Yes; for I consider them contrary to the dictates of true religion, truth, justice, and humanity. 2. So far as I am acquainted with the sentiments of my people, they are of the same mind with myself, in wishing the *Total Abolition* of these laws, and an entirely Free Trade in Corn. 3. We do approve of it. You have our prayers that the Lord of all Grace may direct all your deliberations in the cause of justice for the suffering poor.

1. I am in favour of the Total Abolition of the Corn and Provision Laws, and the Establishment of an entirely Free Trade in Corn. 2. It is my opinion, so far as I am acquainted with the sentiments of our congregation, that they are nearly unanimous in wishing the Total Abolition of these Laws, and an entirely Free Trade in Corn. 3. We do approve of the plan of your meeting, as explained in the accompanying Circular and Minute; we wish you God speed.

* This division includes one from Bute.

Questions.—1. Are you in favour of an entirely Free Trade in Corn? 2. Is your congregation nearly unanimous in wishing an entirely Free Trade in Corn? 3. Do you approve generally of the plan of the Meeting, or have you any suggestions to offer?

1. Yes. 2. Yes. There are some farmers quite opposed to the Corn Laws, and warmly approving of Free Trade, yet stand aloof, under a conscientious apprehension of being ruined by their present high rents with low prices for their grain. 3. I do. And of all lawful means to effect the desired end.

1. Yes. 2. They are. 3. I do. It is hoped the intended meeting will agree to ask nothing less than a Total Abolition of the present Provision and Corn Laws.

1. I do favour the Total Abolition of the Corn and Provision Laws, and the Establishment of Free Trade in Corn. 2. As far as I know, I am of opinion that the greater part of our Congregation are unanimous in wishing the Abolition of these laws and Free Trade in Corn. 3. Instead of inviting Dissenting ministers and members to your meeting, I am of opinion you ought rather to have invited all who are friendly to the cause. May the Lord direct you in all things!

1. Yes. 2. I believe a majority of them are. 3. (No answer given.)

1. The Circular has been laid before the members of the Congregation here, and I have good reason to think that they are unanimous in wishing the speedy Abolition of the Corn Laws; but they cannot pledge themselves to send any delegates to the meeting.

1. Yes. 2. A petition on the subject of the Corn Laws was sent from this place, with 112 signatures, chiefly by members and adherents of the Congregation. All, so far as I know, are Abolitionists. 3. I approve.

1. I am of opinion that there should be a Total Abolition of the Corn and Provision Laws, and an entirely Free Trade in Corn. 2. The people of my Congregation are quite unanimous in wishing the Total Abolition of these Laws and a Free Trade in Corn. 3. I approve of the plan of the meeting, as explained in the Circular.

1. I am. 2. It is. 3. I do.

COUNTY OF AYR.

Answers from 34 Ministers.

Answers.—1. I am MOST DECIDEDLY in favour of both. 2. My Congregation is perfectly unanimous in favour of Total Abolition, and an entirely Free Trade. 3. I do approve generally of the plan of the proposed meeting. I humbly submit, that those Ministers of the Established Church who are known to be friendly to a Total Repeal, should have been asked to attend the meeting. It appears to me also, that although Edinburgh is doubtless the most central place, yet Glasgow would have been a better place, in my fopinion, or giving effect to such a meeting—that there a better attendance of laymen of influence and experience would have been secured, and a greater amount of evidence brought forward, which, of course, is the great thing wanted, in order to tell upon the Government and the public. But I must not trouble you with any farther remarks, as you will see I have answered and signed the above queries, and I have only to express a sincere wish for the speedy success of a Total Repeal of the Provision Laws, and an entirely Free Trade.—Yours truly.

1. Yes. 2. They are unanimous in my opinion. 3. I most heartily approve of the proposed meeting.

1. Yes, decidedly. 2. Yes.

1. I am decidedly in favour of the Total Abolition of these Laws, and wish the speedy establishment of an entirely Free Trade in Corn. 2. Yes,—so far as I know, we have not a Corn Law Advocate amongst us. We have not had a public meeting on the subject; but I have endeavoured to make myself acquainted with their sentiments, and from all I can learn, I believe that they are unanimous in wishing the Abolition of these laws. 3. I cordially approve of it. The names of the gentlemen in the Committee, are a sufficient guarantee to me, that if the proposed meeting do take place, and I sincerely hope it will, whatever is done at it, will be done well.

Questions.—1. Are you in favour of an entirely Free Trade in Corn? 2. Is your congregation nearly unanimous in wishing an entirely Free Trade in Corn? 3. Do you approve generally of the plan of the Meeting, or have you any suggestions to offer.

1. Most decidedly. 2. Unanimous, I believe. 3. Approve.

1. Yes. 2. (no answer.) 3. The number of my people is small, and they are likewise poor. In these circumstances, it will be impossible for me, or any of our Congregation, to attend the proposed meeting. I purpose, however, to agitate the question by all possible means; and a petition, having for its prayer the immediate and entire Abolition of those *most iniquitous* Corn and Provision Laws, will be forwarded so soon as Parliament assembles. My prayer is, that a meeting, large and influential, may be convened, and that the blessing of God may be visible in the unanimity and energy that prevail.

1. Yes. 2. The number of communicants fully 300; and nine-tenths of these, as well as the regular hearers, are favourable. 3. Yes.

1. Yes; and if that cannot be obtained, a modification of these Laws. 2. Not unanimous; the extremes of politics divide us, and the repealers do not feel themselves at liberty to move in this matter in the meantime. 3. I am afraid that responding to your call may throw the apple of discord into some of the Dissenting Congregations, especially in the country, but I have no objections to the movement, where it can be done without injury to the christian community.

1. I cordially agree with the letter and spirit of this query. 2. I have not had an opportunity of meeting with my congregation, but am of opinion, that the great body of them are for the abolition of these Laws, and an entirely Free Trade in Corn. 3. I cordially approve of plan proposed, &c.

1. Yes. 2. Unanimous. 3. Yes.

1. Decidedly in favour of a *Total* Abolition. 2. The Congregation is situated in a rural district, and is made up in a great measure of farmers; but even among them, the opinion is gaining ground, that the Corn Laws ought to be abolished,—other classes in the Congregation entertain strongly this opinion. 3. Yes.

1. Yes. 2. I have taken some pains to ascertain the mind of the Congregation. They are nearly unanimous. Indeed, with the exception of two, perfectly so. 3. Yes.

1. I am. 2. The great majority of them are so. But, as in most other places, the agricultural population are not generally so. 3. I do, though I fear that confining the invitations to Dissenters, may give the meeting a Sectarian character, and thus diminish, in the eyes of many, its just influence. Could not an infusion of true Repealers, although Churchmen, be introduced without any risk of injuring the freedom of Dissenting thought and feeling which may be expected to pervade the meeting on the subject of restrictive Laws respecting human food? The question, I should hope, will be treated *chiefly*, if not *exclusively*, on moral and religious grounds.

1. I am decidedly in favour of the objects referred to in this question. 2. From the shortness of the time allowed for inquiry, I have not had an opportunity of ascertaining the sentiments of the members of my Congregation on the points referred to; but as far as my knowledge goes, I can answer in the affirmative. 3. The plan of the proposed meeting is, in my opinion, excellent. I have carefully considered the Resolutions, and can suggest nothing in the way of improvement, except that *one* member of a congregation, with the minister, is sufficient, as a deputation for representing their sentiments.

1. Yes. 2. Yes. 3. Yes.

1. Most decidedly so. 2. The members of my congregation are generally most desirous that the Corn and Provision Laws should be Totally Repealed. 3. I do. I would humbly submit to the Committee, whether those in every parish who are not Dissenters, and who wish a Total Repeal of the Corn Laws, should not be requested to send a delegate to represent them at the proposed meeting? It appears to me of importance to secure the co-operation of all throughout the country who are friendly to the Abolition of these iniquitous Laws.

1. I am not prepared to answer this question. 2. They are not. 3. I am not prepared to answer this question.

Questions.—1. Are you in favour of an entirely Free Trade in Corn? 2. Is your congregation nearly unanimous in wishing an entirely Free Trade in Corn? 3. Do you approve generally of the plan of the Meeting, or have you any suggestions to offer.

1. A considerable number are in favour of the Total Abolition of the Corn and Provision Laws and an entirely Free Trade in Corn; but on any other commodity, a number would, for the present, be satisfied with a fixed duty. 2. I believe that a large majority of our congregation are for Free Trade in Corn, and every thing else. The last petition which was sent from this place, praying for a revision of the Corn laws, was the most numerously signed that ever went from this town. 3. No.

1. Most certainly, and always have been. 2. With the exception of one or two, my congregation are perfectly unanimous. The communicants are 200.—I may add that out of a population of 7000 in Girvan, only two persons refused to sign the Anti-Corn Law Petition. 3. Entirely.

1. Yes. 2. Nearly unanimous in wishing the Total Abolition of these Laws. 3. Most cordially.

1. Yes. 2. Nearly unanimous—perhaps altogether so. 3. Yes.

1. At a meeting of elders and managers, called to consider your Circular, it appears that a majority are in favour of some alteration in the Corn and Provision Law; but circumstanced as they are, as a congregation without a Pastor, they feel not inclined to interfere with your meeting.

1. Most decidedly. 2. My congregation are *nearly* unanimous in desiring the Total Repeal of the Corn Laws. 3. Yes.

1. (Vacant Charge.) 2. So far as we are acquainted with the sentiments of our congregation, they are nearly unanimous in wishing the Total Abolition of these Laws. 3. We approve generally of the plan of the proposed meeting, as explained in the accompanying Circular and Minute.

1. Yes. 2. Yes. 3. Yes.

1. No. I am desirous to see the Corn Laws altered by such a measure as that proposed by the late Ministry. 2. So far as I am acquainted, either with my congregation or any other, I know none in favour of a Total Abolition of the Corn Laws, but all for an alteration. 3. I approve of every measure of getting the Corn Laws altered, but Total Abolition produces great apathy, or rather hostility, amongst the people; for the general impression is, that Total Abolition would ruin the farmers. The masses are not alive to their own interests. They are deceived by those who hold up the charter as a panacea for all evils. Until there is more union among the people, and a greater eagerness manifested by the multitude, I fear the resolutions and petitions of our order or class will do little good.

1. I am. 2. They are. 3. I do.

1. Yes. 2. Yes. 3. Yes. It is suggested that, along with the Corn Laws, the meeting should entertain the question of the extension of the suffrage.

1. Decidedly in favour of Total Abolition, and an entirely Free Trade in Corn. 2. Nearly unanimous—a few, and only a few, who are Chartists, objected to sign a petition sent to the House of Commons for Total Repeal. 3. Yes. I think meetings and appointments strictly congregational, not advisable.

1. Yes. 2. Yes. 3. Yes.

1. I am, and ever have been, since I understood any thing about these matters. 2. So far as I know, they are unanimous in holding the same views of these matters as I do myself. 3. I do. I would beg most respectfully to suggest that one of the resolutions be so drawn up as to condemn the *class legislation* of this country, which I solemnly believe to be the parent of many of the national evils by which we are afflicted.

1. Yes. 2. Completely unanimous. 3. I approve most heartily of the plan in all its parts. The minute, without any alteration, is, in my judgment, well fitted to promote the objects in view.

1. Decidedly, and strongly 2. There may be two or three not quite hearty in the matter, but such would offer no opposition; and all the others, so far as I know, are strongly in favour of the measure. 3. I do entirely approve.

1. Decidedly so. 2. I have reason to believe they are *quite* unanimous. 3 I very much approve of the plan.

Questions.—1. Are you in favour of an entirely Free Trade in Corn? 2. Is your congregation nearly unanimous in wishing an entirely Free Trade in Corn? 3. Do you approve generally of the plan of the meeting, or have you any suggestions to offer?

COUNTIES OF BANFF AND MORAY.*

Answers from 9 Ministers.

Answers—1. Yes. 2. Yes; such is my opinion. 3. Yes.

1. Decidedly so. 2. I have reason to think that, without exception, they are unanimously so. 3. I do. The whole plan appears excellent.

1. Yes, *decidedly*. 2. In as far as I am aware, though the members reside in a rural district, and the greater number derive their livelihood from agriculture, they are *almost* unanimous *in desiring a Total Repeal*. My people have cheerfully promised to defray my travelling expenses, and I am willing to attend the meeting. 3. Most cordially.

1. Yes; it meets with my cordial approbation. 2. I have no hesitation in saying that they are nearly unanimous. 3. I do: I consider that congregations hold a civil, as well as a religious status in society, and that they can, in complete consistency, plead for, maintain, and defend their civil rights unitedly—even in their congregational capacity—acting as a part of civil society.

1. Yes. 2. Yes. 3. Yes; I hope nothing will take place at the proposed meeting, which would indicate a disposition merely to embarrass the government; but, on the contrary, that matters will be so conducted as to convey the impression that the meeting has just one object, and *only one object*, to gain, viz. the righteous and benevolent relief of the poor and needy.

1. Yes. 2. Nearly unanimous. 3. Yes.

1. Yes; as an individual decidedly so. 2. I am not minutely acquainted with their sentiments on the subject. Most of our town's people are so; others, in the country, in the agricultural interest, entertain opposite sentiments. 3. Yes; it is an orderly business-like manner of ascertaining, and giving expression to public opinion on an important subject, that ought to weigh with the government of the country. All ought to be conducted in a christian, mild, firm, temperate manner. It may be well to guard against the divisions and squabbles of *chartists*, who will try to throw odium upon the whole. It seems highly proper that the meetings should be opened and closed with prayer.

1. Yes, most decidedly. 2. So far as I know, they are; but I have no time to ascertain, so as to be positive. 3. Yes; and if the meeting take place, I wish to give it my best wishes and prayers.

1. I am in favour of the Total Abolition of the Corn Laws, and the establishment of an entirely Free Trade in Corn, &c. 2. They are perfectly unanimous; there is not an individual exception. 3. I approve, and my congregation approves entirely of the course you propose to take. As many petitions should be got up as possible.

COUNTY OF DUMFRIES.

Answers from 19 Ministers.

Answers.—1. At a public meeting, held in my church, on Monday evening last, I was unanimously urged to attend the Corn Law Meeting, to be held at Edinburgh, on the 11th and 12th of January 1842, when I consented to do so; and the church party promised to assist in paying the expenses. I was also requested to engage two friends in Edinburgh, to represent my congregation at said meeting, which I hope you will do for me. The only regret which was felt was, that church *people* had been prevented from attending; and, if the Committee were yet to advertise that they would be received, deputations would appear from all quarters of the kingdom, which would add great weight to the influence of the meeting.

* This division includes one from Inverness.

Questions.—1. Are you in favour of an entirely Free Trade in Corn? 2. Is your congregation nearly unanimous in wishing an entirely Free Trade in Corn? Do you approve generally of the plan of the meeting, or have you any suggestions to offer?

1. Most decidedly in favour of the Total Abolition of the Corn and Provision Laws, and of the importation of Foreign Corn, without any restriction whatever. 2. Yes; I should think that the members and adherents of my congregation are almost unanimous in wishing the Trade in Corn to be absolutely free. 3. I approve generally of the plan of the contemplated meeting, so far as I am acquainted with it. In my opinion, christian ministers and churches are not only guilty of no impropriety, but are eminently in the performance of their duty, when they endeavour, by peaceable and constitutional means, to procure the repeal of laws which prohibit the eaters of bread from buying it from any but British landlords. But they are equally bound to prevent the passing of measures such as that brought forward by the late ministry, which propose that a sum of money should be paid to agriculturists, for liberty to buy corn where it can be got cheapest. Great care should be taken by them, in pursuing these objects, not to identify themselves with any one political party.

1. I am decidedly so. 2. My congregation, though mostly agriculturists, are, I think, nearly unanimous in favour of a great modification, if not a Total Abolition of the Corn Laws. I have moved in the matter a long while ago, and got a petition, largely signed, considering our population, and the whole district being on the * * * estate, as also our village having no feudal right to their houses.—in spite of all, *I got a firm petition numerously and heartily subscribed.* 3. I need not say that I consider the plan excellent. Something must be done. This seems a good way of trying to do it.

1. Yes. 2. Yes. 3. Yes.

1. There is no minister here at present, but I have been appointed by the session to give the following answers. 2. Yes. 3. Yes.

1. Yes. 2. I believe the congregation is unanimous for the repeal. 3. Yes. I have no suggestion to make.

1. While I am an enemy to the Corn Laws, and think it a pity ever they disgraced the statute-book of our country, yet I am not clear about the expediency of petitioning for their immediate and entire abolition. 2. What is the prevailing opinion about the Corn Laws, among the members of the congregation, I cannot certainly say; but I have no reason to think that they are nearly unanimous in thinking that they should be immediately and entirely abolished. 3. Supposing it expedient to petition for the immediate and entire abolition of the Corn Laws, might it not have been better to have included the adherents of the Established Church, as well as the Dissenters?

1. Yes. 2. Nearly unanimous. 3. I approve.

1. Yes. 2. I believe the great majority are so. 3. I do generally, but not in every particular.

1. Yes, Yes, Yes. 2. Yes, Yes, Yes. 3. Yes.

1. I am anxious for the total and *immediate* Abolition of the Corn Laws. 2. My congregation, with one or two exceptions, are in favour of an entirely Free Trade in Corn. The farmers in this parish want neither a sliding scale, nor a fixed duty, but a Total Repeal of the Tax on Bread. 3. I cordially approve of the plan of the proposed meeting, and believe that much good will be effected by it. Nothing occurs, however, in the way of suggesting any improvement.

1. Decidedly in favour of Total Abolition. 2. Nearly unanimous in wishing the Total Abolition of these Laws. 3. I do approve, and have nothing to suggest.

1. Yes. 2. Yes. (3. No answer given.)

1. I am an enemy to the Corn Laws, believing them opposed to reason, scripture, and the rights of man; unworthy of a free country; disgraceful to an enlightened age, and to any system of sound legislation; oppressive, cruel, and unjust. 2. All with whom I have conversed on the subject, are Abolitionists. I consider them unanimous. 3. I approve, and can think of no improvement.

Questions.—1. Are you in favour of an entirely Free Trade in Corn? 2. Is your congregation nearly unanimous in wishing an entirely Free Trade in Corn? 3. Do you approve generally of the plan of the Meeting, or have you any suggestions to offer?

1. I am. I regard the Corn Laws as in their nature and tendency not only the greatest solecism in legislation, but as repudiated alike by the dictates of reason, justice, humanity, and Christianity. 2. With very few exceptions, I should say they are. 3. I do, most unqualifiedly.

1. I certainly am of that opinion. 2. The congregation and elders are also of such an opinion, in as far as I have been able to ascertain. 3. I always approved of the constitutional mode of seeking redress of grievances by petition.

1. Yes. 2. All that I have conversed with are in favour of Total Abolition. 3. Yes. I cannot suggest any improvement on what is contemplated in the minute.

1. I am. 2. My congregation are entirely unanimous in wishing a Total Abolition. 3. I approve.

1. Yes. 2. Yes. 3. Yes.

COUNTY OF EDINBURGH.

Answers from 48 Ministers.

Answers.—1. Am and have ever been. 2. I believe every one of them. 3. I do. I approve of the Resolutions as they are.

1. Most certainly! 2. I know that they are *quite* unanimous. 3. I do. I have no suggestions to offer, except that, in Resolution V. you seem to me to err, in appointing the meetings to take place *each day* at twelve o'clock. That is a good hour for the *first* day, but afterwards the hour should be much earlier.

1. I am. 2. As far as I know, they are nearly unanimous. 3. I do, as far as I have considered it. None have occurred.

1. Most decidedly. 2. I should think a great majority of them coincide with me in these views on this subject. 3. No, and I do not intend being present. I should gladly attend a meeting of friends to Free Trade in Corn, and every thing else, called without reference to *ecclesiastical* standing as ministers or members of churches. I object on the ground both of principle and expediency, to a meeting composed of ministers and members of churches, *as such*, for considering, or acting in reference to, any such question as that of the Abolition of the Corn Laws; but it is very probable that two members of my congregation may be induced to attend the meeting. Did I not object to the principle of the meeting, I should highly approve of the details for its management.

1. Yes. 2. I should think they are; but there are exceptions. 3. Yes.

1. I am, and without hesitation, as a member of society, as a Christian, and a minister of religion. 2. They are. I have a number of farmers, only two of whom, through mistaken views, I had reason to know *were* (I do not say they now *are*) opposed to Total Abolition. The distress of the country, and fears as to the future, tend strongly to enlighten the most selfish and obdurate. 3. Entirely. No improvement occurs to me; I am exceedingly pleased with the terms of the accompanying Minute.

1. Yes. 2. Yes. 3. Yes.

1. Yes. 2. Yes. 3. Yes; but I would prefer the restriction of the invitations to Evangelical Dissenters; or at least that the persons appointed to pray should be selected from their number, and that this be inserted in the rules.

1. I am. 2. My impression is, that they are unanimous, or nearly so. 3. I approve, and have no suggestion to offer.

1. Yes. 2. So far as I know, my congregation are unanimous in the wish. 3. Yes. I have no *important* suggestions to make.

1. Yes. 2. Yes. 3. Yes. I have some scruples in reference to the latter part of Article V. if there be the least likelihood of ministers, who deny the divinity and atonement of Christ, being invited to lead the devotions. Indeed, I think the more honourable and truly liberal course would be to confine the invitation to Evangelical Dissenters.

Questions.—1. Are you in favour of an entirely Free Trade in Corn? 2. Is your congregation nearly unanimous in wishing an entirely Free Trade in Corn? 3. Do you approve generally of the plan of the Meeting, or have you any suggestions to offer?

1. Yes. 2. The general opinion in my congregation is favourable to the Total Abolition of these Laws. There are a few influential farmers, who, although liberal in their general politics, do not go so far, but are neutral or hostile regarding this cause. 3. I do.

1. Yes. 2. Those connected with the agricultural interest, seem to take little interest in the subject. Some are favourable to the Abolition of the present restrictive system; whilst others wish to have some protection. The majority have taken no active part for or against the Corn Laws. Those not connected with the agricultural interest, are unanimously in favour of Free Trade. 3. Before agreeing to attend the meeting, or recommending others to attend it, I must know more precisely who are included in the phrase 'Dissenting Ministers,' employed in the first resolution. At the Manchester Conference, Unitarians, and Roman Catholic priests, were admitted. I can have no objection to join with them, or any class of fellow citizens, in the prosecution of purely civil objects; but the meeting proposed is avowedly a meeting of ministers and members of Dissenting Churches; and I never will, because I cannot, recognize the parties referred to as ministers of the Gospel.

1. Most decidedly,—I would have a Total and immediate Repeal of all these Laws. 2. I think that my congregation may be regarded as almost unanimous in wishing a Total Abolition of the Corn Laws. 3. I am most happy that such a meeting has been thought of, and it has my entire concurrence and approval.

1. I am. 2. Yes. 3. (No answer given.)

1. Yes. 2. There is a diversity of opinion in my congregation on this subject. This is the case especially amongst the farmers, of whom there are upwards of twenty connected with us. Even amongst them, however, I think the general sentiments to be these:—The price of land is much too high,—it must come down,—the Abolition of the Corn monopoly would effect that change. With their present leases the farmers would be sufferers, but allow these to be modified, and the Abolition of the Corn Laws will not ultimately injure them. Others think differently. 3. I decidedly disapprove of confining the invitation *to Dissenters*. It appears to me calculated to divide the liberal interest in Scotland. It will exclude many of the best friends of the cause, and weaken whatever demonstration may be made in the eyes of Government and the country. *Could not tickets of admission be extended beyond two, where* FARMERS *are concerned?* Their interests are deeply involved. The proprietors operate on their fears, and nothing could better tend to enlighten them, or to diffuse information, than attendance on such a meeting.

1. Yes. 2. Yes. 3. Yes.

1. I am decidedly in favour of the Total Abolition of the Corn Laws. 2. They are nearly, I may almost truly say that they are entirely, unanimous, for the Abolition of the Corn Laws. 3. I do approve of the plan of the meeting. At our meeting last evening, the following sentiment met with the approbation of them all, that the *people* of the Established Church resident in Edinburgh, should have been invited, and that, in this cause, the division into Churchmen and Dissenters ought to be avoided as far as possible. May I respectfully suggest, that, though the above opinion cannot be well carried into effect, the Committee should propose a motion to the following effect: 'That while, from circumstances, the meeting is confined to Dissenters, it is gratifying to know, that the great majority of the people belonging to the Established Church, are of the same sentiments, have on former occasions laudably expressed their sentiments; and that this meeting rejoice in the fact, that their brethren in the Establishment cordially unite with them in these measures, and will, in the manner most convenient to themselves, effectually state their opinions on the subject.' I beg also to suggest, that it would be well to fix a time when the evening meeting should terminate, I would say *ten* o'clock precisely.

1. Yes. 2. Yes. 3. I highly approve.

Questions.—1. Are you in favour of an entirely Free Trade in Corn? 2. Is your congregation nearly unanimous in wishing an entirely Free Trade in Corn? 3. Do you approve generally of the plan of the Meeting, or have you any suggestions to offer?

1. I am. 2. My congregation, regularly convened, have expressed their opinion unanimously in favour of the proposed conference on the principles stated. 3. I do, and I feel satisfied with the proposed scheme.

1. Yes. 2. It is. 3. I do.

1. I am. 2. The great majority of my congregation, I have reason to believe, are decidedly in favour of the Total Abolition of the Corn Laws. 3. The proposed meeting has my full approbation, and I have no alteration or improvement to suggest.

1. I am. 2. Not unanimous, this being an agricultural district; but generally, they are in favour of Free Trade. 3. I do.

1. Yes. 2. I cannot answer this question in the affirmative, but am persuaded a considerable number of my congregation wish Total Abolition. 3. Yes.

1. In favour. 2. I should think unanimous. 3. I approve generally.

1. Yes. 2. Yes. 3. Yes.—Would it not be better to have a separate hour for prayer, in case of the presence of persons averse to join in promiscuous prayer as they esteem it?

1. Yes. 2. Unanimous. 3. I approve.

1. I am. 2. Such is my opinion, though it is but fair to state that I have had no very satisfactory means of verifying its accuracy. 3. I do.

1. Yes. 2. I should think that the majority are. 3. Yes.

1. Yes.—I beg to assure you of the deep interest I take in the question of the Corn Laws, as bearing upon the present state of the labouring classes in this country. Something *must* be done, and that speedily, else those who want occasion for delay in settling this matter, will take it from our tardiness. 2. Nearly, not quite. 3. Yes.

1. I am. 2. With very few exceptions; and a few desire a Fixed Duty. 3. I quite approve of it.

1. I am. 2. I believe so. 3. I do, but am inclined to think, three or four meetings would have had a better effect, in Edinburgh, Glasgow, Aberdeen, and Dundee; many more would on the whole have attended. In Resolution IV. I think it should be added,—'from their congregation,' or something to that effect. It struck me on the first reading, that it was a *General Fund* that was recommended. I fear others may think the same and count upon it.

1. Yes. 2. Yes. 3. Yes.

1. Yes. 2. I think so. 3. Yes.—I think it would be as well, instead of having persons only representing *part* of a *congregation*, which may be but a small part, to have them come, perhaps by the suggestion and invitation of the minister, and take their word for the mind of the general congregation on the matter of the Corn Laws.

1. Yes. 2. Yes. 3. Yes.

1. I am. 2. I presume they are nearly unanimous. 3. I do,—but in reference to Resolution 1st in the minute, I disapprove entirely of the ministers and others coming to the meeting as representatives of the congregations with which they are connected. This may give rise to dissensions in congregations, the members of which are not of one mind regarding the Corn Laws. If it is not meant that those who attend the meeting should do so in a representative capacity, Resolution I. is ambiguous, and ought to be altered.

1. Yes. 2. Yes. 3. Yes.

1. I am in favour of a Total Abolition of these Laws, and of the establishment of an entirely Free Trade in Corn. 2. This question, I think, I may with all propriety answer in the affirmative. 3. I beg respectfully to say that it is not my intention to be present at the proposed meeting, nor do I think that any of the members of the congregation to which I belong will attend it; but I would, at same time, take leave to say, that whenever the inhabitants of Edinburgh shall petition Parliament for a Total Abolition of these unjust and oppressive Laws, my name shall be most cheerfully appended to it; and I am sure all the male members of the congregation with which I am connected will with pleasure do so.

Questions.—1 Are you in favour of an entirely Free Trade in Corn? 2. Is your congregation nearly unanimous in wishing an entirely Free Trade in Corn? 3. Do you approve generally of the plan of the Meeting, or have you any suggestions to offer?

1. Yes. 2. The members who are farmers are getting new light on the subject, but in general they are afraid of a change. 3. Yes.

1. Yes. 2. Yes. 3. Yes.

1. Yes: decidedly in favour of the Total Abolition of these Laws, and the establishment of an entirely Free Trade in Corn. 2. There are only a few individuals consisting chiefly of coal-miners—and some are disposed to acquiesce in the Abolition, &c. 3. Yes undoubtedly.—I have no suggestions to make, but entirely agree to the present terms of the Minute sent to me.

1 Yes. I am. 2. Yes, it is. 3. Yes, I do.

1. Yes. 2. It is my opinion that they are very generally in favour of the Total Abolition of the Corn Laws. 3. I approve generally of the plan of the proposed meeting, adhering to my statement delivered at the preliminary meeting, that I and those who may attend will appear as personal friends to the cause, and not *as representatives of a religious body*.

1. Yes. 2. It is. 3. Yes.

1. Yes. 2. Yes. 3. Yes.—I hope there is no necessity for publishing the names, either of the Church, or of the individuals who represent it.

1 I am. 2. It is. 3. I do.

1. Entirely disapproving as I do of the proposed meeting upon various grounds, it is unnecessary for me to enter into particulars.

1. Certainly. 2. Yes. 3. Yes.

COUNTY OF FIFE.

Answers from 54 Ministers.

Answers.—1. My congregation held a meeting last evening, when they were unanimous in their approval of the object of the proposed meeting. They have appointed myself and a member of my session, to represent them at the meeting in Edinburgh.

1. Yes. 2. Yes. 3. Yes.

1. Yes. 2. As far as I know they are unanimous in wishing their Abolition. 3. Most decidedly.—I am not sure of the propriety of limiting the invitations to Dissenting ministers. The number of Established ministers who would attend would probably not be great, but I think a few of the most respectable among them would attend if invited.

1. I am *decidedly* in favour of entirely Free Trade in Corn, and of the same principle in all other interests and services, be they secular or spiritual. 2. I firmly believe they are very nearly unanimous. 3. The gentlemen who have originated this movement deserve Britain's warmest thanks in this hour of her alarming peril. The meeting, I trust, will be distinguished by unanimous and high decision, and Peel must swallow his bitter namesake. National peace and prosperity will thus get a great hitch.

1. Yes. 2. I suppose that on this point they are very nearly unanimous. 3. Yes.—Allow me only to state, that I should wish the Dissenters of Scotland to transact the whole of this important business, not as church members, but in their general capacity as men, Britons, and Christians.

1. Yes. 2. Yes. 3. Yes.

1. I am decidedly in favour of an entirely Free Trade in Corn, and think that the Total Abolition of the Corn and Provision Laws would be a great blessing to the country. 2. Nine-tenths of my congregation are in favour of the Abolition. 3. I do not. [Mainly because Churchmen are excluded and the cause may thereby suffer.]—I would respectfully suggest that the cause would be far better served by sending Mr G. Thompson round the country to lecture on the subject, and by circulating forms of petition, and which might and would be numerously signed in every town and village throughout the land.

Questions.—1. Are you in favour of an entirely Free Trade in Corn? 2. Is your congregation nearly unanimous in wishing an entirely Free Trade in Corn? 3. Do you approve generally of the plan of the Meeting, or have you any suggestions to offer?

1. Yes. 2. As far as I know their sentiments they are unanimous in wishing their Total Abolition. 3. (No answer given.)

1. Yes. 2. Nearly unanimous. 3. I highly approve.

1. I am. 2. I am of this opinion. 3. I do.—If ministers and others come together merely to declaim on the prevailing distress which every body knows, little good will be done. The Committee should take care that persons from the manufacturing districts be prepared with accurate details of their respective localities, and it should be impressed on them to have them *accurate*. Parties are ready to expose errors and overcharged pictures, which exposures would damage your proceedings. The effect of your meeting must depend much on your arrangements with the press.

1. I am decidedly against the Corn Laws, and an enemy to monopolies of every kind. 2. I have reason to believe that *all* of them are against the Corn Laws; that *all* of them are in favour of Total Abolition. Some would prefer a fixed duty, to be gradually reduced till *totally* abolished. 3. So far as I can judge, I approve of it.

1. I am, and most decidedly. 2. Yes. I shall be present, if spared in health. I have not had an opportunity of consulting my congregation, but I have no doubt that some of them will be present at the meeting. 3. I do.

1. Yes, in connexion with a legislative enactment to secure tenants from material injury during existing leases. 2. Yes. 3. Yes. It would perhaps tend to prevent ministers from offending those of their congregations who are afraid of Total Abolition, if it were intimated, that the petitions for it to Parliament shall contain a reference to such a *saving measure* as I have specified in my answer to the first query.

1. Yes, assuredly. 2. The population here, amounting to about a thousand, are generally favourable to the Abolition, as is evident from the fact, that two petitions in favour of it have recently been sent to Parliament, each having nearly 400 signatures. 3. Yes, very much indeed.

1. Yes, decidedly so. 2. I have reason to believe that the great majority are so. . 3. I have several doubts regarding the wisdom and propriety of such meetings.

1. I am. 2. It is. 3. I do not.

1. I am, decidedly and strongly. 2. It is; and as expressed at a regularly called, though very small meeting, held last night, they were perfectly so. 3. I do not. It is suggested by the congregation, that the invitation to attend the meeting, be extended to all the friends of the cause in the Established Church, as well as all other denominations. But few of *her ministers* will attend, it is said. Be it so, the blame of their non-attendance will then rest with *themselves*, while, according to the proposed arrangement, they are furnished with the best apology of leaving the good cause alone. Multitudes of her *members*, besides, are as determined abolitionists as any Dissenters can be. This we know to be the case in our own town, and why exclude *them* from a meeting where there are to be two laymen for every minister? Why not accept, why not ask *their* influence, which, in many cases, from their wealth and station, is much greater than that of Dissenters?

1. In favour for their Total Repeal, and an entire Free Trade in Corn. 2. In a public meeting of the congregation, they were unanimous in wishing the Total Abolition of these Laws, and in having an entirely Free Trade in Corn. 3. I do. I am requested by the congregation to suggest to you the propriety of allowing members of the Established Church an opportunity of appending their names to the petitions to be sent up to both Houses of Parliament. In this neighbourhood, if this is not granted, they will be greatly disappointed.

1. A Total and Immediate Abolition. 2. They are unanimous for some alteration, and with perhaps one or two exceptions, they are for Total Abolition. 3. I do generally.

1. I am. 2. I am of opinion that such is the wish of the congregation, with scarcely an exception. 3. I do.

Questions.—1. Are you in favour of an entirely Free Trade in Corn? 2. Is your congregation nearly unanimous in wishing an entirely Free Trade in Corn? 3. Do you approve generally of the plan of the meeting, or have you any suggestions to offer?

1. Yes. 2. My congregation are unanimous in condemning the Corn and Provision Laws. The same thing may be said of the mass of the population of the town and neighbourhood. 3. Yes. It would be better if the congregations were allowed to choose the substitutes for their lay representatives, either from their own denomination, or from any other Dissenting body.

1. Yes. 2. Yes. 3. Yes.

1. I am. 2. They are, so far as I know, almost unanimous in wishing a Total Abolition of the Corn Laws, &c.; but their opinions are varied as to the most efficient mode in which this may be obtained. 3. I approve generally; however, I disapprove of congregations, as such, moving in the matter.

1. Yes. 2. Unanimous, so far as known to me. Farmers in the congregation have expressed themselves in favour of an entirely Free Trade in Corn. 3. I approve generally of the plan.

1. Yes. 2. It is. 3. I question the propriety of the meeting, especially on the ground of its *sectarian* character; besides, its tendency is to produce dispeace in many congregations.

1. I am. 2. Very many, I believe, wish these laws to be abolished; but some do not. 3. I approve generally. In such a place as this, meetings called to consider the propriety of abolishing the Corn Laws, could not, I am afraid, be restricted to members of any one congregation, without making an invidious distinction among the persons residing in the town who are friendly to the abolition. Would it be a departure from the plan of the proposed meeting, to receive two deputies from a meeting composed of persons not belonging exclusively to any one congregation?

1. I am in favour of a Total Abolition of these Laws, and the establishment of a Free Trade in every thing as well as Corn. 2. I believe that the people composing my congregation are almost unanimous on the subject. 3. I approve.

1. I am very strongly in favour of the Total Abolition of these Laws, and the establishment of a Free Trade in Corn. 2. I know that my congregation are nearly unanimous in wishing Total Abolition, and Free Trade. 3. I approve generally. I think it of importance that every effort should be made prior to the meeting, through the newspapers and otherwise, to disarm, and, if possible, gain, the Chartists. I believe that most of them here will sign an Anti-Corn Law petition. They intend getting up another national petition before the meeting of Parliament. Probably it would be in vain to attempt dissuading them from that.

1. Yes; in favour, &c. 2. Yes; 'tis my opinion. 3. Yes; approve.

1. Yes. 2. I believe that every male member of my church has already signed a petition to that effect, and is prepared to do so again. 3. I highly approve of the plan. I would humbly suggest that, besides having the ordinary meetings opened with prayer, an hour each day should be specially set apart for devotional exercises, to be conducted by persons appointed by the Committee. Might not 11 o'clock, A. M., be a convenient hour for holding such a meeting?

1. I am. 2. Nearly unanimous. 3. I do.

1. I am. 2. So far as I know, my congregation are *nearly* unanimous; *some*, however, are favourable to a *fixed* duty. 3. I do not see the propriety or advantage of making the Abolition of the Corn Laws a Dissenter's question. Would it not be better to have such a meeting as would embrace *all* the friends of abolition? By the proposed meeting, is there not a risk of enlisting sectarian prejudice on the side of monopoly, and giving the upholders of restriction a handle to represent abolition as a Dissenter's question? Can the Manchester meeting be reproduced to advantage on a sectarian platform? Would not the plan of district and departmental meetings be preferable?

1. I am anxious for the repeal of these Laws, and for Free Trade in Corn. 2. They are unanimous in wishing the abolition of these Laws, and an entirely Free Trade in Corn. 3. I do approve.

Questions.—1. Are you in favour of an entirely Free Trade in Corn? 2. Is your congregation nearly unanimous in wishing an entirely Free Trade in Corn? 3. Do you approve generally of the plan of the meeting, or have you any suggestions to offer?

1. Certainly so. 2. Unanimous, with one exception, and have often petitioned for the Total Abolition. 3. I heartily approve.

1. Yes. 2. Yes. 3. I would have preferred the representatives of all churches being summoned, though I believe the result as to attendance would have been the same. I would have put it in the power of our Established brethren to refuse. A few pounds would not have been ill spent in stopping the mouths of our opponents. I regret much that the resolution upon opening the meetings with prayer should have given the meetings a still more sectarian character than it ought to possess. I would deprive no man of the privilege of protesting with me against this monstrous monopoly, because he cannot join with me in supplicating the blessing of Heaven. The experience of the Manchester Conference, and, I may add, of the British and Foreign Bible Society, ought not to have been thrown away.

1. I earnestly desire the Total Abolition of the Corn and Provision Laws, being convinced of their injustice and cruelty. 2. I am persuaded that the congregation of which I am minister are all in favour of the abolition of these Laws, with the exception of one or two. 3. I approve generally of the plan of the proposed meeting. I think it would be better if the meeting in the morning were at 11 o'clock, to adjourn at 3, and meet again precisely at six evening.

1. I am decidedly in favour of both. 2. At a congregational meeting of our church, which took place last night, for a purpose of their own, these two points were also brought before them, and they unanimously and cordially desired a Total and Immediate Repeal of these Laws, and an entirely Free Trade in Corn. 3. I approve of it generally. I wish, however, that it had been found convenient, or practicable, to solicit the attendance of ministers of the Established Church of Scotland. I have no hopes that, though solicited, they would attend. Still, the people would have an opportunity of knowing the value of Endowed charity. Allow me to express my approbation of the judicious and well-concerted nature of your plan.

1. Most decidedly. 2. So far as I am acquainted with the sentiments of my congregation in this, I know not one who does not heartily wish the Total Abolition of the Corn Laws, and an entirely Free Trade in Corn. 3. Generally I do. In Resolution Sixth it is resolved, that the meeting, at the commencement of its first sederunt, shall appoint one or more standing Committees, to arrange the order of business, to prepare resolutions, engage speakers, &c.; and in Resolution Eighth it is resolved, that members addressing the meeting shall keep as closely as possible to the subject of the particular resolutions entrusted to them, &c. Now, in order that the members addressing the meeting may the better be enabled to do so, would it not be possible, at your meeting of the 20th instant (having then ascertained the members who have promised to be present), to engage speakers, and to send them the resolutions upon which you desire them to speak, in order that they may be thoroughly prepared?

1. Yes. 2. They are quite unanimous, as far as I am acquainted with their sentiments. 3. I do; and most heartily wish it God-speed. I have nothing to suggest, except that a public prayer-meeting should be held in one or more of the chapels in Edinburgh, on the mornings of the 11th and 12th January, to implore the righteous and compassionate Jehovah to arise and plead the cause of the poor and the needy; and farther, that the various ministers to whom circulars will be sent after your second preliminary meeting, shall be respectfully requested to enlist their *churches* and *congregations* to abound in prayer to God, that he may be graciously pleased to crown our efforts with success. *Agitation* is good; but it must be combined with *prayer*, or there is little prospect of success.

1. I freely answer this first question in the affirmative; and the following, (2.) as far as my knowledge goes, must be answered in the same manner. 3. As far as I understand it, I heartily approve of it.

Questions.—1. Are you in favour of an entirely Free Trade in Corn? 2. Is your congregation nearly unanimous in wishing an entirely Free Trade in Corn? 3. Do you approve generally of the plan of the Meeting, or have you any suggestions to offer?

1. I have always been of opinion that restrictions on the importation of Corn and Provisions, are alike injurious to the prosperity of nations, and inconsistent with the principles of reason and scripture. 2. I am of opinion that, with a few exceptions of individuals connected with the landed interest, the great body of the congregation are in favour of the principles of Free Trade. 3. As far as I have had leisure to study the plan, it seems well calculated to answer the purpose. It appears to me that, with a view to avoid the appearance of party spirit, it would be an improvement to invite a few of the ministers and members of the Established Church, who are *known* to be *favourable* to the Abolition of the Corn Laws. This, I believe, was done at the Conference in Manchester with good effects. The Rev. Thomas Spencer is of the Church of England.

1. As far as I understand the subject, decidedly so. 2. As far as I know, they are. 3. Yes.

1. Yes. 2. So far as I am acquainted, they are all nearly unanimous in wishing the Abolition of the Corn Laws. 3. I do approve of the plan of the proposed meeting.

1. Yes. 2. We are all, to the best of my knowledge, quite unanimous in wishing Total Repeal. 3. Yes. I have only to express my desire that the Divine blessing may attend all your deliberations, and that ultimately, and speedily, they may be crowned with success.

1. Yes. 2. Yes. 3. Yes.

1. Yes. 2. They are nearly unanimous in wishing them abolished. 3. Yes; and I express my own, and I am sure, my congregation's, earnest wish, that this proposed conference may have a powerful effect in relieving us from that grievous thraldom, occasioned by these wicked laws of man's imposition.

1. Decidedly in favour of Free Trade in Corn, and every thing else. 2. So far as I know, there is but one opinion among us, and it is that expressed above. 3. I have doubts as to the propriety of the plan, chiefly on the ground that the principle on which it is based warrants or demands, not as strongly, perhaps, but as really, the same sort of interference in every other political abuse, as non-employment of the ballot, or limited suffrage, for instance. I will be glad, as a citizen, to lend the aid of purse, or pen, or voice, to the extinction of the evil; but this particular mode of it I have such serious doubts of, that, with all respect for my brethren who act differently, I cannot engage in it.

1. I should be ashamed of myself if I were not, at this time of day, and in the present state of misery and starvation which they have occasioned. 2. I am peculiarly situated; but in regard to all my brethren whose opinions I know, I answer unhesitatingly in the affirmative. 3. I do; and particularly of your plan in the last clause of No. V. on the front of the preliminary arrangements, rather than leaving it to the precarious fate of future discussion. Better stay away, if we cannot join in, or if we hinder, the prayers of our christian brethren. I beg to suggest the propriety of limiting all the speakers, from the commencement till the termination of the proceedings, to the same time; unless in peculiar cases, where the committee of management saw meet to make special and formal exceptions, and announce them to the meeting.

1. A Total Abolition of all restrictions on the importation of Corn, and all other necessaries of life. 2. Quite unanimous in desiring Free Trade in Corn. 3. We do not approve of the proposed meeting, as it has all the appearance of a sectional effort, to the exclusion of a numerous class of our fellow-citizens. That the end wished for will never be gained, but by the united efforts of both Kirkmen and Dissenters. It is very doubtful how far such meetings, even on the broadest basis, can forward the object in view. The proposed meeting has by far too clerical an aspect to allow us taking any part in it.

1. Yes. 2. They are unanimous. 3. Entirely.

1. Yes. 2. Yes. 3. I, and the church, do not approve of a public demonstration, separate from others of our fellow-subjects. We are generally connected with the Anti-Corn Law Society in the district where we reside.

Questions.—1. Are you in favour of an entirely Free Trade in Corn? 2. Is your congregation nearly unanimous in wishing an entirely Free Trade in Corn? 3. Do you approve generally of the plan of the Meeting, or have you any suggestions to offer?

1. Yes, in favour of Total Abolition and Free Trade. 2. Unanimous in the above sentiment. 3. Approve and should like congregational petitions to be recommended.

1. Yes. 2. The congregation of which I am a member are nearly unanimous in wishing the Total Abolition of these laws. 3. Yes. I would suggest the propriety of taking into your consideration, whether the object of the meeting would not be more speedily obtained by at once petitioning for such an extension of the suffrage as would give to all male adults, unconvicted of crime, and of sane mind, a vote in electing members of Parliament.

1. Yes, I am. 2. I believe they are. 3. I do.

COUNTY OF FORFAR.

Answers from 36 Ministers.

Answers.—1. I am. 2. It is my opinion that they are nearly so. 3. I do. No special suggestions occur to me. But I feel deeply the importance of every thing pertaining to the business of the meeting, being, as far as possible, in a state of readiness before it commence, that little time may be lost in discussing what they ought to do.

1. Decidedly so. 2. Nearly unanimous. 3. I approve.

1. and 2. We are, unanimously. 3. I approve.

1. I am. 2. So far as I am acquainted, they wish the Total Abolition of the Corn Laws. 3. I approve.

1. I am. I am opposed to all restrictions and monopolies. 2. I believe they are. 3. I do, very much.

1. I am in favour of Total Abolition, and Free Trade in Corn. 2. It is my opinion, so far as I am acquainted with the sentiments of my people, that they are unanimous in wishing the Total Abolition, and an entirely Free Trade in Corn. 3. I Do approve of the plan of the proposed meeting, as explained.

1 Yes. 2. Yes. 3. I do.

1. I am decidedly in favour of both objects specified in this query. 2. In so far as I am acquainted with the sentiments of my congregation, I believe that all of them, without a single exception, are in favour of both of these objects. 3. I cordially approve.

1. Yes. 2. Yes. 3. Yes.

1. As a private individual, it has long been with me a settled point that those Laws, which are contrary to all natural or just principles, and opposed to the general good, and which in this country have existed in many ways, should be abolished. 2. The greater part of those belonging to the congregation here, are believed to be desirous of the Total Abolition of these laws. 3. We approve highly of the plan of the proposed meeting, but are not sure that the *whole* ministerial and lay force, favourable to the cause, as being *more effective* and *influential*, would not be even more advantageous. We beg to suggest that particular attention should be paid to the arguments brought forward by landed proprietors, the only class almost, as far as our observation goes (though without just cause), decidedly opposed to the Abolition of these Laws.

1. I am in favour of the Total Abolition of the Corn and Provision Laws; but I think that a small fixed duty would be a deal preferable to the present mode. 2. I believe the greater number of my congregation would wish a Total Abolition. 3. Should petitions be sent from towns and counties generally, it might be as likely a way to succeed as the way proposed. The generality of the people belonging to this place depend upon manufacturing linens, and severely feel the low state of trade at present; and the desire for the removal of the Corn and Provision Laws is very general.

1. Yes. 2. Yes. 3. Yes. It is generally the opinion of our congregation, that the time is come to agitate for the abolition of all monopolies.

Questions.—1. Are you in favour of an entirely Free Trade in Corn? 2. Is your congregation early unanimous in wishing an entirely Free Trade in Corn? 3. Do you approve generally of the plan of the Meeting, or have you any suggestions to offer?

1. Yes 2. It is. 3. I do. It occurs to me that invitations might be sent to those ministers of the Establishment whose sentiments are known to be in favour of the object of the meeting.

1. Yes. 2. Yes. 3. Yes.

1. I am. 2. So far as known, they are unanimous. 3. Yes. Would it not be proper to extend the invitation to ministers of the Established Church?

1. Yes. 2. Such is my opinion. 3. I approve.

1. Yes. 2. I believe that they are altogether unanimous in favour of Free Trade, and in opposition to monopoly. 3. I am of opinion that ministers ought very rarely to take a public part in matters not strictly religious or ecclesiastical: and it appears to me that the present is not a time for such persons to push themselves into a prominent position out of their own sphere.

1. Yes. 2. Yes. 3. Yes. I entirely approve of the proposed meeting.

1. I am in favour of the Total Abolition. 2. My congregation (so far as I know) are quite unanimous for their Abolition. 3. I approve of the plan.

1. Yes. 2. Yes. 3. Yes.

1. Yes. 2. They are unanimous. We have already petitioned Parliament, and sent a memorial to the Queen. 3. Yes.

1. Yes, decidedly. 2. Yes. 3. Yes.

1. Yes. 2. I know with certainty that my congregation are unanimous in wishing the Total Abolition of these Laws. 3. Yes.

1. Yes. 2. So far as I know, unanimous in favour of Total Abolition. 3. Approve. Will it be possible to finish the necessary business in *two* days?

1. I am. 2. I presume they are. 3. I do *not*. I think that in all such matters, it is for us to act along with our fellow-citizens as such.

1. Yes 2. I do not believe there is one connected with my church or congregation who does not earnestly wish the Total Abolition of these Laws. 3. Yes. It would have been an useless outlay of money to have sent circulars to *all* the Established Ministers of the country. But might it not have been well to have sent them to the *few* of the ministers who are *known to be friendly*. If this would not have procured their *personal attendance* at the proposed meeting, it might have called forth a few letters from them, and every thing should be made to bear upon our cause, which it is possible for us to bring forward at the present crisis. May I therefore take the liberty of suggesting to you, and the other members of Committee, the propriety (in the event that the meeting is to take place), of sending a special *written* invitation to those ministers connected with the Established Church who attended at the Manchester Conference, and also to those of them who sent favourable letters to that Conference. Notwithstanding the inability of the members of my church to bear my expenses (being almost all weavers, and their trade so bad), I will, if health permit, be present at the proposed meeting, should it be called.

1 Yes. 2. So far as I have had the means of ascertaining. 3. Is not the composition of the meeting somewhat limited and sectarian in being confined to Dissenters? Would it be any improvement to call a meeting of intelligent delegates of the christian public opposed to the Corn Laws without reference to church relation; united with a particular regard to all ministers who approve of the objects of the meeting to countenance it by their presence?

1. Decidedly so. 2. I have no idea, that one of them, male or female, is not of the same opinion on this subject with myself. 3. Yes. Entirely approving of the suggestion, which enables the members of a congregation who are favourable, without committing those who, on any ground whatever may decline to act. I think, that in order to give a defined numerical importance to those delegates, who are not appointed by a unanimous vote of the congregation, they should procure the subscriptions of all the members, male and female, who commission them. Thus the memorials and petitions of the General Convention represent the views, not of so many hundred delegates, but of a reckonable number of citizens by whom they were delegated.

Questions.—1. Are you in favour of an entirely Free Trade in Corn? 2. Is your congregation nearly unanimous in wishing an entirely Free Trade in Corn? 3. Do you approve generally of the plan of the Meeting, or have you any suggestions to offer?

1. I am, *most decidedly*. 2. I am certain they are wholly unanimous in wishing the Corn Laws utterly and for ever abolished. 3 I certainly approve very heartily of a meeting being held such as that proposed in the circular.

1. Most assuredly I am. 2 Yes. 3 Yes.

1. Yes. 2. Yes. 3. No.

1. We are. 2. Not only nearly, but all, without a dissenting voice. 3. Most cordially.

1. Certainly. 2. Certainly. 3. Yes. On Resolution V. I would remark, that I much doubt the propriety of commencing every meeting by prayer, many of our denomination have no freedom in uniting in religious worship in a promiscuous way, and the object in question is purely secular. On Resolution VI. I would remark, that I highly disapprove of the motions to be made by the deputies, being first subjected to the censorship of a Committee; I think that the deputies ought to be entirely unfettered on that point, and a contrary plan will have the appearance of something like a packed jury. With these exceptions, I entirely approve of the general plan.

COUNTIES OF HADDINGTON AND BERWICK.

Answers from 25 Ministers.

Answers.—1. Yes. 2. It is. 3. I do not at present see the propriety of such a meeting.

1. Yes; decidedly. 2. The influential members are supporters of the Corn Laws; but the majority, I believe, are in favour of their Total Abolition. 3. Yes.

1. Yes. 2. It is my opinion, and that of many of my congregation. 3 I do.

1. I am. 2. They are nearly unanimous. But in this agricultural district some few are opposed to the *Total Abolition of these laws*. 3. I do approve *generally* of the plan.

1. Yes. 2. They are nearly unanimous. 3. No; I object to the proposed meeting.

1. Yes; decidedly in favour. 2. They are nearly unanimous. 3. Yes.

1. Yes; decidedly. 2. The majority are, so far as I know their sentiments. 3. Scarcely. I think it too restricted. If dissenters are not called to petition the legislature as churches, nor as dissenters, but as citizens, why not invite other citizens to join them, and thus counteract the influence of dissenters favourable to the Corn Laws, besides presenting the appearance of sectarianism, so injurious to our cause. And it appears to me that sufficient protection to the farmer is not held out by the Repealers. My congregation, like the greater number of dissenting congregations (in this quarter), is supported chiefly by agriculture. Some of them have expended their capital on poor soils, and many pay money rents. They justly dread the loss of their capital between the cupidity of landlords and manufacturers, if the Corn Laws are repealed. Should not more be done to remove these fears by *showing* that your object is not the ruin of agriculture?

1. Yes. 2. Yes. 3. Yes.

1. I am. 2. There may be a few in the congregation in favour of the Corn Laws, but the great majority are, I believe, opposed to them. 3. I do. The arrangements appear to me so judicious, that no improvement suggests itself to me.

1. I am. 2. The majority do. 3. I do.

1. I am in favour of the Total Abolition of the Corn Laws, and a Free Trade in Corn. 2. I am not very perfectly acquainted with the sentiments of my congregation respecting the Corn Laws; but do not think they would be unanimous for Abolition. 3. I approve generally of the plan of the proposed meeting.

Questions.—1. Are you in favour of an entirely Free Trade in Corn? 2. Is your congregation nearly unanimous in wishing an entirely Free Trade in Corn? 3. Do you approve generally of the plan of the Meeting, or have you any suggestions to offer?

1. Yes. 2. The sentiments of the majority of this congregation on the Corn Laws I don't know. Some are strenuous Abolitionists, others are indifferent. I don't know of any supporters of the present system. 3. Yes.

1. Most decidedly, and more, if possible. 2. I know that a considerable number of the congregation are strongly opposed to the Corn and Provision Laws, and have no doubt that Total Abolition is nearly the unanimous wish. 3. I do very cordially, and wish it all manner of success; though circumstances will not admit of my attendance, I sincerely trust that the proposed meeting will take place, and prove a powerful instrument in demolishing the infernal murdering machine, and removing a foul stain from our favoured land.

1. I am in favour of Free Trade in Corn, and in every other needful commodity. 2. I cannot give a decided answer to this question. So far as I know the minds of the congregation on this matter, I would say the most intelligent are in favour of the Repeal of these laws. 3. I do approve generally of the proposed meeting. I would have it to consist of all ministers if possible; but I presume that would be a hopeless case. The legal stipends (of the Established Clergy) will be more powerful in their claims than the voice of famishing thousands.

1. Yes. 2. I cannot speak positively, but should think that, with the exception of the agriculturists, they are nearly so. 3. I certainly do.

1. I am very decidedly in favour of the Total Abolition of these Laws. 2. It would be exceedingly difficult to collect the sentiments entertained on this subject by a congregation composed, like mine, chiefly of farm-servants in the country, or of tradesmen and labourers in the town, dependent less or more on the landlords and tenants of this purely agricultural district. Yet those most likely to know have assured me that the great majority, if not the whole, are for the entire Abolition of the Corn Laws, however they may be prevented, through fear of consequences, from expressing their opinion. 3. I cordially approve of the plan, and shall be happy to do every thing in my power to promote the object it contemplates. I have no suggestions to offer, believing that every thing will be wisely managed by the Committee.

1. I am in favour of the Total Abolition of the Corn and Provision Laws, and the establishment of an entirely Free Trade in every article of commerce. 2. I am not much acquainted with the sentiments of my congregation in reference to the point in question, but, so far as I am, I feel at liberty to say that they are nearly unanimous. 3. Though I cannot be present at the meeting, yet I approve of the plan of it, and am of opinion that, if sufficiently numerous, and properly conducted, it would do much good.

1. We are. 2. We believe they are. 3. While earnestly desiring, and ready to use endeavours for, the Total Abolition of the obnoxious laws, we yet entertain our doubts respecting the propriety of *congregational* effort, and therefore, may not in positive terms approve of the aggregate meeting proposed.

1. I am decidedly in favour of the Total Repeal of these Laws, and have more than once signed petitions to the House of Commons against them. 2. As the great majority of the members of my church are connected with the agricultural interests of the country, I should rather be of opinion that they do not think with me on the subject of the Corn and Provision Laws, but I have had no opportunity of consulting them on the subject, neither will I be able to do it before the 14th instant. 3. I do approve most cordially and fully of the plan of the proposed meeting as explained in the Circular and Minute, and earnestly hope that the Legislature may be persuaded to repeal these iniquitous and oppressive Laws before the gathering storm of the country's indignation burst with unabated fury, scattering firebrands and death all around. I have no suggestion to add to what is so well conceived and expressed in terms of the minute.

Questions.—1. Are you in favour of an entirely Free Trade in Corn? 2. Is your congregation nearly unanimous in wishing an entirely Free Trade in Corn? 3. Do you approve generally of the plan of the Meeting, or have you any suggestions to offer?

1. Yes. 2. Yes. 3. Yes; we highly approve of what is stated in the minute. At a meeting of the elders and managers of this church, held this evening, they resolved that they are happy to learn that this movement has taken place amongst the ministers of the Gospel, and will rejoice to hear of the general meeting contemplated taking place.

1. I am, most decidedly. 2. They are, I am confident, almost unanimous. 3. I fully approve.

1. Yes. 2. Yes. 3. Yes. I have merely to express my regret that ministers of the Establishment were not invited to the projected meeting.

1. I am favourable to their Abolition, and fear that if not soon done, the ruin of this country is certain. 2. I cannot exactly say, but should think they are. 3. I have some doubt of the propriety of Dissenters using their religious influence in this way, and mixing up their churches, as such, with political movements.

1. Yes, if they can be safely accomplished. 2. I believe the majority is. 3. I think, notwithstanding all that has appeared to the contrary, it would have been better had the clergymen of the Establishment been invited. However, I wish you all success.

1. Yes, I am in favour of the *principle*, but not certain that a *Total* Abolition would at *present* be good policy. 2. Yes; the great majority are so. 3. Yes, generally, if not indeed *altogether* so.

COUNTIES OF KINROSS AND CLACKMANNAN.

Answers from 12 Ministers.

Answers.—1. Yes. 2. Yes. 3. Yes.

1. Yes; or at least their immediate alteration, in order to pave the way for their Total Abolition, so soon as this can be prudently done, notwithstanding the unnatural state into which things have been brought by these Laws. 2. There is a diversity of opinion in my congregation upon that subject; but I know not what proportion of them are for or against the Corn Laws. 3. I do not approve of a congregation, *as a church*, meeting to discuss a subject so political in its aspect as that of the Corn Laws; nor do I reckon it expedient to call a meeting, consisting of those of the congregation who hold certain political views, to the exclusion of others, whose views of the same subject are different. I think it is calculated to sow dissension in a congregation. I am of opinion that it is preferable to meet for the consideration of such matters in our capacity as citizens. I have shown the Circular to some of the leading men in my congregation, in case some of them should wish to attend the meeting.

1. In favour. 2. Notwithstanding our rural position, there is a growing opposition to them; some say they do not well understand them. 3. I Generally approve. Should the meeting take place, we object to the hour of meeting being 12 o'clock; there is no reason, they think, in the case of members coming from the country, *expressly for the purpose*, to delay meeting until 12 o'clock; and they wish it to be 10 o'clock for the forenoon meeting.

1. All in favour of a Total Abolition of the Corn and Provision Laws, and the establishment of an entirely Free Trade in Corn. 2. Quite unanimous. 3. We approve of the general plan of the proposed meeting, as detailed in the accompanying Circular.

1. *Decidedly* so. 2. Not unanimous; I have no doubt the vast majority are in favour of Abolition. 3. Approve *very heartily*. So far as I can judge of the plan and the resolutions, they are, in my opinion, very excellent.

1. Most decidedly. 2. They are unanimous. 3. Yes.

1. (Church vacant.) 2. This congregation is nearly unanimous in wishing the Total Abolition of the Corn Laws. 3. (No answer given.)

Questions.—1. Are you in favour of an entirely Free Trade in Corn? 2. Is your congregation nearly unanimous in wishing an entirely Free Trade in Corn? 3. Do you approve generally of the plan of the Meeting, or have you any suggestions to offer?

1. Yes. 2. All belonging to the working class in my congregation are favourable to Total Repeal; but the farmers and proprietors, of whom there are fourteen in my congregation, are favourable to a Fixed Duty, with the exception of two, who are for the Sliding Scale. 3. Yes; but I do not see the propriety of confining it to Dissenting ministers alone. Why not make it the clergy generally, as at Manchester? The Established ministers should be invited, and so make it appear by their refusal who are the friends of the poor.

1. My answer is most decidedly in favour of the abolition of this and of all monopolies. 2. A goodly number of my congregation being proprietors of their farms, hesitate about the matter; but it is my opinion that the greater part have no hesitation whatever. 3. The proposed meeting has my most cordial approbation. The only thing that occurs to me is, that every sederunt of the projected meeting begin and end with prayer, and this without any regard to the usages of Roman Catholics, Unitarians, Swedenborgians, or the Church of England.

1. I have long considered the Corn Laws as an oppressive and intolerable burden on the country. 2. I have reason to believe that the great body of my congregation, if not all, view them in the same light. 3. I consider the proposed measure to be unwise, and inexpedient for accomplishing the great object in view.

1. I am against the Corn Laws, root and branch, and in favour of Free Trade in Corn. 2. I believe the greater part of my congregation have the same views with myself; there are a number of them, however, who I believe have views in favour of the Corn Laws. 3. I do not approve of the plan of the proposed meeting.

1. I am decidedly in favour of Total Abolition. 2. I think the majority are in favour of the Total Abolition. 3. I approve of the plan proposed in the Circular, and wish your Committee and Members may be guided from on high, by Him who hears the lion's roar and the raven's cry for food.

COUNTY OF LANARK.

Answers from 62 Ministers.

Answers.—1. Yes. 2. This is my opinion, as far as I know. 3. I do.

1. I am. 2. So far as I know, they are unanimous for Total Abolition. 3. I approve generally of the plan of the proposed meeting. Would it not be better to begin and close the forenoon sederunt at an earlier hour, say from eleven o'clock to three, instead of from twelve to four? and to suit those who may come from a great distance, would not Wednesday and Thursday be more convenient?

1. I am; because they set limits to a kind Providence, close up the channel of commerce, and must lead to starvation. 2. I am quite sure that they are nearly unanimous; because, during a number of years, a petition from this place has been sent every session to Parliament, in forwarding which my people were the most active. The last petition, in the month of September, had upwards of 1200 signatures. 3. I approve generally. Resolution VI. implies that all men have a great deal of foresight, and prohibits any man from changing his views, or getting more knowledge by discussion. I therefore disapprove of the committee being the sole channel of motion or amendment. The chairman at the moment should have the power of deciding whether motions or amendments are competent; and as the Conference is not a promiscuous rabble, there is no danger of a Chartist or Tory overturn. In order to avoid long speeches, a committee might be appointed to draw out a series of questions on the existence and causes of commercial distress, to be put into the hands of every member of conference. That committee to report on the substance of the answers returned, and thus give the conference at one glance the causes, the symptoms, and the cure of the disease.

Questions.—1. Are you in favour of an entirely Free Trade in Corn? 2. Is your congregation nearly unanimous in wishing an entirely Free Trade in Corn? 3. Do you approve generally of the plan of the Meeting, or have you any suggestions to offer?

1. I am. 2. It is. 3. I should have preferred a general meeting, consisting of delegates from all public bodies who chose to send them, such as town-councils, &c.; and think it would have been more influential. I feel rather averse to churches *as churches*, and individuals in their *ecclesiastical* relationships, meeting to discuss such questions; and nothing but my deep conviction of the magnitude of the evil which results from the Corn Laws, would have induced me to overcome these scruples, or, it may be, prejudices. All the ministers to whom I have spoken seem anxious for some demonstration on the great question, and for general petitioning of a very decided cast. I mean decided as to the terms in which the petitions are expressed. As your circulars are generally issued by this time, you will be able to gather, from the answers returned, what the general feeling is. For myself, while I like as well that churches, as churches, should have as little intercourse with the government or legislature as possible, I feel so anxious to have the Corn Monopoly abolished, and its desolating effects arrested, that I am almost willing to do *any thing*, if it might only tend to ensure such a result, even to vote for the Charter.

1. Yes. 2. Yes. 3. Yes.

1. I am, and have been for many years. 2. I was a delegate from Glasgow to the Manchester meeting in August last, and on my return I called my congregation together, and gave them an outline of our procedure. From the number that attended, and the spirit which they displayed, I would conclude that they are nearly unanimous. 3. I do. I had an opportunity of meeting in Manchester with at least *two* Ministers of the Kirk at the great conference in August. Might not they with some others be invited?

1. Yes. 2. I believe they are almost unanimous in wishing their Abolition. 3. Yes.

1. Yes. 2. Many of them being farmers are afraid of the consequences of such abolition. 3. Yes.

1. Yes; decidedly. 2. It is the opinion of the members of session expressed previously to the Manchester conference, and repeated last night. 3. Yes; and so do the members of session. The elders were called to meet after public worship yesterday, and we were all agreed as to the answers to queries. I would be happy were I able to attend the meeting, and to be of any service. It would be unreasonable on my part to offer any suggestions to those who have considered the matter so deliberately. May God bless your endeavours on behalf of the starving multitude.

1. Yes. 2. It is. 3. I do.

1. Decidedly in favour of this. 2. I cannot say that they are unanimous, but I think they are generally favourable. 3. No. I would highly approve of a meeting of persons from all parts of the country, without reference to their ecclesiastical and religious standing, at which the ministers and members of dissenting churches, in their civil capacity as citizens, might attend; but I object entirely to the plan of the proposed meeting chiefly on two grounds. *First*, That the meeting is to be a meeting of Dissenters only. But I object principally that the proposed meeting is to be a meeting of Dissenters in their *religious* capacity, namely, as ministers and church members; and this in reference to what is a matter not only of general politics, but in existing circumstances, of party politics. I know well that the subject is proposed to be taken up, not on political but purely on moral and religious grounds; nor am I ignorant that such grounds exist. But I know equally well, that there is hardly a question within the wide range of politics which has not religious aspects and bearings, as well as this one. If the church would have the state to refrain from intermeddling with ecclesiastical affairs, let her set the example, by refraining from intermeddling with political affairs.

1. I am. 2. I may say they are so unanimously. 3. I do not.

1. Cordially. 2. So far as I know they are unanimous. 3. Yes. A meeting was held here this evening, and the above answers were agreed to.

Questions.—1. Are you in favour of an entirely Free Trade in Corn? 2. Is your congregation nearly unanimous in wishing an entirely Free Trade in Corn? 3. Do you approve generally of the plan of the Meeting, or have you any suggestions to offer?

1. Most certainly. 2. All but unanimous. 3. Generally. My congregation met last evening, according to intimation from the pulpit, and appointed two of themselves and myself to represent them at the ensuing meeting. I am exceedingly sorry you have not invited the ministers of the Established Church. True, they would not attend; but this, for want of a better, is a good reason for inviting them. It would be the blow of a heavy hammer on the thick head of the Scottish people to drive home the lesson, that an Established Church is opposed to the temporal interests of the community. It were worth while to add another to the many practical proofs that the Teind Law, under which their stipends are payable, is a great Corn Law. I deprecate the sectarian aspect of the gathering; and I am fully persuaded it will detract from the benefit resulting from the meeting. The feeling I refer to may not trouble you in the city: it is quite a different thing in the country. I see already in my own locality the germ of the evil I wish you not to create. You may think it strange, after what I have said, that I should not urge you to send letters to the Kirk Clergy. You might invite them by public advertisement, and it were well to do it. There is another plan which would answer fully my idea, and I humbly beg to suggest it. Address an advertisement to the people of the Church of Scotland, expressing your regret that its ministers, with few exceptions, do not approve of the Anti-Corn Law movement, your cordial satisfaction that the body of its people are in favour of it, your earnest desire that they should co-operate with you in the cause which is not that of party, but of the nation, the united kingdom, yea, of the world; and urging every parish to hold a meeting, and send up a person to represent them at the meeting. As a matter of detail, it were well to prepare the statistics of the Iron Trade in Britain and on the Continent. This is a department of proof of the mischief of the Corn Law, that, as far as my observation extends, has not been sufficiently brought forward.

1. I am. 2. It is. 3. I do. It is my opinion, that unless good reasons be furnished for expecting a large attendance, the proposal should be abandoned, as a feeble expression given in such circumstances would, in my opinion, be unspeakably worse than none at all. To such a resolution as No VI. it is perhaps unnecessary for individuals to commit themselves before the conference assembles.

1. Decidedly in favour. 2. The elders and managers assure me that the congregation are unanimous. 3. I approve. Might not the public meeting commence at eleven instead of twelve, to do the subject more ample justice.

1. Yes. 2. Yes. 3. I do. Though I am quite aware that the 8th resolution precludes the introduction of any discussion *respecting an extension of the elective franchise*, in the contemplated meeting, yet, with the view of securing unanimity in the proceedings of the congregational meeting held this evening, I engaged to report, which I now do, that there is a growing impression on the minds of some of the people, that the Repeal of the Corn and Provision Laws is not likely to be reached, till they and their interests are more fully represented in the legislature of our country.

1. I am, and wish the establishment of Free Trade in Corn every prosperity. 2. They are altogether unanimous in wishing its Abolition. I do not know an exception. 3. I do.

1. Having left home without returning the schedule with which I was furnished by the Committee of Dissenters on the Corn Laws, and anxious that my answers to the queries be forwarded agreeably to request, I take the present method of informing the Committee, that I am agreeable to an Abolition of the Corn Laws; that I think the majority at least of my congregation are favourable to an entirely Free Trade in Corn, and that it is probable that, along with two members of the congregation appointed to represent the others, I will be present at the proposed public meeting in Edinburgh. I have no suggestions to offer on the resolutions of the Committee.

Questions.—1. Are you in favour of an entirely Free Trade in Corn? 2. Is your congregation nearly unanimous in wishing an entirely Free Trade in Corn? 3. Do you approve generally of the plan of the Meeting, or have you any suggestions to offer?

1. Yes, I am. 2. Yes, I believe they are. 3. Yes, I do, and think the state of the country calls for such meetings.

1. I am. 2. I believe there is a majority. Our farmers and proprietors do not. 3. I do.

1. Having no minister, the elders of the Church met, and agreed to give these answers:—2. Yes. 3. Yes.

1, 2. and 3. I have lost your printed circular about the Anti-Corn Law Meeting. I intend to come myself, and probably the session may send some others with me.

1. Yes. 2. I do not know one who is not of the same opinion with myself. 3. I do.

1. I am. 2. The greater proportion of the members of my congregation are agriculturalists, chiefly farmers on a larger or smaller scale; but I know that they are all in principle opposed to the Corn Laws, and would rejoice to see the trade in Corn freed from all restriction. 3. I have carefully considered the circular, and fully approve of the plan proposed.

1. Most certainly. 2. It is. 3. Yes.

1. Yes; coupled with the Abolition of every Tax that falls exclusively upon farmers and proprietors of land; such as cess, teinds, schoolmaster's salary, and that portion of poor rates falling upon proprietors of land exclusively, &c. 2. The great majority; but they are not unanimous in wishing the abolition. 3. The plan seems good; but I have my doubts about the meeting. It brings ministers together rather as politicians than as ministers. I will think of the whole matter, and when the time comes act as duty seems to direct.

1. Yes. 2. They are not nearly unanimous. 3. (No answer given.)

1. I am decidedly in favour of the Total, and if it be found practicable, the Immediate, Abolition of the impolitic and inhuman Corn and Provision Laws. 2. The great majority of the congregation I serve are of my own opinions on this subject. The farmers, in this as well as in most other cases, are most strongly opposed to any movement for alteration or repeal. 3. I most cordially and entirely approve. Owing to my absence at some winter communion occasions, I am late (I trust not too late, however) in notifying my sentiments. I beg you to forgive my seeming indifference or negligence, and oblige.

1. Unquestionably. 2. All but unanimous. 3. Yes.

1. I am decidedly in favour of the Total and speedy Abolition of the Corn and Provision Laws. 2. My congregation is, to the best of my knowledge, without an exception, against these Laws. As a congregation, we have petitioned for three successive years against them. The last petition in May had nearly 800 signatures, and we have resolved to petition again. 3. I approve generally of the plan; but I think the morning meeting should commence at 10 o'clock, instead of 12. Persons coming from a distance would like to state their opinions, and if the sittings are so short, there will be no time for this. I cannot approve of Resolution VI.; it is unjust. The members present cannot know what the Resolutions are, till proposed at the public meeting, and are therefore precluded from expressing their sentiments. No such restriction was imposed at the great meeting in Manchester. The Resolutions alone come through the Committee. This is proper. But no restraint was imposed on any member expressing his dissent, or moving an amendment. True, no amendment was moved to any motion, as every one seemed to meet the universal mind. This Resolution should be altered.

1. Yes. 2. Yes. 3. Yes.

1. Yes; decidedly in favour of it. 2. I am of opinion that our congregation are entirely unanimous in wishing the Total Abolition of the Corn Laws. 3. So far as I am able to judge, I think the plan, to the extent it goes, good.

1. Yes. 2. Yes. 3. Yes.

Questions.—1. Are you in favour of an entirely Free Trade in Corn? 2. Is your congregation nearly unanimous in wishing an entirely Free Trade in Corn? 3. Do you approve generally of the plan of the Meeting, or have you any suggestions to offer?

1. I am; and think Total Abolition the only change worth struggling for. 2. I believe that to be the wish of all in my congregation, who have any knowledge of the *operation* of these Laws. 3. The expediency of the meeting being admitted, I see no objection to the plan proposed for conducting it. If the ministers of a few of the principal towns, were to meet in their respective localities, pass resolutions to get up congregational or district petitions—issue a circular—say from Edinburgh—to their brethren in the country, urging a similar course, as many petitions might be secured as by the more expensive movement of the great central conference.

1. Yes. 2. (No answer given.) 3. I disapprove of the proposed meeting. Churches and ministers seem to me to step out of their proper sphere, when, *as such*, they interfere with the politics of the world. The proposal by which their objection is met, seems to me in no degree to obviate the difficulty. It would directly tend to divide our congregations into two opposing parties, and the churches of our country are already so divided, that it would be neither safe nor proper to throw into the midst of them a new bond of contention.

1. I look upon the Corn Laws as the ruin of the Manufacturing and Commercial interests of this country, and desire their Total Abolition. 2. I believe that the members of my congregation who have attended to the subject are with very few exceptions of the same mind. 3. I regret exceedingly that the circumstances in which my congregation and myself are placed at present, deprive us of the gratification of taking part in the Convention at Edinburgh, the plan of which seems to me altogether fair and prudent.

1. Most decidedly. 2. The opinion of my congregation on this subject is evidenced by their having sent me to represent them at the Manchester Conference. 3. The plan seems, on the whole, well arranged. It seems to me desirable that members should be earnestly *recommended* to provide themselves with *documentary evidence* from their respective localities in support of the statements to be presented by them; the more especially as Anti-Corn Law Advocates are often charged with exaggeration, and the statistics of this great question have as yet been very partially collected.

1. Having received the Anti-Corn Law Circular from Edinburgh, I thought the most regular way of proceeding was to lay it before our session. A meeting of session was held for that purpose yesterday evening; and the Circular, after being read, formed the subject of earnest and prolonged consideration. There was but one opinion expressed as to the impolicy and iniquity of the Corn and Provision Laws, and the obligations resting on all members of the state to seek, by proper means, the Abolition of them. Much regret was also expressed at the idea of our congregation not being represented at any demonstration made to attain that object; and all were of opinion, that the great body of our church members hold the same views. On the other hand, much difficulty was felt as to the proposed mode of giving effect to our sentiments. If these Laws, as being unjust, are to be congregationally opposed, then, it appeared to some members of session, other unjust laws, and laws about the injustice of which there is not the same measure of unanimity, may be obtruded on the attention of our congregations, to the great hazard of disquieting and dividing them. No plan of convening the members was held to obviate this objection, as the same plan could be followed in pushing any other scheme of political reformation. There was another difficulty felt, arising, perhaps, from misapprehension of the intended arrangements. 'Every dissenting minister in Scotland' is to be invited; and in that case, it appeared to some, we must meet with Roman Catholics and Socinians as *Ministers*, or those parties must be excluded, *contrary to the declared constitution of the meeting*. Neither of these alterations was considered agreeable. On these grounds, the session were reluctantly constrained to pause in acceding to the Edinburgh proposals, and to defer an absolute decision, in the hope of such difficulties being somehow removed or mitigated.

Questions.—1. Are you in favour of an entirely Free Trade in Corn? 2. Is your congregation nearly unanimous in wishing an entirely Free Trade in Corn? 3. Do you approve generally of the plan of the Meeting, or have you any suggestions to offer?

1 and 2. In reply to your communication, I have to state that I am in favour of the Abolition of the Corn Laws; that I have reason to believe the greater part of my people are, and that I shall endeavour, with two of my members, to be present at the proposed meeting.—I am, yours, &c.

1. From my heart I hate the Corn Laws, and I firmly believe that the flock like them no better than the pastor. Our session met the other evening, and were unanimous on the subject, *thus far*. I am not against, but decidedly favourable to, the measure of *Christians* speaking out on the subject; and of a confluence of the piety with the policy of the land for sweeping away these wicked laws for ever. I have my doubts as to a dissenting movement, *per se*. Nor can I as yet say whether our congregation will be represented in the Conference. *But I think it altogether probable that it will.* I sincerely wish that it may please God to direct our measures; for I fear we may soon approach a crisis of far greater magnitude than that which presses now.

1. Decidedly. I am in favour of an entirely Free Trade in every thing. 2. I believe my congregation are nearly unanimous in wishing the Abolition of these Laws. A few of the farmers appear to have some fears in consequence of the existing leases, but I have not met with one who approved of the Corn Law itself. 3. I am sorry that the meeting should have a party aspect. The established ministers, as a body, might not have attended, but still, I think, that if ministers, as ministers, ought to be asked, they should not have been passed. I am, however, of opinion, that it would be of importance to have Anti-Corn Law Societies formed throughout the country, from which Delegates could at any time be sent to attend such meetings. Thus, members of all communions might be found to work together; and, in my judgment, the moral effects would be greater than can be expected from meetings of any one class. At the same time, I feel strongly disposed to give up all objections, if, by doing so, I could contribute in any degree to the object desired.

1. I am. 2. There are only a small number who advocate the Corn Law Monopoly. They are but a small fractional part, however. 3. I do most heartily approve of it.

1. I am, decidedly. 2. I believe they are unanimous. I don't know one who would oppose their *Total Abolition*. 3. I do.

1, 2, 3. I am in favour of an entirely Free Trade in Corn; but I do not think that christian congregations, or sessions, or presbyteries, or synods should take up the question; and I have very grave doubts whether a minister of the Gospel, with all the anxiety which he must feel to see the Government do its duty in this matter, can, with advantage to the great work to which he has been set apart, come forward as an advocate for the Abolition of the present system. I especially disapprove of clerical associations for the furtherance of such an object.

1. Yes, if accompanied by an equitable adjustment of the national debt, a commensurate reduction in the amount of taxation, and proper measures for securing a just and satisfactory termination to all existing contracts between landlord and tenant, debtors and creditors, &c., which would be affected by the proposed abolition. Without these, I believe, it would increase the sufferings of the poor, produce unmingled evil, and end in instant revolution. 2. Unanimous, without a single exception. I am thoroughly acquainted with the sentiments of all the members on this subject. 3. No. Such meetings can be productive of no good. 'The Injustice and Immoral tendency of the Corn and Provision Laws' are as well known as you can make them; they have been *experimentally* felt by the people, and meetings to do good, must go to the root of the evil, and endeavour to do away with *exclusive legislation*, and the exercise of *irresponsible power*, the source from whence the Corn. monopoly, and every other oppressive measure, has emanated.

Questions.—1. Are you in favour of an entirely Free Trade in Corn? 2. Is your congregation nearly unanimous in wishing an entirely Free Trade in Corn? 3. Do you approve generally of the plan of the Meeting, or have you any suggestions to offer?

1. I am. 2. Nearly unanimous. 3. I do.

1. I consider the Corn and Provision Laws a piece of the greatest injustice, and am willing to do every thing in my power for the establishment of Free Trade. 2. So far as I know, my congregation are almost without exception of the same mind. 3. I approve cordially of the plan proposed. There is the most anxious desire on the part of the most influential of my people for the repeal of the Provision Laws; but a strong conviction that more information regarding their true nature and operation is needed. Were dissenting ministers *generally* to lift their voices at home, and give this information, as well as *perseveringly* sound the note of condemnation against these Laws, I believe the voice of the country would become far more loud against them, and they would soon be repealed. I confess I do not place much confidence in *merely* meeting to express our opinions together, if we are next to silent when we separate. In this town we are suffering most severely from the operation of these oppressive Laws, and I pray God that your efforts for their repeal may be successful.

1. Most decidedly. 2. I have never directly sounded my congregation on the subject. Unanimity is more than could be affirmed, but I have no doubt of a large majority. 3. Yes. Members will attend, but not as *nominated representatives of the church*, because I hesitate about the propriety of introducing it as a *church question*. I would not say 'no,' but I fear I cannot attend.

1. I am in favour of the Total Abolition of the Corn and Provision Laws, and the establishment of entirely Free Trade in Corn, and every other article of Commerce. 2. As far as I am aware, they are all Corn Law Repealers. 3. I cordially agree to the plan of the proposed meeting. I am unwilling that any division should occur in the meeting; but it is my own opinion, and also that of my congregation, that no alteration of the Corn Laws will ever be effected without an extension of the suffrage. I shall not, however, be absent from the meeting, though this question should not be discussed.

1. Yes, a Total Abolition, and no Restrictions. 2. So far as I am acquainted with the sentiments of my congregation, they are unanimous in wishing a Free Trade in Corn. 3. My best wishes will be with you. May the Disposer of all events guide you in all your deliberations.

1. I am happy to inform you that I, along with two brethren, will attend the proposed conference on the Corn Laws in Edinburgh. We shall come as the representatives of a goodly number, and I have some hope of a newly formed association. Hoping this will not be altogether too late, I am, &c.

1. We are *favourable* to the *Speedy* and *Total Abolition* of the *unjust laws*, by which Free Trade in Corn and Provisions are restricted. 2. We are decidedly unanimous in finding, that the restrictions complained of have already been *hurtful*, and may ultimately prove *ruinous* to all *classes* in our *country*. 3. We approve of the plan as explained, and *gratefully commend all the public-spirited gentlemen* who have given the *healing measure* their *countenance* and AID. The *benevolent spirit manifested*, the *seasonable opportunity embraced*, along with the *very cautious manner*, and *suitable means proposed*, preclude the necessity of any suggestions.

1 Decidedly. 2. It is. 3. I do.

1. Yes. 2. I believe they are unanimous. 3. Yes. I think that in one of the resolutions, the meeting should recommend the transmission of petitions from all factories and public works, and that the attention of employers should be earnestly requested to this. It would be well to propose a short form of petition, which, with modifications according to circumstances, might be adopted by the factories. Were this done, I have no doubt that it would be the means of securing a number of petitions. It would also be of importance to procure from the 'League,' at Manchester, or otherwise, a supply of cheap tracts, which might be purchased by employers, and distributed among their workers.

Questions.—1. Are you in favour of an entirely Free Trade in Corn? 2. Is your congregation nearly unanimous in wishing an entirely Free Trade in Corn? 3. Do you approve generally of the plan of the Meeting, or have you any suggestions to offer?

1. I am favourable to the Total Abolition of these Laws; but would not oppose a Moderate Fixed Duty. 2. Yes. 3. Yes; so far as it accords with my opinion expressed above.

1. Yes. But would wish as little injury done to farmers, &c. as possible in the mode in which the change is effected. 2. After inquiry, I believe they are all desirous of Free Trade in Corn. 3. Yes, they appear to embody all that is necessary for the efficient transaction of the business. I am very glad that this matter has been taken up by you and your friends; we are so depressed by these Laws, that we have difficulty in meeting current expenses, with the utmost economy we can use. The population are chiefly weavers and miners. Hitherto, with great exertions, and the most humble and homely fare, we have been able to provide things honest. When I read your communication to a few of the male members last night, a poor man with a large family offered at once to go, and if no one would aid him, he would surely be able, in one way or another, to meet the expense himself. We will be glad to hear that your plan is approved of by all our brethren. We mean to make a collection to meet the expense; but as we are all poor, and crushed by the wicked Corn and Provision Laws, we may come short, and must look to our more favoured brethren to aid us should it be so.

1. I am. 2. Quite unanimous. 3. I do, upon the whole. It is my opinion, that vote by ballot, short parliaments, and universal suffrage, are essentially necessary in order to the Total Repeal of the Corn Laws; and I would, therefore, suggest that the Edinburgh meeting 'come out' for these openly and at once; and this without naming the Charter or the Chartists.

1. I have long been opposed to the Corn and Provision Laws, as being morally evil, and politically wrong. 2. I cannot exactly state the sentiments of the church. 3. I am not prepared to answer decidedly.

1. Yes. 2. Yes. 3. I do.

1. I am in favour of Total Abolition, but would have gladly accepted the measure of the late ministry as a preliminary. 2. I have no precise means of knowing what are the sentiments of my congregation generally on this point. To say that they have come to an *intelligent* decision on the point is more than I would affirm of the majority of those who will attend the conference. 3. I have considerable doubts respecting the necessity and expediency of the proposed conference; but none as to the duty of immediately attempting to get every Dissenting congregation in Scotland to petition on the subject. I believe Dissenting congregations will be found to have acquiesced, without much examination, in the prevalent opinion, that the Corn Laws are at the foundation of our national difficulties, and will readily sign petitions against them. It would be useful, and I think necessary, that some suggestions were offered to the pastors of churches, respecting the framing of these petitions. I am further of opinion, that every minister who has a vote in a burgh or county represented by a man known to be unfavourable to the Abolition of the Corn Laws, ought (as an elector) to address him in earnest but respectful terms.

1. I am. 2. They are. 3. I do.

COUNTIES OF LINLITHGOW AND DUMBARTON.

Answers from 16 *Ministers.*

Answers.—1. Entirely so. I am persuaded, that these laws, if long retained, will prove as ruinous to land-owners themselves, as they have been, and are, to all other classes of society. 2. I do not know; but suspect not. Farmers have been taught to consider them a protection. 3. I entirely approve; and have confidence both in the men and the measures.

1. Yes. 2. I think the intelligent part of the community unanimous, or almost so, in wishing an entirely Free Trade in Corn. 3. I do.

Questions.—1. Are you in favour of an entirely Free Trade in Corn? 2. Is your congregation nearly unanimous in wishing an entirely Free Trade in Corn? 3. Do you approve generally of the plan of the Meeting, or have you any suggestions to offer?

1. I am; decidedly. 2. So far as I know the sentiments of my people, they are almost unanimous for an alteration of the Corn Laws, and a large majority are for their Total Repeal. 3. I do.

1. It is my firm conviction, that the Corn Laws ought to be abolished without delay. 2. It is my opinion, that those of the congregation here are opposed to the Corn Laws, and that they would rejoice to see them speedily and entirely abolished. 3. I approve of the plan of the proposed meeting. The measures already adopted, if carried out, are calculated to promote the important object in view.

1. I am in favour of the Total Abolition of these Laws, and the establishment of a Free Trade in Corn. 2. I have not had an opportunity of consulting my congregation particularly; but I am persuaded that almost all of them, if not all of them, are in favour of Abolition and Free Trade. 3. I cordially approve of it. I have no suggestions to offer. The terms of the minute seem to me excellent. I hope that the meeting will be an overflowing one, and that it will not be held in vain.

1, 2, and 3. I cordially agree with the design of the proposed meeting. All restrictions on Trade and Provisions I consider to be, at once, contrary to the best interests of men, the welfare of the community, Christianity, and common sense. In my limited sphere and circumstances, it is little I can do; and my various infirmities must prevent or impede attendance on any public meeting. The propriety of it is evident, as making known the circumstances, the necessities, and desires of the nation. With best regards and wishes, &c.

1. Yes. 2. Nearly unanimous. 3. I approve, generally.

1. I am. Yet I have doubts whether a Gradual Repeal might not prove safer than Immediate Abolition. 2. The great majority are decidedly in favour of the Total Abolition of all Restrictions. 3. I cordially approve of the objects and resolutions mentioned in the Circular.

1. I am in favour of these measures. 2. I think they are. 3. I have only to say, that I am apprehensive that agitation and excitement may have an injurious influence on the minds of the lower orders; and would respectfully recommend, that all addresses be delivered in the purest christian meekness; that nothing disrespectful of our laws, or of those in power, be uttered; but that meekness and patience be pressed on all.

1. Owing to some oversight, I did not receive a copy of the first Circular, nor have I ever seen it; and, therefore, I am not aware of the queries that were put, and the suggestions that were asked for. This is my apology for the remarks which I now make. I can state that the great majority of my people, as well as of the liberals around me, are in favour of the Total and Immediate Repeal of the Corn and Provision Laws, and of a Free Trade in Food; as is evident from the fact, that they requested me to attend the Manchester Conference, and paid the expenses of my journey. The district where I reside furnishes a fine example of the working of these Laws, and of the necessity of Free Trade in Food; as, with a population of 12,000, sustained by manufactures, we are surrounded by hills, and are dependent for the greater portion of our food on the importation of Irish Corn. It makes no difference in the principle, whether grain be imported from Ireland or from Poland; and if the importation from Ireland were either fettered by high duties, or prohibited, it would be equivalent to a sentence of starvation or of banishment to three-fourths of the people residing in Dumbarton and the Vale of Leven. The population in this district have increased nearly 5000 within the last ten years, and would go on increasing, were employment and the means of subsistence easily attained; but if matters remain as they are at present, the population will decrease rapidly, as those who can get away are leaving the place, and emigrating to other lands. I trust that, besides other documents, the committee will prepare an address to be issued to the public, explanatory of the principle and operation of the Corn

Questions.—1. Are you in favour of an entirely Free Trade in Corn? 2. Is your congregation nearly unanimous in wishing an entirely Free Trade in Corn? 3. Do you approve generally of the plan of the Meeting, or have you any suggestions to offer?

and Provision Laws. Such a paper would, I am persuaded, be productive of much good. The statements and discussions in the newspapers pre-suppose a degree of knowledge on these points, which intercourse and conversation assure me, is not possessed by many. These Laws seem to them involved in a species of mystery; they know and feel that they are oppressive; but the errors and prejudices which exist in their minds, prevent the public discussions from having the effect on them which they would otherwise produce. This ignorance is not limited to those in the lower ranks of society. What I would take the liberty of suggesting is an address on such topics as the following:—1. The principle and operation of the present scale of duties; showing that they prevent the importation and sale of foreign grain, till the price in this country reaches at least 67s. or 68s. per quarter. 2. The cost of the Corn and Provision Laws: proving, from good testimony and numerical calculations, that this is upwards of L.50,000,000 annually. 3. The persons who get this enormous sum—showing that, with the exception of the small fraction paid to the government on the foreign Corn *actually* sold, the landowners and the monopolists,—the least useful, because the unproductive class,—pocket it. 4. That it is the working classes chiefly who pay this money; the principle here being, that, as families of equal number, whether high or low, consume nearly equal quantities of Corn, the tax presses heavily according to the smallness, and lightly according to the greatness, of the income. 5. The manner in which these Laws limit Trade at home and abroad. They limit the Trade at home to the amount of the money which they cost; on the principle, that whatever money is taken to buy provisions, is withdrawn from manufactures; and whatever, on the contrary, is disengaged and saved from provisions, is expended on articles of manufacture. And they limit our foreign Trade by preventing our merchants from taking the produce of the soil—the only thing which many can give—in exchange for their goods, and by provoking other nations to impose high prohibitory duties on the importation of British manufactures. 6. Answer and remove some objections, as that the Abolition of these Laws would reduce the rate of wages, and that what is paid to the landowners is expended by them in the purchase of goods, while in fact it is utterly lost. 7. Their iniquity; as opposed alike to the revealed will and the Providence of God. 8. The duty of seeking their Immediate and Total Abolition, if we wish to see the people well employed, the interests of education and religion flourishing, the heathen evangelized, and virtue, contentment, and happiness, prevailing in the land. I beg that you will excuse this long letter. The want of the opportunity which the reply to the first Circular would have afforded, and the deep interest which I take in this matter, have induced me thus to trespass on your time and patience. I am fully convinced that the Abolition of these Laws would permanently relieve, and brighten the prospects of the country; and that the continuance of them will exhaust our strength, destroy our active energies, and sink us deeper and deeper in the scale of degradation and suffering.

1. Most decidedly. 2. They are nearly unanimous in the desire for both objects. 3. The plan seems excellent.

1. Most decidedly. 2. I believe that at one time they were almost unanimous on these points; but Chartist orators, and Chartist newspapers, have led numbers of them to suspect that the Abolition of these Laws, and the establishment of a Free Trade in Corn, would lead to the reduction of wages; a subject on which operatives—of which my congregation is chiefly composed—are peculiarly sensitive. Numbers, I think, would sign such a petition; but others will sign for nothing short of the *whole Charter*. 3. I have read these papers carefully throughout, and I approve very highly of every thing therein recommended, and in the meantime, you may rest assured that you have my warmest wishes and prayers for your success.

Questions.—1. Are you in favour of an entirely Free Trade in Corn? 2. Is your congregation nearly unanimous in wishing an entirely Free Trade in Corn? 3. Do you approve generally of the plan of the Meeting, or have you any suggestions to offer?

1. I was cordially in favour of the measure introduced by the late government, and still continue to be so. 2. There may be some little aversion in some quarters, indifference in others, an extended impression in favour of a change, and a respectable number in favour of Abolition. 3. I cordially approve of the proposed meeting The time is come when something energetic requires to be done. The arrangements appear to be admirable and liberal. I much approve of opening the meetings with prayer. Our ultimate trust must still be in God. If your language had been a little less sweeping, it would have included a section of the Liberal party, which it appears to exclude. I trust, if the meeting shall issue an address, they will not, like the committee of another conference, say that we are not suffering under the just judgment of God,—an expression which, though its meaning can be seen, is extremely unhappy.

1. I am, most decidedly. 2. I think I may say they are. The large majority are earnest for the change; the rest are becoming prepared, I think, to acquiesce. 3. I do. I beg leave to express an idea irrelevant, perhaps, to what is required to be noticed here, but bearing on the general object. A numerous class, both of the agricultural and operative manufacturing population never see any of the newspapers, &c. in which Free Trade in Corn is advocated. I have found the circulation of two or three dozen of Noel's Plea for the Poor produce a good effect. Something prepared which could be sold for a penny, advocating the full extent of the change required, presenting concisely the argument according to its present aspects, and combining the power and pathos of Noel, if widely diffused, would do great service.

1. Yes; most decidedly. 2. Yes. 3. Yes. I have no suggestions, being very well satisfied with the gentlemen with whom the preliminary meeting have already lodged the business.

1. Yes; in favour of their Entire Abolition. 2. I have every reason to think that my congregation are heartily unanimous in wishing the Total Abolition of these Corn Laws. 3. As far as I have had time to examine the plan, I perfectly agree with it.

COUNTIES OF CAITHNESS AND ORKNEY.

Answers from 9 Ministers.

Answers.—1. As an enemy of all monopolies, both secular and ecclesiastical, I am decidedly in favour of the Total Abolition of these Laws, and the establishment of an entirely Free Trade in Corn. 2. As far as I am acquainted with the sentiments of the congregation, it is my opinion that they are quite unanimous in wishing the Corn Laws abolished, and Free Trade in Corn established. 3. I very much approve of the plan of the proposed meeting. I think the proposed arrangements are very judicious, and from the names of those I see as the leaders in the movement, I have no doubt but, that if the meeting take place, as I hope it will, these arrangements shall as judiciously be carried into effect.

1. Yes. 2. I cannot speak very positively on this, not having ascertained the general sentiment, but think, so far as the question is understood by them, it is. 3. I do.

1. Yes. I am in favour of Total Abolition. 2. So far as I know, the congregation are unanimously in favour of Total Abolition. 3. I approve generally.

1. Yes. 2. Yes. 3. Yes. Do not Churchmen need Cheap Bread as well as Dissenters? Why are they not invited?

1. Yes; I am. 2. It is my opinion that the great body of the people are in favour of Total Abolition. 3. Yes

1. Yes. 2. Entirely unanimous, so far as I know. 3. I highly approve of it.

Questions.—1 Are you in favour of an entirely Free Trade in Corn? 2. Is your congregation nearly unanimous in wishing an entirely Free Trade in Corn? 3. Do you approve generally of the plan of the Meeting, or have you any suggestions to offer?

1. Yes. 2. As far as I know, they are in favour of Free Trade. 3. Yes.

1. Yes. 2. I know not any except one, who do not wish the Total Abolition of these Laws, and are not desirous of a Free Trade in Corn. 3. I do.

1. I am. 2. It is. 3. I do approve, and have confidence in the wisdom of the Committee. In my communication relating to the meeting at Manchester, I suggested the importance of employing some talented agent to deliver lectures on the subject in all towns in the north, where counter prejudices prevail, and I am still of the same opinion.

COUNTIES OF PEEBLES AND SELKIRK.

Answers from 9 Ministers.

Answers.—1. Most decidedly so. 2. I firmly believe this to be the wish of the majority, and that the minority is daily decreasing in number. 3. I do, very much.

1. On the principles and for the reason stated by Dr Pye Smith, I would plead for Free Trade all over the world in every thing. 3. I could have wished that the scheme had embraced Churchmen as well as Dissenters, some of whom are most zealous in this cause.

1. I am. 2. That part of my congregation, perhaps the most numerous, which is composed of people engaged in agricultural and pastoral pursuits, I believe, are mostly favourable to a protecting duty on Corn. On the other hand, the mechanics and tradesmen are, I believe, generally in favour of Free Trade. 3. I have doubts of either churches or assemblies of ministers, *as such*, discussing such questions; and while I am not certain of the propriety of the meeting referred to in the circular,—while its tendency, if it take place, may be to injure dissenting congregations in the country, by making the influence of landlords, farmers, and others, to bear against them. I never hesitate, in private, to denounce the Corn Laws, and have done so, more than once, from the pulpit.

1. Yes. 2. Yes. 3. Yes. I have sufficient confidence in the gentlemen forming the committee.

1. I am, decidedly. 2. I should think nearly unanimous. There are exceptions certainly. 3. Generally, I do. The latter part of No V. may be questionable as to its propriety. I may harmonize in my views of the Corn Laws, and be able to act in concert regarding them with fellow subjects who could not say Amen to my devotional addresses to our common Creator. Even on the principle of restricting the meeting to Dissenters, I can see no reason for the exclusion of *any class* of Dissenters. And whatever may be alleged as to *clergymen* of the Established Church, I could have wished the meeting to have comprehended such of the members as may be favourable to the Abolition of the Provision Laws.

1. Yes. 2. Yes. 3. I cordially approve of.

1. Yes: and I have proved this, by signing a local petition to that effect, as an inhabitant of this town. 2. I have no doubt that the great majority wish for these measures. I know that they are not unanimous; but how nearly so I cannot tell. 3. No: for it will inevitably be confounded by very many, with a meeting of an ecclesiastical, and even clerical, character. All *such* interference with matters not *strictly and evidently* religious, I have disapproved and opposed, in congregations, presbyteries, and synods, or in any way but as *citizens*. I am far from objecting to *ministers* interfering in that character. On the supposition that I could fall in with the general measure, I should think the arrangements very judicious and proper; except, perhaps, the restriction in Resolution I to *Dissenters;* as many *members*, though very few *ministers* of the Establishment, are friendly to the proposed measures; and the restriction in the latter part of Resolution VI. absolutely requiring the sanction of the Committee.

Questions.—1. Are you in favour of an entirely Free Trade in Corn? 2. Is your congregation nearly unanimous in wishing an entirely Free Trade in Corn? 3. Do you approve generally of the plan of the Meeting, or have you any suggestions to offer?

1. I am; though I would, for the present, submit to the proposal of the Melbourne government. 2. I cannot say 'unanimous,' for I have not ascertained this; but I can say, they are very generally so; and this will be seen. 3. I do approve; and think the measure expedient and proper. No suggestions at present occur to me; and I think the parties in whose hands the affair is, are very fit to conduct it.

1. I am quite clear as to the impolicy of the present Corn Laws; but whether an entirely Free Trade in Corn, or its admission at a low fixed duty, would be best for the country, considering all circumstances, I am not qualified to judge. 2. Perhaps three-fourths of the members of my congregation—being persons depending on trade and manufactures—will be found zealous for the Total Abolition of the Corn Laws. The remaining one-fourth being of the agricultural class, are strongly prejudiced on the other side. 3. I by no means approve of the plan of the conference, in as far as it brings forward ministers and churches, to agitate, in that capacity, a question of national policy; or even in so far as it may call on ministers to take a side, or an active part in a cause, in regard to which their people may be conscientiously of different opinions.

COUNTY OF PERTH.

Answers from 39 Ministers.

Answers.—1. Yes. 2. I should think a decided majority of them are in favour of the Abolition. 3. I Do not wish to express an opinion.

1. I am in favour of the immediate and Total Abolition of these iniquitous Laws. 2. It is my opinion that my small congregation, *without one exception*, are indeed, desirous, for the immediate and Total Abolition of these Laws. 3. Yes.

1. Yes; most decidedly. 2. My opinion is that, with a few exceptions, my people wish the Abolition of these Laws. 3. The meeting proposed is a meeting of *Dissenters*,—the matter to which their attention is to be directed is *political*, and my opinion is, that Dissenters, as such, should confine their united efforts to matters strictly *ecclesiastical*. My opinion is, that petitions should be sent from all parts of the country where they can be obtained. I feel much indebted to you, Gentlemen in Edinburgh, and to yourself in particular, for the care you have exercised, and the labours you have performed, to serve the interests of Dissenters.

1. Yes. 2. If not unanimous, a large majority are. 3. Yes.

1. Decidedly so. 2. Such is my opinion, confirmed by a public meeting held last night. 3. I Approve cordially of the meeting, and the plan on which it is proposed to be conducted; and have nothing to add by way of suggestion.

1. This Congregation at present has no minister. 2. Yes. 3. The congregation cordially approve of the plan of the proposed meeting, and pray that the efforts of those who are labouring to abolish the iniquitous Corn Laws, may be crowned with abundant success.

1 Yes; provided tenants are protected by the Legislature during the current leases. 2. The labouring classes, I believe, are generally so. The farming class would, in general, desire a small fixed duty, to be gradually reduced, until it is totally abolished. 3 If it meets with sufficient encouragement, it may be useful.

1 Yes. 2. Yes. 3. Yes.

1 I am, most decidedly. 2. They are *very* nearly unanimous. 3. I do.

1. I am. 2 I have not made any direct inquiries, but I am inclined to think that none of them are for upholding the system presently practised, and a majority are for Total Abolition. 3 I approve of the plan of the proposed meeting.

Questions.—Are you in favour of an entirely Free Trade in Corn? 2. Is your congregation nearly unanimous in wishing an entirely Free Trade in Corn? 3. Do you approve generally of the plan of the Meeting, or have you any suggestions to make?

1. Yes; decidedly so. 2. I am certain they are nearly unanimous. 3. I do.

1. Yes. 2. Yes. 3. Yes.

1. I am in favour of the establishment of an entirely Free Trade in Corn. 2. Our congregation are nearly unanimous in wishing the Total Abolition of the Corn Laws. 3. I approve highly of the proposed meeting.

1. Most decidedly in favour of it. 2. I believe that ninety-nine out of every hundred of them have the same opinion with myself. 3. I hesitate a good deal about the propriety of Dissenters, or even Christians in general, taking separate ground about any question not ecclesiastical. I would greatly prefer national, to sectional or ecclesiastical agitation; and if it were judged desirable to give prominence, in a general petition, to christian congregations, the names connected with each could be inserted by themselves, and headed by the name of the congregation to which they belong. I question, however, if even this be worth while. It is *fear of man*, rather than *respect for man*, that is to carry the question in our present Parliament, if it be carried at all; and men connected with no church, are more feared than men who are. To me your scheme is, on the whole, less exceptionable than the Manchester one.

1. Yes. 2. Yes. 3. Yes; I very much approve of the plan proposed.

1. Yes. 2. During my limited acquaintance with my congregation, I have heard several express their sentiments decidedly in favour of Total Abolition, but *not one* against it. 3. I must submit strong apprehensions of the prudence of the plan proposed; and I submit to you, whether the plan adopted for the Manchester meeting was not more prudent, as well as generous,—to issue invitations to all denominations, Established as well as Dissenting; and then come who might, the meeting, at any rate, would not have, before the public eye, an entirely sectarian aspect. At the same time, I repose much confidence in the judgment of the Committee, some of whom I have the pleasure of knowing.

1. Yes. 2. Yes. 3. Yes.

1. Yes, I am; believing them to be most injurious to the poor, and, indeed, to the real interests of all. 2. Perhaps the greater number are. 3. I heartily approve of it, and wish it God-speed. I cannot see cause for any suggestions.

1. I am favourable. 2. I believe they are quite unanimous. 3. I do.

1. Yes; *most decidedly*, any thing else will be persevering in an iniquitous course. 2. So far as I can ascertain, my congregation are unanimous, *as far as they understand the subject*. 3. The plan is excellent, and has my entire approbation and gratitude, for the activity of many *worthy characters*.

1. Yes, entirely. 2. They are nearly unanimous. 3. I approve fully of the object, and I am convinced of the necessity of a strong and united effort; but I regret that the movement is confined to Dissenters, as though the Corn and Provision Laws were a Dissenters', and not a national grievance. This aspect of the movement, though not intended, will tend to divide the friends of Total Abolition. This evil may not be much felt where the Dissenting interest is strong; but in places where Dissenters can act efficiently only in union with others holding the same views, the call upon them to appear as a distinct body would, if complied with, be injurious to the common cause. I am of opinion that some plan should have been proposed, with a view to move the whole religious community of Scotland. The crisis is most important. In proportion as the people are depressed by poverty, their power of opposing misrule is diminished. If things continue much longer as they are, either the yoke will be confirmed, or the remedy will be sought, not by a constitutional effort, but by insurrection and revolution.

1. I am. 2. It is. 3. I approve generally. No suggestion occurs to me, unless it were, that a list of questions as to facts should be circulated, on which every minister might prepare himself.

Questions.—Are you in favour of an entirely Free Trade in Corn? 2. Is your congregation nearly unanimous in wishing an entirely Free Trade in Corn? 3. Do you approve generally of the plan of the Meeting, or have you any suggestions to offer?

1. Yes, and of all other monopolies. I adhere to the principle of Free Trade, and do not think that the Abolition of the Corn Laws, apart from other and deeper changes, would secure much benefit to the community. 2. My congregation in general are, of course, against the Corn Laws, and do not anticipate any advantage from their Abolition, but wish more extensive reforms. 3. I do not approve of the plan of the proposed meeting. I regard it as political. The plea of humanity is an argument by which ministers may defend themselves for interfering, as ministers, for the removal of any other civil or political, real or supposed, grievance.

1. I am very anxious for the Total Abolition of the Laws mentioned in the opposite column. 2. The members of my congregation, I believe, are unanimous for the Abolition of these Laws. 3. I cordially approve of the plan proposed.

1. Yes. 2. Yes, so far as I know. 3. Yes.

1. Yes, I am for a Free Trade in Corn, and no monopoly. 2 Our congregation are almost all against monopoly. 3. I highly approve.

1. I am. 2. Nearly, if not quite. 3. I do.

1. 'Mr * * *'s time is so taken up with the better concerns of his people, that he has no time to attend to Corn Laws. The Rev. J. P. Smith is a man of no authority with me; a man that can leave out and take in what he thinks proper of the sacred canon cannot be revered by me.'—[This is given *verbatim*, only suppressing the name of the author. It is presumed the reference to Dr Pye Smith is made in consequence of a printed copy of the letter from that highly-gifted and much-respected minister to Mr Cobden, M.P., having been inclosed in the circulars from the Committee to all the ministers whom they addressed, including the reverend gentleman, whose 'time is so taken up with the better concerns of his people, that he has no time to attend to the Corn Laws.']

1. Yes. 2. Yes. 3. Yes.

1. I am for an entirely Free Trade in Corn. 2. It is my opinion that there is a considerable majority for their *entire* Abolition. 3. I do approve generally. Perhaps, Article VI. is too arbitrary. Several of the friends whom I have consulted think so.

1. Yes. 2 Yes. 3. Yes.

1. I am decidedly in favour of the Total Abolition of the Corn and Provision Laws, &c. 2. The congregation is nearly, if not unanimous in wishing the Total Abolition of these Laws. 3. I most heartily approve of the plan of the proposed meeting.

1. Yes. 2. Yes. 3. Yes. It occurs to me that it would have been as well to have invited every minister, whether of the Establishment or Dissent. Some few went to Manchester from the State churches, and had they been again invited, the people would have had another opportunity of judging how far they desired their real good.

1. I am decidedly in favour of the Abolition of these Laws, &c. 2. It is my opinion that the church I am connected with will be nearly, if not altogether, of the same mind with me on that subject. 3. I do approve the plan proposed, and pray God this matter may be conducted on christian principles, and that the results may be, the good of the nation, and the glory of God.

1. Yes, I am, and would like to see every constitutional measure adopted, in order to obtain so desirable an end. 2. I do think that those of them who are at all acquainted with the subject are unanimous on that point. 3. Yes, I do, because it seems to be the best that could be adopted, considering the circumstances of the case.

1. I am, decidedly. 2. I am sure that they are nearly, if not altogether, unanimous. 3. I do, on the explicit understanding that the meeting does not consist of the representatives of congregations, but only of those members of congregations who are favourable to the object.

Questions.—Are you in favour of an entirely Free Trade in Corn? 2. Is your congregation nearly unanimous in wishing an entirely Free Trade in Corn? 3. Do you approve generally of the plan of the Meeting, or have you any suggestions to offer?

1, 2, 3. Your noble effort has my best wishes and fervent prayers.

1. Most decidedly. 2. Perfectly unanimous. 3. Yes.

1. I am. 2. It is. 3. Yes. I wish the meeting to be conducted in a calm and christian-like spirit. That God may command his blessing on your meeting, is the prayer of yours, &c.

RENFREW.

Answers from 19 Ministers.

Answers.—1. Yes. 2. Yes. 3. Yes.

1. Yes. 2. It is my opinion that they are nearly, if not quite unanimous. 3. Yes.

1. I am decidedly in favour of the Abolition of these Laws, and the establishment of Free Trade in Corn. 2. I think my congregation are nearly unanimous for their abolition. 3. I think your plan thus far less objectionable than that of the Manchester Conference, that it does not exclude from the meeting those who are not ministers; but it retains what appears to me the *prime* mistake of such gatherings, the making of religious societies the instruments or tools of effecting great political changes. All Dissenters protest against bishops being admitted to the House of Lords; why then are Dissenting Ministers to be made political agents? If the Corn Law question is to be regarded as a *religious* question, so may that of the *Charter*. As a citizen, I have shown, and am prepared to show, my political opinions; but I do not occupy my place as a minister to represent any political party. I signed the last petition from the town in which I live, for the abolition of the Corn Laws, and am ready to sign the next. Besides, who are ranked as Dissenters,—the Roman Catholics, the Episcopalians, the Unitarians? By the publication in the newspapers of the Circular to which I am now replying, the Edinburgh Dissenters acted either presumptuously or foolishly.* I say this, because the tone of the document I received pretends to await the judgment of the provinces. [A *member* of the same congregation has since transmitted the following communication]:—At a meeting of members of * * * congregation friendly to the repeal of the Corn and Provision Laws, called by public intimation, the following Resolutions were adopted:—Resolved 1st, That it is the opinion of this meeting that the Corn and Provision Laws are immoral and unjust, and that while the operation of these iniquitous enactments inflicts a national injury, it bears especially against the manufacturing population, and is doubly distressing to Dissenters, inasmuch as it strikes at the prosperity of their ecclesiastical institutions. 2d, That apart altogether from speculative opinions regarding the wisdom of churches, as such, interfering in subjects having political reference, it is the persuasion of this meeting, that a public demonstration, such as the one contemplated, exhibiting, as it will do, the sentiments of the great body of the Dissenters in Scotland, must be productive of the best results. 3d, That in accordance with these views, we appoint Messrs * * * to attend the meeting at Edinburgh, as delegates from this meeting; and, 4th, That a copy of these Resolutions be transmitted to the Secretary of the Edinburgh Committee.

1. Most decidedly in favour of such arrangements. 2. My congregation are unanimous on these points, and ready to accede to any practical measure which is likely to promote the end contemplated by your movement. 3. I do.

[* The Reverend Gentleman who has thus so politely given the Edinburgh Committee the choice of being considered either fools or presumptuous persons, is the only one, of nearly six hundred ministers, who, in answering these Queries, has indulged in any thing like an attack on them; and as he has not condescended to offer any proof that they are obliged to place themselves on either of the horns of the dilemma which his imagination has created for them, they may be excused for declining to make the selection which he requires.

Questions.—Are you in favour of an entirely Free Trade in Corn? 2. Is your congregation nearly unanimous in wishing an entirely Free Trade in Corn? 3. Do you approve generally of the plan of the Meeting, or have you any suggestions to offer?

1. I am. 2. It is. 3. I do. The only suggestion I wish to make is, that I object to the latter part of Resolution VI.; in my opinion it will completely prevent the free expression of opinion in the conference, and will virtually make a farce of the Public Meeting, by placing the whole power of deciding what shall be introduced, in the Committee. I suppose the intention of the clause is to prevent the possibility of Chartists, &c., from introducing extraneous topics into the Conference. I think, however, any danger of that kind is sufficiently provided against by two things,—1st, That none but delegates duly authorised by a congregation can have a place in the Conference; and 2d, That the Chairman has power to prevent the introduction of extraneous topics, motions, or amendments. I think, therefore, the last clause of Resolution VI. should be deleted.

1. Yes. 2. Yes. 3. Yes.

1. Of Total, but not immediate, Abolition of the *Corn* Laws. No sliding scale; but a moderate fixed duty, to be diminished 1s. per annum, till it ceases altogether. Some important existing interests require this; and, perhaps, it is as much as can be obtained in the mean time. 2. A few are of the opinion expressed above; but the great majority of the congregation, I believe, are unanimous in wishing the Total and Immediate Abolition of these Laws, and an entirely Free Trade in Corn. 3. I approve of the proposed plan for conducting the meeting; but why invite Dissenters only, and not all of every denomination and class who are friendly to the object in view? There will be need for them all. I greatly fear that any thing like a full or large conference, at this season, and in the present depressed state of trade, cannot be reasonably expected in *any one* place. Might it not, therefore, be better to try to get similar meetings held, next month, all over the country, say, besides Edinburgh, at Glasgow, Kilmarnock, Dumfries, Kelso, Dundee, Dunfermline, Perth, Aberdeen, &c. Would the sense of the country not be thus more fully brought out? I deem it of vital importance that every opportunity and facility should be afforded to *Farmers* to be present at these meetings, since many of them seem now to be getting their eyes opened, as to the operation of the Corn Laws as to their own interests.

1. We are. 2. All but unanimous. 3. We do.

1. Yes. 2. Yes. 3. Yes.

1. I consider these measures as not only right in themselves, but as essential to the prosperity of Great Britain, viewed as a commercial country. 2. My opinion is, that, while opposition to the Corn Laws has always been general among the members of my congregation, it has been increased by recent events to such a degree, that, with scarcely an exception, they regard the Immediate Abolition of these laws as of vital importance, and would willingly co-operate in any plan by which their abolition is likely to be effected. 3. With all my dislike of commercial restrictions, and all my desire for their removal, I am not convinced of the propriety of the ministers and members of the Christian church, *as such*, interfering in these matters. That the Corn Law question is, in some of its aspects, a religious one, I do not deny; for how few political questions are there which do not touch religion in some of their bearings? But I do not think that it is so directly a religious one, as to bring it fairly within the range of topics which the religious public, *as such*, are entitled to take up. I question, too, whether their interference will tend to promote the object which is contemplated. Yet none will rejoice more sincerely, if the present movement among all classes of the community terminate in the establishment of the principles of Free Trade.

1. Yes. 2. Yes. 3. I do.

1. (Church vacant.) 2. At a meeting held last night in the church, of those friendly to the Total Repeal of the Corn and Provision Laws, it was unanimously resolved that two of their number should attend, as delegates, the meeting to be held in Edinburgh, on 11th and 12th January, 1842. 3. Yes.

Questions.—Are you in favour of an entirely Free Trade in Corn? 2. Is your congregation nearly unanimous in wishing an entirely Free Trade in Corn? 3. Do you approve generally of the plan of the Meeting, or have you any suggestions to offer?

1. Entirely so. 2. They are, as far as I know, unanimous, and have repeatedly expressed their sentiments on the subject. 3. I approve generally of the plan. I have my doubts as to the propriety of inviting every Dissenting minister to the meeting, and, at the same time, forcing on them the necessity of joining in prayers, of which they cannot approve. I could join with an Episcopalian, though he should read his prayers, provided they were evangelical; and with a Roman Catholic, provided he abstained from presenting them through inferior mediators; but I could not join with a Unitarian, and probably none of those could join with me.

1. Yes. 2. So far as I am aware, they are unanimous in wishing the Total Abolition of these Laws. 3. Yes.

1. Yes. 2. Unanimous. 3. Yes. The meeting of the 20th, by mutual consultation, will be more likely to come to a right decision, than by the suggestions of a stranger at a distance. I have written the above answers after consulting with several of the members of the church.

1. Yes. 2. I believe them to be quite unanimous. 3. I approve of the plan generally. The subject of prayer occasioned much discussion at the meeting in Manchester. From the proposed arrangement, it is very likely to occasion the same at the meeting in Edinburgh. For the sake of harmony, I humbly think it would be better *not to propose* the latter part of the fifth resolution. I would not be understood as intending to oppose its adoption, should it be proposed; on the contrary, I shall rejoice should it be harmoniously agreed to. It would be well if some plan could be adopted by which an error in the proceedings at Manchester might be avoided—that of leaving the earlier speakers unrestricted as to time, and allowing the others to do little more than to bow to the chairman and to the meeting, and retire.

1. Yes. 2. Yes. 3. Yes.

1. Yes, decidedly. 2. There is hardly a dissenting voice. 3. I do, except in one particular—that, in place of Dissenting, it should have been *every* minister in Scotland, as was the case at Manchester, which I attended; and I know some who would have attended from the Established Church, who, I am afraid, will consider themselves slighted by *sectarianism*. True, few of these would have attended; but yet some would, and have shamed the rest who opposed or held back in such a holy cause,—that makes the pulse beat high in favour of suffering humanity—'Whoso shutteth his ears at the cry of the poor, himself also shall cry, but shall not be heard.' Although few of them would attend, yet inviting them would tend to show *who were* on the side of suffering humanity—*who* suffered and felt for *the poor*, in the present awful crisis of our country, in which, if our trade and commerce falls, ruin will be the consequence to every interest, whether manufacturing, commercial, or agricultural; and we will then, when too late, have only to repent our folly in our fall, to rise no more at all! Religion and humanity unite their voice with patriotism, justice, and wisdom, as well as expediency, to call aloud for the Total and Immediate Abolition of these starvation Corn and Provision Laws—that should unite all sects, all parties, all men and women, to—in one heart and with one voice—demand their complete abolition, at once and for ever!

1. Yes. 2. Yes. 3. Yes.

COUNTY OF ROXBURGH.

Answers from 15 Ministers.

Answers.—1. I am. 2. In my opinion they are. 3. I do not. I think it wrong in principle and policy, to hold a meeting of Dissenters exclusively. It is fitted to give a *sectarian* aspect to a question which affects all classes equally; and is thus likely to be injurious to the cause of dissent, and obstructive to the repeal of the iniquitous Corn Laws.

Questions.—1. Are you in favour of an entirely Free Trade in Corn? 2. Is your congregation nearly unanimous in wishing an entirely Free Trade in Corn? 3. Do you approve generally of the plan of the Meeting, or have you any suggestions to offer?

1. Yes; but I should think gradually. 2. A few may, but generally they think little about it. 3. (No answer given.)

1, 2, and 3. I decline taking any part in the proposed movement, because, among other things, I disapprove of using our ecclesiastical organization for the accomplishment of objects which I regard as of a civil or political nature; and also, because I disapprove of separating the efforts of ecclesiastical bodies from those of society at large in advocating and enforcing political reforms.

1. I am persuaded that the Abolition of the Corn Laws would be beneficial to all classes of the community. 2. I believe, that with one or two exceptions, our congregation wish the Abolition of the Corn and Provision Laws. 3. As the object of the meeting appears to be one of Justice and Mercy, I can have no objection to its being held. The Resolutions, as far as I can judge, appear to be wise and judicious.

1. I am in favour. 2. They are nearly unanimous. 3. I do approve. If it serve you any thing, it may be mentioned, that there are four or five farmers in this district, *not* in our communion, who pay each about £1500 per annum, who are in favour of the Abolition of the Corn Laws.

1. I am. 2. With very few exceptions, the members of my congregation are decidedly for the Abolition of the Corn Laws. 3. I should have preferred, that instead of an exclusive meeting of Dissenting ministers and deputies from their congregations, there had been a meeting of delegates from all associations and committees in Scotland formed for the repeal of the Corn Laws; because in matters not strictly religious, it appears to me highly desirable that all denominational and religious distinctions should be disregarded and obliterated. But a definite proposal having been submitted for a conference of deputies from the dissenters, I should not like by defeating it to furnish any occasion for the imputation that dissenters were unfavourable or indifferent to the abolition of laws so unjust and pernicious, more especially as it is free from the objection of being clerical, ecclesiastical, or congregational, and joining it does not preclude local organization with fellow-citizens on the broadest basis for the attainment of the same end by public meetings, petitions, &c. Yet if resolved upon, I should propose that the conference receive delegates from any meetings, societies, or classes, seeking the same object, who are willing to conform to its resolutions, especially those for securing the opening of the meetings with prayer, the preservation of order, and the restriction of all discussion to the one subject in hand.

1, Yes. 2. All but unanimous. 3. Yes.

1. I am. 2. It is my opinion that the majority of the members of my congregation are not yet prepared to express publicly their views and wishes relative to a Free Trade in Corn. Many of them, however, wish the Total Abolition of the Corn Laws, and the number, I believe, is rapidly increasing. 3. I do not approve of the plan of the proposed meeting. I think it ought to have been a meeting of those who were in favour of the Total Abolition of the Corn Laws, irrespective altogether of their religious principles and connexions.

1. I am in favour of the Total Abolition of all these, and the Free Trade in Corn. 2. My congregation are quite unanimous in regard to this query. 3. I do

1. I am. 2. It is my opinion. 3. I do approve generally of the plan of the proposed meeting, as explained in the Circular. I feel happy at the purpose of conducting the business in the spirit and exercise of prayer. God must be our counsellor, and his counsel must be sought; and this on such an occasion, not only individually, but also collectively. He must be honoured before men.

1. I am in favour of the Total Abolition of the Corn Laws. 2. I believe the sentiments of the church, of which I am an office-bearer, to be unanimous in wishing the Total Abolition of the Corn Laws. 3. Yes, I do.

Questions.—1. Are you in favour of an entirely Free Trade in Corn? 2. Is your congregation nearly unanimous in wishing an entirely Free Trade in Corn? 3. Do you approve generally of the plan of the Meeting, or have you any suggestions to offer?

1, 2, 3. I have unaccountably mislaid the Circular, but in reply to the Queries, so far as I remember them, I have to state, that I am decidedly opposed to all legislative restrictions on commerce, and particularly to those affecting the trade in Corn; that the sentiments of the great body of my congregation perfectly coincide with my own,—that I cordially approve of the proposed conference. I may add, that the preliminary arrangements seem to me most judicious, and that the only point which appears to me doubtful is the propriety of the preference given to Edinburgh as the place of meeting. Certainly a demonstration equally powerful, in point of the numbers attending the conference, and the depth of public interest taken in its proceedings, would have ten times the moral influence on the government and country coming from Edinburgh, as compared with any other town in Scotland; but many of the very circumstances which would give peculiar weight to a powerful demonstration there, will make it difficult to secure one. Such, for example, as the coldly intellectual character of the place, its comparative disinterestedness, as not being the seat of any great manufacturing interest; the various forms of aristocratic influence which overshadow it, and its vicinity to the principal corn-growing counties, which, I fear, will hamper many ministers of country congregations, in consequence of the delusions abroad, not only amongst the farmers, but even farm-servants, who have got the notion into their heads, that their interests would be injuriously affected by a repeal of the Corn Laws. These circumstances incline me to think that had Glasgow been fixed on as the place of meeting, it would have secured both a much larger attendance, and a more spirit-stirring movement, which would go far to counterbalance the mere weight of the capital. You and your friends, however, have no doubt weighed the matter well, and are infinitely better qualified to judge.

1. Yes; the Total Abolition. 2. The majority of the congregation are, with the exception of a few farmers. 3. Yes.

1. So far as I understand the subject, I decidedly am. 2. That they are not unanimous in wishing the Total Abolition of these Laws I have reason to believe, but as to the proportionate number *for* and *against* them, I am not at all competent to say. 3. I very much doubt the propriety of such a meeting, chiefly on this ground, that it cannot fail to give our churches, which are communities purely spiritual, and constituted for spiritual purposes, a political aspect. A meeting, by delegation, of those in Scotland favourable to the Abolition of these Laws, would, I believe, be of very great importance at the present juncture; but I am clearly of opinion that the representatives composing such a meeting should proceed, not from churches, but from bodies composed of the public generally.

1. I believe all the members here are in favour of a Total Repeal of the Corn Laws. We have no minister at present.

COUNTY OF STIRLING.

Answers from 16 Ministers.

Answers.—1. I am in favour of the Total Abolition of the Corn Laws, &c. 2. The majority wish the Abolition of these Laws. 3. I approve very much of the plan.

1. Most assuredly. 2. This is an agricultural district, and yet the opinion, I believe, is very generally in favour of Free Trade. 3. I can see no objections to it, though to me it would appear an improvement if Churchmen favourable had been invited to co-operate; and if the petitions were drawn out in such terms as might admit of the signature of Churchmen as well as Dissenters.

1. I am decidedly in favour of the Abolition of these Laws. 2. At a meeting of a large number of the members of the congregation, I am authorized to say, that they are very generally in favour of the Abolition of these Laws. 3. I approve. My heart is with the meeting.

Questions—1. Are you in favour of an entirely Free Trade in Corn? 2. Is your congregation nearly unanimous in wishing an entirely Free Trade in Corn? 3. Do you approve generally of the plan of the Meeting, or have you any suggestions to offer.

1. Yes. 2. Yes. 3. Yes.

1. I am favourable to the principles of Free Trade. 2. It is intended to call a meeting of the persons friendly to those principles; then this matter will be submitted to their consideration. 3. I should have preferred if the matter had been taken up without reference to religious denomination at all.

1. I am in favour of the Abolition. 2. So far as I am acquainted with the sentiments of my congregation, they are unanimous in wishing the Total Abolition of these Laws. 3. I approve generally of the plan.

1. I am. 2. It is. 3. I approve of the plan.

1. I am; but should not farmers be relieved of any burdens that fall upon them as such. 2. They are, to my certain knowledge, unanimous, with one or two exceptions. 3. The propriety of churches interfering in this way is not quite clear to me. Ministers and others should respectfully address their representatives on this subject, assuring them that the Corn Monopoly is one of the prime causes of that deeply-rooted disaffection which is spreading among the working-classes, and which is incompatible with permanent safety.

1 Yes; most decidedly. 2. Yes, nearly unanimous. 3. Yes.

1 Yes. 2. A considerable majority wish the Total Abolition, &c.; but, at the same time, that compensation should be given to farmers affected thereby. 3. Yes.

1. Yes. 2. I have no doubt. 3. I do.

1. Yes; but I think it deserves consideration, whether if that shall materially injure tenants, it be not right that they receive an abatement of rent, that the expense of a benefit to the whole community may be borne by that community, and not by a particular class. 2. I believe that the church of which I am a minister is *quite* unanimous for the Abolition. 3. I have doubts as to ministers attending such meetings. Their studies and habits do not fit them for being the best men of business: but, independently of that, they are devoted to a higher department of the King's business, which requires haste and undivided energy. Is not something of this principle brought forward in the saying, 'Let the dead bury their dead; but go thou and preach the Gospel.' The effect, too, may be considered as tending to prejudice, against their ministers, those who may differ from them in this matter. Should they not give themselves wholly to the ministry of the Word and to prayer?

1. Yes. 2 Unanimous. 3. Yes.

1, 2, and 3. I have little doubt but that two members from our congregation will be chosen to attend the anticipated meeting in Edinburgh, as I believe the opinion which generally, if not universally, prevails in our congregation, is in favour of the Abolition of the Corn Laws, and for Free Trade. As for myself, I may say, that while I approve of the object you have in view, and would most readily sign any petition to that effect along with others of the community; still I am not so clear with respect to the propriety of Dissenters and Dissenting Ministers taking such a prominent part in a question of a somewhat political character, and doing this to the exclusion of other denominations; why not include all who are friendly to the object, and thus divest it of the appearance of having a sectarian character? It is probable, however, that I may attend, although at present I cannot give a positive pledge.

1. I am. 2. I think nearly so. 3. I do. Nothing occurs to me of importance.

1. I am decidedly in favour of the Total Abolition, &c. 2. It is my opinion that they are. This fact at least I know, that at the late election, when an appeal was made to the country on the Corn and Provision Laws, of sixty-four voters connected with my congregation, many of them small landed proprietors and farmers, not fewer than fifty-eighty voted for the liberal candidate. 3. I approve generally of the plan, but am not without some doubt of the wisdom of having a meeting for the purpose specified, composed exclusively of Dissenters.

Questions.—Are you in favour of an entirely Free Trade in Corn? 2. Is your congregation nearly unanimous in wishing an entirely Free Trade in Corn? 3. Do you approve generally of the plan of the Meeting, or have you any suggestions to offer?

COUNTIES OF WIGTON AND KIRKCUDBRIGHT

Answers from 17 Ministers.

Answers.—1. I am in favour of the Total Abolition of the Corn and Provision Laws, and wish to have an entirely Free Trade in Corn. 2. I have reason to think that the congregation are nearly, if not altogether, unanimous in wishing the Total Abolition of these Laws, and a Free Trade in Corn. 3. The plan of the proposed meeting seems very good, and it has my approbation. In the case of small congregations, at a great distance, perhaps it might be well to invite them to send *one*, if they are not able to bear the expense of sending *two*, of their members to represent them at the proposed meeting in January.

1. Decidedly so. 2. They are entirely unanimous in wishing the Total Abolition of these Laws. 3. The proposed meeting has my entire approval. May the blessing of God attend it.

1. It is my full conviction that these Laws are iniquitous in every light in which they can be viewed; and that to abolish them every effort ought to be made. 2. I have every reason to think that my congregation unanimously agree in holding the sentiment now expressed. 3. I do so entirely.

1. Decidedly I am. 2. So far as I am acquainted with the sentiments of my congregation on this subject, a goodly number are for a Total Repeal, many for an alteration, and but a very very few indeed for them as they are. 3. Yes. I highly approve of all the measures that have, as yet, been entered into.

1. Decidedly I am. 2. This is an agricultural district; a considerable proportion of the members of my congregation are farmers, and reside in the country. in consists of about 340 members; not less than two-thirds of them are repealers. 3. I approve of the plan of the proposed meeting, and sincerely wish and hope that it may be a large and influential one.

1. Decidedly so. 2. A majority of my congregation are connected with agriculture. Some of my members who are farmers, and others, have doubts as to the *safety* of Abolition. But at a general meeting held last night, nearly all hands were held up in favour of it, and none against it. 3. I do. The only suggestion which occurred to me, was the impropriety of asking Dissenters alone to attend; but I have seen reasons in the *Scotsman* which are quite satisfactory.

1. In favour of the Total Abolition. 2. Some are in favour, and some against. 3. I approve; and trust, in the important matter that may come before the conference, they will be directed by that wisdom which is from above.

1. No minister at present settled in the Secession Church, ———. 2. It is the opinion of the subscribers, that a considerable majority (to speak cautiously) would be in favour of Total Abolition. 3. (No answer given.)

1. I decidedly am. 2 They are nearly so. The district is agricultural, and a few farmers are hostile—but few. 3. I heartily approve of it, and I trust nothing will occur to prevent the meeting, after the publicity that has been given to the proposal.

1. I am. But whether to sweep off these restrictive laws at once, or, in the first instance, by a fixed duty, decreasing annually, may, in my opinion be disputed. 2. I believe them to be unanimous in this opinion. A difference of opinion may exist respecting the method. 3. Generally. Why not give the Ministers belonging to the Establishment an opportunity of assisting in this the cause of humanity and the cause of God? Perhaps few of them would attend. We cant help that. They are *ostensibly* deeply interested in the welfare of the poor. Why deprive them of this fine opportunity of reducing their principles to practice? Or why despise their co-operation in this great work?

Questions.—1. Are you in favour of an entirely Free Trade in Corn? 2. Is your congregation nearly unanimous in wishing an entirely Free Trade in Corn? 3. Do you approve generally of the plan of the Meeting, or have you any suggestions to offer?

1. I heartily join with you in the propriety and necessity of cancelling entirely the Corn Laws. 2. Yes; they are nearly unanimous. 3. I do.

1. Yes. 2. As a congregation, we are unanimous in wishing the Total Abolition of the Corn Laws, and a Free Trade in Corn. 3. Yes.

1. Yes. 2. Yes, I may say unanimous in wishing the Total Abolition. 3. Yes. The projected meetings have my entire and cordial approbation, and, I may also add, of every member of the church, with one single exception.

1. Decidedly so. 2. I have in my congregation nearly thirty land-owners and farmers, all of whom I believe to be decidedly hostile to the existing Corn Laws, and favourable to their Total Abolition. 3. I approve of the meeting. District meetings should be held, and committees formed, say in every County in Scotland, to frame Resolutions, prepare Petitions, and employ any other legitimate means to obtain the Abolition of the Corn Laws. This would give an impetus to the whole kingdom; and, I think, tend to advance the good cause, and diffuse information regarding it.

1. I am. 2. I believe they are nearly unanimous. 3. So far as I have had time to examine the annexed plan of the proposed meeting, I heartily approve of it, and hope it will prove useful.

1. Most decidedly so. 2. I have no doubt that they are quite unanimous in wishing these measures. 3. Very much indeed. I wish you wisdom and great success.

1 and 2. In reply to the Queries annexed, I may state, that so far as I can learn (and I have consulted a considerable number), the Dissenters in this place are unanimous, or nearly so, in wishing the Total Abolition of the Corn Laws, and an entirely Free Trade in Corn. 3. The plan of the proposed meeting seems to meet with their most cordial approbation.

II.—RELIGIOUS BODIES, OF WHICH THERE ARE ONLY A FEW CONGREGATIONS, AND WHO ARE TO BE REPRESENTED AT THE MEETING BY MINISTERS OR MEMBERS OF EACH DENOMINATION.

To these bodies 29 circulars were sent, and from them 21 answers have been received. Eight of their ministers, and twenty-eight of their members, have promised to be present,—making a total of thirty-six, or about one-twentieth part of the whole number who have expressed their intention to attend.

1. Yes. 2. Entirely unanimous. 3. Generally. It may be necessary here to explain that the congregation is arranged upon the principle of not having one minister only, but of every member ministering according to his ability for the good of the whole. Having, therefore, two bishops for the oversight of the church, it is probable that they will attend. Would it not be better, could matters be so arranged, so as to include those who advocate a small fixed duty, as well as those who are in favour of an entirely Free Trade in Corn.

1. Yes, I am. 2. I believe they are. 3. I do.

1. Yes. 2. Quite unanimous. 3. Yes. It is my humble opinion, as well as the unanimous wish of the church over which I have the pleasure to preside, that every minister of the Established Church, and two members of every congregation belonging to said church, should be invited to attend the meeting. I beg leave also to state, as our decided opinion, that the price of provisions would be greatly diminished, and the comfort of the *poor* considerably increased, if ministers would endeavour, by their influence and example, to preserve from destruction the immense quantities of grain consumed in the manufacture of alcoholic agents. This trade is the most fertile source of crime, of wretchedness, and woe among the *poor;* the means by which the gracious bounties of God's providence are most shamefully

Questions.—1. Are you in favour of an entirely Free Trade in Corn? 2. Is your congregation nearly unanimous in wishing an entirely Free Trade in Corn? 3. Do you approve generally of the plan of the Meeting, or have you any suggestion to offer?

abused, and immortal souls debarred from participating of the *bread of life.* Trusting that the Lord, the giver of the fruits of the earth, and the friend of the poor, may lead you and direct your minds to the best methods of promoting this good cause, I have the honour to be, &c.

1. Heartily so. 2. I have laid the matter before a meeting of the church. They are *unanimous* in their opinion of these Laws, as being not only impolitic, but also cruel, oppressive, and unjust. They are at same time, however, as unanimous in preferring another medium than the present for giving expression to their sentiments on this subject,—it being, in their opinion, grossly inconsistent and apparently hypocritical, in men to seek the destruction of a lesser evil, and almost all of them doing nothing for the suppression of a greater one, but rather, by their practice, their influence, their example, and their doctrine, perpetuating and encouraging it. 3. Generally, in as far as it goes; but it is too exclusive, in several respects, to meet our *entire* approval. It being now a well known and undenied fact, that upwards of Forty Millions bushels of Grain are annually destroyed in the production of intoxicating liquors (a quantity more than adequate to the full supply of the nation's wants, if properly used), and being persuaded that the ministers of the gospel, and other influential persons in society, have it in their power to put an end to those drinking customs which require the grain to support them; they would, in their opinion, be acting a part at once more consistent, more wise, more politic, and more christian, were they, in conjunction with their endeavours to get the Corn and Provision Laws abolished, to exert themselves for the suppression of those usages which, in addition to their enormous waste of grain, act powerfully in entailing numberless other evils on the community.

1. I am in favour of Free Trade *in all articles all over the world.* 2. I have no congregation. I belong to a church, which is 'Jesus Christ's congregation.' So far as I know all my brethren the members, who meet with me (though hundreds in this place belong to Christ's church, who do not meet with me), and also the hearers who are not members, would answer this question in the affirmative. 3. I do; only I think two members of each church, either ministers or not, would have been more definite than every Dissenting minister, &c. We have several *ministers*, who labour in word and doctrine, and yet it is doubtful whether you would call them 'Dissenting ministers,' or whether they would desire such a designation. I do not approve of the term, '*the minister*,' it is as unscriptural as '*the pope*,' when applied to an *evangelist* or *bishop*. When you address a minister of the Gospel, do not call him 'Rev.' The only person so denominated in the Holy Scriptures, is Almighty God. Ps. iii. 'Holy and "Reverend" is his name.' A few months ago, I was requested to deliver a lecture or sermon on this text, 'Give us this day our daily bread.' I felt it my duty to comply with the request, and from the effect produced, am led to suggest, that some competent person might deliver a lecture on this text, in every congregation, or town, or village, throughout the kingdom, to which access can be obtained. All Christians in their *public prayers* ought to use this prayer, especially at this time, when the unemployed population of our manufacturing districts cannot obtain their daily bread, because they cannot find daily work, which they would find if the Americans, and other nations, were permitted to bring their Corn into our markets, and buy our cloth, and other manufactured articles, with its price; thus enabling us to 'buy Corn' again. I confess there does appear to me a most revolting inconsistency in any man or minister, praying give us '*Our* daily bread,'—that is, give it not only to me, but to my brethren, of this family, this church, this nation, or this world; for we are commanded to 'pray for all men,'—and who, after he has thus prayed, endeavours to hinder his prayers from being answered, by preventing all the poor of the land, who cannot pay the high prices, induced by the Corn Laws, from obtaining bread. And do not the upholders of the Corn Laws stand

Questions.—1. Are you in favour of an entirely Free Trade in Corn? 2. Is your congregation nearly unanimous in wishing an entirely Free Trade in Corn? 3. Do you approve generally of the plan of the Meeting, or have you any suggestions to offer?

branded, too justly branded with this charge, inasmuch as they endeavour to uphold the interest of the landowner, whatever becomes of the interest of the farmer, the agricultural labourer, the merchant, the manufacturer, and his labourers. In preparing for this mighty contest, however, let us not forget who are our legislators,—the makers of these odious laws. By far the greater number of them are landowners,—lords of the soil, and while self-interest, mistaken self-interest, (for it can never be the real interest of man to riot, or even live, by the very miseries of his fellows) is their governing principle, they may be expected to legislate for themselves. Were all the interests of this great empire fairly represented in the senate of the nation, the agricultural interest would not triumph over the commercial; nor could the present Corn Laws survive another session. There is little prospect, I fear, of an equitable settlement of this great question, while one class of the community only is fully represented in the House of Commons. Class-legislation must cease. The few must not continue to legislate for the many; or, to speak more properly, to legislate for themselves, overlooking the interests of the many. I am, however, no politician, but wishing to see my poor fellow-countrymen have work and adequate wages, and bread at a fair, honest price, I cannot overlook the cause of the Corn Laws, any more than their destroying consequences. I thank you for the candour and frankness manifested in all you have done; and although that very candour has given me confidence to suggest a few changes, you will believe me when I say, that those suggestions are only intended to advance the good cause in which we are all engaged; and that I anticipate from your labours, little else but ultimate success, even should it be remote. Perhaps it would have been well to invite, and even yet to invite, the clergy and members of the civil establishment of religion, to take a part in your proceedings. If only few come, they will be the more welcome; and it does not seem proper to punish the willing by a forced exclusion, merely because the unwilling refuse to do their duty. I very much deprecate the exclusion of able and willing fellow-labourers in this great work, no matter to what section of nominal or real Christians they may be joined. Hoping that we shall never cease to pray fervently, and solemnly, for all the poor as well as the rich, to have daily bread, and that our efforts to obtain it for all, will harmonize with our prayers. I am the friend of the Immediate and Entire Abolition of the Corn Laws.

1. We are. 2. They are unanimous. 3. We do: and, as members of the church, we pray that you may be directed by the Divine Spirit in all your proceedings for the welfare of the British nation.

1. Decidedly so. 2. Their attention has been called to it, and they appear unanimous. 3 I have no objections to the plan, and am not disposed to find fault with any of the proposals, believing the committee will do every thing in their power.

1, 2, and 3. The religious sect to which I belong decline taking any part in the matters embraced in the annexed queries.

1. I am most decidedly in favour of the Total Abolition of these abominable laws, and the establishment of a Free Trade in Corn. 2. The congregation with which I am connected are unanimous in this opinion. 3. I approve fully of the plan of the meeting, and have no suggestions to offer.

1. Yes. 2. Yes. 3. I only object, on *conscientious grounds*, to the opening of the meetings with stated prayer; deeming such an arrangement *illiberal* and *unwise*.

1. Yes; very decidedly. 2. The Friends in this county are not unanimous on the subject; they very generally admit the injustice of these laws; but a part of them being farmers are afraid of injury under existing leases. 3. I do. I do not approve of vocal prayer being always offered at the commencement of meetings of this description, prayer being an important part of Divine worship.

1. We have long wished for the Total Abolition of the Corn and Provision

Questions.—1. Are you in favour of an entirely Free Trade in Corn? 2. Is your congregation nearly unanimous in wishing an entirely Free Trade in Corn? 3. Do you approve generally of the plan of the Meeting, or have you any suggestions to offer?

Laws, and we earnestly desire *Free Trade* in *Corn*. 2. We are unanimous for *Free Trade in Corn*. 3. We do.

1. I am not quite sure but that a very *small fixed* duty may be necessary for our agricultural interests; but I regard our present Corn Laws as unjust and cruel, and desire to see either a great alteration of them, or their Total Abolition. 2. I believe they are. 3. Generally I do. I have no suggestions to offer, but trust you may be directed aright in a matter of so much importance, directly to the suffering thousands of our own country, and indirectly to the world.

1. Decidedly so. 2. They are very nearly, if not entirely unanimous, in that wish. 3. Yes.

1. I am most decidedly so, and have been many years. 2. I have reason to believe they are, though some of them fear the object cannot be accomplished until the masses are more fully represented in Parliament. 3. Generally speaking, I approve of it much; but as regards opening the meetings with prayer, I think it would be best to select one or two Ministers from each denomination present, calling upon them in regular succession, as their names shall stand on the roll.

1. Yes. 2. They are decidedly and unanimously so. 3. I do.

1. Yes. 2. Decidedly so. 3. Yes. As some Ministers of the Established Church are in favour of the Total Abolition, would it not be desirable to give a general invitation to those Established Ministers who are so minded, to attend the meeting?

1. I am in favour of Free Trade in every commodity. 2. I am of opinion that they are unanimous. 3. I object to the exclusion of any christian body. I look on the cause as no way connected with Dissent, more than consent; and am of opinion, that endowed Christians should be invited, and if they will not assist, let the sin lie at their own door.

1. I am decidedly. 2. I should think quite unanimous. 3. I do not approve of a meeting of christian ministers, or churches, *as such*, for the object specified; because, if they can, *in their religious capacity*, assemble and act on a political question, such as the Corn Laws, then, since every political question has its moral and religious aspect, they can equally, when convinced of the injustice and evil effects of certain other political arrangements, meet and act on such matters. Christian ministers and churches may therefore be justified in meeting to consider the extension of the suffrage, the question of the ballot, and other matters which I need not mention, since these might be deemed, and justly deemed, by them intimately connected with the physical, moral, and religious benefit of their countrymen, and a remedy for much misery and vice. I hesitate, therefore, to sanction the principle that, because a political question has a moral and religious aspect, it demands, or requires, the interference of christian ministers, or members of churches, in their *peculiar and exclusive* capacity as ministers and members of churches. I would suggest, that *a general meeting*, of persons influential on account of character and standing in society, to which such citizens as sustain the relation of ministers also may be invited, might remove the objection of various persons to a meeting such as that now contemplated. I should do my utmost to attend any such general meeting, where my appearance would not expose me to the inference which others might please to press upon me (and which I would not be able to parry), that I ought, as the teacher of a christian society, and in my capacity as a minister, to interfere with other political questions, and even to introduce them into my pulpit.

1. Yes. 2. Yes. 3. I generally approve of the plan of the proposed meeting.

1. Yes. 2. Almost unanimous. 3. It meets our approbation as proposed. As we have no stated pastor, I was appointed by our Committee to answer the above Queries. Wishing you every success to your benevolent scheme of ameliorating distress,—I am, &c.

III. RELIGIOUS BODIES OF WHOM ONLY A SMALL PROPORTION ANSWERED THE CIRCULARS, AND NONE OF WHOM HAVE PROMISED TO ATTEND THE MEETING.

These bodies consist (1) of the Reformed Presbyterian Church, to whom thirty-seven circulars were sent, and from whom eleven answers were received; (2) of the Associate Synod of Original Seceders, to whom thirty-three circulars were sent, and from whom six answers were received; and (3) of the Original Burgher Associate Synod, to whom thirteen circulars were sent, and from whom two answers were received. The answers follow in the above order.*

Answers from 19 Ministers.

Questions.—1. Are you in favour of an entirely Free trade in Corn? 2. Is your congregation nearly unanimous in wishing an entirely Free Trade in Corn? 3. Do you approve generally of the plan of the Meeting, or have you any suggestions to offer?

Answers.—1. Very decidedly. My opinions are in favour of Free Trade generally; and of all restrictions, I consider those on *bread* the most intolerable. 2. I have reason to believe they are nearly unanimous in wishing a total abolition of these laws. 3. I do not doubt that such a meeting might have good results. It might serve to blunt the arrows of the unfriendly, if the proceedings could be managed chiefly through the agency of laymen.

1. So far as I understand the subject I am. 2. Some of the farmers may have their doubts, but I believe the majority are in favour of total abolition. 3. I do.

1. 2. 3. It is unnecessary to say what are my particular opinions on the subject of the Corn Laws, as I am not clear that it would be my duty to interfere with them in the manner proposed.

1. 2. 3. Your circular reached me yesterday. My information, in reference to the subject under consideration, is not such as to enable me to express my opinions respecting it in its various bearings with the same confidence as many others. I believe the *existing Corn Laws* to be *decidedly injurious*. But it appears to me that a very great and *hurtful delusion* is cherished, when *these* are represented as almost the *sole cause of the misery* prevailing among many of the inhabitants of this land. And such a representation, besides other evils, is fitted to turn away the minds of those who are suffering, from causes of misery, which it is their duty to remove, and without the removal of which no laws can secure them happiness. I am not yet prepared to pronounce in regard to *the steps* which ought immediately to be taken for the removal of the evils of the Corn Laws themselves. In these circumstances, I do not intend to take any part at the proposed meeting. It is my desire that all the various movements may be directed and overruled to be a happy result for the good of our country.

1. I have been so ever since I was able to form an opinion on the subject. 2. I have never tried any means to ascertain the sentiments of my congregation, as I never talk to them on such points, but as far as I can judge, I think the great majority would favour repeal. 3. I see nothing to object, only I view the determination to invite only Dissenting Ministers as unwise. I think care should be employed to impress the public, when so many ministers are assembled, that the subject is viewed not as one of a party or political character, but as affecting the interests of men generally, both in regard to temporal comfort and to morality.

* It is only an act of justice to these three denominations to explain that their ministers had much less time to return answers to the original queries than those of other Churches, their letters, owing to a misunderstanding amongst the parties who undertook to address them, not having been sent off until eight days after the others.

Questions.—1. Are you in favour of an entirely Free Trade in Corn? 2. Is your congregation nearly unanimous in wishing an entirely Free Trade in Corn? 3. Do you approve generally of the plan of the Meeting, or have you any suggestions to offer?

1. 2. 3. From a variety of circumstances I have been prevented from giving the attention to the subject, which would be necessary to fit me to express a judgment on it to my own satisfaction. The question has never been agitated in my congregation as such, nor is the present a fit time. I believe a great part of the operative class regard the abolition of the Corn Laws as a measure that would contribute greatly to their relief.

1. I am. 2. I should think they are, provided the disadvantages which the present farmers of the land would suffer in consequence of the change be duly considered. 3. Yes. If you wish the farmers to join with you, you must *shew attention* to their interests.

1. The principle of the Corn Laws cannot be justified, but I have doubts as to the expediency of an immediate repeal. 2. There is considerable diversity of sentiment on the subject among my people. Some who were weavers have now become farm-labourers. 3. I have doubts as to the propriety of ministers taking part in these public discussions. In other respects I consider the resolutions to be drawn up with judgment and fairness.

1. Of the present Corn and Provision Laws I entirely disapprove; but instead of a total abolition, I would be satisfied with a SMALL *fixed duty*. 2. I can say nothing in regard to the sentiments of my congregation on this subject, but I should think that they are nearly unanimous in disapproving of the present laws. 3. I approve of strenuous exertions for the abolition of the present laws, &c. but I am not sure as to the propriety of the plan of the proposed meeting. In consequence of the circular being too late in coming to hand, my engagements prevented me from answering the queries till to-day. I need not trouble you with suggestions, &c. as they could not be of any service whatever.

1. I am; but fear in present circumstances, that such a measure would injure, if not ruin, one portion of the community, without essentially benefiting the other. 2. Being scattered over a rural district, I consider them far from being unanimous on that matter. 3. No answer sent.

1. I have not thoroughly studied the subject; but so far as I understand it, I am in favour of a total abolition of the Corn Laws, and of an entirely free trade in corn. 2. Being but a few months the minister of the congregation, I am unable to answer the question. 3. I do most heartily approve of it, if conducted exclusively on scriptural principles. I have no particular suggestions. I shall make the subject a matter of more careful and serious consideration, and shall watch the movements of the association.

1. I am. 2. It is. 3. I do.

1. I am in favour of these measures. 2. So far as I know, my congregation is unanimous in wishing a free trade in corn. 3. With all deference to the respected individuals whose names are contained in the accompanying circular, I may state, that the members of my congregation are averse to the idea of ministers becoming political leaders, and wish me to act in the character of their spiritual guide. Many of them in their different spheres, as members of civil society, are very active in promoting such measures of reform as those now referred to. But I do not think they would approve of the plan of the proposed meeting, as it seems to me an improper blending of civil and ecclesiastical things together.

1. How desirable soever a free trade in corn, abstractly viewed, I consider it unsuitable to the present circumstances of this country. 2. I am persuaded comparatively few of them wish a total abolition of the Corn Laws. 3. I do not approve of ministers coming so prominently forward in a political question, and consider the plan proposed calculated to produce dissension in congregations.

1. Yes. 2. It is. 3. I have not found time to consider it sufficiently. Proceed in a firm and constitutional manner.

1. 2. 3. I, and, I believe, the generality of my congregation, would like to see all taxation on the necessaries of life, whether on food, fuel, clothing, cleanliness, light, or air, abolished; but do not approve of clerical agitation in order to gain this object.

Questions.—1. Are you in favour of an entirely Free Trade in Corn? 2. Is your congregation nearly unanimous in wishing an entirely Free Trade in Corn? 3. Do you approve generally of the plan of the meeting, or have you any suggestions to offer?

1. I duly received your circular on the subject of the Corn Laws, and would have answered it sooner, but waited till I should have an opportunity of laying the matter before my session. They authorise me to state, that they decline sending any representative to the proposed conference. The matter is unquestionably a *civil* one, upon which they will have ample opportunity elsewhere to express their opinion as *citizens*; and though, no doubt, there are few important political questions which have not a moral and religious aspect, and *may* not, in various forms, come under the legitimate review of *ecclesiastical* persons, even regularly assembled in their own courts: yet, in these days, when the limits of ecclesiastical and civil jurisdiction are so generally canvassed, and the importance of strictly maintaining them generally acknowledged, we do apprehend that *ecclesiastical persons* and *associations* should guard against any thing which has the *semblance* of *unnecessarily* overstepping their own proper province. As to the question itself, I believe I may say that I do not know a single member of my flock who is not in favour of the abolition of the Corn Laws. We are, indeed, but a simple people, little versant in political economy, and therefore not forward to express a very strong opinion on subjects about which wiser heads are so much at variance. For my own part, I am neither prepared to subscribe the strong language in which the baneful effects of these laws are often pourtrayed, nor do I expect from their abrogation the degree of relief which many anticipate; but regarding them as a measure which has apparently done no essential service to one class of the community, and has spread irritation and growing discontent among the others, in my humble opinion, it will be the wisdom of the Legislature as speedily as possible to remove them from the statute-book.

1. I am, and always have been, opposed to the Corn Laws; but whether they should be at once and entirely abolished, or the import duty on corn be gradually diminished, and become *nil* at the end of twelve or twenty months hence, I am at a loss to determine. Sudden political changes seem productive of much evil to communities. 2. A number of my congregation are farm-servants, and receive a great part of their wages in grain. These, of course, are higher and lower according to the grain market. Others are employed by the farmers in draining and otherwise improving their land. They certainly would prefer *cheap bread*, but some are afraid if the corn fall much in price, farmers will throw their land into pasture, and dispense with their services. This has been threatened by several farmers in this neighbourhood, and caused some alarm among the labourers. 3. Perhaps I may be permitted to say, that *ministers* seem to have too prominent a part in the matter. "Servants of God in the gospel of his Son," is our character, not politicians; to *save souls* is to be our chief care. 1 Cor. ii. 2; 1 Tim. iv. 15, 16. I beg humbly to suggest, that at the proposed meeting, the chairman,—the business,—committeemen,—and the speakers, should not be ministers, but private gentlemen, who are theoretically and practically acquainted with finance, statistics in corn, home and foreign trade, and the effects of these on society. Acts, vi. 2–4. I consider the Corn Laws a political question, upon which great and good men have long differed widely; and do not see there is greater injustice and immoral tendency in these laws than in other monopolies. It has been asserted, that far more grain is destroyed in the manufacture of intoxicating liquors, than all that is imported from foreign countries. If the people could be persuaded not to use these liquors, they would have cheap bread and more money to buy it with. The manufacture of these liquors, and traffic in them, tend far more, in my opinion, to deeds of villainy and immorality of every kind, than the Corn Laws. In this parish several L.1000's are spent annually on ardent spirits. We have a public-house for each 107 inhabitants, and the quantity of spirits sold in a year is said to be 2½ gallons for every woman and child in the parish. If I thought that free trade in corn would make whisky cheap, I would change my mind, and become a friend to Corn Laws. For great would be the sin committed, and the misery entailed, by lowering the price of intoxicating liquors.

1. Yes. 2. Yes. 3. Yes.

IV. WESLEYAN METHODISTS, WHO GENERALLY DECLINE TO ANSWER THE QUERIES, OR TO ATTEND THE MEETING.

To this body 21 circulars were sent, and from them 8 answers were received.

Answers from 8 Ministers.

Questions.—1. Are you in favour of an entirely Free Trade in Corn? 2. Is your congregation nearly unanimous in wishing an entirely Free Trade in Corn? 3. Do you approve generally of the plan of the Meeting, or have you any suggestions to offer?

Answers.—Sir,—I am extremely sorry that your circular places me under the necessity of saying in reply to the interrogations therein contained, 1. That I cannot admit the right of any one or more individuals to ask by *public circular*, and for *public purposes*, my opinion upon a question which I consider to be a political, rather than a moral one. 2. That I cannot attend the proposed public meeting; because other engagements of a less uncertain kind demand the whole of my time as a minister of Christ. 3. That I cannot meddle with the opinions of my congregation upon any subject, but such as are confessedly moral or religious. But I give full credit for integrity of purpose, and purity of motives, to those whose views *will* sanction what mine *will not*. I am, &c.

1. Yes. 2. Yes. 3. Yes.

1. No. 2. No. 3. I do not approve of the meeting at all.

1. Dear Sir,—In my opinion many of the questions contained in the circular are primarily of a political character, on that ground I beg to be excused from returning any particular answer to them. I remain, &c.

Sir.—I beg respectfully to decline answering the proposed queries.

1. No. 2. I do not know any of them that wish the Total Abolition, &c. 3. No.

1. The foregoing queries involve so many questions that are of a purely *politically* character, that I respectfully beg to be excused from answering them.

1. Mr * * is from home. Yours, &c.

V. ROMAN CATHOLICS, NONE OF WHOM WILL ATTEND THE MEETING, BUT WHO, JUDGING FROM THE ANSWERS RETURNED, ARE NEARLY ALL IN FAVOUR OF TOTAL REPEAL.

To this body 85 circulars were sent, and from them 14 answers have been received. None of the answers are from large towns, with the exception of Greenock. Most of them are from Agricultural districts in remote parts of Scotland.

*Answers from 19 Roman Catholic Priests.**

Questions.—1. Are you in favour of an entirely Free Trade in Corn? 2. Is your congregation nearly unanimous in wishing an entirely Free Trade in Corn? 3. Do you approve generally of the plan of the Meeting, or have you any suggestions to offer?

1. Decidedly so. 2. It is. (A.) Cannot attend. 3. After the Manchester meeting, I am afraid that such meetings do but little good. Petitions numerously signed by every congregation, in my opinion, would do more good than such a meeting.

1. Most certainly. 2. I am certain they are, and have as much need of it as any people in Scotland. (A.) No; on account of the length of journey, and the bad weather in these places, I do not intend being present. (B.) It is not very probable that any of them (his congregation) can go, for they are all so very poor that they cannot afford the expenses for so long a journey. 3. I do so.

* The answers to the two additional queries requesting to know whether they, or any of their people, would attend the meeting, have been given for this body, and also for the Episcopal Church. These answers are marked (A.) and (B.) The other answers are numbered in the usual way 1, 2, and 3.

Questions.—1. Are you in favour of an entirely Free Trade in Corn? 2. Is your congregation nearly unanimous in wishing an entirely Free Trade in Corn? 3. Do you approve generally of the plan of the Meeting, or have you any suggestions to offer?

1. I am in favour of the Total Abolition of the Corn and Provision Laws. 2. So far as I am acquainted with the sentiments of the Catholic congregation here, they are almost unanimous in wishing the Total Abolition of the Corn Laws. (A.) I cannot be present at the meeting. (B.) As our congregation here are almost all of the working classes, it is not probable that any two or even one can attend. Should any Catholic member of the Edinburgh Catholic congregation attend, I have reason to think, they will allow themselves to be represented by any two Catholics in Edinburgh who would be named by them. 3. I approve generally of the plan of the meeting, excepting in so far as mentioned in the end of the 5th resolution, that the meetings shall be opened by prayer by a minister to be named by the chairman. I consider the meeting to be a political one to consider the best means to get rid of an obnoxious law, and I think it ought to be considered as a political meeting. Public prayer in a public assembly, especially when held in a church, is surely considered as part of divine service, and as the meeting is to be composed of dissenters of all denominations, who do not join together in public worship, I think there ought to be nothing of that in the meeting itself; but that the prayer and public worship should be gone through in the morning previous to the hour of meeting, leaving all to attend or not attend as they may judge proper. I have no other remark to make, excepting to say that I think that a petition from a numerous poor Catholic congregation such as this would have no weight by itself, and that any petition going from such a town as this ought to be the petition of all the dissenters in said town. I may however be wrong in that idea, and I leave that consideration to the better judgment of others.

1. Decidedly so. 2. I think they are nearly unanimous. (A.) I find it impossible at the present moment for me to attend. 3. I approve of the plan generally, although there are some things to which I might object.

1. I am an advocate for a low but fixed duty. 2. No. 3. No answer sent.

1. I am. 2. They are, I believe, generally, if not universally, favourable to abolition. (A.) I do not intend because I cannot, be present. (B.) The circumstances of my flock precludes the hope that any two of them will be able to attend, or that they can find others to act as their representatives. 3. I do. The affair being in much abler hands than mine, I see no necessity of suggesting any thing, but attention to the sacred *dictum*: *Quod vis facere fac citò.*

1. Yes. 2. Yes. 3. Yes.

Sir,—I should be sorry to yield to any in my zeal for the interests of the *working classes*. But as I have never studied *Political Economy*, I feel that it would be the height of presumption in me to venture to give an opinion on the subject of the Corn Laws; and being now upwards of seventy years of age, I do not feel that it would be in my power to attend the meetings, nor do I expect that any two members of my congregation will attend. So wishing that God may direct all for the best. I am, &c.

1. I cordially agree with the Total Abolition of the Corn Laws. 2. I believe that this is the general opinion of the people of the country with whom I am acquainted. (A.) I cannot be present. (B.) It is not probable that any two members or substitutes for them will attend the meeting. 3. I do approve of the plan of the minute in all its bearings. The minute appears to me to be so clear and comprehensive, that I have nothing to suggest.

1. Decidedly so. 2. My congregation's composed of farmers and persons almost exclusively engaged in agriculture, are unanimous on the subject. (A.) I am precluded by my official duties from attending. 3. Yes. As prayer is an act of divine worship, I beg leave to state, that the employment of it on this and similar occasions, materially detracts from the attendance of Catholics.

1. I am, heart and soul. 2. My congregation is unanimous in calling for a Total Abolition of the existing Corn Laws. (A.) I am afraid I cannot be present, (B.) I do not think any of my congregation will attend, and I fear few of them have it in their power to appoint substitutes. 3. I do approve generally of the plan, because I see its aim is the general good.

Questions.—1. Are you in favour of an entirely Free Trade in Corn? 2. Is your congregation nearly unanimous in wishing an entirely Free Trade in Corn? 3. Do you approve generally of the plan of the Meeting, or have you any suggestions to offer?

1. Yes. 2. Yes. 3. Yes. A protection duty of a few shillings would not be disagreeable to many of my friends.

1. I would prefer, at least in the first instance, a moderate fixed duty to the Total Abolition of the Corn Laws; and I believe that a majority of those in this quarter favourable to a change, are of the same mind. It will be quite out of my power to be present at the proposed meeting, nor do I think that any of my flock will attend. I am, &c.

1. Yes; for taxes on necessaries are against the poor; taxes on luxuries are only against the great, who can curtail them without hurting life or health. 2. My congregation is in favour of Total Abolition. (A.) From poverty alone I am hindered from attending. (B.) It is not probable that any member can attend, from inability, not from want of will. 3. I approve generally of the plan proposed. I should like that two of the Edinburgh Roman Catholics would take the trouble to represent my congregation, but I do not know to fix upon any individuals by name. Perhaps you Sir might, being in the place, find two. If possible, get different individuals to represent the different interests; the meeting will thereby look more respectable to friends and foes.

VI. THE SCOTTISH EPISCOPAL CHURCH, NONE OF WHOM APPROVE OF THE MEETING, OR WILL ATTEND.

To this body 90 circulars were sent, and from them 21 Answers were received, as follows:—

Questions.—1. Are you in favour of an entirely Free Trade in Corn? 2. Is your congregation nearly unanimous in wishing an entirely Free Trade in Corn? 3. Do you approve generally of the plan of the meeting, or have you any suggestions to offer?

Answers.—Sir,—I have always considered that a Christian Minister should not meddle with politics. I am, Sir, your obedient servant.

1. No. 2. I should think the majority of them are by far too sensible people to wish any thing of the kind. But I never meddle with them in political matters. 3. Neither in general or particular. I would humbly suggest that it would be better to leave the whole matter in the hands of the Legislature, and to forbear from tumultuous agitation on this and all other public affairs, taking care that "supplications, prayers, intercession, and giving of thanks, be made for all men;" *for the Queen, and for all that are in authority,* that we may lead a quiet and peaceable life in all godliness and honesty.

1. Knowing the subject to be of great complexity, and never having had leisure to study it completely, I am not prepared to say that I am in favour of an entirely free trade in Corn. 2. In my intercourse, as a Minister of the Gospel, with my congregation, I have always considered that it was their religious, not their political, principles only, which it was my business to enquire, and hence I am quite ignorant of their sentiments respecting the Corn Trade. 3. I cannot approve of any plan in which Ministers of the Gospel, as Ministers, meet for the purpose of effecting an alteration in commercial law, any more than I could approve of a meeting of lawyers or merchants, as such, for the purpose of remodelling the religion of the country. Doubting the expediency of a Free Trade in Corn, and disbelieving the expediency of Ministers of the Gospel meeting to effect that object, I cannot suggest any thing calculated to promote the objects of the Meeting.

1. I conscientiously believe that nothing could be devised more detrimental to the best interests of the country than the abolition of the Corn Laws, and the substitution of a Free Trade. 2. It is my conviction that my congregation, to a man, repudiate any change in the existing system; and that they have sense enough to detect the quackery of *the few* who have originated the cry of "*Free Trade,*" and to pity *the many* who are deluded by it. 3. Decidedly not.

Questions.—1. Are you in favour of an entirely Free Trade in Corn? 2. Is your congregation nearly unanimous in wishing an entirely Free Trade in Corn? 3. Do you approve generally of the plan of the Meeting, or have you any suggestions to offer?

1. I am *not* in favour of the abolition of the Corn and Provision Laws; and this negative may be considered as answer to all the other queries.

1. No. 2. No. 3. No. I entirely disapprove of such meetings.

1. No. Because much of the land which now grow corn would be let out of cultivation, and as the home supply is the only sure and steady supply, abolition would only produce more unequal prices, and much greater distress, as has been seen before the restrictions. 2. No. Abolition is not required, but emigration on a larger scale to the colonies. More manufactures are produced than are required for the market; hence distress. (A.) No. It is impossible and unnecessary for me to be present. But I and the members of my congregation sincerely sympathize with the distressed objects of the meeting, and with the benevolent feelings which have suggested it. 3. No. Because it seems to be taken for granted that the restrictions are the true cause of the distress, whereas I am of quite a different opinion, as I have shewed above. Only those favourable to abolition are invited. If we would eschew evil, it must be with calmness and common advice. So that if the meeting would find out the true means of mitigating the distress often incident to the manufacturing classes, I would recommend that they should not look entirely to one side of the question. Our population is daily increasing, and therefore requiring a greater supply. By abolition, much of the land in this country must be thrown out of cultivation. The supply from abroad might not be steady, might fail, or those who are now our friends and supply us, might become our enemies, where would we be then?

1. No. 2. It is not. 3. I do not.

1. By no means. 2. I never interfere with my congregation in political matters. 3. Most assuredly not.

1. (No answer given). 2. Not at all unanimous. 3. I do not interfere with any public meetings.

1. No. 2. No. 3. No.

N.B. The subscriber in returning this half-sheet as desired, protests against being addressed as a "dissenting minister; the word *dissenter* being, as he thinks, applicable only to dissentients from the Episcopal Church of the British Empire.

Mr * * * begs to say that he declines answering or signing these queries.

1. No. 2. No. 3. No.

1. I am in favour of every measure that would even *probably* be for the good of the country, but from long and careful attention to the subject, I am fully convinced the abolition of the Corn Laws would be followed by no such beneficial results as some suppose, and therefore I would not meddle in the matter, but leave it entirely in the hands of Government, who must be better acquainted with *all* circumstances bearing on the subject than I can be. And I have full confidence in their efforts to promote the good of *all* classes by every really practicable means. 2. As far as I know, the members of my congregation would, to a man, subscribe to the same sentiments, and reprobate intermeddling in a matter which they would think it better to leave in the hands of those to whom the affairs of the country are entrusted. (A). I do not intend being present at the meeting. It is not only *probable* but *certain* that no two members of my congregation would be found who would go a single mile to attend any meeting on the subject. 3. The *plan* of the proposed meeting may, for aught I know to the contrary, be good enough; but as I do not approve of the *object* of the meeting, nor of the *principle* of interfering on every occasion in matters which properly belong to others, whose duty it is to attend to them. I can in no sense give my sanction to the meeting.

1. I never intermeddle with politic[s] myself, and I believe my congregation wish for nothing less than "an entirely Free Trade in Corn."

1. I have not studied this subject so as to be able to give a very decided opinion; but am inclined to think that the present restrictions on Foreign Corn should be greatly reduced, and nothing retained but what is necessary for the purposes of revenue. 2. No. 3. No. I have not any suggestions to offer. I am obliged for the Tract which was inclosed.

Questions.—1. Are you in favour of an entirely Free Trade in Corn? 2. Is your congregation nearly unanimous in wishing an entirely Free Trade in Corn? 3. Do you approve generally of the plan of the Meeting, or have you any suggestion to offer?

1. I beg to say that I do not wish to connect myself in any public way in regard to the Corn Laws, although I am not against the total repeal of them. 2 I believe that surely some members of my congregation would favour the Total Abolition. (A). I do not intend being present; but probably two members residing elsewhere might be so recommended by one or more of my congregation. 3 In reference to the invitation to attend the meeting, I beg to propose that the Ministers of the Episcopal Communion be not classed as "Dissenting Ministers," but separately designated.

Mr * * * has left * * * * and had nothing to do either there or elsewhere with "Dissenting Ministers;" and has no opinion to express relative to the Corn Laws, except that he would recommend the substitution of some more appropriate subject to the *Ministers* and members, &c. And, above all, that they would not favour him with any further applications. Honesty binds him to return the penny stamp, or he would not have written this letter.

1. I am not favourable to the total abolition of the Corn and Provision Laws, &c. For such a measure I believe would tend to do no good, but the reverse to the whole nation. 2. I am well aware of my congregation's sentiments on this important subject, and they are to a man opposed to the Abolition of the Corn Laws. Their reasons are too numerous and cogent to be stated here. 3. I make no remarks further than to say, that I think Dissenting Ministers would and might be better employed than to lend themselves as agitators and politicians.

1. No. 2. No. 3. No. I am a dissenter from the Established Kirk on religious, not on political grounds.

1. (The schedule returned blank).

APPENDIX.

I. SECESSION AND RELIEF CHURCHES IN THE COUNTIES OF NORTHUMBERLAND, CUMBERLAND, DURHAM, AND WESTMORELAND.

In addressing the first Circular, copies were inadvertently sent to all the Ministers who appeared in the Almanac List of the Secession and Relief Churches, including those who were resident in England. This was contrary to the declared constitution of the Meeting; and, accordingly, when the second Circulars were issued, they were addressed only to ministers resident in Scotland. But the answers to the first Circular which came from Ministers resident in England were thought of considerable value, as shewing the state of public feeling in the border counties, in favour of Total Repeal, and it was therefore resolved to publish them as an Appendix. Twenty-four of these Answers are from Ministers of the Secession, and two from Ministers of the Relief Church.

Answers from 26 Ministers.

Questions.—1. Are you in favour of an entirely Free Trade in Corn? 2. Is your congregation nearly unanimous in wishing an entirely Free Trade in Corn? 3. Do you approve generally of the plan of the Meeting, or have you any suggestions to offer?

Answers.—1. I am of opinion that we should demand and be satisfied with nothing short of a Total Abolition of the Corn and Provision Laws. 2. So far as the sentiments of my congregation are known to me, they disapprove of these laws, as iniquitous in themselves, and injurious to the interests of commerce. More than this I do not feel myself authorized to say. 3. I approve of the plan, and have no suggestions to offer. With best wishes for the success of the good cause, and hoping, as all your deliberations are to be conducted in the spirit of prayer, that you shall be wisely directed in the best steps to take for their speedy and total abolition being obtained, I subscribe myself, &c.

1. Yes. 2. Yes. 3. Yes.

1. Yes. 2. I am not sufficiently acquainted with the sentiments of my congregation. 3. Most cordially.

1. I am. 2. It is. 3. I do. I cordially approve of the proposed meeting in Edinburgh, and hope it will take place. It would give me pleasure to be present, but indisposition prevents me.

1. Most decidedly. 2. The bulk of the congregation, I would suppose, have no very decided opinion on the subject. They are rural, and scattered, and uninfluential individuals, and little conversant with such subjects. Some few have strong opinions on the question, but these are not unanimous. 3. Most cordially. The expression and proclamation of truth and justice can scarcely ever be unseasonable. And as for petitioning, although I am sick of it, and would scarcely be at the trouble to sign a petition to our unwise Legislature, I highly approve of those doing so who think that thereby they can promote the cause of humanity, justice, and liberty.

1. Yes. I am decidedly in favour of the Total Abolition of these laws. They are founded on selfishness, and have been a curse to the nation. 2. So far as I am acquainted with the sentiments of my congregation, they are unanimously in favour of their Total Abolition. And I believe, farther, that the sentiments of ninety-nine-hundredths of the district are of the same description. 3. We do approve of it with all our hearts, and wish you all the success you can reasonably desire. I have almost nothing to suggest. I am happy in being able to state, which I do freely, that an overwhelming majority of the population in this purely agricultural district of the country, are decidedly in favour of a Total Abolition of the Corn Laws, and that among them are to be found a goodly number of the landholders around us: and it is to be supposed that these are exclusively that class of them whose estates are not in circumstances of embarrassment.

1. Yes. 2. Yes. 3. Yes.

Questions.—1. Are you in favour of an entirely Free Trade in Corn? 2. Is your congregation nearly unanimous in wishing an entirely Free Trade in Corn? 3. Do you approve generally of the plan of the Meeting, or have you any suggestions to offer?

1. Yes. I am decidedly in favour of the Total Abolition of the Corn Laws. 2. It is my opinion that, so far as I know the sentiments of the congregation here, that they are in favour of the Total Abolition of the Corn Laws, but they do not openly express these sentiments, because they are more or less connected with the Earl of * * * * * either in the way of business or of employment. 3. I do approve generally of the plan proposed. I am quite satisfied with the whole of the accompanying minute, and have no suggestions of any kind to offer, but wish you all success.

1. Yes; but I think it may be expedient to have a small fixed duty *for a time*; diminishing gradually till it be extinguished. 2. Such are the prevailing sentiments; but my people are not unanimous on the subject. 3. Yes. I have no further remarks to make in reference to the minute; only I may add that petitions to Parliament against the Corn Laws will be forwarded from this place; but whether they may be congregational petitions, or subscribed by the inhabitants of the borough generally, will depend on circumstances.

1. Entirely so. 2. If there be any opponents they are but one or two. 3. Should the meeting adopt short luminous but strong petitions for presentation to the Queen and Parliament, to be transmitted from every congregation, supported by the signatures of male and female members and friends, and if it be agreed that on the same day when presented to rulers on earth, the whole petitioning bodies should assemble in the House of God for prayer, the success would be infallible. Let us hear your counsel, and rest assured of our prayers for your success.

1. Yes. Decidedly. 2. I am certain that they are nearly unanimous in approving of the measures of the late Ministry in reference to the Corn Laws; but having had no opportunity of conversing with any of them since the receipt of your circular, I cannot state with certainty their sentiments respecting an entirely Free Trade in Corn. They are mainly engaged in agricultural pursuits, still I think they will in general be more favourable to a Free Trade than to the present system. 3. Yes.

1. Yes. 2. Yes. 3. Yes. I have no hesitation in stating, that the congregation will concur in any measures which the public meeting may adopt.

1. I am in for the entire Abolition of Corn Laws, and the establishment of Free Trade. Not one so far as I know is not for the Abolition of the Corn Laws 3. I approve of the meeting.

1. I am. 2. They are in favour of a moderate fixed duty in the first instance. 3. I do.

1. Yes. 2. I understand *wholly* unanimous. 3. Yes.

1. Yes. 2. Nearly if not altogether in favour of Total Abolition. 3. I most cordially approve of the plan. Agitate, agitate; I intend to lecture on the subject in all the places where I can get access.

1. Yes. 2. I believe they are. 3 I cordially approve of the meeting.

1. As I reside in England, I will not attend the meeting of Dissenting Ministers to be held on Monday the 20th instant. What will in some measure supersede my attendance is, that an Anti-corn Association is about being formed in this place; and in regard to the queries put, I can reply to the first in the most direct and explicit terms, that I am decidedly against the Corn Laws, and all restrictive laws, and that nine-tenths of my congregation are of the same opinion. And if it were not for an overpowering influence, even the remaining tenth would go along with our sentiments.

1. I am. 2. I am of opinion that they are. 3. I do.

1. I am. 2. They are *nearly*, I have reason to know, if not *all* opposed to the Corn Laws. 3. I most cordially approve of it.

1. I am. 2. I have not consulted them in their collective character, but I believe their general feeling is in favour of an entirely Free Trade in Corn and other provisions. 3. I do.

1. I am most anxious to see these laws abolished. 2. I am sure there are very few belonging to this congregation who would not wish to see the Total Abolition of these Laws. 3. I approve fully of the plan explained in the minute. I have no suggestions to make. I only wish you the Divine blessing in all you attempt for the comfort of the people, and the glory of God.

Questions.—1. Are you in favour of an entirely Free Trade in Corn? 2. Is your congregation nearly unanimous in wishing an entirely Free Trade in Corn? 3. Do you approve generally of the plan of the Meeting, or have you any suggestions to offer?

1. I am, and have been ever since I understood the unjust and oppressive nature of those Laws; and I regard any protection to the agriculturists as a tax to the same amount on the community generally. 2. The district in which I live is almost entirely agricultural; my congregation are all anti-monopolists, since I lectured to them on the subject; although, I believe, many of them would like a small fixed duty, to try it, but only as a step to Total Abolition. 3. I do, and should like that in England instead of one general conference we had county ones. I believe the effect produced would be greater, because the agitation would be more universally diffused. I should have liked to have increased the influence, that it was not confined to Dissenting Ministers and others, but extended to those ministers and members of the Establishment who are at one with us on this question. In such a time of general distress, their co-operation might be depended on more than at another time.

1. I am. 2. Yes. 3. I do.

1. In favour of the Total Abolition of these laws, and the establishment of Free Trade in Corn, not immediately, but by a gradual reduction of duties. 2. I cannot freely say so. But the measures proposed by her Majesty's late Ministers regarding these subjects would have been very generally acceptable. 3. Yes.

1. I am in favour of the Total Abolition of the Corn and Provision Laws, and the establishment of an entirely Free Trade in Corn. 2. All my people live on the estate of * * * [a member of Government,] and yet, so far as I am acquainted with their sentiments, they are favourable to the Total Abolition of these laws, and an entirely Free Trade in Corn. 3. I approve generally of the plan.

II. SECESSION MINISTERS RESIDENT IN LANCASHIRE.

Answers from 6 Ministers.

Questions.—1. Are you in favour of an entirely Free Trade in Corn? 2. Is your congregation nearly unanimous in wishing an entirely Free Trade in Corn. 3. Do you approve generally of the plan of the Meeting, or have you any suggestions to offer?

Answers.—1. I am. 2. I know they are unanimous in this wish 3. I cordially approve of it. I perceive that the invitation is to be confined to Dissenting Ministers. Why exclude Churchmen? They may not attend. In all likelihood they will not attend; but I would give them the *honour* of excluding themselves.

1. Entirely. 2. Nearly unanimous; and in proof of our unanimity we intend, as a congregation, to memorialize the Queen, and to petition Parliament for these objects immediately. 3. I do, generally; but should have wished that invitations had been given to Ministers of the Established Church. Some, as at Manchester, would have attended. It would have been a test of the principles of others.

1. Yes; most decidedly. 2. Yes, with the exception of one family. 3. I do, and wish success to the movement, and a speedy end to the monopoly in corn.

1. Yes. 2. Yes. 3. Yes, I highly approve of it.

1. I am in favour of Free Trade, and regard the present movement not merely in a political point of view, but also as bearing upon the interests of religion. 2. The congregation here are nearly unanimous in wishing the Total Abolition of these Laws. 3. I approve generally of the plan for the proposed meeting.

1. I am most decidedly in favour of *total* and *immediate* abolition. 2. So far as I know the sentiments of my congregation, it is my opinion that they are *entirely* unanimous in wishing a total abolition of the Corn Laws, and an entirely Free Trade in every thing. 3. It has my most cordial approval. The general plan seems to be good; and I think you do well in confining it to Scotland. I consider it of importance, however, that I state it to be the opinion of many of the most enlightened and zealous repealers in this quarter, that Free Trade principles will never be adopted till complete suffrage is obtained; and that the only mode of gaining the former is to secure the latter. I this opinion I fully concur.

No. III. OFFICIAL DOCUMENTS SHOWING THE PROCEEDINGS OF THE DIFFERENT PRELIMINARY MEETINGS, HELD WITH THE VIEW OF GETTING UP THE GREAT PUBLIC MEETING AGAINST THE CORN LAWS.

1. CIRCULAR CALLING THE FIRST PRELIMINARY MEETING.

EDINBURGH, *December* 3, 1841.

SIR,—At a Joint Meeting of the Ministers from Edinburgh, who attended the recent ANTI-CORN LAW CONFERENCE in Manchester,—the Rev. John M'Gilchrist, Alex. Fraser, William Peddie, and James Robertson,—and a Sub-Committee of the EDINBURGH ANTI-CORN LAW ASSOCIATION, consisting of Messrs John Wigham, Jun., James M'Laren, John Gray, Duncan M'Laren, Thomas Russell, and John Howison, it was agreed to call a Preliminary Meeting, consisting of Ministers and Members of Dissenting Congregations in this city and neighbourhood, to consider the propriety of holding a Public Meeting, to which the Minister and two Members of each Dissenting Church in Scotland should be invited, to be held in Edinburgh, on Tuesday the 11th, and Wednesday the 12th, January, 1842, to express their opinion of the injustice and immoral tendency of the Corn and Provision Laws, and to petition for their Total Repeal

You are respectfully requested to attend the preliminary meeting, in Broughton Place Session House, on Monday evening, the 6th instant, at a quarter past eight o'clock, precisely. Cards for this preliminary meeting have been addressed to the minister and two members of different congregations in the city and neighbourhood.—I have the honour to be, Sir, Your very obedient Servant,

D. M'LAREN.

2. MINUTE OF FIRST PRELIMINARY MEETING.

EDINBURGH, *December* 7, 1841.

AT a preliminary Meeting of Ministers and Members of Dissenting Churches, residing in this City and Neighbourhood, held in Broughton Place Session-house this day, to consider the propriety of calling a Public Meeting of Ministers and Members of Dissenting Churches, from various parts of Scotland, to be held in Edinburgh on Tuesday the 11th, and Wednesday the 12th, January, 1842, to express their opinion of the injustice and immoral tendency of the Corn and Provision Laws, and to Petition for their Total Repeal, and an entirely Free Trade in Corn.—Present—Rev. John M'Gilchrist, Rev. Dr Ritchie, Rev. Francis Muir, Rev. Andrew Aitken, Rev. Peter Davidson, Rev. William Peddie, Rev. William Bruce, Rev. William Marshall.—Messrs John Wigham, junior, Adam Black, Duncan M'Laren, Counciller Gray, Commissary Wemyss, John Dunlop, John Wigham, *tertius*, Archibald Thomson, E. Cruickshank, John Ritchie, James M'Laren, John Gray, John Howison, William Miller, William Duncan, Robert Glass, James Durham, William Stark, James Marshall, Francis Richardson, R. S. Grieve, George Johnstone, Andrew Fyfe, Q. Dalrymple, Robert Kerr, Robert Davidson, Charles Peter, J. Pairman, William May, ——— Adie, W. Smith, Thomas Lindsay, D. Bernard, D. Watson, J. Frier, W. Henderson, Slateford; George Thomson, James Hogg, H. Cochrane, W. Dickie, ——— Robb, James Cassie, Alexander M'Lennan, A. Learmonth, Robert Crawford, ——— M'Leod, Thomas Russel, &c.

On the motion of Mr John Wigham, jun., the Rev. John M'Gilchrist was called to the chair. The Meeting having been opened with prayer by the Reverend Dr Ritchie, proceeded to consider the subject for which they had been called together. After much deliberation, it was unanimously Resolved, That a Public Meeting of the kind contemplated, if well attended by the friends of the cause from a distance, was highly desirable, and calculated to do much good; but that, before coming to a final decision on the subject, circulars, with queries, should be sent to Ministers residing at a distance, in order to ascertain their opinions as to the propriety of holding the Meeting, and to know whether they could be present at it; and if the answers should be generally favourable on these points, that the Meeting should then be fixed to take place at Edinburgh on Tuesday the 11th, and Wednesday the 12th, January, 1842.

The Meeting thereafter proceeded to consider to whom, and on what conditions, the invitations to the Public Meeting should be issued (on the assumption that the answers will be favourable), and in what manner its proceedings should be regulated; and after much consideration, the following Resolutions were, in the meantime, agreed to, but with the understanding, that they are to be subject to future revision, when the sentiments of friends residing at a distance, shall be ascertained regarding them:

I. That every Dissenting Minister in Scotland shall be invited by circular to attend the Public Meeting, and that two blank invitations, duly authenticated, shall, at the same time, be enclosed, to be filled up with the names of two Church Members, whom the Minister, and such other Members of his Congregation as he shall think it advisable to call together, either publicly or privately, for that purpose, shall think best qualified to represent their sentiments on this question; that the invitations, so filled up, shall then be delivered to the proper parties, as their credentials for attending the Meeting; and that their names and designations shall, immediately thereafter, be intimated to the Secretary in Edinburgh, to be afterwards appointed.

II. That where it may be inconvenient for members of distant congregations to be present at the Meeting, members belonging to the same denominations, residing in other localities, who can conveniently attend, may be recommended in their room, the invitations being filled up, delivered, and intimated in the manner above provided.

III. That in order, as far as possible, to diminish the expenses of parties leaving their homes, from a distance, to attend the Meeting, and not having friends in Edinburgh with whom they can conveniently reside, the friends of the cause in this city and neighbourhood shall endeavour to provide accommodation, in their own houses, for all persons so situated, during the time of their attendance at the Meeting; and that a small sub-Committee be appointed specially to take charge of this matter, and to get the invitations to the different houses forwarded to visitors, as soon as their names shall be intimated to the Secretary.

IV. That the friends of the cause in each congregation shall be recommended to subscribe to defray the unavoidable travelling expenses of the ministers and members who attend the Meeting.

V. That the Meetings shall take place each day at twelve o'clock *precisely*, adjourn at four P.M., and commence again at half-past six *precisely*; that different Chairmen shall be appointed at each sederunt; and that the Meetings shall always be opened with prayer by ministers selected by the Chairman for the time being, for that purpose.

VI. That the Meeting, at the commencement of its first sederunt, shall appoint one or more standing Committees to arrange the order of business, to frame resolutions, engage speakers, and generally to regulate all other matters,—reporting their proceedings to the Meeting from time to time; and in order to avoid the introduction of subjects not strictly connected with the specific object of the Meeting, it shall not be competent to propose, or put from the chair, any motion or amendment which has not previously been sanctioned by the Committee on whom the public Meeting shall devolve the responsibility of preparing the order of the public business.

VII. That it shall be distinctly understood that the Meeting will be responsible only for the sentiments embodied in the Resolutions and Petitions which shall be sanctioned by its authority; and not for opinions expressed by individual members in moving or seconding these Resolutions or Petitions.

VIII. That Members addressing the Meeting shall keep as closely as possible to the subject of the particular Resolutions entrusted to them,—but communicating at the same time such facts regarding the injurious effects of the Corn and Provision Laws as they may be acquainted with, having reference to the congregations and neighbourhoods with which they are severally connected; and that it shall be the duty of the Chairman for the time being, to prevent the discussions of any other subject than that for which the Meeting was specially called together,—the injustice and immoral tendency of the Corn and Provision Laws, and the duty of strenuously supporting their Total Repeal, and the establishment of an entirely Free Trade in Corn.

IX. That there having been laid before the Meeting draft copies of Letter and Queries proposed to be forwarded to ministers at a distance, along with this Minute, they were severally approved of, and directed to be forwarded.

X. That an adjourned preliminary meeting shall be held, on Monday the 20th instant, in Broughton Place Session-house, at a quarter past eight o'clock in the evening, to make the final arrangements for the public Meeting, if the answers from friends at a distance be generally favourable; and that, in the meantime, the following Committee be appointed, with power to forward the circulars, receive the answers, and make a digest of the same, to be laid before the adjourned Meeting; to propose such alterations on the draft Resolutions as may appear to them advisable, in consequence of any suggestions which may be offered in the answers to the Queries; and generally, with powers to take such other steps as may appear to them advisable for promoting the objects of the meeting. (Here follow the names.)

3. CIRCULAR SENT ALONG WITH THE PRECEDING MINUTE.

EDINBURGH, *December* 7, 1841.

SIR,—I beg to annex copy of Minute of a preliminary meeting of Ministers and Members of Dissenting Churches residing in this city and neighbourhood, held yesterday, to consider the propriety of calling a Public Meeting of Ministers and Members of Dissenting Churches, from different parts of Scotland, to be held in Edinburgh, on Tuesday the 11th, and Wednesday the 12th January, 1842, to express their opinion of the injustice and immoral tendency of the Corn and Provision Laws, and to petition for their Total Repeal, and an entirely Free Trade in Corn.

You will observe from the Minute, that the preliminary meeting unanimously approved of the proposal, in so far as they were entitled to express an opinion on the subject; but a the friends of the cause at a distance are equally interested in the result, it was reselved to fix nothing definitely until their sentiments should be ascertained. With this view, the meeting directed this Circular and Schedule to be sent to you and other Ministers in different parts of Scotland. inquiring whether they approved of the proposed public Meeting, and could make it convenient to be present, &c.

I have, therefore, to beg that you will answer the queries herewith sent. *on the same half sheet of paper*, and return it with your signature, taking care that it is put in the post-office *on or before Tuesday the 14th instant*. On the results of the whole answers will depend whether the meeting will take place or not, as it appeared to be the general opinion of those who were present at the preliminary meeting, that *unless a considerable attendance from a distance was promised*, a meeting of the kind contemplated could not be expected to produce any beneficial results; and, therefore, that the proposal must be abandoned, unless a good attendance can be relied on. If the answers shall be generally favourable, you will be informed, as early as possible, that the meeting is finally determined on; and such other information will, at the same time, be communicated, as may be thought necessary for your guidance.

As it has been ascertained that a number of ministers and members of Dissenting Churches have doubts of the propriety of churches meeting, *as such*, for the discussion of the Corn Laws, or other similar questions, or for the appointment of persons to represent their opinions on such subjects, it has been decided, as you will perceive from the Minute, that meetings andiappointments, *strictly congregational*, are not, in the circumstances, advisable. Hence, meetings may be called in accordance with the Minute, either privately, or by public intimation, in which the invitation shall be restricted to '*those members of the congregation who are in favour of the Total Abolition of the Corn and Provision Laws*, for the purpose of recommending two individuals to represent *their* sentiments at the public meeting to be held on the subject, in Edinburgh, on the 11th and 12th January, 1842;' and thus, it is conceived, the difficulties connected with holding meetings, strictly congregational, will be avoided.—I have the honour to be, Sir, your very obedient servant, (Signed) JOHN M'GILCHRIST.

4. QUERIES SENT ALONG WITH THE PRECEDING MINUTE AND CIRCULAR.

You are respectfully requested to answer and sign the following Queries, and thereafter to tear off the half-sheet, and, as it is already addressed, and has a postage stamp affixed, it requires only to be wafered and dropt into the Post-office. It is particularly requested that this may be done *on or before Tuesday the 14th instant.*

1. Are you in favour of the Total Abolition of the Corn and Provision Laws, and the establishment of an entirely Free Trade in Corn?
2. Is it your opinion, so far as you are acquainted with the sentiments of your congregation, that they are nearly unanimous in wishing the Total Abolition of these Laws, and an entirely Free Trade in Corn?
3. Do you intend being present at the proposed meeting?
4. Is it *probable* that two members of your congregation will attend it? or, if not, Is it *probable* that two members residing elsewhere, who can conveniently attend, will be recommended by members of your congregation to represent their opinions at the meeting?
5. Do you approve generally of the plan of the proposed meeting, as explained in the accompanying Circular and Minute?
6. Be so kind as mention any suggestions which occur to you, with

reference to the terms of the accompanying Minute, or other matters calculated, in your opinion, to promote the objects of the meeting,—it being intended that the draft Resolutions now sent for your perusal, shall afterwards be revised, when the sentiments of friends residing at a distance shall be ascertained regarding them.

5. MINUTE OF SECOND PRELIMINARY MEETING.

At a preliminary Meeting of Ministers and Members of Dissenting Churches, residing in this City and Neighbourhood, held in Broughton Place Session house on the 20th December, 1841, to consider the propriety of calling a Public Meeting of Ministers and Members of Dissenting Churches, from various parts of Scotland, to be held in Edinburgh in January next, to express their opinion of the injustice and immoral tendency of the Corn and Provision Laws, and to Petition for their Total Repeal, and an entirely Free Trade in Corn,—Present—(Here follow the names of fifty-one Ministers and Members who were present.)

On the motion of the Reverend John M'Gilchrist, the Rev. Francis Muir was called to the chair, and the Rev. Peter Davidson opened the meeting with Prayer. The Committee reported that they had forwarded the Circulars as directed by last meeting, the number being 976; and that they had received 569 answers, which they had carefully analyzed, and of which the following is an abstract:—

1. *Bodies who decline taking part in the meeting.*—These comprehend the Episcopalians, to whom 90 Circulars were sent, and from whom 21 answers were received; the Roman Catholics, to whom 85 Circulars were sent, and from whom 14 answers were received; and the Wesleyan Methodists, to whom 21 Circulars were sent, and from whom 8 answers were received; making an aggregate of 196 Circulars and 43 answers. The general import of the answers is, that these bodies decline taking part in the proposed meeting. The answers from the Roman Catholics generally state, in very decided terms, that they and their people are strongly opposed to the Corn and Provision Laws, and in favour of Free Trade: the other bodies generally decline to answer the Queries.

2. *Secession, Relief, Independent, and Baptist Churches.*—The total number of Circulars sent to these four bodies was 670,* and the Answers received from their Ministers 494. It appears, that 459 of these Ministers express decided opinions in favour of the Total Repeal of the Corn and Provision Laws, and the establishment of an entirely Free Trade in Corn; about 12 are in favour either of a small fixed duty, or gradual abolition; and the remaining 33 do not answer this question. It is not a little remarkable, that *not one Minister out of the 494 expresses an opinion in favour of the present Corn Laws.* With regard to the opinions of the people, 431 of the Ministers state that their Congregations are nearly unanimous in approving of the Total Abolition of the Corn and Provision Laws, and Free Trade; and only *three* state that their people are *not* nearly unanimous. Of the remaining 60, about 15 state that their people are either in favour of Gradual Abolition or of a Fixed Duty; and the others omit to answer the question. *Not one Minister states that a*

* All the numbers in this paragraph include the Congregations in the North of England in connection with the Secession and Relief Churches, to whom the *first* circulars were inadvertently addressed; and all the numbers have reference only to the returns as made up on the 20th December. The present publication includes all returns received up to the 30th December, and hence none of the above figures are *now* correct, as compared with the published Answers.

majority of his Congregation approves of these Laws. Again, with reference to the plan of the proposed Meeting, 346 Ministers express their cordial approval; 28 disapprove of it; and 120 either omit to answer the question, or suggest alterations, which considerably qualify their general approval.

3. *Smaller Sects.*—To the smaller sects 110* Circulars were sent; and 32 answers were received from their Ministers and Pastors. These answers show that 23 of their number are decidedly in favour of Total Abolition and Free Trade; *one* is not; and the other 8 either omit to answer the question, or are in favour of a Fixed Duty or Gradual Abolition; and with reference to the opinions of their people, the answers are numerically the same. With reference to the plan of the Meeting, 16 state that they cordially approve of it; *three* that they do not; and the other 13 omit to answer the question—in many instances, apparently from inattention, as appears from the promised attendance at the proposed Meeting, which is 8 Ministers, 26 of their resident Members, and 2 from other places. Many of these Ministers and Pastors, as well as a few of all the other bodies, state that the smallness of the numbers of their people, and the proportionally greater expense of the journey which would fall on each, is the sole cause which prevents them from attending.

4. *Promised attendance at the Public Meeting.*—The number of ministers and members who are likely to attend the meeting cannot certainly be known for some time, as, in numerous instances, the answers state that the subject is under consideration, and the result, from various causes, uncertain. A much larger number plead indisposition, the inclemency of the season, family affliction, and prior engagements, as the causes which prevent their attendance; and in very many instances, they express their deep regret that they are thus precluded from attending a Meeting, the object and plan of which they so cordially approve. But already 712 ministers and members have promised to attend, as appears from the following statement:—

	Ministers.	Resident Members.	Members from other places.	Total of these.
1. Secession Churches,	118	171	95	384
2. Relief Churches,	45	59	26	130
3. Independent Churches,	25	41	44	110
4. Baptist Churches,	19	24	9	52
5. Smaller Sects,	8	26	2	36
Totals,	215	321	176	712

The meeting having heard the foregoing statement, resolved, that, as the attendance promised was so much larger than they had anticipated, the meeting should be held during three days in place of two, as formerly proposed, namely, Tuesday the 11th, Wednesday the 12th, and Thursday the 13th January, 1842, in the Relief Church, South College Street.

[Part of the Minute having reference to the exclusion of the Established Ministers, &c., is here omitted, being copied into the Introduction, pp. 7, 8.]

RESOLUTIONS:—

I. That, with the exception of those religious bodies who have either refused to answer the Queries already circulated, or declined to take part in the proposed meeting, a circular shall be sent to every Dissenting Minister in Scotland, inviting him individually to attend the Public Meeting; and

* This includes the divisions Nos. II. and III. in the present publication, which has been differently arranged from the plan followed in the above Minute. See also note, p. 64, as to the different dates of making up the two returns.

that two blank invitations, duly authenticated, shall, at the same time, be enclosed, to be filled up with the names of two Church Members whom the Minister, and other Members of his Congregation who are in favour of the Total Abolition of the Corn and Provision Laws, and whom he may consult—by calling them together, either publicly or privately, for that purpose —shall consider qualified fairly to represent *their* sentiments, on this question (meetings and appointments *strictly congregational* not being in the circumstances thought advisable); that the invitations shall then be delivered to the parties so recommended, and their names, designations, and residences, intimated to the General Committee in Edinburgh, *if possible*, on or before Thursday the 30th December.

II. That where it may be inconvenient for members of distant congregations to be present at the Meeting, members belonging to the same denominations, residing in other localities, who can conveniently attend, may be recommended in their room, the invitations being duly filled up, delivered, and intimated.

III. That in order, as far as possible, to diminish the expenses of parties leaving their homes, from a distance, to attend the meeting, and not having friends in Edinburgh with whom they can conveniently reside, the friends of the cause in this city and neighbourhood will endeavour to provide accommodation, in their own houses, for all persons so situated, during the time of their attendance at the meeting, *provided their names be transmitted on or before the 30th December;* and that a special Committee be appointed to take charge of this matter, and to get the invitations to the different houses forwarded to visitors, as early as possible; that this special Committee shall be divided into Sub-committees with separate Conveners; that one Sub-committee shall be composed of two members from every Secession congregation in Edinburgh and Leith—Councillor Gray, 60 Princes Street, to be Convener; one shall be composed of two members from every Relief congregation—Mr David Nicolson, 36 Canongate, to be Convener; one shall be composed of two members from every Independent congregation—Mr James M'Laren, 7 Roxburgh Street, to be Convener; one shall be composed of two members from every Baptist congregation—Mr Wm. Miller, 59 George Square, to be Convener; and one shall be composed of members of the Society of Friends, and other small bodies—Mr John Wigham, jun., 10 Salisbury Road, to be Convener; that it shall be the duty of each Sub-committee, in the first instance, to provide accommodation for the ministers and members connected with its own body, and thereafter to assist the other Sub-committees:—Councillor Gray to be Convener of this Special Committee.

IV. That the friends of the cause in each congregation shall be recommended to defray the unavoidable travelling expenses of their own minister, and of those members of their own congregation who attend the meeting.

V. That the Meeting shall take place on Tuesday at eleven o'clock *precisely*, adjourn at four P. M., and commence again at half-past six *precisely;* that on Wednesday the meeting shall take place at 10 o'clock *precisely*, and adjourn at 4 P. M., without resuming again on the same evening, in order to allow members who may be so disposed, an opportunity of attending a Soiree, which is to be held in the evening at half-past 6 o'clock; and that on Thursday the meeting shall take place at 10 o'clock *precisely*, adjourn at 4 P. M., and commence again at half-past 6 o'clock *precisely;* that different Chairmen shall be appointed at each sederunt; and that the Meetings shall be opened with prayer by ministers selected by the General Committee.

VI. That the Meeting, at the commencement of its first sederunt, shall appoint a large standing Committee, with power to sub-commit, in order to arrange the routine of business, to frame resolutions, appoint speakers, communicate with individuals and deputations, who, although not members, may be desirous of addressing the meeting, and, generally, to regulate all other matters,—reporting their proceedings to the Meeting from time to time; and in order to avoid the introduction of subjects not strictly connected with the specific object of the Meeting, it shall not be competent to propose, or put from the chair, any resolution or amendment which has not previously been sanctioned by the Committee on whom the public Meeting shall devolve the responsibility of preparing the public business.

VII. That it shall be distinctly understood that the Meeting will be responsible only for the sentiments embodied in the Resolutions and Petitions which shall be sanctioned by its authority; and not for opinions expressed by individual members in proposing or supporting these Resolutions or Petitions, or by individuals, or deputations from other bodies who, although not members, may be invited to address the Meeting.

VIII. That the Members addressing the Meeting shall keep as closely as possible to the subject of the particular Resolutions entrusted to them,—but communicating at the same time such statistical information and other facts showing the injurious effects of the Corn and Provision Laws, as they may be acquainted with, having reference to the congregations and neighbourhoods with which they are severally connected; that no member shall occupy more than half an hour in addressing the meeting, and that it shall be the duty of the Chairman, for the time being, to enforce this regulation, and prevent the discussion of any other subject than that for which the Meeting was specially called together,—the injustice and immoral tendency of the Corn and Provision Laws, and the duty of strenuously supporting their Total Repeal, and the establishment of an entirely Free Trade in Corn.

IX. That the Chairmen for the five Sederunts of the Meeting shall be selected respectively from Edinburgh, Glasgow, and the other three towns from which the greatest number of Members shall be appointed to attend the Meeting,—the Chairman for Edinburgh to be recommended by the General and Special Committees now elected; and the Chairman from each of the other Towns, to be recommended by a majority of the Members residing in them, whose appointment shall be intimated to the General Committee in Edinburgh, on or before Thursday the 30th December, on which day separate lists of their names shall be forwarded to one of their number in each town, with directions to summon the whole members to Meetings to be held on or before Wednesday the 5th January, for the purpose of recommending Chairmen connected with each town; and in cases where no intimation of such meetings and recommendations shall be received by the General Committee in Edinburgh, on or before the 7th January, it shall be held that the privilege has not been exercised, and it shall be their duty immediately to engage suitable Chairmen to supply such vacancies, without regard to residence in any particular locality, for the purpose of recommending them for election to the Public Meeting.

X. That, as it has been considered necessary, for the proper order of the business, and the success of the Public Meeting, to confer large powers on the Committee proposed to be appointed at its first sederunt, it is desirable that it should be equally and impartially selected, according to some defined rule, from the whole of the towns and districts sending deputies to the Meeting; and that, in order to accomplish this object, it shall be the duty of the General Committee, hereby appointed, to prepare a list of names to form the Committee to be recommended to the Public Meeting, by selecting one member out of every ten, who may attend from the different towns and districts in Scotland, and whose appointment shall be duly intimated on or before the 30th December,—the same rule to be applied to the members resident in this city and neighbourhood; and that in cases where the members residing in any town or district, shall prefer making the selection of every tenth individual of their own number, to leaving it to the General Committee in Edinburgh, it shall be in their power to do so, provided they intimate the names of the persons selected on or before the 7th January.

XI. That in order that the proper business of the Public Meeting may commence without delay or confusion at the appointed time, and in compliance with the wishes expressed in many of the answers to the Queries which have been received from Ministers in distant places, the General Committee be instructed to prepare resolutions, petitions, and other documents for the adoption of the Public Meeting, and generally to arrange the order of the business as far as shall be found practicable; but under the express condition that all the resolutions, petitions, and other documents, shall be submitted to the judgment of the Committee, which shall be appointed by the Public Meeting, and be subject to their revision; and that, for the reasons above stated, the General Committee be farther instructed to engage such number of speakers as they shall judge proper from the Ministers and Church Members who have signified their intention to be present, from the different Districts of Scotland,—but *not exceeding* one-tenth part of the Ministers and one-twentieth part of the Church Members from each of the Religious Bodies composing the Meeting,—and to forward to the speakers so selected, copies of *draft* resolutions, with a request that they will come prepared to speak to them, subject, however, to such modifications as shall be judged expedient by the Committee appointed by the Public Meeting.

XII. That a small number of public men, without regard to their political or religious opinions on other questions, who are known as decided advocates of the Total Abolition of all duties on Corn, and the establishment of an entirely Free Trade, shall be invited by the General Committee to be present at the Public Meeting, to give the members the benefit of their opinion and advice, regarding the moral and religious aspect of the question, its statistics, or its importance in a commercial and financial point of view, and the means best calculated, in their opinion, to promote the cause of Total Abolition and Free Trade.

XIII. That Deputations from Anti-Corn Law Associations, or other bodies having the same object in view—the Total Abolition of all Duties on Corn—may, by permission of the meeting, be admitted and allowed to be heard on the question, without regard to their opinions on other subjects; it being, however, understood, that each application for admission shall be considered on its own merits, and dealt with as the Meeting shall think fit; and that when admitted, only one member of each Deputation shall address the meeting.

XIV. [This Resolution is copied into the Preface.]

XV. That subscriptions to defray the expenses connected with the Meeting, for printing, postages, tickets, door-keepers, and other miscellaneous expenses, shall be received by the Treasurers, Messrs John Howison and John Gray, 2 Drummond Street, and also by the Conveners of the different Committees and Sub-committees; and that they be recommended to endeavour rather to obtain small subscriptions—say sums of five shillings and under—from a large number of persons, than larger subscriptions from a smaller number of persons, in order that the expenses may thus be more equally distributed among the friends of the cause.

XVI. That a ticket, to admit one person, to witness the proceedings of the Public Meeting, shall be presented, through their guests, to each of the families who provide accommodation for a member coming from a distance to attend the meeting; that those families who provide accommodation for two or more members shall receive a proportional number of tickets; and that other friends of the cause who subscribe to the extent of five shillings to defray the necessary expenses connected with the meeting, shall likewise be presented with tickets of admission to witness the proceedings.

The Meeting having considered these Resolutions, approved of the same, and appointed the following General Committee, to carry the foregoing instructions into effect, and with power to take such other steps as may appear to them advisable for promoting the objects of the Meeting—these powers to continue until a new Committee shall be appointed by the Public Meeting, as above provided, when they shall finally cease:—The Ministers who attended the Manchester Conference, namely, the Rev. Dr Ritchie, the Rev. John M'Gilchrist, Francis Muir, William Peddie, Alexander Fraser, James Robertson, Andrew Todd, and William Marshall; together with the Rev. James Kirkwood, James Harper, William Innes, John French, George Johnston, Christopher Anderson, W. L. Alexander, Peter Davidson, James Turnbull, Andrew Thomson, Andrew Arthur, William Bruce, Henry Wight; and also Councillors Black, Renton, Gray, Richardson, Grierson, and Geikie; Deputy Commissary-General Wemyss, Messrs John Wigham, jun., Archibald Thomson, James M'Laren, John Dunlop, Duncan M'Laren, John Gray, William Duncan, John Howison, James Peddie, Thomas Russell, Francis Richardson, R. S. Grieve, Robert Glass, William Miller, Andrew Fyfe, Edward Cruickshank, Robert Davidson, William Stark, Robert Kerr, Robert Crawford, David Nicolson, Charles Spence, William Drummond, James Grant, John Adie, John Neill, William Smith, Robert Anderson, Peter Wilson, Thomas Calder, J. H. Stott, A. D. Campbell, James Mushet, and James Hogg,—with power to add to their number, and to sub-commit from time to time—Mr Duncan M'Laren to be Chairman of the Committee.

(Signed) Francis Muir,
Chairman of the Preliminary Meeting.

6. CIRCULAR SENT ALONG WITH THE PRECEDING MINUTE.

Edinburgh, *Dec.* 23, 1841.

Sir,

I have been directed to transmit to you the enclosed Minute of a meeting of Ministers and members of Dissenting Churches, held here on the 20th instant.

The meeting having freely availed themselves of the suggestions contained in the answers to the queries circulated on the 7th inst. with the first *draft* of the Resolutions, many of the latter have been considerably altered, and other Resolutions have been added, for the purpose of removing some objections, and not a few misconceptions which appear to have prevailed, and in order to render the plan and details of the Meeting more complete. You are therefore requested carefully to peruse the Minute now enclosed, and, in particular, to notice the alterations which have been made on the first Resolution, for the purpose of removing a misconception which appears to have prevailed to the effect, that the Ministers were invited to attend the Meeting in their *official character*, and to express their sentiments *officially as the Ministers of Christian Churches*;—and that each congregation, *as such*, was invited to appoint two Members to represent them at the proposed Meeting *in their strictly congregational character, and as Christian Churches*. No such rule was laid down by the promoters of the Meeting, and if the phraseology formerly employed was in any degree calculated to convey such an impression, the terms of the adjusted Minute, and the explanation now offered, must remove all doubts on the subject.

As the former Circulars contained only a *conditional invitation* to a meeting which was not finally determined on, all the former Answers, with regard to attendance or non-attendance, will be considered as cancelled; and you are, therefore, requested not to trust to any former communication which you may have sent, but immediately to answer the accompanying Queries, *on the same half sheet of paper*, and transmit it by post, if possible, *on or before the 30th December*. If, in consequence of being from home when this Circular reaches your abode, you are prevented from returning an answer before that date, be so kind as write on the *earliest possible day after your return*, and every exertion, in that case, will be made by the Committee to accommodate yourself and the Members of your Congregation who may accompany you.

Those Ministers and Members who have friends in Edinburgh or the neighbourhood, with whom they would prefer to reside—from having been in their houses on former occasions—are requested to communicate with them as early as possible regarding their intentions,—it being considered that all visiters so situated are likely to be more comfortable in the houses of friends to whom they are personally known, than in the houses of those to whom they were previously strangers; but those Ministers who have no preference for themselves, and whose Members are in the same situation, are requested immediately to answer the Queries without making any effort to accommodate themselves by private arrangements; and every exertion will be made by the Committee to provide suitable accommodation for them during the period of the Public Meeting.

If none of the Members of your own congregation can attend the Meeting, and Members resident in this neighbourhood shall be appointed in terms of Resolution II., please to fill in their names, in the accompanying blank invitation; and after certifying the same, *by affixing your signature* where marked for that purpose, transmit it to them at your earliest convenience, and intimate their names to me in answering the annexed Queries. If their names be duly intimated, they will be regularly entered in a book kept for that purpose, and tickets will be prepared for them; but if their names be not intimated, of course, they cannot be entered, and, consequently, no tickets will be prepared for them.

If members of your congregation, although anxious to appoint persons resident here, to represent their opinions at the meeting, shall not be acquainted with the names of properly qualified individuals, you are recommended to forward the blank invitation to any member of this Committee in whom you have confidence, with directions that, after filling in the names of two church members, and ascertaining that they are willing to accept, he shall transmit the document to me, that it may be regularly entered, and tickets prepared. And you will observe that, in this case also, it is indispensable that the invitation *be properly authenticated, by affixing your signature* at the proper place before transmitting it to this City. Unless these requirements be attended to, the names will not be entered, and no tickets will be prepared.

The Tickets will be ready for delivery, at my Warehouse, 329 High Street, on and after the 7th January; and in order to accommodate persons arriving by late coaches, attendance will be given on the Monday evening preceding the Meeting, until half-past 10 o'clock, for the delivery of the Tickets. Ministers and Members coming from a distance will receive, along with their own Tickets, others, to present to the families with whom they reside, in terms of Resolution XVI. To preserve proper order at the Meeting, the door-keepers will be instructed to admit no person whatever without a Ticket.

Unless you have to intimate that you will be present at the Meeting, or that the friends of Abolition in your Congregation will be represented at it, or that you wish to subscribe for copies of the publication referred to in Resolution XIV., it will *not* be necessary to reply to this communication.

I have the honour to be, Sir, your very obedient Servant,

D. M'LAREN,
Chairman of the Committee.

7. QUERIES SENT ALONG WITH THE PRECEDING MINUTE AND CIRCULAR.

1. Do you intend being present at the meeting?

2. If so, have you lodgings provided in the house of a friend, or will you allow the Committee to procure and forward an invitation to you?

3. Will two members of your congregation, or two persons resident in other places, be present in their room?

4. If so, please to fill in their names, designations, and residences opposite:

5. And state whether they have lodgings provided in the houses of friends, or will allow the Committee to procure and forward invitations to them through you?

6. Do you or your friends wish to subscribe for copies of the publication referred to in resolution XIV., which will be ready for delivery with the tickets for the public meeting, and the price of which, to subscribers, will be limited to one shilling?

N.B. It is earnestly requested, that your answers be put into the Post-Office, if possible, *in time to reach Edinburgh on or before the 30th December.*

8. INVITATION TO TWO MEMBERS TO REPRESENT THE FRIENDS OF ABOLITION IN YOUR CONGREGATION.

EDINBURGH, *December* 23, 1841.

GENTLEMEN,

The General Committee for conducting the Public Meeting of Ministers and Members of Dissenting Churches, which is to be held in this City, on the 11th, 12th, and 13th of January 1842,—'To express their opinion of the Injustice and Immoral Tendency of the CORN and PROVISION LAWS, and to Petition for their TOTAL REPEAL and an entirely FREE TRADE in CORN,'—beg that you will attend the same, to represent the opinions of those Members of the Church at ———————— who approve of the object of the Meeting, and the Principles on which it will be conducted, as detailed in the printed Minute of the Preliminary Meeting held on the 20th inst.—I am, Gentlemen, your very obedient Servant,

(Signed) D. M'LAREN,
Chairman of the Committee.

To Mr ————————, residing at ————————;
Mr ————————, residing at ————————.

I approve of the above named individuals being invited to attend the Meeting.

(*The Minister to sign here*) (Signed)————————, *Minister.*

END.

THE

CORN AND PROVISION LAWS

ARRAIGNED, CONVICTED AND DENOUNCED AS INFLICTING POVERTY, DISEASE, AND DEATH; AND PROMOTING IRRELIGION, VICE, AND SEDITION.

A LECTURE:

DELIVERED IN JOHN STREET RELIEF CHURCH, GLASGOW,
ON THE EVENING OF TUESDAY, 29th NOVEMBER, 1842.

UNDER THE AUSPICES OF

THE GLASGOW YOUNG MEN'S FREE TRADE ASSOCIATION.

BY THE

REV. WILLIAM ANDERSON,

OF JOHN STREET RELIEF CHURCH

Published at the request of the Association.

Printed
FOR THE GLASGOW YOUNG MEN'S FREE TRADE ASSOCIATION.

MDCCCXLIII.

The Corn and Provision Laws Arraigned, Convicted and Denounced . . . (1843)

The lectures by Revd William Anderson and Revd Alexander Harvey were part of a series organized by the Glasgow Young Men's Free Trade Association, delivered in the John Street Relief Church on Tuesday evenings in the last weeks of 1842, and published by the Association. Other speakers included Revd Robert Burns (1789–1869, and Revd Andrew Somerville (1800–77).

Revd William Anderson, whose church hosted the lectures was born in Kilsyth, near Glasgow, the son of Revd John Anderson, minister of the local Relief Church and, from 1847, the United Presbyterian Church (formed by the union of the United Secession Church and most of the congregations of the Relief Church).[1] Anderson studied in Glasgow University where he was awarded a LL.D. in 1850, and became minister of his father's congregation. In 1822 he became pastor of the John Street Relief Church, a position he held for the rest of his life.

Anderson, whose eccentricities won him the sobriquet 'daft Willie Anderson', was a popular preacher with a considerable local following. His greatest strength appears to have been the public platform where he spoke against slavery, for oppressed nationalities, for political reform 'in the interests of the people', and for the separation of the Church from the state. Accordingly he defended the introduction of political issues into the pulpit, and encouraged independence of thought and action. On theological matters he was a strong millenarian and a moderate Calvanist, strongly opposed to the Church of Rome.

[1] According to the entry in *D.N.B.* vol. 1, by William Garden Blaikie, Anderson was born in 1799 and dies in 1873. Joseph Irving, *The Book of Scotsmen Eminent*, Paisley: Alexander Gardner, 1881, gives the respective dates as 1800 and 1872.

THE

CORN AND PROVISION LAWS

ARRAIGNED, CONVICTED, &c.

Before I enter on the particular subject which I have been requested to discuss, I shall take the liberty of making a few observations in the way of justifying the part which my brethren and myself act, when in our professional character, as ministers of the Gospel, we thus publicly interfere with the corn and provision laws.

In the course of the last session of parliament, when presenting the Petition of the Conference of Ministers convened at Edinburgh, Lord Brougham, that he might exonerate his conscience, I suppose, of the responsibility for a document so foolish, and that with his superior knowledge of the duties of the pastoral office, he might correct and rebuke the ignorance and impertinence of those men who had so far mistaken their vocation, expressed himself to the effect that Religion has nothing to do with Corn. If his Lordship, who is not much in the habit of affecting the saint, speak in this manner, how much more may we not expect that there should appear pretenders among ourselves,—gentlemen as well as ladies, and merchants as well as clergy, with a great retinue of Conservative operatives, who regard all corn-matters as something much too gross for sharing any part of their pious meditations! I do not caricature. I draw the picture faithfully: and yet, can anything be more preposterous? Corn! why, the half of religion is taken up with it—to be prayerfully dependent on God for it—to observe his laws in our attempt to gain it—to be thankful to Him for its bestowment—to be regulated by his prescriptions in partaking of it—to train up our children in a fitness to gain it honestly for themselves—to help our neighbours in securing their's—and to share our own with the indigent who have none. What a large portion of life is expended on food! And, if religion must be excluded from all concern in it, how little will be left for its regulation! There is nothing else which has a domain so wide as Religion has. She is the Daughter of the Deity, and in the administration of her Father's empire, claims a universal sovereignty. And yet, according to the fancies of some men, there is no other kingdom so narrow, no other authority so circumscribed. They say she has no title authorising her to interfere with our *politics;* none authorising her to interfere with our *science*; none authorising her to interfere with the manner in which a man conducts his *merchandise*; none authorizing her to interfere with the manner in which he makes up his *friendships*, or contracts alliance in *marriage;* and now it seems none authorising her to interfere about his *corn*. What therefore, is left, in which they allow her right to be consulted? Nothing but the systematic assortment of a number of sterile notions which they call *faith*—a little grimace and hearing of lectures which they call *Sabbath-keeping*—and a formal bending of the knees and muttering a few words which they call *prayer*: and having thus purified religion, as they say, of all worldliness, they assume to themselves the character of being peculiarly pious and spiritualized. Lord Brougham, however, will scarcely coincide, I suspect, in his views with such persons; and I feel especially curious about what *he* leaves for the control of religion after he has interdicted her interference with our corn. Perhaps he means the Corn Bill, because that is a *political* subject.* Now, with all my respect, which is not little, for his Lordship's metaphysical acumen, I nevertheless question the possibility of any man making such mental distinctions and abstractions that he can be concerned about the corn itself, either in a secular or religious way, without taking into consideration the Government's law about it. Suppose some one should say that religion has something to do with corn, but nothing to do with the state of the weather, because that is a subject of meteorological science, would he be a more absurd person than he who says that religion may concern itself about corn, but must not interfere with the laws which affect its distribution? Have we not had the demonstration made us full sorely that we are nearly as much dependent for corn on human legislation as on the shining of the sun? And just as it would evince a man a fanatic to pray for corn without having respect to the sunshine and rain; so is that man convicted of fanaticism, or, of what is worse, of insulting Heaven with hypocrisy, who prays that the poor may have bread, when yet he does not pray that God would so influence the hearts of our legislators, that they shall abolish those barbarous laws which obstruct its distribution, after his rain and sunshine have covered the fields with their crops. Here, then, is one respect in which religious men may in their religious character legitimately interfere with these laws—they may make them the subject of their earnest *prayer*. But must the interference stop here?—that would be more scorn-worthy fanaticism than ever. Is not this necessary to genuine religion, that, when at any time we pray that the Lord would accomplish any object, we give ourselves as willing instruments into his hand, by which He may accomplish it, whenever we are capable of furnishing such instrumentality? In other words, that we ourselves work with all our might, and prayerfully wait on Him for prospering our work? If then political men, with their perverse or foolish policy stand in the way of religious men, preventing their acquisition of any object which religion represents as being desirable, they must lay their account with being made the subject of religious men's prayers, that God would change their hearts; or if they continue obstinate, that He would confound their counsels; or, if He will, that He should beat them down, with the rod of his anger, that the cause of righteousness may have its unobstructed march. And, they must lay their account with more than these prayers when we appear before the throne of God, pleading against them with all the interest we have there; they may calculate that with all that energy and zeal which religion inspires, we shall agitate against them, and expose their corruptions to the people till the roar of millions has pronounced their doom, that they shall no longer be stewards of the legislation and government of freeborn, intelligent, and religious men. And when we act in this manner, it is not without our warrant: our Master gave us the example. How ignor-

* Since the text was put up in type I find that the Noble Lord expressed himself thus "that he did not consider the Corn Laws a religious question at all; nor a moral question at all, otherwise than by a remote and strained construction—nor did he see why a conference of Dissenting Ministers, or members of dissenting bodies, should be holden upon this question, any more than upon any other important secular question."

antly some men both think and speak of Christ! How dishonouringly, when they represent Him as having been characterised by nothing but tenderness! Had such been the case, with reverence be it said, his character would have been not only deficient, but culpable: for it indicates both weakness, and a want of upright moral sentiment, to deal tenderly with an obstinate transgressor who has hardened himself against all reasoning, all admonition, all remonstrance, and all petitioning for justice. Accordingly, though words of mercy and encouragement never fell so soothingly from lips, as from those of Christ, on the broken and contrite heart; yet equally never were words of more scorching indignation launched against the heart that was obdurate in sin, and especially the sin of selfishness and oppression of the poor. Let it be a penitent Magdalene who approaches Him: Oh watch and learn of Him! "Woman be of good cheer; thy sins are forgiven; thy faith hath saved thee:" and he lifts her up from her knees and honours her as others would the daughter of a king. How like God! yea, it is God. But watch! *there* is a band of Pharisees. It is God manifest again! "Woe unto you serpents, generation of vipers, how can ye escape the damnation of Hell!" I know that some men say of such a scene that our Lord acted in the character of an inspired prophet, who knew the hearts, and the doom of those wicked men; and that he is not, therefore, in such instances an example to his followers. This is the merest sophistication of men, who neither comprehend Christ's character nor understand their own duty; or who invent apologies for their pusillanimity, and are ashamed of their Master's rudeness as unsuitable to a polished and liberal age! Here was a scene: "*In the audience of all the people,* he said unto his disciples, beware of the scribes who devour widows' houses; the same shall receive greater damnation." If there was prophecy here, was there not equally a designed public exposure of those men, that the people might shake off all respect for them? And what devouring of the substance of widows, I ask, is it possible to imagine those scribes can have practised, which may be paralleled with that, which by means of the Bread Tax the landowners of our country perpetrate, robbing our widows of the half of every loaf for the feeding of their dogs? I, for one, am not afraid of cherishing and expressing the sentiments which were cherished and expressed by Christ; and in the audience of the people I declare my belief and confidence in the God of justice and impartial government, that it will fare no better with oppressors of the present day, than with those of ancient times; and that unless they repent they shall perish under a doom of peculiar woe. Who doubts it? Is there any religion, any faith in the Bible, any belief in the first rudiments of piety existent in the bosom of the man who doubts that God will punish oppression? If you believe it then, why not express it? Try it, and you will be both a better and more useful man for it. A healthiness of influence pervades the spirit when you pass through it the sentiments of Christ; instead of that sickness which comes over the heart when you drug it with the sentimentalism of a spurious religion, or with that hypocritical courtesy which is the bastard offspring of an infidel philosophy. And never shall we have any integrity of public morals on which we can depend, till the Church, purged of her flatteries, and rebuked out of her soft speaking, and her winking at the immoralities of the wealthy and great, shall take her stand and fulfil her vocation in denouncing them boldly, as her Master did the corrupt men of his age; so that the people filled with the scorn of them may eject them from their power; or haply they themselves, under the stern and uncompromising rebuke of religion, may tremble for the threatened judgments of God and repent of their crimes. Instead of there being any just ground for the complaint that ministers of the Gospel sometimes intermeddle with matters political, one of our greatest grievances is, that as a body, they intermeddle with them so seldom, and that, through lack of courage or honesty, they fall so far short of the example which Christ has set them for the performance of their duty. Again, I call for such dealing being given to the oppressors of the present day as Christ administered to the devourers of widows' houses of old. It has been only by walking in his steps in this as in other respects that the Church, as in the times of Luther and Knox, has achieved any signal advantage for the amelioration of the world: and the greater her shame if she surrender her high prerogative of the rebuking of evil-doers just at the time when she may exercise it with such comparative impunity; having little else to fear but the loss of popularity among the corrupt abettors of corrupt placemen; or among women of fantastical faith who being themselves luxuriously fed and elegantly attired, will with such high pretentions to piety pass their imbecile sentences of condemnation on political preachers. The day may come, I do not pray it may, yet I cannot say I strongly deprecate it, when their own poverty will rectify their whining fancies; and convince them that the gospel would be perfect as a system neither of righteousness nor mercy, did it not contain a large department for the rebuke and exposure of those who make the loaf of the widow and fatherless at once so small and so difficult to win.

I shall make only one remark additionally on this subject. The cry against political preaching is not only selfishly raised by those who are the abettors of the corruptions denounced, and who in their turn adopt the practice so soon as the course of politics changes so as to be adverse to their own interests; but it is absurd in this respect, that, on this principle, nothing more would be necessary for arresting the testimony of the pulpit against any sin, but that wicked men should sanction it by a law, so that it would assume the character of political preaching to continue to denounce that which is legalised! They tried this scheme with slavery, and thought by stigmatising us as political ministers they would shame us out of our agitation. How foolishly they miscalculated both the character and influence of their opponents in that question, let the most glorious page of the annals of liberty bear witness; and let them know that the same men are on the field again for the abolition of this other slavery, which we regard as being, if possible, more wicked and oppressive than that against which we erewhile so successfully directed our zeal.

Besides, however, having thus vindicated our conduct in engaging in this agitation in the character of ministers of the Gospel, there are a few explanations which I think it proper to submit on the general question before proceeding to a discussion of the particular topics which have been assigned me as the subject of lecture.

First, all devout men trace the afflictions under which we suffer, in consequence of these Prohibitory Laws which we denounce, to the chastising or avenging hand of Divine Providence. And one of the principal reasons wherefore their evil is prolonged, is that a sinful nation will not penitently confess the righteousness of God's dealing with them in this as well as in many other cases of their complicated calamity. When we admit all this and in our pulpit ministrations contend for it and inculcate it, some persons affect to be unable to see our consistency in agitating for the abolition of the evil: they say that, on our own principles, we seem to be contending against God. Does any Bread-taxer, affecting the piety of a theologian, say so? Let the hypocrite then be told what view we take of the wickedness of the heart of himself and his fellows; just the same which we took of the pestilence of Cholera when it was let loose on us. *That*, too, we were convinced was a visitation of God; but did the conviction lay any embargo on our use of sanatory means for our protection from it? Or, better for illustration—we have been delivered as a punishment of our sins into the hands of a selfish and cruel aristocracy in no other way than Israel of old was delivered of God into the hands of the Philistines. Did the conviction of this prevent those in Israel who feared the Lord, from fighting for the rescue of themselves and their countrymen? Neither will the conviction prevent us from fighting, with such weapons as our religion permits, against our oppressors: and these weapons are not a few; one of them is, that in the audience of the people we denounce them as the devourers of widows' houses. So dealt our Master with the like of them.—But, lest there should be some honest heart perplexed with the difficulty—how we can consistently oppose an evil when we are convinced it is sent as a chastisement by the hand of the Lord, I submit this resolution of it. Almost every affliction—there are but few exceptions, and I am certain the Bread-tax is not one of them—almost every affliction is designed of God to teach three distinct lessons: not only the lesson of humble patience, so long as its pressure is continued; but secondly, faith in God for deliverance; and, consequently, in the third place, activity in the employment of means which he may bless for effecting our deliverance. So that instead of its being the agitators in this question who are to be blamed for want of submission to the will of God, it is those who agitate not, who are to be condemned for want of faith in the Divine mercy, or for holding that faith in a spirit of indolence or cowardice, or a presumptuous fanaticism which expects a blessing without any personal exertion to secure it. Who can doubt that the want of this faith accompanied by activity, is one of the sins wherefore the chastisement has been prolonged?

I explain, in the second place, that we do not accuse the Corn and Provision Laws of being the only cause, but only one of the principal causes of our national distress. This explanation is necessary for the following reasons:—First, that we may defend ourselves from the charge of acting unjustly. There is enough in the conduct of our oppressors to excite our indignation without imputing to their selfish policy a larger measure of evil consequences than can be fairly traced to it. Second, that when we have gained our object, as we soon shall, and when the people feel, that, notwithstanding the abolition of their laws, their afflictions are at best only mitigated and not removed, they may not complain of our having deluded them. We make no promise of a complete redress of their grievances. And Third, that their minds may not be removed from other necessary reforms. The present is only the most pressing of a multitude more, the suspension of attending to which may be followed by the worst consequences. The time when the friends of liberty are engaged in one direction, is often seized on as an opportunity by its enemies to establish and extend corruption in another.

There is especially one respect which I shall notice, for the sake of illustration, in which the Provision Laws are not responsible for the diminished demand for our manufactures. Independently of them, after the establishment of peace in 1815, the nations of the Continent of Europe would have commenced manufacturing for themselves; not on a scale so extensive as they have done, but still on an extensive one. The prognostication of Napoleon Buonaparte is well known; and Montesquieu had long before him in effect uttered the same prediction: "Powers," says he, "established by commerce, may subsist for a long time in their state of mediocrity; but their state of grandeur is of short duration. They elevate themselves little by little without any one observing it; for they do not perform any particular act which creates a noise and which signalizes their prowess: but when affairs have risen to such a pitch that they cannot escape observation, each one becomes eager to deprive that nation of an advantage which it had taken, in a manner, by surprise."* Though not quite so soon, then, as the present day, and perhaps never so completely, yet not long hence, and very widely, must the European market have been circumscribed for the entrance of our goods in consequence of the increase of their own manufactures among the more advanced nations. But for this very reason do we complain more bitterly of the Corn and Provision Laws: First, because they have brought this exclusion on us a quarter, if not half, of a century sooner than it would otherwise have come: and Secondly, because by increasing the hire of the workman that he might be able to purchase his bread, and consequently increasing the price of our goods, they have enabled those more advanced nations to compete with us and undersell us in the markets of other nations; whereas they would have satisfied themselves with the occupation of their own markets at home, and left to us the undisputed possession of the manufacturing commerce of, we may well say, the whole of the rest of the world.

I explain in the third place, that my individual opinion is, that some of our friends have spoken unadvisedly in denouncing the taxation of corn as abstractly and essentially sinful, as if there were no circumstances which could warrant such a proceeding on the part of any government. I am certain that this is a false position for any one to occupy. If the taxation be imposed for the sake of national revenue—for the payment of those who conduct the administration, and dispense justice—for the necessary defences of the country against foreign aggression or internal turmoil—or for the executing of whatever good measure the government may devise for the national benefit, then is the taxation of Corn as lawful as the taxation of any thing else. In certain circumstances it might not be the *wisest* policy, or the most *expedient;* and in our own circumstances I would regard it highly inexpedient; so that as a citizen, on the principles of a wise political economy, I might perchance agitate against the imposition of a fixed duty, however low, although it were declared, and evidently declared with honesty, as having no object but the raising of revenue for the necessities of the government. But in that case I could not as a minister of the Gosple denounce it as an injustice; for there are other circumstances easily conceivable in a nation's condition and economical arrangements, in which a tax on corn, having revenue for its object, would not only be equitable, but the very wisest and most expedient which could be devised.—That representation which has frequently been made—that a corn tax is essentially unjust because it taxes the poor man who consumes as much of it, as heavily as the rich,—is more plausible than sound. It proceeds on the supposi-

* Grandeur et Decadence des Romaines. Chap. iv.

tion is that revenue is drawn from no other source. But if these other things which the wealthy man uses or possesses are proportionably taxed also—his wines, his silks, his horses, and dogs. his house, his property and income, then though he should consume less corn than the working man, so as to contribute less to the national revenue in that direction, yet in other directions he would contribute proportionably to his wealth.

Wherein then lies the grievance of these laws? Evidently in their base partiality, when they have been enacted for the aggrandisement and pampering of one class of the community, at the expense of the interests of all the rest. Were there but a pretence in them that they had a respect to the national revenue for the support of the country's government, so that when we all contributed on the one hand, we would all receive some compensation on the other—were there this pretence in them, it would be some abatement of the wrong. When a knave has injured you, even although you should be convinced that his apology is hypocritical, yet is it some soothing of your indignation when he protests that he intended you no harm But our corn law oppressors will not soften our feelings even with a hypocritical pretence, that they care for any interest of ours; and with unparalleled insolence in as many words declare that their aristocratic pride and lusts need the half of the widow's loaf; and that having the might they care not for the right, but with violent hands will possess themselves of it, obstruct them who dare. Oh these be the men who had they come in the way of the Son of God, would have given him a full opportunity for the display of the indignation of his Godhead! What were the extortions of a pettyfogging Jewish Scribe compared with such enormities as theirs. Let them not felicitate themselves however on their better fortune, that He had departed from this world before they were born, so that they are spared his annoyance. *They* also must yet meet the Son of God, and in form more dreadful than any in which Scribe or Pharisee ever encountered Him. And who of them may not well recoil in terror from the imagination of appearing before his judgment seat, in these garments of violence and oppression which these barbarous laws weave for every man who either legislates or abets them!

Though the corn laws had not produced such calamitous results of national poverty as those under which we at present groan—though they had burdened no man with more than a penny a year, we would nevertheless have complained of them *on principle*. Who, I ask, are the men who thus assume the prerogative of levying a capitation impost over the kingdom for the maintenance of their state? Who, for instance, is the Duke of Buckingham, who glories in being their champion; and who affords a fair enough specimen, I presume, of his class?—Who is he, and what, that he should be privileged to exact from us the materials of his pomp and luxury? Though he were the noblest instance living of a man, the extorted penny, it would not be fit for a Briton to bear with equanimity. But being such a one as he is—look at him! hear him speak! inquire into his well doing! He and his fellows must submit to the scrutiny since they claim to live at our expense. Who then are they, and what? Is there any class in the land which in proportion to their number exhibits so much intellectual imbecility and moral worthlessness? Go tell them,—as our Master once sent his defiance to one like them, that we are weary of the heavy burden of them, and as foul as it is heavy; so that we would feel ourselves guilty in the sight of Heaven did we any longer furnish them with the means of their corruption.

Though it is the abstract iniquity of the principle of the corn laws in exposing which the main strength of our battle lies, so as to make our argument independent of all attempts to refute or weaken our representations of the *amount* of evil which they produce; yet to illustrate the greatness of this amount is perhaps our more popular weapon. The first topic on which I have been requested to discourse is the POVERTY of which they are the baneful cause. Others will illustrate particularly how they effect this; and it is my province to state the argument only generally. It is as follows: First, that these laws, virtually prohibiting the importation of corn from foreign countries, till it has risen in our own market to a famine price, directly increase the price of the poor man's bread—to such an extent that in the annals of these laws there have been several occasions when it cost him double of what it would have done had the importation been free.—And Secondly, that they diminish our commerce, 1st, in the case of some nations which have no money to give for our manufactures, but which would take them in exchange for corn: the loss on our part being double—both that of the cheaper corn, and the more extensive trade; 2nd, in the case of other nations avenging themselves on us by retaliatory tariffs which prohibit or limit the entrance of our manufactures into their markets: as before, our loss here is double again: 3rd, in the case of other nations still who undersell us in the market of the world, in consequence of lower wages being sufficient for the purchase of the food of their workmen than are necessary for the purchase of the food of ours. Here our loss is threefold, for there are some of these nations, which not only would not have attempted competition with us in markets foreign to their own, but would have manufactured less for themselves, so that we lose at once their home trade, their foreign trade, and their cheap corn. For these and a few other reasons we denounce the corn laws—no, it is the wicked men who uphold them that we denounce, as the guilty inflicters of the greater proportion of that cruel poverty by which our land is desolated. Let us now, therefore take a short survey of this calamity.

It would only add another grievance to the already overburdened lot of poverty—for it would be insulting it—to profess to be able to give an adequate description of its woes. All I shall therefore attempt is little more than an enumeration of the principal elements of its misery, with a design of exciting your reflections, and thereby securing from you a deeper detestation of that system of cruelty which is the parent of an offspring so monstrous, and a more resolute determination to have it speedily destroyed.

So complicated as well as numerous are these evils that it is difficult to classify them, but I shall attempt some methodising of them under these two topics—those which are *direct*: and those which are *consequent*. This will produce an illustration nearly the same as that which would result from classifying them—those which are *physical* and those which are *moral*: not precisely so, however; we shall presently see that so strongly influential is poverty of immorality, that it may be represented as directly and necessarily the cause of it, but for extraordinary communications and defences of the grace of God.

Under the First topic, then, I notice primarily the *Hunger* of Poverty—Hunger! What shall we say of Hunger? The strongest appetite of our material constitution:—that which stimulates to nine tenths of human exertion—without which the world would lie down in ignominious sloth—Oh you may be certain that when the creator designed it should be that within us which without fail would secure our activity and the employment of our powers, He made it strong and imperious in its demands—Well, hunger is the denial of this principle's claims—man's life-appetite baulked—its gulph-like vacuity within him unsupplied—its gnawing turned in upon itself through failure of its proper materiel. Even in her of the ladiest and most fairy like form; even in him of the most spiritualised heavenly-mindedness; even in the old man of fourscore years, in whom all other passions have expired, how strong is the appetite for food! What violence is done to nature when it is denied gratification! What disease—what gnawing of rheumatism—what corrosion of cancer—what grinding of stone may be compared with the torment of hunger! How devoutly thankful the greater part of us need be, that we must draw on our imaginations for understanding what hunger is, even in a moderate degree: when all we know of it from experience is, after a plentiful morning's repast, to have had dinner delayed till the evening; or when we were thoughtless children, to have wandered too far from home on the summer holiday, among the hungry grass of the hills, without having made provision for the journey. That is all some of us know of hunger. It can be but few of us who, being healthy, have had the experience of want of food for twelve waking hours, and this only after we had feasted satisfactorily, and when we were sustained by the assured hope of a luxurious meal when we reached home. Never mention it. We know not what hunger is. Think of a healthy man not tasting food for four and twenty hours, and hopeless of relief! think of his fasting being broken only by a crust of bread which instead of appeasing, whets his appetite to greater keenness! think of this experiment on his endurance being prolonged day after day! Hunger such as this made David burst into the sanctuary and perpetrate sacrilege on the shew-bread: Hunger such as this made the mother at Jerusalem fulfil the prophecy and devour her own child: and when subjected to hunger such as this, the Tempter thought he was now sure of victory and made his assault on the Redeemer of the world. And at the present hour there are not only cases to be found among ourselves, but they abound, of hunger nearly as desperate.—But although it should not have proceeded to such extremities—is it not enough, if a man receive only one meal when he should have two, and if that one be so scanty and unsubstantial that he never enjoys the sensation of a gratified appetite, but is always, without respite, a restless hungry man?—Is it not enough that these children who were once the delight of his eyes and the joy of his heart, should now be felt a weariness and a vexation with their cries for food which he is unable to satisfy—that he should deprecate the increase of their number, and that another birth should be anticipated with more grudge than he anticipates a death?—Is it not enough that she who was once his pride, and whose smiling welcome home to himself and their children dispelled all the angry passions which had embittered his heart in the contention with his fellow workmen, or under the challenge of a proud and unfeeling master, should now, with her beauty faded away and her countenance more pale and haggard than his own, only add to his sorrows by her fretfulness and repining?—And she,—although she should not see the father of her children driven to madness—is it not enough, that he who was once the idol of her heart for his manliness and glee, should be so broken down, dispirited, and full of gloomy thoughts, putting aside with contempt all her attempts to soothe him—for shall not even the words of a wife fail in power when addressed to a hungry man beset by hungry children? Is not this enough though poverty should go no further? And who shall be so hard hearted as to increase the misery by denying that this length at least it has gone with thousands of families in our land? And has not that man reason to fear that an avenging God will make the horrors of hunger no longer a matter of imagination for him, but of personal experience, who shall selfishly felicitate himself on the comforts of his own fireside without expending a feeling of commiseration on the surrounding distress, or a benevolent effort for its relief and mitigation? Give me then brethren your first groan of detestation for the barbarity of the system which inflicts so much misery on so many of our fellow citizens, as a pledge of your efforts to have it relentlessly destroyed.

But we have only commenced our tale of woe. Reflect now on the *Cold* of poverty—on the wintry-day with its frost and snow and bitter blast, and the miserable defence of the thin and tattered garb of poverty. And when the shivering victim seeks a shelter in home, what kind of a home has poverty prepared for him? When from its fireless inhospitality he seeks for refuge in his bed—that last resourse of weary and afflicted humanity—think ye that poverty when it has denied him his food will have spared his bed? Were he but *warm in his bed*, so that he might sleep, and for the night forget his sorrows, it would be some mitigation of his wretchedness: but on that bed of straw he lies with that single coverlet over him, hunger within and cold without, in horrid conspiracy to keep him awake—awake to be tempted to doubt, a saint though he be, if there be a God and a Providence. How tempted with doubtings so dark? Because it perplexes him, as it perplexed the saint of old, (Ps. 73.) to reconcile the doctrine of a divine government of the world with the fact, that selfish men should be permitted by their decrees of iniquity, to reduce him and his children to this condition of torment. Brethren, we have assigned us the high task of vindicating the character of the Almighty in the eyes of the poor, by lending ourselves as instruments in the hand of his providence to rescue their bread for them, from the hand of their oppressors: So that seeing our determination and zeal they may have their doubtings changed into thanksgiving—thanksgiving on our account, as being commissioned and invigorated by his grace for the work of their deliverance. Unless this be our conduct they will be tempted still more fiercely—being perplexed to reconcile the fact of our apathy, as professing christians, with the doctrine that the Gospel inspires all who receive it with brotherly affection. These poor men's faith has enough to contend against, when they are subjected to the oppressions of the wicked, without the addition of seeing any lack of sympathetic efforts on our part for their relief; so as to be tempted to denounce all the benevolence of the christian faith as a vain and illusory dream. Let us rise to the vindication of the Gospel, and shew what it makes men in taking the part of the poor against those who oppress them, so that our brethren may not apostatise—singing our war-song with determination,

> That ill men's rod upon the lot
> of just men shall not lie,
> Lest righteous men stretch forth their hand
> unto iniquity.

The Disease and premature Death of poverty follow as a natural consequence.—Hunger is a formidable disease of itself—the Atrophy of Want as the Physicians distinguish it. Men die of it in multitudes; some more quickly when the hunger is extreme, others more slowly, but not less deplorably, by its gradual exhaustion. But especially, it predisposes for the infection of other diseases, and gives scope for the springing up of the seed of constitutional maladies, which abundant and nutritive diet would have enabled the system to suppress.—And then, there is the *cold* of poverty, with its insufficient raiment, and damp and fireless dwelling aggravating the diseases of hunger, and producing a crop of its own.—To consummate the misery and ensure death, poverty denies both physician and medicine to its diseased victims. Its slain are more than the slain of war. We therefore denounce the Corn Laws as a huge system of murder; and what but men of murderous heart, those who uphold them? I for one hesitate not to proclaim them such. So rude am I—so little an adept in metaphysical discrimination, that in such a matter I cannot separate betwixt the instruments and the agents, so as to burden all the guilt on the former, and permit the other to go free. How conveniently some manage to save themselves from the imputation of uncharitableness, and gain for themselves the character of a gentlemanlike preaching of the gospel—assailing systems, but sparing, or apologizing for their upholders! Well, I denounce *them* too as traitorous to the cause of human life, inasmuch as they deal tenderly with those who slay their brethren. How unlike the Master they profess to serve!—who not only guarded his disciples against the leaven of the Pharisees, but exposed to reprobation the Pharisees themselves. Beware, Sirs, how you attempt to improve on the example of Christ. There is a moral neology, ashamed of his zeal, which is equally fatal, and more ignominious than the philosophical neology which is ashamed of his miracles.

Besides the above which are more prominent, as direct evils of poverty, there are some others of no inconsiderable magnitude which we cannot pass without a notice. There is the *shame* of poverty. Next to the pain of an accusing conscience is the pain of shame; and next to guilt, is poverty a cause of shame—the shame of its withered countenance and lean and shrivelled person—the shame of its patched and antiquated raiment—the shame of its mean and ill furnished dwelling—the shame of its ragged children—the shame of its paltry subscription—the shame of turning away without making a purchase, or retiring home without entering like the rest to enjoy the holiday sight—the shame of being dependent on charity and begging for an alms. And who, I again ask, are the men who claim that they should be supported in the pomp of their pride and the luxury of their lusts at the expense of this sore shame of tens of thousands of the most amiable hearts in our land? If the world were possessed of discernment—had it any sense, instead of these men being saluted with signs and greetings of respect when they appear abroad with their equipages so gorgeous, they would be allowed to pass with contempt and neglect as being blazoned with extorted wealth; and sent home to meditate under indications of a nation's scorn, which is the party that needs be ashamed—these who have been spoiled to nakedness, or those who have spoiled them and arrayed themselves in the rapine. See them as they go, dressed in other people's clothes! Is it not enough that for the sake of good order we submit to the laws of such men, whom a chastising providence has permitted to be our legislators, without degrading ourselves by any signs of personal reverence? It is time that both for their benefit and ours they should be disabused of the fancy that we hold in any respect a nobility which is merely one of birth and titles, and which is not sustained by moral integrity.

I shall only further notice, under this department of our subject, the *uselessness* of poverty:—the uselessness of its enervated bodily frame; the uselessness of its down-broken spirit; its uselessness when the contribution is made for works of charity and piety; the uselessness of its ignorance, from want of time, or means or calmness of mind for acquiring knowledge; or when it is learned and wise, its uselessness from being disrespected,—for who invites or listens to the counsel of the poor?—its worse than uselessness—its *burdensomeness* when the maintenance of its victims is fast reducing the wealthy and generous to the level of their own indigence.—Reflect as before—for unless our meditations always revert to this head there will be little practical advantage in them—reflect who and what are the men who by their selfish legislation have beat down our people in millions into this useless and burdensome condition. How spend they that wealth of which God's saints are plundered, and which those saints would turn to such beneficent and holy uses? Meditate on this. There are few points in contemplating the Corn Laws from which they appear so detestable. From what useful hands they have in thousands of instances taken away the wealth, and into what flagitious hands they in instances, not a few, deliver it, to be the means of all abominable wickedness! My heart burns within me when I think of it. My faith in God is put on its trial, if it can sustain itself without staggering, that He should permit that wealth which would be consecrated so largely by His saints to the Mission-work, for example, of the Cross of his Son, should by iniquitous laws be forced from them,, and transferred to men who pamper themselves with it in enormities too shameful to be recorded. The Hertfords and the Frankfords are the many; the Glenelgs and the Morpeths are the few.—There is something besides, however, more full of provocation if possible:—that these laws by reducing men to poverty and rendering them disrespected, should exclude from the counsels not only of secular society, but of the church, some of the best informed, most sagacious, and most sanctified of the people: and leave offices of important trust to be occupied by men of wealth who are neither intellectually nor morally qualified for discharging the duty. It is a sore evil both for the commonwealth and the church; and the Corn Laws or rather their framers and abettors are responsible for its largest share.

When I proceed to sketch with equal brevity the indirect, or moral evil consequences of that poverty which the Corn Laws so widely produce, I feel the need of being on my guard lest I injure the feelings of some of the worthiest of God's saints. There are many who are pious in spite of poverty; and instead of expressing myself so as to cause either themselves or others to suspect their integrity, I felicitate them on the large measure of divine grace which has been bestowed on them; and would hold them up for the admiration of the church; and brave the world with them as witnesses for the faith—that they have been enabled to maintain their virtue in circumstances so trying. For, as has been already noticed, so strongly influential is poverty in producing vice that it may be almost said to be necessarily the cause of it. How worthy then of admiration is he who has withstood its assault! Oh there are some of us for whom it is easy to be thankful and content and of sweetened temper, compared with others! What then shall we say of those others, when from amidst the depths of their poverty they may be heard singing their Psalm of thanksgiving more cheerfully than we? Does it not become us to be abashed in the presence of their greatness? Here now is nobility which we shall honour ourselves in reverencing.

There are few subjects on which so much misconception prevails in the church, as the evil influence of poverty. Political economists far excel christian divines when treating of it. The former expatiate on its baneful effects on morals: whereas the latter will often express themselves as if it were of great spiritual advantage. The source of this error is to be found, I suppose, in a misinterpretation of our Lord's words, when he has pronounced the richest benediction of his religion on the *poor*. That these poor are not *paupers* is evinced by the fact. There are comparatively few of this class religious: and we have as much reason for admiring that grace which will make piety grow among the thorns of destitution and beggary, as for admiring that which will make it flourish among the flowers of wealth. The cases are equally rare. The poor whom Christ blesses with such specialty are the industrious working class as distinguished from the luxurious rich: and the state of facts corresponds with the benediction when thus interpreted. That which we at the present day call poverty—indigent pauperism, is one of the most formidable enemies of virtue.

First, within the Church. By its distraction and cares it incapacitates the mind for meditation and all other exercises of devotion. In the language of Christ it "chokes the word." How many will bear witness that when, being under its pressure, they stood most in need of the disburdening help of prayer, they were the least fitted for the devotional exercise? Whatever be the explanation, it appears to be a fact, that the incapacitating influence of poverty in this respect, is stronger than that of any other affliction—stronger than that of personal disease—stronger than that of the bereavement of a child.—Comparatively, however, the evil would be slight did it proceed no further than this arrestment of spiritual progress—this withering of plants of piety:—What danger there is of the springing up of the poisonous weeds of distrust in the providence of God, and infidel questionings of the truth of that book in which He is represented as being a watchful and tender parent! How difficult it must be to continue to believe in the guardianship of a compassionate God, when a man is assailed by the cries of hungry children, with a wife sitting by more forlorn than a widow, she hungry too, and he himself through manly self-denial for their sakes the hungriest of them all! Who shall expect that any one in such circumstances should bless the name of God? Go feed himself and his family first.—The well-fed Pharisee may mock at the ignorance of experimental religion evinced by such a representation, and tell us that christian faith remembering that scripture "whom the Lord loveth he chasteneth" will extract comfort from the affliction and rejoice in the tribulation. How easy it is to be orthodox in the midst of plenty, and give pious advices about patience to the afflicted. Go feed them first, I say. I know some whose principles have stood the trial—who amid the reverses of fortune, and when plunged into the deepest indigence have persevered in singing their hymn of praise with grateful hearts; but I know not the man, being yet untried, whom I could witness sinking down into abject poverty, without having my fears that he might fall away from the faith. I have seen so much of it.—Then there is the *uncharitableness* of Poverty. Even when it has no ground for charging others with injustice, yet by its envyings when it sees their luxury, and its murmurings that they allow it to pine in want, it will eat all charity out of the heart: how much more when, as in the present case, it has reason to charge them with oppression. As we have already seen, anger is lawful in degree; but how difficult it must be for a hungry man to prevent it from rising to malice, cursing, and revenge?

Besides these more formidable consequences in moral deterioration, within the church, there are other two which demand a notice, however cursory. By casting a man on the bounty of another, poverty destroys his self-respect and breaks down the spirit of independency. That a man should be abased before God is one of the first of feelings to be cherished; but that he should crouch to a fellow creature is to be deprecated fervently. He who depends on another for his support, at the best acts under restraint in obeying the dictates of his own judgment, through fear of displeasing his benefactor; not seldom is he constrained to violate his conscience—voting and canvassing for a candidate whose principles he detests; and forsaking a church which he loves for another which he abhors. It need not be explained how much both civil and religious liberty suffer on this account, even when those who are exposed to the temptation are not in the condition of the abject dependency of poverty, where the power of resistance is still further diminished.—Should I not have given a more prominent place to the evil which I mention last—the manner in which poverty incapacitates a parent for the instruction of his offspring? It requires a lively heart to educate a child. But even to its own father poverty will make a child's prattle, and its curious questions, an annoyance at which he frets.—Over all, to aggravate and consummate the evil of all these, there is the manner in which poverty excludes a man from the House of Prayer where his doubts might be removed, the incipient sin rebuked, or his heart enlivened and encouraged. I therefore charge the upholders of the Corn Laws with being the promoters of Apostasy. They will build churches—will they? They cannot fail to be synagogues of corruption which Bread-taxers erect. Give the people justice so that they may gain their bread in competence, and they will find pastors for themselves who will instruct them both in their duties and their rights.

When the moral dangers of Poverty are so formidable within the church, where there are so many defences, how much more fatal must they be out in the world! My room has already been occupied so extensively that my illustrations here must be even more sketchy than ever.—As a pregnant evil I notice in the first place the obstacles which that poverty, which the Corn Laws generate, places in the way of the *education of the young*. This evil being comprehended in the subject of another Lecture of this course, I shall satisfy myself with making this short remonstrance:—what would it signify though schools were built, and teachers endowed, so that education were proffered gratuitously?—what though the additional boon were proffered of the clothing of the pupils, if yet the parent cannot dispense with the child's labour in the factory to assist him to buy the Bread taxers' high priced loaves? It is consistent that those who starve the body should starve the spirit. But let them be warned; if there is consistency in the cruelty there is also consistency in the danger. A people at once hungry and ignorant form an object of double terror.—On the subject of poverty being the cause of *dishonesty* and *theft*, it is nearly enough that I should refer to the sentiments of an eminent saint who convinced of the strength of the temptation prayed with earnestness "send me not poverty lest I steal." Along with one of the few of the Nobles of that House, whose nobility of mind saves it from the scornful extinction of an indignant nation

* Earl Fitzwilliam.

as a branch of the Legislature, I express my astonishment that the people should preserve their honesty so well in the midst of starvation—a starvation to which many of their oppressors and railers against their morals would not submit for a day, without becoming robbers on the highway, had they courage for the adventure.—I notice in the third place, that Poverty, and consequently the Corn Laws which produce poverty, and consequently the men who uphold the corn laws, demoralise the people with *drunkenness.*—Poverty makes as many drunkards, as drunkenness makes paupers. I am sorry that so little room is left me for the illustration of this. When poverty on the one hand excludes a man from good society and refined enjoyments, and makes him reckless of his character, so that there is little to restrain him in the hour of temptation; on the other, this temptation is strong,—in anxieties which need to be soothed, and in an enervated frame which calls for the excitement of the inebriating potion. True, the relief is but momentary, and the consequence is an increase of misery; but are the poor the only party, who are chargeable with the folly of snatching at momentary pleasure, without regard to future wretchedness? Does not the Bread Taxer, seize on the present pomp and luxury in defiance of the threatened judgments of eternity? Of all the scenes and sayings of horror in a celebrated work of one of our most popular novelists, the following is perhaps the most distressing, as being so true to nature.—" Let me advise you." said Wood, " on no account to fly to strong waters for consolation, Joan. Gin Lane is the nearest road to the churchyard."—" It may be, but if it shortens the distance and lightens the journey, I care not" retorted the widow. " To those who, like me, have never been able to get out of the dark and dreary paths of life the grave is indeed a refuge; and the sooner they reach it the better. The spirit I drink may be poison,—it may kill me,—perhaps it *is* killing me:—but so would hunger, cold, misery,—so would my own thoughts. I should have gone mad without it. Gin is the poor man's friend,—his sole set off against the rich man's luxury. It comforts him when he is most forlorn. It may be treacherous; it may lay up a store of future woe, but it ensures present happiness, and that is sufficient. When I have traversed the streets a houseless wanderer, driven with curses from every door when I solicited alms, and with blows from every gateway where I have sought shelter,—when I have crept into some deserted building, and stretched my weary limbs upon a bulk in the vain hope of repose;—or worse than all, when frenzied with want I have yielded to horrible temptation and earned a meal in the only way I could earn one; when I have felt, at times like these, my heart sink within me, I have drank of this drink, and have at once forgotten my cares, my poverty, my guilt. Old thoughts, old feelings, old faces, and old scenes have returned to me, and I have fancied myself happy,—as happy as I am now." And she burst into a wild hysterical laugh. " Poor creature" ejaculated Wood, " Do you call this frantic glee happiness?"—" It's all the happiness I have known for years," returned the widow, becoming suddenly calm, " and it's short-lived enough as you perceive. I tell you what, Mr Wood," added she, in a hollow voice, and with a ghastly look, " *gin may bring ruin; but as long as poverty, vice, and ill-usage exist, it will be drunk.*" Though it be of his own inditing, Mr Ainsworth was warranted to say, that the widow was roused into eloquence, when he furnished his heroine with this apology. It is no fiction. The upholders of the Corn laws are responsible for the creation of thousands of instances of that which the artist has only copied not fancied.—I notice in the fourth place that poverty is too a terrific extent the cause of profligacy in men and prostitution in women. Under the present commercial depression the streets of our cities swarm with these polluted and polluting characters beyond all former example, and even in our country villages the harlot is no longer a "strange woman." The taxers of bread, making the prospect of supporting a family so fearful, are marked on the forehead with the most hateful of all the signs by which you may know the children of the Apostasy—"forbidding to marry:" and their wives and their daughters are blazoned with jewels at the expense of the most loathsome degradation of their sex.

I must close this enumeration of the moral evils of that Poverty which the corn laws produce, though it might be extended, much farther—only remarking additionally, that, as in a former case, over all there is the manner in which those laws impoverish the saints, so as to disable them for the prosecution of those measures for the dissemination of the Gospel which might stem the torrent of immorality. The bitter reflection returns —what useful hands these laws of iniquity have robbed, of the wealth, to commit it to hands in which it becomes the means of corruption! The evil is twofold and in both of its aspects deplorable—in which to be deplored most it is difficult to determine.

The immorality for which the corn laws—their upholders rather—are responsible I have hitherto traced through that Poverty which they inflict. But there are other directions in which their immoral influence is strong. They in themselves, as we have seen, are a flagrant immorality—an injustice—a cruel oppression. But proceeding as they do from a cruel heart their reflex action is powerful in deepening the cruelty, in the course of defending them.—A principal argument in our exposure of negro slavery was that the system demoralized the tyrant as much as his victim. It is the same with the Corn law slavery. There is not soul of man which ever engaged in its defence without being subjected to a hardening process by which it was rendered to a great extent insensible to human misery.—There is yet another party who, under the present form at least of the Bread tax, are exposed to much moral deterioration; and it is because they are a highly respectable class of men that their principles have not sustained more injury. I refer to our Corn merchants. To what has the Sliding Scale reduced their occupation but a system of gambling? and gambling in the worst possible form—gambling in the trust and with the horrid wish that the chances of harvest may be adverse to their native land—now grudging it the sunshine—and again grudging it the rain! Can any thing be conceived of more deplorable than this?

Finally; the upholders of the Corn laws promote Sedition. They have driven our people in hundreds of thousands from our shores, cursing the land of their birth as a land of oppression, Millions who remain, for other reasons, it is true, but for this above all others have disowned the Legislature as one which they are under any obligations to acknowledge, and are kept in subjection only through fear of military power. And not a few of the ministers of the Gospel—I for one—are perplexed about the principles on which they should inculcate submission for conscience' sake, and not merely for wrath (Rom. xiii. 5.) Were it not the personal character of the reigning Sovereign, who would feel secure respecting the peace of the kingdom? The theory of the constitution is that the nobles stand between, protecting the throne from the shock of the people. The fact is the very reverse. It is Her Majesty who stands between, with the influence of her character as the protector of the coronets of the nobles.

I have done. My charges have been made good. My argument has been too easy. The Corn and Provision laws stand convicted as inflicting on our people to a frightful extent, poverty, disease and death; and as promoting irreligion, vice and sedition. Let their upholders, of every class, look to their accountability both to the nation and the government of God!

⁎ It is but due to state that the foregoing Lecture has been enlarged, and that many of its expressions have been made stronger, since it was originally delivered at the request of the Society under whose auspices it is published; and who, of course, have not had the proof sheets submitted to their inspection; so that they are partially, if at all, responsible for its sentiments, and statements. They are responsible only for having requested the author to give one of the lectures in the course, which they could not well avoid doing, when the lectures were to be delivered in his own chapel. Will this explanation satisfy that lamentable character of whom *Henry* is gone, and only the *lord* remains; so that, if any one tell him of anything offensive to his *piety* in these pages, he may concentrate his denunciations on one who can bear them.

George Brookman & Son, Printers.

THE INFLUENCE

OF

THE PROVISION LAWS

ON

TRADE, WAGES, AND SOCIETY:

A LECTURE

DELIVERED IN JOHN STREET RELIEF CHURCH, GLASGOW,
ON THE EVENING OF TUESDAY, DECEMBER 21st, 1842,

UNDER THE AUSPICES OF

THE GLASGOW YOUNG MEN'S FREE TRADE ASSOCIATION.

BY THE

REV. ALEXANDER HARVEY,
OF CALTON RELIEF CHURCH, GLASGOW.

Published at the request of the Association.

Printed
FOR THE GLASGOW YOUNG MEN'S FREE TRADE ASSOCIATION.

MDCCCXLIII.

Alexander Harvey (1786–1843)[1]

Revd Alexander Harvey (1796–1843)[1] belonged to the Relief Church, and, later, the United Presbyterian Church. He was ordained to the King Street, Kilmarnock congregation in 1822, and removed to Calton Glasgow in 1828. Harvey became Moderator of the Relief Church Synod in 1838.

[1] Irving, *Scotsmen Eminent*, p. 206.

THE INFLUENCE OF THE PROVISION LAWS

ON

TRADE, WAGES, AND SOCIETY.

THE subject for discussion this evening is deeply important in itself and involves the interests of every individual in the community. There is not a single inhabitant in our country who will not be more or less affected by its equitable settlement. It is one therefore which all should carefully study and endeavour to understand in all its bearings on the different classes of which Society is composed. If the corn laws are founded in justice they can bear investigation. The more searching the inquiry, the more deeply will they become rooted in the affections of the people, and it will soon become fruitless to assail them. But if they be based in injustice, and subversive of the prosperity of the country at large, no efforts on the part of those who reap the fruits of this unrighteous monopoly can long protect them from merited destruction. The public attention is now thoroughly awake on this subject. A large and rapidly increasing number in this country, is convinced that these laws are the cause of our deep and widely spread sufferings. Till it be demonstrated that this is a delusion, agitation will never cease till they are repealed. The subject has now acquired that magnitude and importance in the judgment of the community, that it absorbs their chief attention,—renders them indifferent to every other national question,—and therefore it has become the interest of all to procure its settlement as speedily as possible. From its very nature a just decision cannot be obtained from clamour, passion, or fear, but from calm discussion, sound argument, an appeal to facts and the well established principles of a sound political economy. Were party interests and long cherished prejudices laid aside, and the points in debate taken up with an honest desire to arrive at the truth, and a resolute determination to act upon it, when discovered, no one need fear the issue. A speedy settlement would ensue, and prosperity and peace would once more smile on our now agitated and suffering country.

That this subject ought to be examined on these principles and in this spirit all readily admit, but then each party unhappily claims this becoming temper for itself, and loudly bewails the want of it in the opposite. It would be too much to assert that there has been no rashness, violence and impropriety on the side of the repealers, and yet, we may affirm without the slightest exaggeration, that when we take into account the unreasoning obstinacy,—the selfishness,—and the pertinacity with which their supporters continue to impute the basest motives to their opponents,—that their conduct has been dignified, peaceful, and moderate to a marvellous degree. Besides it is no Christian virtue to allow ourselves to be robbed, cheated, and oppressed without remonstrance. It becomes in such circumstances a stern duty to denounce the injustice as much for the sake of those who practice it might be borne, but when millions are suffering with us under the same oppression and thereby reduced to beggary and starvation, the case is entirely altered.—To be silent in this case, or even to maintain in our speech all the calmness of philosophers, when dealing with injustice so monstrous as this were to insult the groans, the tears, and the agonies of outraged humanity and to prove ourselves unworthy to be classed with our species.

If the provision laws have produced but a tenth of the physical suffering and moral mischief which previous Lecturers have attributed to them, and in my opinion justly, then, it is impossible to denounce them too strongly, they deserve to be treated like a ravenous beast which devours at once the people and their food. It is not possible to imagine a more terrible visitation than for a people to be subjected to starvation in the sight of plenty. This is literally the condition of thousands in our land at the present day. They starve not because there is no bread to give them, but because our laws have raised its price beyond the means of the people to purchase it. The misery occasioned by these laws has been long endured with exemplary patience. But it is too much when those who have the means of granting relief stand by and like the Indian savage merely praise the sustained fortitude with which the anguish is borne which they are themselves inflicting. Patience can bear much and long, but it has its limits.—So long as hope sustains the heart it may last, but when once dispair seizes upon the sufferer, it expires. —To this extremity many in the midst of us have already been driven. And what may not be dreaded from hundreds of thousands tormented with gnawing hunger and freezing cold, who are without one refuge to which to flee but the grave? The very selfishness of the monopolist of bread might urge him, were he to act wisely, to join the repealers, and seek a speedy and equitable adjustment of a question that is attracting the attention and enlisting the energies of the wisest and most devoted men in the country.

The department of the subject which has been assigned to me for discussion this evening has less to do with the morality than the political economy of the question. Indeed many have alleged and still boldly assert that religion and morality have nothing to do with the corn laws. If it be meant that these laws have no affinity with religion, give them no sanction but strongly denounce them, I assent. But, if it be intended to insinuate that it is improper to test their injustice by the great principles of morality and religion, then I demur. No nation that lays claim to civilisation can consistently object to have every law on its statute-book tried by this standard, far less the Rulers of Great Britian who claim so boldly the honour of being the guardians and the patrons of the Christian Faith. A nation which calls itself Christian is bound by its own profession publicly to repudiate every practice which the religion of Jesus condemns, and consequently is under the most sacred obligation to see that none of its laws shall run counter to its holy requirements. Consistency demands that either the profession or the unrighteous law be instantly abandoned. Now I am thoroughly satisfied that it has been demonstrated by previous Lecturers to the conviction of every one who knows what Christianity is, that it is impossible to reconcile the one with the other, and that it is difficult to conceive how the love of justice and of the corn law can exist in the same breast. It now becomes my duty to prove that these laws are equally at variance with a sound political economy and the prosperity and peace of this country. It will be readily admitted that I shall completely establish these points if I shall satisfactorily prove that the Provision Laws limit our home and foreign trade—that they lower the rate of wages while they raise the price of food,—and that they produce convulsions in trade and occasion dispeace in society. These are evils of the most enormous magnitude which every wise government will sedulously guard against, and for the existence of which nothing can compensate in such a country as this. To demonstrate these propositions shall be my aim in the sequel of the Lecture.

The first charge which we bring against the Provision Laws is

1. That they limit our trade both at home and abroad. It is surely not necessary that I should prove that the prosperity of this country and the well-being of a large proportion of its inhabitants depend more on a flourishing commerce than even on a prosperous agriculture. Indeed, agriculture depends almost entirely for its success on trade. No nation has ever emerged from barbarism which has not either encouraged manufactures within in its own territory, or exchanged the products of its own soil for those of some other country. We readily admit that it is highly desirable that both agriculture and commerce should flourish in our own land; but then, this important object is not to be secured by protecting the one at the expense of the other. Let both be free, and both will flourish. Let the one be protected and both will languish, and through process of time decay. To affirm, as has been done, that this nation would be as great, powerful, wealthy, and prosperous as it is, though Manchester, Liverpool, and Glasgow, were swept from its surface is the ravings of lunacy. No man out of bedlam will believe it Or, if there be any so credulous in consequence of his ignorance, let him remember that it is to our commerce we are indebted for our navy—our canals—our steam-boats—and our railroads, from which agriculture itself has reaped immense advantages, and the nation a vast superiority over every other. In truth, it is our towns that give to farm produce its chief value, and the cheap rate at which it can be brought to the best market from the most distant parts of the country, has given to land a value which it never could have acquired, but for these improvements. Indeed, the possessor of land is the only individual whose property is improved without capital, skill, or industry, on his part. As our population increase in wealth and numbers, an additional value attaches to the soil. But if these considerations be not sufficient to convince him of the gross absurdity of the statement we are considering, let him examine our population returns, and he will find that more than two-thirds of the inhabitants of this country depend on commerce for subsistence, while not one-third are sustained by husbandry. To destroy our manufacturing towns and villages, would be to banish or starve nearly the one half of our population, and to diminish the value of land more than a half. Before the late war, the agriculturists and those dependent on this branch of industry for labour, were a decided majority of the whole inhabitants; now they are only as one to three. By throwing small farms into large ones, and by the improvement of agricultural implements, fewer hands are employed in cultivating the soil than fifty years ago. And yet, our population has nearly doubled during that period. Nor is there any hope that a greater number of labourers will be employed in rural occupations than at the present moment, unless we return to spade cultivation, which would certainly not be profitable to the proprietor of the soil. While, then, agriculture is not likely to increase the demand for labour, let it be re-

membered that, according to the last census, the population is incresing at the rate of a thousand a day, for whom trade must find employment. Nay, the probability is, that the number of agricultural labourers will yearly decrease from the rapidly increasing practice of farmers only employing unmarried labourers, and from the improvement in the implements of husbandry. And let it likewise be observed, that while with a Free Trade, improvement in machinery increases the demand for labour, its application to husbandry necessarily contract it in that department. This may not appear obvious at first sight, but a little reflection will convince you of its truth. Machinery must be constructed—kept in repair and directed. Articles manufactured by its agency are cheaper than those produced by manual labour alone. Hence, the nation that excels in the application of machinery to the cheap production of articles of clothing will, were trade free, secure to itself the markets of the world. It is true, every new invention which supplants manual labour, will be felt by those employed in it; but the evil would be very temporary. All experience proves, that every new mechanical invention creates much more demand for labour in trade than it destroys. But it is not so in husbandry. The soil cannot be extended like trade—the same work is to be done; but, if it be performed by machinery, then the individuals who are supplanted must search for employment in the manufacturing districts, or be thrown entirely idle. It is clear, then, that a wise and enlightened government will look at the welfare of the great mass of the people; and if its protection could benefit any branch of industry, would extend it in the present state of this country to trade. This is not what we desire. We want no favouritism. We know that so far from proving beneficial, it injures not only the community at large, but ultimately the favoured class themselves. We demand justice for all, and this will be advantageous for all. Besides, we affirm that, while manufacturers and their operatives are injured by the Corn Laws, so likewise are the farmers and their labourers. It is not the object of this lecture to prove this. We would only remark in passing, that, since 1815, there have been no fewer than three Corn Bills passed for the protection of agriculture; and yet, since that period, no fewer than Five Parliamentary Committees have been employed to inquire into the causes of the deep distress under which the farmers were universally labouring. The remedy proposed and adopted was increased protection. And yet, the condition of the farmer is as wretched as ever. More of them have been ruined than among the manufacturers. And the farmers are now beginning to perceive, that they have been cursed, rather than blessed, by the landlords' protection. They are now discovering that the very means which the parliament have adopted professedly for their advantage, have, in reality, created their sufferings; and that Free Trade is as advantageous to them as it is to the manufacturers. In truth, the Provision Laws benefit none but landlords and the Parochial Clergy. The public are beginning to see clearly, that the Provision Laws are a tax imposed on the community for the aggrandizement of the aristocracy; and that the farmers have been made the scape-goat to carry away the odium which must otherwise have attached to them, but which, in future, they must make up their minds to bear themselves, or give up this unrighteous exaction. These observations were necessary to prepare us for perceiving clearly, that if it can be proved that the Provision Laws limit our trade, they must be most pernicious to the community at large. To show you how they most unequivocally do this shall now be my object.

1st. The Provision Laws limit our home trade. It is admitted on all hands, that our home trade is the most valuable and by far the most important. It is conducted at least expense, risk, and trouble. The payments are not only more sure, but more speedy. It forms, likewise, a very large proportion of the whole trade of the country. On these admitted facts, the monopolists of corn endeavour to prove the necessity and importance of their law to secure a prosperous home trade. Could this be established, all opposition to this law should cease. And what is the argument by which they attempt to prove their assertion? They tell us that our agriculturalists are our best customers; and that if we take away their protection they will not be able to purchase our goods. We ask, why? If this be the fact, it only proves incontestibly that the landlords exact from the farmers too high rents. So long as land can be cultivated with profit without rent, no one would suffer but its proprietor; and consequently, it is not the farmers and their labourers on whose custom we are to found our judgment of the soundness of the above allegation, but on that of the thirty thousand landlords themselves. It is clear, were no rents paid, we would only lose the custom of those who are supported by them. And as these form so inconsiderable a proportion of the community, the prosperity of the country could not be greatly affected by their absence from it altogether. As the farmers and their labourers are confessedly suffering under the hardships of the times, it is obvious that they cannot be very good customers; and so far from the law benefiting them, it has in various ways operated most injuriously to their interests. We have now to estimate the effect of the repeal of the provision laws upon the proprietors of land. We shall admit that their rents would be diminished in the first instance, though even this is doubtful, but not certainly to such an extent as to interfere with any of their comforts. They might not be able to keep as many hounds—extensive preserves—or race-horses; but this so far from injuring trade would benefit it. They might not have so much to expend at the gaming table; but they would still have the means of clothing themselves and their families as delicately and magnificently as before. We too, would have fewer absentees. They would be compelled to remain at home and encourage agriculture, by improving their estates and thus benefit both themselves and the country, instead of squandering away among foreigners the resources which are wrung from the toil-worn labourer by their unrighteous law. When I was in Paris last spring, I was assured, on good authority, that there were no fewer than 40,000 English in that city alone. Many of these, no doubt, were mere pleasure hunters and others, because they could live cheaper there than at home. But, were the Corn Laws repealed, you would soon see the greater portion of these in their own country. Provisions would rise abroad, and fall proportionally at home; and those who have gone to economize would speedily discover, that it is as easy to be frugal in their own country as among strangers. At all events, they who live in foreign countries, have no right to tax us on any pretence; far less under that of supporting our home trade.

But there is another answer to this allegation equally conclusive. All will admit that a manufacturer would be better with his goods in his warehouse, than to dispose of them to a customer who should pay him with money previously taken from him. This would be doing business at an absolute loss. The corn law has not indeed brought matters to this pass, but they are verging to it. The manufacturer is first compelled to pay to the British landlords a much larger sum for his food than he could purchase it in other countries, and yet he has to sell him his goods cheaper than they can be bought in any other part of the world. It is clear that, in estimating the worth of such a customer, you must first deduct the extra amount paid to the monopolist for food, as a bounty, before you can ascertain the profit or loss of the transaction. By as much as you have paid to him more for his corn than you could have purchased it in the free market of the world, by so much is the profit diminished, as you cannot sell your goods dearer to him than to another to whom you have paid no bounty. This is bad enough, and yet it is but a part of the injury that is done you. The food you buy has been raised in price by an unjust law, and the goods you have to sell are in a corresponding degree diminished in value, To procure the same amount of food, you have to produce a larger quantity of goods; thus you glut the market and reduce their worth. Besides, to secure a sufficient supply of the necessaries of life, you are compelled to produce more than you can possibly dispose of in the home market, and are obliged to come into competition with other manufacturers in the foreign market, who have no corn law to raise the price of their food. Thus, you perceive, you are compelled to give some of your goods for your own money, and to sell the rest at a reduced rate. Such a state of things must be injurious to our home trade.

Having thus viewed the influence of the corn laws on our home trade, as it relates to our agricultural customers, let us now inquire what influence they exert on the means of the other portions of the community of consuming manufactured products, and we shall find that their ability to purchase these is greatly diminished. Nothing can be more obvious, than that when a man has a very limited income, and this is the case with all our operatives, and he is compelled to expend a larger proportion of it than he would be required to do were food cheap, he has just so much the less to expend on other necessaries. It will not be denied, nay, it is boldly avowed by their advocates, that the very design of the provision laws is to raise the price of food. When bread is dear, the operative has to expend nearly the whole of his earnings on this necessary of life, and has nothing or very little to give for clothes. Thus, when bread is dear, a man who has ten shillings a-week may require to expend five of this sum for this article alone, which, were it not for the corn laws, he might have obtained for three. He is thus prevented from purchasing clothing for himself and family. Hence we find it invariably happen, that when provisions are high priced, a demand for clothing diminishes; the market becomes overstocked; workmen are thrown idle; wages fall; and the evil once commenced, increases at an accelerated rate. We appeal to any person of observation and intelligence if this be not an accurate account of the matter. Were all our industrious artizans clothed as they ought to be, our overstocked warehouses would be completely emptied, and every person willing to work would be in full occupation at remunerating wages. But the provision laws render this impossible. The tax they impose on the people's bread extorts from them a much larger sum than would clothe them and their families in the most comfortable manner. When we look at the number of shoeless persons on our streets—the multitudes everywhere in rags—the empty and bedless rooms of hundreds in our towns—and the crowded apartments in which our industrious population are huddled together—need we wonder that our shoemakers, tailors, cabinet-makers and masons are idle, and that our warehouses are without customers. And if it be asked, Why is this the case? we answer, the people have to give nearly all their earnings for food, and have nothing to expend on other articles. Could the ingenuity of man have invented a system better fitted to paralyze our trade and to pauperize our country?

The abettors of the corn laws indeed try to persuade us that if the money they extort from us be expended in the country, we cannot be injured by them. This looks plausible as a general statement, but we shall find it is far from being true. Admitting that the wealth of the country will not be diminished upon the whole, yet there will be this vast difference, that it will be accumulated in the hands of the monopolists, and will either be expended on foreign delicacies, or hoarded up without the possibility of profitable investment. It is not so much the aggregate wealth of a country that promotes its prosperity, as its free circulation and its equitable distribution throughout the community. If the industrious classes are reduced to wretchedness, or forced to live on the scantiest fare, it matters not what may be theamount of wealth of a few thousands, the trade of the country cannot profit by it. Now, the very tendency of the corn laws is to rob the industrious, and to increase the income of the already sufficiently rich, and consequently to diminish the consumption of manufactured goods in this country. We have said it is not true that it matters not to the prosperity of the country how wealth is acquired, or in what hands it may be placed, provided it be expended in it. This condition, in the present unnatural state of things, can scarcely be complied with. But even though it be expended, it is not on those articles that improve the industry of the country, but on horse-racing and other dissolute practices. Unless a fair proportion of the wealth of the country be expended on its manufactured products, it is clear that its trade can never be in a prosperous state. If a man has to pay twenty shillings more for a quarter of wheat to the home producer than he could procure it from some other country. it is clear that this is just so much lost. Or suppose that he barters his merchandise for wheat. He has to give a much larger amount of goods in the one case than in the other; and consequently has had to produce more, both at an increase of toil and capital, and at the risk of overstocking the market and of suspending his operations altogether. Had he been permitted to exchange his goods for the wheat of the foreign producer, he might not only have procured plenty of bread, but abundance of butter for it likewise. But there is another view of this matter equally important. When more time, labour, and capital are expended on the production of an article than it can be procured for from some other quarter, a loss is incurred To attempt to grow ourselves at a high price what we can buy at a cheaper rate, is just to throw so much money away, and the sum thus expended is just as truly lost to the country as if it had been cast into the sea. The protection afforded by the corn laws is very unequal in its operation, in relation to the landowners themselves. There is great diversity of soil and climate in our own country. Rich soils produce better crops at less expense of cultivation and capital than poor ones; but the protection is not regulated by the quality of the soil. Hence the possessors of rich land chiefly reap the advantage of the protective duty, and the whole amount of the tax is buried in an ungrateful soil to yield a return to no one. No good object can be served by such conduct, but much injury is done to the community. The folly is similar in kind, though vastly greater in degree, to that displayed by the rearer of grapes in a hot-house. when they could be purchased at the third of the expense from the Continent. We have the authority of Sir Robert Peel for affirming that to buy in the cheapest and sell in the dearest market, is the only sure method of securing prosperity. This is sound political economy. But the corn laws compel us to buy in the dearest and sell in the cheapest market, and thus involves those who are forced to carry on this unproductive traffic in ruin. Skill, perseverance and increased exertion may withstand it for a time, but no efforts can ward off the evil for ever. It is needless to remind you how fearfully we are suffering at present under this monstrous system, and there is little hope of relief till we destroy this giant monopoly which is devouring our substance, and restore industry to its natural rights. By robbing the industrious artizans of the fruits of their toil you impoverish your best customers; and you need not marvel if, in such circumstances, you cannot find a market for your goods. The pernicious effects of this restrictive system is first felt by the manufacturer, and then by the operatives he employs. The agriculturists may longer escape. Their protective law gives them a monopoly in the market; and as they cannot produce, on an average of years, sufficient food to meet the wants of the community, their article is kept up in price. But the farmers derive no benefit from the high price of food. They have been tempted to take their farms in the expectation that the corn law will keep it always dear; and consequently, when grain falls in price they are ruined. When food is dear, the workman cannot procure a sufficient supply for himself and his family and other necessary articles besides. And as he must have food, though he should clothe himself in rags, it is in constant demand. But as the evils of the system increase, they must extend to him. The community will at length become too poor even to buy food, and must either be supported as paupers or starve. To this crisis for the present we have come. And hence the farmers with their high rents and cheap markets—cheap, not so much from superabundance as on account of inability to purchase—are beginning to feel that the corn laws will ultimately prove as injurious to agriculture as to trade.

2d. The provision laws restrict our foreign trade. They do so in various ways. It is a universally admitted principle, that no country can continue to sell to another to any extent, unless it also buy from it either directly or indirectly. The Creator has so diversified the earth in its soil, climate, and peculiar productions, that one article necessary for human comfort can be more cheaply produced in one part of the world, and another in some other portion of it. Wisdom consists not in resisting these natural advantages, but in fully availing ourselves of them. It is as foolish as it is impious to restrict the bounties of heaven, and proudly to say that we shall receive as little as possible from other lands. God has given the earth to the children of men: and what better method can be imagined for securing the well-being of the whole human family, than by the reciprocation of mutual benefits. The soil and climate of other lands are more propitious than our own for producing wheat; but, in consequence of our minerals and other circumstances, we have facilities for manufacturing clothing which no other country possesses. We cannot, on an average of years, grow sufficient food for the comfortable subsistence of our large and increasing population; but we can furnish clothing and other articles to any extent, and at a cheaper rate than any nation on the face of the earth. Other countries can supply us with cheaper food than we can obtain at home. Now, were we permitted freely to exchange our manufactures with the Continent and America for their wheat, the advantage would be mutual. But the corn law will not permit this. We want nothing so much as cheap food, and this is the only thing we are not permitted to take. Other countries who are desirous to take our goods have nothing else that we need to give us. Hence, as we cannot take their grain they cannot take our goods; or if they do take them, what is worse, they cannot pay for them. Thus, for instance, we are permitted to take the tobacco and cotton of America in exchange for our products, but not their wheat. Now, the Americans have hitherto taken a larger quantity of our goods than is adequate to pay for the cotton and tobacco which we require. They must either pay the balance in money, or our merchants must lose their property. The latter alternative must ultimately be the result, because no country can continue to pay large sums in specie without utterly deranging their own currency and bankrupting the country. To this condition has America nearly been brought by our corn laws, and consequently our trade with it at present is carried on upon a very limited scale, and on ruinous principles. Immense sums are owing to British merchants, which would instantly be paid were we permitted to take their wheat. And not only would the money due be paid, but a vast extension of trade would immediately take place with that country. Their new tariff, enacted in self defence, would not stand on their statute-books for six months, were our provision laws repealed. The same remarks apply to the Continent, and every other country where food is produced cheaper than in our own.

We have no right to complain of the heavy tariffs of other nations So far from being an injury to us in present circumstances, they are on the whole advantageous No doubt, were it not for these, our merchants might import their goods to any extent into them, but they would not be repaid. No country can long trade to any extent with another, except on the principle of the exchange of their respective products on the principle already explained. Were the rich actually to consume the luxuries of other lands in addition to what they already do, equally to the amount of corn that would be imported, our trade might be as extensive with foreign nations as it would be were our corn laws repealed, but it would still be injured at home. But this they cannot do. Hence we are forced to endure the double evil of a limited foreign market, and compelled to pay a large premium to the landlords for our food—a policy at once unjust and suicidal, inasmuch as it unrighteously exhausts the very means by which the agricultural products of this country can be purchased. The farmers are now beginning to reap the fruits of this system. The present comparative cheap rate of the provision market is not so much to be ascribed to Peel's tariff as to the inability of the people to purchase a sufficiency of the necessaries of life. That the fall in the price of cattle is not owing to importation, is demonstrated from the fact that butter and cheese have fallen in price more in proportion than beef and mutton, and yet no alteration has taken place in the duties imposed on these articles. This conclusion is strengthened by this other fact, that the importation this year of these articles has been considerably less than on previous years. The deficiency in cheese has amounted to 42,487 cwt., and in butter to 46,002 cwt. At the same time it will be found that, from the dryness of the season and the scantiness of the pasture, less has actually been produced at home, Now, to what can we ascribe the fall in price, but to the inability of the people to buy. All their money is necessary to procure bread and potatoes: they cannot obtain beef, butter, and cheese, even at the reduced price.

The Prime Minister and his followers triumphantly adduce the increased exports of last year as a conclusive proof that trade cannot be so bad as the manufacturers allege. There could not be a more absurd conclusion. The prosperity of a country might be more safely estimated from its imports than its exports. The increased exportation ought to be regarded rather as a symptom of disease than an evidence of health, unless it be ascertained that the merchant enjoys profitable returns. The manufacturer may be driven to the foreign market from the impossibility of finding one at home; and, in the very desperation of his circumstances, may be impelled to encounter desperate risks rather than shut up his works and throw all his workers idle. This is the very last expedient which he will adopt so long as he has the slightest hope of a remunerative price. If you doubt this representation, ask the merchants themselves what is the state of the matter, and they will tell you that their goods are warehoused on a foreign shore—that they cannot sell them, because they are not permitted to take in return for them what the foreigners can give, and even those they have sold are in many cases as good as lost, because they have not received payment for them. Of course, this is a state of things which cannot last. The additional exportation may serve in the meantime to keep our workmen a little longer employed, but it will only put off the evil, not ultimately lessen it. At no distant day, if trade is not made free, our exports will gradually diminish, till they cease altogether, and then farewell to the greatness of Britain. The landlords will then discover, when it is too late, that their estates are valueless to them, and that the country is not worth living in.

But it is farther alleged, in defence of our selfish and unjust policy, that foreigners will not take our goods in return for their grain, but demand to be paid for it in gold. Were they to act upon any other principle in the present state of our corn laws they would be fools. They know that we never take their wheat except when dreaded famine drives us to it. They cannot calculate in spring what may be our wants in autumn:—they cannot therefore provide a supply for us. The demand comes upon them unexpectedly, and they have to meet it out of their ordinary stock—a circumstance alike injurious to them and to us. We have to buy from a limited and nearly exhausted stock. Thus the price is raised greatly so soon as it is known that we must become purchasers. The case would be very different were wheat a constant article of trade. There are millions of acres now useless, both on the Continent and in America, of the most fertile land, admirably adapted for growing wheat, which would be brought under cultivation as our demands increased, were we their regular customers. They would soon discover that it would be vastly more profitable for them to grow wheat than to manufacture goods which they could buy cheaper from us than they could produce them at home. By this exchange they would have cheaper clothing and we would have cheaper food, and consequently a more extensive and steadier market for our goods. To this reasoning it is replied, that it is a very inviting speculation, but the proof is demanded in support of its truth. We answer, give us the means of proving it. While we are hemmed in on every side by restrictive laws, and have forced every nation to retaliate against our own selfishness, it is impossible to appeal to facts. Repeal the corn laws, and if the theory of the monopolist be true, the free traders will soon join him in his wish for restriction. At all events we will then have a fair field in which to test the soundness of our reasonings. But so long as you keep our commerce bound by your adamantine laws, it is mockery—it is worse, it is injustice to taunt us with the fancifulness of our opinions

But there is still another way in which our Provision Laws injures our foreign commerce. They provoke other nations to become competitors with us in the same departments of trade. Had we freely taken the wheat of the Continent and America, there is little probability that manufactures would have succeeded in these countries to the extent that they have done. They would have found it more profitable to have cultivated their soil and disposed of its produce in exchange for our goods. This would have been mutually advantageous. They have to foster their manufactures to make them prosper, and we have to give a premium to our agriculturalists. Of course they produce cloth at a loss, and we raise wheat at a great national sacrifice. Both parties are sufferers by this foolish policy. Besides, it ought not to be forgotten, that many of the manufacturing establishments in Belgium, Germany, Russia, Mexico, and America, have been erected by British capital. The machinery has been fabricated by English mechanics, and is superintended by British artizans. Had it not been for these circumstances their establishments would not have reached the same excellence or extent in so short a period. Now, had it not been for the Provision Laws, both the capital and the operatives of this country could have been more profitably employed at home than abroad; and consequently, would never have been engaged in raising up formidable rivals against ourselves. By these means much mischief has already been done to our trade, and much more will speedily ensue from the same cause, if the Corn Law be not immediately repealed, Capitalists will, in greater numbers, betake themselves to other countries, because there is no opening for the profitable investment of their money at home. But if the Provision Laws were repealed, we have nothing to fear from Continental and American rivalry. We have immense national advantages over them for manufacturing, which no skill or industry on their part can ever secure. And when once the agriculturists abroad can find a better and steadier market in England for their wheat than at home, they will not long tolerate those high tariffs which have been imposed for the benefit of their manufacturers, and which compel them to pay so much more for articles of clothing than they could otherwise obtain them. With us the battle is between the aristocracy on the one hand who pocket the profits of monopoly, and the people on the other who pay it. With them the aristocracy and the people would unite against the few monopolist manufacturers, It is clear that, in this case, the contest would not long be doubtful. Let us once secure Free Trade in England, and the same blessing will soon be enjoyed throughout the whole world to the profit of all. I cannot spend more time on this department of the subject, and trust, however, that I have proved to your full conviction, that the Provision Laws greatly limit both our home and foreign trade; and that, therefore, they are most injurious to the prosperity of the country. The next point for consideration is

II. That the Provision Laws lower wages. The law which regulates the price of labour is just beginning to be generally understood. By our political economists it has not been accurately defined, and by the mass of the community it is very imperfectly known. Public attention has of late, been frequently directed to this subject, and correct views in respect to it are rapidly gaining ground. There is no mystery in it. It is at once plain and intelligible, and as certain in its operation as the law of gravitation. The law which regulates the price of everything else, likewise determines the rate of wages; the proportion between the supply and the demand. When any commodity becomes more abundant than needed, it falls in price; when it becomes scarce, it rises in value. This is precisely the case with labour. When there is more work to be done than there are labourers to do it, the price of labour rises. On the contrary, when there are more operatives than there is work to give them, the value of labour diminishes. We need not embarrass ourselves on this subject with the relation between labour and capital. For it is clear that, when capital can be profitably expended on labour it will be so employed: when it cannot, it will be locked up, and remain unproductive. The proportion between the number of labourers and the amount of labour required will invariably regulate its price. This is an invariable rule which even an Act of Parliament could not disturb, except by throwing a number of hands entirely idle when work is scarce or by creating additional ones when it is plenty. It is right that this should be well understood. It is impossible for any length of time, except with the consent of the operatives themselves to depress wages when work is plenty, and it is equally impossible to keep them high when it is scarce, except by withdrawing labourers from the field of competition. When work is plenty masters compete with each other, and wages rise. When work is scarce, workmen underbid each other, and wages fall. You will find, on careful examination, that this is invariably the case. It is possible for the workmen in one department of trade, to keep up their wages, while others are depressed—provided the demand for their labour continue, and they can keep additional workmen from competing with them. But this, in a free country, will soon become impossible; because numbers will press into that trade that is best paid, and gradually bring down their wages to a common level. Though this conclusion is confirmed by all experience, yet there are many who affirm that the rate of wages depends on the price of food. The Corn Law advocates try to make us believe that the price of corn regulates every thing—that it governs wages and all other articles of consumpt. Nothing more absurd. When corn is high, wages are very generally low, and manufactured goods fall in price. If all other articles rose and fell with the price of wheat, and were in the same demand, these laws would neither benefit nor injure any one. They would merely stand as a harmless monument of human folly on the statute book. But, unfortunately, the very opposite is the fact. At the very time that the operative is paying dear for his food, he is compelled, in ordinary circumstances, to sell his own labour cheap, and thus he is robbed in two directions: he has to pay more for his bread than it is worth, were trade free; and he receives less for his labour than its true value, in consequence of the restrictive influence of these laws. Were work as plenty, and wages to rise and fall with the price of food, it would be the same to the operative whatever might be the rate of provisions. As a proof that this is not the case, let us appeal to facts:—In America, in the year 1699, a workman required to toil 137 days to purchase a ton of flour. In 1790, he could procure the same quantity for the labour of 125 days; and in 1841 for the exertions of 78 days. In these instances, wheat and labour have maintained no fixed proportion. The truth is, wheat has regularly fallen, and wages have risen. But it is objected that America is a young rising country; and that no fair conclusion can be drawn from the state of matters there, which can be applied to the circumstances of England. Let us, therefore, see how the case stands at home. In the year 1742, wages in this country were, on an average, six shillings a week; wheat at that period was thirty shillings a quarter; so that, with the labour of five weeks, a workman could purchase a quarter. In 1799, wages were nine shillings, and wheat seventy shillings; so that, to procure the same quantity, nearly eight weeks' labour would be required. In 1841, wheat was seventy shillings, and wages were not, on an average, above eight shillings, and many out of work entirely; so that, even the labourer in full employment would require to toil nine weeks to procure a quarter of wheat. Were we to examine the state of every country throughout the world, we would find that there is no regular proportion between the rate of wages and the price of food. It might have been sufficient to have appealed to your own observation and experience, and to have asked you if you ever knew wages rise and fall with food? Within the last ten years the price of wheat has fluctuated from forty-six shillings to eighty shillings a quarter, but during that period the tendency of wages has been downward. Indeed it would be much nearer the truth to say, the cheaper provisions the higher are wages, not only relatively, but actually, Those, then, who tell you that cheap food would lower wages, not only run in the face of facts, but appear to expect you to believe them in opposition to your own experience. Having shown that there is no necessary connection between the price of food and the rate of wages, I shall now show you how the Provision Laws necessarily lower wages.

They do so by diminishing the amount of labour. There are two methods by which the price of labour may be lowered. Either by lessening its amount or by encreasing the number of workmen, and conversely wages must rise when labour becomes plenty and labourers scarce. If it be true as we have endeavoured to prove, that the provision laws limit both our home and foreign trade, then the consequence follows that they contract the labour market and render work scarce, while their tendency at the same is to increase the population at an accelerated rate, notwithstanding the number they starve and bring to a premature grave. This may be esteemed a paradox, but it has been established as an invariable result, that whenever a community become for any length of time depressed in circumstances they lose self respect—sink in morality—act under the impulse of their animal feelings, and marry young, reckless of consequences. Ireland is a decisive proof of this, and the same fact has been proved beyond contradiction from the condition of our Scotch population by Dr Alison. Here then the corn laws act injuriously in two directions. They first limit the demand for labour, and then force additional competitors into the field and thus greatly lower the value of labour. The slightest reflection must convince any one that this evil must continue to increase unless the corn laws are repealed. Britain is not increasing in size, but our population is increasing at the rate of a 1000 a-day. We had as many acres in 1801, when the population was only 15,000,000, as we have at present now that it is 27,000,000. Agriculture cannot employ a greater number of labourers, the whole increase must then find employment in trade or starve. Our towns dependant on trade are r pidly increasing, our rural population is becoming fewer every census. The people must be miserable if trade do not increase. We cannot afford to allow it to remain stationary. It is clear then that the provision laws if continued will press with augmenting severity every year, more and more depress over trade, diminish the value of labour, and aggravate tho sufferings under which we now groan.

2d. The provision laws likewise force a number of persons prematurely into the labour market. When a parent cannot by his utmost exertions earn sufficient food for himself and his family, rather than allow them to starve, he will try and procure employment for his children. From their tender years and defective education, they ought rather to be at school. All the better emotions of a Father's heart, rouse him to make every exersion, and to submit to every possible sacrifice to spare their youth and to educate them for usefulness, but gaunt famine enters his dwelling—he hears their cries for bread and he has none to give them, and they must either work or perish. In such circumstances he cannot remain long undecided. His children are hurried into the crowded factory, and become at a premature age eager competitors for leave to toil at a scanty remuneration. Had the father good wages and constant employment comparatively few cases of this kind would occur. None indeed except when the parents are dissipated or the children orphants. But in the fearful emergency in which we now are, the most virtuous parents are compelled to draw their chief means of subsistence from the premature labour of their children. These are facts with which every inhabitant in a manufacturing district may be familiar. Labour is not only depreciated in value but the intelligence—morality and religion of the community grievously suffer at the same time. Indeed these laws are the authors of inconceivable mischief in a multitude of ways but it is impossible to attribute to them a particle of good. The wonder is that they should find an advocate, I say not in Britain, but in the world. The nation that supports them deserves to be ranked with cannibals, for they virtually compel the people to devour their own flesh.

3d. There is yet another way in which these laws depreciate the value of labour. By raising the price of bread, they force the labourer to toil longer and work harder than otherwise he would be required to do, for the support of himself and his family. To provide any thing like subsistence in many departments of labour, human strength requires to be tasked to the uttermost. The hours of sleep are abridged, and those of toil lengthened. Even sabbath is grudged because its rest can scarcely be enjoyed without fasting. This incessant toil increases the product of his labour. Thus as the corn laws limit the market on the hand and his over exertion overstocks it on the other, he is entirely thrown idle—cast on the charity of the humane and reduced to absolute pauperism. His children are naked—his house without furniture, and himself in rags. Who that knows any thing of the state of the country at present, will venture to affirm that this is an exaggerated picture of the condition of many of our operatives. Is it resonable—is it just—ought it to be tolerated in a civilized nation, that persons should be compelled to unremitted toil for fourteen or fifteen hours a day, to keep himself and dependants from starving ? And yet there are tens of thousands in the midst of us in this unhappy predicament

Many tell us that the evils under which we are now suffering, are not to be attributed to the Corn Laws, but to over-production. It would be a sufficient answer to reply, that these laws are the very cause of this over-production. But we deny that there is over-production;—the real evil is diminished consumption. The labourer, in dear years, has to give all his earnings for bread, and has nothing to spare for clothes. We ask, are the people too well clothed? Many of them have scarcely a rag to cover their nakedness. Are their dwellings too elegant and their beds too luxurious? Many of them are huddled in garrets or cellars, and have nothing to sleep on but bare boards or a pallet of straw. Are they over-fed? Meagre famine is seen in their faces, and has marked them for its prey. Superabundance should be witnessed in the extravagance of the people, and not read in their destitution. What would you think of the man who first dammed up a river and then complained because it overflowed its banks, and lamented the mischief it was doing, while he carefully guarded the obstruction he had reared? Would you not tell him that he, and not the river, was to blame? You would bid him remove the barrier he had erected, and the stream would return to its natural channel, and instead of causing desolation, it would bring fertility and beauty to the country through which it flowed. So we tell the monopolist you have laid an embargo on our commerce and shut up its outlets, and what right have you to complain that our warehouses are crammed, and yet our people naked. You have forced us by your restrictive laws, to do the work of two days in one to procure the food of one; and why do you pretend to marvel that we go idle and starve the next? Take down your barriers and let trade be free, and we will have no cause to complain, and you will be regaled with the cheerful hum of industry, and be gladdened with the smiles of a busy, but not overwrought—shivering—naked—starving—and discontented people.

Others, again, ascribe the fall of wages and want of employment to the great increase of machinery. We cannot discuss, at present, the effect of machinery on the price of labour. It is a sufficient answer to the above allegation, to state that the wages of those who labour in departments where machinery has never been employed, are lower than in the case of those who take charge of machinery; and a larger proportion of the former are idle than the latter. Thus, masons, tailors, cabinet-makers, shoe-makers, and others, are worse employed than cotton-spinners, and their wages equally depressed. Female sewers, in London, cannot obtain more for making a sailor's shirt than *three-farthings*, or a *penny*. The stocking-frame has not been improved these hundred years; and yet, in England, this class of operatives are in the most wretched condition. The same remarks apply to the Potteries, and to other trades that are not affected by machinery. The fact is, machinery creates rather than diminishes labour. Had it not been for machinery, we could not have endured the pressure of the Provision Laws for the one-half of the time during which they have lasted. Let all our machinery stop throughout the whole country, and the property of the landlords would not be worth one year's purchase.

Again, some of the admirers of the Provision Laws attempt to throw the blame of the reduction of wages on the employer. Those who look merely at the effects of an over-stocked labour market without inquiring into the cause, may be misled by such representations. Not so the intelligent observer. So long as the employer has more work to do than there are hands to perform it, he will seek additional workmen; and, to secure their services, he will tempt them with a larger wage. He will then go to the workman who can make his own price; but when work becomes scarce, the operative has to apply to the employer and to induce him to give him something to do, offers his labour at a reduced rate. It is thus that the workmen come to compete with each other, and necessarily lower the value of their labour. The blame, in these circumstances, is neither attributable to master or workman, but to the cause which reduces them to this condition. It is always best for all parties when work is in demand. It is true, that an avaricious master may, when his own branch of trade is prosperous, and others depressed, enrich himself at the expense of his workers; but this can rarely occur, because he will soon find competitors who will bring him to the natural level. Let us, then, look the real evil in the face, and not be misled by interested parties from assailing the real cause of our sorest sufferings. Be assured that, while the Corn Laws continue in existence, though we may have gleams of prosperity, yet, like sunshine in winter, it will be fitful, and be speedily followed by the hurricane and the storm.

III. The provision laws produce convulsions in commerce and in society.

1st. They produce convulsions in business. We all know from fatal experience that our trade is irregular and unsteady. A few years' prosperity is uniformly followed by deep depression and great stagnation in business. These commercial crises as they are called, are becoming more frequent in their occurrence and of longer duration. These are facts, which none dispute whatever difference of opinion may obtain as to their causes. It has become quite fashionable with a certain class to attribute them to the management of the currency by the Banks. It is alleged, prosperity or adversity depends on the extension or contraction of the circulation of their notes. This is to mistake the symptoms for the disease, and to look at the effects and overlook the cause, an error very common with superficial minds. When trade is bad, it is impossible for the Banks however anxious the directors may be to accomplish it, to keep up the same circulation of money as in prosperous times. They are compelled to contract their issues. Just because there is a diminished demand for goods, there is also less demand for money. It will not account for a stagnation of trade, to say that when ever it takes place, the Banks at the same time limit their circulation. They do this, because money cannot be profitably invested in trade. Before they contract their circulation, the merchant has been previously forced to limit his sales. The state of the Banks is one of the symptoms of bad trade, not the disease which has caused its decay. The chief cause of this we affirm to be the provision laws, and we shall show you how they produce this disastrous result.

Every one knows that the provision market is by far the most fluctuating in the kingdom. The price of wheat since the passing of the corn bill in 1815, has ranged from thirty-six to 94 shillings the quarter. The change is seldom gradual. The scale which regulates the duty, had been more appropriately denominated the *Jumping* then the *sliding-scale*. The price depends on the character of the seasons, and the state of the crops. By the corn bill we are restricted to the home market, till wheat has nearly reached a famine price. Were the trade free, there would always be an abundant supply to meet the demand, and prices would be steady. The harvest is never defective over the whole world at the same time. When there was no corn in Canaan, there was plenty in Egypt. When there is scarcity in Europe, there is abundance in America. There is no marketable article in the world in which all may freely trade, that fluctuates in price as does wheat in Britain. This fluctuation is wholly attributable to our restrictive laws. Our home supplies vary exceedingly from year to year, and hence also the price. Holland is an importing country and has no corn law, and there the price is steady except when we come into the foreign market with our irregular demand. The price would be steady in our own country were the provision laws abolished; but so long as they continue in force, we must lay our account to experience great and rapid changes in the price of food. Now such changes are exceedingly injurious to trade, and it is easy to see how they must be so. To illustrate this, let us inquire how the price of wheat affects our commerce. That the most captious may not be able to question our statement, we shall not fix on extreme prices, but shall take the average price of wheat on a year when trade was good, and the same when it was bad. By ascertaining the respective sums paid on these years for this necessary for life, we shall find the amount which a dear year consumes over a cheap one, and which is of course entirely withdrawn from trade and expended on food. We shall suppose the annual consumpt of wheat in this country, amounts to 16,000,000 of quarters, an estimate much below the truth, some make it as high as 40 millions—for the prosperous year in trade we shall take 1835, and we find that the average price of a quarter of wheat during that year was 39s 4d, but we shall say 40s. For the year of dull trade we shall take 1839, not by any means the worst, but the commencement of the present stagnation. Wheat that year averaged 70s. 6d. but to give the monopolists every advantage, we shall say 70s. making a difference in price on the quarter of wheat of 30s during the two years of good and bad trade. On the former of these years, the country paid only 32 millions for wheat, while on the latter of these years, it paid 56 millions, making a difference of 24 millions sterling. These 24 millions were of course all withdrawn from trade and expended on wheat. Had that sum been expended on the purchase of manufactured goods, it would have kept trade prosperous—work plenty, and wages good, but the operative having to pay so much more for his food, had so much less to give for clothing and furniture, and consequently the market became overstocked. The manufacturer began first to reduce wages—then to put his workers on short time, and last of all to dismiss them altogether. Take a more distant period. In 1817, three years after the passing of the corn bill wheat was ninety-four shillings a quarter, contrast this year with 1822. when wheat was only forty-three shillings. The sum paid for wheat in 1817 exceeded that paid for it in 1822, 42 millions. On the former of these years, and on to 1821, trade was bad and wheat dear. On the latter of these years trade began to revive, and continued prosperous till 1826, when wheat again rose in price and trade declined. These facts, and they might be increased to any extent, clearly prove that we may calculate the fluctuations of trade by the fluctuations of the provision market. It is necessary, however, to observe, that there will always be a certain interval between the rise of wheat and the depression of trade; and, on the contrary, trade will not revive in the month on which wheat becomes cheap. A few months will naturally intervene. But, the results we have stated, will follow just as certainly as the tides do the moon, or the night day. There will be a considerable twilight before our commercial midnight comes, but arrive it must.

But the injury to trade does not entirely consist in the amount of money withdrawn from trade by dear food, though this must be very considerable, but in the great unsteadiness to which it is exposed in consequence of the fluctuations in the price of grain. Our goods and bad seasons often come in series. It is the same with trade. We have not had time to accommodate ourselves to our state of prosperity when we are again plunged in adversity. These rapid transitious are extremely injurious to our commerce, by destroying confidence, periling capital, and limiting trade. The most sagacious cannot calculate the variations of trade, unless he is able to foresee the changes of the weather and the influence which it will exert on the crop. At certain seasons of the year, a knowledge of the state of the barometer is more valuable than of prices current. Hence our merchants are for ever groping in the dark, and involved in dangerous and ruinous speculations, contrary to all their intentions. Thus trade, not only in corn, but in every other article, becomes a species of gambling, by which large fortunes may either be speedily lost or won. This is a system injurious alike to the morality and the prosperity of the country. Let trade in every department be free, and then it would be conducted on fixed principles, rash speculation would be arrested, and the whole community would enjoy prosperity. So long as the present corn law exists, it would be quite chimerical to attempt to prevent convulsions in trade. Remove the cause and the effect will cease.

In addition to the evils enumerated above, as resulting from the provision laws, they transfer periodically a large portion of the gold of this country to the Continent. We have already seen that it is only when food is dear that wheat can be imported under the restrictive system; consequently, when it is needed it must be paid for in specie, and this deranges our currency and renders money scarce—another circumstance most injurious to our trade. Our notes will not circulate on the Continent, but gold is current every where. Hence we find that when we are obliged to import a large quantity of wheat from abroad, the Bank of England is drained of its bullion. Thus there were in that bank, on the 4th May 1838, ten millions of bullion and eleven millions of deposits. During the latter part of that year and the beginning of the next, there were very large importations of foreign wheat; and on 12th December 1839, there were only two and a-half millions in bullion, while the deposits had fallen below six millions. Had the bank not borrowed two and a-half millions from the Bank of France, it would have been compelled to suspend payments. Had this expedient not been adopted, there would scarcely have been a sovereign in its coffers. The same thing occurred under a large importation of wheat from 1828 to 1832. The bullion at that time diminished from ten to five millions. We have fixed on these periods, because they serve to set the injurious working of these laws in a striking light, but the evil is constantly felt in a greater or less degree. The mischief done to the currency and the trade of the country cannot be so easily calculated as the amount of gold transferred from us to our Continental neighbours. The late Chancellor of the Exchequer declared that if the drain of gold had continued much longer in 1839, it would have been impossible to have saved us from national bankruptcy. Had trade in wheat been free, such a state of things could never have occurred. There would have been a sufficient stock in the country, and instead of being compelled to take it from the Continent, had it refused to reciprocate with us on the principles of free trade, we might have obtained an abundant supply from America in return for our goods, and thus both our trade and our gold would have been preserved. But, in present circumstances, the money we give to the Continent for wheat is not only so much lost to us, but gained by them to foster their manufactures to destroy our own. Need we wonder, then, that our trade is thrown into convulsions every few years? This is the inevitable result of our unjust policy, and we must be content to be alternately in prosperity and adversity, with shorter intervals to recruit our strength, till our pernicious system be entirely abolished. Then we shall realize steady markets and prosperous trade. But if our rulers refuse to listen to the righteous demands of the people, then we must just make up our minds to encounter convulsion after convulsion, in closer succession, till the whole framework of society in this country be shivered in pieces.

I have not adverted to the hacknied objection that it would be exceedingly dangerous to be dependent on foreigners for a supply of food. This is a very harmless bugbear which now terrifies nobody. The truth is, that we are already, to a great extent, dependent on foreign supplies, even in the article of provisions, and becoming more and more so every year. Our dependence, under our restrictive system, is dangerous in the extreme, but would be advantageous to all parties were trade perfectly free. We believe free trade would not throw one acre of land in our own country out of cultivation that is already cropped with advantage, but lead to an improved cultivation. Besides, we are dependent entirely on foreign countries for cotton, tea, &c., articles scarcely less necessary to our prosperity than wheat. This gives us no alarm. Even war with China never affected our supply of tea. Why then cherish the fear that we shall ever be deprived of an abundance of wheat, an article which can be profitably cultivated in so many countries, though we were for the future to be wholly dependent on foreigners for our supply. The dread is as unreasonable as that of the monomaniac who starves himself amid plenty, lest he should perish for want on some future day.

2. But the provision laws not only derange our trade, but produce convulsions in society. All grievances excite agitation. The injured very naturally seek for the redress of their wrongs. And it is one of the greatess weaknesses of statesmen that they seldom yield anything to justice, but all to terror. Every monopoly which they have created they hold with tenacious grasp till it actually drops from their hands, through trembling in apprehension at the consequences that may ensue, were they to hold it a moment longer. This conduct is exceedingly unwise and actually holds out a boon to agitation. No deliverance is ever obtained from any serious legal oppression, till the whole country is thrown into a state of high excitement. This state of national fever is very injurious to the industry and trade of the country. These remarks apply to every grievance that is deeply felt. They are, however, peculiarly applicable to the provision laws, inasmuch as they expose our commerce to periodic depressions—throw at stated times thousands out of employment—deprive the operatives of the means of subsistence, and literally kill many with hunger. We cannot wonder that when a large portion of the community is reduced to absolute want or verge on starvation, that they should be easily roused to deeds of violence. and endeavour to retaliate on their oppressors. We indeed rejoice to think that the conviction is becoming very general, that moral force is far more formidable to tyrants than physical, and more sure and valuable in its results. Scarcely anything valuable has ever been gained by violence. We believe it is mainly owing to this growing belief, that the deep and prolonged sufferings of hundreds of thousands in our country during the last

two years have been borne with the fortitude and patience of martyrdom. And yet, unhappily, we have had our *emeutes* which have not been suppressed without bloodshed and the destruction of considerable property. Patience cannot always last. Protracted and hopeless suffering will exasperate the meekest and turn the tamest into a savage. We cannot forget that the French revolution was hastened and rendered more ferocious by the unheeded cries of a famishing multitude for bread. Hunger is a bad reasoner. It is too urgent and too clamorous in its appeals to balance nicely the expediency of its measures. The late violence in the manufacturing districts could not have taken place in a state of prosperous trade. The attempt has been made, but without one particle of success, to fasten the late riots on the corn law repealers. The true authors of them are those who maintain those laws in opposition to the convictions of the vast majority of the nation, and in the face of the misery and wretchedness which they are creating. Those who seek their complete and speedy abolition, are the best friends of the peace and prosperity of their country, and employ the only effective means to prevent the recurrence of such mischievous disturbances. So long as these laws are in existence, we may expect to hear of *Swing* at his nightly work of incendiarism in the agricultural districts, and of frequent strikes and riots in our towns. These evils, every lover of his country must deeply deplore; but property can never be generally respected, nor security enjoyed, in a country in which there are thousands famishing with hunger. It is painful to dwell on this topic, and therefore I shall only add, that from the extent to which the conviction has spread, that these laws are the cause of our greatest sufferings, we can never expect quiet in the country till once they are repealed.

We may feel confident, that firm, temperate, persevering, and peaceful agitation will carry this question as it has done many before. From my conviction of the deeply injurious character of these laws, I exhort you to persevere. The country is, at present, under a course of agitation on this subject, to an extent to which it has never been subjected on any other. The verdict of the millions has gone out against them, and must soon be ratified by the legislature. And, although this tribunal to which you must make your ultimate appeal may be deaf to the claims of justice, yet, be assured, your continued importunity will, ere long, force from it the reply of the unjust judge to the oppressed widow, "We will grant the prayer of the people's petitions for untaxed bread, lest by frequent coming they weary us."

Before concluding, I wish to remind you that it is not the whole subject that has been discussed to-night, but only a single department of it; and, therefore, though you may not have had all your objections met, you are not to suppose that they cannot be satisfactorily answered. I have scarcely glanced at the bearing of the Corn Laws in the agricultural classes of the country. It were easy to show that they are as pernicious to the farmers and their labourers, as to the manufacturing portion of the community; and that ultimately they will prove ruinous to the landlords themselves. They are already in many districts in England paying nearly as much in additional Poor's Rates as they are pocketing from the monopoly in food. And as pauperism increases, and increase it must, unless our trade revive, the whole of their income will, ere long, be absorbed in saving the people from starvation. My object has been to prove, that the Provision Laws limit our home and foreign trade—lower wages, and produce convulsions in business and society. If I have succeeded in convincing you of the truth of these statements, I have surely furnished you with the most powerful inducements to excite you to employ all your energies and influence to secure Free Trade in every thing, but especially in bread, by all moral and constitutional means.

Let me remind you that this is not a party question. It involves the interests and the well-being of all. Whig and Tory, Radical and Chartist, may co-operate to further this cause of justice, humanity, and national prosperity, without merging any of their peculiar principles. Landlords who wish to save their estates—merchants who desire a prosperous business—tradesmen who are solicitous to provide things, honest in the sight of all men—philanthropists who seek the improvement of their species—patriots who love their country—citizens who are anxious to drive misery and famine from our streets—parents who hope to save their children from beggary, ignorance, and crime—and Christians who deplore the insult offered to the benevolence of heaven, and the dishonour done to the Divine Law, ought to unite, notwithstanding their minor differences in one irresistible phalanx, to drive monopoly from our statute book, and to establish immutably, the intercourse of nations on the principles of justice, reciprocal exchange, and lasting peace. Ours is the cause of righteousness, humanity, and religion; and it must prevail. We seek no selfish end; we ask nothing for ourselves but what we demand for all; we have thus a plea that finds a response in every upright mind. The millions are already on our side; the wise and good are with us—religious principles and Christian men are pledged to repeal;—the God of justice smiles on our enterprise. And who are against us? A few aristocrats—some thousands who have a property in the soil. And think you, that they, however closely banded together, can long stem the full tide that is setting in against their monopoly? IMPOSSIBLE! If they do not yield with a good grace, they must either step aside, or allow it to roll over them and be buried in its surges.

There is everything in the nature of the undertaking and in the aspect of the question to cheer us on, and to indicate a speedy triumph. England is rousing from one end to the other—the farmers once against us are now either with us or neutral—the monopolists are quaking for fear, and beginning to desert to our camp—the landlords are setting their house in order and preparing to yield—the citizens of America have indignantly denounced their high tariff; and by their votes in the late elections, have said, by deeds stronger than words—TRADE SHALL BE FREE! This sentiment is echoed by every enlightened Briton. We have but to make another well-directed combined, and united attack on the fortress of monopoly and it is won. In its stead we shall erect a splendid exchange for all nations, and on its topmost pinnacle, set up the banner of victory with this inscription:

"Free as the winds, and boundless as the sea,
Let trade and commerce henceforth always be;
Wherever land is found, or oceans roll,
Or man exists—from Indus to the Pole;
Open to all—with no false ties to bind—
The world shall be the market of mankind."

Economy–Energy–Environment Simulation

Beyond the Kyoto Protocol

Edited by

Kimio Uno

Faculty of Policy Management
Keio University at Shonan Fujisawa Campus, Japan

KLUWER ACADEMIC PUBLISHERS
DORDRECHT / BOSTON / LONDON

Library of Congress Cataloging-in-Publication Data is available.

ISBN 1-4020-0450-8

Published by Kluwer Academic Publishers
PO Box 17, 3300 AA Dordrecht, The Netherlands

Sold and distributed in North, Central and South America
by Kluwer Academic Publishers,
101 Philip Drive, Norwell, MA 02061, U.S.A.

In all other countries, sold and distributed
by Kluwer Academic Publishers, Distribution Centre,
PO Box 322, 3300 AH Dordrecht, The Netherlands

Printed on acid-free paper

Printed and bound in Great Britain by MPG Books Limited, Bodmin, Cornwall.

Contents

Preface

In the policy arena, as well as in the academic world, a new challenge is having to deal with the global community. We are increasingly aware that the world is linked through economy–energy–environment interactions. We are increasingly aware, at the same time, that the emergence of the global community does not imply an integrated harmonious world; rather, it is a community where countries/regions of different interests and values face each other directly. Global governance has to be achieved through actions of national governments under different motives and constraints. We need to have an analytical tool that is capable of producing a global picture, yet with detailed country resolution.

If the world is a better place now compared to 100 years ago in terms of per-capita income, this is due to the industrialization that continued throughout the 20th century. We entered the 21st century knowing that the human aspiration that translates into ever-increasing production may not be tenable in the long run. Sustainability of the global community is at stake. In contrast to incremental decision making through the market mechanism that should lead to some optimal state under some assumptions such as perfect knowledge, smooth movement of resources, no externalities, and so forth, we need to have an analytical tool to provide us with details of the future state of the world. Whether our mode of production, our demand for energy, and our impact on the environment can be sustained over a long period of time cannot be answered based on mere intuition. There are many actors involved. The inter-linkages are complex. Technology is changing.

In a previous publication we pointed to several research agendas (Uno and Bartelmus, eds. 1998):

> Physical-monetary linkages and indicators; International linkages; Inter-temporal comparisons; Technological change; Quality of life and social dimensions; and shift from accounting to modelling.

The current work is a response to this self-imposed agenda. The framework presented here is a database and modelling-simulation system that is capable of projecting the coming decade. It provides detailed country resolution, identifying about 60 countries/regions of the global community. It has a detailed industrial classification, distinguishing 36 branches as a general rule. The focus is placed on the interaction running through economy, energy, and global environment. Physical-monetary linkage is inevitable because production is in general measured in terms of value added and other monetary indicators, including energy and other resource inputs into various activities, whereas energy service has to be specified in physical measurements such as kilocalories or tons of oil equivalent. The impact on global environment has to be in physical units such as volume of CO_2 emissions. International linkages are a must because the economic system is not confined geographically in one country; the country's activities are linked to others through the international flow of goods and services, of money, and of technology. If one country or group of countries imposes energy tax, for instance, the energy-intensive industrial sector may shift to other economies. Sustainability is a long-term issue, rather than being a problem to be tackled with policy measures with a time horizon of one to several years. We must be looking 10 years hence, 50 years, or even farther into the future. It is imperative to obtain the exact time path of economy–energy–environmental development in order to know what the future holds without policy measures or technological change, and what needs to be done now to improve the situation in the future. Technology is a key variable in the long run, determining the mode of production, energy shift and conversion efficiency, and emissions of global warming gases. International technology transfer is one way of softening the sharp conflict between economic development and environmental impact. The empirical evidence pertaining to our performance in economy, energy, and environment is recorded in statistics. More often than not, statistics are collected by national statistical offices following an accounting framework. International organizations sometimes provide collection of data from national sources, but they rarely collect raw data themselves. The statistical accounts compiled annually provide the empirical basis for analysis, but meaningful analysis would have to be based on modelling and policy simulation. The social dimension is not dealt with explicitly in the model framework presented here, but one chapter is devoted to the discussion of the impact of CO_2 tax on employment. It is hoped that the variables included in the current framework will serve as the basis for deriving various social indicators.

Part I is an introduction providing an overview on the sustainability issues in the economy–energy–environment spheres. Part II introduces the tools of analysis employed in this work, pointing out some of the characteristics of our approach, and describing the modelling framework including energy demand, conversion, and fuel substitution; macroeconomic performance and inter-industry relations; and international trade. Object-oriented design of the statistical database and modelling tool is discussed. Part III covers the economic and energy prospects of the global community, and the cases of G7 industrialized countries, developing economies in South-East Asia, China, and Russia are analysed. Finally, the impact of the imposition of CO_2 tax on production and employment is examined. Part IV is a methodology section. Major works by other research groups are examined in terms of the time span, regional and branch coverage, energy sources, assumptions on technology and energy intensity improvements, and the inherent logic in modelling/scenario writing. An attempt is made to compare their numerical results. The Appendix demonstrates the possible integration of a medium-term model such as the one we employ in the current study into a very long-term view covering the period from around 1950 to the year 2100.

This research was supported by Grant-in-Aid for Scientific Research from the Japan Society for the Promotion of Science of the Ministry of Education, Science and Technology of the Japanese Government (Category Code (A)(2), Project Number 10044036). The project was conducted during 1998-2000 with Kimio Uno of Keio University (Institution Number 32612) as the project leader. The publication was supported by Grant-in-Aid for Publication of Scientific Research Results from the Japan Society for the Promotion of Science (Project Number 135331). The subsidy was made available during 2001 with Kimio Uno as the responsible editor.

Last but not least, as the project leader and the editor, I would like to express my appreciation of the project members who have contributed their valuable time to this work. I should particularly mention the effort that went into constructing the infrastructure for the project that included development of simulation programs, a database system, graphic user interface, statistical data, meta data, and model prototypes. I cannot do justice to the effort that constitutes the backbone of the project, but is inevitably less visible in a publication such as this one that places focus on the contents. Construction of infrastructure is indeed crucial in carrying out a project of this scope and, more importantly, making future development possible. The group has also inherited a simulation engine and other important intellectual assets from our predecessors, for which we extend our particular appreciation.

Kimio Uno

Part I

Introduction

1
Economy–energy–environment: COMPASS approach

KIMIO UNO

1. From single-country policy to global governance

In the policy analysis arena there is a keen awareness of the need for global coverage with detailed country resolution. On the one hand we are faced with policy challenges at the global level; on the other hand government decisions at the national level comprise the only way in which resources can be committed to, in order to carry out the policy measures.

Introduced here is a COmprehensive Model for Policy ASSessment (COMPASS) which is an econometric simulation model designed to capture the interaction among 3E spheres encompassing economy, energy, and environment. COMPASS is designed for simulation experiments up to 2010-2020. The model achieves international linkage for 60 countries/regions, covering 99.5% of the world GDP. The country models are based on time-series of a 36-sector input-output framework, the SNA, and financial accounts. They are linked to each other through time-series of 25-commodity trade matrices which explicitly describe annual trade flows among world regions, achieving a global coverage. The model also generates energy balances and CO_2 emissions for individual countries. Thus, the COMPASS provides multi-sector, multi-country information on production, trade, balance of payments, saving and investment flows, energy demand and supply, and environmental impact. It is capable of generating consistent output and price series, together with interest rates, exchange rates, and energy prices. An empirically based econometric method is employed throughout, enabling users to trace the dynamic time path of policy measures, such as increased energy price through the introduction of tradable permits. The model framework we employ may be termed an input-output + econometric model (IOE) following West (1995). The modelling of this magnitude became possible by adopting an object-oriented databasc approach, which comprises a consistent naming convention, accounting rules, and logical structure. The graphic user interface facilitates access to the database, operation of the model, and policy simulation experiments.

The Kyoto Protocol of the UNFCCC, adopted in 1997 by COP-3, set the sage for implcmenting an international format aimed at curtailing CO_2 emissions. The Protocol stipulates a reduction target for Annex I countries to be achieved by around 2010. The problem is that, given the recent trends in energy use, it seems extremely difficult to contain energy consumption to the target level.

K. Uno (ed.), Economy–Energy–Environment Simulation, 3–30.

When signatories to the Framework Convention on Climate Change met in Kyoto in December 1997 at the third Conference of Parties to the Convention (COP-3), the initial position was zero reduction for the United States, EU 15%, and Japan 5% globally but 2.5% for herself. Agreement was reached that the United States, EU, and Japan should reduce the emission of global warming gases by 7%, 8%, and 6%, respectively, by the year 2010. The reduction targets take into account the portion achieved through technology transfer to developing countries. Reduction in developing economies was postponed to future discussion, although a proposal was made requesting their voluntary reduction targets. The COP-4, convened in Buenos Aires in November 1998, ended by adopting an action plan spelling out the future negotiation schedule, without going into substantial discussion on the tradable permits of global warming gases. There still remains the equity issue concerning the initial allocation of the permits, particularly for developing economies and for economies in transition. Technology transfers to developing countries, compensation for oil-producing countries for possible economic losses, and the mechanism for joint implementation are also being disputed. It was agreed that a concrete stipulation pertaining to emission trading be decided in the year 2000. When in fact environment ministers of the Group of Eight met in Japan in preparation for the G8 Summit in Okinawa in July 2000, and as a prelude to the COP-6 meeting in the Hague in November 2000, they could not agree to include a specific time frame in the joint communiqué. While all European Union countries, Japan, and Russia agreed, the two North American countries were reluctant to include the 2002 deadline (Chasek, 2001; Grubb *et al.*, 1999; Mitchell, 1996; Kawashima, 1995; Spector *et al.*, 1994). Thus, we may say that there is a real danger that the COP could degenerate once again into a political process.

One way out of this would be an information system which allows for various policy experiments revealing what would happen if nothing is done and/or if international coordination is realized in order to mitigate emission of GHGs. Our purpose, therefore, is a construction of a simulation model with a dynamic framework. Individual countries have to be explicitly treated in the model as they are the agents that implement policy measures. After all, policy measures will have to be implemented by national governments, sometimes in the face of public resentment or opposition from industrial circles. International repercussion would have to be sought in order to attain sustainability as the global community as a whole, but country resolution of simulation models is indispensable in the political arena.

Compared to the analytical need for which environmental accounting is expected to provide crucial information, current attention is almost solely being devoted to a single-country context. Global linkage would have to be sought in view of the global nature of the most pressing environmental issues such as climate change, resource exhaustion, and the impact of agricultural and forestry activities triggered by international trade (Uno, 2000).

2. What the models should achieve

There are already sufficient models which are operational in estimating the cost of emission reduction. Repetto and Austin (1997) provide a list of focal points of the available models as follows:

(1) The extent to which substitution among energy sources, energy technologies, products, and production methods is possible.
(2) The extent to which market and policy distortions create opportunities for low-cost (or no-cost) improvements in energy efficiency.
(3) The likely rate of technological innovation and the responsiveness of such change to price signals.
(4) The availability and likely future cost of non-fossil, backstop energy sources.
(5) The potential for international 'joint implementation' of emissions reductions.
(6) The possibility that carbon tax revenues would be recycled through the reduction of economically burdensome tax rates.

In addition, there are possible damages (or benefits) which can be avoided by the introduction of carbon tax. They are:

(7) Economic damage from climate change.
(8) The reduction of other air pollution damage associated with the burning of fossil fuels.

Of these, the COMPASS is capable of treating (1), (3), (5), (6) and (8) in whole or in part. Substitution between energy and other factors of production, particularly capital, has been discussed extensively in the literature. Substitution among energy sources can also be analysed in a model depicting energy balances encompassing various sources of primary energy. The rate of technological innovation, or item (3) above, is described in our framework as the changes in input coefficients over time. This does not automatically mean that technological change can be endogenously explained in the model framework. Rather, scenarios may be developed based on technology inventories, which then can be interpreted as alternative input coefficients. Such technology inventories in environmental spheres are available from IPCC (Intergovernmental Panel for Climate Change), IEA (International Energy Agency), UNEP (United Nations Environmental Program), and IIASA (International Institute for Applied Systems Analysis), in addition to various country sources. The assessment of joint implementation, which is item (5) above, is particularly suitable for the model framework at hand. In the arsenal of economic theory, technology is best described in an input-output framework in terms of input coefficients. An alternative technology described in input coefficients, whether they are the ones actually achieved in one country or the ones obtained by hypothetical scenarios, can be shifted to different countries in order to observe economy-wide repercussions. As for (6) above, one can incorporate a channel linking carbon tax revenues to, for example, reduction in social security contributions (Meyer and Ewerhart, 1998). It is also possible to deal with (8) in terms of changes in the imputed damages attributable to, for example, SO_2 (Uno, 1995).

The 1992 'Earth Summit' in Rio de Janeiro called for an integrated approach in achieving long-term sustainable development, and formulated Agenda 21 as its action plan. The UN's System of Integrated Environmental and Economic Accounting, dubbed as SEEA, EU's National Accounting Matrix including Environmental Accounts, or NAMEA, and related statistical systems have been devised during preparations for the Rio Conference. Experience in empirical application and theoretical issues are described in detail in a volume which is an outcome of the Special Conference of the International Association for Research in Income and Wealth (IARIW) held in 1996 (Uno and Bartelmus, 1998). In order to facilitate exchange of views and further development, a group of experts formed a forum called the London Group, named after its first meeting in London (London Group, 1994, 1995, 1996, 1997). The fifth meeting took place in Fontevraud, France, in 1998, followed by the sixth meeting in Canberra, Australia. The thrust of the discussion is directed towards refinement of the SEEA and empirical application of the NAMEA. In other words, development of an environmental accounting so far, however, remains a single-country, static framework.

The SEEA has established itself as the internationally accepted conceptual framework for linking the environmental concerns to the System of National Accounts (Inter-Secretariat Working Group on National Accounts, 1993). Its advantage clearly lies in the fact that it is designed as a satellite to be used in conjunction with the SNA. Likewise, the framework being developed in the European Union focuses on flows and stocks of environment-related goods and services based on the SNA definition (EUROSTAT, 1997; European Commission, 1997). Recent discussion on the integrated environmental and economic accounting in the United States by an expert panel concluded that such effort is solidly based in mainstream economic analysis and that developing a set of comprehensive non-market economic accounts is a high priority for the nation (Nordhaus and Kokkenberg, 1999). The environmental indicators approach, such as represented by listing of indicators (OECD, various years a; United Nations Development Programme, 1997) and decomposition analysis based on indicators (Unander and Schipper, 1998), can be conceived of dealing with summary expression of full accounts. One can pick up numerous other approaches to environmental accounting, but it is now clear that they are composed of more or less similar data sets, if not exactly identical in their formats.

No-one denies the usefulness and urgency of such an effort. Only through such attempts can the conceptual consistency of the framework be guaranteed, and inter-temporal and international comparability of the empirical measurement be obtained.

At the same time, one can look at environmental accounting from its applicability for policy analysis. The development of SNA followed a path where the effort to guarantee conceptual consistency and the need to respond to policy analysis stimulated each other. Environmental concerns cover a wide range of issues, as, for example, reflected in the sustainability issue contained in Agenda 21 (United Nations, 1993a) or the discussion surrounding global climate change (IPCC, 1996a, b).

In addition to domestic policy measures such as carbon tax, which in turn stimulate technological progress or lifestyle change, the Protocol introduced flexibility mechanisms such as Joint Implementation among Annex I parties (Article 6), Clean Development Mechanism among both Annex I and Non-Annex I parties (Article 12), and Emissions Trading among Annex B parties (Article 17). These instruments implemented at a global level (or at least among more industrialized countries/regions) are expected to result in most cost-effective means of realizing the reduction target (Grubb *et al.*, 1999; United Nations, 1997).

The point here is the fact that both the issues at hand and the policy measures go beyond national boundaries. The policy needs clearly point to a simulation model designed to gauge the implication of policy scenarios in a global as well as single-country context, and a statistical framework that is capable of providing globally linked empirical data.

3. Empirical data

The feasibility of a 3E model encompassing economic, energy, and environmental spheres is largely dependent on the availability and organization of the empirical data. The COMPASS is intended to be the basis for policy dialogue. It is therefore deemed important to adopt a transparent framework both theoretically and empirically. The model is based on open data published mostly by international organizations. Limiting the scope of environmental accounting to the global warming issue, the framework should cover economy, energy, and environmental spheres such as the following:

Economy: Final demand, production, income. Input structure, output structure, final demand, value added (including direct taxes and subsidies), output prices. Technological change (=input coefficients), technology transfer, lifestyle shift. Trade balance, trade shares, exporting country, importing country for each branch. Saving-investment balance, flow of funds. Prices, exchange rates, interest rates.

Energy: Total final consumption. Energy conversion. Total primary energy demand. Alternative primary energy sources, fuel substitution. Conversion efficiency.

Environment: CO_2 emissions, emission trade, CO_2 taxes. CO_2 sink.

Those data sets can be set in a logical order as described in Figure 1-1. The COmprehensive Model for Policy ASSessment (COMPASS) is an econometric simulation model designed to capture the interaction among 3E spheres encompassing economy, energy, and environment.

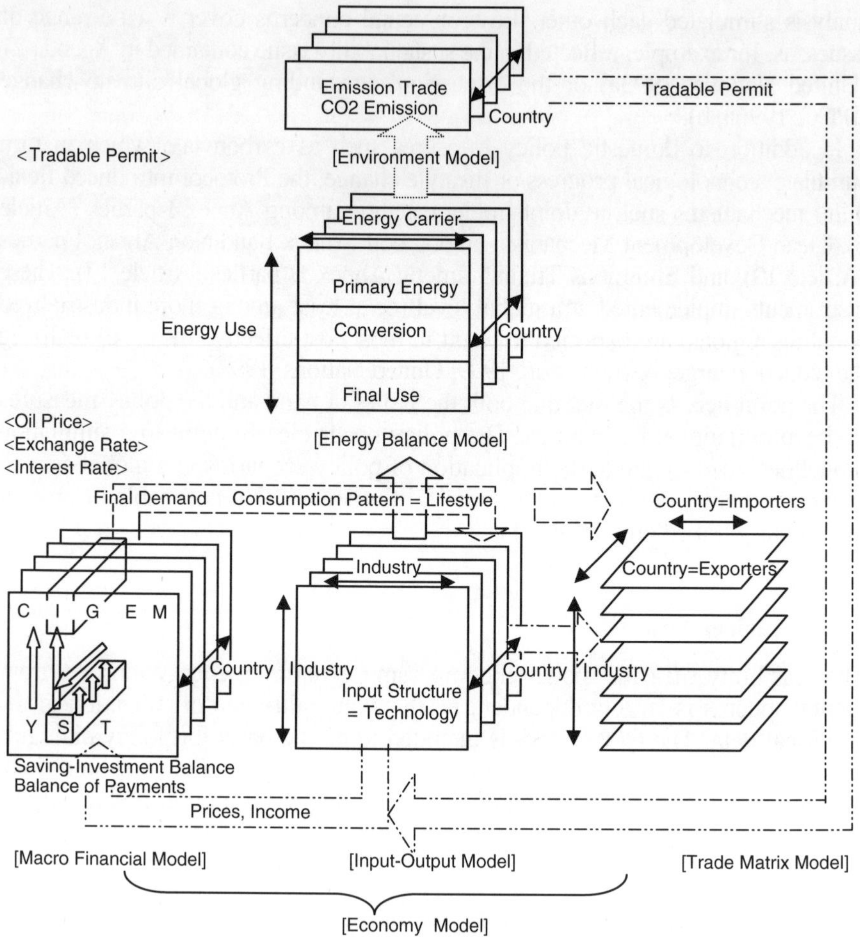

Figure 1-1. Structure of the EEE (economy–energy–environment) COMPASS (COmprehensive Model for Policy ASSessment). The figures represented in the diagram show the relationship among the data sets and refer to one point in time. The model has a dynamic framework.

The regional structure of the model is provided in Table 1-1. This table lists the regions (the term region is preferred over country here due to disputes surrounding the statehood in some cases), their code names in the COMPASS framework, and the model types describing the pertinent regions. The model covers explicit 54 regions and seven additional regions representing 'rest of Asia', etc. The coverage is intended to shed light on all OECD countries, all APEC countries (Peru and Vietnam have recently joined the APEC and are not covered by the current version of the COMPASS), all major energy producers, and most of the bigger developing countries. The model, therefore, is virtually closed globally regarding production of goods and services, foreign trade, financial flows, and energy demand and supply.

The country models are based on time-series of a 36-branch (25 for non-OECD Asian regions) input-output framework, the SNA, financial accounts, and energy balance tables. The term 'branches' is used when referring to disaggregated production activities and the term 'sectors' is reserved to refer to economic agents such as households, enterprises, and government. Branches are linked internationally through time-series of 25-commodity trade matrices that explicitly describe annual trade flows among world regions.

One can envisage COMPASS as a group of regional models linked internationally. Alternatively, one may view it as composed of layers of branch models that are combined to form an integrated global whole, making it possible to carry out branch- (sector)-specific analysis. In order to go beyond the limits of comparative static approach where accounts from mere two data points are compared, and to describe the dynamic time path of final demand, intermediate demand, and international repercussion through trade, relative prices would have to be determined endogenously by the system.

3.1. Time-series input-output tables

Input-output tables are indispensable in the construction of multi-sector models in that they provide consistent structural data ranging from final demand, intermediate inputs (whereas input coefficients describing production technology), value added and income generation, and prices (potentially including CO_2 tax or price hikes reflecting emission trade). One should mention two important developments in this field. One is the publication of input-output tables for the OECD member countries covering the period around 1970 to 1990 (OECD, 1995). Another is a series of bilateral and internationally linked tables for Asian countries by a Japanese source (Institute of Developing Economies 1982, 1992, 1998). The input-output and other pertinent data for China and Russia were provided by country experts. The tables for Asian countries are regularly recompiled into a standard format by the Institute of Developing Economies (1982, 1992, 1998). Among Non-Annex I countries, China is included in the IDE source. Russia and India compile input-output tables regularly, and their conversion to an internationally comparable scheme is not a difficult task. Reflecting the original structure of the tables, the input-output tables for OECD countries have 36 industrial branches, whereas those for Asian countries have 25 in the current version of the COMPASS. Details are depicted in Table 1-2.

A comprehensive framework which describes the structure of an economic system is provided by input-output tables which comprise a part of the SNA. The SEEA also recognizes this as the basis for further extension, although most widely used versions of the SEEA do not employ an input-output framework. Thus, an input-output framework seems to be the natural starting point if environmental accounting should also incorporate inter-industry relations, the relation between final demand (household) and intermediate inputs (industry), international repercussion (imports and exports), and changes in technology and

Table 1-1. COMPASS regional coverage

Serial No.	Region	Region Code	Trade Matrix Code	Region Status				Total Primary Energy Supply (TPES), 1995 (unit: million tonnes of oil equivalent)				
				OECD	APEC	Annex I	OPEC	Coal	Crude Oil	Pet Prod.	Gas	Total
1	Belgium	BE	# = 1	OECD		Annex I		9.10	27.05	−6.07	10.61	52.40
2	Denmark	DK	# = 2	OECD		Annex I		6.45	10.45	−1.14	3.12	20.29
3	France	FR	# = 3	OECD		Annex I		16.06	82.99	3.57	29.57	241.39
4	Germany	DE	# = 4	OECD		Annex I		91.03	106.08	29.63	66.4	338.98
5	Greece	GR	# = 5	OECD		Annex I		8.39	17.33	−3.16	0.04	23.64
6	Ireland	IE	# = 6	OECD		Annex I		3.13	2.32	3.35	2.33	11.35
7	Italy	IT	# = 7	OECD		Annex I		12.33	89.16	5.34	44.84	161.54
8	Netherlands	NL	# = 8	OECD		Annex I		9.19	64.12	−36.74	34.08	73.29
9	Portugal	PT	# = 9	OECD		Annex I		3.60	13.71	−0.02	0	19.25
10	Spain	ES	# = 10	OECD		Annex I		19.51	57.13	−1.47	7.72	103.29
11	UK	GB	# = 11	OECD		Annex I		48.64	100.50	−15.88	65.05	224.49
12	Austria	AT	# = 12	OECD		Annex I		3.29	9.36	1.64	6.31	26.29
13	Finland	FI	# = 13	OECD		Annex I		6.05	9.19	−0.73	2.84	28.85
14	Norway	NO	# = 14	OECD		Annex I		1.02	13.87	−5.86	3.46	23.53
15	Sweden	SE	# = 15	OECD		Annex I		2.79	18.29	−2.29	0.68	50.92
16	Switzerland	CH	# = 16	OECD		Annex I		0.19	4.83	7.63	2.19	25.19
22	Former USSR/RU	USSR	# = 17					193.39	255.70	−34.01	453.03	954.54
	Russia				APEC	Annex I		108.96	191.55	−42.05	306.45	621.48
23	Japan	JP	# = 18	OECD	APEC	Annex I		82.59	230.41	39.16	52.02	497.03
24	Iran	IR	# = 19				OPEC	0.95	56.91	−5.34	28.60	82.47
25	Iraq	IQ	# = 20				OPEC	0.00	24.62	−2.85	3.24	25.09
26	Kuwait	KW	# = 21				OPEC	0.00	47.31	−35.77	4.13	15.67
27	Oman	OM	# = 22				OPEC	0.00	0.00	0.00	0.00	0.00
28	Qatar	QA	# = 23				OPEC	0.00	3.92	−3.09	7.04	7.87
29	Saudi Arabia	SA	# = 24				OPEC	0.00	95.61	−11.90	32.94	83.66
30	Untd Arab Em	AE	# = 25				OPEC	0.00	16.74	−8.17	18.86	24.46
31	Brunei	BN	# = 26		APEC			0	0	0	0	0
32	Hong Kong, China	HK	# = 27		APEC			5.60	0.00	7.49	0.00	13.67

33	India	IN	# = 28					141.98	65.43	16.68	15.59	436.70
34	Indonesia	ID	# = 29		APEC		OPEC	6.36	44.91	−3.09	30.16	124.92
35	Korea Rp	KR	# = 30	OECD	APEC			26.85	89.64	4.46	8.32	148.02
36	Malaysia	MY	# = 31		APEC			1.61	20.36	−1.07	11.10	34.87
37	Philippines	PH	# = 32		APEC			1.16	16.44	1.68	0.01	35.37
38	Singapore	SG	# = 33		APEC			0.02	52.47	−32.50	1.45	21.44
39	Thailand	TH	# = 34		APEC			6.90	27.15	7.46	8.70	71.07
40	Taiwan	TW	# = 35		APEC			17.16	29.42	4.05	3.76	64.38
41	China	CN	# = 36		APEC			658.14	147.95	10.49	16.71	1058.64
42	Australia	AU	# = 37	OECD	APEC	Annex I		37.54	35.15	−0.79	16.74	94.52
43	New Zealand	NZ		OECD	APEC	Annex I		1.19	5.12	0.59	3.83	15.44
44	Papua New Guinea	PG			APEC							
45	Canada	CA	# = 38	OECD	APEC	Annex I		25.36	83.83	−5.66	67.09	232.38
46	USA	US	# = 39	OECD	APEC	Annex I		475.34	824.36	−19.94	508.67	2088.47
47	Brazil	BR	# = 40					11.73	67.01	7.34	4.26	156.36
48	Chile	CL			APEC			2.40	8.71	1.15	1.38	18.68
49	Mexico	MX	# = 41	OECD	APEC			5.43	84.84	−0.11	26.31	133.76
50	Venezuela	VE	# = 42				OPEC	0.21	54.51	−36.88	25.08	47.87
51	Algeria	DZ	# = 43				OPEC	0.52	25.65	−18.06	15.70	24.30
52	Libya	LY	# = 44				OPEC		18.49	−6.75	4.05	15.91
53	Angola	AO	# = 45									
54	Nigeria	NG	# = 46				OPEC	0.09	14.59	−1.08	4.40	83.18

Note: Serial numbers 17-21 are Turkmenistan, Uzbekistan, Kazakstan, Azerbeijan, and other former USSR republics. Serial numbers 55-61 (trade matrix code 47-53) are Rest of Europe, Asia, Oceania, North America, Latin America, Africa, and nes.

Table 1-2. Industrial branch classification of COMPASS

COMPASS IO Models		COMPASS APEC IO Models		Statistical Codes			
No.	Description	No.	Description	Short Code	Standard Code	ISIC Definition	World Trade
1	Agriculture, forestry and fishery			AFF	AG_FO_FI	1	AFF
		1	Paddy	PAD	PADDY		
		2	Other agriculture	OAG	OTH_AGRI		
		3	Livestock	LIV	LIVESTOC		
		4	Forestry	FOR	FORESTRY		
		5	Fishery	FIS	FISHERY		
2	Mining and quarrying			MAQ	MIN_QUAR	2	MAQ
		6	Crude petroleum, natural and liquid gas	CRP	CR_NA_LI		
		7	Other mining and quarrying	OMQ	OTH_MINI		
3	Food, beverages and tobacco	8	Food, beverage and tobacco	FBT	FO_BE_TO	31	FBT
4	Textile, apparel and leather	9	Textile, apparel and leather	TAL	TE_AP_LE	32	TAL
5	Wood and furniture products	10	Wood products and furniture	WAF	WOO_FURN	33	WAF
6	Paper, paper products and printing	11	Paper, paper products and printing	PAP	PA_PP_PR	34	PAP
		12	Chemical products	CHE	CHE_PROD		
7	Industrial chemicals			CHI	IND_CHEM	351 + 352 − 3522	CHI
8	Drugs and medicine			CHD	DRU_CHEM	3522	CHD
9	Petroleum and coal products	13	Petroleum and petro products	PCP	PET_COAL	353 + 354	PCP
10	Rubber and plastic products	14	Rubber products	RPP	RUB_PLAS	355 + 356	RPP
11	Non metallic mineral products	15	Non metallic mineral products	NMP	NOM_MINP	36	NMP
		16	Metal products and primary metals	PMP	MEP_PRIM		
12	Iron and steel			IAS	IRO_STEE	371	IAS
13	Non ferrous metals			NFM	NON_FERR	372	NFM
14	Metal products			MEP	MET_PROD	381	MEP
		17	Machinery	MAC	MACHINER		
15	Non electrical machinery			NEM	NOE_MACH	382 − 3825	NEM
16	Office and computing machinery			OAC	OFF_COMP	3825	OAC
17	Electrical apparatus nec			ELM	ELE_MACH	383 − 3832	ELM
18	Radio, TV and communication eq.			RTC	RA_TV_CO	3832	RTC
		18	Transportation equipment	TET	TRA_EQUI		

19	Shipbuilding and repairing			TES	SHI_REPA	3841	TES
20	Other transportation means			TEO	OTH_TRAM	3842 + 3844 3849	TEO
21	Motor vehicles			TEM	MOT_VEHI	3843	TEM
22	Aircraft			TEA	AIRCRAFT	3845	TEA
		19	Other manufacturing products	AOM	ALO_MANU		
23	Professional goods			PRG	PRO_GOO	385	PRG
24	Other manufacturing			OMA	OTH_MAN	39	OMA
35	Other producers			OTP	OTH_PROD		OTP
25	Electricity, gas and water	20	Electricity, gas, water supply	EGW	EL_GA_WA	4	EGW
26	Construction	21	Construction	CON	CONSTRUC	5	CON
		22	Trade and transportation	TRT	WRT_TRAN		
27	Wholesale and retail trade			WRT	WHO_RETA	61 + 62	WRT
28	Restaurants and hotels			RAH	RES_HOTE	63	REH
29	Transport and storage			TRA	TRA_STOR	71	TRS
		23	Other services	OSE	OTH_SERV		
30	Communication			COM	COMMUNIC	72	COM
31	Finance and insurance			FAI	FIN_INSU	81 + 82	FII
32	Real estate and business services			RAB	REA_BUSI	83	RBS
33	Social and personal services			SPS	CO_SO_PE	9	CPS
34	Government services	24	Government services	GOV	GOV_SERV		GOS
36	Statistical discrepancy	25	Others and discrepancy	SDY	STA_DESC		DSC

lifestyle. Various policy instruments such as emission trading, environmental tax, and the disbursement of revenues can be incorporated (Pearce, 1991; Sand, 1992; Sands, 1995; Sorrell and Skea, 1999). These can be linked to various related statistics such as emission factors (e.g. SO_2, NO_X, waste, water) and employment. It also provides a convenient linkage with various physical indicators.

3.2. System of national accounts

The economic flow between generation of income and final demand is not explicitly described in the input-output tables. This gap is filled by the SNA data. This highly standardized data set is available for most countries in the world and forms the basis for country models. Since input-output tables are available only with some time intervals, SNA data are also employed in estimating the economic structure in the interim years.

The national accounts data are published by the United Nations (United Nations, various years a). Of the original SNA tables, the model incorporates Tables 1.1 and 1.2 (final demand in current prices and constant prices, respectively), 1.3 (cost components of GDP), 1.4 (general government current receipts and disbursements), 1.5 (corporate and quasi-corporate enterprises current income and outlays), 1.6 (households and non-profit institutions current income and outlays), 3.13 (general government capital accumulation account), 3.23 (corporate and quasi-corporate enterprise capital accumulation account), and 1.7 (external transactions).

Needless to say, the SNA reveals a saving-investment balance for individual sectors. The external transactions account describes a country's linkage *vis-à-vis* the rest of the world in terms of merchandise trade, service trade, factor income, and current transfers.

3.3. International financial statistics

Financial variables such as exchange rates and interest rates are obtained from the IMF's *International Financial Statistics*. The items relating to international transactions in this source provide further details on direct investment and portfolio investment, which have gained importance as the global linkage through financial flows becomes increasingly powerful. These and other financial variables included in the model framework help determine the financial solvency of a nation. Foreign direct investment is also a vehicle for technology transfer. The COMPASS distinguishes four institutional sectors, namely: the government sector (*SEG*), the corporate sector (*SEC*), the household sector (*SHE*), and the foreign sector (*SEF*). The corporate sector *SEC* is split into financial and non-financial. The financial corporate sector (*SECB*) consists mainly of: the monetary authority (*MOA*), the deposit money banks (*DMB*), and the other banking institutions and non-bank financial institutions (*SOB*). (See

Chapter 2 for naming convention and Chapter 3 for macro-finance model specification.) They are covered by this statistical source, providing a clue to construct a flow-of-funds account for individual countries. Thus the COMPASS has as its statistical basis several accounting frameworks, a fact which provides a solid basis for consistency among various variables. The cases in question include input-output tables, the SNA, flow of funds, trade matrices, and energy balances.

3.4. Time-series trade matrices

International linkage has to do with commodity trade and financial flows. Trade data are compiled by the United Nations at the detailed commodity level involving several thousand items. International linkage can best be represented by trade matrices identifying exporters and importers for individual commodities. This is not an easy task because reports on bilateral trade from exporters and importers do not necessarily match, due to omissions and/or timing of recording international transactions which necessarily involve transportation. Adjustment to compile consistent matrices is carried out by at least two organizations; one is Statistics Canada and the other is the Institute of Developing Economies in Japan. Financial flows must be examined through SNA (saving and investment) and balance of payment data from the International Monetary Fund.

The country models are linked by time-series of international trade statistics compiled by the UN (United Nations, various years b). Trade matrices have been compiled from the most detailed trade data. The correspondence between production branch classification and trade classification is shown in Table 1-1 above. There are 24 distinct sectors as represented by the COMPASS world trade code plus one dummy sector representing statistical discrepancy.

3.5. Energy balances

Energy data are compiled by the International Energy Agency for both OECD and non-OECD countries (IEA various years, a, b). The energy data are in physical terms (tons of oil equivalent, or toe). IEA also publishes energy price data (IEA various years, c).

The time-series energy balance tables, which is the energy database distinguishing energy sources and energy uses, distinguish the following sectors.

(1) Total primary energy supply (TPES): indigenous production, import, export, stock change.
(2) Energy conversion: electricity plants, etc.
(3) Total final consumption (TFC):
 (3.1) Industry sector: iron and steel; chemical and petrochemical; non-ferrous metals; non-metallic minerals; transport equipment; machinery; mining

and quarrying; food and tobacco; paper, pulp and print; wood and wood products; construction; textile and leather; non-specified.
(3.2) Transport sector: road, rail, etc.
(3.3) Other sector: agriculture, commerce and public service, residential, non-specified.

The energy data are in physical terms (tons of oil equivalent, or toe).

Finally, the accounts should not end as a snapshot at a point of time. From the policy analysis point of view, the focal point is changes over time and, more importantly, the ‘engine’ which is causing such changes. The ‘engine’ in this case may be changes in relative prices, technological progress made possible by R&D and diffusion of new vintage of capital, or policy measures such as taxes and subsidies. Efficiency improvement, fuel shift, lifestyle change, are some examples. However, these factors are typically not an integral part of environmental accounts.

We next examine the possibility of developing an environmental accounting framework that is suitable for policy analysis with a focus on CO_2 emission. This calls for linkage between energy data in value terms and in physical terms. Input-output tables provide a starting point with the most general framework capable of integrating or establishing linkages with statistical framework in specific fields. This occupies a central core in the SNA. Input-output analysis is conducted to provide structural information of an economy in itself or in conjunction with macroeconomic analysis providing information on the level and composition of final demand. The framework is also suitable to deal with technological change (via changes in the input coefficients) and lifestyle (via composition of private consumption such as commodities, energy, and services of various kinds). This can be used for price analysis due to the fact that the framework incorporates indirect taxes and subsidies, making it possible to incorporate energy tax, etc. Input-output analysis can also have a dynamic dimension.

Table 1-3 compares the branch classification of the energy data with the one coming from the input-output tables. The activity classification scheme of the energy balances is shown at the left side of the table. The standardized input-output framework with 36 branch classification, which has been produced for selected OECD countries, is shown at the right corner (shaded). It is then rearranged in order to show the correspondence between the classification scheme for the two data sets. The result is shown in the middle of the table. We note the following points:

(1) One can distinguish three branches in the input-output framework which are directly related to energy. Indigenous production of primary energy carriers corresponds to mining activities related to coal, crude oil, and petroleum in ‘mining and quarrying’ in the input-output framework. Two sectors in the input-output framework, namely ‘electricity, gas and water’ and ‘petroleum and coal products’, correspond to energy conversion activities described in the energy balances.

(2) There is a good match in industrial use of energy, although some of the input-output branches are lumped together in the energy balances.
(3) 'Residential' use of energy in energy balances corresponds to energy components embedded in 'private domestic consumption'.

We note some of the points that are deemed essential in understanding the rearranged input-output table in the context of energy analysis:

(1) Energy conversion activity is represented clearly as the relation among 'energy production mining', 'petroleum and coal products' and 'electricity, gas, and water'. The last of these is understood to include 'heat'. The water supply would have to be removed from this branch in order to focus solely on energy-related activities.
(2) The input structures of energy-related sectors are shown. The input coefficients which are derived from the value table represent the production technology, and provide a clue for accommodating bottom-up technology information in the entire economic structure.
(3) Details of final consumption of energy, attributable to industry (manufacturing, agriculture, etc.), transportation, and private consumption (household) then follow. It is important to note that technology and lifestyle are represented as the input coefficients in various industry branches and converter (i.e., a vector showing the composition of supplying branches) of private consumption, respectively. Energy consumption attributable to the household sector (consumer durables, heating and cooling, and automobiles) can be examined in an economy-wide context. It is often pointed out that changes in technology and lifestyle are the keys in an attempt towards sustainability.
(4) Energy supply is represented by changes in stock, exports, imports, and indigenous production. It is noted that, in terms of the input-output framework, 'changes in stock' assumes a positive sign when the inventory is being increased, but, in terms of energy supply' the same inventory increase should be regarded as negative supply. The same thing applies to 'exports' and 'imports'. In the input-output framework 'exports' is a component of final demand and assumes a positive sign, and 'imports' is the portion of a country's demand being met by foreign supplies and assumes a negative sign. In contrast, in energy balances, 'exports' represent the portion not being made available to domestic use while 'imports' comprise the supply for domestic use.
(5) Policy variables embedded in the input-output framework include 'indirect taxes and subsidies' which is a part of the value-added sphere. This is where taxes on energy or CO_2 emission can be added. A fiscal scheme in which revenue from such taxes can be dispersed as subsidies for employment can also be represented. Depending on the country's trade policy, 'imports' may also include import duties. Trade liberalization entails removal of such measures.

Table 1-3. Branch classification of energy balance tables and input-output tables

Energy Balance Branches		Rearranged IO Branches		Original IO Classification	
IEANo.		IO No.		IO No.	**Industrial Branches**
1	Indigenous production		Output in mining and quarrying		**Final Demand**
2	Imports	IMP	Imports of goods and services	HHC	Private domestic consumption
3	Exports	EXP	Exports of goods and services	GOV	Government consumption
4	Intl. marine bunkers			GFCF	Total gross fixed capital formation
5	Stock changes	energy STK	energy only, Changes in stocks	STK	Changes in stocks
6	**Total Primary Energy Supply (TPES)**			EXP	Exports of goods and services
	Energy Conversion			DFD	Total final demand
7	Transfers			IMP	Imports of goods and services
8	Statistical differences			GO	Gross output
9	Electricity plants	25	Electricity, gas and water		**Intermediate Demand**
10	CHP plants		(excl. water)	1	Agriculture, forestry and fishery
11	Heat plants			**2**	**Mining and quarrying**
12	Gas works			3	Food, beverages and tobacco
13	Petroleum refineries	9	Petroleum and coal products	4	Textiles, apparel and leather
14	Coal transformation			5	Wood products and furniture
15	Liquefaction			6	Paper, paper products and printing
16	Other transformation			7	Industrial chemicals
17	Own use			8	Drugs and medicines
18	Distribution losses			**9**	**Petroleum and coal products**
19	**Total Final Consumption (TFC)**			10	Rubber and plastic products
20	**Industrial sector**			11	Non-metalic mineral products
21	Iron and steel	12	Iron and steel	12	Iron and steel
22	Chemical and petrochemical	7	Industrial chemicals	13	Non-ferrous metals
23	of which petrochemical feed	8	Drugs and medicines	14	Metal products
		10	Rubber and plastic products	15	Non-electrical machinery
24	Non-ferrous metals	13	Non-ferrous metals	16	Office and computing machinery
25	Non-metallic minerals	11	Non-mettalic mineral products	17	Electric apparatus, nec
26	Transport equipment	19,	20, 21, 22	18	Radio, TV and comm. equipment
27	Machinery	14,	15,16,17,18, 23	19	Shipbuilding and repairing
28	Mining and quarrying		Energy use in Mining and quarrying	20	Other transport

29 Food and tobacco	3 Food, beverages and tobacco	21 Motor vehicles
30 Paper, pulp, and print	6 Paper, paper products and printing	22 Aircraft
31 Wood and wood products	5 Wood products and furniture	23 Professional goods
32 Construction	26 Construction	24 Other manufacturing
33 Textile and leather	4 Textiles, apparel and leather	**25 Electricity, gas and water**
34 Non-specified industry	24 Other manufacturing	26 Construction
35 **Transport sector**	29 Transport and storage	27 Wholesale and retail trade
36 37, 38, 39, 40, 41		28 Restaurants and hotels
42 Non-specified services		29 Transport and storage
43 **Other sectors**		30 Communication
44 Agriculture	1 Agriculture, forestry and fishery	31 Finance and insurance
45 Commerce and public serv.	25, 27, 28, 30, 31, 32, 33, 34	32 Real estate and business services
46 Residential	part of HHC part of private domestic consumption	33 Community, social, personal services
47 Non-specified	{ 35 Other producers	34 Producers of government services
	{ 36 Statistical discrepancy	35 Other producers
48 **Non-energy use**		36 Statistical discrepancy

Note: Italics characters represent terms from the energy balance tables.

Energy balance tables consist basically of three parts: total primary energy supply (TPES), energy conversion (basically into 'electricity' and 'petroleum and coal products', and total final consumption (TFC). In addition, there is a small portion of energy carriers going into non-energy use. Some of the analytical points relating to energy balances are as follows:

(1) Fuel substitution can be represented as the time-series change in the individual shares in primary energy supply. We have witnessed declines in coal, increase in petroleum, and emergence of gas. Depending on the country's energy policy, a considerable portion of energy supply is borne by the nuclear sector. Introduction of non-polluting renewable sources of energy is a focal point in recent years, including combustion of urban wastes for power and heat generation. The shift can be explained by the relative prices of various energy carriers and R&D effort directed to this end.
(2) Energy conversion efficiency can be observed as the ratio between inputs of primary energy and output secondary energy (i.e. electricity). The efficiency has improved in some countries owing to R&D activities and capital formation embodying new technology.
(3) Energy intensity which is represented by energy inputs per unit production in individual economic branches or for the whole economy is also represented in the balance table. This parameter is typically explained by the relative price of energy *vis-à-vis* the price of output in respective branches.

Energy balance tables are intended to describe the energy supply being made available for domestic use, whereas input-output tables identify demand regardless of whether it originates domestically or across national boundaries. Reflecting the difference in point of view, export of energy assumes a negative sign in energy balance tables whereas it represents a positive final demand item in an input-output framework, and *vice-versa* for energy imports. The energy transformation from primary to secondary appears with a negative sign and electricity output has a positive sign in the IEA *Energy Balances*. In the input-output framework, transformation is represented with a positive sign, and electricity output with a negative sign in order to be able to say that the sum of transformation and final consumption equals primary energy supply.

4. The philosophy of the COMPASS approach

The purpose of the project is to construct a robust test-bed for simulation experiments concerning global policy issues. The COMPASS approach is based on a set of guiding principles which include the following:

Policy relevance: COMPASS is a policy model. Efforts have been made to identify major players which determined the scope of the model in terms of regions, economic branches, and relevant variables in economy-energy with its implication on energy prices, energy conservation, trade patterns, international relocation of energy-intensive activities, employment profiles, and economic performance in general. This may also lead to re-examination of the tax system as a whole (Oates, 1995).

Global closure: COMPASS is an international model. It distinguishes as many countries/regions as possible, within the constraints of data availability and other unavoidable factors. As a policy model rather than a mere academic exercise it is necessary to provide information to decision makers in individual countries/regions. However, more often than not we are faced with policy issues with global implications. Trade liberalization, international capital movements, and global environmental concerns are a few examples. In a single-country model we are obliged to assume economic trends in trading partners, exchange rate, world prices for various commodities, and international financial flows. With inclusion of economies representing more than 99% in terms of world GDP, trade flows, and energy production and consumption, the model is closed globally with respect to production of goods and services (as represented in trade balance), financial resources (as represented in saving-investment balance), and energy (production and final use). The COMPASS generates consistent international commodity prices and domestic prices at the disaggregated level. It also generates financial flows both within a country and internationally, making it clear whether or not an investment fund is forthcoming from either domestic or international sources. It has a very detailed energy model, using physical quantities as well as values, tracing the domestic flow from final use through conversion to supply of primary energy, which then goes into international trade of coal, oil, and gas, determining energy prices.

Bottom-up combined with top-down: The macroeconomic performance results from activities at the branch level. COMPASS is based on input-output tables and corresponding trade matrices precisely for this reason. Also, behavioural equations are intended to describe the actual decision rules at the branch level. The model traces the response of economic agents to price signals (price of goods and services at branch level, exchange rate, interest rate, and energy prices), but perfect knowledge and market clearing are not assumed *a priori*. On the contrary, the model reveals the disequilibrium which may emerge in the economic system and how it is resolved over time through adjustment on the part of individual economic agents induced by changing relative prices.

Full integration: COMPASS is intended to be a test-bed for various policy experiments. A model focusing on one particular issue is only able to provide partial views. The scope of COMPASS in contrast extends over economy–energy–environment interactions. The economic part consists of a macro-financial model, an input-output model, and a world trade model. It covers the flow of goods and services both domestically and internationally. It deals with saving-investment balance at local as well as global levels. With full integration of various aspects, any single issue can be analysed from a system-wide perspective.

Accounting consistency: Most models are built around the variables of interest. This has an advantage of making the model small and simple. COMPASS, in contrast, tries to generate various accounting tables which provide a system-wide perspective and are widely used by policy-related institutions. The cases in question include SNA with sectoral balances, balance of payments, flow of funds, input-output tables, energy balances, and trade matrices against which individual variables can be examined from the system-wide point of view.

Transparency: In order to serve as a test-bed for various policy experiments, COMPASS is based on generally accepted theory employing internationally open data. Different theoretical orientation or sensitivity analyses regarding a particular policy variable can be accommodated by changing the relevant portion of the model framework.

Operationality: In some modelling environments, data and parameters are parts of a very large programme, making it difficult to make the necessary adjustment when a model specification is altered. Easy operation is also an indispensable attribute required of a model which is used as a platform for various simulation experiences. The model framework may be very large and complex, but the operation has to be simple when one considers the number of simulation runs to test, for example, sensitivity of the world economy to various trade arrangements. COMPASS employs identical logical sequences in model development and simulation runs regardless of whether one is dealing with macro and financial part, input-output model, energy and environment block, or trade linkages.

Coping with time path: In policy analysis it is imperative to be able to tell the course of development over time if certain measures are taken. A framework which only describes what will happen when equilibrium is attained does not provide the required answer. There are models which project into the year 2100, for instance, but they have to rely on heavy assumptions on the parameters. COMPASS has a dynamic structure which provides information along the time horizon. It is based on econometrically estimated parameters from 1970 to around 1995, and it is capable of projecting annually into the future until 2010 (at the maximum 2020).

Coping with non-linearity: Econometric and other quantitative models are based on the assumption of linearity and COMPASS is no exception. In reality, however, there are non-linear relations, but one would be misguided if one concluded that econometric models cannot properly describe non-linearity and hence cannot adequately describe the reality. There are various non-linear relations which can be linearly approximated. Johnston (1963) lists semilog transformation (corresponding to a constant rate of growth), double-log transformation (corresponding to the assumption of constant elasticity), reciprocal transformation (corresponding to an assumption of an asymptotic level), logarithmic, reciprocal transformation (to accommodate threshold levels, etc.). In addition, proper disaggregation, such as attempted in COMPASS, reduces the cases of seemingly non-linear relations at the aggregate level. For example, energy consumption may show a kink at the macroeconomic level whereas at a disaggregated level individual branches behave the same as before but the weights are changing (e.g. manufacturing shrinking and services becoming dominant).

Coping with structural change: Models are often accused of their inability to deal with structural change. This is precisely why COMPASS is constructed at disaggregated levels. It also explicitly treats economic sectors such as household, industry, government, and the rest of the world in three distinct spheres: (1) goods and services, (2) financial flows, and (3) energy. Thus, it is possible to examine the structural change of the economy (input-output relations), trade structure (trade matrices explicitly stating exporters and importers for an individual commodity), balance of payments (trade and capital flows), energy (primary energy supply through energy conversion to final use) and policy tools (taxes and subsidies), among others.

Coping with lack of historical data: There is no way of overcoming the lack of past data. COMPASS bypasses the problem by borrowing and estimating. Borrowing the historical experience elsewhere has its limits, of course, but may shed light on the future course of events in the countries/regions undergoing rapid industrialization, for example. Estimating the past data based on available column sums or row sums of a matrix is acceptable and even desirable because there can exist only one set of variables which satisfies the accounting balance.

Model as a black box: As models become larger and more complex they are often treated as a black box, and only the main results are published. Model results are only as good as the assumptions that are fed to the model, but the influence of such exogenous information to the solution is often not discussed. Looking at the main results is of course interesting, but one has to be able to obtain information on how the rest of the economy looks. COMPASS graphic user interface (GUI) allows model-builders and model-users to examine macro-financial models, input-output models, energy models, and trade models in terms of their structure, assumptions, and econometrically obtained parameters.

Impact on employment: Trade liberalization and environmental preservation may affect employment levels and change occupational profiles. Policy makers in many countries are worried about the impact on employment just as they are concerned about the trade balance and the levels of GDP. The model presented here does not provide precise information on employment, although this point can be remedied. See Chapter 11.

5. Comparisons with other models

The COMPASS focuses on medium-term analysis, not short-term (cyclical) or long-term (general equilibrium) analyses, but traces how the paths would evolve in different regions and in different industrial branches responding to the introduction of policy measures (such as tradable permit or carbon tax), technological change (such as new input structure and better conversion efficiency), and lifestyle shift (such as service orientation or energy conservation effort).

The COMPASS framework, because of its branch disaggregation and regional breakdown, and because of its simultaneous equation system, allows bottom-up and top-down interaction. The inclusion of branch prices (36 branches), final demand prices (consumption, investment, government spending, exports, and imports), exchange rate, interest rate, and various energy prices as endogenous variables, and the adjustment mechanism by economic agents based on relative prices are described explicitly.

The model treats world petroleum prices as exogenous variables, but equilibrium world petroleum prices are calculated within the model in order to monitor the market forces behind the assumed price levels. Technology factors such as production technology (described by input coefficients), energy substitution (among different energy carriers), and changes in energy intensity are fully explained endogenously. The model can project input-output tables and energy balances in the future, providing structural information of the world community.

COMPASS has feedback channels running through economy–energy–environment spheres. Its framework is disaggregated almost to the maximum extent that is feasible from the data point of view. COMPASS incorporates, and is capable of endogenously generating, a relevant accounting scheme, including national income accounting, flow of funds (being tested) and saving-investment balance, input-output tables, trade matrices, and energy balance tables. It can also generate prices for individual industrial branches, final demand, and energy. Exchange rates and interest rates are endogenously determined. Technological factors are represented as changes in input coefficients and changes in energy intensity for an industry over time because they represent new production methods requiring different material use. COMPASS also provides information at detailed country levels, an advantage over various other models.

An object-oriented approach is maintained throughout the project, ranging from naming convention, statistical database, model-building software, and simulation engine. Consistent use of meta data makes the construction and maintenance of large-scale models mainly systematic (Soltes, 1999). Because of this approach, the inclusion of other regions in the model framework can be systematically accomplished.

Table 1-4 presents a comparison of COMPASS with other models with a focus on the interaction involving economy, energy, and environment; for details see Chapter 12.

6. Policy analysis

Some of the characteristics of COMPASS are summarized below, after cross-checking with other models. The model can be used as a test-bed for various policy scenarios.

6.1. *Lifestyle*

Lifestyle can be regarded as a reflection of changing personal values and income levels. Although an econometric model is ill-suited for dealing with people's values, it can at least deal with changing consumption patterns which presumably reflect changing lifestyle in addition to income effects. COMPASS accommodates this variable by allowing the model-builders to apply different branch make-up of private consumption vector in the final demand quadrant of the input-output tables (Parikh *et al.*, 1991; Rayner and Malone, 1998; Redclift and Benton, 1994; Schipper *et al.*, 1996; Wier *et al.*, 2001. See also Van Asselt *et al.*, 1995). Needless to say, one can specify a consumption function for individual branches if appropriate data (such as panel data providing consumption expenditures by household income bracket) are available if the purpose of the analysis is to measure the consumption pattern under changing income and price levels.

One way to mitigate the collision between the human aspiration and the global environment is to seek an alternative lifestyle which is more amenable to sustainability. The empirical foundation in this regard will be final consumption expenditures by function for government and private sectors provided by Tables 2.3 and 2.4 of the SNA. A different expenditure pattern signifies a different environmental impact, e.g. in terms of energy consumption. Particularly important is the household expenditures on durable goods, which form a linkage point between consumption and technology, such as represented by energy efficiency. Consumer durable goods as the stock determines a large portion of energy consumption that appears in the account as expenditure on fuel and power.

6.2. *Alternative technology*

Despite the fact that technological factors have become the central focus of the policy debate, the treatment of technology in economic theory is rather blurred. COMPASS is based on a time-series of input-output tables, and the input-output framework describes the input structure (which is the production technology *per se*) for individual branches of the economy. Technological change can be described by the changes in input coefficients over time. In the case of energy, the model includes extra variables such as substitution among primary energy sources and conversion efficiency.

In the COMPASS framework, technology is represented at four major points:

(1) input coefficients in the input-output models,
(2) conversion efficiency of primary energy to secondary energy in the energy models,
(3) the selection among different energy carriers also in the energy models,
(4) changes in energy intensity over time.

The input coefficients describe the composition of material and service inputs into respective branches of the economy. In other words they describe the

Table 1-4. Methodological comparison of economy–energy–environment projections

Model Names	Reference	Modeling Logic	Projection Period	Economy-Energy Linkage	Prices	Regions	Energy Sources	Industrial Branches	Commodity Trade Linkage	Emission Trading
3E COMPASS	**Uno *et al.* (2002)**	**IO + Econometric**	**2010 (annual)**	**Endogenous**	**Endogenous**	**61**	**6**	**36**	**Yes (53*53 matrices** for 26 commodities)	**Yes**
Adam Rose-Brand Steven	Rose & Stevens (1999)	General equilibrium, optimization	25 years	Economy exogenous	No	14	1	1	No	Yes
AIM	National Institute for Environmental Studies	Top-down world, bottom-up technology	2100	Economy exogenous	No	19	No	Varied	No	No
APEC Energy Outlook	APERC (1996)	Scenarios	2010	Economy exogenous	Exogenous	6	6	3	No	No
ASF	IPCC (2000)	Demand-supply adjustment by price	2100	Economy exogenous	Yes	9	Numerous	1	No	No
Decomposition	Unander & Schipper (1999)	Decomposition of indicators + scenarios	2010	Economy exogenous	No	7	Various	Various	No	No
DEMETER	van der Zwaan *et al.* (2000)	Optimization	2100	Partly endogenous (leaning-by-doing)	Yes (taxes, subsidies)	No	Carbon energy	No	Yes	Yes
ECN Study	Sijm *et al.* (2000)	Cost curves and demand curves	2010	Economy exogenous	No	30	Not explicit	Not explicit	No	Yes
EDGE Model	Jensen *et al.* (2000)	General equilibrium	2030	Endogenous	Yes (emission)	8	5	7	Yes	Yes
G-cubed	Bagnoli, McKibbin, & Wilcoxen (1996)	General equilibrium, econometric	2020	Endogenous	Yes	8	4	12	Yes (8*8 matrices for 12 commodities)	No
GemWTraP	Bernard & Vielle (1999)	General equilibrium, optimization	2020	Economy exogenous	Yes	7	5	12	No	Yes

GREEN	OECD (1994b)	IO + Econometric	2010 2050	Endogenous	Endogenous	12	5	11	Yes, bilateral flows	No
GTAP	Hertel & Tsigas (1997)	General equilibrium, I-O	No time series	Endogenous	Yes	24	5	37	Yes (31 commodities)	No
IEA Energy Model	Vouyoukas (1993)	Econometric	2005 (annual)	Economy exogenous	Exogenous	10	14	3	No	No
IFs: International Futures	Hughes (1999)	System dynamics	2100	Economy exogenous	No	20	6	5	Yes (pooled approach)	No
IIASA and WEC	Nakicenovic *et al.* (1998)	Scenarios	2100	Economy exogenous	No	11	5	No	No (assumption)	No
IMAGE 2.0	Alcamo (1994)	Elasticity	2100	Economy exogenous (= IPCC)	No	13	6	5	No	No
IPCC Special Report	IPCC (2000)	Scenarios	2100	Economy exogenous	No	No	6	No	No	No
MARIA	IPCC (2000)	Non-linear optimization	2100	Economy exogenous	Yes	8	9	3	No	No
MARKAL Models	Loulou & Kanudia (2000)	Partial equilibrium	Varies	International permits	Yes	Stand alone	Varies	Varies	Some models with regional linkage	Yes
MARKAL MATTER	Gielen & Kram (2000)	Linear programming	2060	Price dependent demand	Yes	No	25	No	No	No
MERGE	Manne, Mendelsohn, and Richels (1995)	General equilibrium, optimization	2200	Economy exogenous (= IPCC)	No	5	2	3	No	No
MESSAGE	IPCC (2000)	Dynamic linear programming	2100	Economy exogenous	No	10	Numerous	1	No	No
MIDAS	Capros *et al.* (1996)	Bottom-up technology	10 years	Economy exogenous (= HERMES)	Yes	4 independent	5	11	No	No
MiniCAM	IPCC (2000)	Partial equilibrium	2100	Economy exogenous	Yes	11	7	3	No	No

Table 1-4. continued

Model Names	Reference	Modeling Logic	Projection Period	Economy-Energy Linkage	Prices	Regions	Energy Sources	Industrial Branches	Commodity Trade Linkage	Emission Trading
MS-MRT	Bernstein *et al.* (1999b)	General equilibrium, optimization	2030	Economy exogenous	No	10	4	6	Yes	Yes
New Earth	Nishio, Fujii & Yamaji (2000)	Non-linear optimization	2020	Economy exogenous	No	10	9	No	No	Yes
The PRIMES	European Commission (1995)	Optimization type, Partial equilibrium	2030	Endogenous	Yes	12	4	12	No	No
Rains-Asia	Resource Management Association (1996)	Scenarios	2020	Economy exogenous	No	23	17	6	Not explicit	No
RICE	Nordhaus & Yang (1996)	General equilibrium, optimization	2200	Economy exogenous	No	10	1	1	No	No
WEPS	Energy Inf. Admin., USDE (1997a)	Scenarios	2020	Economy exogenous, elasticity assumptions	No	16	6	1	No	No
World Energy Outlook	International Energy Agency (1998b)	Scenarios	2020	Economy exogenous	Yes	10	8	4	No	No
World Model	Duchin & Lange (1994)	IO + Scenarios, bottom-up technology	2020	Economy exogenous	Relative price of oil	16	3	44	Yes (39 commodities)	No
WorldScan	Bollen *et al.* (1999)	General equilibrium, optimization	2100	Endogenous	Yes	12	4	11	Yes (two-way trade)	Yes

Note: For detailed discussion of each projection, see Chapter 12. Quantitative results are summarized in Table 12-25.

prevailing production processes. One can therefore experiment econometrically on how the changes in relative prices of one input (say, energy) affect the corresponding coefficients. Alternatively, based on information from a technology inventory which provides perspectives for innovation, one can try to insert input coefficients representing future technology scenarios. Internationally, experiments on technology transfers can be conducted by transplanting the actual input structure in industrialized countries to developing economies (Rosenberg, 1997; Sakurai *et al.*, 1996; Wallace, 1995).

In addition, it will be possible to include consumer durables in the model framework, and the effect of improved energy efficiency of automobiles, air conditioners, refrigerators, etc. can be examined.

6.3. Tradable permits

The COP is a very complex political process and it is not realistic to replicate the installment of various rules and fine-tuning of numerical targets to be implemented in a precise time span. The purpose of the simulation experiments regarding tradable permits must be as follows.

(1) Calculate the base trend without introduction of new policy measures such as tradable permits and carbon tax. The COMPASS, with its empirically estimated parameters incorporated in a multi-sector, multi-country framework and global closure regarding production and trade on the real side and saving and investment on the financial side, is a powerful tool for this purpose.

(2) Experiment with tradable permits based on the CO_2 emission targets which are given in the Kyoto Protocol. With some exceptions regarding developing economies and the economies in transition, every country will be initially granted that amount of permit that is equal to the actual emission. Subsequently the permit will be reduced following the path leading to the reduction target. On the individual regional level, government will be in a position to impose an energy tax (if the country is a buyer) or allocate the surplus (if the country is a seller). It is likely that most of the industrialized countries will find themselves buying the permits. A rising tax rate reduces energy demand and, thus, CO_2 emissions. On the global level, new energy demand and corresponding price of the permit is calculated. If the emission of the country is higher, it has to purchase permits on the international market; if the emissions are lower, the country can sell to the market. The price of the permits is set at a level where market clears by equilibrating demand and supply. Simulation will be conducted regarding the direct effect of changing energy prices. The effect may vary among regions, giving room for conflicts of interest.

(3) Examine the secondary effect of the introduction of tradable permits (and other policy measures) on industrial structure, trade patterns, government finance, employment, etc.

It should be remembered that simulation experiments are not forecasts. They are the basis for our awareness of the required policy measures and the needs for new technological development.

Part II

The framework of analysis

2
Object-oriented database and modelling system

DIRK VANWYNSBERGHE and FRANK HOHMANN

1. Introduction

This chapter sets up the time-series conventions for the database and the modelling engines used in COMPASS in the framework of international cooperation. The project provides the users with a set of tools that allow users, to understand the whole process and to be able to achieve the model in a well-defined number of steps within the limits of predefined time horizon and budget. The project offers a set of predefined prototype working models that are dubbed as Quickdyme versions for IO, Quickmac for SNA and Financial macro modelling, and Worldtrad for world trade linkage at commodity level. They allow users to complete the data set-up, test the consistency of the basic data, build more and more realistic models in transparent and standardized steps and to present and analyse the simulation results.

Why use a database concept? Data can be presented in two concepts: a *data set* concept (a file concept), and a *data base* concept (either a relational database system or an object-oriented database system). Although the *difference between set and base* is fundamental, the state of the art of the technology for IO modelling does not allow using a *unified* concept for the entire project scope. Why? As we shall see, *from the client's point of view, the raw data source side and the productivity side*, one needs a database approach. However, *from the model-builder and model engine's viewpoint*, only data sets are used for both input and output.

The COMPASS model links economy, energy, and environment (3E) in a consistent way. The data used in the framework come from a number of selected sources. Such a global system uses, for representative comparison and efficiency reasons as much as possible, widely recognized and standardized sources of data. Thus, data come in the first place from international sources (such as UN, IMF, World Bank, OECD, and IEA, among others), but also from a number of precious national sources (e.g. the Institute of Developing Economies in Japan). All these sources use database systems and transfer their data by classical database interface output formats. None of these is directly readable by the available model engines. Furthermore, one of the important pillars of the success of such a project in general, and of this one in particular, is the unified and standardized way in which the data are supplied, used and delivered. Such a way can only be achieved in a database concept.

K. Uno (ed.), Economy–Energy–Environment Simulation, 33–53.

Why are data sets still there? On the other hand, the individual model-builders and model engine constructors consider data as numbers in a file read by the model in one format or another. As model updates and simulation experiments always involve data, an unbridgeable gap tends to be innocently built in from the start by the model building. This gap has never been recognized by the model-builders who basically have no experience with database-organized information.

A data set file contains mainly numerical data and series names in a specific format for both the numerical data and for the name of the series. Special characters may be introduced to indicate the end of a series, e.g. a semicolon. Typically such a series will contain numerical values for each of the time periods but nothing else on the non-numerical level. Sometimes the file name may give some hint as to the type of data and the data source. Only the maker of the file will know what the data are, what the units are and so on. Another user cannot find any such information except in forms not linked to the data points. In a nutshell, everything is in the head of the maker and nothing is really shared with the potential user.

The solution is theoretically simple: use a database concept (RDMS or its improved version) for the whole scope of the project, meaning from data preparation, and model-building step to the output analysis (decision) step. Unfortunately, today almost all (if not all) modelling engines need data sets as input, and all of them use data sets (files) as output. This conceptual difference, together with the limited/unreliable performance of data-set-oriented software applications, has almost killed the classical model market and replaced it by robust but naïve and over-simplified database explorations combined with spread-sheet extrapolations. In day-to-day business obtaining the results is the dominant concern rather than how you are structured logically internally. Models are great tools but to the decision-makers they look like infantile instruments.

2. Does IO go the dinosaur's way?

Today's interactive computer applications basically consist of objects on a screen that are responding to standardized kind of actions from the user. These standards do not depend on the designer of the application or on the type of application, but are only reflecting the state-of-the-art technology in graphical user interfaces (GUI). With the introduction of the remote terminal all computer applications started to exploit the interaction between subjects (e.g. user, designer), an input device, and the application software. Nowadays the input device consists of the objects on the screen that can be activated by keystrokes, mouse clicks and very soon by voice. In the earlier days these objects on the screen were very primitive and rather cryptic, and the possible action of the user was limited, and to a large extent depended on the execution process of the application program. The program managed the users rather than the other way round. The application had a pre-programmed procedural execution and in the best case a structural program did achieve the predefined task. The users could not do anything that had not been pre-programmed, nor could they vary the run stream by any creative intervention. This solution puts too many constraints on the application both from the designer's viewpoint and from the user's viewpoint. The situation has changed drastically in recent years and is still in a turbulent revolution.

The input-output analysis has an inherent problem when looked at from this perspective. Input-output models were no exception in the past, but nowadays lag far behind the above-described fundamental changes. Building and using an input-output model is still a lifetime task for the few individuals who have the time, money and patience to struggle through that process. Maintaining and updating the models is such a labour-intensive and exclusive task that most of them are in constant construction and almost never reach the operational phase. The lucky few, once there, are so difficult to operate that in most cases only the designer or model-builder can use them. Why is this so?

We see the problem coming from three different angles:

(1) The IO technology is complicated because it runs through from IO table, static model, dynamic model, to econometric model. Standards in the naming are not available or not integrated with macroeconomics, social accounting, energy and environment.
(2) The data needed both in the numerical sense and in the conceptual sense are very demanding and difficult to handle. IO started with numbers and has never moved out from this short-sighted view. Most of the meta data are not at all recorded or referenced and only exist in the brain, and in some cryptic notes made by the model-builder.
(3) The available computer software is not designed as an engine and does not pay much attention to a user-friendly data preparation, model design, model operation, or an update of both the data and the model. It is usually built together with one particular model and will probably never reach the operational phase of its lifecycle. Maintenance and update of the software are typically not part of the project design.

The result is that only a few experts are able to handle IO models; transfer of their know-how is difficult; with a result that fewer and fewer junior people can be found. The misunderstanding of the IO model has also brought some mistrust – not least from colleague economists – and the usage of this powerful technology is far below its potential.

Is there another way of doing things to remedy these drawbacks? The object-oriented future is the way to go. We believe there is indeed a way that is based on an object-oriented approach in the design, the database, the programming and the use of standardized IO models. Clearly the origin of the problem cannot be with individuals, but with the conceptual approach to models and their extremely poor implementation as objects. One can define an object as the realization of every working concept. It consists of many smaller objects in itself. The user does not have to know how an object performs its tasks, but just how to send messages so that the object executes by itself the appropriate method that gives the expected result for the action of the user. The action of the user is limited to keystrokes and clicks. The user action will create events. The events will execute methods that will manipulate data (known as properties of the object on which the action is directed).

It should be possible to bring IO models to the state-of-the-art user interfaces for data preparation, for the model building, for model using and for the analysis phase of all data input and output. The major steps solved in the project are at three levels: the software level: *Compass GUI;* the IO model level: *Compass IO;* the policy and management conclusion level: *Compass PM.* What is of most importance to see is how each of these fields integrates into the whole COMPASS project, and how each step is necessary to achieve the following one. The policy and management considerations cannot be studied without such an integrated and productive approach.

3. The database (DB) and the database management system (DBMS)

Data can be presented in two concepts: a *data set* concept (system-wise a file concept), and a *data base* concept (system-wise either a relational database system or an object-oriented database system). Although the difference between set and base is fundamental, the state-of-the-art technology for IO modelling does not allow us to use a *unified* concept for the entire project scope. Why?

A *relational database* stores information in the form of *tables* that contain *related information for the same topic*. A table is not stored in a file as such, but all tables and their relations are stored in a special file: the database file. One can say that *the type of information* is stored as *the column headers* also called fields, and that each *individual data point* will be a *record or row* in that table. Each record or row will contain the relevant value for each of the column headers that fit together for that individual data point. It should be clear that not only numerical data but also non-numerical data are stored in the same table. The order of the rows or records in a table does not matter and a retrieval of the data will be in a random order. However, *sort* and *search values* (alphanumerical ones with placeholders) can be put on each column of the table to sort and to look for a specific type of information. Also, such values can be used as *filters to retrieve* only the information that satisfies these criteria. The database management system, and not the application program, will keep track of all changes and the update; insertion and deletion of data will be done by that system. The database is independent of the operating system (platform) used and can be accessed by standard software other than the application. A copy of the database will not work on another computer if not properly installed. The way the data are stored is unusable for human beings, but extremely well adapted for computer treatment through the DBMS. Therefore, the non-DBMS user needs an interface to retrieve, input, update, delete explore, analyse, export and use the data in all kind of applications. Compass GUI is such software specially built for international modelling and linkage.

3.1. Client expectations: database-oriented

The model users, distinct from model-builders, are exclusively used to database-delivered information (not in a file but in an information system and today even in a decision system). They do not want, or do not have the time or the resources, to become involved with any of the data set considerations nourished so privately by the model-builders.

3.2. Data sources: database dominance

The COMPASS model links economy, energy, and environment in a consistent way. The data used come from a number of *selected sources*. Such a system uses for comparison and efficiency reasons as much as possible widely recognized and standardized *international* data. All these sources use database systems and transfer their data by classical database interface output formats. None of these is readable by the available IO model engines.

3.3. Productivity interest: database oriented

Furthermore, one of the important pillars of the success of such a project in general, and of this one in particular, is the unified and standardized way in which the data *are supplied, used and delivered*. Such a method can only be in a database concept.

3.4. IO model world: data set dominance

On the other hand, the individual model-builders and model-engine constructors consider data as numbers in a file read by the model in one format or another. As model update, simulation and output always involve data, an unbridgeable gap was unwittingly built in from the start by the model-builders. This gap was never recognized by the model-builders who basically have no experience with database-organized information (except negative ones). A data set file contains numerical data for a given series as single time-series or as matrix. The series will be presented in a special format for the numerical data and for the name of the series. Special characters may be introduced to indicate the end of a series. Typically such a series will contain numerical values for each of the time periods and nothing else on the non-numerical, information level. Only the maker of the file will know the data at the meta level, i.e., what the data are, what the units are, what the sources are, and so on. Another user cannot find any information on that except in a form not linked to the data points. Some comments may be added to the file for information, but they do not make part of the data used by the engine.

3.5. Communication interest: data set preference

From a communication point of view, data files are very efficient for transfer both on hard carriers and on networks. The export of database results is mainly done by files; however, the structure of the information usually reflects a database concept, and not a time-series concept, requiring some interfaces.

3.6. The theoretical solution

The solution is theoretically simple: use a database concept (RDMS or a better one) for the whole scope of the project, meaning from the model-building step to the output analysis (decision) step. Unfortunately, today almost all (if not all) modelling engines need data sets as input and all of them use data sets (files) as output. This conceptual difference, together with the limited capabilities and/or unreliable performance of data set-oriented software applications, have almost killed the classical model market and replaced it by robust but naïve and over-simplified database explorations combined with spread-sheet extrapolations.

3.7. The COMPASS compromise: a central database with automated data set interface for different engines

The data approach is the first step to show maturity for many reasons. COMPASS started with a new approach on the data side: first taking into account the user's understanding and preferences as the major objective, and second taking the technical limitations only as the constraints to be worked around.

The basic raw data are harvested in the basic raw data system (BRDS). This contains the full set of all available international data of the selected data sources and for the selected data domains and the equivalent national data for some countries with insufficient international coverage (for whatever reason), e.g. China and the Russian Federation, among others. For efficiency reasons the basic raw data from the BRDS are automatically transferred to the model raw data system (MRDS) that contains only the data needed for the model system. Here data correction and data manipulation is already done. Up to that level all data are stored in database management systems and use standard database engines. However, for the modelling, one has to create the specific data input sets needed by the model engines that is in a particular case. For this reason the MRDS creates in an automated way the data sets for the different modelling engines used. They are referred to as modelling engine data files (MEDF) and are stored in specific formats and in predefined directories designated by the model system and the model engines. The models themselves will then read this engine data set and create the model system data files (MSDF) for each specific model engine.

4. Standardization in IO: naming conventions

The naming conventions proposed here are for the starting versions of the models, and more elaborate models will have these variables as totals of more detailed ones developed by the experienced user. Only the classical variables should be standardized fully. Names of the series refer in the first place to a classical input-output table and should be easy to remember and have as much relation as possible to the English definition. We should do away with the pure mathematical conventions once used like *x* or *q* for gross output – there is no *x* or *q* in the definition, *y* for value added – there is also no *y* in value added, and so on. Exceptions should only exist for generally excepted concepts such as gdp or GDP. Names of other variables (non-input-output series) used in the database and model could be chosen more freely as long as they use the standard rules and do not conflict with the input-output names. However, as a number of models for different countries are developed within this software, using the same names for all countries does give the result a greater portability.

The naming principles are for the *modelling software developers* and for the *model developers* starting to use the versions of the database and model simulation engine known under the name Quickdyme. The modelling software will internally use these names. If the user also uses the same names for his data input, then no C++ code will have to be changed in the Quickdyme versions of the model. Experienced users can proceed as they did before. These names will be the ones used in the central database for all countries and in the different versions of Quickdyme. So understanding number 1 says that *if the user accepts* the naming conventions, then no C++ code must be changed for the all Quickdyme versions because externally used names are fully consistent with internally used names.

Time-series can be *single series* like an exchange rate, *vectors* (n × 1) like the exports for each of the branches in the model, or *matrices* (n × n) like the intermediate flows from each branch of origin to each branch of destination. The naming rules should be so that the user (and the system) sees immediately if the variable is a single series, a vector or a matrix. The vector series of dimension 1 × 1 are vectors for the software but single series for the user. They will have special names to be recognized immediately; we minimize their use to an absolute minimum.

Names for *vectors* and *matrices* have a *three-digit* root for the meaning, e.g. intermediate demand, household consumption, investment, etc.; *prefixes* for the different types within the root, such as shares, coefficients, prices, bridges, etc.; and *suffixes* for detail in the root, e.g. rural household consumption, urban household consumption, or for groups such as heavy industry, high-technology branches. Such names are: *prefix_root_suffix.*

The *single series* will use much the same conventions for vectors and matrices, but should have a name (like the root) *that is more than 5 characters long* so that one can immediately see that this is not a vector or a matrix.

Three-digit roots can never end in an integer, as branch numbers will be added automatically by the software. So suffixes for branches such as *1, 2, 3, n* are not needed, and if integers are used in the root for other reasons, then they should end in an '_' being part of the root. So forget integers in the root.

Names should immediately show if the variables are in real terms or in nominal terms (in more general terms, whether the variables in question are not affected by the price system or are affected – employment is like a vector in real terms), and whether they have unit dimensions or not (e.g. coefficients or shares, or growth rates, or percentage changes). A special rule will be worked out for series that are mixed, e.g. valued added in current prices divided by output in constant price.

The simpler the system is, the better it can be applied, and the shorter the names – if they have meaning for the user – the better. No full logical system has been found so far, so a final list will have to be agreed on. This list will be kept constantly up to date and new names – including exceptions – will be added. All new ideas are welcome.

Some series involve a mixture of current and constant prices such as value added in current prices per unit of output in constant prices. So we need a way to formalize this type of data. We will use the prefix (see below for prefixes) to express the first series in the root and the second series can be either silent (not referenced in the root, and then it should always be in the same form as the first one), or the second series might be referenced in the root, and then it can speak for itself. An example:

C_voo: unit value added defined as value added in current prices per unit of output in constant prices. Here the '*C_*' is in CAPS to indicate that the first digit of the root (it must be small because this is a vector) is in current prices, the second digit is *o* to indicate the operation 'over' or element-by-element divide and small because it goes together with the second series, in constant prices, output giving the '*o*' as third digit of the root.
C-vOO: would stand for value added in current prices 'over' output in current prices. We do not use this series, but it is given to clarify the rules.

The same rules are valid for the '*s_*' and '*S_*' referring to the first digit of the root being in constant or in current prices. The second series, if present in the root, can declare itself by the CAPS or small attribute. The same principle can be used for '*b_*' and '*B_*' for the first digit of the root.

As a general rule one could say that, in this type of mixed series made by operations, if the second series is not mentioned it is always in the same form as the first one. So if the first one is constant the 'silent' second one is also constant and *vice-versa.* If this is not the case the root should mention the two series involved. If more than two series are involved, as in the definition of domestic demand = output + imports − exports, we will omit the operators, e.g.:

omx: domestic demand in constant prices defined as output (*o*) + imports (*m*) − exports (*x*);
opm: domestic demand in constant prices defined as output (*o*) plus (*p*) imports (*m*);
oPM: would stand for the same series but in current prices.

The concept behind this special series is that the user knows the definitions rather well so that the operators can be omitted. The basic included series should as much as possible be mentioned.

5. Naming format

The proposed format is '*prefix_root_suffix*', prefixes and suffixes can be omitted but if present should always be linked to the root by '_'.

5.1. The root

The root is three digits long for *matrices* and *vectors*, at least six digits for *single series*. Digits 4 and 5 are left open for future extensions of the root. The first digit in the three-digit root is in CAPS for a matrix (e.g. '*A*') and small (e.g. '*a*') for a vector. All other remaining digits of the root after the first one are in CAPS for *current prices* and small for *constant prices*. We have more constant price series in the input-output model than current price series.

The meaning of the first digit of the root is as follows:

a: intermediate
f: final
c: private or household consumption
g: public or governmental
m: imports
i: investment
n: iNventory changes
x: eXports
h: otHer final demand
o: output
v: value added
w: wages
l: other Labour income and alike (social security contributions)
u: operating sUrplus
s: subsidies
t: indirect Taxes
d: depreciation
r: other or Residual of value added
k: capital stock
e: employment
p: productivity
y: income
z: discrepancy
d: Domestic *demand* distinguished from domestic d as *origin* of goods.

So final demand has $f(c,g,i,n,x,h,z)$; *m* stands for imports, value added has $v(w,l,u,t,s,d,r)$, *o* stands for output and *k* for capital stock while *e* indicates employment and *p* productivity. The final demand minus imports, much used in input-output analysis, has to be formed by the *f* as first digit; as explained later the second cannot be *m* (imported) nor *d* (domestic), so we propose *fim* standing for **f**inal demand m**i**nus **im**ports.

The meaning of the second digit in the root indicates either the origin of the goods and services, e.g. :

m: for iMported
d: for Domestic
t: for Total = imported + domestic.

The operation done on the series involved:

p: plus (+),
i: mInus (−)
o: over meaning an element-by-element division
x: meaning an element-by-element multiplication.

So to give the vector in constant prices of total resources = output + imports we can use the name *opm*, another free character to help the user to remember the name easily.

The meaning of the last digit in the root is:

t or ***T***: if the vector or matrix represents an *aggregate or a total*. In the simple model only the total series can be included, but at a later phase detail may be added by the builder, e.g. for household consumption, governmental consumption, investment, etc. The series ending with *t* in the root will always continue to exist and the detail will be added to the root by '_*p*' where *p* stands for partition in that root (see later: suffixes) So we have *fdt* for the final demand domestic total vector in constant prices, *fmt* for the final demand imported total in constant prices and *ftt* for the sum of *fmt* and *fdt*.

tot or ***TOT***: in the case of the *calculated total* of a vector – of which the root may or may not already be ending in at (like *fdt, fmt, ftt* defined above-, then the word 'tot' is added to the root to stress the fact that this single series is a vector (1 × 1) in vam software, e.g. *fdttot, fmttot, ftttot*.

5.2. *The prefixes*

The use of prefixes should be seen as types that are made on the same root, e.g.:

*p*_ for prices and deflator, p90_out would stand for 1990-based output price indices, and p89_xtt for 1989-based export prices;
*c*_ for coefficients, so *c_Att* would be the technical coefficient matrix, *c_Amt* the import coefficient matrix and *c_Adt* the domestic coefficient matrix;
*s*_ for shares, so *s_ctt* would be the budget shares for household consumption based on the constant prices;
*d*_ for percentage changes; and
*g*_ for growth rates.

5.3. *The suffixes*

In general suffixes should be seen as subcategories of the root, e.g. partitions, or other details of a group:

- *_p*: for a partition of the root meaning that the sum over all '*_p*' for the same root will give the total for this root (always goes together with a series ending in *t* in the third digit of the root);
- *_d*: for detail of the root that is not a partition; and
- *_g*: for groups in the root with overlapping possibilities.

Other usage will be added later. The basic understandings for naming conventions can be compared to the grammar rules in a language. There will, however, as in every language, be some exceptions to the rules. We tried to minimize these.

6. GUI

This section presents some of the results already achieved, and highlights the development going on in the Compass GUI part of the project. There are a number of very senior IO model-builders unable to approach the performance of a junior person with no economic training, no database understanding but only standard user interface techniques. In less than one hour the junior person outperformed all of them, reading in IO tables for 10 different countries for four years each, domestic and imported flows, and outputting all those data to the application software in machine-readable form. The reason was that the possible actions on each object were clear from the graphical environment settings. In particular the display objects, the action objects and the clicking of the objects informed the user (but not the so-called specialist) of all possibilities and options.

The user can perform mouse actions (all clicking, dragging and dropping) and keyboard actions (alphanumerical input, short keys, and hot key and function key input) all conforming to the Windows standard. He is presented standard Windows user interfaces such as *edit lines, drop down and combo boxes, check boxes, tabs and so on*. In particular the use of the shift key and the Ctrl key is normalized on Windows. This together with a standard menu and toolbar approach allows any new user with Windows experience to navigate through the application with any prior information and most of the training to be done by Windows.

Figure 2-1 represents the conceptual design of the COMPASS database. Meta data are the key to an integrated relational database based on an object-oriented principle. The need for meta data stems from the following factors:

(1) Various organizations compile statistical data sets, and very often definitions, measuring units, etc., are not an integral part of the numerical information.

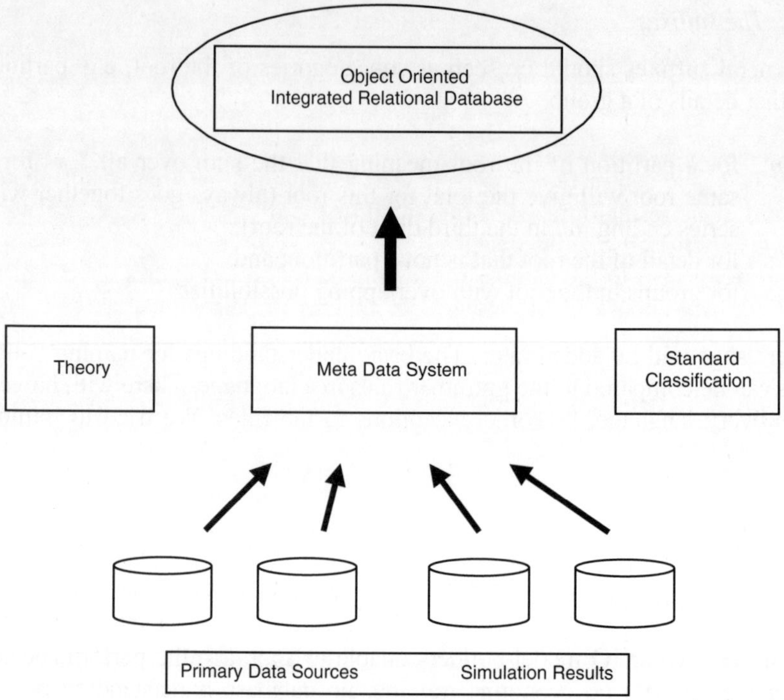

Figure 2-1. Conceptual scheme of COMPASS database.

(2) Data are published with various reporting intervals, such as monthly, quarterly, annual, five-year intervals, or varying intervals.
(3) Data take various forms such as matrix, vector, or scalar and even within the same kinds of data they come in various formats.
(4) They are made available in various information media, including printed form, floppy disks, CD-ROMs, and on-line service.
(5) Data refer to various measuring units such as value (yen, dollar, ECU, etc.; current prices vs. constant prices, etc.; thousand or million or billion, etc.), physical unit (ton, toe or ton of oil equivalent, cubic metres, litres, barrels, kcal, kW, kWh, joule, etc.), index (with various base years), ratio (income per capita, output per hour, etc.), among others.

Meta data are needed to fill statistical discrepancies among data sets, to establish linkage among them, and to enable data conversion. It is often necessary to bridge conceptual differences among data sets (examples are sample survey *vs.* aggregate value such as household data *vs.* national accounts data; establishment base *vs.* activity base *vs.* commodity base, such as production based on business survey, input-output tables, and international trade).

The COMPASS database is a relational database in the true sense of the word: each data point is stored in the database management system and is accessible in any output format. Thus, for example, one can look at the input-output data in a matrix form for a particular point in time or in a time-series of a particular cell or a vector. This provides enormous flexibility for the data users. This is in contrast to many so-called 'databases' that are actually sequential files. This results in a fixed-output format and poses a severe limit to the cross-disciplinary use of the data.

The user access to the database is facilitated by GUI. Figure 2-2 shows how the users may choose from among data spheres (input-output, macro-finance, trade, and energy; ENE is chosen in the example) and regions. By clicking on Show Result, the users have easy access to the data. It is noted that, in the case of COMPASS, data generated by simulation are also stored in the database and can be accessed in exactly the same manner as the historical series. Needless to say, the data thus obtained can be exported to spreadsheets. Figure 2-3 shows model-building steps. As above, users choose from among the spheres and regions (country/region lists are provided; Japan is chosen in the example). The model-building process in broken down into easy-to-understand steps (in the case of a macro-financial model, they consist of the following:

(1) prepare model data: according to model specification, standard query language (SQL) is automatically issued and data are retrieved from the database;
(2) check model data: data are checked for accounting/definitional consistency;
(3) model final demand: final demand equations are run;
(4) model income: likewise, income equations are run;
(5) model balance of payments: balance of payments equations are run that link macroeconomic variables to financial ones;
(6) model monetary market: financial equations are run.

These steps vary according to the spheres to look at because model structures are different, but principles are the same. This is followed by 'Make Stand-alone Model', 'Make COMPASS Linkage Run', and 'Show Results'. In the process, essential files in each step are shown so that users are able to look at individual programs. They are the files actually used in the model-building and simulation runs so it is possible to alter the programs, including the years to look at, functional forms, logical flow, etc. Thus, although COMPASS is a fairly large system with complex logical flow and data manipulation, it is also a transparent system in which each step is open to users.

Figures 2-4 to 2-7 are the results of the data query in respective fields. Figure 2-8 shows that, behind the scenes, SQL is issued by the system to gain access to the data. User query through the GUI is translated into SQL automatically, and data are retrieved from the database that are stored on hard disks.

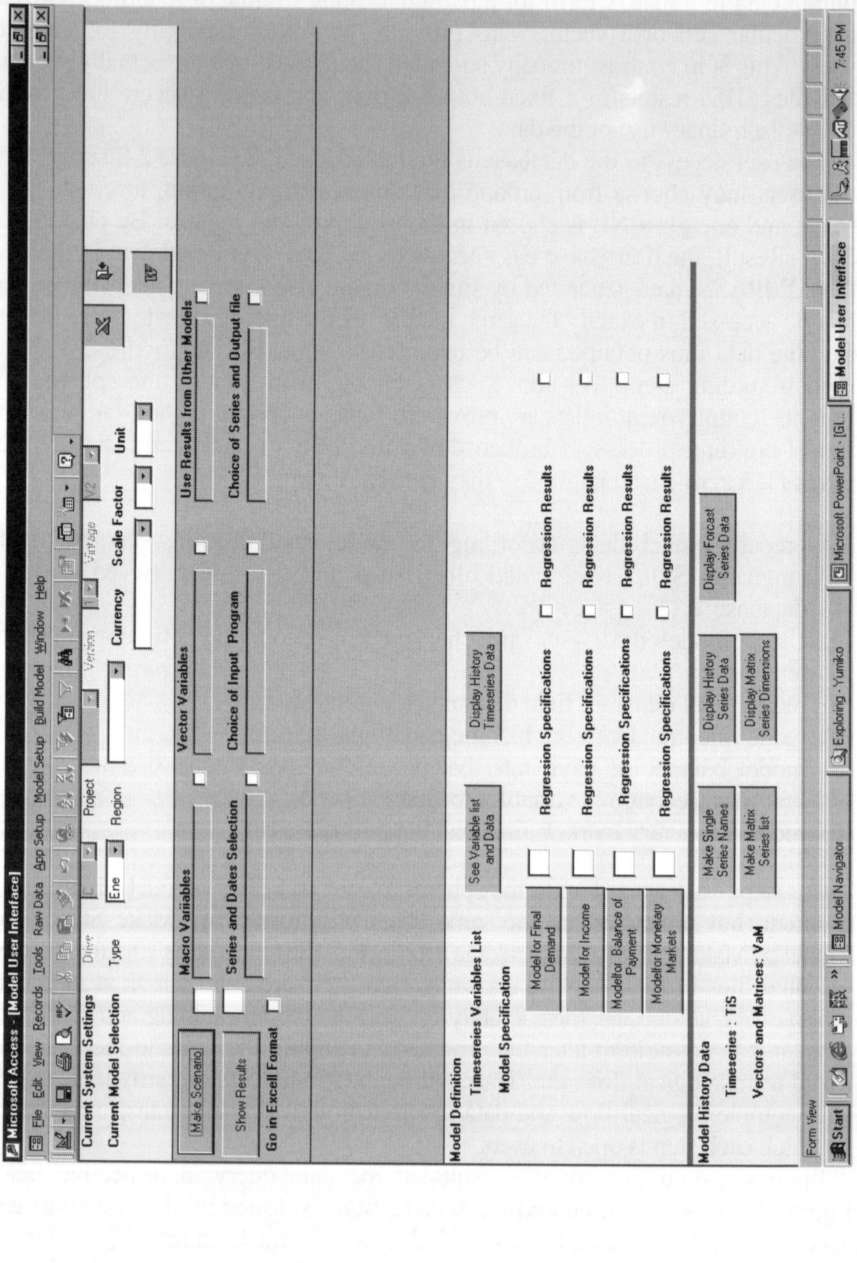

Figure 2-2. GUI for database access.

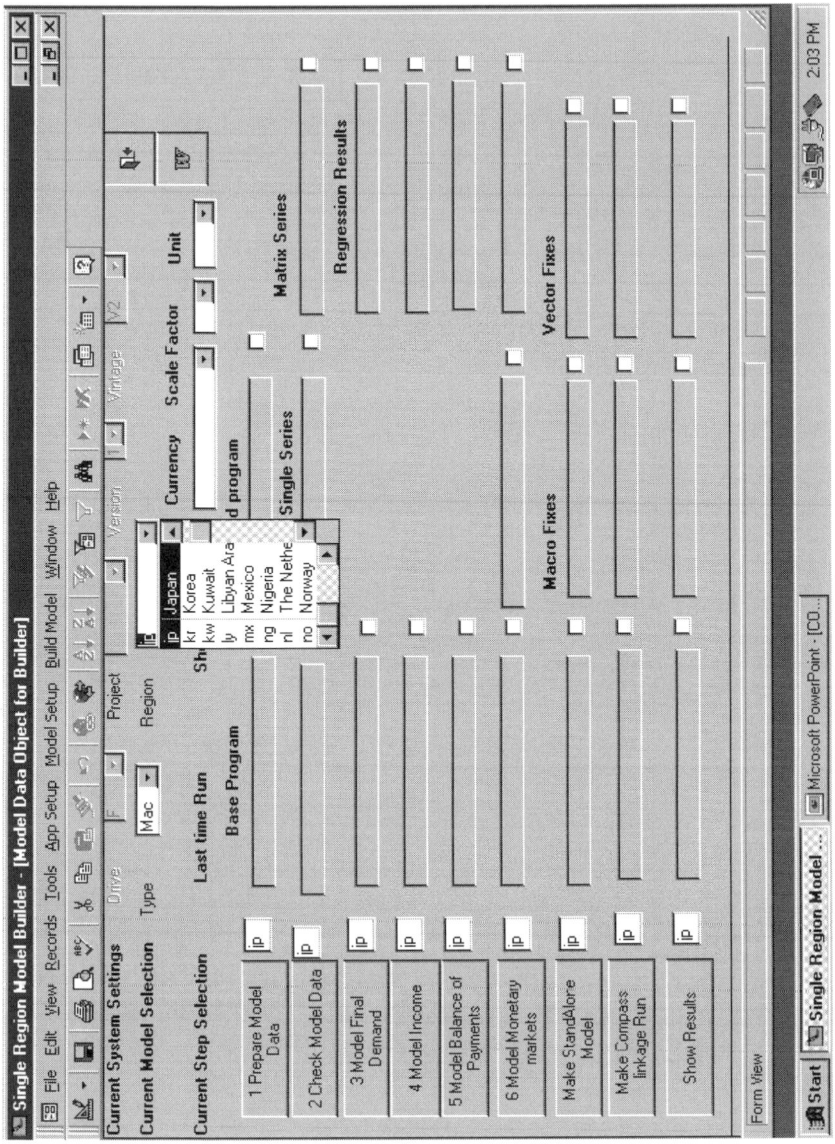

Figure 2-3. GUI for model building.

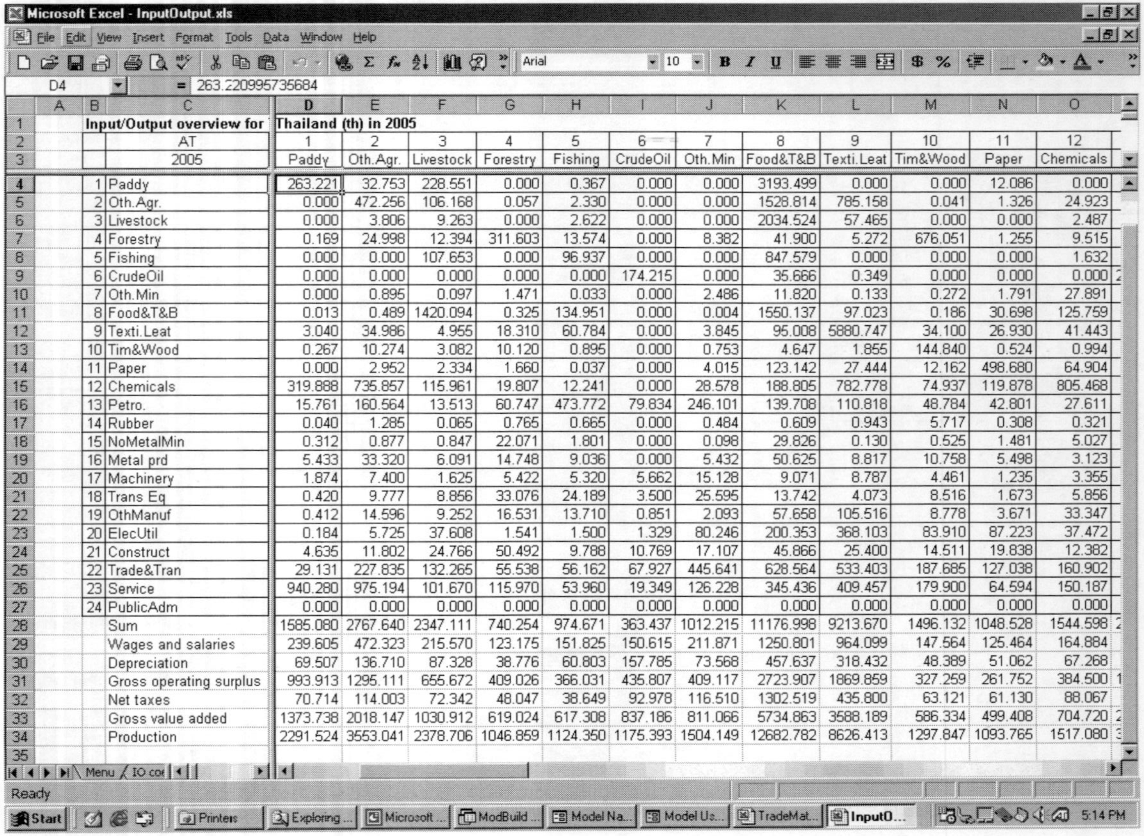

		1	2	3	4	5	6	7	8	9	10	11	12
	Input/Output overview for AT 2005	Paddy	Oth.Agr.	Livestock	Forestry	Fishing	CrudeOil	Oth.Min	Food&T&B	Texti.Leat	Tim&Wood	Paper	Chemicals
1	Paddy	263.221	32.753	228.551	0.000	0.367	0.000	0.000	3193.499	0.000	0.000	12.086	0.000
2	Oth.Agr.	0.000	472.256	106.168	0.057	2.330	0.000	0.000	1528.814	785.158	0.041	1.326	24.923
3	Livestock	0.000	3.806	9.263	0.000	2.622	0.000	0.000	2034.524	57.465	0.000	0.000	2.487
4	Forestry	0.169	24.998	12.394	311.603	13.574	0.000	8.382	41.900	5.272	676.051	1.255	9.515
5	Fishing	0.000	0.000	107.653	0.000	96.937	0.000	0.000	847.579	0.000	0.000	0.000	1.632
6	CrudeOil	0.000	0.000	0.000	0.000	0.000	174.215	0.000	35.666	0.349	0.000	0.000	0.000
7	Oth.Min	0.000	0.895	0.097	1.471	0.033	0.000	2.486	11.820	0.133	0.272	1.791	27.891
8	Food&T&B	0.013	0.489	1420.094	0.325	134.951	0.000	0.004	1550.137	97.023	0.186	30.698	125.759
9	Texti.Leat	3.040	34.986	4.955	18.310	60.784	0.000	3.845	95.008	5880.747	34.100	26.930	41.443
10	Tim&Wood	0.267	10.274	3.082	10.120	0.895	0.000	0.753	4.647	1.855	144.840	0.524	0.994
11	Paper	0.000	2.952	2.334	1.660	0.037	0.000	4.015	123.142	27.444	12.162	498.680	64.904
12	Chemicals	319.888	735.857	115.961	19.807	12.241	0.000	28.578	188.805	782.778	74.937	119.878	805.468
13	Petro.	15.761	160.564	13.513	60.747	473.772	79.834	246.101	139.708	110.818	48.784	42.801	27.611
14	Rubber	0.040	1.285	0.065	0.765	0.665	0.000	0.484	0.609	0.943	5.717	0.308	0.321
15	NoMetalMin	0.312	0.877	0.847	22.071	1.801	0.000	0.098	29.826	0.130	0.525	1.481	5.027
16	Metal prd	5.433	33.320	6.091	14.748	9.036	0.000	5.432	50.625	8.817	10.758	5.498	3.123
17	Machinery	1.874	7.400	1.625	5.422	5.320	5.662	15.128	9.071	8.787	4.461	1.235	3.355
18	Trans Eq	0.420	9.777	8.856	33.076	24.189	3.500	25.595	13.742	4.073	8.516	1.673	5.856
19	OthManuf	0.412	14.596	9.252	16.531	13.710	0.851	2.093	57.658	105.516	8.778	3.671	33.347
20	ElecUtil	0.184	5.725	37.608	1.541	1.500	1.329	80.246	200.353	368.103	83.910	87.223	37.472
21	Construct	4.635	11.802	24.766	50.492	9.788	10.769	17.107	45.866	25.400	14.511	19.838	12.382
22	Trade&Tran	29.131	227.835	132.265	55.538	56.162	67.927	445.641	628.564	533.403	187.685	127.038	160.902
23	Service	940.280	975.194	101.670	115.970	53.960	19.349	126.228	345.436	409.457	179.900	64.594	150.187
24	PublicAdm	0.000	0.000	0.000	0.000	0.000	0.000	0.000	0.000	0.000	0.000	0.000	0.000
	Sum	1585.080	2767.640	2347.111	740.254	974.671	363.437	1012.215	11176.998	9213.670	1496.132	1048.528	1544.598
	Wages and salaries	239.605	472.323	215.570	123.175	151.825	150.615	211.871	1250.801	964.099	147.564	125.464	164.884
	Depreciation	69.507	136.710	87.328	38.776	60.803	157.785	73.568	457.637	318.432	48.389	51.062	67.268
	Gross operating surplus	993.913	1295.111	655.672	409.026	366.031	435.807	409.117	2723.907	1869.859	327.259	261.752	384.500
	Net taxes	70.714	114.003	72.342	48.047	38.649	92.978	116.510	1302.519	435.800	63.121	61.130	88.067
	Gross value added	1373.738	2018.147	1030.912	619.024	617.308	837.186	811.066	5734.863	3588.189	586.334	499.408	704.720
	Production	2291.524	3553.041	2378.706	1046.859	1124.350	1175.393	1504.149	12682.782	8626.413	1297.847	1093.765	1517.080

Figure 2-4. Sample output of the COMPASS database: input-output table simulation for Thailand in 2005.

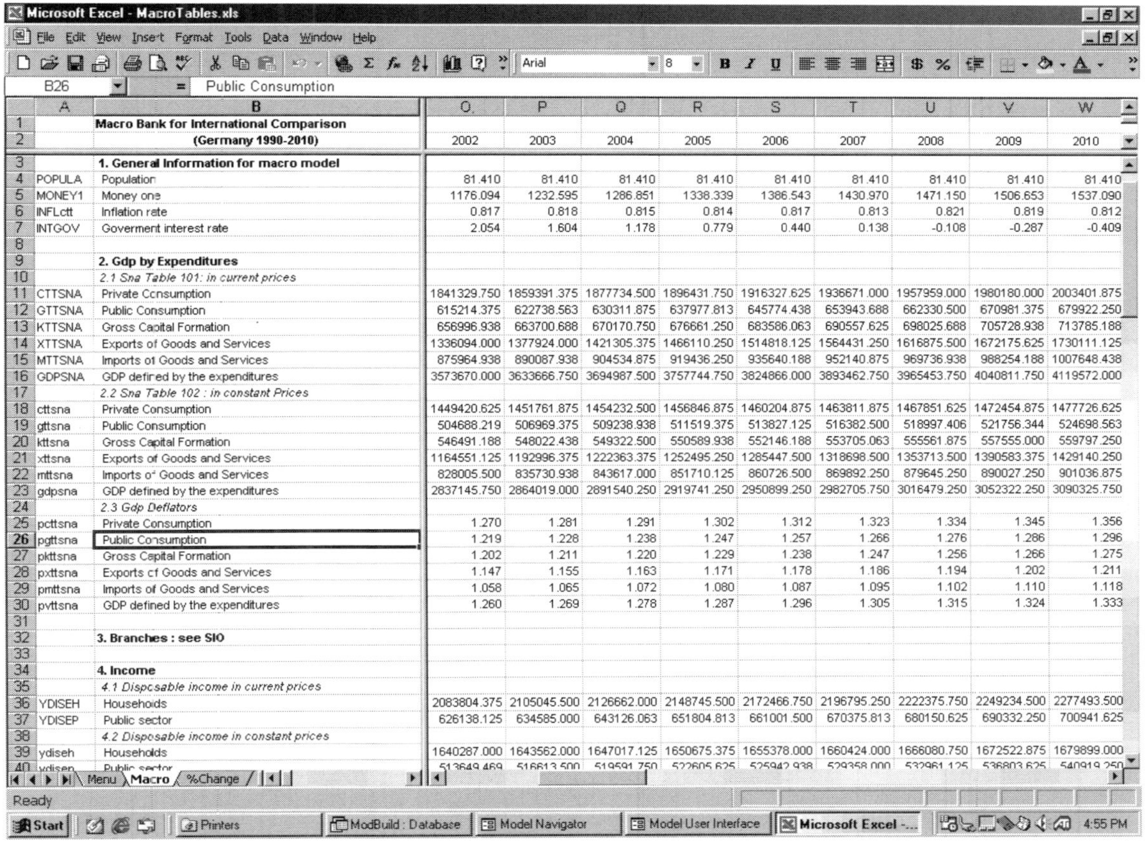

		2002	2003	2004	2005	2006	2007	2008	2009	2010
	Macro Bank for International Comparison (Germany 1990-2010)									
	1. General Information for macro model									
POPULA	Population	81.410	81.410	81.410	81.410	81.410	81.410	81.410	81.410	81.410
MONEY1	Money one	1176.094	1232.595	1286.851	1338.339	1386.543	1430.970	1471.150	1506.653	1537.090
INFLctt	Inflation rate	0.817	0.818	0.815	0.814	0.817	0.813	0.821	0.819	0.812
INTGOV	Goverment interest rate	2.054	1.604	1.178	0.779	0.440	0.138	-0.108	-0.287	-0.409
	2. Gdp by Expenditures									
	2.1 Sna Table 101: in current prices									
CTTSNA	Private Consumption	1841329.750	1859391.375	1877734.500	1896431.750	1916327.625	1936671.000	1957959.000	1980180.000	2003401.875
GTTSNA	Public Consumption	615214.375	622738.563	630311.875	637977.813	645774.438	653943.688	662330.500	670981.375	679922.250
KTTSNA	Gross Capital Formation	656996.938	663700.688	670170.750	676661.250	683586.063	690557.625	698025.688	705728.938	713785.188
XTTSNA	Exports of Goods and Services	1336094.000	1377924.000	1421305.375	1466110.250	1514818.125	1564431.250	1616875.500	1672175.625	1730111.125
MTTSNA	Imports of Goods and Services	875964.938	890087.938	904534.875	919436.250	935640.188	952140.875	969736.938	988254.188	1007648.438
GDPSNA	GDP defined by the expenditures	3573670.000	3633666.750	3694987.500	3757744.750	3824866.000	3893462.750	3965453.750	4040811.750	4119572.000
	2.2 Sna Table 102 : in constant Prices									
cttsna	Private Consumption	1449420.625	1451761.875	1454232.500	1456846.875	1460204.875	1463811.875	1467851.625	1472454.875	1477726.625
gttsna	Public Consumption	504688.219	506969.375	509238.938	511519.375	513827.125	516382.500	518997.406	521756.344	524698.563
kttsna	Gross Capital Formation	546491.188	548022.438	549322.500	550589.938	552146.188	553705.063	555561.875	557555.000	559797.250
xttsna	Exports of Goods and Services	1164551.125	1192996.375	1222363.375	1252495.250	1285447.500	1318698.500	1353713.500	1390583.375	1429140.250
mttsna	Imports of Goods and Services	828005.500	835730.938	843617.000	851710.125	860726.500	869892.250	879645.250	890027.250	901036.875
gdpsna	GDP defined by the expenditures	2837145.750	2864019.000	2891540.250	2919741.250	2950899.250	2982705.750	3016479.250	3052322.250	3090325.750
	2.3 Gdp Deflators									
pcttsna	Private Consumption	1.270	1.281	1.291	1.302	1.312	1.323	1.334	1.345	1.356
pgttsna	Public Consumption	1.219	1.228	1.238	1.247	1.257	1.266	1.276	1.286	1.296
pkttsna	Gross Capital Formation	1.202	1.211	1.220	1.229	1.238	1.247	1.256	1.266	1.275
pxttsna	Exports of Goods and Services	1.147	1.155	1.163	1.171	1.178	1.186	1.194	1.202	1.211
pmttsna	Imports of Goods and Services	1.058	1.065	1.072	1.080	1.087	1.095	1.102	1.110	1.118
pvttsna	GDP defined by the expenditures	1.260	1.269	1.278	1.287	1.296	1.305	1.315	1.324	1.333
	3. Branches : see SIO									
	4. Income									
	4.1 Disposable income in current prices									
YDISEH	Households	2083804.375	2105045.500	2126662.000	2148745.500	2172466.750	2196795.250	2222375.750	2249234.500	2277493.500
YDISEP	Public sector	626138.125	634585.000	643126.063	651804.813	661001.500	670375.813	680150.625	690332.250	700941.625
	4.2 Disposable income in constant prices									
ydiseh	Households	1640287.000	1643562.000	1647017.125	1650675.375	1655378.000	1660424.000	1666080.750	1672522.875	1679899.000
ydisep	Public sector	513649.469	516613.500	519591.750	522605.625	525942.938	529358.000	532961.125	536803.625	540919.250

Figure 2-5. Sample output of the COMPASS database: macroeconomics simulation for Germany to 2010.

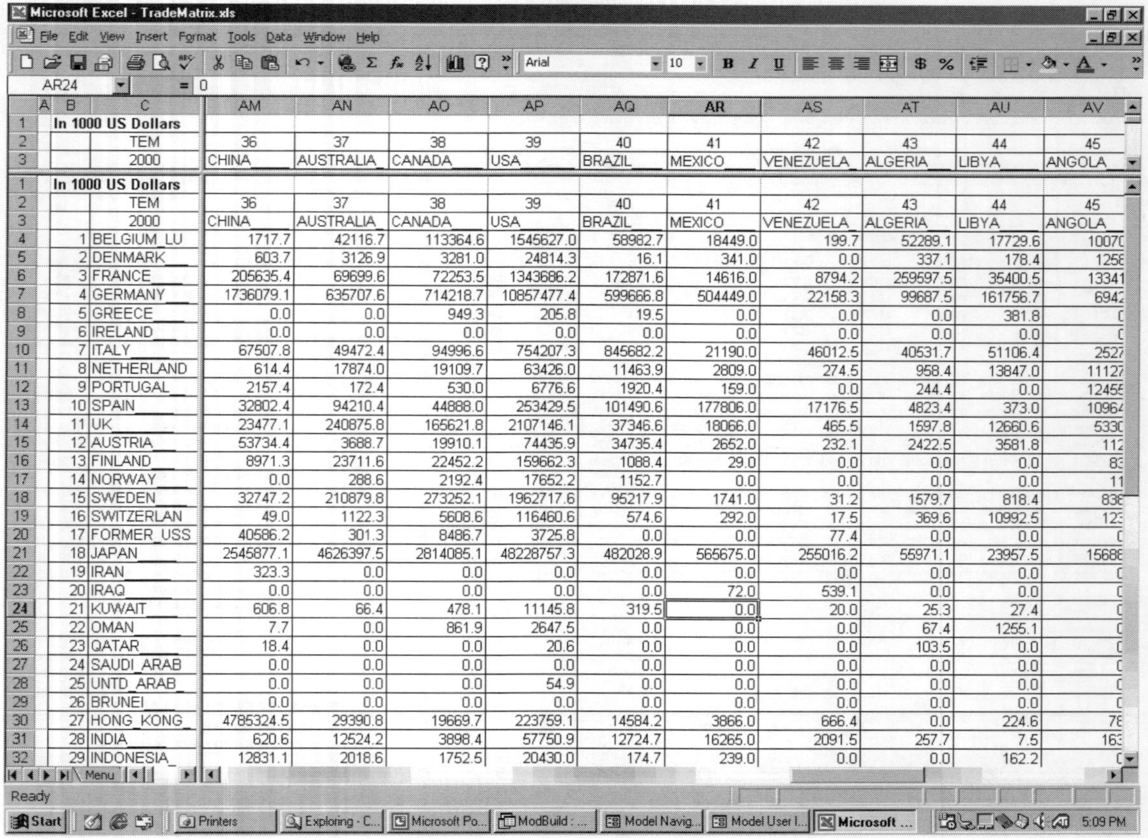

	B	C	AM	AN	AO	AP	AQ	AR	AS	AT	AU	AV
1	In 1000 US Dollars											
2		TEM	36	37	38	39	40	41	42	43	44	45
3		2000	CHINA	AUSTRALIA	CANADA	USA	BRAZIL	MEXICO	VENEZUELA	ALGERIA	LIBYA	ANGOLA
4	1	BELGIUM_LU	1717.7	42116.7	113364.6	1545627.0	58982.7	18449.0	199.7	52289.1	17729.6	1007(
5	2	DENMARK	603.7	3126.9	3281.0	24814.3	16.1	341.0	0.0	337.1	178.4	125(
6	3	FRANCE	205635.4	69699.6	72253.5	1343686.2	172871.6	14616.0	8794.2	259597.5	35400.5	13341
7	4	GERMANY	1736079.1	635707.6	714218.7	10857477.4	599666.8	504449.0	22158.3	99687.5	161756.7	694:
8	5	GREECE	0.0	0.0	949.3	205.8	19.5	0.0	0.0	0.0	381.8	(
9	6	IRELAND	0.0	0.0	0.0	0.0	0.0	0.0	0.0	0.0	0.0	(
10	7	ITALY	67507.8	49472.4	94996.6	754207.3	845682.2	21190.0	46012.5	40531.7	51106.4	252
11	8	NETHERLAND	614.4	17874.0	19109.7	63426.0	11463.9	2809.0	274.5	958.4	13847.0	1112
12	9	PORTUGAL	2157.4	172.4	530.0	6776.6	1920.4	159.0	0.0	244.4	0.0	1245
13	10	SPAIN	32802.4	94210.4	44888.0	253429.5	101490.6	177806.0	17176.5	4823.4	373.0	1096
14	11	UK	23477.1	240875.8	165621.8	2107146.1	37346.6	18066.0	465.5	1597.8	12660.6	533(
15	12	AUSTRIA	53734.4	3688.7	19910.1	74435.9	34735.4	2652.0	232.1	2422.5	3581.8	11
16	13	FINLAND	8971.3	23711.6	22452.2	159662.3	1088.4	29.0	0.0	0.0	0.0	8
17	14	NORWAY	0.0	288.6	2192.4	17652.2	1152.7	0.0	0.0	0.0	0.0	1
18	15	SWEDEN	32747.2	210879.8	273252.1	1962717.6	95217.9	1741.0	31.2	1579.7	818.4	83
19	16	SWITZERLAN	49.0	1122.3	5608.6	116460.6	574.6	292.0	17.5	369.6	10992.5	12
20	17	FORMER_USS	40586.2	301.3	8486.7	3725.8	0.0	0.0	77.4	0.0	0.0	(
21	18	JAPAN	2545877.1	4626397.5	2814085.1	48228757.3	482028.9	565675.0	255016.2	55971.1	23957.5	1568
22	19	IRAN	323.3	0.0	0.0	0.0	0.0	0.0	0.0	0.0	0.0	(
23	20	IRAQ	0.0	0.0	0.0	0.0	0.0	72.0	539.1	0.0	0.0	(
24	21	KUWAIT	606.8	66.4	478.1	11145.8	319.5	0.0	20.0	25.3	27.4	(
25	22	OMAN	7.7	0.0	861.9	2647.5	0.0	0.0	0.0	67.4	1255.1	(
26	23	QATAR	18.4	0.0	0.0	20.6	0.0	0.0	0.0	103.5	0.0	(
27	24	SAUDI_ARAB	0.0	0.0	0.0	0.0	0.0	0.0	0.0	0.0	0.0	(
28	25	UNTD_ARAB	0.0	0.0	0.0	54.9	0.0	0.0	0.0	0.0	0.0	(
29	26	BRUNEI	0.0	0.0	0.0	0.0	0.0	0.0	0.0	0.0	0.0	(
30	27	HONG_KONG	4785324.5	29390.8	19669.7	223759.1	14584.2	3866.0	666.4	0.0	224.6	7
31	28	INDIA	620.6	12524.2	3898.4	57750.9	12724.7	16265.0	2091.5	257.7	7.5	16
32	29	INDONESIA	12831.1	2018.6	1752.5	20430.0	174.7	239.0	0.0	0.0	162.2	(

Figure 2-6. Sample output of the COMPASS database: trade matrix simulation for motor vehicles in 2000.

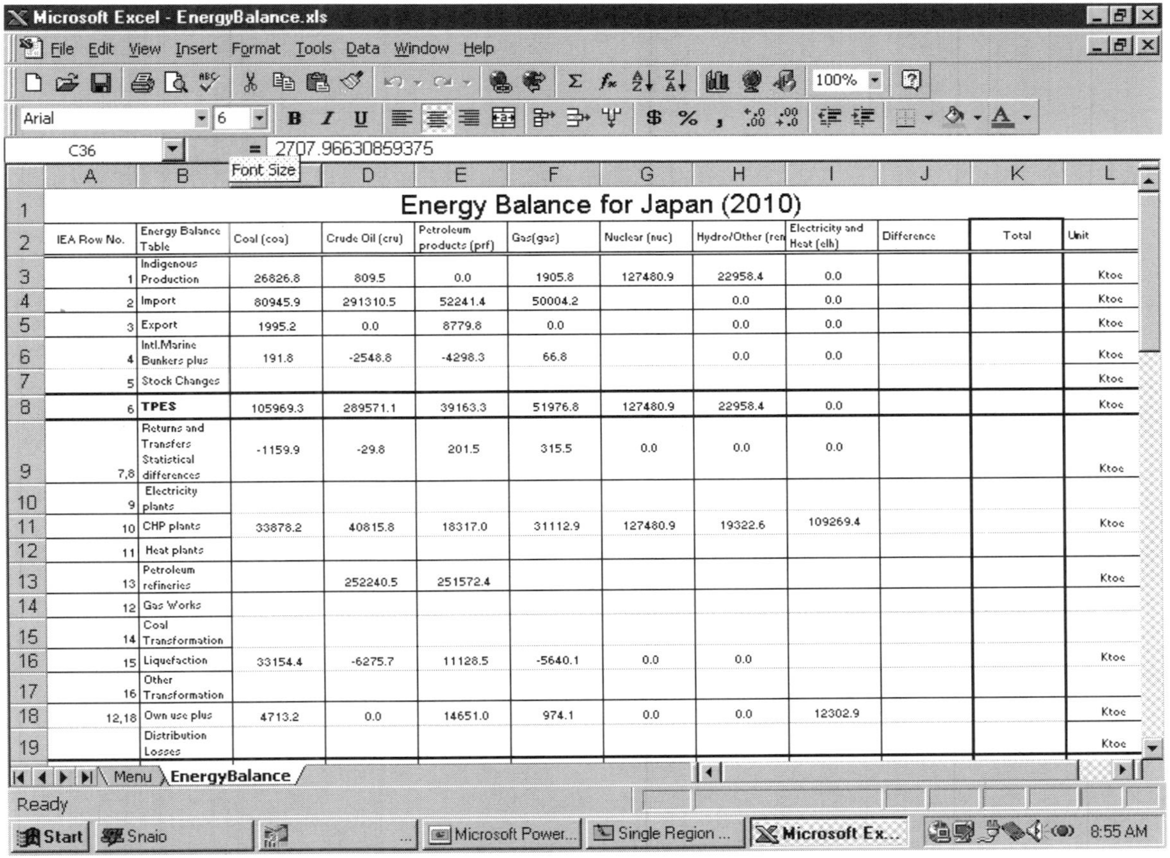

Energy Balance for Japan (2010)

IEA Row No.	Energy Balance Table	Coal (coa)	Crude Oil (cru)	Petroleum products (prf)	Gas(gas)	Nuclear (nuc)	Hydro/Other (ren	Electricity and Heat (elh)	Difference	Total	Unit
1	Indigenous Production	26826.8	809.5	0.0	1905.8	127480.9	22958.4	0.0			Ktoe
2	Import	80945.9	291310.5	52241.4	50004.2		0.0	0.0			Ktoe
3	Export	1995.2	0.0	8779.8	0.0		0.0	0.0			Ktoe
4	Intl.Marine Bunkers plus	191.8	-2548.8	-4298.3	66.8		0.0	0.0			Ktoe
5	Stock Changes										Ktoe
6	**TPES**	105969.3	289571.1	39163.3	51976.8	127480.9	22958.4	0.0			Ktoe
7,8	Returns and Transfers Statistical differences	-1159.9	-29.8	201.5	315.5	0.0	0.0	0.0			Ktoe
9	Electricity plants										
10	CHP plants	33878.2	40815.8	18317.0	31112.9	127480.9	19322.6	109269.4			Ktoe
11	Heat plants										
13	Petroleum refineries		252240.5	251572.4							Ktoe
12	Gas Works										
14	Coal Transformation										
15	Liquefaction	33154.4	-6275.7	11128.5	-5640.1	0.0	0.0				Ktoe
16	Other Transformation										
12,18	Own use plus	4713.2	0.0	14651.0	974.1	0.0	0.0	12302.9			Ktoe
	Distribution Losses										Ktoe

Figure 2-7. Sample output of the COMPASS database: energy balance simulation for Japan in 2010.

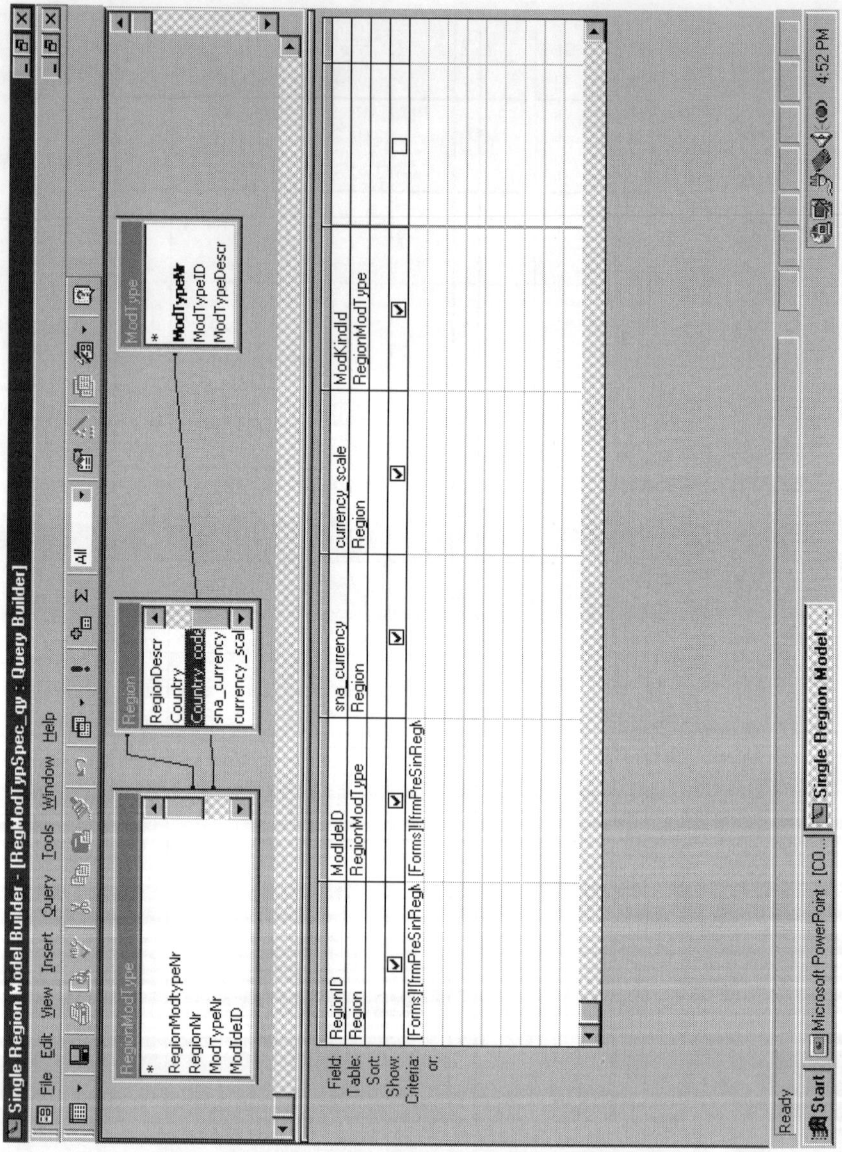

Figure 2-8. Database query.

7. Final words

It is demonstrated in this chapter that an object-oriented database and modelling system for COMPASS serves as:

(1) Model-building tool covering from a single country/region model to a globally linked model.
(2) Scenario description tool allowing changes in exogenous/policy variables, including overriding results from simulation runs.
(3) Simulation tool by which projection results are obtained and compared taking international and inter-industrial repercussions into account.
(4) Accounting tool where original data and/or simulation results can be put into an accounting framework such as System of National Accounts (SNA) and balance of payments, System of Input-Output, Energy Balances, and Trade Matrices where internal consistency can be examined. In other words, the iteration process is repeated until accounting consistency is obtained throughout the global system.

The database and simulation infrastructure such as this is indispensable to make a research project of the scope and magnitude of COMPASS. The advantages of the system are demonstrated in the following chapters.

3
IO, macro-finance, and trade model specification

BERND MEYER and CHRISTIAN LUTZ

1. Introduction

This chapter provides an overview of the model-structure of the economic part of the system focusing on the regional linkages. COMPASS is a world system, but it has a special focus on the APEC region. COMPASS is the only disaggregated model with double international linkage consisting of a multisectoral trade model and a linkage of the capital flows. The input-output structure will easily allow its detailed extension to energy and environmental modelling. This will be the third international linkage. This will be described in a later chapter.

We need information concerning the policy options that can avoid environmental catastrophes as well as conflict between nations. There seems to be no doubt that in the 21st century Asia will be the region with leading economic growth rates. This will have severe consequences for worldwide energy demand and global warming. COMPASS is modelling the economy–energy–environmental interdependencies worldwide, but with focus on the APEC countries. COMPASS will be an instrument that can be used to answer any questions which arise.

The main difference between COMPASS and other global economic-environmental models (see for example Edmonds *et al.*, 1994; Burniaux *et al.*, 1992) derives from the specific historical question which COMPASS addresses itself. The specific structure of production and consumption in the individual countries has to be described based on actual performance of the countries in focus, which needs an econometric analysis of the behaviour of the agents. This forbids open parametric modelling as is usual with CGE modelling.

Another important difference between COMPASS and other global models is the relationship between the macro-models and the input-output models. The usual way is a top-down modelling as in the GIO model (Duchin and Smyshlyaev, 1995). In this case the components of final demand are determined by the macro-systems and thc input-output model gives only the sectoral structure. This means that structural change has no influence on final demand and it further produces inconsistency, because the solution of the input-output system implies value added, which may differ from the macro estimated GNP (see Grassini, 1995). COMPASS has a bottom-up structure, in which the generation of income in the sectors of the economy adds up to macroeconomic income figures.

K. Uno (ed.), Economy–Energy–Environment Simulation, 55–68.

A third difference concerns the linkage between the regions. The trade linkage is usually done in the following way: imports for good *i* are summed up to a world import of good *i*, and a region's export is a constant or variable share of world import (Nyhus, 1991; Duchin and Smyshlyaev, 1995). Instead of this procedure we will establish a multisectoral bilateral trade model with endogenized shares such as the one constructed by Ma (1996), which was used for the first time as part of the INFORUM International System (Nyhus *et al.*, 1996).

The linkage of capital flows is neglected in most models. There is a big variety of modelling approaches (Klein and Krelle, 1983) because with the full representations of the balance of payments of the regions the question of endogenization of exchange rates arises. For COMPASS the link of the capital flows is very important, because the restrictions of a clearing global capital market have to underlie the forecast for the rapidly growing APEC countries. We will try a modelling that endogenizes the exchange raes and uses the US interest rate to equalize worldwide capital demand and supply.

2. The general architecture

A first view of the system from a distance, as shown in Figure 3-1, gives the impression of a wheel: its axis is given by the multisectoral bilateral trade model.

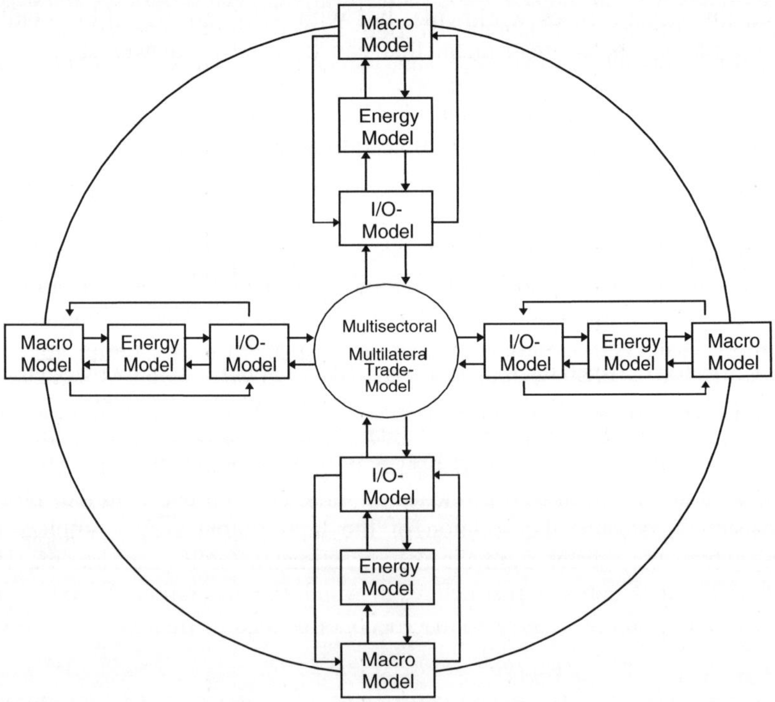

Figure 3-1. The Compass wheel.

The spokes are the country models consisting of an I/O model, an SNA (system of national accounts) system, and a financial model and their linkages between each other and the trade model. The tread is the linkage through the capital flows.

The trade model is based on trade matrices describing bilateral trade flows at the commodity levels. It obtains from each of the country models a vector of export prices and vector of import volumes, and it gives back to the country models a vector of export volumes and a vector of import prices.

The input-output model describes the production technology as reflected in the input structure of individual industrial activities at the disaggregated level. It gives the components of primary inputs such as labour income, operating surplus, depreciation, and indirect taxes and the vector of imports to the SNA system, where these streams are aggregated.

The SNA system depicts the redistribution of income between enterprises, government, households, and the rest of the world. It further calculates the aggregates of the components of final demand and gives them back to the input-output models. The SNA system receives the exports from the trade model and imports from the input-output model. It also obtains value added from the input-output model and computes disposable income and net lending figures, among others. The SNA system contains the balance of payments with exports and imports of goods and services and an explicitly modelled net flow of capital.

The financial model depicts the capital flows, the balance of the Central Bank, and the interest rates. The US interest rate is calculated by the condition that all capital flows sum up to zero. This is the condition which links all country models on the macro level, expressed by the 'tread' of the wheel in Figure 3-1.

3. The input-output models

The real import of good i $fm_i(\mathrm{t})$ (we omitted the country index) is depending on its relative price $p_i(\mathrm{t})/q_i(\mathrm{t})$ measured in the countries' currency and final demand $f_i(\mathrm{t})$ of good i:

$$fm_i(\mathrm{t}) = fm_i[p_i(\mathrm{t})/q_i(\mathrm{t}), f_i(\mathrm{t})] \tag{1}$$

By definition we obtain the vector of real final demand minus imports of finished goods. With D as the matrix of domestic input coefficients and y as the vector of real gross production we get:

$$y(\mathrm{t}) = [E - D(\mathrm{t})]^{-1} [f(\mathrm{t}) - fm(\mathrm{t})]; \quad E\text{: unit matrix} \tag{2}$$

The input coefficients are assumed to be exogenous variables, without losing generality to endogenize them as needed. The domestic input coefficient d_{ij} is defined as:

$$d_{ij}(\mathrm{t}) = a_{ij}(\mathrm{t}) * [1 - m_{ij}(\mathrm{t})] \tag{3}$$

a_{ij} is the technical coefficient and m_{ij} is its share of imports. The matrix AM of the coefficients for imported inputs has the elements:

$$am_{ij}(\mathrm{t}) = a_{ij}(\mathrm{t}) * m_{ij}(\mathrm{t}) \tag{4}$$

The relation between indirect taxes minus subsidies and real output may be constant:

$$T_j \cdot (t) = \alpha_j * y_j \cdot (t); \quad \alpha_j > 0 \tag{5}$$

The same hypothesis is assumed for depreciation

$$D_j \cdot (t) = \beta * y_j \cdot (t); \quad \beta_j > 0 \tag{6}$$

Wages w_j are depending on a macro-productivity term of the preceding period and the consumer price index of the last period.

$$w_j(t) = w_j[gnp(t-1)/H(t-1);\ p_c(t-1)] \tag{7}$$

H: total working hours
p_c: consumer price index
gnp: gross national product

The labour input (measured in hours) h_j is explained by the real wage rate, a time trend and gross production.

$$h_j(t) = h_j[w_j(t)/p_j(t), y_j(t), t] \tag{8}$$

The labour input coefficient is given by:

$$z_j(t) = h_j(t)/y_j(t) \tag{9}$$

and the salaries with:

$$l_j(t) = w_j(t) * h_j(t) \tag{10}$$

The vector of unit cost u is defined as:

$$u(t) = D'(t) * p(t) + AM'(t) * q(t) + Z(t) * w(t) + \alpha + \beta \tag{11}$$

D: matrix of domestic input coefficients
AM: matrix of input coefficients of imported goods
Z: diagonal matrix of labour input coefficients
w: vector of wages
α: vector of indirect taxes minus subsidies per unit of output
β: vector of depreciation per unit of output

The price of sector j is now dependent on its unit cost:

$$p_j(t) = p_j[u_j(t)] \tag{12}$$

This approach allows us to estimate different prices for the row of the input-output table. If the data allow, we could estimate different prices for final consumption and intermediate inputs, all explained in a regression by unit cost.

Now the balance of the columns of the input-output table can be used to calculate operating surplus g as a residual.

$$g_j(t) = p_j(t) * y_j(t) - u_j(t) * y_j(t) \tag{13}$$

Most of the industrialized countries in Asia, Europe, and North America are represented by an input-output model. The global economy can be considered to consist of layers of different economic activities, with different resource requirements and environmental implications. This is particularly important in that the model is capable of tracing the effect of structural change of the economies. It is widely known that industrial branches are characterized by widely diverse energy requirement per unit output, implying that environmental impact may be mitigated through structural change.

The dynamic input-output models have its inputs final demand items such as consumption and investment generated in the macro models. The export vector is given by the trade model. The import vector is determined by the final demand of good (*i*) and the relative price measured in the country's currency. The sector disaggregation of final demand vector is treated as share variables. The input coefficients in the basic model are treated as exogenous variables, but are subject to various policy experiments including treatment as endogenously determined variables (e.g., depending on energy prices) or exogenous scenario variables (e.g., diffusion of a particular technology in the future or international technology transfer affecting input coefficients).

4. The macro-financial models

The macro models refer to a combined SNA-financial framework. The SNA system receives generated value added from the input-output system, distributing it to private households, enterprises, government, and the rest of the world. Disposable income is then calculated, which in turn determines the levels of consumption. The model has investment functions. The cost component of GDP such as indirect taxes, depreciation, wages and operating surplus are obtained from the input-output model. Where detailed information is lacking, a simplified model framework (macro simulator) has been prepared, largely based on trend information.

The financial model converts the balance of current account *SUR* into dollars dividing it by the exchange rate of the countries' currency per dollar:

$$CUR^l(\mathrm{t}) = SUR^l(\mathrm{t})/e^l(\mathrm{t}) \tag{14}$$

The balance of capital account is dependent on the balance of current account and the interest rate and the rate of inflation of country *l* and of other countries, which are linked by autonomous capital flows with country *l*.

$$CAP_l(\mathrm{t}) = CAP^l[CUR^l(\mathrm{t}), rl(\mathrm{t}), r^w(\mathrm{t}), \pi^l(\mathrm{t}), \pi^w(\mathrm{t})] \tag{15}$$

r^l = interest rate of country *l*
r^w = interest rate, country *w*
π^l = rate of inflation, country *l*
π^w = rate of inflation, country *w*

The difference of inflation rates shall be a proxy for exchange rate expectations. The standard specification for the exchange rate e of country l is:

$$e^l(\mathrm{t}) = e[r^l(\mathrm{t}), r^w(\mathrm{t}), \pi^l(\mathrm{t}), \pi^w(\mathrm{t})] \quad (16)$$

In some countries additionally the exchange rate of a dominating currency such as DM or the yen are important variables. The relation between the net foreign assets of the country and its reserve money may also influence the market valuation of the currency. In very rapidly inflating countries the relation between the gdp deflator and the US gdp deflator gives a very good explanation of the exchange rate.

The overall balance in dollars is given by definition:

$$ALL^l(\mathrm{t}) = CUR^l(\mathrm{t}) + CAP^l(\mathrm{t}) \quad (17)$$

Multiplying by the exchange rate yields the change of the central bank's net foreign assets in the currency of country l.

$$\Delta NFA^l(\mathrm{t}) = ALL^l(\mathrm{t}) * e^l(\mathrm{t}), \quad (18)$$

The stock of net foreign assets follows.

$$NFA^l(\mathrm{t}) = \Delta NFA^l(\mathrm{t}) + NFA^l(\mathrm{t}-1). \quad (19)$$

The stock of net domestic assets NDA is explained by a monetary/policy-reaction function, which describes the efforts of the central bank to let the monetary base grow parallel to needs coming from the real and the price development:

$$NDA^l(\mathrm{t}) = NDA^l[gdp(\mathrm{t}), p(\mathrm{t}), NFA(\mathrm{t})] \quad (20)$$

gdp = gross domestic product
p = deflator of gdp

We expect a negative sign for the coefficient of NFA, because we assume that the central bank in the case of a monetary expansion caused by foreign influence will try to stabilize the monetary base.

We then get, by definition, the reserve money:

$$RM^l(\mathrm{t}) = NDA^l(\mathrm{t}) + NFA^l(\mathrm{t}) \quad (21)$$

The country interest rates can be calculated solving a simple Keynesian money market:

$$MD^l(\mathrm{t}) = p^l(\mathrm{t}) \cdot MD^l[gdp^l(\mathrm{t}), r^l(\mathrm{t})] \quad (22)$$

$$MS^l(\mathrm{t}) = m^l(\mathrm{t}) * [RM(\mathrm{t})] \quad (23)$$

$$MD^l(\mathrm{t}) = MS^l(\mathrm{t}) \quad (24)$$

MD = money demand
MS = money supply
RM = reserve money

m = money multiplier
gdp = gross domestic product
p = deflator of gdp
r = rate of interest

The equilibrium condition is that the sum of all capital flows is zero. From iteration to iteration the interest rate is rising (falling), if there is a demand surplus (deficit) in the international capital market.

The clearing of the international capital market formally can be written as follows:

$$DIFF(t) = \sum_{l=1}^{n} NFC^{l}(\mathrm{t}) \tag{25}$$

$$CAL(\tau) = \begin{cases} -ETA & \text{if } DIFF > ALPHA \\ 0 & \text{if } -ALPHA < DIFF < ALPHA \\ +ETA & \text{if } DIFF < -ALPHA \end{cases} \tag{26}$$

$$ETA, ALPHA > 0$$

$$r^{w}(\mathrm{t}, \tau) = r^{w}(\mathrm{t}, \tau - 1) + CAL(\tau) \tag{27}$$

$$\tau = \text{iteration index}$$

DIFF is the demand suplus of the world capital flows. If *DIFF* is bigger than a very small number *ALPHA*, which is an acceptable deviation from a cleared capital market, the US interest rate is raised by an *ETA*, and in the next iteration the capital import of the countries will be reduced.

The balance of payments bridges the SNA to the financial model. The balance of capital account is explained by interest rate and inflation rates, while the exchange rates remain constant. The country interest rate can be calculated by solving a set of money market equations representing demand and supply of money. In future versions the interest rate in the United States is obtained by equalizing global demand and supply of the capital flows.

Explicit inclusion of saving-investment balance at the global level, as well as within individual countries, is deemed essential in a long-term growth model such as the COMPASS. The model does not have the explicit production function in the framework, largely due to the unavailability of reliable capital stock series for many of the countries in question. If the model is driven by the demand side alone, without proper consideration to the supply side, growth would continue almost indefinitely in a developing economy context where actual constraints lie with supply capacity which can only be enhanced through capital formation. The COMPASS examines whether a country's desire to invest is actually feasible under its own capacity to save and its ability to use someone else's savings channelled through global capital flow.

5. The trade model

The trade model will have the following structure:

$$x_l^i(t) = \sum_{k=1}^{n} S_{lk}^i(t) * m_k^i(t) \tag{28}$$

i: goods index
l, *k*: country index
n: number of countries
x: exports in constant dollars
S_{lk}^i: trade share of country *l* in the imports of country *k* for product *i*
m: imports in constant dollars

with

$$S_{lk}^i(t) = S_{lk}^i\left[\tilde{p}_l^i(t)/\tilde{p}(t), t\right] \tag{29}$$

$\tilde{p}_l^i$: price of good *i* in the exporting country *l* in dollars
$\tilde{p}^i(t)$: world market price of good *i* in dollars
t: time trend

The import prices for good q^i_k in country *k* are compiled as weighted averages of the export prices of the different exporting countries:

$$\tilde{q}_k^i(t) = \sum_{l=1}^{m} S_{lk}^i(t) * \tilde{p}_l^i(t) \tag{30}$$

q_k^i: import price of good *i* in country *k* in dollars

The COMPASS is designed to capture the interdependencies among regions of the world through merchandise trade, service trade, primary income flows, financial flows, energy, and the environment. The trade model is intended to focus on the linkages of the global community through trade. The trade flow is disaggregated to 25 commodity classes. Input-output models and macro models are specified in order to facilitate such linkage.

A single-region model offers the values of import demand and export prices (as represented by the domestic output price) to the trade model. Exchange rates are also generated by the country macro models. The trade model in turn picks up the import demand and allocates the demand among exporters according to trade share. The trade shares and world prices will be determined by an iteration process based on the relative prices and a time-trend variable, subject to two constraints:

(1) The sum of shares from all sources in a given commodity class must add up to 1.
(2) Total imports in the world equals total exports in the world.

Key variable at play is the export prices supplied by the country models, adjusted for exchange rate to obtain prices expressed in dollar terms. World import price (i.e. in terms of US$) is generated based on the export prices and trade shares, which is then converted to import prices in terms of national currency. The national macro models use the results of the trade model concerning allocated exports and world prices (i.e. import prices) to obtain new import levels and export prices. Iteration between the country models and the trade model is continued until convergence is obtained with desired margin.

6. Details of the SNA system

This chapter gives a listing of the equations of a SNA system, that takes generated income from an input-output system, transforms it by distribution between enterprises, households, government and rest of the world into disposable income of private households and the government, which are determinants of private and public consumption. It further shows capital formation, the balance of payments with trade and capital flows, and the financial system with the balance of the central bank. The interdependent internationally linked SNA system will allow estimation of a world interest rate.

This section gives the numbers of the tables from the UN statistics which are needed to calculate the entire system. The variable names are based on the naming conventions explained in an earlier chapter. The reader will find all definitions and the main and typical specifications of the regressions functions of the system, although it is not possible to show here all of the alternative specifications. A regression function always has the name of the dependent variable as the name of the function and its arguments in brackets. For brevity the country codes are omitted for all variables. The equations are organized following the structure of the UN statistics.

fin_dem.re1: final demand

Table 1.2. Expenditure on the GDP in constant prices

1.	Government Expenditure	
	gttsna(t) = gttsna[ydisep(t), . . .]	(1)
2.	Private Consumption	
	cttsna(t) = cttsna[ydiseh(t), INTLEN(t), . . .]	(2)
3.	Gross Capital Formation	
	kttsna(t) = kttsna[(GCFSEP(t) + GCFSEC(t))/pkttsna(t), . . .]	(3)
4.	Exports	
	*xttsna(t) = rxttsnasio * xttsio(t)*	(4)
5.	Imports	
	mttsna(t) = mttsna[mttsio(t), . . .]	(5)
	Real GDP:	
	gdp(t) = gttsna(t) + cttsna(t) + kttsna(t) + xttsna(t) − mttsna(t)	(6)
Prices for Components of Final Demand		
	Deflator of Government Expenditures	
	pgttsna(t) = pgttsna[p_outsio(t), . . .]	(7)

Table 1.2. continued

Deflator of Private Consumption	
pcttsna(t) = pcttsna[p_outsio(t), . . .]	(8)
Deflator of Investment	
pkttsna = pkttsna[p_outsio(t), . . .]	(9)
Deflator of Exports	
pxttsna(t) = pxttsna[p_outsio(t), . . .]	(10)
Deflator of Imports	
pmttsna(t) = pmttsna[p_outsio(t), . . .]	(11)
Rate of Iflation (Private Consumption)	
*INFLCTT(t) = 100.0 * (pcttsna(t) − pcttsna(t−1))/pcttsna(t−1)*	(12)
Expenditure on the GDP in Current Prices	
*GTTSNA(t) = gttsna(t) * pgttsna(t)*	(13)
*CTTSNA(t) = cttsna(t) * pcttsna(t)*	(14)
*KTTSNA(t) = kttsna(t) * pkttsna(t)*	(15)
*XTTSNA(t) = xttsna(t) * pxttsna(t)*	(16)
*MTTSNA(t) = mttsna(t) * pmttsna(t)*	(17)
Nominal GDP:	
GDP(t) = GTTSNA(t) + CTTSNA(t) + KTTSNA(t) + XTTSNA(t) − MTTSNA(t)	(18)
Price of GDP:	
pvttsna(t) = GDP(t)/gdp(t)	(19)

dis_inc.re1: income

Table 1.3. Cost components of the GDP

1. Indirect Taxes, Net	
*TSTSNA(t) = RTSTSNASIO * TSTSIO(t)*	(20)
2. Consumption of Fixed Capital	
*DETSNA(t) = RDETSNASIO * DETSIO(t)*	(21)
3. Compensation of Employees, Paid by Resident Producers	
*WATSNA(t) = RWATSNASIO * WATSIO(t)*	(22)
4. Operating Surplus	
URTSNA(t) = GDP(t) − TSTSNA(t) − DETSNA(t) − WATSNA(t)	(23)

Table 1.4. General government current receipts and disbursements

Receipts	
1. Operating Surplus	
URTSEP(t) = URTSEP[URTSNA(t), . . .]	(24)
2. Property and Entrepreneurial Income	
YPRSEP(t) = YPRSEP[YPPSEP(t) + YPPSEC(t) + YPPSEH(t) + YPPSEF(t)]	(25)
3. Taxes	
A. Indirect Taxes	
TTTSNA(t) = TTTSNA[GDP(t), . . .]	(26)
B. Direct Taxes	
DITSEP(t) = DITSEH(t) + DITSEC(t)	(27)
C. Social Security Contributions	
SORSEP(t) = SORSEP[SOPSEH(t), . . .]	(28)
4. Other Current Transfers + 3.D Compulsory Fees, Penalties	
OTRSEP(t) = OTRSEP[OTPSEH(t), . . .]	(29)
Disbursements	
1. Government Final Consumption Expenditure	
GTTSNA(t): see equation (13)	

Table 1.4. continued

2. Property Income
   $YPPSEP(t) = YPPSEP[INTGOV(t) * NLESEP(t), YPPSEP(t-1), \ldots]$ (30)
3. Subsidies
   $SUTSNA(t) = TTTSNA(t) - TSTSNA(t)$ (31)
4. Other Current Transfers
   A. Social Security Benefits and B. Social Assistance Grants
   $SOPSEP(t) = SOPSEP[SOPSEH(t), YDISEP(t), \ldots]$ (32)
   C. Other
   $OTPSEP(t) = OTPSEP[SOPSEH(t), OTPSEH(t), \ldots]$ (33)
   Net Saving
   $SAVSEP(t) = URTSEP(t) + YPRSEP(t) + DITSEP(t) + TTTSNA(t) + SORSEP(t) + OTRSEP(t) - GTTSNA(t) - YPPSEP(t) - SUTSNA(t) - SOPSEP(t) - OTPSEP(t)$ (34)
   Disposable Income in Current Prices
   $YDISEP(t) = GTTSNA(t) + SAVSEP(t)$ (35)
   Disposable Income in Constant Prices
   $ydisep(t) = YDISEP(t)/pgttsna(t)$ (36)

Table 3.13. General government: capital accumulation account, total finance of accumulation

Finance of Gross Accumulation

1. Gross Saving
   A. Consumption of Fixed Capital
   $DETSEP(t) = DETSEP[DETSNA(t), \ldots]$ (37)
   B. Net Saving
   $SAVSEP(t)$: see equation (34)
2. Capital Transfers
   $CTRSEP(t) = CTRSEP[CTPSEH(t) + CTPSEC(t) + CTPSEF(t), \ldots]$ (38)

Gross Accumulation

1. Gross Capital Formation
   $GCFSEP(t) = GCFSEP[(INTGOV(t) - INFLCTT(t), YDISEP(t), \ldots]$ (39)
2. Purchases of Land
   $PULSEP(t) = PULSEP(t)$ (40)
3. Purchases of Intangible Assets
   $PUASEP(t) = PUASEP(t)$ (41)
4. Capital Transfers
   $CTPSEP(t) = CTPSEP[GDP(t), \ldots]$ (42)
   Net Lending
   $NLESEP(t) = SAVSEP(t) + CTRSEP(t) + DETSEP(t) - GCFSEP(t) - CTPSEP(t) - PULSEP(t) - PUASEP(t)$ (43)

Table 1.5. Current income and outlay of corporate and quasi-corporate enterprises

Receipts

1. Operating surplus
   $URTSEC(t) = URTSEC[URTSNA(t), \ldots]$ (44)
2. Property and Entrepreneurial Income Received
   $YPRSEC(t) = YPRSEC[YPPSEP(t) + YPPSEC(t) + YPPSEH(t) + YPPSEF(t), \ldots]$ (45)
3. Current Transfers
   $OTRSEC(t) = OTRSEC[OTPSEP(t) + OTPSEC(t) + OTPSEH(t) + OTPSEP(t), \ldots]$ (46)

Table 1.5. continued

Disbursements

1. Property and Entrepreneurial Income

$$YPPSEC(t) = YPPSEC[YPPSEC(t-1), INTGOV(t) * NLESEC(t), URTSNA(t), \ldots] \quad (47)$$

2. Direct Taxes

$$DITSEC(t) = DITSEC[URTSEC(t), YPRSEC(t), \ldots] \quad (48)$$

3. Other Current Transfers

$$OTPSEC(t) = OTPSEC[GDP(t), \ldots] \quad (49)$$

4. Net Saving

$$SAVSEC(t) = URTSEC(t) + OTRSEC(t) + YPRSEC(t) - YPPSEC(t) - DITSEC(t) - OTPSEC(t) \quad (50)$$

Table 3.2.3. Corporate and quasi corporate enterprise capital account finance

Finance of Gross Accumulation

1. Gross Saving

A. Consumption of Fixed Capital

$$DETSEC(t) = DETSEC[DETSNA(t), \ldots] \quad (51)$$

B. Net Saving

SAVSEC(t): see equation (50)

2. Capital Transfers

$$CTRSEC(t) = CTRSEC[CTPSEH(t) + CTPSEC(t) + CTPSEP(t) + CTPSEF(t), \ldots] \quad (52)$$

Accumulation

1. Gross Capital Formation

$$GCFSEC(t) = GCTSEC[URTSEC(t), INTGOV(t) - INFLCTT(t), \ldots] \quad (53)$$

2. Purchases of Land

$$PULSEC(t) = PULSEC(t) \quad (54)$$

3. Purchases of Intangible Assets

$$PUASEC(t) = PUASEC(t) \quad (55)$$

4. Capital Transfers

$$CTPSEC(t) = CTPSEC[GDP(t), \ldots] \quad (56)$$

Net Lending

$$NLESEC(t) = SAVSEC(t) + CTRSEC(t) + DETSEC(t) - GCFSEC(t) - PULSEC(t) - PUASEC(t) - CTPSEC(t) \quad (57)$$

Table 1.6. Current income and outlay of households and non-profit institutions

Receipts

1. Compensation of Employees, Received

A. From Resident Producers

$$WDRSEH(t) = WDRSEH[WATSNA(t), \ldots] \quad (58)$$

B. From Rest of the World

$$WMRSEH(t) = CERSEF(t) \quad (59)$$

Total

$$WTRSEH(t) = WDRSEH(t) + WMRSEH(t) \quad (60)$$

2. Operating Surplus

$$URTSEH(t) = URTSEH[URTSNA(t), \ldots] \quad (61)$$

3. Property and Entrepreneurial Income

$$YPRSEH(t) = YPRSEH[YPPSEP(t) + YPPSEC(t) + YPPSEH(t) + YPPSEF(t), \ldots] \quad (62)$$

4. Current Transfers

A. Social Security Benefits and B. Social Assistance Grants

$$SORSEH(t) = SORSEH[SOPSEP(t), \ldots] \quad (63)$$

Table 1.6. continued

C. Other
$OTRSEH(t) = OTRSEH[OTPSEP(t) + OTPSEC(t) + OTPSEH(t) + OTPSEF(t), \ldots]$ (64)

Disbursements

1. Private Consumption
   $CTTSNA$: see equation (14)
2. Property Income
   $YPPSEH(t) = YPPSEH[INTGOV(t) * CTTSNA(t), YPPSEH(t-1), \ldots]$ (65)
3. Direct Taxes and other Transfers
   A. Social Security Contributions
   $SOPSEH(t) = SOPSEH[WATSNA(t), \ldots]$ (66)
   B. Direct Taxes
   $DITSEH(t) = DITSEH[WATSNA(t) + YPRSEH(t), \ldots]$ (67)
4. Other Current Transfers + 3.C. Fees, Fines and Penalties
   $OTPSEH(t) = OTPSEH[WATSNA(t), \ldots]$ (68)
5. Net Saving
   $SAVSEH(t) = WDRSEH(t) + YPRSEH(t) + URTSEH(t) + SORSEH(t) + OTRSEH(t) - CTTSNA(t) - YPPSEH(t) - SOPSEH(t) - DITSEH(t) - OTPSEH(t)$ (69)
   Disposable Income in Current Prices
   $YDISEH(t) = CTTSNA(t) + SAVSEH(t)$ (70)
   Disposable Income in Constant Prices
   $ydiseh(t) + YDISEH(t)/pcttsna(t)$ (71)

bal_pay.re1: balance of payments

Table 1.7. External transactions on current account

Payments to the Rest of the World

1. Imports of Goods and Services
   $MTTSNA(t)$: see equation (17)
2. Factor Income to the Rest of the World
   A. Compensation of Employees
   $CEPSEF(t) = CEPSEF[WATSNA(t), \ldots]$ (72)
   B. Property and Entrepreneurial Income
   $YPPSEF(t) = YPPSEF[YPPSEP(t) + YPPSEC(t) + YPPSEH(t), \ldots]$ (73)
3. Current Transfers to the Rest of the World
   $OTPSEF(t) = OTPSEF[OTPSEP(t) + OTPSEC(t) + OTPSEH(t), \ldots]$ (74)
4. Surplus of the Nation on current Transactions
   $SURSEF(t) = RECSEF(t) - MTTSNA(t) - CEPSEF(t) - YPPSEF(t) - OTPSEF(t)$ (75)

Receipts from the Rest of the World

1. Exports
   $XTTSNA(t)$: see equation (16)
2. Factor Income from Rest of the World
   A. Compensation of Employees
   $CERSEF(t) = CERSEF[WATSNA(t), \ldots]$ (76)
   B. Property and Entrepreneurial Income
   $YPRSEF(t) = YPPSEP(t) + YPPSEC(t) + YPPSEH(t) + YPPSEF(t) - YPRSEP(t) - YPRSEC(t) - YPRSEH(t)$ (77)

Table 1.7. continued

3. Current Transfers from the Rest of the World

$$OTRSEF(t) = OTPSEP(t) + OTPSEC(t) + OTPSEH(t) + OTPSEF(t) - OTRSEP(t) - OTRSEC(t) - OTRSEH(t) \quad (78)$$

Payments to the Rest of the World Plus
Surplus of the Nation and Current Transactions

$$PAYSEF(t) = MTTSNA(t) + YPPSEF(t) + CEPSEF(t) + OTPSEF(t) + SURSEF(t) \quad (79)$$

Receipts from the Rest of the World

$$RECSEF(t) = TTSNA(t) + CERSEF(t) + YPRSEF(t) + OTRSEF(t) \quad (80)$$

Current Account

$$CURBAL(t) = CURBAL[SURSEF(t)/NACUSD(t), \ldots] \quad (81)$$

Net Capital Exports

$$CAPBAL(t) = CAPBAL[(INTGOV(t) - INFLCTT(t)), INFLCTTus(t), INTGOVj(t), \ldots] \quad (82)$$

mon_mar.re1: financial system

Change of Foreign Assets of the Central Bank

$$ALLBAL(t) = CURBAL(t) + CAPBAL(t) \quad (83)$$

Exchange Rate

$$NACUSD(t) = NACUSD[INTGOV(t), INTGOVj(t), INFLCTT, \ldots] \quad (84)$$

Foreign Assets, Net of the Central Bank in National Currency

$$ASS(t) = [FORASS(t-1), ALLBAL(t) * NACUSD(t), \ldots] \quad (85)$$

Claims on Central Government

$$CLAGOC(t) = CLAGOC[RESMON(t), \ldots] \quad (86)$$

Claims on Deposit Money Banks

$$CLAMBK(t) = CLAMBK[RESMON(t), \ldots] \quad (87)$$

Central Government Deposits

$$GOVDEP(t) = GOVDEP[RESMON(t), \ldots] \quad (88)$$

Other Deposits

$$OTHDEP(t) = OTHDEP[RESMON(t), \ldots] \quad (89)$$

Reserve Money

$$RESMON(t) = [gdp(t), pvttsna(t), TTREND(t), \ldots] \quad (90)$$

Money M1

$$MONEY1(t) = MONEY1[RESMON(t), INTDIS(t), \ldots] \quad (91)$$

Interest on Government Yields

$$INTGOV(t) = INTGOV[MONEY1(t), GDP(t), \ldots] \quad (92)$$

Discount Rate

$$INTDIS(t) = INTDIS[INFLCTT(t), \ldots] \quad (93)$$

Lending Rate

$$INTLEN(t) = INTLEN[INTDIS(t), INTLEN(t-1), \ldots] \quad (94)$$

4
Endogenized trade shares in a global model

BERND MEYER and CHRISTIAN LUTZ

1. Introduction

Globally integrated modelling is achieved by employing trade matrices for linking country models. In the case of COMPASS this is achieved by having time-series for trade matrices of 25 commodity groups linking 53 countries and regions. In addition to country models that are estimated econometrically based on empirical data, trade matrices themselves are available over time in response to changing relative prices (endogenous in the model) and other factors. This chapter focuses on an attempt to empirically explain the trade shares.

Prices play an important role for energy demand and supply. In the first place the shares of the different energy carriers are dependent on their relative prices. Secondly, the energy intensities in factor demand of the industries and in household consumption are following price signals. Finally, energy prices influence production costs of all intermediate and final products and have an impact on product prices and demand for the different intermediate and final products. So a shock of energy prices will not only have a direct impact on energy demand, but also have indirect effects resulting from changes in the structure of the economy.

In a global context this means that the competition of the different economies is hit by energy price changes, because countries have a very different usage of energy carriers, energy intensities in production, and very different structures of intermediate and final demand.

In general energy forecasting needs an exact forecast of the world economic developments, and in times of globalization this can be achieved only by a realistic anticipation of structural change in international trade.

Global energy problems should be discussed in a multisector-multicountry context. The multisector approach is necessary, because energy influences structural change of the economies and is on the other hand dependent on it reflecting different energy intensities among industrial sectors. A regional modelling concept is useful, because of the big differences in the economic structures and the energy markets. From the view of modelling policy decisions the regions should be politically defined as countries. This makes sense, because policy decisions reflect the structures of the economies in question.

The global model COMPASS (Meyer and Uno, 1999; Uno *et al.*, 1999) fulfils these requirements. It depicts the interdependencies of prices and volumes on the

K. Uno (ed.), Economy–Energy–Environment Simulation, 69–80.

different stages of production and consumption for 53 countries and links the economies by a multisector global trade model. This chapter focuses on the latter part of the model.

In section 2 we first give a short overview of the role of the trade modelin the system COMPASS and continue with the alternatives of modelling trade in section 3. In the literature three approaches for modelling bilateral trade are discussed: the first is the hypothesis of given structures in international trade, which can be rejected with a short review of the facts. The second is modelling import functions based on the Armington hypothesis. This approach is used – for example – in the general equilibrium model GTAP (Hertel and Tsigas, 1997). The third approach is modelling export shares. In global multisector models this approach was first realized in the INFORUM system (Ma, 1996; Nyhus *et al.*, 1996). In section 3 we discuss the different approaches and prefer the third.

In section 4 the logical structure of the trade model of COMPASS is presented. Results of the econometric estimations of the functions of the trade model are discussed in section 5. Section 6 shows that trade matters: we present the results of two simulations with the whole COMPASS system with constant *versus* price-dependent trade shares. We compare the impacts of a price shock for primary energy on GDP and CO_2 emissions for the G7 countries. The results show that modelling of trade plays an important role in depicting the interdependency of energy, economy and environment.

2. The role of the trade model in the global 3E system COMPASS

The structure of the global energy-economy-environment model COMPASS is depicted in Figure 3-1 in the previous chapter: it shows a wheel, in which the bilateral trade model is the axis. The spokes are the country models, which always consist of a macro model and for most OECD and APEC countries of an input-output model and an energy model. The tyre represents the linkage of the countries via the global equality of savings and investments.

A deeper insight into the linkage of the trade model with the other parts of the system is shown in Figure 4-1 for one specific country. The global trade model receives a vector of import volumes and export prices from every country model. For every country it calculates a vector of export volumes and import prices.

The input-output models consist of 36 sectors. They obtain the vector of export volumes and import prices from the trade model and aggregated investment and private and public consumption figures from the macro models, and distribute these to 36 sectors. From the energy models they receive prices for the energy carriers. The input-output models calculate the vectors by industry of gross production, intermediate demand, the vector of imports and the vectors for the different components of primary inputs. The input-output models further estimate the vector of unit costs and the vector of prices.

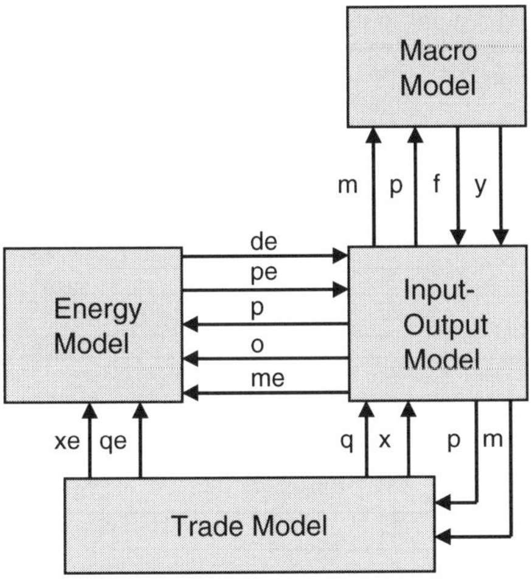

f: aggregate components of final demand	de: vector of energy demand
p: pice vector	pe: vector of energy prices
q: vector of import prices	qe: vector of energy import prices
x: export vector	xe: vector of energy exports
m: import vector	me: vector of energy imports
o: output vector	

Figure 4-1. The linkage of the trade model and the other models for one specific country.

The macro models aggregate primary income, import volumes and prices coming from the input-output models. They show the redistribution of income between the government, households, enterprises and foreign countries and calculate the disposable income for these institutions, which are important determinants of private and public consumption. The macro models further depict monetary markets and calculate the interest rate and other determinants of investment. The accounting system of the macro models further contains the balance of payments.

The energy models receive the vector of gross production by industry and final demand by branches as well as industry prices, energy import volumes from the input-output models. The trade model delivers energy import prices and energy export volumes to the energy models. The energy models calculate primary and secondary energy demand for seven carriers in detail, the conversion of energy and CO_2 emissions of the different fossil energy carriers. Based on energy import prices the energy models further determine wholesale and retail prices for the energy carriers, which are delivered to the input-output models.

The 53 countries of the model include all OECD countries, all APEC countries, all OPEC countries, Russia and India (see Table 4-1). For the moment the

Table 4-1. Countries and regions in the trade matrices

1	Belgium and Luxemburg	19	Iran	37	Australia
2	Denmark	20	Iraq	38	Canada
3	France	21	Kuwait	39	USA
4	Germany	22	Oman	40	Brazil
5	Greece	23	Qatar	41	Mexico
6	Ireland	24	Saudi Arabia	42	Venezuela
7	Italy	25	United Arab Emirates	43	Algeria
8	Netherlands	26	Brunei	44	Libya
9	Portugal	27	Hong Kong	45	Angola
10	Spain	28	India	46	Nigeria
11	United Kingdom	29	Indonesia	47	Rest of Europe
12	Austria	31	Korea	48	Rest of Asia
13	Finland	31	Malaysia	49	Rest of Oceania
14	Norway	32	Philippines	50	Rest of North America
15	Sweden	33	Singapore	51	Rest of South America
16	Switzerland	34	Thailand	52	Rest of Africa
17	Former USSR	35	Taiwan	53	Rest of Continents
18	Japan	36	China		

structure discussed above is realized for the most important OECD and APEC countries. The others are represented only in the trade model and with macro models, from which 18 models are simple macro simulators.

All oil-, gas- and coal-producing countries, the bigger developing countries and the industrialized countries are explicitly part of the system. Additionally seven regions are defined, which include the countries not explicitly mentioned, so that the system closes on the global level. It is guaranteed that energy demand and supply can be depicted in a global dimension simultaneously with goods and capital markets.

3. Alternatives of modelling bilateral trade

In multisector systems the trade model transforms the vector of import volumes of the different countries into the export volumes of delivering countries. Of course a simple hypothesis is that the regional structure of the imports of the different countries is constant. In that case we would only need information concerning the regional structure of the imports for every country for one year. Given this information the exports of every country could be calculated by definition.

A look at the dynamics of international trade raises some doubts. Table 4-2 compares the shares of some selected countries in total world exports. We see, that China, Thailand and Hong Kong have rapidly growing shares coming from a very low level. But most of the G7 countries also have rising trade shares.

Table 4-3 shows that on the industry level the dynamics of international trade are even stronger. Here we see for the strongly expanding product group 'office and computing machinery' the same picture as for the totals concerning China, Thailand and Hong Kong, but now the shares of some G7 countries such as

Table 4-2. World export demand in US$: shares of selected countries (in %)

	1980	1996
China	1.083	3.080
Thailand	0.342	1.039
Hong Kong	1.064	3.332
France	5.081	5.401
Germany	8.594	10.107
Italy	3.543	4.880
UK	5.952	5.109
Japan	6.232	6.969
Canada	3.505	4.313
USA	11.281	11.825
Rest	53.322	43.944

Table 4-3. World export demand of office and computing machinery in US$: shares of selected countries (in %)

	1980	1996
China	0.041	2.176
Thailand	0.024	2.491
Hong Kong	3.870	6.497
France	6.321	2.479
Germany	10.592	3.848
Italy	4.027	2.239
UK	8.785	5.672
Japan	14.427	14.431
Canada	1.008	3.235
USA	31.378	18.708
Rest	19.526	38.222

USA, Germany, UK and Italy are shrinking. We are convinced that this dynamic cannot be depicted by a trade matrix with constant shares, where every change in the regional structure of exports has to be explained by the regional structure of the import vector.

A more elaborate approach was presented by Armington (1969). He postulated that the share of country l in imports of country k of good i depends on the price for good i, that country l is taking in country k relative to the average of the import prices of good i over all delivering countries. He further set the hypothesis that the corresponding price elasticity might be independent from the delivering country.

$$s_{kl}^{i}(t) = b_{kl}^{i} \cdot \left(q_{kl}^{i}(t) / q_{kl}^{i}(t)\right)^{\mu_k^i} \tag{1}$$

s_{kl}^{i} = share of imports of good i in country k delivered from country l
b_{kl}^{i} = positive constant parameter
q_{kl}^{i} = import price of good i in country k from country l in US$
q_{k}^{i} = average of import prices in country k over all delivering countries in US$
μ_{k}^{i} = price elasticity of imports of good i in country k.

The hypothesis is a critical one: it supposes that, for example, the price elasticity of imported cars in Germany would be the same for Japanese, Korean, American, French and Italian cars. But for many goods consumers have preferences with respect to the delivering country.

The advantage of the hypothesis is that price elasticities can be estimated without having time-series of the shares of the delivering countries. A time-series of the total imports of good *i* in country *k* is enough.

For an econometric estimation of the Armington hypothesis see for example Brenton (1989). Often model-builders do not estimate on their own, but take estimated price elasticities from literature. They need only one observation of the shares and the relative import prices for one year. With the predetermined price elasticity they can calculate the parameters *b* of equation (1). This procedure is called calibration. With a time-series for the import prices they can use equation (1) to forecast the import shares. In this way bilateral trade relations are modelled in the GTAP system (Hertel, 1997; Hertel and Tsigas, 1997) and in many other CGE models.

If we want to achieve a better representation of the preferences of the agents we have to estimate specific price elasticities for the delivering countries. To execute the regressions we need a data set, which is at least by factor 15 bigger than in the Armington case. We reject the Armington hypothesis, because we want to have a more adequate analysis and an explicit econometric test of the used equations. This is not possible in the described calibration procedure of CGE modelling.

If we change our perspective from the importing to the exporting country, the share of the imports of good *i* in country *k* coming from country *l* obviously is the share of the exports of country *l* of good *i* to country *k* in the imports of good *i* in country *k*:

$$x_l^i(t) = \sum_{k=1}^{n} s_{lk}^i(t) \cdot m_k^i(t) \tag{2}$$

s_{lk}^i = share of exports of country *l* in the imports of good *i* of country *k*
x_l^i = nominal exports of good *i* in country *l*
m_k^i = nominal imports of good *i* in country *k*.

Following earlier work by Klein and Van Petersson (1973), Moriguchi (1973), Hickmann and Lau (1973) and Gana *et al.* (1979), Ma (1996) specified the following function for the endogenization of the trade shares:

$$\log\left(s_{lk}^i(t)\right) = a_{lk}^i + b_{lk}^i \cdot \log\left[\left(p_l^i(t)/q_k^i(t)\right)\right] + c_{lk}^i \cdot \log\left(K_l^i(t)/K_w^i(t)\right) + d_{lk}^i \cdot t \tag{3}$$

p_l^i = export price of good *i* in country *l* in US\$
q_k^i = import price of good *i* in country *k* in US\$
K_l^i = capital stock invested in production of good *i* in country *l*
K_w^i = capital stock invested in production of good *i* in the world.

Using this approach Ma estimated price elasticities that change with the exporting and the importing country. The capital stocks are indicator variables, which will measure the influence of changes in the quality of the production in the delivering country and its competitors. The time trend has to catch other continuously developing influences. His good results encourage us to follow his approach.

4. The logical structure of the trade model in the COMPASS system

As stated above in equation (2) the exports of the model are calculated as follows:

$$x_l^i(t) = \sum_{k=1}^{n} s_{lk}^i(t) \cdot m_k^i(t) \tag{4}$$

x_l^i = nominal exports of country l of good i
s_{lk}^i = share of exports of country l in the imports of good i of country k
n = number of countries (53)
m_k^i = nominal imports of country k of good i.

Here s_{lk}^i is the nominal share of the export of country l in the imports of country k of good i depending on the export price of country l relative to the average of the import prices of good i in country k and a time trend.

$$s_{lk}^i(t) = s_{lk}^i\left[p_l^i(t)/q_k^i(t), t\right] \tag{5}$$

s_{lk}^i = share of exports of country l in the imports of good i of country k
p_l^i = price of good i in the exporting country l in US$
q_k^i = import price of good i in country k in US$
t = time trend.

Since capital stocks by industries were not available for the different countries, we had to reduce Ma's specification.

The import prices of good i in country k are calculated as weighted averages of the export prices of the different countries. The weights are given with the trade shares

$$q_k^i(t) = \sum_{l=1}^{n} s_{lk}^i(t) \cdot p_l^i(t) \tag{6}$$

q_k^i = import price of good i in country k
s_{lk}^i = share of exports of country l in the imports of good i of country k
p_l^i = price of good i in the exporting country l.

For a better understanding of the role of the trade model in energy modelling we take a look at the logical flow in the case of a rise in oil prices, for example. In equation (6) rising export prices in oil-producing countries increase the import prices for oil in the other countries. This will influence wholesale prices and retail prices in the energy models, which will induce substitution and changes in energy intensities in the energy models of the different countries. The input-output models transform the price changes for energy carriers in domestic price changes for the different goods and calculate reactions on product demand including import demand. From here we come back to the trade model, where in equation (4) the world exports for the different goods are calculated, using trade shares that have been changed by the adjusted relative prices as equation (5) of the trade model shows. The change of the exports then feeds back into the country models and induces further reactions on macro variables, production of industries, demand for commodities and energy demand.

Ma's trade model is part of the INFORUM system (Nyhus *et al.*, 1996). This consists of about 100 product groups compared to only 25 in COMPASS, but only 13 countries compared to 53 in COMPASS. The INFORUM system is limited to only a part of global trade.

5. Empirical results of the estimation of trade shares

The database of the empirical work comprises time-series of trade matrices of Statistics Canada with about 6000 product groups of the producing sectors from 1980 to 1996 in US dollars. Services are not included. We aggregated these raw data to the 25 product groups of the two-digit classification scheme of the OECD input-output tables. The data were also adjusted, so that the identities of the trade matrix in equation (2) are not violated.

We estimated the nominal trade shares by the logarithmic function of (5) with the ordinary least squares (OLS) estimation. The estimated equation can be written as:

$$\log\left(s_{lk}^{i}(t)\right) = \beta_{1,lk}^{i} + \beta_{2,lk}^{i} \cdot \log\left(p_{l}^{i}(t)/q_{k}^{i}(t)\right) + \beta_{3,lk}^{i} \cdot \log(t) \tag{7}$$

The trade shares were estimated automatically using a C++ program. With 25 product groups and 53 times 53 trade shares for each group not less than 70,225 trade shares had to be analysed. In the program equation (7) and also its alternatives without a time trend (8) or without price dependency (9) were estimated:

$$\log\left(s_{lk}^{i}(t)\right) = \beta_{1,lk}^{i} + \beta_{2,lk}^{i} \cdot \log\left(p_{l}^{i}(t)/q_{k}^{i}(t)\right) \tag{8}$$

$$\log\left(s_{lk}^{i}(t)\right) = \beta_{1,lk}^{i} + \beta_{3,lk}^{i} \cdot \log(t) \tag{9}$$

If at least one value of the time-series was zero, the trade share would be set constant at the level of the last observation. Afterwards, the three equations (7), (8) and (9) were estimated for the remaining variable trade shares. For each trade share the selection procedure was the following: first, the estimated value of the price elasticities $\beta_{2,lk}^{i}$ was restricted to economic plausibility. Because the trade shares are nominal this price elasticity had to be less than 1. On the other hand extreme price elasticities lower than −10 were rejected:

$$-10 \leq \beta^{i}_{2,lk} \leq 1 \tag{10}$$

Secondly, the selection followed econometric criteria: the *t*-values for the estimated coefficients had to be above 2 or below −2. The Durbin-Watson statistic had to be between 1.1 and 2.9. If more than one of the three equations above accomplished these restrictions, the program would choose the estimation with the highest R^2. If all specifications failed, trade share in question would be kept constant in the simulation period.

The algorithm above is applied for 25 product groups and 53 countries; this means for 70,225 time-series. As 42,588 of the time-series have one or more zero values, 27,637 trade shares were estimated. A total of 12,564 equations (45.5% of the non-zero trade shares) hold the restrictions discussed above and the trade shares can be endogenized. Altogether 9300 trade shares (one-third of the non-zero trade shares) are explained only with a time trend, 8.0% depend only on prices and 3.8% are determined by prices and trends. So price dependency is given for 3264 of the trade shares.

Table 4-4 shows these results in detail. The most price-dependent commodity groups are drugs and medicines (14.3%), food beverages and tobacco (14.0%) and wood and furniture products with 13.6%. In mining and quarrying only 6.7% of the trade shares depend on relative prices.

6. The relevance of endogenized trade shares: results of simulations with the whole system

The econometric analysis of price dependency of trade shares has shown that over all sectors not more than 12% of the non-zero trade shares are price-dependent. A look at the sector details shows further that the energy products do not belong to the group with the strongest price dependency. Does this mean that prices do not matter?

Without information regarding the importance of the price-dependent shares for the solution of the system the answer is difficult. Of course, there is the expectation that bigger shares are more price-dependent than smaller ones. In this regard the price-dependent trade volume might be much bigger than 12%. However, the importance of a trade share is not only given with its number; it also depends on the import total of that good in the observed country, with which the share is multiplied to obtain the export of the delivering country. Importance of the trade shares in energy analysis further depends on the product group and its direct and indirect relevance for the energy markets.

It seems that the identification of important trade shares is rather difficult. Therefore, another approach is chosen, which uses all information that is hidden in the whole COMPASS system: first, a simulation is run with an energy price shock with constant nominal trade shares and then the same simulation is repeated with endogenized trade shares. A comparison will then give

Table 4-4. Results of the estimation of the import shares

		Number of Coefficients	At Least One Value of the Series is Zero	Estimated Coefficients				Constant Coefficients
				Only with Trend	Only with Prices	Prices and Trend	Total	
1	Agriculture, forestry and fishery	2809	1445	498	118	56	672	692
2	Mining and quarrying	2809	1753	429	48	23	500	556
3	Food, beverages and tobacco	2809	1198	534	155	70	759	852
4	Textile, apparel and leather	2809	1251	485	123	82	690	868
5	Wood and furniture products	2809	1733	320	97	49	466	610
6	Paper, paper pro. and printing	2809	1473	451	100	61	612	724
7	Industrial Chemicals	2809	1342	546	124	52	722	745
8	Drugs and medicine	2809	1609	433	128	43	604	596
9	Petroleum and coal products	2809	2047	252	72	23	347	415
10	Rubber and plastic products	2809	1755	409	70	38	517	537
11	Non metallic mineral products	2809	1628	396	98	39	533	648
12	Iron and steel	2809	1706	390	76	48	514	589
13	Non ferrous metals	2809	1820	333	68	37	438	551
14	Metal products	2809	1415	442	127	36	605	789
15	Non electrical machinery	2809	1345	519	110	71	700	764
16	Office and comp. machinery	2809	1879	289	80	37	406	524
17	Electrical apparatus nec	2809	1490	453	106	50	609	710
18	Radio, TV and com.Equipment	2809	1695	373	96	33	502	612
19	Shipbuilding and repairing	2809	2327	106	28	8	142	340
20	Other transportation means	2809	2214	168	43	18	229	366
21	Motor vehicles	2809	1687	381	75	57	513	609
22	Aircraft	2809	2310	130	35	16	181	318
23	Professional goods	2809	1433	452	129	54	635	741
24	Other manufacturing	2809	1258	501	104	49	654	897
25	Electricity, gas and water	2809	2775	10	3	1	14	20
	Total	70,225	42,588	9300	2213	1051	12,564	15,073

an answer. Of course, the case of constant nominal shares also implicitly assumes price dependency, because the real shares have a price elasticity of −1. So we actually compare two model versions with price-dependent trade shares.

In the business-as-usual (bau) scenario the price for crude oil is fixed at the level of $22 and the price for coal is also constant for the period 2000-2010. In the alternative scenario the oil price grows by 4% per year, an increase of about 50% against the bau in 2010, and the price for coal in every country follows the path of the price for refined petroleum. We choose these two prices because in our trade matrix petroleum and coal are a combined product group.

Which effects can be expected? On the energy markets the price shock induces substitution between energy carriers: in final energy demand gas and renewable energy carriers, and in electricity production nuclear energy and renewables will expand their shares. Rising energy prices will reduce the energy intensities of the sectors. Both effects diminish CO_2 emissions. GDP will be reduced, because higher energy prices will raise the output prices of the sectors and this diminishes the demand for goods. This is the reason for a further reduction of CO_2 emissions.

Table 4-5 shows that for all countries our expectations are fulfilled. However, the results are very different in the countries. Let us first consider the results for constant nominal trade shares: in the US we observe the strongest reduction of GDP and compared to this a relatively low reduction of CO_2. This is plausible, since a low reduction of CO_2 indicates a low reduction of energy demand and a stronger impact on costs, prices of goods and GDP. In general this relation also holds for the other countries. Only for Japan is the picture different. The reaction of CO_2 emissions is very low. The reason is that, in Japan, energy efficiency follows strong long-run trends and is not price-elastic. The low impact on GDP in Japan can be explained by low reactions of the countries' goods prices on changes in energy costs.

In the case of endogenized trade shares the effects on CO_2 emissions do not change drastically, but the impacts on GDP are very different for the US, France and Canada. In the US and Canada we have a 30% and a 26% lower reduction of GDP, whereas in France the reduction of GDP is 40% higher than

Table 4-5. Effects of higher energy prices in G7 countries: deviations of GDP and CO_2 emissions from the BAU scenario in the year 2010 (in percent)

	Constant Trade Shares		Endogenous Trade Shares	
	GDP	CO_2	GDP	CO_2
USA	−1.74	−3.01	−1.25	−2.88
Japan	−0.63	−1.36	−0.58	−1.29
Germany	−1.08	−8.90	−0.99	−8.42
France	−1.14	−6.62	−1.60	−6.82
Italy	−0.58	−11.70	−0.43	−11.83
Great Britain	−0.97	−9.27	−1.00	−9.58
Canada	−0.93	−4.68	−0.69	−4.38

in the case of constant nominal shares. One interpretation may be that in the US and Canada the price-elasticity of the exports is on average less than one in absolute terms, and in France on the average more than one. However, there are many other effects, such as changes in the sectoral and regional import structures, which are responsible for the result.

7. Conclusions

Global 3E (energy-economy-environment) studies have to analyse questions in a multicountry and multisector approach. The multisector approach is necessary, as changes in energy demand and supply have drastic impacts on the structure of the economy. The multicountry approach is useful because global policy is done by the governments of actually existing countries and not of artificial country groups in regions. Policy decisions are always predisposed by the structure of the economy, that has to be modelled. In consequence we get a huge system with a large number of countries. This chapter shows that, also in the global context of 53 explicitly modelled countries, the endogenization of trade shares is possible without the restrictions of the Armington hypothesis, typically used for CGE modelling.

As we could show, endogenized trade shares have an influence on the impacts of energy prices on the economy. The deviations from the bau scenario in the case of constant shares and in the case of endogenized shares are different. Of course we are presenting results from work in progress. Further work will show how a variation of the economic and econometric restrictions on the estimation of the trade share functions influences the results.

The impact of the different modelling approaches (constant *versus* endogenized shares) on the levels of exports and GDP in both scenarios is not discussed. There are very strong differences in respect to the sector and the regional structure of the world economy, but this is beyond the aim of this chapter.

5
Developing an energy balance simulation model

YUMIKO UMEHARA

1. The need for an energy balance model

The COMPASS energy balance model is constructed on the basis of the 36 sectors of an input-output and macro econometric model with the financial and trade balances. The economic models of COMPASS cover 60 countries/regions in the world. They are all constructed on the basis of the original object-oriented database system that stores all the data sets required for modelling such as IO, SNA, financial, trade and energy statistics. The energy balance model, as one of the modules in COMPASS, retrieves the IEA (International Energy Agency) energy balance table from the COMPASS database system. Then it simulates the energy balance and compiles the energy balance table for the future.

Policies to combat climate change require country- and sector-specific analysis of the greenhouse gas mitigation opportunities. Nevertheless recent research focuses on international aspects, such as the impacts of the Kyoto Mechanism. Although there are many energy-economics models in the world, the engineering models lack economic disaggregation, whereas economic models tend to lack energy end-use and process descriptions. Assessment of both policy measures geared towards specific activities together with international environmental framework calls for description of economy and energy in detailed disaggregation levels. The energy balance model contains seven energy sources for primary, transformation, utility and three end-use sectors, namely the (1) industry, (2) transportation, and (3) residential/commercial sector including agriculture. It can be used as the energy material flow model, and as the energy-environmental policy simulation tool both at aggregate and disaggregate levels. The important aspects embedded in energy balance modelling are the potential of technological change and the fuel switching towards de-carbonized society, that are likely to be induced by any policy to increase energy costs. These are econometrically estimated and employed in the simulation. This model is operated together with the COMPASS international team. COMPASS (Comprehensive Model for Policy Assessment) is a dynamic modelling system to capture multi-country and multi-sector interactions. This chapter presents the development of the energy balance model.

In literature on energy modelling the observed correlation between the economic development stage and energy intensity trends often leads to the

K. Uno (ed.), Economy–Energy–Environment Simulation, 81–98.

assumption of AEEI (autonomous energy efficiency improvement). AEEI is entirely apart from any conservation induced by rising energy prices. Recent comparison of six widely used models produced AEEI ranging from 0% to 1% per year. This implies a difference of 2.5 billion tons of carbon by 2020. The difference widens to 42 billion tons of carbon by 2100, a figure 7 times higher than the 1990 emissions level. The numerical value of the AEEI is highly controversial and remains problematical.

It is our view that modelling attempts based on assumed AEEI, or those based on AEEI measured at highly aggregate level, such as GDP and total energy consumption, are highly inadequate.

In contrast, the work presented here is based on detailed energy balance tables that are compiled annually by the IEA for a large number of countries. Energy balance tables consist of three parts: primary energy supply, energy conversion, and final use in industry, transport, and residential and other sectors. Of the primary energy sources, coal, crude oil, petroleum, natural gas, nuclear, hydro and others are distinguished. Electricity is generated by converting primary energy. The COMPASS examines economy-energy interactions at three points in the energy balance tables; namely (1) energy intensity change, defined as the energy consumption per output in respective industrial branches; (2) energy conversion efficiency, depicting the ratio between input of primary energy sources into electricity generation and the obtained electricity; and (3) the substitution among primary energy sources. Of these, (1) and (3) are econometrically examined, while (2) is an exogenous technological parameter.

In the model, relative energy price and output determine the energy intensity in three end-use sectors. Energy intensity is interpreted to represent the technology levels of a pertinent industrial branch at a given time.

The demand for electricity, in turn, determines the amount of transformation needed. The electricity generation is modelled with the conversion efficiency explained by time trend.

The share of each fuel in total primary energy supply, as well as in electricity generation, is also dependent on the relative price of the fuels in each sector. Shares of nuclear and new and renewables (hydro and others) are exogenous. The shares of remaining fuels are rescaled in the model so that the total share adds up to unity.

The economic variables such as relative prices of energy and production level of individual industrial branches are provided by the input-output/macro/financial/trade models. The link between input-output and commodity trade of energy-related products is important since this link enables endogenization of world oil prices. This becomes possible by utilizing a model incorporating the main OECD members, APEC members, Russia, oil-exporting countries, and other developing countries.

2. Objectives and features

2.1. Objectives

Considering that there are a number of existing energy-economics models operational today, it is imperative that the advantage of the COMPASS modelling approach, particularly focusing on the energy balance model, should be clarified before describing its structure. There are three major objectives in developing an energy balance model.

First, COMPASS aims at depicting a dynamic time path of interaction between energy production (seven energy sources) and consumption (three end-use sectors) in a disaggregated way. It gives both monetary and physical magnitudes of energy supply/demand in combination with the input-output model. Such materials/energy balance modelling is partly based on accounting frameworks represented by a system of integrated environmental and economic accounts (SEEA), known as green GNP. This framework consists of material inputs delivered by the natural environment, transformations within the economy, i.e. extraction, conversion, manufacturing, consumption, and material outputs (residuals) such as wastes etc. (Uno, 1995). However, such an accounting is only a snapshot of the interaction between economy and environment. The dynamic change of environmental and related activities can be described by a time-series comparison of such a framework. The idea of the negative outputs returning to the natural environment is not specifically treated in monetary value in our framework. Currently, only the CO_2 emissions are modelled, the cost of which is an externality for the whole globe to be internalized by social economic systems. The model is built on a country-by-country basis, and gives a global dynamic picture in linkage with the commodities trade of fossil coal, oil, and gas.

Secondly, COMPASS includes the technology aspect explicitly. The energy-input structure of industrial productions, household activities, transportation or commercial services, describes the level of energy production and transformation technology together with the end-use technology. For example, energy production technology can be observed as conversion efficiency. Similarly, technology in the iron and steel sector, for example, can be represented by energy intensity. However, unit consumption of energy in households, or in transportation services, cannot be calculated as the energy required to cook or light, or a passenger to travel, which represent the end-use technologies in a real sense. The development of internationally comparable physical data of durable stock representing 'lifestyle', is needed to study technologies in a modelling framework.

Thirdly, and most importantly, COMPASS captures dynamic interactions between technology, market mechanisms, and government policy on a sectoral basis. The energy balance model, combined with the IO/SNA, financial and trade balance models, distinguishes indirect taxes and subsidies for individual sectors in addition to inputs of material and labour in production processes. It is particularly important that, in practice, prospect policy measures to reduce CO_2 emissions are in most cases sector-specific. Indeed, little study has been done on linking the disaggregated analysis of driving force of the emissions with the policy options at domestic level, while keeping international comparability in mind. One of the few studies conducted to look into the existing low-cost mitigation opportunities on a country basis is the disaggregated decomposition analysis by Unander and Schipper (1999). They distinguished the activity effect, energy service effect, intensity effect, and fuel mix effect as causes of the domestic CO_2 emissions. This enables one to draw a picture of where the energy is still used inefficiently, and where the policies can be most effectively adopted, but there is no feedback regarding the policy impact of economic activities on energy aspect within this framework itself. The energy balance model, through the full disaggregation of the sectors that are linked internationally, is able to test the policy scenarios in the industry, transportation, residential/commercial (agriculture, public sectors are included), and energy sectors.

Let us try to clarify the features of the energy balance model as a tool for assessing policy measures to combat climate change. Repetto and Austin (1997) provided a list of focal points of the available models as follows:

(1) The extent to which substitution among energy sources, energy technologies, products, and production methods is possible.
(2) The extent to which market and policy distortions create opportunities for low-cost (or no-cost) improvements in energy efficiency.
(3) The likely rate of technological innovation and the responsiveness of such change to price signals.
(4) The availability and likely future cost of non-fossil, backstop energy sources.
(5) The potential for international 'joint implementation' of emissions reductions.
(6) The possibility that carbon tax revenues would be recycled through the reduction of economically burdensome tax rates.

Currently the COMPASS is designed to capture all of these except (4). The main features of the model are that it explicitly estimates the (1) substitution among energy sources, and (3) the price responsiveness of technological change. The model is also able to generate world and domestic energy prices when it is fully integrated with the energy sectors in an IO model. This is a great advantage since energy prices for non-OECD countries are not fully available from the IEA database. The removals of price distortions, a part of (2) that arises mostly from subsidies, specifically play significant roles in reducing CO_2 emissions in EITs (economies in transition) and developing countries. The assessment of joint implementation, which is item (5), can be described as the technology (input coefficients/energy intensity) transplanted to EITs. Either energy intensity or the input coefficient can be easily transferred across countries/sectors. Finally, item (6) is important in assessment of the market-based policies such as carbon tax or permits trading. The impacts of a rise in energy price will lower carbon intensity, and a change in mark-up price will affect all energy-using sectors through cost functions. The impact can also be observed as the second-round effects in the monetary policy response to control inflation in linkage with the macro-financial model.

2.2. *Theoretical standpoint*

(a) Type of model

The model that we present can be classified as a multi-sector econometric energy balance model. This type of model cannot be mapped into a conventional model categorization.

The most widely known categorization of energy-economics models draws a distinction between an *economic* and an *engineering* model. A *top-down* model has a detailed description of the economy depending on specific parameters. The other type, called *bottom-up*, entails the individual consumption pattern of energy and related technologies (IPCC, 1996b). Repetto and Austin (1997) point out that the top-down models typically assume that all cost-effective improvements in energy efficiency have already been realized, an assumption contradicted by actual experience. On the other hand the bottom-up models have found inefficiencies in energy use to the degree that around 20% of current carbon emissions could be eliminated at no cost.

The two modelling approaches have often been cited as alternatives, but recent developments show both approaches are supplementary. The MARKAL (Loulou and Kanudia, 2000) and the AIM (National Institute for Environmental Studies) are examples of such models integrating both types. Such integrated models allow us to consider the possibility of choices among a menu of technologies, under a certain constraint on economic activity. The parameters for the economic part can be modified if the result from the technology model diverges from assumptions at the macroeconomic levels. This approach serves to increase the consistency of potential technological progress in the economic context, thus the results may not be too optimistic. Weyant (1999) categorized the models presented at the energy modelling forum in their economic model types and energy/carbon model types (see Table 5-1). In the presented categories, the COMPASS energy balance model may be mapped into the last row of an economic model type; however, an energy model type may lie between energy demand/supply sectors and technology detail. We will discuss our modelling approach in economy and energy together with a theoretical background.

(b) Multi-sector econometric model

For convenience of describing this modelling approach let us compare it with CGE (computable general equilibrium model). In COMPASS the energy

Table 5-1. Model types

Economy Model	Energy/Carbon Model: Energy Supplies & Demands by Sector	Energy Technology Detail	Carbon Coefficients
Aggregate Production/Cost function		CETA MERGE3 GRAPE	FUND RICE
Multi-sector General Equilibrium	MIT-EPPA WorldScan G-Cubed	ABARE-GTEM AIM MS-MRT SGM	
Multi-sector Macroeconometric	Oxford		

Source: Weyant *et al.* (1999).

supply/demand is expressed in monetary value in an IO framework, and in physical volume in an energy balance model. Together with IO, SNA-financial, and trade balance they comprise a multi-sector economic and energy flow model. Let us first clarify the type of economic model of the COMPASS. The system includes employment, financial markets, international capital flows, and monetary policy. According to West (1995), the model can be termed as the IOE (input-output + econometric model). CGE provides the optimal solution by assuming consumers and producers allocate their resources in order to maximize their welfare or profits. Although it is convenient in analytical terms, IOE does not assume the equilibrium in the market (Meyer and Uno, 1999a; Ayres, 1994), which does not reflect the real world. It does not necessarily assume perfect knowledge in the market place, thus it describes economy in 'as is base' and reflecting the reality of the economic behaviour, without *a priori* assumptions not based on empirical evidence. What mostly makes IOE differ from CGE is that IOE is a dynamic modelling approach. Therefore, IOE is capable of depicting time paths of the endogenous variables reacting to the exogenous impacts on economic systems. Thus, with the energy balance model, not only can we test the impacts of certain policy measures, but we can also explore how the objective of such a policy is being met with the passage of time.

(c) Energy model and technological change

Many energy-economics models employ production functions, which assume the factors of production are continuously variable and substitutable (Allen, 1968). However, whether substitutability exists between energy and capital is controversial. Some observers claim that energy and capital are complementary in the short run, and substitutable in the long run; others conclude there is no such evidence. Slade *et al.* (1993) summarize the reasons for such divergence in research outcomes. They note that the important difference in the observation lies in the estimation of capital stock. The substitution between energy and other factors, commonly presented as ESUB, lies between 0.3 and 0.7 across the models (Azar, 1996). The higher this value is, the easier it is to reduce CO_2 emissions. Austin and Repetto (1997) argue that, despite being more or less disaggregated, models differ in the assumed ease of substitution among products and technologies in response to cost change, and it is difficult for modellers to get it right.

Let us briefly look at the organization of the energy-models employing production functions at an aggregated/disaggregated level. In the DICE model (Nordhaus, 1994) there is only one product: world output, and two factors of production: capital and labour inputs. In the Global 2100 (Manne and Richels, 1992) that encompasses the subdivided regions of the world, the electrical energy and non-electrical energy, capital, and labour have the constant elasticity of substitution. The MARKAL is an engineering model in which the production function allows substitution between the pair capital-labour and energy. The two-level CES (constant elasticity of substitution) function (Kosaka and Yano, 1999) separates labour from capital for the substitution for energy inputs. The nested-CES functions are employed by a multi-sector general equilibrium model such as OECD GREEN (Burniaux *et al.*, 1992), GemWTrap (Bernard and Vielle, 1999), among others. In any of these models the production factors substitution plays a central role in the formulation of energy demand functions and consequently determines the costs required for reducing emissions.

The well-established production functions are unquestionably theoretically satisfying. Nevertheless, we do not use such a function in linking between energy and economy in the model. We consider, though, that marginal, but econometrically estimated technological change (shifts in isoquants), rather than constant substitution (movements alongside an isoquant), need to be modelled. Currently in COMPASS, the input coefficients (*aij*) are yet to be modelled to shift according to the change in labour and material costs. Higher productivity presents lower labour cost in producing the same value, and mark-up pricing is being implemented. In the energy balance model the technological change is considered to occur by the change in relative prices of energy to labour and material costs.

In addition, there is no internationally comparable capital stock data. We will keep exploring the quality and availability of R&D data from individual country sources. It is an important step to discuss in enhancing the model, since it relates to the discussion of endogenous technological change. Rather, at this stage, we try to observe the price responsiveness of energy intensity – a change in mixed form of the technologies and production processes – that is not radical, but surely more than marginal in nature.

2.3. *Energy intensity*

In the model we use estimated price elasticity of energy intensities at end-use sectors, testing the hypothesis of price-induced technological change. It is probable that the rate of technological change and its price responsiveness varies across countries and sectors. As for energy efficiency improvement, such variations may be due to differences in the existing energy tax, share of carbon-intensive fuel, and the energy intensity level. If the rise in relative price induces the inefficient technologies to retire and investments are made towards installing more energy-efficient ones, the emissions can be reduced efficiently. This approach allows the model to look into the low-cost opportunities spreading across the economy in the long run in response to the initial market signals, whereas socioeconomic adjustment requires some time lags. The reasons we employ such an approach are as follows.

Energy intensity can be interpreted as an *ex-post-facto* realization of selected technology. In reality, the causes of the fall/rise in energy intensities are complex. They include technological improvements in individual energy use, structural shifts in energy systems, inter-fuel substitutions, economic structural change from more to less energy-intensive industries, and changing lifestyles. Not necessarily all, but many, of these factors affecting energy efficiency improvement form the long-term trend in energy intensity. Therefore, whether the economy can lower energy intensities constitutes an important key in mitigating any greenhouse gas emissions. Most of today's domestic climate change measures/policies are directed towards efficiency improvement.

Nakicenovic *et al.* (1998) found that the energy intensities are lower at higher per-capita GDP, except for the former USSR. They attribute the result, first, to more efficient energy conversions and end-use technologies that become affordable, and second, to the higher quality of energy carriers made available by the energy sector. The observed correlation between the economic development stage and energy intensity trends leads to the assumption of the AEEI in conventional energy-economic modelling. The AEEI of 0.5% per year results in an energy conservation growth at 0.5% less than GDP, and is entirely apart from any conservation induced by rising energy prices.

The OECD model comparison project (Dean and Hoeller, 1992) conducted sensitivity analyses of the model outcomes by standardizing essential assumptions. The six widely used models were compared including CRTM (Rutherford, 1992), ERM by Edmonds-Reilly (Barns *et al.*, 1992), OECD GREEN (Burniaux *et al.*, 1992), IEA model (Vouyoukas, 1992), Global 2100 (Manne-Richels, 1992) and WW (Whalle-Wigley, 1992). They found that AEEI ranges from 0% to 1%, resulting in a gap of 2.5 billion tons of carbon by 2020, which increases to 42 billion tons of carbon by 2100. This is nearly 7 times larger than the emissions level in 1990. The emission abatement cost is crucially sensitive to the baseline emission level where highly controversial AEEI assumption plays a key role.

Jorgenson and Wilcoxen (1993) recognized in the neoclassical approach that the economy could be more energy-using, contrary to the conventional wisdom of autonomous conservation, if the relative price stays constant. Azar and Dowlatabadi (1999) pointed out that AEEI is not an appropriate measure of technological change since the energy efficiency improvement is not likely to be captured unless specific policies are adopted. They claimed that, for heavy industries, energy costs are the major concerns, and they must figure prominently in economic activity for technological change to reduce energy intensity. Such discussions arise in the wake of the evolutionary theory of economics, in which the technological change is considered to occur in the economic disequilibrium, which creates incentives for new technological development and thus drives economic growth (Ayres, 1994).

As will be discussed in the next section the estimated elasticity is constant, by taking the double-log specification, and is applied to the energy balance simulation for the future. In this approach the change in elasticity itself has not yet been studied in the current framework of our energy balance model.

2.4. Energy substitution

The term energy substitution needs to be clearly defined here; it refers to the inter-energy substitution induced by price change. There are few descriptions of the model specification regarding the constant elasticity for inter-energy substitution. The GREEN model distinguishes the elasticity for old vintages and new vintages. The parameter for the inter-energy elasticity is 0.25 for old and 2.0 for new vintages. It is assumed to be 10.0, quite large, between conventional and backstop technologies. The parameter is uniform across countries and energy use sectors. The Oxford model (Cooper *et al.*, 1999), which is similar in sector disaggregation to COMPASS, presents the elasticity for electricity generation. The parameters are modified by technology models so that the 'coal, oil, and gas total' and 'nuclear/non-fossil fuel' elasticity of 0.5 includes a 0.2 technological gain, which is not likely to be reversed.

If elasticity is high or it is easier for an economy to de-carbonize, and whether the models treat non-fossil or backstop energies, matters greatly in cost evaluation. For example models that exclude backstop technologies overstate the economic impact of carbon tax because the economy is assumed to rely indefinitely on conventional fuels even after their costs were higher than the costs at which alternative energy sources would be profitable (Repetto and Austin, 1997). The major backstop technologies for production of electricity include: solar photovoltaics and thermal, fluidized-bed combustion, integrated gasification/combined cycle, geothermal, wind, and fuel cells. The most important drawback is their cost relative to a conventional combustion system, i.e. the capital costs of coal combustion are between $1260 (1983 US$/kW) and $1580, whereas the solar thermal system cost is about $2000 to $3000. The costs are expected to decline in the earlier stage of diffusion, alongside the curve of learning by experience. There are also possibilities that other relatively inexpensive technologies can also substitute for heavy fuels. Fuel switching to new energies can be prompted by the future prospective of returns to investment, supported by government subsidies. However, entering into new technologies is highly uncertain and may not be very promising for the medium-term contribution to CO_2 abatement. In most of the energy markets, fossil fuel 'lock-in' could be persistent, in particular with relatively low oil prices. In such a case it is possible that the renewable energy technologies remain restricted to niche markets.

3. The model design

3.1. Energy balance and sectors

The development of an energy model is based on the time-series of the IEA energy balance table that are reworked and stored in the database system of COMPASS. The structure of the energy table in the model is shown in Table 5-2 together with standard variables names used in the database and modelling. This consists of seven energy sources for primary, secondary, and final consumption. We added the line 'Additional*' for convenience of modelling.

Let us first describe the construction of the table. TPES (total primary energy supply) is equal to the sum of domestic production, import, and stock change minus export (IEA Row no. 1-5). It is also equal to TFC (total final consumption) plus all the inputs for energy transformation and own use and losses (expressed as a negative) plus all the inputs for energy transformation and own use and losses (expressed as a negative) and $\pm$ statistical difference (no. 7-18). The transformation includes electricity generation, etc. (no. 9-12), petroleum refinery (no. 13), coal transformation (no. 14), liquefaction of gas (no. 15), and other transformation (no. 16). TFC consists of energy use in Industry, Transportation, and Residential/Commercial sectors plus Non-energy use.

Industry, Transportation, and Residential/Commercial sectors contain consumption of each fuel, represented with the prefix *ind*, *tra*, and *pro*, respectively. These end-use sectors are grouped with the IO 36 sectors according to the International Industrial Classification Rev. 2 and Rev. 3 as is shown in Table 5-3 (United Nations, 1990). We need to combine Rev. 2 and Rev. 3 because the recent IEA data are classified according to Rev. 3, but the COMPASS classification has not yet been updated. This grouping enables us to link the whole energy balance table with the IO table. In the near future, the supply of seven fuels will be grouped with the energy sectors in IO, such as petroleum and coal products, mining and quarrying, and electricity and gas.

3.2. Logical structure

The flow chart of the energy balance model is drawn in Figure 5-1. The economic variables coming from IO/macro/financial and trade models drive energy-related materials consumption, as is indicated in the figure as IO model. The arrow shows the dependence of the variables; the arrows with double lines show that variables are used in regressions, and arrows with thick lines indicate

Table 5-2. Energy balance table in the model

IEA No.	Energy Balance Table	Coa	Crude Oil	Petroleum	Gas	Nuclear	Hydro/ Other	Electricity and Heat	Difference	Total	Unit
1	Indigenous production	Outcoa	outcru	outprf	outgas	outnuc	outren	outelh			Ktoe
2	Import	Mttcoa	mttcru	mttprf	mttgas	mttnuc	mttren	mttelh			Ktoe
3	Export	Xttcoa	xttcru	xttprf	xttgas	xttnuc	xttren	xttelh			Ktoe
4	Intl. marine bunkers plus	Nttcoa	nttcru	nttprf	nttgas	nttnuc	nttren	nttelh			Ktoe
5	Stock changes										Ktoe
6	*Total Primary Energy Supply*	Petcoa	petcru	petprf	petgas	petnuc	petren	petelh			Ktoe
7,8	Returns and transfers Statistical differences	Sdtcoa	sdtcru	sdtprf	sdtgas	sdtnuc	sdtren	sdtelh			Ktoe
9	Electricity plants							ougelh =			
10	CHP plants	Inecoa	inecru	ineprf	inegas	inenuc	ineren	(ougele) + (oughea)			Ktoe
11	Heat plants										
13	Petroleum refineries		inpcru	ourprf							Ktoe
12	Gas works										
14	Coal transformation										
15	Liquefaction	Otfcoa	otfcru	otfprf	otfgas	otfnuc	otfren				Ktoe
16	Other transformation										
12,18	Own use plus	Loocoa	loocru	looprf	loogas	loonuc	looren	looelh			Ktoe
	Distribution losses										Ktoe
19	*Total Final Consumption*	Ftecoa	ftecru	fteprf	ftegas	ftenuc	fteren	fteelh		fteorg = ftedes	Ktoe
Aditional*	***Energy use***	Feecoa	feecru	feeprf	feegas		feeren	feeelh			Ktoe
20	***Industry sector***	Indcoa	indcru	indprf	indgas		indren	indelh		feeind	Ktoe
21	Iron and steel (ias)										Ktoe
22,23	Chemical (che)										Ktoe
24	Non-ferrous metals (nfm)										Ktoe
25	Non-metalic minerals (nmp)										Ktoe
26	Transport equipment (tre)										Ktoe
27	Machinery (mac)										Ktoe
28	Mining and quarrying (maq)										Ktoe
29	Food and tobacco (fbt)										Ktoe
30	Paper, pulp and printing (pap)										Ktoe

Table 5-2. continued

IEA No.	Energy Balance Table	Coa	Crude Oil	Petroleum	Gas	Nuclear	Hydro/ Other	Electricity and Heat	Difference	Total	Unit
31	Wood and wood products (waf)										Ktoe
32	Construction (con)										Ktoe
33	Textile and leather (tal)										Ktoe
34	Non-specified Industry (oth)										Ktoe
35,36,37, 38,39,40, 41,42	***Transport sector*** Air, road, rail, Internal navigation and non-specified transport	Tracoa	tracru	traprf	treagas		traren	traelh		feetra	Ktoe
43	***Tertiary sector***	Procoa	procru	proprf	progas		proren	proelh		feepro	Ktoe
44	Agriculture										Ktoe
45,46,47	Public/commerce, residential										Ktoe
48,49, 50,51	***Non-energy use***	Fnecoa	fnecru	fneprf	fnegas					fnetot	Ktoe
52	Electricity generated	Geecoa		geeprf	geegas	geenuc	geeren			geetot	Gwh
55	Heat generated	Gehcoa		gehprf	gehgas	gehnuc	gehren	(gehele) + (gehhea)		gehtot	TJ
Aditional*	Electricity and heat generated	Gencoa		genprf	gengas	gennuc	genren	genelh	gendif	gentot	Ktoe

Source: COMPASS working paper Umehara (1999).

Note: GWh*0.0086 is equal to Mtoe. TJ*0.002388 is equal to Mtoe.

Table 5-3. Sector integration of input-output and energy balance (end-use level)

Total Final Energy Consumption	IEA ISIC (Rev. 2)	IEA ISIC (Rev. 3)	COMPASS IO Branches Description
Industry sector			
1 Iron and steel	371		12 Iron and steel
2 Chemical	351, 352, 354, 355, 356		7 Industrial chemicals 8 Drugs and medicine 9 Petroleum and coal products 10 Rubber and plastic products
3 Non-ferrous metals	372		13 Non-ferrous metals
4 Non-metallic minerals	36		11 Non-metallic mineral products
5 Transport equipment	384		19 Ship building and repairing 20 Other transport 21 Motor vehicles 22 Aircraft
6 Machinery	38		14 Metal products 15 Non-electrical machinery 16 Office and computing machinery 17 Electrical apparatus, 18 Radio, TV and communication equipment 23 Professional goods
7 Mining	23, 29		2 Mining and quarrying
8 Food processing, beverages and tobacco	31		3 Food, beverages and tobacco
9 Pulp paper and printing	34		6 Paper, paper products and printing
10 Wood and wood products	33		5 Wood products and furniture
11 Construction	50		26 Construction
12 Textiles and leather	32		4 Textiles, apparel and leather
13 Non-specified	****	25, 33, 36, 37	24 Other manufacturing
Transport sector	****	60, 61, 62	29 Transport and storage
Air			
Road			
Rail			
Internal navigation			
Non-specified transport			
Other sectors			
Agriculture Public/commerce Residential Non-specified other		01, 02, 05 41, 50, 51, 52, 55, 63, 64, 65, 66, 70, 71, 72, 73, 74, 75, 80, 85, 90, 91, 92, 93, 95 and 99	1 Agriculture, forestry and fishing 25 Electricity and gas and water (Water Only) 27 Whole sale and retail trade 28 Restaurants and hotels 30 Communication 31 Finance and insurance 32 Real estate and business services 33 Community, social and personal services 34 Producers of government services
Non-energy use	****	****	****

Sources: Compiled by the present author based on IEA (various year a,b); OECD (1995a); and United Nations (1990).

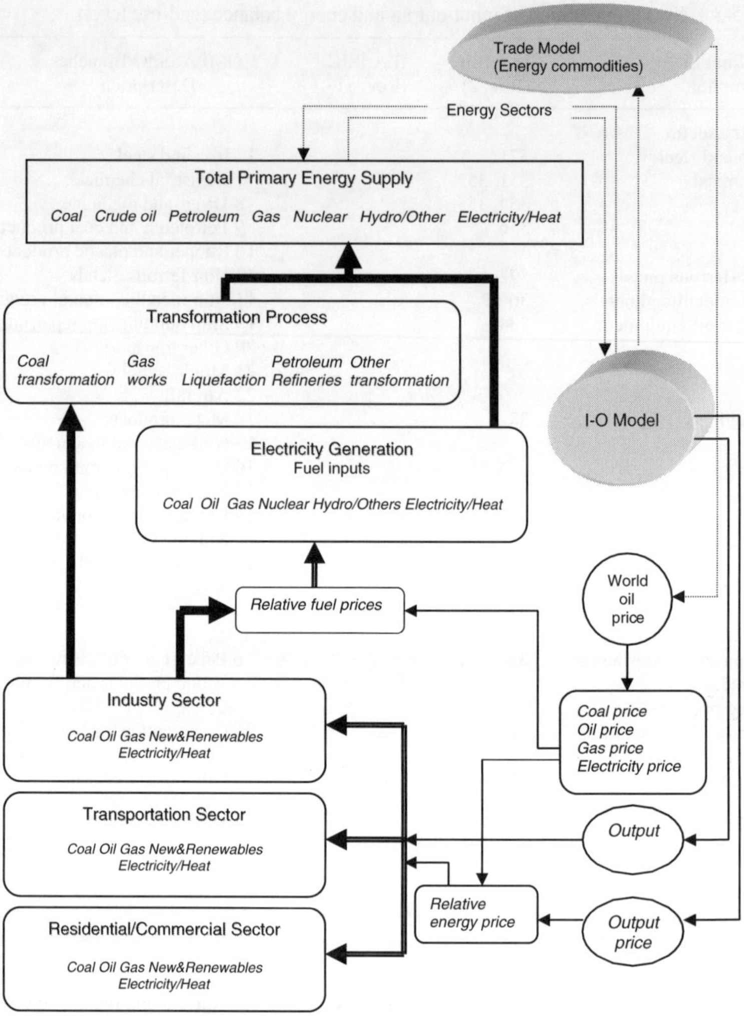

Figure 5-1. Structure of energy balance model.

that the aggregations are done by energy sources. A dotted line indicates the links with economic spheres. This is important for future development since this link enables us to endogenize the world oil price when other regions of the world, including oil-exporting countries, are incorporated in an energy balance model. When this is achieved this will be the third global closure within the COMPASS framework, including commodity trade, international financial transactions, and world energy flow.

In the model the relative energy price and *output* determine the energy intensity levels in three end-use sectors, which represent the technology defined here as the energy consumption per unit sector *output*. Energy consumption in end-use sectors is calculated as the estimated energy intensity multiplied by the *output*. Then final energy demand/supply is determined through transformation and electricity generation.

Shares of each fuel in the end-use sectors, as well as in electricity generation, are also dependent on the relative price of the fuels in each sector. Shares of nuclear and new and renewables (hydro/others) are exogenous. Electricity generation is also modelled with conversion efficiency depending on time trend. With the share of nuclear and new and renewables given by policy, the remaining shares of the rest of the fuel inputs are recalculated so the total share adds up to unity.

3.3. *Equations*

(a) Price equations

Price indexes for coal, oil, gas are used to calculate the weighted energy price index in three end-use sectors and utility sector.

$$pe_{ij(t)} = p_{j(t)} \times s_{ij(t)} \tag{1}$$

$$pe_{i(t)} = \sum_j pe_{ij(t)} \tag{2}$$

Pe = Energy price index (1990 = 100)
i = End-use sectors; Industry, Transportation, Residential
j = Energy carriers: Coal, Oil, Gas, Electricity

The weighted output price indexes are obtained in the input-output models (modelled in I-O).

Unit cost of production is determined by the unit price of domestic and imported products, labor, plus indirect tax minus subsidies minus depreciation per unit of output.

$$u_{(t)} = D'_{(t)} \times p_{(t)} + AM_{(t)} \times q_{(t)} + Z_{(t)} \times w_{(t)} + a + b \tag{3}$$

D = matrix of domestic input coefficients
AM = matrix of input coefficients of imported goods
Z = diagonal matrix of labour input coefficients
w = vector of wages
a = vector of indirect taxes minus subsidies per unit of output
b = vector of depreciation per unit of output
p = vector of domestic price
q = vector of import price.

The price of sector *i* is now dependent on the unit cost of sector *i*.

$$p_{i(t)} = p_i[u_{i(t)}] \tag{4}$$

(b) Energy intensity equation

$$\log \frac{E_{i(t)}}{X_{i(t)}} = a + \beta \log\left(\frac{Pe_{i(t)}}{P_{i(t)}}\right) + t \tag{5}$$

E_i = Energy consumption in sector *i* (unit: Ktoe)
X_{it} = Output in sector *i*
t = Time trend.

Now we have the estimated energy intensity, then multiply it by the *production output* is equal to the energy demand in sector *i*.

$$E_{i(t)} = X_{i(t)} \times \frac{E_{i(t)}}{X_{i(t)}} \tag{6}$$

(c) Energy substitution equation

$$s_{ij} = f\left[\log\left(s_{ij(t-1)}\right), \log\left(\frac{pe_{ij(t)}}{pe_{i(t)}}\right)\right] \tag{7}$$

(d) Final energy consumption equations

$$E_{c(t)} = \sum_i (s_{ic(t)} E_{i(t)}) \tag{8}$$

$$E_{o(t)} = \sum_i (s_{io(t)} E_{i(t)}) \tag{9}$$

$$E_{g(t)} = \sum_i (s_{ig(t)} E_{i(t)}) \tag{10}$$

$$E_{e(t)} = \sum_i (s_{ie(t)} E_{i(t)}) \tag{11}$$

(e) Transformation and conversion equations

$$e_{tc(t)} = r_c E_{c(t)} \tag{12}$$

$$e_{to(t)} = r_o E_{o(t)} \tag{13}$$

$$e_{tg(t)} = r_g E_{g(t)} \tag{14}$$

$$s_{uj_{(t)}} = \log\left(\frac{p_{uj}}{p_u}\right) \tag{15}$$

$$e_{uc(t)} = S_{uc}E_{e(t)} \tag{16}$$

$$e_{uo(t)} = S_{uo}E_{e(t)} \tag{17}$$

$$e_{ug(t)} = S_{ug}E_{e(t)} \tag{18}$$

(f) Fuel inputs equations for electricity generation

Fuel *j* input is determined by the relative price of the fuel over weighted price of fuels in the electricity sector.

(g) Total primary energy supply equation

$$F_c = e_{tc} + e_{uc} \tag{19}$$

$$F_o = e_{to} + e_{uo} \tag{20}$$

$$F_g = e_{tg} + e_{ug} \tag{21}$$

$$F_c = E_e \tag{22}$$

(h) Carbon emission equations

The carbon coefficient (MMTC/Mtoe) of coal is 1.08, oil is 0.84 and gas is 0.64.

$$C_{ic(t)} = c_c E_{ic(t)} \tag{23}$$

$$C_{io(t)} = c_o E_{io(t)} \tag{24}$$

$$C_{ig(t)} = c_g E_{ig(t)} \tag{25}$$

4. Energy balance table and the model

The logical flow of the energy model is as follows. Economic agents (utilities, industry, and consumers) react to changes in relative prices of energy to the price of the branch output (i.e., elasticity of energy intensity in terms of $pei_i = pene/pout$ i) and relative prices among primary energy sources (i.e. elasticity of energy substitution in terms of coal prices *vs*. average energy price, or crude oil price *vs*. average energy price, etc.) is explained in the model. It is not treated as exogenous assumptions. In a simulation experiment these can be made policy variables, and can be forcefully made to take particular values coming from a scenario. The same thing can be said about technology (input coefficients are endogenous or can be policy variables through R&D or technology transfers), trade pattern (country shares are endogenous depending on prices or R&D, but can be determined by policy through liberalization), industrial structure (final demand = lifestyle is endogenous but can be changed by environmental policy, and output of each industrial branch can be endogenous or imposed for the sake of a policy experiment), and cost structure (production cost is endogenously explained, but, with the introduction of emission trade, new cost components can be added).

The emission of CO_2 can be calculated based on technically given parameters for different fossil fuels (APERC, 1998).

Coal: 1.08 tC/toe
Gas: 0.64 tC/toe
Oil: 0.84 tC/toe

The price for tradable permits is obtained by the market-clearing process. Define the demand surplus of world CO_2 emission rights. If the demand for the permit is bigger than the supply the price of the permit is raised by a very small fraction. The demand will be reduced by a small margin in the next iteration. The iterative process determines the clearing of the international energy market. In the input-output framework carbon tax can be treated as indirect tax which is represented in the value-added sphere.

In summary, the logical flow of the energy block is from final consumption through conversion to primary energy demand. Econometrically estimated variables are energy consumption by different industrial sectors and the selection among different energy carriers. Technological parameters are the conversion efficiency from primary energy to secondary. The economic block (see Chapter 3) generates prices of output in individual branches (*p* or *pout*) whereas energy prices in respective branches are derived from exogenously given prices for primary energy carriers and their shares in energy use in the branch in question.

Part III

Economy–energy–environment, 2010

6
Policy agenda

YUMIKO UMEHARA

1. Kyoto and beyond

The global climate change issue is gaining ever-growing attention as the seriousness of the greenhouse effect becomes widely recognized. This poses a serious challenge to the global community. For one, global warming itself is a serious threat, in addition posing a shift of our mindset from economic growth to sustainability of the way of life and the resource base. Second, for lack of a global policy agent and a global market mechanism encompassing environmental spheres, we are left with a situation in which we are faced with a threat on a global scale. We are not equipped with an effective mechanism for decision making and policy implementation except for national governments that are, at best, responsible for domestic constituencies of the current generation.

Since the beginning of the industrialization in the late 19th to early 20th century, a series of new innovative technologies has contributed to the high productivity growth. The appearance of new technologies has eliminated environmental problems while creating new ones. However, activities with heavy reliance on the burning of fossil fuels outpaced sequestration of GHGs (greenhouse gases) by the eco-system. This caused the dramatic rise in CO_2 (carbon dioxide) emissions. The concentration of CO_2 reached 340 ppmv (1/million in volume) in 1980. This is expected to double to 560 ppmv possibly as early as 2030, and could lead to a rise in global mean temperatures unprecedented in human history. The industrialized countries have disproportionately increased the accumulation of CO_2. Nevertheless, LDCs (less developed countries) are vital in contemplating any long-term solution. The most commonly used reference scenario of CO_2 emissions trajectory, IPCC's IS92a, indicates that LDCs' total emission level will reach the level of industrialized nations by the year 2037. Therefore, the methods by which the global society addresses the climate change issue involve issues such as the division of responsibilities and differing capabilities to respond. Climate change is unique in the human history of pollution in that it is caused by all human activities, and the consequences are uniform over the globe as a whole.

The Framework Convention to Climate Change (UNFCCC) was signed in 1992 at the United Nations Conference on Environment and Development

K. Uno (ed.), Economy–Energy–Environment Simulation, 101–110.

(UNCED). The objective of the Convention is:

> to achieve stabilization of greenhouse gas concentrations in the atmosphere at a level that would prevent dangerous interference induced by human activities in a time-frame sufficient for ecosystems to adopt to climate change, and secure food production so the economic development proceed in a sustainable manner (Article 2).

It requires the parties to take precautionary measures to anticipate, prevent, or minimize the causes of climate change and mitigate its adverse outcomes cost-effectively. The parties should also take into account the benefit of present and future generations, on the basis of equity and in accordance with their common but differentiated responsibilities.

After the Earth's Summit conference in 1992, a series of COP (Conferences of the Parties) took place to materialize the UNFCCC. The Kyoto Protocol, adapted in 1997 at COP-3, was the first stage of the international framework that enforces the emission limitations on Annex-I parties – most of the industrialized countries (UNFCC, 1997). Table 6-1 shows the target reduction from the 1990 emission levels for the major Annex I parties. At the time of writing this chapter, the Protocol has been signed by 84 countries and is subject to ratification. However, only a few of the small island countries have so far ratified. The negotiations are likely to become more difficult, as discussions of the implementation of the Protocol are sensitive to a number of complex interest groups.

When environmental ministers from G8 countries met in Otsu City in Japan, in April 2000, one of the events leading to the Summit in Okinawa in July 2000, the most heavily debated point was whether to set a concrete date for putting the Kyoto Protocol into effect. The Protocol, which was adopted at the Third Conference of the Parties (COP-3) in Kyoto in December 1997, obliges industrialized countries to reduce greenhouse gas emissions in order to mitigate global warming. The United States and Canada could not agree to include a specific deadline to ratify the Protocol because of domestic legislative procedures. All European Union countries, Japan, and Russia agreed that the Kyoto

Table 6-1. Kyoto targets and 1996 CO_2 emissions, G7 countries

	Target in 2010 (1990 = 100)	1996 Emission (1990 = 100)
Canada	94	110
USA	93	109
Japan	94	111
France	100	101
Germany	79	93
Italy	92	110
UK	87.5	100

Protocol should be ratified as soon as possible. The joint communiqué stated that 'We confirm our commitment to ensure that results achieved at COP-6 help promote the ratification and entry into force of the Kyoto Protocol as soon as possible. For most countries, this means no later than 2002.' The Sixth Conference of the Parties (COP-6) to the UN Framework Convention on Climate Change was held in the Hague, Netherlands, in November 2000, but had to re-convene in Bonn in July 2001 in an effort to come to an agreement on the details of implementing the Protocol in order to resolve major differences among participants. The US has shown considerable reluctance in following up the consensus achieved in Kyoto. Japan demonstrated unwillingness, recognizing that meeting the target would be extremely difficult given the current excess emissions by the target date, in addition to the fact that its energy efficiency is already highest in the world, leaving less room for future reduction. The EU as a group of countries strongly committed to the implementation phase, admitted carbon sequestration sinks for Japan and Canada, and contributed to keep the Protocol alive. The focus of COP-7 that met in Marrakesh, Morocco, in November 2001 was whether the participating countries could agree on the rules for compliance. Earlier in the year, a top official of the US said that the treaty would impose an excessive burden on US industries and that it is inappropriate to exempt developing countries, including China and India, from the mandatory emissions targets. Since then, the United States started to contemplate its own way of approaching the generally-agreed need to reduce greenhouse gas emissions, but not through a single international agreement. Japan opted to treat the emission targets as 'politically' binding, but not 'legally' binding, before the treaty is formally ratified next year. In the end, it has decided to ratify the Protocol even without waiting for US participation. Russia also agreed after obtaining a concession that doubles the credits it could claim for carbon absorption of its forests and agricultural land. The Rio Plus 10 meeting is scheduled to be held in 2002, marking the 10th anniversary of the 1992 Earth Summit in Rio De Janeiro and laying the groundwork for future environmental issues.

2. Policy issues

The innovative element of the Protocol is to introduce flexibility mechanisms such as 'Joint Implementation (Article 6)', 'Clean Development Mechanism (Article 12)', and 'Emissions Trading (Article 17)'. Such international cooperative modes of emission abatement contribute greatly to reducing the economic burden of the countries with high abatement costs under the set of specific targets. However, these mechanism are supplemental and major reductions of GHGs will have to be achieved domestically by each party (Figure 6-1). Therefore, the selection of appropriate policy measures is currently being sought by governments. Despite the fact that the measures should be based on our understanding on the greenhouse effect, and its potential consequences, economic considerations should play an important role in choosing the means of achieving the target. For instance, the

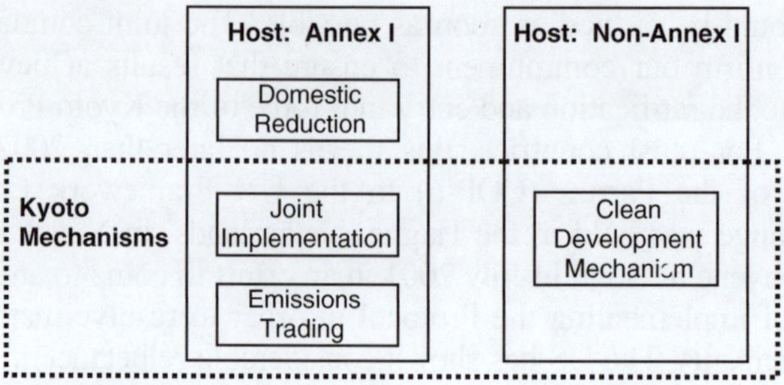

Figure 6-1. Kyoto mechanisms.
Source: Sijm *et al.*, 2000.

Best Practice already proposed by the UK government includes the Climate Change Levy, which will be imposed on industrial sectors, but not on transport of the household sector with consideration to social equity. Within industries, energy-intensive sectors will be given lower rates of levy so that they will not lose competitiveness. How would this affect economy and environment at the sectoral level? What would be the consequence if Japan, for instance, took the same step towards levying on industries? Are there any low-cost mitigation opportunities? The interaction between technology, market mechanism, and government policy needs to be studied in more detail. The energy balance model presented here is built in response to such needs coming both from the policy designing process and international policy coordination.

The specified limits on GHG emissions in the Kyoto Protocol would reduce the Annex I countries' average annual emissions between 2008 and 2012 to about 5% below the 1990 level. The basket of the six key GHGs are included – CO_2, CH_4, N_2O, halocarbons, perfluorocarbons, and sulphur hexafluoride, which are not controlled by the Montreal Protocol. The quantified reduction targets for Annex I countries and the required reductions from the reference case (IOE99) are shown in Table 6-2. All industrialized countries except Australia are required to reduce emissions, whereas economies in transition, such as Eastern Europe and the former Soviet Union, are projected to have excess emissions over target by 374 MMTC (million metric tons of carbon). The industrialized countries are allowed to enter the 'emission reduction units' among themselves, and of 'certified emission reduction' under the clean development mechanism. Such flexible mechanisms contribute greatly to reducing the global net cost of mitigating GHGs. However, since the differentiated targets are likely to result in heavy economic burdens if the mechanisms do not operate effectively, many studies focused on the cost-effectiveness of the different trading regimes.

Who will be the buyers and who will be the sellers in international emission trading? A variety of model results on the cost of Kyoto targets are presented and studied in the work by the EMF (Energy Modeling Forum) (Weyant, 1999). The costs differ in great extent across the variety of models presented.

Table 6-2. Projected 2010 emission and required reduction of Annex I parties

Region and Country	1990 Emission (MMTC)	2010 Reference Case (MMTC)	2010 Kyoto Target MMTC)	Change from Reference Case, 2010 (%)
Annex I Industrialized				
United States	1384	1790	1252	−30
Canada	126	162	118	−27
Western Europe	936	1021	862	−16
Japan	274	322	258	−20
Australia	90	133	97	−14
Total Annex I Industrialized	2772	3408	2586	−24
Transitional (EE/FSU)				
Former Soviet Union	991	666	990	49
Eastern Europe	299	270	320	18
Total EE/FSU	1290	935	1309	40
Total	4062	4344	3895	−10

Source: Energy Information Administration, US Department of Energy (1999).

Table 6-3. Model types

	Energy/Carbon Model		
Economy Model	Energy Supplies & Demands by Sector	Energy Technology Detail	Carbon Coefficients
Aggregate Production/Cost function		CETA MERGE3 GRAPE	FUND RICE
Multi-sector General Equilibrium	MIT-EPPA WorldScan G-Cubed	ABARE-GTEM AIM MS-MRT SGM	
Multi-sector Macroeconometric	Oxford		

Source: Weyant *et al.* (1999).

Comparing the results in all 13 models, Japan is faced with the highest carbon price, indicating the highest marginal abatement cost. The average carbon tax required to meet the target for Japan under a No Trading (NT) regime is around \$400/tc (1990 US\$/metric ton of carbon). The average for the USA and CANZ (Canada/Australia/New Zealand) lies between \$150 and \$200, and the EU average ranges from \$200 to \$300. The differences in carbon prices reflect pre-existing energy prices, share of coal, amount of energy produced domestically, and the required reduction in emissions given the baseline emission growth (Bernstein *et al.*, 1999). Russia, where actual emission is less than the target level, will be the only seller. All of the model results concluded that there is a great cost reduction under Annex I Trading (AI) than under NT. A rough overview shows the cost drop to 1/4 for Japan, 1/3 for EU, and 1/2 for USA and CANZ with the equalized carbon price for AI parties. Under Global Trading

(GT), the equalized global carbon price may be less than \$50, in which case the costs can be halved compared to the AI case. This is due to additional sales of emission right by non-Annex I countries. This kind of model exercise gives excellent insights into policy making in broader perspective.

3. The players

Annex I countries refers to the UNFCC Climate Convention list and include all OECD members and countries with economies in transition. All other countries are referred to as non-Annex I countries. (Annex B countries, not touched upon here, refer to the Kyoto Protocol lists and include those developed countries that have accepted the target for their GHG emissions and include OECD members, Central and Eastern Europe, and Russia.)

Faced with the increased energy cost in meeting the Kyoto targets, energy-intensive industries may shift to non-Annex I countries where the energy costs are lower, in which case the reduction of GHGs can be readily offset. It is pointed out that GHG emissions in non-Annex I countries might increase in response to mitigating efforts in the Annex I countries, representing ‘carbon leakage’. On the part of the industrialized countries, this means significant production reduction and employment loss. Full global trading eliminates leakage because all regions then face emissions caps. In this context participation by the developing countries to emissions trading is another critical issue to be addressed. This needs to be discussed in relation to the equity issue. Therefore the economic trends in countries that did not sign the Protocol, represented by South-East Asia and China in our analysis, are an important policy issue.

In the former Soviet Union and some East European countries, emissions in the target year are expected to be lower than in the 1990 base. The term ‘hot air’ points to the difference between the assigned amount of GHG emissions and the actual level in the 2008-2012 target year. This represents the emissions reduction caused by the decline in the economy, but not by energy efficiency improvements. If Russians can sell the difference to the international emission permit market they can realize a windfall gain. If this happens, Annex I countries would not be obliged to reduce GHG emissions domestically. The economic performance of Russia in the future is to be carefully looked at in this context.

3.1. The scenarios for industrialized countries

Compared to the 1990 level the United States is required to reduce emissions by 7% in 2010. Of this, the United States expects to achieve a 4% cut through domestic measures, sink, and reduction of GHGs other than CO_2, and the remaining 3% through emission trading, JI (joint implementation), and CDM (clean development mechanism). It is estimated that actual emissions would far exceed the target, necessitating a reduction of 30%. In order to secure low-cost measures the United States requires the participation of developing countries in the scheme.

The European Union aims at reducing the emission of global warming gas by 8% from the 1990 level. In reality, however, the emission in 2010 will be 7% larger than the 1990 figure. In other words, a 15% reduction will be required around the year 2010 in order to honour the commitment made at Kyoto. Energy requirement per unit of economic activity would be reduced at an annual rate of 1.5% or more till the year 2020, reflecting the structural change of the market and technological progress, whereas on the supply side, nuclear plants will be closed successively. Reflecting divergent reduction responsibilities within Europe, the EU's response will be based on national policies within individual members, and common measures are regarded only as supplementary. The EU will initiate consultation to individual members regarding emission trading, and expects to come up with a framework for emission trading within the European Union by 2005. Already, in some countries, a domestic scheme is being drawn up, despite the fact that this is the first attempt at a market solution to emission reduction.

Japan is committed to a 6% reduction. Actually, it is projected that CO_2 emission will be considerably higher than the target, reflecting a slower pace of energy saving under lower energy prices. If the economy recovers from the current slump an 18% reduction will be required from the projected level in 2010. Originally, it was envisaged that 1.8% of the 6% reduction would be achieved through emission trading, and the remaining portion by utilizing CO_2 sink and voluntary action plans drawn up by industries such as automobile and household appliances. Further effort will be required in order to meet the commitment, such as early implementation of emission trading, and expansion of JI with developing countries, among others.

In models assuming identical AEEI (autonomous energy efficiency improvement), or ESUB (substitution between energy and other sectors) for that matter, across the countries, only comparable differences can be found deductively in simple economic assumptions such as GDP or population. On the contrary, with the estimated price/output elasticity of energy intensity change, together with the inter-energy substitution, policy simulation can be done on the ground of observed underlying differences. Therefore, the approach at the disaggregated sector level based on empirically observed parameters is inductive, while not losing sight of an international overview.

3.2. South-East Asia

Asian economies exhibited high economic growth. This was attributable to favourable macroeconomic performance leading to a cycle with high saving leading to high investment ratio and high output growth, accompanied by high productivity and quality improvement, leading to successful penetration into the world market. Favourable international economic conditions also contributed. At an earlier stage, foreign economic assistance helped build up a social infrastructure (World Bank, 1993). More recently, foreign direct investment worked as the vehicle for financial resources as well as technological transfer.

In the mid-1990s, inflow of portfolio investment followed the economic success of the region, only to show that international exposure in this aspect could be reversed. The Asian economic crisis followed, shifting an overly optimistic outlook into excessively pessimistic views. As the economies entere the new millennium the situation looks more stable. 'Recovery is taking hold in much of Asia, and the upswing trend observed to date is likely to continue in the second half of 1999 through the year 2000. The acute phase of the Asian crisis is now over. However, many challenges posed by the Asian crisis remain' (APEC, 1999). The report points to two opposing views on the causes of the crisis. 'The panic camp' holds that the crisis was a self-fulfilling panic caused by the inherent instability of international financial markets. 'The home-grown camp' holds that the crisis was home-grown in the sense that crisis-affected economies had their own problems. Neither camp would contend that its view applies in a pure form, and there are views in between. A broad common understanding that emerged contends that 'financial instability, particularly, volatility of short-term capital flows play an important role. Economies had such problems as financial sector weaknesses and inflexible exchange policy that left them vulnerable to reversals of capital flows.' A recent report testifies on these accounts. 'The Asian crisis can be characterized as a capital account crisis, the origin of which was large inflows of private capital relative to the underlying current account deficit and of a largely short-term nature, followed by a sudden and massive reversal of capital flows. The magnitude of the swing in capital movement from massive inflows to sudden reversal accounted for about 11 percent of the DGP of crisis-hit Asian economies. In this capital account crisis, it was large swings in capital account balances that first caused the large current account deficits in 1995-1996, then the shift suddenly to large current account surpluses in 1998-1999, not the other way around as in previous conventional crisis.' (Asian Policy Forum, 2000; see also Yoshitomi and Shirai, 2000.)

The fact remains that the economies in South-East Asia represent the fastest-growing part of the world economy, implying, in turn, that energy demand in this region would continue to grow. One potential long-term constraint to growth, or indeed a cause of short-term disruption, would be insecurity in energy supply as reflected in large swings in international energy markets and capping of GHG emissions (including CO_2 emission, which is inseparably linked to energy consumption) imposed by the international community. We take up the economic structure and energy balance of Thailand, Malaysia, Singapore, the Philippines, Indonesia, Taiwan (Chinese Taipei), and Korea.

3.3. China

Currently, global warming gas emission is largely attributable to industrialized countries; within several decades, China, India, and other developing countries will emerge as the largest contributors. It is expected that Chinese growth will be somewhat lowered, and India's somewhat heightened, and both will continue to grow at an annual rate of 5% or so in the years to come. Chinese energy supply is heavily dependent on coal, and demand is largely for industrial use, but this pattern will quickly change. Energy supply will shift to oil and larger demand will originate in transportation and household sectors. India will become the world's most populous nation in the first half of the 21st century. Coupled with an increase in income, India will witness a rapid shift to commercial energy. Both China and India are cautious not to turn emission reduction to growth constraint. This points to the room for policy coordination such as technology transfer between industrialized countries and the big late-comers.

Literature suggests that past economic growth rates record in China had been biased upward, not because of intentional manipulation but because of statistical peculiarities reflecting price structure under central planning (Wu, 1998; Maddison, 1998a, State Statistical Bureau and Hitotsubashi University, 1997; see also OECD, 1996). The difference in view will also affect the trajectory of this enormous economy. A particularly important factor in deciding the future growth of the Chinese economy is the availability of financial resources. As Chinese official views hold, there would not be a shortage of final demand in terms of capital formation, household consumption, or government spending. Rather, the constraint on continued expansion is likely to be posed by the lack of investment funds. The international flow of financial resources would be crucial.

The chapter on China (Chapter 9) discusses some of the alternative estimates of the Chinese economy in the past, present, and future, and prepares a basis for simulation experiments at the global level that takes into account alternative paths of Chinese development. The main author of the chapter on China is an experienced multi-sector econometric model-builder and in a position to provide long-term structural analysis to the Chinese government. As for the macroeconomic performance, the author adheres to the official position that the economy will continue to grow at an annual rate of 10% in the foreseeable future. The structural change of the Chinese economy will be discussed and simulation results presented.

3.4. The case of Russia

The former Soviet Union and Eastern Europe are included in Annex I but are not subject to reduction obligations. Due to economic slumps, and a shift from coal to cleaner natural gas, these countries have increased the sellable emission right. When emission trading is conducted with Annex I they will obtain $45 billion income in 2010 according to one calculation. In drawing up an economic recovery plan, therefore, revenues from emission trading will be a positive factor to be considered in addition to crude oil exports.

Russia shifted to SNA in the early 1990s, at the time of the economic reform (Kuboniwa, 1997). The analysis contained in Chapter 10 employs input-output tables and macroeconomic data from the post-reform period. Russia is also a major producer of crude oil and gas, the price of which is a major factor determining the Russian balance of payments. A low international energy price has had an adverse effect on Russian economic reconstruction. Moreover, the economic downturn resulted in less than sufficient investment in the energy sector in Russia.

In this context the recovery scenario is examined. Institutional characteristics of the Russian economy have improved drastically through the measures taken during the past decade (Kuboniwa and Gavrilenkov, 1997; for the past growth record, see Maddison, 1995, 1998b). The situation in 1997 showed some positive development in terms of the macroeconomic aggregate. The 1998 financial crisis inflicted a severe blow to the Russian economy, resulting in a decline in GDP. Due to higher oil and gas prices, and promotion of exports, partly contributed by import-substitution in manufacturing, the economic growth rate was 3.2% in 1999, followed by more than 8% growth in 2000.

Looking into the future, there can be optimistic views that anticipate acceleration. This version of the prospect is based on the smooth progress of structural reform and the promotion of business activities and capital formation. The devaluation of the ruble in financial crisis gave an impetus for import-competing manufacturing industries. In addition, one may envisage that the sudden drop in economic activities in the wake of the financial crisis in 1998, on top of the continued decline in the 1990s, provides room for quick recovery. The inflow of direct foreign investment and advanced technology is an additional factor that can be counted on in the medium to long term. In contrast, pessimistic views stem from the prospect of lagging structural reforms. Distorted economic structure and low international competitiveness, the lack of an effective legal infrastructure, underdeveloped financial institutions, bureaucratic and corrupt administration, among others, are often listed as the factors adversely affecting the course of economic reform. This version of the view also anticipates continued inflation due to lack of hard budget constraints and explicit/implicit subsidies to enterprises.

It is noted that the dividing line between the optimistic views and pessimistic ones hinges on the prospect of economic reforms, which is a domestic factor, and not on an external factor such as the drop in international oil and gas prices or an economic crisis due to more financial turbulence. In other words, both optimists and pessimists assume that current improvement in the international economic environment represented by higher energy prices is expected to continue. The fact remains that the future of the economic performance of Russia is contingent upon the international economic environment.

Against this backdrop in Chapter 10, two economists from Russia provide an assessment of the reform process in the 1990s, describe the economic records at the turn of the century to 2004, and describe the official long-term social and economic program until 2010.

7 Price-induced energy intensity and inter-energy substitution of G7 countries

YUMIKO UMEHARA

1. Price-induced energy intensity

In this chapter, first the estimation results of energy intensity and energy substitution of G7 countries are described. Secondly, the assumptions embedded into energy balance simulation are explained. Then the chapter shows the results of the future energy balance table and CO_2 emission simulation up to 2010.

Let us look at the energy intensity of the Industry, Transportation and Tertiary sectors shown in Tables 7-1a, b, and c. The general trend in all sectors shows that the intensities have been declining during the period from 1980 to 1995. A slight increase observed from 1980 to 1985 was mostly due to the relatively low oil price after oil shocks in the 1970s. Amongst the seven countries, Canada and the USA show relatively high energy intensity, indicating a lower energy efficiency level compared to other countries. The reasons for this must be multiple; however, a major part of the inefficient use of energy could be attributable to abundant domestic production of energy, and hence the lower price of energy. Intensities in Japan are the lowest throughout the observation here, followed by European countries.

We now compare the observed energy intensity levels and trends (Tables 7-1a, b, and c) with estimated price elasticities (Tables 7-2a, b, and c) for respective sectors. In Table 7-1a, the Industry sector from 1980 to 1995, Germany and the USA have lowered the intensity by 0.5% per year and Canada has reduced by 0.4% per year. Japan has decreased 0.3% per year, and the rest show negligible or no improvement.

Let us look in parallel at the estimated price and output elasticity of intensity shown in Table 7-2a. An output elasticity of -0.5 indicates that the rise in production output by 1% will result in a 0.5% decline in energy intensity. During a course of economic development, such an energy efficiency improvement is a general incidence, as already discussed in the previous chapter. Our results show that the parameters of USA, France, and Germany are bigger than -1. The rest are between -0.5 and -1 except Japan which is -0.43. These figures do not contradict the conventional assumption of AEEI. However, the price effects on intensity are not taken into account in such an assumption. In

K. Uno (ed.), Economy–Energy–Environment Simulation, 111–134.

Table 7-1a. Energy intensity change of G7 countries: Industry sector (Mtoe/billion US$ of 1990)

	1980	1985	1990	1995
Canada	0.26	0.27	0.22	0.19
France	0.08	0.14	0.07	0.06
Germany	0.13	0.19	0.08	0.05
Italy	0.07	0.11	0.06	0.07
Japan	0.09	0.09	0.05	0.04
UK	0.08	0.12	0.08	0.07
USA	0.20	0.17	0.14	0.12

Table 7-1b. Energy intensity change of G7 countries: Transportation sector (Mtoe/billion US$ of 1990)

	1980	1985	1990	1995
Canada	1.73	1.73	1.43	1.57
France	0.67	1.09	0.53	0.48
Germany	1.73	2.25	0.91	0.54
Italy	0.48	0.79	0.49	0.54
Japan	0.74	0.81	0.38	0.25
UK	0.59	1.05	0.44	0.41
USA	1.75	1.31	0.97	0.88

Table 7-1c. Energy intensity change of G7 countries: Residential/Commercial sector (Mtoe/billion US$ of 1990)

	1980	1985	1990	1995
Canada	0.15	0.15	0.12	0.13
France	0.06	0.10	0.05	0.05
Germany	0.13	0.20	0.08	0.05
Italy	0.03	0.07	0.04	0.05
Japan	0.05	0.05	0.03	0.03
UK	0.08	0.12	0.06	0.06
USA	0.09	0.08	0.07	0.08

this analysis, most importantly, the price responsiveness of energy intensity is estimated separately.

We were able to observe significant results except for the USA. A price elasticity of -0.1 indicates that if the energy price rises by 1% with the price of other inputs staying constant, then the intensity will fall by 0.1%. The larger the parameter is, efficiency could be improved with relatively lower costs. The results interestingly indicate that the elasticity is high in Canada of -0.34, reflecting the low cost improvement possibility. Japan showed the lowest elasticity of -0.1, and the highest elasticity observed was in Italy, -0.53, followed by -0.47 in Germany.

Table 7-2a. Estimated parameters of energy intensity equations: Industry sector (figures in parentheses are *t*-values)

	Price Elasticity	Output Elasticity	Adjusted RSQ	DW
Canada	−0.34	−0.54	0.86	0.84
	(−3.20)	(−6.45)		
France	−0.22	−1.40	0.82	1.07
	(−1.70)	(−7.00)		
Germany	−0.47	−1.55	0.97	1.30
	(−2.26)	(−20.68)		
Italy	−0.56	−0.74	0.95	0.84
	(−3.58)	(−10.64)		
Japan	−0.10	−0.43	0.83	1.69
	(−2.25)	(−6.45)		
UK*	−0.15	−0.62	0.98	2.46
	(−2.1)	(−8.0)		
USA	−0.44	−1.70	0.85	1.33
	(−0.77)	(−5.17)		

* U.K is the results include the time trend of which parameter is −1.19 (−5.6).

Table 7-2b. Estimated parameters of energy intensity equations: Transportation sector (figures in parentheses are *t*-values)

	Price Elasticity	Output Elasticity	Adjusted RSQ	DW
Canada	−0.47	−0.53	0.88	1.71
	(−5.56)	(−6.59)		
France	−0.18	−0.13	0.82	2.18
	(−7.47)	(−4.92)		
Germany	−0.04	−0.42	0.94	1.63
	(−1.15)	(−13.12)		
Italy*	−0.09	−0.79	0.79	1.05
	(−1.22)	(−3.55)		
Japan	−0.09	−0.25	0.65	0.72
	(−1.95)	(−3.98)		
UK*	−0.26	−0.80	0.99	1.69
	(−7.98)	(−26.71)		
USA	−0.01	−0.58	0.97	1.04
	(−0.25)	(−13.60)		

* Italy, U.K, includes time trend of which parameter is 2.32 (3.91), 1.76 (10.42) respectively.

In the Transportation sector intensities are very high in Canada and the USA and in Germany, as shown in Table 7-1b. It should be remembered that the intensity in this sector does not represent energy consumption per physical service such as passengers/kilometre. Output in this sector is the monetary evaluated transportation services. Thus, a country with relatively low provision for public transportation service may end up having a high intensity level. USA

Table 7-2c. Estimated parameters of energy intensity equations: Residential/Commercial sector (figures in parentheses are *t*-values)

	Price Elasticity	Output Elasticity	Adjusted RSQ	DW
Canada*		−1.17	0.83	1.28
		(−2.21)		
France	−0.18	−0.13	0.82	2.18
	(−7.47)	(−4.92)		
Germany	−0.43	−1.19	0.97	1.33
	(−2.25)	(−16.60)		
Italy*		−1.00	0.79	1.40
		(−2.14)		
Japan*		−0.59	0.94	2.23
		(−2.09)		
UK*		−0.84	0.98	1.32
		(−27.68)		
USA	−0.21	−0.89	0.92	2.04
	(−1.70)	(−6.53)		

* Canada includes time trend of which parameter is 2.05 (1.20), Italy 1.15 (1.08), Japan 2.54 (5.03). UK does not include time trend.

intensity in this sector has declined by 0.5% per year, the same change as in the Industry sector, whereas Canada still shows the level achieving only 0.1% per year during the period from 1980 to 1995. EU countries' reductions in annual intensity are at about the same level as in 1995, an average of 0.5% per year. Again in Japan, the level is the lowest, and Japan has reduced the intensity level by 0.3% per year. In estimating the elasticity in the Transportation sector we tested equations with time trend, the results of which showed an overall trend of intensity rise in most of the countries without price consideration. Table 7-2b shows that the price elasticity in this sector is lower than in the Industry sector in France and Germany, but higher in Canada. The elasticity is at about the same level as that observed in the Industry sector for Japan. The result for the USA was not significant. The highest elasticity was observed in Canada, −0.47, followed by the UK with −0.26. France was −0.18, and Italy and Japan showed −0.09. The lowest elasticity was observed in Germany.

Now, let us look at Table 7-1c. In the Tertiary sector energy intensity is lowest in Japan, and again highest in Canada in 1995. Second highest is the USA, followed by the UK, and France, Germany, and Italy have the same intensity level. Germany has lowered intensity by 0.5% per year, and the rest of the countries by 1% per year, except Italy which showed 1% per year increase. The fall in intensity level was significant from 1985 to 1990 in France, the UK, and Germany. However, only Germany continued to reduce the level from 1990 to 1995. In this sector, elasticity of price was only observed in France, −0.18; Germany, −0.43 and the USA, −0.21 (Table 7-2c).

2. Price-induced inter-energy substitution

Tables 7-3a, b, and c show the estimated price elasticity of energy share. The figures show the point change in share; e.g. if the price of coal rises relative to the weighted price of energy the share would fall by the point shown in the 'energy total' of the group 'coal'. For example, in Table 7-3a, 0.06 in the first row for Japan means that if the share of coal was 30% in this sector, the relative price rise by 1% will push down the share to 29.4%. We also estimated the cross-energy price elasticity. For instance, coal price rise relative to oil price of Japan in the Industry sector will cut the share of coal by 0.04 point.

In the Industry sector, the share of coal in 1995 is: Canada 5%, France 10%, Germany 12%, Italy 6%, UK 15%, Japan 12%, USA 7%. Since coal is the most carbon-intensive energy the shift away from coal to less intensive energy

Table 7-3a. Estimated parameter of energy share equation: Industry sector: price elasticity of inter-energy substitution (percentage change in share)

	Canada	USA	Japan	France	Germany	Italy	UK
Coal							
Energy total	*	*	−0.06	−0.04	−0.10	*	*
Oil	*	*	−0.04	−0.03	−0.04	*	*
Gas	−0.04	*	−0.08	−0.03	−0.05	*	*
Electricity	*	*	−0.09	−0.09	−0.44	*	*
Oil							
Energy total	−0.06	*	−0.53	*	−0.29	−0.58	*
Gas	*	*	*	−0.30	*	−0.36	*
Electricity	*	*	−0.16	*	−0.03	*	*
Gas							
Energy total	−0.07	−0.26	*	−0.08	−0.03	*	*
Electricity	−0.03	−0.05	*	−0.04	*	*	*

* indicates that no significant results were observed.

Table 7-3b. Estimated parameter of energy share equation: Transportation sector: price elasticity of inter-energy substitution (percentage change in share)

	Canada	USA	Japan	France	Germany	Italy	UK
Coal							
Energy total	**	**	**	**	**	**	**
Oil	**	**	**	**	**	**	**
Gas	**	**	**	**	**	**	**
Electricity	**	**	**	**	**	**	**
Oil							
Energy total	*	*	−0.09	−0.15	−0.18	−0.16	*
Gas	−0.02	*	−0.003	*	−0.005	*	−0.008
Electricity	*	*	−0.002	*	−0.004	−0.005	*
Gas							
Energy total	−0.03	−0.01	**	**	**	−0.002	**
Electricity	−0.04	−0.01	**	**	**		**

** indicates that the fuel is not used in this sector.

Table 7-3c. Estimated parameter of energy share equation: Residential/Commercial sector: price elasticity of inter-energy substitution (percentage change in share)

	Canada	USA	Japan	France	Germany	Italy	UK
Coal to							
Energy total	*	*	−0.009	−0.01	*	*	*
Oil	*	*	−0.007	−0.01	*	*	*
Gas	*	*	*	*	*	*	*
Electricity	*	*	*	*	*	*	*
Oil to							
Energy total	−0.05	−0.02	−0.10	*	−0.25	*	*
Gas	*	−0.02	*	−0.05	*	*	*
Electricity	*	*	−0.15	*	*	*	−0.05
Gas to							
Energy total	*	−0.11	*	*	−0.08	−0.14	*
Electricity	*	−0.05	*	*	−0.02	−0.09	*

contributes greatly to CO_2 emission reduction. Germany had the biggest share of coal of 23% in 1990, and decreased by 2% per year to 1995. The USA has also decreased by 1% per year in the same period. Table 7-3a shows that in Japan, France, and Germany, the price elasticity of coal share was observed to a great extent. The price of coal relative to electricity was especially large in Germany, at 0.44. For the USA, Italy, and the UK, no significant results were observed. The share of oil is: France 33%, Canada 27%, Germany 31%, Italy 28%, Japan 50%, UK 33%, USA, 26% in 1995. The share is by far the highest in Japan. The elasticity of oil to energy price in this sector is high. Japan, Germany, and Italy have −0.53, −0.29, and −0.58, respectively. The share of gas in 1995 is: Canada and France 28%, Germany 29%, Italy 40%, Japan 5%, UK 32% and USA 35%. Italy has the largest share, followed by the USA and UK and other EU countries. Use of gas in Japan is only 5% of total energy in the Industry sector. The elasticity of gas price to energy price was large in the USA at −0.26. The biggest and smallest user of gas in the Industry sector is Italy, and Japan did not show significant results. Canada and USA showed −0.07 and −0.08, respectively.

In the Transportation sector the elasticity is generally smaller than in the Industry sector. There is no coal used in this sector for all seven countries. The oil is almost all the energy used in this sector, more than 90%. In the USA and UK, almost 99% is oil. The elasticity of oil to energy is large in Germany at −0.18, and France −0.15, Italy −0.16, and Japan −0.09, as shown in Table 7-3b. Gas is only a small portion in this sector; the largest share is 10% in Canada and the lowest is 0% in Japan, Germany, France, and the UK. Canada and the USA show −0.03 and −0.01, respectively; Italy shows a small elasticity of −0.002.

In the Residential/Commercial sector the coal share is 1% for Canada, France, and Japan; 3% in Italy; 4% in Germany and 5% in the UK. Table 7-3c shows that the elasticity of the relative price of coal to energy total is about −0.01 for France and Japan. No significant results were observed for other countries. The share of oil is: largest in Japan, 46%; 36% in Germany, 30% in France, 25% in Italy, 20% in Canada, and 14% and 12% in the UK and USA, respectively. Elasticity is large in Germany at −0.25, and Japan at −0.1. Canada and the USA show −0.05 and −0.02. One of the few observed results for the UK is the elasticity of oil price to electricity price at −0.05. The share of gas is very large in the UK at 56%, followed by 47% in Italy and 42% in the USA. France shows 20% and this is as small as 10% in Japan. The elasticity of gas price to energy price is −0.14 in Italy, −0.11 in the USA, and −0.08 in Germany.

We have also estimated the elasticity of electricity price to energy price in the three end-use sectors. However, we have only endogenized the share of electricity recently, and the results are almost as acceptable after briefly evaluating the parameters statistically. Careful tests on the level of significance are still necessary; therefore we do not include the results in this chapter. The share of 'New & Renewables' is calculated as the residual in the three sectors. The share of inputs in the electricity generation sector is also estimated for each fuel depending on relative price, except for policy variables such as 'Nuclear' and 'New & Renewables'. The results of the regressions are good in overall fit for every fuel share; nevertheless serial correlation may exist. In addition the significance of each estimated parameter also needs to be tested in this sector.

3. Major findings

Considering the difficulty of estimating the price elasticity of energy intensity change, we were quite successful in obtaining the results we expected. The parameters were observed at each of three different end-use sectors in respective countries, providing cross-country overview, and this helps to a great extent to understand the outcomes of the policy simulation studies to be done in the near future. In models assuming the same AEEI or ESUB across countries, only a comparable difference can be found deductively in simple economic assumptions such as GDP or population. In contrast, with an econometrically estimated price/output elasticity of energy intensity change based on empirical data, together with inter-energy substitution, policy simulation can be done on the grounds of already observed underlying differences. Therefore, our simulation approach at disaggregated sectors is inductive, while not losing sight of the international overview.

In the Industry sector the price responsiveness of energy intensity was quite a bit larger than we had expected. Autonomous technological change was also observed. The relative price-induced substitution of other energy for coal was observed in Japan, France and Germany, and the larger possibility of substitution of electricity for coal was especially indicated. In Canada a growing production of natural gas has resulted in substitution for coal. In France and Italy the substitution of natural gas for oil was observed. Germany and Japan also showed the potential substitution of electricity for oil. In the USA, the substitution of electricity for gas was observed. We need to look further into the UK as it showed no significant results. The pre-existing distorted energy market (such as coal subsidization) may be the reason that we were unable to observe price-induced energy substitution in this country.

In the Transportation sector the price elasticity showed that the fuel prices have induced energy efficiency improvements. The output elasticity also proved that increased output resulted in efficient use of energy. However, the positive elasticity observed with the time trend in all countries showed that, apart from economic factors, the change in quality of the service preferred by consumers resulted in more energy using. One of the reasons can be attributed to the increased purchases of recreation vehicles that are suitable for the lifestyle of modern-day people, but requiring more fuel to drive a kilometre. The substitution possibility in this sector is rather small, given the fact that a large part of the energy used is oil. Nevertheless, we have observed that greater use of gas and electricity is encouraged. For instance, the substitution of gas for oil was observed in Canada, Japan, Germany and the UK. Electricity has also substituted for oil in Japan, Germany, and Italy, and for gas in Canada and the USA. In France the parameters did not specify exactly from what fuel, but substitution for oil was also observed.

In the Tertiary sector the price elasticity of energy intensity was observed only in France, Germany, and the USA. We need to analyse further why other countries did not show significant results. The more disaggregation in this sector is needed because it is probable that inclusion of the Residential sector together with public, commerce, and other activities may explain the reasons, as it has always been speculated that this particular sector is the most price-unresponsive sector. It should be noted that the output elasticity was quite large in all countries. In the whole Tertiary sector, the expanding service activities accounted for most of the increasing output. Therefore, improved energy efficiency in, for instance, commercial buildings may have contributed towards lowering the intensity. In this sector substitution for oil was observed in all countries except Italy. Compared to the shift from coal to oil observed in Japan and France, this contributes greatly to CO_2 reduction. For example, substitution of gas for oil was observed in the USA and France. In Japan and the UK electricity substituted for oil and, though not specified in detail, other fuel substitution was observed in Canada and Germany. Further substitution of electricity for gas was observed in Italy, the USA, and Germany.

4. Energy balance and CO_2 emission simulation 2010

Before starting any policy simulation we need to test the performance of the model. To this end we have simulated a baseline energy balance and CO_2 emissions of G7 countries. By feeding a world oil price assumption of IEA projection – the most commonly used price in energy models – the model should be able to produce results similar to those presented in the IEA energy outlook. Up to the present we have simulated to the year 2010. The shares of 'Nuclear' and 'New & Renewables' in electricity production are also given from the policy review, also done by IEA. Estimated parameters described in the previous section are employed in the simulation model. Since this is a model of time-series balance table, we are able to obtain every year table for the simulated period; however, we show the results only for 2010.

4.1. Assumptions

The world oil price is projected to rise to $25 in 2010 from $12 in 1998. In the energy balance model the prices of domestic fuels are dependent on the world oil price, therefore the relative prices will also be forecast as the baseline case. Policy scenarios for share of 'Nuclear' and 'New & Renewables' are shown in Table 7-4. Share of Nuclear will stay constant from 1995 to 2010 in Canada. It is assumed to decline in Germany, the USA and most notably in the UK. France will continue to produce nuclear energy and the share in electricity production will rise by a small fraction. Japan is also assumed to expand nuclear generation, although the growth rate is set lower than originally proposed by the Japanese government. Share of 'New & Renewable' energy in generation will stay constant in Canada at 60%, Italy 17%, Japan about 10%, the USA about 10%, and the UK 32%. In France this share will decline to 10%, and Germany is assumed to increase the share to 15%, which is three times larger than in 1995.

4.2. Baseline energy balance simulation 2010

The COMPASS simulation results of the energy balance for G7 countries in 2010 are listed in Tables 7-5a to g. They are presented in the identical format of energy balance tables by the IEA. The baseline simulation experiment was conducted based on a fully linked COMPASS including macro/finance, IO, trade, and the energy balance models. They should be regarded as the test run

Table 7-4. Scenarios for the energy balance model: share of Nuclear and New & Renewables in electricity generation

	Nuclear 1995	Nuclear 2010	New & Renewables 1995	New & Renewables 2010
Canada	0.17	0.17	0.60	0.60
France	0.77	0.80	0.15	0.10
Germany	0.24	0.20	0.05	0.15
Italy	0.00	0.00	0.17	0.17
Japan	0.29	0.35	0.10	0.11
UK	0.26	0.13	0.32	0.32
USA	0.19	0.13	0.11	0.09

Table 7-5a. Simulated energy balance for Canada, 2010

IEA Row No.	Energy Balance Table	Coal (coa)	Crude Oil (cru)	Petroleum Products (prf)	Gas (gas)	Nuclear (nuc)	Hydro/Other (ren)	Electricity and Heat (elh)	Total	Unit
1	Indigenous production	49,215.4	113,207.9	0.0	149,702.6	33,001.4	47,871.0	0.0	392,998.3	Ktoe
2	Import	6956.5	49,898.5	6821.2	551.7	0.0	0.0	638.3	64,866.1	Ktoe
3	Export	23,588.7	60,516.2	12,413.8	64,707.8	0.0	0.0	3736.2	164,962.7	Ktoe
4	Intl. marine bunkers plus	1188.8	783.0	•68.0	1032.4	0.0	0.0	0.0	2936.2	Ktoe
5	Stock changes									Ktoe
6	**TPES**	33,772.0	103,373.1	•5660.6	86,578.8	33,001.4	47,871.0	•3097.9	295,837.8	Ktoe
7,8	Returns and transfers	663.4	0.0	2858.3	•1511.9	0.0	0.0	0.0		Ktoe
	Statistical differences									
9	Electricity plants									
10	CHP plants	26,137.1	1283.0	554.8	7417.3	33,001.4	37,748.6	62,899.0		Ktoe
11	Heat plants									
13	Petroleum refineries		102,090.1	101,618.3						Ktoe
12	Gas works									
14	Coal transformation									
15	Liquefaction	1655.0	0.0	0.0	3139.2	0.0	0.0			Ktoe
16	Other transformation									
12,18	Own use plus	233.2	0.0	8582.0	9979.2	0.0	0.0	9091.9		Ktoe
	Distribution losses									Ktoe
19	**TFC**	6410.1	0.0	89,679.2	64,531.2	0.0	10,122.4	50,709.2	221,452.1	Ktoe
20 through 34	**Industry sector (ind)**	5687.4	0.0	16,745.7	28,083.8	0.0	10,299.8	19,650.7	80,467.5	Ktoe
35 through 42	**Transport sector (tra)**	315.6	0.0	54,871.5	6691.7	0.0	313.2	453.6	62,645.7	Ktoe
43	**Other sectors (pro)**	62.1	0.0	11,511.8	29,755.7	0.0	2454.8	30,604.8	74,389.3	Ktoe
44	Agriculture									Ktoe
45,46,47	Public/commerce, residential, etc.									Ktoe
48,49,50,51	**Non-energy use**	344.9	0.0	6550.2	0.0				6895.1	Ktoe
52	Electricity generated	110,950.4		6094.6	41,052.7	126,324.3	438,830.0		725,082.6	Gwh
55	Heat generated	0.0		1177.2	18,141.7	3372.3	0.0	0.0	22,691.1	TJ
Additional	Electricity and heat generated	9541.7		552.2	3963.8	10,944.4	37,739.4	0.0	62,899.0	Ktoe

Table 7-5b. Simulated energy balance for France, 2010

IEA Row No.	Energy Balance Table	Coal (coa)	Crude Oil (cru)	Petroleum Products (prf)	Gas (gas)	Nuclear (nuc)	Hydro/Other (ren)	Electricity and Heat (elh)	Total	Unit
1	Indigenous production	48,884.6	2998.4	0.0	3731.6	26,585.6	7593.9	0.0	89,794.0	Ktoe
2	Import	9578.5	108,053.9	22,339.7	28,101.3	0.0	97.5	246.0	168,416.9	Ktoe
3	Export	465.2	445.6	15,537.7	616.2	0.0	0.0	6252.3	23316.9	Ktoe
4	Intl. marine bunkers plus	919.6	257.4	•3232.2	•708.9	0.0	9.1	0.0	•2755.0	Ktoe
5	Stock changes									Ktoe
6	**TPES**	58,917.6	110,864.1	3569.8	30,507.8	26,585.6	7700.5	•6006.3	232,139.1	Ktoe
7,8	Returns and transfers	103.8	0.0	5214.5	•788.7	0.0	•180.7	0.0		Ktoe
	Statistical differences									
9	Electricity plants									
10	CHP plants	50,711.9	0.0	20,260.1	•3860.8	26,585.6	0.0	43,866.2		Ktoe
11	Heat plants									
13	Petroleum refineries		110,864.2	111,566.0						Ktoe
12	Gas works									
14	Coal transformation									
15	Liquefaction	2798.4	0.0	2325.9	•34.3	0.0	0.0			Ktoe
16	Other transformation									
12,18	Own use plus	540.6	0.0	5787.9	447.5	0.0	0.0	6690.7		Ktoe
	Distribution losses									Ktoe
19	**TFC**	4970.6	0.0	91,976.4	33,166.7	0.0	7519.8	31,169.2	168,802.6	Ktoe
20 through 34	**Industry sector (ind)**	4591.3	0.0	16,712.2	13,003.6	0.0	347.9	8827.8	43,482.9	Ktoe
35 through 42	**Transport sector (tra)**	293.9	0.0	57,165.4	0.0	0.0	293.9	1029.0	58,782.2	Ktoe
43	**Other sectors (pro)**	85.4	0.0	13,013.8	20,163.0	0.0	12,635.5	21,312.3	67,210.1	Ktoe
44	Agriculture									Ktoe
45,46,47	Public/commerce, residential, etc.									Ktoe
48,49,50,51	**Non-energy use**	0.0	0.0	5084.9	0.0				5084.9	Ktoe
52	Electricity generated	197,885.3		237,074.1	−26,901.8	102,014.4	0.0		51,0072.1	Gwh
55	Heat generated	0.0		0.0	0.0	0.0	0.0	0.0	0.0	TJ
Additional	Electricity and heat generated	17,018.1		20,388.4	−2313.6	8773.2	0.0	0.0	43,866.2	Ktoe

Table 7-5c. Simulated energy balance for Germany, 2010

IEA Row No.	Energy Balance Table	Coal (coa)	Crude Oil (cru)	Petroleum Products (prf)	Gas (gas)	Nuclear (nuc)	Hydro/Other (ren)	Electricity and Heat (elh)	Total	Unit
1	Indigenous production	81,035.9	3609.1	0.0	23,572.7	34,527.9	8958.2	0.0	151,703.8	Ktoe
2	Import	12,228.3	125,637.8	44,809.9	55,311.9	0.0	0.0	3417.2	241,405.1	Ktoe
3	Export	1970.6	779.0	14,470.8	2395.3	0.0	0.0	3002.4	22,618.1	Ktoe
4	Intl. marine bunkers plus	2424.1	251.2	−710.7	−1323.3	0.0	0.0	0.0	641.3	Ktoe
5	Stock changes									Ktoe
6	**TPES**	93,717.7	128,719.0	29,628.4	75,166.1	34,527.9	8958.2	414.9	371,131.2	Ktoe
7,8	Returns and transfers	1545.0	0.0	−6704.6	−1293.6	0.0	0.0	0.0		Ktoe
	Statistical differences									
9	Electricity plants									
10	CHP plants	80,377.8	0.0	422.8	12,177.7	34,527.9	7644.8	57,017.7		Ktoe
11	Heat plants									
13	Petroleum refineries		128,719.0	129,281.1						Ktoe
12	Gas works									
14	Coal transformation									
15	Liquefaction	3675.3	0.0	6390.4	−718.8	0.0	0.0			Ktoe
16	Other transformation									
12,18	Own use plus	1244.4	0.0	7338.7	2801.5	0.0	0.0	8754.8		Ktoe
	Distribution losses									Ktoe
19	**TFC**	9965.2	0.0	138,052.9	59,612.1	0.0	1313.4	48,677.8	257,621.5	Ktoe
20 through 34	**Industry sector (ind)**	4085.2	0.0	24,363.7	20,952.5	0.0	134.6	17,768.4	67,304.4	Ktoe
35 through 42	**Transport sector (tra)**	404.0	0.0	78,481.9	3.5	0.0	405.5	1810.8	81,105.7	Ktoe
43	**Other sectors (pro)**	5271.5	0.0	31,138.3	38,656.1	0.0	1265.2	29,098.6	105,429.7	Ktoe
44	Agriculture									Ktoe
45,46,47	Public/commerce, residential, etc.									Ktoe
48,49,50,51	**Non-energy use**	204.5	0.0	4068.9	0.0				4273.5	Ktoe
52	Electricity generated	324,252.8		1906.0	41,634.5	132,437.5	55,577.1		555,807.9	Gwh
55	Heat generated	206,324.3		10,919.9	129,581.3	583.1	38,615.5	0.0	386,024.0	TJ
Additional	Electricity and heat generated	32,812.8		424.7	6675.0	11,403.5	5701.8	0.0	57,017.7	Ktoe

Table 7-5d. Simulated energy balance for Italy, 2010

IEA Row No.	Energy Balance Table	Coal (coa)	Crude Oil (cru)	Petroleum Products (prf)	Gas (gas)	Nuclear (nuc)	Hydro/Other (ren)	Electricity and Heat (elh)	Total	Unit
1	Indigenous production	−4398.8	5497.2	0.0	33,206.8	0.0	6724.6	0.0	41,029.8	Ktoe
2	Import	13,101.3	78,054.2	24,395.0	28,553.3	0.0	231.5	3324.9	147,660.2	Ktoe
3	Export	91.0	414.0	17,010.6	31.1	0.0	0.0	106.2	17,652.9	Ktoe
4	Intl. marine bunkers plus	−773.1	178.8	−2043.1	−224.6	0.0	0.0	0.0	−2861.9	Ktoe
5	Stock changes									Ktoe
6	**TPES**	7838.4	83,316.3	5341.4	61,504.4	0.0	6956.1	3218.7	168,175.3	Ktoe
7,8	Returns and transfers statistical differences	−25.3	0.0	108.5	−0.2	0.0	0.0	0.0		Ktoe
9	Electricity plants									
10	CHP plants	4241.9	0.0	8850.1	12,021.8	0.0	5747.4	19,504.6		Ktoe
11	Heat plants									
13	Petroleum refineries		83,315.6	82,984.3						Ktoe
12	Gas works									
14	Coal transformation									
15	Liquefaction	1487.3	0.0	5090.6	−42.9	0.0	162.4			Ktoe
16	Other transformation									
12,18	Own use plus	420.2	0.0	5425.9	668.3	0.0	0.0	2996.7		Ktoe
	Distribution losses									Ktoe
19	**TFC**	1663.7	0.0	69,067.6	48,857.0	0.0	1046.3	19,726.6	140,361.1	Ktoe
20 through 34	**Industry sector (ind)**	1192.6	0.0	8259.0	21,442.0	0.0	168.6	11,080.0	42,142.3	Ktoe
35 through 42	**Transport Sector (tra)**	246.5	0.0	47,625.1	295.8	0.0	246.3	836.5	49,250.2	Ktoe
43	**Other sectors (pro)**	114.5	0.0	10,922.3	27,119.2	0.0	1034.0	7810.1	47,000.2	Ktoe
44	Agriculture									Ktoe
45,46,47	Public/commerce, residential and non-specified other									Ktoe
48,49,50,51	**Non-energy use**	110.1	0.0	2261.0	0.0				2371.1	Ktoe
52	Electricity generated	18,657.8		102,498.9	60,281.4	0.0	42,837.5		224,275.7	Gwh
55	Heat generated	0.0		0.0	0.0	0.0	9082.8	0.0	9082.8	TJ
Additional	Electricity and heat generated	1604.6		8814.9	5184.2	0.0	3900.9	0.0	19,504.6	Ktoe

Table 7-5e. Simulated energy balance for Japan, 2010

IEA Row No.	Energy Balance Table	Coal (coa)	Crude Oil (cru)	Petroleum Products (prf)	Gas (gas)	Nuclear (nuc)	Hydro/Other (ren)	Electricity and Heat (elh)	Total	Unit
1	Indigenous production	29,011.4	809.5	0.0	82.4	119,193.6	21,702.2	0.0	170,799.0	Ktoe
2	Import	80,945.9	292,669.4	52,241.4	50,004.2	0.0	0.0	0.0	475,860.8	Ktoe
3	Export	1995.2	0.0	8779.8	0.0	0.0	0.0	0.0	10,775.0	Ktoe
4	Intl. marine bunkers plus	191.8	−2548.8	−4298.3	66.8	0.0	0.0	0.0	−6588.5	Ktoe
5	Stock changes									Ktoe
6	**TPES**	108,153.9	290,930.1	39,163.3	50,153.4	119,193.6	21,702.2	0.0	629,296.1	Ktoe
7,8	Returns and transfers	−1230.9	−31.2	205.7	315.5	0.0	0.0	0.0		Ktoe
	Statistical differences									
9	Electricity plants									
10	CHP plants	31,649.2	38,000.0	17,053.3	29,287.8	119,193.6	18,066.5	102,166.0		Ktoe
11	Heat plants									
13	Petroleum refineries		256,585.1	255,905.5						Ktoe
12	Gas works									
14	Coal transformation									
15	Liquefaction	35,184.2	−6581.0	11,357.2	−5640.5	0.0	0.0			Ktoe
16	Other transformation									
12,18	Own use plus	5001.8	0.0	14,952.0	974.2	0.0	0.0	11,503.1		Ktoe
	Distribution losses									Ktoe
19	**TFC**	35,087.8	2894.3	251,912.0	25,847.5	0.0	3635.8	90,662.8	410,040.1	Ktoe
20 through 34	**Industry sector (ind)**	31,883.4	2894.3	79,725.2	10,941.8	0.0	3299.9	44,935.0	173,679.7	Ktoe
35 through 42	**Transport sector (tra)**	528.3	0.0	102,424.7	52.9	0.0	529.3	2319.1	105,854.3	Ktoe
43	**Other sectors (pro)**	2676.0	0.0	43,604.6	14,852.7	0.0	1548.9	43,408.7	106,091.0	Ktoe
44	Agriculture									Ktoe
45,46,47	Public/commerce, residential, etc.									Ktoe
48,49,50,51	**Non-energy use**	0.0	0.0	26,157.6	0.0				26,157.6	Ktoe
52	Electricity generated	158,041.2		197,118.7	152,734.4	457,370.8	142,557.1		1,183,174.6	Gwh
55	Heat generated	509.5		2341.8	8769.3	0.0	0.0	5671.6	17,292.1	TJ
Additional	Electricity and heat generated	13,603.7		17,008.1	13,344.6	39,333.9	12,259.9	135.4	102,166.0	Ktoe

Table 7-5f. Simulated energy balance for the United Kingdom, 2010

IEA Row No.	Energy Balance Table	Coal (coa)	Crude Oil (cru)	Petroleum Products (prf)	Gas (gas)	Nuclear (nuc)	Hydro/Other (ren)	Electricity and Heat (elh)	Total	Unit
1	Indigenous production	31,002.6	13,6481.3	0.0	76,376.1	22,877.2	2377.9	0.0	269,115.1	Ktoe
2	Import	11,007.8	44,348.0	8774.3	1505.3	0.0	0.0	1404.9	67,040.3	Ktoe
3	Export	862.7	88,308.1	22,298.3	869.0	0.0	0.0	2.0	112,340.1	Ktoe
4	Intl. marine bunkers plus	5507.9	920.1	−2359.0	768.0	0.0	0.0	0.0	4837.0	Ktoe
5	Stock changes									Ktoe
6	**TPES**	46,655.6	93,441.2	−15,883.0	77,780.4	22,877.2	2377.9	1402.9	228,652.2	Ktoe
7,8	Returns and transfers	−112.3	0.0	3715.5	−2915.8	0.0	0.0	0.0		Ktoe
	Statistical differences									
9	Electricity plants									
10	CHP plants	45,573.7	−14,866.5	−3892.6	14,717.1	22,877.2	1957.6	30,197.9		Ktoe
11	Heat plants									
13	Petroleum refineries		108,307.7	107,439.7						Ktoe
12	Gas works									
14	Coal transformation									
15	Liquefaction	262.2	0.0	1402.2	0.0	0.0	0.0			Ktoe
16	Other transformation									
12,18	Own use plus	46.6	0.0	7751.3	5174.3	0.0	0.0	5000.6		Ktoe
	Distribution losses									Ktoe
19	**TFC**	660.8	0.0	90,011.3	54,973.3	0.0	420.2	26,600.2	172,665.8	Ktoe
20 through 34	**Industry sector (ind)**	344.0	0.0	13,612.0	14,269.0	0.0	76.1	9739.5	38,040.5	Ktoe
35 through 42	**Transport sector (tra)**	316.8	0.0	61,699.1	0.0	0.0	316.8	1022.6	63,355.3	Ktoe
43	**Other sectors (pro)** }	0.0	0.0 }	6560.2 }	40,704.3	0.0 }	380.9 }	15,838.1 }	63,483.4	Ktoe
44	Agriculture									Ktoe
45,46,47	Public/commerce, residential, etc.									Ktoe
48,49,50,51	**Non-energy use**	0.0	0.0	8140.1	0.0				8140.1	Ktoe
52	Electricity generated	199,092.3		−44,899.9	82,350.6	87,784.5	17,556.9		351,138.2	Gwh
55	Heat generated	0.0		0.0	0.0	0.0	0.0	0.0	0.0	TJ
Additional	Electricity and heat generated	17,121.9		−3861.4	7082.2	7549.5	1509.9	0.0	30,197.9	Ktoe

Table 7-5g. Simulated Energy Balance for United States, 2010

IEA Row No.	Energy Balance Table	Coal (coa)	Crude Oil (cru)	Petroleum Products (prf)	Gas (gas)	Nuclear (nuc)	Hydro/Other (ren)	Electricity and Heat (elh)	Total	Unit
1	Indigenous production	629,338.6	399,990.1	0.0	454,728.3	201,225.3	116,812.5	0.0	1,802,094.8	Ktoe
2	Import	5300.3	386,926.9	41,954.8	65,771.0	0.0	31.9	4021.4	504,006.2	Ktoe
3	Export	54,746.3	2383.9	38,758.3	3533.0	0.0	0.0	786.6	100,208.0	Ktoe
4	Intl. marine bunkers plus	−6744.8	5019.6	−23,141.3	10,772.1	0.0	22.8	0.0	−14071.7	Ktoe
5	Stock changes									Ktoe
6	**TPES**	573,147.8	789,552.6	−19,944.8	527,738.4	201,225.3	116,867.1	3234.8	2,191,821.2	Ktoe
7,8	Returns and transfers	1775.0	0.0	43,901.9	−5956.8	0.0	−0.6	0.0		Ktoe
	Statistical differences									
9	Electricity plants									
10	CHP plants	536,909.1	0.0	−20,172.4	157,049.6	201,225.3	88,098.6	342,290.4		Ktoe
11	Heat plants									
13	Petroleum refineries		789,552.6	793,449.1						Ktoe
12	Gas works	11,125.5	0.0	0.0	0.0	0.0	0.0			Ktoe
14	Coal transformation									
15	Liquefaction									
16	Other transformation									
12,18	Own use plus	656.3	0.0	53,734.0	45,224.5	0.0	0.0	54,125.6		Ktoe
	Distribution losses									Ktoe
19	**TFC**	26,231.9	0.0	783,844.7	319,507.6	0.0	28,767.9	291,399.7	1,449,751.6	Ktoe
20 through 34	**Industry sector (ind)**	26,310.9	0.0	83,867.8	109,513.4	0.0	41,880.1	71,616.2	327,188.5	Ktoe
35 through 42	**Transport sector (tra)**	3048.8	0.0	585,714.5	18,228.7	0.0	2439.1	336.3	609,767.4	Ktoe
43	**Other sectors (pro)** }	2872.1	0.0 }	41,384.6 }	191,765.4 }	0.0 }	16,519.6 }	219,447.1 }	471,988.9	Ktoe
44	Agriculture									Ktoe
45,46,47	Public/commerce, residential, etc.									Ktoe
48,49,50,51	**Non-energy use**	0.0	0.0	72,877.8	0.0				72,877.8	Ktoe
52	Electricity generated	2,253,272.5		−206,953.3	638,703.1	772,143.6	429,223.9		3,886,389.5	Gwh
55	Heat generated	142,727.3		−103,601.3	267,498.7	0.0	30,933.5	0.0	337,558.2	TJ
Additional	Electricity and heat generated	197,189.8		−20,272.0	61,316.3	66,404.3	37,651.9	0.0	342,290.4	Ktoe

of the model rather than projection. Annual results are obtained, but we report here only on the terminal year of the simulation. The results are consistent with the IEA studies in magnitude and direction of energy demand/supply pattern change. The results proved the high performance and quality of the energy balance model.

Let us look at the simulation for Canada. The total TPES is 296 Mtoe compared to the IEA of 280 Mtoe. The difference comes from the larger supply of coal and nuclear results in our model. Breaking down on the sectors, total consumption in end-use sectors shows almost the same results as IEA, except that our model resulted in more energy use growth in the Tertiary sector, notably electricity consumption. As for France, the total TPES is 232 Mtoe, less than 281 Mtoe of IEA. The difference comes from nuclear, which is smaller in our model. Industry consumption of energy is also smaller. This is due to the lower electricity demand in our model, whereas consumption values in Transportation and the Tertiary sector are both larger compared to IEA. Simulation for Germany indicates that the total TPES is 371 Mtoe, larger than the 350 Mtoe of IEA. Our results show more oil and renewable supply, and less supply of nuclear than in IEA. Consumption in Industry is smaller in our results, mostly due to the smaller supply of coal. The other two sectors show more consumption, coming from a larger demand for gas and electricity, especially in the Tertiary sector. The total TPES of the UK is 229 Mtoe, which is less than the 249 Mtoe of IEA. This difference is due to the smaller supply of oil and gas, although coal supply is larger than IEA. Transportation and the Tertiary sector consumption values are almost the same as in IEA; however, they are less in Industry in our results. Italy's total TPES is 163 Mtoe, whereas IEA forecast is 188 Mtoe. Smaller supplies of coal and gas are reasons for the difference. The Transportation sector is larger than in IEA, while Industry and Tertiary are a little less. According to the results of Japan the total TPES is very large in our results of 629 Mtoe, compared to 562 Mtoe of IEA. This is due to the very high *output price* coming from the IO model of Japan. We need to look into the IO model and modify it if any inappropriate specification is adopted. The consumption values by the Industry and Tertiary sectors are almost the same as in IEA, although more electricity use in the Industry but less in the Tertiary sector is indicated. Transportation consumption reaches the level of the Tertiary sector in our model. Lastly, total TPES of the USA is 2191 Mtoe, compared to 2583 Mtoe of IEA. Supplies of gas and 'New & Renewables' are larger in our results, and the rest are smaller. Industry and Transportation consumption values of energy are greater in IEA, and the Tertiary sector shows almost the same results.

We have briefly looked at the energy balance simulation results and, except for the large difference in TPES in Japan and the USA, other forecasted countries showed almost the same magnitude as reported by IEA. However, the objective of this observation is not to compare the results with other studies, rather to check the consistency in general as already stated. It is surprisingly that the forecasts with the energy balance model and IEA show the results in great similarity to detail, if one looks at the two results in parallel. Therefore, we conclude that the energy balance simulation up to 2010 was very successfully done.

4.3. Baseline CO_2 emission simulation to 2010

Now we have simulated the energy balance, next comes the CO_2 emission simulation. The simulated Total emission, Utility emission (electricity production), Industry emission, Transportation emission, and Tertiary emission values are shown from Figure 7-1a to Figure 7-1g for respective G7 countries. The baseline emission is based on the baseline energy balance; therefore the assumptions and scenario for nuclear and renewables are also embedded into the simulation here. Therefore, in this baseline case, no additional energy or environmental policy is incorporated.

Let us look at Figure 7-1a. Canada is forecasted to increase total CO_2 emission as is indicated as Carbon Emission, by 2.2% per year from 1990 to 2010. Deducing other emissions shown in the figure from total gives the emission from other transformation processes. The annual increase of emission at each sector is 1.6% per year in the Utility sector, 3.8% per year in Industry, 1.9% per year

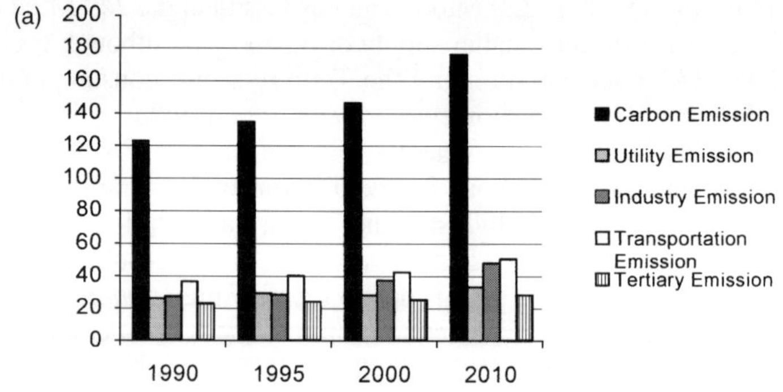

Figure 7-1a. Baseline CO_2 emission simulation: Canada (MMTC).

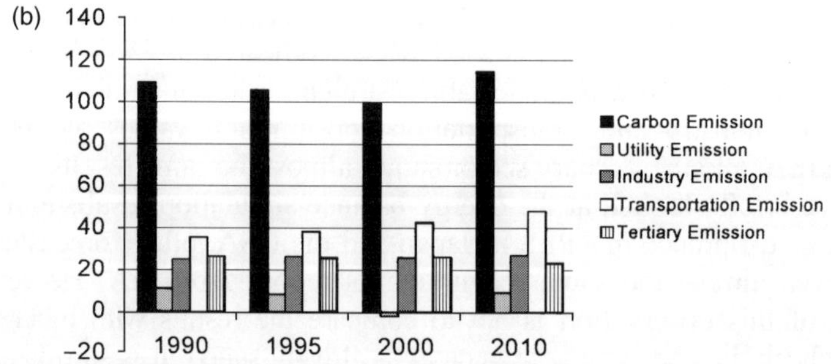

Figure 7-1b. Baseline CO_2 emission simulation: France (MMTC).

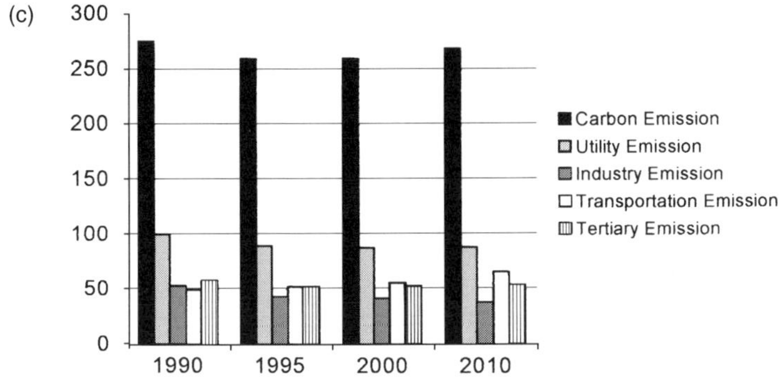

Figure 7-1c. Baseline CO_2 emission simulation: Germany (MMTC).

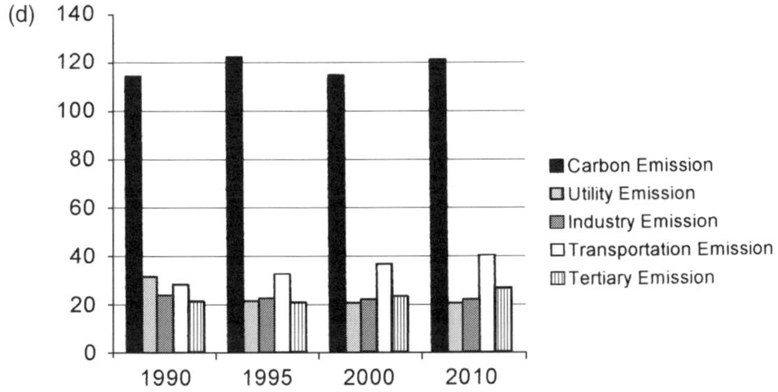

Figure 7-1d. Baseline CO_2 emission simulation: Italy (MMTC).

in Transportation, and 1.5% per year in the Tertiary sector. In order to achieve the Kyoto target of 6% reduction from 1990 level, Canada has to reduce almost 30% from this baseline emission in 2010. The reduction opportunities still lie in energy efficiency improvement and substitution. However, emission from the Transportation sector may be a big challenge because of the vast land area of this country.

Figure 7-1b is the simulation results of France. A large contribution by the extremely large share of nuclear energy can be seen in the very small total emission growth. From 1990 to 2010 total emission increased by 0.2% per year, and Industry sector emission grows at 0.5% per year. The largest increase is seen in the Transportation sector at 1.8% per year. Utility and Tertiary sector emission declines by −0.6% per year and −0.4% per year, respectively. The negative Utility emission in 2000 shows that a variable in the model may not be correctly calculated for this year, and we will have to investigate what is causing such results. As for the Kyoto target, France is obliged to reduce its future

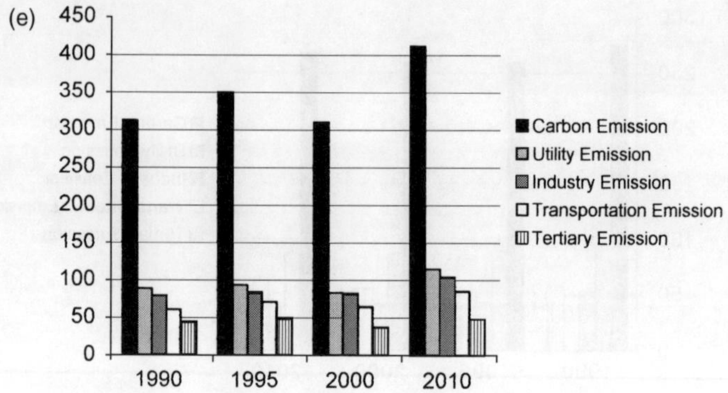

Figure 7-1e. Baseline CO_2 emission simulation: Japan (MMTC).

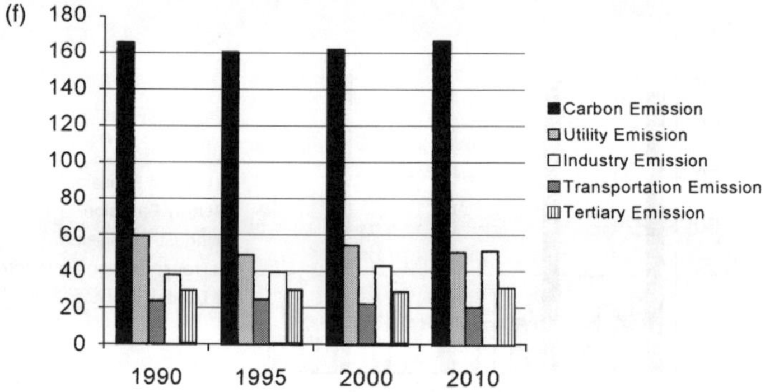

Figure 7-1f. Baseline CO_2 emission simulation: United Kingdom (MMTC).

emission level to the 1990 level as part of a burden-sharing agreement with other European Union member states. Therefore, the target will probably not cast a heavy economic burden on this country.

Figure 7-1c shows the CO_2 emission of Germany. In this country all sectors will reduce CO_2 emission during the period from 1990 to 2010 except the Transportation sector. Germany is required to reduce its emission by 21% from the 1990 level. This seems quite ambitious. The price responsiveness of technological change was quite large in this country, in all end-use sectors. In addition the heavy reliance on coal that is subsidized by the government indicates there are low cost mitigation opportunities. Whether Germany can enter the unregulated energy market and a make healthy policy mix, such as promotion of nuclear and renewables, is crucial. The efficiency improvement in office buildings and housing, and voluntary agreement, tax on petrol and diesel, promoted modal shift in transportation-related activities are expected to contribute greatly towards reducing emission. Nevertheless, whether Germany can meet the target is not clear, and government needs to coordinate the policies better.

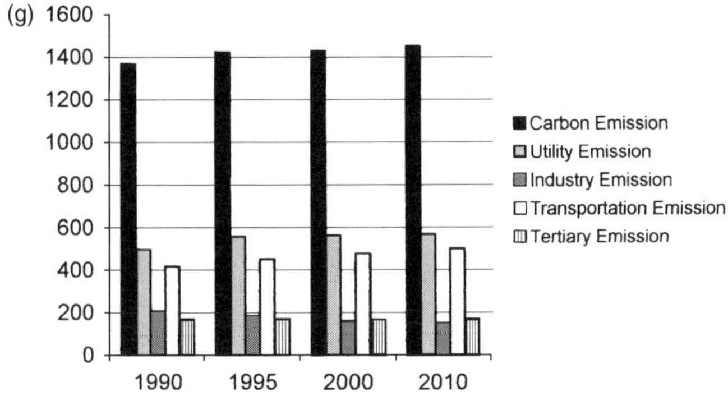

Figure 7-1g. Baseline CO_2 emission simulation: USA (MMTC).

The CO_2 emission of Italy is shown in Figure 7-1d. The total emission is forecast to increase at 0.4% per year from 1990 to 2010. The emission from Utility is expected to decline at 1.8% per year, and Industry is going to reduce emission at 0.4% per year. Increasing sectors are Transportation and Residential/Commercial, 2% and 1.2% respectively. Italy is targeting to reduce emission by 8% from the 1990 level. The high price elasticity of energy intensity, and price-induced substitution of gas for oil observed in Industry indicate that the low cost reduction opportunities are still to be found in this sector. At the same time, energy intensity in the Transportation sector has risen from 1990 to 1995, with the positive time trend indicating that the energy intensity is not declining regardless of relative price changes. At initial observations, the challenge seems to lie in emission reduction by the Transportation sector. In the Residential/Commercial sector the price-induced substitution of electricity to gas was observed, although technological change was only captured in output elasticity. Since Italy is not a nuclear-producing country, with growth of renewables supply probably remaining marginal, gas and electricity are going to play an important role both in terms of energy mix policy and climate change.

Figure 7-1e shows the emission forecast for Japan. Because of the rapid expansion of *output price* obtained from the IO model we have simulated energy balance with a larger figure for each of TPES, resulting in a higher level of emission in 2010. It is also questionable that the base year emission in 1990 is already higher in our simulation by more than 30 MMTC than the outlook by EIA, shown in Table 6-2 in Chapter 6. In Japan the emission from Utility is larger than in other sectors presented, despite the fact that the simulation results include the possibility of nuclear expansion, at a maximum 20% increase from present. As discussed in section 1 above, the potential low cost opportunities in this country seem hard to find, which observation is consistent with the outcomes from the model exercises introduced in Chapter 6. To meet the Kyoto target requires many efforts both on supply and demand sides. However, considering that 70% of the total energy supply depends on imports, and the shift to gas is limited due to there being no connection to pipelines across the surrounding seas, reduction by the supply side should not be viewed optimistically. In addition, whether the supply of renewables could augment as drastically as expected in the government plan remains questionable. The top-runner in end-use sectors and voluntary agreement in Industry are expected to contribute to CO_2 emission reduction, the effects of which are also unknown. In this respect, the government of Japan is faced with a big challenge in coordinating and institutionalizing measures to induce more energy-efficient technologies and cleaner energies to enter the market.

Figure 7-1f shows the emission of the UK. CO_2 emission in this country is forecast to stay almost at the same level as in 1990, except the rise in the Transportation sector at 1.7% per year during the period from 1990 to 2010. The UK has the emission reduction target at 12.5% below the 1990 level. The share of coal has declined to a great extent due to the privatization in 1994, and government considers reducing emissions through greater reliance on renewables and combined heat and power. In addition, government expects that nuclear energy proportion will decline steadily. How to meet the target and its own domestic aim of fuel diversity and energy security, without lowering the social equity figure, is one of the challenging tasks for this country.

Figure 7-1g shows the emission simulation of the USA. Total emission is forecast to increase by 0.3% per year. The Utility emission also increases by 0.75% per year, and Transportation increases by 1.0% per year. The Tertiary sector also increases by 0.17% per year, while the Industry sector emission declines by 1.2% per year. In section 3, we observed that the price elasticity of energy intensity was found only in the Tertiary sector in this country; whereas price-induced energy substitution, especially the shift from oil to gas, and gas to electricity, was observed in all sectors. In fact, fuel switching is an important factor in mitigating CO_2 emissions. Currently it is faced with trade-offs, whether to keep the energy prices low through competitive market while imperatives lie in climate change consideration.

5. Conclusion

Although the assessment of the domestic policy measures to tackle climate change was not an objective of this chapter, we were already able to draw a cross-country/sector picture of low cost mitigation opportunities and its challenges. This is one of the advantages of the energy model, as stated earlier, that it starts with disaggregated analysis of energy use and process, demand and supply. Now we are convinced of the validity of theories about price-induced technological change. The inter-energy substitution that lies behind the modelling was also proved to apply for the observed period. On top of that, we have tested the credibility of data, and the performance of the model, which were also proved good. We easily found from the simulated result whether something strange was occurring in variables, thanks to the very well-organized object-oriented database system and transparent modelling process. The assessment of domestic policy measures is to be conducted in the near future, and this will be able to provide great insights into how the country could/should meet the Kyoto target with its own domestic priorities in other policies. Especially, and most importantly, the policy such as a domestic carbon tax would induce technological change both in energy and end-use sectors through price signals, which are the important framework in our model.

It is already possible to conduct carbon tax simulation after baseline simulations were successfully done (see Chapter 11 for the effect of carbon tax on employment in G7 countries), The mechanism within the model of simulating such a policy is as follows. First, an imposed carbon tax rate will be added onto the energy price as mark-up percentages increase. The tax is imposed on each energy carrier according to their carbon content. The fraction of energy price increase is also added onto the price functions of energy sectors in the IO model (functions (3) and (4) in Chapter 5). The rise in energy costs will change the economic structure and international trade, and consequently change the *output* and *output prices*. The change in these two variables will affect the relative price of energy back into the energy balance model, the level of which induces the energy intensity change and inter-energy substitution. Therefore, the energy demand would decline as a result of the carbon tax. As described previously, the rate of changes in *output* (cost of CO_2 reduction) in relation to the rate of energy efficiency improvement and fuel switching are critically dependent on the estimated price elasticity of these elements. Therefore, a country with high price elasticity of energy intensity and energy substitution will probably result in a lower requirement level of carbon tax.

It should be noted here that it is crucially important to enable the model to handle international aspects of climate change policies, as discussed in Chapter 6. Despite the fact that the international mechanisms such as emissions trading should be supplemental to domestic policy measures, it is imperative that the parties design the mix of available policy options. There should be more insight into available opportunities and economic cost together with related impacts on socioeconomic trade-offs such as inflation or unemployment. We turn to this topic in Chapter 11.

It should be stressed as the concluding remark that, although it is not an easy task for economists to better capture the economic costs together with the economic benefits, the policy should be directed towards long-term benefit. If better technologies come into operation they will, in most cases, contribute greatly to operate and produce required services more efficiently than before. Such innovation augmentation could surely change the pattern of energy use in our society. However, such technological change is not likely to be continually induced unless the properly designed policy measures send price signals to users. The policies cannot be derived from models, but they should not be designed on human intuition. This is because the climate change issue is likely to affect not only the parties required to reduce GHGs, but also the whole globe, especially the developing countries within a very long time frame. We hope that the energy balance model will contribute to capture economy–energy–environment interaction and its policy implications, and thus to stimulate discussions on the economic analysis of policy measures to avoid climate change in a more in-depth way.

8
The case of South-East Asia

DIRK VANWYNSBERGHE, YUMIKO UMEHARA, and KIMIO UNO

1. Object-oriented approach to model building

Asia is diverse. The various countries differ in terms of per-capita income, size of the economy, and structure. In this chapter we take up countries in East and South-East Asia, namely Thailand, Malaysia, Singapore, Indonesia, the Philippines, Taiwan (Chinese Taipei), and Korea. They constitute a distinct group of countries in the global community despite all the differences among them; they have rapidly emerged in the world trade scene and proved to be the most dynamic engine of the world economy (Jung *et al*., 2000; Pesaran *et al*., 1998; World Bank, 1993; World Bank, various years b; ADB, various years b). Asian economic outlook is available in ADB, various years a; World Bank, various years a. Today, Korea is an OECD member. Taiwan is legally a part of China but its position as an economic entity is distinct. All of the countries that we take up are the core members of the APEC (Asia Pacific Economic Cooperation) (see Table 1-1 in Chapter 1).

The South-East Asian countries have succeeded in catching up with the West through their industrialization drive. This chapter looks into the energy and environment of the region. Despite its importance in the long run this issue tends to be neglected in the face of more urgent, short-term concerns. Because of their geographical proximity the relation with Japan is crucial. In other words the Asian economies are linked with the Japanese economy through trade, direct investment, and technology transfer, particularly after the 1985 realignment of the yen *vs*. the US dollar.

Energy analyses were conducted systematically for the G7 countries in Chapter 7. In this chapter it is intended to carry out a comparable work for Asian economies. Although physical data are available for those countries, price data are not.

In our object-oriented approach to database construction and model building, data set is an object and logic is an object. For energy analysis we need three main data. First is the physical quantity of energy, disaggregated by energy source and by final use. The empirical basis of the analysis is provided by the International Energy Agency's *Energy Statistics and Balances of Non-OECD Countries* (Korea is an OECD member) (IEA, various years b). This source provides energy balance

K. Uno (ed.), Economy–Energy–Environment Simulation, 135–144.

tables in an identical format as for OECD members, with slight differences in the order of listing. After adjusting for this difference, the data set for non-OECD countries can be treated in the same manner as the data set for OECD members.

Second is the output price of economic branches so that relative price can be derived. This is obtained from the economy model of COMPASS.

Third is the energy prices corresponding to the final use categories, which are not readily available. The problem is the energy prices. In the case of the OECD countries data are available from the IEA *Energy Prices and Taxes* (IEA, various years c). For Asian countries (and other developing economies) this is not the case. This chapter starts by describing the process of preparing energy price data, an indispensable step in attempting an econometric analysis of responses of economic agents to price signals. For global energy and environmental policy analysis, price parameters are deemed important in that they foretell the effectiveness of energy tax and other price-based policy instruments.

With energy data in physical terms and energy price data that comprise the basis for calculating relative prices of energy for different final uses, we can employ the standard model specification developed in the preceding chapter as the logical object. In other words we apply the equation specification object developed for G7 countries to the data objects coming from Asian countries.

2. Energy prices for Asian countries

The models that exist at present do not utilize full information of market signals with which economic agents are confronted, namely changing relative prices of energy. In contrast, the COMPASS approach emphasizes the price-responsiveness of the economic agents. This is deemed important in view of the preference on market-oriented policy measures such as carbon tax in achieving a sustainable development path.

Energy prices for Asian countries are required, to improve the simulation models for selected Asian countries.

The energy balance model for G7 countries developed in Chapter 7 focuses on three major parts of the energy balances, namely: (1) energy intensity (defined as energy consumption per output), (2) conversion efficiency of primary energy into electricity, and (3) energy substitution among different carriers. Of these, parameters concerning (1) and (3) are econometrically estimated, whereas (2) is a technological parameter (explained by time trend in the baseline simulation). In the case of South-East Asian countries we focus on energy intensity in three end-use sectors, i.e. Industry, Transportation, and Residential/Commercial sectors. The shift among primary energy sources (including preference on domestially produced energy) is not a pure market phenomenon but more or less a policy decision in Asian countries.

2.1. *The estimation procedure*

Energy prices

It is noted that Japan, and more recently Korea, are OECD members from Asia. Japan is analysed together with other G7 countries in Chapter 7. Korea is included in Asian countries for this study because of its development stage which, until recently, characterized this country as in a rapid industrialization phase, rather than a mature phase characterized by service orientation, etc. Taiwan, a region of China according to the official status in the international community, is treated as an independent economic entity within the framework of COMPASS. This is justified on the grounds of its relative independence from mainland China in economic terms, at least up until recently, and its significance in terms of economic size. Thus, Asian countries/regions in this study are as follows: Thailand, Malaysia, Singapore, Indonesia, Philippines, Taiwan, and Korea. China is analysed separately in Chapter 9 on the grounds that energy use there can hardly be conceived of as activities of independent economic agents; rather, it is largely determined by central planning.

For Asian countries the energy balance tables are available from IEA *Energy Balances for Non-OECD Countries*. Alternatively, and particularly for the period from 1970 to 1992, the Asian Development Bank has published annual tables for a wide range of countries under its jurisdiction (ADB, 1994). The ADB work is now integrated into the IEA work. This source, which provides time-series price data by energy carrier, is the basis of our energy analysis. The ADB source provides time-series energy prices per physical unit (such as baht/ton, baht/kWh) for various energy categories. What we need in the model is energy price for the final use sectors (i.e. Industry, Transportation, Household, Commerce, etc.). For this, prices by energy carrier are bundled together according to the share in the final use. The energy balance tables are also utilized in calculating the shares of various energy sources for respective final use. The base year is 1990. The shares of energy categories in the base year, obtained above, are multiplied by the time-series price data in order to estimate energy prices in different final use sectors.

The problem is that the ADB price data end in 1992. The availability of data thereafter varies among countries/regions. For a limited number of countries/regions (to be specific, Korea, Taiwan, and Thailand, among other developing economies), data are published in the IEA33 *Energy Prices and Taxes*. Thus, the availability of energy price data is as shown in Table 8-1.

Where data are not available, it is conceivable (1) to 'borrow' the data from neighbouring economies where the development phase and other economic characteristics are more or less similar, and use a dummy variable for 1993 onwards in the regression analysis in order to accommodate any data discontinuity, if necessary; or (2) to use the international price of oil, natural gas, and coal, adjusted by the exchange rates (local currency per US$, from *International Financial Statistics*).

Table 8-1. Availability of energy price data

	1973-1992	1992-1998
Thailand	OK	OK
Indonesia	OK	OK
Philippines	OK	n.a.
Malaysia	OK	n.a.
Taiwan	Partial (1982-1992)	OK
Korea	Partial (1980-1991)	OK
Singapore	n.a.	n.a.

Energy use data correspond to (1) Industry, (2) Transport, (3) Residential, (4) Public/Commerce, (5) Agriculture, (6) Others, and (7) Non-energy use. In the case of energy analysis for G7 countries attempted earlier, items (3) through (7) were combined into one category labelled 'Residential/ Commercial'. However, in order to reflect the response of economic agents to changing price signals it may be desirable to focus on items (3) and (4), without mixing them with other activities.

2.2. *1990 weights from the energy balances*

We use the shares of individual energy sources in total as the weights to aggregate into energy prices. The procedure to have access to the IEA energy balances is shown in Figures 8-1 and 8-2.

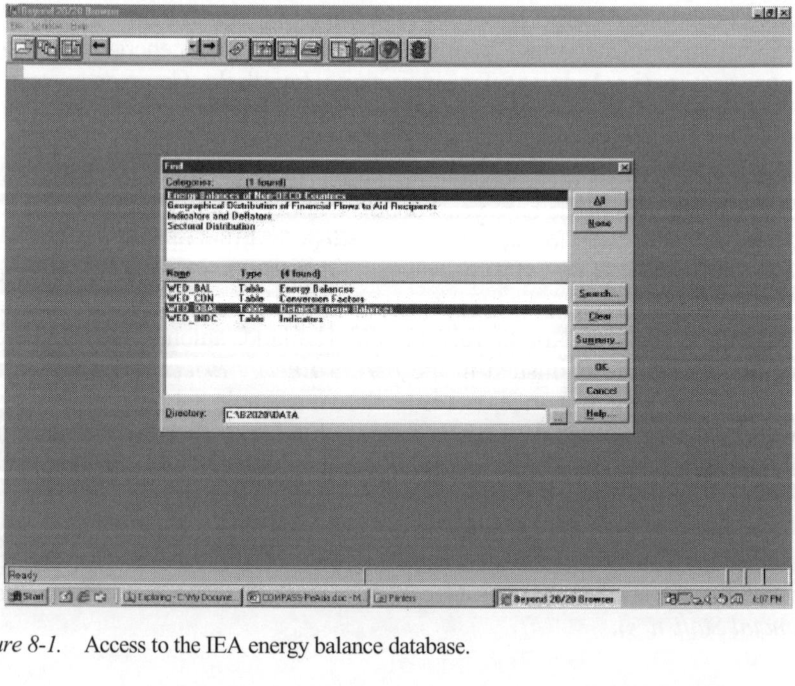

Figure 8-1. Access to the IEA energy balance database.

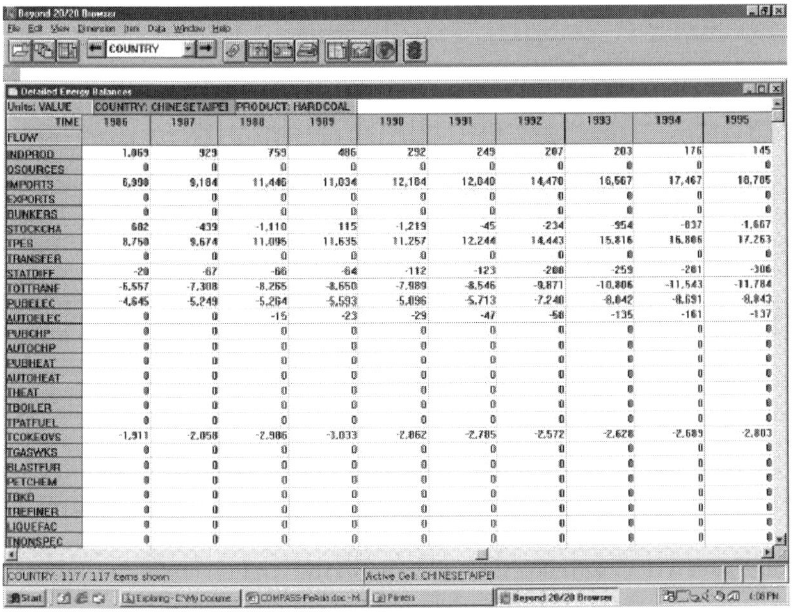

Detailed Energy Balances

Units: VALUE | COUNTRY: CHINESETAIPEI | PRODUCT: HARDCOAL

TIME / FLOW	1986	1987	1988	1989	1990	1991	1992	1993	1994	1995
INDPROD	1,069	929	759	486	292	249	207	203	176	145
OSOURCES	0	0	0	0	0	0	0	0	0	0
IMPORTS	6,900	9,184	11,446	11,034	12,184	12,040	14,470	16,567	17,467	18,705
EXPORTS	0	0	0	0	0	0	0	0	0	0
BUNKERS	0	0	0	0	0	0	0	0	0	0
STOCKCHA	682	-439	-1,110	115	-1,219	-45	-234	-954	-837	-1,667
TPES	8,750	9,674	11,096	11,635	11,257	12,244	14,443	15,816	16,806	17,263
TRANSFER	0	0	0	0	0	0	0	0	0	0
STATDIFF	-20	-67	-66	-64	-112	-123	-200	-259	-281	-306
TOTTRANF	-6,557	-7,308	-8,265	-8,650	-7,989	-8,546	-9,871	-10,806	-11,543	-11,784
PUBELEC	-4,645	-5,249	-5,264	-5,593	-5,096	-5,713	-7,240	-8,042	-8,691	-8,843
AUTOELEC	0	0	-15	-23	-29	-47	-58	-135	-161	-137
PUBCHP	0	0	0	0	0	0	0	0	0	0
AUTOCHP	0	0	0	0	0	0	0	0	0	0
PUBHEAT	0	0	0	0	0	0	0	0	0	0
AUTOHEAT	0	0	0	0	0	0	0	0	0	0
THEAT	0	0	0	0	0	0	0	0	0	0
TBOILER	0	0	0	0	0	0	0	0	0	0
TPATFUEL	0	0	0	0	0	0	0	0	0	0
TCOKEOVS	-1,911	-2,058	-2,986	-3,033	-2,862	-2,785	-2,572	-2,628	-2,689	-2,803
TGASWKS	0	0	0	0	0	0	0	0	0	0
BLASTFUR	0	0	0	0	0	0	0	0	0	0
PETCHEM	0	0	0	0	0	0	0	0	0	0
TBKB	0	0	0	0	0	0	0	0	0	0
TREFINER	0	0	0	0	0	0	0	0	0	0
LIQUEFAC	0	0	0	0	0	0	0	0	0	0
TNONSPEC	0	0	0	0	0	0	0	0	0	0

COUNTRY: 117 / 117 items shown | Active Cell: CHINESETAIPEI

Figure 8-2. IEA database search results.

In Figure 8-2 the selector window at the top left (now showing COUNTRY in this example) will allow users to select among country, product, flow, time, and units. The left and right arrows allow the users to move within each category (i.e. from country to country, product to product, or year to year).

2.3. Deriving estimated time-series of energy price data

The next step is to establish a linkage between price data and the weights.

Note that price data in terms of physical units have been converted to index numbers (1990 as 1.00). The shares of individual energy products have been obtained above. The sum of products of index and weights should generate energy price series. This process is repeated for Industry, Transportation, Household, Commerce and Public, etc. They have to be aggregated into an identical classification of energy sources. In the COMPASS database and model the following categories are used:

1. Coal (coa)
2. Crude oil (cru)
3. Petroleum products (prf)
4. Gas (gas)
5. Nuclear (nuc)

6. Hydro/Other (ren)
7. Electricity and heat (elh)

Difference
Total

Up to 1992 the above procedure can be followed for most of the Asian countries. From 1993 onwards the availability of price data differs among countries, whereas energy balance tables are available uniformly. Where price data are lacking our strategy is to 'borrow' the price data from neighbouring countries. However, countries have experienced different rates of inflation that reflect into different energy price movements over the years, making simple 'borrowing' unjustifiable. One way out of this may be, for the 'lending' country, where data availability is better, to use a GDP deflator as the general price level, and adjust the energy price series relative to the general price level (i.e. *Pe*/*P*, where *Pe* is the energy price and *P* the GDP deflator) for individual countries/regions. The 'borrowing' country will use the relative prices in the regression analysis (and not the energy price series alone). A dummy variable may be needed to absorb any discontinuity in the relation among variables.

For countries/regions where data are available after 1993 (from IEA's *Energy Prices and Taxes*, rather than ADB series for 1973-992), price data have been derived by the following procedure.

Tabulate current prices per physical unit.
Convert into index (1990 as 1.00).
Obtain weights for individual energy sources for the base year, based on IEA's *Energy Balances for Non-OECD Countries* (in the process it was found that inclusion of 'New Energy' leads to wrong results (Singapore, Taiwan, and Korea are the exceptions), total elements being larger than the total, presumably due to misplaced decimals. 'New Energy' data have been omitted. 'Crude Oil' is omitted because only in Thailand does it have a minor share).
Time series data on energy prices are obtained by multiplying weights and price series. (Not all prices for components under energy products are available. Thus, we were obliged to use different items for different countries/regions. The estimated data are included for the period 1992 on.)

The same formula as above is applied for earlier years. This gives better continuity, but at the cost of not including some components where data are available for earlier years but not so for the period 1992 on.

3. Regression results

The preliminary results of regression runs for the Industry sector are reported in Table 8-2a, for the Transportation sector in Table 8-2b, and for Household sector in Table 8-2c. They are preliminary in the sense that energy price data in respective countries are, as we have explained above, not in an ideal situation, although probably there is not much room for improvement given the availability of raw

Table 8-2a. Estimated parameters on energy equations for Asia, Industry sector

	Price Elasticity (*t*-value)	Output Elasticity (*t*-value)	Adjusted RSQ	DW
Thailand	−2.28 (−2.40)	−0.24 (−1.20)	0.44	1.34
Malaysia	−1.38 (−7.41)	*	0.88	1.25
Singapore	−4.66 (−3.87)	−0.35 (−0.86)*	0.61	1.24
Indonesia	*	*	*	*
Philippines	*	*	*	*
Taiwan	−0.21 (−1.24)	−0.33 (−2.74)	0.75	1.59
Korea	*	*	*	*

* indicates that no significant results were observed.

Table 8-2b. Estimated parameters on energy equations for Asia, Transportation sector

	Price Elasticity (*t*-value)	Output Elasticity (*t*-value)	Adjusted RSQ	DW
Thailand	−0.67 (−5.86)	*	0.85	1.78
Malaysia	−1.26 (−6.01)	*	0.89	0.96
Singapore	−0.11 (−0.80)	*	*	*
Indonesia	−0.34 (−0.77)*	*	*	*
Philippines	−0.39 (−1.79)	*	0.74	1.07
Taiwan	−0.35 (−2.38)	*	0.87	1.95
Korea	−0.25 (−1.49)	*	0.88	1.22

* indicates that no significant results were observed.

data for the East-Asian countries. They are preliminary also in the sense that we have employed the functional form developed and tested for G7 countries in Chapters 5 and 7 without searching for the best-fit equations. It is customary in a model-building process to first start from a theoretically accepted standard form and then, after looking at the results, try out alternative functional forms, alternative data, different time lags, and so forth. We chose this approach here in order to experiment with the object-oriented approach in model specification.

The results are mixed. One notable thing is that, in the case of the Transportation sector, although price elasticity is empirically measured for all countries, output elasticity is not. Output elasticity is intended to capture the size effect: it is expected that, as the activities in question expand in scale, there would be

Table 8-2c. Estimated parameters on energy equations for Asia, Residential sector

	Price Elasticity (*t*-value)	Output Elasticity (*t*-value)	Adjusted RSQ	DW
Thailand	*	−0.71 (−3.08)	0.79	0.77*
Malaysia	−0.58 (−12.19)	−0.40 (−3.39)	0.97	0.62*
Singapore	−0.86 (−3.70)	−0.65 (−3.51)	0.56	0.63*
Indonesia	−0.70 (−1.64)	−1.29 (−2.88)	0.84	1.90
Philippines	*	0.67 (−6.22)	0.81	1.05
Taiwan	−0.19 (−1.25)	−0.10 (−0.66)*	0.38	0.65*
Korea	*	−0.28 (−1.89)	0.89	0.65*

* indicates that no significant results were observed.

efficiency gains. If our observation is correct there is no such effect in the case of transportation. This may very well be true in the Asian context where a mass-transit system and large-scale cargo transportation network tend to be lacking. If we look at the Industry sector we realize that there are cases where the scale effect is captured together with responsiveness to relative price change. In the Residential sector price elasticity is observed for four countries out of seven, and output elasticity is uniformly observed, and also significant, in most of the countries under consideration.

4. Simulation experiment

It is necessary to examine the performance of the model before actually conducting policy analysis. We have carried out a simulation experiment by incorporating the energy balance models for South-East Asia into the globally linked COMPASS covering economy–energy–environment spheres. Just as we did in Chapter 7, which dealt with the industrialized countries of G7, we examine whether the simulation results are consistent with other studies in terms of the magnitude and direction of change. The models for South-East Asia focus on changes in energy intensity in response to price signals. As the reference case we chose energy demand and supply outlook for the APEC (APERC, 1998).

This publication is composed of energy balance tables for the APEC, which include all of the countries covered by the energy balance model that is developed in this chapter. The publication includes three cases including baseline, environmentally friendly scenario, and protracted case scenario. We base our comparison on the baseline scenario. The outlook is provided for 1995 (actual), 2000, 2005, and 2010. Our simulation results are available on an annual basis but we only look at year 2010, the terminal year of the experiment.

Let us look at the simulation for Thailand. The total TPES in 2010 is calculated to be 87.4 Mtoe whereas APERC predicts 95.9 Mtoe. In terms of primary energy supply the COMPASS scenario is more optimistic about the introduction of renewables by 2010. We share a similar view regarding the rapid introduction of natural gas, whereas we are more reserved about oil and petroleum products. In the final consumption (TFC) in general, we tend to believe that there would be more energy saving in Industry and Transportation. The Malaysian economy is projected to hover throughout the decade at the level that prevailed during 1998-2000 period, which is lower than in 1995. We predict a lower number than APERC, that predicts 77.2 Mtoe in 2010. Singapore is a small state with market orientation and, perhaps reflecting this, the results from two sources are almost identical. The COMPASS simulation experiment generates 25.7 Mtoe compared to 25.3 from the APERC. Indonesia is a country for which it is extremely difficult to predict the future based on price signals because of the hyperinflation that country has gone through and political turbulence that the country is experiencing. Our macroeconomic indicators predict that the Indonesian economy will be 7% larger in 2010 compared to the 1995 level, and this should be reflected in energy demand. Our problem with Indonesia also lies on the energy supply side. It seems we have an exaggerated view on the availability of gas and renewables in that country if we believe country experts who have produced the APERC projections. As for the Philippines, COMPASS is more optimistic than the APERC, predicting 58.1 Mtoe compared to 48.8 Mtoe in 2010. We believe the Industry sector will be more energy saving while the Residential sector will be using twice as much energy as is predicted by the APERC. We share the similar view concerning the Transportation sector. COMPASS and the APERC have different views on Taiwan. The major difference is that we believe the economy there will become much more energy efficient than is predicted by the APERC. The TFC in Taiwan was 33.4 Mtoe in 1990 and 44.3 Mtoe in 1995 according to COMPASS (or 42.2 Mtoe in 1995 in the APERC). The figure for 2010 is 35.6 Mtoe for COMPASS compared to 84.6 Mtoe for APERC. Industry will be three times as lean in 2010. For Korea we share a common view with the APERC. The TFC in 2010 is predicted to be 179.5 Mtoe by COMPASS whereas the comparable figure from the APERC is 178.0. The number for the Residential sector is identical, and that for the Transportation sector is more or less the same, although we believe the Industry sector will be more energy efficient than is assumed by the APERC. The major difference is found in the energy supply: we believe more gas could be used in Korea and we are more optimistic about the introduction of nuclear energy there. This is again a national policy issue rather than a model assumption.

The comparisons generally prove that the simulation of energy balance tables can actually be done for developing economies. We have limited our modelling attempt to the energy intensity in the final use sectors including Industry, Transportation, and Residential, and excluded the shift among energy sources which was one of the focal points in modelling G7 countries. The reason is that, in the Asian context, the choice among primary energy sources is often a policy decision rather than market phenomena participated by many 'atomic' agents.

5. In lieu of conclusion

The COMPASS approach in database construction and model-building is characterized by an object-oriented approach. Although this concept was established nearly two decades ago among database theoreticians, and some database development tools have become available in the market in the past decade, the content side is still lagging in actually implementing the concept in the empirical context. Statistics the world over are still published in a more or less segmented and self-contained user interface which, once faced with a need to produce an integrated database, proves to be inflexible. What is more lagging is the application of the object-oriented approach to model-building and simulation. It is evident, however, when one wants to develop an empirically based model for the global community with detailed country resolution as well as industrial branch classification encompassing enormous economy–energy–environment spheres, a traditional approach, where a single country model is developed and then international linkage is attempted, cannot be followed. We have tried to fill this gap.

We have demonstrated that the object-oriented approach to database and modelling is indeed possible and effective. The COMPASS approach in model-building is to develop a prototype such as we did in Chapters 5 and 7 for the energy balance model and apply the logic to other cases. This is the focal point of this chapter. It can now be said that the experiment went rather well, although considerable refinement in the regression analysis must follow. We can reasonably hope that this approach can be used more extensively in future developments of the model.

9
The case of China

WANG YINCHU and ZUO LI

1. Progress in the national economy

The Chinese economy has grown at a fast rate since 1978 when the policy of economic reform and openness commenced. The GDP values in nominal, the GDP per capita in nominal, the GDP indexes in real terms and the GDP per-capita index in real terms, from 1978 to 1997, are shown in Table 9-1. It can be seen that, in real terms, the GDP in 1997 was 5.82 times the 1978 GDP. During the period from 1978 to 1997 the average yearly growth rates of GDP and GDP per capita were 9.8% and 8.4%, respectively. The average GDP growth rate is 6.5% higher than the world average growth rate in the same period, 7.3% higher than the developed countries, 6.5% higher than other developing countries, 1.9-3.5% higher than Singapore, Korea, Chinese Taiwan, Malaysia and Indonesia, all of which showed high economic growth rates in the same period.

As a result of the high speed of economic development, Chinese integrative national power increased greatly, the industrial structure improved significantly and Chinese people's quality of life improved considerably.

According to the World Development Report of the World Bank, the Chinese GDP value was 252.23 billion US dollars in 1978 and 1055.4 billion US dollars in 1997. The position of Chinese GDP in the top ten countries in the world was raised from 8th in 1978 to 7th in 1997, as shown in Table 9-2. From the table it can also be seen that the difference between the Chinese GDP and the one of the 6th country (Italy) of the top ten countries has reduced from 36% (1 − 252230/393950) in 1978 to 8.7% (1 − 1055400/1155400) in 1997.

Meanwhile, Chinese foreign trade value increased considerably. The total amount of Chinese foreign trade was 20.64 billion US dollars in 1978 and China held the position of 27th in the world order. Exports were 9.75 billion US dollars and this showed the share of 0.81% in total world export and 28th position. In 1997 Chinese foreign trade had extended to 325.1 billion US dollars and was 15.8 times the 1978 level. The position in world trade rose to 10th. Export values reached 182.7 billion US dollars and this was 18.7 times the 1978 export value. Export share increased to 3.3% of world total; the international reserve also increased greatly from 0.17 billion US dollars in 1978 to 139.9 billion US dollars in 1997. China was then in second position in the world, and just below Japan. The development of Chinese foreign trade 1978-1997 is shown in Table 9-3.

K. Uno (ed.), Economy–Energy–Environment Simulation, 145–161.

Table 9-1. The GDP and per-capita GDP of China in the past 20 years

Year	GDP at Current Price, 100 Million Yuan	Per Capita GDP at Current Price, Yuan	GDP Index at Comparable Price, Preceding Year = 100	Per Capita GDP Index at Comparable Price, Preceding Year = 100
1978	3624.1	172.8	111.7	110.2
1979	4038.2	184.2	107.6	106.1
1980	4517.8	205.0	107.8	106.5
1981	4860.3	211.1	105.2	103.9
1982	5301.8	236.7	109.3	107.5
1983	5957.4	264.9	111.1	109.3
1984	7206.7	327.1	115.3	113.7
1985	8989.1	406.9	113.2	111.9
1986	10,201.4	475.6	108.5	107.2
1987	11,954.5	544.9	111.5	109.8
1988	14,922.3	661.0	111.3	109.5
1989	16,917.8	786.0	104.2	102.5
1990	18,598.4	1147.5	104.2	102.3
1991	21,662.5	1409.7	109.1	107.7
1992	26,651.9	1681.8	114.1	112.8
1993	34,560.5	2123.2	113.1	112.2
1994	46,670.0	2685.9	112.6	111.4
1995	57,494.9	3054.7	109.0	109.3
1996	66,850.5	3494.0	109.8	108.4
1997	73,142.7	3797.2	108.5	107.7

Table 9-2. International comparison of GDP (M. = Million US$, R. = Rank)

	1980		1985		1990		1995		1997	
	M.	R.	M.	R.	M.	R.	M.	R.	M.	R.
US	2,587,100	1	3,946,600	1	5,392,200	1	6,952,020	1	7,690,100	1
Japan	1,039,980	2	1,527,900	2	2,942,890	2	5,108,540	2	4,772,300	2
Germany	819,140	3	624,970	3	1,488,210	3	2,415,764	3	2,319,500	3
France	651,890	4	510,320	4	1,196,780	4	1,536,089	4	1,526,600	4
Britain	522,850	5	454,300	5	975,150	6	1,105,822	5	1,220,200	5
Italy	393,950	6	358,670	6	1,090,750	5	1,086,932	6	1,155,400	6
Canada	253,350	7	346,030	7	570,150	7	568,928	9	583,900	9
China	252,230	8	265,530	8	364,900	10	697,647	7	1,055,400	7
Brazil	237,930	9	188,250	9	414,060	9	688,085	8	773,400	8
Spain	198,320	10	164,250	11	491,240	8	558,617	10	570,100	10
Mexico	166,700	11	177,360	10	237,750	13	250,038	13	348,600	16

Along with the rapid development of the economy, the Chinese industrial structure was adjusted towards the direction of maturity. The ratios among primary industry, secondary industry and tertiary industry were 28.1:48.2:23.7 in 1978. These figures changed to 19.1:50.0:30.9 in 1997. The change was basically consistent with the development of industrial structure throughout the world, i.e. the ratio of primary industry decreasing and the ratios of secondary and tertiary industries increasing. In the sector of primary industry, the situation of farming production was the major part (the ratios in 1978 among farming, forestry, animal

Table 9-3. Total imports and exports (unit: US$ 100 million)

Year	Total Imports & Exports	Total Exports	Total Imports	Balance
1978	206.4	97.5	108.9	−11.4
1980	381.4	181.2	200.2	−19.0
1985	696.0	273.5	422.5	−149.0
1986	738.5	309.4	429.1	−119.7
1987	826.5	394.4	432.1	−37.7
1988	1027.9	475.2	552.7	−77.5
1989	1116.8	525.4	591.4	−66.0
1990	1154.4	620.9	533.5	87.4
1991	1356.3	718.4	637.9	80.5
1992	1655.3	849.4	805.9	43.5
1993	1957.0	917.4	1039.6	−122.2
1994	2366.2	1210.1	1156.1	54.0
1995	2808.6	1487.8	1320.8	167.0
1996	2898.8	1510.5	1388.3	122.2
1997	3251.6	1827.9	1423.7	404.2

husbandry and fishery were 80:3:15:2); these changed to 58:4:28:10 in 1997. As regards secondary industry, China experienced light industry having priority to develop, with the result that light and heavy industries developed in synchronization. The problem of a shortage of daily goods was solved first and the market boomed. The bottleneck problem of the supply capacity of infrastructure sectors such as energy, raw materials production, transportation and communication has been solved to some degree. In the sector of tertiary industry, finance, insurance and real estate developed rapidly. This changed the traditional situation in which tertiary industry mainly consisted of commerce and restaurants. Table 9-4 shows the history of Chinese industrial structure change from 1978 to 1997.

The fast growth of the economy led to a fast increase in residents' income. The per-capita net income of rural households increased from 133.6 yuan in 1978 to 2090 yuan in 1997. As regards price factors, the average yearly growth rate was 8.1%. The per-capita disposable income of urban households rose from 343.4 yuan to 5160 yuan. Adjusting for price factor the average yearly growth rate was 6.2%. The urban and rural household saving deposit was 4628 billion yuan; adding cash in hand and various securities, household financial assets exceeded 6000 billion yuan at the end of 1997. Along with increased income, the life quality of the population has obviously been improved. Household consumption levels increased from 184 yuan in 1978 to 2677 yuan in 1997. The yearly growth rate was 7.7% in real terms. The consumption structure has also showed much change. The Engel coefficient (the ratio between food expenditure and total expenditure) of rural households decreased from 67.7% in 1978 to 55.1% in 1997. The Engel coefficient of urban households decreased from 57.4% to 46.4% during the same period. Table 9-5 shows details of increasing household income.

Table 9-4. Industrial structure changes (%)

Year	GDP	Primary Industry	Secondary Industry	Tertiary Industry
1978	100	28.1	48.2	23.7
1979	100	31.2	47.4	21.4
1980	100	30.1	48.5	21.4
1981	100	31.8	46.4	21.8
1982	100	33.3	45.0	21.7
1983	100	33.0	44.6	22.4
1984	100	32.0	43.3	24.7
1985	100	28.4	43.1	28.5
1986	100	27.1	44.0	28.9
1987	100	26.8	43.9	29.3
1988	100	25.7	44.1	30.2
1989	100	25.0	43.0	32.0
1990	100	27.1	41.6	31.3
1991	100	24.5	42.1	33.4
1992	100	21.8	43.9	34.3
1993	100	19.9	47.4	32.7
1994	100	20.2	47.9	31.9
1995	100	20.5	48.8	30.7
1996	100	20.4	49.5	30.1
1997	100	19.1	50.0	30.9

Table 9-5. Per-capita annual income of households (unit: yuan)

Year	Rural	Index (1978 = 100)	Urban	Index (1978 = 100)
1978	133.6	100.0	343.4	100.0
1980	191.3	139.0	477.6	127.0
1985	397.6	268.9	739.1	160.4
1986	423.8	277.6	899.6	182.5
1987	462.6	292.0	1002.2	186.9
1988	544.9	310.7	1181.4	182.5
1989	601.5	305.7	1375.7	182.8
1990	686.3	311.2	1510.2	198.1
1991	708.6	317.4	1700.6	212.4
1992	784.0	336.2	2026.6	232.9
1993	921.6	346.9	2577.4	255.1
1994	1221.0	364.4	3496.2	276.8
1995	1577.7	383.7	4283.0	290.3
1996	1926.1	418.2	4838.9	301.6
1997	2090.1	437.4	5160.3	311.9

2. The economic problems

Chinese economic development was not plain sailing. For example, China was successful in controlling the fast growth of the population and in transferring the labour force from agriculture to secondary and tertiary industries in the past 20 years. However, China is still under very great pressure from the size of the population, especially in rural areas. This is a long-term problem. There were other problems in the past 20 years, including the following four points that are prominent.

(1) The forming of the unified market was slow and the efficiency of resource allocation was low. China is in the process of changing its economic system. In this process, on the one hand, the traditional system is losing its dominant position. On the other hand, the new market economic system is not fully in place. Local protectionism fragmented the market in reality. This had a bad impact on raising the efficiency of resource configuration. It did not achieve equilibrium in various regional developments in China. There are quite large and obvious differences between the north and the south, between shoreland and backland. There are conflicts and contradictions among developed and undeveloped regions. Local governments involved in the competition process have distorted the competition among enterprises; therefore, the market was segmented and the efficiency of the national economy was lost.
(2) The inequality of wealth resulted in social dissatisfaction. It was pointed out in many research reports that income distribution was becoming increasingly unequal when reforms because deeper. According to the World Bank the Gini coefficient of China was 28.8 in 1981 and reached 38.8 in 1995 (*Sharing the Increasing Income*, World Bank, 1998). The difference in the occupancy of state-owned assets and the difference in the right of using state-owned assets were important factors in expanding the difference of household incomes. They were also important reasons behind social dissatisfaction.
(3) The relative surplus happened under conditions in which the development level was not high. Even though Chinese household income and consumption levels increased during the reform and opening-up process, it is still at a comparatively low level compared to developed countries. According to the World Bank (*World Development Report, 1998/99*), the GDP per capita of China was 860 US dollars in 1997. This means that China has just stepped over the threshold of middle-low-income countries. However, due to the lopsidedness of income distribution, a relative surplus, from consumption materials to production materials, is currently extant. From the point of view of society as a whole the increase in urban household income and saving deposit is insufficient to support purchases of housing and cars; the increase in rural household income and saving deposit is insufficient to support the purchase of modern household goods, further restricting the development of the Chinese economy.
(4) The excess consumption of natural resources and pollution of the environment. The rapid development of the Chinese economy also consumed an ever-increasing amount of natural resources and caused deterioration the living environment. Farming land was reduced significantly. The per-capita area of cultivated land in 1997 was 60% of that in 1957. The water shortage

problem became very serious in many cities and rural areas. The efficiency of resource use, such as energy consumption per unit of output, was much lower than the advanced level of the world. Pollution from waste water, waste gas and solid waste is seriously destroying environmental quality.

3. The economic prospects

From the external point of view the Chinese economy will benefit from the maintained increase in the world economy and the fast process of economic globalization in the next 10 years. At the same time, from the internal point of view the Chinese economy will benefit from the setting up of a market economic mechanism and improvement in government management ability in the macro-economy in next decade. Under these conditions China has her long-term development goals. They are:

(1) To advance the integrative national power.
(2) To increase the ability of international competition.
(3) To improve people's life quality.
(4) To promote sustainable development.

With these goals, and a proper scenario, the COMPASS China model provides the prospect of the Chinese economy from 2000 to 2010.

The Chinese economy will maintain its high speed of development the next ten years. GDP values, in nominal, will reach 16,587 and 30,700 billion Chinese yuan in 2005 and 2010, respectively. The yearly average growth rates, in real terms, will be 7.20% from 2001 to 2005 and 7.23% from 2006 to 2010. The GDP per capita will reach 12,259 Chinese yuan in 2005 and 21,386 Chinese yuan in 2010. According to the exchange rate in year 2000 the GDP value will be 3712 billion US dollars in 2010, which will mean China reaching the 4th position among the top ten countries in the world, behind the US, Japan and Germany, if all the other countries which are in front of China at present have yearly growth rates of about 3.0% from 2001 to 2010. However, due to the huge population, the GDP per capita of China in 2010 will be 2586 US dollars, which will still be lower than the world average level. Table 9-6 shows the details.

Table 9-6. GDP in next 10 years

Year	2000	2005	2010	2000-2005	2005-2010
GDP (Billion Yuan)	9343.9	16,587.4	30,700.2		
GDP index in real term	100	141.60	200.75	7.20%	7.23%
GDP in 2000 USD	1129.9	2005.7	3712.2		
GDP per capita	7306	12,259	21,386		
GDP per capita index in real term	100	133.8	178.84	6.00	5.97%
GDP per capita in 2000 USD	884	1482	2586		

Table 9-7. Industrial structure changes to 2010

Year	Primary Industry	Secondary Industry	Tertiary Industry
2000	16.9	49.6	33.5
2001	16.3	50.0	33.7
2002	15.8	50.0	34.2
2003	15.5	49.8	34.7
2004	15.1	49.8	35.1
2005	14.8	49.9	35.3
2006	14.7	49.7	35.7
2007	14.3	49.8	35.8
2008	14.0	49.4	36.6
2009	13.8	48.9	37.3
2010	13.5	48.6	37.9

The Chinese economy is still in the process of industrialization. The change in industrial structure is one of the main sources to accelerate the growth of the economy. Table 9-7 shows the changes in industrial structure from 2000 to 2010. It can be seen that the share of primary industry in GDP will continue to decline, from 16.9% in 2000 to 13.5% in 2010. The share of secondary industry will show a slight increase and reach a peak value of 50% in the period from 2001 to 2005. This share will show a slight decrease in the subsequent five years. On the other hand the share of tertiary industry in GDP will show a stable increasing trend, from 33.5% in 2000 to 37.9% in 2010.

Adjustment of the internal structure of agriculture will continue. The share of farming will continue to go down, that of forestry will keep the same value as before, while animal husbandry and fishery will go up in the next ten years. The gross output ratios of farming, forestry, animal husbandry and fishery will be about 53:4:31:12 in 2005 and 51:4:33:12 in 2010.

As for the internal picture of manufacturing industry, the structure will show the following changes, as shown in Table 9-8.

(1) In the energy production aspect the share of coal mining in whole industry gross output will go down from 1.45% in 2000 to 1.34% in 2010 while the share of the production of crude petroleum and natural gas will go up from 0.93% in 2000 to 1.0% in 2010. Meanwhile, the share of electricity production and supply, including hot water and steam, in the whole industry gross output will go up from 3.53% in 2000 to 3.80% in 2010; the share of petroleum refining will increase from 2.95% in 2000 to 3.47% in 2010.

(2) The share of food processing will increase from 5.09% in 2000 to 5.77% in 2010, which means the degree of processing food will be greater than before. The increase in the share of beverage shows the Chinese people will have more drinks, such as milk, fruit juice, and so on. At the same time the share of tobacco production will decrease from 1.59% in 2000 to 1.37% in 2000.

(3) The traditional industrial sectors, such as textiles and, wearing apparel production, among others, will tend to decrease their shares, but still keep

Table 9-8. Structure changes of industry to 2010 (gross output, selected sectors)

Sector	2000	2005	2010
Coal mining	1.45	1.39	1.34
Crude petroleum and natural gas	0.93	0.97	1.00
Food process & manufacturing	5.09	5.47	5.77
Beverages	3.28	4.22	5.14
Tobacco manufacture	1.59	1.47	1.37
Textiles	7.67	7.11	6.88
Wearing apparel	3.00	2.78	2.69
Leather, fur and their products	1.95	1.97	2.07
Paper and paper products	1.70	1.65	1.61
Printing industries	0.86	0.93	0.97
Cultural, education, sports articles	0.63	0.71	0.77
Petroleum refineries	2.95	3.30	3.47
Chemical industries	6.35	6.61	6.86
Medicines	1.81	1.86	1.88
Chemical fibers	1.04	1.16	1.28
Rubber products	1.08	1.05	1.03
Plastic products	2.35	2.49	2.62
Primary iron and steel	5.22	4.39	3.71
Primary non-ferrous metals	1.59	1.24	1.01
Metal products	4.17	3.77	3.42
Ordinary machinery	7.35	6.90	6.43
Motor vehicles	5.48	6.27	6.73
Electric machinery and instrument	4.55	4.34	4.17
Electronic and communication equip.	4.55	4.08	3.84
Electricity, steam and hot water	3.53	3.72	3.80
Production and supply of water	0.29	0.32	0.34

large ratios, more than 9.5%, in the whole industry gross output. Meanwhile, the leather, fur and their product will increase the share, reflecting the change of demand for clothes.

(4) The shares of chemical industry, medicine, chemical fibre and plastic production, will increase continuously. Rubber production will maintain almost the same share. Including the situation of petroleum refining, we can conclude that the share of heavy chemical industry will rise in the Chinese economy in next ten years.

(5) The shares of primary iron and steel, primary non-ferrous metals, metal products and ordinary machinery will go down and the share of motor vehicles will go up. This is a reasonable change in manufacturing structure. However, the decrease in shares of electric machinery and electronic products is not consistent with the globally observed development trend. This reflects the fact that there is a shortage in supply capacity of electric machinery and electronic products, suggesting the need to strengthen investment in these sectors.

Within the tertiary industry sector the structure changes towards the direction of raising the tertiary industry level. Table 9-9 shows the changes in shares of selected sectors in the whole tertiary industry gross outputs.

Table 9-9. Structure changes of tertiary industry to 2010 (gross output, selected sectors)

	2000	2005	2010
Railway transportation	2.07	1.66	1.42
Highway transportation	8.77	9.22	9.85
Air transportation	1.07	1.10	1.14
Communications	2.58	2.91	3.18
Commerce	30.50	28.41	27.62
Restaurants	7.65	8.20	8.04
Finance and insurance	13.95	14.61	15.83
Real estate and social services	12.31	13.47	14.47
Health care, sports and social welfare	4.09	3.70	3.24
Education, culture, arts, radio, film, TV	5.14	4.67	4.23
Scientific research and technical services	3.33	2.57	2.04

The share changes in transportation, i.e. the railway decreasing while highway and air increase, reflect the general trend of the development speed of different transportation modes. The traditional commerce service goes down significantly, but still has a high share. Along with the change of lifestyle, restaurant service will raise its share continuously. Communication, finance and insurance, as well as real estate and social services, will increase their shares steadily. It should be noticed that the sectors of health care and social welfare, education and culture service, scientific research and technical services will lose their shares. This points to the fact that the development speed of these sectors is slower than the whole tertiary industry. It also foretells that there is a possibility that some aspects of social development will lag behind in economic development if there are no special policy measures in place.

After successfully resisting the Asia financial crisis and joining the WTO, Chinese foreign trade will maintain its tendency to increase. The average yearly growth rate of exports and imports, in real terms, will be more than 10%, which is larger than the GDP growth rate. However, comparing the positive values of the net export from 1998 to 2003, net export will become negative from 2004. Table 9-10 shows a forecast of total imports and exports in current prices.

The import and export structures will also change. Shares of imported crude petroleum and petroleum refining in total imports will increase, while the share of metal manufacturing (primary iron and steel, primary non-ferrous metals and metal products) will decrease. The import share of machine manufacturing (ordinary machinery, electric machinery and instruments, motor vehicles, electronic and communication equipment) will keep its high value, which is around 50%. The export share of primary products (agriculture, mining) in total export will go down while the share of textile products, including clothes, will go up. The export share of machinery equipment and electronic products will go up.

As a result of the fast economic growth household income and consumption levels are expected to rise quickly. The per-capita net income of rural households will increase from 2700 yuan in 2000 to 7500 yuan in 2010. Adjusting for the

Table 9-10. Exports and imports to 2010 (current prices, 100 million Chinese yuan)

Year	Export	Import	Net Export
2000	17,767	15,898	1869.1
2001	20,642	19,332	1309.4
2002	23,956	22,900	1056.2
2003	27,771	27,043	727.9
2004	32,158	32,159	−1.6
2005	37,196	37,647	−450.7
2006	42,977	43,828	−851.6
2007	49,600	50,457	−856.8
2008	57,180	58,645	−1464.2
2009	65,846	68,358	−2512.0
2010	75,741	79,493	−3752.2

price factor the average yearly growth rate will be 7%. The per-capita disposable income of urban households will rise from 7000 yuan in 2000 to 13,000 yuan in 2010. As regards the price factor, the average yearly growth rate will be 5.5%. Household consumption levels will increase from 3530 yuan in 2000 to 10,500 yuan in 2010. The yearly growth rate will be 6% in real terms. The consumption structure will improve continuously, and the Engel coefficient of rural households will decrease from 52.4% in 2000 to 43% in 2010, while that for urban households will decrease from 44.8% in 2000 to 32% in 2010.

4. Progress in the energy sphere

Energy is the important physical basis of economic and social development. In the procedure of economic opening and reform since 1978 the energy industry has made a great contribution to Chinese economic achievement.

(1) The capacity of energy production extended rapidly and the position in world energy rose continuously. In the process of economic development the Chinese government placed the energy industry as the highest priority sector in the investment list in order to increase the capacity of energy production. From 1978 to 1997 the output of primary energy increased from 628 million tons to 1324 million tons of standard coal equivalent. Of this total the output of coal increased from 618 million tons to 1387 million tons; the output of crude oil increased from 104 million tons to 163 million tons; the output of natural gas increased from 13,730 million cubic metres to 24,110 cubic metres; and the output of hydropower increased from 44,600 million kWh to 196,000 million kWh. Nuclear power came into use in 1995 and its output was 14,420 million kWh. Details are shown in Table 9-11.

Following its development in the past 20 years, China has become one of the biggest countries in the world in energy production. The output of primary energy is number 3 in the world and in excess of 10% of the world total. From

Table 9-11. Production of primary energy

Year	Coal Production, 100 Million Tons	Crude Oil, 100 Million Tons	Natural Gas, 100 Million Cube Meters	Power, 100 Million KWh	
				Hydro-power	Nuclear Power
1978	6.18	1.04	137.30	446	
1980	6.20	1.06	142.70	582	
1985	8.72	1.25	129.30	924	
1990	10.80	1.38	152.98	1267	
1995	13.61	1.50	179.40	1906	128
1996	13.97	1.57	201.14	1880	143
1997	13.87	1.63	241.10	1960	144

Table 9-12. Total production of energy and its composition

Year	Total Energy Production, 10,000 Tons of SCE	As Percentage of Total Energy Production (%)			
		Coal	Crude Oil	Natural Gas	Hydro-power
1978	62,770	70.3	23.7	2.9	3.1
1980	63,735	69.4	23.8	3.0	3.8
1985	85,546	72.8	20.9	2.0	4.3
1986	88,124	72.4	21.2	2.1	4.3
1987	91,266	72.6	21.0	2.0	4.4
1988	95,801	73.1	20.4	2.0	4.5
1989	101,639	74.1	19.3	2.0	4.6
1990	103,922	74.2	19.0	2.0	4.8
1991	104,844	74.1	19.2	2.0	4.7
1992	107,256	74.3	18.9	2.0	4.8
1993	111,059	74.0	18.7	2.0	5.3
1994	118,729	74.6	17.6	1.9	5.9
1995	129,034	75.3	16.6	1.9	6.2
1996	132,616	75.2	17.0	2.0	5.8
1997	132,410	74.1	17.3	2.1	6.5

1978 to 1997 the position of coal production rose from number 3 to number 1 in the world, while the position of crude oil production rose from number 8 to number 5. The position of generated electricity rose from number 7 to number 2. The improvement in energy supply greatly alleviated the bottleneck restriction on economic development.

(2) The structure of energy starts to change and the demand for clean energy increases. Tables 9-12 and 9-13 show the structure changes in energy production and consumption. It can be seen that, while coal still shows a high ratio in energy structure, the demand for clean energy shows an increasing tendency. The structure change of energy consumption showed that the ratio of coal had decreased since 1991, whereas the ratio of crude oil and natural gas had increased since 1996. The continuously increasing demand from the domestic market for crude oil products stimulated the import of crude oil. China has become a net import country of crude oil since 1993. There is a trend towards increasing the import of crude oil.

Table 9-13. Total consumption of energy and its composition

Year	Total Energy Consumption, 10,000 Tons of SCE	As Percentage of Total Energy Production (%)			
		Coal	Crude Oil	Natural Gas	Hydro-power
1978	57 144	70.7	22.7	3.2	3.4
1980	60 275	72.2	20.7	3.1	4.0
1985	76 682	75.8	17.1	2.2	4.9
1986	80 850	75.8	17.2	2.3	4.7
1987	86 632	76.2	17.0	2.1	4.7
1988	92 997	76.2	17.0	2.1	4.7
1989	96 934	76.0	17.1	2.0	4.9
1990	98 703	76.2	16.6	2.1	5.1
1991	103 783	76.1	17.1	2.0	4.8
1992	109 170	75.7	17.5	1.9	4.9
1993	115 993	74.7	18.2	1.9	5.2
1994	122 737	75.0	17.4	1.9	5.7
1995	131 176	74.6	17.5	1.8	6.1
1996	138 948	74.7	18.0	1.8	5.5
1997	138 173	71.5	20.4	1.7	6.2

The increasing demand for clean energy stimulated the development of the industry of electricity production and supply. From 1978 to 1997 the power-generating capacity increased from 57 million kW to 237 million kW. The total electricity generated from 256,600 million kWh increased to 1,135,553 million kWh.

(3) The efficiency of energy use improved considerably and the coefficient of energy elasticity decreased continuously. Simultaneously with developing energy resource, China paid more attention to the popularization of the technology of saving energy and made considerable efforts towards that end. From 1980 to 1995 energy consumption per-capita GDP decreased, with a yearly average of 4.4%. The total energy saved was about 620 million tons of standard coal equivalent. The improvement in efficiency of energy use helped aided economic development under the condition of limited energy resources. Since the commencement of reform and opening, China's coefficient of energy elasticity has decreased continuously. The average level of the coefficient was 1.67 from 1971 to 1975. This decreased to 0.96 in the period from 1976 to 1980. In the period from 1981 to 1990 the coefficient further decreased to 0.56. The average level in the period from 1991 to 1997 was 0.50.

(4) Energy consumption per capita showed an obvious rise. Table 9-14 shows the situation of primary energy consumption per capita in China. This shows that primary energy consumption per capita rose from 594 kilograms of standard coal equivalent in 1978 to 1165 kilograms of standard coal equivalent in 1997. However, it is still at a low level. There is quite a large difference compared with developed countries and some developing countries. In 1996 primary energy consumption per capita in China was half of the world

Table 9-14. Per capita energy production and consumption (unit: kilogram of standard coal equivalent)

Year	Production	Consumption
1978	652	594
1980	646	611
1985	808	724
1986	820	752
1987	835	793
1988	863	838
1989	902	860
1990	909	863
1991	905	896
1992	915	932
1993	937	979
1994	991	1024
1995	1065	1083
1996	1084	1135
1997	1071	1118

average. It was less than 10% of the level of the USA, Canada and Korea, less than 20% of the level of Japan, Germany, France and the UK. Furthermore, the ratio of energy used for general living was low, being about 11%.

5. Problems in the energy sphere

(1) The relationship between energy development and national economy development is not harmonized. From the history of developed countries' economic development and the trend of present world development, there is a pronounced relationship between energy consumption level per capita and economic development level. To date there is no such precedent in the world of reaching high a economic development level with very low energy consumption per capita. In other words, under the technology and consumption mode that prevails at present, a high level of energy consumption per capita is necessary for reaching the economic development level of industrialization. Since energy consumption per capita is still at a very low level, and there is a huge population in China, the demand for energy will show a big increase during the process of modernization. However, the development speed of the energy industry is not adequate for the development speed of the national economy. In the period from 1978 to 1997 the average yearly growth rate of GDP was 9.8% and the average yearly growth rate of energy production was 4.1%. The coefficient in energy elasticity was 0.42. The improvement in energy efficiency had positive promotional effects in decreasing the coefficient of energy elasticity. However, from the long-term point of view, the prolonged shortage of energy had restrained the demand for energy. To realize the elevation of economic and social development levels it is necessary that the energy industry shows faster development.

(2) The structure of energy production is not fit for the demand from economic development. The shortage of high-quality energy is the main concern. The energy structure in which coal plays the main part has not changed fundamentally in China in recent years. However, the demand for clean energy rises steadily. That high-quality energy plays a major part in the energy structure is a consequence of social and economic development. In a relatively closed energy system such as China the production structure and consumption structure of energy are basically the same. Compared with the increasing demand for high-quality energy, the production structure in which coal plays a major part will become worse in satisfying the demand. This is one of the main difficulties in developing the energy industry in China.

(3) The efficiency of energy use is low. The energy consumption per unit of output in China is higher not only than that of developed countries, but also than the average level of other developing countries. There are several reasons for this, e.g.: (a) the share of manufacturing industry in GDP is higher than in other developing countries; (b) solid fuel comprises the main energy source, which lowers energy efficiency; (c) a low technical and management level in energy use. Improvement in the efficiency of energy use depends not only upon progress in technology, improvement in management, and adjustment in the industrial structure, but also on elevation of national policies.

(4) A contradiction between demand and supply of energy in rural areas emerges. There are 850 million people living in rural areas in China; 70% of the energy for the livelihood of the rural people is biology-nature energy. This destroys the forest vegetation in vast areas. Mass of straw cannot be returned to the field, and this lowers the amount of organic material in soil. Furthermore, the electrification level is low in the countryside and there are about 100 million people who have no chance to use electricity. Third, the energy consumption of agriculture reaches a high level along with the increase in output per unit of land area. To meet these demands is a big task in energy supply in China.

(5) The environment problem resulting from energy production is serious. Development of the energy industry with the energy structure where coal plays the main part places huge pressure on the environment. Coal has a share of about 75%, and 80% of this is burned directly. The SO_2, CO_2 and soot created from burning coal result in air pollution of the fuliginous type. The extension of SO_2, hydronitrogen and volatile hydrocarbon harmed the environment and caused some regional acidification, which was due to emissions that were not fully treated. The acid rain area accounts for 29% of the country's land area. As the biggest country in coal consumption in the world, the volume of greenhouse gas emission was at the position of number 2 in the world according to the report of IEA in 1997. If there is no big change in energy structure, along with the increasing demand for energy, the volume of greenhouse effect gas emission will double and become

number 1 in the world in 2020. The environmental issue will be one of the important factors restricting energy development in China.

6. The energy prospect

(1) Energy consumption will increase continuously in China. Even considering the factors of technical progress in energy saving, changes in industrial structure and improvement in production management, total energy consumption in China will increase continuously along with the rapid economic development and the considerable improvement in people's quality of life. According to our analysis the total energy consumption of China in 2010 will be 2050 million tons of standard coal equivalent and this is 1.49 times the 1997 energy consumption. The average yearly growth rate is 3.12%. Coal consumption will be 1800 million tons in 2010, i.e. 1.29 times the 1997 coal consumption, or an average yearly growth rate of 1.98%. Crude oil consumption will be 370 million tons in 2010, i.e. 1.88 times the 1997 crude oil consumption. The average yearly growth rate is 4.96%. Natural gas consumption will be 60,000 million cubic metres in 2010, i.e. 3.07 times the 1997 natural gas consumption with an average yearly growth rate of 9.02%. Electricity consumption will be 2560 billion kWh in 2010, i.e. 2.27 times the 1997 electricity consumption, with an average yearly growth rate of 6.50%.

(2) Coal will still from the main part of the structure of energy consumption. Since the limitation in energy resource, the main part of the structure of energy consumption in China will still be coal. This type of energy consumption framework was formed for long time because China thought it was a great threat to the national security to import energy in large quantities, especially crude oil and natural gas, and therefore took the strictly autarkic energy guarantee strategy at all times. The large part played by coal will see no essential change in next 10 or 20 years. To reduce the pressure on environment and transportation, new large investments in energy transportation system, such as pipelines for coal slurry, will be carried out. The carefully washed coal will be widely used and its ratio in total coal consumption will rise from 20% at present to more than 50% in 2010.

(3) It will be imperative to greatly extend the imports of crude oil and natural gas. The demand for crude oil and natural gas, which exceeds its supply, will be another basic character of China's energy market in the future. China is one of the countries in which there is a lack of crude oil resources. Expansion of the imports of crude oil will continue and the ratio between net imports and total consumption of crude oil will rise from 20% in 1997 to 33% in 2010. China becoming a main importer of crude oil will have an important influence on the international oil market. This is probably good news and a new opportunity for international oil companies and for many oil-producing countries.

Table 9-15. Forecast of power supply capacity to 2010

		2000		2010	
			%		%
Thermal Power	Capacity (million kW)	235	76.87	413.8	77.24
	Output (billion kWh)	1175	83.17	2069.0	82.33
Hydropower	Capacity (million kW)	67.5	22.08	100.0	18.66
	Output (billion kWh)	220.0	15.57	318.0	12.66
Nuclear Power	Capacity (million kW)	2.7	0.88	20.0	3.73
	Output (billion kWh)	16.2	1.15	120.0	4.78
New Energy	Capacity (million kW)	0.5	0.17	2.0	0.37
	Output (billion kWh)	1.6	0.01	5.8	0.23
Total	Capacity (million kW)	305.7	100	535.8	100
	Output (billion kWh)	1412.8	100	2512.8	100

(4) The supply capacity of electricity will increase to meet the demand for it. The forecast for power supply capacity is shown in Table 9-15. It can be seen that the main part of the power supply will still be generated from burning fuel (coal, oil and gas), which is more than 80% of the total. The capacity of power-generating units of thermal power will increase from 235 million kW in 2000 to 413.8 million kW in 2010. The average yearly growth rate is 5.85%. The capacity of power-generating units of hydropower will increase from 67.5 million kW in 2000 to 100 million kW in 2010. The average yearly growth rate is 4.1%. Nuclear power capacity will increase from 2.7 million kW in 2000 to 20 million kW in 2010. Its share in the total capacity of power-generating units will rise from 0.9% in 2000 to 3.7% in 2010. The capacity of power-generating units using other new energy, such as wind and solar, will increase from 0.5 million kW in 2000 to 2.0 million kW in 2010. The total capacity of power-generation units will increase from 305.7 million kW in 2000 to 535.8 million kW in 2010. The total output of power could reach 2512.8 billion kWh in 2010, which is close to the demand for electricity consumption (2560 billion kWh).

(5) Air pollution is serious in some regions. As mentioned earlier, the main source of energy in China is coal. Due to a lack of strong consciousness in protecting the blue sky, people did not pay attention to the elimination of soot in many factories. SO_2 emissions increased from 1550 million tons in 1990 to 1970 million tons in 1997. Air pollution is serious in some regions. Acid rainfall sometimes occurred. Meanwhile, CO_2 emissions rose from 670 million tons in 1990 to 750 million tons in 1997.

Air pollution will be controlled and the air quality will be improved in the next ten years based on the factors listed below:

(1) The energy structure will change continuously in the direction of reducing coal usage. This can be seen from section 4 of this chapter.

(2) Investment in equipments to eliminate smoke and particles will increase, since stricter air-protection measures will be implemented. SO_2 emissions will be reduced from 21.5 million tons in 2000 to 18.0 million tons in 2010.
(3) CO_2 emissions will still increase from 780 million tons in 2000 to 850 million tons in 2010. However, comparing the growth rate of the CO_2 emission from 1990 (670 million tons) to 2000 and the expanded scale and maturity of the economy, the growth rate of CO_2 emissions will slow down and CO_2 emissions per unit of GDP will decrease greatly. According to a forecast report from the Research Team on Sustainable Development, China Academy of Sciences, CO_2 emissions will reach a peak value (900 million tons) in 2020 and go down from that point on.

10
The case of Russia

ALEXEY KOLTSOV and VLADIMIR VOLKOV

1. Results of eight years of the Russian economy reforming

During eight years of reforms, in relatively short terms, the critical mass of changes carried out makes the reforms irreversible. The Russian economy has passed from a centrally operated economic system to a different one, though this one is very far from the systems established in developed market economies. This time large-scale privatization was carried out in Russia. In 1999, according to one evaluation, more than 75% of GDP was produced in the non-state sector of the economy. The share of production for which prices and tariffs are adjusted at the federal level did not exceed 15-16% of GDP. Securities and currency markets were formed, despite some problems, and are functioning, as well as financial institutions including the banking sector. The state monopoly in foreign trade was abolished, and Russian participation in world markets of commodities, capitals and services has become more active.

In 1997 it seemed changes in operation of the Russian economy had begun to produce positive results. Rates of inflation were reduced in 1997 to less than 1% per month. In the middle of the year interest rates have begun to decline values which allowed enterprises to make money borrowings for implementation of efficient projects in the real sector of the economy. After the deep decline which continued during some seven years, growth of real volumes of GDP and industrial production was observed. This happened mainly because of money borrowings by enterprises to increase their circulating capital.

However, the financial and economic crisis, with its sharpest phase coming in August 1998, has shown up the fragility and instability of positive changes in the Russian economy which were obtained beginning in 1997. The ruble was devalued sharply, and as a result the rate of inflation increased significantly, production declined sharply, the real incomes and standard of living of the population decreased perceptibly, the crisis in bank liquidity sharpened, and the confidence of investors and population in state and financial institutions was undermined. As regards the main macroeconomic parameters Russia was thrown back for some years (see Table 10-1).

At the same time the crisis had some positive consequences (admittedly through high prices), because it 'on appearance' has removed some accumulated deformations and disproportions which could not be removed by the government or the Bank of Russia.

K. Uno (ed.), Economy–Energy–Environment Simulation, 163–184.

Table 10-1. Macroeconomic parameters of the Russian economy in the 1990s (1992-1999, percentage of the previous year)

	1992	1993	1994	1995	1996	1997	1998	1999	1999 to 1991, %
Gross Domestic Product	85.5	91.3	87.3	95.9	96.6	100.9	95.1	103.2	62.5
Inflation (consumer's prices index, %):									
by the end of year	2609	940	315	231	122	111	184	136.5	6080 times
In average per month	31.2	20.5	10	7.2	1.7	0.9	5.2	2.6	
Industrial production	82	86	79.1	96.7	96	102	94.8	108.1	54.1
Price index of industrial production producers:									
by the end of year	3378.0	995	333	275	126	107.5	123	167	8570 times
In average per month	34.0	21.1	10.6	8.8	1.9	0.6	1.75	4.4	
Agriculture production	90.6	96	88	92	94.9	101.5	86.8	102.4	60.3
Investment in basic capital	60	88	76	90	82	95	93.3	104.5	27.4
Retail trade	100.3	101.6	100.2	93.6	99.5	103.8	96.7	92.3	88.1
Value of payable services to population	82	70	62	82	94	105.6	99.5	107.4	30.9
Real disposable income per capita	52	116	113	85	100.1	105.3	83.7	85.2	43.5
Unemployment (% to economically active population, by the end of year):									
by the ILO methodology	–	6.0	7.8	9	10	11.2	13.3	12.2	
officially registered	0.8	1.1	2.2	3.2	3.4	2.8	2.6	1.7	
Exports	–	111	113.2	120	109.3	99.6	84.4	100.7	139.5*
Imports	–	103.1	114	120.6	112.9	107	81.1	67.2	93.3*

* 1999 to 1992, %

Source: Here and below (if this is not stipulated specially) the actual data are from the Russian Statistic Committee.

Analysis of the August 1988 crisis usually begins for external reasons – change for the worse of the world markets, conjuncture of fuels, and the negative impact of the 'Asian' financial crisis. Certainly these factors have complicated the financial-economic situation. However, the reasons for the crisis are to a marked degree associated not with external reasons but with fundamental problems of the Russian economy which were not overcome during reforms.

Generalized comprehension of the Russian economy leads to the following observations that may be called lessons of reforms:

(1) Persistent problems of budget balancing, delays with structural and tax-budget reforms that have caused an avalanche-type growth of state debt, which has determined the long duration of difficulties experienced by Russia in this most important area. At the same time the good performance of financial institutions, which was supported not as a result of their operations with real sectors of economy but as a result of the high profitability of operations with state securities (really – at the expense of state budget) turned out to be an illusion and has disappeared for many banks, along with removal of the short-term state obligations pyramid. A result of the crisis was removal of disproportion by high prices.
(2) Errors in the exchange rate policy of the Bank of Russia, especially immediately before the crisis. As a result of perceptible strengthening of the ruble to dollar real exchange rate (when internal inflation is taken into account) the ruble exchange rate was evidently abnormally high. However, the Bank of Russia has continued to support the ruble exchange rate persistently, even under significant worsening of Russian trade and international payment balances with a strong negative impact of the abnormally high ruble exchange rate on domestic production. In this context overcoming the crisis by ruble devaluation (though it would be better to 'release' the ruble gradually) also had positive consequences.
(3) Inefficiency of foreign trade and tariff policy in combination with exchange rate policy has made the situation worse in a number of very important directions. In particular, the inconsistency between final demand and production was increased sharply, which was characterized by a deeper decline in production compared with consumption. At the same time the moderate dynamics of household consumption was supported, first of all, through increased imports and state loans. The volume of imports depended on exports of fuels and raw materials, causing production for domestic market to 'shrink'.
(4) Hypertrophied concentration on macroeconomic policy and insufficient attention to the reforms at micro level (in terms of real actions, if not openly declared) was one of the most important reasons which hindered the removal of structural disproportion, through the growth of production and improved efficiency.

(5) Weakness of state social policy, long-standing social problems at the periphery of reforms, and perceived intangibility of reform results for most of the population.
(6) Keen regional problems are not solved; this is manifested, in particular, in significant differentiation of Russian regional social and economic development, in insufficient sharing of authorities between federal and regional government bodies and interaction among them.
(7) Inconsistency of reforms, in particular, 'fluctuations' in carrying out macroeconomic and stabilizing policies when periods of rigid financial and monetary-credit policy are followed by periods of significant slackening, and vice-versa. This lowered the level of confidence in government from potential investors and population, a barrier not so easy to break.
(8) Serious problems with formation of the market economy norms based on laws and rules (mainly because of keen disparities between presidential and government structures from one side, and State Parliament (Duma) from the other side), as well as the inefficiency of laws and rules enforcing mechanisms. This, in particular, relates to the disability of the legal system protecting the rights for owners and investors, insufficient anti-monopoly regulation and measures aimed at formation of competitive environment, non-completion of laws and rules for accomplishment of private ownership rights for land and immovable fixed properties.
(9) The simplified notion on the quick transition from administrative-command system to market economy in Russia as well as on complexity of associated problems); heightened expectations of rapid, positive, and almost automatic results from inclusion into the market mechanism. Unfulfilled expectations led to 'fatigue from reforms'.

The reasons for the real sector economic revival, and for rapid financial budget improvement, can be traced to the impact of ruble devaluation and favourable world markets for fuels. Physical values of exports were raised essentially (more than 10% compared to previous year), and imports reduced. As a result the GDP growth rate for 1999 was 5.4% compared to the previous year, and the growth rate of industrial production was 11.0%.

For a period since the beginning of ruble devaluation to the end of 1999, the dollar on the Russian market strengthened two times in real terms. Along with that, the tendency of some (reasonable from our point of view) ruble strengthening was observed: as a whole the ruble/dollar exchange rate has grown at 30.8% with inflation rate equal to 36.5%.

2. The Russian economic outlook: 2000 and the first half of 2001

During the year 2000 and the first half of the current year the trends in improvement of the economic and financial situation that appeared during the post-crisis period of 1998-1999, on the whole, continued. This reflected in positive dynamics

Table 10-2. Macroeconomic parameters of the Russian economy, 2000-2001 (percentage compared to the appropriate period of the previous year)

	2000	2001 1-st half	2001 (estimate)
Gross Domestic Product	108.3	105.0	105.5
Inflation (consumer's prices index,%):			
by the end of year	20.2	12.7	18
In average per month	1.5	2.0	1.4
Industrial production	111.9	105.5	105.5
Price index of industrial production producers:			
by the end of year	31.6	8.8	16.5
In average per month	2.3	1.4	1.3
Agriculture production	107.0	101.0	106
Investment in basic capital	117.4	107.2	106.0
Retail trade	108.7	109.5	110.0
Value of payable services to population	106.0	103.0	103.0
Real disposable income per capita	109.3	104.7	105.5
Exports	139.5	106.3	101.0
Imports	113.5	120.5	112.5

of the most macroeconomic figures in 2000-2001 (see Table 10-2). GDP and industrial production growth continued, and the growth rate in 2000 was the highest during the past 30 years. Investments into fixed capital increased with a high rate of growth, first at the expense of the enterprises' own resources, and because of the inflow of foreign direct investments into the Russian economy.

A rise of budget incomes was significant. The year 2000 was the first time from the commencement of reforms when the surplus of the federal budget had been reached, and this tendency has continued in the current year. Usage of barter and other non-monetary accounts in 2000 and the first half of the current year has diminished substantially.

Dynamics of real income and consumption of goods and services by the population rose; population savings increased. Under the conditions of overall economic revival the unemployment rate reduced.

In spite of continued capital outflow from the country high volumes of external trade balance enabled the government of Russia to serve external debt almost without additional loans from international finance organizations.

At the same time positive tendencies in social-economic development in 2000 and the first half of 2001 were to a great extent based on favourable international trade situation and the consequences of ruble devaluation, although some activation of governmental measures took place in this period (particularly in budget, tax and custom spheres, de-bureaucratization of the economy, etc.).

Under monetary growth stimulated by the Bank of Russia making intensive purchases of foreign currency from the exporters to prevent excessive strengthening of the ruble, inflation has been rather high. For all that, in spite of the current growth in real supply of money in the economy, the period of its active bank investments into production has not come materialized. Financial results of enterprise activity (in the real sector of the economy) have gradually worsened.

Under some positive shifts in population living conditions, differentiation of the population by incomes and consumption remains significant, with a very high poverty rate. The situation in the agricultural sector remains unstable, especially in livestock breeding. Reduction in cattle numbers continued, mainly because of low provisions of feed.

GDP volume in the first half of 2001 increased by 5.0% compared to the corresponding period in 2000 and, according to estimations of the Ministry of Economic Development and Trade of Russia, will increase for the whole of 2001 by 5.5% (in 2000 this figure was 8.3%). The part of economic growth based on ruble devaluation and import substitution is gradually shrinking.

Despite growth of real income of the population, and especially investments into fixed capital, in the structure of final demand characterized by used GDP the share of exports remains high. As a whole more than a third of GDP growth in 2000 was based on external factors. At the same time a component of internal demand and its share in the structure of used GDP has gradually extended.

Volume of **industrial production** in the first half of 2001 increased by 5.5% compared to the corresponding period of the previous year (after a growth rate of 11.9% in 2000). High growth of industrial production in 2000 was also stimulated by improvements in financial conditions of enterprises (increase of balanced profit and monetary resources in current assets, reduction of quantity of unprofitable enterprises). For the whole of 2000 the inflation rate was 20.2% and in the first half of 2001 it was 12.7%.

Federal budget incomes during January-December 2000, as estimated by the Russian Ministry of Finance, amounted to 16.0% of GDP and was much higher compared to 1999 (comparable figure for last year amounted to 13.4% of GDP). In the current year the gradual increase of volume of federal budget earnings with respect to GDP has been taking place (it comprised 17.9% of GDP in the first half of 2001). **Expenses of federal budget** during January-December 2000 were financed at the volume of 14.6% of GDP and 14.5% of GDP in the first half of the current year.

During January-December 2000 18% of all expenses of the federal budget were spent to serve government debt (in the first half of the current year this figure was 22.2%). Disbursements for the external debt service were 67.2% of volume of percentage expenses in 2000 (82.2% in the first half of 2001). **Federal budget profit** was 1.4% of GDP in 2000 and 3.4% of GDP in the first half of the current year. So the budget policy has been rather austere since the crisis.

The state of **balance of payments** during 2000 and the first half of the current year remained stable. According to data (2000 year) and estimations (the first half of 2001 year) from the Bank of Russia, in 2000 and the first half of the current year the surplus of current account operations was US$ 46.3 billion and US$ 21.2 billion, respectively. The global market environment was favourable for the development of the external economic sphere, significant export and trade balance growth. New foreign capital investments have not improved, and this resulted in a reduction of external liabilities of economy. Negative balance of financial account became US$ 37.5 billion in 2000 and US$ 11.0 billion in the first half of 2001, respectively. Official gold and hard-currency reserves in Russia by 1 July 2001 amounted to US$ 35.1 billion approximately, which is the maximum since the beginning of reforms. This considerably exceeds internationally accepted standard of 3-month reserve sufficiency (in comparison with import of goods and non-factor services).

3. Features of Russian industry and international comparisons

Some positive tendencies as a result of reform measures are observed in the dynamics and structure of Russian industrial production during 1998-2000.

To bring the Russian economy out of crisis the Government of the Russian Federation and the Bank of Russia during the last months of 1998 realized some measures on stabilization of the social-economic situation, money circulation and state finances. The most important measures were as follows:

(1) elimination of many of the payment defaults in the bank system by inter-bank clearing,
(2) normalization of the situation on the currency market,
(3) reduction of import customs duties for many commodities of everyday consumer demand,
(4) some emergency measures, ensuring steady food supplies to the population, having a special purpose financing and state support of the investment process.

Negotiations with foreign investors were begun on conditions of adjustment and restructuring of the Russian internal debt, resident obligations and others.

These measures have allowed enterprises to stabilize and even to increase volumes of production, including export-oriented products, along with reducing barter operations. As a result rates of production decline are significantly slowed compared with the corresponding period of the previous year, but taking into account the seasonal component since the October 1998 declining trend in production was reversed.

In 1999 the positive changes of main production-economic activity indexes of industry enterprises which have been marked in the last months of 1998 continued. The index of physical volume of total industrial production as a whole was 108.1%, including: July 112.8%, August 116%, September 120.2%, October 110.3%, and December 111.1% compared with the corresponding period of the previous year. The economic performance of the last months of 1998 was associated basically with the compensation effect – in August 1998 production was at a rate of 88.4%, in September 1998 it was 85% and in October 88.3% compared to the corresponding months of 1997.

The increase in total industrial production was caused mainly by increasing exports and the development of imports-substitution processes that promoted growth of the domestic products share on the home market. An increase in volume of production in machine building has brought an increase in demand on the product of adjacent sectors – metallurgy, chemistry and oil chemistry, and an improvement in the situation in the investment complex that has caused growth of construction materials production, forestry and woodworking industry production. The tendency of the fuel and raw materials sectors share to decrease continued.

In 2000, basically, because of a demand increase on the home market on domestic products and activations of export, the growth rate of production was 109.2% compared with the previous year, or 111.9% compared with the 1997 (in 1999 it was 108.1% and 102.5%, respectively).

The growth of industrial production during 1999-2000 was caused by the following factors:

(1) Expansion of internal demand because of budget incomes increase, improvement of enterprises' financial conditions, growth of population incomes and expenses, trade turnover and capital investment.
(2) Increase in the competitive advantages of domestic commodity producers, defined, first of all, by home product price and quality.
(3) Import-substitution processes, which have caused a growth in demand for the domestic product and, accordingly, growth of production in many industrial sectors.

However, rates of production growth are slowed at the end 2000-beginning of 2001. In the first quarter of 2001 the growth rate was 103.3% compared with the corresponding period of the previous year. Together with that, in April of the current year the growth rate was 5.2%. As a whole in 2001 the expected growth rate of production is 4.5%. Decline in growth rates is stipulated basically by cessation of impact of the growth-promoting in 1999-2000 associated with the devaluation of the ruble (export-promoting) and import-substitution processes.

Growth of industrial production was not accompanied by qualitative changes in the structure of industry, goods or services. Russian-produced goods have won in the competitive struggle in the home market, not due to superior quality, but simply because they are cheaper compared with imported ones. At present, when economic environment becomes less favourable, we observe a trend of imports increasing because of the low competitiveness of domestic goods.

As before, the raw materials orientation of the economy prevails, high energy and other resources consumption per unit of production remains, and efficiency of 'human capital' use is also low.

Lack of financial resources continues, stipulated by low profitability and insufficient amortization. The absence of ownership protection particularly for minor shareholders and foreign investors remains. as well as negative impact on production has lack of separate types of raw materials, half-finished products and others.

3.1. Production trends

As mentioned above, some positive tendencies as a result of progress reform measures are observed in the dynamics and structure of the Russian industrial production during 1998-2001. Prolongation of these historical changes taking into account the main tendencies of the perspective development of the Russian economy allows to evaluate the medium-term perspectives of industrial production to 2004 (Table 10-3 and Figures 10-1(a-d), where indexes of industrial production are shown).

Figure 10-1a shows that in 1999-2001 recovery was begun, with growth of electricity and fuels production being slower than growth of total industrial production. Extrapolation of these tendencies leads to faster growth of total industrial production compared with growth of electricity and fuels production.

The growth of chemistry and oil chemistry production, which is mainly the manufacturing sector (Figure 10-1b), is faster than growth of total industrial production, and growth of iron and non-iron metallurgy production is slower than growth of total industrial production.

The production of the basic manufacturing sector – machinery and metal-working sector (Figure 10-1c) – grows faster compared with total industrial

Table 10-3. Growth rates of the industrial production by sectors (percentage of previous year)

	1997	1998	1999	**2000**	2001	2002	2003	2004
Industry, total	1.020	0.95	1.11	**1.12**	1.05	1.05	1.06	1.05
Electricity	0.980	0.98	0.99	**1.02**	1.03	1.03	1.03	1.03
Fuels	1.003	0.98	1.03	**1.05**	1.02	1.01	1.01	1.01
Iron metallurgy	1.100	0.92	1.17	**1.16**	1.02	1.02	1.02	1.02
Non-iron metallurgy	1.060	0.95	1.10	**1.15**	1.02	1.02	1.02	1.02
Chemistry and oil chemistry	1.040	0.93	1.24	**1.13**	1.06	1.07	1.08	1.08
Machinery and metal-working industry	1.040	0.93	1.17	**1.20**	1.07	1.09	1.10	1.09
Forestry, wood-working and cellulose-paper industry	1.009	1.00	1.18	**1.13**	1.05	1.05	1.06	1.06
Construction materials industry	0.960	0.94	1.10	**1.13**	1.08	1.08	1.08	1.08
Light industry	0.980	0.89	1.12	**1.21**	1.07	1.06	1.05	1.05
Food industry	0.992	0.98	1.04	**1.14**	1.09	1.09	1.09	1.09

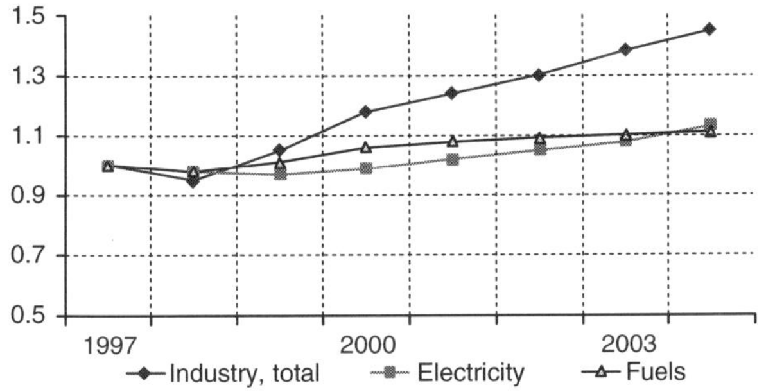

Figure 10-1a. Indexes of production by sectors; 1997 = 1.

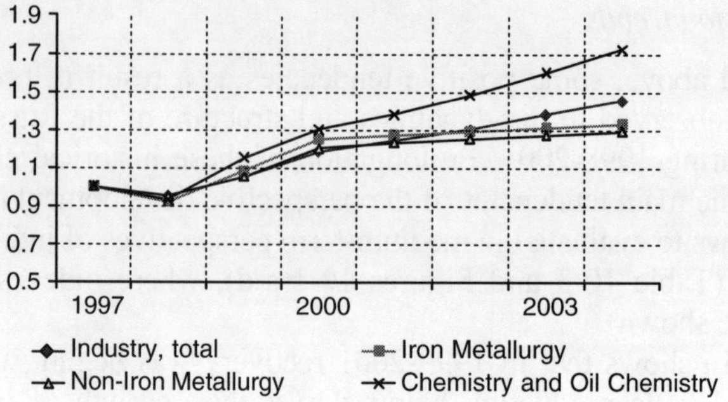

Figure 10-1b. Indexes of production by sectors; 1997 = 1.

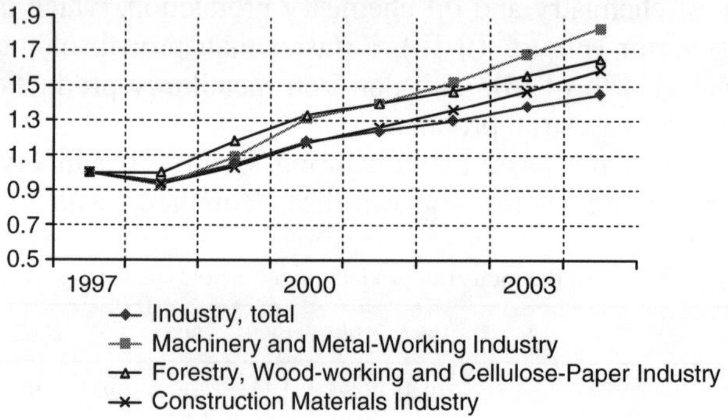

Figure 10-1c. Indexes of production by sectors; 1997 = 1.

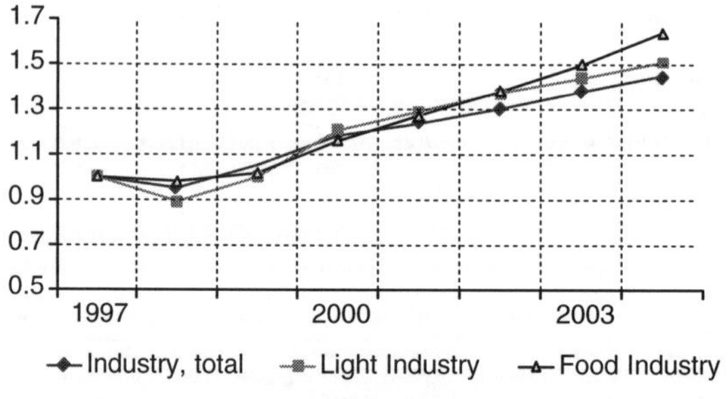

Figure 10-1d. Indexes of production by sectors; 1997 = 1.

production and all sectors. At the same time growth of forestry, woodworking and cellulose-paper industry production, which is partially manufacturing and partially produces raw materials (raw wood), is approximately as fast as growth of total industrial production. The growth of the construction materials industry, which produces the raw materials partially, is also approximately equal to total industrial production.

Table 10-4. Shares of production by sectors in total industrial production (%)

	1997	1998	1999	**2000**	2001	2002	2003	2004
Electricity	17.1	17.0	10.1	**9.1**	9.0	8.8	8.6	8.4
Fuels	17.4	15.5	16.9	**19.9**	19.3	18.6	17.9	17.2
Iron metallurgy	7.9	7.7	8.3	**9.0**	8.7	8.4	8.1	7.8
Non-iron metallurgy	5.5	7.6	10.1	**10.1**	9.8	9.6	9.2	8.9
Chemistry and oil chemistry	7.2	7.3	7.3	**6.4**	6.5	6.6	6.7	6.9
Machinery and metal-working industry	18.8	18.0	19.2	**18.6**	19.0	19.7	20.5	21.2
Forestry, wood-working and cellulose-paper industry	3.7	3.9	4.8	**4.5**	4.5	4.5	4.5	4.6
Construction materials industry	4.1	3.5	3.0	**3.1**	3.2	3.3	3.3	3.4
Light industry	1.8	1.8	1.7	**1.7**	1.7	1.7	1.7	1.7
Food industry	12.4	13.3	14.6	**12.6**	13.1	13.6	14.0	14.5

Light industry and the food industry (Figure 10-1d) are the main producers of consumer commodities. The growth of the food industry is the same as the growth of total industrial production and growth of light industry production, where the biggest decline during the reform years was observed, is slower than the growth of food industry production.

Such dynamics of production, when growth of manufacturing sectors is faster than growth of non-manufacturing and raw materials-producing sectors, resulted in some positive **structural shifts** in industrial production (Table 10-4).

This analysis allows us to draw the following main conclusions concerning the dynamics and structure of industrial production in Russia during 1997-2004.

First, the growth of total industrial production and industrial production by sectors will be continued but with decreasing rates after 2000, that is associated with delay of the import-substitution by home-made products processes and aggravation of conditions for exporters at external markets caused by rapprochement of internal and world prices as well as delay (or even falldown) in world oil prices, which is one of the most important Russian export commodities.

Second, most manufacturing sectors are growing faster compared with fuels and raw materials-producing sectors, with coincidence of growth tendencies (but with different rates) for total industry and its sectors.

Third, because of such production dynamics, some positive structural shifts are observed associated with decrease or stabilization of raw materials-producing and non-manufacturing sectors production shares and increase in manufacturing sectors production shares.

3.2. International comparisons: production

More detailed characteristics of the Russian economy give a comparative analysis of production, exports and imports structures (shares in GDP) for G7 countries, China and Russia, which is based on the input-output tables of these countries for 1995 using the OECD 36-sector classification.

The structure of production for selected G7 countries plus China and Russia by sectors in 1995 is shown Tables 10-5a, b, and c.

The Russian economy has large shares (8-9%) compared with G7 countries for food products, mining, and agriculture, and only China has larger share of agriculture (around 12%). This reflects the fact that Russia ıs a large producer of oil and gas, forestry, food including beverages and tobacco, fishery and livestock, and is evidence of the important role that these sectors play in the Russian economy on the one hand, and raw materials orientation of the economy as a whole on the other.

Table 10-5a. International comparison of economic structure in 1995, production (unit: %)

Industrial Branches	Germany	Japan	USA	Canada	China	Russia
1 Agriculture	1.72	2.17	2.66	3.67	12.38	9.18
2 Mining	0.56	0.18	1.87	4.17	3.46	7.53
3 Food	5.45	4.81	4.10	4.45	6.26	8.97
4 Textiles	1.64	1.82	1.46	1.40	8.12	3.23
5 Wood and wood products	1.33	0.87	1.07	1.96	1.43	1.93
6 Paper	1.86	2.60	3.02	4.14	1.52	0.67
7 Chemicals	3.59	2.49	2.60	2.22	3.93	3.64
8 Medicine	0.00	0.70	0.49	0.36	0.76	0.42
9 Petroleum and coal products	1.35	1.23	1.72	1.78	1.63	0.20
10 Rubber plastics	1.45	1.64	1.08	1.00	1.85	0.13
11 Nonmetallic mineral products	1.25	1.32	0.67	0.82	4.29	2.33
12 Iron and steel	1.45	3.30	1.11	1.24	4.22	4.15
13 Nonferrous metals	0.55	0.68	0.74	1.68	1.50	3.08
14 Metal products	2.33	2.03	1.56	1.83	2.54	1.12
15 Machinery	4.25	3.19	2.16	1.31	4.21	2.69
16 Office and computing machinery	0.56	1.24	0.67	0.39	0.97	0.67
17 Electrical machinery	3.90	2.26	0.92	0.74	2.51	1.01
18 Radio TV communication equipment	0.00	2.89	1.28	1.07	0.98	0.78
19 Ship building and repairs	0.15	0.24	0.16	0.14	0.34	1.23
20 Other transportation equipment	0.00	0.32	0.17	0.21	0.16	0.62
21 Motor vehicles	5.16	4.69	2.55	5.39	3.66	2.75
22 Aircraft	0.34	0.06	1.31	0.70	0.34	0.95
23 Personal goods	0.58	0.53	1.28	0.25	0.72	0.45
24 Other manufacturing	1.52	0.51	0.40	0.41	0.83	1.06
25 Electricty	2.73	2.12	2.51	2.23	3.13	8.78
26 Construction	6.67	9.12	7.14	8.90	8.32	9.59
27 Whole and retail trade	9.01	9.77	11.11	9.41	6.48	1.14
28 Restaurants and hotels	1.86	2.88	2.97	2.64	1.26	0.49
29 Transportation	3.13	5.96	3.74	4.56	2.63	4.12
30 Communication	1.53	1.02	1.77	1.67	0.45	1.76
31 Finance and insurance	4.35	4.10	5.18	8.36	1.57	3.30
32 Real estate business	17.17	10.40	14.50	3.76	4.32	0.95
33 Social and personal services	3.55	6.93	10.93	4.82	0.92	7.50
34 Government	6.11	3.51	5.18	0.38	2.29	3.30
35 Other activivites	2.11	1.27	−0.07	11.93	0.00	0.30
36 Discrepancy	0.80	1.16	0.00	0.00	0.00	0.00

Table 10-5b. International comparison of economic structure in 1995, exports (unit: %)

Industrial Branches	Germany	Japan	USA	Canada	China	Russia
1 Agriculture	0.83	0.09	3.87	3.62	5.47	0.89
2 Mining	0.36	0.03	1.24	10.15	1.52	24.04
3 Food	4.70	0.46	4.81	4.22	4.35	3.81
4 Textiles	4.24	1.60	1.68	1.20	27.53	1.38
5 Wood and wood products	1.17	0.09	1.22	4.06	3.10	5.07
6 Paper	2.18	0.65	4.52	8.68	0.17	1.35
7 Chemicals	11.69	4.93	6.16	3.44	1.18	9.39
8 Medicine	0.00	0.22	0.85	0.17	0.95	1.08
9 Petroleum and coal products	0.67	0.47	2.26	1.57	0.43	0.16
10 Rubber plastics	3.05	1.56	1.57	1.49	2.30	0.32
11 Nonmetallic mineral products	1.54	1.02	0.72	0.63	2.81	0.33
12 Iron and steel	2.70	3.35	1.35	1.25	0.50	13.04
13 Nonferrous metals	1.81	0.66	1.52	5.63	0.47	15.14
14 Metal products	2.19	1.33	3.94	2.29	2.78	1.29
15 Machinery	14.34	10.68	6.35	3.13	18.73	3.10
16 Office and computing machinery	1.91	6.82	4.37	1.73	4.01	0.77
17 Electrical machinery	10.28	5.84	3.03	1.15	3.93	1.16
18 Radio TV communication equipment	0.00	13.75	4.78	3.14	4.10	0.90
19 Ship building and repairs	0.52	1.95	0.35	0.06	0.82	1.42
20 Other transportation equipment	0.00	1.24	0.32	0.64	0.38	0.71
21 Motor vehicles	16.06	20.34	7.91	22.55	0.33	3.16
22 Aircraft	1.10	0.20	7.25	2.62	0.10	1.10
23 Personal goods	1.61	2.85	3.15	0.62	8.86	0.01
24 Other manufacturing	3.31	0.70	0.84	0.75	0.59	0.49
25 Electricty	0.20	0.05	0.11	0.40	0.01	0.72
26 Construction	0.38	0.00	0.04	0.02	0.00	0.16
27 Whole and retail trade	3.74	4.61	7.54	3.01	0.00	0.71
28 Restaurants and hotels	0.47	0.81	0.08	1.85	0.28	0.30
29 Transportation	5.89	8.65	8.37	2.14	2.62	4.93
30 Communication	0.41	0.09	0.63	0.40	0.48	2.11
31 Finance and insurance	0.07	0.96	3.14	1.02	0.06	0.11
32 Real estate business	1.50	1.05	4.06	1.65	1.12	0.01
33 Social and personal services	0.96	0.10	1.99	1.02	0.01	0.69
34 Government	0.12	0.00	0.00	0.00	0.00	0.11
35 Other activities	0.00	0.09	0.00	3.70	0.00	0.01
36 Discrepancy	0.00	2.75	0.00	0.00	0.00	0.00

The share of petroleum and coal products in Russia is one of the lowest between all countries in spite of the large oil mining constituent (Figure 6). This is explained by the large amount of oil exports and the relatively low internal prices of petroleum products compared with world prices.

Russia and China have the largest share (around 4%) of iron and steel production compared with G7 countries and this is further confirmation of the raw materials and half-finished orientation of the Russian economy as a whole. This is also confirmed by the relatively high share in Russia (more than 2%) of non-metallic mineral products; China has the largest share of this sector (around 4%).

The share of machinery for Russia, which is one of the basic manufacturing sectors and determines the technological level of all sectors of the economy and the possibility of producing high-quality and competitive commodities, is

Table 10-5c. International comparison of economic structure in 1995, imports (unit: %)

Industrial Branches	Germany	Japan	USA	Canada	China	Russia
1 Agriculture	5.81	6.44	1.75	1.59	4.34	3.68
2 Mining	5.14	18.00	7.65	4.22	2.18	2.49
3 Food	6.60	9.72	3.99	4.01	0.76	19.13
4 Textiles	9.11	6.00	8.77	5.43	3.50	16.74
5 Wood and wood products	1.95	2.22	1.65	1.43	2.04	1.81
6 Paper	2.98	1.23	2.54	3.16	1.49	0.64
7 Chemicals	9.39	4.02	3.44	4.41	7.91	6.13
8 Medicine	0.00	0.96	0.93	0.67	0.35	0.70
9 Petroleum and coal products	4.59	4.60	3.47	1.50	0.63	0.07
10 Rubber plastics	2.72	0.91	1.94	2.48	0.79	0.21
11 nonmetallic mineral products	1.84	0.73	1.16	1.23	0.41	1.47
12 Iron and steel	2.72	1.53	2.04	1.56	2.19	3.87
13 Nonferrous metals	3.11	4.82	1.27	2.18	1.65	1.88
14 Metal products	1.45	0.62	2.03	4.36	0.51	2.76
15 Machinery	5.97	4.40	5.93	7.63	27.48	6.62
16 Office and computing machinery	3.67	1.67	3.72	4.03	4.65	1.66
17 Electrical machinery	9.48	1.48	3.36	3.04	5.13	2.48
18 Radio TV communication equipment	0.00	2.61	8.69	5.25	5.52	1.93
19 Ship building and repairs	0.17	0.12	0.16	0.16	0.82	3.03
20 Other transportation equipment	0.00	0.10	0.37	0.54	0.08	1.52
21 Motor vehicles	8.14	2.54	14.76	20.11	11.17	6.76
22 Aircraft	1.72	1.32	1.58	1.45	2.55	2.35
23 Personal goods	1.59	1.24	3.21	1.63	5.73	0.56
24 Other manufacturing	3.05	1.05	3.23	2.24	1.17	1.05
25 Electricty	0.24	0.01	0.37	0.36	0.32	0.07
26 Construction	0.19	0.00	0.00	0.05	0.00	2.34
27 Whole and retail trade	0.92	0.76	2.40	1.07	3.38	1.48
28 Restaurants and hotels	0.50	5.43	0.00	3.51	0.49	0.64
29 Transportation	2.90	5.84	0.65	2.57	1.83	3.08
30 Communication	0.65	0.13	0.00	0.46	0.47	1.32
31 Finance and insurance	0.12	1.77	0.65	2.74	0.01	0.19
32 Real estate business	2.51	2.44	0.31	3.10	0.45	0.02
33 Social and personal services	0.74	0.69	0.14	1.82	0.00	0.75
34 Government	0.00	0.00	0.00	0.00	0.00	0.19
35 Other activities	0.00	0.07	12.57	0.00	0.00	0.37
36 Discrepancy	0.00	4.54	0.00	0.00	0.00	0.00

comparable with this one for all countries, and equal to around 2.7%. Shares of other countries vary from around 1.3% for Canada to more than 4% in Germany. This sector should be developed to around 4% as is the case in Germany and China. The share of metal products for Russia (i.e. the manufacturing sector) (around 1%) is less compared with shares for all other countries, which vary from around less than 1.5% for the UK to around 2.3% for Germany. This sector, as well as machinery, should be rapidly developed to improve the structure of the Russian economy in the direction of a manufacturing sectors share increase. On the other hand, in Russia production of the non-ferrous metals sector, which is mostly non-manufacturing, amounts to 3% of GDP compared with a range from 0.5% for Germany to around 1.5% for Canada and China.

Russia is a small producer of high-technological commodities such as production of the radio, TV and communications sector. The share of this sector (less than 1%) is the lowest of all countries being compared. The situation with electrical devices is a little better and the share of this sector production for Russia (1%) is more than for the USA and Canada, and less than for other countries. The largest producers in this area are Japan (more than 2%), China (2.5%) and Germany (around 4%). A rather better situation concerns the production of office and computing machinery, of which the share for Russia is around 0.5%, i.e. more than for Italy, France and Canada, and approximately equal to the share for the USA and Germany and less than for Japan, China and the UK (around 1%).

The share of motor vehicles production in Russia, which is around 3%, is comparable with the USA, more than in Italy and the UK and less than in Canada, Japan, Germany, France and China.

The electricity, gas and water supply sector production plays a large role in the economies of all countries. In Russia the share of this production is around 9%, that is three or four times more compared with G7 countries and China, and is indirect evidence of excessive inputs of these resources. Some measures towards their preservation are urgent.

A very low share of the restaurants and hotels sector in Russia, which is less than 0.5% and much lower compared with all countries, is evidence of its underdevelopment, and the low attention paid to this sector, which may be a large source of revenue. Poor development of market services in Russia is indicated by the very low share of the wholesale and retail trade sector (around 1%) which is much less compared with other countries (around 11% for the USA, around 10% for Italy, the UK and Japan, etc.) Much construction activity in Russia shows the biggest share of the construction sector (around 10%), that is more than for all countries being compared (from 6-7% for USA, Germany and Italy to 8-9% for the UK, China, Canada and Japan.

A sufficiently high level of financial and insurance activity in Russia is confirmed by the relatively high share of this sector, which is over 3%, i.e. more than in China and a little less than for the USA, Japan, Germany and Italy (4-5%). The biggest share is characteristic for France, Canada and the UK (7-8%). The share of the communication sector in Russia (around 2%) is comparable with those for the USA, Canada, Germany and the UK, a little greater than for France, Italy and Japan (around 1%) and significantly less than for China (around 0.5%). The development of a transportation system, judging by the shares, is sufficiently high in Russia and comparable with all other countries (3-4%) except Japan, where this share is more, and accounts for around 6%, and China where this share is the least (less than 3%).

The government services sector in Russia is sufficiently large (around 3%) and is more compared with Canada, China and Italy and less compared with other countries (from around 4% for Japan and to around 9% for France). The social and personal services sector in Russia is more than twice as big compared with the government service sector and its share accounts for around 7%, i.e. greater than the shares for Canada, Japan, Germany, France and China, and lower than those for the USA, UK and Italy, where it is largest (around 14%).

3.3. International comparisons: exports

The structure of Russian exports, which depends strongly on production, is very similar to the industrial structure, as shown in Table 10-5b. Russia is the largest exporter of mining products (first of all oil and gas) which accounts for almost 25% of total exports. The share of mining products is noticeable for Canada (10%) and the UK (around 5%) and for other countries is significantly less. As for food exports Russia is a very small exporter of agricultural products (around 1% of total exports) because of the poor level of agricultural development and shortages of these products.

Iron and steel exports in Russia take a large share, which is around 13% of total exports, and much less than for all other countries. For Canada and the USA this share is around 1% and around 3% for Japan, Germany, Italy, France and the UK. The lowest exporter of iron and steel products is China (less than 1%). Russia is the lowest exporter of non-metallic mineral products and rubber and plastics products (shares are less than 1%). Shares of these products for other countries are not significant (in the limits 1-3%).

Russia is a relatively small exporter of machinery and metal products, and these shares are around 3% and 1% of total exports, correspondingly. Canada is a similar (by the share) exporter of machinery, and other countries have much bigger shares of these exports (from around 6% for the USA and France to 14% for Germany and over 18% for Italy). As regards metal products exports, all countries have small shares in total exports, which range from around 1% for Japan to 4% for Italy and the USA. On the other hand, Russia is a large exporter of non-ferrous metals, with the share of total exports being around 15%, the second position is taken by Canada, around 5%, and all other countries have shares which range from less than 1% for China, Italy and Japan to around 2% for France, the UK and Germany.

Russia is also the lowest exporter of such high-tech products of manufacturing sectors as Radio, TV and communications, electrical machines and office computers. The exports share of these products for Russia is around 1% while shares of these range from around 3% of radio, TV and communications products exports for Canada to around 14% for Japan. The shares of electrical devices exports range from around 1% for Canada to around 10% for Germany, and of office computers shares of exports which range from around 2% for Canada, Germany, Italy and France to over 6% for Japan.

All G7 countries are large exporters of motor vehicles. The shares of these products exports are range from around 8% for the USA to 20% for Japan, and around 22% for Canada, while such shares for Russia are around 3%, and for China less than 1%.

3.4. International comparisons: imports

Imports are important to supplement the national economies with insufficient internal demand for production of goods and services. The structure of imports for selected G7 countries, Russia and China by OECD sector classification is shown in Table 10-5c.

Russia is a largest importer of food because of low agriculture and food industry efficiency, and the share of food imports is around 19%, that is much more compared with all other countries. The lowest food imports share is for China (less than 1%). These shares for other countries range from 8% for Italy to around 10% for Japan. Being a large exporter and producer of mining products Russia, along with China, are small importers of these products i.e. around 2%. The largest importers of mining products are Italy (around 19%) and Japan (around 18% of total imports). Russia is also a relatively small importer of agricultural products (around 4% of total imports). The lowest importers of these products are Canada and the USA (less than 2%) and the UK (2%), and the largest ones are Italy (7%) and Japan (6%).

Russia is the lowest (almost zero) importer of petroleum and coal products. For other countries the share of these products varies from 0.5% for China to 4.5% for Japan, Germany and Italy. The shares of drugs and medicine exports are small for all countries and do not exceed 1%. On the other side, all countries, including Russia (whose share of these products is 6%), are large importers of industrial chemicals, that is more compared with Canada, the USA and Japan (3-4%) and less compared with the UK, China, France, Italy and Germany (around 7-9%).

Russia, Canada, France and China are the largest importers of machinery products (with shares around 6-7% for the first three countries and over 25% for China). These shares are less for other countries (around 6% for the USA, Germany and France) and are the least for Italy and Japan (around 4%). All countries are small importers of metal products and suitable shares do not exceed 3% (for Russia around 3%), except Canada, for which these shares account for around 4%). The same situation occurs with non-ferrous metals – shares of these products imports do not exceed 3% (except Japan, around 5%) and for Russia this share accounts for around 2%.

Russia is a moderate importer of radio, TV and communications equipment and its share accounts for 2%, while other countries are bigger importers (over 2% for Japan, around 5% for Italy, Canada and France, 6% for the UK and around 9% for the USA). Imports of electrical devices are over 2% for Russia, which is more compared with Italy and Japan (around 1%, respectively), less than for other countries (around 3% for the USA, Canada, France and the UK) and China and Germany (5% and over 9%, respectively). Russia is a small importer of office computers and the share of this import is around 1.5%, that is similar to that for Japan, and for other countries this share is more (around 3% for Germany and the USA, and around 4% for Canada, France, the UK and China).

Motor vehicle imports into Russia and Italy are around 7%; that is more than into Japan (around 2.5%) and less than into Germany (around 8%). Much larger importers are the UK and France (8-9%), China (around 11%) and the largest ones are the USA and Canada (15% and 20%, respectively). Russia is the largest importer of other transportation means (less than 2%) and for other countries these shares are insignificant (less than 1%). The same situation is characteristic for shipbuilding and repairing: Russia and China are the largest importers of this sector products (around 3% and 1%, respectively) and for all other countries these shares are insignificant and less than 1%.

4. Long-term social and economic programme of the government of the Russian Federation

In June of 2000 the government generally approved the Long-Term (to 2010) Social and Economic Policy Guidelines. In July the government adopted a social policy and economy modernization action plan for 2000-2001 designed to secure the completion of strategic developmental milestones laid down in the Guidelines.

4.1. Current state assessment and selection of a development path

Despite a number of major negative trends, Russia currently finds itself in a completely new environment opening up a 'window of opportunity' for solving the fundamental problems of this country. The political situation has become stable, and the economy is showing signs of recovery.

Russia still boasts significant potential for accelerated growth. Its tremendous intellectual capital, the basic market institutions framework in place, vast natural resources, core components of production and communication infrastructure and the accumulated financial savings all add up to favourable preconditions for national renewal.

In the medium-term perspective we need to prevent a further gap between Russia and industrialized nations, and in the longer-term context to restore and strengthen Russia's status as one of the leaders in global development. In order to capitalize on this 'window of opportunity' we must identify a path that will lead to the realization of Russia's potential and balanced growth. There are three realistic development options.

The first scenario includes deregulation of virtually all areas of economic activity, opening up the country to the outside world and privatization of most social functions. This scenario can lead to significant economic growth. However, it is the least probable one, given the impossibility of the quick creation of an institutional market framework which is critical for a liberal economy, and the inability of most Russian enterprises to compete on an equal footing with foreign market players.

The second scenario presumes more direct involvement of the state in the regulation of economic and social relations, which will necessitate a major increase in tax collection and investment activity of the state. This will hardly create a favourable environment which would encourage entrepreneurial activities. This option also implies the preservation of a closed economy, which will make it impossible to participate in the international division of labour and may lead to further technological lagging behind industrialized nations. Any attempts to increase the effective tax burden will result in additional capital flight and further criminalization of the economy and society. Broader functions of the government will make the state machine even less manageable than it is now.

The third, modernization, scenario is based on the idea of freeing up private initiative and strengthening the role of the state in promoting a favourable business environment, including financial and social stability, and is a balanced combination of the elements of the other two strategic options. Instead of a social state (paternalism) and privatization of social functions (radical liberalism), a 'subsidiary' state is created to provide social guarantees to the extent that society is unable to do so on its own. Instead of complete isolation or openness, the focus is on Russia's active integration into the world community and economy while protecting the interests of Russian producers from unfair competition on the part of foreign market players.

4.2. Goals of long-term policy

The primary goal of the government's long-term policy is to ensure sustained improvement in the general standard of living, reduce social inequality, safeguard and promote Russia's cultural values, and restore the economic and political role of Russia within the world community.

The Russian Government and general public face the following key challenges:

(1) implement social reform, institute a new social contract (based on trust between citizens and the state, employees and employers, business entities and individuals);
(2) reform the state system;
(3) modernize the economy.

By now Russia has a market framework in place, but in order to be able to function efficiently it also requires a seamless operation of market support infrastructure, including the judicial system, compliance enforcement, law-enforcement institutions and federal relations. The strengthening of the state or the *reform of the state system* is a prerequisite condition for modernization of the economy. However, the critical necessity of reforming the state system is stipulated not only by economic growth requirements, but first and foremost by the need to safeguard the rights, freedoms and safety of citizens and to secure public trust in authorities.

The programme's goals are achievable only provided there is *economic modernization*. The only way to bridge the gap between Russia and the most developed nations, and to create the basis for enhancing the standards of living, is economic growth at a rate higher than the growth of the world economy. Such growth can be secured by combining the accumulation of intellectual and capital resources with their more efficient utilization and freeing up entrepreneurial initiative. A reduction of the administrative and tax burden on businesses will ensure (as early as at the first stage) a return on the short-term resources for growth achieved through increasing labour productivity and utilization of idle but viable production capacity. At the second stage economic freedom will result in increased efficiency of investments, the promotion of which will become the focus of economic policy. The major components of the economy modernization programme include, first of all, the creation of a favourable investment climate, sensible budgetary policy and structural reform.

The *social policy* goal is to complete transition from the paternalist to subsidiary state model. This implies accessible and free-of-charge basic social services for all citizens, first and foremost in the area of education and health care; re-allocation of social expenses of the state in favour of the most vulnerable members of the public while reducing support for reasonably prosperous households; gradual elimination of social inequality; and providing individuals with opportunities for a higher level of social consumption from the sources of personal income.

The critical areas of social policy during economic modernization are: first, the support of vulnerable social groups and secondly, investments in human development, primarily in education which is a prerequisite condition for Russia to become competitive within the globalized, information-based and dynamic world economy.

4.3. Expected main quantitative results of the long-term programme

The implementation of the programme is expected to ensure GDP growth at a minimum annual average rate of 5% during a 10-year period. By 2010 the GDP should increase by approximately 70% (compared to 1999). In dollar terms GDP will grow by a factor of 2.5 by 2010, calculated at the current exchange rate.

The funding of economic growth will greatly depend on reduced capital flight. If capital flight declines two-fold, investments can be increased by approximately one-third provided that capital remains in the country and is used for investment purposes.

Gross savings in 2000-2010 will amount to approximately 30% of GDP, enabling Russia to retain high growth potential throughout the planned period. This implies that economic growth, at least in the medium-term perspective, should be accompanied by increased investments in capital assets outpacing the pattern of consumption. Thus, this strategy is focused on the maximum utilization of growth potential to make the national economy attractive for long-term investors. Foreign investments will constitute another source of funding.

The period of investment growth outpacing consumption may continue for at least 6-8 years. By the end of the decade the growth of investments and economic growth in general may slow down to a certain extent.

The implementation of the programme will make it possible to gradually overcome distortions in the distribution of *personal income* and, in addition to general growth in disposable income, increase the percentage of medium-level income social groups in total personal income. This will create a basis for sustained mass domestic demand and transition to a qualitatively new growth pattern, with consumption outpacing investment.

As a result, by the end of the decade the pattern of private consumption will steadily outpace investments so that in 2010 consumption will grow at a somewhat higher rate than GDP. Overall, GDP growth will lag behind both consumption and gross savings. This lag will be offset by reduced net exports and, consequently, reduced capital flight.

A decline in *net exports* and the resulting reduction of the current account balance may start as early as in 2001, triggered by both decreasing exports due to the anticipated unfavourable situation on the world commodity markets comprising traditional Russian exports, and increasing imports, including the import of investment resources. However, this trend will have no destabilizing effect on the economy as it will be accompanied by reduced capital flight. By 2004 the balance of trade and the current account balance will decline to less than $20 billion and $10 billion, and by 2010 to under $10 billion and $5 billion, respectively.

Notably, in the nearest decade the ruble will be becoming stronger in real terms and market rate will approximate purchasing power parity, thus encouraging imports which may grow two-fold over 10 years. By 2010 we may expect growth in the real ruble rate by a factor of at least one-third.

In parallel, there are expectations of a stable accumulation of foreign currency reserves by monetary authorities (Bank of Russia).

Judging from the present-day *sectoral structure of the Russian economy*, the GDP development pattern during the next few years will be largely shaped by the development of the manufacturing sector. Information and communication sectors, which are expected to grow at a presumably higher rate, account for some 2% of GDP. Although an increase in the scope of those and other market services in the medium-term perspective is likely to accelerate GDP growth, the above sectors will not yet become dominant. A noticeable increase in the export of services can be expected only by the end of this decade, so the traditionally negative value of the balance of services may approximate zero.

Net exports may fall to 5-7% of GDP by 2004 and may total some 2-3% of GDP by the end of this decade. Investments in capital assets will account for some 26-27% of GDP by 2010 and will tend to fall gradually thereafter. Consumption as a percentage of GDP will remain almost unchanged until 2004 – an increased percentage of gross savings will be offset by a proportionate decrease in net exports. Following 2004 there will be a steady growth of consumption which may exceed 70% as a percentage of GDP. This ratio is well over the percentages of 1991-1995 and approximates the proportions of 1996-1998 (however, in those years Russia's high percentage of consumption was maintained at the expense of external borrowings).

In parallel, state consumption as a percentage of GDP will gradually decline while growing in real terms, albeit at a pace which is expected to be significantly slower than the GDP growth rate. These developments will be accompanied by a reduction of the nominal tax burden and state debt which is not being served at present. As a result private consumption will grow at least 80% provided that overall consumption grows at a slightly faster rate than GDP.

A reduction of expanded production as a percentage of GDP will help to redistribute resources available to the private sector more efficiently. The state will be able to perform its obligations regarding *the repayment and servicing of its foreign debt*. Those expenses as a percentage of GDP will gradually decline as a consequence of GDP growth in real terms and a stronger national currency. Interest expenses will account for less than 3% of GDP by 2010. Non-interest expenses as a percentage of GDP will account for some 30% of GDP by the end of the period.

Beginning from 2004, *inflation* will stay at less than 10%, despite the higher rate of increase in money supply which will be offset by increased demand for money as a result of economic growth and the substitution of non-monetary forms of settlements with monetary ones.

The development of financial markets within the deficit-free budget policy framework will also help contain the pressure of money supply on price levels, so a potential 'excessive' inflow of foreign capital may be counterbalanced by issuing financial instruments with relatively low yields. Increased monetization of the economy will contribute to higher capitalization of the banking system, and the share of debt in the structure of investments will grow gradually.

11
Carbon tax and labour compensation – a simulation for G7

BERND MEYER and CHRISTIAN LUTZ

1. The scenario

A worldwide harmonized climate policy needs target lines for the greenhouse gas emissions of all countries. One perspective is to establish a world market for pollution rights, on which only governments are suppliers and demanders. To reach the national targets every country might introduce energy taxes. World climate policy will only be successful if the burden to reach the targets is acceptable for the different countries. In this chapter we use the system to calculate the maintenance costs for the group of G7 countries, which are the most important energy users.

We assume that, in each of the G7 countries, a carbon tax is introduced, which has the following characteristics. Every producer and importer of fossil energy carriers has to pay taxes in relation to the CO_2 emissions which are set free when the specific energy carrier is burned. Producers and importers of fossil energy carriers raise their prices due to the tax payment. The governments start with a tax rate of 1 US dollar in 2001 per ton of CO_2 and raise the tax rate linearly to 10 dollars in 2010. The governments use the tax revenue to lower social security contributions. The idea – implemented in the environmental fiscal reform in Germany starting in 1999 – is to raise energy costs and to lower labour costs in the hope of obtaining rising employment as a second dividend of climate policy.

The taxes will raise the prices of the different energy carriers depending on their carbon concentration. Coal is levied more than petroleum and gas. The relation is about 4:3:2. Nuclear and renewable energy is not taxed at all. Higher energy prices will reduce energy demand and carbon emissions. Further energy prices will spread all over the economy and raise the prices of all goods depending on their direct and indirect energy inputs. On the other hand wages will be reduced, because the government uses the tax revenue to lower social security contributions. This effect lowers costs, and thus prices, especially in the labour-intensive sectors. Structural change will be induced, which favours labour-intensive industries and depresses energy-intensive industries.

The aggregate impact on the economy cannot be predicted without a model simulation, the reactions on GDP and employment depend on contrary effects.

K. Uno (ed.), Economy–Energy–Environment Simulation, 185–189.

Of course, the economies will develop in different ways, because of their different structures of production. This will induce further effects on other contries via international trade.

2. Specification of the labour market in COMPASS

Since the labour market plays a specific role in the analysis, we want to discuss the model structure here in more detail. We assume that in every sector and every country the nominal wage of the sector depends with elasticity 1 on the actual price of the sector and its productivity trend. The real labour input coefficient is dependent on the real wage rate with a negative elasticity. Because of data restrictions we were not able to estimate these elasticities econometrically. For Germany the elasticities of labour demand on the real wage for most industries are close to -0.7 (Meyer *et al.*, 1999). We assume this value for all industries in all countries.

For every country and every sector we specify the following labour market model. The model is sector- and country-specific, but we omit sector and country indices.

Real wage rate is growing exogenously:

$$\log(w/p) = \log a + g * t \quad a > 0, g > 0 \tag{1}$$

w = nominal wage rate, index 1990 = 100
p = price index of output, 1990 = 100
t = time.

Real labour demand is dependent on output, the real wage rate and a time trend:

$$\log L = \log b + \log x + \beta^*\log(w/p) + v^*t \quad b>0, \ \beta<0, \ v<0. \tag{2}$$

L = real labour input measured in 1990 wage rates
x = real gross production.

(1) in (2):

$$\log(w^*L) = \log b + \log x + \beta \log(w/p) + v^*t + \log a + g^*t + \log p \tag{3}$$

$$\log(w^*L/p^*x) = \log b + (1+\beta)^*\log a + [(1+\beta)^*g + v]^*t \tag{4}$$

Assuming $\beta = 0.7$, an experience from estimations with German data, $g = 1.5$ or 2.0, a plausible long-run growth rate for real wages, can be calibrated in equation (1) by data of 1990, when w and p are 1 and g and t are given. Running the regression

$$\log(w^*L/p^*x) = a_0 + a_1{}^*t \quad a_0 = b^*a^*\exp(1+\beta), \ a_1 = (1+\beta)^*g + v \tag{5}$$

v and b can be identified by the regression results.

3. Simulation results

A uniform tax rate of up to 10 US$/t CO_2 in 2010 induces different tax revenues in G7 countries. In the US carbon taxes reach in 2010 about 60 billion US$, about 1% of GDP. In the other countries taxes are much lower. In Japan the carbon tax amounts to 12 billion US$ or 0.25% of GDP, because of the already high energy productivity of the Japanese economy. Energy efficiency in European countries is much higher than in the USA, but much lower than in Japan. In 2010 carbon taxes reach 9 billion US$ in Germany and 0.5% of GDP, in France (4/0.4), Italy (3/0.5) and Britain (5/0.7) the carbon tax is similiar. Canada (6/1.0) with its low energy productivity is comparable to the USA. Over all G7 countries the carbon tax reaches about 100 billion US$ in 2010. So the USA would bear about 60% of the tax.

Impacts on the different G7 countries are shown in Table 11-1. Carbon emissions are reduced by around 5% against the business as usual in six countries. In the USA and Canada energy consumption is obviously less price-dependent than in European countries. Higher taxes as a percentage of GDP have more pressure on overall prices in northern America than in Europe. GDP is at the same time affected much more. On the labour market two different effects can be seen. Lower labour costs induce more employment, whereas lower GDP reduces employment. For the four European countries the labour cost effect is more important. Especially Germany, France and Italy, that still suffer from high unemployment, can improve the situation on the labour market. For the USA and Canada both effects more or less equalize. Japan, compared to the other countries, shows different effects. Energy productivity has shown almost no price dependency in the past. Higher energy prices reduce carbon emissions only slightly. As the taxes are low compared to GDP, impacts on GDP and labour are relatively small.

A comparison of the effects on the industry level shows some general features of the carbon taxes. The production decline of petroleum and coal products is the strongest. Construction, on the other hand, is reduced only slightly. Except for Italy and Britain the reduction in all other countries is below average.

4. Environmental tax reform: the concept and its realization

We have just discussed the impact of a carbon tax on economy and environment as we find it in textbooks. Of course from the ecological point of view it

Table 11-1. Effects of carbon taxes on GDP, labour, prices and emissions in G7: percentage differences against the business as usual in 2010

	USA	Japan	Germany	France	Italy	Great Britain	Canada
GDP	−1.72	−0.23	−0.35	−0.31	−0.34	−0.75	−1.61
Labour	0.08	0.27	0.89	0.90	0.93	0.56	0.19
Output prices	1.82	0.60	0.52	0.38	0.66	0.77	1.92
Carbon	−5.38	−1.14	−4.5	−4.18	−6.11	−4.31	−5.90

Table 11-2. Output effects of carbon taxes on different sectors in G7: percentage differences against the business as usual in 2010

	USA	Japan	Germany	France	Italy	Great Britain	Canada
Food processing	−2.02	−0.27	−0.32	−0.36	−0.29	−0.69	−1.83
Petroleum and coal products	−2.87	−0.33	−0.82	−0.50	−0.47	−2.42	−3.67
Iron and steel	−1.35	−0.28	−0.33	−0.45	−0.48	−0.82	−1.60
Machinery	−1.06	−0.22	−0.26	−0.29	−0.48	−0.72	−1.11
Motor vehicles	−1.41	−0.42	−0.33	−0.47	−0.40	−0.74	−1.92
Construction	−1.01	−0.02	−0.13	−0.21	−0.39	−0.78	−1.06
All industries	−1.74	−0.18	−0.32	−0.33	−0.35	−0.75	−1.71

is the most effective way to tax primary energy consumption, because it induces improvements in energy efficency on all stages of production and in the energy transformation processes. Since we have assumed that all G7 countries introduce the carbon tax, the following problems could be avoided.

If a single country introduces such an ecotax, the problem might arise that energy imports could rise. To avoid this substitution, imports also have to be taxed. This will work for primary energy but not for electricity, because in this concept electricity is not taxed. Nevertheless, the price for electricity in the domestic country will rise, because the costs for primary energy increase. So there will be growing imports of electricity, because in the foreign countries we have stable prices for electricity. If our country in question belongs to the European Union the possible reaction – taxation only on energy imports – is forbidden, because it would be a discrimination.

Further restrictions derive from conflicts between the environmental and general economic targets. Very often several regions or branches of the economy have to be sheltered. So we should not be surprised, that the political process creates environmental taxes with a confusing variety of tax rates and exemptions, that are differentiated for energy carriers and user groups.

This is the case for Denmark, Finland, the Netherlands, Norway, Sweden and Germany. For the latter country a model simulation study (Bach *et al.*, 2001) is available, which calculates the impact of the German Environmental Tax Reform on economy and environment. It might be interesting to compare our results of the textbook carbon tax for Germany with that of a real-world tax with all its exemptions and differentiations. This comparison makes sense, since the tax revenue is of a comparable order and the tax is also used to reduce payments for social security.

The tax revenue that will be reached in Germany with the 'real-world ecotax' in the year 2003 is about 15 billion US$. In our simulation of a textbook taxation tax revenues for the last simulation period for Germany amount to 10 billion US$. The effect on GDP is nearly the same with −0.35% in our simulation and −0.43% in the 'real-world case'.

Since the German Environmental Tax Reform is aimed to the end-use of energy, and hits primarily households, we have relatively strong negative production effects for labour-intensive consumer industries and service sectors. So in spite of the stronger wage reductions the employment effects are, at 0.5%, a little bit weaker than in the textbook simulation (0.89%).

The rise of production prices is correlated with the level of taxation. In the 'real-world case' we have as an average of all industries 0.64% higher prices and in the textbook case 0.52%.

The emissions of CO_2 are affected not only by the level of taxation, but also by its design. In the textbook case the tax rate per ton CO_2 is the same for all energy carriers. This means that the 'dirtiest' carrier coal has the highest taxation; thus its consumption will be reduced most strongly. In the German Environmental Tax Reform coal is not taxed at all. Further industries with a high energy intensity are excluded from tax payment. This difference in the design of the tax explains why the CO_2 emissions induced by the German Environmental Tax Reform reduce only at 2.3%, whereas in the textbook case this figure is 4.6%.

Summarizing, we see that the results of both simulations for Germany seem to be consistent, which also gives strong confirmation of the results of our analysis for the other countries.

Part IV

Methodologies

12
Energy projections: comparison of methodologies

KIMIO UNO

1. Introduction

The global-warming issue has passed through several phases, starting from scientific fact-finding to the worldwide recognition of the nature of the issue as constituting a sustainability of human society and the ecosystem, then to the debate on options open to the world community and presently to the phase of policy formulation and implementation. It has been established that CO_2 constitutes the largest contributor among major greenhouse gases and its emission is largely traced to energy use. Of the greenhouse gases (GHGs) with direct effect on radiative forcing, CO_2 contributes 64% of 1990 emissions to global warming. Of this, 80% is attributed to energy use, with other factors such as deforestation and changing land use and cement production contributing 17% and 3%, respectively. Combustion of fossil fuels is also blamed for emissions of CH_4 and N_2O with direct effects on radiative forcing and CO and NO_x with indirect effects on radiative forcing. This explains strong interest in evaluating CO_2 emission potentials and in limiting greenhouse gas emissions in general, and CO_2 emissions in particular. This review provides an overview of energy projections conducted by various research groups from the methodological point of view.

The purpose of this review is two-fold. First, it is intended to highlight the main features of COMPASS compared to the existing energy projection framework. Second, methodological comparison in itself is useful in interpreting the projection outcomes. The capabilities, as well as the limits, of models are already embedded in the model framework itself. It is imperative to make explicit (1) scope of the model, (2) the theoretical standpoint, and (3) assumptions that went into the simulation experiment. In addition, the main thrust of the individual modelling exercise is represented in accompanying tables reproduced from the original literature.

We may summarize some of the characteristics of COMPASS as follows, after cross-checking with other models.

(1) COMPASS has feedback channels running through economy–energy–environment spheres.
(2) Its framework is disaggregated almost to the maximum extent that is feasible from the data point of view.

K. Uno (ed.), Economy–Energy–Environment Simulation, 193–298.

(3) COMPASS incorporates, and is capable of endogenously generating, a relevant accounting scheme, including national income accounting, balance of payments and saving-investment balance, input-output tables, trade matrices, and energy balance tables. It can also generate prices for individual industrial branches, final demand, and energy. Exchange rates and interest rates are endogenously determined.
(4) Technological factors are represented as changes in input coefficients for each industrial branch and changes in energy intensity.
(5) An object-oriented approach is maintained throughout the project, ranging from naming convention, statistical database, model-building software, and simulation engine, making the construction and maintenance of large-scale models considerably systematic.

The main exogenous variables needed for the current version of COMPASS are as follows:

(1) Population.
(2) Exchange rate (this can be endogenized).
(3) Service trade (commodity trade is fully explained by the model) .
(4) Unit labour cost ((wage rate * employment) / output, or wage rate * labour productivity) at branch level (this can be endogenized, but this variable is often determined by wage policy).
(5) US interest rate.
(6) World oil price (model also calculates world oil prices to monitor the market force)

The scope of the COMPASS extends over economy, energy, and environmental spheres:

Economy: Input structure, output structure, final demand, value added, prices. Technological change (input coefficients, conversion efficiency, shares among primary energy sources), technology transfer, lifestyle shift. Balance of payments, trade shares matrices, exporting country, importing country for each branch. Saving-investment balance, flow of funds. Exchange rates, interest rates.

Energy: Total final consumption (TFC), energy conversion, total primary energy supply (TPES), required energy supply, energy trade, energy prices (global as well as domestic).

Environment: CO_2 emissions, emission trade. (Price change through emission trade, CO_2 taxes, etc.)

It is planned to present the raw data and simulation results in various formats, among them internationally linked environmental accounting.

COMPASS also provides information at detailed country levels, an advantage over various other models that provide information at aggregated regional groups. Analytical needs exist concerning developing countries and oil-producing countries as well as for developed industrial countries, to evaluate the impact of policy measures that are in most cases implemented by individual governments.

2. Comparison of methodologies

The methodology used can be broadly categorized as follows. In general the word *projection* is used to mean future outcome based on econometric or other quantitative analysis which relies on observed behaviour in the past, adjusted by evolutionary perspectives in order to take account of discontinuities such as introduction of new technology, new lifestyle, or new policy instruments. *Scenarios* refer to examination of potential alternative development over time, or a series of sensitivity analysis, contingent upon various assumptions pertaining to variables in question, presented in objective terms. The word *outlook* can be more judgemental observation pertaining to the future course of events, not necessarily based on formal analytical framework. In contrast, *forecast* and *prediction* are used interchangeably, and are inclined to deterministic description of future outcomes presented as a single, point estimate. *Prescription* emphasizes suggestions for policy response to an anticipated future situation, with or without quantitative description. *Goal* or *target* refers to policy objectives, with the implication that its realization is desirable. *Model solution* or *simulation result* refers to quantitative outcomes of a mathematically or econometrically formulated system of causal relationship, both during the observation period and in the future, without judgemental observation. It is noted, however, that underlying assumptions of models could be highly judgemental and subjective, without empirical foundation.

2.1. Scenarios

Projection based on various sources, without formal modelling. Studies by international organizations, with periodical updates, are often of this type (e.g. IEA, EIA, APERC. For a systematic examination of scenarios, see Kram *et al.*, 2000). IPCC report (IPCC, 2000b) as well as IIASA's work (IIASA, 1995) also belong to this category. There is a case where technological scenarios are incorporated into an IO model (World Model by Duchin and Lange, 1994). The work based on various elasticities can also be classified in this group, or it can be viewed as a hybrid of scenario writing and econometric modelling (IMAGE 2.0).

Scenarios can be more structured by decomposition of indicators. In other words, definitional identity can be broken down into relations among various indicators, whereby projection of individual components can be synthesized into a single, consistent projection (Unander and Schipper, 1998, 1999).

2.2. Computable general equilibrium (CGE) models

This approach, which assumes market-clearing equilibrium for individual economic agents as well as at macro level, dominates the academic scene. The term 'general equilibrium', however, is used to refer to a variety of approaches by different researchers. One can properly distinguish two schools in this camp: one using parameters from one specific point in time and seeking optimization over time under certain constraints, and the other using econometric models based on time-series observations employing market-clearing assumptions (i.e. disequilibrium is not dealt with by assumption). This approach can solve for optimality for a very long period of time, with a result that all long-term projections (typically 2100 as the terminal year) are of this variety.

2.3. *Input-output plus econometric models*

This approach employs the input-output framework, sometimes from one point in time and sometimes in time-series, to describe the structure of the economy, which is combined with a model embodying econometrically estimated parameters (COMPASS, GREEN, and G-cubed). It is thus capable of detailed intersectoral description as well as macroeconomic analysis. West (1995) referred to this type as IOE, as opposed to static IO and CGE. The availability of empirical data for econometric estimation limits its ability to project into the future, and models based on this methodology usually look at 10 to 20 years into the future. In return, it can deliver a time path of various structural adjustments as well as responses to disequilibrium in the system.

We have examined the models with focus on economy–energy–environment interaction. It is noteworthy that many models with energy-environment orientation treat the linkage with economy as exogenous. In other words they take the economic projection/scenario from an independent source and build energy and environmental analyses based on it. Naturally, the feedback from energy-environment spheres to the economy is typically lacking. The framework that closes this feedback channel employs an econometric modelling approach (COMPASS, GREEN, G-cubed, and Oxford Model; GTAP employs IO; the PRIMES is a group of country models).

The number of regions that are explicitly treated in the analysis range from several to about 60. The relation among them can best be described by trade matrices (COMPASS, GREEN, Duchin and Lange, WorldScan, GTAP, G-cubed). Some models use a pooled approach rather than describing the trade structure (International Futures). Other works do not specify the global linkage through trade. There are some cases where international linkage through financial flow is incorporated in the model framework. Most models, however, ignore this aspect despite the fact that growth potentials of various regions are constrained by global availability of financial resources. It is important to recognize that any investment plan and public policy has to be financed to be viable, including those in energy and environmental spheres.

The environmental impact of trade liberalization is actively discussed, with the discussion at the WTO as the backdrop. We have examined various studies as to their applicability to fields other than energy. Agriculture, forest products, and various service activities are the cases in question. The frameworks which demonstrate considerable flexibility include COMPASS, E3ME (Barker, 1998, 1999; Barker *et al.*, 1999), World Model (Duchin and Lange, 1994), GemWTraP (Bernard and Vielle, 1999, 2000), GTAP (Hertel and Tsigas, 1997), G-cubed (Bagnoli *et al.*, 1996), and IMAGE 2.0 (Alcamo, 1994a, b), followed by GREEN and International Futures. Other works employ an analytical framework strictly limited to energy-environment spheres.

The Kyoto Protocol calls for global effort aimed at curtailing CO_2 emissions to the 1990 levels among Annex I countries, and there are several approaches that trace the effects of international emission permit trading, such as MS-MRT (Bernstein *et al.*, 1999), GemWTraP (*ibid.*), Rose-Stevens Model (Rose and Stevens, 1999), and WorldScan (Bollen *et al.*, 1999), with COMPASS trailing. It is interesting to note that they were all published in 1999, except for pioneering work RICE by Nordhaus which came out in 1996.

3. Summary of models and projections

The field of economy-energy modelling and forecasting is developing rapidly, and the list is not intended to be comprehensive. This review is based on published materials that were available to the author at the time of writing, and may not reflect the current development of individual projects. The description is solely the responsibility of the author of this chapter.

In the following, particular emphasis is placed on the examination of economy-environmental linkage. Quantitative results are not emphasized; rather, the focal points of various projects are presented so that the whole array of methodologies will be exhibited. The review will also reveal that the end-results are contingent upon a set of assumptions that went into the analysis, as well as the scope of the conceptual framework being employed.

In order to facilitate comparisons, individual models are described in terms of the following aspects:

(1) Time span: target year of the analysis.
(2) Regions: regional details provided.
(3) Branch classification: economic sectors (industry, household, etc.) and disaggregation of industry sector into branches.
(4) Energy sources: primary energy, secondary energy.
(5) Scenarios: purpose of the simulation runs and a set of major assumptions.
(6) Technology: treatment of technology in the model framework in view of the importance of the technological factor.
(7) Energy intensity improvements: related to technology, but more precisely on energy.
(8) Lifestyle: consumption pattern, modal shift of transportation, recycling, among other things, related to economy–energy–environment.

(9) Policy tools: introduction of new policy measures and how this is incorporated in the model.
(10) Environment linkage: impact of economic activities and energy consumption on environment, with particular emphasis on CO_2 emissions.
(11) Economic linkage: feedback from energy and environment to economy.
(12) Modelling logic: theoretical background of the model, causal flow among economy–energy–environment, the method of achieving global linkage.

The specific references in the original work pertaining to the above points are referred to with page numbers. The summary is intended to highlight methodological characteristics as well as main findings of the original work. The results of methodological comparisons are listed in Table 1-4 in Chapter 1. The quantitative projections into the future are summarized in Table 12-25 below.

COMPASS (Comprehensive model for policy assessment)

Source

(A) Uno, Kimio (ed.). *Economy–Energy–Environment Simulation: Beyond the Kyoto Protocol*. Dordrecht: Kluwer Academic Publishers, 2002.

Time span: Annual to 2010-(2020).
Regions: 61 (54 countries plus 7 aggregate regions).
Branch classification: 36 for IO countries, 26 world trade for OECD (20 for APEC).
Energy sources: 6 (coal, crude oil, petroleum products, gas, nuclear, new and renewables) plus secondary (petroleum products, gas, and electricity and heat).
Scenarios: Alternative development in technology described through changes in input coefficients, changes in energy intensity (which is endogenous but can be exogenized for experiment), world oil price development (equilibrium world oil prices endogenously calculated but without direct feedback to the model). Policy simulation has not been attempted.
Technology: Scenario pertaining to input coefficients. Technology transfer through input coefficients.
Energy: Final consumption of energy endogenous. Substitution among energy carriers (shares) endogenous. Energy intensity improvements endogenous.
Lifestyle: (Endogenous household consumption).
Policy tools: Carbon tax, emissions trading.
Economic linkage: GDP for individual regions endogenous. International trade endogenous (endogenous trade matrices also tested), energy export and import endogenous. Prices, exchange rates, domestic energy prices endogenous. Saving-investment balance for the region and the world as a whole endogenous.
Environment linkage: Carbon emissions endogenous.

Modelling logic: Econometric models based on time-series IO tables, trade matrices, energy balances, financial flows, linked internationally through trade, price changes, and exchange rates.

Summary

COmprehensive Model for Policy ASSessment (COMPASS) is an econometric simulation model designed to capture the interaction among 3E spheres encompassing economy, energy, and environment. COMPASS is designed for simulation experiments up to 2020, but current experiment focuses on the period up to 2010. The COMPASS is characterized by regional and structural details based on econometrically obtained parameters, which enables the model to trace the actual time-path of the global economy. The model achieves international linkage for about 60 regions, covering 99.5% of the world GDP and energy consumption. The country models are based on time-series of a 36-sector input-output framework, the SNA, and financial accounts. The linkage is achieved through time-series of 25-commodity trade. The model also generates energy balances and CO_2 emissions for individual countries. The energy-related parameters include final consumption demand (industry sector, transport sector, and other sectors including residential, etc.) and substitution among energy carriers. The COMPASS closes the world in terms of goods and services (production and trade), financial flows (saving and investment), and energy supply and demand.

The COMPASS focuses on medium-term transition, not short-term (cyclical) analysis or long-term (general equilibrium) analysis, but traces how the paths would evolve in different regions and in different industrial branches responding to introduction of policy measures (such as tradable permit or carbon tax), technological change (such as new input structure and better conversion efficiency), and lifestyle shift (such as service orientation or energy conservation effort).

The COMPASS framework, because of its branch disaggregation and regional breakdown, and because of its simultaneous equation system, allows bottom-up and top-down interaction. The inclusion of branch prices (36 branches), final demand prices (consumption, investment, government spending, exports, and imports), exchange rate, interest rate, and various energy prices as endogenous variables, the adjustment mechanism by economic agents based on relative prices are described explicitly. The model treats world petroleum prices as an exogenous variable, but equilibrium world petroleum prices are calculated within the model in order to monitor the market forces behind the assumed price levels. Technology factors such as production technology (described by input coefficients), energy substitution (among different energy carriers), and changes in energy intensity are fully explained endogenously. The model can project input-output tables and energy balances in the future, providing structural information of the world community.

The energy block will be linked to environmental block via carbon emission factors (Asia Pacific Energy Research Centre, 1998, p.22)

Coal: 1.08 tC/toe
Gas: 0.64 tC/toe
Oil: 0.84 tC/toe

The policy experiments using the energy model for environmental analysis (CO_2 emissions, tradable permits, and AIJ (activities implemented jointly)) are being formulated.

Adam Rose-Brand Stevens model

Sources

(A) Adam Rose and Brandt Stevens. 'A Dynamic Analysis of the Efficiency and Equity of Tradable Greenhouse Gas Emission Permits.' Paper presented at the Joint Meeting organized by the International Energy Agency, Energy Modelling Forum, and the international Energy Workshop (IIASA), 16-18 June 1999, Paris.
(B) Adam Rose and Brandt Stevens. 'A Dynamic Analysis of Fairness in Global Warming Policy: Kyoto, Buenos Aires, and Beyond.' *Journal of Applied Economics*, 1998.
(C) Adam Rose, B. Stevens, J. Edmonds, and M. Wise. 'International Equity and Differentiation in Global Warming Policy: An Application to Tradable Emission Permits.' *Environmental and Resource Economics*, 12 (1), 1998.

Time span: 25-year time horizon (A, p.2). 1990 as the base year (A, p.27).
Regions: 14 (Africa, Australia and New Zealand, Canada, China, Eastern Europe, Former Soviet Union, India, Japan, Latin America, Middle East, Asian Tigers, South Asia, United States, Western Europe) (A, p.2, p.4).
Branch classification: No.
Energy sources: No disaggregation.
Scenarios: Stepwise, from the most basic (emission quotas for Annex B countries as set forth in the Kyoto Protocol to a globally comprehensive and fully dynamic CO_2 emissions trading) (A, p.10).
Technology: Positive and increasing marginal cost as percentage of abatement increases (A, p.8).
Energy intensity improvement: Not explicit.
Lifestyle: No.
Policy tools: Banking, inter-period trading, interregional trading.
Economic linkage: The number of constraints, which is 364 under business as usual case, is reduced to one as trading extends temporally and spatially (A, p.2, p.9).

Environment linkage: Benefit functions are tied to CO_2 concentration levels in climate equations (A, p.2).
Modelling logic: Nonlinear programming model, incorporating 364 constraints (A, p.2). The objective function is to minimize total global abatement cost which is endogenous.

Summary

Scenarios consist of the following (A, pp.10-11).

(1) No trading (Kyoto based emission quotas for Annex B countries).
(2) Trading by Annex B countries only (Kyoto-based tradable quotas):
  (a) trading among countries or groups (interregional trading)
  (b) banking
  (c) banking and borrowing (complete inter-period trading)
  (d) interregional and inter-period trading
  (e) interregional and inter-period trading and intergenerational equity.
(3) Trading among Annex B countries and developing countries (equity-based quotas for developing countries):
  (a) interregional trading (no harm to developing countries)
  (b) banking
  (c) banking and borrowing
  (d) interregional (no harm) and inter-period trading
  (e) timing of developing country emission reduction commitments
  (f) interregional and inter-period trading and intergenerational equity.

It is concluded that 'the greatest efficiency gains in the design of a GHG tradable permit policy stem from utilizing the low-cost mitigation options of developing countries (even if no additional mitigation is forthcoming from this group itself) and then from requiring emission reductions from developing countries at some future date' (A, p.25).

Inter-period permit trading (banking or borrowing) yields relatively small incremental gains. This is partly due to assuming constancy of mitigation costs for each country/region over time. Even if mitigation costs decreased by 1% per year over time, relative gains from inter-period trading improve only a factor of one- to two-fold (A, p.25).

In the case with interregional permit trading, compared to banking and inter-period trading cases, mitigation costs are lowered for each Annex B country whereas gross benefits for each country stay the same (A, p.13). The inclusion of developing countries into permit trading enlarges the global gains. In this case, however, Eastern Europe and the FSU are permit buyers rather than permit sellers (A, p.16).

AIM: Asian-Pacific integrated model

Sources

(A) National Institute for Environmental Studies, Japan. 'Asian-Pacific Integrated Model AIM' (mimeo). No publication date given.
(B) Intergovernmental Panel on Climate Change. *Special Report on Emissions Scenarios*. Cambridge: Cambridge University Press, 2000.
(C) Tsuneyuki Morita *et al. Global Carbon Dioxide Emission Scenarios and Their Basic Assumptions: 1994 Survey*. CGER-1101-94. Tsukuba: Center for Global Environmental Research, National Institute for Environmental Studies, 1994.

Time span: 2000-2100, with 5-year steps before 2030, and 2050, 2075, and 2100 subsequently (B, p.336).
Regions: 19 regions (A, p.21). 17 regions for the bottom-up and land equilibrium models (Economies in transition, OECD-West, USA, Oceania, Japan, Korea, Indonesia, Thailand, Malaysia, Other East Asia, India, Other South Asia, China, Other Centrally Planned Asia , Middle East, Africa, Latin America), 9 regions for the energy-economy model (B, pp.336, 338).
Branch classification: Varies by country (typically, industrial sector, residential sector, commercial sector, transportation sector, power plant).
Energy sources: Detailed.
Scenarios: Economic growth ranging from 1.1% to 3.0% per annum to 2100 (A, p.13). As defined in the Special Report on Emissions Scenarios (SRES) (B, p.5).
Technology: Technology selection from 100 alternatives, based on purchase prices and fuel costs, and the timing of replacement (A, p.19).
Energy intensity improvements: Varied but not explicit.
Lifestyle: No.
Policy tools: Not explicit. The case of carbon tax (30,000 yen per tC) is discussed for Japan (A, p.23).
Environment linkage: Modules on SO_2 emissions and deposition (A, pp.39-42), desulfurization (A, pp.43-44), climate change (A, pp.51-53), global carbon cycle (A, pp.55-57), water resources (A, pp.61-66), natural ecosystems (A, pp.67-70), malaria (A, p.71). CO_2 and other GHGs (B, p.336).
Economic linkage: Integrated bottom-up national models and top-down global model (A, p.3).
Modelling logic: Economic spheres based on country macro models and global linkage. Feedback from economy to energy is through technological selection which is endogenized. Various independent modules covering details on energy-environmental spheres, including spatial description.

Summary

AIM is a computer simulation model for scenario analyses of GHG emissions an the impacts of global warming, with focus on the Asia-Pacific region. The project was started in 1991 by the National Institute for Environmental Studies, Tsukuba, Japan, Dr Tsuneyuki Morita as the leader, with funding from the Environmental Agency of the Japanese government. The AIM model was used to provide global and regional emission scenarios to the IPCC. The new version links bottom-up models, traditionally the strong point of the AIM, with top-down models (an energy economy model based on Edmonds-Reilly-Barns model, and a land equilibrium model. The bottom-up components are linked with top-down models through a linkage module (B, p.29, pp.336-338). See Figure 12-1.

The entire project consists of three major models, focusing on emission processes (AIM/emission), climate change process (AIM/climate), and the impact analysis (AIM/impact) (B, p.336).

The emission model consists of several national models and provides predictions on the emission of several global warming gases. This in turn is linked to a rest-of-the-world model. Assumptions on population, economic trends, and government policies are entered into the model, providing estimates of energy consumption, land use, etc. The country model contains a module that generates end-use energy demand by multiplying the energy service by an energy efficiency factor. This factor is derived by a series of assumptions about the introduction of new technologies which is induced by energy prices. The energy selection sub-module decides which particular technologies will be introduced from the arsenal of more than 100 technologies. Energy demand estimates are then linked to a top-down economic model.

Economic scenarios entered into the emission model assume annual growth rates of 1.1% to 3.0% by the end of the 21st century, or an expansion of 3 to 25 times. A population growth rate is assumed to be 0.7%, although the estimates for the year 2100 range from 3.6 billion (due to higher death rates attributable to environmental pollution) to 109.4 billion (based on the current fertility rate).

It is predicted that China will become the largest emitter of CO_2 before 2025. India will become the fourth largest emitter, following the United States and former Soviet Union. Japan is placed fifth. The Asian-Pacific share of global CO_2 emissions, which currently stands at 25%, will reach 36% in 2025 and 50% by the end of the next century.

The emission model has a land use change model to take account of the effects of deforestation on CO_2 levels and CH_4 emissions. The climate change model deals with carbon cycles and climatic phenomena. The mean global value of temperature changes is calculated, which then becomes the input into the regional models.

The impact model examines the interaction between the emission and climate change models. It calculates the impact on primary industries (water supply, agriculture, forest products, etc.) and human health.

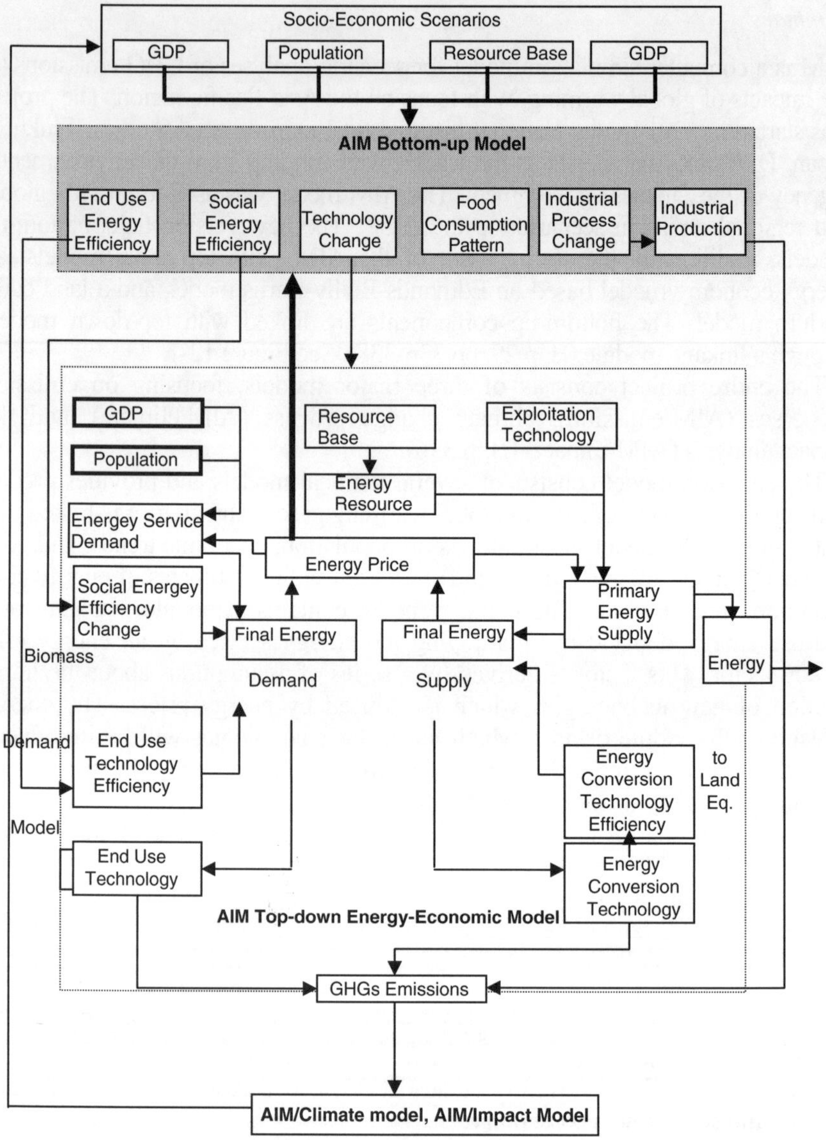

Figure 12-1. Bottom-up and top-down linkage in AIM.

Source: Intergovernmental Panel on Climate Change (2000). Modified by the present author to focus on bottom-up top-down linkage.

Asia-Pacific GIS provides a spatial dimension to the AIM.

Regarding policy tools, the report says as follows referring to the CO_2 emission model for Japan. 'In order to reduce emissions to the 1990 level with a single carbon tax, a high tax rate of 30,000 yen/tC is required. … An alternative would be to use the revenues from the tax to subsidize investment in energy-efficient technologies. In this case, the tax rate would only need to be 3,000 yen/tC. This combination of tax and subsidy policies can be evaluated with a two-dimensional optimization technique. The AIM model can solve for these sophisticated algorithms internally' (A, p.23).

APEC energy outlook by APERC

Sources

(A) Asia Pacific Energy Research Centre. *APEC Energy Demand and Supply Outlook*. Tokyo, 1998.
(B) Australian Bureau of Agricultural and Resource Economics. *The MEGA-RARE Model: Interim Documentation*. Canberra, 1996.

Time span: 2010 (A, p.iii).
Regions: 6 (United States, Other Americas (Canada, Chile, Mexico), China, Other East Asia (Hong Kong (China), Japan, Korea, Chinese Taipei, Oceania (Australia, New Zealand, and Papua new Guinea), and Southeast Asia (Brunei Darussalam, Indonesia, Malaysia, the Philippines, Singapore, Thailand) (A. p.1). 30 in the model (B).
Branch classification: 3 (industrial sector, transportation sector, and residential and commercial sector (A, pp.4-7). 37 in the model (B).
Energy sources: 6 (coal, oil, natural gas, hydro, nuclear, new and renewable energy (NRE)) and electricity (A, pp.9-14).
Scenarios: 3 scenarios: baseline based on MEGABARE model; protracted crisis scenario (PCS); and environmentally friendly scenario (EFS) (A, p.iii).
Technology: Not directly included in the framework; assumed in energy intensity improvements below.
Energy intensity improvements: Assumed. See Table 12-1.
Lifestyle: No.
Policy tools: Not directly included in the framework. Infrastructure requirements, regulatory reform as background information. (A, pp.17-18).
Environment linkage: CO_2 from coal, gas, and oil are derived based on emission factors (A, p.22).
Economic linkage: No feedback. Economic scenarios are from a separate global model MEGABARE.
Modelling logic: Scenarios in energy sphere. Economic performance as exogenous.

Summary

The APEC Energy Action Programme adopted at the APEC Economic Leaders Meeting in November 1995 assigned the task of compiling an Asia-Pacific

Table 12-1. Energy intensity assumptions and energy requirement in APEC

	Actual	B98			EFS		
	1995	2000	2005	2010	2000	2005	2010
Energy Intensity (TPEC / GDP)(toe per million 1987 US$)							
APEC	0.39	0.39	0.38	0.36	0.38	0.35	0.32
United States	0.39	0.37	0.35	0.33	0.36	0.33	0.30
Other Americas	0.57	0.55	0.52	0.51	0.53	0.49	0.45
China	1.20	1.02	0.88	0.77	0.94	0.78	0.67
Other East Asia	0.20	0.21	0.20	0.19	0.20	0.19	0.18
Oceania	0.36	0.39	0.37	0.37	0.37	0.34	0.32
Southeast Asia	0.53	0.56	0.53	0.52	0.54	0.50	0.47
Total Final Energy Consumption (Mtoe)							
APEC	3130.2	3486.8	3901.2	4368.5	3412.8	3699.2	4039.4
United States	1507.3	1651.0	1766.3	1880.9	1632.8	1700.9	1767.3
Other Americas	284.5	316.3	368.6	435.4	307.9	345.9	392.2
China	623.4	750.9	882.1	1014.3	716.6	808.9	922.3
Other East Asia	505	538.3	601.3	675.1	530.1	577.6	629.6
Oceania	83.9	95.4	110.8	130.1	93.5	104.3	116.8
Southeast Asia	126.1	134.8	172	232.8	131.8	161.7	211.3
Net Energy Imports by APEC Region							
APEC	691.1	829.8	1064.6	1327.8	656.5	654.2	647.0
United States	439.4	531.3	629	708.4	490.4	498.7	482.5
Other Americas	−168.6	−185.3	−158.1	−108.6	−198.0	−193.5	−179.9
China	−12.0	49.4	99.5	121.4	−31.3	−46.5	−68.0
Other East Asia	580.4	634.3	708.4	788.3	609.4	645.3	676.0
Oceania	−94.7	−120.2	−139.8	−148.4	−126.4	−154.2	−181.7
Southeast Asia	−53.7	−79.9	−74.4	−33.2	−87.6	−95.5	−81.7

Source: APERC (1998).

Economic Cooperation (APEC) regional energy outlook to the Asia-Pacific Energy Research Centre (APERC) which was established in 1996. Energy experts from the APEC countries (United States, Canada, Chile, Mexico, China, Hong Kong (China), Japan, Korea, Taiwan (Chinese Taipei), Australia, New Zealand, Papua New Guinea, Indonesia, Malaysia, Philippines, Singapore, Thailand, and Brunei Darussalam are stationed at the APERC.

The projection consists of three scenarios. First, 1998 baseline scenario (B98) is built around the GDP growth projections from the MEGABARE model provided by the Australian Bureau of Agricultural and Resource Economics (ABARE). The MEGABARE model has been developed at ABARE to provide a global perspective on major policy issues facing Australia, such as enhanced greenhouse effect and trade liberalization under the Uruguay Round and APEC initiatives. It looks especially into international flows of commodities and capital from a global perspective. Second, a protracted crisis scenario provides a more pessimistic view assuming continued economic turmoil in Asia, with more severe ramifications for APEC economies. Third, the environmentally friendly scenario (EFC) is based on the same GDP as the baseline scenario but assumes improved energy efficiency throughout the region and switching of fuels in order to minimize the use of carbon-intensive fuels.

It is indicated that the APEC region's demand for energy is expected to outpace its energy production by a wide margin, pointing to the region's growing energy import. The policy conclusions drawn are four-fold: (1) securing adequate energy supplies to meet growing energy demand when the economies in the region recover from the current downturn; (2) minimizing environmental degradation resulting from energy production and use; (3) using energy resources efficiently; and (4) promoting infrastructure investment and regulatory reform in the energy sector (A, pp.15-19).

'APERC's outlook projects CO_2 emissions to increase 42 per cent in the period to 2010 and increase by 22 per cent under the more energy efficient EFS case' (A, p.15). 'The APEC forum is ideally suited for development cooperative policies that encourage investment in energy conservation practices and facilitate the introduction of new and more efficient technologies.' 'The EFS case highlights the gains from energy efficiency improvements across the APEC region with reduction in TPEC in 2010 of 10 per cent, net energy imports of 51 per cent and CO_2 emissions of 14 per cent' (A, pp.16-17).

ASF: the atmospheric stabilization framework

Sources

(A) Intergovernmental Panel on Climate Change. *Special Report on Emissions Scenarios*. Cambridge: Cambridge University Press, 2000.
(B) D. Lashof and D. A. Tirpak. *Policy Options for Stabilizing Global Climate*. Washington, DC: US Environmental Agency, 1990.
(C) W.J. Pepper *et al.* 'No-policy Greenhouse Gas Emission Scenarios: Revising IPCC 1992.' *Environmental Science and Policy*, 1998.

Time span: 2100.
Regions: 9 (Africa, Centrally Planned Asia, Eastern Europe and Newly Independent States, Latin America, Middle East, OECD-East, OECD-West, South East Asia and Oceania, USA) (A, p.339).
Branch classification: Energy plus agriculture and forestry.
Energy sources: Various.
Scenarios: As defined in the Special Report on Emissions Scenarios (SRES) (A, p.5).
Technology: Conversion efficiency.
Energy intensity improvement: Implicit in conversion efficiency.
Lifestyle: No.
Policy tools: Tax policies by region.

Economic linkage: Supply and demand of energy, energy supply prices, secondary energy prices, agricultural products (A, p.339).
Environment linkage: Energy, agricultural, and deforestation models leading to estimation of GHGs, which then feeds into atmospheric model.
Modelling logic: Energy supply and demand adjusted by price iteration.

Summary

The ASF study is conducted by the ICF Consulting in the USA.

The ASF treats GHG emissions from energy, agricultural, and deforestation origins, feeding into an atmospheric model. The supply and demand for energy is achieved by energy price adjustments. Energy prices differ by region and by type of energy, reflecting market conditions, supply constraints, conversion costs, etc. An iterative process is employed to determine supply prices. The producer prices, in turn, determine the secondary energy prices in each region. The secondary prices reflect interregional transportation cost, refining and distribution costs, and regional tax policies. The electricity price reflects relative proportions of each fuel, secondary prices of those fuels, and conversion efficiency (A, p.339).

The ASF agricultural model is driven by population and GNP growth, and estimates the production of major agricultural products. It is linked to the ASF deforestation model which estimates the land deforested annually as a function of population growth and agricultural demand.

The ASF GHG emission model uses results from energy, agricultural, and deforestation models to estimate GHG emissions in each region. The ASF atmospheric model then estimates the GHG concentrations and corresponding radiative forcing and temperature effects (A, p.339).

Decomposition of energy scenarios by Unandar *et al.*

Sources

(A) Fridtjof Unander and Lee Schipper. 'Which Road from Kyoto? Decomposition of Emission Scenarios.' Paper presented at the Joint Meeting organized by the International Energy Agency, Energy Modeling Forum, and the international Energy Workshop (IIASA), 16-18 June 1999. Paris 1999.
(B) Fridtjof Unander and Lee Schipper. 'Past and Future Trends in CO_2 Emissions from Energy Use: The Indicator Approach.' *ENER Bulletin* No.22. European Network for Energy Economic Research, 1998.
(C) International Energy Agency. *Energy Efficiency Initiative. Energy Policy Analysis*, Volume 1. Paris: OECD, 1998.

Time span: 1972, 1990, 1994, 2000, 2010 (A, p.2).
Regions: 7 (Australia, Denmark, Germany, Japan, Norway, United Kingdom, United States) (A, p.8); 6 additional countries in (B).

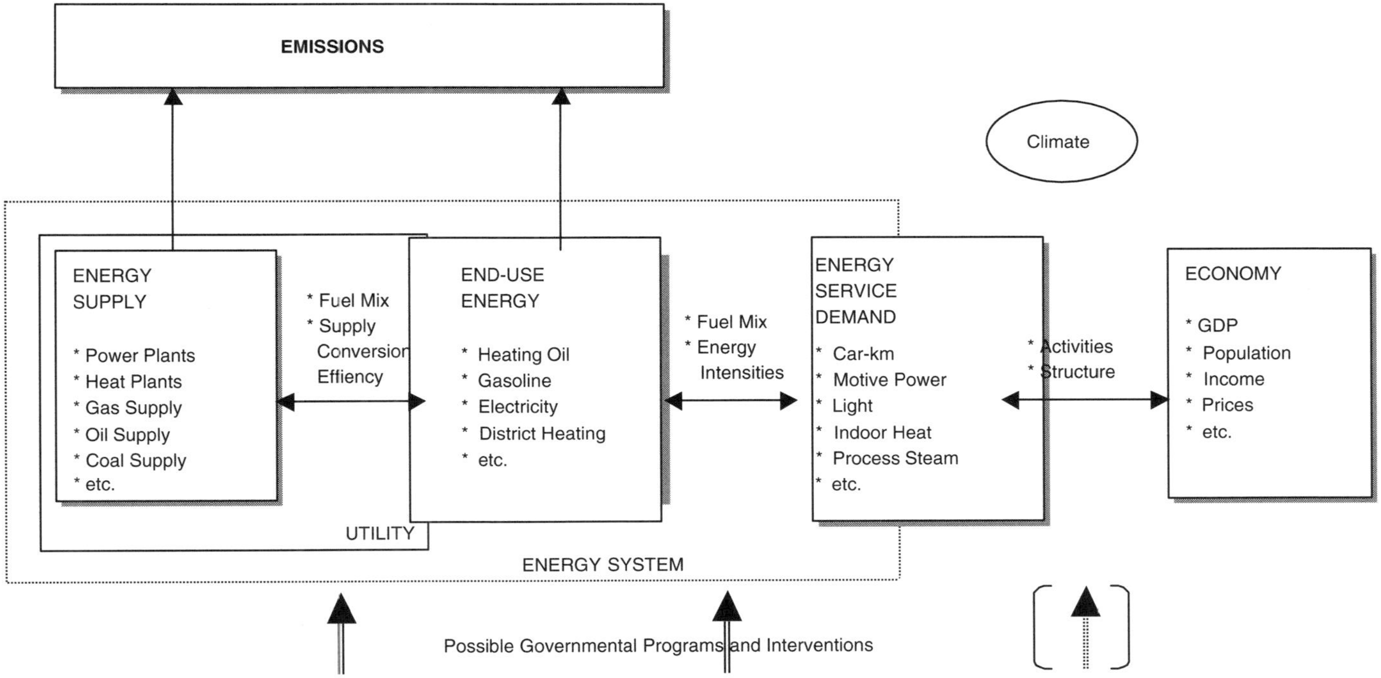

Figure 12-2. Decomposition model of energy-emission indicators, Unander and Schipper.
Source: Unander and Schipper (1999).

Table 12-2. Decomposition results (unit: annual average rate of change)

	Actual Emissions	GDP	Emissions/ GDP	Activity	Structure	Utility Fuel Mix	Energy Intensity	Final Fuel Mix	Carbon Intensity	Energy Services
1973-1990										
Denmark	−0.1	1.8	−1.9	1.1	0.3	−0.1	−2.3	0.5	−1.9	1.50
Norway	−0.9	3.3	−4.2	1.4	−0.1	−0.1	−0.3	−1.7	−2.1	1.30
W. Germany	−0.6	2.2	−2.9	1.4	0.6	−1.1	−2.2	0.3	−2.8	2.00
UK	−0.7	2.0	−2.8	1.0	0.2	−0.5	−1.8	0.4	−1.8	1.20
USA	0.2	2.7	−2.5	1.9	0.1	−0.4	−1.8	0.1	−2.0	2.00
Japan	0.9	3.7	−2.9	2.7	0.0	−0.8	−1.8	0.3	−2.1	2.70
Australia	2.5	3.0	−0.4	2.0	1.0	−0.4	−0.7	0.5	−0.5	3.00
1990-1994										
Denmark	0.0	1.6	−1.6	0.6	0.4	−1.2	0.3	0.0	−0.8	1.00
Norway	−1.1	3.0	−4.0	0.7	−0.8	0.0	−0.5	−0.5	−0.6	−0.10
W. Germany	0.6	1.8	−1.2	0.3	1.0	−0.3	−0.3	0.0	−0.6	1.30
UK	−2.4	0.9	−3.2	0.3	0.2	−2.3	−0.6	0.2	−2.7	0.50
USA	0.9	2.3	−1.3	1.8	0.7	−0.6	−0.8	0.1	−1.3	2.50
Japan	1.6	1.4	−0.2	−0.4	0.8	−0.3	1.5	0.1	1.2	0.40
Australia	1.5	3.3	−1.7	1.4	0.5	0.0	−0.4	0.1	−0.3	2.00

Source: Unander and Schipper (1999).

Branch classification: Nearly three dozen activities and economic branches (A, p.1). Manufacturing, other industries, households, services, travel, freight are specifically discussed (A, pp.9-10, p.12).

Energy sources: Final energy mix, utility fuel mix described as carbon intensity of fuel *j* used in sub-sector *i* (A, p.1, p.5).

Scenarios: Decomposition method used for constructing scenarios in terms of economic/energy/emissions futures originating in various agreements reached at COP-3 or from national sources (A, pp.10-12).

Technology: Energy intensity exogenous.

Energy intensity improvement: End-use energy intensities specified from various sources (A, p.1, p.5, p.10).

Lifestyle: Can be partially reflected in the term representing overall activity levels and sectoral structure.

Policy tools: Policies can be directed towards:

(1) more efficient end-use energy,
(2) changes to end-use fuels with lower carbon contents,
(3) supply side such as improvement of conversion efficiency, moves to renewable energy and low-carbon fuels,
(4) reduced activity levels, and
(5) changes in the structure of energy use, such as improving public transportation (A, p.6).

Economic linkage: Overall activity and sectoral structure (A, p.5).

Environment linkage: Energy intensity and the carbon contents of each fuel (A, p.5).

Modelling logic: Decomposition. Emissions are related to four multiplicative terms (sectoral activity levels, shares of sub-sectors, energy intensity in each sub-sector, and carbon contents of each fuel) (A, p.5). See below.

Summary

'We calculate the relative importance [of] changes in energy intensities, final fuel mix, utility fuel mix, sectoral activity level and structure had on energy use and carbon emissions over time' (A, p.1). The decomposition analysis is not applicable to the past experience. 'The approach will identify what kinds of changes must take place in both fuel mix and energy intensities to achieve a given level of energy use and emissions in a future year. Some important information can be based on results from calculations with energy and macroeconomic models.' At the same time, 'this approach can help bring together results from top-down and bottom-up analysis in a very transparent manner' (A, p.10). The decomposition of changes in CO_2 emission can be summarized by the relation as follows:

$$G = A * Si * Ii * Fij$$

where

G = missions in a sector,
A = overall sectoral activity (as value added in manufacturing),
S = share of output by sub-sector i,
I = energy intensity of each sub-sector i (e.g. energy use/real value added)
F = carbon content of each fuel j used in sub-sector i.

'Carbon intensity' refers to the product of the terms I and F, and 'energy services' can be defined as the product of A and S (A, p.5).

'It is important to separate the components of the carbon intensity effect (which is related to energy efficiency and fuel choices) from those related to people and enterprises' demand for energy service, since they change for different reasons and in response to different stimuli, as energy prices' (A, pp.5-6).

It is observed that, between 1970 and the mid-1990s, falling energy intensities, shifts away from coal and oil, and (in some countries) a reduction of energy-intensive manufacturing contributed to lowering emissions per unit of output. The trend has been slowed or reversed due to renewed economic growth, slowdown in the decline in energy intensities, and growth in the size and power of personal vehicles (A, p.13). If Kyoto targets are to be met, 'most IEA countries would need to decarbonize faster than any previous time period, at a time when oil prices are at historically low levels' (A, p.13).

DEMETER: the DEcarbonisation model with endogenous technologies for emission reductions

Source

(A) B.C.C. van der Zwaan, R. Gerlagh, G. Klaassen, and L. Schattenholzer. 'Endogenous Technological Change in Climate Change Modelling.' Paper presented at the Joint EMF/IEA/IIASA Meeting, Stanford University, June 2000.

Time span: 2100.
Regions: No.
Branch classification: No.
Energy sources: Carbon energy.
Scenarios:

	Temperature Constraint	Endogenous Technology	Endogenous Energy Demand
BAU	no	yes	yes
METH1	2C	yes	no
METH2	2C	yes	no
METH3	2C	no	yes
METH4	2C	yes	no

Technology: Technological change as a function of cumulative capacity (A, p.3). Two different energy technologies (carbon and carbon-free) (A, p.5).
Energy intensity improvement: Not assumed, but explained by learning-by-doing. The cost of the carbon-free technology depends on the cumulative capacity installed (A, p.5).
Lifestyle: No.
Policy tools: Indirectly, through subsidies for investments in non-carbon renewables, such as solar, biomass and wind (A, p.18). Subsidies are not incorporated in the model itself.
Economic linkage: Production function incorporates $A(t)$, representing the level of technological progress for the capital/labour composite, and $B(t)$, representing the specific level of energy technological progress or energy technology stock. $B(t)$ is chosen so as to reproduce an exogenous path for the AEEI (A, p.6).
Environment linkage: Impact on optimal CO_2 abatement and carbon tax levels of introducing endogenous technological change in a macroeconomic model.
Modelling logic: An optimization programme is solved in which the objective function of the total discounted sum of consumption is to be maximized (A, p.8).

Summary

'We employ a macroeconomic model that distinguishes between two different energy technologies (carbon and carbon-free), which, as in the bottom-up case, are subject to learning-by-doing. The costs of the carbon-free technology depend on the cumulative capacity installed' (A, p.5). 'The bottom-up and top-down approaches of endogenizing technological change are fundamentally different, both having their advantages. The purpose of this paper is to utilize the advantages of both approaches by combining them in a single model' (A, p.5).

'Effects of emission reduction measures and endogenous technological progress on energy demand are now explicitly reflected' (A, p.5).

'Our results are stronger than suggested by existing bottom-up and macroeconomic models. Earlier reductions are warranted since in contrast to bottom-up models total energy demand reductions are included as an additional carbon abatement option.' 'The model results show that the development of carbon-free technologies turns out to be the most important emission reduction option. The inclusion of endogenous technological progress implies that earlier investments in the non-fossil carbon-free technology are warranted, than traditional models suggest' (A, p.18).

Simulation results show that large differences start to occur between taxes among four scenarios. The carbon tax in METH1 and METH3 increases rapidly during the second half of the 21st century and reaches values of around 450 \$/tC and 380 \$/tC, respectively, in the year 2100. In METH2 and METH4, which incorporate learning-by-doing, the cost of energy produced by non-fossil fuel is lower, the carbon taxes increase much more moderately, carbon taxes reach approximately 230 $/tC and 175 $/tC, respectively, in 2100.

ECN (The Netherlands energy research foundation) study on the Kyoto mechanism

Source

(A) J.P.M. Sijm *et al*. 'Kyoto Mechanism: The Role of Joint Implementation, the Clean Development Mechanism and Emissions Trading in Reducing Greenhouse Gas Emissions.' Patten, the Netherlands: Netherlands Energy Research Foundation, 2000.

Time span: 2010.

Regions: 30 (Western Annex I (23: Netherlands, Belgium, Germany, Italy, Sweden, Finland, Denmark, France, Greece, Portugal, Spain, United Kingdom, Austria, Ireland, Luxembourg, Switzerland, Norway, Japan, USA, Australia, Canada, New Zealand, Iceland), CEE+FSU Annex I, Latin America, Africa, Asia, FSU non-Annex I, Middle East, Oceania) (A, p.38).

Table 12-3. Emission trends, Kyoto targets, and reduction commitments of western Annex I countries (unit: Mt)

	Emissions			Reduction Requirements	
	1990 (Mt)	2010 (Mt)	Kyoto Target (Mt)	(Mt)	(% of 2010 Emissions)
Netherlands	225	258	212	47	18
Belgium	130	144	120	24	16
Germany	1203	976	951	25	3
Italy	511	592	478	113	19
Sweden	67	76	69	7	9
Finland	64	83	64	19	23
Denmark	73	79	58	21	27
France	501	515	501	14	3
Greece	101	147	126	22	15
Portugal	68	86	84	2	3
Spain	294	358	338	19	5
United Kingdom	752	699	658	42	6
Austria	79	86	69	17	20
Ireland	53	69	60	9	13
Luxembourg	16	12	12	0	0
Switzerland	53	66	49	17	26
Norway	43	52	44	8	16
Japan	1333	1587	1253	334	21
USA	6187	7751	5754	1997	26
Australia	423	496	456	40	8
Canada	340	402	320	82	20
New Zealand	69	105	69	36	34
Iceland	3	4	3	1	29

Source: J.P.M. Sijm *et al*. (2000).

Table 12-4. Domestic reductions and emission trade effects

	Reduction Requirements (Mt)	Domestic Reductions (Mt) Case A	Domestic Reductions (Mt) Case B	Trade in Emission Credits (Mt) Case A	Trade in Emission Credits (Mt) Case B	Trade (% of Requirements) Case A	Trade (% of Requirements) Case B
Netherlands	47	19	10	−27	−36	59	78
Belgium	24	8	4	−16	−20	66	84
Germany	25	59	29	34	4	−135	−14
Italy	113	25	11	−88	−102	78	90
Sweden	7	2	1	−5	−6	76	87
Finland	19	7	3	−13	−17	65	86
Denmark	21	4	2	−17	−19	83	91
France	14	36	17	22	3	−158	−22
Greece	22	11	6	−10	−16	48	74
Portugal	2	7	4	4	1	−183	−49
Spain	19	28	14	9	−5	−48	26
United Kingdom	42	20	10	20	10	−48	−23
Austria	17	5	3	−13	−14	73	80
Ireland	9	6	3	−3	−6	29	64
Luxembourg	0	0	0	0	0	n.a.	n.a.
Switzerland	17	3	3	−14	−15	80	84
Norway	8	3	2	−6	−7	70	78
Japan	334	57	48	−278	−286	83	86
USA	1997	734	341	−1263	−1656	63	83
Australia	40	23	13	−17	−27	43	69
Canada	82	31	18	−51	−64	63	78
New Zealand	36	21	9	−15	−27	43	76
Iceland	1	1	0	−1	−1	81	108
CEE + FSU Annex I	0	254	900	254	900	n.a.	n.a.
Latin America	0	151	177	151	177	n.a.	n.a.
Africa	0	113	68	113	68	n.a.	n.a.
Asia	0	1116	1001	1116	1001	n.a.	n.a.
FSU non-Annex I	0	96	41	96	41	n.a.	n.a.
Middle East	0	57	159	57	159	n.a.	n.a.
Oceania	0	1	0	1	0	n.a.	n.a.

Note: In Case A, reduction options at negative marginal costs in non-Annex I and CEE/FSU Annex I countries are excluded from the analysis, whereas this potential is included in Case B.

Source: J.P.M. Sijm *et al.* (2000).

Branch classification: Not explicit.
Energy sources: Not explicit, but the ones leading to CO_2 emissions.
Energy intensity improvement: Not explicit.
Lifestyle: No.
Policy tools: Flexibility mechanisms as stipulated in the Kyoto Protocol (A, p.8).
Economic linkage: Baseline emissions in 2010 assumed, and contrasted to the Kyoto Targets (A, p.33).
Environment linkage: CO_2 emissions, equilibrium price for emission credits, average cost before and after international trade (A, p.37).
Modelling logic: No formal model. Based on cost curves and demand curves.

Table 12-5. Costs effects of using emissions trading

	Reduction Cost before Trade (mUS$95)	Reduction Cost after Trade (mUS$95)		Net Gains of Trade (mUS$95)		Net Gains (% of GDP 2010)	
		Case A	Case B	Case A	Case B	Case A	Case B
Netherlands	506	266	117	240	389	0.04	0.07
Belgium	298	147	64	151	234	0.04	0.06
Germany	20	−69	19	88	1	0.00	0.00
Italy	7551	764	320	6788	7232	0.46	0.49
Sweden	128	46	19	82	109	0.03	0.04
Finland	266	122	54	144	212	0.09	0.13
Denmark	859	143	58	715	800	0.31	0.35
France	11	−50	9	60	1	0.00	0.00
Greece	162	115	53	47	109	0.04	0.09
Portugal	0	−13	0	13	0	0.01	0.00
Spain	33	19	29	14	4	0.00	0.00
United Kingdom	595	−88	−19	683	614	0.05	0.04
Austria	1167	104	43	1063	1125	0.34	0.36
Ireland	46	40	20	6	26	0.01	0.03
Luxembourg	0	−1	0	1	0	0.00	0.00
Switzerland	1061	111	44	950	1017	0.23	0.25
Norway	242	49	20	193	222	0.10	0.11
Japan	32222	2179	864	30043	31357	0.45	0.47
USA	28830	12154	5341	16676	23490	0.18	0.25
Australia	371	196	92	175	278	0.04	0.06
Canada	1090	474	205	616	886	0.08	0.11
New Zealand	282	192	93	90	190	0.13	0.28
Iceland	14	10	5	4	9	0.04	0.10
Total Western Annex I	75753	16911	7449	58842	68304	0.20	0.23
CEE + FSU Annex I	0	−1029	−2557	1029	2557	0.09	0.23
Total Annex I	75753	15882	4892	59871	70861	0.20	0.23
Latin America	0	−580	−442	580	442	0.02	0.02
Africa	0	−432	−138	432	138	0.06	0.02
Asia	0	−4277	−2347	4277	2347	0.08	0.05
FSU non-Annex I	0	−370	−68	370	68	0.17	0.03
Middle East	0	−217	−444	217	444	0.02	0.03
Oceania	0	−5	−1	5	1	0.05	0.01
Total Non-Annex I	0	−5881	−3439	5881	3439	0.06	0.03
World	75753	10002	1453	65751	74299	0.16	0.18

Source: J.P.M. Sijm *et al.* (2000).

Summary

This is a work by ECN (the Netherlands Energy Research Foundation) at Petten, the Netherlands, which is an independent market-oriented organization for research, development, and consultancy in energy and related fields.

The study analyses the ‘potential role of the Kyoto Mechanism in meeting the commitments of Annex I countries to limit their greenhouse gas (GHG) emissions in the period 2008-2012’ (A, p.2). The Kyoto Mechanism or ‘flexible instruments’ include Joint Implementation, the Clean Development Mechanism, and Emissions Trading.

Table 12-6. GHG emissions 1990-2010 by region

	GHG			CO_2		
	1990 (Mt)	2010 (Mt)	Growth (%)	1990 (Mt)	2010 (Mt)	Growth (%)
Western Annex I	12,588	14,645	16	9920	11,702	18
CEE/FSU Annex I	4885	4813	−1	4124	3962	−4
Total Annex I	17,473	19,458	11	14,044	15,664	12
Latin America	2141	2572	20	1021	1284	26
Africa	1589	2877	81	767	1876	145
Asia	7290	10,535	45	4051	6337	56
FSU non Annex I	1232	1330	8	341	442	30
Middle East	1113	1702	53	838	1317	57
Oceania	9	13	40	4	4	5
Total non-Annex I	13,374	19,028	42	7022	11,260	60
World	30,848	38,486	25	21,065	26,924	28

Source: J.P.M. Sijm *et al.* (2000).

Following Skea (1999), the authors point to the distinction between the 'what' flexibility, the 'when' flexibility, and the 'where' flexibility (A, p.8).

'What' flexibility:	basket of six greenhouse gases (GHGs)consideration of sinks
'When' flexibility:	base year choice banking/early crediting
'Where' flexibility:	joint implementation (JI) clean development mechanism (CDM) emissions trading (ET)

Those flexibility mechanisms have been introduced in order

(1) to reduce the abatement costs of the Annex I countries as well as
(2) to encourage the sustainable development of non-Annex countries by means of technology transfers and institutional capacity building, and
(3) to facilitate an agreement among all countries involved.

At first sight these commodities seem to be traded on separate markets, which are distinguished institutionally by different systems of governance, monitoring, validation, etc. In fact, however, these markets are closely interrelated as they deal in the same basic commodity, namely additions to – or subtractions from – the amount of GHG emissions assigned to Annex I countries for the period 2008-2012 (p.16). The term 'emission credits' is used as the collective concept for credits generated and transferred by JI, CDM and/or ET. It is assumed that this basic commodity is traded on an integrated market (p.21).

A spreadsheet model has been developed to simulate a market for trading *emission credits* in order to indicate the potential role and cost impact of each Kyoto Mechanism separately and, subsequently, for all mechanisms together in a global setting.

As a first step, data have been gathered or estimated with regard to:

(1) National or regional GHG emissions in a reference year (i.e. 1990/1995) and a future year (i.e. 2010, as representative of 2008-2012). By means of these data and certain reduction targets – such as the Kyoto commitments for 2010 – national or regional reduction requirements have been calculated in terms of physical quantities of GHG emissions.
(2) The potential and costs to reduce GHG emissions in a certain country or region. These data have been used to determine individual *cost curves* for the reduction of GHG emissions in a particular country or region. Subsequently, these individual curves have been added up and combined into aggregated cost curves covering several or all GHGs, countries and/or regions. Marginal cost curves for reducing CO_2 emissions are available for most western Annex I countries. These curves have been derived from ETSAP and COHERENCE studies, based on detailed energy and technology bottom-up models such as MARKAL and EFOM (p.24).
(3) Finally, this process of adding up cost curves has resulted in the construction of a world-wide cost curve for the reduction of all GHG emissions (p.21).

The *demand curve* of emission credits depends on the amount of emissions that a country is obliged to reduce according to the Kyoto Protocol. This curve is represented by a vertical line.

By aggregating the supply and demand curve of all countries concerned, the same procedure has been used to determine the equilibrium price on the international market of emission credits.

EDGE model

Source

(A) Jesper Jensen *et al.* 'The Economic Effects of the European Ceilings Proposal.' Paper presented at the Joint EMF/IEA/IIASA Meeting, Stanford University. 20-22 June 2000.

Time span: 2030.
Regions: 8 (European Union; United States; New Zealand, Australia, and Canada; Japan; Eastern Europe and Former Soviet Union; China; Major Oil Exporters; Rest of the World).
Branch classification: 7 (coal, petroleum, crude oil, natural gas, electricity, energy intensive sectors, other sectors).
Energy sources: 5 (coal, petroleum, crude oil, natural gas, electricity).
Scenarios:
Annex B trade:
No trade: No trade. Only domestic abatement.

Proposal B: The European proposal excluding trade with non-Annex B countries.
Hot air: The European proposal excluding trade with non-Annex B countries and no restriction on hot air.
Annex B: Free trade between Annex B countries.

Global trade:
No trade: No trade. Only domestic abatement.
Proposal G: The European proposal including trade with non-Annex B countries.
Global: Free global trade (A, p.12).

Technology: Production processes are represented by nested constant elasticity of substitution (CES) functions to characterize the choices between: (1) the region-specific imports and (2) the composite import goods and the domestically produced good (A, p.9).

Energy intensity improvement: Autonomous energy efficiency improvement to match growth in GDP and emissions is assigned (A, p.11).

Lifestyle: No.

Policy tools: International trade in emission reductions, and a set of concrete ceilings for selling and buying emission reductions for all Annex B countries.

Economic linkage: Interregional flows of goods and services.

Environment linkage: Climate policy analysis (A, p.9). The model reproduces a set of paths for emissions growth, GDP growth, energy production, and energy prices (A, p.11).

Modelling logic: Applied general equilibrium model (A, p.4).

Summary

EU members have proposed a set of guidelines for emissions reductions trade within the Kyoto Protocol. The European proposal limits imports of emission reductions by Annex B countries to 50% of the total abatement requirements and eliminates exports of hot air. The economic effects of the European proposal are analysed using the EDGE model.

'In the short run, the proposal drives up global prices for emission reductions, because the elimination of hot air reduces the supply of emission reductions. In the longer run, the proposal drives down global prices for emission reductions because binding import ceiling on emission reductions reduce the demand for emission reductions' (A, abstract).

The benchmark steady-state is based on 1995 data from the GTAP database.

The only greenhouse gas in the current version is carbon dioxide. Incorporation of other greenhouse gases and sinks is planned (A, p.10).

The model is under construction and all results are preliminary (A, p.4). The work is part of the project 'Quantitative Instruments for the Analysis of Global

Environmental Issues', an environmental modelling project financed by the Environmental Directorate-General of the European Commission.

G-cubed

Source

(A) Philip Bagnoli, Warwick J. McKibbin, and Peter J. Wilcoxen. 'Future Projections and Structural Change.' In N. Nakicenovic, W.D. Nordhaus, R. Richels, and F.L. Toth, eds. *Climate Change: Integrating Science, Economics, and Policy*. CP096-1. Laxenburg, Austria: International Institute for Applied Systems Analysis, 1996.

Time span: 1990-2020 (A, p.185).
Regions: 8 (USA, Japan, Australia, Other OECD, China, LDCs, Eastern Europe and the Former USSR (EEB), Oil Exporting Developing Countries (OPEC)) (A, p.188).
Branch classification: 12 (Electric utilities; Gas utilities; Petroleum refining; Coal mining; Crude oil and gas extraction; Other mining; Agriculture, fishing, and hunting; Forestry and wood products; Durable manufacturing; Non-durable manufacturing; Transportation; Services) (A, p.188).

Table 12-7. Emission stabilization taxes by the year 2000 (unit: US$1990 per ton of carbon)

	1995	2000	2010
USA			
Scenario 1	2.80	16.80	44.80
Scenario 2	1.40	8.40	22.40
Japan			
Scenario 1	10.50	63.00	168.00
Scenario 2	5.50	33.00	88.00
Australia			
Scenario 1	3.80	22.80	60.80
Scenario 2	2.60	15.60	41.60
Other OECD			
Scenario 1	6.80	40.80	108.80
Scenario 2	3.70	22.20	59.20
China			
Scenario 1	1.15	6.90	18.40
Scenario 2	0.24	1.44	3.84
Developing Countries			
Scenario 1	2.60	15.60	41.60
Scenario 2	1.15	6.90	18.40
Eastern Europe and former USSR			
Scenario 1	1.15	6.90	18.40
Scenario 2	0.35	2.10	5.60

Source: Bagnoli, McKibbin, and Wilcoxen (1996).

Energy sources: Electricity, gas, petroleum, coal (A, p.188).
Scenarios: Scenario1: sectoral productivity growth the same across sectors; Scenario 2: Differential sectoral productivity growth (A, pp.196-203).
Technology: Assumed labour productivity growth (A, p.194).
Energy intensity improvement: Falls in industrial economies, gradually rising beyond 2000; in China and other developing countries, rises initially and then falls over time; in Eastern Europe and Former Soviet Union, more movement due to structural changes. This is assumption, or 'speculation' (A, p.196).
Lifestyle: No.
Policy tools: Carbon taxes, recycling of revenue (A, p.202).
Economic linkage: Carbon taxes (A. p.202), changes in prices (A, p.182).
Environment linkage: The effect of differential sectoral growth on carbon emissions.
Modelling logic: Econometric multisector general equilibrium model (A, p.181, p.184, p.187). Neoclassical growth model (A, p.184).

Summary

The authors point out that projecting energy use based on simple extrapolations of GDP is misleading, and set out to test the sensitivity of the aggregate outcomes to the assumptions about sectoral productivity performance (A, p.181). Of the sources of growth including (1) increases in labour, capital, and other inputs; (2) increases in the quality of these inputs; (3) technical change; (4) improvements in the way that inputs are allocated across industries; and (5) reallocation of inputs among countries, the authors put particular emphasis on (4) and (5) (A, p.185).

The eight regions are linked by flow of goods and assets. Flow of goods are determined by bilateral trade matrices. There is one 8*8 trade matrix for each of the 12 sectors in the model (A, p.190). Capital flows respond to interest arbitrage relations and exchange rates which float freely (A, p.190). The model includes foreign direct investment as well as short-term financial capital (A, p.191).

Producing sectors choose inputs and level of investment so as to maximize stock market values, subject to a multiple-input production function (capital, labour, energy, and materials as inputs) and a cost of adjustment model for the capital stock and prices (A, p.188). The parameters of the production technology are estimated from the input-output tables and price data for the USA (A, p.188). Each industry is assumed to have the same energy, materials, and substitution elasticities regardless of its location in the world. However, the share parameters for regions outside the USA are derived from input-output tables for respective regions and correspond to individual countries.

In Scenario 1 the global emissions rise from 5388 million tons of carbon in 1990 to 15,378 million tons in 2020 (A, p.196). In Scenario 2 the comparable figures are 9818 million tons in 2020, or a decrease of almost 5500 million tons compared to Scenario 1. This is attributable to the fact that 'without rising labor productivity in the energy sectors, energy becomes relatively scarce, which reduces the growth of downstream industries' (A, p.201).

The paper notes that 'different assumptions about the sectoral composition of growth have dramatic effect on the size of the taxes necessary to stabilize carbon emissions in each region' (A, p.203). 'By 2010 the stabilizing tax in the USA is $44.80 (1990 US$) per ton of carbon in Scenario 1 and $22.40 per ton of carbon under Scenario 2' (A, p.202).

GemWTraP: General equilibrium model for assessment of world tradable permits, a new version of GEMINI-E3 (General equilibrium model of international-national-interaction for economy–energy–environment)

Sources

(A) Alain L. Bernard and Marc Vielle. 'Efficient Allocation of a Global Environment Cost between Countries: Tradable Permits VERSUS Taxes or Tradable Permits AND Taxes? An Appraisal with a World General Equilibrium Model.' Paper presented at the Joint Meeting organized by the International Energy Agency, Energy Modelling Forum, and the International Energy Workshop (IIASA), 16-18 June 1999, Paris.
(B) Alain L. Bernard and Marc Vielle. 'Preliminary Results of Sensitivity Analysis on Leakage with GEMINI-E3/GemWTraP.' Paper presented at the Joint EMF/IEA/IIASA Meeting, Stanford, 20-22 June 2000.

Time span: 1990-2020, with yearly steps (A); 2000-2040 (B).
Regions: 7 countries/regions (France, Other European Countries (EU11), USA, Japan, Former Soviet Union (FSU), Energy Exporting Countries (EEC), Rest of the World (ROW).
Branch classification: 12 for France and EU11, 8 for USA, Japan, FSU, EEC, and ROW. 3 institutional sectors (households, firms, and government).
Energy sources: 5, including coal, gas, electricity, crude oil, refined oil products.
Scenarios: Pure domestic taxation: without permit trading;
Iso-Tax OECD: equalization of carbon taxes in OECD countries, on the basis of total abatement of OECD in Kyoto Protocol;
Iso-Tax OECD with hot air: equalization of carbon taxes in OECD countries, on the basis of total abatement of Annex I countries;
Iso-CMA OECD: equalization of marginal abatement cost in OECD;
Iso-CMA with hot air: equalization of marginal abatement cost in OECD countries, on the basis of total abatement of Annex I countries; and
Iso-Tax Annex I: equalization of carbon taxes in Annex I countries, on the basis of total abatement of Annex I countries (A, pp. 7-8).

Sensitivity analysis on leakage for energy-intensive sectors (EIS), based on different values of the elasticity of substitution between imports and domestic production (Armington elasticity, or AE):

Sct0: Domestic taxes and AE in EIS equal to			0;
Sct3 (central scenarios):		”	3;
Sct6:	”	”	6;
Sct9:	”	”	9;
Scp0: Tradable permits and AE in EIS			0;
Scp3:	”	”	3;
Scp6:”		”	6;
Scp9:	”	”	9;

ScPworld: Like Scp3, and commitment by non-Annex I countries to BaU CO_2 emissions;

Scpworldm10: like Scp3, and commitment by non-Annex I countries to 10% below BaU CO_2 emissions.

Technology: Not explicit. Costs of adjustment are not taken into account (A, p.16).

Energy intensity improvement: Decreases at about 0.8 to 1.0% in various regions/countries (A, p.21).

Lifestyle: Linear expenditure system.

Policy tools: Indirect taxation and social contributions, 13 categories with rates differentiated: by commodity (taxes on production, on imports); by sector (social contributions, subsidies); by sector × commodity (intermediate consumption); by commodity × institutional sector (final demand); by commodity × sector × IS (investment).

Economic linkage: Annual growth of energy consumption and GDP for 1995-2020 assumed constant (A, p.21). Endogenous real rates of interest (determined by equilibrium between saving and investment) and endogenous exchange rates (determined by constraints on foreign trade deficits and surpluses).

Environment linkage: Elasticities of substitution between imports and domestic production; between capital, labour, and energy; between individual fuels; and between commodities.

Modelling logic: Dynamic general equilibrium model.

Summary

'Internalizing externalities such as pollution can be equivalently performed by taxes or tradable permits. This is not any more the case when there are "distortions", i.e. in an economy which cannot be considered as first-best Paretian.' The paper compares trade of pollution permits based on costs (marginal abatement costs) and on market prices (carbon taxes) (A, p.1). 'As any country would not pay for a pollution right more than it costs to him, and should not sell for less, marginal abatement cost is more likely to be the base for exchanges of permits. A market operating on this base has then for result that marginal abatement costs are equalized across countries, but this is not the case for carbon taxes. Implementing such a market supposes that only governments are traders, or if private agents are the operators, that governments set corresponding taxes (or subsidies) such as the total price paid by firms (eventually households) reaches the desired level' (A, p.3).

Important parameters in the model are the elasticities of substitution. Values of elasticities of substitution were determined according to various sources and econometric estimations (A, p.20). Production function is nested CES with fixed factors for fossil fuel sectors. Import function is nested with domestic production.

The model outputs, by country and annually, include:

(1) carbon taxes, marginal abatement costs, and price of tradable permits;
(2) effective abatement of CO_2 emissions, net sales of tradable permits;
(3) total net welfare loss (net loss from terms of trade, pure deadweight loss of taxation, net purchases of tradable permits);
(4) macroeconomic aggregates including real exchange rates and real interest rates; and
(5) sectoral data such as production and factors of production (A, p.19).

The results of Iso-Tax and Iso-MAC scenarios show that 'abatement in OECD countries is maximum when they cannot benefit from the "contribution" of FSU through the hot air resource. When they benefit from both Hot Air and the additional abatement of FSU induced by a carbon tax (at the same level as OECD countries), abatement is minimum and marginal abatement costs are then very low (from 50 to 100 ECUs in 2010, instead of 140 to 300 in the scenarios of domestic taxes in OECD.' 'Relatively to Iso-Tax scenarios, Iso-MAC equilibria yield a higher abatement for the USA and lower for other OECD countries, but the difference is negligible' (A, p.11). The paper then examines the scenarios of tradable permits where transfers related to sales or purchases of permits are taken into consideration (A, pp.12-16).

Sensitivity analysis on leakage is carried out corresponding to different values of the elasticity of substitution between imports and domestic production (Armington assumption, or Armington elasticity). The analysis is applied to a specific sector or group of sectors, namely energy-intensive sectors (B, p.2).

'Sensitivity analysis on the Armington elasticity confirms that leakage increases with substitutability in international markets of energy intensive goods, but remains of a limited extent when implementation of the Kyoto Protocol incorporates trade of permits between Annex I countries. Total world emissions of CO_2 also increase, mainly through the shifting of production in energy intensive industries from countries induced to reduce carbon intensity of their products toward countries which do not have the same incentive.' In simulation of 'Enlarged Kyoto' scenarios, 'Annex I countries would benefit – and not suffer – from a commitment by non-Annex I countries to stabilize their emissions. Losers would then be energy exporting countries, but this already appears in simulation of Kyoto scenarios' (B, p.16).

Table 12-8. Iso-Tax and Iso-MAC scenarios (abatement in million tons of carbon, costs and taxes in ECUs, 1990)

	2010			2020		
	Abat.	MAC	Tax	Abat.	MAC	Tax
Domestic Taxes						
France	20	292	169	33	514	358
EU 11	220	322	256	297	459	395
USA	522	140	107	663	187	148
Japan	75	228	149	111	336	240
Total or average	838	199	0	1104	285	0
Iso-Tax OECD without HA						
France	18	257	140	24	348	208
EU 11	150	196	140	202	270	208
USA	597	177	140	776	255	208
Japan	73	217	140	103	298	208
Total or average	838	186	0	1104	264	0
Iso-Tax OECD with HA						
France	11	154	65	17	253	145
EU 11	88	107	65	148	186	203
USA	399	92	65	624	167	219
Japan	44	120	65	78	203	181
Total or average	542	98	0	868	175	0
Iso-Tax ANNEX 1						
France	7	102	33	10	161	64
EU 11	51	65	33	87	110	64
USA	262	53	33	430	91	64
Japan	26	76	33	49	118	64
FSU	191	61	33	280	92	64
Total or average	537	59	0	857	96	0

Source: Bernard and Veille (1999).

Table 12-9. Additional emissions of CO_2 by non-Annex I countries and FSU (unit: million metric tons of carbon)

	2010	2020	2030	2040
Sct0	87	131	185	250
Sct3 (reference)	105	157	217	287
Sct6	116	173	238	312
Sct9	124	184	255	332
Scp0	35	66	105	151
Scp3	37	70	110	158
Scp6	40	73	115	165
Scp9	41	76	120	171
Total corresponding emissions in the base line scenario (incl. FSU)	5270	6846	8535	9814
Total abatement by OECD countries	829	1065	1235	1416

Source: Bernard and Vielle (2000).

Further analysis would require a model with a higher disaggregation by sector, where production functions need not resort to the Armington assumptions. Vintage production functions are promising candidates (B, p.16).

GREEN: General equilibrium environmental model by OECD

Sources

(A) Organisation for Economic Cooperation and Development. *GREEN: the Reference Manual.* Paris: OECD, 1994.
(B) Andrew Dean and Peter Hoeller. 'Costs of Reducing CO_2 Emissions: Evidence from Six Global Model.' Paris: OECD, 1992.
(C) Jean-Marc Burniaux, Giuseppe Nicoletti, and Joaquim Oliveira-Martins. 'GREEN: A Global Model for Quantifying the Costs of Policies to Curb CO_2 Emissions.' *OECD Economic Studies*, No.19, Winter 1992.

Time span: Five-year intervals up to 2010, twenty-year intervals to 2050 (C, p.51).
Regions: 12 (United States, Japan, EC, Other OECD, Central and Eastern Europe, the Former Soviet Union, Energy-Exporting LDCs, China, India, Dynamic Asian Economies, Brazil, Rest of the World) (C, p.52).
Branch classification: 11 (1. Agriculture; 2. Coal mining; 3. Crude oil; 4. Natural gas; 5. Refined oil; 6. Electricity, gas, and water distribution; 7. Energy-intensive industries; 8. Other industries and services; 9. Carbon-based back-stop; 10. Carbon-free back-stop; 11. Carbon-free electric back-stop) (C, p.52).
Energy sources: 5 (coal, crude oil, natural gas, refined oil products, electricity, gas and water distribution) and 3 back-stop, non-conventional energy sources (C, pp.52-53).
Scenarios: GREEN and five other global models compared based on output growth and population (B).
Technology: Back-stop energy technologies (C, p.53).
Energy intensity improvements: Sensitivity analysis conducted on autonomous energy efficiency parameter (AEEI), by assuming growth rate of AEEI of 1% per annum and 0.5% per annual (B, pp.26-27).
Lifestyle: Consumer sectors (1. Food, beverages and tobacco; 2. Fuel and power; 3. Transport and communication; 4. Other goods and services) (C, p.52).
Policy tools: Carbon tax, energy tax, tradable permits (constraint at the world level, initial quotas for each country, a single world price as the shadow price of carbon) (C, pp.61-62).
Environment linkage: CO_2 emissions.
Economic linkage: Full trade links in a trade sub-model with separate specification for each bilateral flow (C, pp.62-63).

Modelling logic: Econometric model with policy tools. Sensitivity analysis on energy efficiency.

Summary

The model focuses on energy use and CO_2 emissions. The production side of regional models describes the supply of fossil fuels and their use, as well as non-fossil energy inputs into the production process. Carbon-based back-stop includes liquid synthetic fuel derived from coal or shale; carbon-free back-stop includes liquid fuel such as derived from biomass; and carbon-free electric back-stop refers to carbon-free electricity not derived from hydro or nuclear fission sources (e.g. nuclear fusion, solar or wind). They become available at a given identical time period in all regions and their prices are exogenous and identical across regions.

The decisions by producers are described in several steps: (1) choose the mix between (a) intermediate inputs and (b) composite input including primary factors and energy; (2) divide among labour and other primary factors; (3) choose the mix between energy and the capital plus fixed factor bundle; (4) allocate the energy bundle among coal, oil, gas, refined oil products, and electricity; (5) decide the mix between conventional and back-stop technologies; (6) determine the mix between capital and the fixed factor; and (7) allocate intermediate and energy inputs among domestic supply and imports.

GREEN incorporates full trade linkages between all regions of the world. Country models are based on input-output data, providing sufficient sectoral detail. The model is suitable for the analysis of the international competitiveness issue and of the impact of different agreements to curb CO_2 emissions. Changes in government budget by the introduction of carbon tax are compensated by offsetting changes in the income tax rate, which amounts to lump-sum transfer to households.

The model is a simple recursive type. The dynamic feature comes from the saving decisions which affect the accumulation of productive capital and future economic growth. The capital stock is sector specific and distinction is made between old and new capital vintages. The model is closed by equating gross investment to net saving. The equilibrium search produces the world price of oil as well as prices of coal, gas, and the carbon-free resources. It is also possible to solve for the carbon or energy tax needed to satisfy the constraint on carbon emissions.

GTAP: Global trade analysis project model of global trade

Sources

(A) Thomas W. Hertel and Marinos E. Tsigas. 'Structure of GTAP.' In Thomas W. Hertel, ed. *Global Trade Analysis, Modeling and Applications*. Cambridge: Cambridge University Press, 1997.

Table 12-10. Average bilateral applied tariff (unit: percentage of cif values)

Exporting Countries	Importing Countries							
	AUS	NZL	CAN	US	JPN	KOR	EU	IDN
AUS	0.0	15.0	5.3	4.3	1.7	10.5	2.5	5.3
NZL	10.7	0.0	2.9	2.3	5.1	11.8	3.8	11.3
CAN	14.3	18.4	0.0	3.2	3.1	9.9	4.8	5.5
US	15.9	23.1	7.1	0.0	3.1	16.5	4.2	12.1
JPN	18.9	32.2	7.6	5.2	0.0	18.3	9.1	14.3
KOR	17.8	23.0	9.8	6.1	6.9	0.0	7.1	18.0
EU	15.4	21.8	8.9	4.5	7.1	18.0	0.0	16.2
IDN	8.9	17.3	9.2	7.5	3.2	9.3	7.9	0.0
MYS	13.8	15.6	7.6	4.4	2.6	12.2	7.1	12.3
PHL	14.8	25.7	11.9	8.7	5.1	14.1	10.0	10.8
SGP	16.1	42.3	6.3	3.8	5.2	20.1	9.7	11.0
THA	8.5	13.6	9.2	6.6	6.1	15.6	8.2	9.7
CHN	19.8	35.0	12.7	6.2	7.0	14.4	5.9	11.1
HKG	17.1	34.5	15.2	11.1	6.8	20.5	10.2	18.9
TWN	15.2	28.0	8.5	5.9	8.2	19.2	7.2	18.9
ARG	9.2	6.7	8.5	5.1	4.7	21.4	10.0	3.9
BRA	15.3	19.8	8.3	5.6	3.4	13.5	6.7	10.8
MEX	10.3	12.2	6.8	4.0	1.6	12.2	2.6	11.0
LAM	10.3	5.5	3.1	4.5	2.8	7.1	6.6	4.1
SSA	4.1	3.2	1.3	1.1	3.2	6.2	3.9	5.8
MNA	5.7	1.8	1.6	2.0	0.6	5.7	2.8	1.4
EIT	13.5	20.6	6.8	5.1	3.3	14.6	5.5	8.4
SAS	10.1	20.8	16.2	10.3	3.9	12.6	8.6	6.8
ROW	19.4	24.2	5.0	4.3	3.8	13.4	5.7	10.3

Source: Hertel and Tsigas (1997).

Note: This table represents part of the original table.

(B) Mark Gehlhar *et al*. 'Overview of the GTAP Data Base.' In Thomas W. Hertel, ed. *Global Trade Analysis, Modeling and Applications*. Cambridge: Cambridge University Press. 1997.
(C) Carlo Perroni and Randall Wigle. 'Environmental Policy Modeling.' In Thomas W. Hertel, ed. *Global Trade Analysis, Modeling and Applications*. Cambridge: Cambridge University Press. 1997.

Time span: 1992 as the base year. No time-series.

Regions: 24 (Australia, New Zealand, Canada, United States of America, Japan, Republic of Korea, EU-12, Indonesia, Malaysia, Philippines, Singapore, Thailand, People's Republic of China, Hong Kong, Taiwan, Argentina, Brazil, Mexico, Rest of Latin America, Sub-Saharan Africa, Middle East and North Africa, Eastern Europe and Former Soviet Union, South Asia, Regions not elsewhere classified.

Branch classification: 37 (Paddy rice; Wheat; Grains; Non-grain crops; Wool; Other livestock; Forestry; Fishing; Coal; Oil; Gas; Other minerals; Processed rice; Meat products; Milk products; Other food products; Beverages and tobacco; Textiles; Wearing apparel; Leather, etc.; Lumber and wood; Pulp, paper, etc.; Petroleum and coal products; Chemicals, rubber, and plastics;

Nonmetallic mineral products; Primary ferrous metals; Nonferrous metals; Fabricated metal products; Transport equipment; Machinery and equipment; Other manufacturing; Electricity, water, and gas; Construction; Trade and transport; Other services (private); Other services (government); Ownership of dwellings (A, p.75).

Energy sources: Coal, oil, gas, petroleum and coal products, electricity (A, p.75).

Scenarios: Various policy applications (A, pp.191-346).

Technology: Embedded in input-output structure of the base year (1992).

Energy intensity improvement: GTAP docs not currently incorporate environment (C, p.305). Parameters to be specified by model users (A, p. 40).

Lifestyle: Embedded in consumer behaviour in final demand.

Policy tools: GTAP does not account for macroeconomic policies and monetary phenomena (A, p.52).

Economic linkage: Input-output tables (1992) linked by bilateral trade (A, pp.74-76).

Environment linkage: No. See (C) for possible extension in this direction.

Modelling logic: General equilibrium (A, p.29). Partial equilibrium closures can be examined by selectively omitting some equations (A, p.13).

Summary

The GTAP model describes the accounting for household, business firms, global transportation sector, and global banking sector (supply of investment goods and aggregate savings).

The database underlying the GTAP consists of bilateral trade, transport, and protection matrices that link 24 countries/regions (B, p.74). The regional databases are derived from country input-output tables. The input-output tables from the latest available year are updated to conform to the 1992 trade and macroeconomic data (B, p.75). Trade data are obtained from the United Nations and adjustments were made at the 4-digit SITC level prior to aggregation to 31 merchandise sectors (B, p.77).

The GTAP database, and a standard modelling framework built on it, is not in itself focused on particular policy issues including energy and environment. Rather, it is intended to be a collection of fully documented and publicly available data and a standard modelling tool.

It is suggested that at least four types of economy-environment interaction be made explicit in the model:

(1) Changes in the relative valuation of public goods compared to private goods.
(2) Changes in relative prices.
(3) Changes in consumption patterns caused by changes in environmental quality.
(4) Interactions between abatement activities taken by firms and private mitigating activities (C, p.307).

It is also pointed out that the models that lack abatement activities 'miss the interaction between abatement activities and other activities of the economy' (C, p.307). For this reason, a generalized algebraic modelling system was employed to 'calculate the "shocks" to GTAP that are necessary to achieve a given combination of emission fees and abatement.' These shocks are fed to GTAP, resulting changes in sectoral output, etc. are calculated, which are then used as inputs in the third step (C, p.309).

IEA energy model

Sources

(A) E. Lakis Vouyoukas. 'IEA Medium Term Energy Model.' OECD, *The Costs of Cutting Carbon emissions: Results from Global Models*. Paris. 1993.
(B) E. Lakis Vouyoukas. 'World Energy Outlooks.' In Jean-Baptiste Lasourd, Jacques Percebois, and François Valette, eds. *Models for Energy Policy.* London: Routledge. 1996.
(C) International Energy Agency. *World Energy Outlook to the Year 2010.* Paris: OECD, 1998b.

Time span: Annual to 2005 (A, p.107; B, p.127).
Regions: 10 (OECD North America, OECD Europe, OECD Pacific, Africa*, Asia*, Latin America*, Middle East*, East Europe*, Soviet Union*, China**)(*: less detailed. **: exogenous) (A, p.109).
Branch classification: 3 (Transportation, industry, other) (A, p.109). No description of industrial structure (A, p.108).
Energy sources: Eight oil products (gasoline, diesel, kerosene, gas, oil, heavy fuel oil, bunkers, other), seven other products (industrial gas, other gas, industrial coal, coke, other coal, industrial electricity, other electricity) (A, p.109).
Scenarios: Reference case, 1%, 2%, 3% reduction per annum in emission, stabilization case close to the 1990 level (A, pp.114-116). See Table 12-11.
Technology: Exogenous; slow introduction (A, p.108).
Energy intensity improvements: Detailed. Short- to medium-term rigidities of energy markets is the focus (A, p.108).
Lifestyle: No.
Policy tools: Carbon tax (A, p.109, pp.111-118).
Economic linkage: Macroeconomy exogenous, no economic cost estimates (A, p.107; B, p.127). Crude prices exogenous (A, p.108). Feedback between oil prices and GDP is possible (A, p.109). The data for non-OECD regions weak in end-use prices and their link to primary fuel prices (A, p.108).
Environment linkage: CO_2 emissions (A, p.110).
Modelling logic: Energy model with econometrically estimated parameters, with adjustment factors complementing econometric forecasts (A, p.107). Treats macroeconomy exogenously (B, p.127).

Table 12-11. Carbon tax and emission reduction due to substitution, total OECD

	1990	1995	2000	2005
Reference case:				
Energy (MTOE)	4184.6	4508.1	4776.3	5011.1
Emissions (million tons carbon)	3043.0	3274.7	3466.5	3631.9
One percent reduction case:				
Energy	4184.6	4327.3	4428.0	4520.9
Emissions	3043.0	3091.5	3113.1	3138.8
Reduction in emissions %		−5.8	−10.8	−14.6
Reduction in energy %		−4.1	−7.6	−10.3
Substitution %		1.7	3.2	4.3
as % of total reduction		28.9	29.6	29.4
Two percent reduction case:				
Energy	4184.6	4145.9	4088.2	4070.0
Emissions	3043.0	2923.1	2803.0	2736.3
Reduction in emissions %		−11.4	−21.2	−28.3
Reduction in energy %		−8.4	−15.6	−20.8
Substitution %		3.0	5.7	7.5
as % of total reduction		26.3	26.8	26.5
Three percent reduction case:				
Energy	4184.6	3859.1	3717.3	3657.1
Emissions	3043.0	2668.8	2480.7	2384.6
Reduction in emissions %		−20.5	−33.5	−42.1
Reduction in energy %		−15.5	−25.1	−31.5
Substitution %		4.9	8.4	10.6
as % of total reduction		24.0	25.1	25.1
Stabilization case:				
Energy	4184.6	4251.4	4333.6	4417.2
Emissions	3043.0	3019.7	3023.9	3043.2
Reduction in emissions %		−8.1	−13.7	−17.7
Reduction in energy %		−5.9	−9.7	−12.6
Substitution %		2.2	3.9	5.1
as % of total reduction		7.7	28.8	28.7

Source: Vouyukas (1993).

Summary

The model consists of four interdependent sub-models (final demand sub-model, transformation sub-model, supply sub-model, and price sub-model) and one self-contained sub-model (activity sub-model which converts exogenous assumptions on GDP etc. into sector-level activity variables).

The final demand sub-model solves for final energy demand based on the sector activity, the end-user price, and assumptions on sector-specific variables (saturation, technology, etc.). The transformation or power generation sub-model converts the demand for final electricity into primary fuel demand based on the structure of the electricity industry in each region, conversion efficiencies, and assumptions about non-fossil fuels (nuclear, hydroelectric, geothermal). The supply sub-model generates a set of primary fuel supplies, on the basis of output of the price sub-model and assumptions on reserves, discovery rates and other relevant variables (A, p.109).

It is claimed that the strength of the IEA model lies in (a) the detailed modelling of end-use consumer prices and their link to primary prices, and (b) the incorporation of rigidities in the current energy system of OECD regions (A, p.118).

Based on simulation results, the conclusion is reached that 'any reduction in emissions is likely to originate from a reduction in energy rather than from substitution in favor of less polluting fuels'. 'The model suggests that reducing emissions from current levels would require the imposition of implausibly high taxes and historical experience would suggest that this is likely to be very costly' (A, p.119).

IFs: International futures, the third generation

Source

(A) Barry B. Hughes. 'The International Futures (IFs) Modeling Project.' *Simulation and Gaming*, Vol. 30, No. 3, September 1999.

Time span: 1990s-2100 (A, p.305).
Regions: 20 in the model, 162 in the database (A, p.304).
Branch classification: 5 (agriculture, materials, energy, industry, services) (A, p.307).
Energy sources: 6 (oil, gas, coal, nuclear, hydroelectric, other renewables (e.g. photovoltaic, biomass, and wood) (A, p.307).
Scenarios: Variety of scenario interventions, including technological advance, multipliers on investment rates, tax rates, export levels, and other economic variables. Itis possible to intervene in systems concerning energy, agriculture, and environment (A, p.315). Change individual parameters. Change more than 20 functional relations within IFs by specifying analytic functions of choice (A, p.309). A parameter representing absorption of atmospheric CO_2 by oceanic and other sinks can be altered (A, p.319). Scenarios on feedback of CO_2 on agricultrue (A, p. 319).
Technology: Technological advance by assumption (A, p.315).
Energy intensity improvement: To be changed by scenarios (A, p.318).
Lifestyle: No.
Policy tools: Tax on fossil fuel use (A, p.317).
Economic linkage: Economic module encompasses the partial equilibrium analyses from the agriculture and energy modules (A, p.307).
Environment linkage: CO_2 emission (A, p.318).
Modelling logic: System dynamics. 'It is a general equilibrium model that does not assume exact equilibrium will exist in any given year; instead, the model chases equilibrium over time' (A, p.307).

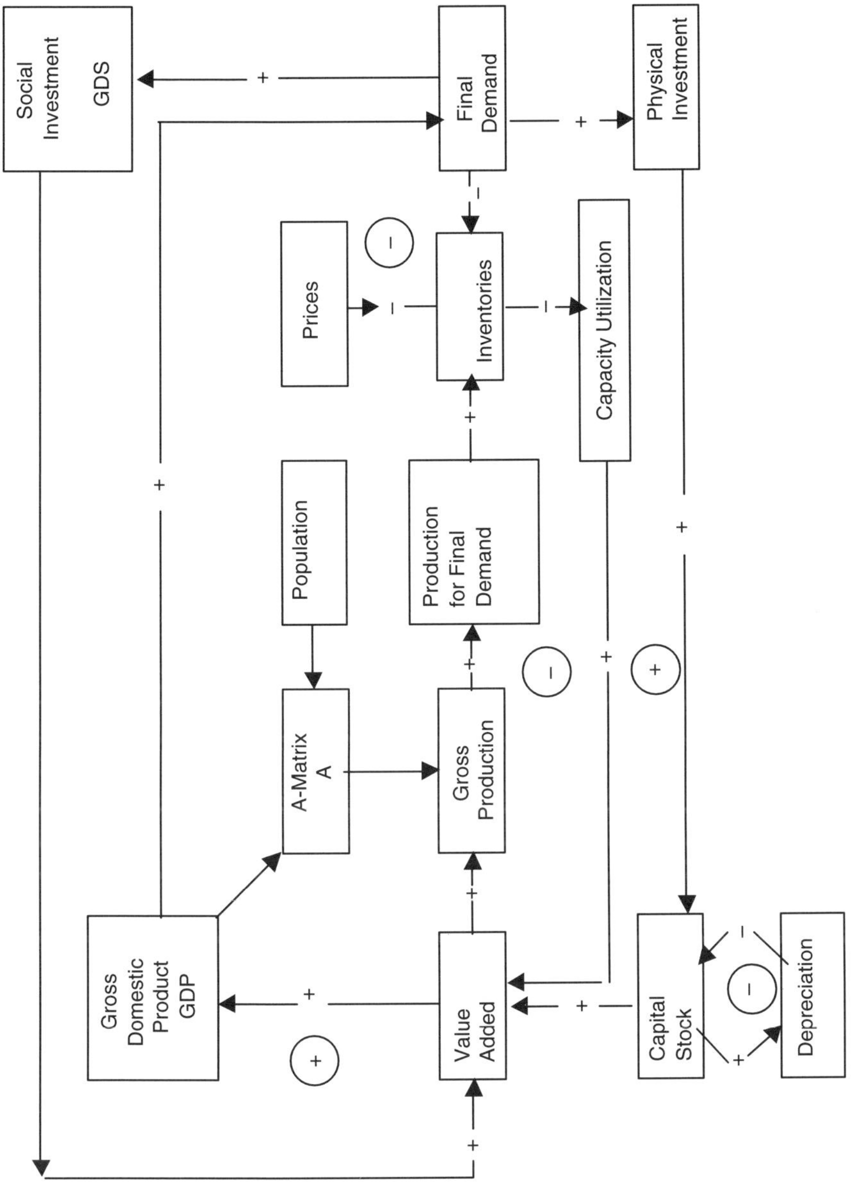

Figure 12-3. Economic module of International Futures.
Source: Hughes (1999).

Summary

The purpose of IFs is as a world model intended to analyse demographic, economic, energy, agricultural, environmental, and sociopolitical systems into the 21st century. It provides 200 variables across 20 countries and regions. In particular, the model looks at (1) the possible transition towards sustainability in the 21st century, and (2) aspects of sociopolitical change within countries and in the global system (A, p.304). It allows 'cross-sectional and limited longitudinal analysis of relationships among hundreds of variables across 162 countries' (A, p.305). IFs responds to the need to 'analyze long-term global change and human leverage with respect to that change' (A, p.310).

IFs consists of six modules (A, pp.306-308):

(1) Population module: represents 19 cohorts. Fertility, mortality, life expectancy are calculated.
(2) Agriculture module: production, consumption, and trade, price changes.
(3) Energy module: production of 6 energy types, consumption and trade at the aggregate level. Price changes. Known and ultimate reserves.
(4) Economic module: 5 sectors (see above). International trade uses the pooled rather than the bilateral approach.
(5) Sociopolitical module: fiscal policy including taxing and government spending. The spending categories are military, health, education, foreign aid, and a residual.
(6) Environment module: tracks the level of atmospheric CO_2, the area of forest land, the use of fresh water, and reserves of fossil fuels.

The model needs more detailed specification on the energy demand. 'It will be useful to elaborate the demand-side of the energy model by sector (household, transportation, etc.)' (A, p.424).

The model stresses 'feedback loops in reinforcing processes'. 'First, we can examine trends in population and economics … . Second, we can shift our perspective on … the specifics of agriculture, food, and environmental systems … . Those who have looked at human development with the first perspective are quite optimistic about the future, whereas those who adopted the second perspective are more skeptical.' IFs is able to integrate both perspectives (A, p.311).

'The IPCC itself builds two scenarios, a doubling and a quadrupling of global energy demand … . Even the 4-fold demand increase at the high end of IPCC forecasts for 2100 seems optimistically low, but IFs adopts something close to it for the base case.' Nuclear energy is described as becoming 'more expensive as the full costs of the nuclear fuel cycle, including long-term disposal of nuclear wastes, appropriately become part of costing'. The costs of renewable energy, while continuing to fall, will remain relatively high. 'Fossil fuels remain relatively plentiful and therefore not particularly expensive. There is an extreme global scarcity of political will to tax and discourage fossil fuel use' (A, p.317). As a result, 'We will have doubled atmospheric CO_2 (to about 600 ppmv) by 2050 and ... it will continue to rise slowly' (A, p.319).

IIASA and WEC's global energy perspective

Source

(A) Nebojsa Nakicenovic, Arnulf Grüber, and Alan McDonald. *Global Energy Perspectives.* Cambridge: Cambridge University Press, 1998.

Time span: 2020-2100 (A, p.5).
Regions: 11 world regions (North America, Latin America and the Caribbean, Sub-Saharan Africa, Middle East and North Africa, Western Europe, Central and Eastern Europe, Newly independent states of the former Soviet Union, Centrally planned Asia and China, South Asia, Other Pacific Asia, Pacific OECD (A, pp. 257-260).
Branch classification: No.
Energy sources: 5 (coal, oil, gas, nuclear, renewables) (A, pp.119-124).
Scenarios: See Table 12-12.
Technology: By assumption. Turnover of capital plays role (A, p.vii; pp.113-118).
Energy intensity improvements: By assumption, 0.8% to 1.4% (A, p.xiii).
Lifestyle: By assumption (floor space, appliances, passenger km) (A, p.95).
Policy tools: Environmental tax in case C (A, p.6). CO_2 emission constraint in case C (A, p.6).

Table 12-12. IIASA and WEC: three global energy scenarios in 2050 and 2100

	Case A High Growth	Case B Middle Course	Case C Ecologically Driven
Population (Billion)			
1990	5.3	5.3	5.3
2050	10.1	10.1	10.1
2100	11.7	11.7	11.7
Gross World Product (Trillion US$ in 1990 prices)			
1990	20	20	20
2050	100	75	75
2100	300	200	220
Global Primary Energy Intensity Improvement (% per year)			
1990-2050	−0.9	−0.8	−1.4
1990-2100	−1.0	−0.8	−1.4
Primary Energy Demand (gigatons of oil equivalent)			
1990	9	9	9
2050	25	20	14
2100	45	35	21
Net Carbon Emissions (giga tons of carbon)			
1990	6	6	6
2050	9 to 15	10	5
2100	6 to 20	11	2

Source: Nakicenovic *et al.* (1998).

Environment linkage: Endogenous carbon emissions.
Economic linkage: Gross world product by assumption (3 cases) (A, p.6). International trade by assumption (A, p.105). Prices and exchange rates outside the scope.
Modelling logic: Technology scenarios.

Summary

This work provides the future scenarios on world production, energy demand, and carbon emissions for the years 2050 and 2100 jointly conducted by the International Institute for Applied Systems Analysis (IIASA) and World Energy Council (Nakicenovic *et al.*, 1998).

Case A represents a scenario built around high rates of economic growth (2% per annum in OECD and double that pace in the developing countries) and rapid improvement in energy intensity (0.9% to 2050 and 1.0% during 2050-2100). Although there are a subset of assumptions under this scenario, it is suggested that technological change potential may make it possible to tap the vast oil and gas occurrences, an outcome which is contrary to the conventional wisdom which foresees exhaustion of fossil fuels. There is also a possibility of resorting to coal as the backstop fossil fuel, or to shift to large-scale introduction of renewables and a new generation of nuclear power plants, leading to a transition to a post-fossil-fuel age.

Case B is intended to describe a more pragmatic development, assuming more modest economic growth and technological change than Case A. In reality this reflects economic transition in Eastern Europe and the former Soviet Union and differentiated economic performance in the South.

Case C is labelled as 'ecologically driven'. In addition to an optimistic outlook as regard technology and geopolitics, it assumes 'unprecedented progressive international cooperation focused explicitly on environmental protection and international equity'. It assumes incentives to energy producers and consumers for more energy-efficient behaviour, green taxes, international agreements in environmental and economic spheres, and technology transfer. The growth in the South will be stimulated through substantial resource transfers from industrialized countries. As a result, CO_2 emission in the year 2100 will be contained to 2 GtC, or 1/3 of today's level. Scenario C incorporates two alternative scenarios concerning nuclear fuels: it either finds greater social acceptability through introduction of safe and small-scale new-generation reactors, or provides transient technology to be phased out by the end of the 21st century.

IMAGE 2.0: Integrated model to assess the greenhouse effect

Sources

(A) J. Alcamo. 'Modeling the Global Society-Biosphere-Climate System: Part 1: Model Description and Testing.' In Joseph Alcamo, ed. *IMAGE 2.0,*

Integrated Modeling of Global Climate Change. Dordrecht: Kluwer Academic Publishers, 1994a.
(B) J. Alcamo *et al.* 'Modeling the Global Society-Biosphere-Climate System: Part 2: Computed Scenarios.' In Joseph Alcamo, ed. *IMAGE 2.0, Integrated Modeling of Global Climate Change.* Dordrecht: Kluwer Academic Publishers, 1994b.
(C) Intergovernmental Panel on Climate Change. *Special Report on Emissions Scenarios*. Cambridge: Cambridge University Press, 2000.
(D) de Vries, "Greenhouse Gas Emissions in an Equity-, Envivonment- and Service-Oriented World: An IMAGE-Based Scenario for the 21st Century." *Technological Forecasting & Social Change.* 63 (2-3).

Time span: 1970-1990-2100 (A, p.1, p.18). Time steps vary (A, p.4).
Regions: 13 (Canada, USA, Latin America, Africa, OECD Europe, Eastern Europe, CIS (Former Soviet Union), Middle East, India (including Bangladesh, Bhutan, India, Myanmar, Nepal, Pakistan, Sri Lanka), China (including China, Korea DPR, Kampuchea, Laos, Mongolia, Vietnam), East Asia (Indonesia, Korea, Malaysia, Philippines, Thailand), Oceania, Japan) (A, p.5; C, p.341).
Branch classification: 5 (Industry, Transportation, Residential, Commercial, Other) (A, p.6).
Energy sources: 6 (coal, gas, oil, fuel wood, other biomass, electricity) (A, p.6).
Scenarios: Latest simulation scenarios as defined in the Special Report on Emissions Scenarios (SRES) (C, p.5). Earlier scenarios included:

(1) Conventional wisdom scenario, incorporating no assumptions about climate-related policies. Driving forces are partly based on the assumptions of the IS92 scenarios of the Intergovernmental Panel on Climate Change (IPCC).
(2) Biofuel crops scenario, differing from (1) above in their 'assumptions about how/where modern biofuels are grown'. Scenario (2) requires new cropland.
(3) No biofuels scenario, where biofuels are removed from (1) above and replaced by oil.
(4) Ocean realignment, investigating the consequences of a major change of the ocean's circulation pattern (B, pp.38-39).

Technology: Assumed efficiency of electricity and heat generation, improving from the 1990 level to 0.50 in 2100 in OECD regions, Eastern Europe, CIS, and Middle East; and to 0.45 in 2100 in other regions (B, p.45). Effectiveness of improved energy efficiency is examined (A, p.6).
Energy intensity improvement: Autonomous energy efficiency improvements, which are region specific. (B, p.45).
Lifestyle: No.
Policy tools: Introduction of biofuels (B, p.38).

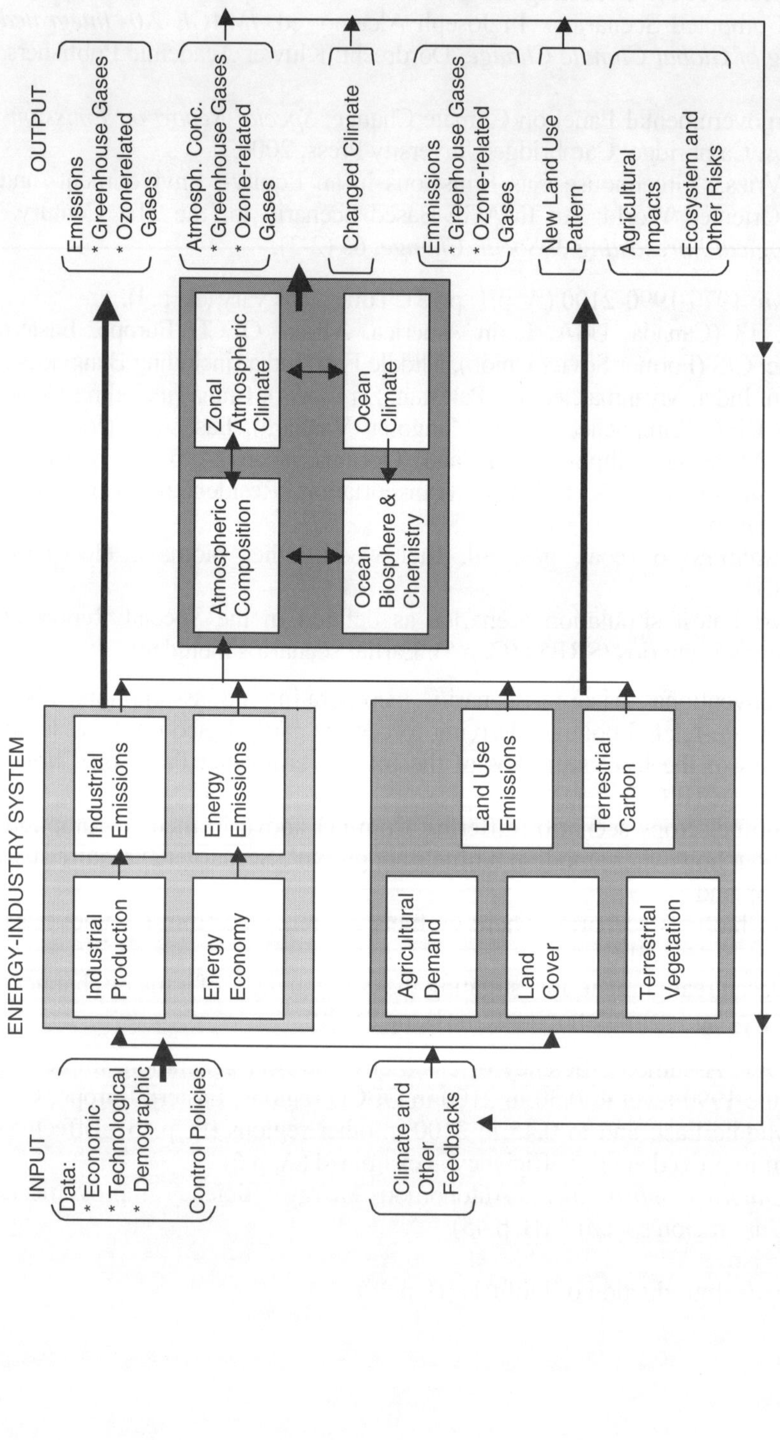

Figure 12-4. Flow chart of IMAGE 2.0.
Source: Alcamo *et al.* (1994).

Table 12-13. IMAGE 2.0 scenario results

Year, Scenario	Carbon Cycle (PgC)			Methane Emissions	Atmospheric Concentration					Average Surface Temperature (Degrees C)	
	CO_2-Emissions from Energy/Industry	Net Biosphere Flux*	Ocean Flux*	($TgCH_4$)	CO_2 (ppm)	CH_4 (ppm)	Trop. O_3	Chage of Agricultural Area (1000 km^2)	Change of Forest Area (1000 km^2)	Northern Hemisphere	Southern Hemisphere
1990	6.1	−1.2	−1.6	492	358	1.7	...	26.2	47.2	14.2	
							**	**	**	***	***
2050											
Conventional Wisdom	15.2	−7.2	−3.0	688	522	2.5	11.6	9%	−26%	plus 1.4	plus 1.0
Biofuel Crops	15.2	−6.0	−3.1	692	534	2.6	12.6	30%	−32%	1.5	1.0
No Biofuels	17.0	−7.5	−3.2	677	539	2.4	9.0	9%	−26%	1.4	1.0
Ocean Realign.	15.2	−4.5	−3.1	686	563	2.6	12.7	12%	−27%	0.0	1.1
2100											
Conventional Wisdom	24.0	−8.2	−4.2	778	777	2.3	10.0	14%	−27%	2.4	1.8
Biofuel Crops	24.0	−6.7	−4.5	793	821	2.4	12.0	65%	−31%	2.7	2.0
No Biofuels	29.2	−8.9	−4.8	746	857	1.7	(+ or −) 0.2	15%	−27%	2.4	1.9
Ocean Realign.	24.0	−6.7	−4.1	778	863	2.4	11.7	18%	−28%	1.2	2.0

* Minus sign indicates net sink.
** Percentages are relative to 1990.
*** 2050 and 2100 are absolute changes in degrees C relative to 1990.

Source: Alcamo *et al.* (1994).

Policy tools: Introduction of biofuels (B, p.38).

Economic linkage: Economic growth and population are exogenous (A, p.41). Regional population and GNP are the main driving forces of the model (A, p.7). Estimates of future population and economic growth are taken from the IPCC IS92s (B, p.39).

Environment linkage: Elasticity functions that relate activity levels of each sector with end-use energy consumption (A, p.7). Energy conservation function relates energy prices with the motivation for energy conservation (A, p.7). CO_2, CH_4, N_2O, and other greenhouse gas emissions are calculated by emission coefficients (A, p.7).

Modelling logic: The IMAGE Targets Image Energy Regional (TIMER) simulation model is a system dynamic model, with investment decisions in energy efficiency, electrical generation, and energy supply (based on anticipated demand, relative prices, institutional and informational delays) (C, p.340). Observed and assumed elasticity linking variables and modules (A, p.41).

Summary

IMAGE 2.0 is an integrated model designed to simulate the global society-biosphere-climate dynamics. The model consists of three subsystems:

(1) The Energy-Industry System (EIS): includes energy economy model, energy emissions model, industrial production and industrial emissions model. Computes the emissions of greenhouse gases in 13 world regions as a function of energy consumption and industrial production.

(2) The Terrestrial Environment System (TES): composed of agricultural demand model, terrestrial vegetation model, land cover model, terrestrial carbon model, and land-use emission model. Simulates the changes in global land cover on a grid-scale ($0.5° \times 0.5°$ latitude-longitude) and the flux of CO_2 and other greenhouse gases from the biosphere to the atmosphere.

(3) The Atmosphere-Ocean System (AOS): contains atmospheric composition model, zonal atmospheric climate model, ocean climate model, and ocean biosphere/chemistry model. Calculates the build-up of greenhouse gases in the atmosphere, the resulting zonal average temperature and precipitation patterns (A, p.3, pp.6-18; C, p.340).

It is expected that 'this approach can provide new scientific information and new policy information linking human activity with its consequences on the global biosphere and climate' (A, p.1).

Elasticity functions, energy conservation function, and other parameters are obtained from the 1970-1990 period (A, p.5, p.7). Energy-related scenario variables include value added of industrial output, value added of commercial services, public consumption, number of passenger vehicles, fuel mix, fuel prices, efficiency of primary energy conversion, autonomous efficiency improvements, and emission factors (B, p.40).

IPCC special report on emissions scenarios

Source

(A) Intergovernmental Panel on Climate Change. *Special Report on Emissions Scenarios*. Cambridge: Cambridge University Press, 2000.

Time span: 2100.
Regions: Mostly global aggregate; some tables provide figures by region (A, p.196, p.221) which distinguish 4 (OECD90, REF (Central and Eastern Europe and Former Soviet Union), ASIA, and ALM (Africa and Latin America), with totals for the world, developed countries, and developing countries. Detailed world region definition is given (A, pp.332-333). Underlying models typically distinguish around 10 regions (A, p.338).
Branch classification: No at the scenario level. Underlying models have branch disaggregation (A, pp.336-346).
Energy sources: 3 for resource use (coal, oil, gas), 6 primary sources (coal, oil, gas, nuclear, biomass, other renewables), 6 final energy (non-commercial, solids, liquids, gas, electricity, others) (A, pp.358-580).
Scenarios: As defined in the Special Report on Emissions Scenarios (SRES). Scenario 'families' are as follows (A, pp.4-5):
A1 story *line*: a world of very rapid economic growth, global population that peaks in mid-century and declines thereafter, and the rapid introduction of more efficient technologies. The A1 story line and scenarios assume 'convergence among regions, capacity building, and increased cultural and social interactions, with substantial reduction in regional differences in per capita income'.
A1F1: fossil fuel intensive.
A1T: predominantly non-fossil fuel.
A1B: balance across all sources.
A2 story line: a very heterogeneous world, with continuously increasing global population. Economic development is primarily regionally oriented and per-capita economic growth and technological change are fragmented and slower than in other story lines.
B1 story line: a convergent world, with the same population trends as in A1. Rapid changes in economic structure towards a service and information economy, with reductions in material intensity and introduction of resource-efficient technologies.
B2 story line: emphasis is on local solutions to economic, social, and environmental sustainability. Increasing global population at a lower rate than in A2, intermediate levels of economic development, and slower and diverse technological change than the A1 and B1.
Technology: By assumption in various scenarios.
Energy intensity improvement: Embedded in six underlying models.

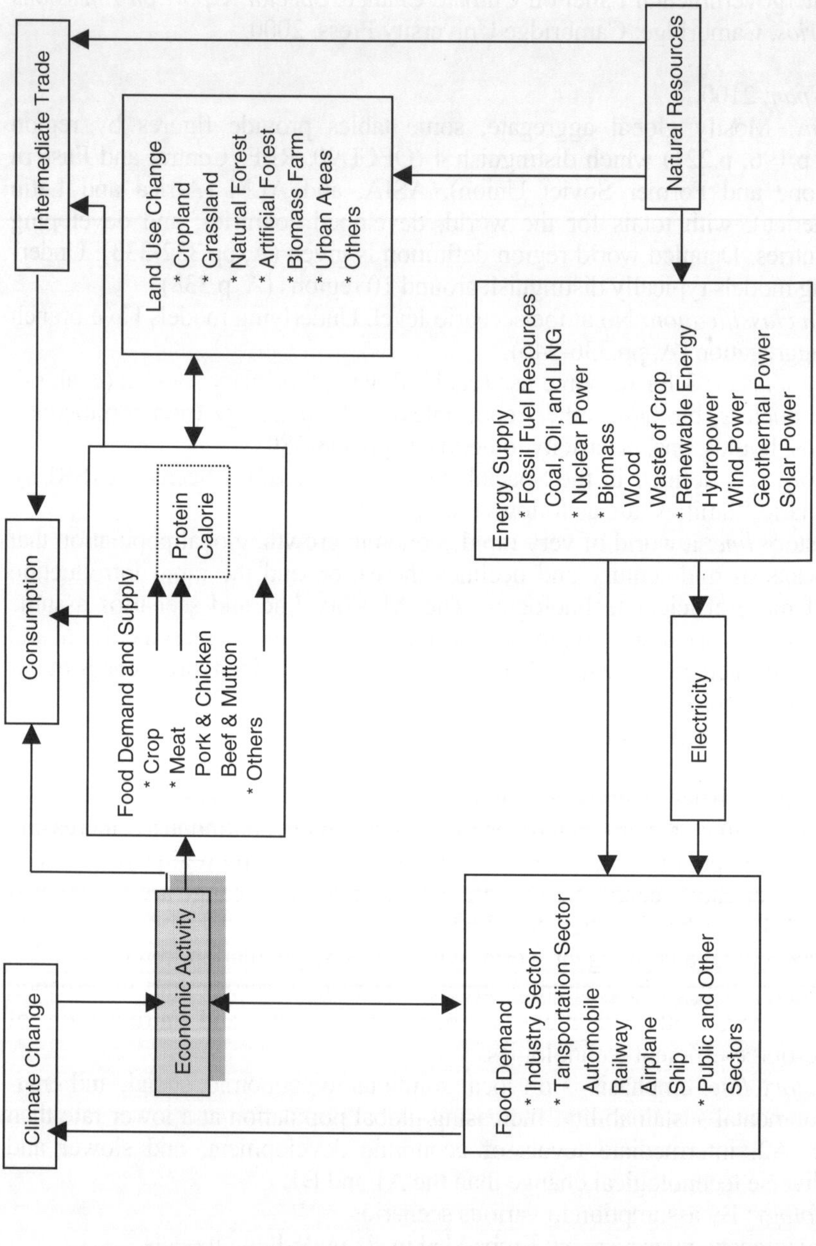

Figure 12-5. Structure of the MARIA model of one region.
Source: Intergovernmental Panel on Climate Change (2000).

Lifestyle: Embedded in some models.
Policy tools: No.
Economic linkage: Economic growth and population dynamics by exogenous assumptions.
Environment linkage: Detailed energy (resource use, primary energy, final use), cumulative CO_2 emissions, anthropogenic emissions of GHGs, land use.
Modelling logic: Scenarios (as above) based on six global models.

Summary

In 1992 the IPCC released emission scenarios to be used for driving global circulation models to develop climate change scenarios. The so-called IS92 scenarios were pathbreaking. They were the first global scenarios to provide estimates for the full suite of greenhouse gases. In response to a 1994 evaluation of the earlier IPCC IS92 emissions scenarios, the 1996 Plenary of the IPCC requested preparation of a *Special Report on Emissions Scenarios*, which was made available in 2000.

Table 12-14. IPCC emission outlook based on 26 harmonized scenarios

		Scenarios					
	Actual	A1			A2	B1	B2
Scenario Group		A1F1	A1B	A1T	A2	B1	B2
Final energy intensity (10^6J/US$)							
1990	16.7						
2020		9.4	9.4	8.7	12.1	8.8	8.5
2050		6.3	5.5	4.8	9.5	4.5	6.0
2100		3.0	3.3	2.3	5.9	1.4	4.0
Primary energy (10^8J/yr)							
1990	351						
2020		669	711	649	595	606	566
2050		1431	1347	1213	971	813	869
2100		2073	2226	2021	1717	514	1357
Share of coal in primary energy (%)							
1990	24						
2020		29	23	23	22	22	17
2050		33	14	10	30	21	10
2100		29	4	1	53	8	22
Share of zero carbon in primary energy (%)							
1990	18						
2020		15	16	21	8	21	18
2050		19	36	43	18	30	30
2100		31	65	85	28	52	49

Note: Overview of main secondary scenario driving forces in 1990, 2020, 2050, and 2100.
The range across different scenarios in the six scenario groups, provided in the original source, is omitted here.

Source: Intergovernmental Panel on Climate Change, *Special Report on Emissions Scenarios* (2000).

The new set of scenarios contained in this new publication is based on four sets of scenarios, which developed into 6 scenario groups (see above). Altogether 40 scenarios have been prepared (termed as SRES (Special Report on Emission Scenarios) scenarios. '26 scenarios were "harmonized" to share agreed common assumptions about global population and GDP development' (A, p.29).

Six global models have been employed to quantify story lines into 2100. Six models are 'representative of different approaches to modelling emissions scenarios and different integrated assessment frameworks in the literature and include so-called top-down and bottom-up models' (A, p.29). They are:

(1) Asian Pacific Integrated Model (AIM).
(2) Atmospheric Stabilization Framework Model (ASF).
(3) Integrated Model to Assess the Greenhouse Effect (IMAGE).
(4) Multiregional Approach for Resource and Industry Allocation (MARIA).
(5) Model for Energy Supply Strategy Alternatives and Industry Allocation (MESSAGE).
(6) Mini Climate Assessment Model (MiniCAM).

They are described individually in this survey.

MARIA: Multiregional approach for resource and industry allocation model

Source

(A) Intergovernmental Panel on Climate Change. *Special Report on Emissions Scenarios*. Cambridge: Cambridge University Press, 2000.

Time span: 2100.
Regions: 8 (NAM (USA and Canada), Japan, Other OECD countries, China, ASEAN countries (Indonesia, Malaysia, Philippines, Singapore, Korea, Thailand), SAS (India, Bangladesh, Pakistan, Sri-Lanka), EEFSU (Eastern Europe and the Former Soviet Union), and ALM (Africa and Latin America).
Branch classification: Energy demand consists of industry, transportation, and other public uses.
Energy sources: 9 (fossil (coal, natural gas, oil), biomass, nuclear power, renewable energy technologies (hydropower, solar, wind, geothermal)) (A, p.343).
Scenarios: As defined in the Special Report on Emissions Scenarios (SRES) (A, p.5).
Technology: Nuclear fuel recycling technologies, carbon sequestration technologies are taken into account (A, p.343).
Energy intensity improvement: No.
Lifestyle: No.
Policy tools: No.
Economic linkage: Future GDP growth is projected by potential growth rates (the products of two exogenous assumptions – population and per-capita

GDP growth) and endogenously determined energy costs and prices. Market prices are determined endogenously on the basis of model-calculated shadow prices (A, p.343).

Environment linkage: Energy (long-term profiles of fuel mix changes), food and land use, global warming.

Modelling logic: Intertemporal non-linear optimization model.

Summary

The origin of the model is the Dynamic Integrated Model of Climate and Economy (DICE) model (Nordhaus, 1994). The cost coefficients of energy conversion technologies are extracted from the GLOBAL 2100 model (Manne and Richels, 1992). The latest version of the model incorporates Rogner's estimates on fossil resource availability (Rogner, 1997) (A, p.343). The Global Warming Subsystem is based on Wigley's model for the emission-concentration mechanism (Wigley *et al.*, 1994).

The Food and Land Use module assesses the potential contribution of biomass. Forests are a source of biomass and wood products, but their function as a carbon sink is evaluated (A, p.344).

MARIA is designed for macro-level evaluation, and does not provide information on industrial structural change (A, p.344).

MARKAL models

Sources

(A) Richard Loulou and Amit Kanudia. 'Economic Indicators from a Multi-sector, Multi-region Bottom-up MARKAL Model'. Paper presented at the Joint EMF/IEA/IIASA Meeting, Stanford University, June 2000.
(B) Dolf Gielen and Tom Kram. 'Meeting UNFCCC Target via Materials Policies.' Paper presented at the Joint EMF/IEA/IIASA Meeting, Stanford University, June 2000.

Time span: Depends on the model versions.

Regions: More than 30 stand-alone models (A, p.5). Italy (country model), Matter (EU), Nordic, North America are among 15 participating models in ACROPOLIS (Assessing Climate Response Options through POLIcy Simulations) organized by IEA and EC collaboration project. MARKAL-Europe and MARKAL-US are among 14 models participating in Energy Modelling Forum study on Technology and Global Climate Change Policies.

Branch classification: Depends on the model versions.

Energy sources: Depends on the model versions.

Scenarios: Restricted or extended carbon trade, etc., depending on the model versions.

Technology: More than 5000 technologies in total (A, p.7).

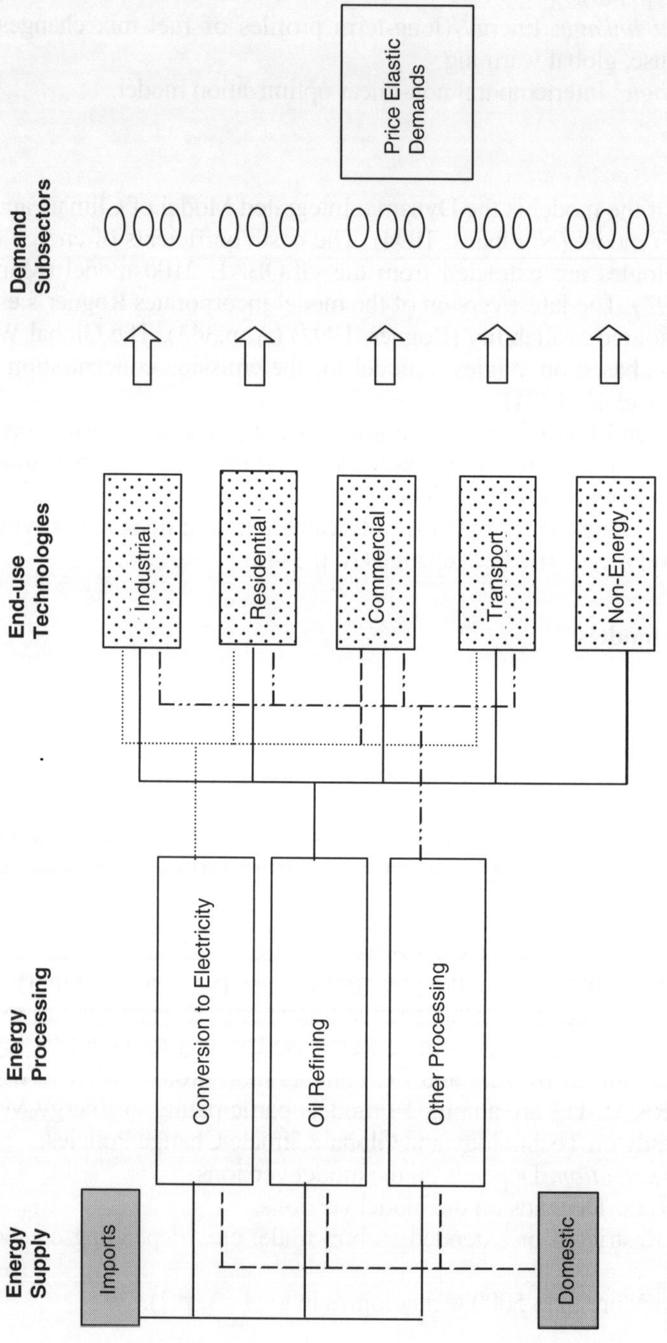

Figure 12-6. MARKAL reference system.
Source: Loulou and Kanudia (2000).

Energy intensity improvement: Embedded in choice of technology.
Lifestyle: No.
Policy tools: International permits (the case of North American MARKAL) (A, p.12).
Economic linkage: Commodity prices are derived based on marginal cost pricing. Equilibrium is based on least total cost (A, p.7).
Environment linkage: Through energy processing and use technologies. Scenarios include energy-related trade (the case of model for Canada)(A).
Modelling logic: Dynamic inter-temporal linear programming.

Summary

The MARKAL linear programming model was developed 20 years ago within the international IEA/ETSAP (International Energy Agency/Energy Technology Systems Analysis Programme) framework. More than 50 institutes in 27 countries use MARKAL as of today, it is reported (B, p.4). MARKAL consists of more than 30 stand-alone models. Most OECD countries and several LDCs are modelled, as well as several multi-regional models (A, p.5).

The economy is modelled as a system represented by processes and physical and monetary flows between these processes (B, p.4). Each piece of equipment is described by its technical parameters, cost parameters, and life duration. Capital turnover is tracked at the technology level (often at plant level) (A, p.7).

This is a technology rich, bottom-up model.
The last generation of the model is capable of producing economic information, such as:

(1) impact on sectors' output (physical and value),
(2) impact on sectors' value added (value),
(3) impact on product prices ($/ton),
(4) impact on trade (ton and value),
(5) impact on consumption (value), and
(6) impact on welfare (net social surplus) (A, p.3).

Future work includes TIMES (The Integrated Markal-Efom System, which is a world-wide, extended partial equilibrium model, with 15-20 regions, and endogenous trade (up to 10 commodities). This attempt, an ongoing project by ETSAP (above), is intended to embody all advances in MARKAL developments (A, p.26).

MARKAL MATTER

Source

(A) Dolf Gielen and Tom Kram. 'Meeting UNFCCC Target via Materials Policies.' Paper presented at the Joint EMF/IEA/IIASA Meeting, Stanford University, June 2000.

Time span: 1980-2000-2060.
Regions: Western Europe as a single region.
Branch classification: No; 150 materials, 100 products, and 30 categories of waste materials covered (A, pp.5-6).
Energy sources: 25 energy carriers. Final energy includes electricity, heat, and biomass (through incineration of waste) (A, p.5).
Scenarios: Constraints are set, representing the demand for products and services, the maximum introduction rate of new processes, the availability of resources, environmental policy goals for energy use and for emissions (A, p.4).
Technology: Processes are characterized by their physical inputs and outputs of energy and material, by their costs, and by their GHG emissions. The model contains a database of several hundred processes, covering the whole life cycle of both energy and materials (A, p.4).
Energy intensity improvement: No. Imbedded in selection of processes.
Lifestyle: No.
Policy tools: GHG policies are represented by emission penalties. The penalty levels have been selected in order to represent a broad spectrum of policy targets. The 20 EURO level corresponds with a 20% emission reduction compared to the base case, and the 200 EURO level corresponds with a 75% emission reduction.
Economic linkage: The demand is price dependent (A, p.4).
Environment linkage: The model is used to calculate the least-cost system configuration for the whole time period, meeting product and service demands and meeting emission reduction targets (A, p.4).
Modelling logic: Linear programming model (A, p.4).

Summary

'The relation between materials production and energy use has received a lot of attention because 60-80% of industrial energy use occurs during materials production. Apart from production, materials transportation represents another 5-10% of total energy use.' 'Little attention has been paid as of yet to energy and environmental strategies that focus on materials consumption. Changes in materials consumption can affect energy use and environmental impacts in other parts of the materials life cycle' (A, pp.1-2).

The MARKAL MATTER model has been built to capture the Western European energy and materials system in order to analyse the dematerialization potentials in detail. The work dates back five years, with participation of a large number of institutes and individuals. Detailed information regarding sub-modules for specific materials and products groups is made available.

In this study, materials include all substances excluding energy carriers and excluding food and fodder (A, p.1). Lifestyle changes can have a very significant impact on energy use and GHG emissions, but the analysis in this study is limited to engineering potentials for existing products. Three types of

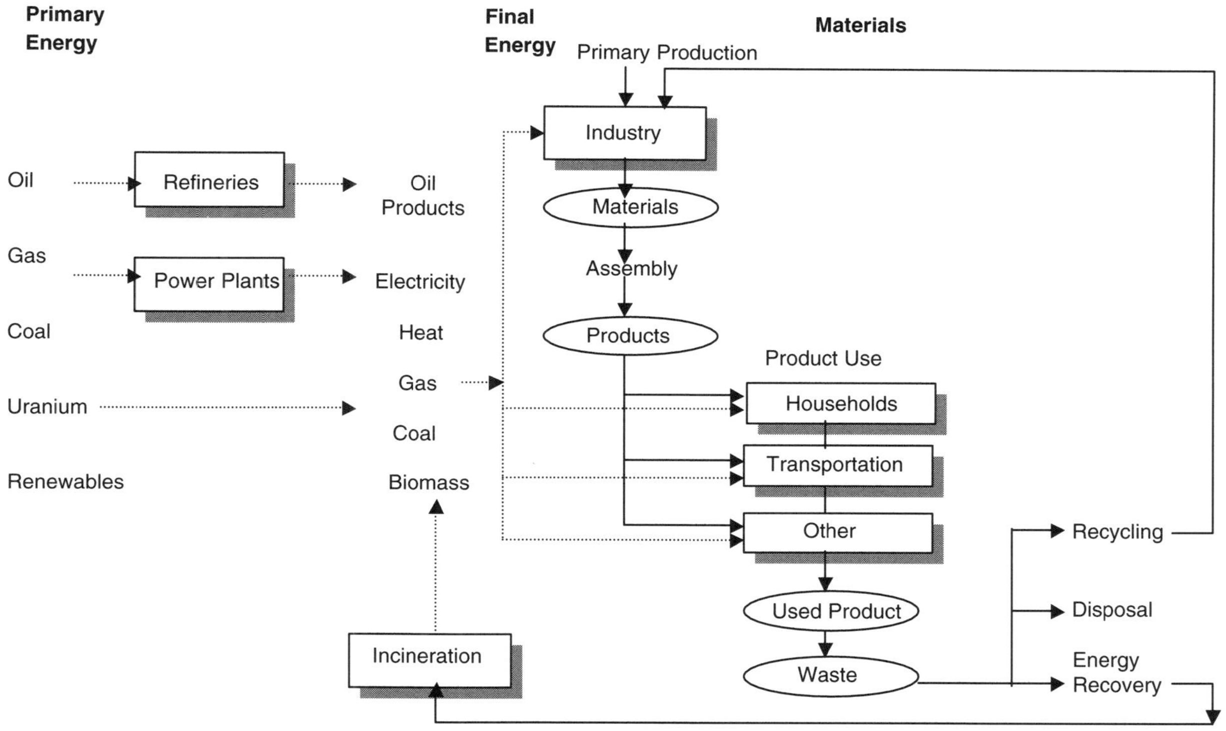

Figure 12-7. MARKAL MATTER energy and materials system model.

Note: Dotted lines represent energy flows; continuous lines represent materials flows.

Source: Gielen and Kram (2000); modified by the present author.

Table 12-15. Design-for-environment technology strategies

Strategy		Description
1	Increased resource efficiency	Reduced losses during materials production
2	Increased materials efficiency	Improvements of the chemical or physical materials quality Reduced variation in materials quality More diverse materials standardization Reduced materials losses during product manufacturing Less materials intensive product design
3	Increased product efficiency	Increased product life More efficient product use, e.g. shared car ownership Development of multi-functional products
4	Recycling/energy recovery of waste materials	Increased waste recovery Increased waste recycling (including cascading) Increased energy recovery
5	Reuse of waste products	Increased product recovery increased product reuse
6	Substitution of natural resources	Renewable organic feedstocks
7	Substitution of materials	Renewable materials (e.g. wood products) Less CO_2 intensive materials Materials with superior physical characteristics Recyclable materials
8	Substitution of products	Less material intensive products Products that require less maintenance Products with longer life, or multifunctional products

Source: Gielen and Kram (2000).

dematerialization strategies are considered explicitly; i.e. (1) increased efficiency of materials use; (2) materials substitution; and (3) recycling/energy recovery (A, p.3).

According to the calculation results, ‘up to 800 Mt GHG emissions reduction (20% of 1990 emission levels) can be achieved through changes in materials consumption’ (A, p.1). ‘The modelling results suggest a 67% emission reduction potential in the materials system’ (A, p.13).

‘Dematerialization strategies result in emission reduction in other parts of the system than where the action takes place. As a consequence, the analysis must consider a number of linked processed simultaneously.’ ‘Two important differences exist between materials use and energy use. First, materials can be recycled and energy can be recovered from organic waste materials, while energy is used and released into the environment.... A life cycle approach is required for proper analysis, instead of a chain approach for energy. Second, materials are stored in products during the product life span. A time lag exists between materials consumption and waste release. As a consequence, proper analysis of materials strategies requires a dynamic approach, contrary to energy analysis.’ ‘The GHG impact of dematerialization depends on energy system characteristics, e.g. the GHG intensity of materials production and the GHG intensity of electricity production. As a consequence an integrated energy and materials systems approach is required, resulting in complex models' (A, p.2).

MERGE: Model for evaluating regional and global effects of GHG reduction policies

Sources

(A) Alan Manne, Robert Mendelsohn, and Richard Richels. 'MERGE: a Model for Evaluating Regional and Global Effects of GHG Reduction Policies.' *Energy Policy*. Vol. 23, No. 1 (1995).
(B) Alan Manne and Richard Richels. 'The Greenhouse Debate: Economic Efficiency, Burden Sharing and Hedging Strategies.' *The Energy Journal*, Vol. 16, No. 4 (1995).
(C) Alan Manne and Richard Richels. 'International Carbon Agreements, EIS Trade and Leakage.' Paper presented at the Joint EMF/IEA/IIASA Meeting, Stanford University, June 2000.

Time span: 1990 to 2200, with 10-year steps from 1990 to 2050, and 25-year steps during the rest of the projection period (A, p.19).
Regions: 5 (the USA, other OECD nations (Western Europe, Japan, Canada, Australia, and New Zealand), the Former USSR, China, and the rest of the world (A, p.19). 9 (USA, OECD-Europe, Japan, CANZ, EEFSU, China, India, Mexico plus OPEC, and the rest of the world) (C, Figure 2).
Branch classification: Energy (electric and non-electric), and an aggregate outside energy (A, p.20).
Energy sources: Electric, non-electric (A, p.20).
Scenarios: Five policy scenarios, i.e.:

(1) business as usual,
(2) a tax on carbon emissions starting at $1/tonne in 2000 and increasing at 5%/year,
(3) a tax on carbon emissions starting at $5/tonne in 2000 and increasing at 5%/year,
(4) stabilizing global CO_2 emissions at 1990 levels, and
(5) stabilizing concentrations of CO_2 in the atmosphere at near current levels.

Technology: Output depends on four inputs (capital, labour, electric and non-electric energy). There are constant returns to scale. There is a unit elasticity of substitution between (1) capital and labour, and (2) electric and non-electric energy. There is a constant elasticity of substitution between (1) and (2).

Energy intensity improvement: There are autonomous energy-efficiency improvements (AEEI) that are summarized by the scaling factor (A, p.21).
Lifestyle: There is a single representative producer-consumer. Savings decisions are made so as to maximize the sum of the discounted utility of consumption (A, p.19).
Policy tools: Tax on carbon emissions (A, p.26).
Economic linkage: Up to 2100 the growth rates represent the average of higher and lower rates in the IPCC's Working Group III. From 2100 onward it is assumed that per-capita growth rates will decline over time, but that the gap between the industrialized countries and the rest of the world will continue to be substantial (A, p.21).
Environment linkage: Energy-economy interactions, resource exhaustion, and the introduction of new technologies (A, p.20).
Modelling logic: General equilibrium model (A, p.19).

Summary

MERGE consists of three major submodels: (1) Global 2200 which is used to assess the economy-wide costs of alternative emission constraints; (2) the climate submodel with focus on greenhouse gases such as carbon dioxide (CO_2), methane (CH_4), and nitrous oxide (N_2O); and (3) the damage assessment submodel which carries out global climate cost-benefit analyses.

Global 2200: This CGE model is composed of 2800 linear and non-linear constraints and 3800 variables, many of which are subject to individual upper bounds (A, p.23). The GDP growth is a key determinant of energy demand. The rate of GDP growth depends on both population and per-capita productivity trends (A, p.21). Potential per-capita projections are made based on constant energy prices. 'Energy consumption need not grow at the same rate as the GDP. Over the long run, they may be decoupled' (A, p.21). These possibilities are represented in Global 2200 through two parameters, ESUB (the elasticity of price-induced substitution) and AEEI (autonomous energy efficiency improvements). ESUB is approximately equal to the absolute value of the price elasticity of demand. The values for ESUB are set at 0.40 for the United States and for the other OECD members. In the other regions of the world, it depends on long-term structural changes in the political and economic system. We have therefore set ESUB at 0.30 for these other three regions' (A, pp.21-22).

AEEI, which represents non-price efficiency improvements, may be brought about, for example, by deliberate changes in public policy, shifts in the economic mix away from manufactured goods and towards services (A, p.22). For most regions and time periods, AEEI of 0.5% per year is assumed regardless of GDP growth rate (A, p.22).

Climate model: The emission of anthropogenic greenhouse gases is divided into energy and non-energy. Energy-related emissions of CO_2, CH_4, and N_2O

Table 12-16. Identification of technologies by MERGE

A. Electricity Generation

Existing Technologies:	Description		
HYDRO	Hydroelectric, geothermal, and other renewables		
GAS-R	Remaining initial gas fired		
OIL-R	Remaining initial oil fired		
COAL-R	Remaining coal fired		
NUC-R	Remaining initial nuclear		
New Technologies:		Earliest possible introduction date (a)	Estimated US cost (b) (Mills.kWh)
GAS-N	Advanced combined cycle, gas fired	1995	34.3(c)
COAL-N	New coal fired	1990	51.0(d)
ADV-HC	High cost carbon free	2010	75.0
ADV-LC	Low cost carbon free	2020	50.0

a Estimated year when technology could provide 0.1 trillion kWh (approximately 20 GW of installed capacity at 60% capacity factor). For the other OECD region, we assume that the technology could provide 0.2 trillion kWh by this date.

b Based on 1990 dollar.

c Based on price of gas in 1990. Gas prices are projected to rise over time.

d Estimated costs are assumed to be 10 mills/kWh higher in the other OECD region due to higher fuel costs.

Table 12-16. continued

B. Non-electric Energy Supplies

Technology Name	Description	Carbon Emission Coefficient (Tons of Carbon per GJ of Crude Oil Equivalent)	Unit US Cost per GJ of Crude Oil Equivalent (1990 Dollars)
OIL-MX	Oil imports or exports	0.0199	3.70 in 1990 rising over time
CLDU	Coal – direct uses	0.0241	2.00
OIL-LC	Oil – low cost	0.0199	2.50
GAS-LC	Natural gas – low cost	0.0137	2.75(a)
OIL-HC	Oil – high cost	0.0199	3.00
GAS-HC	Natural gas – high cost	0.0137	4.25(a)
RNEW	Renewables	0.0000	6.00
SYNF	Synthetic fuels	0.0400	8.33
NE-BAK	Nonelectric backup	0.0000	16.67

a To allow for gas distribution costs, $1.25 per GJ is added to the wellhead price.

Source: Manne, Mendelsohm, Richels (1995).

are projected by fuel type for each period up to 2200, whereas emissions from other sources are exogenous to the model (A, pp.23-25).

Damage assessment submodel: Global cost-benefit analysis has to deal with damage in terms of (1) marketed goods and (2) non-marketed factors such as biodiversity, environmental quality, and human health. 'Many cost-benefit calculations ignore the issue altogether and confine their analyses to economically measurable consequences only' (A, p.25). The paper deals with this issue through a willingness-to-pay approach. 'The issue is framed in the context of how much the consumers in each region would be willing to pay to avoid ecological damages. Each region values ecological damages independently of where such damage occurs, whether they occur within or outside their own boundaries. The S-shaped function implies, however, that lower income regions will place a lower value on such losses than higher income regions' (A, p.26). 'Rather than advocate any particular set of numbers, we will explore the implications of alternative valuations' (A, p.26).

Changing location of production: MERGE has been modified to include the possibility of changes in the location of production of the energy-intensive sectors (EIS). EIS is an aggregate composed of ferrous and non-ferrous metals, chemicals, non-metallic minerals, paper, pulp and print. It does not include petroleum refining (C, p.1).

The GTAP database is employed to estimate initial EIS demand in each region (C, p.1).

'For projecting the impact of the Kyoto Protocol, each region is taken to be self-sufficient in EIS at base year energy prices. Each of the nine MERGE regions is sufficiently large to be nearly self-sufficient with respect to EIS. Changes in the location of production are attributed primarily to changes in the cost of energy. At base year prices in the USA about 85% of the cost of EIS consisted of non-energy inputs (labour and capital charges, shipping, iron ore, etc.), and 15% of the cost consisted of energy inputs. ... Under these conditions, a doubling of energy prices would imply only a 15% increase in the cost of EIS. This is why it is assumed that the demand for EIS is inelastic with respect to the price of energy. For projecting future demands, the income elasticity for EIS is taken to be 0.5' (C, p.1).

The analysis is constructed upon the Heckscher-Ohlin fraction, which is the relative price of imports at which domestic supplies drop to zero. 'The intercept of the non-energy supply curve for EIS in each region may be described as a Heckscher-Ohlin fraction. If this intercept is unity, EIS is viewed as a perfectly homogeneous commodity. Small change in energy cost will then lead to large changes in the international location of production. If the intercept is less than unity, the supply function is less elastic, and the changes in location will be less dramatic' (C, p.1).

The Kyoto Protocol 'exempts non-Annex B countries from any obligation to restrict greenhouse emissions. Accordingly, they will have an artificial incentive to produce EIS – even though their energy and carbon coefficients may be higher than in Annex B. This is bound to exacerbate the problem of leakage – that is, an increase in non-Annex B emissions associated with a reduction in those of Annex B.' 'Annex B reductions will impose downward pressure upon international oil and gas prices. This will lower the export earnings of two of our major regions: EFFSU (Eastern Europe + Former Soviet Union) and MOPEC (Mexico + OPEC). These lower prices would stimulate the importing countries to increase their consumption of oil and gas' (C, p.3).

Major findings are: (1) Leakage is a distinct possibility. (2) During the early decades of the 21st century, leakage would be associated primarily with EIS trade; during the middle decades, leakage would be associated primarily with trade in oil and gas. (3) Leakage ratios are sensitive to the numerical values of the EIS trade parameters (C, p. 4).

MESSAGE: Model for energy supply strategy alternatives and their general environmental impact

Sources

(A) Intergovernmental Panel on Climate Change. *Special Report on Emissions Scenarios*. Cambridge: Cambridge University Press, 2000.
(B) S. Messner and M. Strubegger. *User's Guide for MESSAGE III*, WP-95-69. International Institute for Applied Systems Analysis. Laxenburg, Austria, 1995.

Time span: 2100.
Regions: 10 (Former Soviet Union, Eastern Europe, Western Europe, North America, Pacific OECD, Pacific Asia, South Asia, Centrally Planned Asia, Middle East and North Africa, Sub-Saharan Africa, and Latin America) (A, p.338).
Branch classification: Energy sector and industrial emission sources only, and agricultural and land-use related emissions are not included.
Energy sources: Detailed.
Scenarios: As defined in the Special Report on Emissions Scenarios (SRES) (A, p.5). Scenario Generator (SG) model derives energy demand path consistent with historical dynamics and with the specific scenario features, such as high or moderate economic growth or rapid or gradual energy intensity improvements. Empirically estimated equations of trends are employed (A, p.341).
Technology: Menu of technologies is given. The model calculates cost-minimal supply structure under a set of constraints (A, p.341).
Energy intensity improvement: Incorporated in scenarios.
Lifestyle: No.
Policy tools: Not explicit.

Economic linkage: Exogenous assumptions about per-capita economic growth and population by region.
Environment linkage: Energy system structure, including energy demand, supply, and emissions patterns (A, p.341).
Modelling logic: Dynamic linear programming model.

Table 12-17. Selected energy technologies represented in MESSAGE

Technology Aggregates	Including
Centralized Electricity Generation:	
Coal conventional	Conventional coal power plants with DESOX (fuel gas desulfurization, FGD) and DENOX (flue-gas denitrification)
IGCC	Integrated coal Gasification Combined Cycle
Coal fuel cell	Coal-based high-temperature fuel cell (internal reforming)
Oil	New standard oil power plant (Rankine cycle, low Nox, and with FGD); existing crude oil and light oil engine-plants; light oil combined cycle power plants
Gas standard	Standard gas power plant (Rankine cycle, potential for cogeneration)
NGCC	Natural Gas-fired Combined cycle power plant with DENOX
NGFC	Natural Gas-powered high-temperature Fuel Cell, cogeneration possibilities
Bio	New biomass-fired power plant (Rankine cycle, cogeneration possibilities), advanced biomass plants (gasified biomass is burned in combined gas turbines)
Nuclear	Conventional, existing nuclear power plants
Advanced nuclear/other	Nuclear high-temperature reactors for electricity and hydrogen co-production, future inherently safe nuclear reactor designs, and other future zero-carbon electricity-generating technologies for base load
Hydro	Hydropower plants (low and high cost)
Wind	Wind power plant
Other renewables	Geothermal power plant (cogeneration potential); grid-connected solar photo-voltaic power plant (no storage); solar thermal power plants with storage, and solar thermal power plant for hydrogen production
Decentralized Electricity Generation:	
Hydrogen fuel cell	Decentralized stationary and mobile hydrogen fuel cells (cogeneration systems or off-hours electricity generation)
Photo-voltaics	On-site solar photo-voltaic power plant in the residential and/or commercial sectors, and in the industrial sector
Synfuels:	
Coal synliquids	Light oil and methanol production from coal
Biomass synliquids	Ethanol production from biomass
Gas synliquids	Methanol production from natural gas
Syngases	Syngases from various sources, including biomass and coal gasification
Hydrogen H2 (1)	Hydrogen production from fossil fuels (coal or gas)
Hydrogen H2(2), (3)	Non-fossil hydrogen production: H2(2): from biomass and electricity H2(3): from nuclear and solar

Source: IPCC (2000).

Summary

MESSAGE is an energy systems engineering model, and is one of the six models that constitute IIASA's integrated modelling framework, which includes:

(1) Scenario Generator (SG) model,
(2) Linked MESSAGE (bottom-up type) and MACRO (top-down type),
(3) Regional Air Pollution Impacts Model (RAIMS),
(4) Basic Linked System of National Agricultural Models (BLS),
(5) Model for Assessment of GHG-Included Climate Change (MAGICC), and
(6) General Circulation Model (GCM) (A, p.342).

MESSAGE is a bottom-up type model that calculates cost-minimal supply structure under the constraints of resource availability, the set of given technologies, and the demand for useful energy. It generates energy demand, supply, and emission patterns that are consistent with the development produced by the SG. MACRO, on the other hand, is a top-down model, built on the Global 2100 model (Manne and Richels, 1992). Solution is obtained by maximizing the inter-temporal utility function in each world region. It establishes the relationship between macroeconomic development and energy use. MESSAGE and MACRO are linked and used in tandem (A, p.341).

In one of the scenarios (B2 market), it is reported that the price-induced energy demand savings are 8% by 2020, 23% by 2050, and 30% by 2100 (A, p.341). In addition, the MESSAGE model was used to quantify four scenario groups of the A1 story line and a number of scenarios of the B1 story line of the SRES.

In the B2 market, shadow prices for international trade are calculated as follows (A, p.342) (1990 US$/GJ):

Year	Gas	Coal	Oil
2020	0.4	0.3	0.5
2050	0.7	0.4	1.1
2100	0.7	1.1	2.3

MIDAS: Multinational integrated demand and supply

Source

(A) P. Capros, P. Karadeloglou, L. Mantzos, and G. Mentzas. 'The Energy Model MIDAS.' In Jean-Baptiste Lasourd, Jacques Percebois, and François Valette, eds. *Models for Energy Policy*. London: Routledge, 1996.

Time span: 10 years (A, p.41).
Regions: United Kingdom, Italy, France, and Germany (A, p.43).

Table 12-18. Policy analysis that can be studied with MIDAS

Crude-oil prices	Impacts of international crude-oil price shocks
Fiscal policy	Changes of tax-rates on energy products and sectors
Investment programs	Impact on energy demand and supply and on equilibrium energy prices of alternative technological and utilities investment programs; impact of nuclear programs
Demand policy	Direct and secondary impacts of incentives and measures in the energy demand side
Impact of growth	Energy system impacts and secondary effects of macro-economic policy and forecasts
Sectoral policy	Energy system impact evaluation of specific energy sectoral policies (natural gas, mining, refineries, etc.)
Environmental policy	Carbon tax policy, impacts evaluation and potential assessment of pollution abatement equipment and reduced emission technologies
Forecasts	Consistent construction of future EUROSTAT balances and price-lists; e.g. Energy 2010 studies of CEC
EC issues	Tax harmonization, EC unified market analysis, elimination of trade barriers

Source: Capros, Karadeloglou, Mantzos, and Mentzas (1996).

Branch classification: Electricity use of the MIDAS Demand model has iron and steel, non-ferrous metals, chemicals, building materials, paper and pulp, other industries, space heating, cooking and water, specific uses, transport, exports (A, pp.49-50).

Energy sources: Electricity, petroleum, coal, natural gas, synthetic gas (A, p.44).

Scenarios: Technological characteristics. As a single-country model it has no international linkages.

Technology: Described in detail in sub-models on electricity production, petroleum refining, coal mining, natural gas distribution, synthetic gas and coal production.

Energy intensity improvement: Not explicit.

Lifestyle: As reflected in energy use.

Policy tools: Fiscal policy, investment programme, demand policy (A, p.46).

Economic linkage: Crude oil prices, demand policy (A, p.46).

Environment linkage: Environmental policy, e.g. carbon-tax policy, pollution abatement, reduced emission technologies (A, p.46).

Modelling logic: Bottom-up technology model. Macroeconomic variables are exogenous.

Summary

MIDAS is developed under the auspices of CEC/DG-XII (A, p.41). The complete MIDAS model is available for the United Kingdom, Italy, France, and Germany.

MIDAS is linked to the macroeconomic model HERMES and a sub-model that evaluates CO_2 emissions (A, p.41, p.43).

MIDAS is a country-specific energy model for European countries covering both demand and supply of energy. The energy demand sub-model is an econometric system using relative prices of energy to estimate energy demand and energy substitution by sector. Energy supply consists of five sub-models; namely electricity generation, petroleum refining, natural gas and synthetic gas, coal mining and coke-oven plants (A, p.41).

The paper offers interesting observations about price determination. 'Models built for the USA energy system generally retain a price-adjustment formulation. … On the contrary, European energy models … such as MIDAS retain quantity adjustment formulation. This difference reflects the diverse conditions that prevail in energy markets' (A, p.43). 'If the market clearing price p^* is calculated such that $D = S$, then the market is formulated as a price adjusted one. Such a formulation corresponds to a perfectly competitive market. … If the market has an oligopolistic or monopolistic character and competiton does not operate perfectly, supply firms may adopt a cost mark-up pricing policy. In this case, prices are a function of supply, i.e. $p = p(S)$ while demand and supply are rationed by each other at the given level of prices so that $D = S = min\{D(p), S(p)\}$. ... This market clearing formulation is called quantity-adjustment. If we further assume excess supply in the market, … we may calculate this case, prices are a function of supply, i.e. $p = p(S)$ while demand and supply are rationed by each other at the given level of prices so that $D = S = min\{D(p), S(p)\}$. ... This market clearing formulation is called quantity-adjustment. If we further assume excess supply in the market, … we may calculate a rate of capacity utilization as $U = S/S^*$ where $S^* = S(P)$. This rate may influence prices, i.e. $p = p(S, U)$, representing the disequilibrium pressures exerted on price formulation' (A, p.43).

MiniCAM: The mini climate assessment model

Source

(A) Intergovernmental Panel on Climate Change. *Special Report on Emissions Scenarios*. Cambridge: Cambridge University Press, 2000.

Time span: 2100.

Regions: 11 (Centrally Planned Europe, OECD-Europe, Canada, USA, Oceania, Japan, South East Asia, Centrally Planned Asia, Middle East, Africa, Latin America) (A, p.338). A 14-region version is being prepared (A, p.344).

Branch classification: 3 (industrial, transportation, residential/commercial).

Energy sources: 7 (coal, oil, gas, nuclear, hydro, solar, and biomass) (A, p.344).

Scenarios: As defined in the Special Report on Emissions Scenarios (SRES) (A, p.5).

Technology: Labour productivity increase in the long term as part of scenario exercise (A, p.344).

Energy intensity improvement: Represented by the improvement in end-use energy efficiency (A, p.345). 'Fuel-specific rates of technical change are available for primary fuel production and conversion, as are technical change coefficients for each category of electricity production' (A, p.344).

Lifestyle: No.

Policy tools: No.

Economic linkage: Prices adjust energy supply and demand. Population times aggregate labour productivity exogenous. The resultant estimate of GNP is corrected for changes in energy prices using GNP/energy elasticity. Detailed age breakdown and labour force participation rates to deal with population scenarios (A, p.344).

Environment linkage: Global GHG emissions; agriculture, forestry and land use; climate change; impacts of climate change through damage functions.

Modelling logic: FRB is a partial equilibrium model.

Summary

MiniCAM is being developed by the Global Change Group at Pacific Northwest Laboratory. It has recently expanded to deal with emissions of GHG gases (A, p.344). The MiniCAM framework integrates ERB model for global GHG emission estimates (Edmonds *et al.*, 1994, 1996), MAGICC model for climate change assessment (Wigley and Raper, 1993), the SCENGEN tool to deal with regional climate changes (Hulme *et al.*, 1995), and the Manne *et al.* (1995) damage functions to examine the impacts of climate change (A, p.344).

Energy demand is estimated for 3 categories of activities (residential/commercial, industrial, and transportation) as a function of price and income. Energy services are provided by 4 secondary fuels (solids, liquids, gases, and electricity), demand for which depends on their relative costs and the improvement in the end-use energy efficiency. Demand for primary fuels is determined by the relative costs of transforming them into the secondary fuels (A, p.344).

The energy supply sector provides both renewable and non-renewable resources. The cost of fossil resources relates to the resource base by grade. This practice allows the model to test the importance of fossil fuel constraints. Unconventional fuels such as oil shale and methane hydrates are potentially available at high cost, or after extensive technology development. The cost of production includes both technical and environmental factors (A, p.345).

Biomass is supplied by the agriculture sector, and provides the linkage with the land-use model and the energy model.

MS-MRT: Multi-sector, Multi-region trade model

Sources

(A) Paul M. Bernstein, W. David Montgomery, Thomas F. Rutherford, and Gui-Fang Yang. 'Effects of Restrictions on International Permit Trading.' *Energy Journal*, May 1999.

Table 12-19. Carbon permit trade

	2010						
	Permit Price (1995$ / Ton)			Permit Purchases (Million of Tons of Carbon)		Permit Purchases (Billion of 1995 Dollars)	
Countries/Regions	NT	A1	GL	A1	GL	A1	GL
USA	274	89	30	305.0	461.8	27.3	13.2
JPN	482	89	30	57.4	81.1	5.1	2.4
EUR	211	89	30	103.5	165.1	9.2	5.0
OOE (other OECD)	246	89	30	40.1	61.9	3.6	1.9
SEA (south-east Asia)	0	0	30	0.0	−49.0	NA	−1.5
OAS (other Asia)	0	0	30	0.0	−12.0	NA	−0.4
CHI (China & India)	0	0	30	0.0	−274.6	NA	−7.5
FSU (Eastern Europe & former SU)	0	89	30	−506.0	−311.8	−45.2	−9.4
MPC (Mexico & OPEC)	0	0	30	0.0	−58.3	NA	−1.8
ROW	0	0	30	0.0	−91.3	NA	−2.8

Countries/Regions	2030						
	Permit Price (1995$ / Ton)			Permit Purchases (Million of Tons of Carbon)		Permit Purchases (Billion of 1995 Dollars)	
	NT	A1	GL	A1	GL	A1	GL
USA	353	224	32	180.4	709.40	40.4	22.5
JPN	526	224	32	108.5	183.90	24.3	5.8
EUR (EU of 15)	431	224	32	184.8	429.00	41.4	13.6
OOE (other OECD)	505	224	32	59.1	141.20	13	4.5
SEA (south-east Asia)	0	0	32	0	−123.30	NA	−3.9
OAS (other Asia)	0	0	32	0	−37.60	NA	−1.2
CHI (China & India)	0	0	32	0	−901.30	NA	−28.6
FSU (Eastern Europe & former SU)	50	224	32	−532.8	−6.10	−119.5	−0.2
MPC (Mexico & OPEC)	0	0	32	0	−153.80	NA	−4.9
ROW	0	0	32	0	−241.40	NA	−7.7

Source: Bernstein, Montgomery, Rutherford, and Yang (1999).

(B) Paul M. Bernstein, W. David Montgomery, and Thomas Rutherford. 'Global Impacts of the Kyoto Agreement: Results from the MS-MRT Model.' Paper presented at the Joint Meeting organized by the International Energy Agency, Energy Modeling Forum, and the International Energy Workshop (IIASA), 16-18 June 1999b, Paris.
(C) Paul Bernstein. 'MS-MRT Model Enhancements and Results.' Paper presented at the Joint EMF/IEA/IIASA Meeting, Stanford University, June 2000.

Time span: 2000 to 2030 with 5-year intervals (A, p.223).
Regions: 10 (United States, Japan, Europe Union of 15, Other OECD, Eastern Europe and Former Soviet Union, China and India, South East Asia (Korea, Singapore, Taiwan, Thailand, and Malaysia), Other Asia, Mexico and OPEC, Rest of the world) (A, p.224). New version incorporates 9 global regions, 35 individual countries (C, p.2).
Branch classification: 6, including 4 energy forms (oil, coal, natural gas, electricity) and 2 non-energy goods (energy intensive sectors and all other goods) (A, p.224).
Energy sources: 4 (oil, coal, natural gas, and electricity) (A, p.224).
Scenarios: (1) No-trade scenario where the emissions permits are tradable within each Annex I region but not across regions; (2) the Annex I trading scenarios where permits are tradable across Annex I countries; and (3) the global trading scenarios where the permits are tradable throughout the world (A, p.232, p. 234). 10%, 30%, and 50% ceiling on satisfying country's emissions obligation through purchase of emissions permits (A, p.241).
Technology: Represented by key elasticities. See below.
Energy intensity improvement: Assumed (A, p.233).
Lifestyle: Infinitely-lived representative agent allocates region's entire lifetime income in different time periods in order to maximize welfare (A, p.227). The consumer faces the choice between current consumption and future consumption purchased via savings (A, p.227).
Policy tools: Emissions trading along three scenarios. See above.
Economic linkage: The business-as-usual growth rates from MERGE by Alan Manne and Richard Richels. The energy production and consumption forecasts as well as regional emissions from the Department of Energy Information Center's.
International Energy Outlook, 1998 (A, p.233). Key elasticities are assumed (oil supply price elasticity, Armington elasticity, demand elasticity, interfuel elasticity of substitution, and the cost of the carbon-free backstop technology) (A, p.233). New version includes fully dynamic treatment of investment, saving, and capital flows (C, p.2).
Environment linkage: Emissions trading.
Modelling logic: Dynamic, general equilibrium model (A, p.222).

Summary

The work is intended to respond to some of the key questions concerning the Kyoto Protocol.

Distribution of economic impacts across regions: how will developing countries be affected by emission limits adopted by the industrial countries? How will the cost of reducing emissions be distributed among countries?

Carbon leakage and effects on international competition: how will energy-intensive industries be affected when some countries agree to binding emission limits and others do not? How large will leakage of carbon emissions from participating to non-participating countries be?

Effects of international emission permit trading: how will emission limits and international permit trading affect the terms of trade and capital flows between countries? Who will be the buyers and sellers of permits in an international permit trading system? Will developing countries be made better or worse off by participating in a system of international permit trading? (B, pp.2-3).

'Countries have argued extensively over the equitable structuring of an international permit trading protocol. The United States has advocated unrestricted emissions trading, extended as rapidly as possible to include key non-Annex I countries. The European Union and a number of developing countries have proposed tight restrictions on emissions trading and oppose any efforts to include non-Annex I countries. Russia has made it clear that its participation in the Kyoto Protocol is contingent on its unrestricted ability to sell permits to other Annex I counties' (A, p.222).

The paper considers several different Annex I trading regimes (A, pp.241-242):

(1) Ceilings on percentage of a country's emissions obligation that may be satisfied through the purchase of emissions permits. 10%, 30%, and 50% limits are suggested.
(2) Impacts of prohibiting the East European and Former Soviet Union region from selling its 'hot air'. 'Hot air' or paper tons refer to the positive difference between the Kyoto emissions targets for the EE/FSU and its actual forecasted emissions. This resulted from its economic decline since 1990.
(3) The case where EE/FSU exercise some market power and charge a monopoly price for its emissions permits.
(4) Restrictions on sales where countries are allowed to sell only 30% of the amount they would sell under unrestricted Annex I trading.
(5) Comparisons of full global trading with clean development mechanism (CDM).

Of the alternative measures of economic impacts (including change in consumers surplus measured by the equivalent valuation, the discounted present value of consumption, GDP, and direct costs), the paper employs the intertemporal equivalent variation (A, p.237).

MS-MRT is based on the GTAP database (C, p.2).

New Earth 21 (Sometimes referred to as DNE21 or Dynamic New Earth)

Source

(A) Kenichiro Nishio, Yasumasa Fujii, and Kenji Yamaji, 'Analysis of the Kyoto Mechanisms using a Global System Model DNE21.' Paper presented at the Joint EMF/IEA/IIASA Meeting, Stanford University, June 2000.

Time span: Up to 2020 with a two-year step.
Regions: 10 (North America, Latin America, Western Europe, Former USSR and Eastern Europe, Middle East and Northern Africa, Subsaharan and Southern Africa, South and East Asia, China, Japan, Oceania) (A, p.2).
Branch classification: No.
Energy sources: 9 primary (natural gas, oil, coal, biomass, photovoltaics, wind and other renewables, hydro, geothermal, nuclear). 4 secondary (gaseous fuel, liquid fuel, solid fuel, electricity), where liquid fuel is decomposed into 3 (gasoline, light fuel oil, and heavy fuel oil) (A, p.3).
Scenarios: Constraints represent supply-demand balances, energy and CO_2 balances in the various types of energy processing plants, several inter-temporal dynamics such as depletion of fossil fuel resources and limitations on the maximum growth rates of annual fuel production.
Technology: Detailed description of conversion from primary energy sources to secondary energy carriers.
Energy intensity improvement: No. Embedded in technology selection.
Lifestyle: No.
Policy tools: Emission trading, clean development mechanism, banking and borrowing of emission reduction (A, pp.4-5).
Economic linkage: Future energy demands are exogenously given (A, p.3).
Environment linkage: CO_2 emission reductions.
Modelling logic: Multi-period inter-temporal nonlinear optimization. Objective function is defined as the sum of the discounted total energy system costs distributed over time (5% discount rate) (A, p.2).

Summary

New Earth 21 is an engineering process model.

Two sets of analysis are provided based on mathematical formulation of the Kyoto Mechanisms. Formulations correspond to:

Case 0: without the Kyoto Mechanism with Kyoto Mechanism
Case 1: No trading
Case 2: Emissions trading

Case 3: Emissions trading + clean development mechanism
Case 4: Emissions trading + clean development mechanism (including the banking)

The first analysis concerns the potential of the Kyoto Mechanism in the first commitment period, i.e. 2000 to 2008-2012 (6 representative time points). The whole annual emission in case 0 (BAU) reaches 9000 Mt-C/year by 2012, implying 1.5 times as much as that of 1990. The average emission of Annex I regions during the 1st commitment period is 4873 Mt-C/year (21% over 1990 levels). In Case 2 the emission increases a little by the so-called hot air of FSSU and Eastern European countries. In Cases 3 and 4 a noticeable amount of emission credits will be transferred from non-Annex I regions to Annex I regions. Furthermore, the banking of CDM stimulates the reduction of non-Annex I regions during the interim period (A, pp.5-6).

The second analysis includes both the 1st and the 2nd commitment period, and the time horizon is extended to 2000 to 2018 (9 representative time points). Here, CDM action during the interim period enables Annex I regions to bank the emission reductions from the 1st commitment period to the 2nd commitment period. Various cases are simulated (A, pp.7-8).

The PRIMES project, European Commission

Sources

(A) European Commission, Directorate-General XII Science, Research and Development, *The PRIMES Project*. EUR 16713 EN. Brussels and Luxembourg: European Commission. 1995.

Time span: 1990-2030 (A, p.11).
Regions: 12 European Union countries (Belgium, Denmark, France, Germany, Greece, Ireland, Italy, Luxembourg, the Netherlands, Portugal, Spain, and the United Kingdom) (A, p.11).
Branch classification: Residential, commercial, industry (6 sub-sectors: iron and steel, non-ferrous metals, building materials, chemicals, paper and pulp, and other industries), transport (4 transport modes) (A, p.14).
Energy sources: Coal (3 types), oil (4 different refineries), natural gas (regional detail), electricity (A, p.14).
Scenarios: Operate on decision variables. See below.
Technology: 50 thermal generation technologies, all renewables. 2 technology vintages for residential sector, 2 technology vintages for commercial sector, 4 fuels for industry sector, 4 transport modes and different car technologies in transport sector (A, p.14).
Energy intensity improvement: Embedded in technology penetration structure by fuel use.
Lifestyle: Embedded in 'individual agents' behavior'.

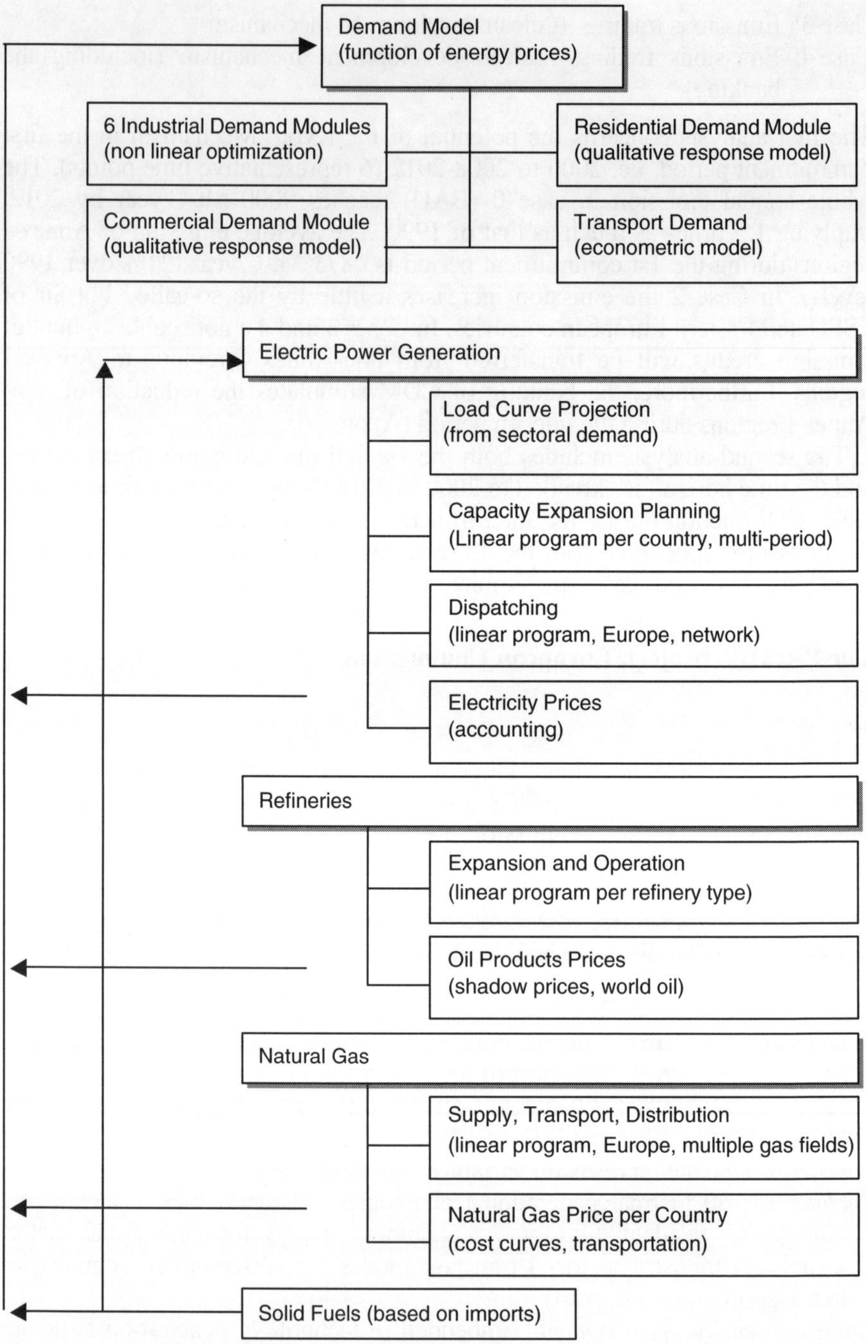

Figure 12-8. General model structure of PRIME.

Source: European Commission (1995).

Policy tools: Standards, taxes, tradables (A, p.67). Third-party access for electricity (A, p.12). Decision variables introduced in the optimization routine (A, p.18).

Economic linkage: Market clearing energy prices, individual agents' behaviour (A, p.12).

Environment linkage: Emissions of CO_2, SO_x, and NO_x (A, p.14, p.67).

Modelling logic: Partial equilibrium (A, p.11). Non-linear optimization (A, p.18).

Summary

'PRIMES is a partial equilibrium model for the European energy system and market, including environmental applications' (A, p.7). 'The PRIMES model combines the detailed "bottom-up" technological approach ... with an accurate presentation of the different energy markets and the feedback between supply and demands as determined by market prices' (A, p.12).

'PRIMES is developed under JOULE II, which is a programme on non-nuclear energy (1991-1994). The general objective of the JOULE II is 'to contribute to the development of (1) economically viable and environmentally safer energy options, and (2) energy saving technologies. The programme covers four areas, namely: (1) analysis of strategies and modelling, (2) minimum emission power reduction from fossil fuels, (3) renewable energy sources, and (4) energy utilization and conservation. The sub-programme, 'analysis of strategies and modelling', focuses on 'the utilization of Community-wide models to analyze the different energy, environmental and related economic policies.' (A, pp.5-6).

Under the JOULE II programme, other models such as GEM-E3, E3-ME, WARM, MEGAPESTES, POLES, and SAFIRE have been developed besides PRIMES (A, p.7).

Compared to previous models available to the European Commission, PRIMES differs in the following points.

(1) Formation of energy prices is explicitly considered. It calculates price equilibria in each energy market.
(2) Market clearing mechanisms are the main explanatory force in the model, making it suitable for providing realistic trends towards the liberalization of European energy markets.
(3) The behaviour of individual agents is recognized, removing the central planning paradigm.
(4) Details about technologies are contained in both supply and demand (A, pp.11-12).

The decision variables (fuel switching, cogeneration, exploitation of renewable energy, use of recycled material and scrap, consumption of by-products, and heat recovery) represent a number of options in satisfying demand while minimizing costs. 'The optimisation process is also constrained by upper limits on pollutant emissions, but measures can be taken to alleviate this constraint by either investing in pollution abatement equipment and/or by purchasing pollution permits' (A, p.18).

The prototype model focuses on: (1) global warming and (2) acid deposition and ambient quality. For this purpose, energy-related emissions of CO_2, NO_x, and SO_2 are investigated (A, p.67).

The following policy instruments are considered in the prototype.

(1) A minimum abatement percentage compared to a reference level.
(2) Prescriptive technological standards or fuel quality.
(3) Emission or product charges.
(4) Tradable permits (A, p.69).

This is in contrast to the main instruments actually used at EU or national levels which are 'command and control' type, such as emission standards, technology standards for motor vehicles (imposition of catalytic converter), and fuel quality standards (regulation of sulphur content) (A, p.69).

RAINS-Asia

Sources

(A) Resource Management Association. *RESGEN: Regional Energy Scenario Generator for Asia*. Madison, 1996.
(B) Markus Amman and Jhuzer Dhoondia. *RAINS-Asia User's Manual*. Washington, D.C.: International Bank for Reconstruction and Development, 1994.

Time span: 2000-2010-2020.
Regions: 23 plus sea lanes (Bangladesh, Bhutan, Brunei, Cambodia, China, Hong Kong, India, Indonesia, Japan, Korea (North), Korea (South), Laos, Malaysia, Mongolia, Myanmar, Nepal, Pakistan, Philippines, Sea lanes, Singapore, Sri Lanka, Sri Lanka, Taiwan, Thailand, Vietnam). 94 sub-national regions.
Branch classification: 6 (fuel production and conversion, power plants and district heating, household and other consumers, transport, industry, non-energy use) with sub-divisions by process.
Energy sources: 17 (brown coal/lignite (high grade), brown coal/lignite (low grade), hard coal (high grade), hard coal (medium), hard coal (low quality), derived coal, other solid (low S), other solid (high S), heavy fuel oil, medium distillates (diesel, light fuel oil), light fraction (gasoline, kerosene, naphtha, LPG), gas, renewable (solar, wind, small hydro), hydro, nuclear, electricity, heat).
Scenarios: Default base case energy scenario is based on country projections of energy consumption as much as possible (A, p.47). Low energy scenario assumes the overall energy intensity improvement by 26%.

Table 12-20. RAINS-Asia energy consumption projection by country (unit: petajoules)

	1990	2000	2000	2010	2010	2020	2020
Country		Base	Low	Base	Low	Base	Low
Bangladesh	805	1062	1019	1554	1427	2363	1965
Bhutan	22	31	30	41	40	58	56
Brunei	62	130	122	171	149	229	178
Cambodia	101	183	161	354	258	757	454
China	30255	50527	433438	73518	59132	101016	75348
Hong Kong	422	662	619	912	762	1211	980
India	15812	22908	20192	36932	29764	63622	48368
Indonesia	3739	6247	5879	9250	7769	13684	10139
Japan	17866	22606	20188	25679	20914	28809	21536
North Korea	1764	3186	2826	4980	3923	7910	5455
South Korea	3594	6264	5814	9497	7793	13449	9744
Laos	38	56	55	82	79	121	108
Malaysia	1060	1953	1928	3457	3186	6031	4686
Mongolia	151	193	178	260	212	361	266
Myanmar	309	426	421	577	567	737	719
Nepal	270	357	336	467	425	615	514
Pakistan	1436	2531	2359	4353	3910	7361	6391
Philippines	585	1082	948	1921	1820	3113	2401
Sea Lanes	163	208	208	266	266	343	343
Singapore	342	645	641	1130	1061	1731	1522
Sri Lanka	190	399	285	502	372	632	432
Taiwan	2094	3334	2910	4796	4241	6843	5771
Thailand	1688	3292	2903	5693	4482	9326	6697
Vietnam	772	1186	1176	2118	1926	3801	3358
Total	83594	129468	114669	188528	154476	274121	207431

Note: Base refers to base case scenario, and Low to efficiency/low energy scenario.

Source: Resource Management Association (1996).

Technology: Energy intensities, fuels and power plant specifications, and locations.

Energy intensity improvement: For each of the 23 countries, base case (business-as-usual) and energy efficiency scenarios are provided (A, p.32). The efficiency improvements through 2020 are based on the experiences of industrialized countries during the period 1973-1983 as they responded to the sharp rise in energy prices (A, p.48).

Lifestyle: No.

Policy tools: Technology-driven cost-curves, free and competitive market for the exchange of emission control technology.

Economic linkage: No feedback. Country GDP and sub-national GDP needed (A, p.34). GDP is disaggregated into end-use sectors (industrial, commercial, agriculture, residential, non-energy, transportation) (A, p.35).

Environment linkage: Energy, sulphur.

Modelling logic: Based on socioeconomic assumptions (population and economic activity), energy and sulphur deposition details are generated (A, p.31).

Summary

The Regional Air Pollution INformation and Simulation (RAINS) model was developed as a tool for the integrated assessment of alternative strategies to reduce acid deposition in Europe (B, p.3) The RAINS-Asia, developed under collaboration of the World Bank, the Asian Development Bank, and the IIASA, contains technical and economic details of about 250 (B, p.4) or 355 (A, p.7) of the largest point sources in Asia. The model consists of three modules (energy-emissions (ENEM), acid deposition (ATMOS), and ecosystems impact (IMPACT) (B, p.8).

Although the model as a whole is designed to examine sulphur deposition, the energy-emissions module has general applicability to energy projection models.

'Regional and national potentials for emission control and the associated costs are estimated on the basis of detailed data on the most commonly used emission control technologies. The cost evaluation is based on the international operating experiences of pollution-control equipment, by extrapolating them to the country-specific situation. … Some important country-specific factors that have a strong impact on abatement costs include the sulfur content of fuels, plant capacity utilization regime, and boiler sizes.' 'A free and competitive market for the exchange of emission control technology is assumed' (B, p.5). 'The RAINS model also computes national cost curves that rank the abatement measures by their cost-effectiveness. Due to country-specific factors, such as energy-use patterns and technical infrastructure, national cost curves show significant differences among countries' (B, p.5).

Sulphur deposition is calculated on a 1 degree by 1 degree grid (B, p.6).

RAINS-Asia is accompanied by a regional scenario-developing database tool called Regional Energy Scenario GENerator (RESGEN) for Asia.

In the base case scenario the average energy consumption per capita increases by a factor of 2.25 by 2020, or about 50% of the current average for Europe and 20% of the USA. The energy intensity of the Asian economy as a whole decreases 3.5%. Under the low energy scenario the overall energy intensity improves by about 26%, to a level close to the industrialized countries in the 1980s (A, p.50).

RICE: Regional integrated model of climate and the economy

Sources

(A) William Nordhaus and Zili Yang. 'A Regional Dynamic General Equilibrium Model of Alternative Climate-Change Strategies.' *The American Economic Review*, September 1996.
(B) William Nordhaus. *Managing the Global Commons: The Economics of the Greenhouse Effects*. Cambridge, MA: MIT Press, 1994.

Time span: 1990-2100-2200. Solutions are provided with 10-year intervals up to 2100.

Table 12-21. Major input parameters for the RICE Model

	Cost Intercept	Climate Damage Intercept	CO_2 Emissions, 1990		Population	Per Capita Output	CO_2 Ratio, 2100
			Land-use	Industrial			
Region	(a)	(b)	(c)	(d)	(e)	(f)	(g)
United States	0.07	0.01102	0.010	1.360	0.294	68.8	0.119
Japan	0.05	0.01174	0.000	0.292	0.125	89.1	0.063
China	0.15	0.01523	0.136	0.669	1.656	9.9	0.512
European Union	0.05	0.01174	0.100	0.872	0.427	63.0	0.074
Former Soviet Union	0.15	0.00857	0.000	1.066	0.366	18.9	0.322
Rest of World	0.10	0.02093	1.730	1.700	6.738	18.1	1.185

a The intercept of cost function equals the fraction of annual output required to reduce net CO_2 emissions to 0.
b The intercept of climate-damage function equals the reduction in annual net output from an increase of 2.5 degres C in global mean temperature.
c Emissions are measured in billion of tons of carbon per year. Land-use emissions are primarily from deforestation.
d Emissions are measured in billion of tons of carbon per year. Industrial uses primarily from burning fossil fuels.
e Population is in billions of people.
f Gross domestic product (GDP) is measured at 1990 market exchange rates in thousands of 1990 US dollars.
g The ratio is industrial CO_2 emission to GDP (tons of carbon per $1000 of output in 1990 US dollars).

Source: Nordhaus and Yang (1996).

Regions: 10 (the United States, Japan, China, the European Union, Former Soviet Union (FSU), India, Brazil and Indonesia, 11 large countries, 38 medium-sized countries, and 137 small countries). Each of the first 5 regions are treated as single decision maker. Regions 6 through 10 are sometimes treated as the rest of the world (A, p.743).

Branch classification: No.

Energy sources: No breakdown. Expressed in terms of CO_2 emissions.

Scenarios: Three strategies are compared. They are: (1) a market approach, (2) a global cooperation approach, and (3) a noncooperative or nationalistic approach (A, p.743, p.749, p.761).

Technology: Level of technology is exogenous. Emissions-reduction cost function, marginal atmospheric retention ratio of CO_2 emissions, elasticity of output with respect to capital, etc. are parameters (A, p.763). Hicks-neutral technological change, approximately at the observed rates for 1960-1990 generates each region's income. After 1990, growth rates are assumed to decline exponentially (A, p.741).

Energy intensity improvement: Expressed in terms of CO_2 emissions reduction, which is assumed.

Lifestyle: No.

Policy tools: Control rates for CO_2 emissions, carbon taxes (A, p.751). Policy variables include gross investment and rate of emissions reduction (A, p.763).

Economic linkage: Endogenous variables include consumption (per-capita and total), damage from greenhouse warming, atmospheric temperature relative to pre-industrial levels, among other things, are endogenous (A, p.762). Population is exogenous (A, p.763), taken from the United Nations projections (A, p.744). *Environment linkage*: The economic choices faced by countries are: (1) to consume goods and services, (2) to invest in productive capital, and (3) to slow climate change through reducing CO_2 emissions (A, p.743).

Modelling logic: Optimization-type dynamic general-equilibrium model (A, p.761). The model solves for the intertemporal general equilibrium. For algorithm for finding the cooperative solution, see A, pp.745-748, and for noncooperative solution, see A, p.748.

Summary

'Most existing models of global climate change take the vantage point of the Global Commoner engaged in determining how nations *should* design sensible strategies. The RICE model takes a positive point of view by asking how nations would in practice choose climate change policies in light of economic trade-offs and national self-interest' (A, p.742). The model 'emphasizes the implications of the fact that while climate change is a global externality, the decision makers are national and relatively small' (A, p.762). Countries may not undertake costly efforts today for three reasons: (1) the benefits are 'so conjectural'; (2) they occur so far in the future; and (3) no individual countries can have significant impact upon the pace of global warming (A, p.762).

Three alternative solution concepts are developed. (1) Market approach: this strategy assumes that there is no correction for the climate change. Consequently, there is no abatement of CO_2 emissions. (2) Cooperative approach: countries undertake policies that reduce greenhouse-gas emissions efficiently. (3) Noncooperative approach: this case corresponds to a situation where each country sets its CO_2 emissions controls to maximize its own economic welfare assuming that other countries' strategies are invariant to a country's policies (A, p.749).

'There are major gains to taking an efficient cooperative approach to coping with global warming as opposed to the noncooperative approach. The net economic gains from an efficient policy has a discounted value of $433 billion relative to the market scenario, while noncooperative policy has a gain of only $43 billion' (A, p.762). In the efficient solution, carbon taxes are identical in all regions, which is calculated to be about $6 per ton of carbon in the year 2000. The control rates will differ, however, because of different costs of reducing CO_2 emissions. ... These results indicate that there will be substantial inefficiencies in any policy (such as that currently in force under the Framework Convention) that equalizes emissions control rates across countries or does not allow trading of emissions permits' (A, p.761).

DICE (the Dynamic Integrated model of Climate and the Economy) is an earlier model whereby policies are taken so as to maximize the generalized level of consumption now and in the future (Nordshaus, 1994). Output is explained by Cobb-Douglas production function, where the elasticity of output with respect to capital is assumed to be 0.25 (B, p.12). Total factor productivity term starts from an empirically observed value during 1965-1975, but is assumed to decline by half every six decades in the years to come (B, pp.13-14). The model specifies in sequence the linkage between the GHG emissions to economic activity, accumulation of GHG in the atmosphere, the relationship accumulation of GHGs and increased radiative forcing, radiative forcing and climate change, the impact of climate change on human and natural systems, and the cost of reducing GHG emissions (B, pp.15-19). The rate of reduction of emissions relative to uncontrolled emissions is determined by the optimization (B, p.15). Series of coefficients are employed representing the impact of CO_2 doubling on output by sector, including agriculture, energy, coastal activities, and other (B, p.51). No change in relative prices is assumed.

WEPS: World energy projection system by EIA

Sources

(A) Energy Information Administration, US Department of Energy. *World Energy Projection System Model Documentation.* DOE/EIA-M050(97). Washington, DC, 1997.

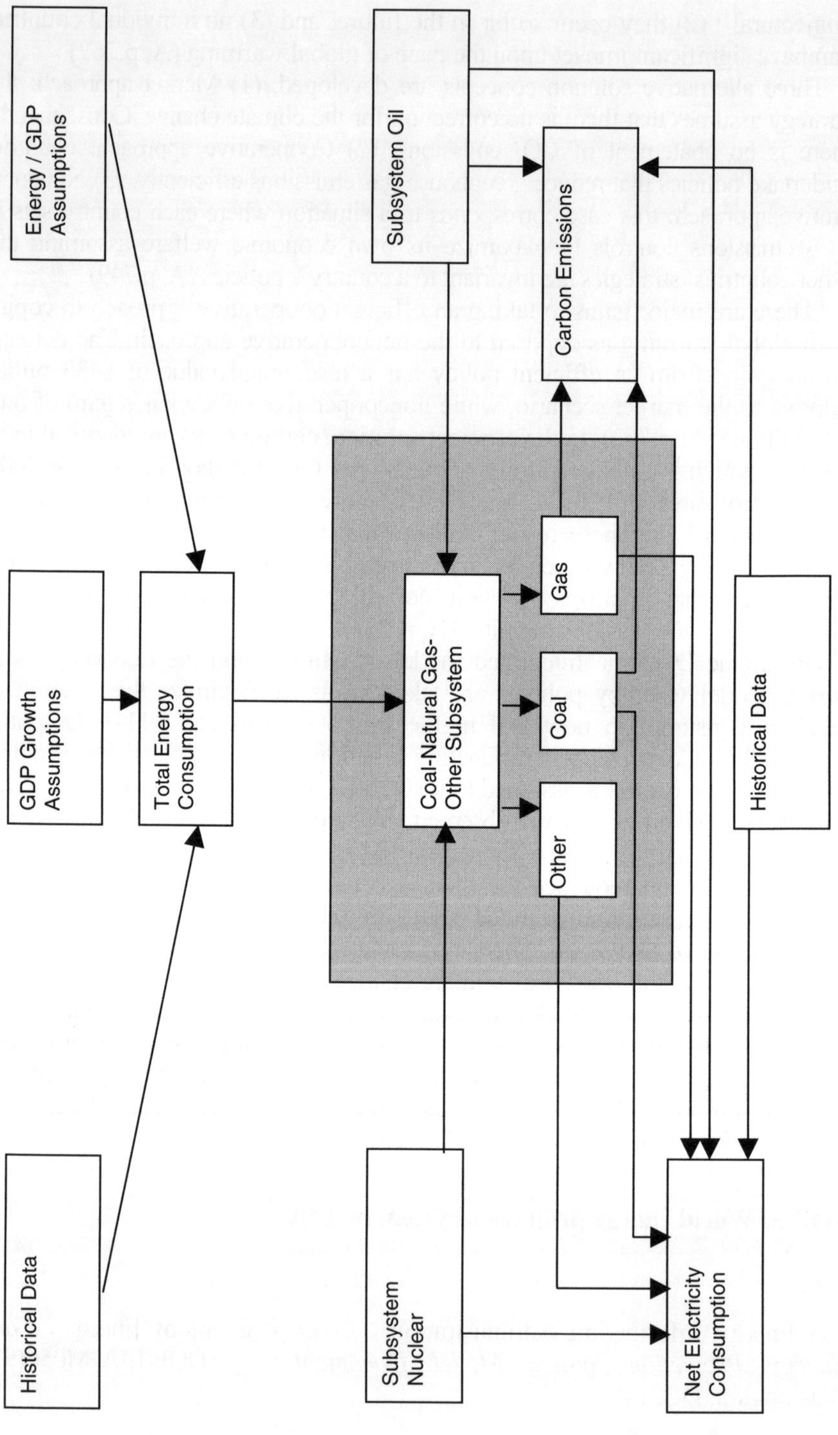

Figure 12-9. World energy consumption system interaction in WEPS.
Source: Energy Information Administration, US Department of Energy (1997a).

(B) Energy Information Administration, US Department of Energy. *International Energy Outlook 1999*. DOE/EIA-0484(99). Washington, DC, 1999.

Time span: 1990-2020 with 5-year intervals (A, p.26).
Regions: 7 individual countries (United States, Canada, Mexico, Japan, China, India, and Brazil) and 9 regions including North America (Canada, Mexico, and the United States), Western Europe, Pacific (Japan, Australia, New Zealand, etc.), developing Asia (China, India, and other Asia), Middle East, Africa, and Central and South America (Brazil and other Latin America), Eastern Europe, and the former Soviet Union (A, p.1, p.4).
Branch classification: No. Embedded in sub-models.
Energy sources: Oil, natural gas, coal, nuclear, hydroelectricity and other renewable sources, electricity (A, p.26).
Scenarios: High and low economic growth, high and low electricity consumption (A, p.27).
Technology: Embedded in assumptions on energy intensity, conversion factors, etc. (A, p.15, p.26).
Energy intensity improvement: By independent models and assumptions (A, p.26; B. p.14, pp.131-134).
Lifestyle: No.
Policy tools: No.
Economic linkage: Future elasticity assumptions (A, p.15).
Environment linkage: Carbon emissions (A, p.26).
Modelling logic: Scenarios incorporating high and low economic growth.

Table 12-22. Projected 2010 emission and required reduction of Annex I parties

Region and Country	1990 Emission (MMTC)	2010 Reference Case (MMTC)	2010 Kyoto Target (MMTC)	Change from Reference Case, 2010 (%)
Annex I Industrialized				
United States	1384	1790	1252	−30
Canada	126	162	118	−27
Western Europe	936	1021	862	−16
Japan	274	322	258	−20
Australia	90	133	97	−14
Total Annex I Industrialized	2772	3408	2586	−24
Transitional (EE/FSU)				
Former Soviet Union	991	666	990	49
Eastern Europe	299	270	320	18
Total EE/FSU	1290	935	1309	40
Total	4062	4344	3895	−10

Source: Energy Information Administration (1999).

Summary

The WEPS provides projection of total energy consumption by world regions based on an assumed relationship to gross domestic product. 'Econometric techniques are not used to determine changes in relationships over the projection period' (A, p.28). The model is used to provide an accounting framework that produces consistent world energy consumption balances from diverse sources of information. The data are in terms of physical units (such as tons and kilowatt hours).

WEPS is described as 'an integrated set of personal-computer-based spreadsheets containing data compilations, assumption specifications, descriptive analysis procedures, and projection models'. 'WEPS provides projections of total world primary energy consumption, as well as projections of energy consumption by permit type (oil, natural gas, coal, nuclear, and hydroelectric and other renewable sources), and projections of net electricity consumption. Carbon emissions resulting from fossil fuel use are derived from the energy consumption projections' (A, p.1, p.26). The files are updated annually.

The system is composed of total energy consumption subsystem, high and low economic growth subsystem, oil subsystem, nuclear energy subsystem, coal-natural gas-other allocation system, carbon emissions subsystem, high and low carbon emissions subsystem, electricity consumption subsystem, and high and low electricity subsystem. Oil consumption projections are from the International Energy Module of the National Energy Modeling System (NEMS). Nuclear generation projections are supplied by the International Nuclear Model. International coal trade is accepted from NEMS Coal Export Sub module (A, pp.26-27).

IEA's *Energy Balances of OECD Countries* and *Energy Balances and Statistics of Non-OECD Countries* are among the input data. WEFA's *World Economic Outlook* is employed as the economic projections. Projections produced by the WEPS are published in EIA's annual report *International Energy Outlook*. See B. The results are reported in Table 6-2 of this volume.

About the energy prospect in relation to the Kyoto Protocol, the EIA's annual report writes as follows. 'Additional uncertainty arises from the commitments being made by developed countries under the Kyoto Protocol of the Framework Convention on Climate Change. If those commitments are realized, energy demand could actually be reduced over the next decade. Such a development could lower total world energy consumption in 2010 by more than 10 percent relative to the reference case projection presented here. … The protocol identifies stringent targets for reduced greenhouse gas emissions in developed countries; however, neither policies nor technologies to achieve the targets have been identified for implementation, nor have countries ratified the agreement. Thus, the Kyoto Protocol is viewed in this report as a factor heightening uncertainties and the need for collateral analysis of the IEO99 reference case rather than one that *per se* alters it (B, p.8).

World energy outlook by the international energy agency

Source

(A) International Energy Agency. *World Energy Outlook*. Paris: OECD. 1998.

Time span: 1995-2010-2020.
Regions: 10 (OECD: North America, Europe, Pacific; Non-OECD: Transition Economies, Africa, China, East Asia, South Asia, Latin America, Middle East) (A, p.26, p.147).
Branch classification: Electrical services (final consumers), mobility (transport), stationary services (heating in buildings and industrial processes), power generation (A, p.25).
Energy sources: 8 (A, p.26).
Scenarios: Continued trends and policies.
Technology: Detailed description for individual energy sources (A, pp.63-174).
Energy intensity improvement: Embedded in analyses.
Lifestyle: Embedded in 'electrical services' and 'mobility'.
Policy tools: Scale of regulation and 'carbon value' that need to be included into fossil fuel prices in order to meet Kyoto commitment (A, p.26).
Economic linkage: Energy prices (A, p.26).
Environment linkage: Limitations imposed by finite recoverable reserves (A, p.26).
Modelling logic: Scenarios on energy supply (including reserves) and demand. There is an underlying world energy model (A, p.3) Fuel prices not formally modelled (A, p.26).

Summary

'Our aim is not to foretell the future. ... Instead, we see this publication as an opportunity to identify and discuss the main energy issues that could arise over this period. ... Because the *Outlook* now projects twenty-five years ahead, we have paid particular attention to the relationship between cumulative oil production to date and estimates of oil reserves. Our analysis of the current evidence suggests that world oil production from conventional sources could peak during the period 2010 to 2020. There will be no shortage of liquid fuels if this happens because reserves of unconventional oil are large' (A, p.3).

The business-as-usual case assumes energy policies existing before the Kyoto Conference will be continued and no account is taken for many flexibility mechanisms in the Protocol. 'This can be described as an illustration of how energy demand, supply, and prices are likely to develop if recent trends and current policies continue' (A, p.24).

Without such new policies the *Outlook* projects that, between 1995 and 2020, world energy demand will grow by 65% and CO_2 emission by 70%. The underlying assumption is the growth of world economy at 3.1% per annum, which is

Table 12-23. World oil and gas supply and prices, mid-1990s-2020

A. Oil Supply 1996-2020

Conventional Oil Reserves of 2.3 trillion barrels	(Million barrels per day)		
	1996	2010	2020
Total Demand for Liquid Fuels	72.0	94.8	111.5
Total Natural Gas Liquids, Processing Gains and Identified Unconventional Oil	9.3	15.9	20.1
Conventional Crude Oil			
Middle East OPEC	17.2	40.9	45.2
World excluding Middle East OPEC	45.5	38.0	27.0
Total Crude Oil	**62.7**	**79.0**	**72.2**
World Liquids Supply excluding Unidentified Unconventional Oil	72.0	94.8	92.3
Balancing Item – Unidentified Unconventional Oil	0.0	0.0	19.1

B. Natural Gas Production and Net Imports	(Mtoe)		
Indigenous Production	1995	2010	2020
OECD North America (including Mexico)	592	759	764
OECD Europe	199	276	238
OECD Pacific	31	77	68
Transition Economies	585	809	1116
China	17	57	81
Rest of World (excluding Mexico)	395	750	1208
World	**1818**	**2727**	**3474**
Net Imports	1995	2010	2020
OECD North America (including Mexico)	−2	−2	−2
OECD Europe	104	230	387
OECD Pacific	42	42	64
Transition Economies	−74	−162	−281
China	0	0	0
Rest of World (excluding Mexico)	−76	−114	−174

C. World Fossil Fuel Prices, BAU Assumptions	1995	1998-2010	2015-2020
IEA Crude Oil Import Price ($ 1990/bbl)	15	17	25
OECD Steam Coal Import Price ($ 1990/ton)	40.3	42	46
US Natural Gas Wellhead Price ($ 1990/thousand cubic ft.)	1.35	1.7*	3.5
Natural Gas Import Price into Europe ($ 1990/toe)	89.9	103	150
Japan LNG Import Price ($ 1990/toe)	125.6	141	210

Note: * refers to 1998-2005.

Source: International Energy Agency (1998b).

close to the actual record since 1971 (1990 US$, purchasing power parity). It is suggested that 'two-thirds of the increase in energy demand over the period 1995-2020 comes from China and other developing countries' (A, p.19).

The dependence on oil supplies from the Middle East will increase and oil prices could rise during the period. The *Outlook* says that 'the probability of supply disruptions and price shocks could rise'. As 2020 approaches, it is predicted that unconventional sources (such as shale oil, tar sand, and conversion from coal, biomass, and gas) will start to play their roles (A, p.19).

The report identifies several sources of uncertainties including the following.

(1) Economic output and structure, population growth.
(2) Technical change and capital stock turnover.
(3) Human attitudes and behaviour.
(4) Fossil fuel supplies and extraction costs.
(5) Energy market developments.
(6) Energy subsidies.
(7) Changing environmental objectives and policies.

Regarding energy subsidies, the report writes: 'In many developing countries, energy prices are set at levels well below the full cost of supply. ... Over time, prices are expected to rise. ... This change permit the privatization of state-owned facilities and encourage foreign investment in energy supplies.' On environmental aspects, the report adds that 'Perhaps the greatest unceertainty ... is that surrounding the policy choices that governments will make to meet the commitments they entered into in Kyoto' (A, p.24).

As for the Kyoto Protocol, the *Outlook* says that 'it is not possible to prepare a projection that meets the Kyoto targets because the countries involved have not yet announced the policies they intend to use'. Two sets of analyses are presented in this regard: (1) the scale of regulation that would be required to meet the Kyoto commitments; and (2) the carbon value that needs to be built into fossil fuel prices to meet the Kyoto targets (A, p.26).

World model for the future of the environment

Source

(A) Faye Duchin and Glenn-Marie Lange. *The Future of the Environment. Ecological Economics and Technological Change.* New York and Oxford: Oxford University Press, 1994.

Time span: 2020 at decade intervals.

Regions: 16 (1. High-income North America; 2. Newly industrializing Latin America; 3. Low-income Latin America; 4. High-income Western Europe; 5. Medium-income Western Europe; 6. Eastern Europe; 7. Former Soviet Union; 8. Centrally Planned Asia; 9. Japan; 10. Newly industrializing Asia;

11. Low-income Asia; 12. Major oil producers; 13. Northern Africa and other Middle East; 14. Sub-Sahara Africa; 15. Southern Africa; 16. Oceania (A, p. 6, pp.199-201).

Branch classification: 44 industrial (A, p.6, pp.203-204), 39 trade (A, pp.205-206).

Energy sources: Fossil fuels (oil, gas, coal) (A, p.32).

Scenarios: *Our Common Future* (OCF) scenario constructed from scattered information contained in the Brundland Report, vs. reference scenario (no technological change after 1990), alternative technological scenarios.

Technology: Details in Table 12-24.

Energy efficiency improvements: Details in Table 12-24.

Lifestyle: Reflected in the percentage of the population in living in cities (A, p.192).

Policy tools: Alternative technologies, rather than carbon tax (A, p.7).

Economic linkage: GDP and population are exogenous. Imports are from a single world trade pool rather than being specified by bilateral flows. A balance of payments deficit is assumed to be covered by an inflow of short-term capital. Price vector is used to sum up GDP. Relative price change of petroleum can be captured. Net inflow of economic aid, long-term capital, and foreign earnings are specified (A, p.193).

Environment linkage: 3 types of emissions (carbon dioxide, sulphur oxides, nitrogen oxides) based on sulphur contents, types of production processes, etc. (A, pp.51-71).

Modelling logic: Static input-output model, extended by the explicit representation of investment and international exchanges (A, p.191).

Summary

On the methodological issue the authors write: 'A conventional textbook might describe the economist's objective as identifying those alternatives, and in the process determining the corresponding "right" prices, that ensure optimal allocation of resources and maximum utility for consumers in a global economy in equilibrium. This theoretical position, and the actual models that are based on it (general equilibrium models), are appealing for their comprehensiveness and simplicity of objective. However, any theory or model of an economy has its shortcomings, and some of the major ones of this perspective are that a real economy is never in equilibrium; that social welfare is not the same as the "utility" of consumers; and that most environmental problems cannot reasonably be associated with prices that would make it possible to simply add them to calculations of utility because any such prices would be arbitrary. The challenge we have tried to face is to go beyond criticism of mainstream economic models, and beyond qualitative description alone, to build a formal framework that is capable of representing the activities of a real economy and to arrive at quantitative results which avoid these shortcomings' (A, p.6).

Table 12-24. Technology scenarios in 2020 relative to 1990

1. Petroleum price	$44 by 2020
2. GDP and population	
3. Household energy:	
A. In-house use	Small increase in investment requirements
B. Developed	50 percent energy savings
C. Developing	200-400 percent increase in energy per capita (including fuel for transportation); greater increases in electricity per capita
4. Transportation:	
A. Motor vehicles	Changing material inputs, 20 percent increase in fuel efficiency
B. Transportation services	50 percent less fuel per mile
C. Households	50 percent less fuel per mile, 16-450 percent expansion in vehicles per capita in developing countries
5. Electricity:	
A. Fuel mix	Displacement of 15 percent of coal and oil by gas in most regions Unchanged share of non-thermal electricity in most regions after 2000
B. Conversion efficiency:	
Developed (including pollution control)	15 percent improvement 20 percent incease in capital
Eastern Europe, former Soviet Union, and other regions	25 percent improvement 20-25 percent increase in capital
6. Emissions:	
A. Carbon	Reduction of emissions only through lower energy use
B. Sulfur and nitrogen:	
Developed	Scrubbers provide 90 percent removal after combustion; 10 percent increase in electricity use and 10 percent increase in capital; installation in 100 percent of power plants in Japan, 50 percent in Europe, 20 percent in Eastern Europe, 25 percent in former Soviet Union, 33 percent in North America; installation in 50 percent of industries in Western Europe and Japan; 30 percent reduction of coal sulfur in Eastern Europe and former Soviet Union through coal washing; Sulfur content of petroleum products

Table 12-24. continued

	reduced 33-50 percent; 33-50 percent reductions of nitrogen with 100 percent installation of catalytic converters in motor vehicles
Developing	No use of scrubbers; 35 percent decrease in coal sulfur content in centrally planned Asia and low-income Asia due to increased coal washing with increase in capital requirements; little use of catalytic converters
7. Industrial conservation:	Small increase in investment requirements
Developed	20 percent energy saving on average
Eastern Europe and former Soviet Union	20-50 percent energy savings (depends on sector)
Developing	20-50 percent energy savings (depends on sector); 10-30 percent of fossil-fuel use displaced by electricity
8. Construction:	
A. Maintenance vs. new construction	Share increase of 50 percent
B. Materials	Copper inputs decrease by 33 percent; aluminum inputs increase 15-33 percent; wood inputs unchanged; cement inputs decrease 15-25 percent; finished chemical inputs (mainly paint) increase 35 percent
Developed	Steel inputs decrease 25 percent
Developing	Steel inputs decrease 50 percent, more highly processed inputs
9. Metal-fabricating sectors	Virgin material inputs decrease 15 percent
10. Paper	Recycled content reaches 60 percent in developed regions
11. Electronics:	
A. Investment	
Most regions	Value share in total investment goods rises to 56 percent
Poorest regions	Share remains at 1990 value
B. Production	
Developed and newly industrializing	65 percent decrease in inputs
Other regions	45 percent decrease in inputs
12. Capital coefficients	
Developing regions	Increase in various sectors

Source: Duchin and Glenn-Lange (1994).

'The World Model does not attempt to determine a unique and optimal path to sustainable development, but simply to evaluate the implications of a set of technical and organizational choices that are made outside the model (by the Brundtland Report, in this case). 'The first stage of analysis needs to focus on the implications of the technological options for achieving specific targets. If the objectives still appear desirable, the economic incentive needed to make the shift voluntary can be explored at a later stage' (A, p.7). What the authors have in mind is introduction of carbon tax, for example.

Thus, the authors provide details on technological potentials of main activities of industry, including electric power generation, industrial energy conscrvation, processing and fabrication of metals, construction, cement, pulp and paper, chemicals, household energy conservation, and motor vehicles.

'The *Our Common Future* (OCF) (World Commission on Environment and Development, 1987) scenario reduces emissions of the three pollutants that are tracked below what they would be under the Reference scenario. But the problem is that these emissions still increase substantially between 1990 and 2020; in particular, annual carbon emissions rise by 60 percent' (A, p.8).

'In addition, the locus of pollution shifts decisively from the industrial countries, where historically most of it has originated, to the developing countries, where most of the world's people live and where most of the future increase in population will take place' (A, p.8).

If the objectives of sustainable development spelled out in the Brundland Report are to be realized, authors argue, the need for motorized transport has to be reduced through new design of communities, and reliance on renewable sources for energy and materials would have to be promoted.

WorldScan

Source

(A) Johannes Bollen, Ton Manders, and Hans Timmer. 'The IPCC Stabilisation Scenarios.' Paper presented at the Joint Meeting organized by the International Energy Agency, Energy Modeling Forum, and the International Energy Workshop (IIASA), 16-18 June 1999; Paris, 1999.

Time span: 1995-2100.
Regions: 12 (United States, Western Europe, Japan, Rest of the OECD, Eastern Europe, Former Soviet Union, Middle East and North Africa, Sub-Saharan Africa, Latin America, China, South-East Asia, South Asia and Rest).
Branch classification: 11 in WorldScan core (agriculture, services, trade and transport, electricity, intermediate goods, consumer goods, capital goods, oil, natural gas, coal, other raw materials (A, p.4, p.5), with further disaggregation of 'raw materials' and 'utility' in carbon extension of the model.
Energy sources: Coal, gas, oil, electricity (A, p.4).

Scenarios: Scenario A1 is the case with emphasis on global technological convergence and strongly intensified trade linkages (A, p.10).
Technology: Fixed technology trend. Overall technology differs across countries. Catch up is possible by adopting foreign technology (A, p.5).
Energy intensity improvement: Sharp decarbonization after 2050.
Lifestyle: Scenario A1 assumes income maximization (A, p.10). Dualistic economy is assumed (A, p.5).
Policy tools: (1) immediate action (global permit market by 2030) vs (2) delayed response (by 2050) (A, pp.10-11).
Economic linkage: Permit price, which drops sharper in the early action scenario compared to the delayed response (A, p.18). Technology transfers related to the relocation of energy-intensive industries.
Environment linkage: Timing of new entrants into permit trading altering the cost-benefit of participating countries (A, pp.13-15).
Modelling logic: Applied general equilibrium model (A, p.1).

Summary

WorldScan is based on neoclassical theories of growth and international trade. The emphasis is placed on long-term analysis (A, p.4). The model is benchmarked to the GTAP database.

In addition to neoclassical specification, the model has the following extensions:

(1) An Armington trade specification, explaining two-way trade and allowing market power to determine trade patterns in the medium run, while allowing Hecksher-Ohlin mechanisms in the long run;
(2) Imperfect financial capital mobility;
(3) Consumption patterns depending upon per-capita income, and developing towards a universal pattern;
(4) A Lewis-type low-productivity sector in developing regions, from which the high-productivity sector can draw labour, enabling high growth for a long period (A, p.5).

As for the policy experiments, the authors write: 'We show how a specific burden sharing rule yields different regional target profiles, if the global policy either calls for an early action or a delayed response. It is shown that by applying system of tradable permits to achieve a global constraint, new partners can be attracted to join the abatement coalition. But it is also shown that some countries within the abatement coalition might be against entry of any new partners' (A, p.1). Welfare triggers are used to force entrance of new members to the Annex I group of countries. The welfare target is set at $10,000 per capita (A, p.10).

The overall conclusion by the authors is that 'stabilization of greenhouse gases in the atmosphere at 550 ppmv can be achieved at moderate costs'. 'Model simulations show that there might be conflicting interests due to income transfers

Table 12-25. Economy–energy–environment in the 21st century: simulation/scenario results from main projects

Model / Scenario Names	Sub Title	References	Item	Unit	Year 1990	1995	2000	2005	2010	2020	2050	2100
6 model results on C emission (AEEI 1% Case)		Dean & Hoeller (1992)										
CRTM	Carbon Rights Trade Model	Rutherford (1992)	Carbon	billion tons	6.003		6.931		8.031	9.327	11.337	35.863
ERM(1)	Edmonds-Reilly Model	Barns *et al.* (1992)			5.767			6.709		8.180	11.838	22.579 (2095 figure)
GREEN(1)	OECD Model	Oliveira-Martins (1992)			5.815		7.071	7.704	8.705	10.806	18.998	
IEA	IEA Model	Vouyoukas (1992)			5.919		7.316	7.932				
MR(2)	Global 2100	Manne (1992)			6.003		6.748		7.581	8.681	11.356	26.039
WW	Whalley-Wigle Model	Whalley & Rigle (1992)			Average 1990-2100 25.2							65.5
APEC Energy Outlook	APEC Energy Demand	APERC (1998)	Final Energy Consumption	Mtoe								
	APEC Total		B98 Baseline			3130.2	3486.8	3901.2	4368.5			
			Env.Friendly Scenario				3412.8	3699.2	4039.4			
	United States		B98 Baseline			1507.3	1651.0	1766.3	1880.9			
			Env.Friendly Scenario				1632.8	1700.9	1767.3			
	Other Americas		B98 Baseline			284.5	316.3	368.6	435.4			
			Env.Friendly Scenario				307.9	345.9	392.2			
	China		B98 Baseline			623.4	750.9	882.1	1014.3			
			Env.Friendly Scenario				716.6	808.9	922.3			
	Other East Asia		B98 Baseline			505.0	538.3	601.3	675.1			
			Env.Friendly Scenario				530.1	577.6	629.6			
	Oceania		B98 Baseline			83.9	95.4	110.8	130.1			
			Env.Friendly Scenario				93.5	104.3	116.8			
	Southeast Asia		B98 Baseline			126.1	134.8	172.0	232.8			
			Env.Friendly Scenario				131.8	161.7	211.3			

Table 12-25. continued

Model / Scenario Names	Sub Title	References	Item	Unit	1990	1995	2000	2005	2010	2020	2050	2100
			Env.Friendly Scenario				656.5	654.2	647.0			
	United States		B98 Baseline			439.4	531.3	629.0	708.4			
			Env.Friendly Scenario				490.4	498.7	482.5			
	Other Americas		B98 Baseline			−168.6	−185.3	−158.1	−108.6			
			Env.Friendly Scenario				−198.0	−193.5	−179.9			
	China		B98 Baseline			−12.0	49.4	99.5	121.4			
			Env.Friendly Scenario				−31.3	−46.5	−68.0			
	Other East Asia		B98 Baseline			580.4	634.3	708.4	788.3			
			Env.Friendly Scenario				609.4	645.3	676.0			
	Oceania		B98 Baseline			−94.7	−120.2	−139.8	−148.4			
			Env.Friendly Scenario				−126.4	−154.2	−181.7			
	Southeast Asia		B98 Baseline			−53.7	−79.9	−74.4	−33.2			
			Env.Friendly Scenario				−87.6	−95.5	−81.7			
ECN Study CO_2 Emissions	Western Annex I	Sijm *et al.* (2000)	CO_2	Mt	9920				11702			
	CEE/FSU Annex I				4124				3962			
	Total Annex I				14044				15664			
	Latin America				1021				1284			
	Africa				767				1876			
	Asia				4051				6337			
	FSU non Annex I				341				442			
	Middle East				838				1317			
	Oceania				4				4			
	Total non-Annex I				7022				11260			
	World				21065				26924			

ECN Study		Sijm *et al.* (2000)	Greenhouse gases	Mt GHG		
Emissions Trends	Netherlands		Emissions		225	258
			Kyoto Target			212
	Germany		Emissions		1203	976
			Kyoto Target			951
	Italy		Emissions		511	592
			Kyoto Target			478
	France		Emissions		501	515
			Kyoto Target			501
	United Kingdom		Emissions		752	699
			Kyoto Target			658
	Japan		Emissions		1333	1587
			Kyoto Target			1253
	USA		Emissions		6187	7751
			Kyoto Target			5754
	Australia		Emissions		423	496
			Kyoto Target			456
	Canada		Emissions		340	402
			Kyoto Target			320
				Mt CO2		
	Western Annex I				9920	11702
	CEE/FSU Annex I				4124	3962
	Total Annex I				14044	15664
	Latin America				1021	1284
	Africa				767	1876
	Asia				4051	6337
	FSU non Annex I				341	442
	Middle East				838	1317
	Oceania				4	4
	Total non-Annex I				7022	11260
	World				21065	26924

Table 12-25. continued

Model / Scenario Names	Sub Title	References	Item	Unit	Year 1990	1995	2000	2005	2010	2020	2050	2100
G-cubed	Emission Stabilization Taxes	Bagnoli, McKibbin, Wilcoxen (1996)	Emission Stabilization Taxes	US$/t Carbon								
	Scenario 1 (Base Line)											
	USA					2.80	16.80		44.80			
	Japan					10.50	63.00		168.00			
	Australia					3.80	22.80		60.80			
	Other OECD					6.80	40.80		108.80			
	China					1.15	6.90		18.40			
	Developing Countries					2.60	15.60		41.60			
	Eastern Europe & Former USSR					1.15	6.90		18.40			
	Scenario 2 (Energy Scarcity)											
	USA					1.40	8.40		22.40			
	Japan					5.50	33.00		88.00			
	Australia					2.60	15.60		41.60			
	Other OECD					3.70	22.20		59.20			
	China					0.24	1.44		3.84			
	Developing Countries					1.15	6.90		18.40			
	Eastern Europe & Former USSR					0.35	2.10		5.60			
IEA Energy Model	Medium Term Energy Model	Vouyukas (1993)										
	Energy		Reference Case	MTOE	4184.6	4508.1	4776.3	5011.1				
			Stabilization Case	MTOE	4184.6	4251.4	4333.6	4417.2				
	Emissions		Reference Case	Mil. Tons C	3043.0	3274.7	3466.5	3631.9				
			Stabilization Case	Mil. Tons C	3043.0	3019.7	3023.9	3043.2				
IIASA-WEC	Global Energy Scenarios											
	Gross World Product	Nakicenovic *et al.* (1998)		Trillion US$, 1990 prices								
			High Growth		20						100	300
			Middle Course		20						75	200
			Ecologically Driven		20						75	220

Primary Energy Demand	Nakicenovic *et al.* (1998)		Giga tons of oil equivalent				
		High Growth		9		25	45
		Middle Course		9		20	35
		Ecologically Driven		9		14	21
Carbon Emissions, Net	Nakicenovic *et al.* (1998)		Giga tons of Carbon				
		High Growth		6		9 to 15	6 to 20
		Middle Course		6		10	11
		Ecologically Driven		6		5	2
International Energy Outlook	Energy Information Admin., US Dept. of Energy (1997b)	Carbon Emissions	Mil. Tons				
Annex I Industrialized Countries		IOE Reference Case		2772	3408		
		Kyoto Protocol Target			2586		
North America		IOE Reference Case		1472	1952		
		Kyoto Protocol Target			1370		
United States		IOE Reference Case		1346	1790		
		Kyoto Protocol Target			1252		
Canada		IOE Reference Case		126	162		
		Kyoto Protocol Target			118		
Western Europe		IOE Reference Case		936	1021		
		Kyoto Protocol Target			862		
Industrialized Asia		IOE Reference Case		364	435		
		Kyoto Protocol Target			354		
Japan		IOE Reference Case		274	322		
		Kyoto Protocol Target			258		
Australasia		IOE Reference Case		90	113		
		Kyoto Protocol Target			97		

Table 12-25. continued

Model / Scenario Names	Sub Title	References	Item	Unit	Year 1990	1995	2000	2005	2010	2020	2050	2100
	Transitional (EE/FSU)		IOE Reference Case		1290				935			
			Kyoto Protocol Target						1309			
	Former Soviet Union		IOE Reference Case		991				666			
			Kyoto Protocol Target						990			
	Eastern Europe		IOE Reference Case		299				270			
			Kyoto Protocol Target						320			
	Total		IOE Reference Case		4062				4344			
			Kyoto Protocol Target						3895			
IMAGE 2.0	Scenario Results	Alcamo *et al.* (1994)										
	CO_2 Emissions from Industry		Conventional Wisdom	Pg C	6.1						15.2	24.0
			Biofuel Crops								15.2	24.0
			No Biofuels								17.0	29.2
			Ocean Realignment								15.2	24.0
	Atmospheric Concentration		Conventional Wisdom	ppm	358						522	777
			Biofuel Crops								534	821
			No Biofuels								539	857
			Ocean Realignment								563	863
	Average Surface Temperature,		Conventional Wisdom	Centigrade							plus 1.4	2.4
	Northern Hemisphere		Biofuel Crops								1.5	2.7
			No Biofuels								1.4	2.4
			Ocean Realignment								0.0	1.2
IPCC Special Report	A1F1 Fossil fuel intensive case	IPCC (2000)	Primary energy	10**18 J/yr	351					669	1431	2073
	A1B Balance across sources				351					771	1347	2226
	A1T Predominantly non-fossil				351					649	1213	2021
	A2 Heterogenous world				351					595	971	1717
	B1 Convergent world				351					606	813	514
	B2 Local solution, diverse tech.				351					566	869	1357

MESSAGE	Scenario A1B, World	IPCC (2000)								
	Population			Million	5262	6117	6888	7617	8704	7056
	Final Energy									
	Non-commercial			EJ	38	28	22	16	5	0
	Solids			EJ	42	58	59	67	48	15
	Liquids			EJ	111	125	160	204	357	254
	Gas			EJ	41	48	67	85	164	96
	Electricity			EJ	35	47	70	107	311	859
	Others			EJ	8	10	20	38	122	525
	Total				275	316	398	517	1005	1749
	Primary Energy			EJ						
	Coal			EJ	91	105	120	157	210	192
	Oil			EJ	128	155	172	198	281	138
	Gas			EJ	71	85	128	178	378	350
	Nuclear			EJ	7	9	12	19	84	358
	Biomass			EJ	46	47	63	87	204	475
	Other Renewables			EJ	8	13	29	52	240	1172
	Total			EJ	352	415	524	689	1397	2683
	Anthropogenic Emissions									
	Fossil Fuel CO_2			GtC	5.99	6.90	8.31	10.56	16.47	13.83
	Other CO_2 (land-use changes)			GtC	1.11	1.07	1.04	0.26	−0.02	0.00
	Total CO_2			GtC	7.1	7.97	9.36	10.81	16.45	13.83
	Cumulative Resources Use									
	Coal			ZJ	0.0	0.9	2.0	3.2	9.0	19.0
	Oil			ZJ	0.0	1.4	3.0	4.7	11.4	25.2
	Gas			ZJ	0.0	0.7	1.6	2.9	10.3	31.9
	Cumulative CO_2 Emissions			GtC	7.1	82.4	169.1	269.9	695.1	1544.4
MS-MRT	Carbon Permit Trade	Bernstein *et al.* (1999b)								
	Permit Price			1995$ / ton						
	USA		No trade				274			
			A1 trade				89			
			Global trade				30			

Table 12-25. continued

Model / Scenario Names	Sub Title	References	Item	Unit	Year							
					1990	1995	2000	2005	2010	2020	2050	2100
	Japan		No trade						482			
			A1 trade						89			
			Global trade						30			
	Europe		No trade						211			
			A1 trade						89			
			Global trade						30			
	Other OECD		No trade						246			
			A1 trade						89			
			Global trade						30			
	South East Asia		No trade						0			
			A1 trade						0			
			Global trade						30			
	Other Asia		No trade						0			
			A1 trade						0			
			Global trade						30			
	China		No trade						0			
			A1 trade						0			
			Global trade						30			
	Former Soviet Union		No trade						0			
			A1 trade						89			
			Global trade						30			
	Mexico and Oil Producers		No trade						0			
			A1 trade						0			
			Global trade						30			
	Rest of the World		No trade						0			
			A1 trade						0			
			Global trade						30			
	Permit Purchases	Bernstein *et al.* (1999b)										
	USA		A1 trade						305.0			
			Global trade						461.8			

	Japan	A1 trade				57.4	
		Global trade				81.1	
	Europe	A1 trade				103.5	
		Global trade				165.1	
	Other OECD	A1 trade				40.1	
		Global trade				61.9	
	South East Asia	A1 trade				0.0	
		Global trade				−49.0	
	Other Asia	A1 trade				0.0	
		Global trade				−12.0	
	China	No trade				0.0	
		A1 trade				−274.6	
	Former Soviet Union	A1 trade				−506.0	
		Global trade				−311.8	
	Mexico and Oil Producers	A1 trade				0.0	
		Global trade				−58.3	
	Rest of the World	A1 trade				0.0	
		Global trade				−91.3	
RAINS-Asia	Energy Consumption	Resource Management Association	Petajoules				
	China	Base		30255	50527	73518	101016
		Low			433438	59132	75348
	India	Base		15812	22908	36932	63622
		Low			20192	29764	48368
	Indonesia	Base		3739	6247	9250	13684
		Low			5879	7769	10139
	Japan	Base		17866	22606	25679	28809
		Low			20188	20914	21536

Table 12-25. continued

Model / Scenario Names	Sub Title	References	Item	Unit	Year 1990	1995	2000	2005	2010	2020	2050	2100
	South Korea		Base		3594		6264		9497	13449		
			Low				5814		7793	9744		
	Malaysia		Base		1060		1953		3457	6031		
			Low				1928		3186	4686		
	Philippines		Base		585		1082		1921	3113		
			Low				948		1820	2401		
	Singapore		Base		342		645		1130	1731		
			Low				641		1061	1522		
	Taiwan		Base		2094		3334		4796	6843		
			low				2910		4241	5771		
	Thailand		Base		1688		3292		5693	9326		
			Low				2903		4482	6697		
	Asia Total		Base		83594		129468		188528	274121		
			Low				114669		154476	207431		
World Energy Outlook												
Oil Supply		IEA (1998)		Mil. Barrels/day		1996						
	Total Demand for Liquid Fuels					72.0			94.8	111.5		
	Natural Gas Liquids, etc.					9.3			15.9	20.1		
	Crude Oil					62.7			79.0	72.2		
	Middle East OPEC					17.2			40.9	45.2		
	World excl. Middle East OPEC					45.5			38.0	27.0		
	Unidentified Unconventional Oil					0.0			0.0	19.1		
Natural Gas	Indigenous Production	IEA (1998)		Mtoe		1995						
	OECD North America incl. Mexico					592			759	764		
	OECD Europe					199			276	238		
	OECD Pacific					31			77	68		

Transition Economies				585	809	1116
China				17	57	81
Rest of World excl. Mexico				395	750	1208
World				1818	2727	3474
Net Imports						
OECD North America incl. Mexico				−2	−2	−2
OECD Europe				104	230	387
OECD Pacific				42	42	64
Transition Economies				−74	−162	−281
China				0	0	0
Rest of World excl. Mexico				−76	−114	−174
Crude Oil Import Price, IEA	IEA (1998)		$ 1990 / bbl	15	17	25
Natural Gas Import Price into Europe	IEA (1998)		$ 1990 / toe	89.9	103	150
CO_2 Emissions by non Annex I and FSU	Bernard and Vielle (2000)	Base line scenario	Mt C		5270	6846

from permit trade'. 'The entrance of new members, e.g. the Middle East, has a negative impact on the position of some of the Annex I countries (Eastern Europe and Former Soviet Union). We see that EEFSU will become a net importer of permits after entrance of Latin America and the Dynamic ASEAN economies (A, pp.18-19).

In a recent paper the focus is on carbon leakage. 'Leakages occur as a result of trade in energy carriers and trade in energy-intensive products. ... Trade in energy leads to lower energy prices in developing countries, making production there more energy-intensive. Energy-intensive industries may reallocate from Annex-B countries to developing countries, making imports in Annex-B countries more energy-intensive.' 'We analyze technology transfers related to the relocation of energy-intensive industries. It is shown that these transfers mitigate the leakage and increase the efficiency in global energy use'.

'Leakage occurs mainly within the developing countries. However, we show that carbon leakage can also occur in the former Soviet Union, which is part of the Annex-B group, because their agreed emission limits are above their emissions in a business-as-usual scenario. Typical value for the leakage rate turns out to be around 20 percent, if one analyzes the impact of the Kyoto Protocol with a time horizon of 20 years.'

4. What do we know about the future?

Table 12-25 summarizes the numerical results for the future from various studies on economy–energy–environment spheres. The results are cited directly from the original sources that we examine in this chapter in order to show similarity and divergence of experts' opinion. It is noted that not all studies provide numerical data for the future.

APPENDIX: A very long-term view of the global community

DIRK VANWYNSBERGHE and KIMIO UNO

1. Introduction

A 50-year time span is nearly the maximum at the detailed level of econometric analysis. However, the economy–energy–environment interaction would have to be placed under a much longer perspective. Apart from a concerted effort towards database construction and model-building based on the data from 1970 to 2000 that comprise earlier chapters of this volume, the COMPASS project has produced a series of research memos concerning long-term performance of the global community. Taken together, the data set covers the period from 1820 to 2100.

A long-term historical view on the performance of individual economies from 1820 to the present is available from Maddison (1995), together with demographic trends. His work has the advantage that per-capita income is PPP (purchasing power parity) adjusted, so that cross-section comparisons across countries are possible for any time in the 180 years of time span, together with time-series analysis within a single economy. The results from our study up to 2020 are fitted onto Maddison's long-term trend. This reveals the long-term economic trends, with their implication on energy consumption and GHG emissions.

2. The needs for a long-term perspective

Apart from a concerted effort towards database construction and model-building based on the data from 1970 to 2000, the COMPASS project has produced the following research memo concerning long-term performance of the global community. Taken together, the data set covers the period from 1820 to 2100, based both on data compilation by Angus Maddison from various country sources (1820-1990) and the updates by the COMPASS project (1991-1997/1998), those generated by econometric modelling and simulation (1995-2010) and scenarios (2000-2100).

It is clear that the econometric method, which is restricted by the availability of historical data as the basis of determining the functional forms and parameters of individual components of the vast feedback system running through the global community, is not sufficient to provide a global view in the longer term. First,

K. Uno (ed.), Economy–Energy–Environment Simulation, 299–305.

there are countries/regions for which historical data are lacking, or do not provide guidelines for the future. China and Russia, for example, have a long history of central economic planning, which came to an end abruptly, and are now in a long process towards a free market. Their performance, together with that of many others, exerts a profound impact on the global community in the future, but their future is full of uncertainties. Various future scenarios would have to be examined. Second, while more rigorous econometric modelling and simulation can be applied for the recent past, and probably 10 to 20 years into the future, such short- to medium-term analysis would have to be put into a longer-term perspective. Third, relative positioning in the global community may provide additional insights into the potentials of individual countries/regions. Here, catching up and saturation of industrial growth, among others, seem to be relevant considerations (Fei and Ranis, 1964; Rosenberg and Birdzell, 1986; Rostow, 1990; Schmalensee *et al*., 1998; Sathaye and Ketoff, 1991, among others).

The basis of the work is Maddison (1995), which discusses the economic performance (PPP-adjusted GDP, demography, and PPP-adjusted per capita-GDP) of individual countries (56 representative sample countries and 143 non-sample countries) between 1820 and 1992. Recently, this work has been extended into the last millennium and updated to the most recent year (Maddison, 2001). Prior to the start of the project COMPASS, Keio University Uno Laboratory had obtained permission from Angus Maddison for the use of his data set for educational and research purposes on campus, and was supplied with data and text on electronic media. Keio University also invited Angus Maddison as a Special Invited Professor for lecture and collaborative work. Based on the above, a country/regional classification has been modified in order to be consistent with the one used in the COMPASS project. This step is important for the COMPASS approach because it covers the world exhaustively by including non-individually distinguished economies in Rest of Europe, Rest of Asia, etc. so that the total of countries/regions would truly be a global total. Subsequently, the time span has been extended to cover the period 1991 to 1997/1998 based on GDP indexes published in *International Financial Statistics* (IMF, various years), supplemented by GDP data from the IEA (originally from the World Bank) (IEA, various years b). For the period from around 1995 to 2010 we refer to actual records, short-term projections by various international organizations (ADB, various years a; APEC; 1999; EBRD, 1998 and 2000; OECD, various years c; United Nations ESCAP, various years; World Bank, various years a, among others), and the COMPASS simulation results. For 2010 to 2100 the projection is generated by a Scenario Writer. This is a graphic user interface (GUI) based on a widely used spreadsheet that allows users to operate on key parameters. The COMPASS database for this purpose provides data annually for 199 countries/regions, with an explicit classification scheme that leads to the COMPASS classification of about 60 countries/regions. Data are then aggregated to 13 countries/regions in order to facilitate presentation of the global perspective.

3. Brief examination of the data

As an illustration, data sheets have been compiled covering the period 1950-2100. They are:

Population
PPP-adjusted GDP
PPP-adjusted per-capita GDP.

The table provides two sums, one representing the trend value and the other based on a scenario. The trend values do not depend on subjective judgement but are the extension of an actual trend that prevailed up to the present. On the other hand, since scenario parameters are user-defined, as explained above, the projection figures listed in the following tables are for illustration only, and not a point estimate of the future. Two kinds of sums are compared in terms of percentage difference from the trend. Looking at the population projections for the year 2100, the scenario value (11,274 million) is 11.3% lower than the trend value (12,709 million). This view is consistent with the recent downward revision of world population projections by major international organizations (United Nations, 1991 and 1998; United States Bureau of Census, 1996; Wexler, 1996; World Bank, 1996; Zaba and Clarke, 1994, among others). However, in the case of Japan, it is assumed in the scenario that the present population growth rate would be maintained throughout the 21st century. This of course is not possible from current birth rates. A large amount of population inflow from abroad is implicitly assumed.

Turning to PPP-adjusted GDP per-capita projection, the scenario value for the year 2100 (8993 US$) is 31% higher than the trend value (6825 US$). Needless to say, these numbers are nothing but supposition. However, the supposition comes from various external information items regarding individual country/ region performance in the future, as well as in the recent past. For example, Japan's growth rate in terms of per-capita GDP will be low throughout the projection period, reflecting the difficulty in shifting the top-down planning on the real side of the economy to the bottom-up decision making and resource allocation on the financial side. However, in the latter half of the 21st century growth is assumed to resume at a faster pace when the institutional set-up is altered from the one fitted for catching up to the one where innovation is the key to the success. It is also noteworthy to examine the relative performance of China and Russia. At present the per-capita GDP of China is about one-half of that of Russia. By the end of the 21st century China will enjoy per-capita GDP that slightly exceeds that of Russia. This is attributable to China's success in shifting to a market-oriented development pattern. China has declared its intention to double the size of its economy in the coming decade (*People's Daily*, 13 March 2001). Whether this is possible cannot be judged simply by an econometric method because the historical record is not long enough and/or detailed enough to enable empirical examination. It is helpful to

Appendix Table 1. Population trends, 1950-2100

			1950	1960	1970	1980	1990	2000	2010	2020	2050	2100
A. Population size (unit: 1000)												
RAFN	1	Africa	173,484	217,939	281,089	367,950	492,935	582,213	686,087	763,962	994,085	1,542,537
CNHN	2	China	548,725	670,070	822,274	986,298	1,139,380	1,261,284	1,385,396	1,435,947	1,549,581	1,830,569
EASN	3	South East Asia	74,794	98,981	132,263	166,899	200,774	232,040	267,021	290,310	356,280	509,777
RASN	4	Other Asia	182,318	225,633	283,781	360,925	459,158	500,694	544,674	575,762	663,826	834,451
EURN	5	Europe	413,494	453,470	495,788	529,693	558,056	594,112	633,236	675,268	809,615	1,076,350
FSUN	6	Former Soviet Union	180,050	214,350	242,757	265,542	288,734	325,067	365,869	399,845	502,568	718,672
INDN	7	India	359,000	434,000	541,000	679,000	848,000	959,136	1,078,442	1,144,852	1,321,119	1,719,393
JAPN	8	Japan	83,563	94,053	104,334	116,800	123,540	127,984	132,607	137,486	152,848	181,224
NAMN	9	North America	166,047	198,625	226,432	251,883	276,600	301,889	328,491	347,061	400,364	502,599
OCEN	10	Oceania	13,899	17,598	21,661	25,614	30,079	35,858	42,757	48,389	65,552	107,999
OPRN	11	Oil Producers	246,324	312,910	402,666	524,191	668,213	772,159	888,856	966,830	1,188,631	1,697,683
SAMN	12	Other South America	71,990	91,669	115,808	143,509	175,281	207,051	243,959	271,783	353,659	550,432
UNIN	13	Unidentified	0	0	0	0	0	0	0	0	0	0
		Total	2,513,688	3,029,298	3,669,852	4,418,304	5,260,750	5,899,488	6,597,392	7,057,493	8,358,127	11,271,688
		COMPASS trend	2,513,688	3,029,298	3,669,852	4,418,304	5,260,750	5,813,302	6,502,917	7,192,531	9,261,375	12,709,447
		Percentage off from trend						1.5%	1.5%	−1.9%	−9.8%	−11.3%
B. Population shares (unit: percent of world total)												
RAFN	1	Africa (%)	6.90	7.19	7.66	8.33	9.37	9.87	10.40	10.82	11.89	13.69
CNHN	2	China (%)	21.83	22.12	22.41	22.32	21.66	21.38	21.00	20.35	18.54	16.24
EASN	3	South East Asia (%)	2.98	3.27	3.60	3.78	3.82	3.93	4.05	4.11	4.26	4.52
RASN	4	Other Asia (%)	7.25	7.45	7.73	8.17	8.73	8.49	8.26	8.16	7.94	7.40
EURN	5	Europe (%)	16.45	14.97	13.51	11.99	10.61	10.07	9.60	9.57	9.69	9.55
FSUN	6	Former Soviet Union (%)	7.16	7.08	6.61	6.01	5.49	5.51	5.55	5.67	6.01	6.38
INDN	7	India (%)	14.28	14.33	14.74	15.37	16.12	16.26	16.35	16.22	15.81	15.25
JAPN	8	Japan (%)	3.32	3.10	2.84	2.64	2.35	2.17	2.01	1.95	1.83	1.61
NAMN	9	North America (%)	6.61	6.56	6.17	5.70	5.26	5.12	4.98	4.92	4.79	4.46
OCEN	10	Oceania (%)	0.55	0.58	0.59	0.58	0.57	0.61	0.65	0.69	0.78	0.96
OPRN	11	Oil Producers (%)	9.80	10.33	10.97	11.86	12.70	13.09	13.47	13.70	14.22	15.06
SAMN	12	Other South America (%)	2.86	3.03	3.16	3.25	3.33	3.51	3.70	3.85	4.23	4.88
UNIN	13	Unidentified (%)	0.00	0.00	0.00	0.00	0.00	0.00	0.00	0.00	0.00	0.00
		Total (%)	100.00	100.00	100.00	100.00	100.00	100.00	100.00	100.00	100.00	100.00

Appendix Table 2. PPP-adjusted GDP trends, 1950-2100

			1950	1960	1970	1980	1990	2000	2010	2020	2050	2100
A. GDP size (unit: million 1990 US$)												
RAFN	1	Africa	148,945	221,796	345,893	489,039	640,438	961,342	1,485,263	2,185,114	3,305,810	5,971,580
CNHN	2	China	339,278	595,012	914,681	1,485,014	3,158,584	4,591,094	6,828,857	9,666,577	13,230,693	19,373,900
EASN	3	South East Asia	79,668	133,760	267,034	564,847	1,107,139	1,439,990	1,880,907	2,330,600	3,176,603	4,626,809
RASN	4	Other Asia	120,650	182,089	288,798	457,985	668,280	836,043	1,052,133	1,306,657	1,661,231	2,418,440
EURN	5	Europe	1,605,502	2,583,386	4,122,351	5,602,413	6,880,591	7,573,061	8,354,521	9,216,940	10,754,040	14,838,993
FSUN	6	Former Soviet Union	510,243	843,434	1,351,818	1,709,174	1,987,995	2,487,467	3,130,777	3,886,534	4,945,518	7,185,033
INDN	7	India	214,288	318,928	474,804	637,189	1,115,999	1,675,136	2,587,390	3,805,636	5,754,684	9,809,482
JAPN	8	Japan	156,546	364,791	985,736	1,531,612	2,291,456	2,408,457	2,532,351	2,663,519	3,107,292	4,754,846
NAMN	9	North America	1,554,502	2,173,848	3,296,743	4,553,212	5,986,653	6,592,379	7,224,326	7,804,908	9,941,286	14,473,055
OCEN	10	Oceania	79,641	117,044	189,073	257,935	345,206	448,773	586,062	725,830	986,406	1,438,489
OPRN	11	Oil Producers	363,590	637,136	1,144,297	2,098,329	2,504,906	3,514,624	5,014,503	6,799,527	9,057,917	12,727,253
SAMN	12	Other South America	199,308	285,647	444,682	651,474	706,805	989,719	1,408,785	1,904,501	2,595,454	3,779,228
UNIN	13	Unidentified	0	0	0	0	0	0	0	0	0	0
		Total	5,372,159	8,456,871	13,825,910	20,038,224	27,394,051	33,518,084	42,085,875	52,296,341	68,516,934	101,397,110
		COMPASS trend	5,372,159	8,456,871	13,825,910	20,038,224	27,394,051	31,214,683	36,767,020	42,319,357	58,976,368	86,738,053
		Percentage off from trend						7.38%	14.47%	23.58%	16.18%	16.90%
B. GDP shares (unit: percent of world total)												
RAFN	1	Africa (%)	2.77	2.62	2.50	2.44	2.34	2.87	3.53	4.18	4.82	5.89
CNHN	2	China (%)	6.32	7.04	6.62	7.41	11.53	13.70	16.23	18.48	19.31	19.11
EASN	3	South East Asia (%)	1.48	1.58	1.93	2.82	4.04	4.30	4.47	4.46	4.64	4.56
RASN	4	Other Asia (%)	2.25	2.15	2.09	2.29	2.44	2.49	2.50	2.50	2.42	2.39
EURN	5	Europe (%)	29.89	30.55	29.82	27.96	25.12	22.59	19.85	17.62	15.70	14.63
FSUN	6	Former Soviet Union (%)	9.50	9.97	9.78	8.53	7.26	7.42	7.44	7.43	7.22	7.09
INDN	7	India (%)	3.99	3.77	3.43	3.18	4.07	5.00	6.15	7.28	8.40	9.67
JAPN	8	Japan (%)	2.91	4.31	7.13	7.64	8.36	7.19	6.02	5.09	4.54	4.69
NAMN	9	North America (%)	28.94	25.71	23.84	22.72	21.85	19.67	17.17	14.92	14.51	14.27
OCEN	10	Oceania (%)	1.48	1.38	1.37	1.29	1.26	1.34	1.39	1.39	1.44	1.42
OPRN	11	Oil Producers (%)	6.77	7.53	8.28	10.47	9.14	10.49	11.91	13.00	13.22	12.55
SAMN	12	Other South America (%)	3.71	3.38	3.22	3.25	2.58	2.95	3.35	3.64	3.79	3.73
UNIN	13	Unidentified (%)	0.00	0.00	0.00	0.00	0.00	0.00	0.00	0.00	0.00	0.00
		Total (%)	100.00	100.00	100.00	100.00	100.00	100.00	100.00	100.00	100.00	100.00

Annex Table 3. PPP-adjusted per-capita GDP, 1950-2100

			1950	1960	1970	1980	1990	2000	2010	2020	2050	2100
A. PPP-adjusted per capita GDP (unit: 1990 US$)												
RAFN	1	Africa	859	1,018	1,231	1,329	1,299	1,651	2,165	2,860	3,325	3,871
CNHN	2	China	618	888	1,112	1,506	2,772	3,640	4,929	6,732	8,538	10,584
EASN	3	South East Asia	1,065	1,351	2,019	3,384	5,514	6,206	7,044	8,028	8,916	9,076
RASN	4	Other Asia	662	807	1,018	1,269	1,455	1,670	1,932	2,269	2,503	2,898
EURN	5	Europe	3,883	5,697	8,315	10,577	12,330	12,747	13,193	13,649	13,283	13,786
FSUN	6	Former Soviet Union	2,834	3,935	5,569	6,437	6,885	7,652	8,557	9,720	9,840	9,998
INDN	7	India	597	735	878	938	1,316	1,747	2,399	3,324	4,356	5,705
JAPN	8	Japan	1,873	3,879	9,448	13,113	18,548	18,818	19,097	19,373	20,329	26,237
NAMN	9	North America	9,362	10,944	14,560	18,077	21,644	21,837	21,992	22,489	24,831	28,796
OCEN	10	Oceania	5,730	6,651	8,729	10,070	11,477	12,515	13,707	15,000	15,048	13,320
OPRN	11	Oil Producers	1,476	2,036	2,842	4,003	3,749	4,552	5,642	7,033	7,620	7,497
SAMN	12	Other South America	2,769	3,116	3,840	4,540	4,032	4,780	5,775	7,007	7,339	6,866
UNIN	13	Unidentified	0	0	0	0	0	0	0	0	0	0
		Total	2,137	2,792	3,767	4,535	5,207	5,682	6,379	7,410	8,198	8,996
		COMPASS trend	2,137	2,792	3,767	4,535	5,207	5,370	5,654	5,884	6,368	6,825
		Percentage off from trend						5.81%	12.83%	25.94%	28.73%	31.81%
B. Per capita GDP levels (unit: percent of world average)												
RAFN	1	Africa (%)	40.17	36.45	32.66	29.31	24.95	29.06	33.94	38.60	40.57	43.03
CNHN	2	China (%)	28.93	31.81	29.53	33.20	53.24	64.07	77.27	90.85	104.15	117.65
EASN	3	South East Asia (%)	49.84	48.41	53.59	74.62	105.90	109.23	110.42	108.34	108.76	100.89
RASN	4	Other Asia (%)	30.96	28.91	27.01	27.98	27.95	29.39	30.28	30.63	30.53	32.22
EURN	5	Europe (%)	181.68	204.07	220.70	233.21	236.78	224.36	206.82	184.20	162.03	153.25
FSUN	6	Former Soviet Union (%)	132.60	140.95	147.81	141.92	132.22	134.69	134.14	131.17	120.04	111.14
INDN	7	India (%)	27.93	26.32	23.30	20.69	25.27	30.74	37.61	44.86	53.14	63.42
JAPN	8	Japan (%)	87.66	138.93	250.78	289.14	356.20	331.22	299.36	261.44	247.99	291.66
NAMN	9	North America (%)	438.05	392.04	386.46	398.58	415.65	384.35	344.75	303.49	302.90	320.11
OCEN	10	Oceania (%)	268.11	238.25	231.70	222.04	220.40	220.28	214.87	202.43	183.56	148.06
OPRN	11	Oil Producers (%)	69.07	72.94	75.43	88.26	71.99	80.11	88.44	94.91	92.96	83.34
SAMN	12	Other South America (%)	129.54	111.62	101.92	100.10	77.44	84.13	90.52	94.57	89.52	76.32
UNIN	13	Unidentified (%)	0.00	0.00	0.00	0.00	0.00	0.00	0.00	0.00	0.00	0.00
		Total (%)	100.00	100.00	100.00	100.00	100.00	100.00	100.00	100.00	100.00	100.00

learn from other countries' experience in the similar stage of economic development, and to be able to judge China's relative size in the global community and/or its per-capita income in the future is actually tenable. In the meantime, Russian income growth is assumed to recover from the current negative or very low level growth to positive and sustained growth. Like Japan the future success will depend on fundamental changes in the institutional set-up.

The scenario adopted here is based on the view that population growth will be contained in the future, whereas per-capita income will grow faster than the record in the recent past. Thus, in terms of aggregate GDP, higher-than-trend expansion is implied. At this point in research no deeper examination of scenario parameters has been conducted, and care should be taken not to take the figures provided as the COMPASS projection. It should be stressed that they are the test result of the Scenario Writer software.

4. The long-term view as the reference for medium-term simulation runs

Projection from 2000 to 2100 is therefore based on the historical trends of individual countries/regions, adjusted by the most plausible new development in the future. In order to be able to go back into history and to look far into the future, we have to adopt a suitable methodology focusing on key parameters such as per-capita GDP and population trends. Methodologically, this can be considered as a scenario type. In fact, the COMPASS Scenario Writer allows users to insert their own scenarios on global perspectives. This work has a clear advantage in providing a global view, even when the user's scenarios are confined to specific countries/regions or to a specific time horizon.

COMPASS simulation is based on an econometric method covering the economy–energy–environment interaction at detailed industrial description disaggregated to 36 branches, with country/region resolution of about 60. Its observation period is from 1970 to mid-1990, and its projection period is from mid-1990 to 2010/2020.

The Scenario Writer gives a long-term perspective of the global community for the period 1950 to 2100. Angus Maddison's original work goes back to 1820. The very-long term view of the global community running from 1820 to 2100 provides a reference baseline for judging the sustainability of the global environment while satisfying human aspirations.

Bibliography

Abramovitz, M. (1986). 'The Search for the Sources of Growth: Areas of Ignorance, Old and New.' *Journal of Economic History*, 52(2), pp.217-243.

Adelman, M.A. and Lynch, M.C. (1997). 'Fixed View of Resource Limits Creates Undue Pessimism.' *Oil and Gas Journal*, April, pp.50-60.

Ahmed, K. (1994). *Renewable Energy Technologies. A Review of the Status and Costs of Selected Technologies*. Washington, DC: World Bank.

Alcamo, J., ed. (1994). *IMAGE 2.0: Integrated Modelling of Global Change*. Dordrecht: Kluwer Academic Publishers.

Alcamo, J., Kreileman, E., and Leemans, R., eds. (1998). *Global Change Scenarios of the 21st Century. Results from the IMAGE 2.1 Model*. London: Elsevier Science.

Alcamo, J., Shaw, R., and Hordijk, L. (1990). *The RAINS Model of Acidification: Science and Strategies in Europe*. Dordrecht: Kluwer Academic Publishers.

Allen, R.G.D. (1968). *Economic Theory: A Mathematical Treatment*. New York: St. Martin's Press.

Amman, M. and Dhoondia, J. (1994). *RAINS-Asia User's Manual*. Washington, DC: World Bank.

Andersen, E.S. (1994). *Evolutionary Economics: Post-Schumpeterian Contributions*. London: Pinter.

Armington, P.S. (1969). *A Theory of Demand for Products Distinguished by Place of Production*. International Monetary Fund Staff Papers, Vol. 16, pp.159-176.

Asian Development Bank (ADB) (various years a). *Asian Development Outlook*. Hong Kong: Oxford University Press.

Asian Development Bank (ADB) (various years b). *Key Indicators of Developing Asian and Pacific Countries*. Hong Kong: Oxford University Press (China) Ltd.

Asian Development Bank (ADB) (1994). *Energy Indicators of Developing Member Countries of Asian Development Bank*. Manila.

Asian Policy Forum (2000). *Policy Recommendations for Preventing Another Capital Account Crisis*. Tokyo: Asian Development Bank Institute.

Asia Pacific Economic Cooperation (APEC) Secretariat (various issues). *APEC Energy Statistics*. Tokyo: Institute of Energy Economics, Energy Data and Modelling Center.

Asia-Pacific Economic Cooperation (APEC) (1999). *APEC Economic Outlook*. Singapore: APEC Secretariat.

Asia Pacific Energy Research Centre (APERC) (1998). *APEC Energy Demand and Supply Outlook*. Tokyo.

Australian Bureau of Agricultural and Resource Economics (1996). *The MEGARARE Model: Interim Documentation*. Canberra: ABARE.

Ayres, R.U. (1994). 'On Economic Disequilibrium and Free Lunch.' *Environmental and Resource Economics*, 4, pp.435-454.

Azar, C. (1997). 'Managing the Global Commons: The Economics of Climate Change by W.D. Nordhaus.' *Environmental Values*, 6(1), pp.106-108.

Azar, C. and Dowlatabadi, H. (1999). 'A Review of Technical Change in Assessment of Climate Policy.' Prepared for the *Annual Review of Energy & Environment*, 24.

Azar, C. and Rodhe, H. (1997). 'Targets for Stabilization of Atmospheric CO_2.' *Science*, Vol. 276.

Bach, S., Bork, C., Kohlhaas, M., Lutz, C., Meyer, B., Praetorius, B., and Welsch, H. (2001). *Die ökologische Steuerreform in Deutschland. Eine modellgestützte Analyse ihrer Wirkungen auf Wirtschaft und Umwelt*. Heidelberg: Physica-Verlag.

Bagnoli, P., McKibbin, W.J., and Wilcoxen, P.J. (1996). 'Future Projections and Structural Change.' In Nakicenovic, N., Nordhaus, W.D., Richels, R., and Toth, F.L., eds. *Climate Change: Integrating Science, Economics, and Policy*. CP096-1. Laxenbourg, Austria: International Institute for Applied Systems Analysis.

Baranzini, M. and Scazzieri, R., eds. (1990). *The Economic Theory of Structure and Change*. Cambridge: Cambridge University Press.

Barker, T. (1998). 'The Use of National Accounts in Modelling Greenhouse Gas Mitigation.' Paper presented at the 25th General Conference of the International Association for Research in Income and Wealth, Cambridge. August.

Barker, T. (1999). 'Achieving a 10% Cut in Europe's Carbon Dioxide Emissions Using Additional Excise Duties: Coordinated, Uncoordinated and Unilateral Action Using the Econometric Model E3ME.' *Economic Systems Research*, 11, pp.401-422.

Barker, T., Gardiner, B., Chao-Dong, H., Jennings, N., and Cshurich, C. (1999). *E3ME Version 2.2 (E3ME22) User's Manual*. Cambridge: Cambridge Econometrics.

Barns, D.W., Edmonds, J.A., and Reilly, J.M. (1992). 'Use of the Edmonds-Reilly Model to Model Energy-related Greenhouse Gas Emissions.' OECD Economics Department Working Paper No.113. Paris: OECD.

Baron, R., Bosi, M., Lanza, A., and Pershing, J. (1999). 'A Preliminary Analysis of the EU Proposals on the Kyoto Mechanisms.' Paper presented at the IEA-EMF-IEW workshop. Paris.

Baumol, W.J. (1995). 'Environmental Industries with Substantial Start-up Costs as Contributors to Trade Competitiveness.' *Annual Review of Energy and the Environment*, 20, pp.71-81.

Benhaïm, J. and Schembri, P. (1996). 'Technical Change: An Essential Variable in the Choice of Sustainable Development Trajectory.' In Faucheux, S., Pearce, D., and Proops, J., eds. *Models of Sustainable Development*. Cheltenham: Edward Elgar.

Bernard, A.L. and Vielle, M. (1999). 'Efficient Allocation of a Global Environment Cost between Countries: Tradable Permits VERSUS Taxes or Tradable Permits AND Taxes? An Appraisal with a World General Equilibrium Model.' Paper presented at the Joint Meeting organized by the International Energy Agency, Energy Modeling Forum, and the International Energy Workshop (IIASA), June, Paris.

Bernstein, P. (2000). 'MS-MRT Model Enhancements and Results.' Paper presented at the Joint EMF/IEA/IIASA Meeting, Stanford University, June.

Bernstein, P.M., Montgomery, W.D., Rutherford, T.F., and Gui-Fang Yang (1999a). 'The Effects of Restrictions on International Permit Trading: the MS-MRT Model.' *Energy Journal*, Special Issue, pp.221-256.

Bernstein, P.M., Montgomery, W.D., and Rutherford, T.F. (1999b). 'Global Impacts of the Kyoto Agreement: Results from the MS-MRT Model.' Paper presented at the Joint Meeting organized by the International Energy Agency, Energy Modeling Forum, and the International Energy Workshop (IIASA), June, Paris.

Bohm, P. (1999). 'An Emission Quota Trade Experiment among Four Nordic Countries.' In Sorrell, S. and Skea, J., eds. *Pollution for Sale: Emissions Trading and Joint Implementation*. Cheltenham: Edward Elgar.

Bollen, J., Manders, T., and Timmer, H. (1999). 'The IPCC Stabilisation Scenarios.' Paper presented at the Joint Meeting organized by the International Energy Agency, Energy Modeling Forum, and the International Energy Workshop (IIASA), 16-18 June, 1999; Paris.

Bos, E. and Vu, M.T. (1994). *World Population Projections: Estimates and Projections with Related Demographic Statistics*, 1994-1995 edition. Washington, DC: World Bank.

Boulding, K.E. (1968*). Beyond Economics, Essays on Society, Religion, and Ethics*. Ann Arbor: University of Michigan Press.

Brenton, P.A. (1989). 'Modeling Bilateral Trade Flows: An Empirical Analysis Using Disaggregate Commodity Data.' *Journal of Policy Modeling*, No. 11, pp.547-567.

Brown, L.R. *et al.*, eds. (various years). *State of the World*. London: Earthscan.

Burniaux, J.-M. (1999). 'Burden Sharing Rules in Post-Kyoto Strategies: A General Equilibrium Evaluation Based on the GREEN Model.' Paper presented at the IEA-EMF-IEW workshop, Paris.

Burniaux, J.M., Nicoletti, G., and Oliveira-Martins, J. (1992). 'GREEN. A Global Model for Quantifying the Costs of Policies to Curb CO_2 Emissions.' *OECD Economic Studies*, No. 19/Winter.

Capros, P. *et al.* (1995). 'GEM-E3 Computable General Equilibrium Model for Studying Economy-Energy-Environment Interactions for Europe.' DG-XII. The European Commission.

Capros, P., Karadeloglou, P., Mantzos, L., and Mentzas, G. (1996). 'The Energy Model MIDAS.' In Lasourd, J.-B., Percebois, J., and Valette, F., eds. *Models for Energy Policy*. London: Routledge.

Chasek, P.S. (2001). *Earth Negotiations, Analyzing Thirty Years of Environmental Diplomacy*. Tokyo, New York, Paris: United Nations University Press.

Chenery, H., Robison, S., and Syrquin, M., eds. (1986). *Industrialization and Growth: A Comparative Study*. Oxford: Oxford University Press.

Cline, W.R. (1999). 'Discounting the Very Long Run.' In Portney, P.R. and Weyant, J.P., eds. *Discounting and Intergenerational Equity*. Washington, DC: Resources for the Future.

Cohen, W.M. and Levintal, D.A. (1989). 'Innovation and Learning: Two Faces of R&D.' *Economic Journal*, 99, pp.569-596.

Constanza, R., ed. (1991). *Ecological Economics: The Science and Management of Sustainability*. New York: Columbia University Press.

Cooper, A., Livermore, S., Rossi, V., Wilson, A., and Walker, J. (1999). 'A Cross-Country Quantitative Investigation using the Oxford Global Macroeconomic and Energy Model.' *Energy Journal*, Kyoto Special Issue, pp.335-364.

Darmstadter, J., Dunkerley, J., and Alterman, J. (1977). *How Industrial Societies Use Energy – A Comparative Analysis*. Resources for the Future. Baltimore: Johns Hopkins University Press.

Dean, A. and Hoeller, P. (1992). 'Costs of Reducing CO_2 Emissions: Evidence from Six Global Models.' Economics Department Working Paper No. 122. GD(92)140. Paris: Organisation for Economic Co-operation and Development.

De Jong, A. and Zalm, G. (1991). 'Scanning the Future: A Long-term Scenario Study of the World Economy 1990-2015.' OECD: *Long-term Prospects of the World Economy*, Paris, pp.27-74.

Demeny, P. (1990). 'Population.' In Turner II, B.L. *et al*., eds. *The Earth as Transformed by Human Action*. Cambridge: Cambridge University Press.

De Vries, B., Janssen, M., and Beusen, A. (1999). 'Perspectives on Global Energy Futures – Simulations with the TIME Model.' *Energy Policy*, 27, pp.477-494.

De Vries, B., Bollen, J., Bouwman, L., den Elzen, M., Janssen, M., and Kreileman, E. (2000). 'Greenhouse Gas Emissions in an Equity-, Environment- and Service-Oriented World: An IMAGE-based Scenario for the 21st Century.' *Technological Forecasting & Social Change*, 63(2-3).

De Vries, H.J.M., Olivier, J.G.J., van den Wijngaart, R.A., Kreileman, G.J.J., and Toet, A.M.C. (1994). 'Model for Calculating Regional Energy Use, Industrial Production and Greenhouse Gas Emissions for Evaluating Global Climate Scenarios.' *Water, Air, Soil Pollution*, 76, pp.79-131.

Dicken, P. (1986). *Global Shift, Industrial Change in a Turbulent World*. London: Paul Chapman.

Dornbusch, R. and Poterba, J.M. (1991). *Global Warming: Economic Policy Responses*. Cambridge, MA: MIT Press.

Douglas, M., Gasper, D., and Thompson, M. (1998). 'Human Needs and Wants.' In Rayner, S. and Malone, E.L., eds. *The Societal Framework*. Columbus, OH: Battelle Press.

Dowlatabadi, H. (1995). 'Integrated Assessment Models of Climate Change: An Incomplete Overview.' *Energy Policy*, 23(4/5), pp.289-296.

Downing, R.J., Ramankutty, R., and Shah, J.J. (1997). RAINS-ASIA, An Assessment Model for Acid Deposition in Asia. Washington, DC: World Bank.

Duchin, F. and Lange, G.-M. (1994). *The Future of the Environment: Ecological Economics and Technological Change*. New York and Oxford: Oxford University Press.

Duchin, F. and Smyshlyaev, A. (1995). 'Development and the Environment: Extending the Global Input-Output-Modelling System'. In Klein, L.R. and Fu Chen Lo, eds. *Modelling Global Change*. Tokyo: United Nations University Press.

Economic and Social Commission for Asia and the Pacific (various years). *Economic and Social Survey of Asia and the Pacific*. New York: United Nations.

Economic and Social Commission for Asia and the Pacific (ESCAP) (1991). *Energy Policy Implications of the Climate Effects of Fossil Fuel Use in the Asia-Pacific Region*. ST/ESCAP/1007. Bangkok: ESCAP.

Economic Commission for Europe (1992). *East-West Energy Efficiency*. New York: United Nations.

Edmonds, J.A. and Barns, D.W. (1992). 'Factors Affecting the Long-term Cost of Fossil Fuel CO_2 Emissions Reduction.' *International Journal of Global Energy Issues*, 4(3), pp.140-166.

Edmonds, J., Wise, M., and MacCracken, C. (1994). *Advanced Energy Technologies and Climate Change. An Analysis Using the Global Change Assessment Model (GCAM)*. PNL-9798, UC-402. Richland, WA: Pacific Northwest Laboratory.

Edmonds, J., Wise, M., Pitcher, H., Richels, R., Wigley, T., and MacCracken, C. (1996). 'An Integrated Assessment of Climate Change and the Accelerated Introduction of Advanced

Energy Technologies: An Application of MiniCAM 1.0.' *Mitigation and Adaptation Strategies for Global Change*, 1(4), pp.311-339.

Energy Information Administration, US Department of Energy (1997a). *World Energy Projection System Model Documentation*. DOE/EIA-M050(97). Washington, DC.

Energy Information Administration, US Department of Energy (1997b). *Annual Energy Outlook 1998 with Projections to 2020*. DOE/EIA-0383 (98). Washington, DC: EIA.

Energy Information Administration, US Department of Energy (1999). *International Energy Outlook 1999*. DOE/EIA-0484(99). Washington, DC.

Engelman, R. (1994). *Stabilizing the Atmosphere: Population, Consumption and Greenhouse Gases*. Washington, DC: Population Action International.

EUREC Agency (1996). *The Future of Renewable Energy. Prospects and Directions*. London: James & James.

European Bank for Reconstruction and Development (EBRD) (1998). *Transition Report 1998*. London: EBRD.

European Bank for Reconstruction and Development (EBRD) (2000). *Transition Report Update*. London: EBRD.

European Commission, Directorate-General XII Science, Research and Development (1995). *The PRIMES Project*. EUR 16713 EN. Brussels and Luxembourg: European Commission.

European Commission (1997). *Methodological Problems in the Calculation of Environmentally Adjusted National Income Figures*, Vol. One and Vol. Two. Studies for the European Commission Directorate General XII.

EUROSTAT (Statistical Office of the European Communities) (1997). *Material Flow Accounting. Experience of Statistical Institutes in Europe*. Luxembourg.

Fankhauser, S. (1995). *Valuing Climate Change. The Economics of the Greenhouse*. London: Earthscan.

Faucheux, S., Pearce, D., and Proops, J. (1996). *Models of Sustainable Development*. Cheltenham: Edward Elgar.

Fei, J.C.H. and Ranis, G. (1964). *Development of the Labor Surplus Economy, Theory and Policy*. Homewood, IL: Richard D. Irwin.

Fischer, G. and Rosenzweig, C. (1996). 'The Impacts of Climate change, CO_2 and SO_2 on Agricultural Supply and Trade.' WP-96-5. Laxenburg, Austria: International Institute for Applied Systems Analysis.

Fischer, G., Frohberg, K., Keyzer, M.A., and Parikh, K.S. (1988). *Linked National Models: A Tool for International Policy Analysis*. Dordrecht: Kluwer Academic Publishers.

Fiksel, J. (1996). *Design for Environment: Creating Eco-efficient Products and Processes*. New York: McGraw-Hill.

Førsund, F.R. (1995). 'Input-Output Models, National Economic Models, and the Environment.' *Handbook of Natural Resource and Energy Economics*, Vol. I. Amsterdam: Elsevier Science Publishers.

Freeman, C. (1982). *The Economics of Industrial Innovation*. Cambridge, MA: MIT Press.

Freeman, C. (1990). 'The Economics of Technical Change.' *Cambridge Journal of Economics*, 18, pp.463-514.

Freeman, C., ed. (1996). *Long Wave Theory*. Cheltenham: Elgar Reference.

Gaffin, S.R. (1998). 'World Population Projections for Greenhouse Gas Emissions Scenarios.' *Mitigation and Adaptation Strategies for Global Change*, 3(2-4), pp.133-170.

Gana, J.L. *et al.* (1979). 'Alternative Approaches to Linkage of National Econometric Models.' In Sawyer, J.A. ed., *Modelling the International Transmission Mechanism*. Amsterdam: North Holland.

Gehlhar, M. *et al.* (1997). 'Overview of the GTAP Data Base.' In Hertel, T.W., ed. *Global Trade Analysis, Modeling and Applications*. Cambridge: Cambridge University Press.

Gielen, D. and Kram, T. (2000). 'Meeting UNFCCC Target via Materials Policies.' Paper presented at the Joint EMF/IEA/IIASA Meeting, Stanford University, June.

Giovannini, B. and Baranzini, A., eds. (1997). *Energy Modelling: Beyond Economics and Technology*. Geneva: International Academy of the Environment and Geneva: Centre for Energy Studies of the University of Geneva.

Glenn, J.C. and Gordon, T.J., eds. (1997). *State of the Future: Implications for Actions Today*. The Millennium Project. Washington, DC: American Council for the United Nations University.

Grassini, M. (1995). 'Comments on Chapter 5.' In Klein, L.R. and Fu Chen Lo, eds. *Modelling Global Change*. Tokyo: United Nations Press.

Greene, D.L. and Santini, D.J., eds. (1993). *Transportation and Global Climate Change*. Washington, DC: American Council for an Energy-Efficient Economy.

Greening, L.A., Davis, W.B., Schipper, L.J., and Khrushch, M. (1997). 'Comparison of Six Decomposition Methods: Application to Aggregate Energy Intensity for Manufacturing in Ten OECD Countries.' *Energy Economics*, 19(3), pp.375-390.

Gregory, K. and Rogner, H.H. (1998). 'Energy Resources and Conversion Technologies for the 21st Century.' *Mitigation and Adaptation Strategies for Global Change*, 3(2-4), pp.171-229.

Grubb, M., Vrolijk, C., and Brack, D. (1999). *The Kyoto Protocol: A Guide and Assessment*. London: Royal Institute of International Affairs, Energy and Environmental Programme.

Grueber, A. (1998). *Technology and Global Change*. Cambridge: Cambridge University Press.

Gürer, N. and Ban, J. (1997). 'Factors Affecting Energy-Related CO_2 Emissions: Past Levels and Present Trends.' *OPEC Review*, XXI(4), pp.309-350.

Hall, G. and Howell, S. (1985). 'The Experience Curve from the Economist's Perspective.' *Strategic Management Journal*, 6, p.197.

Hertel, T.W., ed. (1997). *Global Trade Analysis, Modeling and Applications*. Cambridge: Cambridge University Press.

Hertel, T.W. and Tsigas, M.E. (1997). 'Structure of GTAP.' In Hertel, T.W., ed. *Global Trade Analysis, Modeling and Applications*. Cambridge: Cambridge University Press.

Hickman, B.G. and Lau, L.J. (1973). 'Elasticities of Substitution and Export Demand in a World Trade Model.' *European Economic Review*, 4, pp.347-380.

Higgins, M. and Williamson, J.G. (1997). 'Age Structure Dynamics in Asia and Dependence on Foreign Capital.' *Population and Development Review*, 23(2), pp.261-293.

Hogan, W.W. and Jorgenson, D.W. (1991). 'Productivity Trends and the Cost of Reducing CO_2 Emissions.' *Energy Journal*, 12, pp.68-85.

Hufschmidt, M.M., James, D.E., Meister, A.D., Bower, B.T., and Doxon, J.A. (1983). *Environment, Natural Systems, and Development. An Economic Valuation Guide*. Baltimore and London: Johns Hopkins University Press.

Hughes, B.B. (1999). 'The International Futures (IFs) Modeling Project.' *Simulation and Gaming*, 30(3), September.

Hulme, M., Jiang, T., and Wigley, T. (1995). *SCENGEN: A Climate Change SCENario GENerator: Software User Manual*, Version 1.0. Climate Change Research Unit, School of Environmental Sciences. Norwich: University of Anglia.

Institute of Developing Economies (IDE) (1982). *International Input-Output Table for ASEAN Countries, 1975*. Tokyo.

Institute of Developing Economies (IDE) (1992). *Asian International Input-Output Table 1985*. Tokyo.

Institute of Developing Economies (IDE) (1998). *Asian International Input-Output, 1990*. Tokyo.

Intergovernmental Panel on the Climate Change (IPCC) (1992a). *Climate Change 1992 – The Supplementary Report to the IPCC Scientific Assessment*. Houghton, J.T., Callandar, B.A., and Varney, S.K., eds. Cambridge: Cambridge University Press.

Intergovernmental Panel on the Climate Change (IPCC) (1992b). *Climate Change 1992 – The Supplementary Report to the IPCC Impacts Assessment*.

Intergovernmental Panel on the Climate Change (IPCC) (1992c). *Climate Change: The IPCC 1990 and 1992 Assessment*.

Intergovernmental Panel on the Climate Change (IPCC) (1994). *IPCC Guidelines for National Greenhouse Gas Inventories*, 3 volumes. London: IPCC WGI Technical Support Unit.

Intergovernmental Panel on the Climate Change (IPCC) (1995). *Climate Change 1994 – Radiative Forcing of Climate Change and an Evaluation of the IPCC IS92 Emission Scenarios*. Cambridge: Cambridge University Press.

Intergovernmental Panel on the Climate Change (IPCC) (1996a). *Climate Change 1995 – The Science of Climate Change*. Contribution of Working Group I to the Second Assessment Report. Cambridge: Cambridge University Press.

Intergovernmental Panel on the Climate Change (IPCC) (1996b). *Climate Change 1995 – Impacts, Adaptations, and Mitigation of Climate Change: Scientific-Technical Analyses – Contribution of Working Group II to the Second Working Group II to the Second Assessment Report*.

Intergovernmental Panel on the Climate Change (IPCC) (1996c). *Climate Change 1995 – Economic and Social Dimensions of Climate Change – Contribution of Working Group III to the Second Assessment Report.*
Intergovernmental Panel on the Climate Change (IPCC) (2000). *Special Report on Emissions Scenarios*. Cambridge: Cambridge University Press.
International Energy Agency (IEA) (various years a). *Energy Statistics and Balances of OECD Countries*. Paris: OECD.
International Energy Agency (IEA) (various years b). *Energy Statistics and Balances of Non-OECD Countries*. Paris: OECD.
International Energy Agency (IEA) (various years c). *Energy Prices and Taxes*. Paris: OECD.
International Energy Agency (IEA) (1995). *Energy Policies of the Russian Federation*. Paris: OECD.
International Energy Agency (IEA) (1997a). *Indicators of Energy Use and Efficiency: Understanding the Link between Energy and Human Activity*. Paris: OECD.
International Energy Agency (IEA) (1997b). *Renewable Energy Policy in IEA Countries*. Vol. I and Vol. II. Paris: OECD/IEA.
International Energy Agency (IEA) (1998a). *Enhancing the Market Deployment of Energy Technology. A Survey of Eight Technologies*. Paris: IEA.
International Energy Agency (IEA) (1998b). *World Energy Outlook*. Paris: OECD.
International Energy Agency (IEA) (1998c). *Energy Efficiency Initiative. Energy Policy Analysis*, Vol. 1. Paris: OECD.
International Energy Agency (IEA) (1999). *Non-OECD Coal Fired Power Generation – Trends in the 1990s*. London: IEA Coal Research.
IIASA (International Institute for Applied Systems Analysis) – WEC (World Energy Council) (1995). *Global Energy Perspectives to 2050 and Beyond*. Laxenburg, Austria: International Institute for Applied Systems Analysis.
International Monetary Fund (IMF) (various years). *International Financial Statistics Yearbook*. Washington, DC.
International Monetary Fund (IMF) (various years). *Balance of Payments Statistics Yearbook*. Washington, DC.
International Monetary Fund (IMF) (various years). *World Economic Outlook*. Washington, DC.
International Monetary Fund (IMF) (1993). *Balance of Payments Manual*. Washington, DC.
Inter-Secretariat Working Group on National Accounts (1993). *System of National Accounts 1993*. Brussels, New York, Paris, Washington, DC.
Ishiguro, M. and Akiyama, T. (1995a). 'Energy Demand in Five Major Asian Developing Countries, Structure and Prospects.' World Bank Discussion Paper. Washington, DC: World Bank.
Ishiguro, M. and Akiyama, T. (1995b). 'Electricity Demand in Asia and the Effects on Energy Supply and the Investment Environment.' Policy Research Working Paper 1557. Washington, DC: World Bank.
Jensen, J. *et al.* (2000). 'The Economic Effects of the European Ceilings Proposal.' Paper presented at the Joint EMF/IEA/IIASA Meeting, Stanford University. 20-22 June.
Johansson, O. and Schipper, L.J. (1997). 'Measuring the Long-Run Fuel Demand of Cars: Separate Estimations of Vehicle Stock, Mean Fuel Intensity, and Measured Annual Driving Distances.' *Journal of Transport Economics and Policy*, 31(3), pp.277-292.
Johansson, T.B., Kelly, H., Reddy, A.K.N., and Williams, R.H. (1993). *Renewable Energy: Sources for Fuels and Electricity*. Washington, DC: Island Press.
Jorgenson, D.W. and Wilcoxen, P. (1993). 'Energy, the Environment, and Economic Growth.' In Kneese, A.V. and Sweeney, J.L., eds. *Handbook of Natural Resource and Energy Economics*. Amsterdam: Elsevier.
Johnston, J. (1963). *Econometric Methods*. New York: McGraw-Hill.
Jung, T.Y., La Rovere, E.L., Gaj, H., Shukla, P.R., and Zhou, D. (2000). 'Structural Changes in Developing Countries and Their Implication to Energy-Related CO_2 Emissions.' *Technological Forecasting & Social Change*, 63(2-3).
Kanoh, T. (1992). 'Toward Dematerialization and Decarbonization. Science and Sustainability.' *Selected Papers on IIASA's 20th Anniversary*. Laxenburg, Austria: International Institute for Applied Systems Analysis.
Katseli-Papaefstratiou, L.T. (1979). *The Reemergence of the Purchasing Power Parity Doctrine in the 1970s*. Special Papers in International Economics No. 13. Princeton: Princeton University Press.

Kawashima, Y. (1995). 'The Drafting Process of the Framework Convention on Climate Change and Factor Analysis of the Structure of Confrontation among Nations.' *Kankyo Joho Kagaku Ronbunshu* (J), pp.139-144.
Kelley, A. (1988). 'Economic Consequences of Population Change in the Third World.' *Journal of Economic Literature*, 26(4), pp.685-728.
Kemp, R. (1997). *Environmental Policy and Climate Change*. Cheltenham: Edward Elgar.
Klein, L.R. and Krelle, W., eds. (1983). 'Capital Flows and Exchange Rate Determination.' *Journal of Economics*, Supplementum 3.
Klein, L.R. and Van Peterssen, A. (1973). 'Forecasting World Trade within Project LINK.' In Ball, R.J., ed. *The International Linkage of National Economic Models*, Amsterdam: North-Holland.
Kneese, A.V. and Sweeney, J.L. (Vol. I and II 1985, Vol. III 1993). *Handbook of Natural Resource and Energy Economics*. Amsterdam: Elsevier.
Kolsrud, G. and Torrey, B.B. (1992). 'The Importance of Population Growth in Future Commercial Energy Consumption.' In White, J.C., ed. *Global Climate Change: Linking Energy, Environment, Economy and Equity*. New York: Plenum.
Kosaka, H. and Yano, T. (1999). 'An Empirical Analysis of Carbon Dioxide Emissions: Developing and Energy Model by Panel Data.' Mimeo. Keio University at Shonan Fujisawa Campus.
Krackeler, T., Shipper, L., and Sezgen, O. (1999). 'Carbon Dioxide Emissions in OECD Service Sectors: The Critical Role of Electricity Use.' *Energy Policy*, 26(15), pp.1137-1152.
Kram, T. (2000). *The MATTER Project. Integrated Energy and Materials Systems Engineering for GHG Emission Mitigation*. Petten, the Netherlands: ECN.
Kram, T., Morita, T., Riahi, K., Roehrl, R.A., van Rooijen, S., Sankovski, A., and de Vries, B. (2000). 'Global and Regional Greenhouse Gas Emissions Scenarios'. *Technological Forecasting & Social Change*, 63(2-3).
Kuboniwa, M. (1997). 'Input-Output Analysis of the Russian Economy (1).' (J) *Sangyo Renkan*. Business Journal of PAPAIOS, Vol. 7, No. 4.
Kuboniwa, M. and Gavrilenkov, E. (1997). *Development of Capitalism in Russia: The Second Challenge*. Tokyo: Maruzen Co.
Lashof, D. and Tirpak, D.A. (2000). *Policy Options for Stabilizing Global Climate*. Washington, DC: US Environmental Agency.
Latin American Energy Organization (1999). *Energy-Economic Statistics and Indicators of Latin America and the Caribbean*. Quito, Ecuador.
Lazarus, M.L., Greber, L., Hall, J., Bartels, C., Bernow, S., Hansen, H., Raskin, P., and von Hippel, D. (1993). *Towards a Fossil Free Energy Future: The Next Energy Transition*. A Technical Analysis for Greenpeace International. Boston: Stockholm Environmental Institute Boston Center.
Lind, R.C. (1995). 'Intergenerational Equity, Discounting, and the Role of Cost-Benefit Analysis in Evaluating Global Climate Policy.' *Energy Policy*, 23, pp.379-389.
London Group (1994). *National Accounts and the Environment*. Papers and Proceedings from a Conference, London, England. March. Ottawa: Statistics Canada.
London Group (1995). *Second Meeting of the London Group on Natural Resource and Environmental Accounting*. Conference Papers. Washington, DC: US Department of Commerce, Bureau of Economic Analysis.
London Group (1996). *Third Meeting of the London Group on Natural Resource and Environmental Accounting*. Proceedings volume. Stockholm: Statistics Sweden.
London Group (1997). *National Accounts and the Environment*. Papers and Proceedings from a Conference, Ottawa, Canada. June. Ottawa: Statistics Canada.
Loulou, R. and Kanudia, A. (2000). 'Economic Indicators from a Multi-sector, Multi-region Bottom-up MARKAL Model'. Paper presented at the Joint EMF/IEA/IIASA Meeting, Stanford University, June.
Lutz, C. (1998). *Umweltpolitik und die Emission von Luftschadstoffen: eine empirische Analyze für Westdeutschland*. Berlin: Dunker & Humbolt.
Lutz, W., ed. (1996). *The Future Population of the World: What Can We Assume Today?* 2nd edition. London: Earthscan.
Lutz, W., Sanderson, W., and Scherbov, S. (1997). 'Doubling of World Population Unlikely.' *Nature*, 387(6635), pp.803-805.
Ma, Q. (1996). 'A Bilateral Trade Model for the INFORUM International System.' Unpublished Ph.D. dissertation. Paper presented at the 3rd World INFORUM Conference, Lodz.

MacCracken, C.N., Edmonds, J.A., Kim, S.H., and Sands, R.D. (1999). 'The Economics of the Kyoto Protocol.' *Energy Journal*, special issue.

MacKellar, F.L., Lutz, W., Prinz, C., and Goujon, A. (1995). 'Population, Households and CO_2 Emissions.' *Population and Development Review*, 21(4), pp.849-865.

Maddison, A. (1989). *The World Economy in the 20th Century*. Paris: Development Centre of the Organisation for Economic Co-operation and Development.

Maddison, A. (1991). *Dynamic Forces in Capitalist Development, A Long-Run Comparative View*. Oxford and New York: Oxford University Press.

Maddison, A. (1995). *Monitoring the World Economy 1820-1992*. Development Centre of the Organisation for Economic Co-operation and Development. Paris: OECD.

Maddison, A. (1998a). *Chinese Economic Performance in the Long Run*. Development Centre Studies. Paris: OECD.

Maddison, A. (1998b). 'Measuring the Performance of a Communist Command Economy: An Assessment of the CIA Estimates for the U.S.S.R.' *Review of Income and Wealth*, 44(3), pp.307-323.

Maddison, A. (2001). *The World Economy: A Millennial Perspective*. Development Centre Studies. Paris: OECD.

Mahlman, J.D. (1997). 'Uncertainties in Projections of Human-Caused Climate Warming.' *Science*, 278, November.

Manne, A. (1992). 'Global 2100: Alternative Scenarios for Reducing Carbon Emission'. OECD Economics Department Working Paper No. 111. Paris: OECD.

Manne, A.S. and Richels, R.G. (1992). *Buying Greenhouse Insurance, The Economic Costs of CO_2 Emissions Limits*. Cambridge, MA: MIT Press.

Manne, A. and Richels, R. (1994). 'The Costs of Stabilizing Global CO_2 Emissions: A Probabilistic Analysis Based on Expert Judgements.' *Energy Journal*, 15(1), pp.31-56.

Manne, A. and Richels, R. (1995). 'The Greenhouse Debate: Economic Efficiency, Burden Sharing and Hedging Strategies.' *Energy Journal*, 15(4), pp.1-37.

Manne, A. and Richels, R. (1997). 'On Stabilizing CO_2 Concentrations – Cost-effective Emission Reduction Strategies.' *Environmental Modeling and Assessment*, 2, pp.251-265.

Manne, A. and Rutherford, T.F. (1994). 'International Trade, Capital Flows and Sectoral Analysis: Formulation and Solution of Intertemporal Equilibrium Models.' In Cooper, W.W. and Whinston, A.B., eds. *New Directions in Computational Economics*. Dordrecht: Kluwer Academic Publishers.

Manne, A., Mandelsohn, R., and Richels, R. (1995). 'MERGE: A Model for Evaluating Regional and Global Effects of GHG Reduction Policies.' *Energy Policy*, 23(1), pp.17-34.

McDevitt, T.M. (1996). *World Population Profile*. Report WP/96. US Bureau of Census. Washington, DC: Government Printing Office.

McKibbin, W.J. and Wilcoxen, P.J. (1999). 'Permit Trading under the Kyoto Protocol and Beyond.' Paper presented at the Joint Meeting organized by the International Energy Agency, Energy Modeling Forum, and the International Energy Workshop (IIASA). June, Paris.

Messner, S. and Strubegger, M. (1995). *User's Guide for MESSAGE III*, WP-95-69. International Institute for Applied Systems Analysis. Laxenburg, Austria.

Meyer, B. and Ewerhart, G. (1998). 'Multisectoral Policy Modelling for Environmental Analysis.' In Uno, K. and Bartelmus, P., eds. *Environmental Accounting in Theory and Practice*. Dordrecht: Kluwer Academic Publishers.

Meyer, B. and Uno, K. (1999a). 'Global Econometric 3E-Modelling: The System COMPASS.' In Sydow, A. and Jin-Yi Yu, eds. *1999 International Conference on Mission Earth*. San Diego: Society for Computer Simulation International.

Meyer, B. and Uno, K. (1999b). 'COMPASS – Ein globales Energie-Wirtschaftsmodell.' *ifo-Studien*. 45(4), pp.703-718.

Meyer, B., Bockermann, A., Ewerhart, G., and Lutz, C. (1999). *Marktkonforme Umweltpolitik. Wirkungen auf Luftschadstoffemissionen, Wachstum und Struktur der Wirtschaft*. Heidelberg: Physica-Verlag.

Mitchell, J.V. (1996). *The New Geopolitics of Energy*. Washington, DC: Brookings Institution.

Mori, S. (2000). 'The Development of Greenhouse Gas Emissions Scenarios Using an Extension of the MARIA Model for the Assessment of Resource and Energy Technologies.' *Technological Forecasting & Social Change*, 63(2-3).

Moriguchi, C. (1973). 'Forecasting and Simulation Analysis of the World Economy.' *American Economic Review*, 63(2), pp.402-409.

Morita, T. *et al.* (1994). *Global Carbon Dioxide Scenarios and their Basic Assumptions*. Tsukuba: Center for Global Environmental Research, National Institute for Environmental Studies.

Nakicenovic, N., Nordhaus, W.D., Richels, R., and Toth, E.L. (1996). *Climate Change: Integrating Science, Economics, and Policy*. CP-96-1. Laxenburg, Austria: International Institute for Applied Systems Analysis.

Nakicenovic, N., Grueber, A., and McDonald, A. (1998). *Global Energy Perspectives*. Cambridge: Cambridge University Press.

National Institute for Environmental Studies, Japan. 'Asian-Pacific Integrated Model AIM.' (mimeo). (No publication date given.)

National Research Council (1986). *Population Growth and Economic Development: Policy Questions*. Washington, DC: National Academy Press.

Nishio, K., Fujii, Y., and Yamaji, K. (2000). 'Analysis of the Kyoto Mechanisms using a Global System Model DNE21,' Paper presented at the Joint EMF/IEA/IIASA Meeting, Stanford University, June.

Nordhaus, W. (1994). *Managing the Global Commons, the Economics of Climate Change*. Cambridge, MA: MIT Press.

Nordhaus, W.D. and Kokkenberg, E.C., eds. (1999). *Nature's Numbers, Expanding the National Economic Accounts to Include the Environment*. Washington, DC: National Academy Press.

Nordhaus, W.D. and Popp, D. (1997). 'What is the Value of Scientific Knowledge? An Application to Global Warming Using the PRICE Model.' *Energy Journal*, 18(1), pp.1-45.

Nordhaus, W.D. and Yang, Zili (1996). 'A Regional Dynamic General Equilibrium Model of Alternative Climate-Change Strategies.' *American Economic Review*, September.

Nyhus, D. (1991). 'INFORUM International System'. *Economic Systems Research*, 3(1), pp.55-64.

Nyhus, D., Ma, Q., and Wang, Q. (1996). 'A First Attempt at Linking INFORUM National Models by a Multisectoral Bilateral World Trade Model.' Paper presented at the Fourth INFORUM World Conference, Tokyo.

Oates, W.E. (1995). 'Green Taxes: Can We Protect the Environment and Improve the Tax System at the Same Time?' *Southern Economic Journal*, 61(4), pp.915-922.

Odell, P.R. (1999). 'Dynamics of Energy Technologies and Global Change.' *Energy Policy*, 27, pp.737-742.

Onishi, A. (1999). *FUGI Global Model 9.0 M 200/80: Integrated Global Model for Sustainable Development*. Tokyo: Soka University Institute for Systems Science.

Organisation for Economic Co-operation and Development (OECD) (various years a). *OECD Environmental Data, Compendium*. Paris: OECD.

Organisation for Economic Co-operation and Development (OECD) (various years b). *International Direct Investment*. Paris: OECD.

Organisation for Economic Co-operation and Development (OECD) (country reports, various years c). *OECD Economic Surveys*. Paris: OECD.

Organisation for Economic Co-operation and Development (OECD) (1992a). *Long-term Prospects for the World Economy*. Paris: OECD.

Organisation for Economic Co-operation and Development (OECD) (1992b). *Climate Change: Designing a Tradeable Permit System*. Paris: OECD.

Organisation for Economic Cooperation and Development (OECD) (1994a). *Assessing the Environmental Effects on Trade*. Paris: OECD.

Organisation for Economic Co-operation and Development (OECD) (1994b). *GREEN: The Reference Manual*. Paris: OECD.

Organisation for Economic Co-operation and Development (OECD) (1995a). *The OECD Input-Output Database*. Paris: OECD.

Organisation for Economic Co-operation and Development (OECD) (1995b). *Global Warming, Economic Dimensions and Policy Responses*. Paris: OECD.

Organisation for Economic Co-operation and Development (OECD) (1996). *China in the 21st Century*. Paris: OECD.

Organisation for Economic Co-operation and Development (OECD) (1997a). *The World in 2020: Towards a New Global Age*. Paris: OECD.

Organisation for Economic Co-operation and Development (OECD) (1997b). 'The WorldScan Model: Background and Simulations for Linkages II' (mimeo). Development Centre.
Organisation for Economic Co-operation and Development (OECD) (1997c). *Indicators of Energy Use and Efficiency. Understanding the Link between Energy and Human Activity*. Paris: OECD.
Organisation for Economic Co-operation and Development (OECD) (1997d). *Enhancing the Market Deployment of Energy Technology, A Survey of Eight Technologies*. Paris: OECD.
Organisation for Economic Co-operation and Development (OECD) (1997e). *Energy Technologies for the 21st Century*. Paris: OECD.
Organisation for Economic Co-operation and Development (OECD) (1998a). *Twentyfirst Century Technologies: Promises and Perils of a Dynamic Future*. Paris: OECD.
Organisation for Economic Co-operation and Development (OECD) (1998b). *Eco-Efficiency*. Paris: OECD.
Organisation for Economic Co-operation and Development (OECD) (2000a). *Instruments and Technologies for Climate Change Policy: an Integrated Energy and Materials Systems Modelling Approach*. ENV/EPOC/GEEI(99)15. Paris: OECD.
Organisation for Economic Co-operation and Development (OECD) (2000b). *Assessing the Environmental Effects of Trade Liberalisation Agreement, Methodologies*. Paris: OECD.
Parikh, J., ed. (1996). *Energy Models for 2000 and Beyond*. New Delhi: Tata McGraw Hills.
Parikh, J.K., Parikh, K.S., Gokarn, S., Painuly, J.P., Saha, B., and Shukla, V. (1991). *Consumption Patterns: The Driving Forces of Environmental Stress*. Report prepared for the United Nations Conference on Environment and Development (UNCED), IGIDR-PP-014. Mumbai, India: Indira Ghandi Institute for Development Research.
Parson, E.A. and Fishervanden, K. (1997). 'Integrated Assessment Models of Climate-Change.' *Annual Review of Energy and the Environment*, 22, pp.589-628.
Pearce, D.W. (1991). 'The Role of Carbon Taxes in Adjusting to Global Warming.' *Economic Journal*, 101, pp.938-948.
Peck, S.C. and Teisberg, T.J. (1992). 'CETA: A Model for Carbon Emission Trajectory Assessment.' *Energy Journal*, 13(1), pp.55-77.
Peck, S.C. and Teisberg, T.J. (1995). 'International CO_2 Emissions Control – An Analysis Using CETA.' *Energy Policy*, 23(4), pp.297-308.
Pepper, W.J., Barbour, W., Sankovski, A., and Braaz, B. (1998). 'No-Policy Greenhouse Gas Emission Scenarios: Revisiting IPCC 1992.' *Environmental Science and Policy*, 1, pp.289-312.
Perroni, C. and Wigle, R. (1997). 'Environmental Policy Modeling.' In Hertel, T.W., ed. *Global Trade Analysis, Modeling and Applications*. Cambridge: Cambridge University Press.
Pesaran, M.H., Smith, R.P., and Akiyama, T. (1998). *Energy Demand in Asian Developing Economies*. A World Bank Study. Oxford: Oxford University Press.
Portney, P.R. and Wayant, J.P., eds. (1999). *Discounting and Intergenerational Equity*. Washington, DC: Resources for the Future.
Price, L., Michaelis, L., Worell, E., and Khrushch, M. (1998). 'Sectoral Trends and Driving Forces of Global Energy Use and Greenhouse Gas Emissions.' *Mitigation and Adaptation Strategies for Global Change*, 3(2-4), pp.263-319.
Rayner, S. and Malone, E.L. (1998). *Human Choice and Climate Change*, Vol. 1: *The Social Framework*. Columbus, OH: Battelle Press.
Redclift, M. and Benton, T. (1994). *Social Theory and the Global Environment*. London and New York: Routledge.
Repetto, R. and Austin, D. (1997). *The Costs of Climate Protection: A Guide for the Perplexed*. Washington, DC: World Resources Institute.
Resource Management Association (1996). *RESGEN: Regional Energy Scenario Generator for Asia*. Madison.
Reynolds, T.S. and Cutliffe, S.H., eds. (1997). *Technology and the West*. Chicago: Chicago University Press.
Rogner, H.H. (1996). *An Assessment of World Hydrocarbon Resources*. WP-96-56. Laxenburg, Austria: International System for Applied Systems Analysis.
Rogner, H.H. (1997). 'An Assessment of World Hydrocarbon Resources.' *Annual Review of Energy Environment*, 22, pp.217-262.
Roodman, D. (1996). *Paying the Piper: Subsidies, Politics, and the Environment*. Worldwatch Paper 133. Washington, DC: Worldwatch Institute.

Rose, A. and Stevens, B. (1998). 'A Dynamic Analysis of Fairness in Global Warming Policy: Kyoto, Buenos Aires, and Beyond.' *Journal of Applied Economics*, 1.
Rose, A. and Stevens, B. (1999). 'A Dynamic Analysis of the Efficiency and Equity of Tradable Greenhouse Gas Emission Permits.' Paper presented at the Joint Meeting organized by the International Energy Agency, Energy Modeling Forum, and the International Energy Workshop (IIASA), 16-18 June. Paris.
Rose, A., Stevens, B., Edmonds, J., and Wise, M. (1998). 'International Equity and Differentiation in Global Warming Policy: An Application to Tradable Emission Permits.' *Environmental and Resource Economics*, 12(1).
Rosenberg, N. (1994). *Exploring the Black Box: Technology, Economics, and History*. Cambridge: Cambridge University Press.
Rosenberg, N. (1997). 'Economic Development and the Transfer of Technology: Some Historical Perspectives.' In Reynolds, T.S. and Cutcliffe, S.H., eds. *Technology and the West*. Chicago: Chicago University Press.
Rosenberg, N. and Birdzell, L.E. (1986). *How the West Grew Rich: The Economic Transformation of the Industrial World*. London: I.B. Tauris & Co.
Rostow, W.W. (1990). *The Stages of Economic Growth*. 3rd edition. Cambridge: Cambridge University Press.
Rotmans, J. and de Vries, H.J.M., eds. (1997). *Perspectives on Global Futures: The TARGETS Approach*. Cambridge: Cambridge University Press.
Rotmans, J., van Asselt, M.B.A. *et al.* (1994). *Global Change and Sustainable Development. A Modelling Perspective for the Next Decade*. GLOBO Report Series No. 4. The Netherlands: National Institute of Public Health and Environmental Protection.
Rutherford, T. (1992). 'The Welfare Effects of Fossil Carbon Restrictions: Results from a Recursively Dynamic Trade Model'. OECD Economics Department Working Papers No. 112. Paris: OECD.
Sakurai, N., Ioannidis, E., and Papacontantinou, G. (1996). 'The Impact of R&D and Technology Diffusion on Productivity Growth: Evidence for 10 OECD Countries in the 1970s and 1980s.' Directorate for Science, Technology and Industry. OECD/GD(96)27 Paris.
Sands, P.H., ed. (1992). *The Effectiveness of International Environmental Agreements: A Survey of Existing Legal Instruments*. United Nations Conference on Environment and Development (UNCED). Cambridge: Grotius.
Sands, P. (1995). *Principles of International Environmental Law I. Framework, Standards and Implementation*. Manchester and New York: Manchester University Press.
Sathaye, J. and Ketoff, A. (1991). 'CO_2 Emissions from Major Developing Countries: Better Understanding the Role of Energy in the Long Term.' *Energy Journal*, 12(1), pp.161-196.
Schipper, L., Hass, R., and Sheinbaum, C. (1996). 'Recent Trends in Residential Energy Use in OECD Countries and Their Impact on Carbon Dioxide Emissions: A Comparative Analysis of the Period 1973-1992.' *Journal of Mitigation and Adaptation Strategies for Global Change*, 1, pp.167-196.
Schipper, L., Ting, M., Khrushch, M., and Golove, W. (1997). 'The Evolution of Carbon Dioxide Emissions from Energy Use in Industrial Countries: An End-Use Analysis.' *Energy Policy*, 25(7-9), pp.651-672.
Schmalensee, R., Stoker, T., and Judson, R. (1998). 'World Carbon Dioxide Emissions: 1950-2050.' *Review of Economics and Statistics*, LXXX(1), pp.15-27.
Schneider, S.H. (1990). *Global Warming: Are We Entering the Greenhouse Century*? Cambridge: Lutterworth Press.
Schwartz, P. (1991). *The Art of the Longview: Three Global Scenarios to 2005*. New York: Doubleday.
Sijm, J.P.M. *et al.* (2000). 'Kyoto Mechanisms: The Role of Joint Implementation, the Clean Development Mechanism and Emissions Trading in Reducing Greenhouse Gas Emissions.' Petten, the Netherlands: Netherlands Energy Research Foundation.
Sivasubramonian, S. (1998). 'Twentieth Century Economic Performance of India.' Paper prepared for the 25th General Conference for Research in Income and Wealth, Cambridge, England, 23-29 August.
Skea, J. (1999). 'Flexibility, Emissions Trading and the Kyoto Protocol.' In Sorrell, S. and Skea, J., eds. *Pollution for Sale: Emissions Trading and Joint Implementation*. Cheltenham: Edward Elgar.

Slade, M.E., Kolstad, C.D., and Weiner, R.J. (1993). 'Buying Energy and Nonfuel Minerals: Final, Derived, and Speculative Demand.' In Kneeze, A.V. and Sweeney, J.L., eds. *Handbook of Natural Resource and Energy Economics*. Amsterdam: Elsevier.

Soltes, D. (1999). 'Metadata and Metainformation – Old Concepts and New Challenges.' *IASSIST Quarterly*, 23(1), pp.12-14.

Sorrell, S. and Skea, J., eds. (1999). *Pollution for Sale: Emissions Trading and Joint Implementation*. Cheltenham: Edward Elgar.

Spector, B.I., Sjøstedt, G., and Zartman, I.W. (1994). *Negotiating International Regimes: Lessons Learned from the United Nations Conference on Environment and Development (UNCED)*. London: Graham & Trotman.

State Statistical Bureau of the People's Republic of China, and Institute of Economic Research, Hitotsubashi University (1997). *The Historical National Accounts of the People's Republic of China 1952-1995*. Tokyo: Hitotsubashi University.

Timmer, H. (1998). 'WorldScan – A World Model.' *Quarterly Review Netherlands Bureau of Economic Policy Analysis*, 3, pp.37-40.

Unander, F. and Schipper, L. (1998). 'Past and Future Trends in CO_2 Emissions from Energy Use: The Indicator Approach.' *ENER Bulletin* No. 22. European Network for Energy Economic Research.

Unander, F. and Schipper, L. (1999). 'Which Road from Kyoto? Decomposition of Emission Scenarios.' Paper presented at the Joint Meeting organized by the International Energy Agency, Energy Modeling Forum, and the International Energy Workshop (IIASA), 16-18 June, Paris.

United Nations (various years a). *National Accounts Statistics: Main Aggregates and Detailed Tables*. New York.

United Nations (various years b). *International Trade Statistics Yearbook*. New York.

United Nations (1990). *International Standard Industrial Classification of All Economic Activities, Third Revision*. Series M No. 4, Rev. 3. New York.

United Nations (1991). *Consequences of Rapid Population Growth in Developing Countries*. New York.

United Nations (1993a). *Agenda 21: The United Nations Programme of Action from Rio*. New York: United Nations Department of Public Information.

United Nations (1993b). *Integrated Environmental and Economic Accounting*. New York: United Nations Statistical Division.

United Nations (1997). *Critical Trends: Global Change and Sustainable Development*. No. ST/ESA/255. New York.

United Nations (1998). *World Population Projections to 2150*. UN Department of Economic and Social Affairs. New York: United Nations.

United Nations Development Programme (UNDP) (1997). *Human Development Report 1997*. New York: Oxford University Press.

UNFCCC (1992). *United Nations Framework Convention on Climate Change. Convention Text*. UNEP/WMO Information Unit of Climate Change (IUCC) on behalf of the Interim Secretariat of the Convention. Geneva: IUCC.

UNFCCC (1997). *Kyoto Protocol to the United Nations Framework Convention on Climate Change*. FCCCC/CP/L7/Add.1. December. New York: United Nations.

United States Bureau of Census (1996). *World Population Profile 1996*. WP/96. Washington, DC: US Government Printing Office.

United States Environmental Protection Agency (1990). *Policy Options for Stabilizing Global Climate*. Report to Congress. Washington, DC.

Uno, K. (1995). *Environmental Options: Accounting for Sustainability*. Dordrecht: Kluwer Academic Publishers.

Uno, K. (2000). 'Environmental Effects of Trade Liberalization Agreements: the COMPASS Approach.' OECD Proceedings. *Assessing the Environmental Effects of Trade Liberalisation Agreements, Methodologies*. Paris: OECD.

Uno, K. and Bartelmus, P., eds. (1998). *Environmental Accounting in Theory and Practice*. Dordrecht: Kluwer Academic Publishers.

Van Asselt, M., Rotmans, J. *et al.* (1995). *Uncertainty in Integrated Assessment Modelling: a Cultural Perspective Based Approach*. GLOBO Report Series No. 9. The Netherlands: National Institute of Public Health and the Environment.

Van der Zwaan, B.C.C., Gerlagh, R., Klaassen, G., and Schattenholzer, L. (2000). 'Endogenous Technological Change in Climate Change Modelling.' Paper presented at the Joint EMF/IEA/IIASA Meeting, Stanford University, June.

Viguier, L. (1999). 'Emissions of SO_2, NO_x, and VO_2 in Transition Economies: Emission Inventories and Divisa Index Analysis.' *Energy Economics*, 20(2), pp.59-75.

Vouyoukas, E.L. (1992). 'Carbon Taxes and CO_2 Emissions Targets: Results from the IEA Model'. OECD Economics Department Working Papers No. 114. Paris: OECD.

Vouyoukas, E.L. (1993). 'IEA Medium Term Energy Model.' OECD, *The Costs of Cutting Carbon Emissions: Results from Global Models*. Paris.

Vouyoukas, E.L. (1996). 'World Energy Outlooks.' In Lasourd, J.-B., Percebois, J., and Valette, F., eds. *Models for Energy Policy*. London: Routledge.

Wallace, D. (1995). *Environmental Policy and Industrial Innovation: Strategies in Europe, the USA, and Japan*. London: Earthscan.

West, G.R. (1995). 'Comparison of Input-Output, Input-Output + Econometric and Computable General Equilibrium Impact Models at the Regional Level.' *Economic Systems Research*, 7(2).

Wexler, L. (1996). *Improving Population Assumptions in Greenhouse Emissions Models*. WP-96-099. Laxenburg, Austria: International Institute for Applied Systems Analysis.

Weyant, J.P. (1997). 'Technological Change and Climate Policy Modelling.' Paper prepared for the Workshop on Induced Technological Change and the Environment. Laxenburg, Austria: International Institute for Applied Systems Analysis.

Weyant, J.P., ed. (1999). 'The Costs of the Kyoto Protocol: a Multi-Model Evaluation.' *Energy Journal*, special issue.

Weyant, J.P. and Hill, J.N. (1999). 'Introduction and Overview.' *Energy Journal*, special issue, pp.vii–xliii.

Whalley, J. and Wigle, R. (1992). 'Results for the OECD Comparative Modelling Exercise from the Whalley-Wigle Model'. OECD Economics Department Working Papers, No. 121. Paris: OECD.

White, J.C., ed. (1992). *Global Climate Change: Linking Energy, Environment, Economy, and Equity*. New York and London: Plenum Press.

Wier, M., Lenzen, M., Munksgaard, J., and Smed, S. (2001). 'Effects of Household Consumption Patterns on CO_2 Requirements.' *Economic Systems Research*, 13(3), pp.259-274.

Wigley, T.M.L. and Paper, S.C.B. (1993). 'Future Changes in Global Mean Temperature and Sea Level'. In Warwick, R.A., Barrow, E.M., and Wigley, T.M.L., eds. *Climate and Sea Level Change Observations, Projections and Implementation*. Cambridge: Cambridge University Press.

Wigley, T.M.L. *et al.* (1994). *Model for the Assessment of Greenhouse-gas Induced Climate Change*, Version 1.2. Climate Research Unit, University of East Anglia, UK.

Wigley, T.M.L., Richels, R., and Edmonds, J.A. (1996). 'Economic and Environmental Choices in the Stabilisation of Atmospheric CO_2 Concentrations.' *Nature*, 379, pp.240-243.

World Bank (various years a). *Global Economic Prospects and the Developing Countries*. Washington, DC.

World Bank (various years b). *World Development Report*. Oxford: Oxford University Press.

World Bank (various years c). *Global Development Finance, Analysis and Summary Tables*. Washington, DC: World Bank.

World Bank (1993). *The Asian Miracle, A World Bank Policy Research Report*. Washington, DC: World Bank.

World Bank (1996). *Long-term Trends of World Population '94/95 (1990-2150)*. Washington, DC: World Bank.

World Bank (1998). *Global Development Finance* (Formerly published as the *World Debt Tables*). *Analysis and Summary Tables. Country Tables.* Washington, DC.

World Business Council for Sustainable Development (WBCSD) (1997). *Exploring Sustainable Development: WBCSD Global Scenarios 2000-2050*. London: WBCSD.

World Commission on Environment and Development (1987). *Our Common Future*. Oxford and New York: Oxford University Press.

World Energy Council (WEC) (1998). *Survey of Energy Resources*. London: WEC.

World Energy Council and the International Institute for Applied Systems Analysis (1995). *Global Energy Perspectives to 2050 and Beyond*. Laxunburg, Austria: IIASA.

World Resources Institute (WRI) (1997). *Resource Flows: The Material Basis of Industrial Economies*. Washington, DC: WRI.

Wu, H.X. (1998). 'An Alternative Estimation of Chinese Industrial Performance, 1949-95.' Paper prepared for the 25th General Conference of the International Association for Research in Income and Wealth. Cambridge, England.

Yoshitomi, M. and Shirai, S. (2000). *Technical Background Paper for Policy Recommendation for Preventing Another Capital Account Crisis*. Tokyo: Asian Development Bank Institute.

Zaba, B. and Clarke, J., eds. (1994). *Environment and Population Change*. Liege, Belgium: Derouaux Ordina Editions.

COMPASS working papers

Koltsov, A. and Volkov, V. (1998). 'Comparison: SNA and IO Table for Russia, 1995.' December 1998 Workshop, Keio University.

Lutz, C. (1998). 'The Linkage of Trade and 18 IO Country Models: A Historical Price Simulation.' December 1998 Workshop, Keio University.

Lutz, C. (1998). 'User Manual for the Macroeconomic System.' December 1998 Workshop, Kcio University.

Meyer, B. and Ewerhard, G. (1998). 'Multisectoral Policy Modelling for Environmental Analysis.' In Uno, K. and Bartelmus, P., eds., *Environmental Accounting in Theory and Practice.* Dordrecht: Kluwer Academic Publishers.

Meyer, B. and Uno, K. (1998). 'The Internationally Linked Dynamic Input-Output Model COMPASS: The Logical Structure.' Paper presented at the Twelfth International Input-Output Conference, held 18-22 May, 1998, New York.

Meyer, B. and Uno, K. (1999). 'Global Econometric 3E-Modelling: The System of COMPASS.' Paper presented at 1999 Western MultiConference, San Francisco, January 17-20, 1999. Sydow, A. and Jin-Yi Yu, eds., *1999 In International Conference on Mission Earth.* San Diego: The Society for Computer Simulation International.

Meyer, B., Bockermann, A., and Lutz, C. (1999). 'The Endogenization of Trade Shares in the Global Model COMPASS.' APEC Energy Project, Keio University.

Miketa, A. (1998). 'Price Dependency of Energy Input: Experiment Based on OECD IO Tables and Energy Balances.' Paper presented at the Twelfth International Input-Output Conference, 18-22 May, New York.

Miketa, A. (2000). 'Maddison Data Update, 1991-1997/1998.' Uno Laboratory. Keio University.

Umehara, Y. (1998). 'The Energy/Environmental Model for 3E-COMPASS.' December 1998 Workshop, Keio University.

Umehara, Y. (1999). 'Modeling Energy Balances for Policy Simulation.' Paper presented at a joint meeting of the International Energy Agency, The Energy Modeling Forum, and the International Energy Workshop, held 16-18 June, Paris. Revised September 1999.

Uno, Kimio (1998a). 'Identifying Research Priority.' In Uno, K. and Bartelmus, P., eds., *Environmental Accounting in Theory and Practice.* Dordrecht: Kluwer Academic Publishers.

Uno, K. (1998b). 'Policy Application of Global Economy-Energy-Environment (3E) Accounting and Modelling.' Paper presented at the Twelfth International Input-Output Conference, 18-22 May, New York.

Uno, K. (1998c). 'From Single-Country Accounting to Global Modelling.' Paper presented at the Fifth Meeting of the London Group on Natural Resources and Environmental Accounting, Fontevraud, 25-29 May, 1998.

Uno, K. (1999a). 'Energy Projection: Comparison of Methodologies (preliminary).' Paper presented at a joint meeting of the International Energy Agency, The Energy Modeling Forum, and the International Energy Workshop, 16-18 June, Paris. Revised October 1999.

Uno, K. (1999b). 'Environmental Effects of Trade Liberalization Agreements: The COMPASS Approach.' Paper presented at the OECD Joint Workshop on Trade and Environment, 26-27 October, Paris.

Uno, K. (1999c). 'Environmental Accounting, Policy Analysis, and Global Governance.' Paper prepared for the Sixth Meeting of the London Group on Natural Resources and Environmental Accounting, 15-19 November, Canberra.

Uno, K. (2000). 'An Analysis of Global Ecological Linkages using an Input-Output Database.' Paper presented at an International Workshop Globalization and the World Economy: Changes and Challenges, 14 December, Hitotsubashi University.

Uno, K. (2001). 'Very Long Term Demographic and PPP-Adjusted Economic Data for the World Community.' Project Report. Keio University SFC Research Institute.

Uno, K. and Meyer, B. (1999). 'Data Structure and Logical Flow of the 3E (Economy-Energy-Environment) Model COMPASS (Comprehensive Model for Policy Assessment).' Paper presented at a joint meeting of the International Energy Agency, The Energy Modeling Forum, and the International Energy Workshop, 16-18 June, Paris.

Uno Laboratory (1999). '3E COMPASS, Economy-Energy-Environment Comprehensive Model for Policy ASSessment.' COMPASS-single-manual. Keio University.

Vanwynsberghe, D. and Wang, Y. (1996). 'Quickdyme, Installation Files.' Center of Excellence, Keio University.

Vanwynsberghe, D. and Wang, Y. (1996). 'Quickdyme Modelling, the Naming Conventions.' Center of Excellence, Keio University.

Vanwynsberghe, D. (1997). 'Naming Convention, the Quickdyme Approach.' Center of Excellence, Keio University.

Vanwynsberghe, D. (1997). 'The Integral Project User Manual Time Series.' Keio University.

Vanwynsberghe, D. (1998). 'The Sector, the Branch, the SNA and the Financial Definition.' COMPASS Modelling Project, Keio University.

Vanwymsberghe, D. (1998). 'Object-oriented Approach in International Input-Output Models.' Paper presented at the Twelfth International Input-Output Conference, 18-22 May, New York.

Vanwynsberghe, D. (1998). 'COMPASS Regions and Branches.' December 1998 Workshop, Keio University.

Vanwynsberghe, D. (1998). 'World Trade Branches and SITC Codes.' December 1998 Workshop, Keio University.

Vanwynsberghe, D. (1998). 'COMPASS Financial Account Framework and Variable Names.' December 1998 Workshop, Keio University.

Vanwynsberghe, D. (1998). 'From Input-Output over Macro Economic Aggregates to Financial Accounts FIOM.' December 1998 Workshop, Keio University.
Vanwynsberghe, D. (2001). 'Long-Term Data on Economy, Demography, and Energy.' Uno Laboratory, Keio University.
Vanwynsberghe, D. and Wang, Y. (1997). 'Quickdyme, Make Country SNAIO Database System Manual.' Center of Excellence, Keio University.
Vanwynsberghe, D. and Wang, Y. (1997). 'Macro Models, Make Country Macro Models.' Center of Excellence, Keio University.
Wang, Y. (1996). 'GETAIJ & PUTAIJ, a Program for Analysing the Elements of a Matrix.' Center of Excellence, Keio University.
Wang, Y. (1996). 'MUDAN III, A Multi-sector Model for China.' Center of Excellence, Keio Univertity.
Wang, Y. (1997). 'Quickdyme, Country Model Software.' Center of Excellence, Keio University.
Wang, Y. (1998). 'From Data Preparation to Construction of Simulation Models.' Paper presented at the Twelfth International Input-Output Conference, held 18-22 May, 1998, New York.
Wang, Y. (1998). 'What's New in Quickdyme Version 2 and the Present Situation of IO Models.' December 1998 Workshop, Keio University.
Wang, Y. (1999). 'An Approach to Determine Gross Output Price Index from Value Added Price Index.' APEC Energy Project, Keio University.
Wang, Y. (1999). 'Price Equation for the National Model Linked with Trade Model.' APEC Energy Project, Keio University.

Notes on Contributors

Frank Hohmann has studied computer science and business administration at the University of Osnabruuck (Diplom Betriebswirt 1994). Since 1996 he supported GWS mbH as a freelance consultant and since 1999 he has been working as a databank and software expert for GWS.

Alexey Koltsov is doctor of economics and serves as the Head of Division, Summarizing Department for Industry and Science and Technologies, Russian Federation. He is responsible, among other things, for structural and medium-term analysis and forecasting of the Russian economy.

Zuo Li is the Director, the Development Forecasting Department of Jiangsu Information Center, China. She graduated from Northeast Univerisity in 1982 and started economic modelling and analysis in 1985, and has been working in the field of multi-sector modelling since 1995.

Christian Lutz is vice-director of GWS mbH. He studied economics at the University of Tuubingen (Diplom Volkswirt 1993) and at the University of Osnabruuck (PhD in economics 1997). Since 1997 he has been research fellow at the GWS. The focus of his research has been economics of energy, air emissions, land use, and international trade.

Bernd Meyer is professor of macroeconomic theory at the University of Osnabruuck and director of the GWS mbH. In 1997 he was visiting professor at the Department of Policy Management at Keio University, Japan. Since 1996 he has been a member and since 1999 chairman of the Council of Advisors for Economic and Environmental Accounting for the German Ministry of Environment. His research in the last years concentrates on the construction and application of macroeconomic and interindustry simulation and forecasting models with a focus on environmental questions.

Yumiko Umehara is the National Program Director of LEAD (Leadership for Environment and Development) Japan Program. She is a fellow of the LEAD Program that is headquartered in London. She obtained MA from the Graduate School of Media and Governance in 2000 and has been a researcher at the Keio University Research Institute at Shonan Fujisawa Campus (SFC). Her academic papers on multi-sector energy balance model have been presented at Energy Modelling Forums at IEA (1999) and Stanford University (2000), and OECD Joint Workshop on Trade and Environment (1999).

Kimio Uno is Professor of Media and Governance at Keio University, Japan. Previously he taught at the Graduate School of Environmental Science at University of Tsukuba. He obtained PhD in economics from University of Illinois in 1973 and was a visiting fellow at Yale University. He served as a consultant to the United Nations Conference on Environment and Development and the United Nations University on various occasions. He worked as research associate at the International Institute for Applied Systems Analysis (IIASA). He chairs a government committee on environmental accounting.

Dirk Vanwynsberghe is a consultant in system integration at Economic Research International in Belgium. He holds MA in applied economics and commercial engineering from University of Leuven. With his expertise in energy areas and database construction, his international experience includes assignment at UNIDO, Chase Econometrics, and consulting and teaching in various parts of the world.

Vladimir Volkov is doctor of economics and currently the Deputy Head of Macroeconomic Analysis and Forecasting Department, Ministry of Economic Development and Trade, Russian Federation. His responsibility focuses on short-term macroeconomic analysis.

Wang Yinchu is Vice-Director of the Economic Information Center, Jiangsu Province, China. He graduated from Nanjing University in 1977 and has been working in the field of economic modelling and analysis since 1977. He has worked on multi-sector modelling and analysis for China since 1992.

Disclaimer

Project Support: The project has been supported by the following sources.

Institute of Energy Economics: 'Construction of APEC Energy Network', Keio University Shonan Fujisawa Campus Research Institute, 1995-1999.

Japan Society for the Promotion of Science, Grant-in-Aid for International Research Collaboration: 'Global Scenario on Energy and Environment', 1998-2000.

Ministry of Education, Database Construction Subsidy Scheme: 'Comprehensive Model for Policy Assessment', Keio University, 1997-1999.

Ministry of Education, Center of Excellence: 'Creative Digital Media, Its Impact on the New Century', Keio University Shonan Fujisawa Campus Research Institute, 1996-2000.

Economic Planning Agency, Japan and Ministry of Economy, Russian Federation: 'Joint Research Project on the Russian Economic Reform', 1996-2000.

3E Research Institute: 'Energy, Environment, and Economy'. Keio University, Japan and Tsinghua University, China, project supported by the JETRO and the NEDO of the Japanese Government, 2000-2004.

Keio University Shonan Fujisawa Campus Research Institute research grant: 'Very Long Term Demographic and PPP-Adjusted Economic Data for the World Community', 2000.

Ministry of Education and Science, Hightech Research Center Project: 'Next Generation Cyber Space', 2000-2002.

Japan Society for the Promotion of Science, Grant-in-Aid for Publication of Scientific Research Results, Database: 'Global Economy Energy Environment Database (Global 3E)', 2001.

Japan Society for the Promotion of Science, Grant-in-Aid for Publication of Scientific Research Results, Academic Publication: 'Economy-Energy-Environment: A Global Perspective', 2001.

Index

Economy & Environment

1. F. Archibugi and P. Nijkamp (eds.): *Economy and Ecology: Towards Sustainable Development.* 1989 ISBN 0-7923-0477-2
2. J. Bojö, K.-G. Mäler and L. Unemo: *Environment and Development: An Economic Approach.* 1990 ISBN 0-7923-0802-6
3. J. B. Opschoor and D. W. Pearce (eds.): *Persistent Pollutants: Economics and Policy.* 1991 ISBN 0-7923-1168-X
4. D.J. Kraan and R. J. in 't Veld (eds.): *Environmental Protection: Public or Private Choice.* 1991 ISBN 0-7923-1333-X
5. J.J. Krabbe and W.J.M. Heijman (eds.): *National Income and Nature: Externalities, Growth and Steady State.* 1992 ISBN 0-7923-1529-4
6. J. Bojö, K.-G. Mäler and L. Unemo: *Environment and Development: An Economic Approach* (revised edition). 1992 ISBN 0-7923-1878-1
7. T. Sterner (ed.): *Economic Policies for Sustainable Development.* 1994 ISBN 0-7923-2680-6
8. L. Bergman and D.M. Pugh (eds.): *Environmental Toxicology, Economics and Institutions.* The Atrazine Case Study. 1994 ISBN 0-7923-2986-4
9. G. Klaassen and F.R. Førsund (eds.): *Economic Instruments for Air Pollution Control.* 1994 ISBN 0-7923-3151-6
10. K. Uno: *Environmental Options: Accounting for Sustainability.* 1995 ISBN 0-7923-3513-9
11. K. Uno and P. Bartelmus (eds.): *Environmental Accounting in Theory and Practice.* 1997 ISBN 0-7923-4559-2
12. J.C.J.M. van den Bergh, K.J. Button, P. Nijkamp and G.C. Pepping: *Meta-Analysis in Environmental Economics.* 1997 ISBN 0-7923-4592-4
13. S. Faucheux, M. O'Connor and J. v.d. Straaten: *Sustainable Development: Concepts, Rationalities and Strategies.* 1998 ISBN 0-7923-4884-2
14. P. Kågeson: *Growth versus the Environment: Is there a Trade-off?.* 1998 ISBN 0-7923-4926-1
15. J.C.J.M. van den Bergh and M.W. Hofkes (eds.): *Theory and Implementation of Economic Models for Sustainable Development.* 1998 ISBN 0-7923-4998-9
16. J.N. Lekakis (ed.): *Freer Trade, Sustainability, and the Primary Production Sector in the Southern EU: Unraveling the Evidence from Greece.* 1998 ISBN 0-7923-5151-7
17. M. Boman, R. Brännlund and B. Kriström (eds.): *Topics in Environmental Economics.* 1999 ISBN 0-7923-5897-x
18. S.M. de Bruyn: *Economic Growth and the Environment.* An Empirical Analysis. 2000 ISBN 0-7923-6153-9
19. C. Kraus: *Import Tariffs as Environmental Policy Instruments.* 2000 ISBN 0-7923-6318-3
20. K. Uno (ed.): *Economy - Energy-Environment Simulation. Beyond The Kyoto Protocol.* 2002 ISBN 1-4020-0450-8

Economy & Environment

21. J. Beghin, D. Roland-Horst and D. Van der Mensbrugghe (eds.): *Trade and the Environment in General Equilibrium: Evidence for Developing Economies*. 2002
ISBN 1-4020-0479-6

KLUWER ACADEMIC PUBLISHERS – DORDRECHT / BOSTON / LONDON